Southern Africa

Deanna Swaney
Mary Fitzpatrick
Paul Greenway
Andrew Stone
Justine Vaisutis

LONELY PLANET PUBLICATIONS
Melbourne • Oakland • London • Paris

SOUTHERN AFRICA

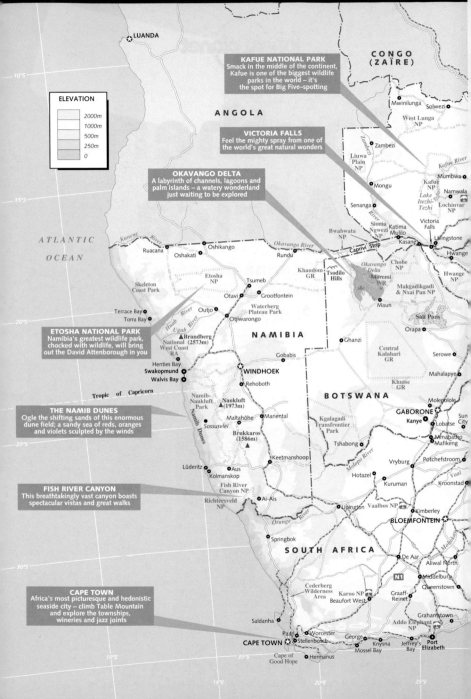

KAFUE NATIONAL PARK
Smack in the middle of the continent,
Kafue is one of the biggest wildlife
parks in the world – it's
the spot for Big Five–spotting

VICTORIA FALLS
Feel the mighty spray from one of
the world's great natural wonders

OKAVANGO DELTA
A labyrinth of channels, lagoons and
palm islands – a watery wonderland
just waiting to be explored

ETOSHA NATIONAL PARK
Namibia's greatest wildlife park,
chocked with wildlife, will bring
out the David Attenborough in you

THE NAMIB DUNES
Ogle the shifting sands of this enormous
dune field; a sandy sea of reds, oranges
and violets sculpted by the winds

FISH RIVER CANYON
This breathtakingly vast canyon boasts
spectacular vistas and great walks

CAPE TOWN
Africa's most picturesque and hedonistic
seaside city – climb Table Mountain
and explore the townships,
wineries and jazz joints

ELEVATION

2000m
1000m
500m
250m
0

CONGO
(ZAÏRE)

ANGOLA

ATLANTIC
OCEAN

NAMIBIA

BOTSWANA

SOUTH AFRICA

○ LUANDA

Mwinilunga ○   Solwezi ○
West Lunga
NP
Zambezi ○
Liuwa
Plain
NP   Mumbwa ○
Kafue
NP   Namwala ○
Mongu ○   Lake
Itezhi-   Lochinvar
Tezhi   NP
Senanga ○
Sioma
Ngwezi   Katima
Bwabwata   NP   Mulilo   Victoria
National   ○   ○   Falls
NP   Capavi Strip Kasane ○   ○ Livingstone
Ruacana ○   Rundu ○   Chobe Hwange ○
Oshikango ○   Okavango NP   Hwange
Oshakati ○   Khaudom Tsodilo Delta   NP
Etosha   GR   Hills Moremi
NP   Tsumeb ○   WR
Otavi ○   ○ Grootfontein   Makgadikgadi
Terrace Bay ○   Outjo ○   Waterberg   & Nxai Pan NP
Torra Bay ○   Plateau Park   Maun ○
Otjiwarongo ○   Salt Pans
▲Brandberg   Orapa ○
(2573m)   Ghanzi ○
National
West Coast   Central
RA   Kalahari
Gobabis ○   GR   Serowe ○
Henties Bay ○
Swakopmund ○   ○ WINDHOEK   Mahalapye ○
Walvis Bay ○
Rehoboth ○   Khutse
GR   Molepolole ○
Tropic of Capricorn
Namib-   Naukluft   GABORONE ○
Naukluft   ▲(1973m)   Kgalagadi   Kanye ○   Sun
Park   Transfrontier   Lobatse ○ City
Maltahöhe ○ ○ Mariental   Park   ○ Mmabatho
Sossusvlei ○   Mafikeng
Brukkaros   Tshabong ○
(1586m)   Vryburg ○   Potchefstroom ○
Keetmanshoop ○   Hotazel ○
Lüderitz ○   ○ Aus   Kroonstad ○
Kolmanskop ○   Kuruman ○
Fish River   Kimberley ○
Canyon NP   Upington ○ Vaalbos NP ○
Richtersveld ○ Ai-Ais   Orange River   BLOEMFONTEIN ○
NP
Springbok ○
De Aar ○
Aliwal North ○
N1   Middelburg ○
Cederberg   Karoo NP ○   Graaff-   Queenstown ○
Wilderness   Beaufort West ○ Reinet ○
Area   Grahamstown ○
Addo Elephant
Saldanha ○   George ○   NP
Paarl ○ Worcester ○   Knysna ○ Jeffrey's Port
CAPE TOWN ○ Stellenbosch ○   Mossel Bay ○ Bay Elizabeth ○
Cape of   ○ Hermanus
Good Hope

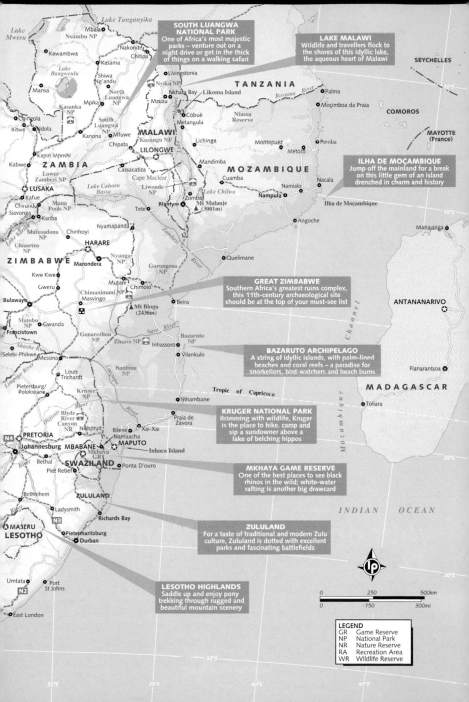

SOUTH LUANGWA NATIONAL PARK
One of Africa's most majestic parks – venture out on a night drive or get in the thick of things on a walking safari

LAKE MALAWI
Wildlife and travellers flock to the shores of this idyllic lake, the aqueous heart of Malawi

ILHA DE MOÇAMBIQUE
Jump off the mainland for a break on this little gem of an island drenched in charm and history

GREAT ZIMBABWE
Southern Africa's greatest ruins complex, this 11th-century archaeological site should be at the top of your must-see list

BAZARUTO ARCHIPELAGO
A string of idyllic islands, with palm-lined beaches and coral reefs – a paradise for snorkellers, bird-watchers and beach bums

KRUGER NATIONAL PARK
Brimming with wildlife, Kruger is the place to hike, camp and sip a sundowner above a lake of belching hippos

MKHAYA GAME RESERVE
One of the best places to see black rhinos in the wild; white-water rafting is another big drawcard

ZULULAND
For a taste of traditional and modern Zulu culture, Zululand is dotted with excellent parks and fascinating battlefields

LESOTHO HIGHLANDS
Saddle up and enjoy pony trekking through rugged and beautiful mountain scenery

LEGEND
GR   Game Reserve
NP   National Park
NR   Nature Reserve
RA   Recreation Area
WR   Wildlife Reserve

0   250   500km
0   150   300mi

www.lonelyplanet.com

your online travel community

350+ DESTINATION PROFILES · 5,000+ TRAVEL POSTS DAILY · 50,000+ MEMBERS

WEEKLY COLUMNS & INTERVIEWS · MONTHLY ADVISORIES · STORIES FROM AROUND THE WORLD

ONLINE SHOP · TRAVEL SERVICES · BEST TRAVEL WEBSITE: WEBBY AWARDS

lonely planet

Contents – Text

THE BEATS OF SOUTHERN AFRICA 113

LESOTHO 142

MALAWI 162

MOZAMBIQUE 246

NAMIBIA 306

SOUTH AFRICA 402

SWAZILAND 577

4 Contents – Text

Contents – Maps

6 Contents – Maps

The Authors

Deanna Swaney

After her university studies, Deanna hit the road and has been addicted to travel ever since. Despite an erstwhile career in computer programming, she managed intermittent forays away from the corporate bustle of midtown Anchorage, and at first opportunity, made a break for South America where she wrote Lonely Planet's *Bolivia* guide. Subsequent travels steered her through a course of diverse countries, and resulted in six more 1st editions for Lonely Planet: *Tonga, Samoa, Iceland, Greenland & the Faroe Islands, Zimbabwe, Botswana & Namibia, Norway* and *The Arctic*. She has also co-authored updates of *Brazil, Mauritius, Réunion & Seychelles, Madagascar & Comoros* and *Russia, Ukraine & Belarus*, and contributed to numerous shoestring guides.

Deanna now divides her time between travelling, hiking, writing and looking for time to work on various construction projects around her home base in Alaska's Susitna Valley.

Mary Fitzpatrick

After finishing university in Washington, DC, her home town, Mary set off for several years working in Europe. Her fascination with languages and cultures soon led her further south to sub-Saharan Africa, where she has been for much of the past decade, including over three years in Mozambique. Elsewhere, Mary's journeys have taken her on foot through remote Malagasy villages, on rickety pick-ups along dusty roads in the Sahel, and on bicycle through Tibet and south-western China. Mary has authored or co-authored numerous other Africa titles for Lonely Planet, including *Mozambique, Tanzania, East Africa, West Africa* and *Africa on a shoestring*.

Paul Greenway

Gratefully plucked from the blandness and security of the Australian Public Service, Paul has worked on over 20 Lonely Planet guides including *Jordan, Botswana,* and *Bulgaria*. During the rare times that he's not travelling – or writing, reading or dreaming about it – Paul relaxes (and pretends he can play) heavy rock, and eats and breathes Australian Rules Football.

Andrew Stone

In his childhood, Andrew travelled with family to a few exotic destinations (post-independence Zambia, pre-revolution Iran, post-Jimi Hendrix Isle of Wight) before settling in southern England.

After a brief career as a journalist on obscure weekly trade magazines, he moved to Hong Kong, where he persuaded two different publishers to let him write guidebooks. He began writing for Lonely Planet soon afterwards.

A South African mother and sister-in-law have given him plenty of good excuses to fly south and he has been a regular visitor to South Africa and the region since 1990. Needless to say, he jumped at the chance to explore more of South Africa, Lesotho and Swaziland for this edition.

Justine Vaisutis

Justine first became addicted to the nomadic lifestyle when she lived in South Africa and South Korea as a little tacker. Growing up in the exotic city of Canberra further augmented her love for travel. After completing an Arts degree in Third World Development Studies, she decided it was more enjoyable to save the world by writing about it, so she hit the study books again in pursuit of a noble career as a travel writer.

Justine lives in Australia, where she spends as much time as possible satisfying her other passions – anything remotely related to wildlife or cinema. This is her first job for Lonely Planet.

FROM THE AUTHORS

Deanna Swaney

While covering Namibia and Botswana over a dozen years, I've been fortunate enough to meet and foster friendships with many Namibians, Batswana, South Africans and others who've graciously assisted with my coverage of their spectacular countries.

The Namibia chapter of this book was greatly enhanced by Aulden & Rachael Harlech-Jones, Mush and Ephraim, all at the Cardboard Box in Windhoek; Crazy Kudu Mike Godfrey in Windhoek; Chris at Outside Adventures in Windhoek; Louis & Riette Fourie at Fish River Lodge; Frenus & Sybille Rorich in Swakopmund; Willem & Piet Swiegers at Klein Aus; Way-Out Willie and Mild Milligan for various adventures; Val & Weynand Peypers in Rundu; Ralph & Sharon Meyer-Rust at Lianshulu; Rob & Marianne Lowe at Zebra River; and Dave van Smeerdijk & Rowan Calder at Wilderness Safaris. Love and thanks to all of you.

Similarly, in Botswana, thanks to Tiaan & Sabine for their hospitality in Maun; Steve Caballero & Sarah Rhodes, for yet another great Tsodilo holiday; Jonathon Gibson in Kasane; Ralph Bousfield & the whole Jack's Camp/Planet Baobab gang; and Colin McVey & Cecilia Mooketsi in Gaborone.

For their help In South Africa, I also want to thank Genene Park in Cape Town; Marie & Grant Burton at Groenfontein; and Sandra & Detlef at Oak Lodge. Of course, I must also thank Jon Murray and Hilary Rogers in Melbourne, who so expertly set the stage for this project, as well as my co-authors, who supplied their work in good time and always answered queries promptly.

Finally, love to Dean, Kim, Lauren, Jennifer and Earl Swaney in Fresno; Rodney, Heather, Bradley, Eric and 'forthcoming' Leacock in Colorado Springs; and of course to Dave Dault, with whom I shared all sorts of adventures in magical Southern Africa.

Mary Fitzpatrick

Thanks most of all to Rick for the support, enthusiasm and encouragement.

I'd also like to extend many thanks to Lesley Sitch and Bart van Straaten in Pemba; to Ibraimo Arrafa Ali of the Mozambique Island tourist information centre; to Sidney Bliss for his ongoing generosity and assistance in Maputo; to Qian Jia Qi for the good company on the road between Mtwara and Pemba; and, to Fanny Viret and Lucas Chambers for the meal and for lending me a tent when we all got stuck on the banks of the Rovuma. Finally, a big debt of gratitude to all the VSOs who helped me out, especially Sander and Laetitia in Marracuene, and Lee Webster, Emma Johnson, Mark Learwood and Benoît Faure in Nampula.

I'd like to dedicate my portion of this book to Valdomiro.

Paul Greenway

Special thanks to Lubasi Lubasi from the Zambia National Tourist Board; Val Bell from the Bulawayo & District Publicity Association; Wade Seymour in Lusaka; and Clive, Liz & Roy in Kariba.

Andrew Stone

A thousand thanks must go first of all to the Hodnett clan for a thousand kindnesses. To Tracey for loaning me her car and letting me drive the thing almost to destruction, to Rosa for putting me up in her beautiful house and making me so welcome and to Mark, Rene, David and Margo for all their help.

To Jabulani Sithebi, thanks for your help in the research and for your extremely pleasant company covering scary downtown Jo'burg and to Laura Malan thanks for showing me the bright lights of Melville.

To David, Margie and Sue Ritchie in Cape Town special thanks. After eight weeks on the road, dusty, tired and saddlesore, you have no idea how I appreciated your hospitality.

Around South Africa I'd also like to thank: Maxine and the party animals at Harry's and Delagoa for a wonderful weekend in Graskop; to all the folk at Malealea Lodge in Lesotho for their help and a wonderful stay; to all at Bucanneers in Cintsa for running an outstanding hostel and especially to Sean for his help with the Wild Coast research; to all at Cape Tourism for their help and impressive efficiency.

Finally, thanks to Mum and Dad for going to so much trouble smoothing various administrative wrinkles for me.

Justine Vaisutis

My biggest thank you for this project goes to my partner in crime – Alan Murphy, without whose driving, commentary, singing, dancing, washing, laughing and overwhelming support, Malawi simply would not have been as much fun. For keeping me sane most of the time via the information super highway I thank my sister Aidy.

On the road I was inundated with kindness, generosity and support and in particular I would like to thank: Claire, Paul and Liz in Nkhata Bay, Tash at Usisya, Charlie and Nairuth at Ruarwe, Nick at Chizumulu (ok just one more green), Monica, Thomas, Adela and Will at Likoma, Robyn and Ed at Nyika, Gerard at Mzoozoozoo, Chris at Central African Wilderness Safaris and Mark at Doogles.

Others along the way who made this trip so much more enjoyable include Melinda from Canada, both Jos from England and Melanie from home – what are you doing here??!!

I also want to thank both Hilary Rogers and Deanna Swaney who were both incredibly supportive. And lastly, every bit of work I did for this book is dedicated to my wonderful and enigmatic father, for instilling in me a great love for all things African.

This Book

The 1st edition of *Southern Africa* was written and researched by David Else, Jon Murray and Deanna Swaney. The 2nd edition was coordinated by David Else with updated chapters from Joyce Connolly, Mary Fitzpatrick, Alan Murphy and Deanna Swaney.

This 3rd edition of *Southern Africa* was coordinated by Deanna Swaney who also updated Botswana, Namibia and the introductory chapters. Andrew Stone updated the South Africa, Lesotho and Swaziland chapters, Justine Vaisutis updated Malawi, Mary Fitzpatrick updated Mozambique again, and Paul Greenway updated Zambia and Zimbabwe and wrote the new Victoria Falls chapter. The 'Beats of Southern Africa' special colour section was written by in-house research editor, Anastasia Safioleas, and Quentin Frayne prepared the Language chapter.

FROM THE PUBLISHER

This 3rd edition of *Southern Africa* was commissioned in Lonely Planet's Melbourne office by Hilary Rogers with the help of Jon Murray (while Hilary was out of the office on an authoring expedition). This edition was project managed by Huw Fowles and Chris Love. Tasmin Waby coordinated all the editing, proofing and indexing. Craig MacKenzie, Gabrielle Wilson, Helen Yeates, John Hinman, Lou McGregor and Paul Harding edited and proofread various chapters. Meg Worby and Ann Seward kindly assisted with indexing. The talented Chris Thomas prepared the climate charts and coordinated the cartography, with assistance from Csanad Csutoros, James Ellis, Valentina Kremenchutskaya, Natasha Velleley, Daniel Fennessy, Anneka Imkamp and Sarah Sloane. The images used in this book were supplied by LPI. The cover was designed by Gerilyn Atterbery. The book was laid out by Jacqui Saunders with assistance from Birgit Jordan and Sally Darmody. Jacqui also designed the colour pages. Mark Germanchis and David Burnett assisted with all the technical hitches along the way. And for that we have to say a big thank you! Finally, thanks also to Brigitte Ellemor, Shahara Ahmed, Kate McDonald and Adriana Mammarella for their guidance throughout production.

Thanks

Many thanks to the travellers who used the last edition and wrote to us with helpful hints, useful advice and interesting anecdotes:

DK & Sue Adams, Giuliani Adolfo, Jeff & Alison Allan, Alison Allgaier, Michelle Antici, Terry Aspinall, Daniel Barber, Eileen Barrett, Geoff Barton, Henk Bekker, Wim Berghius, Andrew Bergwald, Sarah & Gianluca Bisi, Steve Blair, Gerda Bogaards, Paolo Boglietti, Rory Bolton, Joerg Bongen, Peter Boodell, Bob & Anne Bown, Lucienne Braam, Andre Brown, Debbie Bruk, Hayley Cameron, Alan & Lynne Charlton, Stephen Cheng, Cindy Choua, Jo Coley, WA Constable, Etelka Corten, Saudra Cox, Edward Crean, Emily Cross, Jody Culham, Monique Cuthbert, Trish Daly, Laury de Jong, Zelna de Villiers, Emma Dean, Hilary Dean-Hughes, John Delaney, Peter Demey, Elissa Dennis, Pam Dennison, Andre DeSimone, Rob Dirven, Charly Dolman, Lunay Dreyer, Anne Easterling, Albrecht W Eberts, Gary Edgar, Roderick Eime, Ian Emerson, Aurelia Erhardt, Bernard Farjounel, Julie Fisher, Mark Foster, Peter Foster, Mike French, Anja Frensen, Mary Garlicki, Elizabeth Garrett, Ewan Gatherer, Audrey Gaughran, Willaim Giles, Lee Gillyon, Ben Giola, Christian Goltz, Maria Gonzalez-Beato, Michael Graf, Adin Greaves, Vasily V Grebennikov, Ronny Groenteman, Marc Grutering, Lee Gullick, Sally Hagen, Andrew Hamling, Wolfgang Hamm, Veronica Harris, Keith Hart, Robin Hartle, Charles Hartwig, Kate Harvie, Rex Haught, Bernd Heidemann, Sharon Herkes, Rona Hiam, Gary W Hickman, Richard Hill, Peter Hiller, Dr Steffen Himmelmann, Sarah Horton, Derek Huby, Glenda Hudson, David Hulshuis, Corey Innes, Bridgett James, Michael Jennings, Martin Jones, Catherine Junor, Raviv Karauk, Clare Kerr, Paul Kilfoil, Giel Klanker, Heiko Koch, David Koetsier, Andreas Konieczny, Noshir Lam, Sandy Lam, Chris Lanyon, Sally & George Larson, Marc Le Dilosquer, Andre Lotz, Catarina Lyden, Brian MacCormaic, Maria Cecilia Macatangga, MJ Mackay, Bernard Madigan, Maureen Maguire, Richard Mahoney, Dale Malmskog, Hamish Mansbridge, Karl Martin, Silvia & Stefano Mazzocchio, Gordon Mcewan, Nicole Mcintyre, Hugh McNaughtan, Elizabeth McSweeney, Basia Meder, Matthias Meixner, Markella Mikkelsen, Natasha & Paul Milijasevic, Kai Monkkonen, Karin Moor, Jonathan Morgan, Siiri Morley, Tom Morris, Heather Mothershead, Claudia Mueller, Afke Mulder, Anneke Naerebout, John Oldham, Hans Opmeer, Jenny Orchard, Volker & Rolf Ostheimer, Ivo Oud, Vittorio Paielli, Ellen Pansegrau, Dirk Jan Parlevliet, Sanjeev Parmar, Nina, Kiran & Maya Patel, Giorgio Perversi, Charlie Pointer, Jessica Posner, Jim Potter, Claudio Predan, Anja Priess, James Prior, Trevor Purchase, Peter Ras, Marco Reinhoudt, Jacqueline Remmelzwaal, Jan Doeke Rinzema, John Riordan, Leslie Robin, Mary Robinson, Jenny Roche, Keith Rodwell, Nick Rooker, Kerstin Rosen, Anny Ruesink, Richard & Caroline Rule, Bobby Russell, Vic Russell, Monika Rutishauser, Reinhard Schmidt, David Sharp, Sharon Shewmake,

Kim Shockley, J Simonis, Gerald Sing-Chin, Eric Slenters, Ryan Slimmon, Peter Sloth-Madsen, Jonathan Smith, Joost & Conny Snoep, Kathy Snow, Krzysztof Sobien, Paul Spaans, Tim Spicer, Mike Stapleton, Richard Stokes, Jon Taylor, Michel Tio, Alex & Becca Tostevin, Camille Unnerstall, Dirk Van Camp, Zannie van der Walt, Corne van Dongen, Johannes van Eeden, Caren van Halen, Marieke van Schaik, Slavica & Jilles van Werkhoven, Erwin van Wijk, Marcel van Zonneveld, Jan Venema, Sean Vermooten, Manuel Villanueva, Esther Visser, Vanessa Ward, E Warmer, Steph Weeks, Camilla Wickstrom, Vincent Wiegers, Sanne Wijnhorst, Eddie Wilde, Brian Wilkes, Jean A Wilsen, Sean & Dympna Wilson, Joseph Winter, Jan Witkiewicz, Andreas Wladis, Katherine Wolf, Alastair Womack, Robert Wotton, Susan Wright, Ian Young, Julie Zeitlinger, Andrea Zeus, Michael Ziemba, Corrine Zondag.

Foreword

ABOUT LONELY PLANET GUIDEBOOKS

The story begins with a classic travel adventure: Tony and Maureen Wheeler's 1972 journey across Europe and Asia to Australia. There was no useful information about the overland trail then, so Tony and Maureen published the first Lonely Planet guidebook to meet a growing need.

From a kitchen table, Lonely Planet has grown to become the largest independent travel publisher in the world, with offices in Melbourne (Australia), Oakland (USA), London (UK) and Paris (France).

Today Lonely Planet guidebooks cover the globe. There is an ever-growing list of books and information in a variety of media. Some things haven't changed. The main aim is still to make it possible for adventurous travellers to get out there – to explore and better understand the world.

At Lonely Planet we believe travellers can make a positive contribution to the countries they visit – if they respect their host communities and spend their money wisely. Since 1986 a percentage of the income from each book has been donated to aid projects and human rights campaigns, and, more recently, to wildlife conservation.

Although inclusion in a guidebook usually implies a recommendation we cannot list every good place. Exclusion does not necessarily imply criticism. In fact there are a number of reasons why we might exclude a place – sometimes it is simply inappropriate to encourage an influx of travellers.

UPDATES & READER FEEDBACK

Things change – prices go up, schedules change, good places go bad and bad places go bankrupt. Nothing stays the same. So, if you find things better or worse, recently opened or long-since closed, please tell us and help make the next edition even more accurate and useful.

Lonely Planet thoroughly updates each guidebook as often as possible – usually every two years, although for some destinations the gap can be longer. Between editions, up-to-date information is available in our free, monthly email bulletin *Comet* (W www.lonelyplanet.com/newsletters). You can also check out the *Thorn Tree* bulletin board and *Postcards* section of our website which carry unverified, but fascinating, reports from travellers.

Tell us about it! We genuinely value your feedback. A well-travelled team at Lonely Planet reads and acknowledges every email and letter we receive and ensures that every morsel of information finds its way to the relevant authors, editors and cartographers.

Everyone who writes to us will find their name listed in the next edition of the appropriate guidebook. The very best contributions will be rewarded with a free guidebook.

We may edit, reproduce and incorporate your comments in Lonely Planet products such as guidebooks, websites and digital products, so let us know if you don't want your comments reproduced or your name acknowledged.

How to contact Lonely Planet:
Online: e talk2us@lonelyplanet.com.au, W www.lonelyplanet.com
Australia: Locked Bag 1, Footscray, Victoria 3011
UK: 72-82 Rosebery Ave, London, EC1R 4RW
USA: 150 Linden St, Oakland, CA 94607

Introduction

In Southern Africa, it's the sheer, awe-inspiring landscapes combined with a relatively harmonious cultural diversity that strikes most visitors. The region brims with a wealth of unforgettable sights, sounds and experiences: from Johannesburg's gleaming high-rises to the Okavango Delta's pristine wetlands; from Zambia's traditional villages and Malawi's idyllic lakeshore to Mozambique's tropical beaches; and from Namibia's world-renowned dunes to Lesotho's wild mountain country. And then there's Victoria Falls, shared by Zimbabwe and Zambia, which indisputably ranks as one of the natural wonders of the world.

Through the deserts, rainforests, farmlands, vineyards, savannas and mountains you can travel by car, horse, local bus, luxury train or on the bed of a *bakkie* (pickup truck). Alternatively, travel by steamboat across Lake Malawi, explore Botswana's tranquil waterways by *mokoro* (dugout canoe) or hit an adrenaline high rafting through the Zambezi rapids below Victoria Falls.

In the bush, you can look for elephants in the desert or penguins on the beach, or experience simple traditional villages of mud-and-grass-huts. Alternatively, head for the urban areas and explore the vibrant townships or comfortable city suburbs;

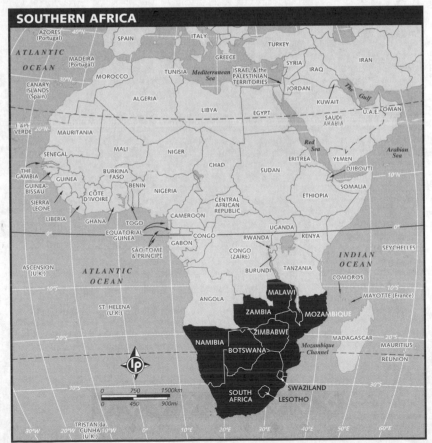

SOUTHERN AFRICA

appreciate the cultural richness of the Zulu, Ndebele, Lozi, Herero, Owambo, Xhosa, Makonde and Himba; or visit the world-renowned National Parks – including Kruger, Etosha and Hwange – with their menagerie of African wildlife and splendidly varied birds and flowers.

While you're soaking up the spectacular sights, cultures and wildlife, however, don't forget to allow some time to relax, observe and experience the ambient spirit of Africa on its own terms. This is one place that really gets its grips into visitors and residents alike, and for some, it never lets go. Stand alone on a foggy shoreline; walk on a country highway with nothing to shelter you but the big sky; stroll along a sand river through the wildest bush; venture into a dunefield and enter the realms of fantasy; or gaze across the sunburnt plains and witness a scene unchanged since humans first emerged aeons ago.

For the writers who have compiled this book, deciding what to omit was nearly as difficult as deciding what to include. While we hope to introduce you to many of the well-known wonders of the region and a few of its hidden delights, use this book as a guide only. Keep yourself open to your own discoveries, and remember that spontaneous travel experiences are normally the most rewarding and memorable.

Facts about the Region

This chapter describes the more general aspects of Southern Africa. For colonial and modern history of the individual countries, see the relevant country chapters.

HISTORY

Southern Africa contains many archaeological records of the world's earliest human inhabitants. While scientists and researchers dispute exactly who evolved into whom, and when, most accept that the first 'hominids' (upright-walking humanlike creatures) became established in the savannas of East and Southern Africa nearly four million years ago. In Southern Africa, evidence of early hominids over three million years old have been discovered in South Africa's Mpumalanga Province, and in Malawi,

---

Ancient Rock Art

There's a lot of speculation about the origins of the ancient rock paintings and engravings found around Southern Africa, but there's no reliable way of dating them without destroying them. For the archaeologist, there are considerable difficulties in relating the paintings to the cultural sequences preserved in soil layers of caves and rock shelters, but recent advances in radiocarbon dating are beginning to shed some light.

Thanks to tools and animal remains left around major sites and the scenes depicted, it's surmised that the artists were nomadic hunter-gatherers, without knowledge of agriculture or pottery. For that reason, the works have been attributed to the early San people.

Most rock paintings reflected people's relationship with nature. Some rock paintings are stylised representations of the region's people and animals, but the majority are realistic portrayals of hunters, giraffes, elephants, rhinos, lions, antelopes and so on in rich red, yellow, brown and ochre.

Common themes include the roles of men and women, hunting scenes and natural medicine. The latter includes examples of trance dancing and spiritual healing using the San life force, known as nxum, which was invoked to control aspects of the natural world, including climate and disease. All these elements still feature in San tradition.

As with similar cave art found in Europe, it has been speculated that the animal paintings were intended to somehow ensure an abundance of those animals. However, this concept hasn't been noted in any present-day African culture, and there's no evidence of ancient ties with Europe. Furthermore, few of the animals portrayed would have served as food for the ancient San.

Although the earliest works have long faded, flaked and eroded into oblivion, the dry climate and sheltered granite overhangs have preserved many of the more recent paintings. Anthropological studies have used the content, skill level and superposition of the paintings to identify three distinct periods.

The earliest paintings seem to reflect a period of gentle nomadism during which people were occupied primarily with the hunt. Later works, which revealed great artistic improvement, suggest peaceful arrivals by outside groups, perhaps Bantu or Khoi-Khoi. The final stage indicates a decline in the standard of the paintings; either due to a loss of interest or a loss of facility with the genre, or these are imitations of earlier works by more recently arrived peoples.

Red pigments were ground mainly from iron oxides, which were powdered and mixed with animal fat to form an adhesive paste. The whites came from silica, powdered quartz and white clays, and were by nature less adhesive than the red pigments. For this reason, white paintings survive only in sheltered locations, such as well protected caves. Both pigments were applied to the rock using sticks, the artists' fingers and brushes made from animal hair.

The most poignant thing about rock art is that it remains in the spot where it was created. Unlike in a museum, sensitive viewers may catch a glimpse of the inspiration that went into the paintings. Although rock art is found all over Southern Africa, the best examples are probably in Matobo National Park, Domboshawa and Ngomakurira, all in Zimbabwe; the Tsodilo Hills in Botswana; Twyfelfontein in Namibia; and Giant's Castle in South Africa.

archaeologists have found remains thought to date back as far as 2.5 million years.

Most scientists agree that by about two million years ago, changing climatic and environmental conditions resulted in the evolution of several hominid species, including *Homo habilis* and *Homo erectus*. By about 1.5 to one million years ago, the latter apparently became dominant and developed basic tool-making abilities, evolving into *Homo sapiens* (modern humans). It's believed that these early Africans lived a nomadic existence, eventually migrating to inhabit other parts of the world, where local factors determined the racial characteristics of each group.

Today, remains of temporary camps and stone tools are found throughout Southern Africa, and one site in Namibia suggests that 750,000 years ago, these early people were hunting elephants and cutting up carcasses with large stone axes. By 150,000 years ago, people were using lighter spear heads, knives, saws and other tools for their hunting and gathering activities. (Archaeologists classify this period of tool making as the Stone Age, subdivided into the Early, Middle and Late stages, although the term applies to the people's level of technological development, rather than to a specific epoch.)

Early Khoisan Inhabitants

By about 30,000 years ago, the humans in Southern Africa had developed an organised hunting and gathering society. Use of fire was universal, tools were more sophisticated – made from wood and animal products as well as stone – and natural pigments were used for personal adornment. These Boskop people (named after the site in South Africa where their remains were discovered) are believed to be the ancestors of the San people (also called Bushmen), who still exist in isolated pockets today. Physical features of the San include a relatively small build (average males are about 1.3m tall), yellow to light-brown skin, slightly slanted eyes and dark hair growing in 'clumps' of tight curls.

By about 20,000 years ago, the San had made significant technological progress. Tools became smaller and better designed, which increased hunting efficiency and allowed time for further innovation and artistic pursuits. This stage is called the Microlithic Revolution because it was characterised by

The Bantu

The Bantu peoples could more accurately be called 'Bantu-speaking peoples' since the word 'Bantu' actually refers to a language group rather than a specific race. However, it has become a convenient term of reference for the black African peoples of Southern and Eastern Africa, even though the grouping is as ill-defined as 'American' or 'oriental'. The Bantu ethnic group is comprised of many subgroups or tribes, each with their own language, customs and traditions.

the working of small stones. The remains of microliths are often found alongside clear evidence of food gathering, consumption of shellfish and working of wood, bone and ostrich eggshell.

By about 10,000 years ago, the San began producing pottery. The artistic traditions of these people are also evidenced by the paintings that can be seen today in rock shelters and caves all over Southern Africa (see the boxed text 'Ancient Rock Art' later in this chapter). Despite these artistic and technical developments, the San had no knowledge of metal working, and thus remain classified as Stone Age people.

During this same period (around 8000BC), the San came under pressure from another group called the Khoikhoi (or Khoi-Khoi), known in more recent times as Hottentots. Their precise origins are uncertain, but most scientists agree that the San and Khoikhoi share a common ancestry, and that differences were slight, based more on habitat and lifestyle than significant physiological features. (The Khoikhoi were more sedentary, which may have allowed them to develop larger physiques.) They also shared a language group, characterised by distinctive 'click' sounds. Today these two peoples are regarded as one, termed Khoisan or Khoi-San, and are found only in remote parts of Namibia and Botswana. (For more information, see the boxed text 'The San' in the Botswana chapter; some details are also given in the Namibia chapter.)

The Bantu Migration

While the Khoisan were developing in Southern Africa, in West Africa another group with larger body types and darker skin was emerging: the Bantu. By around 3000 to 4000 years ago, they had developed iron-working skills which enabled them to make tools and weapons.

Their skills led to improved farming methods and the ability to migrate into the domains of neighbouring groups. Over 2000 years ago, this group, which is now known as the Bantu, moved into the Congo Basin and over the next thousand years, spread across present-day Uganda, Kenya and Tanzania and migrated south into Zambia, Malawi, Mozambique and other parts of Southern Africa. The term 'migration' when used in this context refers not to a specific or sudden upheaval, but to a sporadic and very slow spread over many hundreds of years. Typically, a group would move from valley to valley, or from one water source to the next. This process inevitably had a knock-on effect, as weaker tribes were constantly being 'moved on' by invaders from other areas.

At first, the Bantu in Southern Africa apparently lived in relative harmony with the original Khoisan inhabitants, trading goods, language and culture. However, as Bantu numbers increased, some Khoisan were conquered or absorbed by this more advanced group of peoples, while the remainder of the Khoisan hunters and gatherers were pushed further and further into areas that were less attractive for farming by the Bantu incomers.

Early Bantu Kingdoms

A feature of the Bantu culture was its strong social system, based on extended family or clan loyalties and dependencies, and generally centred around the rule of a chief. Some chiefdoms developed into powerful kingdoms, uniting many disparate tribes and covering large geographical areas.

One of the earliest Bantu kingdoms was Gokomere, in the uplands of Zimbabwe. The Gokomere people are thought to be the first occupants of the Great Zimbabwe site, near present-day Masvingo. Between AD 500 and 1000 the Gokomere and subsequent groups developed gold-mining techniques and produced progressively finer-quality ceramics, jewellery, textiles and soapstone carvings. Cattle herding became the mainstay of the whole community.

Early Traders

Meanwhile, from the latter half of the 1st millennium, Arabs from the lands around the Red Sea were sailing southwards along the eastern seaboard of Africa. They traded with the local Bantu inhabitants, who by this time had reached the coast, buying ivory, gold and slaves to take back to Arabia.

Between AD 1000 and 1500 the Arab-influenced Bantu founded several major settlements along the coast, from Mogadishu (in present-day Somalia) to Kilwa in southern Tanzania, including Lamu (Kenya) and Zanzibar (Tanzania). In Kenya and Tanzania particularly, the Bantu people were influenced by the Arabs, and a certain degree of inter-marriage occurred, so that gradually a mixed language and culture was created, called Swahili, which remains intact today. From southern Tanzania the Swahili-Arabs traded along the coast of present-day Mozambique, establishing bases at Quelimane and Ilha de Moçambique.

From the coast the Swahili-Arabs pushed into the interior, and developed a network of trade routes across much of East and Southern Africa. Ivory and gold continued to be sought after, but the demand for slaves grew considerably, and reached its zenith in the early-19th century when the Swahili-Arabs and dominant local tribes are reckoned to have either killed or sold into slavery 80,000 to 100,000 Africans per year.

Later Bantu Kingdoms

About the same time, quite separate from the development along the coast, the Bantu societies in the African interior were becoming increasingly organised. As early as the 11th century, the inhabitants of Great Zimbabwe had consolidated their position and come into contact with Arab-Swahili traders from the coast. Great Zimbabwe became the capital of the wealthiest and most powerful society in Southern Africa – its people the ancestors of today's Shona people – and reached the zenith of its powers around the 14th century (see History in the Zimbabwe chapter).

To the north, between the 14th and 16th centuries, another Bantu group called the Maravi (of whom the Chewa became the dominant tribe) arrived in Southern Africa from the Congo Basin and founded a powerful kingdom covering southern Malawi and parts of present-day Mozambique and Zambia. At about the same time the Tumbuka and the Phoka groups migrated into the north of Malawi, although their traditions do not agree on their origins (see History in the Malawi chapter).

During the 16th and 17th centuries, another Bantu group called the Herero migrated from the Zambezi Valley into present-day Namibia, where they came into conflict with the San and competed with the Khoikhoi for the best grazing lands. Eventually most indigenous groups (including the Damara, whose origins are unclear) submitted to the Herero. Only the Nama people, thought to be descended from early Khoikhoi groups, held out (see History in the Namibia chapter for more).

The power of the Bantu kingdoms started to falter in the late 18th and early 19th centuries, as two significant events had a tumultuous effect on the whole Southern African region. The first was a major dispersal of indigenous tribes, called the *difaqane*, and the second was a rapid increase in the number of European settlers.

The Difaqane

The *difaqane* (meaning 'forced migration' in Sotho, or *mfeqane*, 'the crushing', in Zulu) was a period of immense upheaval and suffering for the indigenous peoples of Southern Africa. It originated in the early 19th century when the Nguni tribes in modern KwaZulu-Natal (South Africa) changed rapidly from loosely organised collections of chiefdoms to the more centralised Zulu Nation. Based on its highly disciplined and powerful warrior army, the process began under Chief Dingiswayo, and reached its peak under the military commander Shaka Zulu.

Shaka was a ruthless conqueror and his reputation preceded him. Not surprisingly, tribes living in his path chose to flee, in turn displacing neighbours and causing disruption and terror across Southern Africa. Tribes displaced from Zululand include the Matabele, who settled in present-day Zimbabwe, while the Ngoni fled to Malawi and Zambia. Notable survivors were the Swazi and Basotho who, forged powerful kingdoms that became Swaziland and Lesotho.

European Colonisation & Settlement

Although there had been a European presence in Southern Africa for several hundred years, in 1820 the British Cape Colony saw a major influx of settlers. Around 5000 individuals were brought from Britain on the promise of fertile farmland around the Great Fish River, but in reality to form a buffer between the Boers (to the west of the river) and the Xhosa (to the east) who competed for territory. Within a few years many retreated to safer settlements to pick up the trades they had followed in Britain, and places such as Grahamstown developed into commercial and manufacturing centres.

From this point, European settlement rapidly spread from the Cape Colony to Natal and later to the Transvaal – especially after the discovery of gold and diamonds. In many cases Europeans were able to occupy land abandoned by African people following the difaqane (see History in the South Africa chapter for more information).

From South Africa, over the next 100 to 150 years, an ever-increasing number of Europeans settled in areas that became the colonies of Swaziland, Nyasaland (Malawi), Northern and Southern Rhodesia (Zambia and Zimbabwe), Bechuanaland (Botswana), Basotholand (Lesotho), German South West Africa (Namibia) and Portuguese East Africa (Mozambique). With this change, Southern Africans would never again be permitted to follow entirely traditional ways.

GEOGRAPHY

Except in the coastal regions, Southern Africa consists of a plateau rising from 1000m to 2000m, with escarpments on either side. Below the escarpments lies a coastal plain, which is narrowest in Namibia and widest in southern Mozambique.

The highest part of the region is Lesotho (often called the Kingdom in the Sky), and the neighbouring Drakensberg area, where many peaks rise above 3000m, including Thaban-Ntelenyana (3482m), which is the highest point in Southern Africa. Other highland areas include the Nyika Plateau (in northern Malawi and northeastern Zambia), Mt Mulanje (in southern Malawi), Eastern Highlands (between Zimbabwe and Mozambique) and the Khomas Hochland (Central Namibia). Lower and more isolated hills include the characteristic inselbergs of Namibia and South Africa's Karoo, and the lush Zomba Plateau in central Malawi.

Rivers of Southern Africa

Due to a general dearth of water over much of the region, Southern Africa's few perennial rivers attract not only people but wildlife. As a result, most of the region's national parks and many of its recreation sites lie along their banks.

The best-known of these is, of course, the Zambezi, which rises in Angola, then enters north-western Zambia and forms a short border between Namibia and Zambia before plummeting over the world-famous Victoria Falls. From there, it forms the border between Zambia and Zimbabwe, raging through Batoka Gorge to the artificial Lake Kariba. Beyond Kariba dam, it's joined by the Kafue before passing between Zimbabwe's Mana Pools and Zambia's Lower Zambezi National Parks. After the Luangwa flows in, it enters Mozambique, gets detained briefly behind the Lago Cahora Bassa dam, and then drains into the Indian Ocean north of Beira.

Other main rivers in Southern Africa include the Kunene (between Namibia and Angola), which flows into the Atlantic; the Okavango, which rises in Angola and flows across part of Namibia before it enters Botswana and spreads out into the Okavango Delta, the Limpopo, whose various source tributaries rise in Botswana and South Africa and form the border between South Africa and Botswana, then Zimbabwe, before entering Mozambique and reaching the Indian Ocean near Maputo; and the Orange, which rises in Lesotho and flows westwards across South Africa (where it's joined by the Vaal), eventually forming the border between Namibia and South Africa before flowing into the Atlantic at Alexander Bay.

The most prominent break in the Southern African plateau is the Great Rift Valley – a 6500km-long fissure where the continent of Africa is literally 'breaking apart' as tectonic forces attempt to rip the continent in two. This enormous fault in the Earth's crust runs from the Jordan Valley (between Israel and Jordan) in the north, and southward through the Red Sea, where it enters Ethiopia's Danakil Depression. At this point, it heads south across Kenya, Tanzania and Malawi, dividing in two at one stage, to form the great lakes of East Africa. This spreading zone ends at the present site of Lake Kariba, between Zimbabwe and Zambia.

CLIMATE

In Southern Africa, summer runs from about November to March/April, while winter is from May to July/August. By March and April, temperatures and rainfall drop and by May, the much drier winter season begins (snow may even fall on the highlands of South Africa and Lesotho). Through June and July the weather remains dry: warm on the coast but with a huge temperature range in the interior – from 20°C in the day to below freezing at night.

From August, temperatures begin to rise and by October, most of the region is hot, and the first rains are arriving in the north-ernmost regions.

In the Western Cape, which is the only part of Southern Africa to experience a Mediterranean (that is, winter rainfall) climate, the pattern is different. Here, summers are warm and sunny, while winter brings typically changeable and often rainy weather.

ECOLOGY & ENVIRONMENT

Environmental issues in Southern Africa are similar to those faced by the rest of the world: habitat and wildlife destruction, alien plant introduction, deforestation, soil erosion, water degradation and industrial pollution are all increasingly pertinent.

All over Southern Africa, an ever-growing human population places demands on the land and other natural resources. To conserve these resources – and the region's wild areas and ecosystems – most experts agree that population growth must be contained by improving education (especially for women) and raising living standards by fostering economic growth.

Many Africans believe conservation for its own sake is a luxurious Western notion that the people of Southern Africa simply cannot afford. To concede the benefits of conservation, locals need to see some of these benefits, and that's where tourism comes in. If the money earned from visitors coming to enjoy the animals and the environment stays in the pockets of locals (or in the country as a whole), then this will encourage wildlife and environmental protection.

Commercial hunting is also a form of tourism that stimulates local economies and thereby fosters 'conservation-minded' attitudes. In some parts of Southern Africa, areas of land are set aside for hunting, and hunters are charged 'trophy fees' to shoot animals.

The Ivory Debate

A major issue all over Southern Africa concerns elephant conservation, and both sides of the argument have an emotional following. Foreign interests generally hold that elephant herds should be conserved (or preserved) for their own sake or for aesthetic reasons; the local sentiment maintains that the elephant must justify its existence on long-term economic grounds – 'sustainable utilisation' – for the benefit of local people or for the country as a whole. In fact, the same arguments can be applied to most other wildlife.

Since the 1970s various factors have led to an increase in elephant poaching in many parts of Africa. By the late 1980s the price of 1kg of ivory (US$300) was three times the *annual* income of over 60% of Africa's population. Naturally, the temptation to poach was great, although the real money was made not by poachers – often villagers who were paid a pittance for the valuable tusks – but by the dealers, who acted with the full knowledge (and support) of senior government figures. In East Africa and in some Southern African countries – notably in Zambia – elephant populations were reduced by up to 90% in about 15 years. But in other Southern African countries where parks and reserves are well-managed – notably Zimbabwe, South Africa, Botswana and Namibia – elephant populations were relatively unaffected.

In 1990, following a massive campaign by conservation organisations, a world body called the Convention on International Trade in Endangered Species (Cites) internationally banned the import and export of ivory. It also increased funding for antipoaching measures.

Although elephant populations recovered in some ravaged areas, Southern African human populations continued to grow, and another problem surfaced. Elephants eat huge quantities of foliage but in the past, herds would eat their fill then migrate to another area, allowing time for the vegetation to regenerate. However, an increasing human population pressed the elephants into smaller and smaller areas – mostly around national parks – and the herds were forced to eat everything available. In many places, the bush began to look as if an atom bomb had hit.

In some places, park authorities are currently facing elephant overpopulation. While Botswana has the most serious problem, some parts of Namibia's Caprivi region are suffering from the spillover from Botswana. Proposed solutions include relocation (where herds are permanently transplanted to other areas) and a pioneering contraception project, in which breeding cows are injected with a 'pill' equivalent. The only other alternative is to cull herds, sometimes in large numbers; this seems a bizarre paradox, but illustrates the seriousness of the problem, and at present the other options remain experimental and limited in their effect.

As a side effect, culling provided large quantities of legal ivory, which in the past could have been sold to raise funds for elephant management. However, the Cites ban stopped that. With the renewed culling programmes, some Southern African countries called for the trade to be legalised again, in order to fund conservation projects. They argued that in this way, the elephant would again become a valuable resource and provide local governments and people with the incentive to ensure its survival.

In March 1999, Botswana, Namibia, South Africa and Zimbabwe were permitted by Cites to resume strictly controlled ivory exports. Despite these measures, opponents of the trade warned that elephant poaching would increase in other parts of Africa, as poached ivory could now be laundered through the legal trade. Sure enough, 1999 saw an increase in poaching all over Africa – from Kenya to Gabon – and in late 1999, a Zimbabwean newspaper reported that 84 elephants had been poached in Zimbabwe that year.

Opponents of the trade protested loudly, but the Zimbabwean government, for one, dismissed the opposition by attributing it to animal rights campaigners attempting to sabotage the trade. Either way, it is still too early to say if the resumed trade will have overall financial benefits in Southern Africa. The ban came under review again in mid-2000, and efforts by Botswana, Namibia, South Africa and Zimbabwe to expand the ivory trade were unsuccessful.

This is unacceptable to many people, however for people who lack other resources the trophy fees are large (thousands of US dollars for animals such as elephants or lions) and an invaluable source of income. Paradoxically, the financial benefits of hunting tourism encourages the management and protection of these animals and their environment.

The Communal Areas Management Programme for Indigenous Resources (Campfire) is a project in Zimbabwe where local villagers 'own' the elephants and other animals that inhabit their traditional lands, and they can generate funds from controlled hunting or photographic safaris run there.

Similarly, in Namibia, the Save the Rhino Trust (SRT) promotes conservation education and public sponsorship of individual animals to provide local people with alternative sources of income. Namibia also has a system of community camps sponsored by the Namibia Community-Based Tourism Association (Nacobta). In Botswana, several communities in the Okavango Delta have set up their own tourism bases, including the popular Okavango Polers Trust. The idea is that the presence of wildlife will draw more vitiors and bring income to their areas.

In Zambia, the Admanc programme and the South Luangwa Area Management Unit (Slamu) scheme allow local people to benefit financially from their wildlife populations, getting a share from revenue paid by tourists and hunters.

Income is also generated by the jobs that hunting and wildlife tourism create, such as guides, game rangers, tour guides and various posts in the associated hotels, lodges and camps. Further spin-offs include the sale of crafts and curios.

For information on field guides for Southern Africa, see Field Guides under Books in the Regional Facts for the Visitor chapter.

FLORA

The following rundown of major vegetation zones (arranged roughly south to north, and from the coasts to the inland areas) is greatly simplified, but provides a useful overview.

Southern Africa's distinctive fynbos zone occurs around the Cape Peninsula and along the south coast of South Africa, interspersed with pockets of temperate forest, where you'll find trees such as the large yellowwood, with its characteristic 'peeling' bark.

The west coast of Southern Africa consists largely of desert, which receives less than 100mm of precipitation per year. Vegetation consists of tough grasses, shrubs and euphorbias, plus local specialities, including the bizarre *welwitschia* (a miniature conifer) and *kokerboom* (a type of aloe).

Along the east coast of Southern Africa, the natural vegetation is coastal bush – a mixture of light woodland and dune forest; high rainfall has also created pockets of subtropical forest.

In South Africa's Karoo, typical vegetation includes grasses, plus bushes and succulents that bloom colourfully after the rains. Much original Karoo vegetation has been destroyed since the introduction of grazing animals and alien plants.

To the east lie the temperate grasslands of the 'highveld' and to the north, a vast arid savanna, characterised by acacia scrub which takes in most of central Namibia, much of Botswana, and the northern parts of South Africa.

To the north and east is the woodland savanna, consisting of mainly broadleaf deciduous trees. Dry woodland, dominated by mopane trees, covers northern Namibia, northern Botswana, the Zimbabwean Lowveld and the Zambezi Valley. In wetter areas – central Zimbabwe, northern Mozambique and most of Zambia and Malawi – the dominant vegetation is moist woodland, or *miombo*. A mix of the two, which occurs in northeastern South Africa and central Mozambique is known as mixed woodland, or 'bushveld'.

Small pockets of high ground all over the region have a vegetation zone termed afromontane, which occurs in highland areas where open grasslands are interspersed with heathland and isolated forests.

FAUNA

Wildlife-viewing is undoubtedly one of Southern Africa's main attractions, and it won't disappoint. Nowhere else on earth are there such varieties and quantities of large mammal species (for information on the most prominent of these, see the 'Wildlife Guide' special section in this book). While nearly everyone thrills at the sight of large animals, the region also supports a wonderful array of birds, reptiles, amphibians and

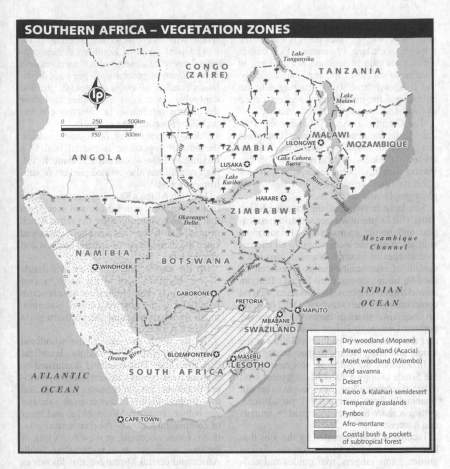

SOUTHERN AFRICA – VEGETATION ZONES

Legend:
- Dry woodland (Mopane)
- Mixed woodland (Acacia)
- Moist woodland (Miombo)
- Arid savanna
- Desert
- Karoo & Kalahari semidesert
- Temperate grasslands
- Fynbos
- Afro-montane
- Coastal bush & pockets of subtropical forest

even insects (but often in less-appreciated quantities).

We won't attempt to describe each of the boggling number of fauna species you're likely to see, but a large number of useful local and international field guides do (see Field Guides under Books in the Regional Facts for the Visitor chapter).

Birds

Birds rate highly among the many attractions of Southern Africa. For sheer abundance and variety, few parts of the world offer as much for the bird-watcher, whether expert or beginner. Southern Africa is host to nearly 10% of the world's bird species – over 900 species have been recorded in the region. More than 130 are endemic to Southern

Africa or are near-endemic, also being found only in adjoining territories to the north.

This astonishing variety can be attributed to the number of habitats. The climate ranges from cool temperate with winter rainfall in the southwest, to a hot tropical zone with summer rains in the northeast.

These habitats are well defined and can be separated into eight main categories: forest; savanna-woodland; fynbos; grassland-semidesert; Karoo (South Africa's desert-like interior); the Namib Desert; freshwater areas (rivers, marshes, lakes, pans, and their adjoining shores); and seashore areas (including areas of brackish water where fresh water meets salt water in lagoons and estuaries).

All the national parks and reserves are home to a great range of birdlife, especially

Wildlife Viewing

Whether you're viewing wildlife from a vehicle or on foot, early morning or evening are the best times, as this is when most animals are active. The following tips will help you get the most out of watching them:

- Wildlife viewing is generally best in the dry season, when sparse vegetation opens up the view and thirsty animals congregate around water sources.
- Be patient – take time to notice the environment. After spotting an animal, stop to look around and you'll usually notice a lot more activity. Staking out a waterhole for several hours will almost always reward you with a greater understanding of what's going on
- If another vehicle has beat you to a hot spot, whatever is happening, it's polite to stay back and not block their view.
- Warthogs, baboons, zebras, giraffes and many antelope species happily associate with each other, so it's common to observe several species at one time. However, the presence of feeding herbivores does not preclude the possibility of a predator in the vicinity, so be alert for stalking lions.
- If you want to observe wildlife, don't dazzle it with shocking pink, fluorescent yellow or even (unlikely in Africa), freshly scrubbed white. Wear natural earthy colours and avoid bright jewellery that can catch the sunlight.
- Don't startle animals with any quick movements.
- Don't forget your binoculars, which will allow you to turn a speck in the distance into something that's somewhat more interesting, and will also enhance bird-watching opportunities.

Mana Pools, Victoria Falls, Hwange and Gonarezhou National Parks in Zimbabwe; Etosha, Mudumu and Mamili National Parks in Namibia; and Chobe National Park and virtually any part of the Okavango Delta in Botswana.

In South Africa, bird-watching is especially fruitful at Kruger and Pilanesberg National Parks in the northeast; Ndumo and Mkuzi Game Reserves, Lake St Lucia and Oribi Gorge in KwaZulu-Natal; and Karoo, West Coast and Bontebok National Parks in Western Cape.

In Malawi, the areas around Lake Malawi are rewarding, as are the various woodlands of Liwonde, Kasungu and Lengwe National Parks. Although not a reserve, the Elephant Marsh in Southern Malawi also has particularly rich birdlife.

In Zambia, top-class bird-watching areas include the plains of Barotseland and the swamps of Lake Bangweulu, as well as Kafue, South Luangwa and Lochinvar National Parks.

Mozambique has over half of all bird species identified in Southern Africa; on Inhaca Island alone, about 300 bird species have been recorded. The Chimanimani Mountains, Mt Gorongosa, Mt Namúli and Bazaruto Archipelago are of particular note for bird-watching.

Reptiles

Southern Africa's most notable reptile is the Nile crocodile. Once abundant in lakes and rivers across the region, today its numbers have been greatly reduced by hunting and habitat destruction, and it is now classed as 'threatened'. Female crocodiles lay up to 80 eggs at a time, depositing them in sandy areas above the high-water line. After three months incubation in the hot sand, the young emerge. Newly hatched crocs are avocado green in colour; as they age, they darken to nearly black. Many live up to 70 years.

Southern Africa has a complement of both venomous and harmless snakes, but most fear humans and you'll be lucky to even see one. The largest snake – although generally harmless to humans – is the python, which grows to over 5m in length. The puff adder, which inhabits mainly mountain and desert areas, grows to about 1m long. Like all reptiles it enjoys sunning itself, but it is very slow and sometimes trodden on by unwary hikers – with very unpleasant results.

Other seriously dangerous snakes include the fat and lazy gaboon viper; the black mamba, which inhabits dry areas; the boomslang, which lives in trees; the spitting cobra, which needs no introduction; and the zebra snake, which is one of the world's most aggressive serpentine sorts. If you're

Close Encounters

Although you'll hear plenty of horror stories, the threat of attack by wild animals in Africa is largely exaggerated and problems are extremely rare. However, it is important to remember that most African animals are *wild* and that wherever you go on safari, particularly on foot, there is always an element of danger.

The tips below will further diminish your chances of a close encounter of the unpleasant kind, and on organised safaris you should always get advice from your guide.

- Buffaloes are usually docile in a herd, but lone individuals can be unpredictable, making them particularly dangerous. If you encounter a buffalo while walking in the bush, back away quietly and slowly. If it charges, climb the nearest tree or dive into the bush and 'run like a rat'.
- Elephants certainly aren't bloodthirsty creatures, but they are large, and it's said that an elephant never forgets. Those who have had trouble from humans previously may feel the need to take revenge. If an elephant holds its trunk erect and sniffs the air, it probably detects your presence and may charge rather than retreat. In this case you should be the one who retreats – but move away slowly. When camping, don't keep fresh fruit in your tent, as it tends to attract elephants and may invite them to explore further.
- Hippos aren't normally vicious, but they may attack if you get too close or come between them and the water, or between adults and young. It's true that hippos kill more humans in Africa than any other animal. When boating or canoeing, steer well away from them, and never pitch a tent in an open area along vegetated riverbanks, as it's probably a hippo run.
- Crocodiles also present risks, and when they're snoozing in the sun, they look more like logs or branches. Never swim, paddle or even collect water without first making a careful assessment of what's occupying the water in question. Local advice is best but if it's not available, assume the worst.
- Hyenas are potentially dangerous, although they're normally just after your food. They aren't particularly fussy either: they'll eat boots and equipment left outside a tent, and have been known to gnaw right through vehicle tyres! However, there are plenty of frightening tales of hyenas attacking people sleeping in an open tent – although this is rare, it's still wise to zip up.
- Leopards are normally active only at night, so you're unlikely to encounter one on foot, although some have become accustomed to humans and may approach lodges and camp sites after dark. Only very rarely do they present any threat to humans.
- Lions have also been known to investigate lodges and camp sites. If you're camping out in the bush, zip your tent up completely. If you hear a large animal outside, lie still and don't try to leave your tent. While walking in the bush, if you encounter a lion try to avoid an adrenalin rush (easier said than done) and don't turn and run. If you act like prey, the lion could respond accordingly.
- Rhinos tend to be wary of humans, although they may charge vehicles that get too close. If you are caught out on foot and can't immediately climb a tree, face the charge and step to one side at the last moment in bullfight style (again, easier said than done).

tramping in snake country, be sure to watch your step and keep away from anything you don't recognise as nonvenomous.

Lizards are ubiquitous from the hot and dusty Kaokoveld (Namibia) to the cool highlands of the Nyika Plateau (Malawi), and from the bathroom ceiling to the kitchen sink. The largest of these is the water monitor, a docile creature that reaches over 2m in length and is often seen lying around water holes, perhaps dreaming of being a crocodile. Two others frequently seen are chameleons and geckos – the latter often in hotel rooms; they are quite harmless and help to control the bug population.

NATIONAL PARKS

The term 'national park' actually has a very precise definition in Southern Africa, but is often used as a catch-all term to include wildlife reserves, forest parks, or any government conservation area; there are also several privately-owned reserves, as well as a growing number of transfrontier parks, which combine adjacent parks in adjoining countries. Most parks in Southern Africa conserve habitats and wildlife species and provide recreational facilities for visitors. South African parks are among the best-managed in the world, and most of the rest are quite good, although Zimbabwean parks are rapidly declining and those in Mozambique are still being developed.

In most parks and reserves harbouring large (and potentially dangerous) animals, visitors must travel in vehicles or on an organised safari, but several do allow hiking or walking with a ranger or safari guide.

Nearly all parks charge an entrance fee, and in almost all cases foreigners pay substantially more than local residents or citizens. This may rankle some visitors – and some parks are seriously overpriced – but the idea is that residents and citizens pay taxes to the governments that support the parks, and therefore are entitled to discounts.

Park Accommodation

Most parks and reserves contain accommodation, so you can stay overnight and take wildlife drives in the early morning and evening. Accommodation ranges from simple camp sites to luxury lodges run by companies that have concessions inside the parks. Prices vary to match the quality of facilities. In some countries you can just turn up and find a place to camp or stay; in other countries reservations are advised (or are essential at busy times). For details, see individual country chapters.

GOVERNMENT & POLITICS

The politics of Southern Africa were dominated through the 1980s by South Africa's declared state of emergency, continued implementation of the apartheid laws and political disruption of neighbouring states. To counter this, the other Southern African countries formed the Southern African Development Coordination Conference (SADCC) or as it is unofficially known, the 'Frontline States'. Notable exceptions were Malawi, which refused to ostracise South Africa, and Botswana, which considered itself a Frontline State but continued to trade openly with South Africa. Both were well rewarded with valuable aid from Pretoria.

Since the 1994 democratic elections, South Africa is back in the fold. Several South African state and private-sector organisations have teamed up with counterparts in neighbouring countries to further trade links and intragovernmental contacts, and South Africa is now a leading member of the renamed Southern African Development Community (SADC). South Africa has also been re-admitted to the British Commonwealth, which includes most other countries in the region. Intriguingly, Mozambique has also joined the Commonwealth, though it was never a British colony.

For further information – including the latest on the lamentable situation in Zimbabwe – see the individual country chapters.

EDUCATION

All the countries in Southern Africa have state education systems that follow patterns established by their colonial powers, ie, a primary stage for all children, a secondary stage for most and a tertiary stage for a few academic achievers or for the wealthy.

Officially, those who pass relevant examinations can go to secondary school and university. In reality, which children go to school and how far up the ladder they progress is determined by their family income rather than by academic performance; poor children may not be able to afford school fees or extra items such as uniforms and books, and may be kept away from school to work in the fields or to provide income from other employment.

Across the region, these problems are compounded by restrictions on government revenue available for education. The end result is simply not enough schools to cater for the number of children – particularly in rural areas. Many schools have to operate two 'shifts', with one lot of children studying in the morning, and another in the afternoon. Even so, classes may hold over 100 pupils, sitting three or four to a desk and sharing books and pens. At the same time, teachers are grossly underpaid. Consequently, literacy rates across Southern Africa are low.

A tragic side note to this discussion illustrates another serious problem. In some areas, sexual abuse of girls by teachers is an enormous problem, and as a result, many girls are reluctant to attend school. The perpetrators often cite low wages and poor working conditions as justification for partaking of this perceived 'fringe benefit'. Sadly, national and local governments and individuals have so far done little to express their intolerance for such unacceptable behaviour.

National Parks in Southern Africa

Nearly all the world-famous national parks in the region offer excellent wildlife-viewing, and among the lesser-known parks and reserves are some real gems. The latter are usually smaller and often quieter than their more famous counterparts, with rewarding wildlife viewing and bird-watching opportunities.

Botswana

Makgadikgadi & Nxai Pan – vast and remote, this is the site of Southern Africa's last great wildlife migrations

Chobe – a large and varied park with both a wildlife-rich riverfront and broad savanna plains. It's particularly known for its large elephant herds.

Moremi – this beautiful park takes in a portion of the expansive and stunning Okavango Delta

Central Kalahari – Botswana's largest national park takes in the widest horizons you'll ever likely to see

Malawi

Liwonde – a well-managed lowland park that is growing in status and has good elephant viewing

Mt Mulanje – the 'island in the sky', with sheer peaks and excellent hiking

Nyika – unique montane grassland area, with endless views and splendid horse riding

Lengwe – this lovely park in southern Malawi protects a range of antelopes (including the rare nyala), as well as diverse bird species

Mozambique

Bazaruto Archipelago – a tropical paradise of reefs and islands and beaches, and opportunities for sailing and diving

Great Limpopo Transfrontier – the former Limpopo National Park has been combined with South Africa's Kruger and Zimbabwe's Gonarezhou parks to form this enormous conservation area. Mozambique's portion was devastated by war, but has now been stocked with wildlife from elsewhere.

Namibia

Waterberg Plateau Park – this sky island features walking tracks and a repository for endangered wildlife

Fish River Canyon – Africa's grand canyon presents one of the most spectacular scenes on the continent and Namibia's most popular hiking track. Surrounding lodges offer diverse activities.

Etosha – this vast park is one of Africa's most renowed wildlife-viewing venues – and deservedly so. It features an enormous pan and numerous water holes, and is one of the best places in the region to see black rhinos.

Namib-Naukluft – one of the world's largest national parks, this stunning and magical desert wilderness takes in world-famous sand dunes and wild desert mountains with excellent hiking.

SOCIETY & CONDUCT

In Southern Africa, two societies and cultures (Western and African) run in parallel, and they rarely cross. As you might expect, in a Western situation social customs are similar to those in Europe, although often a touch more formal – but at the same time more friendly – than in other parts of the Western world. For example, Afrikaners will often shake hands and say their name, even if you're only meeting them briefly. While you'll meet locals of European origin and 'Europeanised' black Africans all over the region, the societies and cultures are predominantly African (see under Social Graces in the Regional Facts for the Visitor chapter for more information).

Happily, short of public nudity or openly vocal criticism of the government, there aren't really any unforgivable faux pas that must be avoided (for foreigners, anyway). However, in most places, any open displays of affection are frowned upon and show insensitivity to local sentiments.

RELIGION

Most people in Southern Africa follow Christianity or traditional religion, often

National Parks in Southern Africa

South Africa

Drakensberg – this mountain region may be low on 'big game', but it's high on awe-inspiring mountain scenery and extensive hiking opportunities

St Lucia – this coastal wetland in a remote part of the country presents a unique ecosystem of global significance

Tsitsikamma – a lovely coastal park with forests, fynbos, beaches, rocky headlands and a world-renowned hiking trail

Hluhluwe-Umfolozi – near the Zulu heartland, this bushland park is best-known for its rhino populations

Kgalagadi Transfrontier – recently combined with Botswana's Mabuasehube-Gemsbok National Park, this wild corner of the Kalahari is now one of Africa's largest protected areas. The desert landscape supports a surprising amount of wildlife.

Kruger – South Africa's most popular national park covers an enormous area and offers the classic wildlife experience, along with comfortable and well-organised facilities

Zambia

Kafue – massive and genuinely wild, with an impressive range of habitats and wildlife

Kasanka – pioneering, privately managed park, noted for sightings of the rare sitatunga antelope

Lower Zambezi – spectacular setting, escarpments and plains, plus the great river itself. It's best appreciated on multi-day canoe trips.

South Luangwa – this wild and pristine wildlife park is growing more popular, but many still consider it 'Africa's best-kept secret'

Mosi-oa-Tunya – taking in both Zambia's portion of Victoria Falls and a small game park, this park is one of the country's most visited attractions

Zimbabwe

Chizarira – with three distinct environments and spectacular scenery, this is certainly Zimbabwe's most beautiful wildlife park, and visitors are likely to have it to themselves

Matusadona – with both lakefront and mountain habitats south of Lake Kariba, this rewarding wildlife park is known for its enormous buffalo herds and lion populations

Nyanga, Vumba, Chimanimani – these three parks in the misty Eastern Highlands offer mountain retreats and excellent hiking opportunities

Zambezi National Park – this accessible park immediately west of Victoria Falls enjoys large wildlife populations and great canoeing opportunities

Hwange – Zimbabwe's best-known wildlife park holds one of the densest wildlife populations in Africa. It's conveniently close to Victoria Falls.

Mana Pools – combines the Zambezi Escarpment, a swathe of bushland and beautiful riverine scenery to create a varied wildlife experience. Canoe safaris are popular.

---

combining aspects of both. All the Western-style Christian churches are represented (Catholics, Protestants, Baptists, Adventists etc) – most of which were introduced in colonial times by European missionaries. Many indigenous Christian faiths have also been established, ranging from a small congregation meeting in a simple hut to vast organisations with millions of followers such as the Zion and Apostolic churches in Zimbabwe and South Africa.

Islam is also followed in some areas. People brought to South Africa by colonial authorities from India or Malaysia brought their religion with them, and in Malawi and on the Mozambique coast, Islam was originally introduced by Swahili-Arab traders.

There are many traditional religions in Southern Africa, but no great temples or written scriptures. For outsiders, beliefs can be complex (and to the Western mind, illogical) as can the rituals and ceremonies that surround them. Most traditional religions are animist – based on the attribution of life or consciousness to natural objects or phenomena – and many accept the existence of a Supreme Being, with whom communication

Dress Codes

Currently, none of the Southern African countries have any dress regulations. Malawi was once a celebrated exception because women visitors were required by law to wear skirts that covered the knees, while men were required to have short hair and tidy beards. This came about when former president Hastings Banda learned that locals were offended by women wearing shorts, especially in the Muslim north. (Oddly enough, this didn't prevent the government putting out glossy tourist brochures advertising Lake Malawi beaches with photos of bikini-clad babes.) The law was dropped in 1994, but it remains insensitive to wander around with most of your legs showing (except on lake beaches, or for hiking or sports).

If you do wear skimpy clothing in most parts of the region, don't be surprised if kids laugh, adults treat you with disdain and in the case of women, some young guns see you as easy prey. Naturally this doesn't apply on most beaches or in private lodges.

However the tropical sun is still a factor to consider; from a practical perspective, keeping reasonably covered with loose-fitting clothing may decrease your risk of sunburn or heatstroke. Look around – the only people wearing shorts or tatty clothes are kids, labourers and the poor. It should then be clear why some officials and other locals treat scruffy, bare-legged travellers with contempt.

is possible through the intercession of ancestors. Thus, ancestors play a particularly strong role. Their principal function is to protect the tribe or family, and they may on occasion show their pleasure (eg, a good harvest) or displeasure (eg, a member of the family becoming sick).

Witchcraft

Within many traditional African religions, there is a belief in spells and magic (usually called witchcraft or in some places, *mutu*), which is a complex subject, and may be hard for Westerners to appreciate or understand. In brief simplistic terms it goes like this: physical or mental illnesses are often ascribed to a spell or curse having been put on the sufferer. Often, a relative or villager is suspected of being the 'witch' who placed the curse, usually for reasons of spite

or jealousy. A traditional doctor, also called a diviner or witchdoctor, is then required to hunt out the witch and cure the victim. This is done in different ways in various parts of the region, and may involve the use of herbs, divining implements, prayers, chanting, dance or placing the spell in a bottle and casting it into a remote spot (if you find such a bottle in the bush, don't touch it!).

However, services do not come free of charge, and many witchdoctors demand high payments – up to US$20, in countries where an average month's earnings may be little more than this. It's a sad fact that the 'witches' who are unearthed are frequently those who cannot defend themselves – the sick, the old or the very poorest members of society. There are even reports of very young children being accused by witchdoctors of harbouring evil spirits.

Regional Facts for the Visitor

This chapter describes general aspects of travel in the Southern African region. For specifics about travel in the individual countries, see the relevant chapters.

SUGGESTED ITINERARIES

Southern Africa is a large and diverse region, and your itinerary will of course depend on your available time and money. The other main factor affecting your trip will be your form of transport. Many travellers use buses and trains for their entire trip, which are economical and adventurous, but also slow and will almost certainly require a bit of hitching to reach most sites of interest. A rental car cuts these delays and is also near-essential for access to national parks.

Many travellers combine public transport with a few days or weeks in a rental car, sometimes teaming up with others to split the costs. It's also possible to purchase a car in Southern Africa, tour the region, and then sell it. For details, see the Getting Around the Region chapter near the start of the book and the Getting Around sections in individual country chapters.

The Quick Trip

It's unlikely that international visitors will come to Southern Africa just for one week, but those who do tend to fly into Cape Town, or another large city, and spend the entire time exploring that city and its immediate hinterlands.

If you're short on time, it's advisable to limit yourself to one or two places rather than just skim the surface in a mad rush to fit in more sites. For 10 days or two weeks, the 'four corners' area of Zimbabwe, Zambia, Botswana and Namibia is packed with highlights and lends itself well to a short visit. The best (and most economical) point to fly in to is probably Vic Falls, via Harare or Johannesburg. From there, you can cross over to Livingstone to see the Zambian side of the falls. After this, you have a range of choices: Chobe National Park (from Kasane, Botswana) or the Okavango Delta (from Maun, Botswana); one or two of the national parks in Zambia (such as Kafue or Lower Zambezi); one or two national parks in Zimbabwe (Mana Pools, Hwange,

Matusadona or Matobo); or a traverse of Namibia's Caprivi Strip to reach Botswana's Okavango Panhandle.

Another option for two weeks might be the South African parks and coast of Kwa-Zulu-Natal, possibly combined with a quick jaunt into Kruger National Park, Lesotho, Swaziland or southern Mozambique. South Africa's spectacular Western Cape is also filled with interest; perhaps begin in Cape Town and make a circuit through the Winelands and the Garden Route.

Alternatively, head straight for Malawi, which is a compact country that lends itself to a two-week visit. Logically, this would be combined with a visit to Zambia's South Luangwa National Park, which is readily accessible from Lilongwe.

One to Three Months

With one month to travel, your possibilities increase to three or four of the options listed under The Quick Trip. With two months and your own set of wheels, you could probably buzz around all these places. By public transport (maybe including a regional flight) you'd do well to choose a region (Zimbabwe, Botswana and Namibia; South Africa, Lesotho and Swaziland; or Malawi, Zambia and Mozambique) and see it well. Alternatively, combine Mozambique with eastern South Africa, or Namibia with western South Africa.

In The Big Trip, following, we suggest a six-month 'grand tour', but those with half that time may want to consider doing just half the circuit.

The Big Trip

Those who are able to spend six months or more in Southern Africa will have time to discover many of its wonders – and may even extend their itineraries to spend 'just a few more days' in a place they've visited and fallen in love with. For those who don't have that luxury but want to see the regional highlights, the following grand tour takes in must-see sites, as well as places the authors have especially enjoyed. Detailed itineraries for each country are included in the relevant country chapters to help you plan side trips beyond this suggested Big Trip route.

The Top 10 Highlights

Southern Africa contains many of the world's most inspiring wonders, so it's worth noting some of the region's icons, which few will want to miss. At the risk of omitting someone's favourite spot, we've come up with a list of 10 must-see sites. This section will provide a bit of direction for those who want to plan a rewarding trip. Note that all these sites – plus plenty more places which may be equally worthwhile – are thoroughly covered in the individual country chapters. For more inspiration, see the Highlights list at the start of every country chapter.

Victoria Falls (p594) If Southern Africa has one world-renowned destination, it's Victoria Falls, which is shared by Zimbabwe and Zambia. Each side enjoys a distinctive and contrasting character, and most visitors will want to see both. Adrenaline junkies will find joy in the boggling variety of activities on offer here, including a plunge down the world's wildest commercially rafted river.

Cape Town (p435) One of the world's most beautifully located cities, Cape Town is *the* place in Southern Africa to indulge your senses: taste fine wines and food inside gracious old Cape Dutch wineries; hear tales of imprisonment on Robben Island; tramp the breathtaking Cape Peninsula; or admire the views from Table Mountain's summit (and then abseil or paraglide off it).

Okavango Delta (p125) The world's largest inland delta, formed where the Okavango River flows into Botswana's Kalahari sands, the Okavango Delta is a convoluted maze of lethargic waterways, rich wetlands and palm islands. This watery wonderland creates a paradise for vegetation and wildlife, as well as the people who have inhabited it for centuries.

Kruger National Park (p531) Huge, varied and thick with wildlife big and small, Kruger National Park is justifiably renowned. It's well run, affordable and boasts all of the Big Five animals. Sip a sundowner above a lake of belching hippos; take a night drive in search of elusive leopards; or if you have the time, hike, camp and track wildlife with rangers.

Most of this trip is accessible by public transport, but in wildlife parks and several other cases (eg, Sossusvlei in Namibia and the Okavango Delta in Botswana), you'll need to hire a vehicle or join a safari.

Normally, it's best to fly into either Johannesburg or Cape Town. This tour begins in Cape Town, but because it's a circuit, it's also possible to begin in Jo'burg. It can be done in either direction, obviously, but here it's described counter-clockwise.

After a good look around Cape Town, the Cape Peninsula and the Winelands, head east onto the Garden Route, possibly detouring north at George to visit Oudtshoorn, the Swartberg Pass and Prince Albert. Continuing east, it's worth a stop at Tsitsikamma Coastal National Park before continuing to Durban via Grahamstown, Transkei, and the Wild Coast. From Durban, head inland to Ladysmith and the Natal Drakensberg Range, then cross into Lesotho at dramatic Sani Pass. From there, you can explore Lesotho and either return the way you came, or make your way to Maseru and take better roads back to Ladysmith and then to Mbabane, Swaziland.

After a look around Swaziland, make a beeline for Jo'burg and Pretoria (or skip them altogether and make your way from Mbabane to Nelspruit).

At this stage you'll of course want to visit Kruger National Park. After returning to Nelspruit, you can enter Mozambique (for this trip, be sure to have a multi-entry visa) and head straight for Maputo. Heading up the coast, it's worth stopping at Vilankulo for a visit to the idyllic Bazaruto Archipelago. (If you want to go straight to Ilha de Moçambique, hop on a plane – via Beira, with almost certain delays – to Nampula, or first travel to Beira overland and fly from there.)

The next leg is to Chimoio, where you cross the border to Mutare, in Zimbabwe, possibly hiking in Chimanimani and Nyanga National Parks and the Bvumba Mountains. From Mutare, take a bus to Masvingo for a visit to the ruins of Great Zimbabwe before heading north to Harare. After a look around the capital city, find transport to Blantyre, in Malawi, via Mozambique (transit visa required).

A great side trip from Blantyre would be to Mt Mulanje for a bit of hiking. Then

The Top 10 Highlights

Lake Malawi (p196) The vast crystalline waters of Lake Malawi offer some of the finest swimming, snorkelling, kayaking, diving and boating activities in the whole of Africa. Along its shores, you can also go horse riding, hiking and exploring – or just lazing. The atmosphere along the lakeshore varies from pure party to remote isolation, and views are always exquisite.

The Namib Dunes (p368) Along the western coast of Namibia stretches an enormous dunefield, featuring 300m-high sand mountains with unforgettable colours and a sense of utter desolation. Although they're accessible in several places, most travellers head for the dramatic and colourful vleis around Sossusvlei.

Ilha de Moçambique (p293) With its time-warp atmosphere, fascinating cultural blend, and azure surrounding waters, Ilha de Moçambique is one of Southern Africa's most exotic destinations. It has a good selection of accommodation and relatively easy access – once you reach the coast. Cross the bridge from the mainland and you'll step back four centuries.

Etosha National Park (p345) One of the great wildlife parks of Africa, Etosha consists of dusty plains and bushland surrounding an immense ephemeral pan. For intense wildlife-viewing it can't be beaten, and changing seasons – especially the dramatic arrival of the first rains – are the stuff of David Attenborough documentaries. What's more, comfortable facilities make it accessible to almost everyone.

Great Zimbabwe (p726) The greatest medieval city in sub-Saharan Africa, Great Zimbabwe provides clear evidence of a sophisticated civilisation. You can stay near the ruins or along the mighty Lake Mutirikwe nearby; otherwise, enjoy a day trip from the charming town of Masvingo.

Kafue National Park (p655) Zambia's largest national park, Kafue National Park is classic wildlife country. It is the best place to admire the Big Five, as well as cheetahs and numerous antelopes. Reasonably accessible from Lusaka, most lodges and camps in Kafue can arrange wildlife drives, boat trips or walking safaris with armed rangers.

retrace your steps and head for Liwonde, where you can visit Liwonde National Park. If you want to reach Ilha de Moçambique, plan on a strictly backpacker-standard journey. First, head for the Mangochi–Mandimba border crossing, at the southern end of Lake Malawi, into Mozambique. There you'll have to hitch on a daily truck to Cuamba, then take the slow train to Nampula, where morning minibuses will get you to Ilha de Moçambique. Then you'll have to retrace your steps to Liwonde, in Malawi, or – if one-way is gruelling enough – splash out on the weekly flight between Nampula and Blantyre. Alternatively, head up the coast into Tanzania (visa required) and return to Malawi via the road to Lake Malawi.

Once you're back in Malawi, aim north towards Lilongwe via Monkey Bay, Senga Bay and other Lake Malawi highlights. It's also worthwhile making a side trip to northern Malawi to visit Nkhata Bay and Nyika National Park.

Back in Lilongwe, cross over into Zambia and spend a couple of days at South Luangwa National Park. After marvelling at the wildlife, retrace your steps as far as Chipata and

then continue to the Zambian capital, Lusaka. Along the way, you may want to make a side trip to Lower Zambezi National Park for a canoe safari before returning to Lusaka for a return excursion to fabulous Kafue National Park. Back in Lusaka, continue southwest to Livingstone.

At this stage, it's worth spending a bit of time visiting this 'four corners' area of Zimbabwe, Zambia, Botswana and Namibia. After crossing into Zimbabwe, it's worth a side trip by rail to Bulawayo, via Hwange National Park, for a visit to Matobo National Park. In Bulawayo, you can either choose to return directly to Vic Falls and there find transport to Kasane, in Botswana, or cross over into Francistown, in Botswana, and then take minibuses to Nata and Kasane.

From Kasane, you can visit elephant-rich Chobe National Park, then decide whether you want to reach Maun by minibus (via Nata), join an overland safari through Chobe National Park, or take a short flight. Once in Maun, beside the Okavango Delta, you can do a *mokoro* (dugout canoe) trip in the Eastern Delta, take a safari in Moremi Wildlife Reserve, or splash out on a fly-in

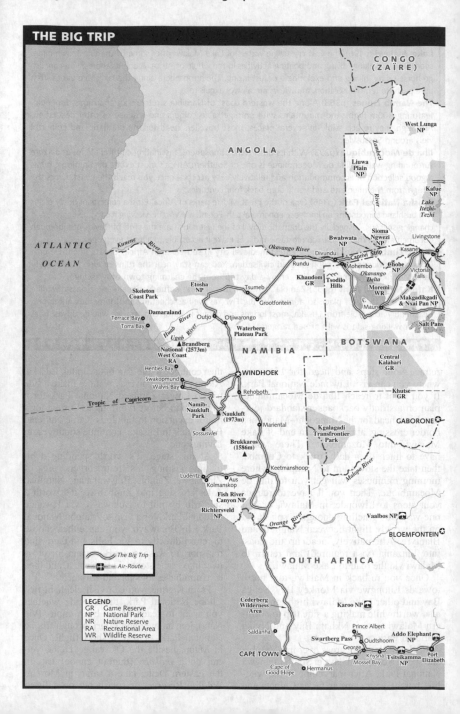

THE BIG TRIP

CONGO (ZAÏRE)

ANGOLA

ATLANTIC OCEAN

West Lunga NP

Liuwa Plain NP

Kafue NP

Lake Itezhi-Tezhi

Livingstone

Bwabwata NP

Sioma Ngwezi NP

Kasane

Kunene River

Okavango River

Divundu

Caprivi Strip

Rundu

Mohembo

Okavango Delta

Chobe NP

Victoria Falls

Skeleton Coast Park

Etosha NP

Tsumeb

Khaudom GR

Tsodilo Hills

Moremi WR

Makgadikgadi & Nxai Pan NP

Terrace Bay

Damaraland

Outjo

Grootfontein

Otjiwarongo

Maun

Salt Pans

Torra Bay

Huab River

Ugab River

▲Brandberg National (2573m)

West Coast RA

Waterberg Plateau Park

NAMIBIA

BOTSWANA

Central Kalahari GR

Hentiesbaai

WINDHOEK

Swakopmund

Walvis Bay

Rehoboth

Khutse GR

Tropic of Capricorn

Namib-Naukluft Park

Naukluft (1973m)

Mariental

Kgalagadi Transfrontier Park

GABORONE

Sossusvlei

Brukkaros (1586m)

Keetmanshoop

Malopo River

Lüderitz

Aus

Kolmanskop

Fish River Canyon NP

Vaalbos NP

Richtersveld NP

Orange River

BLOEMFONTEIN

SOUTH AFRICA

The Big Trip

Air-Route

LEGEND
GR   Game Reserve
NP   National Park
NR   Nature Reserve
RA   Recreational Area
WR   Wildlife Reserve

Cederberg Wilderness Area

Karoo NP

Saldanha

Prince Albert

Swartberg Pass

Oudtshoorn

Addo Elephant NP

CAPE TOWN

George

Knysna

Tsitsikamma NP

Port Elizabeth

Cape of Good Hope

Hermanus

Mossel Bay

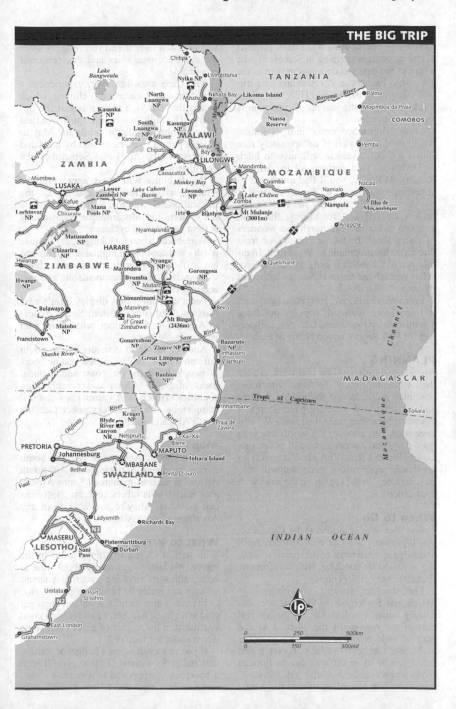

trip into the Inner Delta. From Maun, take a minibus clockwise around the delta towards Namibia, perhaps stopping in Sepupa to take a boat to Seronga and do a *mokoro* trip in the Okavango Panhandle. A rewarding side trip will take you to the Tsodilo Hills (no public transport), which the San people maintain is the site of creation.

From Mohembo, cross into Namibia, where public transport is unfortunately rare (those without a vehicle will have to hitch to Divundu – and perhaps all the way to Rundu). At Rundu, you'll find minibuses to Grootfontein and then to Tsumeb, which is the gateway to Etosha National Park (safari or hire car only). After visiting the park, you can either drive through the wonders of Damaraland, or take a minibus or train directly to Swakopmund or Windhoek. In either place, it's worth joining an inexpensive safari to reach the dunes at Sossusvlei before returning to Windhoek.

From Windhoek, you can take a bus south to Cape Town, with side trips by bus from Keetmanshoop to Aus and Lüderitz, and perhaps to Fish River Canyon National Park.

PLANNING

Anyone with limited time will want to plan their trip carefully, while those with more time may prefer to just follow their whims and take life at a leisurely pace, stopping whenever something takes their fancy. Whichever style you choose, it's worth carrying good maps and a willing sense of adventure. Lonely Planet's *Read This First: Africa* is an invaluable predeparture guide that will help travellers new to the region hit the road with confidence.

When to Go

Unless your visit is limited to the Cape area, you'll probably want to visit between April and August, when most of the region is basking in temperate sunshine, with comfortable (but often very chilly) nights.

The shoulder seasons of February to March and September to October are also usually quite comfortable in the central part of the region. In the north, you can plan on inclement weather from November to March; the heat can be oppressive and travel can be more difficult due to flooded rivers and washed-out roads. Wildlife-viewing is also less rewarding than in the winter

(and some parks close completely), but bird-watching is at its best, and you're likely to see the most dramatic skies and thunderstorms imaginable.

The Cape area, however, experiences a Mediterranean (winter rain) climate, which means that the high season is just the opposite. The high season in Cape Town runs from October to March, while the May to August period is characterised by rains and blustery winds. April and September can go either way.

Beach bums will most appreciate the winters, which are warm and dry on the tropical coasts. Summer is often extremely hot or wet, and Mozambique occasionally suffers devastating cyclones.

Winter is also best for hiking, again because it's dry and cool in the highlands and not too hot in the lowlands. In the summer, however, there's more water available, and rain is rarely constant.

For a dazzling floral display, don't miss Namaqualand (northwestern South Africa) in August and September, when there's an indescribable show.

Another factor to consider is the South African school holidays, when vast numbers of people head for the coast and national parks of South Africa and neighbouring countries. Hotels and camp sites can fill completely, and prices skyrocket (see the South Africa chapter).

Maps

The Automobile Association (AA) of South Africa produces a useful map of South Africa (as well as numerous South African area maps), plus others covering Botswana and Namibia. They're available from any AA shop in South Africa.

What to Bring

With such a variety of things to do in the region, it's hard to generalise about what to bring, although anything you find yourself without can easily be bought along the way.

Even in warm months, highland areas get cold at night, so a jacket, a pullover or a good sweatshirt, a hat, a pair of gloves and some warm socks are required.

If you're travelling on a budget or visiting national parks without facilities, you'll need a backpack (as opposed to a suitcase), tent, sleeping bag and sheet liner (which may also come in handy at budget hotels). Other essentials include a basic medical kit; torch and batteries; mosquito repellent and net; water bottle and water purifying tablets or filter (see Health later in this chapter).

For overnight hiking, a camping stove is essential, as fires are not allowed in many areas. One that runs on petrol will be the least hassle (don't rely on finding refined 'white gas' such as Shellite or Coleman fuel), but methylated spirits for Trangia-type stoves can usually be found in supermarkets, hardware shops or pharmacies. Butane 'gaz' cartridges can be bought in most cities, but the supply is unreliable.

RESPONSIBLE TOURISM

Tourism has a substantial effect on the destinations most frequented by foreign visitors. While some of these are absolutely beneficial, providing local income and incentive for environmental conservation, other aspects of tourism can seriously disrupt local economies. Across East and Southern Africa, local people may lose access to their lands because tourism focuses on wildlife, and there's a perception that wildlife and human activities are incompatible. What's often forgotten is that Africans have managed to live in harmony with their environment for thousands of years, and only an increase in the human population has caused a shift in the balance.

Ivory Souvenirs

Ivory carvings sold in tourist shops around the region, especially in Zimbabwe, Namibia and South Africa, will come with a certificate, which may or may not be genuine, stating that they came from a legally killed elephant. It is not illegal to buy these souvenirs, but it *is* currently illegal to carry ivory products into countries that are signatories to the Convention on International Trade in Endangered Species (Cites) agreement – which includes virtually all Western countries. In other words, you won't be allowed to take your ivory souvenir back home. Consider the environmental impact of a purchase. By buying ivory and other wildlife products (even certified items) you bolster the market and thereby encourage the illicit trade in endangered animals.

In popular tourist areas, the sheer number of visitors also puts a strain on the local environment. It's ironic that although tourists count on observing healthy wildlife populations, pristine landscapes or rich cultural traditions, tourists and tour companies – even those who claim to be 'ecofriendly' – often do little to sustain them. The following guidelines may help you decide the approach you wish to take:

- Save precious natural resources. Avoid establishments that clearly consume limited resources such as water and electricity at the expense of local residents.
- Support local enterprise. But when buying locally made souvenirs, avoid items made from natural material – wood, skin, ivory etc – unless they come from a sustainable source (admittedly, this is difficult to check).
- Recognise land tenure. Indigenous people who use the land are entitled to it by international law, whether or not local governments respect that law.
- Ask permission before taking close-up photographs of people, and if payment is requested, either pay up or put the camera away.
- Please don't give money, sweets or pens to children as it encourages begging, demeans the child and often insults the parents. A donation to a recognised project – a health centre or school – is a more meaningful way to help.
- Respect for local etiquette earns respect. Politeness is a virtue in all parts of the world, but different people have different ideas about what's polite.
- Learn something about the history and current affairs of a country, which will help you understand its people.
- Be patient, friendly and sensitive. Remember that you are a guest.

These guidelines are based on those issued by the British organisation **Tourism Concern** (☎ 020-7753 3330; W *www.tourismconcern .org.uk; Stapleton House, 277-281 Holloway Rd, London N7 8HN*). Another UK-based body is **Action for Southern Africa** (☎ 020-7833 3133; W *www.actsa.org; 28 Penton St, London N1 9SA*), which campaigns for (among other things) sustainable tourism throughout the region. In the USA, **Indigenous Tourism Rights International** (☎ 651-644 9984, fax 644 2720; W *www .tourismrights.org; 366 N Prior Ave, Suite 205, Saint Paul, MN 55104*) is a similar organisation which aims to preserve and protect local lands and cultures.

For further information on responsible tourism, see Ecology & Environment in the Facts about the Region chapter.

VISAS & DOCUMENTS
Passport
Visitors require a valid passport to enter every country covered in this book. To accommodate visas and border stamps, you'll need at least one or two empty pages per country you intend to visit, especially if your itinerary calls for multiple border crossings. If your passport is close to full, get a new one or pick up an insert – but apply for it well in advance. If your passport is due to expire, replace it before you leave home, as some officials won't admit you unless your passport is valid at least three (or even six) months beyond the end of your stay. Long-term travellers who intend to visit countries beyond Southern Africa may also want to change a passport that contains stamps from countries such as Libya, Cuba, South Korea, Taiwan or (especially) Israel.

Visas
Visa requirements change according to your nationality. More details about who needs what are given in the individual country chapters and on Lonely Planet's website (**w** www.lonelyplanet.com), which also has links to other visa sites.

Travellers from North America, Australasia or most of Western Europe don't require visas for South Africa, Lesotho, Swaziland, Namibia, Botswana or Malawi. Everyone requires a visa for Zimbabwe, but visitors from most Western countries can buy one at the border or airport. For Zambia, everyone requires a visa, but they're available at borders (with the possible exception of the one on the Tazara rail line from Tanzania); visas are free if you're 'introduced' to the country by a Zambian safari company or accommodation option. To visit Mozambique, everyone needs a pre-issued visa from a Mozambican embassy or consulate.

If you're from Asia, Africa, Eastern Europe or Latin America, you should check with the local embassies of the countries you intend to visit, as some may only accept visas issued in your home country. This may also apply to travellers of Asian descent (even those with a Western passport),

who may require visas even though their black or white compatriots don't. Note also that some visas have limited validity – that is, in some cases you're required to enter the country in question within a specified time period.

Travel Insurance
In general, all travellers need a travel insurance policy, which will provide some sense of security in the case of a medical emergency or the loss or theft of money or belongings. Travel health insurance policies can usually be extended to include baggage, flight departure insurance and a range of other options.

Claims on your travel insurance must be accompanied by proof of the value of any items lost or stolen (purchase receipts are the best, so if you buy a new camera for your trip, for example, hang onto the receipt). In the case of medical claims, you'll need detailed medical reports and receipts. If you're claiming on a trip cancelled by circumstances beyond your control (illness, airline bankruptcy, industrial action etc), you'll have to produce all flight tickets purchased, tour agency receipts and itinerary, and proof of whatever glitch caused your trip to be cancelled.

Other Documents
Depending on which countries you're visiting, you may need the following: a vaccination certificate to show you have all the right jabs (see Health later in this chapter); a driving licence, and perhaps an International Driving Permit (for the rare occasions when it may be required to hire a vehicle), as well as a youth hostel card and a student or youth identity card (such as ISIC), which may be good for discounts on flights, long-distance buses and visits to sites of interest (especially museums).

Copies
Before leaving home, make several photocopies of your passport photo page, visas, travellers cheque numbers, air tickets and credit cards. Carry one copy with you, separate from the originals and your other valuables; give one copy to your travelling companion; and leave one copy at home with friends, in case they need to fax it to you in an emergency.

Your Own Embassy

It's important to realise what the embassy of your country of citizenship can and can't do to help you if you get into trouble while travelling.

Generally, embassies aren't much help in emergencies if the trouble is even remotely your own fault. Remember that you are bound by the laws of the country you're visiting and your embassy won't be sympathetic if you're accused of a crime and wind up in jail, even if your actions would have been legal in your home country.

EMBASSIES & CONSULATES

If you're on a long trip or have a flexible itinerary, you can get your visas from embassies as you go. Most of the Southern African countries have embassies in neighbouring countries, and these are listed in the country chapters.

Embassies of most travellers' home countries (UK, USA etc) in Southern Africa are listed in the individual country chapters. Where home countries have no embassy, often a consul is appointed, who is not a full-time diplomat but has certain diplomatic responsibilities. Australia, Canada and New Zealand have few embassies in Southern Africa, but limited emergency assistance is available from the British High Commission.

Also listed in country chapters are embassies, consulates or high commissions of Southern African countries in a number of home countries. Readers from countries not listed should use the phone directory of their own capital city to check which Southern African countries are represented.

MONEY

Details on specific currencies, exchange rates and places to exchange money are given in the individual country chapters. Although the Botswana pula is somewhat stable, due to fluctuations in other currencies we've quoted prices in US dollars in this book.

Exchanging Money

Throughout the region, you can exchange currency at banks and foreign exchange bureaus, which are normally found near borders, in larger cities and in tourist areas. You can also change money at some shops and hotels (which almost always give very poor rates).

For the fewest headaches, carry US dollars, which are accepted all over Southern Africa. Also usually acceptable are UK pounds or euros. Australian dollars, Canadian dollars, and other currencies may be accepted at banks and airport exchange bureaus in South African cities. The South African rand is also widely recognised throughout the region, but it's not worth changing your currency into rand before converting it to kwacha, pula or whatever.

At border crossings where there is no bank, unofficial moneychangers are usually tolerated by the authorities. It's always important to be alert though, as these guys can pull all sorts of stunts with poor exchange rates, folded notes and clipped newspaper sandwiched between legitimate notes.

Cash & Travellers Cheques Most travellers carry a mix of cash and travellers cheques, although cash is more convenient. It's wise to purchase a range of travellers cheque denominations so you don't have to exchange US$100 in a country where you need only half that. When exchanging travellers cheques, many places want to check your purchase receipts (the ones the travellers cheque company told you to always keep separate), but carry them with you only when you want to change money. Just be sure to have photocopies of them, along with the international numbers to call in case of loss or theft.

Due to counterfeiting, few places accept US$100 notes unless they have a light machine to check validity.

Credit & Debit Cards Most credit and debit cards can be used in automated teller machines (ATMs), which are found all over South Africa, Botswana and Namibia. In other countries, they're found only in capital cities and larger towns, and may not be reliable.

Credit cards work for purchases all over South Africa, Namibia and Botswana, and in tourist establishments in other countries. You can also use credit cards to draw cash advances (but even in South Africa this can take several hours). Credit cards cannot be

The Fine Art of Bargaining

In some African countries, bargaining over prices – often for market goods – is a way of life. In Africa, commodities are considered to be worth whatever their seller can get for them.

In markets selling basic items such as fruit and vegetables, some sellers will invariably quote higher prices to foreigners. If you pay their first price – whether out of ignorance or guilt about how much you have compared to locals – you may be considered foolish, and will also do a disservice to fellow travellers by creating the impression that all foreigners are willing to pay any price named! You may also harm the local economy: by paying high prices you put some items out of the locals' reach. And who can blame the sellers – why sell something to a local when foreigners will pay twice as much? In such cases, you may need to bargain over the price.

That said, away from cities and tourist areas, many sellers will quote you the same price that locals pay, so don't always expect to be quoted inflated prices.

At craft and curio stalls, bargaining is very much expected. The vendor's aim is to identify the highest price you're willing to pay. Your aim is to find the price below which the vendor will not sell. Decide what you want to pay or what others have told you they've paid; your first offer should be about half this. At this stage, the vendor may laugh or feign outrage, while you plead abject poverty. The vendor's price then starts to drop from the original quote to a more realistic level. When it does, you begin making better offers until you arrive at a mutually agreeable price.

And that's the crux – *mutually agreeable*. You hear travellers all the time moaning about how they got 'overcharged' by souvenir sellers. When things have no fixed price, nobody really gets overcharged. If you don't like the price, it's simple: don't pay it. Note also that once a seller has accepted an offered price, they'll consider it a contract and at that point, you're obligated to purchase the item for that price. To just walk away at this point would be considered inexcusably rude.

Some people prefer to conduct their bargaining in a stern manner, but a friendly and spirited exchange will probably produce better results. There's no reason to lose your temper – if the effort seems a waste of time, politely take your leave. Sometimes sellers will call you back, as very few will pass up the chance of making a sale, however thin the profit.

Remember the sellers are under no more obligation to sell to you than you are to buy from them. You can go elsewhere, or (if you really want the item) accept the price. This is the raw edge of capitalism!

used to purchase petrol anywhere in the region.

Whatever card you use, it's not wise to rely totally on plastic, as computer or telephone breakdowns can leave you stranded. Always have some cash or travellers cheques as backup.

Black Market In some parts of the world, artificially fixed exchange rates in the bank mean you can get more local money for your hard currency by changing on the so-called black market. Not only is this illegal, it's also potentially dangerous. In most of the region, currency deregulation has eliminated the black market, and Zimbabwe is the only country that still has artificial controls. If someone approaches you anywhere in the region offering substantially more than the bank rate, they almost certainly have a well-formulated plan for separating you from your money. In Zimbabwe, where a thriving – and

very risky – black market still exists, you'll also have to beware of police stings aimed at foreigners attempting to circumvent their disastrous system.

Costs

Generally speaking, prices in Southern Africa are around 50% to 75% of what they are in Europe, Australasia or North America. However, the low value of the rand at the time of writing made South Africa, Lesotho, Swaziland and Namibia much better value than that, and the crisis in Zimbabwe has caused foreign currency prices to plummet. Botswana is always considerably more expensive, while Malawi, Zambia and Mozambique offer a wide range of options, from dirt cheap to exceptionally expensive. In general, locally produced items will be good value wherever you go, while imported goods may be twice what they cost in the West (thanks to import duties).

Accommodation costs less than US$1 per night for basic local resthouses, US$3 to US$10 for camping, US$5 for hostel dorms, and US$25 to US$50 for mid-range hotels. Expect to pay from US$100 to ozone layer rates for top-end establishments. Doubles are almost always cheaper per person than singles.

Transport options are equally varied: you can hitch for free or go by chartered plane at something like US$10 per minute. Most people, however, use buses or trains, which are inexpensive by Western standards.

Taking all these aspects into account, serious backpackers may get by on an average of US$10 per day, including accommodation, food and transport, although US$15 allows more flexibility. For a bit more comfort, US$20 to US$25 per day is a reasonable budget for day-to-day living expenses. To stay in mid-range hotels, eat well and travel in comfort when possible, you're looking at around US$50 per day or more.

Along with these basic costs, you'll have to consider visa and national park fees, plus the cost of any tours or activities (eg, wildlife safaris or white-water rafting). To hire a car, you'll find the cheapest deals in South Africa, where some companies will allow you to take the vehicle into neighbouring countries for a minimal extra charge. Especially in Namibia, it's wise to plan on hiring a car or taking a budget safari, which will be necessary to reach sites of interest.

More detailed cost rundowns are provided in individual country chapters.

Tipping

When it comes to tipping, every country is different. Generally, it isn't necessary in small local establishments, mid-range restaurants, backpackers lodges, hotels or fast-food places, but in any upmarket restaurant that doesn't automatically include a service charge (which isn't obligatory if the service has been poor), it may be appropriate. There is a grey area between mid-range and up-market restaurants, because tipping is rarely expected from locals but may be expected of foreigners. On the other hand, wealthier Africans may sometimes tip even at smaller restaurants, not because it's expected, but as a show of status.

At safari lodges and on tours, everyone is expected to leave a blanket tip to be divided among the staff. Safari guides are typically tipped separately.

Taxi drivers aren't normally tipped, but may expect about 10% from well-heeled travellers; in larger cities, even backpackers may be expected to fork over a bit extra.

If you're driving – especially in cities – you are expected to tip parking guards, who'll watch your car while you're away (in a few cases, this is a protection racket, but they're mostly legitimate). However, there's no need to tip the guys who wave you into the parking space you were going to take anyway.

POST & COMMUNICATIONS
Post & Telephone

Post, telephone and fax services are good in South Africa, Botswana and Namibia, pretty good in Swaziland, and range from OK to bad in Zimbabwe, Mozambique, Malawi, Lesotho and Zambia. In all countries, service between towns tends to be more reliable than service to and from rural areas.

If you need to receive mail, the poste restante service has letters sent to a main post office, usually in a capital city, where they are held for you to collect. Letters should be addressed clearly with your family name in capitals, to Poste Restante, General Post Office, (insert city). To collect your mail, you need your passport, and may have to pay a small fee. Letters sometimes take a few weeks to work through the system, so have them sent to a place where you're going to be for a while.

In addition to local telephone cards, in South Africa you may want to try the ekno Communication Card, which provides cheap international calls, a range of messaging services and free email (see the South Africa chapter for details on how to join).

In Southern Africa, mobile phones are very popular, but can typically only be used within 10km to 20km of a major city or town. Airports often have a counter where you can rent a mobile phone for the duration of your stay.

Email & Internet Access

Most capital cities (and some large towns) in the region have at least one Internet café, and many hotels and backpackers hostels also offer these services. Hourly rates vary, but you should plan on around US$2 to US$4 per hour. Note that some equipment is fairly antiquated, so getting your mail may be frustratingly slow.

DIGITAL RESOURCES

The World Wide Web is a rich resource for travellers. You can research your trip, hunt down bargain air fares, book hotels, check on weather conditions or chat with locals and other travellers about the best places to visit (or avoid!).

The Lonely Planet website (**w** www.lonely planet.com) has several pages of information on each country in Southern Africa, postcards from other travellers and the Thorn Tree notice board, where you can ask questions before you go or dispense advice when you get back. The subwwway section links you to useful travel resources elsewhere on the Web, and you can also find travel news.

Other useful websites include:

Africa Insites (**w** www.africa-insites.com) A very good brochure-style site, concentrating on tourism in Southern Africa, with useful links to other relevant sites

AfricaNet (**w** www.africanet.com) A site covering many different aspects of Africa, including tourism

BackPacker (**w** www.backpackafrica.com) This site has a South Africa bias, but lists lots of travel-related companies and has a live booking system and useful links

Getaway to Africa (**w** www.getawaytoafrica.com) The site of *Getaway* magazine; includes a Travellers Talk forum for up-to-date advice on hotels, road conditions etc, as well as ads for destinations and tour companies

iafrica.com (**w** www.iafrica.com) This diverse South African–dominated site includes travel, news and lifestyle sections, plus links to sites on other Southern African countries

Just Backpacking Southern Africa (**w** www.back packing.co.za) Aimed at budget travellers in East and Southern Africa, although South Africa–biased; includes hostel lists, Internet café details, news, forums and links to other relevant sites

Africa Politics Online (**w** www.africapoliticsonline .com) This site provides news and political stories from all over

Political Africa (**w** www.politicalafrica.com) Here you'll find the latest Africa stories from various news services around the world

BOOKS

This section lists publications covering most of Southern Africa. Books on individual countries are listed in the relevant country chapters. Note that many books have dif-

ferent publishers in different countries, and that a hardcover rarity in one country may be a readily available paperback in another, so we haven't included publishers in this list (unless relevant). In any case, bookshops, libraries and online booksellers search by title or author.

Lonely Planet

If you're looking for more in-depth coverage, Lonely Planet also publishes *South Africa, Lesotho & Swaziland*; *Zimbabwe*; *Botswana*; *Namibia*; *Zambia*; *Malawi*; and *Mozambique*. If you're travelling the entire continent, you may want to check out *Africa on a shoestring*, which covers the entire continent. Lonely Planet also publishes guides to a number of other African countries, as well as *Trekking in East Africa*, which includes routes in Malawi.

Guidebooks

Hiking Trails of Southern Africa by Willie & Sandra Olivier covers major backpacking routes in South Africa and Namibia.

If walking is your game, the *Complete Guide to Hiking Trails in Southern Africa* by Jaynee Levy describes more than 350 trails in South Africa (plus another 50 or so in Namibia, Botswana, Swaziland, Lesotho, Zimbabwe and Malawi), from short nature strolls to major expeditions in wild areas.

Pan-continental motorcyclists should grip the *Adventure Motorbiking Handbook* by Chris Scott. It contains lots of information on riding through Africa.

The *Illustrated Guide to Southern Africa* (Readers Digest) and *Secret Southern Africa* (AA of South Africa) are large-format books full of photos, maps and touring descriptions. Both books are recommended for motoring around the region.

Travel

The following suggestions involve several countries in Southern Africa (country-specific titles are mentioned under Books in the individual country chapters).

Grains of Sand by Martin Buckley is a travelogue describing the author's travels through the deserts of the world, including both the Namib and the Kalahari.

The Electronic Elephant by Dan Jacobson describes a journey through South Africa, Botswana and Zimbabwe. It combines frequently depressing contemporary encounters with fascinating historical flashbacks.

In Quest of Livingstone by Colum Wilson & Aisling Irwin tells the story of two British travellers who follow the renowned missionary-explorer through Tanzania and Zambia on mountain bikes. It combines contemporary observations with flashbacks to Livingstone's own journals.

South from the Limpopo by Dervla Murphy chronicles the famously eccentric and beer-swilling author's cycling trip through South Africa. This is a sequel to *The Ukimwi Road* which describes a cycling trip from Kenya to Zimbabwe.

History & Politics

Africa by Phyllis Martin and Patrick O'Meara is the nearest you'll get to a pocket library, with scholarly but accessible essays on a wide range of subjects including history, religion, colonialism, sociology, art, popular culture, law, literature, politics, economics and the development crisis.

Africa: Dispatches from a Fragile Continent by Blaine Harden provides provocative and pessimistic reading on several topics, such as the failure of African political leadership. In any case, the author maintains that African values endure and will eventually save the day.

Chris Munion's *Banana Sunday – Datelines from Africa* contains humorous accounts of this journalist's coverage of various African wars.

Blood on the Tracks by Miles Bredin chronicles an essentially hopeless journey between Angola and Mozambique. It's a tale of war, bureaucracy, corruption and inefficiency neatly outlining the problems faced by modern Africa.

In *The History of Southern Africa*, Kevin Shillington objectively and sensitively discusses Botswana, Namibia, South Africa, Lesotho and Swaziland, covering prehistory plus African and colonial history.

The title *Introduction to the History of Central Africa: Zambia, Malawi, and Zimbabwe* by AJ Wills is misleading – this 500-page work is comprehensive and generally considered the best on the region.

The Scramble for Africa: White Man's Conquest of the Dark Continent from 1876 to 1912 by Thomas Pakenham details the colonial history of Africa in well-written

and entertaining prose. It was one of the first studies to tell both sides of the story and has become established as the standard work on the topic.

Masters of Illusion: The World Bank and the Poverty of Nations by Catherine Caufield discusses the influence that the global development lending agency has had on poor countries around the world.

Literature

Literature by country-specific authors is listed under Arts in individual country chapters; other novels are presented under Books.

Being There, edited by Robin Malan, is a good introductory collection of short stories from Southern African authors written since 1960.

The Heinemann Book of African Poetry in English, edited by A Maja-Pearce, includes poetry by writers from several African countries including Zimbabwe and South Africa. Another recommended poetry anthology is *The Penguin Book of Modern African Poetry*, edited by Moore & Beier.

The Penguin Book of Southern African Stories, edited by Stephen Gray, features stories (some of which are thousands of years old) from around the region. The stories are deliberately not classified by original language to show the similarities and common threads in various literary traditions.

The excellent *Traveller's Literary Companion to Africa*, edited by Oona Strathern, includes over 250 prose and poetry extracts from all over Africa, with an introduction to the writing of each country, plus a list of 'literary landmarks' – real features that appear in novels written about the country.

Field Guides

Southern Africa's incredible floral and faunal diversity has inspired a large number of field guides for visitors and wildlife enthusiasts. In the UK, an excellent source for wildlife and nature titles is **Subbuteo Natural History Books Ltd** (☎ *0870-0109 700, fax 0109 699;* **w** *www.wildlifebooks.com*). International mail orders are welcome. In the USA, try the **Adventurous Traveler Bookstore** (☎ *800-282 3963;* **w** *www.adventuroustraveler.com*) or **Nature Co** (☎ *800-227 1114*). In Australia, check out **Andrew Isles Natural History Books** (☎ *03-9510 5750;* **w** *www.andrewisles.com*).

Robert's Birds of Southern Africa by Gordon Lindsay is a bird-watching requisite, but it's not a featherweight volume.

Ian Sinclair's Field Guide to the Birds of Southern Africa by Ian Sinclair is a comprehensive work with colour plates of all avian species in the region. An abridged version, the *Illustrated Guide to the Birds of Southern Africa*, concentrates on commonly observed species.

Newman's Birds of Southern Africa by Kenneth Newman is a comprehensive work on the region's avifauna; all species are identified in colour or black-and-white illustrations.

Field Guide to the Mammals of Southern Africa by Chris & Tilde Stuart is a well-illustrated field guide to just about every furry thing you're likely to encounter in this part of the world. A handy pocket version of this book, also written by the Stuarts, is *Southern, Central & East African Mammals.* Haltenorth & Diller's *Field Guide to Mammals of Africa Including Madagascar* is a good portable choice with lots of colour plates.

Field Guide to the Snakes and Other Reptiles of Southern Africa by Bill Branch is the one to consult if you want to know what it is that's slithering underfoot – and whether or not it's dangerous.

South African Frogs by Neville Passmore and Vincent Carruthers has all the answers for frogophiles. It concentrates on South Africa, but includes most species found north of the border.

The Field Guide to the Butterflies of Southern Africa by Igor Migdoll isn't totally comprehensive, but you probably won't encounter a butterfly that isn't included in this guide.

Complete Guide to Freshwater Fishes of Southern Africa by Paul Skelton is a favourite with anglers.

Flowers of Southern Africa by Auriol Batten is less a field guide than a large-format celebration of major flowering species, illustrated with colourful paintings.

Trees of Southern Africa by K Coates provides the most thorough coverage of the subcontinent's arboreal richness, illustrated with colour photos and paintings.

Medicinal Plants of South Africa provides background on regional medicinal plants; it's available from **Briza Publications** (☎ 12-329

3896, fax 329 4525; **W** www.briza.co.za) in South Africa.

General

Images of Power by D Lewis-Williams & T Dowson is a fascinating study of the art of the San people, utilising modern scientific techniques and rediscovered records of discussions between the San and early European settlers.

Raymond Bonner's *At the Hand of Man* discusses conservation issues and the destruction of African wildlife, holding that conservation will only work if African people see real benefits themselves.

Zambezi: Journey of a River by Michael Main is a very readable combination of history, geography, geology, anthropology, careful observation, humour, rumour and myth, following the Zambezi River through Zambia, Angola, Zimbabwe and Mozambique, with side-tracks into Malawi.

NEWSPAPERS & MAGAZINES

News magazines that cover the continent include *Africa Now, Africa Today, Business Africa* and the best, BBC's *Focus on Africa.* These are available from newsagents in South Africa, and from bookshops in capital cities in other countries.

Getaway magazine covers travel in Southern Africa, with articles ranging from epic 4WD trips to active and not-so-active tours all over the region. It also includes reviews of lodges and other tourism-oriented topics. The useful advertising section provides ideas on where to go and what to do. Outdoor adventure buffs will like *Out There*, which features articles on the African wilds and how to enjoy them.

The beautiful, glossy *Africa Geographic*, published bimonthly, should be considered an essential subscription for every Africa buff. Bird-watchers will also want to read the excellent bimonthly *Africa Birds & Birding.* For subscriptions to these magazines contact **Africa Geographic** (☎ 27-21-686 9001, fax 686 4500; **W** www.africa-geographic.com; Black Eagle Publishing, PO Box 44223, Claremont 7735, South Africa).

PHOTOGRAPHY & VIDEO
Film & Equipment

In South Africa, the availability of film, video tapes and equipment is good, and prices are roughly on a par with those in Europe. In Namibia, you'll find slide film in Windhoek and Swakopmund, but in other countries, availability of any sort of film is restricted to cities and tourist centres, and prices are higher. The best advice is to carry a supply of film and any special requirements from home.

The sunlight in Africa is intense, so most people find Fujichrome Velvia 50, Kodachrome 64 or any 100ISO (ASA) film perfectly adequate, with a 200ISO film suitable for long-lens or evening shots. Useful photographic accessories might include a small flash, a cable or remote shutter release, filters and a cleaning kit. Also, remember to take spare camera batteries.

Some African airports may have old X-ray machines, so it's always wise to request a hand check of your film and camera equipment. Even newer film-safe models can affect high-speed film (1000ISO and higher), especially if it passes through several checks during your trip (the effects are cumulative). Travellers coming from the USA should carry all film and camera equipment in their hand luggage, as new anti-terrorism X-ray machines for checked baggage are not film safe.

Blank video tapes are available in capital cities and large towns, but qualities and formats vary, and African tapes won't work on North American machines. You can recharge batteries in hotels and lodges as you go, but you'll need a charger, plug adaptors and applicable transformers for the countries you're visiting.

For more information, check out Lonely Planet's *Travel Photography*.

Wildlife Photography

To score some excellent wildlife photos, a good lightweight 35mm SLR automatic camera with a lens between 210mm and 300mm – and a modicum of skill – should do the trick. Video cameras with zoom facility may be able to get closer and digital cameras will perform all sorts of magic. If your subject is nothing but a speck in the distance, resist wasting film but keep the camera ready. An early start is advisable because most wildlife is active during the cooler hours. When photographing animals, take light readings on the subject and not the brilliant African background or your

shots will be underexposed. The best times to take photos on sunny days are the first two hours after sunrise and the last two before sunset, both of which take advantage of the low sun's colour-enhancing rays. Filters (eg, ultraviolet, polarising or skylight) can also produce good results; ask for advice in a good camera shop.

TIME

In the southern summer, Southern Africa is two hours ahead of UTC (Universal Time Coordinate, formerly called GMT, or Greenwich Mean Time). The only Southern African country with daylight-saving time is Namibia, which turns its clocks forward one hour in September, and back one hour in April.

In the southern winter, however, the region is on the same time as British Summer Time (daylight savings time).

ELECTRICITY

Electricity in Southern Africa is generated at 220V to 240V AC. The exceptions are Pretoria (250V) and Port Elizabeth (220/250V) in South Africa. Most plugs have three prongs (or pins), either round or rectangular ('square') in section. In South Africa, round-pin plugs are used. Outside South Africa, British-style square three-pin plugs are common. Few continental European or North American plug adaptors will cope, and you may have to buy a plug locally (eg, at a hardware store or travel agency) and connect it yourself if you plan to use your own electrical equipment. A voltage adaptor is also needed for US appliances.

country	pins	plug shape
Botswana	2	round
Lesotho	3	round
Malawi	3	square
Mozambique	3	square
	2 & 3	round
Namibia	2 & 3	round
South Africa	3	round
Swaziland	3	round
Zambia	3	square
Zimbabwe	3	square/round

WEIGHTS & MEASURES

All the countries covered in this book use the metric system. To convert between metric and imperial units, refer to the conversion chart at the back of the book.

LAUNDRY

Although laundrettes (laundromats) are rare, you'll find them in larger cities, and many camping grounds, backpackers hostels and guest houses have laundry sinks or washing machines. Otherwise, finding someone to wash your clothes is fairly simple; at cheaper hotels, a staff member will do the job, or find somebody else who can. The charge is usually per item, and often negotiable. At top-end and mid-range hotels, you'll pay around US$1 per item, and very upmarket lodges may include laundry in their rates.

TOILETS

There are two main types of toilet in Africa: the Western style, with a toilet bowl and seat; and the African style, which is a squat toilet with a hole in the floor. Standards of both types vary tremendously, from pristine to nauseating.

In rural areas, long-drop squat toilets are built over a deep hole in the ground, where waste matter decomposes naturally as long as people avoid depositing rubbish (including tampons or sanitary pads, which should be disposed of separately).

There's also a bizarre hybrid, in which an unplumbed Western toilet is perched over a long-drop hole. As you can imagine, the lack of running water can turn these into an unspeakable horror.

HEALTH

Travel health depends on your predeparture preparations, your daily health care while travelling and how you handle any medical problem that may develop. While the potential dangers can seem quite frightening, in reality few travellers experience anything more than an upset stomach.

Before You Go

If you're booking a wildlife safari while in Southern Africa, remember to alert the operator to any medical condition you may have that could present problems – such as diabetes, epilepsy, a heart condition or bee-sting allergy. It won't stop you going, but could make matters easier if the guide knows of your condition if there is a problem.

Medical Kit Check List

Following is a list of items you should consider including in your medical kit – consult your pharmacist for brands available in your country.

☐ **Antibiotics** For travel in remote areas; see your doctor before you leave home (these must be prescribed) and carry the prescription with you

☐ **Antifungal cream or powder** For fungal skin infections and thrush

☐ **Antihistamine** For allergies (eg, hay fever, to ease the itch from insect bites or stings, and to prevent motion sickness)

☐ **Antiseptic (such as povidone-iodine)** For cuts and scrapes

☐ **Aspirin or paracetamol (acetaminophen in the USA)** For pain or fever (note that aspirin isn't recommended for anyone under 18)

☐ **Bandages, Band-Aids (sticking plasters) and other wound dressings**

☐ **Calamine lotion, sting relief spray or aloe vera** To ease irritation from sunburn and insect bites or stings

☐ **Cold and flu tablets, throat lozenges and nasal decongestant**

☐ **Insect repellent, sunscreen, lip balm and eye drops**

☐ **Kit containing sterile syringes** Injections aren't generally a problem, but these may provide peace of mind in rural areas

☐ **Loperamide or diphenoxylate (Lomatil or Imodium)** As a stopgap measure to control diarrhoea on long journeys; not to be taken if there's fever or a bloody stool

☐ **Prochlorperazine or metaclopramide** For nausea and vomiting

☐ **Rehydration mixture** To reverse dehydration in the case of severe diarrhoea; it's especially important if you're travelling with children

☐ **Scissors, tweezers and a thermometer** Note that mercury thermometers may not be carried on planes

☐ **Water purification tablets or iodine**

Predeparture Planning

Immunisations It is recommended you seek medical advice at least six weeks before travel, and be aware that children and pregnant women are often at greater risk of health problems while travelling. Discuss your requirements with your doctor. Plan ahead for getting your vaccinations, as some require more than one injection, and others should not be given simultaneously. Note that some vaccinations are advised against during pregnancy or for people with allergies – these are both matters to be discussed with your doctor.

Carry proof of your vaccinations, especially yellow fever, as this may be required to enter some countries. Vaccinations to consider for this trip include the following (for more on the individual diseases, see later in this section):

Diphtheria & Tetanus Vaccinations for these two diseases are usually combined and are recommended for everyone. After an initial course of three injections (usually given in childhood), boosters are necessary every 10 years.

Hepatitis A Vaccines for Hepatitis A (eg, Avaxim, Havrix 1440 or VAQTA) provide long-term immunity (possibly more than 10 years) after an initial injection and a booster at six to 12 months. Alternatively, an injection of gamma globulin can provide short-term protection against hepatitis A – two to six months, depending on the dose given. It is not a vaccine, but is a ready-made antibody collected from blood donations. It is reasonably effective and, unlike the vaccine, it is protective immediately, but because it is a blood product, there are concerns about its long-term safety. Hepatitis A vaccine is also available in a combined form, Twinrix, with hepatitis B vaccine. Three injections over a six-month period are required, the first two providing substantial protection against hepatitis A.

Hepatitis B Travellers who should consider vaccination against hepatitis B include those on a long trip, as well as those visiting countries where there are high levels of hepatitis B infection, where blood transfusions may not be adequately screened, or where sexual contact or needle sharing is a possibility. Vaccination involves three injections, with a booster at 12 months. More rapid courses are available if necessary.

Meningococcal Meningitis Vaccination is recommended for travellers to certain parts of Asia, India, Africa and South America. A single injection provides protection against the major epidemic forms of the disease for three years. Protection may be less effective in children under two years.

Polio Everyone should keep up to date with this vaccination, which is normally given in childhood. A booster every 10 years maintains immunity.

Rabies Vaccination should be considered if you will spend a month or longer in a country where rabies is common, especially if you will be cycling, handling animals, caving or travelling in remote areas. It is also recommended for children (who may not report a bite). Pretravel rabies vaccination involves three injections over 21 to 28 days.

If someone who has been vaccinated is bitten or scratched by an animal, they will require two booster injections of vaccine; those not vaccinated require more.

Tuberculosis (TB) The risk of TB to travellers is usually very low, unless you will be living with or closely associated with local people in high risk areas – which include some parts of Southern Africa. Vaccination against TB is recommended for children and young adults living in these areas for three months or more.

Typhoid Vaccination against typhoid may be required if you are travelling in Africa for more than a couple of weeks. It is now available either as an injection or as capsules to be taken orally. A combined hepatitis A and typhoid vaccine has been launched, but its availability is still limited – check with your doctor to find out its status in your country.

Yellow Fever A yellow fever vaccine is now the only vaccine that is a legal requirement for entry into certain countries, usually only enforced when coming from an infected area. Vaccination is recommended for travel in areas where the disease is endemic (including parts of Africa). To get the vaccination you may need to go to a special health centre.

Malaria Medication Antimalarial drugs do not prevent you from being infected, but kill the malaria parasites during a stage in their development and significantly reduce the risk of serious illness or death. Expert advice on medication should be sought, as there are many factors to consider, including the area to be visited, the risk of exposure to malaria-carrying mosquitoes, the side effects of medication, your medical history, and whether you are a child or an adult or pregnant. Travellers to isolated areas in high risk countries should definitely carry a treatment dose of medication for use if symptoms occur.

Health Insurance Make sure that you have adequate health insurance. See Travel Insurance under Visas & Documents earlier in this chapter for details.

Travel Health Guides Lonely Planet's *Healthy Travel Africa* is a handy pocket-sized guide, packed with useful information on pretrip planning, emergency first aid, immunisation and disease information, and what to do if you get sick on the road. Lonely Planet's *Travel with Children* also includes advice on travel health for younger children.

There are also a number of excellent travel health sites on the Internet. The Lonely Planet website (w www.lonelyplanet.com) has links to the WHO and the US Center for Disease Control & Prevention.

Other Preparations Make sure you're healthy before you leave home. Have your teeth and eyes checked, and be sure to carry spare glasses or contact lenses, if necessary, and a copy of any optical prescriptions.

If you require a particular medication take an adequate supply, as it may not be available locally. Take part of the packaging showing the generic name rather than the brand, which will make it easier to replace. To avoid problems, carry a legible prescription or letter from your doctor to show that you legally use the medication.

Basic Rules
Food There is an old adage which says: 'If you can cook it, boil it or peel it you can eat it – otherwise forget it.' Vegetables and fruit should be washed with purified water or peeled where possible. Beware of ice cream which is sold in the street or anywhere it might have been melted and refrozen; if there's any doubt (eg, a power cut in the last day or two), steer clear. Shellfish such as mussels, oysters and clams should be avoided (steaming does not make tainted shellfish safe). Also avoid undercooked meat, particularly in the form of mince.

If a place looks clean and well run and the vendor also looks clean and healthy, then the food is probably OK. In general, places that are packed with travellers or locals will be fine, while empty restaurants are questionable. The food in busy restaurants is cooked and eaten quite quickly with little standing around and is probably not reheated.

Water The number one rule is *be careful of the water* and especially ice. If you don't know that the water is safe, assume the worst. Reputable brands of bottled water or soft drink are generally fine, although in some places bottles may be refilled with tap water. Only use water from containers with a serrated seal – not tops or corks. Take care with fruit juice, particularly if water may have been added. Milk should be treated with suspicion as it is often unpasteurised, though boiled milk is fine if it

is kept hygienically. Tea or coffee should also be OK, since the water should have been boiled.

Water Purification The simplest way to purify water is to boil it thoroughly. Vigorous boiling should be satisfactory; however, it should be boiled longer at higher altitudes, where water boils at a lower temperature and bugs are less likely to be killed.

Consider purchasing a water filter for a long trip. There are two main kinds of filter. Total filters take out all parasites, bacteria and viruses and make water safe to drink. They're expensive, but can be more cost effective than buying bottled water on a long trip. Simple filters (which can even be a nylon mesh bag) remove dirt and larger foreign bodies to prepare it for treatment with chemical solutions. When buying a filter, it's very important to read the specifications so you'll know exactly what sort of contaminants it can remove. Simple filtering will not remove all dangerous organisms, so if you cannot boil water it should be treated chemically. Chlorine tablets will kill many pathogens, but not some parasites like giardia and amoebas. Iodine is more effective in purifying water and is available in tablet form. Follow the directions carefully and remember that too much iodine can be harmful.

Medical Problems & Treatment
Self-diagnosis and treatment can be risky, so you should always seek medical help. An embassy, consulate or five-star hotel can usually recommend a local doctor. Although we do give drug dosages in this section, they are for emergency use only. Correct diagnosis is vital. In this section we have used the generic names for medications – check with a pharmacist for brands available locally.

Note that antibiotics should ideally be administered under medical supervision. Take only the recommended dose at the prescribed intervals and use the whole course, even if you feel better earlier. If you have any serious reactions to an antibiotic, stop taking it immediately, and don't use it at all if you're unsure that it's the right one. If you're allergic to commonly prescribed antibiotics (such as sulphates or penicillin), carry this information (eg, on a bracelet).

Environmental Hazards

Heat Exhaustion Dehydration and salt deficiency can cause heat exhaustion. Take time to acclimatise to high temperatures, drink sufficient liquids and do not do anything too physically demanding.

Salt deficiency is characterised by fatigue, lethargy, headaches, giddiness and muscle cramps; salt tablets may help, but adding extra salt to your food is better.

Anhidrotic heat exhaustion is a rare form of heat exhaustion that is caused by an inability to sweat. It tends to affect people who have been in a hot climate for some time, and can progress to heatstroke. Treatment involves removal to a cooler climate.

Heatstroke This serious, occasionally fatal, condition can occur if the body's heat-regulating mechanism breaks down and the body temperature rises to dangerous levels. Long, continuous periods of exposure to high temperatures and insufficient fluids can leave you vulnerable to heatstroke.

The symptoms are feeling unwell, not sweating very much (or at all) and a high body temperature (that is 39° to 41°C; 102° to 106°F). Where sweating has ceased, the skin becomes flushed and red. Severe, throbbing headaches and lack of coordination will also occur, and the sufferer may be confused or aggressive. Eventually the victim will become delirious or convulse. Hospitalisation is essential, but in the interim get victims out of the sun, remove their clothing, cover them with a wet sheet or towel and then fan continually. If they're conscious, administer fluids.

Hypothermia Too much cold can be just as dangerous as too much heat. Hypothermia occurs when the body loses heat faster than it can produce it and the core temperature of the body falls. It is surprisingly easy to progress from very cold to dangerously cold due to a combination of wind, wet clothing, fatigue and hunger, even if the air temperature is above freezing. To avoid hypothermia it is best to dress in layers; silk, wool and some artificial fibres are all good insulating materials. A hat is important, as a lot of heat is lost through the head. A strong, waterproof outer layer (and a 'space' blanket for emergencies) is essential. Carry basic supplies, including food containing simple sugars to generate heat quickly, and fluid to drink.

Symptoms of hypothermia are exhaustion, numb skin (particularly toes and fingers), shivering, slurred speech, irrational or violent behaviour, lethargy, stumbling, dizzy spells, muscle cramps and violent bursts of energy. Irrationality may take the form of sufferers claiming they are warm and trying to take off their clothes.

To treat mild hypothermia, first get the person out of the wind and rain, remove their clothing if it's wet and replace it with dry, warm clothing. Provide hot liquids – not alcohol – and some high-kilojoule, easily digestible food. Do not rub victims: instead, allow them to slowly warm themselves. This should be enough to treat the early stages of hypothermia. The early recognition and treatment of mild hypothermia is the only way to prevent severe hypothermia, which is a critical condition.

Prickly Heat An itchy rash caused by excessive perspiration trapped under the skin, prickly heat usually strikes people who have just arrived in a hot climate. It may help to keep cool, bathe often, keep your skin dry and use a mild talcum powder. Alternatively, resort to air-conditioned accommodation.

Sunburn In the tropics, the desert or at high altitude, sunburn is a real risk, even on cloudy days. Use a sunscreen, a hat, and a barrier cream for your nose and lips. Calamine lotion or a commercial after-sun preparation are good for mild sunburn. Protect your eyes with good quality sunglasses, particularly if you're near water, sand or snow.

Infectious Diseases

Diarrhoea Simple things like a change of water, food or climate can all cause a mild bout of diarrhoea, but a few rushed toilet trips with no other symptoms is not indicative of a major problem.

Dehydration is the main danger with any diarrhoea, particularly in children or the elderly, in whom it can occur quite quickly. Under all circumstances *fluid replacement* (at least equal to the volume being lost) is essential. Good choices include weak black tea with a little sugar; soda water; or soft drink allowed to go flat and diluted 50% with clean water. With severe diarrhoea, a rehydrating solution is preferable to replace minerals and salts lost. Commercial oral rehydration salts (ORS) should be added to boiled or bottled water. In an emergency, dissolve six teaspoons of sugar and a half teaspoon of salt in a litre of boiled or bottled water. You need to drink at least the same volume of fluid that you are losing in bowel movements and vomiting. Urine is the best guide – if you have small amounts of urine, or it's deep yellow in colour, you need to drink more fluid. Keep drinking small amounts often and stick to a bland diet as you recover.

Gut-paralysing drugs such as loperamide or diphenoxylate can be used to bring relief from the symptoms, but they don't actually cure the problem. Only use these drugs if you do not have access to toilets, eg, if you *must* travel. Note that these drugs are not recommended for children under 12 years.

In certain situations antibiotics may be required: diarrhoea with blood or mucus (dysentery), diarrhoea accompanied by fever, profuse watery diarrhoea, persistent diarrhoea not improving after 48 hours and severe diarrhoea. These suggest a more serious underlying problem, and in these cases, gut-paralysing drugs should be avoided.

With serious diarrhoea, a stool test may be necessary to diagnose what bug is involved, so it's wise to seek medical help urgently. Where this is not possible, the recommended drugs for bacterial diarrhoea (the most likely cause of severe diarrhoea in travellers) are norfloxacin 400mg twice daily for three days or ciprofloxacin 500mg twice daily for five days. These are not recommended for children or pregnant women. The drug of choice for children would be co-trimoxazole with dosage dependent on weight. A five-day course is given. Ampicillin or amoxycillin may be given in pregnancy, but medical care is necessary.

Two other causes of persistent diarrhoea in travellers are giardiasis and amoebic dysentery. **Giardiasis** is caused by a common parasite, *Giardia lamblia*. Symptoms include stomach cramps, nausea, a bloated stomach, watery, foul-smelling diarrhoea and frequent gas. It can appear several weeks after you have been exposed to the parasite, then the symptoms may disappear for a few days before returning. This can go on for several weeks.

Amoebic dysentery, caused by the protozoan *Entamoeba histolytica*, is characterised by a gradual onset of low-grade diarrhoea, often with blood and mucus. Cramping abdominal pain and vomiting are less likely than in other types of diarrhoea, and fever may not be present. It will persist until treated and can recur and cause other health problems.

You should seek medical advice if you think you have giardiasis or amoebic dysentery, but where this is not possible, tinidazole or metronidazole are the recommended drugs. Treatment is a 2g single dose of tinidazole or 250mg of metronidazole three times daily for five to 10 days.

Fungal Infections These infections are encouraged by moisture and occur more commonly in hot weather. They are usually found on the scalp, between the toes (athlete's foot) or fingers, in the groin and on the body (ringworm). Ringworm, which is not a worm but a fungal infection, is contracted from infected animals or other people.

To prevent fungal infections wear loose, comfortable clothes, avoid artificial fibres, wash frequently and dry yourself carefully. If you do have an infection, wash the infected area at least daily with a disinfectant or medicated soap and water, and rinse and dry well. Apply an antifungal cream or powder, such as tolnaftate. Try to expose the infected area to air or sunlight as much as possible, and wash all towels and underwear in hot water and let them dry in the sun.

Hepatitis This is a general term for inflammation of the liver, and is a common disease worldwide. Several different viruses are responsible for hepatitis, and they differ in the way they're transmitted. Symptoms – which are similar in all forms of hepatitis – include fever, chills, headache, fatigue, feelings of weakness, and aches and pains, followed by loss of appetite, nausea, vomiting, abdominal pain, dark urine, light-coloured faeces, jaundiced (yellow) skin and yellowing of the whites of the eyes. People who have had hepatitis should avoid alcohol for some time after the illness, as the liver needs time to recover.

Hepatitis A is transmitted by contaminated food and drinking water. You should seek medical advice, but the only treatment is rest, lots of fluids, light eating and avoidance of fatty foods. **Hepatitis E** is transmitted in the same way as hepatitis A; it can be particularly serious in pregnant women.

There are about 300 million chronic carriers of **hepatitis B**, which is spread through contact with infected blood, blood products or body fluids. Transmission can occur through sexual contact, unsterilised needles, blood transfusions, or contact with blood via small breaks in the skin. Other risky situations include shaving, tattooing or body piercing with contaminated equipment. The symptoms of hepatitis B may be more severe than those of type A and the disease can lead to long-term problems such as chronic liver damage, liver cancer or a long-term carrier state. **Hepatitis C and D** are spread in the same way as hepatitis B and can also lead to long term complications.

Vaccines are available against hepatitis A and B, but not other types. The best preventative measures are to follow basic rules about food and water (hepatitis A and E) and avoid risky situations (hepatitis B, C and D).

HIV & AIDS Infection with the human immunodeficiency virus (HIV) may lead to acquired immune deficiency syndrome (AIDS), which is fatal. Any exposure to blood, blood products or body fluids may put the individual at risk. The disease is often transmitted through sexual contact or dirty needles – vaccinations, acupuncture, tattooing and body piercing are potentially as dangerous as intravenous drug use. HIV/AIDS can also be spread through infected blood transfusions; some developing countries don't screen blood used for transfusions. Of the countries in this book, only South Africa, Botswana and Namibia have reliable blood supplies. If you do need an injection, ask to see the syringe unwrapped in front of you, or take a needle and syringe pack with you.

Fear of HIV infection should never preclude treatment for serious medical conditions.

Intestinal Worms These parasites are most common in rural, tropical areas. Different worms infect people in different ways. Some may be ingested on food such as undercooked meat (eg, tapeworms) and some enter through the skin (eg, hookworms). Infestations may not show up for some time,

and although they are generally not serious, they can cause severe long-term health problems if left untreated. When you return home, consider having a stool test, then determine the appropriate treatment for any problems.

Meningococcal Meningitis This serious disease can be fatal and there are recurring epidemics in sub-Saharan Africa. It's usually spread by close contact with people who carry it in their noses and throats, and pass it on through coughs and sneezes.

The first symptoms include fever, severe headache, sensitivity to light, and neck stiffness which prevents nodding forward. There may also be purple patches on the skin. Death can occur within a few hours, so urgent medical treatment is essential. Treatment is large doses of penicillin given intravenously, or chloramphenicol injections.

Schistosomiasis Also known as bilharzia, this disease is transmitted by minute flukes that infect freshwater snails found in rivers, streams, and lakes, and particularly behind dams. The flukes multiply and are eventually discharged into the water. The fluke enters through the skin and attaches itself to your intestines or bladder. The first symptom may be a general feeling of unwellness, or a tingling or light rash around the area where it entered. Weeks later a high fever may develop. Once the disease is established, it may cause abdominal pain and blood in the urine. However, the infection often causes no symptoms until the disease is well established (several months to years after exposure) and damage to internal organs is irreversible.

The best prevention is to avoid swimming or bathing in fresh water where bilharzia is present; running water isn't usually a problem, but avoid swimming in dams or other stagnant water. If you do get wet, dry off quickly and dry your clothes.

A blood test is the most reliable way to diagnose the disease, but the test will not show positive until a number of weeks after exposure. Treatment is usually with a product known as biltricide, which is available in pharmacies all over affected areas of Africa.

Sexually Transmitted Infections (STIs) HIV/AIDS and hepatitis B can be transmitted through sexual contact – see the relevant sections earlier for more details.

The Devastation of AIDS

Africa is plagued by wars, famines, natural disasters and political unrest, but AIDS remains the greatest problem it has ever faced, and the statistics are shocking. Since the mid-1990s, AIDS has been the leading cause of death in Africa; more than 30 million people across the continent will die of the disease by 2020. Around 90% of the world's AIDS sufferers live in Africa – a continent suffering wider humanitarian crises, with deficient health services and limited resources for HIV/AIDS prevention, care and treatment.

According to the United Nations' AIDS body, UNAIDS, the sub-Saharan region, by far the worst-affected part of Africa, is home to 29.4 million people living with HIV/AIDS. Women account for 58% of sufferers. Ten million young people (aged 15 to 24) and almost three million children under 15 are living with HIV.

National adult HIV prevalence has risen higher than thought possible in Botswana (38.8%), Lesotho (31%), Swaziland (33.4%) and Zimbabwe (33.7%). The rates in other Southern Africa countries are as follows: Namibia, 22.5%; Zambia, 21.5%; South Africa, 20.1%; and Malawi, 15%.

The Southern African region loses 836,000 adults and children to AIDS each year and there are an estimated 2.5 million orphans under the age of 15 who have lost their mother or father or both parents to AIDS. Even in prosperous South Africa, 1500 people become infected every day.

There are many possible reasons why AIDS has taken such a hold in Africa compared with the West. Migration of people in search of work and to escape wars and famine, a general lack of adequate health-care and prevention programs, and social and cultural factors – in particular the low status of women and their lack of empowerment in many African societies – are all believed to have played a role in the rapid spread of HIV/AIDS. While South Africa, Botswana and Namibia have done a relatively good job of educating their populace about HIV/AIDS risks, some politicians refuse to encourage HIV education, citing racially motivated 'outside conspiracies'. This does little to alter the attitudes of local people who consider HIV/AIDS (and, in many cases, sex) a taboo subject.

In nations with high infection rates, the socioeconomic effects are overwhelming. Unlike many diseases that mostly affect the weak, HIV/AIDS predominantly hits the most productive members of society – young adults.

In Southern Africa, it's particularly rife among those who are educated and have relatively high earnings or mobility. Thus, teachers, truck drivers and civil servants (and their stay-at-home wives) are at greater risk than those with a more stationary lifestyle. This has a huge impact on family incomes, and on food production and local economies in general, meaning that Africa faces the loss of a large proportion of whole generations. This is creating a population age profile that will no longer resemble the usual pyramid, but rather an hourglass, representing a generation of orphans and elderly.

Treating sufferers is a great burden for already underfunded health services. The increasing number of orphans whose parents die from AIDS increases strain on the state and on extended families. The high cost of drug therapies is out of reach of most sufferers, and although a few Western pro-grammes now provide affordable treatment, there's not yet any effective cure for the disease. It will be many years before the benefits of these programmes become visible in the statistics.

Africa faces massive challenges, with UNAIDS predicting that the AIDS death toll will continue to rise before peaking around the end of this decade. It is a desperate battle with severe social and economic costs that are yet to make their impact fully known.

Other STIs include gonorrhoea, herpes and syphilis; common symptoms include sores, blisters or rashes around the genitals, and discharges or pain when urinating. In some STIs, such as wart virus or chlamy-dia, symptoms may be less marked or not observed at all, especially in women. Chlamydia infection can cause infertility in men and women before any symptoms have been noticed. Syphilis symptoms eventually disappear completely but the disease continues and can cause severe problems in later years. While abstinence from sexual contact is the only 100% effective prevention, using condoms is usually effective. Gonorrhoea, syphilis and other STIs are typically treated with antibiotics, but each one requires a different regimen.

Typhoid A dangerous gut infection caused by contaminated water and food, typhoid always requires medical attention. In its early stages sufferers may sense the beginnings of a bad cold or flu: headache, body aches and a fever which rises a little each day up to around 40°C (104°F) or more. Whereas the pulse is elevated with a normal fever, it is relatively slow in the presence of typhoid. Other possible symptoms include vomiting, abdominal pain, diarrhoea or constipation.

In the second week, the high fever and slow pulse continue and a few pink spots may appear on the body, accompanied by trembling, delirium, weakness, weight loss and dehydration. Resulting complications may include pneumonia, perforated bowel or meningitis.

Insect-Borne Diseases

While most insect-borne diseases pose little risk for travellers, there is a risk of contracting malaria or dengue fever. For information on other insect-borne diseases, see under Less Common Diseases at the end of this health section.

Malaria This serious and potentially fatal disease is spread by the *anopheles* mosquito. Those travelling in endemic areas should take special caution to avoid mosquito bites and take any doctor-prescribed prophylaxis. Before you travel, seek medical advice to find the right medication and dosage.

Symptoms of malaria typically begin with a vague feeling of ill-health and a loss of appetite, then progress to spells of fever, chills and sweating, headache, diarrhoea and abdominal pains. If malaria is suspected, seek medical help immediately; without treatment malaria can rapidly grow more serious and can be fatal.

A variety of medications is available, including mefloquine, Fansidar and Malarone. If medical care is not available, malaria tablets (as well as tetracycline and several other antibiotics) can be used but you must use a different treatment from the one you were taking as a prophylaxis.

Travellers are advised to prevent mosquito bites at all times. The main messages are:

- Wear light-coloured clothing
- Wear long trousers and long-sleeved shirts
- Use mosquito repellents containing the compound DEET on exposed areas (prolonged overuse of DEET may be harmful, especially to children, but its use is considered preferable to being bitten by disease-transmitting mosquitoes)
- Avoid perfumes or aftershave
- Use a mosquito net impregnated with mosquito repellent (permethrin) – it may be worth taking your own
- Impregnating clothes with permethrin effectively deters mosquitoes and other insects

Dengue Fever Unlike the *anopheles* (malaria-carrying) mosquito, the *Aedes aegypti* mosquito, which transmits the dengue virus, is most active during the day and is found mainly in urban areas and around human dwellings. Signs and symptoms of dengue fever include a sudden onset of high fever, headache, joint and muscle pains (hence its old name, 'breakbone fever'), and nausea and vomiting. A rash of small red spots sometimes appears three to four days after the onset of fever. In the early phase of illness, dengue may be mistaken for other infectious diseases, including malaria and influenza. Minor bleeding (such as nose bleeds) may occur in the course of the illness, but this does not necessarily mean that you have progressed to the potentially fatal dengue haemorrhagic fever (DHF – commonly known in Africa as Congo fever). This is a severe illness, characterised by heavy bleeding, which is thought to be a result of secondary infection from a different strain (there are four major strains). Recovery, even from simple dengue fever, may be prolonged, with tiredness lasting for several weeks.

If you suspect dengue fever, seek medical attention as soon as possible, mainly to exclude malaria. There's no specific treatment for dengue, but aspirin should be avoided to minimise the risk of haemorrhaging. There is no vaccine against dengue fever. The best prevention is to avoid mosquito bites – for advice, see the Malaria section earlier.

Cuts, Bites & Stings

See Less Common Diseases later in this section for details of rabies, which is passed through animal bites.

Cuts & Scratches Minor injuries should be washed well and treated with an antiseptic such as povidone-iodine. Where possible avoid bandages and Band-Aids, which can keep wounds moist. Coral cuts are notoriously slow to heal and if they are not adequately cleaned, small pieces of coral can become embedded in the wound.

Bedbugs & Lice Bedbugs live mainly in dirty mattresses and bedding, evidenced by spots of blood on bedclothes or on the wall. They leave itchy bites in neat rows. Calamine lotion or a sting relief spray may help.

All lice cause itching and discomfort. They make themselves at home in your hair (head lice), your clothing (body lice) or in your pubic hair (crabs). They're transmitted by direct contact with infected people by sharing combs, clothing and the like. Use medicated powders or shampoos to kill the lice and wash infected clothing in very hot, soapy water, then leave it in the sun to dry.

Bites & Stings Bee and wasp stings are usually more painful than dangerous, but travellers who are allergic to bee or wasp stings should always carry the required emergency treatment with them. Calamine lotion or a sting relief spray will give relief, and ice packs will reduce the pain and swelling. Some spiders are quite dangerous, but in Africa, scorpions present a greater risk. Always check your shoes, clothing and boots before putting them on, and avoiding putting your hands into dark logs before checking what's there.

Leeches & Ticks Leeches, which love damp conditions, attach themselves to your skin to suck your blood. They often wind up on trekkers' legs and in their boots. Don't pull them off, as the bite may become infected; apply salt or a lighted cigarette until they fall off. Because the leech injects an anticoagulant to keep the blood flowing, wounds are likely to bleed more than usual. After cleaning the wound, apply pressure until the bleeding stops. Insect repellent may keep leeches away.

Those walking through the bush should check occasionally for ticks, as they can cause skin infections and other more serious diseases. If a tick is found, press down around the tick's head with tweezers, grab the head and gently pull upwards. Avoid pulling the rear of the body as this may squeeze the tick's gut contents through the attached mouth parts into the skin, increasing the risk of infection and disease. Chemical applications will not make the tick let go, and are not recommended.

Snakes To minimise your chances of being bitten always wear boots, socks and long trousers when walking through undergrowth where snakes may be present. Don't put your hands into holes and crevices, and be careful when collecting firewood.

Snake bites do not cause instantaneous death and antivenins are usually available. Immediately wrap the bitten limb tightly, as you would for a sprained ankle, and then attach a splint to immobilise it. Keep the victim still and seek medical help, if possible. Do all you can to get a positive identification of the snake, but don't attempt to catch it! A good field guide may prove invaluable (see Field Guides under Books earlier in this chapter). Tourniquets and sucking out the poison are now comprehensively discredited.

Less Common Diseases

The following diseases pose a small risk to travellers, and are therefore only mentioned in passing. Naturally, anyone who suspects any of these things should seek medical advice.

Cholera Outbreaks of cholera, which is marked by a severe, watery diarrhoea, are generally widely reported, so you can avoid such problem areas. *Fluid replacement is the most vital treatment* – the risk of dehydration is severe, and you may lose up to 20L of fluids a day. If you can't reach a hospital, begin taking tetracycline; the adult dose is 250mg four times daily (but it isn't recommended for pregnant women or children under nine years). While tetracycline will help shorten the illness, adequate fluids are required to save lives.

Filariasis This is a mosquito-transmitted parasitic infection found in many parts of Africa. Possible symptoms include fever, pain and swelling of the lymph glands; inflammation of lymph drainage areas; swelling of a limb or the scrotum; skin rashes; and blindness. Treatment is available to eliminate the parasites from the body, but damage already caused may not be reversible. Seek medical advice promptly if you suspect the infection.

Leishmaniasis This group of parasitic diseases is transmitted by sandflies, which are found in many parts of Africa. Cutaneous leishmaniasis affects the skin tissue causing ulceration and disfigurement, and visceral leishmaniasis affects the internal organs. Seek medical advice, as laboratory testing is required for diagnosis and correct treatment. Avoiding sandfly bites is the best precaution. Bites are usually painless, itchy and yet another reason to cover up and apply repellent.

Rabies This fatal viral infection is found in many countries, and is transmitted in the saliva of infected animals, especially dogs, cats, bats and monkeys. Any bite, scratch or even lick from an animal should be cleaned immediately and thoroughly. Scrub with soap and running water, and then apply alcohol or iodine solution. Medical help should be sought promptly to receive a course of injections to prevent the onset of symptoms and death.

Sleeping Sickness The tsetse fly, which is found in many areas of Southern Africa, can carry trypanosomiasis, or sleeping sickness. It's slightly larger than an ordinary housefly and is recognisable by its scissorlike wings. Only a small proportion of tsetse flies carry the disease, but it can be fatal without treatment. No protection is available except avoiding tsetse fly bites. The flies are attracted to large moving objects such as safari buses, and to perfume, aftershave and bright colours (especially blue). The first sign of infection is swelling of the bite – usually after five or more days – followed within two or three weeks by fever.

Tetanus This disease is caused by a bacteria *(Clostridium tetani)* which lives in soil and in the faeces of horses and other animals. It enters the body via breaks in the skin. The first symptom may be discomfort in swallowing, or stiffening of the jaw and neck; this is followed by painful convulsions of the jaw and whole body, and is most often fatal. It's easily prevented by vaccination, which is good for five to 10 years.

Tuberculosis (TB) This is a bacterial infection usually transmitted from person to person by coughing but which may be transmitted through consumption of unpasteurised milk. Milk that has been boiled is safe to drink, and the souring of milk to make yogurt or cheese also kills the bacilli. Because close household contact is usually required to pass along the disease, travellers are usually not at great risk. You may want to have a TB test before you travel, as it will help diagnose the disease later if you become ill.

Typhus Spread by ticks, mites or lice, typhus begins with fever, chills, headache and muscle pains followed a few days later by a body rash. There is often a large painful sore at the site of the bite, and nearby lymph nodes are swollen and painful. Typhus can be treated under medical supervision. Seek local advice on areas where ticks pose a danger and always check your skin carefully for ticks after walking in an endemic area. Insect repellants may help, and hikers in tick-infested areas may want to impregnate their boots and trousers with benzyl benzoate and dibutylphthalate.

Yellow Fever This viral disease is endemic in many African and South American countries and is transmitted by mosquitoes. The initial symptoms are fever, headache, abdominal pain and vomiting. Seek medical care urgently and drink lots of fluids.

SOCIAL GRACES
Greetings
A few straightforward courtesies may greatly improve a foreigner's chances of acceptance by the local community, especially in rural areas. In Southern Africa, pleasantries are taken quite seriously, and it's essential to greet or say goodbye to someone entering or leaving a room. Learn the local words for hello and goodbye and use them unsparingly. In rural Zimbabwe, verbal greetings are often accompanied by a clap of the hands. For those out of earshot, it is customary to offer a smile and a pleasant wave, even if you're just passing in a vehicle.

Emphasis is also placed on handshakes. The African handshake consists of three parts: the normal Western handshake, followed by the linking of bent fingers while touching the ends of upward-pointing

Gifts

If you visit a remote community, please tread lightly and leave as little lasting evidence of your visit as possible. In some African societies, it isn't considered impolite to ask others for other items one may desire. If you're besieged with requests, it's perfectly acceptable to refuse without causing offence. If you start feeling guilty about your relative wealth and hand out all your earthly belongings, you may be regarded as very silly indeed. As for gift-giving, reciprocation of kindness is one thing but superficial altruism is another. Indiscriminate distribution of gifts from outside, however well intentioned, tends to create a taste for items not locally available, erodes well established values, robs people of their pride, and in extreme cases, creates villages of beggars.

On the other hand, when you're offered a gift, don't feel guilty about accepting it, as refusal may bring shame on the giver. To receive a gift politely, accept it with both hands and perhaps bow slightly. If you're receiving some minor thing you've asked for, such as a salt shaker or a pen, or getting back change at a shop, receive it with your right hand while touching your left hand to your right elbow; this is the equivalent of saying thanks. Spoken thanks aren't common and local people tend to think Westerners say thank you too often and too casually, so don't be upset if you aren't verbally thanked for a gift.

---

thumbs, and then a repeat of the conventional handshake. In Botswana, offer your right hand for a conventional handshake while holding your right elbow with your left hand. Often, people continue to hold hands right through their conversation.

Status

As in most traditional societies, the achievement of old age is an accomplishment worthy of respect, and elders are treated with deference – their word should not be questioned and they should be accorded utmost courtesy. Teachers, doctors, and other professionals often receive similar treatment.

Likewise, people holding positions of authority – immigration officers, government officials, police, village chiefs, and so on – should be dealt with pragmatically. Officials in South Africa, Botswana, and Namibia are not as sensitive as those in most neighbouring countries and are normally refreshingly open and friendly. However, if you cross them or strike a nerve, all that may change. It is one thing to stand up for your rights, but blowing a fuse, undermining an official's judgement or authority, or insulting an ego may only serve to waste time, tie you up in red tape and inspire closer scrutiny of future travellers.

Children rate very low on the social scale. They are expected to do as they're told without complaint and defer to adults in all situations. For example, it is considered rude for a child to occupy a seat in a bus if adults are standing. Foreigners are normally exempted.

Similarly, Southern Africa is largely still a male domain, and black African men will not normally give up a seat to a woman, never mind that she is carrying a baby and luggage and minding two toddlers. Local whites, however, generally follow Western conventions.

Visiting Villages

When visiting rural settlements, it's a good idea to request to see the chief to announce your presence and ask permission before setting up camp or wandering through a village. You will rarely be refused permission. Women should dress and behave modestly, especially in the presence of chiefs or other highly esteemed persons.

Visitors should also ask permission before drawing water from community bore holes. If you do draw water at a community tap or bore hole, avoid letting it spill on the ground, especially in desert areas, where it's as precious as gold. If you wish to wash your body or your clothing, fill a container with water and carry it elsewhere.

Lone travellers may be looked upon with suspicion – women because they should be at home rearing families, and men because, in many areas, foreigners are potentially spies for right-wing factions. It may help to carry photographs of your family or evidence of a profession not linked to espionage.

Food Etiquette

Most travellers will have the opportunity to share an African meal sometime during

Sexual Harassment

Although sexual harassment is less of a problem for women travellers in Southern Africa than it is in some parts of the world, women travellers (especially those travelling alone) may have to deal with unwanted suitors. This will usually be no more than unpleasant meetings with lewd officials or tenacious admirers who won't take 'no' for an answer.

Interest on the part of local men normally stems from the fact that local women rarely travel alone, and a single foreign woman is an unusual sight. Thanks to imported TV and Hollywood films, Western women are sometimes perceived as being 'loose' and 'easy'.

It's disappointing but true: what you wear will influence how you're treated. Most African women dress conservatively, so if you wear something significantly different from the local norm you will draw attention to yourself. In the minds of some men, unusual dressing will be seen as provocative. Watch what other women wear and follow suit; cover your upper arms, and keep your thighs covered. (See the boxed text 'Dress Codes' in the Facts about the Region chapter.)

Ideally, avoid visiting isolated areas alone. If you do find yourself alone in an uneasy situation, stick your nose in a book or invent an imaginary husband who will be arriving shortly. Although as a traveller you would be very unlucky to encounter any serious problems, it's worth trying to understand the grim context of sexual violence in Southern Africa. The statistics are horrifying, particularly in South Africa. The most recent Human Rights Watch statistics available at the time of research revealed that three out of 10 women surveyed in the Jo'burg area reported that they had been victims of sexual violence in the previous year (1998); one in four young men questioned reported having had sex with a woman without her consent by the time he had reached 18. It's going to be a huge undertaking to debunk this culture of violence towards women and girls, all the more so as President Thabo Mbeki continues to criticise the statistics, calling them inflated and speculative.

their stay and will normally be given royal treatment and a seat of honour. Although concessions are sometimes made for foreigners, table manners are probably different from what you're accustomed to. The African staple, maize or sorghum meal, is the centre of nearly every meal. It is normally taken with the right hand from a communal pot, rolled into balls, dipped in some sort of sauce or relish – meat, beans or vegetables – and eaten. As in most societies, it is considered impolite to scoff food, or to hoard it or be stingy with it. If you do, your host may feel that he or she hasn't provided enough. Similarly, if you can't finish your food, don't worry; the host will be pleased that you have been satisfied. Often, containers of water or home-brew beer may be passed around from person to person. However, it is not customary to share coffee, tea or bottled soft drinks.

WOMEN TRAVELLERS
Attitudes Towards Women

Generally speaking, women travellers in Southern Africa will not encounter serious gender-related problems. In fact, compared with North Africa and the Middle East (especially Morocco, Egypt and Turkey), South America, and many Western countries, the region is relatively safe and unthreatening for women travellers (but see the boxed text 'Sexual Harassment' later for the other side of the equation concerning local women).

Southern Africa is one of the few places in the developing world where women can meet and communicate with local men – of any race – without automatically being misconstrued. That's not to say that sexual harassment against travellers never happens, but local white women (mostly South Africans, Namibians, Zambians and Zimbabweans) have done much to refute the idea that women of European descent are willing to hop into bed with the first taker.

That said, when it comes to evening entertainment, both black and white societies in Southern Africa are very much conservative, traditional and male-dominated. Therefore, women travellers may face a few glass walls and ceilings. Many bars are male only (by law of the establishment, or by law of tradition), and even where women are 'allowed', cultural conventions often dictate that women don't enter without a male companion. If you ignore these conventions, be aware that accepting a drink from a local man is usually construed as a come-on (much as it would be in many other parts of the world). However distasteful that may seem to liberated Westerners, trying to buck the system may lead to an uncomfortable situation – or worse.

To avoid attracting unwanted attention, it's best to solicit and follow local female advice on which places are acceptable. While some white women may try to discourage you from any sort of nightlife (citing one or two horrendous events they recall), local black women generally have a more realistic picture of what's going on.

It may be difficult to connect with some local women – especially older women, who may have received very little education and therefore speak little English. Similarly, women with young children are normally expected to stay home and attend to domestic duties, which leave them little time to socialise with outsiders. On the other hand, in recent years an increasing number of girls have been permitted to stay in school while boys are sent away to work. Female literacy is becoming more prevalent all over the region and as a result, many of the employees in government offices – including tourist offices – are educated, young to middle-aged women. In rural areas, most of the teachers and healthcare workers are also women.

For women who do meet someone they like, or who wish to sample local hospitality, never forget that in Africa, HIV/AIDS presents a threat that's unimaginable in the West. Local sex workers are almost always infected, and men may see a foreign woman as a safe alternative. Don't be naive, don't do anything stupid and at the very least, always use a condom.

Other Considerations

Mugging remains a threat, mainly because local low-life sees women – especially lone women – as easy targets. Your best defence is to simply avoid risky areas (see Dangers & Annoyances in the individual country chapters), especially at night.

While the countries in this region are considerably safer than some other parts of the world, hitching is not recommended and hitching alone is foolish. If you decide to thumb it, you should refuse a lift if the driver is drunk (a sadly common condition) or the

car is chock-a-block with men (eg, a military vehicle). Use common sense and things should go well.

Tampons and sanitary napkins are sold in pharmacies and supermarkets in major towns. They may also be available from shops at hotels and upmarket safari lodges.

Female travellers may like to contact the global organisation called **Women Welcome Women World Wide** (☎/fax 01494-465441; **w** www.womenwelcomewomen.org.uk; 88 Easton St, High Wycombe, Bucks HP11 1LT, UK), which fosters international friendship by enabling women of different countries to visit one another.

GAY & LESBIAN TRAVELLERS

All the countries covered in this book are conservative in their attitudes towards gay men and lesbians, and homosexuality is rarely discussed sensibly in public. In traditional African societies, gay sexual relationships are a cultural taboo, although some homosexual activity – especially among younger men – does occur.

In the past several years, the presidents of Zimbabwe and Namibia have both spoken out publicly and venomously against homosexuals. In 2001, President Sam Nujoma of Namibia famously said:

In Namibia we don't allow lesbianism or homosexuality...We will combat this with vigour... Police are ordered to arrest you and deport you and imprison you...Those who are practicing homosexuality in Namibia are destroying the nation. Homosexuals must be condemned and rejected in our society.

While this may seem both alarming and deluded, observers see it – along with Zimbabwean president Robert Mugabe's vociferous diatribes against homosexuals – as just a way of deflecting attention from greater governmental problems.

Officially, male homosexual activity is illegal in all the countries in this book, except South Africa (where larger cities – especially Cape Town – enjoy a growing gay scene) and Lesotho. Lesbian activities are illegal in Malawi, Namibia, Swaziland and Zimbabwe, and are ignored in other countries because officials aren't really aware of them.

In most places open displays of affection are generally frowned upon, whatever your orientation. Please be sensitive to local sensibilities.

DISABLED TRAVELLERS

People with mobility limitations will not have an easy time in Southern Africa. Even though there are more disabled people per head of population here than in the West, facilities are few. In South Africa and the capitals of some other countries, some official buildings have ramps and lifts, but these are probably not the sort of places you want to visit!

For the imaginative, Zambezi raft trips, *mokoro* trips in the Okavango Delta (where at least one mobility disabled person works as a *mokoro* poler) wildlife drives and cruises, lie-down sandboarding in the Namib Dunes (if you can reach the top on a quad bike), and other activities won't be inaccessible. In almost all cases, safari companies – including budget operators – are happy to accommodate travellers with special needs, so it never hurts to ask! One company specialising in accessible tours is listed under Disabled Travellers in the South Africa chapter.

Most wheelchair users find travel easier with an able-bodied companion, and happily, travel in Southern Africa does offer a few advantages compared with other parts of the developing world: footpaths and public areas are often surfaced with tar or concrete, rather than with sand, mud or gravel; many buildings (including safari lodges and national park cabins) are single storey; assistance is usually available on domestic and regional flights; and car hire is easy in South Africa, Namibia and Botswana; and with permission, vehicles can be taken to neighbouring countries.

Organisations

In the US, **Mobility International** (☎ 541-343 1284, fax 451-343 6812; Ⓦ www.miusa.org; PO Box 10767, Eugene OR 97440) advises disabled travellers on mobility issues. It primarily runs educational exchange programmes, and some include African travel. Also in the US, assistance and advice are available from the **Society for Accessible Travel and Hospitality** (☎ 212-447-7284, fax 725 8253; Ⓦ www.sath.org; 347 Fifth Ave, Suite 610, New York NY 10016). A one-year subscription to its quarterly magazine, *Open World*, costs US$45.

In the UK, a useful contact is the **Royal Association for Disability & Rehabilitation** (☎ 020 7250 3222, fax 7250 0212; Ⓦ www.radar.org.uk; 12 City Forum, 250 City Rd, London EC1V 8AF).

SENIOR TRAVELLERS

Southern Africa is generally good for senior travellers (on the assumption that they want to rough it less than the younger folk), with facilities such as comfortable and amenable hotels and restaurants generally available. Many senior South Africans (mostly whites) tour their own country – there is a thriving caravan scene – and visit many of the neighbouring countries independently or with organised package tours.

Unfortunately, few hotels or tour companies offer senior discounts, but if you ask, you can get discounts on most regional airlines, as well as long-distance bus companies (such as InterCape Mainliner). Discounts are also available on many (already negligible) museum admissions.

The **American Association of Retired Persons** (AARP, ☎ 800-424 3410; Ⓦ www.aarp.org; 601 E St NW, Washington DC 20049), is an advocacy group for US residents over 50 years of age and a good source of travel bargains. Non-US residents can get one-year memberships for US$10.

TRAVEL WITH CHILDREN

Southern Africa presents few problems specific to children, and while health concerns are always an issue, food and lodging are mostly quite familiar and manageable. What's more, foreigners with children are usually treated with great kindness, and a widespread local affection for the younger set opens up all sorts of social interaction for travelling families.

In South Africa, away from the coast, many resorts, hotels and national park lodges and camping grounds have a wide range of facilities for children. Many families hire camper vans in South Africa to tour the region. There are fewer child-orientated facilities in the other countries, but here the attractions usually provide entertainment enough: large wild animals in the national parks are a major draw, and even bored teenagers have been known to enjoy Vic Falls and its adrenaline activities. Namibia also lends itself to family travel by campervan, and the attractions – such as the wildlife of Etosha National Park, or the world's biggest sandbox at Sossusvlei – are entertainment in themselves.

In tourist hotels and lodges, family rooms and chalets are normally available for only slightly more than doubles. Otherwise, it's normally easy to arrange more beds in a standard adult double for a minimal extra charge. On public transport children are expected to pay for their seats unless they spend the entire journey on their parents' laps.

In Southern Africa, compared with some other parts of the world, there are few nasty diseases to worry about, and good (if expensive) medical services are almost always within reach. On the downside, distances between sites of interest can be long, especially on public transport, so parents may well need to invent creative games or provide supplementary entertainment. Children will normally enjoy having their own small backpacks to carry favourite toys or teddies, books, crayons and paper, or even a Nintendo Game-Boy (but not for use on wildlife drives, where it'd be too noisy, or on local buses, where few children have access to such technological wonders).

Outside major towns in South Africa, do not plan on finding pasteurised milk, formula, or disposable nappies. They may be available sporadically, but this is the exception rather than the rule.

For more advice and anecdotes, see Lonely Planet's *Travel with Children*.

DANGERS & ANNOYANCES

It is very important not to make sweeping statements about personal safety in Southern Africa. While some areas are undeniably risky, most places are completely safe. Essentially, violent robbery is much more prevalent in cities and towns than in rural or wilderness areas. But even towns can differ; there's more of a danger in those frequented by foreigners than in places off the usual tourist track. Details are provided in the individual country chapters.

Street Smarts

The main annoyances you'll come across in Southern Africa are the various hustlers, touts, con artists and scam-merchants who recognise tourists as easy prey. Although these characters aren't always dangerous,

their aim is to get at your valuables. Awareness, vigilance and suitable precautions are advisable, and should help you deal with them. The following are just several of the inventive ways some scoundrels separate travellers from their money.

Remember Me? A popular trick in tourist areas is for local lads to approach you in the street and say, 'Hello, it's me, from the hotel, don't you recognise me?' You're not sure. You don't really remember him, but then you don't want to seem rude, so you stop for a chat. After a few more pleasantries comes the crunch: How about a visit to his brother's souvenir shop? Or do you wanna buy some grass? Need a taxi or a tour? By this time you're hooked, and you'll probably end up buying or arranging something you don't really want. The best way to avoid the trap is to be polite but firm. If you don't remember the person, make that clear, and tell them you'd rather be left alone. You could ask 'which hotel' after the first greeting, but the guy may really work there, or at least have noticed you coming out.

The Friendly Stranger *Never* accept sweets, snacks or drinks from strangers, however friendly or respectable they may appear. The incidence of druggings, followed by robbery (and worse), is well documented. Refuse politely and complain of a stomach upset or allergy that would preclude your accepting the proffered gift. This cannot be stressed strongly enough!

Dud Sounds You buy some cassettes from a booth in the market, or from the young guys who walk the streets selling from a box. When you open the case, you'll find a blank tape or a recording by a completely different artist. This may well be due to faulty technology, but it's often a deliberate trick. When you buy tapes, always try to listen to them first – and remember that purchasing bootleg tapes is a crime all over the world.

Sponsorship Tourists are often approached by young people carrying sign-up sheets, requesting sponsorship for their school, sports team, youth club, grandmother's liver transplant or other apparently worthwhile causes. The sheets will invariably include the names of 'generous' foreigners who have donated US$100 or more. These are almost invariably a scam; ignore them and politely take your leave.

Safety Tips
Some simple precautions will hopefully ensure that you have a trouble-free journey. Travellers who exercise due caution rarely have problems. The precautions suggested in this section are particularly relevant to cities, although some might apply to other places too.

- On the streets, don't make yourself a target. Carry as little as possible. Consider leaving your daypack and camera in your hotel room if the room is safe. Even passports, travellers cheques and credit cards are sometimes safer left behind – particularly if the hotel has a reliable security box.
- Don't wear jewellery or watches, however inexpensive they may be. Use a separate wallet for day-to-day purchases, and keep the bulk of your cash out of sight, preferably hidden in a pouch under loose-fitting clothing.
- Walk purposefully and confidently, and never look like you're lost (even if you are!). Don't obviously refer to this guidebook. Tear out the pages you need, or duck into a shop to have a look at the map to get your bearings.
- At night, don't walk in the back streets, or even some main streets; take a taxi – a couple of dollars for the fare could save you a lot of pain and trouble.
- Don't fall into the trap of thinking all robbers are on the street. Although most hotels are reputable, some travellers have left money in a safe, only to find that less reputable staff members with a spare key have helped themselves. Often this trick involves taking just a few notes, in the hope that you won't notice. To avoid this, store your valuables in a safe inside a pouch with a lockable zip, or in an envelope you can seal.
- Travellers occasionally report stuff going missing from hotel rooms, and especially from shared hostel dorms. Travellers often leave handy little items like pocketknives, film or jewellery scattered all over the bed or floor, making it very convenient for hostel or hotel staff to help themself. Similarly, there are travellers around who are not averse to 'liberating' other people's possessions. The moral: keep your gear hidden in a bag that isn't easily carried off.

ACTIVITIES
Southern Africa's climate and landscape make the region ideal for numerous outdoor activities – from peaceful and relaxing to energetic and downright terrifying. **Wildlife**

viewing and **bird-watching** are two of the main activities that attract visitors. Details on the region's fascinating wildlife and national parks are provided in the Facts about the Region chapter, the Wildlife Guide and in the individual country chapters. For direction on organising wildlife safaris, see Organised Tours in the Getting Around sections of each country chapter. See also Safaris at the end of this section.

Numerous other activities are available for active visitors (ie, you can hire gear, arrange tuition, get permits etc) and all are covered in more detail in the relevant country chapters. The following list is not exhaustive, but may provide some ideas:

Air sports (Paragliding, parachuting, microlighting) South Africa, Zambia, Namibia
Beaches (if you count these as an activity) South Africa, Mozambique, Namibia, Malawi
Bungee jumping Zambia, Zimbabwe
Canoeing & kayaking (*mokoro* trips) Zimbabwe, Zambia, Namibia, South Africa, Malawi, Botswana
Cycling South Africa, Zimbabwe, Malawi, Zambia
Diving & snorkelling South Africa, Mozambique, Malawi
Fishing (deep-sea & surf) South Africa, Namibia, Mozambique
Fishing (river & lake) South Africa, Botswana, Zimbabwe, Malawi, Zambia
Hiking South Africa, Lesotho, Namibia, Zimbabwe, Malawi
Horse riding South Africa, Namibia, Zimbabwe, Lesotho, Zambia, Malawi
Rock climbing South Africa, Malawi, Zimbabwe, Namibia
Sandboarding Namibia
Sea kayaking Namibia, South Africa
Surfing South Africa, Mozambique
White-water rafting South Africa, Zimbabwe, Zambia, Namibia
Windsurfing (sailboarding) South Africa, Mozambique, Malawi

Cycling
Mountain bikes can be hired from hotels or tour companies in several tourist areas around Southern Africa, but you can also hire local-style sit-up-and-beg steel roadsters. These are good for getting around towns (especially flat ones) or exploring rural areas at a leisurely pace. For information on bringing your own bike to Southern Africa, see the regional Getting There & Away chapter.

Diving & Snorkelling

The best diving and snorkelling in the region is along the coast of Mozambique. It's also excellent along South Africa's Indian Ocean coast, which has good coral formations. Lake Malawi offers some of the best freshwater diving in the world, and is a particularly popular (and inexpensive) place to learn.

Football

Football (soccer) is Africa's most popular participation and spectator sport. If you want to play, the universities and municipal stadiums are the best places to find a good-quality game, but nearly every town in Africa has pitches where informal matches are played most evenings (in coastal areas, the beach works equally well). Foreigners are usually warmly welcomed and joining in a game is one of the best ways to meet the locals. Bring along your own ball (which could be deflated for travelling) and you'll be the hit of the day.

Otherwise, the ball may be more suitable for tennis, or it may be half-deflated or just a round bundle of rags, and each goal a couple of sticks, not necessarily opposite each other. You may have to deal with puddles, ditches and the odd goat or donkey wandering across the pitch, but the game itself is taken very seriously, and play is fast and furious, with the ball played low.

Hiking

Across Southern Africa there are many excellent opportunities for hiking, and this is one of the most popular activities in the region. Some hiking guidebooks are listed under Books, earlier in this chapter.

Trails Most hiking trails in Southern Africa are established and maintained by national park authorities, conservation bodies and private landowners. In South Africa, Namibia and some other countries you must pay a fee to use the trail, which covers the use of camp sites or accommodation (ranging from simple shelters to comfortable cabins) along the route. These trails are sometimes called overnight hikes; routes that take more than one day. Typically, you can only do the route in one direction (some are traverses while others are circular), and to preserve the condition of the trail, only a limited number of people are allowed to hike on any one day. In fragile areas, departures are only permitted once or twice per week, and even day and time of departure is sometimes stipulated. You must complete the trail in the set number of days and may not link two days together (except perhaps the last two) or stay extra nights at any camp site or hut, so they never become overcrowded.

Some trails have their own regulations. For example, few hikes allow fires (hikers need to carry camping stoves), and most are limited to parties of no fewer than three and no more than 10 people. For some of Namibia's tougher routes, participants must provide a doctor's certificate of health.

In South Africa and Namibia, popular multiday hiking trails typically require a reservation through the national parks office or other relevant authority. Only the popular classics such as the Otter Trail and Fish River Canyon are likely to be fully booked. In South Africa, you can sometimes find a slot when someone else has cancelled (this is no longer allowed in Namibia unless it's privately arranged).

Once space has been confirmed, you are issued with a permit. This is sent by post if you have a local address, or is held ready for collection at the national park headquarters. You can pay in advance with a credit card, or on arrival. Included in the price may be an information sheet or map of the route. You must turn up at the start of the trail on the arranged date and report to the 'officer-in-charge'. You'll also have to fill in a register (with details of the number of people in your party, experience, equipment, colour of backpacks), to be used in case of an emergency. Although this sounds like an incredibly complicated way to just take a walk, travellers who have completed the popular routes – especially in South Africa – recommend them highly.

Because of the bureaucracy surrounding the national parks' routes in Namibia, a growing number of private landholders have established their own long-distance routes, and many are just as rewarding as the well-known ones, but tend to cost a bit more. The best of these are outlined under Activities in the Namibia chapter.

Day Hikes For many visitors, hiking is the most convenient way to explore the region

Desert Hiking

While desert areas of Southern Africa – especially parts of Namibia, Botswana and South Africa – offer a host of hiking opportunities, the conditions are quite different from those to which most visitors are accustomed. Tramping through this lonely country is a wonderful experience, but hiking isn't recommended during the heat of the summer months, when temperatures can exceed 40°C. In national parks, summer hiking is officially forbidden, and most hiking trails are closed from November or December to April or May.

In the desert heat, hikers should carry 4L of water per person per day (an excellent way to carry water is in 2L plastic Coke bottles, which are available all over the region). The most effective way to conserve water isn't necessarily to drink sparingly. Before setting off in the morning (assuming that water is available at your overnight stop), flood your body's cells with water. That is, drink more water than you feel you can possibly hold! After a few hours, when you grow thirsty, do the same again from the supply you're carrying. Believe it or not, with this method you'll actually use less water and feel less thirsty than if you drink sparingly all day long.

Another major concern is the desert sun, which can be brutal. Wear light-coloured and lightweight clothing; use a good sunscreen (at least UV Protection Factor 30); and never set off without a hat that shelters your neck and face from the direct sun.

If the heat is a major problem, it's best to rise before the sun and hike until the heat becomes oppressive. You may then want to rest through the heat of mid-day and begin again after about 3pm. (Note, however, that summer thunderstorms often brew up at around this time and may continue into the night.) During warmer months, it may also be worthwhile timing your hike with the full moon, which will allow you to hike at night.

Because many trails follow canyons and riverbeds, it's important to keep a watch on the weather. Rainy periods can render normally dry kloofs and streambeds impassable, and rivers with large catchment areas can quickly become raging torrents of muddy water, boulders and downed trees. Never camp in canyons or dry riverbeds, and always keep to higher ground whenever there's a risk of flash-flooding.

---

on foot. Day hikes can range from 3km rambles to 20km marathons. In many parks and reserves, a number of day-hiking routes can be accessed from a single point (usually the park headquarters or a main camp), following a set route, with arrows, markers and distance indicators. Maps are often available, but these vary in quality from excellent to dangerously confusing. Although you won't get right out in the wilderness, you don't have to worry about reservations, pre-planning or carrying loads of gear.

One last point – in South Africa and Namibia the Afrikaans word *wandelpad* seems to refer to any kind of trail. Therefore, it's best to check the English translation, just to make sure your planned day-walk doesn't turn into a week's expedition.

4WD Trails

One of the most popular activities with locals in Southern Africa is taking off through the bush in 4WD vehicles. Historically, 4WD trips were limited to rugged wilderness tracks

through the remotest areas of the region. Recently, because of encroaching development and possible environmental degradation, 4WD enthusiasts with their own vehicles can now enjoy an increasing number of designated 4WD trails throughout South Africa, Namibia and Botswana. They're very popular, and prospective participants may have to book up to a year in advance. You must pay a daily fee and are obligated to travel a certain distance each day and stay at prespecified camp sites. Major routes are discussed in the relevant chapters.

Safaris

In most places in Southern Africa, large animals are confined to national parks (or similar conservation areas), and the only way to see them is by vehicle – this is both by law and by default, as there's rarely any public transport. If you don't have a vehicle (motorcycles and bicycles don't count), your only option is to join an organised safari.

Minimum Impact Camping

Wilderness campers should help to preserve Southern Africa's beauty and foster goodwill by heeding the following guidelines:

- Always carry out your rubbish (including cigarette butts), unless it can be burnt completely. Do not leave cans or silver foil (including the inner lining from drinks and soup packets) in the fire. Some hikers bury rubbish, but this is generally a no-no, as animals may smell the food and dig it up, or it may be exposed by soil erosion during rain.
- Select a well-drained camp site and, especially if it's raining, use a waterproof groundsheet. Don't dig trenches, which lead to more erosion.
- In some areas you have to camp at designated areas. In others you can camp where you like, but along popular tracks and trails try to set up camp in established sites.
- Use toilet facilities if they are available. Otherwise, select a site at least 50m from water sources and bury wastes at least several inches deep. If possible, burn the used toilet paper or carry it in a couple of strong plastic bags until it can be burnt or disposed of properly.
- Use only biodegradable soap products, which are available in bar form from Cape Union Mart shops in South Africa, Namibia and Botswana (you'll probably have to carry biodegradable liquid soaps from home). Also, use natural temperature water where possible. When washing up with hot water, avoid pollution and damage to vegetation either by letting the water cool to outdoor temperature before pouring it out or dumping it in a gravely place away from natural water sources and vegetation.
- Wash dishes and brush your teeth well away from watercourses
- When building a fire, try to select an established site and keep fires as small as possible. Use only fallen dead wood, and when you're finished, make sure ashes are cool and buried before leaving the site. (See also the boxed text 'Firewood' in the Namibia chapter.)

The term 'safari' (which means 'we go' in Swahili) may conjure up the image of a single-file procession of adventurers and porters stalking through the bush behind a large elephant gun, but modern usage is broader and may extend to bushwalking, river rafting, horse riding, canoeing, playing golf or just warming a seat on a train or vehicle. That said, most safaris involve wildlife viewing, which is most often done from a vehicle with open sides, large windows, or a pop-up roof to allow clear views and photographic opportunities. A driver (who doubles as guide) comes with the vehicle.

The range of wildlife-viewing safaris available in Southern Africa is enormous. They can last from a day to a month, and participants may camp outside and cook over an open fire or stay in luxury lodges and be served gourmet meals. You could charter a safari customised for your group's interests or join an already established group or pre-scheduled safari. You could spend a frantic day ticking species off a list or spend hours by a single waterhole watching the comings and goings.

And of course, there's also a range of prices available. The best value will be participation safaris, in which clients muck in to pack and unpack the vehicle, put up their own tents, and help with cooking and washing up. These are typically good value, and are almost always highly rewarding, especially when you get off the beaten track. At the other end of the spectrum, you can pay US$300 to US$400 per person per day and enjoy all the comforts of home, with a camp staff to take care of all the chores.

Lots of overseas agencies (see the Getting There & Away chapter) cobble together programmes using local operators, but these are typically quite expensive. Packages are generally more economical when organised on site (the exception is for safaris involving upmarket lodges, which are often block-booked by overseas agents who can get deals that are lower than rack rates). Locally, the best places to organise safaris are Cape Town, Windhoek and Harare, and the tourist towns of Livingstone and Vic Falls. For details, see Organised Tours in the Getting Around sections of the individual country chapters, and (where relevant) under the places themselves.

If you're on a real shoestring budget and can't afford even the cheapest of safaris, you'll probably be frustrated by the rules and regulations that appear to be designed specifically to keep you out of the parks. There is no public transport, and hitching is forbidden. Even in parks where walking is permitted, you usually have to start from the park headquarters, which is only accessible by vehicle. Hitching is prohibited *inside* the parks, but hours spent waving your thumb at the entrance gate may result in a lift that takes you where you want to go. Plan on long waits and have plenty of food and water.

ACCOMMODATION

In all the countries covered in this book, you'll find a wide range of overnight options. In towns and cities, top-end hotels offer clean, air-conditioned rooms with private bathrooms, while mid-range hotels typically offer fans instead of air-con. At the budget end, rooms aren't always clean (and may be downright filthy), and bathrooms are usually shared and may well be in an appalling state. Often, your only source of air will be a hole in the window. Many cheap hotels double as brothels, so if this is your budget level don't be surprised if there's a lot of coming and going during the night.

The good news is that in towns and cities on the main backpacker trail, there's usually at least one backpackers hostel, and in some places – such as Harare and Cape Town – you'll have a wide choice. These are usually straightforward, no-frills places, with space for camping, dormitories and a few private doubles, all at very affordable prices. Many also have a TV room, swimming pool, bar, restaurant and email and phone service, as well as a travel desk where you can book tours and safaris. Several of the smarter places accept credit cards.

Another option for the budget conscious are resthouses run by local governments or district councils. These are found all over the region, and many date from colonial times. Some are very cheap and less than appealing; others are well-kept and good value. In resthouses and other cheap hotels, definitions of single and double rooms are not always consistent. It may be determined by the number of beds rather than the number of people.

Therefore it is not unusual for two people to share a single room (which may have a large bed), paying either the single rate or something just a bit higher. If you want to save money, it's always worth asking.

Camping is also a popular option, especially in national parks, at coastal and lakeshore areas and in more expensive places, such as Botswana. Some camping grounds are quite basic, while others have a range of facilities, including hot showers and security fences. Wild camping (ie, not on an official site) is another option, but security can be a problem and wild animals are always a concern, so choose your tent site with care (see also the boxed text 'Minimum Impact Camping' earlier).

Many places offer self-catering facilities, which may mean anything from a fridge and a hotplate in the corner to a full kitchen in every unit. In some cases, guests will have to supply their own cooking implements – and perhaps even water and firewood.

In the national parks and wildlife reserves, there's a wide choice of accommodation, ranging from simple camping grounds to cabins, chalets, bungalows and luxurious camps and lodges. It's important to note that 'camp' doesn't necessarily denote a camp site, although it may. This sort of camp is normally a well-appointed upmarket option run by the private company that has won the concession for a set period of time (usually 10 years). Its structures are necessarily temporary, in compliance with local law, so accommodation is usually in tents or chalets made from natural materials. Contact numbers for these places will be at their office in a larger town, and are for bookings and inquiries only, not for direct contact with the lodge or camp.

In cities and towns, many hotels charge for a bed only, with perhaps breakfast included. In more expensive places, this means a full buffet breakfast with all the trimmings, while cheaper places offer just a light breakfast and coffee. In upmarket lodges and camps, the rates will typically include accommodation plus half-board, activities (wildlife drives, boat trips etc) and perhaps even house wine and beer. It may also include laundry and transfers by air or 4WD (although these are usually extra).

In Zimbabwe, Zambia and sporadically in other countries, hotels and lodges charge in tiers. That is, overseas visitors pay international rates (full price), visitors from other Southern African countries pay a regional rate (say around 30% less) and locals get resident rates (often less than half the full rate). Most places also give discounts in the low season. In this book, where possible we've quoted the international high season rates, including the value added tax (VAT), which ranges from 10% to 30%. If you intend staying at mostly top-end hotels and lodges, it's worth contacting a travel agent at home or in the capital of the country you're visiting to see if any special deals are available.

FOOD

While local cuisine isn't exactly exciting, you'll always find something to eat. For shoestring travellers, takeaway snacks (street food) are sold at roadsides, bus stations or markets. Options may include bits of grilled meat, deep-fried potato or cassava chips, roasted corn cobs, boiled eggs, peanuts (locally called ground nuts), biscuits, cakes and fried dough balls, which approximate doughnuts. Prices are always dirt cheap (unfortunately, often with the emphasis on dirt).

For something more substantial but still inexpensive, try a food stall (also called a tea stall), which is a basic eatery housed in a shack or hut. They're typically found in markets, bus stations, and around industrial areas or any part of town with low rent and a good passing trade. The most common meal is the regional staple, boiled maize meal, which is called *mielie pap* in South Africa and Namibia, *sadza* in Zimbabwe, and *nshima* or *nsima* in countries further north (in North America, it would be called 'grits', but the Southern African version is usually more finely ground). In Botswana, the standard is known as *bogobe*, in which sorghum replaces the maize. When fresh and well cooked, all varieties are both tasty and filling, and are usually eaten with a relish, which is either very simple (eg, boiled vegetable leaves) or something more substantial, such as a stew of beef, fish, beans or chicken.

Meals at food stalls are served in a bowl, and while some locals prefer to eat with their hands, spoons are normally available. You may eat standing up, or at a simple table with chairs. The main meal is at noon, so most cheap eateries are closed in the evening. In the morning you can buy coffee or tea (with or without milk – the latter is cheaper) and bread, sometimes with margarine, or maybe a slightly sweetened breadlike cake.

A grade above the food stalls are the takeaways and cheap restaurants in cities, large towns, and areas frequented by tourists. These tend to be slightly larger, cleaner and with better facilities. You can buy traditional meals of *mielies* and relish, or Western dishes, such as beef or chicken served with rice or chips (fries). In coastal and lakeside places, fish is also available. South Africa, Namibia and Botswana are also sprouting a range of fast-food joints – particularly places specialising in fried or *peri peri* (hot chilli) chicken. Wimpy, McDonald's, Whistle Stop and the like are becoming more ubiquitous, and in new shopping malls you'll even find fast-food Thai, seafood and Middle Eastern outlets.

Up another level are cheap to mid-range restaurants, with tablecloths, menus and waitstaff, where meals cost from US$3 to US$5. Many serve traditional food as well as chicken and chips, but also dish up more elaborate options, such as steaks, pies, fish dishes, pasta and something that resembles curry over rice. *Samoosas* (parcels of meat or vegetables wrapped in pastry; elsewhere called samosas) are common, as are burgers, pizzas and other Western-style foods. In tourist-oriented towns (Vic Falls, Livingstone, Nkhata Bay etc) you'll find many of the goodies you may be craving from home, including such backpacker specials as chocolate thick shakes, burritos and banana pancakes.

Moving up the scale to the mid-range, you'll typically pay US$5 to US$10 per person for the standard beef, chicken, fish, lamb and other dishes, but the price is justified by better quality, presentation, location and cleanliness. Meals in these places may emphasise beef or game (especially in South Africa, Namibia and Botswana), and may be influenced by a country's former colonial power or a prominent ethnic group (eg, German in Namibia, Portuguese in Mozambique, British in Botswana, Indian in South Africa or Zambia).

At top-end hotels and restaurants in cities and tourist areas, you'll find straightforward international standards, including plenty of steak places as well as French, British and Italian options. Most cities also have speciality restaurants serving genuine (or at least pretty close) Indian, Thai, Chinese, Lebanese, Mexican or ethnic African (such as Ethiopian or West African) cuisine.

Vegetarian

Vegetarianism isn't widely understood in Africa, and many locals think a meal is incomplete unless at least half of it once lived and breathed. That said, if you're not worried about variety or taste, finding inexpensive vegetarian options isn't that difficult. In the cheapest places, you may have to stick to the *mielies* and greens. A step above that would be eggs and chips (which may be fried in animal fat) with whatever vegetables may be available. Those who eat fish should have even more luck, but note that many places will even serve chicken as a vegetarian dish, on the notion that it's not really meat. Nearly all mid-range and upmarket restaurants offer some sort of genuine vegetarian dish, even if it's just a vegetable omelette or pasta and sauce. In larger cities and towns, a growing number of places specialise in light vegetarian cuisine – especially at lunch time – and of course, Lebanese, Indian and Italian restaurants usually offer interesting meat-free choices.

Self-Catering

All over Southern Africa you'll find fresh fruit and vegetables for sale at shops, markets and roadside stalls. This is useful if you're self-catering, and of course you can eat a lot of things raw (but see the advice on washing and peeling in the Health section earlier in this chapter).

Depending on the season, your diet can include bananas, pineapples, paw-paw (papaya), mangoes, avocados, tomatoes, carrots, onions and potatoes. Tinned and packaged foods are found at shops in small towns and villages, and in supermarkets in the cities.

DRINKS
Nonalcoholic Drinks

You can buy tea and coffee in many places, from top-end hotels and restaurants to humble local eating houses. International soft drinks such as Coke and Pepsi are widely available. As always, price reflects the standard of the establishment rather than the taste in your cup.

Alcoholic Drinks

In bars, hotels and bottle stores you can buy beer and spirits – either imported international brands or locally brewed drinks. South African and Namibian beers are available throughout the region, and in many areas they dominate local markets. Wonderful South African wines are widely available, as is a growing range of extremely popular spirit coolers.

Traditional beer of the region is made from maize, brewed in the villages and drunk from communal pots with great ceremony on special occasions, and with less ado in everyday situations. This product, known as *chibuku* (or shake-shake), is commercially brewed in many countries and sold in large blue paper cartons, or by the bucket-full. It's definitely an acquired taste, and it does pack a punch.

Getting There & Away

This chapter describes access possibilities to Southern Africa from other parts of the world. Regional access is described in the Getting Around the Region chapter. Details on travel between and around individual countries are provided in their respective chapters.

AIR
Airports
You can fly to any major city in Southern Africa from anywhere in the world, but some routes are more popular (and therefore usually cheaper) than others. The most useful airports for visitors are Johannesburg (South Africa), Cape Town (South Africa), Windhoek (Namibia), Harare (Zimbabwe), Lusaka (Zambia) and Lilongwe (Malawi). Gaborone (Botswana) is an especially pricey access point. Victoria Falls is best-accessed via Harare or Johannesburg.

Your access point need not necessarily be the nearest point to your intended destination. For example, it's often cheaper to fly into South Africa, from where you can take a short hop to Harare, Windhoek or Lusaka for less than a direct flight. On the other hand, bargain deals to Namibia, Zimbabwe or Zambia may be cheaper than a direct flight to South Africa. Advance research will greatly improve your chances of finding an economical airfare, so start looking early.

Tickets
When buying your air ticket, you may want to check out 'open-jaw' deals – ie, flying into one country and out of another. Sometimes though, even if you want to do a linear trip (starting in Cape Town and finishing in Harare, for example), it may be easier and cheaper to get a standard return (eg, in and out of Cape Town) and a one-way regional flight (Harare to Cape Town) at the end of your trip.

Purchasing tickets online is a growing trend. Many airlines now have their own web sites that allow you to book and purchase tickets with a credit card, but you'll generally get better deals through the various web sites specialising in discounted tickets:

w www.cheaptickets.com
w www.flynow.com
w www.lowestfare.com
w www.priceline.com
w www.travel.yahoo.com
w www.travelocity.com

At the moment, w www.flynow.com seems to come up with the lowest fares, but that could change at any time.

Airlines
Most major European airlines serve Southern Africa, including British Airways, KLM–Royal Dutch Airlines, Lufthansa Airlines, Swiss, Alitalia, Air France, Virgin and TAP Air Portugal. Additionally, Emirates, Kenya Airways, South African Airways, Air Namibia and LAM (Linhas Aereas de Moçambique) fly between Europe and the region, and unlikely-sounding carriers such as Ethiopian Airlines often offer good-value services between Europe and many parts of Africa.

Although several airlines fly between the USA (Atlanta) and Southern Africa, many prospective visitors find it less convenient, but considerably cheaper, to fly via Europe. From Australia, Qantas and other airlines have regular services from Sydney and Perth to both Harare and Johannesburg.

Australia & New Zealand Airlines flying from Australia to Southern Africa include Qantas, Air Zimbabwe and South African Airways. If flying between New Zealand and Southern Africa you must go via Australia. The best place to start looking for cheap deals are the ads in major weekend newspapers. Standard return flights between Australia and Southern Africa (usually Jo'burg, Cape Town or Harare) start at around A$1750.

Two well-known agencies for cheap fares in Australia are:

Flight Centre (☎ 131 600, w www.flightcentre
.com.au) This agency has offices throughout Australia
STA Travel (☎ 03-9349 2411, Australia-wide 131 776, w www.statravel.com.au) Offices are in all major cities and on many university campuses

These agencies are also represented in New Zealand:

Flight Centre (☎ 09-309 6171, W www.flight centre.co.nz) This agency has many branches throughout the country

STA Travel (☎ 09-309 0458, W www.statravel.co .nz) STA Travel has a main office in Auckland, and has offices in Hamilton, Palmerston North, Wellington, Christchurch and Dunedin

In addition, the following agencies specialise in Africa travel:

Africa Travel Company (☎ 02-9264 7661) Level 1, 69 Liverpool St, Sydney 2000, NSW

Africa Travel Shop (☎ 09-520 2000) 21 Remuera Rd, Newmarket, Auckland

African Wildlife Safaris (☎ 03-9696 2899, fax 9696 4937, e office@africasafaris.com.au) 1/259 Coventry St, South Melbourne 3205, Vic. Cobbles together custom tours to Namibia and the entire region. The focus is on wildlife safaris.

USA & Canada From North America, the cheapest high-season flights are currently between Atlanta and Johannesburg, which start at US$1818 return. To reach one of the other capitals, such as Harare, Lilongwe or Maputo, you can get a connection from Jo'burg for around US$200 more. It may be cheaper to fly on an economy hop from the USA to London (on British Airways or Virgin Atlantic) or Amsterdam (on KLM), and then buy a discount ticket from there to Southern Africa. Canadians also will probably find the best deals travelling via Atlanta or London.

North Americans won't get the great deals that are available in London, but discount agencies watch out for the best airfare bargains:

Air Brokers (☎ 800-883 3273 or 415-836 8718, fax 836 8719, W www.airbrokers.com) This is a consolidator that can come up with good rates on complicated itineraries

Council Travel (☎ 800-226 8624 or 617-528 2091, W www.counciltravel.com) This student travel agency does inexpensive bookings

High Adventure Travel/Airtreks (☎ 877-247 8735 or 415-912 5600, e travel@airtreks.com, W www.airtreks.com) 442 Post St, 4th Floor, San Francisco, CA 94102. This company specialises in round-the-world travel – itineraries including Southern Africa start at around US$2000.

Premier Tours & Travel (☎ 215-893 9966, fax 893 0357, e info@premiertours.com, W www .premiertours.com) 217 S 20th St, Philadelphia, PA 19103. See Organised Tours, later in this chapter.

Spector Travel (☎ 800-879 2374 or 617-338 0111, fax 338 0110, e africa@spectortravel .com, W www.spectortravel.com) 2 Park Plaza, Boston, MA 02116. This company combines tours with discounted airfares.

STA Travel (☎ 800-329 9537, e go@statravel .com, W www.statravel.com) This organisation, which isn't limited to students, has offices all over the USA

Travel Avenue (☎ 800-333 3335, fax 800-838 4376, e fareinfo@travelavenue.com, W www .travelavenue.com) This company books flights and tours, then returns a portion of their commission to travellers in the form of a rebate.

Travel Cuts (☎ Canada-wide 866-246 9762, W www.travelcuts.com) This is the Canadian student travel association

UK & Ireland Numerous airlines fly between Britain and Southern Africa, and you'll occasionally find excellent rates, especially through a budget travel agency that has access to a ticket consolidator. For a high-season return ticket, plan on UK£500 to UK£700 between London and Jo'burg, depending on the quality of the airline, service and routing. At the time of writing, the cheapest fares between London and Jo'burg were with Emirates, via Dubai (UK£516). Other return air fares from London include: Harare (UK£550 to UK£650), Windhoek (UK£550 to UK£650), Lilongwe (UK£600 to UK£800) and Maputo (around UK£800 to UK£1000). The least expensive point of arrival will probably be Jo'burg, although an increasing number of flights arrive in Cape Town, which is a safer introduction to Africa.

London is normally the best place to buy a ticket, but specialist agencies elsewhere in the UK can provide comparable value. Also, check ads in weekend newspapers, travel magazines and listings in freebie magazines (especially the *SA Times*, which is aimed at South Africans in the UK).

Some companies listed under Organised Tours (later in this chapter) also sell flights, and some of the agents listed here also sell tours and safaris:

Africa Travel Centre (☎ 020-7387 1211, fax 7383 7512, e info@africatravel.co.uk, W www.africa travel.co.uk) 21 Leigh St, London WC1H 9QX

Bridge the World (☎ 0870-444 7474, fax 020-7813 3350, ℯ sales@bridgetheworld.com, ᴡ www.bridgetheworld.com) 45-47 Chalk Farm Rd, Camden Town, London NW1 8AJ

North-South Travel (☎ 01245-608291, ℯ Brenda@northsouthtravel.co.uk, ᴡ www.northsouthtravel.co.uk) Moulsham Mill Centre, Parkway, Chelmsford CM2 7PX. At this experienced agency profits support development projects overseas

STA Travel (☎ 0870-1600 599, ℯ help@statravel.co.uk, ᴡ www.statravel.co.uk) STA Travel has branches in London, Manchester, Bristol and most large university towns

Trailfinders (☎ 020-7938 3939, ᴡ www.trailfinders.co.uk) This popular company has several office in London, as well as Manchester, Bristol and several other cities

Travel Mood (☎ 0870 4449911, fax 0870 4449610, ᴡ www.travelmood.com) 214 Edgware Rd, London W2 1DH

Continental Europe You can fly to Southern Africa from any European capital, but the main hubs are Amsterdam and Frankfurt, and to a lesser extent Zurich and Lisbon (for Maputo). The most popular routes are generally the cheapest, which means that Jo'burg or Cape Town will normally be destinations of choice. Specialist travel agencies advertise in newspapers and travel magazines, so check there for advertisements before ringing around.

There are bucket shops by the dozen in Paris, Amsterdam, Brussels, Frankfurt and other places. Many travel agents in Europe have ties with STA Travel, where you'll find cheap tickets that may be altered once without charge. STA Travel and other discount outlets in major transport hubs include:

Alternativ Tours (☎ 030-881 2089, fax 030-883 5514, ℯ info@alternativtours.de) Wilmersdorferstrasse 94, Berlin

CTS (☎ 06-687 2672, ᴡ www.cts.it) Corso Vittoria Emanuele 11, 297 Rome

Kilroy Travels *Germany* (☎ 030-310 0040, ℯ germany.sales@kilroytravels.de, ᴡ www.kilroytravels.com) Hardenbergstrasse 9, D-10623 Berlin
Holland (☎ 020-524 51 00, fax 020-524 51 5; ℯ amsterdam.sales@kilroytravels.com, ᴡ www.kilroytravels.com) Singelstraat 413-415, Amsterdam

International Student & Youth Travel Service (☎ 01-3233 7676, ℯ info@isytstravel.gr, ᴡ www.isytstravel.gr) Nikis 11, 10557 Athens

Malibu Travel (☎ 020-638 6059, ℯ malfares@etn.nl, ᴡ www.etn.nl/malibu/) Damrak 30, Amsterdam

SSR (☎ 01-261 2954, ᴡ www.ssr.ch) Leonhardstrasse 5-10, CH-8001 Zürich

STA Travel (☎ 069-70 30 35, ℯ frankfurt.uni@statravel.de, ᴡ www.statravel.de) Bokenheimer Landstr. 133, D-60325 Frankfurt

Voyages Wasteels (☎ 08-36 68 22 06, 01-43 25 38 20, ℯ parisstmichel@wasteels.fr, ᴡ www.voyages-wasteels.fr) This agency has 66 offices all over France

Asia The most logical way to travel between southern or Southeast Asia and Africa is to fly. From Delhi (India), the cheapest fare to Jo'burg is around US$1200 return. From Bangkok, which has bucket shops galore, the easiest and cheapest routing is SAA's nonstop flight to Jo'burg, which starts at US$1300 return.

In India, recommended discount agencies in New Delhi include **Cozy Travels** (☎ 2331 2873; BMC House, 1N Connaught Place) and **Tan's Travel** (☎ 2332 1490; 72 Janpath). In Kolkata (Calcutta), try **Travellers' Express Club** (20 Mirza Ghalib St) and in Mumbai (Bombay), there's the renowned **Transway International** (☎ 2262 6066; ᴡ www.transwayinternational.com; Pantaky House, 8 Maruti Cross Lane).

Africa Many travellers on trans-Africa trips fly some sections, either because time is short or simply because the routes are virtually impassable. Some sample fares are given in the relevant country chapters.

The overland route between East Africa and Southern Africa is extremely popular, but it's also easy to find a flight between Nairobi (Kenya) and Harare or Jo'burg. Alternatively, it's a short hop between Dar es Salaam (Tanzania) and Lilongwe, which avoids a gruelling overland stretch. Coming from Cairo (Egypt) or Ethiopia, most flights to Southern Africa go via Nairobi.

If you're travelling from West Africa, you have to fly as the overland route is blocked by war in Democratic Republic of Congo (Zaïre). Travellers also tend to avoid Nigeria and Congo-Brazzaville. The most popular flight is from Abidjan (Côte d'Ivoire) to Jo'burg. You can also fly from Abidjan to Nairobi (Ethiopian Airways has one-way flights for around US$600) and then reach Southern Africa from there.

Travellers with Specific Needs

If you have special needs of any sort – you're on crutches, vegetarian, kosher, halaal, allergic to peanuts, in a wheelchair, visually impaired, taking the baby, terrified of flying, or whatever – you should let the airline know as soon as possible so it can make arrangements. It's also wise to remind the airline when you reconfirm your booking (at least 72 hours before departure) and again when you check in at the airport.

Airports and airlines can be surprisingly helpful, but they do need advance warning. If you're disabled, most international airports in Europe (although not all in Southern Africa) will provide escorts where needed, and most have ramps, lifts and accessible toilets. Aircraft toilets may well present problems, so anyone with concerns should discuss this with the airline at an early stage and, if necessary, with their doctor.

Deaf travellers can ask for airport and in-flight announcements to be written down for them (but outside South Africa, airports in the region probably won't offer this service). Blind travellers may have to travel separately from their guide dogs (which would travel in a container in the baggage hold with other animals). Note that guide dogs are subject to the same quarantine laws (eg, six months in isolation) as any other animal when entering or returning to countries currently free of rabies, such as Britain or Australia.

Children aged under two normally travel for 10% of the standard fare (or free, on some airlines), as long as they don't occupy a separate seat, but don't have a baggage allowance. 'Skycots' should be provided by the airline if requested in advance; these will take a child weighing up to about 10kg. Children between two and 12 years can usually occupy a seat for half to two-thirds of the full fare, and do get a baggage allowance. Strollers/prams can often be taken as hand luggage (but aren't recommended for use in Southern Africa).

LAND
Border Crossings

The most frequented routes into Southern Africa are from Tanzania into Malawi at Songwe (see the Malawi chapter for details) and from Tanzania into Zambia at Nakonde (see the Zambia chapter). The rarely used crossing point from [...] bique provides an e[...] the region, but is d[...] packer standard.

Other countries b[...] African region are [...] (Zaïre), which are both troubled areas, but the far south of Angola (along the Okavango and Kunene Rivers) and south-eastern Congo (Zaïre) remain relatively unaffected. From Angola, the main border crossings into Namibia are at Ruacana and Oshikango, and from Congo (Zaïre), at Chilabombwe into Zambia. Due to safety issues, few travellers use these options, but improving conditions, in Angola at least, may change that.

Overland to Southern Africa

However you travel (by car, bike or public transport), if you're planning to reach Southern Africa overland, your first decision should be which of the main routes through Africa you want to take.

From North & West Africa Although tensions are easing in southern Algeria, most trans-Sahara travellers still use the Morocco and Mauritania route into Senegal and the rest of West Africa. Due to unrest, the route from Algeria into Mali and Niger is still not recommended. Once through West Africa, your route to Southern Africa will next be blocked by more unrest in Congo (Zaïre). This means a flight – probably from Accra (Ghana) or Lagos (Nigeria) to Nairobi (Kenya), from where you can follow the route outlined under From East Africa.

From Northeast Africa The Nile Route through northeast Africa starts in Egypt, and goes into Sudan (either via Lake Nasser or via the Red Sea from Suez or Hurghada); note, however, that these days it's extremely difficult to score a Sudanese visa. Southern Sudan is blocked to overland travellers due to civil war, so most people fly from Cairo (Egypt) or Khartoum (Sudan) to Kampala (Uganda) or Nairobi, or overland from northern Sudan through Eritrea and Ethiopia to Nairobi, where again you can follow the route outlined under From East Africa.

From East Africa From Nairobi, the most popular route runs via Mombasa (Kenya) or

Tanzania) to Dar es Salaam (Tan-
. From here, drivers follow the Great
th Road, and those without wheels take
ie Tanzania–Zambia Railway (Tazara);
both lead to Kapiri Mposhi (Zambia), which
is within easy reach of Lusaka, Livingstone
and Victoria Falls. Alternatively, get off at
Mbeya (in southern Tanzania) and enter
northern Malawi at Songwe. Another option from Dar es Salaam takes you across
the country to Kigoma on Lake Tanganyika,
then by steamer to Mpulungu (Zambia), from
where you can continue overland to Lusaka
and beyond.

Other possibilities from Nairobi include
travelling through Uganda, Rwanda and
Burundi (currently not recommended, due
to unrest), catching the Lake Tanganyika
steamer from Bujumbura (Burundi; if it's
running), and connecting with the previously outlined route at Mpulungu (Zambia). When the troubles have ended, this
route will be a rewarding option. Currently,
however, once you've survived this section
you may not feel like travelling further.

Car & Motorcycle

Driving from Europe to Southern Africa
is a major undertaking. The main points
to emphasise include the incredibly long
distances, the appalling nature of most
roads, and the constant challenge of dealing with police and/or border officials. Overland drivers will have to be mechanically
competent and carry a good collection of
spares. You'll also need vehicle registration
papers, liability insurance, a driving licence
and international drivers' permit, as well as
a *carnet de passage*, effectively a passport
for the vehicle and temporary waiver of
import duty, designed to prevent car import
rackets. Your local automobile association
can provide details.

Your home liability insurance won't be
valid in many countries, and some require
international drivers to purchase expensive
(and effectively useless) insurance when
crossing borders. In most cases, this is just
a racket, and no matter what you spend on
local insurance, you'll effectively be travelling uninsured.

Several guidebooks for trans-African
drivers are suggested under Books in the
Regional Facts for the Visitor chapter.
You might also want to check the website

w www.sahara-overland.com for information about crossing the Sahara.

Bicycle

Cycling is a cheap, convenient, healthy, en-
vironmentally sound and, above all, fun way
to travel. It can also be addictive. It's quite
straightforward to take your bike onto a plane
and use the bike to get around on the ground.
For air travel, you can dismantle the bike and
box it up. Bike boxes are available at airports
and most bike shops. If you're willing to risk
damage to your bike, it's also possible to de-
flate the tyres, remove the pedals and turn the
handlebars sideways, then just wheel the bike
up to the check-in desk (if your bike doesn't
hold up to baggage handlers, it probably
won't survive Africa!) Some airlines don't
charge to carry a bike, and don't even include
it in the weight allowance. Others charge an
extra handling fee of around US$50.

Outside of South Africa, you'll have difficulty buying hi-tech European or American
spares, so bring anything essential along with
you, and know how to make repairs. Plan for
frequent punctures, and take lots of spare
inner tubes. Because automobile tyres are
constantly being repaired, patches and glue
are available almost everywhere. However,
it may be worth carrying a spare tyre, in
case of a really devastating blow-out. For
more on cycling, see Bicycle in the Getting
Around chapter

Overland Tours

Although overlanding across Africa from
Europe or the Middle East has become quite
difficult due to the various 'roadblocks'
imposed by unrest, some overland tour
operators still take up the challenge. Some
begin in Morocco and head down through
Mauritania, Mali, Niger and onward as far
as possible. Others take the easier option and
begin in Kenya.

While these trips are popular, they're
designed mainly for inexperienced travellers who feel uncomfortable striking out on
their own or for those who prefer guaranteed
social interaction to the uncertainties of the
road. If you have the slightest inclination towards independence or would feel confined
travelling with the same group of 25 or so
people for most of the trip (although quite a
few normally drop out along the way), think
twice before booking an overland trip.

Increasingly, many overland companies also offer shorter-haul transport - a sort of backpackers' bus and transfer service. Independent travellers may join overland trucks for a daily rate, plus food kitty contributions. This is a particularly useful way to transfer quickly between Nairobi and Southern Africa.

For information and recommendations on the latest offerings, attend travel fairs, check ads in adventure travel magazines and ask around discount travel agencies. For information on short-haul overland truck trips, see the Getting Around the Region chapter.

SEA

For most people, reaching Southern Africa by sea is not a viable option. The days of working your passage on commercial boats have vanished, although a few travellers do manage to hitch rides on private yachts along the east coast of Africa from Mombasa (Kenya) to Mozambique or South Africa.

Alternatively, several cargo shipping companies sail between Europe and South Africa, with comfortable cabins for public passengers. The voyage between London and Cape Town takes about 16 days, with stops in the Canary Islands, and the one-way trip costs from around £1000, all inclusive. See **Strand Voyages** (*☎ 020-7240 8111, fax 7836 4039; e business@strandtravel.co.uk, w www.strandtravel.co.uk; Charing Cross Shopping Concourse, Strand, London WC2N 4HZ)* for details.

ORGANISED TOURS

Literally hundreds of tour and safari companies now organise package tours to Southern Africa, but it always pays to shop around for details and deals. Especially in Europe, it's becoming increasingly popular to look for late bookings, which may be advertised in travel sections of weekend newspapers, or even at special late bookings counters in some international airports. If you prefer a more independent approach, you can pre-book flights and hotels for the first few nights, then join tours locally (see Organised Tours in the Getting Around chapter).

The best place to begin looking for reputable agencies are weekend newspapers or travel magazines, such as *Wanderlust* in the UK and *Outside* or *National Geographic Adventure* in the US. It's also useful to attend travel fares or ask around discount travel agencies.

Speciality magazines for flower, bird-watching, wildlife-viewing, railway, and other buffs may also include advertising for tours focusing on their own areas of interest. Following is a list of possibilities:

Australia

Adventure World (☎ 02-8913 0755, fax 9956 7707, e info@adventureworld.com.au, w www.adventureworld.com.au) Organises tours, safaris, car hire and hotel packages all over Southern Africa

African Wildlife Safaris (☎ 03-9696 2899, fax 9696 4937, e office@africansafaris.com.au, w www.africanwildlifesafaris.com.au) This agency sells discounted tickets and designs mainly wildlife safaris around Southern Africa

Peregrine Travel (☎ 03-9663 8611, fax 9663 8618, e simon.cameron@peregrine.net.au, w www.peregrine.net.au) This Africa specialist cobbles together safaris for all budgets (starting at A$3635 for a two-week circuit).

France

Makila Voyages (☎ 01-42 96 80 00, fax 42 96 18 05, e info@makila.fr, w www.makila.fr) This upmarket company organises tours and safaris all over East and Southern Africa

UK

Discover the World (☎ 01737-218800, fax 362341, e sales@discover-the-world.co.uk, w www.discover-the-world.co.uk) This company runs exclusive wildlife-oriented tours to various sites worldwide, including a number of Southern African itineraries

Explore Worldwide Ltd (☎ 01252-760000, fax 760001, e info@exploreworldwide.com, w www.exploreworldwide.com) Organises group tours through Zimbabwe, Botswana and Namibia, focusing on adventure and hands-on activities

In the Saddle (☎ 08700-133983, fax 01256-338641, e rides@inthesaddle.com, w www.inthesaddle.com) This company appeals specifically to horse aficionados, including a range of adventurous horseback routes

Naturetrek (☎ 01962-733051, fax 736426, e info@naturetrek.co.uk, w www.naturetrek.co.uk) This company's aim is to get you to where the animals are. It offers specialised wildlife-viewing itineraries.

Temple World (☎ 020-8940 4114, fax 8332 2456, e jane@templeworld.com, w www.templeworld.co.uk) This sophisticated and recommended company organises middle to upper-range tours to the best of the region

USA

Adventure Center (☎ 800-227 8747 or 510-654 1879, fax 654 4200, **e** lp@adventure center.com, **w** www.adventurecenter.com or www.farandwide.com) This travel specialist organises adventure tours worldwide, and is the US agent for several overland operators, including Guerba, Dragoman and Karibu

Africa Adventure Company (☎ 800-882 9453 or 954-491 8877, fax 491 9060, **e** info@africa -adventure.com, **w** www.africa-adventure.com) These top safari specialists can organise any sort of Southern Africa itinerary

Africa Travel Center, Explorers Travel Group (☎ 800-631 5650 or 732-542 9006, fax 542 9420, **e** explorers@monmouth.com) This is a travel and resource centre for prospective Africa travellers: flights, hotels, overland tours, safaris, custom tours, visas and insurance.

Born Free Safaris (☎ 800-472 3274, fax 818-753 1460, **e** bornfreesafaris@att.net, **w** www.born freesafaris.com) Safaris, trekking cultural tours and flights

Bushtracks (☎ 800-995 8689 or 650-326 8689, fax 463 0925, **e** info@bushtracks.com, **w** www.bushtracks.com) This US sales agent is quite expensive, but cobbles together a variety of unforgettable experiences

Premier Tours & Travel (☎ 215-893 9966, fax 893 0357, **e** info@premiertours.com, **w** www.premiertours.com) Premier sells discount tickets and organises inexpensive participation camping safaris all over Southern Africa

Voyagers (☎ 800-633 0299 or 607-273 4321, fax 273 3873, **e** explore@voyagers.com, **w** www.voyagers.com) This company specialises in photographic and wildlife-viewing safaris

Wilderness Travel (☎ 800-368 2794 or 510-558 2488, fax 558 2489, **e** info@wildernesstravel .com, **w** www.wildernesstravel.com) This company offers guided group tours with an emphasis on down-to-earth touring, including hikes, treks and other hands-on pursuits

Getting Around the Region

This chapter briefly outlines the various ways of travelling around Southern Africa. For specifics, see the Getting Around in each of the individual country chapters.

AIR

Distances are great in Africa, and if time is short, regional flights can considerably widen your options. For example, after touring South Africa for a while you could fly from Cape Town to Victoria Falls and then tour Zimbabwe or southern Zambia. Alternatively, fly to Lilongwe, which is a good staging point for trips around Malawi or eastern Zambia, or to Windhoek, which opens up all the wonders of Namibia.

Even within a country, tight schedules can be accommodated with short hops by air. Both domestic and regional flights are usually operated by both state airlines and private carriers, and except in Botswana, the competition generally keeps prices down to reasonable levels.

Sometimes the only practical way into remote parks and reserves is by air, and charter flights provide easy access to national park or remote lodge airstrips. Although these are normally for travellers on less restrictive budgets, access to the best of the Okavango Delta is possible only by charter flight.

The following list includes regional airlines with domestic and intra-Southern Africa routes.

Air Botswana (☎ 267-395 3823, 390 5500, fax 397 4802, **W** www.airbotswana.com.bw
Air Malawi (☎ 265-1-620811, fax 620042, **W** www.airmalawi.net
Air Namibia (☎ 264-61-299 6444, fax 299 6154, **W** www.airnamibia.com.na)
Air Zimbabwe (☎ 263-4-253751, fax 705251, **W** www.airzimbabwe.com)
British Airways Comair (☎ 27-11-921 0111, fax 973 3913, **W** www.comair.co.za)
Linhas Aereas de Moçambique (☎ 258-1-426001, 465810, **W** www.lam.co.mz/english)
Mid Airlines (☎ 263-4-791143)
National Airlines (☎ 27-21-934 0350)
South African Airways (☎ 27-11-978 1111, 0861-359722, **W** www.flysaa.com)
South African Express (☎ 27-11-978 5577, fax 978 5578, **W** www.saexpress.co.za)
Zambian Airways (☎ 260-1-271133, fax 223227, **W** www.africa-insites.com/zambianairways/)

BUS
International Bus

Long-distance buses (coaches) operate regularly between most Southern African countries. Most routes are covered by fairly basic, cheap and often slow services; major links include between Francistown (Botswana) and Bulawayo (Zimbabwe), Gaborone (Botswana) and Johannesburg (Jo'burg; South Africa), Harare (Zimbabwe) and Blantyre (Malawi), and Harare and Lusaka (Zambia). From Cape Town and Jo'burg, larger and more comfortable buses also run to Maseru (Lesotho), Mbabane (Swaziland), Maputo (Mozambique) and Windhoek (Namibia). This includes prominent **Intercape Mainliner** (**W** www.intercape .co.za) which runs a variety of convenient routes between South Africa, Botswana and Namibia.

For bus travellers, border crossings can be tedious while customs officials search through huge amounts of luggage. It's particularly slow if you are crossing from South Africa to Zimbabwe, or Zimbabwe to Malawi, but may go more smoothly in the other direction. Minibus services may be more efficient, as fewer passengers will mean less time at the border.

There are also several international bus services especially designed for backpackers and other tourists. These companies normally use comfortable 16-seat buses and have helpful drivers, on-board music and pick-ups/drop-offs at main tourist centres and backpackers' hostels. Among these are the twice-weekly services between Jo'burg and Victoria Falls, via Bulawayo, offered by **Zim Travel** (**e** zimtravl@iafrica.com, **W** www.gozimbabwe.co.za).

For more information on bus travel between countries, see Getting There & Away in the individual country chapters, or seek out the latest information at backpackers hostels and budget travel agents throughout Southern Africa.

Overland Trucks

Lots of companies run overland camping tours in trucks converted to carry passengers. Sometimes the trucks finish a tour, then run straight back to base to start the next one. Often, drivers are happy to carry 'transit' passengers. This is not a tour, as such, but can be a comfortable way of transiting between Vic Falls and Jo'burg, or Harare and Nairobi (Kenya), for around US$20 per day, plus food kitty contributions. Those looking for rides should check around truck stops in well-known tourist areas, such as Cape Town, Jo'burg, Harare, Victoria Falls, Windhoek or Lilongwe or visit backpackers' hostels (where these companies invariably leave stacks of brochures).

National Bus & Local Transport

Within individual countries, public bus services range from basic to luxurious. In addition to the typically spluttering big buses, many countries also have minibuses, which are faster, more frequent and perhaps even more dangerous due to their speed. See the individual country chapters for more details.

In Southern Africa, there's a notable lack of long-distance shared service taxis (such as the seven-seat Peugeots that are so popular in other parts of Africa). Some travellers occasionally get a group together and hire a city taxi for a long trip, but this is rare.

In rural areas, the frequency of bus services drops dramatically. In such cases, public transport may be limited to the back of a pick-up truck (ute). Everyone pays a fare to the driver – which is normally comparable to the bus fare for a similar distance. This can be great fun – however uncomfortable – and it's often your only option.

TRAIN

Rail travel around Southern Africa focuses on the South African network and its offshoots into Botswana, Mozambique, Namibia, Swaziland, Zimbabwe and Zambia – but currently the only cross-border railway services are the Tazara line between Zambia and Tanzania and the line between Keetmanshoop (Namibia) and Upington (South Africa).

Travelling by train within the various countries is still a decent option – and it's almost always fun – but can be a slow way to go. For details, see under Train in the Getting Around sections of individual country chapters.

CAR & MOTORCYCLE

Minimal information on bringing your own wheels to Southern Africa is found in the regional Getting There & Away chapter earlier in this book. More information on getting around, and other matters related to car and motorcycle travel, is provided under Getting Around in the individual country chapters.

Rental

Car rental isn't cheap, but can be a very convenient way to travel, especially if you're short of time or want to visit national parks and other out-of-the-way places. Costs can be mitigated by mustering a group to share the rental and petrol, and will open up all sorts of opportunities. In all the countries covered by this book, to hire a vehicle you must be at least 21 years old (in some cases as old as 25).

A list of local car-rental firms is included in the Getting Around sections of country chapters. They're usually accessible on email, and it pays to book before you leave home. If you're visiting more than one country, check whether you're able to cross borders with a rental vehicle. This is usually allowed by South African companies, which will let you take vehicles into Namibia, Botswana, Lesotho and Swaziland, as well as Zimbabwe, with payment of an additional

---

To Go or Not To Go?

A dangerous traffic quirk in Southern Africa concerns the use and significance of indicator lights. When a car comes up behind a slow vehicle, wanting to overtake, the driver of the slower vehicle will often flash one indicator to let the other driver know whether or not it's safe to overtake. Logically, the left indicator would mean 'go' (that is, it may potentially be turning left, and the way is clear) and the right would mean 'don't go' (it may potentially be turning right, indicating that the way is not clear). Unfortunately, quite a few confused drivers get this backwards, creating a potentially disastrous situation for a trusting driver in the vehicle behind. The moral is: ignore the well-intentioned signals and never overtake unless you can see that the road ahead is completely clear.

cross-border fee (usually around US$100). Companies advertising the lowest daily rates will typically also require payment of a per-kilometre fee, so if you're doing a lot of driving, you'd do better to pay extra for an unlimited mileage deal. Also, check on the fees for other items such as tax, damage and insurance, all of which can add considerably to the final bill.

In South Africa and Namibia you can hire campervans (RVs) that accommodate two to six people. With additional payment, these come with as much equipment as you may need for demanding safaris. In most countries, you can also opt for a 4WD vehicle, which will typically cost around US$150 per day with unlimited mileage.

Purchase

An increasing number of travellers opt to buy a car, tour the region, then sell it at the end of their trip. Although you need a relatively large amount of money up front, you can expect to get at least some of it back, and travelling this way can work out a lot cheaper than car rental – especially if costs are split among several people.

For visitors, South Africa is the best place to buy a car (other countries place restrictions on foreign ownership, have stiff tax laws, or simply don't have the choice of vehicles). Also, South African registered vehicles don't need a *carnet de passage* to visit any of the countries covered by this book. Travelling through Botswana, Lesotho, Namibia and Swaziland is easy, while for Malawi, Mozambique, Zimbabwe and Zambia you'll easily get temporary import permits at the border.

It's usually cheaper to buy privately, but for tourists it is often more convenient to go to a dealer. For some idea about prices, check the newspapers. The *Cape Times* has ads every day – especially on Thursday – and the weekend *Argus* also presents a good selection.

Some dealers might agree to a buy-back arrangement – if you don't trash the car, you can reasonably expect to get about 60% of your purchase price back after a three-month trip, but you need to check all aspects of the contract to be sure this deal will stick. **Wayne Motors** (☎ *021-465 2222; 21 Roeland St, Cape Town*) will guarantee a buy-back price in advance. **Drive Africa**

(☎ *021-447 1144, fax 4388262;* e *cb-talbot@ driveafrica.co.za*) specialises in buy-back sales for tourists.

Whoever you're buying from, make sure that the car details correspond with the ownership papers and check the owner's name against their identity document. Before buying, consider getting the car independently tested – the Automobile Association (AA) has a test station in Cape Town and charges about US$60 for a full test (you don't need to be a member).

A roadworthy certificate – which will come with cars sold by a reputable dealer – is required when you register the change of ownership and pay for a road-licence disk. (Note that there are a lot of unscrupulous testers around – a roadworthy certificate doesn't necessarily mean your car is safe.)

You'll be lucky to find a decent vehicle for much less than US$2500, and realistically, you should expect to pay around US$3500 for a 10-year-old Toyota Corolla or VW Golf in reasonable condition. If you want to go off-road, a Land Rover will cost anything from US$5000 to US$10,000. Alternatively, look for a 'bakkie', such as a 2WD Toyota Hi-Lux, which should cost around $8000. Before you finalise purchase, you should get a certificate issued by the police to prove the vehicle isn't stolen.

To register your newly purchased vehicle, go to the applicable **Motor Vehicle Registration Division**, where you can collect a change of ownership form to complete, and also enquire about other necessary documents. The charge to re-register is about US$20.

Insurance against theft or damage is highly recommended. Again the AA will provide the best advice. To purchase insurance, foreigners will normally need a South African driving licence (and in order to get that, you'll need an international driving permit).

Driving in Southern Africa

Whatever vehicle you drive, prepare to deal with some of the world's worst, fastest and most arrogant and aggressive drivers. In all the countries covered in this book, traffic officially drives on the left – but that may not always be obvious, so be especially prepared on blind corners and hills.

The good news is that most main roads in Southern Africa are in fair to excellent

Bush Driving

While Southern Africa has a good network of sealed roads, driving on unsealed roads requires special techniques and appropriate vehicle preparation. (See also the 'Gravel Roads' boxed text under Getting Around in the Namibia chapter).

- For rough road conditions, you'll need a robust, high-clearance vehicle, but you'll only have to engage the 4WD when driving in sand or mud, or over boulder-sized rocks.
- In especially rocky conditions, have someone get out and direct the driver over the route of least resistance.
- At river crossings, always check the water depth and bottom conditions before starting across. It will be obvious that sand, stones and gravel are preferable to mud and muck!
- Make sure your vehicle is in good running order before you start. Carry tools, spares and equipment, including towrope, torch, shovel, fan belts, vehicle fluids, spark plugs, wire, jump leads, fuses, hoses, a good jack and a wooden plank to act as a base in sand. A second spare tyre is highly advised, and even a third if you've got room. You could also carry tyre levers, a tyre pump, spare tubes and repair kit, but mending punctures in the bush is much harder than the manuals imply, and should be avoided if possible. And of course you'll need the expertise to handle and install all this stuff…
- Wrap tools and heavy objects in blankets or padding. Pack supplies that are likely to be pitched around in strong plastic or metal containers and strap everything down tightly on the roof or in the back. Keep breakable items with you in the cab. Once you're on unsealed roads, dust permeates everything – so tightly wrap food, clothing and camera equipment in strong dust-proof containers.
- When calculating fuel requirements, estimate your intended distance and then double it to allow for getting lost and emergencies. For serious off-roading, remember to allow for petrol consumption up to four times higher than in normal conditions – especially on sandy tracks.
- In indestructible containers, carry at least 5L of water per person per day – allowing for delays and breakdowns. Extra petrol should be carried in strong, leak-proof jerry cans.
- Take the best maps you can find, plus a GPS or compass that you know how to use. Take readings periodically to make sure you're still travelling in the right direction. To get an accurate compass reading, stand at least 3m from the vehicle.

condition, and are passable to even small compact cars. In Malawi, Zambia and Mozambique, however, you may be slowed down considerably by sealed roads that haven't seen any maintenance for many years and are plagued with bone-crunching and tyre-bursting potholes. On lesser roads, standards vary considerably, from relatively smooth highways to dirt tracks (for details, see the 'Bush Driving' boxed text later in this chapter).

Tree branches on the road are the local version of warning triangles, and usually indicate a broken-down vehicle ahead. If you come up behind someone on a bicycle, hoot the horn as a warning and offer a friendly wave as you pass. This isn't considered offensive, and the cyclist will appreciate the heads up.

On rural highways, always be on the lookout for children playing, people selling goods, seeds drying or animals wandering around on the loose. Livestock are always a concern, and hitting even a small animal can cause vehicle damage, while hitting something large – like a cow or a kudu – can be fatal (for both the driver and the animal). If you see kids with red flags on the road, it means they're leading a herd of cows. Slow down, even if you can't see any cows (especially if you can't see any cows).

These things become much harder to deal with in the dark. Additionally, many vehicles have faulty lights – or none at all – so avoid driving at night if at all possible.

BICYCLE

On a bicycle, travellers will often be on an equal footing with locals, and will have plenty of opportunities to meet and visit with people in small towns and villages along the way. Pointers on bringing a bike

Bush Driving

Bush Tracks

Bush tracks rarely appear on maps and their ever-changing routes can utterly confound drivers. Some provide access to remote cattle posts or small villages and then disappear, often to re-emerge somewhere else. Some never re-emerge, leaving you stranded.

• Take care driving through high grass – seeds can block radiators and cause overheating. Dry grass next to the exhaust pipe can also catch fire. Stop regularly and remove plant material from the grille or exhaust.

Sand

In sandy conditions you may be following a faint track – often just the wheel marks of previous vehicles – or driving across completely bare wilderness. Either way, driving is easier if the air is cool (usually mornings), as the sand is more compact at these times.

• Tyre pressure should be low – around half that for normal road conditions. To prevent bogging or stalling, move as quickly as possible and keep the revs up, but avoid sudden acceleration. Shift down a gear before you reach deep sandy patches, not when you're in them.

• Allow the vehicle to wander along the path of least resistance when negotiating a straight course through rutted sand. Anticipate corners and turn the wheel slightly earlier than you would on a solid surface – this will allow the vehicle to slide smoothly around.

Pans

Many of the rules for bush-track or sand driving apply here, but some extra points are worth making.

• First, never drive on a pan unless you know exactly what you're doing. If you do venture onto a pan, stick to the edges until you're sure it's dry.

• Even if the pan *seems* dry, it can still be wet underneath – vehicles can break through the crust and become irretrievably bogged. Foul-smelling salt can mean the pan is wet and potentially dangerous. If in doubt, follow the tracks of other drivers (unless, of course, you see bits of vehicles poking above the surface).

• If you do get bogged and have a winch, anchor the spare wheel or the jack - anything to which the winch may be attached - by digging a hole and planting it firmly in the muck. Hopefully you'll be able to anchor it better than the pan has anchored the vehicle.

on the plane are found under Bicycle in the regional Getting There & Away chapter.

For getting around, traditional touring bikes will cope with most sealed roads (and some good dirt roads) with little trouble, but narrow tyres are normally unsuitable and to get off the main routes, you'll need a mountain bike with fat tyres. On sandy roads, however, even balloon tyres won't help, and you'll wind up pushing the bike.

A cyclist's greatest cause for alarm will be motorists. Cyclists are usually regarded as second-class road users, so make sure you know what's coming up behind you and always be prepared to make an evasive swerve onto the verges. For this purpose, a rearview-mirror (handlebar or helmet mounted) will prove invaluable.

Other factors to consider are the heat, the long distances, and finding places to stay. Aim to travel in cool, dry periods,

and carry at least 4L of drinking water. If you get tired, or simply want to cut out the boring bits, bikes can easily be carried on buses or trucks – although you'll need to pay an extra luggage fee, and be prepared for some rough handling as your beloved machine is loaded onto a roof rack.

A good source of information may be your national cycling organisation. In Britain, the **Cyclists' Touring Club** (☎ 01483-417217, fax 426994; e cycling@ctc.org.uk; w www .ctc.org.uk) provides cycling advice and also organises group cycling tours. In the USA, the **International Bicycle Fund** (☎/fax 206-767 0848; e ibike@ibike.org; w www.ibike.org) organises socially conscious tours and provides information.

If you don't have a bike but fancy a few days cycling, you'll normally be able to hire a bike locally, especially in tourist areas. Otherwise, local people in villages and towns are often willing to rent their bikes for the day. Ask at your hotel or track down a bicycle repair shop (every town market has one).

HITCHING

Hitching is a way of life in Southern Africa, and visitors may well have the opportunity to join the throng of locals looking for lifts. While this is a good way to get around places without public transport (or even with public transport), there is a protocol involved. As a visitor, you're likely to x take precedence over locals (especially with white drivers), but if other people are hitching, it's still polite to stand further along the road so they'll have the first crack (that is, unless there's a designated hitching spot where everyone waits).

Another option is to wait around petrol stations and try to arrange lifts from drivers who may be going your way. If you do get a lift, be sure to determine what sort of payment is expected before you climb aboard. In most cases, plan on paying just a bit less than the equivalent bus fare.

As in any other part of the world, hitching is never entirely safe, and we therefore don't recommend it. Travellers who hitch should understand that they are taking a small but potentially serious risk.

ORGANISED TOURS

Travellers are faced with a boggling array of organised tour options in Southern Africa, and the only problem will be selecting something. In addition to the very convenient hop-on-hop-off bus services in South Africa, there are plenty of budget tours and safaris available to take you to the regional highlights. You'll have the most options in Cape Town, Jo'burg, Victoria Falls, Livingstone, Maun, Windhoek and other places frequented by tourists. As with all tours, the range of options is enormous: they can last from two days to three weeks and can involve camping and mucking-in to luxury shuttles between five-star lodges. Vehicles may be private aircraft, Kombi vans, no-frills safari trucks or comfortable buses with air-con and chilled wine in the fridge.

For countries with a choice of locally-based tour companies, a selection is listed under Organised Tours in the Getting Around sections of those country chapters, with further choices also under some specific destinations. Some countries may have only a limited selection of operators, which are often attached to local travel agencies or budget hotels. For details, see specific destinations in the individual country chapters.

Local tour operators which run tours around Southern Africa include:

Wayfarer Adventures (☎/fax 021-715 0875, e gillw@freemail.absa.co.za, w www.allworld -vacation.com/wayfarer-adventures) Wilderness adventure travel throughout Southern Africa, including Land Rover tours around Namibia

Which Way? (☎ 021-845 7400, fax 845 7401, e whichway@iafrica.com) This popular local overland company does 'mobile party' camping safaris throughout Southern Africa

Wilderness Safaris (☎ 011-807 1800, fax 807 2110, e enquiry@wilderness.co.za, w www .wilderness-safaris.com) This company offers a range of tours in all Southern African countries. In addition to the standard luxury lodge-based tours in remote areas, it offers fly-in safaris and activity-based trips.

Wildlife Guide

CARNIVORES

Genet Small-spotted (or common) genet (*Genetta genetta*); large-spotted (or rusty-spotted) genet (*Genetta tigrina*; pictured)

Relatives of the mongoose, genets resemble long, slender domestic cats and have a pointed fox-like face. The two species in the region are very similar, but can be differentiated by the tail tips (white in the small-spotted genet and black in the large-spotted). They are solitary animals, sleeping by day in abandoned burrows, rock crevices or hollow trees and emerging at night to forage. Very agile, they hunt equally well on land or in trees, feeding on small rodents, birds, reptiles, nestlings, eggs, insects and fruits.

Size: length 85cm to 110cm; weight 1.5kg to 3.2kg. **Distribution:** the small-spotted genet is widespread in Namibia, Botswana, southwestern Zimbabwe and most of South Africa; the large-spotted genet is common in the rest of the region, with a slight overlap. **Status:** very common, but strictly nocturnal.

Mongoose

Though common, most mongooses are solitary and are usually seen fleetingly. The slender mongoose (*Galerella sanguinea*) is recognisable by its black-tipped tail, which it holds aloft when running. A few species, such as the dwarf mongoose (*Helogale parvula*), the banded mongoose (*Mungos mungo*; pictured) and the meerkat (*Suricata suricatta*) are intensely sociable. Family groups are better at raising kittens, spotting danger and when confronting a threat: collectively, mongooses can intimidate enemies. Insects and other invertebrates are their most important prey.

Size: ranging in size from the dwarf mongoose at length 40cm, weight up to 400g; to the white-tailed mongoose (*Ichneumia albicauda*) at length 120cm, weight up to 5.5kg. **Distribution:** throughout the region. **Status:** common where they occur; sociable species are diurnal, solitary species are nocturnal.

Aardwolf *Proteles cristatus*

Smallest of the hyena family, the aardwolf subsists almost entirely on harvester termites and almost never consumes meat. Unlike other hyena species, it does not form clans or den communally; rather, it forms loose associations between pairs and forages alone. The male assists the female in raising the cubs, mostly by babysitting at the den while the mother forages. The aardwolf is persecuted in the mistaken belief that it kills stock, and may suffer huge population crashes following spraying for locusts (this spraying also wipes out the termites, its major prey).

Size: shoulder height 40cm to 50cm; length 80cm to 100cm; weight 8kg to 12kg. **Distribution:** throughout the region as far north as southern Zambia, but absent from Mozambique and Malawi. **Status:** uncommon; nocturnal, but occasionally seen at dawn and dusk.

Leopard *Panthera pardus*

The leopard is the supreme ambush hunter, using infinite patience to stalk within metres of its prey before attacking in an explosive rush. It eats everything from insects to zebras, but antelopes are its primary prey. The leopard is highly agile and hoists its kills into trees to avoid losing them to lions and hyenas. It is a solitary animal, except during the mating season, when the male and female stay in close association for the female's week-long oestrus. A litter of up to three cubs is born after a gestation of three months and the females raise them without any assistance from the males.

ARIADNE VAN ZANDBERGEN

Size: shoulder height 70cm to 80cm; length 160cm to 210cm; weight up to 90kg. **Distribution:** widespread throughout the region except for central South Africa. **Status:** common but, being mainly nocturnal, it is the most difficult of the large cats to see.

Lion *Panthera leo*

The lion lives in prides of up to about 30, the core comprising between four and 12 related females, which remain in the pride for life. Males form coalitions and defend female groups from foreign males. The lion is strictly territorial, defending ranges of between 50 and 400 sq km. Young males are ousted from the pride at the age of two or three, entering a period of nomadism that ends at around five years old, when they are able to take over their own pride. The lion hunts virtually anything, but wildebeests, zebras and buffaloes are the mainstay of its diet.

MITCH REARDON

Size: shoulder height 120cm; length 250cm to 300cm; weight up to 240kg (male), 160kg (female). **Distribution:** occurs in all major parks in the region, but is rare outside them. **Status:** common in parks; mainly nocturnal, but easy to see during the day.

Cheetah *Acinonyx jubatus*

The world's fastest land mammal, the cheetah can reach speeds of at least 105km/h but becomes exhausted after a few hundred metres and therefore usually stalks prey to within 60m before unleashing its tremendous acceleration. The cheetah preys on antelopes as well as hares and young wildebeests and zebras. Litters may be as large as nine but in open savanna habitats, most cubs are killed by other predators, particularly lions. Young cheetahs disperse from the mother when aged around 18 months. The males form coalitions, while females remain solitary for life.

ALEX DISSANAYAKE

Size: shoulder height 85cm; length 180cm to 220cm; weight up to 65kg. **Distribution:** widespread (but at low densities) throughout the region; absent from most of South Africa and increasingly restricted to protected areas elsewhere. **Status:** uncommon, with individuals moving over large areas; active by day.

Caracal *Felis caracal*

Sometimes also called the African lynx due to its long tufted ears, the caracal is a robust, powerful cat that preys predominantly on small antelopes, birds and rodents but is capable of taking down animals many times larger than itself. Like most cats, it is largely solitary. Females give birth to one to three kittens after a 79 or 80-day gestation and raise the kittens alone. It is territorial, marking its home range with urine sprays and faeces. The caracal has a wide tolerance for habitat but prefers semi-arid regions, dry savannas and hilly country; it is absent from dense forest.

Size: shoulder height 60cm; length 95cm to 120cm; weight up to 13kg. **Distribution:** throughout the region. **Status:** fairly common, but largely nocturnal and difficult to see.

Brown hyena *Hyena brunnea*

Once considered endangered, the brown hyena is relatively numerous in the arid southwest of the region. It is a poor hunter and subsists largely by scavenging, visiting kill remains left by other animals and carrying off large parts to cache for later. It occasionally kills small animals and is partial to ostrich eggs and fruit. The brown hyena forages alone, although groups numbering as many as 12 cooperate to raise young and defend territories. It is primarily nocturnal and generally difficult to see, though viewing is possible in the Kgalagadi Transfrontier Park (South Africa–Botswana).

Size: shoulder height 80cm; length 120cm to 160cm; weight 28kg to 43kg. **Distribution:** throughout Botswana, Namibia except the southeast, the extreme southwest of Zimbabwe and northern South Africa. **Status:** widespread in semi-arid areas, but uncommon elsewhere.

Spotted hyena *Crocuta crocuta*

Widely reviled as a cowardly scavenger, the spotted hyena is actually a highly efficient predator with a fascinating social system. Females are larger and dominant to males and even have male physical characteristics, the most remarkable of which is an erectile clitoris rendering the sexes virtually indistinguishable at a distance. The spotted hyena is massively built and appears distinctly canine, but is more closely related to a cat than to a dog. It can reach speeds of up to 60km/h and a pack can easily dispatch adult wildebeests and zebras. The lion is its main natural enemy.

Size: shoulder height 85cm; length 120cm to 180cm; weight up to 80kg. **Distribution:** occurs throughout the region, but is common only in protected areas; absent or rare in most of South Africa and Namibia. **Status:** common where there is suitable food; mainly nocturnal, but also seen during the day.

Bat-eared fox *Otocyon megalotis*

The huge ears of this little fox detect the faint sounds of invertebrates below ground, before it unearths them in a burst of frantic digging. The bat-eared fox eats mainly insects, especially termites, but also fruit and small vertebrates. It is monogamous and is often seen in groups comprising a mated pair and offspring. Natural enemies include large birds of prey, spotted hyenas, caracals and larger cats. It will bravely attempt to rescue a family member caught by a predator by using distraction techniques and harassment, which extends to nipping larger enemies on the ankles.

DAVE HAMMAN

Size: shoulder height 35cm; length 75cm to 90cm; weight up to 5kg. **Distribution:** widespread in Namibia, Botswana, western Zimbabwe and throughout South Africa (except for the east). **Status:** common, especially in national parks; mainly nocturnal, but often seen in the late afternoon and early morning.

Cape fox *Vulpes chama*

Southern Africa's smallest canid, the dainty Cape fox forms monogamous pairs but usually forages alone. It feeds on insects, small mammals and reptiles. In some parks, individuals visit tourist barbecues to scrounge for food and eventually become very tame. In farming areas the Cape fox is wrongly blamed for losses of lambs and goat kids and is heavily persecuted as a result.

ABI

Size: shoulder height 30cm to 33cm; length 75cm to 90cm; weight up to 4kg. **Distribution:** drier parts of Namibia, western South Africa and southern Botswana. **Status:** common; seen mostly at night or in the early morning, especially in the summer months, when they are often seen close to their breeding burrows.

Serval *Felis serval*

A tall, slender and long-legged cat, the serval resembles a miniature cheetah. Its tawny to russet-yellow coat is dotted with large black spots, forming long bars and blotches on the neck and shoulders. Other distinguishing features include very large upright ears, a long neck and a relatively short tail. The serval generally eats vegetation near water and is most common on floodplain savannas, wetlands and woodlands near streams. It feeds primarily on rodents, including mice, vlei rats, cane rats and hares, as well as birds, small reptiles and sometimes the young of small antelopes.

DAVID WALL

Size: shoulder height 60cm; length 95cm to 120cm; weight up to 13kg. **Distribution:** northern Namibia, northern Botswana, eastern South Africa and widespread in other areas. **Status:** relatively common, but mainly nocturnal; sometimes seen in the early morning and late afternoon.

WILDLIFE GUIDE

African wild cat *Felis lybica*

The progenitor of the household tabby, the African wild cat was originally domesticated by the Egyptians. African wild cats differ from domestic cats in having reddish backs to their ears, proportionally longer legs and a generally leaner appearance. They crossbreed freely with domestic cats close to human habitation and this is probably the greatest threat to the wild species. Wild cats subsist mainly on small rodents, but also prey on birds, insects and species up to the size of hares. They are solitary except when mating and when females have kittens.

Size: shoulder height 35cm; length 85cm to 100cm; weight up to 6kg. **Distribution:** throughout the region. **Status:** common, nocturnal, although sometimes spotted at dawn and dusk.

Wild dog *Lycaon pictus*

The wild dog's blotched black, yellow and white coat, and its large, round ears, make it unmistakable. It is highly sociable, living in packs of up to 40, though 12 to 20 is typical. Marvellous endurance hunters, the pack chases prey relentlessly to the point of exhaustion, then cooperates to pull down the quarry. The wild dog is widely reviled for killing prey by eating it alive, but this is in fact probably as fast as any of the 'cleaner' methods used by other carnivores. Mid-sized antelopes are its preferred prey, but it can kill animals as large as a buffalo. The wild dog requires enormous areas and is one of the most endangered large carnivores in Africa.

Size: shoulder height 65cm to 80cm; length 105cm to 150cm; weight up to 30kg. **Distribution:** fairly widespread in Botswana, but restricted to major parks elsewhere. **Status:** highly threatened, with numbers declining severely from a naturally low density.

Cape clawless otter *Aonyx capensis*

Very similar to European otters but much larger, the Cape clawless otter has a glossy chocolate-brown coat and a white or cream-coloured lower face, throat and neck. Unlike most otters, only its hind feet are webbed, and the front feet end in dexterous, human-like 'fingers' with rudimentary nails. The otter is normally active during early morning and evening, though it becomes nocturnal in areas where it is hunted by humans. Its main foods include fish, crabs and frogs, as well as marine molluscs in seashore habitats. Its only known natural enemy is the crocodile.

Size: length 105cm to 160cm, including a 50cm tail; weight up to 28kg. **Distribution:** all large freshwater bodies and rivers in the region, as well as eastern and southern coastlines. **Status:** uncommon throughout its distribution, and very shy; seen usually in the early morning and late afternoon.

Honey badger (or ratel) *Mellivora capensis*

Africa's equivalent of the European badger, the honey badger has a reputation for a vile temper and ferocity. While stories of it attacking animals the size of buffaloes are probably folklore, it is pugnacious and astonishingly powerful for its size. Normally active between dusk and dawn, it is omnivorous, feeding on meat, fish, frogs, scorpions, spiders, reptiles, small mammals, roots, honey, berries and eggs. In some parks, the honey badger becomes used to scavenging from bins, presenting the best opportunity for viewing this normally elusive animal.

Size: length 90cm to 100cm; weight up to 15kg. **Distribution:** widespread, although absent from central South Africa and Lesotho. **Status:** generally occurs in low densities; mainly nocturnal.

Black-backed jackal *Canis mesomelas*

This jackal relies heavily on scavenging but is also an efficient hunter, taking insects, birds, rodents and even the occasional small antelope. It also frequents human settlements and takes domestic stock. As a result, it is persecuted by farmers but is very resilient and can be seen widely on farms. The black-backed jackal forms long-term pair bonds, and each pair occupies a home range varying from 3 to 21.5 sq km. Pups are born in litters of one to six, and are often looked after by their siblings from an older litter as well as their parents.

Size: shoulder height 35cm to 50cm; length 95cm to 120cm; weight up to 12kg. **Distribution:** throughout the region. **Status:** very common and easily seen; active both night and day.

Side-striped jackal *Canis adustus*

Resembling the black-backed jackal but with a distinctive white-tipped tail, the side-striped jackal is the most omnivorous of all jackals, commonly eating wild fruit, maize, eggs and invertebrates, as well as meat. It forages alone or in pairs, in a territory that it defends from other pairs. It has a varied vocal repertoire, including an explosive yap and an owl-like hoot.

Size: shoulder height 35cm to 50cm; length 95cm to 120cm; weight up to 12kg. **Distribution:** extreme northern Namibia, northern Botswana, throughout Zimbabwe, Zambia and Malawi, extreme eastern and northeastern South Africa. **Status:** widespread but not abundant; active at night and in the early morning.

UNGULATES (HOOFED ANIMALS)

Rock dassie *Procavia capensis*

The rock dassie (also known as the hyrax) occurs practically everywhere there are mountains or rocky outcrops. It is a sociable animal and lives in colonies of up to 60 individuals. Despite its resemblance to a large, robust guinea pig, the dassie is actually related to the elephant. It feeds on vegetation, but spends much of the day sunning itself on rocks or chasing other rock dassies in play. Where it has become habituated to humans it is often quite tame, but otherwise it dashes into rock crevices when alarmed, uttering shrill screams.

ARIADNE VAN ZANDBERGEN

Size: length 60cm; weight up to 5.5kg. **Distribution:** throughout the region, but absent from dense forest. **Status:** common and easy to see, especially where it has become habituated to humans.

Rhinoceros White rhinoceros *(Ceratotherium simum; pictured)*; black rhinoceros *Diceros bicornis*

Poaching for rhino horn has made the rhino Africa's most endangered large mammal. The white rhino is a grazer and prefers open plains, while the black rhino is a browser, living in scrubby country. While the white rhino is generally docile, the black rhino is prone to charging when alarmed. Its eyesight is extremely poor. The white rhino is the more sociable species, forming cow-calf groups numbering up to 10. The black rhino is solitary and territorial, only socialising during the mating season.

RICHARD I'ANSON

Size: (white) shoulder height 180cm, weight 1200kg to 2000kg; (black) shoulder height 160cm, weight 800kg to 1200kg. **Distribution:** restricted to protected areas, mainly in the parks of South Africa and Namibia. **Status:** black rhinos are endangered; white rhinos are threatened, but well protected in South Africa.

Warthog *Phacochoerus aethiopicus*

The warthog's social organisation is variable; groups usually consist of one to three sows with their young. Males form bachelor groups or are solitary, only associating with the female groups when a female is in season. The distinctive facial warts can be used to determine sex – females have a single pair of warts under the eyes whereas males have a second set further down the snout. The warthog feeds mainly on grass, but also eats fruit and bark. In hard times, it will burrow with its snout for roots and bulbs. It rests and gives birth in abandoned burrows or in termite mounds.

ABI

Size: shoulder height 70cm; weight up to 105kg, but averages 50kg to 60kg. **Distribution:** widespread in the region; absent in deserts, in South Africa restricted to the northeast. **Status:** common and easy to see.

African elephant *Loxodonta africana*

The African elephant usually lives in small family groups of between 10 and 20, which frequently congregate in much larger herds at a common water hole or food resource. Its society is matriarchal and herds are dominated by old females. Bulls live alone or in bachelor groups, joining the herds when females are in season. A cow may mate with many bulls during her oestrus. An adult's average daily food intake is about 250kg of grass, leaves, bark and other vegetation. An elephant's life span is about 60 to 70 years, though some individuals may reach 100 or more.

LUKE HUNTER

Size: shoulder height up to 4m (male); weight 5 to 6.5 tonnes. **Distribution:** mostly restricted to parks in northern Namibia, northern Botswana, northern Zimbabwe, northern South Africa, southern and central Zambia and southern Mozambique. **Status:** very common in some parks, but very rare elsewhere.

Zebra Burchell's zebra *Equus burchelli* (pictured); mountain zebra *Equus zebra*

The Burchell's zebra has shadow lines between its black stripes whereas the mountain zebra lacks shadows and has a gridiron pattern of stripes just above its tail. Both are grazers, occasionally browsing on scrub. The social system centres around small groups of related mares over which stallions fight fiercely. Stallions may hold a harem for as long as 15 years but single mares are often lost to younger males gradually building up their own harem. Zebras are preyed upon by large carnivores, with lions their main predators.

ROB DRUMMOND

Size: shoulder height 140cm to 160cm; weight up to 390kg. **Distribution:** The Burchell's zebra is found throughout the region; the mountain zebra is found in southern South Africa and scattered throughout Namibia. **Status:** Burchell's zebra is common; mountain zebra is far less numerous.

Hippopotamus *Hippopotamus amphibius*

The hippo is found close to fresh water, spending most of the day submerged and emerging at night to graze on land. It can consume about 40kg of vegetable matter each evening. It lives in large herds, tolerating close contact in the water, but forages alone when on land. Adult bulls defend territories against each other and most males bear the scars of conflicts. Cows with babies are aggressive towards other individuals. The hippo is extremely dangerous on land and kills many people each year, usually when someone inadvertently blocks the animal's retreat to the water.

DAVID WALL

Size: shoulder height 150cm; weight up to 2000kg (males are larger than females). **Distribution:** Zambia, Malawi, Mozambique and extreme eastern South Africa; also along the Zambezi, Chobe and Cunene River system. **Status:** common in major watercourses.

ROB DRUMMOND

Common (or grey) duiker *Sylvicapra grimmia*

One of the most common small antelopes, the duiker is usually solitary, but is sometimes seen in pairs. The common duiker is a greyish lightbrown in colour, with a white belly and a dark brown stripe down its face. Only males have horns, which are straight and pointed, and rarely grow longer than 15cm. This duiker is predominantly a browser, often feeding on agricultural crops. This habit leads to its being persecuted outside conservation areas, though it is resilient to hunting. The duiker is capable of going without water for long periods, but will drink whenever water is available.

Size: shoulder height 50cm; weight up to 21kg. **Distribution:** very widespread throughout the region except on Namibia's Skeleton Coast. **Status:** common, active throughout the day, except where disturbance is common.

DAVID WALL

Klipspringer *Oreotragus oreotragus*

A small, sturdy antelope, the klipspringer is easily recognised by its curious tiptoe stance – its hooves are adapted for balance and grip on rocky surfaces. The widely spaced 10cm-long horns are present only on the male. The klipspringer normally inhabits rocky outcrops; it also sometimes ventures into adjacent grasslands, but always retreats to the rocks when alarmed. This amazingly agile and sure-footed creature is capable of bounding up impossibly rough rock faces. Male and female klipspringers form long-lasting pair bonds and occupy a territory together.

Size: shoulder height 60cm; weight up to 13kg. **Distribution:** on rocky outcrops and mountainous areas throughout the region; absent from dense forests. **Status:** common.

DENNIS JONES

Steenbok *Raphicerus campestris*

The steenbok is a very pretty and slender small antelope; its back and hindquarters range from light reddish-brown to dark brown with pale underparts markings. The upper surface of its nose bears a black, wedge-shaped 'blaze', useful for identification. Males have small, straight and widely separated horns. It is a solitary animal and only has contact with others during the mating season. The steenbok is active in the morning and evening.

Size: shoulder height 50cm; weight up to 11kg. **Distribution:** widely distributed throughout the region in all habitats, except desert areas. **Status:** common where it occurs.

Giraffe *Giraffa camelopardalis*

The name 'giraffe' is derived from the Arabic word *zarafah* (the one who walks quickly). Both sexes have 'horns', short projections of skin-covered bone. Despite the giraffe's incredibly long neck, it still has only seven cervical vertebrae – the same number as all mammals, including humans. The giraffe browses on trees, exploiting a zone of foliage inaccessible to all other herbivores except elephant. Juveniles are prone to predation and a lion will take down even fully grown adults. The giraffe is at its most vulnerable at water holes and always appears hesitant when drinking.

ARIADNE VAN ZANDBERGEN

Size: height up to 5.2m (male); weight 900kg to 1400kg. **Distribution:** northeastern South Africa, southern Zimbabwe, southern Mozambique, southern Zambia, northern Botswana and northern Namibia. **Status:** common where it occurs and easy to see.

Impala *Aepyceros melampus*

Often dismissed by tourists because it is so abundant, the impala is a unique antelope with no close relatives. Males have long, lyre-shaped horns averaging 75cm in length. It is a gregarious animal. Though males defend female herds during the oestrus, outside the breeding season males congregate in bachelor groups. The impala is known for its speed and ability to leap; it can spring as far as 10m in one bound, or 3m into the air. It is common prey of lions, leopards, cheetahs, wild dogs and spotted hyenas.

JASON EDWARDS

Size: shoulder height 90cm; weight up to 70kg. **Distribution:** widespread in the northeast of the region, with an isolated population in northern Namibia. **Status:** very common and easy to see.

Springbok *Antidorcas marsupialis*

Southern Africa's only gazelle, the springbok is extremely common in the arid areas of the subregion. It can survive without being near a water source (it gets enough water in its food), but may move large distances to find new grazing. It is one of the fastest antelopes and has a distinctive bounding gait called 'pronking', which it displays when it sees predators. Both sexes have ridged, lyre-shaped horns. Cheetahs are its main predators, though lions can be more of a threat in some areas of Namibia.

JASON EDWARDS

Size: shoulder height 75cm; weight up to 50kg. **Distribution:** Namibia, southern Botswana and northwestern South Africa. **Status:** very common and easy to see.

Black wildebeest (gnu) *Connochaetes gnou*

The black wildebeest once migrated across Southern Africa in enormous herds, but hunting decimated its populations and it is now restricted to a few parks in South Africa. The loud 'ge-nu' sound the black wildebeest makes when alarmed is the source of its other name, 'gnu'. Young males form bachelor groups, while older males defend territories onto which they herd passing groups of females. Herds are prone to dissolve into cavorting madness if surprised or threatened.

Size: shoulder height 140cm; weight 230kg. **Distribution:** confined to a few ranches and reserves in central South Africa. **Status:** endangered but easy to see wherever it occurs.

Blue wildebeest *Connochaetes taurinus*

The blue wildebeest is gregarious, forming herds up to tens of thousands strong, often with zebras and other herbivores. In Southern Africa, numbers are much reduced and huge herds are rare. Males are territorial and attempt to herd groups of females into their territory. The wildebeest is a grazer, and moves constantly in search of good pasture and water. Because it prefers to drink daily and can survive only five days without water, the wildebeest will migrate large distances. During the rainy season it grazes haphazardly, but in the dry season it congregates around water holes.

Size: shoulder height 150cm; weight 250kg. **Distribution:** occurs in all major parks in the region. **Status:** very common but mostly restricted to protected areas.

Hartebeest Red hartebeest *Alcelaphus buselaphus* (pictured); Lichtenstein's hartebeest *Sigmoceros lichtensteinii*

The hartebeest is a red-to-tan-coloured, medium-sized antelope recognisable by its long, narrow face and short, stout horns, present in both sexes. The distinctly angular and heavily ridged horns form a heart shape, hence the name from 'heart beast' in Afrikaans. The hartebeest feeds on grass and prefers open plains, but is also found in sparsely forested woodlands. It is a social animal and often associates with other herbivores such as zebras and wildebeests. Its major predators include big cats, hyenas and wild dogs.

Size: shoulder height 125cm; weight 120kg to 150kg. **Distribution:** (red) northwestern South Africa, central Botswana and Namibia; (Lichtenstein's hartebeest) some parks in Zambia, Malawi, Zimbabwe and South Africa. **Status:** (red) common where they occur; (Lichtenstein's hartebeest) very rare.

Tsessebe *Damaliscus lunatus*

The tsessebe is similar to the hartebeest but darker, with glossy violet-brown patches on the rear thighs, front legs and face. The horns, carried by both sexes, curve gently up, out and back. A highly gregarious antelope, it lives in herds and frequently mingles with other grazers. During the mating season, bulls select a well-defined patch, which they defend against rivals, while females wander from one patch to another. The tsessebe is a grazer, and although it can live on dry grasses, it prefers flood plains and moist areas that support lush pasture. It is capable of surviving long periods without water as long as sufficient grass is available.

Size: height at shoulder 120cm; weight 120kg to 150kg. **Distribution:** northeastern South Africa, southwestern Zimbabwe, northern Botswana and southwestern Zambia. **Status:** common where it occurs.

Bontebok & blesbok Bontebok *Damaliscus dorcas* (pictured)

Closely related subspecies, the bontebok and the blesbok are close relatives of the tsessebe. The best way to tell them apart is to look at their colour: the blesbok has an overall dullish appearance and lacks the rich, deep brown-purple tinge of the bontebok. Both species graze on short grass and, as with many antelope, males are territorial, while females form small herds. Both sexes have horns.

Size: shoulder height 90cm; weight up to 80kg. **Distribution:** both subspecies are endemic to South Africa; the bontebok is confined to the extreme southwest, while the blesbok is widespread in the central region. **Status:** the bontebok is rare, but is easy to see where it occurs; the blesbok is common.

Gemsbok (oryx) *Oryx gazella*

Adapted for arid zones, the gemsbok can tolerate areas uninhabitable by most antelopes. It can survive without being near a water source (it gets enough water in its food) and can tolerate extreme heat. A solid, powerful animal with long, straight horns present in both sexes, it is well equipped to defend itself and has been known occasionally to kill attacking lions. Herds vary from five to 40 individuals. The gemsbok is principally a grazer, but also browses on thorny shrubs unpalatable to many species.

Size: shoulder height 120cm; weight up to 240kg. **Distribution:** most of Namibia, Botswana and northern South Africa. **Status:** common where it occurs, but often shy, fleeing from humans.

Greater kudu *Tragelaphus strepsiceros*

The greater kudu is Africa's second-tallest antelope and the males carry massive spiralling horns, much sought after by trophy hunters. It is light grey in colour with between six and 10 white stripes down the sides and a white chevron between the eyes. The kudu lives in small herds comprising females and their young, periodically joined by the normally solitary males during the breeding season. It is primarily a browser and can eat a variety of leaves, but it finds its preferred diet in woodland-savanna with fairly dense bush cover.

Size: shoulder height 150cm; weight up to 250kg. **Distribution:** throughout the region, but absent from most of central South Africa. **Status:** common.

Eland *Taurotragus oryx*

Africa's largest antelope, the eland is a massive animal. Both sexes have horns about 65cm long, which spiral at the base and sweep straight back. The male has a distinctive hairy tuft on the head, and stouter horns than the female. The eland prefers savanna scrub, feeding on grass and tree foliage. It drinks daily, but can go for a month or more without water. It usually lives in groups of around six to 12, normally comprising several females and one male. Larger aggregations (up to a thousand) sometimes form at localised 'flushes' of new grass growth.

Size: shoulder height 170cm; weight up to 900kg (male). **Distribution:** distributed mostly in woodlands and semidesert. **Status:** naturally low density, but relatively common in its habitat and easy to see.

African buffalo *Syncerus caffer*

The African buffalo is the only native cow of Africa. Both sexes have distinctive curving horns that broaden at the base and meet over the forehead in a massive 'boss'; those of the female are usually smaller. It has a fairly wide habitat, but requires areas with abundant grass, water and cover. The African buffalo is gregarious and may form herds numbering thousands. Group composition is fluid and smaller herds often break away, sometimes rejoining the original herd later. Although it is generally docile, the buffalo can be very dangerous and should be treated with caution.

Size: shoulder height 1.4m; weight up to 820kg (male). **Distribution:** widespread but large populations now occur only in parks. **Status:** common; can be approached where it is protected.

PRIMATES

Bushbaby Greater (or thick-tailed) bushbaby
(*Otolemur crassicaudatus; pictured*); lesser bushbaby
Gulag moholi

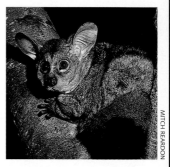

Named for its plaintive wailing call, the bushbaby is actually a primitive primate. Both species have small heads,
large rounded ears, thick bushy tails and the enormous
eyes that are typical of nocturnal primates. The greater
bushbaby has dark brown fur, while the tiny lesser bushbaby is very light grey with yellowish colouring on its legs.
Tree sap and fruit are the mainstay of their diet, supplemented by insects as well as, in the case of the greater
bushbaby, lizards, nestlings and eggs.

MITCH REARDON

Size: (greater bushbaby) length 80cm, including a 45cm tail, weight up to 1.5kg; (lesser bushbaby) length
40cm, weight 150g to 200g. **Distribution:** the greater bushbaby is restricted to the region's east; the
lesser bushbaby to South Africa, Mozambique and Namibia. **Status:** common, but strictly nocturnal.

Vervet monkey *Cercopithecus aethiops*

The most common monkey of the woodlands, the vervet
is easily recognisable by its grizzled grey hair and black
face fringed with white. The male has a distinctive bright
blue scrotum, an important signal of status. Troops may
number up to 30. The vervet monkey is diurnal and
forages for fruits, seeds, leaves, flowers, invertebrates and
the occasional lizard or nestling. It rapidly learns where
easy pickings can be found around lodges and camp sites,
but becomes a pest when it gets habituated to being fed.
Most park authorities destroy such individuals, so avoid
feeding them.

ARIADNE VAN ZANDBERGEN

Size: up to 130cm long, including a 60cm tail; weight 3.5kg to 8kg. **Distribution:** widespread in woodland-savanna throughout the region; absent only from deserts. **Status:** very common and easy to see.

Chacma baboon *Papio ursinus*

The dog-like snout of the chacma baboon gives it a more
aggressive appearance than most other primates. When
you see the interactions within a troop, it's difficult not to
make anthropomorphic comparisons. The chacma baboon
lives in troops of up to 150 animals, and there is no single
dominant male. It is strictly diurnal and forages for
grasses, fruits, insects and small vertebrates. The baboon
is a notorious opportunist and may become a pest in camp
sites, which it visits for hand-outs. Such individuals can
be very dangerous and are destroyed by park officials, so
don't feed them.

ABI

Size: shoulder height 75cm; weight 25kg to 45kg. **Distribution:** throughout the region. **Status:** common
in many areas; active during the day.

RODENTS

GALLO IMAGES/ANTHONY BANNISTER

Springhare *Pedetes capensis*
In spite of its name and large ears, the springhare is not a hare, but a rodent. With its powerful, outsized hind feet and small forelegs, it most resembles a small kangaroo and shares a similar hopping motion. The springhare digs extensive burrows, from which it emerges at night to feed on grass and grass roots. Reflections of spotlights in its large, bright eyes often give it away on night safaris. Although swift, it is preyed upon by everything from jackals to lions.

Size: length 75cm to 85cm; weight 2.5kg to 3.8kg. **Distribution:** widespread throughout most of the region; favours grassland habitats with sandy soils. **Status:** common, but strictly nocturnal

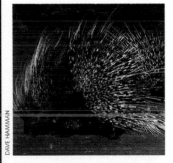

DAVE HAMMAN

Cape porcupine *Hystrix africaeaustralis*
The prickly Cape porcupine is the largest rodent native to Southern Africa. Its spread of long black-and-white banded quills from the shoulders to the tail makes it unmistakable. For shelter, it either occupies caves or excavates its own burrows. The porcupine's diet consists mainly of bark, tubers, seeds, and a variety of plant and ground-level foliage. The young are born during the hot summer months in litters of between one and four.

Size: length 75cm to 100cm; weight 10kg to 24kg. **Distribution:** throughout the region. **Status:** nocturnal, but occasionally active on cooler days; difficult to see.

MITCH REARDON

Cape ground squirrel *Xerus inauris*
The ground squirrel is a sociable rodent living in colonial burrows, which it often shares with meerkats. It feeds on grass, roots, seeds and insects, but readily takes handouts from people in tourist camps. The ground squirrel is well adapted to its dry surroundings; it does not need to drink, and extracts all the moisture it requires from its food. It has an elegant fan-like tail, which it erects when alarmed and also uses as a sunshade.

Size: length 45cm; weight up to 1kg. **Distribution:** Namibia, northern South Africa and southern central Botswana. **Status:** common; active throughout the day.

Title page: Reticulated giraffes *(Giraffa camelopardalis)* by Mitch Reardon

Botswana

Botswana, formerly known as Bechuanaland, is an African success story. A long-neglected British protectorate, Botswana achieved its timely independence under democratic rule in 1966 and soon after discovered three of the world's richest diamond-bearing formations. It enjoys politically and ideologically enlightened nonracial policies along with high health, educational and economic standards which, with the exception of South Africa, are unequalled elsewhere in sub-Saharan Africa.

Its modern veneer, however, belies the fact that much of Botswana remains a country for the intrepid, not to mention relatively wealthy, traveller. This largely roadless wilderness of vast spaces – savanna, desert, wetlands, salt pans and myriad traditional villages - requires time, effort and above all else lots of cash to enjoy to its fullest.

Facts about Botswana

HISTORY

For a detailed account of the early history of the whole Southern African region, including Botswana's precolonial history, see History in the Facts about the Region chapter.

Early History

Botswana's first people were the San (formerly known as 'Bushmen'), who have inhabited Southern Africa for at least 30,000 years. They were followed by the Khoikhoi (formerly known as 'Hottentots') who are thought to have originated from a breakaway San group. The language group of both peoples is collectively called Khoisan.

During the 1st or 2nd century AD the Bantu people migrated from the north. Relations between the Khoisan and Bantu societies appear to have been peaceful and there's evidence that they traded, intermarried and mixed freely. The Bantu group known as the Tswana migrated from present-day South Africa sometime during the 14th century to colonise the country's southeastern

Botswana at a Glance

Area: 582,000 sq km
Population: 1.61 million
Capital: Gaborone
Head of State: President Festus Mogae
Official Languages: English & Setswana
Currency: pula (P)
Exchange Rate: US$1 = P5.18

Highlights

- Okavango Delta and Moremi Wildlife Reserve – exploring these watery, wildlife-packed wonderlands

- Wild Kalahari – marvelling at its vast spaces and incredible night skies

- Tsodilo Hills – wandering through the 'Wilderness Louvre' of ancient San paintings in Botswana's most inspiring wild landscape

- Chobe National Park – exploring this huge wildlife-rich reserve, with its magnificent riverfront, inland marsh and savanna zones

- Makgadikgadi & Nxai Pans National Park – experiencing the grassland and salt pan wilderness of Makgadikgadi and enjoying Botswana's best wet season wildlife viewing at Nxai Pan

- Kgalagadi Trans-Frontier Park – striking into the wilderness on a 4WD camping safari in search of the Kalahari's enigmatic wildlife

strip, and today forms Botswana's largest population group.

In 1818 the confederation of Zulu tribes in South Africa set out to conquer or destroy all tribes and settlements in its path, causing waves of disruption throughout Southern Africa. Tswana villages were scattered and some were pushed into the dead heart of the Kalahari. In response to this aggression, the Tswana regrouped and developed a highly structured society. Each Tswana nation was ruled by a hereditary monarch and the king's subjects lived in the central town or satellite villages. Each clan was allocated its own settlement, which was under the control of village leaders. By the second half of the 19th century some of these towns had grown to a considerable size.

Early Colonial Era

The orderliness and structure of this town-based society impressed the early Christian missionaries, who arrived in 1817. None of them managed to convert great numbers of Batswana (at the time, this referred only to people of Tswana nationality) but they advised the Tswana, sometimes wrongly, in their dealings with the Europeans who followed – explorers, naturalists, traders, miners and itinerant opportunists.

From the late 1820s the Boers, dissatisfied with British rule in the Cape Colony, began their Great Trek across the Vaal River (the Cape Colony's frontier). Confident that they had heaven-sanctioned rights to any land they might choose to occupy in Southern Africa, 20,000 Boers crossed the Vaal River

into Tswana and Zulu territory and established themselves as though the lands were unclaimed and uninhabited (indeed many were, having been cleaned out earlier by Zulu factions or the tsetse fly). At the Sand River Convention of 1852 Britain recognised the Transvaal's independence and the Boers informed the Batswana that they were now subjects of the South African Republic. The Boer leader MW Pretorius notified the British that the Tswana were acquiring weapons from white traders and missionaries and preparing for war with the Boers.

The British Protectorate

Prominent Tswana leaders Sechele I and Mosielele refused to accept white rule and incurred the wrath of the Boers. After heavy losses of life and land, the Tswana sent their leaders to petition the British for protection. Britain, however, was in no hurry to support lands of dubious profitability and offered only to act as arbitrator in the dispute. By 1877, however, the worsening situation provoked the British annexation of the Transvaal and launched the first Anglo–Boer War.

Violence continued until the Pretoria Convention of 1881 when the British withdrew from the Transvaal in exchange for Boer allegiance to the Crown. In 1882 Boers again moved into Tswana lands and subdued Mafeking (now Mafikeng), threatening the British route between the cape and possible mineral wealth in what is present-day Zimbabwe.

Again, the Tswana lobbied for British protection and in 1885, thanks to petitions from John Mackenzie (a friend of the Christian Chief Khama III of Shoshong), Britain resigned itself to the inevitable. Lands south of the Molopo River became the British Crown Colony of Bechuanaland and were attached to the Cape Colony while the area north became the British Protectorate of Bechuanaland.

A new threat to the Tswana chiefs' power base came in the form of Cecil Rhodes and his British South Africa Company (BSAC). By 1894 the British had all but agreed to allow him to control the country. An unhappy delegation of Tswana chiefs, Bathoen, Khama III and Sebele, accompanied by a sympathetic missionary, WC Willoughby, sailed to England to appeal directly to Colonial Minister Joseph Chamberlain for

continued government control but their pleas were ignored. As a last resort, they turned to the London Missionary Society (LMS) who in turn took the matter to the British public. Fearing the BSAC would allow alcohol in Bechuanaland, the LMS and other Christian groups backed the Christian Khama. Public pressure mounted and the British government was forced to concede.

At this stage, the chiefs grudgingly accepted that their rites and traditions would be affected by Christianity and Western technology. The cash economy was by now firmly in place and the Tswana were actively participating in it. The capital of the protectorate was established at Mafeking (now Mafikeng, in present-day South Africa) and a system of taxes was introduced. Each chief was granted a tribal 'reserve' in which he was given jurisdiction over all black residents and the authority to collect taxes; the chiefs would retain a 10% commission on all money collected. The sale of cattle, oxen and grain to the Europeans streaming north in search of farming land and minerals provided the basis of the protectorate's economy.

This system didn't last long, however. The construction of the railway through Bechuanaland to Rhodesia (Zimbabwe) and an outbreak of foot-and-mouth disease in the 1890s destroyed the transit trade. By 1920 maize farmers in South Africa and Rhodesia were producing so much grain that Bechuanaland no longer had a market. In 1924 South Africa began pressing for Bechuanaland's amalgamation into the Union of South Africa. When the Tswana chiefs refused, economic sanctions destroyed what remained of their beef market.

In 1923 Chief Khama III died and was succeeded by his son Sekgoma, who died after serving only two years. The heir to the throne was four-year-old Seretse Khama, and the job of regent went to his 21-year-old uncle, Tshekedi Khama, who was later criticised by colonial authorities for his handling of several local disputes according to tribal law.

Resident commissioner of the protectorate Sir Charles Rey determined that no progress would be forthcoming as long as the people were governed by Tswana chiefs and proclaimed them all local government officials and answerable to colonial magistrates. So great was the popular opposition to the

move – people feared that it would lead to their incorporation into South Africa – Rey was ousted from his job and his proclamation annulled.

During WWII, 10,000 Tswana volunteered for the African Pioneer Corps to defend the British Empire. After the war Seretse Khama went to study in England where he met and married Ruth Williams, an Englishwoman. This breach of tribal custom infuriated not only Tshekedi Khama but also the entire tribe, the South African authorities and the British, and Seretse Khama was exiled in Britain. In 1956 after renouncing his right to power, he was permitted to return to Botswana with his wife and set up residence.

Nationalism & Independence

The first signs of nationalist thinking among the Batswana occurred in the late 1940s; during the 1950s and early 1960s all Africa experienced political change as many former colonies gained their independence, and by 1955, it had become apparent that Britain was preparing to release its grip on Bechuanaland. University graduates returned from South Africa with political ideas, and although the country had no real economic base, the first Batswana political parties surfaced and began thinking about independence.

Following the Sharpeville Massacre in 1960, South African refugees Motsamai Mpho of the African National Congress (ANC) and Philip Matante, a Johannesburg preacher affiliated with the Pan-Africanist Congress (PAC), together with KT Motsete, a teacher from Malawi, formed the Bechuanaland People's Party (BPP). Its immediate goal was independence for the protectorate.

In 1962 Seretse Khama and Ketumile 'Quett' Masire formed the more moderate Bechuanaland Democratic Party (BDP), and were later joined by Chief Bathoen II of the Ngwaketse. The BDP formulated a schedule for independence, drawing on support from local chiefs and traditional Batswana.

They promoted the transfer of the capital into the country (from Mafikeng to Gaborone), drafted up a new nonracial constitution and set up a countdown to independence, to allow a peaceful transfer of power. General elections were held in 1965 and Seretse Khama was elected president. On 30 September 1966 the country, now called the Republic of Botswana, peacefully gained its independence.

Seretse Khama, who was knighted shortly after independence, was no revolutionary; because of Botswana's economic dependence on its neighbours, he adopted a neutral stance (at least until near the end of his presidency) towards South Africa and Rhodesia. Nevertheless, Khama refused to exchange ambassadors with South Africa and officially disapproved of apartheid in international circles.

Botswana was economically transformed by the discovery of diamonds near Orapa in 1967. The mining concession was given to South Africa's De Beers, with Botswana taking 75% of the profits.

Although most of the population remains in the low income bracket, thanks to this mineral wealth, Botswana now possesses enormous foreign currency reserves. Its economic dependence upon its southern neighbour is waning, and South Africa remains an active trading partner.

Sir Seretse Khama died in 1980, but his Botswana Democratic Party still commands a substantial majority in parliament. Dr Ketumile 'Quett' Masire, who served as president for 18 years, and Festus Mogae, who took the helm in March 1998 with the voluntary retirement of Dr Masire, have continued in their predecessor's path (while the government cautiously follows pro-Western policies). President Mogae, who holds an honours degree in economics from Oxford University, is fiscally astute and carries on the conservative traditions of his predecessors. While the BDP is well-ensconced, there is also considerable urban support for the opposition party, the Botswana National Front, which supports redistribution of wealth and a centrally regulated economy.

Botswana now has one of the world's highest rates of economic growth, but it still suffers from unemployment, urban drift, a high birth rate and one of the world's highest HIV infection rates. In 2000 the country suffered devastating floods that left 70,000 people homeless, while droughts in recent years have caused considerable suffering, especially in the western part of the country. Despite these challenges, Botswana remains a peaceful nation that continues to be a bright and hopeful spot on the African continent.

GEOGRAPHY

With an area of 582,000 sq km, landlocked Botswana extends 1100km from north to south and 960km from east to west, making it about the same size as Kenya or France and somewhat smaller than Texas.

Most of the country lies at an average elevation of 1000m and consists of a vast and nearly level sand-filled basin characterised by scrub-covered savanna. The Kalahari (Kgalagadi), a semi-arid expanse of wind-blown sand deposits and long, sandy valleys covers nearly 85% of Botswana, including the entire central and southwestern regions. In the northwest the Okavango River flows in from Namibia and soaks into the sands, forming the Okavango Delta, which covers an area of 15,000 sq km. In the northeast are the great salty clay deserts of the Makgadikgadi Pans.

CLIMATE

Although it straddles the Tropic of Capricorn, Botswana experiences extremes in both temperature and weather. It's mainly dry, but does have a summer rainy season, which runs roughly from November to March. (In January and February 2000, record rainfalls and subsequent flooding paralysed much of the country.)

From late May to August, rain is rare anywhere in the country. Days are normally clear, warm and sunny, and nights are cool to bitterly cold. In the Kalahari, below freezing temperatures at night are normal in June and July and, where there's enough humidity, frosts are common.

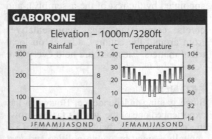

ECOLOGY & ENVIRONMENT

While much of Botswana is largely wide, open and pristine, it does face several ecological challenges. The main one revolves around its 3000km of 1.5m-high 'buffalo fence', officially called the 'veterinary cordon fence' – a series of high-tensile steel wire barriers that cross some of the country's wildest terrain. The fences were first erected in 1954 to segregate wild buffalo herds from domestic free-range cattle and thwart the spread of foot-and-mouth disease. However, it hasn't been proven that the disease is passed from species to species and the fences not only prevent contact between wild and domestic bovine species, but also prevent other wild animals from migrating to water sources along age-old seasonal routes. While Botswana has set aside large areas for wildlife protection, they don't constitute independent ecosystems, and migratory wildlife numbers (particularly wildebeest, giraffe and zebra) continue to decline. Cattle ranching is a source of wealth and a major export industry, but all exported beef must be disease-free, so understandably ranchers have reacted positively to the fences, and the government tends to side with the ranchers.

Botswana also has water issues. From the time of the first European colonists, both settlers and developers have been eyeing the Okavango Delta as a source of water to transform northwestern Botswana into a lush, green farmland. Nowadays, pressure from population growth, mining interests and increased tourism – particularly around Maun – are straining resources and placing the delta at the crux of a debate between the government, ranchers, engineers, developers, tour operators, rural people and conservationists. In 1985 a plan was put forward to dredge the Boro River and divert water into a series of dams and irrigation projects, but an international outcry highlighted the need for a complete environmental impact study (formulated in 1991). In the end, officials agreed to explore alternative water plans while keeping the dredging issue open as a contingency plan if no other solutions are found. Over the past decade, Maun's population has continued to grow, placing further strain on the area's water resources. Whether or not the dredging issue will resurface in the near future remains to be seen.

FLORA & FAUNA

If you are looking for the Africa of your dreams – vast open savannas with free-ranging wildlife – Botswana may well be the best destination for you. Most of the country is covered with scrub brush and

BOTSWANA

savanna grassland, although small areas of deciduous forest (mopane, msasa and Zambezi teak) thrive on the Zimbabwean border. The Okavango and Linyanti wetlands of the northwest are characterised by riverbank and swamp vegetation, which includes reeds, papyrus and water lilies as well as larger trees such as acacia, jackalberry, leadwood and sausage trees.

Because the Okavango Delta and the Chobe River provide an incongruous water supply, nearly all Southern African mammal species, including such rarities as pukus, red lechwes, sitatungas and wild dogs, are present in Moremi Wildlife Reserve, parts of Chobe National Park and the Linyanti Marshes. In the Makgadikgadi & Nxai Pan National Park, herds of wildebeest, zebra and other hoofed mammals migrate between their winter range on the Makgadikgadi plains and the summer lushness of the Nxai Pan region.

National Parks & Reserves

Botswana's national parks are among Africa's wildest, characterised by open spaces where nature still reigns supreme, and although they do support a few private safari concessions, there's next to no infrastructure and few amenities.

The major parks include the Central Kalahari Game Reserve, Chobe National Park, Khutse Game Reserve, Kgalagadi Transfrontier Park (an amalgamation of Botswana's former Mabuasehube–Gemsbok National Park and South Africa's Kalahari–Gemsbok National Park), Makgadikgadi & Nxai Pans National Park and Moremi Wildlife Reserve. The North-East Tuli Game Reserve is not a national park, but rather is cobbled together from several private reserves.

Fees for parks (except for Kgalagadi Transfrontier Park) for nonresidents are US$22/13 (P120/70) per day for individual travellers/licensed safari participants, plus US$5.50 (P30) per person for camping; foreign/Botswana-registered vehicles pay US$10/2 per day. Children and Botswana residents and citizens get substantial discounts (residents of Botswana pay US$6/4 per day to enter/camp and citizens pay US$2/1). At Kgalagadi Transfrontier Park, everyone pays US$4 per day to enter and nonresidents pay US$6 to camp plus US$37 per day to use the wilderness 4WD tracks (see the Kalahari section later in this chapter).

You can book accommodation in the national parks by post, phone, fax, email or in person up to one year prior to your intended visit. Contact the office of the **Department of Wildlife & National Parks (DWNP) Reservation Office** (☎ 318 0774, fax 318 0775; e dwnp@gov.bw; PO Box 131, Government Enclave, Khama Cres, Gaborone; open 7.30am-12.45pm & 1.45pm-4.30pm Mon-Fri). You can also book through the **Maun Office** (☎ 686 1265, fax 686 1264; PO Box 20364, Boseja, Maun), beside the police station. Chobe National Park bookings are also available from the **Kasane Office** (☎ 625 0235, fax 625 1623), in Kasane.

When booking, include the name of the park, the camping ground, the dates of arrival and departure, the total number of campers and whether they are citizens, residents or nonresidents of Botswana. Payment in Botswana pula or by credit card must be received within one month or you forfeit the booking.

GOVERNMENT & POLITICS

Botswana is one of Africa's success stories, with a stable multiparty democracy that oversees the affairs of a peaceful and neutral state. Freedom of speech, press and religion are constitutionally guaranteed.

The government has three divisions: the executive branch, headed by the president, 11 cabinet ministers and three assistant ministers; the legislative branch, made up of the parliament (which comprises the president and the assembly, which is in turn made up of the speaker, the attorney general, 40 elected MPs and four special members appointed by the rest of the assembly); and the judicial branch. A 15-member house of chiefs, comprising tribal representatives from around the country, advises on local tribal matters. Elections are held every five years.

ECONOMY

Since gaining independence, Botswana has experienced one of the world's fastest-growing economic rates (between 11% and 13% annually), aided by stable politics and vast natural resources. Most of the natural wealth is based on mineral resources, specifically diamonds. Copper and nickel are mined near Selebi-Phikwe, gold is still mined around Francistown; limited amounts of coal are taken from near Palapye; and soda

The San

The San people have probably inhabited Southern Africa for at least 30,000 years, but unfortunately, their tenure hasn't yielded commensurate benefits. There's evidence that they peacefully coexisted – and probably even traded and intermarried with – early Bantu groups who later arrived from the north. However, the pressure of the Bantu numbers eventually changed that situation. Some San people made themselves quite unpopular by purloining Bantu herders' cattle. Others probably attempted integration with the Bantu communities, but the San almost invariably wound up as slaves.

Some San abandoned their traditional hunting grounds and sought unpopulated areas to continue their nomadic ways, but the choice of amenable unpopulated areas quickly diminished.

Historically, the San had no collective name for themselves, but there's evidence that some referred to themselves as 'the harmless people' or in similarly self-deprecating terms. The early Europeans in Southern Africa knew them as 'Bushmen', which stuck for several centuries. The Tswana generally refer to them by the rather derogatory name Basarwa – essentially 'people from the sticks'. The word 'San' originally referred to the language of one group of indigenous people in Southern Africa (the entire language group was known as Khoisan), and it's currently the most acceptable name, despite the fact that it probably originates from words meaning 'wild people who can't farm'. On the other hand, the San now commonly refer to themselves by their clan name (eg, Ju/hoansi, !Kung etc) or Ncoakhoe, meaning 'the Red People'.

Some researchers have suggested that the San historically lived in a state of 'primitive affluence'. That is, they had to work only a short time each day to satisfy all their basic needs. At certain times and locations this might have been true, but during some seasons and in some conditions life could be harsh, for their sandy dry environment was above all very unpredictable.

Traditionally, this nomadic hunting and gathering society travelled in small family bands, following water, wildlife and edible plants. They had no chiefs or system of leadership, possessed no land, animals, crops or personal effects, and respected the individualism of their members. Women spent much of their time caring for children and gathering edible or water-yielding plants, while the men either hunted or helped with the food gathering.

According to one myth, the San are unable to distinguish colour because San languages contain few colour-related words. In fact, the languages are more concerned with tangibles than abstracts, so it's simply considered unnecessary to linguistically separate an object from its attributes. Similarly, there is no word for 'work', which is a fundamental facet of living and therefore requires no separate designation.

Another myth is that the San possess extremely keen senses of hearing, eyesight and direction. Although their awareness of their surroundings certainly seems phenomenal to the technology-dependent world, anthropological studies have determined that these attributes have been learned out of necessity and aren't any sort of physiological adaptation. It's generally agreed that just about anyone, given the right circumstances and healthy faculties, can develop a similar awareness.

Of the remaining 55,000 or so San, approximately 60% live in Botswana, 35% in Namibia and the remainder are scattered through South Africa, Angola, Zimbabwe and Zambia. Tragically, most modern San work on farms and cattle posts or languish in squalid alcohol-plagued settlements centred on bore holes in western Botswana and northeastern Namibia.

One recent contentious political issue in Botswana has been the forced relocation in March 1998 of the San from the Central Kalahari Game Reserve, which was set aside as a traditional hunting and gathering ground for them in 1961. In spite of vocal protests from the San, who realised that removal from their traditional lands would likely result in what would amount to indentured servitude on private ranches or cattle posts, they were shifted from the village of Xade to a settlement called New Xade – which has neither water nor permanent buildings – outside the reserve. They were advised that failure to move would result in less government money for health and educational facilities.

Officially, this action was justified due to the need to support wildlife preservation, tourism development and the need to 'rescue the Bushmen from their way of life and integrate them into mainstream Batswana society'. Cynics might also suggest that vast expanses of potential cattle grazing land and suspected diamond deposits within the reserve might also have played a role.

Through such grass-roots organisations as The First People of the Kalahari in Botswana and the Nyae Nyae Farmers' Cooperative in Namibia, some hopes for the future have emerged. For more information on the San and their current situation contact **Survival International** (☎ 020-7242 1441; w www.survival -international.org; 11-15 Emerald St, London WC1N 3QL UK), which is active on this issue.

ash (sodium carbonate) and salt are extracted from Sua Pan.

Because Botswana is mostly arid, ranching is the only significant agricultural enterprise. Subsistence farmers depend mostly on cattle, sheep and goats, and grow maize, sorghum, beans, peanuts, cottonseed and other dry-land crops.

POPULATION & PEOPLE

Of Botswana's 1.61 million people, about 60% claim Tswana heritage. Botswana also has one of the world's most predominantly urban societies. The bulk of the population is concentrated in the southeastern strip of the country between Lobatse and Francistown. A small number of Europeans and Asians live mainly in Gaborone, Maun and Francistown. Other groups include the Herero, Mbukushu, Yei, San, Kalanga and Kgalagadi, who live mainly in the west and northwest.

ARTS
Arts & Crafts

The original Batswana artists managed to convey individuality, aesthetics and aspects of Batswana life in their utilitarian implements. Baskets, pottery, fabrics and tools were decorated with meaningful designs derived from tradition. Europeans introduced a new form of art, some of which was integrated and adapted to local interpretation, particularly in weavings and tapestries. The result is some of the finest and most meticulously executed work in Southern Africa.

Literature

As indigenous languages have only been written since the coming of the Christian missionaries, Botswana lacks an extensive literary tradition. What survives of the ancient myths and poetry of the San, Tswana, Herero and other groups has been handed down orally and only recently written down.

Botswana's most famous modern literary figure was Bessie Head (who died in 1988), who settled in Sir Seretse Khama's village of Serowe and wrote works that reflected the harshness and beauty of African village life and the Botswanan landscape. Her most widely read works include *Serowe – Village of the Rain Wind*, *When Rain Clouds Gather*, *Maru*, *A Question of Power*, *The Cardinals*, *A Bewitched Crossroad* and *The Collector of*

Treasures; the last is an anthology of short stories. Welcome recent additions to Botswana's national literature are the works of Norman Rush, which include the novel *Mating*, set in a remote village, and *Whites*, which deals with the country's growing number of expatriates and apologists from South Africa and elsewhere.

LANGUAGE

English is the official language of Botswana and the medium of instruction from the fifth year of primary school. The most widely spoken language, however, is Setswana, which is the first language of over 90% of people.

Facts for the Visitor

SUGGESTED ITINERARIES

Botswana's tourist highlight is the Okavango Delta, and if you have only a week, this is where you'll want to focus. Choose Maun or the Okavango Panhandle (the northwestern extension of the Okavango Delta) as your base and organise a *mokoro* (dugout canoe) trip through the wetlands, followed by a wildlife-viewing trip through Moremi Wildlife Reserve.

With a month (and lots of money), you can hire a 4WD or use a reputable safari company and see the best of the country: do a *mokoro* trip in the Okavango Delta; visit Moremi and Chobe; camp and hike in the Tsodilo Hills; cruise on the Okavango Panhandle; and explore the furthest reaches of the Kalahari.

The Big Trip

Due to the costs, many travellers skip Botswana on their big trip around Southern Africa, but there are still options. The best route to visit the highlights will first take you to either Kasane, which is readily accessible to or from Zambia or Zimbabwe, or Shakawe, near the Namibian border. A recommended route between these two would include a wildlife drive or cruise in Chobe National Park, and a *mokoro* trip from either Maun or Seronga.

Those headed to or from Namibia will find at least one daily bus for each of the four public transport segments between Maun and Windhoek (Maun–Ghanzi–Buitepos–Gobabis–Windhoek). Coming from South Africa via Gaborone or from Zimbabwe

via Francistown, you'll have lots of long open stretches before reaching the visitor highlights.

Travel Tips

To travel economically in Botswana, you'll need a tent; most lodges along the road system have camp sites with full facilities.

The direct route between Kasane and Maun through Chobe entails two days of tough 4WD-driving. Via Nata, it's an easy six-hour drive or eight-hour bus ride (with a connection in Nata) on a good sealed road.

PLANNING
When to Go

In winter (late May through August) days are normally clear, warm and sunny, and nights are cool to cold. Wildlife never wanders far from water sources so sightings are more predictable than in the wetter summer season. This is also the time of European, North American and – most importantly – South African school holidays, so some areas can be busy especially between mid-July and mid-September.

In summer (October to April), wildlife is harder to spot and rains can render sandy roads impassable. This is also the time of the highest humidity and the most stifling heat; daytime temperatures of over 40°C are common.

Maps

The most accurate country map is the *Shell Tourist Map of Botswana*, which shows major roads and includes insets of tourist areas and central Gaborone. It's sold in a packet with a small tourist guide in bookshops all over the region. Almost as good is Rainbird Publishers 1:2,500,000 *Explorer Map Botswana*. The 1:1,750,000 *Republic of Botswana*, published by Macmillan, also contains insets of Gaborone and the tourist areas. The detailed *ContiMap 1:1,100,000* is a decent road map that sells for US$10.

The **Department of Surveys & Mapping** (☎ 395 6015; Old Lobatse Rd, Private Bag 0037, Gaborone) publishes topographic sheets, city and town plans, aerial photographs, geological maps and Landsat images for US$2 to US$4 per sheet. For geological mapping, contact **Geological Surveys** (☎ 533 0327, fax 533 2013; e geosurv@global.bw; Private Bag 0014, Lobatse).

TOURIST OFFICES

The continually improving **Department of Tourism office** (☎ 395 3024, fax 390 8675; e botswanatourism@gov.bw; 2nd floor, Standard Chartered Bank Building, The Mall, Private Bag 0047, Gaborone) dispenses tourist information and distributes brochures, maps and the annual *Botswana Focus* and *Discover Botswana* magazines. The offices in **Kasane** (☎ 625 0357) and **Maun** (☎ 686 0492) are also becoming more useful.

Botswana has no dedicated overseas tourist offices, but the following private agencies have been contracted to market the country internationally:

Interface International (☎ 030-42 25 60 26, fax 42 25 62 86, e pgeddesinterface@t-online.de) Petersburgerstr 94, D-10247, Berlin, Germany
Kartagener Associates Inc (☎ 516-858 1270, e kainyc@att.net) 631 Commack Rd, Suite 1A, Commack, NY 11725, USA
Southern Skies Marketing (☎ 01344-636430, fax 020-8987 0488, e botswanatourism@ southernskies.co.uk) Index House, St George's St, Berks SL5 7EU, UK

VISAS & DOCUMENTS
Visas

Visas are not required by citizens of most Commonwealth countries, most European countries or the USA; however, Israelis do need visas. On entry, everyone is granted a 30-day stay.

Visa Extensions Extensions are available for up to three months (for contact details of the immigration office, see Information in the Gaborone section). You may be asked to show an onward air ticket or proof of sufficient funds for your intended stay. For more than a three-month extension, apply to the **Immigration & Passport Control Officer** (☎ 361 1300, fax 355 2996; cnr State Hour Dr & Khama Cres, PO Box 942, Gaborone) before your trip.

Working visas are also available for non-residents – see Work later in this section.

Driving Licence & Other Documents

Travellers may drive using their home driving licence for up to six months (non-English language licences must be accompanied by a certified English translation). Those entering by vehicle need current registration

papers and third-party insurance valid in the Southern African Customs Union. On entry, foreign-registered vehicles are subject to a road safety levy of US$2 (P10).

EMBASSIES & CONSULATES
Botswanan Embassies & High Commissions

Botswana has embassies and high commissions in Namibia, South Africa, Zambia and Zimbabwe (see the relevant country chapters), as well as in the following countries. Where Botswana has no diplomatic representation, information and visas are available through the British high commission.

EU (☎ 32-2-732 2070, fax 735 6312) 169, Ave de Tervuren, B-1150 Brussels, Belgium
UK (☎ 020-7499 0031, fax 7495 8595) 6 Stratford Place, London W1N 9AE
USA (☎ 202-244 4990, fax 244 4164) 1531-33 New Hampshire Ave NW, Washington, DC 20008

Embassies & High Commissions in Botswana

All of the following are in Gaborone:

Angola (☎ 390 0204, fax 397 5089, e angola emb@info.bw) 5131 Nelson Mandela Rd, Private Bag BR111, Broadhurst
France (☎/fax 397 3863) 761 Robinson Rd, PO Box 1424
Germany (☎ 395 3143, fax 395 3038) 3rd floor, Professional House, Broadhurst, PO Box 315
Namibia (☎ 397 2685) BCC Bldg, 1278 Lobatse Rd, PO Box 1586
UK (☎ 395 2841, fax 395 6105) Queen's Rd, Private Bag 0023, The Mall
USA (☎ 395 3982, fax 395 6947, e pausemb3@ botsnet.bw) Government Enclave, Embassy Dr, PO Box 90
Zambia (☎ 395 1951, fax 395 3952) Zambia House, The Mall, PO Box 362
Zimbabwe (☎ 391 4495, fax 390 5863) Orapa Close, PO Box 1232

CUSTOMS

Botswana is a member of the Southern African Customs Union, which allows unrestricted carriage of certain items between member countries duty free. However, extra petrol and South African alcohol (more than 2L of wine and 1L of beer or spirits) are subject to duty. From outside the union, you can import up to 400 cigarettes, 50 cigars and 250g of tobacco duty free. Edible animal products such as untinned meat, milk

and eggs are confiscated at the border (and also at veterinary cordon fences between the northwestern province of Ngamiland and the rest of the country).

MONEY
Currency

Botswana's unit of currency is the pula (meaning 'rain'), which is divided into 100 thebe (meaning 'raindrops'). Bank notes come in denominations of P5, P10, P20, P50 and P100, and coins in denominations of 5t, 10t, 25t, 50t, P1, P2 and P5.

Exchange Rates

At the time of print, exchange rates for the pula were as follows:

country	unit		pula
Australia	A$1	=	P3.43
Canada	C$1	=	P3.83
euro zone	€1	=	P6.09
Japan	¥100	=	P4.40
Malawi	MK1	=	P0.05
Mozambique	Mtc100	=	P0.02
New Zealand	NZ$1	=	P2.99
South Africa	R1	=	P0.65
Tanzania	Tsh100	=	P0.52
UK	UK£1	=	P8.63
USA	US$1	=	P5.18
Zambia	k100	=	P0.10
Zimbabwe	ZW$1	=	P0.63

Exchanging Money

Full banking services are available in all main towns, but avoid the banks around the middle or end of the month, when the queues are formidable. To change cash, both Barclays and Standard Chartered banks charge 3% commission, while the former charges 3% to change travellers cheques and the latter, 1.25%. Fortunately, foreign exchange bureaus exist in Gaborone, Maun, Selebi-Phikwe and Kasane, and are typically more efficient for cash and travellers cheques.

Credit Cards Most major credit cards (especially Visa and MasterCard) are accepted at tourist hotels and restaurants in the larger cities and towns, but not petrol stations. Barclays and Standard Chartered banks in Gaborone, Lobatse, Maun, Francistown and Kasane do Visa or MasterCard over-the-counter cash advances of up to P3000 per day without commission. If you have a pin number, you can use most

Standard Chartered bank ATMs to withdraw up to P1000 per day. Note that most hotels and restaurants add 10% to 12% to the bill for credit card payment (and don't bother arguing that credit card companies forbid such practices – no-one wants to hear about it).

Costs

Travelling cheaply in Botswana isn't impossible, but if you can't afford a flight into the Okavango, a day or two at Moremi Wildlife Reserve or Chobe National Park, or a 4WD trip through the Kalahari, you may want to think twice before visiting. Safari lodges – especially those in the Okavango Delta and Chobe National Park – are for the most part exclusive haunts of the wealthy, and you'll rarely find anything for less than US$600, double. Hotels, camping, car hire, domestic air flights, meals, alcohol and self-catering prices are comparable to those in Europe, North America and Australasia, and although buses and trains are quite economical (US$1 per hour of journey time), they won't take you to the most interesting parts of the country.

Tipping

In most places a service charge is added as a matter of course, but the official policy of courting upmarket tourists only has increased expectations. At remote safari lodges, it's wise to leave a blanket tip with the management to be divided among the staff (say US$20 to US$25 for a stay of three days). *Mokoro* polers always expect to be tipped, and clients may well be reminded of that fact several times – about US$2.50 per poler per day is a good standard. Taxi drivers generally aren't tipped.

POST & COMMUNICATIONS
Post

Although generally reliable, postal services can be extremely slow, so allow at least two weeks for delivery to an overseas address. Postcards to all Western countries cost P1.80 and letters up to 10g cost P2.50 to Europe and P3 to Australasia and North America. Designate an airmail letter by clipping one corner off the envelope.

Poste restante is available all over the country, but is most reliable in Gaborone; to pick up mail you must present your passport or photo ID. To post or receive parcels, go to the parcel office and fill out the customs forms. Parcels may be plastered with all the sticky tape you like, but in the end they must be tied up with string and sealing wax, so bring matches to seal knots with the red wax provided.

Telephone

Botswana's country code is ☎ 267; there are no internal area codes, so when phoning from outside Botswana, dial ☎ 267 followed by the phone number. From Botswana, the international access code is ☎ 00, which should be followed by the country code, area code (if applicable) and telephone number.

Reliable coin and card telephone boxes are found at Botswana Telecom and post offices, and in shopping centres in all major towns. Phonecards in denominations of P20, P25 and P40 are sold at Botswana Telecom, post offices and some petrol stations and shops. Alternatively, numerous enterprising individuals with mobile phones have set up small 'phone shops' where you can make calls.

Note that Botswana is currently changing from six- to seven-digit telephone numbers (in this chapter, we've included the new numbers whenever possible). If you use the old number, a recording will provide the new one.

Email & Internet Access

Internet and email access is now available at Internet cafés in Gaborone, Maun, Francistown, Kasane and Ghanzi, and it's relatively fast and inexpensive. The most popular ISP is botsnet.bw (Ⓦ www.botsnet.bw), based in Gaborone.

DIGITAL RESOURCES

Following is a list of helpful websites:

Botswana Government (Ⓦ www.gov.bw) Contains current news and links to business and government departments
Info Botswana (Ⓦ www.info.bw) Includes links to tourism operators, plus the latest news and weather
On Safari (Ⓦ www.onsafari.com) Gives details on tour companies and lodges in Botswana and Southern Africa
University of Botswana (Ⓦ www.ub.bw) Provides information on history, archaeology, politics, society and tourism

BOOKS
Guidebooks
African ADrnturer's Guide to Botswana, by Mike Main, concentrates on off-road information, including GPS coordinates, for those venturing into the great unknown with their own vehicles. It's available in better bookshops around Southern Africa.

Travel
Lost World of the Kalahari, by Laurens van der Post, is a classic work dealing with the San people and contains some wonderful background on the Tsodilo Hills. The author's quest for an understanding of San religion and folklore is continued in *Heart of the Hunter* and *The Voice of the Thunder*.

Starlings Laughing, by June Vendall-Clark, is a memoir describing the end of the colonial era in Southern Africa. The author spent many years in the Maun area.

Cry of the Kalahari, by Mark & Delia Owens, is an entertaining and readable account of an American couple's seven years studying brown hyenas in the Central Kalahari.

With My Soul Amongst Lions and *Last of the Free*, by Gareth Patterson, carries Joy and George Adamson's *Born Free* legacy from Kenya to Mashatu, in Botswana's Tuli Block. These rather tragic tales may make depressing reading for anyone inspired by Adamson's early efforts and visions.

History & Culture
Ditswammung – The Archaeology of Botswana, by P Lane, A Redi and A Segobye, is a weighty tome, compiled by the Botswana Society, and is the definitive work for archaeology buffs.

History of Botswana, by T Tlou & Alec Campbell, is the most readable account of Botswana's history, from the Stone Age to modern times.

A Marriage of Inconvenience: The Persecution of Seretse and Ruth Khama, by Michael Dutfield, details the negative responses to the marriage of Ngwato heir and Botswana's first president, Sir Seretse Khama, and Englishwoman Ruth Williams in the 1950s.

General
Kalahari – Life's Variety in Dune and Delta, by Michael Main, and *Okavango – Jewel of the Kalahari*, by Karen Ross, study the faces of the Kalahari and the Okavango Delta, respectively, with particular attention to their vegetation, wildlife and geological and cultural histories. They're full of personality and good colour photos.

A Story Like the Wind, by Laurens van der Post, is an entertaining, fictional treatment of a meeting between European and San cultures. Its sequel is *A Far Off Place*.

The Sunbird, by Wilbur Smith, is a light read telling two fanciful and highly entertaining tales about the mythical 'lost city of the Kalahari'.

NEWSPAPERS & MAGAZINES
The government-owned *Daily News*, published by the Department of Information and Broadcasting, is distributed free in Gaborone and includes government news, plus major national and international news. The *Midweek Sun* (Wednesday), the *Botswana Gazette* (Wednesday) and the *Botswana Guardian* (Friday) take a middle-of-the-road political stance and are good for national news. For something more political, see the left-leaning *Mmegi/Reporter*, published on Wednesday. Of more interest to visitors is the *Botswana ADrrtiser*, distributed at hotels and shops. Also, look for the *Ngami Times* in Maun; the *Metro* and *Northern ADrrtiser* in Francistown; the *Central ADrrtiser* in Eastern Botswana; and the *Phikwe Bugle* in Selebi-Phikwe.

Air Botswana's in-flight magazine, *Marung* (the name means 'In the Clouds') includes articles on travel, local arts and culture. It's available free from Air Botswana offices and the tourist office in Gaborone. International news magazines are sold at most bookshops and hotel gift shops.

RADIO & TV
Nationwide programming is provided by Radio Botswana, broadcasting in both English and Setswana. Botswana has one television station, the Gaborone Broadcasting Corporation (GBC), which transmits nightly from 5pm to 9pm and provides a blend of foreign programming (mostly British and American), news, sports and occasional local productions. Most hotels provide MNET, with a cocktail of international cable channels, including CNN, Sky, BBC World and MTV.

HEALTH

As a relatively wealthy country, Botswana enjoys high standards of healthcare, and the several of the large hospitals in Gaborone and Francistown are comparable to any in Western Europe. In main towns, you'll also find dental services and good pharmacies. For remote rescues; **MedRescue** (☎ *390 1601*).

General health information is covered under Health in the Regional Facts for the Visitor chapter.

DANGERS & ANNOYANCES

The greatest dangers in Botswana are posed by natural elements, combined with a lack of preparedness.

While police and veterinary roadblocks, bureaucracy and bored officials may become tiresome, they're mostly just a harmless inconvenience. The officers are normally looking for stolen vehicles or meat products. Although theft occurs, Botswana enjoys a very low crime rate compared to other African (and many Western) countries. However, don't leave valuables in sight in your vehicle, especially in Gaborone.

The Botswana Defence Force (BDF) takes its duties seriously and is best not crossed. The most sensitive base, which is operated jointly with the US government, lies in a remote area off the Lobatse road, southwest of Gaborone. Don't stumble upon it accidentally! Also, avoid the State House in Gaborone, especially after dark.

BUSINESS HOURS

Normal business hours are from 8am to 5pm (often with a one- or two-hour closure for lunch). On Saturday shops open around 8am and close at noon or 1pm; on Sunday there's scarcely a whisper of activity anywhere. In larger towns, banking hours are from 9am to 3.30pm Monday to Friday and 8.30am to 11am Saturday. Post offices are open from 8.15am to 4pm (closing for lunch between 12.45am and 2pm). Government offices are open 7.30am to 12.30pm and 1.45pm to 4.30pm Monday to Friday.

PUBLIC HOLIDAYS & SPECIAL EVENTS

Public holidays in Botswana include:

New Year's Day 1 January
Day after New Year's Day 2 January
Easter March/April – Good Friday, Holy Saturday and Easter Monday
Labour Day 1 May
Ascension Day April/May
Sir Seretse Khama Day 1 July
President's Day July
Botswana/Independence Day 30 September
Day after Independence Day 1 October
Christmas 25 December
Boxing Day 26 December

Botswana stages few major celebratory events. **Gaborone's Maitisong Festival** (☎ *367 1809, fax 358 4946;* **w** *www.info.bw /~maitisong*), in March or April, features local and regional music, dance and drama. Celebrations are held all over the country on Sir Seretse Khama Day, President's Day and Botswana/Independence Day.

ACTIVITIES

Since Botswana is largely a high-budget, low-volume tourist destination, activity tourism focuses on the softer or more expensive options: wildlife viewing, 4WD safaris, *mokoro* trips and the like. If you're really flush with cash, the sky is the limit, and you can choose between elephant or horseback safaris in the Okavango, learning to fly in Maun, quad-biking on the Makgadikgadi Pans, or hiring a 4WD and heading out into the Kalahari. Hiking opportunities are limited to the Tsodilo Hills in the northwest and several small ranges in the eastern and southeastern parts of the country. Wildlife hikes can also be arranged for guests of Okavango Delta lodges or participants on *mokoro* safaris.

WORK

Botswana is developing rapidly and the education system cannot produce enough skilled professionals in several fields. Those with training and experience as medical doctors, secondary school teachers, professors, engineers and computer professionals will find the warmest welcome. Most foreigners choose to remain in or around Gaborone, Francistown or Maun, but if you're willing to work in the bush, your chances of employment will increase. Foreigners are normally granted a three-year renewable residency permit. Applications must be submitted from outside the country to the **Department of Immigration**

(☎ 361 1300, fax 355 2995; PO Box 942, Gaborone).

Numerous NGOs and international volunteer organisations – the Peace Corps, VSO etc – are also active in Botswana, and accept volunteer placements.

ACCOMMODATION

Accommodation (with the exception of camp sites) is subject to a 10% accommodation bed tax. Payment by credit card normally requires an additional charge of 10% to 12%. Rates given in this chapter are for cash payments only.

Camping

Quite a few hotels and lodges along the road system have camp sites with varying amenities for around US$7 per person, which normally includes access to the lodge bar and swimming pool. Wild camping is permitted only outside national parks, private land and government freehold lands. If you can't escape local scrutiny, visit the local *kgosi* (chief) or police station to request permission to camp and get directions to a suitable site.

In national parks, the typically rudimentary camps have little more than *braai* (barbecue) pits and flush toilets; many are simply clearings in the dust. However, you can't just turn up at the park gates and get a camp site; they must be prebooked through National Parks & Wildlife Reserves offices (see National Parks & Reserves in the Facts about Botswana section).

Safari Camps & Lodges

Most safari camps and lodges are found around Chobe National Park, the Tuli Block, the Linyanti Marshes, the Moremi Wildlife Reserve and all over the Okavango Delta. They range from tiny tented camps to large complexes of brick or reed chalets. With a very few exceptions, prices for accommodation, meals and activities start at US$300/400 per person in low/high season, and lone travellers may also pay a single supplement of up to US$200. Rates listed in this chapter are for high season – March to September – and almost always include meals and activities.

While a few lodges are accessible by car or 4WD, most Okavango Delta camps are accessed only by air, which will add around US$150 to US$200 to your bill. All remote camps and lodges require prebooking, but some road-accessible options around Kasane and Maun may accept walk-ins.

Hotels

Every town has at least one hotel, and larger towns and tourist areas offer several in different price ranges. However, you won't find anything as cheap as in most other African countries, and the less expensive hotels in Botswana sometimes double as brothels. There's a shortage of decent accommodation in Gaborone, so it pays to book ahead.

FOOD

Although eating out isn't particularly exciting – Botswana has no great national cuisine to knock your socks off – self-caterers will find the pickings among the best in Africa. Restaurants normally serve up decent, if unimaginative, fare. Vegetarian and international cuisines haven't really caught on, but in Gaborone, Francistown and Maun, you'll find Chinese, Indian, French and Italian options. In smaller towns, expect little menu variation: chicken, chips, beef and greasy fried snacks are the norm.

Forming the basis of most traditional Batswana meals are *mabele* (sorghum) or *bogobe* (sorghum porridge), or the increasingly popular imported *mielies* (maize) and *mielie pap* (maize porridge). All of these are typically served with some sort of meat relish and eaten with the fingers.

Open markets aren't as prevalent as in neighbouring countries, but Gaborone, Francistown and Maun do have growing informal markets where you'll find inexpensive produce and other staples.

DRINKS

A range of 100% natural fruit juices from South Africa are sold in casks in supermarkets in the major cities and towns. You'll also find a variety of tea, coffee and soft drinks.

Botswana's main domestic drop is the very light St Louis Special Light lager (you can't drink it fast enough to feel it). You'll also find Castle, Lion and Windhoek Lager (from Namibia), as well as a growing range of spirit coolers. Some of the more popular traditional alcoholic drinks are less than legal, including mokolane wine, a potent swill made from distilled palm sap. Another is *kgadi*, made from a distilled brew of brown sugar and berries or fungus. Other home-brews include the

Traditional Foods in Botswana

Traditionally, the Tswana staple was beef; the Yei depended on fish; and the Kalanga ate mainly sorghum, millet and maize; while the Herero subsisted on thickened, soured milk. Nowadays, most people get their food from agriculture or the supermarket, but before South African imports arrived, people herded animals and looked to the desert, which dished up a diverse array of wild edibles to augment their staple foods.

Historically, Batswana men were responsible for fishing or tending the herds – and lived mainly on meat and milk – while women were left to gather and eat wild fruits and vegetables. In remote areas, people still supplement their diets with these items. A useful desert plant is the *morama*, an immense underground tuber that contains liquid and is a source of water. Above ground, the *morama* grows leguminous pods that contain edible beans. Other desert delectables include marula fruit, plums, berries, tubers and roots, tsama melons, wild cucumbers and honey.

A fungus that grows on the *Grewia flavia* bush is related to the European truffle. In San mythology, these so-called Kalahari truffles are thought to be the eggs of the lightning bird because their presence is revealed by rings of cracked soil around the bush after electrical storms. The bush itself produces a small shrivelled berry, used locally to make *kgadi* wine. The nutritious and protein-rich mongongo nut, similar to the cashew, is eaten raw or roasted, and has historically been a staple for some San groups.

Traditional people – mainly the San – still gather wild animal products, such as birds and their eggs, small mammals and reptiles and even ant eggs. Mopane worms, caterpillarlike inhabitants of mopane trees, are normally gutted and cooked in hot ash for about 15 minutes. Alternatively, they're boiled in salt water or dried in the sun to be later deep-fried in fat, roasted or eaten raw.

---

common *bojalwa*, an inexpensive, sprouted sorghum beer that is also brewed commercially; a wine made from fermented marula fruit; light and nonintoxicating *mageu*, made from mielies or sorghum mash; and *madila*, a thickened sour milk.

SHOPPING

The standard of Botswana handicrafts is generally very high, particularly the beautifully decorative Botswana baskets that were originally produced in Ngamiland. In Gaborone, they're sold at Botswanacraft on The Mall and at other cooperatives. A range of basketware is available in Maun curio shops; alternatively, in Shorobe, Francistown and the Okavango Panhandle villages of Gumare or Etsha 6 you can buy directly from the artists and craftspeople – you'll pay less and also contribute directly to the local economy.

In the western regions, you'll find excellent quality San jewellery and leatherwork, including leather aprons, ostrich eggshell beads (which cannot be imported into some countries) and strands of seeds, nuts, beads and bits of carved wood.

Beautiful and reasonably priced weavings and textiles are available from cooperatives at Odi and Francistown. Other cooperatives at Maun, and Gabane and Thamaga (both

near Gaborone), make and sell original pottery pieces.

Note that in theory, an export permit is required for any item made from animal products, including ostrich eggshells, animal skins and feathers. If you purchase an item from a handicraft outlet, it will have been registered upon acquisition but anything bought directly from locals must technically be registered with **Director of Veterinary Services** (☎ *355 0617; Private Bag 0032, Gaborone*).

Getting There & Away

This section covers travel between Botswana and its neighbouring countries only. Information on travel to Southern Africa from elsewhere in Africa or from other continents is outlined in the regional Getting There & Away chapter.

AIR

Surprisingly few international airlines serve Botswana, as most international travellers use Johannesburg (Jo'burg) as a gateway to the region and to a lesser degree, Victoria Falls via Harare, Zimbabwe. Sir Seretse

Khama International Airport in Gaborone is the country's largest, and is home to the national carrier, **Air Botswana** (w *www.air botswana.co.bw*), which flies to and from Jo'burg (US$167) several times daily and Harare (US$304) three times weekly (with connections to Lusaka, Zambia). It also connects the private Limpopo Valley Airport, at Mashatu Game Reserve in the Tuli Block, with Jo'burg (US$288). Air Botswana regularly offers special promotions between Gaborone and Harare, as well as between Jo'burg and Harare, Limpopo Valley, Maun and Kasane; these often include accommodation and car hire. See the website for the latest details.

The international air departure tax of US$9 (P50) is included in ticket prices.

LAND
Border Crossings

Overland travel to or from Botswana is usually straightforward. At border crossings, arriving travellers are often requested to clean their shoes, even those packed away in their luggage, in a disinfectant dip to prevent them carrying foot-and-mouth disease into the country. Vehicles must also pass through a pit filled with the same disinfectant.

Border opening hours change all the time, but major crossings between Botswana and Namibia or South Africa generally open sometime between 6am and 8am and close sometime between 6pm and 10pm. The main crossings between Botswana and Zimbabwe are open from 6am to 8pm and the Kazungula ferry to Zambia runs from 6am to 6pm. Minor crossings, such as the many across the Limpopo and Molopo Rivers between Botswana and South Africa, are normally open between 8am and 4pm, but close in periods of high water. Some minor crossings close for lunch from 12.30pm to 1.45pm.

Namibia

The three main border crossings are at Ngoma Bridge, Mahango–Mohembo and Mamuno–Buitepos. Note that during the winter months (late May to August), Namibia is one hour behind Botswana.

Bus There's at least one daily combi between Ghanzi and Mamuno (US$3, three hours), on the border, but from there, you'll have to wait for a minibus on to Gobabis or

Windhoek. Unfortunately, on the Namibian side they only run when full, so you may have to hole up on the border at the useful East Gate Petrol Station & Rest Camp (see under Buitepos in the Namibia chapter).

At 7.30am on Monday **Audi Camp** (☎ *Maun 686 0599*, ☎ *Windhoek 0811-272870*) runs a useful shuttle service from Maun to Windhoek (US$55, 10 hours), via Ghanzi. From Windhoek, it departs at 7.30am on Wednesday. Pre-booking is essential.

Although the Intercape Mainliner bus between Windhoek and Victoria Falls passes through Kasane, passengers may not embark or disembark in Botswana. There are no cross-border buses through the Mahango–Mohembo border crossing.

Hitching From Kasane the sealed 54km transit route through Chobe National Park to Ngoma Bridge is relatively well travelled, and doesn't require payment of park fees. Nearly everyone refuels at Kasane, so you may want to look for lifts at the Shell petrol station, which also serves as the bus terminal. There's no longer any serious strife in Namibia's Caprivi region, so hitching isn't inordinately risky, but the stretch between Kongola and Divundu still sees little traffic.

To hitch along the Trans-Kalahari Highway from Ghanzi to Gobabis (Namibia), inquire about lifts at the Kalahari Arms Hotel or the Oasis petrol station, both in Ghanzi. Most people head out in the morning. To improve your chances, you can also hitch with a Gaborone-bound vehicle to New Junction, 40km south of Ghanzi, and wait there; be sure you have lots of water.

South Africa

Most overland traffic between Botswana and South Africa passes through the Ramatlabama, Tlokweng or Pioneer border crossings. Other border crossings serve back roads across the Limpopo River, in the Tuli Block, and the Molopo River in Southern Botswana; some of these are impassable to 2WD vehicles, and may be closed altogether during periods of high water.

Bus & Minibus Minibuses between Gaborone and Jo'burg (US$12, six hours) leave when full, 6am to 5.30pm, from the northwest corner of the main bus terminal.

Minibus services also connect Lobatse with Mafikeng (US$3, 1½ hours) and between Palapye and Jo'burg (US$14, eight hours), via Martin's Drift.

Intercape Mainliner (☎ *Gaborone 357 4294; Kudu Shell, Queen's Rd;* ☎ *Pretoria 012-654 4114; 108 Klerk St)* travels daily between Gaborone and Jo'burg (US$18, six hours), leaving Gaborone at 6.30am and Jo'burg Station at 3.30pm.

Hitching Between Botswana and South Africa, hitching is straightforward, especially at the main border crossings, but you may be expected to pay for lifts.

Zimbabwe

The two most commonly used borders are at Ramokgwebana–Plumtree and at Kazungula, west of Victoria Falls. There's also a lesser-used back-road crossing at Pandamatenga.

Bus Between Francistown and Bulawayo (US$3.50, three hours), buses leave five to seven times daily in either direction. Alternatively, take a combi from Francistown to Ramokgwebana (US$1.50, 1½ hours), on the border, and then another combi to Bulawayo.

Golden Bridge also has a bus service on Monday and Friday from Maun to Gweru (US$11, 10 hours), via Bulawayo (US$5, eight hours). It returns from Gweru on Wednesday and Sunday. The same company also runs a nightly bus from Gaborone (US$5, 10 hours).

Between Kasane and Victoria Falls (US$42, two hours), **UTC** (☎ *Vic Falls 4225)* operates a morning transfer service. In Kasane, Thebe River Safaris and Chobe Safari Lodge also offer Victoria Falls transfers (US$28, two hours). If they don't have enough passengers, ask them to ring around and find a bus that is going. In Victoria Falls, Gareth McDonald at the **Victoria Falls Backpackers' Lodge** (☎ *Vic Falls 2209;* e *matopo@telcovic.co.zw; 357 Gibson Rd)* runs inexpensive transfers (US$10 per person) to Kazungula, but doesn't cross the border. Taxis between Victoria Falls and the Kazungula border cost around US$30.

Although the Intercape Mainliner bus service between Victoria Falls and Windhoek passes through Kasane, passengers cannot embark or disembark in Botswana.

Train Due to Zimbabwe's failure to pay its share of the costs for the rail link between Gaborone and Bulawayo, this service no longer operates, and it's unlikely to resume as long as Zimbabwe's political and economic crises continue.

Hitching Between Francistown and Bulawayo via the Ramokgwebana–Plumtree border crossing hitching is fairly easy. Mornings are best for hitching into Botswana, while most afternoon traffic is headed towards Bulawayo. From Kasane to Victoria Falls, it's best to wait for a lift at the Kazungula border post; from Victoria Falls to Kasane, wait at the Kazungula road turn-off 1.5km southeast of the town centre.

RIVER
Zambia

Botswana and Zambia (along with Zimbabwe and Namibia) share what's certainly the world's shortest international border – a single point in the middle of the Zambezi River. Direct travel between the two countries is on the Kazungula ferry, which operates from 6am to 6pm daily and costs US$0.50 per person and US$7.50 for motorbikes, US$12 for cars and US$20 for larger vehicles. If there's a long queue or the ferry isn't operating, it's not difficult to reach Livingstone via Victoria Falls, Zimbabwe.

If you're hitching from Kasane–Kazungula or the Zambian shore of the Zambezi, ask truck drivers about lifts to Livingstone.

Getting Around

Botswana's small population means that its public transport service is quite limited. Its single train line offers a limited but reliable service, but Air Botswana domestic services are expensive and bus routes are largely restricted to the main highways.

AIR

The national carrier, **Air Botswana** (☎ *395 2812, fax 397 4802;* w *www.airbotswana.co .bw; PO Box 92, Gaborone)*, operates scheduled domestic flights between Gaborone, Francistown, Maun and Kasane. The best fares are available with 14-day advance purchase (Apex) tickets, but the airline also runs occasional special packages between

Gaborone and Maun which include accommodation and car hire; see the website for details. Note that one-way fares may be higher than return fares, and that discounts are available for children. Passengers have a baggage allowance of just 20kg and the domestic departure tax of US$2.50 is included in ticket prices.

Under normal conditions Air Botswana flies at least once daily (except Sunday) between Gaborone and Francistown (US$100) and at least once daily between Gaborone and Maun (US$156), with connections to and from Kasane (US$157) on Monday, Wednesday, Friday and Sunday.

Air Charter

Air charter provides the best – and sometimes the only – access to remote villages and tourist lodges, and also provides sightseeing options. Travel agencies and safari lodges, especially those in the Okavango Delta, arrange flights for their clients, but individual charters can usually be booked with one day's notice. They typically charge an hourly rate (US$160 to US$225 for a five-seater plane) plus a per kilometre rate (about US$0.90 per km) for a return trip to the destination (so they can return to home base once you're dropped off). If a booked charter has empty seats, you may be able to hop on for a set fare (agree beforehand whether you pay the charter company or the folks chartering the plane). This is great for access to remote villages but you can't fly into safari lodges without also booking a return trip. Note that charter passengers have a baggage allowance of 10kg.

Major charter companies include:

Delta Air (☎ 660044, fax 686 1682, 686 1791, e ddsmaun@info.bw) PO Box 39, Maun
Kalahari Air Services (☎ 395 1804, fax 391 2015, e kasac@info.bw) Sir Seretse Khama International Airport, PO Box 41278, Gaborone
Mack Air (☎/fax 686 0675, e mack.air@info.bw) Private Bag 329, Maun
NAC Executive Charters (☎ 397 5257, fax 397 5258, e les@info.bw) Sir Seretse Khama International Airport, Private Bag SK6, Gaborone
Ngami Air (☎ 686 0530, fax 686 0593) PO Box 119, Maun
Northern Air (☎ 686 0385, fax 686 0379, e nair@kerdowney.bw) PO Box 40, Maun
Okavango Helicopters (☎/fax 686 0664, e okavangoheli@dynabyte.bw) Private Bag 161, Maun

Swamp Air (☎ 686 0569, fax 686 0040, e swampair@info.bw) Private Bag 13, Maun

BUS & MINIBUS

Buses and minibuses travel regularly along all major highway routes in Botswana, but services are less frequent in the western part of the country than along the eastern corridor. With few exceptions, small villages are served only if they lie along major highways. On the most popular runs, minibus services operate according to demand and depart when full, while buses follow a fixed schedule. Botswana's small population means that its public transport service is quite limited. In all cases, there are no advance bookings; tickets are sold only on board.

Note that there's no bus service through Chobe National Park between Kasane and Maun but safari companies offer three-day 4WD safaris via Moremi Wildlife Reserve (see Organised Tours later in this section).

TRAIN

Although it's slow, train travel is an inexpensive, relaxing and effortless way to traverse the vast and dusty scrublands of eastern Botswana. The domestic train line runs between Ramatlabama on the South African border and Ramokgwebana on the Zimbabwe border, and was once part of the now-defunct Johannesburg–Bulawayo rail route. Currently, passenger services only extend between Francistown and Lobatse, with main halts in Mahalapye, Palapye and Gaborone. There's also a single-class commuter service between Gaborone and Lobatse (US$1.50).

Botswana Railways (☎ 471 1375, fax 471 1385; Private Bag 00125, Gaborone) runs two services between Gaborone and Francistown – the quicker day train and the lumbering overnight train (also with service to and from Lobatse). The day train offers two classes: 'club' (1st class) and economy (2nd class), while the night train has 1st (with four berths), 2nd (with six berths) and economy class (with seats only). Both sleeper classes have communal toilets and hot showers, and include bedding. There's also a dining car and bar, but never leave your belongings unattended in your cabin.

Timetables, reservations and tickets are available at Gaborone and Francistown; bookings are essential for 1st and 2nd class sleepers.

CAR & MOTORCYCLE

To get the most out of Botswana, you'll need a vehicle. Road journeys normally fall into one of three categories: a high-speed rush along the excellent sealed road system; an uncertain rumble over a rapidly decreasing number of dusty secondary roads; or a wilderness expedition in a sturdy, high-clearance 4WD vehicle with a good GPS system. While conventional motorcycles perform well on the sealed roads and high-powered dirt bikes can be great fun on desert tracks, neither are permitted in national parks or reserves.

Driving is on the left. The national speed limit on sealed roads is 120km/h, while through towns and villages it normally drops to 60km/h or 80km/h – and the police have radars. Seat-belt use is compulsory in the front seat, and it's worth noting that your insurance policy becomes invalid if you have an accident while under the influence of alcohol.

In open areas, especially at night, be wary of animals. In theory, livestock owners are responsible for keeping their animals off the road, but in practice, unfenced cattle, goats, donkeys and sheep wander wherever they want, and especially like to graze on the road verges. If you hit one, your distress – and the likely vehicle damage – would be compounded by a typically fruitless search for the owner and lots of red tape to file a complaint. Along major highways, elephants and kudus also present driving hazards.

Rental

Hiring a vehicle – especially a 4WD – will allow you the freedom to explore some of Africa's most pristine wilderness areas. Unless you're in a group, this option will be out of reach for budget-conscious travellers because rates are high, distances are great and the per kilometre charges rack up quickly. A credit card is needed for the refundable deposit.

To hire a vehicle, the minimum age ranges from 21 to 25 years, and you'll need a valid driving licence from your home country, which is good for up to six months. With permission and the proper paperwork, some international car hire companies will let you take a vehicle to other countries in the Southern Africa Customs Union, as well as Zimbabwe (this is currently discouraged). For an extra US$200 you may even be able to drop it off in Jo'burg (South Africa) or Windhoek (Namibia).

As a guide, plan on paying around US$20 per day (or US$32 per day with 200 free kilometres per day for a minimum of six days), plus US$0.30 per kilometre, for the least expensive Toyota or VW Golf. For a 4WD Toyota Hilux (the standard 4WD rental vehicle), you'll pay US$65 per day (US$120 per day with 200 free kilometres per day for a minimum of six days), plus US$0.70 per kilometre. Note that it's far less expensive to hire a vehicle in South Africa and drive it across the border.

With all car hire, check the paperwork carefully and examine the vehicle before accepting it; make sure the 4WD engages properly and that you understand how it works. Also check the vehicle fluids and other workings – the Kalahari is a harsh place to learn that the company has overlooked something important. The following agencies in Gaborone also maintain small offices in other large towns:

Avis (☎ 391 3093, fax 391 2550, **w** www.avis .com) PO Box 790 Gaborone, Sir Seretse Khama International Airport
Budget (☎ 390 2030, fax 390 2028, **w** www .budget.co.za) Sir Seretse Khama International Airport, LTD Bag SK5, Gaborone
Holiday (☎ 686 2429) Holiday Safaris, Maun Airport
Imperial (☎ 390 7333, **w** www.imperialcar rental.co.za) LTD Bag SK10, Gaborone, Sir Siretse Khama International Airport
Tempest (☎ 390 0011, **w** www.tempestcarhire .co.za) PO Box 80169, Gaborone, Sir Seretse Khama International Airport

BICYCLE

Botswana is largely flat but that's the only concession it makes to cyclists. Distances are great, the sun can be intense, water is scarce and villages sparse. On the typically flat and straight sealed roads, vehicles tend to crank up the speed and when a semitrailer passes at 150km/h, cyclists may unwittingly be blown off the road. What's more, bicycles aren't permitted in wildlife reserves, and most of Botswana's back roads and tracks are almost invariably just parallel ruts in deep sand. If you're undaunted, please write and let us know how it went!

BOTSWANA

HITCHING

Because public transport is somewhat erratic, hitching is relatively safe and fairly common. On main routes, there should be no major problems, but ascertain a price before climbing aboard. Most drivers expect the equivalent of bus fare.

Hitching the back roads isn't as straightforward. If you're hitching along the Trans-Kalahari Highway, through the Tuli Block or from Maun to Kasane through Chobe National Park, carry camping gear and enough food and water for several days of waiting. For trips even further afield (eg, through the Makgadikgadi Pans or to Gcwihaba Caverns), remember that vehicles pass no more than once or twice a day at most, so try to arrange a lift in advance through a nearby lodge.

LOCAL TRANSPORT

Taxis, which may be cars or minibuses, are recognisable by their blue number plates and circulate along set routes around major towns. Private taxis (known as 'special taxis') rarely cruise the streets for fares, but rather operate from taxi stands or by radio dispatch. Similarly, few taxis hang around the airports, but flights are met by courtesy vans for guests of upmarket hotels and lodges. These are free for lodge guests but others can normally negotiate a fare with the driver. To charter a taxi for sightseeing around an urban area, plan on around US$25 to US$35 per day.

ORGANISED TOURS

In general, it's cheaper to arrange tours through Botswanan tour companies than through overseas agents, but don't expect to just turn up and find a tour within a couple of days. Tour companies typically require a minimum number of passengers and need time to organise accommodation, transport and so on.

Most Botswanan tour companies are based in Maun and, to a lesser extent, Kasane and Gaborone.

Because the government promotes organised tours over individual travel, it offers tour discounts on national park entry fees. The following list includes major tour operators:

Afro-Trek (☎/fax 686 0177, Ⓦ www.afrotrek.com) Private Bag 058, Maun. This popular, inexpensive option runs one-/two-/three-day *mokoro* trips

in the Eastern Delta for US$55/85/110 with at least two people, clients must supply their own food and camping gear. It also does day trips to the Delta (US$55 to US$75, depending on the number of participants), all-inclusive four-day camping safaris to Moremi, Chobe, the Central Kalahari or Makgadikgadi Pans (US$440) and bird-watching hikes along the Thamalakane River (US$20 for two hours).

Afro Ventures (☎ 27-11-809 4300, fax 809 4400, Ⓦ www.ccafrica.com), Private Bag X27, Benmore 2010, South Africa. These folks run Nxabega Camp in the Okavango Delta.

Audi Camp Safaris (☎ 686 0599, fax 686 0581, Ⓦ www.audicamp.bizland.com) Private Bag 28, Maun. Audi Camp offers budget *mokoro* trips in the Eastern Delta (three days US$145/220 without/with meals) and Okavango Panhandle fly-in safaris (two days US$275/450 without/with meals). It also does several all-inclusive trips from Maun: day trips to Moremi (US$225), two-/three-day Moremi safaris (US$425/525), five-day Moremi and Chobe safaris (US$850), and two-/seven-day safaris in the Central Kalahari Game Reserve (US$325/1070).

Crocodile Camp Safaris (☎ 686 0265, fax 686 0793, Ⓦ www.botswana.com) PO Box 46, Maun. This company, on the banks of the Thamalakane River, does one-/two-day trips to the Eastern Delta (US$75/120), fly-in day trips to the Inner Delta (US$185) and day trips to Moremi (US$80), as well as custom trips to Chobe, the Central Kalahari, Makgadikgadi & Nxai Pans, Mabuasehube etc. Participation safaris start at around US$150 per person per day.

Desert & Delta Safaris (☎ 686 1243, fax 686 1791, Ⓦ www.desertanddelta.com) Private Bag 198, Maun, 44 Old Kilcullen Rd, PO Box 130555, Bryanston 2074, South Africa. This company runs the plush Moremi-area lodges Camp Moremi, Camp Okavango and Xugana, as well as Savute Lodge and Chobe Game Lodge, both in Chobe National Park.

Elephant Back Safaris (☎ 686 1260, fax 686 1005, Ⓦ www.elephantbacksafaris.com) Ngami Data Bldg, Private Bag 332, Maun. This frightfully posh and expensive option operates Abu's Camp in the Okavango Delta, and features bush rides on former circus elephants.

Ghanzi Trail Blazers (☎/fax 659 6169, Ⓔ jabutler@global.bw) PO Box 35, Ghanzi. This small company runs San culture tours around the wildest Kalahari.

Gunn's Camp Safaris (☎ 686 0023, fax 686 0040, Ⓔ gunnscamp@info.bw) Private Bag 33, Maun. This is the last budget option in the Inner Delta, and it also offers relatively inexpensive three-/four-/five-/six-day Inner Delta *mokoro* trips (US$316/386/456/526) from Gunn's Camp

and its affiliated Bush Camp, near Chiefs Island. These include flights from Maun and park fees, but clients must provide their own food and camping gear.

Island Safaris (☎ 686 0300, fax 686 2932, ⓔ island@info.bw) PO Box 116, Maun. This company runs Island Safari Lodge and operates *mokoro* trips in the Eastern Delta (one-day US$80/130 for one/two people, two days US$140/220, three days US$185/270).

Ker & Downey (☎ 686 0375, fax 686 1282, ⓦ www.kerdowney.com) PO Box 27, Maun. This company is Botswana's most exclusive luxury operator, running numerous upmarket camps around the Okavango Delta.

Kwando Safaris (☎ 686 1449, fax 686 1457, ⓦ www.kwando.com) PO Box 550, Maun. This company runs the Kwando Lagoon and Kwando Lebala camps in the Linyanti region, as well as Kwara Lodge, near Moremi.

Okavango River Lodge (☎ 686 3707, ⓔ free wind@info.bw) Private Bag 28, Maun. These friendly folks run good-value one-/two-/three-day *mokoro* trips in the Eastern Delta for US$60/90/120 with two people.

Okavango Tours & Safaris (☎ 686 1154, fax 686 0589, ⓦ www.okavango.bw) PO Box 39, Maun. This company's speciality is lodge-based tours in the delta. It is also the agent for Oddball's Palm Island Luxury Lodge and Delta Camp.

Phakawe Safaris (☎/fax 686 4377, ⓦ www .phakawe.demon.co.uk) The Pumpkin Patch, Private Bag 0385, Maun. This recommended company, housed in the very orange building called the Pumpkin Patch, runs informal participation safaris through Botswana's wildest regions for US$135 per day, including meals and camping. They'll take you beyond even the unbeaten track for a rare experience of Botswana at its best: Moremi, Chobe, the Okavango Delta, Makgadikgadi Pans (including Kubu Island), Nxai Pan, the Central Kalahari Game Reserve, Gcwihaba Caverns, the Aha Hills and the Tsodilo Hills.

Thebe River Safaris (☎ 71-868800, ☎/fax 625 0314, ⓦ www.theberiversafaris.co.za) PO Box 5, Kasane. One of Botswana's best-value companies, Thebe River organises Chobe wildlife drives and cruises (US$35), custom overland safaris with varying degrees of luxury (US$100 to US$165 per day with at least four people) and one- to three-day Chobe camping safaris (US$80 to US$280 with at least two people). An all inclusive seven-day participation safari through Chobe and Moremi costs US$700.

Uncharted Africa Safaris (☎ 241 2277, fax 241 3458, ⓔ office@uncharted@co.bw) PO Box 173, Francistown. This company operates two wonderful safari camps – Jack's Camp and San Camp – in the Makgadikgadi Pans, as well as the

mid-range Planet Baobab, near Gweta. A range of activities are available from all camps, and it specialises in surprises.

Wilderness Safaris (☎ 686 0086, fax 686 0632, ⓦ www.wilderness-safaris.com) Private Bag 14, Maun. This well-heeled subsidiary of South Africa's Wilderness Safaris operates a boggling number of diverse upmarket lodges around the Okavango Delta, Chobe National Park, the Linyanti region and all over Southern Africa.

Gaborone

pop 250,000
Botswana's capital, Gaborone, may be best described as a sprawling village suffering from the growing pains, drabness and lack of definition that accompany an abrupt transition from rural settlement to modern city. It has a few sites of interest for visitors, but it's one of Africa's most expensive capitals, and merits only a day or two on your regional itinerary.

History
In 1964, when the village of Gaborone (named for an early Tlokwa chief) was designated as the future capital of independent Botswana, the task of designing the new city was assigned to the Department of Public Works, which never envisaged a population of more than 20,000. By 1990, however, the population was six times that, and Gaborone is now among the world's fastest-growing cities, with an increasing population of 250,000.

Orientation
Although it now has a distinct skyline, Gaborone (normally affectionately shortened to Gabs) lacks any real central business district, and the action focuses on its shopping malls. Most government ministries and offices are concentrated around the Government Enclave along Khama Crescent, at the head of the main mall. While several shopping centres serve local neighbourhoods, the enormous Kgale Centre and Riverwalk Malls provide the widest range of retail outlets and restaurants.

Maps The *Botswana Map Pack* (US$5) includes a detailed map of Gaborone and other urban centres. The *Gaborone City Centre Street Map*, published by Shell, is a viable

BOTSWANA

GABORONE

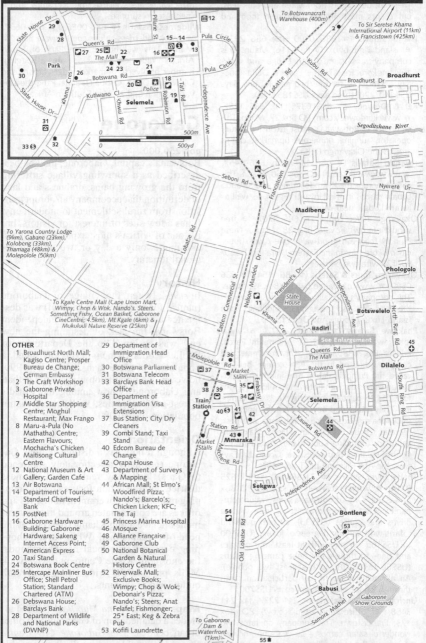

OTHER
1 Broadhurst North Mall; Kagiso Centre; Prosper Bureau de Change; German Embassy
2 The Craft Workshop
3 Gaborone Private Hospital
7 Middle Star Shopping Centre; Moghul Restaurant; Max Frango
8 Maru-a-Pula (No Mathatha) Centre; Eastern Flavours; Mochacha's Chicken
9 Maitisong Cultural Centre
12 National Museum & Art Gallery; Garden Cafe
13 Air Botswana
14 Department of Tourism; Standard Chartered Bank
15 PostNet
16 Gaborone Hardware Building; Gaborone Hardware; Sakeng Internet Access Point; American Express
20 Taxi Stand
24 Botswana Book Centre
25 Intercape Mainliner Bus Office; Shell Petrol Station; Standard Chartered (ATM)
26 Debswana House; Barclays Bank
28 Department of Wildlife and National Parks (DWNP)

29 Department of Immigration Head Office
30 Botswana Parliament
31 Botswana Telecom
33 Barclays Bank Head Office
36 Department of Immigration Visa Extensions
37 Bus Station; City Dry Cleaners
39 Combi Stand; Taxi Stand
40 Edcom Bureau de Change
42 Orapa House
43 Department of Surveys & Mapping
44 African Mall; St Elmo's Woodfired Pizza; Nando's; Barcelo's; Chicken Licken; KFC; The Taj
45 Princess Marina Hospital
46 Mosque
48 Alliance Française
49 Gaborone Club
50 National Botanical Garden & Natural History Centre
52 Riverwalk Mall; Exclusive Books; Wimpy; Chop & Wok; Debonair's Pizza; Nando's; Steers; Anat Felafel; Fishmonger; 25° East; Keg & Zebra Pub
53 Kofifi Laundrette

alternative. Both are sold in local bookshops. The free tourist office map, *Gaborone & its Surroundings*, details local sites of interest, but depicts only major streets.

PLACES TO STAY
4 Citi-Camp Caravan Park
10 Gaborone Sun Hotel &
   Casino; Barclays Bank
19 Brackendene Lodge
21 Cresta President Hotel;
   Terrace Restaurant;
   Botswanacraft
32 Boiketlo Lodge
38 Gaborone Hotel
47 Lolwapa Lodge
51 Riverside Lodge
55 Cresta Lodge; Chatters
   Restaurant

PLACES TO EAT
5 Bull & Bush Pub
6 Maharaja Restaurant
22 King's Takeaway
23 KFC

EMBASSIES & CONSULATES
11 Angolan Embassy
17 Zambian High
   Commission
18 French Embassy
27 British High Commission
   & British Council
34 US Embassy
35 Zimbabwean High
   Commission
41 South African Embassy
54 Namibian High
   Commission

Information

Tourist Office The **Department of Tourism** (*☎ 355 3024, fax 330 8675; *e* botswanatourism@gov.bw; 2nd floor, Standard Chartered Bank Building, The Mall; open 7.30am-12.30pm & 1.45pm-4.30pm Mon-Fri*) has greatly improved over the past couple of years and does its best to help with specific queries.

Immigration Office The **Department of Immigration** (*☎ 361 1300, fax 395 2996; cnr State House Dr and Khama Crescent*), handles inquiries, but visa extensions are available only at the small office (*☎ 395 2969; Nelson Mandela Dr*), immediately north of the Molepolole flyover.

Money Major branches of Barclays Bank and the slightly better value Standard Chartered Bank have foreign exchange facilities and ATMs. The quickest place to change cash or travellers cheques is the Barclays Bank branch (*open 8am-5pm Mon-Fri, 8am-noon Sat*) at the Gaborone Sun Hotel (which takes a 2.5% commission on travellers cheques) or at the several bureaus de change, including the **Prosper Bureau de Change** (*☎ 390 5358; Kagiso Centre, Broadhurst North Mall*) and **Edcom Bureau de Change** (*☎ 391 1123; Omega House*), near the train station. There is also currency exchange at the Barclays branch (*☎ 361 2476; open 6am-8.15pm daily*) at Sir Seretse Khama international airport.

The American Express representative is **SAA City Centre** (*☎ 395 2021; Gaborone Hardware, The Mall*).

Post & Communications The main post office (*The Mall; open 8.15am-1pm & 2pm-4pm Mon-Fri, 8.30am-11.30am Sat*) has the most reliable poste restante address, and also has coin and card phones. Phonecards are sold at the post office, Botswana Telecom, and most shops and supermarkets. In shopping areas and around the train station, you'll find plenty of mobile phone stands charging competitive rates for phone calls.

The most economical Internet and email access is at **PostNet** (*open 8am-7pm Mon-Fri,*

8am-3pm Sat-Sun; US$2/hr), on The Mall, which also offers fax and phone services.

Bookshops Botswana's best bookshop is **Exclusive Books** *(Riverwalk Mall)*, with a range of literature, nonfiction, travel books and numerous regional works. The **Botswana Book Centre** *(The Mall)* specialises in international literature as well as novels, reference books, school texts, magazines and souvenir publications. **Kingston's** *(Broadhurst North Mall)* sells popular novels, textbooks, magazines and stationery. For used books, see **J&B Books**, upstairs from Woolworth's at Broadhurst North Mall.

Laundry With a coin-operated laundry, **Kofifi Laundrette** is on Allison Crescent. Otherwise, try your hotel's (typically expensive) laundry service or **City Dry Cleaners** *(Gaborone bus station; Molepolole Rd)*.

Camping Equipment You'll find basic outdoor equipment, including butane cartridges, at **Gaborone Hardware** *(☎ 395 2611; The Mall)*, but your best option is the South African chain, **Cape Union Mart** *(Kgale Centre Mall)*.

Medical Services For anything serious, head for the **Gaborone Private Hospital** *(☎ 390 1999; Segoditshane Way)*, opposite Broadhurst North Mall. Consultations by appointment cost US$18.

Emergency The central police station *(☎ 395 1161; Botswana Rd)* is opposite the Cresta President Hotel. General emergency numbers include **police** *(☎ 999)*, **ambulance** *(☎ 997)* and **fire** *(☎ 998)*. Local and bush rescue services are available from **MedRescue** *(☎ 911)*.

Things to See
The **National Museum & Art Gallery** *(☎ 397 4616, fax 390 2797; Independence Ave; Private Bag 0014; admission free; open 9am-6pm Tues-Fri, 9am-5pm Sat-Sun)* is a repository of stuffed wildlife and cultural artefacts, including displays on San crafts, material culture and hunting techniques, traditional and modern African and European art, and ethnographic and cultural exhibits. The extension, the **National Botanical Garden & Natural History Centre**

(☎ 397 3860; Okwa Rd, The Village; open 7.30am-12.30pm & 1.45pm-4.30pm Mon-Fri), opposite the Gaborone Club, is a rather unimpressive garden that's slated for improvement in the next few years.

The **Gaborone Game Reserve** *(☎ 358 4492; admission US$0.20, plus per vehicle US$0.40; open 6.30am-6.30pm daily)*, 1km east of Broadhurst, is accessible only by private vehicle (no bikes or motorcycles). It's home to a variety of grazers and browsers, and makes a nice break from the city bustle. Access is from Limpopo Dr; turn east immediately south of the Segoditshane River.

Orapa House *(☎ 395 1131; cnr Nelson Mandela Dr & Khama Crescent)*, owned by Debswana, is designed to make use of natural daylight – without direct sunlight – for the purpose of sorting and grading diamonds from the world's largest diamond mine at Jwaneng. If you have time and aren't put off by red tape, you can muster a group and arrange a tour.

Activities
The **Gaborone Club** *(☎ 395 6333; Okwa Rd)* offers swimming, tennis, squash and lawn bowling for members, but guests must be accompanied by members. On the other hand, visitors are welcome at the **Gaborone Golf Course** *(☎ 391 2262; Chuma Dr)*, which charges US$10 per day for temporary membership, including access to the pool, bar and restaurant. Greens fees are an additional US$3/6 for nine/18 holes.

Places to Stay – Budget
Citi-Camp Caravan Park *(☎ 7244 6067, ☎/fax 391 1912; e citicamp@info.bw; camping per person US$6, electric hook-ups US$2, doubles US$30)*, 15 minutes' walk from the centre, provides a friendly option for travellers with camping sites and budget chalets. At night, frogs provide riveting performances and the adjoining rail line thrills train-spotters and keeps lesser noises at bay. The enormous and very convincing ponderosa pine beside it, which can be seen from all over the city, is in fact a mobile phone tower.

Boiketlo Lodge *(☎ 395 2347; Khama Crescent; singles/doubles US$12/20)* is cheap, noisy and poorly signposted, but also very convenient to the centre. You'll find it opposite the Botswana Post Building near the corner of Kaunda Rd.

For other camping options, as well as mid-range accommodation, see also Mokolodi Nature Reserve and Kopong (Country Horse Safaris) under Around Gaborone, later in this section.

Places to Stay – Mid-Range

There's a large number of informal B&Bs in the neighbourhood south of the National Museum and west of the South Ring Rd. You may also want to try one of the following:

Lolwapa Lodge (☎ 72-226504, ☎/fax 318 4865; e lolwapalodge@yahoo.com; Plot 2873 Ext 10, Mobutu Dr, Private Bag 286; singles/ doubles US$30/38) has simple rooms with use of cooking facilities; rates include breakfast.

Brackendene Lodge (☎ 391 2886, fax 390 6246; e felomena@it.bw; PO Box 621; singles/doubles without bathroom from US$26/30, with bathroom US$29/33), three minutes' walk from The Mall, is currently undergoing total renovation, but it still offers decent accommodation. Meals are available on request.

Riverside Lodge (☎ 392 8802, fax 392 8837; PO Box 1771, Tlokweng; doubles US$40 with breakfast) is a spartan but amenable place near the river in Tlokweng.

Yarona Country Lodge (☎ 391 3634, fax 397 4914; e psimon@global.bw; Plot 989 Mogoditshane; PO Box 2436; singles/doubles from US$44/57) makes a quiet garden retreat 5km from the city centre. To get there, take Mogoditshane taxi route 4.

Gaborone Hotel (☎ 392 2777, fax 392 2727; e gabhot@info.bw; singles/doubles from US$46/57), north of the train station and opposite the bus terminal, has a great bar, a takeaway and live (loud) music at weekends. For credit card payment, add 20% to the rates.

Places to Stay – Top End

Cresta Lodge (☎ 375375, fax 300635; Samora Machel Dr, Private Bag 00126; e cresta lodge@info.bw; singles/doubles US$90/105) serves as a quiet and comfortable mid-range option with a top-end price. From the hotel, a walking track leads to the scenic Gaborone Dam.

Gaborone Sun Hotel & Casino (☎ 395 1111, fax 390 2555; e gabsres@sunint.co.za; Julius Nyerere Dr; standard/luxury doubles US$122/151), once highbrow, has now been humbled by competition. It's still quite posh, however, and features a casino, swimming pool, golf course and several restaurants.

Cresta President Hotel (☎ 395 3631, fax 395 1840; e crestabs@iafrica.com; The Mall, PO Box 200; standard singles/doubles US$72/89) offers friendly, central accommodation, plus English/continental buffet breakfasts for US$8.50/7.50 in the attached Terrace Restaurant, overlooking The Mall.

Places to Eat

Devotion to fast food almost qualifies as a religion in Gaborone, and enlightenment is best found at the city's major malls. Gaborone boasts a wide range of fast-food options, including **KFC** (The Mall & the African Mall); **St Elmo's Woodfired Pizza**, **Nando's**, **Barcelo's** and **Chicken Licken** (the African Mall); **Max Frango** (Middle Star Shopping Centre); **Mochacha's Chicken** and **Eastern Flavours** (Maru-a-Pula Shopping Centre); **Debonair's Pizza** (Broadhurst North Centre); **Wimpy**, **Chop & Wok**, **Nando's**, **Steers** and **Something Fishy** (Kgale Centre); and **Wimpy**, **Chop & Wok**, **Debonair's Pizza**, **Nando's**, **Steers** and **Anat Felafel** (Riverwalk Mall).

For more substantial meals, Riverwalk also has the notable seafood restaurant, **Fishmonger** (mains US$6-10); the Asian-oriented **25° East** (mains US$5-9, sushi US$2-4); and the lively **Keg & Zebra Pub** (mains US$4-7). At Kgale Centre the **Ocean Basket** (mains US$5-7) fills the seafood niche.

King's Takeaway (☎ 395 2792; The Mall), which serves up inexpensive burgers, chips and snacks, is a favourite lunch spot for government office workers.

Terrace Restaurant (☎ 395 3631; The Mall), on the terrace of the Cresta President Hotel, serves healthy lunches, including spinach quiche, cream of asparagus soup and vegetable curries, as well as meat-oriented fare. Afterwards, you can linger over a rich and frothy cappuccino and eclairs while surveying the passing Mall scene below. In the evening it does grill specials.

The Kgotla Restaurant & Coffee Shop (☎ 395 6091; above Woolworth's, Broadhurst North Mall; breakfast from US$4, other meals US$4-7; closed Monday) deserves its popularity, serving up great breakfasts, vegetarian fare and coffee specialities.

Brazilian Cafe (☎ 317 0227; Kagiso Centre, Broadhurst North Mall; light meals US$3-7; open 9am-5pm daily) appeals to coffee

addicts with a variety of European-style coffee specialities. It also serves late breakfasts and light lunches daily.

Taj (☎ 391 3569; African Mall; buffet lunch US$8) dishes up Indian, Mauritian and continental cuisine and excellent salads, and does a buffet lunch seven days a week.

Da Alfredo (☎ 391 3604; Broadhurst North Mall; open for lunch & dinner daily) specialises in seafood and Italian cuisine, serving lunch, dinner and takeaways.

Moghul (☎ 397 5246; Middle Star/Nyerere Dr shopping centre; Indian buffet lunch US$9, mains US$4-7) serves Indian, Pakistani and Chinese fare, with an especially popular Indian buffet lunch.

Diamond Creek Spur (☎ 390 1266; Kagiso Centre, Broadhurst North Mall; mains US$5-7), an outlet of the popular South African chain of Spur steak houses, does breakfast (from 9am), as well as lunch and dinner. Specialities include a very nice salad bar and ice cream and fudge brownie desserts.

Bull & Bush Pub (☎ 397 5070; mains US$5-10), which is probably Gaborone's best and most popular eatery, is the place to go for a British twist or a nice patio meal. From Nelson Mandela Rd, look for the west-pointing sign reading 'Police Housing Bull & Bush'. The extensive menu offers everything from beef, pizza and pasta to elaborate vegetarian starters and main dishes.

Entertainment

Bull & Bush Pub (☎ 397 5070) – see Places to Eat – is the expatriate hang-out, with great pub meals, a variety of mind-numbing drinks and sports on the big-screen TV. On some weekends, it also has a DJ or stages live music performances.

Nightspark (Broadhurst North Mall; weekend admission US$2) features all sorts of musical acts and is popular with middle-class Batswana youth.

Waterfront (Gaborone Dam) south of the city, occasionally hosts live performances.

Alliance Française (☎ 395 1650; Pudulogo Way) frequently screens classic films.

Gaborone CineCentre (☎ 391 0807; Kgale Centre; admission US$4), with seven screens, shows first-run films every afternoon and evening.

Maitisong Cultural Centre (☎ 397 1809; e maitisong@info.bw; ticket office open 8am-6pm Mon-Fri), at Maru-a-Pula Secondary School, has a 450-seat theatre that provides a venue for cultural events from Shakespeare to Batswana musical productions. A list of upcoming events is posted on a bulletin board at the ticket office.

Shopping

For shoppers, Gaborone is a series of shopping malls, headed up by the lovely Riverwalk Mall and the enormous Kgale Centre. Lesser options include Broadhurst North/ Kagiso Centre, The Mall and the increasingly seedy Maru-a-Pula (No Mathatha), Nyerere (Middle Star) and African Malls.

Botswanacraft Marketing (☎ 392 2487, fax 392 2689; w www.botswanacraft.bw; Plot 20716, New Broadhurst Industrial Estate, Western Bypass; PO Box 486), at the corner of Magochanyama Rd and Parakarungu Way, deals in a selection of material arts and crafts from around Botswana, with outlets at its headquarters, on The Mall and at the airport. Several nearby villages also feature worthwhile craft centres.

The Craft Workshop (☎ 395 6364; 5648 Nakedi Rd, Broadhurst Industrial Estate) combines a number of souvenir outlets, with a fun flea market on the last Sunday of each month. It's accessed on the Broadhurst 3 minibus.

Getting There & Away

Air From Sir Seretse Khama International Airport, 14km from the centre, Air Botswana operates scheduled domestic flights to and from Francistown (US$100), Maun (US$156) and Kasane (US$157).

The **Air Botswana office** (☎ 390 5500, fax 395 3928; Botswana Insurance Company House, The Mall; open 8am-12.30pm & 1.45pm-5pm Mon-Fri) also serves as an agent for other regional airlines.

Bus Intercity buses and minibuses to Lobatse (US$1.20, 1½ hours), Mahalapye (US$2.50, three hours), Palapye (US$4, four hours), Serowe (US$4, five hours), Francistown (US$5, six hours), Selebi-Phikwe (US$6, six hours), Ghanzi (US$10, 11 hours) and Jo'burg (except the Intercape Mainliner, which runs from the Kudu Shell petrol station beside The Mall – see the Getting There & Away section earlier in this chapter) use the main bus terminal, over the Molepolole flyover from the town centre. It also offers local services to Kanye (US$1.50, two

hours), Jwaneng (US$4, three hours), Manyana (US$0.80, 1½ hours), Mochudi (US$1, one hour), Thamaga (US$0.80, one hour) and Molepolole (US$1.20, one hour) – also called 'Moleps'. To reach Maun, Shakawe or Kasane, use the Francistown bus and change there; for Mamuno, take a Ghanzi bus. Buses operate according to roughly fixed schedules and minibuses leave when full.

Train The day train departs for Francistown daily at 10am (US$7/3.50 club/economy, 6½ hours) and the night train, with 1st- and 2nd-class sleepers, leaves at 9pm (US$24/20/5 1st/2nd/economy, 8¼ hours). Coming from Francistown, the overnight service continues to Lobatse (US$1, 1½ hours) early in the morning, with only economy class seats available from Gaborone. For current information, contact **Botswana Railways** (☎ 395 1401).

Hitching To hitch north, catch the Broadhurst 4 minibus from any shopping centre along the main city loop and get off at the standard hitching spot at the northern end of town. There's no need to wave down a vehicle – anyone with space will stop for passengers. Plan on around US$6 to Francistown, where you can look for onward lifts to Nata, Maun and Kasane.

Getting Around
To/From the Airport The only reliable transport between the airport and town is the courtesy minibuses operated by the top-end hotels for their guests. If there's space, nonguests may talk the driver into a lift, but you'll have to tip at least US$6 to US$8. Taxis rarely turn up at the airport; if you do find one, you'll pay anywhere from US$3 to US$12 per person to the centre.

Minibus Packed white minibuses, recognisable by their blue number plates, circulate according to set routes and cost US$0.30 (P1.50). They pick up and drop off only at designated lay-bys marked 'bus/taxi stop'. The main city loop passes all the main shopping centres except the new Riverwalk Mall and the Kgale Centre, which are on the Tlokweng and Kgale routes, respectively.

Taxi A number of companies operate conventional private hire taxis, known as 'special

taxis', which charge around US$3 around the city centre and US$4.50 to the environs. Try **City Cab** (☎ 312 1031), **Goody-Goody Cab** (☎ 397 4522), **Town Cab** (☎ 318 0380) or **Unique Cab** (☎ 391 6696).

AROUND GABORONE
Kopong
Country Horse Safaris (☎ 71-234567, 390 9091; Lentsweletau Rd; camping per person US$5, doubles US$25) is a friendly Swedish-run place specialising in horse riding, but it also offers inexpensive accommodation. From Gaborone, drive 16km northwest on the Molepolole Rd to Metsemotlhaba and turn northeast on Lentsweletau Rd towards Kopong. The guesthouse is on this road 10km north of Kopong village; otherwise, phone for a lift from Kopong or Metsemotlhaba, both of which are accessible by minibus from Gaborone.

Odi
This small village (pronounced **Oo**-dee) is best-known for its internationally-acclaimed **Odi Weavers** (☎ 339 2268; PO Box 954, Gaborone; open 8am-4.30pm Mon-Fri, 10am-4.30pm Sat-Sun), which produces and sells a range of locally made weavings, tapestries, bedspreads and cushions. Take a northbound minibus from Gaborone and get off at Odi Junction; from here, you'll probably have to hitch the final 7km to the workshop.

Mochudi
Mochudi, one of Botswana's most fascinating villages, was first settled by the Kwena in the mid-1500s, as evidenced by ruined stone walls in the hills. In 1871 came the Kgatla people, who had been forced from their lands by northward-trekking Boers. The Cape Dutch-style **Phuthadikobo Museum** (☎ 577 7238, fax 574 8920; admission free, donations suggested; open 8am-5pm Mon-Fri, 2pm-5pm Sat-Sun), established in 1976, is one of Botswana's best, with displays on the village and its Kgatla history. After visiting the museum, it's worth spending an hour appreciating the variety of designs in the town's mud-walled architecture.

Buses to Mochudi depart from Gaborone when full. By car, head north to Pilane and turn east; after 6km, turn left at the T-junction and then right just before the hospital, into the historic village centre.

Thamaga

The delightful but unexciting village of Thamaga is home to the **Botswelelo Centre** (☎ 499 9220; Molepolole Rd; tours US$0.30; open 8am-5pm daily), also called Thamaga Pottery. This nonprofit community project was started by missionaries in the 1970s and now sells a wide range of creations for good prices. Tours must be booked in advance. Buses run frequently from the main bus terminal in Gaborone (US$0.80, one hour).

Molepolole

The tongue-twisting name of this hillside village (pronounced **mo**-lay-po-**lo**-lay) is often sensibly shortened to 'Moleps'. The main attraction, the **Kgosi Sechele 1 Museum** (☎ 592 0917; Gaborone Rd; open 9am-noon & 2pm-4pm Tues-Fri, 11am-4pm Sat), is housed in the 1902 police station and features traditional housing, paintings, historic photos and David Livingstone memorabilia. It's reputed that Chief Sechele was the only person the missionary Livingstone ever managed to convert to Christianity. This was accomplished after Livingstone visited the Kobokwe Cave (5km from town along the Thamaga road) and survived, despite dire warnings from local shamans that to approach the cave would bring about a speedy death.

You may also want to visit the **Shacter & Namder Diamond Factory** (☎ 592 0815; Thamaga Rd), which is Botswana's only diamond-cutting venue.

Mafenya-Thala Hotel (☎ 595 0522; e cia ron@mega.bw; Gaborone Rd; singles/doubles US$37/48) offers comfortable and well-decorated rooms. Camping is also sporadically possible and the attached restaurant serves up classy meals.

Minibuses run frequently from the main bus terminal in Gaborone (US$1, 1½ hours).

Mt Kgale

The 'sleeping giant', Mt Kgale, overlooks Gaborone, and you can easily hike to the summit for a sweeping view over the capital. Take any Lobatse bus or head out along the new Lobatse road to the car park (opposite an obvious satellite dish, just beyond the Kgale Centre Mall). Cross the white concrete stile and follow the track through a shallow gully to the trail of whitewashed stones that lead to the summit. Due to recent robberies, it's wise not to walk alone or carry anything of value.

Mokolodi Nature Reserve

The 5000-hectare **Mokolodi Nature Reserve** (☎ 316 1955; W www.mokolodi.com; admission US$2, plus per vehicle US$3.50; camping per adult/child US$11/6, educational centre dorm beds US$15 with breakfast, 3-/6-bed chalets US$88/105; open 7.30am-6pm daily), 12km south of Gaborone, concentrates on wildlife education for school children. This scenic reserve also protects a full complement of Botswana's wildlife, including white rhino reintroduced from South Africa. Guided three-hour ranger walks cost US$44; horse tours are US$11 per hour; two-hour day/evening wildlife drives are US$22/33; and special wildlife-tracking walks range from US$61 for giraffes to US$72 for rhino. In addition to the comfortable chalets, there's an excellent restaurant and bar. Transfers from the centre/airport costs US$28/44 for up to four people. Otherwise take a Lobatse minibus 12km south of Gaborone and get off at the turning 2.5km south of the Mokolodi village turn-off. From there, it's 1.5km west to the reserve entrance.

Lobatse

Despite its nice setting 68km south of Gaborone, Lobatse is one of Botswana's dullest places, and is known mainly as the site of the national mental hospital, the Supreme Court and the country's largest abattoir. It does, however, boast a range of shady, exotic trees (willow, Italian poplar, eucalyptus, piñon etc) and the beautiful, thatch-roofed St Mark's Anglican Church.

You can change money at the ASA Bureau de Change, at the BP petrol station on the main road from Gaborone.

Cumberland Hotel (☎ 533 0281, fax 533 2106; W www.cumberlandhotel.net; singles/doubles US$33/48) has decent and longstanding digs.

Rest Inn (☎ 550 6999, fax 533 4044; PO Box 668; singles/doubles US$27/38) offers a very pleasant – and cheaper – alternative; all rooms have satellite TV.

You'll find inexpensive meals at **Mochacha's Chicken Village** and **Village Pie & Bake**, on the main street, and **Chicken Licken** and **Cookie's Takeaway**, on the street parallel to the train line.

Minibuses run frequently between Gaborone and Lobatse, and there's also a morning train from Gaborone.

Kanye

The sprawling village of Kanye, set amid beautiful hills, serves as a pleasant stopover along the Trans-Kalahari Highway.

Motse Lodge *(☎ 548 0363, 71-659964, fax 548 0370;* **e** *motselodge@botsnet.bw; Plot 1258, Sepojane Ward, Private Bag MK 24; camping per person US$3.80, rondavels US$9, singles/doubles with breakfast US$40/ 60)* is a wonderful, friendly option, with a pool and conference facilities, that makes a stop in Kanye worthwhile. If you're in town, don't miss it.

Ko Gae Café *(☎ 544 1323; Kanye Mall; open 7.30am-10.30pm daily; traditional fare US$1.50-3, burgers US$3, mains from US$4.50)* offers large servings of tasty traditional and international fare, with vegetarian options.

Mmakgodumo Restaurant *(☎ 544 1511; RIIC Compound; open 10am-10pm Mon-Thur, 10am-11pm Fri, 3pm-11pm Sat, 3pm-10pm Sun; mains US$6-8, weekday specials US$4)*, run by the Rural Industries Commission, serves excellent meals and features live music at weekends.

Eastern Botswana

Although in the winter months it appears to be a desert zone, the scrubland strip along the South African and Zimbabwean borders is more amenable to agriculture and human habitation than most other parts of Botswana. It's not lush by any stretch, but still receives most of Botswana's rainfall and in summer, takes on a pleasantly green cloak.

MAHALAPYE

Mahalapye has little to offer but spacious skies, distant horizons and a welcome break from the highway between Gaborone and Francistown. Since it's mainly a refuelling stop for vehicles and travellers, there are lots of petrol stations, shops and takeaway places.

The **Oasis Lodge** *(☎ 471 2081, fax 471 2082; Madiba Rd; singles/doubles from US$26/30, log cabin US$17/19)* is 4km west of town, but it's the most comfortable place around. The more expensive rooms have satellite TV, air-conditioning and a fridge.

Kaytee's *(☎ 471 0795)*, 'the pride of Botswana', at the southern end of town, does takeaway and à la carte meals.

SELEBI-PHIKWE

Before 1967 Selebi-Phikwe was little more than a cattle post, but it's now Botswana's third-largest community. In the early 1960s, the twin copper-nickel-cobalt deposits of Selebi and Phikwe, 14km apart, were discovered and developed by Bamangwato Concessions Ltd (BCL). Mining commenced in 1973 and the mines now have a combined annual total output of 2.5 million tonnes of ore.

For information, see the helpful **Botswana Tourism Department** *(☎ 261 1023, fax 261 1021; open 8am-4pm Mon-Fri)*, on The Mall.

Bosele Hotel & Casino *(☎ 261 0675, fax 261 1083;* **e** *resbosele@cresta.co.bw; Tshekedi Rd; singles/doubles US$82/108)* is the standard place to stay in the centre.

Syringa Lodge *(☎ 261 0444, fax 261 0450; Airport Rd; doubles US$63)* may be out of town, but the rooms, pool, gardens and attached steak house make up for any inconvenience.

TULI BLOCK

The strip of freehold farmland known as the Tuli Block extends for 350km along the northern bank of the Limpopo River from Buffels Drift to Pont Drift, reaching widths of 10km to 20km. It was originally held by the Ngwato tribe, but shortly after the Bechuanaland Protectorate was established in the 1880s, it was ceded to the BSAC for a railway, which was never constructed.

The main attraction is the 90,000-hectare **North-East Tuli Game Reserve**, which is dominated by the private 45,000-hectare **Mashatu Game Reserve** and the 7500-hectare **Tuli Game Reserve**. As Africa's largest private wildlife reserve, it's an excellent place to view big cats, antelopes and large herds of elephants, as well as the stately mashatu tree *(Xanthocercis zambeziaca)* and impressive landscapes: savanna, rock kopjes, river bluffs, riverine forests and tidy villages.

Botswana's easternmost village, **Pont Drift**, is also a border crossing. When the Limpopo cannot be forded because it is too deep, passengers are ferried across on the rustic Pont Drift cableway (US$4.50). Immediately beyond the immigration post is the Mashatu reception centre. Except for the small exclave east of the Motloutse

BOTSWANA

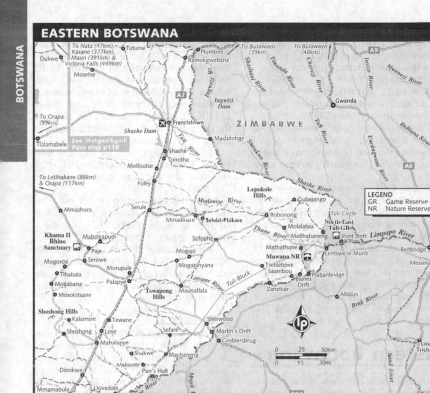

EASTERN BOTSWANA

LEGEND
GR Game Reserve
NR Nature Reserve

crossing, Mashatu is open only to guests of the Mashatu lodges.

The sandy Motloutse (Large Elephant) River, 27km west of Pont Drift, rarely flows; as you plough through the riverbed, notice the bizarre dolerite dike known as **Solomon's Wall** that flanks the river.

Places to Stay

Mashatu Lodge (☎ 27-011-789 2677, fax 886 4382; w www.mashatu.com; PO Box 2575, Randburg 2125, South Africa; single/double chalets US$225/300, bush camp US$188/250), with luxury-class chalets and a tented camp in the bush, offers superb wildlife-viewing. It's one of Botswana's more affordable luxury lodges, and the rates include accommodation, meals,

wildlife drives and transfers from the Tuli Lodge air strip or the Pont Drift cableway.

Tuli Lodge (☎ 264 5303, fax 264 5344; w www.tulilodge.com; PO Box 83, Lentswe le Muriti; standard singles/doubles US$171/250, luxury lodges US$245/353, Kolobe tented camp US$102/160, Fish Eagle self-catering house US$296) occupies a green riverine oasis beside the Limpopo, amid lovely red rock scenery. It consists of a shady main lodge, tented camp and a self-catering complex 2km upstream; rates at all three include meals, two wildlife drives, a wildlife walk and transfers from the airport or cableway. They'll also organise three-day walking safaris (US$307), horse riding (US$40), canoeing on the Limpopo (US$40) and additional wildlife drives (US$14).

Getting There & Away

Mashatu and Tuli Lodges support a scheduled Air Botswana flight between Jo'burg, Kasane and the Limpopo Valley Airport at Mashatu. Most Tuli Block roads are well-graded gravel and are negotiable by 2WD, but the Motloutse River crossing west of Pont Drift may require 4WD.

By minibus, you can reach Sherwood and Martin's Drift from Palapye, and Bobonong and Molalatau from Selebi-Phikwe, but the only public transport to Mashatu is by air.

PALAPYE
pop 23,000

Originally called Phalatswe, ('Many Impalas' in Sekgalagadi and 'Large Impalas' in Setswana), Palapye is a thriving town along the Gaborone–Francistown road. Its commercial heart is the Engen shopping complex on the main highway, but the centre is actually 5km away, near the train station.

Camp Itumela (☎ 71-806771; Palapye Station; camping per person US$3.50, single/double chalets US$18/21, caravans US$16/30), behind the train station, enjoys a quiet setting with a pool, bar and lots of shade. It's warmly recommended.

Desert Sands Motel (☎ 492 4360, fax 492 4361; PO Box 2; singles/doubles from US$40/45), on the main highway, features a Wimpy bar that doubles as a dining room.

For just a quick bite, try **Chicken Licken**, **Nando's**, **Pie City** or **Tla Pitseng Takeaways** (which also serves as the bus station), all in the Engen shopping complex.

Buses run frequently from Gaborone and Francistown, and there are two train services daily.

SEROWE

Sprawling Serowe, Botswana's largest village, has served as the Ngwato capital since Khama III moved it from Phalatswe (Palapye) in 1902.

The **Khama III Memorial Museum** (☎ 463 0519; admission free; open 7.30am-4.30pm Tue-Fri, 11am-4pm Sat) outlines the history of the Khama family. Displays include the personal effects of King Khama III and his descendants, as well as artefacts depicting the Serowe's history. There is also a growing natural history exhibition, featuring a large collection of African insects and a display on snakes of the area.

The 12,000-hectare **Khama II Rhino Sanctuary** (☎ 463 0713, fax 463 5808; w www.khamarhinosanctuary.org; PO Box 10; admission US$2 plus per vehicle US$3; camping per adult/child US$5/2, double chalets US$40-50), 28km northwest of Serowe, serves as a safe haven for 16 of Botswana's remaining rhinos. Day/evening wildlife drives are US$40/60 for up to four people, plus US$12 for a guide; nature walks cost US$8 and rhino tracking is US$20. Minibuses between Serowe and Rakops will drop you at the entrance (US$1); from there, reserve officials provide transport to the camp site or chalets.

Places to Stay & Eat

Serowe Hotel (☎ 463 0234, fax 463 0203; e welcomebs@botsnet.bw; PO Box 150; singles/doubles from US$38/44), on the Palapye side of town, is a comfortable travellers' oasis with a nice pool and gardens.

Lentswe Lodge (☎ 463 4333, fax 463 4332; e lentswe@mopane.bw; PO Box 32057; doubles US$52), on the Botalaote hilltop 3km along a very rough road from the Serowe Hotel, is as unusual as the view is beautiful. The sign at the entrance warns that 'Every part of Lentswe Lodge is dangerous', so you're on your own here! Meals are available (breakfast/lunch/dinner US$7/8/12), and they can also arrange local excursions, including a trip to Moremi Falls (US$43/87 for one/two days).

For meals, try either the **Serowe Hotel** or **Grandma's Kitchen** (main road near The Mall).

Getting There & Away

From the bus terminal at The Mall, buses run frequently to Palapye (US$0.80, one hour), 46km away, but there are also direct services to and from Francistown (US$3, 2½ hours) and Gaborone (US$4, five hours).

FRANCISTOWN
pop 95,000

Francistown was originally a gold-mining centre, but industry and commerce now prevail, and the town has become a booming retail and wholesale shopping mecca.

Information

The excellent booklet *Exploring Tati*, by Catrien van Waarden, provides enough

BOTSWANA

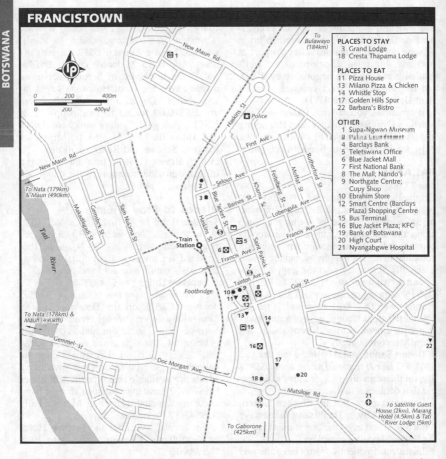

FRANCISTOWN

PLACES TO STAY
3 Grand Lodge
18 Cresta Thapama Lodge

PLACES TO EAT
11 Pizza House
13 Milano Pizza & Chicken
14 Whistle Stop
17 Golden Hills Spur
22 Barbara's Bistro

OTHER
1 Supa-Ngwao Museum
2 Polina Laundromat
4 Barclays Bank
5 Teletswana Office
6 Blue Jacket Mall
7 First National Bank
8 The Mall; Nando's
9 Northgate Centre;
    Copy Shop
10 Ebrahim Store
12 Smart Centre (Barclays
    Plaza) Shopping Centre
15 Bus Terminal
16 Blue Jacket Plaza; KFC
19 Bank of Botswana
20 High Court
21 Nyangabgwe Hospital

historical information on local sites to transform this desultory town into a fascinating place. It's available for US$4.50 at the Supa-Ngwao Museum or through **Marope Research** (PO Box 910, Francistown).

The Barclays and First National Banks along Blue Jacket St, among other banks, have ATMs and foreign exchange facilities. For Internet and email access, go to the **Copy Shop** (☎ 241 0177; Northgate Centre; open 8am-8pm daily; US$2/hr). Laundry service is available at the **Polina Laundromat** (Blue Jacket St), at the eastern end of Blue Jacket St. The place to buy camping gear is **Ebrahim Store** (☎ 241 4762; Francis Ave).

The **Nyangabgwe Hospital** (☎ 241 1000, emergency ☎ 997) lies immediately east of

the Thapama roundabout. The **police station** (☎ 241 2221, emergency ☎ 999; Haskins St) lies at the northern end of Blue Jacket St.

Supa-Ngwao Museum

The main site of tourist interest is the basic Supa-Ngwao cultural and historical museum (☎/fax 240 3088; **e** snm@info.bw; New Maun Rd; admission free but donations suggested; open 8am-5pm Mon-Fri, 9am-5pm Sat). It's housed in a 100-year-old Government Camp, which includes a prison and a police canteen. Displays include local and regional culture and history, as well as visiting art exhibitions.

[Continued on page 117]

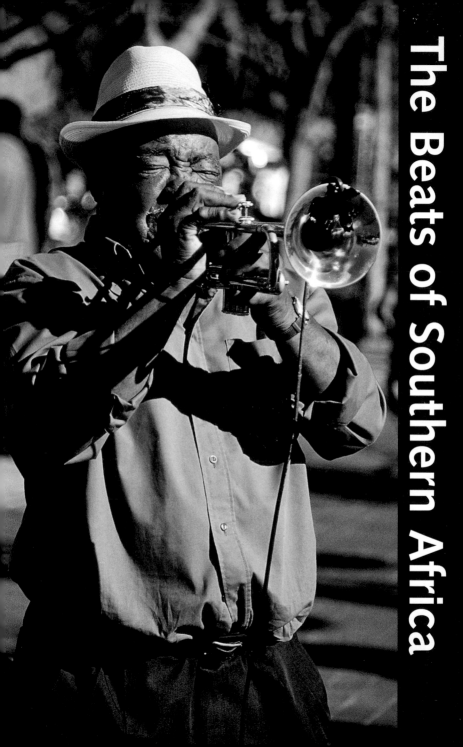

The Beats of Southern Africa

The Beats of Southern Africa

RICHARD I'ANSON

DI JONES

RICHARD I'ANSON

Title page: Jazz trumpeter, Victoria & Alfred Waterfront, Cape Town, South Africa (photo by Craig Pershouse)

Top: Hard-hat wearing troupe, Johannesburg, South Africa

Middle: Local band playing instruments made from oil cans, fishing line and drums, Malealea Lodge, Lesotho

Bottom: Mural, South Africa

THE BEATS OF SOUTHERN AFRICA

So you think you know nothing about Southern African music. Well, ever danced yourself silly to the 1952 classic *Wimoweh* by The Weavers? Perhaps Paul Simon's ground-breaking *Graceland* album lurks somewhere in your record collection? Or how about Malcolm McLaren's mega-1980s hit *Double Dutch*? All these (and many, many more) have been inspired by the celebrated music of Southern Africa.

In the case of The Weavers and Paul Simon, *Zulu a capella*, the wonderfully elegant singing style of the Zulu working class, was the inspiration. *Double Dutch* came courtesy of the infectious *mbaqanga* beats of South African outfit The Boyoyo Boys.

Zulu a capella and *mbaqanga* are just two of many musical genres. Over the centuries Southern Africa's staggering ethnic diversity has produced a complicated family tree of music and vocal styles. Begin at the very top and expect to follow an at-times complicated, but always exhilarating, musical path.

South Africa

As early as the late 19th century, urbanisation in Cape Town and Johannesburg attracted American musicians to visit. It wasn't until the 1920s, when a government-imposed curfew resulted in rowdy all-night concerts, that contemporary South African music really began to flourish. (These night concerts only finished once daybreak signalled the end of curfew.)

From these night concerts came *marabi*, with its lashings of Dixieland jazz. But by the 1950s, *marabi* had transmuted into jive, after fusing with American swing to produce African jazz. (Hunt down the *Dark City Sisters/Flying Jazz Queens* album for a marvellous collection of songs from this time.)

Right: Musicians perform in the street, Johannesburg, South Africa

RICHARD I'ANSON

113

Almost simultaneously, the imaginatively named pennywhistle jive began to spread from townships to the city centres. But not before rebellious white youths caught on to this new sound and renamed it *kwela*. (The Black Mambazo even had an international hit with their *kwela*-inspired single *Tom Hark*.) The addition of saxophone and, during the 60s the electric guitar, only added to the jive mix (and gave birth to the term *mbaqanga*, which later turned into *mqashiyo*, the Zulu word for 'bounce'). Think Mahlathini and the Mahotella Queens, and The Boyoyo Boys.

During the late 1960s and early 70s, American soul music became popular in South Africa. Synthesiser-propelled disco promptly followed. It wasn't until the end of apartheid in the early 1990s that the government established a number of radio stations and a television station. With it came a strict quota guaranteeing a certain percentage of South African music was played, sparking a renaissance in the South African music scene.

However, the end of apartheid brought the end of international boycotts, which saw a deluge of overseas influences. And while US hip hop has since flooded the South African market, drum 'n' bass has given rise to the fashionable *kwaito* sound. Taking its cue from the Detroit dance sound (but slowed down to what has been termed *slow jam*) it's the current sound of choice for South African youths.

Our Pick If the teenage stylings of *kwaito* doesn't grab you, try the Soweto String Quartet. Formed in the late 1980s by a classically trained trio of brothers, it initially attracted criticism for its traditional European sounds. The group has since begun to experiment with African rhythms, and a deal with a major label company ensured its worldwide exposure. Albums are available through BMG.

Zimbabwe

Not until the war of independence ended in 1978 were Zimbabwean musicians inspired to write and record their own songs. Based on traditional Shona sounds (but performed using Western instruments) they produced what was called *chimurenga*. This has formed the basis for much of the popular music you'll hear in Zimbabwe today.

One way to tap into what's current and popular is to take your own radio and tune in to one of the Shona stations.

As well as the popular Shona and Shangaan styles, there is a strong market for Congolese (Zaïrean) *kwasa kwasa* music, which tends to be based on the rhumba beat.

The recorded music you will generally hear in pubs and discos will be a mix of mainstream American artists, dance, funk and pop.

Our Pick Thomas Mapfumo was imprisoned in 1977 for his controversial songs, and later released when he agreed to perform for the ruling party. This all changed following Zimbabwe's liberation in 1980, when Mapfumo formed Blacks Unlimited and released *Lion in the Bush*, a celebration of his country's new-found independence.

Malawi

Gospel may appear to be the music style of choice in Malawi, but delve a little deeper and you'll find a rich musical history. For starters, Malawi jazz has only ever been played on acoustic instruments by untrained musicians. And the backbone of most musical styles to come out of Malawi has been the women-at-the-mortar sound, essentially the catchy rhythm produced by the unanimous pounding of the pestle at dinner time.

Our Pick When in Malawi today, look out for the music of the Alleluya Band. Featuring Lucius Banda and his older brother Paul Banda, the band's music is hugely popular in Malawi. The band originally featured Paul on vocals, but his younger brother Lucius took over in the early 1990s. Lucius' deliberately controversial songs were the first to introduce the reggae beat, and have since gone on to influence a slew of Malawi reggae outfits.

Mozambique

The beat Mozambique mostly swings to is *marrabenta*, an infectious rhythm not dissimilar to calypso. First played during the colonial period, musicians unable to afford their own guitars would fashion them out of wood and fishing wire; tunes were then bashed out in an energetic and contagious flurry. Mistrusted by the Portuguese, *marrabenta* flourished as a musical form after independence.

For something a little more traditional, *timbila* orchestras are found all along the coast. Played on traditional instruments similar to the xylophone, 30-plus *timbila* orchestras make for an awesome spectacle.

Our Pick Have a listen to Ghorwaen's *Majurugenta* album, widely available on Peter Gabriel's Real World record label.

Right: Young busker, Cape Town, South Africa

RICHARD I'ANSON

Zambia

During the mid-70s, guitar-playing President Kenneth Kaunda issued a decree that no less than 95% of music on radio was to be Zambian in origin. Hundreds of bands were established as a result. During this time the rumba-inspired *kalindula* was formed. This urban dance style went on to dominate for decades.

An economic crisis during the 90s led to the collapse of the music industry in Zambia, opening the floodgates to music from all around the world. Most *kalindula* bands broke up during this time. But this meant newer generations of musicians influenced by a variety of overseas sounds emerged. Reggae, *ragga* and hip hop are not uncommon influences in contemporary Zambian music.

Our Pick For some good old *kalindula*, Larry Maluma embodies the spirit of Zambian music. His album *Nuff is Enough* is widely available through most world-music stores.

[Continued from page 112]

Places to Stay

Marang Hotel *(☎ 241 3991, fax 241 2130; e marang@info.bw; km5 Matsiloje Rd, PO Box 807; camping per person US$5, singles/doubles US$80/92, budget double rondavels US$36)*, 5km from the centre, is a friendly, long-standing favourite in Francistown, with a shady pool, a casino and a bar and restaurant. You can camp on the beautiful grassy lawns near the Tati River or stay in rondavels.

Tati River Lodge *(☎ 240 6000, fax 240 6080; w www.info.bw/~trl; km5.5 Matsiloje Rd; camping per person US$5, singles/doubles from US$71/86)* offers standard rooms and more expensive self-catering chalets, as well as a riverside camp site.

Satellite Guest House *(☎ 241 4665, fax 240 2115; singles/doubles US$27/35)* is a quirky option in a walled compound. From the Thapama roundabout, take the Matsiloje turnoff for 2.5km and follow the signs.

Grand Lodge *(☎ 241 2300, fax 241 2309; cnr Haskins St & Selous Ave, PO Box 1713; singles/doubles with toilet & shower US$30/34)* is an option if you prefer the town centre. It's newly refurbished.

Cresta Thapama Lodge *(☎ 241 3872, fax 241 3766; e thapama@global.bw; Thapama roundabout cnr Blue Jacket St & Doc Morgan Ave; singles/doubles with breakfast from US$90/111)* may be Francistown's most up-market hotel, but the rather stuffy atmosphere is less than upbeat.

Places to Eat

Marang Hotel *(☎ 241 3991; English/continental breakfast US$8/6; dinner US$12)* offers excellent value for breakfast, and in the evening there's a salad bar and fixed menu.

Barbara's Bistro *(☎ 241 3737; Francistown Sports Club; open noon-2pm & 7pm-11pm Mon-Sat)* serves up tasty and inexpensive lunches and dinners in a quiet, leafy setting.

Whistle Stop *(Blue Jacket St; breakfast US$3, mains US$2.50-4)* does excellent breakfasts, burgers, chicken, fish, steak and ice-cream desserts.

Pizza House *(☎ 241 6099; Haskins St; pizzas from US$4)* bakes up wood-fired pizzas, as well as chicken, kebabs and pasta.

Golden Hills Spur *(Blue Jacket St opposite Cresta Thapama Hotel; open 9am-9pm daily; mains US$5-8)* belongs to the popular South African Spur chain, and, predictably, specialises in steaks and other standards.

Milano Pizza & Chicken *(☎ 241 0077; behind Barclays Plaza; pizzas & pasta from US$4)*, off the Blue Jacket Plaza car park, serves up a wide range of pizza, pasta and chicken dishes, which are also available as takeaway orders.

There are also several fast food options, including **Nando's** *(The Mall)* and **KFC** *(Blue Jacket Plaza)*.

Getting There & Away

Air Botswana *(☎ 241 2393; Francis Ave)* flies between Francistown and Gaborone (US$100) at least once daily, except Sunday.

From the main bus terminal, between the train line and the Blue Jacket Plaza, bus and minibus services connect Francistown with Nata (US$3, two hours), Maun (US$7.50, five hours), Gaborone (US$6.50, six hours), Serowe (US$3, 2½ hours), Selebi-Phikwe (US$2, two hours) and Bulawayo, Zimbabwe (US$2.80 to US$3.50, two hours).

The overnight train to Gaborone (US$24/20/5 1st/2nd/economy, 8¼ hours) leaves at 9pm and the day train (US$7/3.50 club/economy, 6½ hours) leaves at 10am.

Makgadikgadi Pans

Botswana's great salt pans, Sua and Ntwetwe Pans, collectively comprise the 80,000-sq-km Makgadikgadi Pans and are like no other landscape on earth. Especially during the sizzling heat of late winter days, the stark pans take on a disorienting and ethereal austerity. Heat mirages destroy all sense of space or direction, and imaginary lakes shimmer and disappear, ostriches fly and stones turn to mountains and float in mid-air.

In September herds of wildebeests, antelopes and zebras begin moving into the thirsty grasslands west of the pans to await the first rains. Although the water is short-lived, animals gravitate towards depressions, which retain stores of water.

Then around December, the deluge begins. The fringing grasses turn green and the herds of wildlife migrate to partake of the bounty. As if from nowhere, millions of flamingoes, pelicans, ducks, geese and other water birds arrive at the mouth of the

BOTSWANA

MAKGADIKGADI PANS

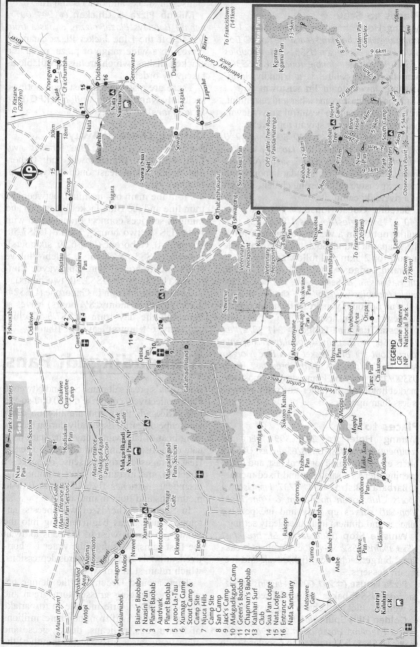

Around Nxai Pan

Kgama-Kgama Pan · 13.5km · Eastern Pan Complex · 9.6km · 10.6km · Off Cattle Trek Route to Paradamatenga · Baobab North Camp · Bore Hole · 6.4km · 5.8km · South Camp · Baobab 12.6km · Baobab Tree · 4.1km · Nxai Pan · 9.1km · Park Headquarters · 5.54km · Observation Point

To Francistown (141km) · River · X'hongwane · Nata Rv · Cha'chumtsha · Didibakwe · Semowane · Dukwe · Veterinary Cordon Fence · To Kasane (287km) · Nata · Nata Sanctuary · Tsagake · Kwadii-ze · Lepasha · Nata Delta · Sowa · Sowa (Sua) Pan · Sowa (Sua) Spit · Zoroga · Zoroga · Sigara · Thatatshukudu · Sowa/Sua Pan · Bojatau · Xurathiwa Pan · Kubu Island · Tshitsane Pan · Ntokoksa Pan · Tshwagong · Veterinary Checkpoint · Veterinary Checkpoint · Mmatshumo · To Francistown (203km) · Lethakane · Nwetwe Pan · Ntokoksa Pan · Ntlokwane Pan · To Serowe (178km) · Tshuxaba · Odiakwe · Gweta · Gutsa Pan · Galetladi Island · Mmatshumo · Meditsenyane · Gutlago · Ntlokwane Pan · Rhysna Pan · Orapa · Prohibited Area · See Inset · Oodakwe Quarantine Camp · Park Gate · Nxai Pan Section · Kudiakum Pan · Park Headquarters · Veterinary Cordon Fence · Sokoro Katsha Pan · Njarc Pan · Chikutsa Pan · Mopipi · Makalamabedi · Prohibited Area · Nkai Pan Section · Main Entrance to Makgadikgadi Pans Section · Makgadikgadi & Nxai Pans NP · Makgadikgadi Pans Section · Tamtiga · Daibui Pan · Toromoje · Mopipi Dam · Phorokwe · Lake Kau (Dry) · Kaokare · Makolwane Gate (Main Entrance to Nkai Pan Section) · Matima · Mosemiaoto · Xumaga · Xumaga Gate · Morotobolo · Dikwalo · Tsoe · Rakops · swanatsha · Xorodomo Pan · To Maun (82km) · Motopi · Senagom River · Boteti River · Nxwee · Senagom · Molosi · Xumo · Mabe · Mabe Pan · Gidikwe Pan · Gidikwe · Matswee Gate · Central Kalahari GR

LEGEND
GR Game Reserve
NP National Park

1 Baines' Baobabs
2 Nxasini Pan
3 Planet Baobab Aardvark
4 Planet Baobab
5 Leroo-La-Tau
6 Xumaga Game Scout Camp & Camp Site
7 Njuca Hills Camp Site
8 San Camp
9 Jack's Camp
10 Makgadikgadi Camp
11 Green's Baobab
12 Chapman's Baobab
13 Kalahari Surf Club
14 Sua Pan Lodge
15 Nata Lodge
16 Entrance to Nata Sanctuary

Nata River in Sua Pan to build their nests along the shoreline, feeding on the algae and tiny crustaceans, which have lain dormant in the salt awaiting the rains.

NATA

Nata, the main refuelling stop for cars and buses between Kasane, Francistown and Maun, is little more than a dust hole with four petrol stations, two bottle stores and a couple of lodges.

Sua Pan Lodge (☎ 621 1263; camping per person US$5, single/double rondavels US$30/40) has fuel pumps and a bottle store and takeaway, while the **Northgate Shop & Takeaway** (open 6am-10pm daily), over the road, sells groceries, serves up chicken and chips and claims to be organising an Internet café. It also serves as the bus station.

Nata Lodge (☎ 621 1210, fax 621 1265; W www.natalodge.com; PO Box 10; camping per person US$5.50, 2-/4-bed chalets US$69/77, 4-bed tents US$57), 10km from Nata on the Francistown road, occupies an oasis of monkeythorn, marula and mokolane palms. Meals (US$6 to US$12) and drinks are very pleasant at the shady outdoor restaurant and bar, and two-hour sunrise or sunset trips to Nata Sanctuary cost US$16.

THE PANS

The more accessible of the two big pans, Sua Pan, is mostly a single sheet of salt-encrusted mud and algae stretching across the lowest basin in northeastern Botswana. *Sua* means 'Salt' in the language of the San, who once mined it and sold it to the Kalanga. Except during the driest years, flocks of water-loving birds gather during the wet season to nest at the delta where the Nata River flows into the northern end of Sua Pan.

To the west lies the wilder and more convoluted Ntwetwe Pan, which is surprisingly littered with ancient Stone-Age tools. During rainy periods, small pools attract birdlife to its perimeter.

Nata Sanctuary

A beautiful 230-sq-km wildlife refuge at Sua Pan, Nata Sanctuary (☎ 71-656969; admission & camping for residents/nonresidents US$3.50/5; open 7am-7pm daily) has a range of birdlife, as well as antelopes and other grassland animals. It's 15km southeast of Nata. In the dry season, you don't need 4WD, but high clearance is advisable.

Kubu Island

Near the southwestern corner of Sua Pan lies the original desert island. Except for just one tenuous finger of grass, the alien-looking outcrop of 20m-high Kubu Island (originally Lekhubu, 'to the rock') with its ghostly baobabs lies surrounded by a sea of salt. At its southern edge sits an Iron Age stone enclosure that was the inspiration for the myth of the Lost City of the Kalahari. You can camp on the salt or at the otherworldly camp site on the island, but no water is available. Campers must register with the Game Scouts on the site and groups are expected to provide a 'donation' (US$5.50 per person) to the National Museums & Monuments, but be sure to ask for a receipt.

To get there, you need 4WD. The route is signposted 'Lekhubu' from the Nata–Maun road, 24km west of Nata; after 65km, you'll reach desultory Thabatshukudu village, on a low ridge. South of here, the route skirts a salt pan and after 15km passes a veterinary checkpoint; 1.5km south of this barrier is the signposted left-turn toward the island, which is about 20km away.

Places to Stay

Jack's Camp (☎ 241 2277, fax 241 3458; W www.unchartedafrica.com; singles/doubles US$625/930), run by Uncharted Africa Safaris, is one of the company's two incredible – and highly recommended – safari camps at the northern end of Ntwetwe Pan. Jack's Camp is named for the grizzled Africa hand, Jack Bousfield, who built a homestead on this site and was the father of the charismatic present manager, Ralph Bousfield. The nearby **San Camp** also enjoys a tranquil setting surrounded by mokolane palms. Accommodation at either camp is in 1940s East African–style tents, and rates include full board, most drinks, wildlife drives, guides, park fees and quad bike (ATV) trips; tax and community levy is also included. If they're in your price range, don't miss these amazing places, where the surprises just keep coming. For the same rates, you can also do quad bike trips to Kubu Island; add US$35 per person and they'll do mobile safaris around the country. Air/4WD transfers from Maun/Gweta cost US$110/150 per person.

Makgadikgadi Camp (☎ 686 0796; e sales@botswana.com; singles/doubles US$450/625) offers comfortable, all-inclusive packages amid mokolane palms near the edge of Ntwetwe Pan. Due to wet weather, it's closed from December to February.

Getting There & Away

To explore the pans on your own, you need 4WD and a good map and GPS system, as well as common sense and confidence in your driving and directional skills. Drive only in the tracks of other vehicles, and keep to the edges of the pan.

GWETA

Gweta, 100km west of Nata, is a popular refuelling and travellers' rest stop; the onomatopoeic name was derived from the croaking of large bullfrogs (Pyxicephalus adspersus), which bury themselves in the sand until the rains provide sufficient water for them to emerge and mate.

Fuel is available in the village and it's a good spot to look for lifts into the Makgadikgadi & Nxai Pan National Park.

Gweta Rest Camp (☎/fax 612220; e gweta@info.bw; camping per person US$4, singles/doubles without bathroom US$20/25, with bathroom US$27/32) provides an affordable respite in thatched rondavels. Meals are available here.

Planet Baobab (camping per person US$4, single/double rondavels US$35/51, 4-bed huts US$73, beehive huts US$18/26), in a stand of giant baobabs 4km east of Gweta, is brought to you by the same people who run Jack's Camp and San Camp. A worthwhile excursion is to the bizarre fossil formations at Nxasini Pan (US$25); camping (US$64) and quad-biking (US$41) trips to Ntwetwe Pan include transport, bedrolls, a barbecue and breakfast. Even if you don't stay here, check out their enormous concrete aardvark along the main road.

All buses between Nata and Maun call in at Gweta.

MAKGADIKGADI & NXAI PANS NATIONAL PARK

West of Gweta, the main road between Nata and Maun slices through Makgadikgadi & Nxai Pans National Park. Because they complement each other in enabling wildlife migrations, Makgadikgadi Pans Game Reserve

---

Mokolane Palms

Dotted around the Makgadikgadi & Nxai Pans National Park are islands of mokolane palms (Hyphaene petersiana). The solid white nuts from the palms are popular with elephants, and can also be carved and used for jewellery and art. The fronds are the main component in the beautiful baskets made all over Botswana. The palms are also tapped for sap, which is allowed to ferment, or is distilled into a potent liquor known as 'palm wine'. The specimens in the Makgadikgadi region are officially protected from thirsty sap-tappers, but elsewhere in Botswana, over-exploitation and increasing numbers of cattle, which nibble the young shoots, have brought it under serious threat.

---

and Nxai Pan National Park were established concurrently in the early 1970s and combined into one park in the mid-1990s, with the hope of protecting their unique ecosystem. Access to either unit is by 4WD only.

Makgadikgadi Pans Section

The 3900-sq-km Makgadikgadi Pans Game Reserve section of the park takes in grasslands and beautiful savanna country. During the winter dry season, animals concentrate around the Boteti River, but between February and April huge herds of zebra and wildebeest migrate north to Nxai Pan, only returning to the Boteti when the rains cease in early May.

Nxai Pan Section

The Nxai Pan National Park section takes in over 4000 sq km. The grassy expanse of Nxai Pan is most interesting during the rains, when large animal herds migrate from the south and predators arrive to take advantage of the bounty. In the southern part of the park is the stand of hardy trees known as Baines' Baobabs, which were immortalised by artist and adrnturer Thomas Baines on 22 May 1862, when he painted them for posterity.

Places to Stay

The Xumaga Camp Site, at the Game Scout camp near Xumaga village, is Makgadikgadi's main public camping ground. There are also two camp sites atop the Njuca Hills, 20km from the Game Scout Camp,

with a pit toilet but no water. The nearest supplies are at the bush shops in Gweta and Xumaga villages.

In the Nxai Pan section, from the **Game Scout Camp**, **North Camp** lies 8km north across the Pan (it may be inaccessible during the wet) and **South Camp** is 1.5km to the east. All these sites must be pre-booked through DWNP in Maun or Gaborone, and drivers must be totally self-sufficient.

Leroo-La-Tau (☎ 686 8407; W www.bot swana.co.za/leroo-la-tau-botswana.html; PO Box 38, Xumaga; camping per person US$4, singles/doubles US$450/600, but off-season US$275/370) occupies the banks of the Boteti River, 6km north of Xumaga. In summer, it becomes a lush oasis, rich in birdlife, while in the dry winter season it attracts thirsty wildlife. Rates include meals, wildlife drives and walking tours; vehicle transfers from Maun cost US$100 for up to six people.

Chobe National Park

Chobe National Park, which encompasses 11,000 sq km, is home to Botswana's most varied wildlife. The riverfront strip along the northern tier, with its perennial water supply, supports the greatest wildlife concentrations, but when they contain water, the lovely Savuti Marshes of the Mababe Depression in western Chobe also provide prime wildlife habitat and attract myriad water birds. Rarely-visited Ngwezumba, with its pans and mopane forests, is the park's third major region, and Chobe's northwestern corner just touches the beautiful Linyanti Marshes.

The northern park entrance lies immediately west of Kasane and is accessible to conventional vehicles. However, to proceed through the park or approach from Maun, you need high-clearance 4WD. Due to mud and flooding, Savuti may be inaccessible from January to March.

KASANE & KAZUNGULA

Kasane sits in a riverine woodland at the meeting of four countries – Botswana, Zambia, Namibia and Zimbabwe – and the confluence of the Chobe and Zambezi Rivers. It's also the gateway to Chobe National Park and, as such, this town of just a few thousand people is a focus of activity in northern Botswana. Immediately to the east, the tiny

settlement of Kazungula serves as the border crossing between Botswana and Zimbabwe, and the landing for the Kazungula ferry, which connects Botswana with Zambia.

Information

Kasane's friendly **tourist office** (☎ 625 0357; open 7.30am-12.45pm & 1.45pm-4.30pm Mon-Fri) dispenses basic information. Although the Barclays Bank changes cash and travellers cheques, it's much quicker to use the Kasane Bureau de Change (open 8am-4.30pm Mon-Fri, 8am-1pm Sat) in the Audi Centre.

The **post office** lies about 300m north of Chobe Safari Lodge; you'll find public phones here, at the airport and in Kazungula village. In the Audi Centre, the **Kool Khaya I-Café** (☎ 625 0736; open 8am-5pm Mon-Fri, 8am-1pm Sat; US$3.50/hr) offers email and Internet access.

Those travelling to lodges on Namibia's Mpalila Island must pass through the Kasane Immigration Post (☎ 625 0133); otherwise, anyone leaving Botswana here will pass through Ngoma Bridge (☎ 625 0491) to Namibia, the Kazungula road border post (☎ 625 0252) to Zimbabwe or the Kazungula Ferry (☎ 625 0420) to Zambia.

Kazungula Crocodile Farm

The Kazungula Crocodile Farm (admission US$3.50; open 10.30am-12.30pm & 2.30pm-4pm Mon-Fri) will introduce you to the region's toothy types. It's just north of the main road about 1km west of Kazungula.

Places to Stay

All of the following places can organise Chobe wildlife drives and cruises, as well as other excursions.

Thebe River Camping (☎ 625 0314; e thebe@info.bw; Kazungula Rd; camping per person US$8) provides a green riverside setting, along with a bar, meals and Chobe wildlife drives and cruises (US$14).

Liya Guest Lodge (☎ 71-756903, ☎/fax 625 1450; e liyaglo@botsnet.bw; 1198 Tholo Crescent, PO Box 212; singles/doubles from US$38/56) is a warm, friendly and very economical family-run option on the hillside.

Sedudu Guest House (☎ 625 1748, fax 625 0284; PO Box 82; singles/doubles US$37/51, single caravans US$31) is a simple place

BOTSWANA

CHOBE NATIONAL PARK

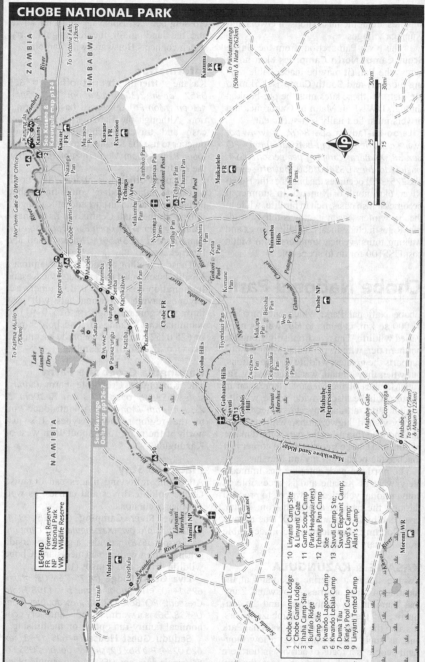

LEGEND
FR Forest Reserve
NP National Park
WR Wildlife Reserve

1 Chobe Savanna Lodge
2 Chobe Game Lodge
3 Ihaha Camp Site
4 Buffalo Ridge
   Camp Site
5 Kwando Lagoon Camp
6 Kwando Lebala Camp
7 Duma Tau
8 King's Pool Camp
9 Linyanti Tented Camp

10 Linyanti Camp Site
    & Linyanti Gate
11 Game Scout Camp
    (Park Headquarters)
12 Tchinga Pan Camp
    Site
13 Savuti Camp Site;
    Savuti Elephant Camp;
    Lloyd's Camp;
    Allan's Camp

along the main road; meals (US$6 to US$8) are provided on request.

Garden Lodge (☎ 625 0551, fax 625 0577; *w www.thegardenlodge.com; Private Bag K48; doubles US$89*), which really occupies a garden, is Kasane's most beautiful economical option.

Chobe Safari Lodge (☎ 625 0336, fax 625 0437; *w www.chobesafarilodge.com; PO Box 10; camping US$6.50, doubles US$70-89*) has a camp site, basic rondavels, simple rooms and riverview suites. The dining room does a buffet breakfast (US$9) and in the evening, puts on a generous buffet *braai* (US$14) in the garden.

Mowana Lodge (☎ 625 0300, fax 625 0301; *e mowana@info.bw; PO Box 266; all inclusive singles/doubles US$255/450, double room only US$90*) is a beautiful riverside lodge that makes the most of the open air and superb views.

Chobe Marina Lodge (☎ 625 2220, fax 625 2224; *e reservations@chobe.botsnet.bw; Private Bag K83; singles/doubles with breakfast US$158/210, room only US$72/98, self-catering for 4 people US$165*) is an architecturally appealing place with lovely artwork and an artificial river, right in the heart of Kasane. Meals are available and Chobe wildlife drives and cruises cost US$22, plus safari park fees. Regional residents get substantial discounts.

For further options see also Mpalila Island in the Namibia chapter.

Places to Eat
The Old House (☎ 71-425383; *snacks US$2-3, mains US$5-7; closed Mon*) is Kasane's only real restaurant; here you'll find everything from steak and fish to chicken and vegetarian options.

Sava's Superette, diagonally opposite the petrol station, is the place to go for self-catering.

Hot Bread Shop (*Madiba Shopping Centre*) does bakery goods.

Getting There & Away
Air Botswana connects Kasane's airport to Maun (US$100) and Gaborone (US$157).

Minibuses to Nata (US$8, three hours), with connections to Maun and Francistown, run when full from the Shell petrol station bus terminal. Between Kasane and Victoria Falls (US$42, two hours), **UTc** (☎ Vic Falls 4225) operates a morning transfer service. Thebe River Camping, Mowana Lodge and Chobe Safari Lodge also run Victoria Falls transfers (US$40, two hours). All these options usually pick up booked passengers at hotels and guest houses between 9.30am and 10am.

CHOBE RIVERFRONT
The Chobe Riverfront is packed with wildlife, and for most visitors, appreciation of this natural wonderland will entail a river cruise or a wildlife drive. The most obvious feature of the landscape is the damage done by the area's massive elephant herds, but virtually every Southern African mammal species, except the rhino, is represented here. You can also see puku, a rare antelope species. In addition, the abundance and variety of birdlife in this zone of permanent water is astonishing.

Activities
A great way to enjoy Chobe is on a **river trip** or **wildlife drive**. The best time to cruise is late afternoon, when hippos amble onto dry land and the riverfront fills with elephants heading down for a drink and a romp in the water. All hotels and lodges arrange 2½- to three-hour wildlife drives and cruises in the morning and afternoon for US$14 to US$22, plus safari discounted park fees. Note that if you take a morning wildlife drive you can also do an afternoon 'booze cruise' and pay park fees for only one day.

Places to Stay
Ihaha Camp, inside Chobe National Park, is a lovely place about 15km west of the now-disused Serondela Camp, with toilets, cold showers and lots of wildlife. Unfortunately, it has recently become a target of thieves from over the river, so campers must remain vigilant.

Chobe Game Lodge (☎ 650340, fax 650223; *e cgl@info.bw; singles/doubles US$520/780, suites US$630/1000*), in the national park, managed to attract the likes of Richard Burton and Elizabeth Taylor on the occasion of their second wedding. Rates include meals, park fees, and as many wildlife drives and river trips as you'd like, and suites have private pools.

Buffalo Ridge Camping (☎ 625 0430, fax 625 0223; *camping per person US$5.50*) lies

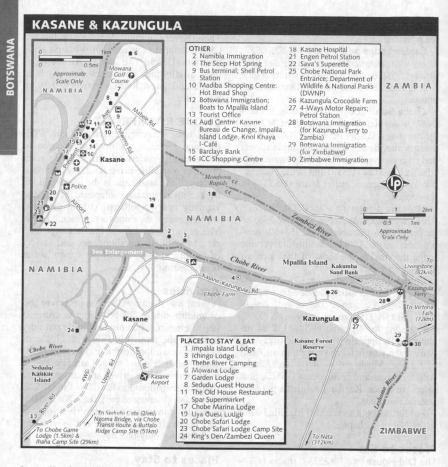

KASANE & KAZUNGULA

OTHER
2 Namibia Immigration
4 The Seep Hot Spring
9 Bus terminal; Shell Petrol Station
10 Madiba Shopping Centre; Hot Bread Shop
12 Botswana Immigration; Boats to Mpalila Island
13 Tourist Office
14 Audi Centre; Kasane Bureau de Change, Impalila Island Lodge, Kool Khaya I-Café
15 Barclays Bank
16 ICC Shopping Centre
18 Kasane Hospital
21 Engen Petrol Station
22 Sava's Superette
25 Chobe National Park Entrance; Department of Wildlife & National Parks (DWNP)
26 Kazungula Crocodile Farm
27 4-Ways Motor Repairs; Petrol Station
28 Botswana Immigration (for Kazungula Ferry to Zambia)
29 Botswana Immigration (for Zimbabwe)
30 Zimbabwe Immigration

PLACES TO STAY & EAT
1 Impalila Island Lodge
3 Ichingo Lodge
5 Thebe River Camping
6 Mowana Lodge
7 Garden Lodge
8 Sedudu Guest House
11 The Old House Restaurant; Spar Supermarket
17 Chobe Marina Lodge
19 Liya Guest Lodge
20 Chobe Safari Lodge
23 Chobe Safari Lodge Camp Site
24 King's Den/Zambezi Queen

immediately uphill from the Ngoma Bridge border crossing, near the western end of the Chobe transit route.

Getting There & Away
The northern park entrance lies 5km west of Kasane and is accessible by conventional vehicle (some Chobe Riverfront drives require 4WD), but to reach Savuti or other places in the interior of the park requires 4WD and high clearance. To transit between Kasane and the Namibian border at Ngoma Bridge is free of charge.

SAVUTI
Savuti's flat expanses make an obligatory stop for safaris and overland trips between Kasane and Maun. Gobabis Hill, south of

the Savuti gate near the Savuti Channel, bears several sets of 4000-year-old rock art, which are probably of San origin. The wildlife populations, particularly elephants and antelopes, can seem overwhelming, especially after heavy rains. Due to potential high water, Savuti is normally closed (and inaccessible) between January and March.

Average folk can stretch their budget to spend a night at the national park camp site, but for the private camps here, only millionaires need apply.

Places to Stay
Savuti Camp Site, with flush toilets, hot showers and plenty of shade, is what park rangers call a 'rough camp', meaning it's

prone to nocturnal invasion by wildlife, especially elephants, baboons and hyenas.

Savuti Elephant Camp (☎ 686 0351; e gtres@iafrica.com; singles/doubles US$691/1118), run by Gametrackers in Maun, offers luxurious tented accommodation beside the Savuti Channel.

Lloyd's Camp (☎ 686 0351, fax 686 0571; singles/doubles US$735/1190) proffers both exotic cuisine and excellent guides.

Allan's Camp (☎ South Africa 27-11-884 2504, fax 884 3159; singles/doubles US$535/810) has thatched A-frame chalets and emphasises wildlife drives; the adjacent Savuti South Camp has the same rates.

Getting There & Away
Under optimum conditions, it's a four- to six-hour drive from Kasane to Savuti. The road is passable by 2WD as far as Kachikau, but after it turns south into the Chobe Forest Reserve, the road deteriorates into parallel sand ruts that require high-clearance 4WD. Coming from Maun, you'll need 4WD to proceed north of Shorobe.

LINYANTI MARSHES
West of Chobe, on the Botswana–Namibia border, lies the Kwando area, which is dominated by the 900-sq-km Linyanti Marshes. The area may be reminiscent of the Okavango Delta, but it's actually just a broad, flooded plain along the Linyanti River, which is home to large herds of elephants and buffaloes. As yet, there's no easy access, but several concessionaires run luxury camps.

Places to Stay
Linyanti Camp, beside the river, lies within Chobe National Park and is run by the government. Amenities include flush toilets, hot showers and lots of elephants.

Linyanti Tented Camp, Duma Tau & King's Pool (W www.wilderness-safaris.com; singles/doubles US$490/800 to US$625/990), all owned by Wilderness Safaris (see the Getting Around section earlier in this chapter), provide luxurious accommodation in one of Botswana's remotest wilderness areas. Rates include beds, meals, transfers and activities.

Kwando Lagoon (☎ 686 1449, fax 686 1457; W www.kwando.co.za; singles/doubles US$765/1158) and **Kwando Lebala Camp** (prices and details as for Kwando Lagoon) occupy a huge private concession in one of Botswana's wettest and wildest areas. Along with outstanding waterfront accommodation (in tents), the rates include meals, activities and fly-in transfers from Maun. Kwando Lagoon can also be booked through a symbiotic programme with the even more beautiful Lianshulu Lodge, over the river in Namibia (see Places to Stay under Mudumu National Park in the Namibia chapter).

Getting There & Away
With a 4WD vehicle, you can reach Chobe's Linyanti Camp along a very rough track from Savuti. Otherwise, air transfers are organised by individual lodges; Kwando Lagoon Camp is also accessible by river from Lianshulu Lodge in Namibia.

The Okavango Delta

The 1430km Okavango River rises in central Angola, then flows southeast across Namibia's Caprivi Strip before entering Botswana east of Shakawe. There, 18.5 billion cubic metres of water annually spread and sprawl like an open palm across the flat landscape as they're consumed by the thirsty air and swallowed by the Kalahari sands. Eventually, the river loses itself in a 16,000-sq-km maze of lagoons, channels and islands. In this desert country, the incongruous waters of the resulting wetland – best-known as the Okavango Delta – attract myriad birds and other wildlife, as well as most of Botswana's tourists.

MAUN
Maun, an agglomeration of mud huts and sprouting office buildings, is a schizophrenic combination of traditional Botswana and the burgeoning safari industry that drives the town's economy. It's a safe bet that the dusty old town that preceded the sealed road from Nata is gone forever and that Maun's future lies in Okavango Delta tourism.

Orientation
Central Maun contains most of the restaurants, shops and travel agencies, while the village of Matlapaneng, 10km northeast of the centre, has most of the budget lodges and camp sites. In between are the Sedia Hotel and several other tourist-oriented businesses.

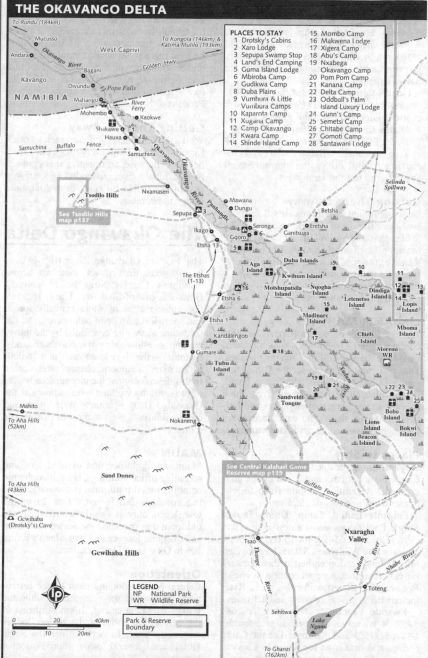

THE OKAVANGO DELTA

PLACES TO STAY
1 Drotsky's Cabins
2 Xaro Lodge
3 Sepupa Swamp Stop
4 Land's End Camping
5 Guma Island Lodge
6 Mbiroba Camp
7 Gudikwa Camp
8 Duba Plains
9 Vumbura & Little
  Vumbura Camps
10 Kaparota Camp
11 Xugana Camp
12 Camp Okavango
13 Kwara Camp
14 Shinde Island Camp
15 Mombo Camp
16 Makwena Lodge
17 Xigera Camp
18 Abu's Camp
19 Nxabega
   Okavango Camp
20 Pom Pom Camp
21 Kanana Camp
22 Delta Camp
23 Oddball's Palm
   Island Luxury Lodge
24 Gunn's Camp
25 Semetsi Camp
26 Chitabe Camp
27 Gomoti Camp
28 Santawani Lodge

LEGEND
NP   National Park
WR   Wildlife Reserve

Park & Reserve
Boundary

0   20   40km
0   10   20mi

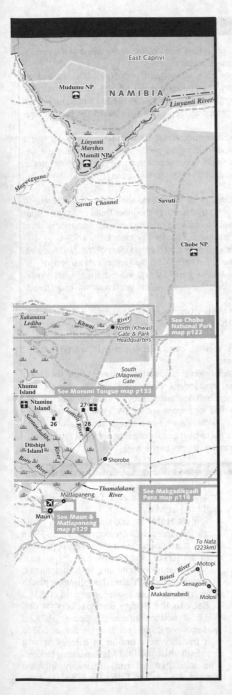

Information

The **tourist office** (☎ 686 0492; Tsheke Tsheko Rd; open 7.30am-12.30pm & 1.45pm-4.30pm Mon-Fri) is improving, and you'll also find good information at the town's many tour companies (see Getting Around earlier in this chapter) and the Matlapaneng lodges. To book national parks camp sites, go to the **Department of Wildlife & National Parks** (☎ 686 1265, fax 686 1264; open 7.30am-12.30pm & 1.45pm-4.30pm Mon-Sat, 7.30am-noon Sun); the reservations office is housed in a caravan behind the main building.

The Mall has branches of Barclays Bank and Standard Chartered Bank, but the fastest exchange services, including credit card cash advances, are with **Sunny Bureau de Change** (☎ 662786; Ngami Centre; open 7am-6pm daily) or **Civette Bureau de Change** (behind Nando's; open 7.30am-5.30pm Mon-Fri, 7.30am-1pm Sat-Sun).

The **post office** (open 8.15am-1pm & 2.15pm-4pm Mon-Fri, 8.30am-11.30am Sat) is near The Mall. Email and Internet access are available at the **Afro-Trek I-Café** (Sedia Hotel; US$5.50/hr) or **PostNet** (Score Centre; US$6/hr; open 9am-6pm Mon-Fri, 9.30am-3pm Sat).

The pharmacist at the **Okavango Pharmacy** (☎ 686 2049) does consultations (US$2) and malaria blood tests (US$7.50); for other problems, see the **Delta Medical Centre** (☎ 686 1411; e pak@info.bw; Tsheko Tsheko Rd).

Things to See

The **Maun Environmental Education Centre** (☎ 686 1390; admission free; open 7.30am-12.30pm & 1.45pm-4.40pm daily), on the eastern bank of the Thamalakane River, aims to provide school children with an appreciation of nature. If you're in town, it's worth an hour or so rambling around the bush here.

The **Nhabe Museum** (☎ 686 1346; donations welcome; open 9am-5pm Mon-Fri, 9am-4pm Sat), housed in a historic building, features art exhibitions and outlines the natural history and cultures of the Okavango. Peripheral activities include local theatre presentations and sales of locally produced arts and crafts.

Organised Tours

Most delta lodges are affiliated with specific agencies and lots of safari companies run

The Okavango Delta

Sprawling like an open palm across northwestern Botswana, the Okavango Delta is one of the world's most impressive ecosystems and Botswana's premier attraction.

Visitors to Botswana find it difficult to resist the calming spell of this watery wilderness and its extraordinary environments. In this desert country, the abundant water attracts vast quantities of wildlife – elephants, zebras, buffaloes, wildebeests, giraffes, hippos, antelopes and innumerable birds – and also provides largesse for the several groups of people that have fished and hunted here from time immemorial.

Generally, the best months to visit are July to September, when the weather is dry, water levels are high – and the prices skyrocket into the ozone. Because most people visit at this time, these are the prices quoted in this book, so if you're travelling off-season consider these jaw-dropping rates a worst case scenario. The Okavango Delta is usually subdivided into four areas:

Eastern Delta This part of the delta, which focuses on the lower Boro and Santandadibe Rivers, is more accessible – and therefore cheaper to reach – from Maun than from the Inner Delta or Moremi. You can easily base yourself in Maun and enjoy the delta by mokoro on a day or overnight trip, or on a chartered fly-in trip, for far less than the cost of staying in a Moremi or Inner Delta Lodge.

Inner Delta The area west, north and immediately south of Chiefs Island (part of Moremi) features classic delta scenery and is rich in wildlife. Accommodation here – with only one or two exceptions – is in frightfully expensive camps and lodges that are accessed only by expensive charter flights. While most of these places will provide a fabulous and unforgettable experience, you'll wish you could forget that you had to mortgage the house to stay there.

Moremi The most popular destinations lie within Moremi Game Reserve, the largely wetland region that includes Chiefs Island and Moremi Tongue. This is the only protected area within the delta, so wildlife is plentiful, but daily entry fees are high and surrounding lodges charge much the same rates as those in the Inner Delta. The good news is that several basic and relatively affordable DWNP camp sites are dotted along the park's 4WD road network.

Okavango Panhandle The swampy, papyrus-lined finger that stretches northwest from the Inner Delta is culturally the Delta's most interesting area. Most lodges here – while typically more affordable than in the other areas – cater mainly to anglers, and don't really provide a classic delta experience. On the other hand, it's the most accessible area for anyone with a 2WD vehicle or travelling on public transport, and because the area is dotted with villages, some enterprising locals have set up local camp sites and offer cheaper mokoro trips. Motorboat and fishing trips are extra attractions, and anyone with a 4WD can also enjoy the contrasting deserts to the west.

---

mokoro trips and 4WD safaris, so it's wise to check around before choosing one (see Organised Tours under Getting Around, earlier in this chapter). **Travel Wild** (☎ 686 0822, fax 686 0493; e travelwild@dynabyte.bw), opposite the airport, serves as a central booking and information office for lodges, safaris and other adventures.

Places to Stay

Sedia Hotel (☎/fax 686 0177; w www.sedia -hotel.com; camping per person US$5, double tents US$19, single/double rooms US$66/76, double chalets from US$108), 7km out on the Shorobe (Matlapaneng) Rd, is an economical option and the attached outdoor restaurant

(mains US$9-12, pizzas US$4-6) is a favourite night out in Maun.

Riley's Hotel (☎ 686 0320, fax 686 0580; singles/doubles with breakfast US$90/118), a rather sterile place near the river, is popular with upmarket tour groups.

Most budget options are in Matlapaneng, 10km northeast of Maun; the following places offer transfers from town for around US$10.

Back to the Bridge Backpackers (☎ 686 2037; e hellish@info.bw; Hippo Pools, Old Matlapaneng Bridge; camping per person US$5) is a friendly new option in a leafy setting beside the historic Old Matlapaneng Bridge. The management runs four-day mokoro trips in the Eastern Delta for US$100. Free

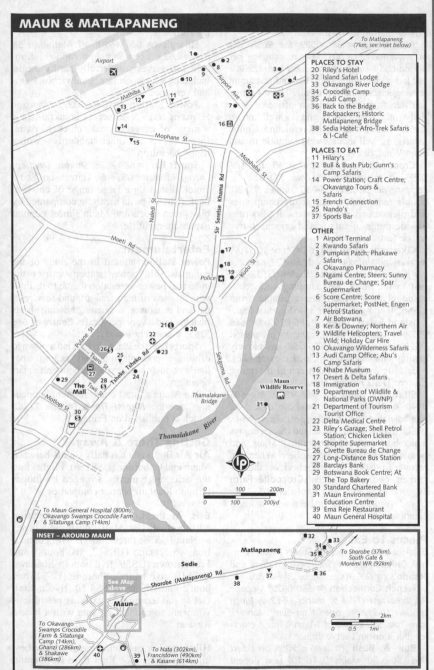

MAUN & MATLAPANENG

To Matlapaneng
(7km, see inset below)

Airport

PLACES TO STAY
20 Riley's Hotel
32 Island Safari Lodge
33 Okavango River Lodge
34 Crocodile Camp
35 Audi Camp
36 Back to the Bridge
   Backpackers; Historic
   Matlapaneng Bridge
38 Sedia Hotel; Afro-Trek Safaris
   & I-Café

PLACES TO EAT
11 Hilary's
12 Bull & Bush Pub; Gunn's
   Camp Safaris
14 Power Station; Craft Centre;
   Okavango Tours &
   Safaris
15 French Connection
25 Nando's
37 Sports Bar

OTHER
1 Airport Terminal
2 Kwando Safaris
3 Pumpkin Patch; Phakawe
   Safaris
4 Okavango Pharmacy
5 Ngami Centre; Steers; Sunny
   Bureau de Change; Spar
   Supermarket
6 Score Centre; Score
   Supermarket; PostNet; Engen
   Petrol Station
7 Air Botswana
8 Ker & Downey; Northern Air
9 Wildlife Helicopters; Travel
   Wild; Holiday Car Hire
10 Okavango Wilderness Safaris
13 Audi Camp Office; Abu's
   Camp Safaris
16 Nhabe Museum
17 Desert & Delta Safaris
18 Immigration
19 Department of Wildlife &
   National Parks (DWNP)
21 Department of Tourism
   Tourist Office
22 Delta Medical Centre
23 Riley's Garage; Shell Petrol
   Station; Chicken Licken
24 Shoprite Supermarket
26 Civette Bureau de Change
27 Long-Distance Bus Station
28 Barclays Bank
29 Botswana Book Centre; At
   The Top Bakery
30 Standard Chartered Bank
31 Maun Environmental
   Education Centre
39 Ema Reje Restaurant
40 Maun General Hospital

Mathiba St
Airport Ave
Mophane St
Motshaba St
Sir Seretse Khama Rd
Naledi St
Moeti Rd
Kudu St
Police
Pulane St
Tsaro St
Tsheke Tsheko Rd
Tswii St
The Mall
Mottopi St
Sekgoma Rd
Thamalakane Bridge
Maun Wildlife Reserve
Thamalakane River

To Maun General Hospital (800m);
Okavango Swamps Crocodile Farm
& Sitatunga Camp (14km)

0   100   200m
0   100   200yd

INSET – AROUND MAUN

Matlapaneng

Sedie

Shorobe (Matlapaneng) Rd

See Map above

Maun

To Okavango
Swamps Crocodile
Farm & Sitatunga
Camp (14km),
Ghanzi (286km),
& Shakawe
(386km)

To Nata (302km),
Francistown (490km)
& Kasane (614km)

To Shorobe (37km),
South Gate &
Moremi WR (92km)

0   1   2km
0   0.5   1mi

pick-ups arc available on request from the Power Station in town.

Audi Camp *(☎ 686 0599, fax 686 0581; W www.audicamp.bizland.com; camping per person US$4, single/double tents from US$20/26)* has a swimming pool, bar and restaurant serving snacks and full meals. There's a free transfer from their in-town office at 5pm daily (otherwise US$3), and it's well known for its Eastern Delta, Moremi and Chobe safaris, as well as its weekly shuttle to and from Windhoek (US$55).

Crocodile Camp *(☎ 686 0265, fax 686 0793; e sales@botswana.com; PO Box 46; camping per person US$4.50, singles US$20, double tents US$35)* has shady camp sites and pleasant riverside chalets. It also runs a wide range of safaris and organises live music fests.

Okavango River Lodge *(☎/fax 686 3707; e freewind@info.bw; Private Bag 28; camping per person US$3, singles/doubles US$32/37)*, just to the north, has camping and good-value chalets. Meals are available from US$6.50 and golfing for a US$2 'dust fee'.

Island Safari Lodge *(☎ 686 0300, fax 686 2932; e island@info.bw; camping per person US$5, singles/doubles US$53/58)* has a lovely setting with shady but rock-hard camp sites. Meals are available and it can also arrange Eastern Delta *mokoro* trips.

Sitatunga Camp *(☎ 686 4539, fax 686 4540; e groundhogs_@hotmail.com or e delta rain@dynabyte.bw; camping per person US$4)*, which mainly attracts overland trucks, enjoys a nice bush setting 14km south of Maun, and boasts a serious party atmosphere. When you recover from the hangover, check out the restaurant, pool and adjacent **Crocodile Farm** *(e sitatunga@info.bw; admission US$1.80; closed Wed)*. Access is best with a high-clearance vehicle.

Places to Eat
Fast-food choices include **Steers** *(Ngami centre)*, **Chicken Licken** *(Shell petrol station)* and **Nando's** *(☎ 686 3006; Tsheke Tsheko Rd)*.

French Connection *(☎ 680 0625; Mopane Rd; breakfast US$3-5, snacks US$2-5, lunch specials US$12.50; open 8am-5pm Mon-Fri, 8am-3pm Sat)* is one of Maun's finest eateries, but it doesn't serve dinner.

Bull & Bush *(☎ 686 2905; breakfast US$3.50-5.50; mains US$6-10)* is a decent option near the airport. It lacks the range of

its sibling pub in Gaborone, but does have its own ambience.

Hilary's *(☎ 686 1610; off Mathiba I St; mains US$3; open 8am-4pm Mon-Fri, 8am-2pm Sat)* serves wonderfully earthy meals, including vegetarian fare, sandwiches, soups and very nice sweets.

Power Station *(☎ 686 2037; Mophane St; mains US$5.50-8)* serves breakfast, plus a menu of burgers, steak, chicken, pasta, Indian dishes and other standards – with a trippy backdrop.

Sports Bar *(☎ 686 2676; Shorobe (Matlapaneng) Rd, mains US$4-6)*, 1km east of Sedia Hotel, dishes up a large range of chicken, beef, fish and pasta meals, accompanied by big-screen sports and Maun's most popular expatriate nightlife.

Entertainment
Power Station, housed in the ruins of the enigmatic old power station, carries the industrial power-generation theme to its limit with all sorts of industrial art, and features a bar and restaurant, a cinema showing sports matches and a very nice **Crafts Centre** *(☎ 686 3391; e craftcentre@info.bw)*.

Sports Bar (see Places to Eat) is a renowned drinking, pool-playing and raging spot that's popular with expats, pilots and safari operators.

For Maun's latest entertainment happenings, see the *Ngami Times* *(☎ 686 2236)*, which is published on Friday.

Getting There & Away
Air Air Botswana has daily flights between Maun and Gaborone (US$156). Flights into the delta are typically arranged by lodges through local air charter companies.

Bus At the Long-Distance Bus station northeast of The Mall you'll find buses to Nata (US$6; three hours), with connections to Kasane (US$12, six hours) and Francistown (US$9, five hours); Shakawe (US$10, five hours); Shorobe (US$1, one hour); and Ghanzi (US$4.50, five hours). Get to the terminal as early as possible if you want to connect in Nata with a bus to Kasane.

Hitching For eastbound travellers, the best hitching spot is the Ema Reje Restaurant, on the Nata road.

Travelling by Mokoro

Most visitors to the Okavango spend at least some time travelling by *mokoro* (plural, *mekoro*), a shallow-draught dugout canoe hewn from ebony or sausage tree log (or, more recently, moulded from fibreglass). The *mekoro* are poled from a standing position and their precarious appearance belies their amazing stability. A *mokoro* normally accommodates the poler, two passengers and their food and camping equipment.

While one-day trips are possible in the Eastern Delta (with a return drive lasting several hours from Maun), or a more expensive fly-in trip, most people prefer a multiday trip, where travellers ride for several days with the same poler, breaking their journey with walks on palm islands and moving between established camps or wild camping along the way. In this case, the quality of the experience depends largely upon the skill of the poler, the meshing of personalities and the passengers' enthusiasm.

The importance of finding a competent poler cannot be overstated, especially when you're expecting them to negotiate labyrinthine waterways or lead you on bushwalks through wildlife country. The keenest polers can speak at least some English; warn you about dangers (never swim without first asking the poler!); recognise and identify plants, birds and animals along the way; explain the delta cultures; and perhaps even teach clients how to fish using traditional methods.

If you're organising a budget *mokoro* trip, inquire in advance whether you're expected to provide food for your poler. Even if they do bring their own supplies, many travellers prefer to share meals. The polers may, for example, provide a sack of *mealie meal* (ground maize) and cooking implements while travellers supply the relishes: tins of curries, stews and vegetables. If you have arranged to provide your poler's meals, the standard daily rations are 500g of mealie meal, 250g of white sugar, six tea bags and sufficient salt and powdered milk.

Although it's still possible to negotiate with independent polers, most visitors organise *mokoro* trips through delta lodges or Maun safari companies, or through the Okavango Polers Trust in Seronga.

Getting Around

Local minibuses between town and Matlapaneng (US$0.30) run when full from the bus terminal and airport; taxis cost around US$4.

EASTERN DELTA

The area normally defined as the Eastern Delta takes in the wetlands between the southern boundary of Moremi Wildlife Reserve and the buffalo fence along the Boro and Santandadibe Rivers, off the Shorobe road north of Matlapaneng. If you can't swing the air fare into the Inner Delta, this provides an accessible alternative.

Mokoro trips in the Eastern Delta are mainly organised by Maun lodges and tour companies (see the Getting Around section earlier in this chapter), and while they're handy, it's important to use a reputable company and insist on an experienced poler, who knows the area and understands clients' interests.

Places to Stay

Gomoti Camp *(Crocodile Camp Safaris; singles/doubles US$237/360)* is a tented camp on the Gomoti River, midway between Maun and Moremi Reserve. Rates include road transfers from Maun, but it is readily accessible from the Maun–Moremi road.

Chitabe Camp *(Okavango Wilderness; singles/doubles US$650/900)* is on the Santandadibe River near the southern borders of Moremi; it also has the affiliated Chitabe Trails Camp, on a nearby island. The area supports the Wild Dog Conservation Fund and there's a good chance of seeing wild dogs here.

INNER DELTA

Roughly defined, the Inner Delta occupies the areas west of Chiefs Island and between Chiefs Island and the base of the Okavango Panhandle. While most lodges here charge jaw-dropping rates, there are a couple of mid-range options.

Mokoro trips through the Inner Delta are almost invariably arranged with licensed polers affiliated with specific camps. They operate roughly between June and December, depending on the water level. To see the most wildlife, travellers will have to pay park

fees to land on Chiefs Island or other parts of Moremi. Also, be sure to advise the poler if you'd like to break the trip with bushwalks around the palm islands.

Relatively inexpensive *mokoro* trips are available from Oddball's and Gunn's Camp, while more upmarket lodges also run *mokoro* trips between permanent camps and offer some degree of luxury.

Places to Stay – Mid-Range

Oddball's Palm Island Luxury Lodge *(Okavango Tours & Safaris; singles/doubles US$220/360)* occupies a less-than-exciting woodland beside an airstrip, but it's within a short stroll of some nice delta scenery. It's no longer a backpackers' option, but remains less painfully priced than other nearby choices. Air transfers cost US$130 per person.

Gunn's Camp *(Gunn's Camp Safaris; camping per person US$10, single/double luxury tents US$350/400)* is beside the upper Boro River on palm-studded Ntswi Island. The camping ground has hot showers, flush toilets, *braais*, a basic shop and bar. Rates for the 'luxury tents' include meals, drinks and wildlife-viewing. No-frills one-day *mokoro* trips are US$90 for two people and three-/four-/five-/six-day *mokoro* trips cost US$316/386/456/526 per person, with a minimum of two people (for one person, add 30%), including park fees and return flights from Maun. Those not on packages pay US$176 for return flights.

Semetsi Camp *(Crocodile Camp Safaris; single/double dome tents US$207/268)* is a luxury tented camp on a palm island opposite Chiefs Island. Rates include meals, *mokoro* trips and wildlife-viewing activities.

Places to Stay – Top End

Duba Plains *(Okavango Wilderness; singles/doubles US$625/990; w www.dubaplains.com)* is a tented camp situated in a remote savanna region north of the main delta. All-inclusive rates include wildlife drives, *mokoro* trips and walks.

Vumbura Camp *(Okavango Wilderness; singles/doubles US$625/990; w www.vumbura.com)* is a twin camp to Duba Plains at the transition zone between the savannas and swamps north of the delta. It's one of the most remote delta camps and the region is known for large buffalo herds. Its twin camp, **Little Vumbura**

(w www.littlevumbura.com) occupies a nearby island.

Delta Camp *(Okavango Tours & Safaris; singles/doubles US$520/840)* is beautifully situated beside a flowing channel near the southern end of Chiefs Island. Rates include catered *mokoro* trips and guided walks; for a treat, request a night in the tree house. Transfers from Maun cost US$120.

Kanana Camp *(Ker & Downey; singles/doubles US$650/900)* occupies a watery site in a maze of grass- and palm-covered islands. It's a good base for wildlife-viewing by *mokoro* around Chiefs Island.

Xigera Camp *(Okavango Wilderness; w www.xigera.com; singles/doubles US$625/990)* in a remote permanent wetland region of the Inner Delta, is known for its birdlife and the sitatungas, as well as other wildlife. Rates are for tented accommodation, meals and activities. Night drives should be permitted soon.

Nxabega Okavango Camp *(Afro Ventures; singles/doubles US$525/750)* offers beautiful tented accommodation, with sundecks overlooking the Okavango Delta floodplains.

Pom Pom Camp *(Ker & Downey; singles/doubles US$490/800)* is a remote, tented property that is accessible via air or bush track from the southwestern end of the delta. It's a particularly good area for birdwatching and short *mokoro* trips.

Abu's Camp *(Elephant Back Safaris; singles/doubles 5 nights US$10,800/16,500)* was the brainchild of operator Randall Moore, who brought three circus-trained African elephants from North America to ferry visitors around on their backs. However, this novelty doesn't come cheap – you're paying US$2160/3300 per day or US$1.50/2.30 per minute. Think about that when you're lying around relaxing!

MOREMI WILDLIFE RESERVE

Moremi Wildlife Reserve *(open 6am-6.30pm daily Mar-Sept, 5.30am-5.30pm daily Oct-Feb)*, encompassing 3000 sq km, was set aside in the 1960s to protect the most wildlife-rich part of the Okavango Delta. The park has a distinctly dual personality, with large areas of dry land rising between vast wetlands. The two most prominent dry features are Chiefs Island, deep in the Inner Delta (see earlier in this chapter), and the Moremi Tongue, comprising the reserve's

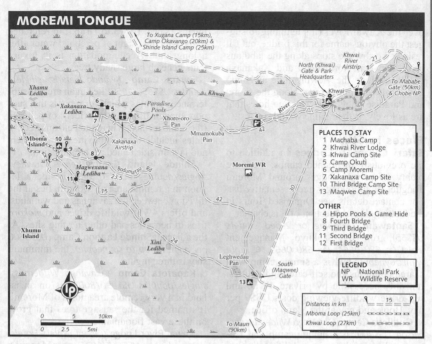

MOREMI TONGUE

To Xugana Camp (15km),
Camp Okavango (20km) &
Shinde Island Camp (25km)

Khwai
River
Airstrip

North (Khwai)
Gate & Park
Headquarters

To Mababe
Gate (50km)
& Chobe NP

Khwai

Xhamu
Lediba

Khwai

River

Xakanaxa
Lediba

Paradise
Pools

Xhoro-oro
Pan

Mmamokuba
Pan

Mboma
Island

Xakanaxa
Airstrip

Moremi WR

Magwexana
Lediba

Bodumatsu Rd

Xhumu
Island

Xini
Lediba

Leghwedau
Pan

South
(Maqwee)
Gate

PLACES TO STAY
1 Machaba Camp
2 Khwai River Lodge
3 Khwai Camp Site
4 Camp Okuti
6 Camp Moremi
7 Xakanaxa Camp Site
10 Third Bridge Camp Site
13 Maqwee Camp Site

OTHER
4 Hippo Pools & Game Hide
8 Fourth Bridge
9 Third Bridge
11 Second Bridge
12 First Bridge

LEGEND
NP National Park
WR Wildlife Reserve

Distances in km
Mboma Loop (25km)
Khwai Loop (27km)

0   5   10km
0   2.5   5mi

To Maun
(90km)

northeastern extent. Habitats range from mopane woodland and thorn scrub to dry savanna, riverbank woodlands, grasslands, floodplains, marshes, permanent waterways, lagoons and islands.

South Gate

Moremi's south entrance, aptly known as South Gate, lies 84km northeast of Maun. Here visitors pay park fees; just inside the entry gate is a camping ground with showers and a shady picnic area.

Third Bridge

Third Bridge is literally the third log bridge after entering the reserve at South Gate, 48km away. The bridge, which crosses a very sandy-bottomed pool on the Sekiri River, is rustically beautiful and is used by wildlife (particularly lions) as well as vehicles. It may look inviting, but the crocodile threat precludes swimming. Also don't camp on the bridge or sleep in the open as lions are common.

Camp sites, on either side of the bridge, lack facilities so use common sense when cooking and performing ablutions. Burn your rubbish, bury solid waste well away

from the water, use a basin when washing up and pour waste water into the sand.

Mboma Island

The grassy savanna of Mboma Island – actually just a long extension of the Moremi Tongue – covers 100 sq km and contrasts sharply with surrounding landscapes. The sandy Mboma Loop route turns off 2km west of Third Bridge and makes a pleasant loop trip.

Xakanaxa Lediba

Around Xakanaxa Lediba are several private camps, as well as a public camping ground, which occupies a narrow strip of land surrounded by marsh and lagoon. With one of the largest heronries in Africa, it's a bird-watcher's paradise. Potential sightings include marabou and saddle-bill storks; egrets; wood, sacred and glossy ibis; and seven species of heron; as well as lots of mammals.

North Gate

North Gate, with a developed camping ground, is the road entrance for southbound traffic coming from Chobe. Vehicles enter

the park on a long and clattery log bridge over the Khwai River (it's tempting to suggest the obvious name for this bridge, but I'll resist). Worthwhile stops along the fabulous drive between North Gate and Xakanaxa Lediba include the viewing hide at Hippo Pools, where hippos crowd along the shore, and Paradise Pools, two watering holes that are as lovely as their name would suggest.

Places to Stay

Safari Camps & Lodges In addition to the previously mentioned camps, there are plenty of private lodges around Moremi Tongue; the following is a representative list. For contact details, see Organised Tours in the Getting Around section of this chapter.

Santawani (camping or 2-bed chalets US$55), run by Sankuyo Management Trust (☎ 680 0664, fax 680 0665; e santa wani@dynabyte.bw) is a simple camp with shared ablutions and self-catering facilities. It's only accessible by private 4WD, and self-drive wildlife-viewing costs US$9 per day. Book and pay at the Maun office.

Gudikwa Camp (Okavango Wilderness; per person US$300) is a unique camp that features cultural rather than wildlife activities. Here you'll visit villages, learn about local arts and meet the peoples who've occupied the Okavango Delta for thousands of years.

Camp Moremi (Desert & Delta; singles/doubles US$520/780) sits in a savanna environment beside Xakanaxa Lediba, amid gaint ebony trees. Activities include wildlife drives, bird-watching trips and sundowner cruises. Rates include meals in an elevated dining room, transfers and activities. Access is via Xakanaxa air strip and 4WD.

Camp Okuti (Ker & Downey; singles/doubles US$445/590), on bird-rich Xakanaxa Lediba, accommodates 14 guests in thatched bungalows. Rates include meals, wildlife drives, boat trips and guided walks. Park fees and air transfers (US$99) cost extra.

Camp Okavango (Desert & Delta; singles/doubles US$520/780) is a lovely camp set amid sausage and jackalberry trees on Nxaragha Island. If you want the Okavango served up with silver tea service, candelabras and fine china, this is the place. There's a minimum stay of two nights – and meticulous attention to detail.

Xugana Camp (Desert & Delta; singles/doubles US$520/780) is in an area frequented by ancient San hunters, and in fact, the name means 'Kneel Down to Drink', in reference to the welcome sight of perennial water after a long hunt. Accommodation is in luxury tents beneath large shady trees.

Kwara Camp (Kwando Safaris; singles/doubles US$650/1150) lies in an area of subterranean springs which form pools that support enough fish to attract flocks of pelicans (the name means 'Where the Pelicans Feed'). Rates include meals, activities, air transfers and lagoon-side tented accommodation.

Shinde Island Camp (Ker & Downey; singles/doubles US$720/990), beside a lagoon in a remote area of Moremi, lies at the division between the savannas and wetlands, and offers 4WD wildlife drives and mokoro trips to heronries and other nesting sites. At the adjacent **Shinde Lagoon Camp** (US$3600 per night for up to six people), the minimum stay is three nights.

Kaparota Camp (Okavango Wilderness; singles/doubles US$490/800) lies on an island in a very remote area north of Moremi. It's named for the sausage trees that grow on these vast floodplains.

Khwai River Lodge (Orient Express Hotels; singles/doubles US$645/1026), near Moremi's North Gate, allies itself more with dryland Moremi than the water world of the Okavango. It boasts friendly staff, a swimming pool, bar, shop and tented accommodation. Air transfers from Maun cost US$160, but it's also accessible by 4WD.

Machaba Camp (Ker & Downey; singles/doubles US$650/900) sits along the Khwai River, just outside Moremi's North Gate. The name reflects the local word for the sycamore fig trees that shelter the tents. The surrounding waters attract large numbers of animals, including elephants, antelopes and zebras.

Mombo Camp (Okavango Wilderness; w www.mombo.co.za; singles/doubles US$1090/1780) and its sister camp **Little Mombo** are off the northwestern corner of Chiefs Island. No – the price isn't a misprint – they're almost the most expensive and exclusive lodges in the delta. Yes, it's actually on Chiefs Island – inside Moremi – and the wildlife viewing is excellent.

Getting There & Away

There's no public transport to Moremi, so you'll need a 4WD vehicle or a drive-in or

fly-in safari. If you're booked into one of the delta camps, air, road or boat transport is normally arranged by the camp, but usually for an additional charge.

THE OKAVANGO PANHANDLE

In northwestern Botswana, the Kalahari sands meet the Okavango Delta. In the Okavango Panhandle, the river's waters spread across the valley on either side to form vast reed beds and papyrus-choked lagoons. Here a cosmopolitan mix of people (Mbukushu, Yei, Tswana, Herero, European, San and refugee Angolans) occupy clusters of fishing villages and extract their livelihoods from the rich waters. They're also increasingly catering to the growing numbers of visitors to the region, where *mokoro* trips and accommodation are more affordable than in other parts of the Okavango Delta.

The Etshas

The Etshas, a refugee settlement constructed for Mbukushu refugees from the war in Angola, was divided into 13 parts based on clan and social structure carried over from Angola. In Etsha 6 it's worth visiting the **House of the River People** (*admission US$1.50*), a museum and cultural centre featuring the traditions and artistry of the Bayei, Mbukushu and San people of the Okavango region. The adjacent Okavango Basket Shop is an excellent place to buy Ngamiland baskets, pottery and carvings.

Etsha Guesthouse & Camping (*Etsha 6; camping per person US$3, singles US$9*) has four thatched guest lodges, each with two single beds, a *braai* stand and communal facilities. Very basic snacks are available at **Ellen's Cafe** (*Etsha 6*), beside the Shell petrol station.

From the main highway, sealed spur routes turn off to Etsha 6 and Etsha 13. Motorists normally drop by Etsha 6 to buy fuel or pick up supplies at the Etsha 6 Cooperative. Buses between Maun and Shakawe normally call in several times daily.

Seronga

As the rest of the delta grows more expensive, the Okavango Panhandle is currently booming, thanks largely to the **Okavango Polers Trust** (☎ 687 6861, fax 687 6939; ⓦ www.okavango.co.bw; Private Bag 109, Maun) in the small, traditional village of

Seronga. The aim of this local cooperative is to allow clients to pay less for *mokoro* trips (US$28 per day for two people) and polers to earn more than they could through a lodge or agency. The trust also looks after quality control issues, with varying degrees of success.

There's no longer a daily bus from Mohembo to Seronga, but it's almost always possible to hitch from the free Okavango River ferry in Mohembo. Plan on paying about US$0.80 for a lift.

When they're operating, water taxis run along the Okavango between Sepupa Swamp Stop and Seronga (US$3, two hours); transfers from the Seronga dock to Mbiroba Lodge, 3km away, cost US$9. Otherwise, Sepupa Swamp Stop charters 18-passenger boats for US$90.

Shakawe

For travellers, the sleepy outpost of Shakawe serves as a Botswanan entry or exit stamp, or a staging point for trips into the Tsodilo Hills or fishing or *mokoro* trips in the Okavango Panhandle. The heart of Shakawe is **Wright's Trading Store**, with a self-service supermarket and bottle shop, and it can often exchange pula for Namibian dollars or South African rand. Just opposite at **Mma Haidongo's Nice Bread Bakery** you can buy excellent home-made bread for US$1.

Several buses connect Shakawe with Maun (US$10, five hours) several times daily, with stops in Gumare, Etsha 6 and Sepupa. There's also a petrol station (no sign) east of the main road immediately before the turning into the centre (but don't count on it too heavily).

Places to Stay

Panhandle camps are mostly mid-range and have until recently catered mainly for the sport-fishing crowd. However, that's changing with the increase in travellers looking for affordable delta trips.

Drotsky's Cabins (☎ 687 5035, fax 687 5043; ⓔ drotskys@info.bw; camping per person US$10, single/double A-frames US$60/108, 4-person chalets US$120) is a lovely, welcoming lodge and camping ground set amid a thick riverine forest with fabulous bird-watching and fine views across the reeds and papyrus. Meals are available and

BOTSWANA

it also rents boats (from US$30/108 per hour/day) and can arrange tours.

Sepupa Swamp Stop (*☎/fax 687 7073, 686 2992; e swampstop@maun.info; camping per person US$4, single/double tents US$28/37*) offers riverside camping, clean facilities and a friendly atmosphere. Boat hire costs US$14/91 per hour/day, houseboat trips are US$28/150 (plus fuel) for up to eight people, and transfers to Seronga cost US$90 for up to 18 people.

Land's End Camping (*☎ 687 6852; Seronga; camping US$4, 4-bed cottage US$110*) offers a clean, green spot to camp in Seronga village.

Mbiroba Camp (*☎ 687 6861, fax 687 6939; e mbiroba@okavango.co.bw; w www .okavango.co.bw; PO Box 24, Seronga; camping US$4.50, rondavels US$9 for 3 people, singles/doubles US$37/46*), with a bar, traditional restaurant and comfy two-storey chalets, is the usual launch point for *mokoro* trips with the Okavango Polers' Trust. It's about 3km from Seronga village.

Guma Island Lodge (*☎ 687 4022; e gumacamp@info.bw; camping per person US$5, double chalets US$500*) lies east of Etsha 13, on the Thaoge River. Fishing is the focus at this decent-value camp, which profiles itself as a family resort. Chalet rates include half-board, boat trips, fishing tackle hire and *mokoro* trips. The final 16km from Etsha 13 requires a 4WD, but the lodge provides safe parking facilities and transfers from Etsha 13 (around US$45 per trip).

Makwena Lodge (*☎ 687 4299, fax 687 4302; camping per person US$5.50, backpackers' singles/doubles US$30/45, chalets with/without meals & activities US$100/28*) is operated by Drotsky's Cabins. It's on Qhaaxhwa ('Birthplace of the Hippo') Lagoon, at the base of the panhandle, but it more closely resembles the Inner Delta. Inexpensive *mokoro* trips can be arranged and those without a 4WD can pre-arrange transfers from Etsha 6 (US$10 per person).

Xaro Lodge (*☎ 687 5035, fax 687 5043; e drotskys@info.bw; PO Box 115, Shakawe; singles/doubles US$51/77*), accessible by river transfer (US$10) from the affiliated Drotsky's Cabins, is a friendly camp that focuses on fishing, but also makes a great remote retreat. Accommodation is in tidy chalets.

GCWIHABA CAVERNS (DROTSKY'S CAVE)

In the !Kung language, the name of this decorated cavern system in the Gcwihaba Hills means 'Hyena's Hole'. They weren't brought to European attention until the mid-1930s when the !Kung showed them to a Ghanzi farmer, Martinus Drotsky, and for years they were known as Drotsky's Cave. The two entrances are 300m apart but the route through the cave is about 800m.

There are no lights and no indication of which route to take, so you must carry several powerful torches as well as emergency lights, such as matches and cigarette lighters. The hardest part is a short, vertical climb down into a pit and then up the other side to a shelf, where there's a tight squeeze before you emerge in a large room. The nearest water is the borehole at Nxainxai (variously spelt Cae Cae, Xai Xai and Cgae Cgae) village.

However inconvenient it may be, visitors are advised to check in with the village of Nxainxai before visiting the caves, as villagers claim ownership of the caves and gates may be installed to prevent visitors entering without paying local guides and admission fees (around US$5 per person) through the Dutch-organised Cgae Cgae Tlhabolo Trust.

Tours to the cave (and to the nearby Aha Hills) can be arranged in Maun, but only with enough people paying enough money. Self-drivers need a 4WD with high clearance, long-range petrol tanks, water reserves and camping equipment. Take an unsignposted turn-off 2km northwest of Tsau and follow the roving track for about 90km to the signposted turn-off to the Xhaba borehole. Turn south here and after 27km you'll reach the borehole; another 27km gets you to the caverns. Alternatively, you can approach from the Aha Hills (see Aha Hills, following).

AHA HILLS

Straddling the Botswana–Namibia border, the 700-million year old limestone and dolomite Aha Hills rise 300m from the flat, thorny Kalahari scrub. They're scenic enough, but the foremost attraction is their end-of-the-world remoteness and utter silence, due mainly to the almost total absence of water. You can camp anywhere along the main track, and basic supplies and water are

available at Nxainxai and Gcangwa, where there's an unremarkable and overpriced **Community Camp Site** (☎ 686 0539; camping per person US$13).

Two taxing 4WD routes lead to the Aha Hills. One follows the Gcwihaba Caverns route (see earlier), and the other turns west from the Maun–Shakawe road, north of a small bridge near Nokaneng. From there, it's 190km west to the Aha Hills.

TSODILO HILLS

The four Tsodilo Hills (Male, Female, Child and North Hill) rise abruptly from a rippled, oceanlike expanse of desert and are threaded with myth, legend and spiritual significance for the San people, who believe this was the site of Creation. More than 2750 ancient rock paintings have been discovered at well over 200 sites. And as in most of Southern Africa, the majority of these are attributed to ancestors of today's San people.

There's now a **museum** near Main Camp extolling the undeniably spiritual nature of the hills, as well as several unmarked tracks that pass the main paintings and sacred sites. Normally, local San people will guide groups for around US$13 per day.

Places to Stay

Visitors can camp at either the **Main (Rhino)**, **Malatso**, **Makoba Woods camping grounds**, or at wild **camp sites** around

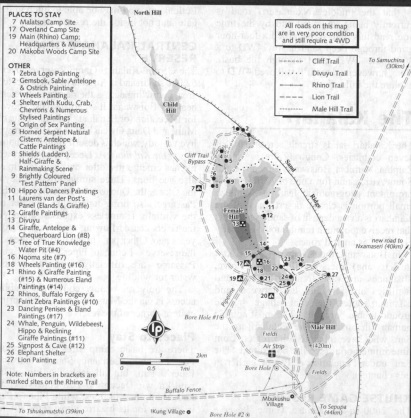

TSODILO HILLS

PLACES TO STAY
7 Malatso Camp Site
17 Overland Camp Site
19 Main (Rhino) Camp; Headquarters & Museum
20 Makoba Woods Camp Site

OTHER
1 Zebra Logo Painting
2 Gemsbok, Sable Antelope & Ostrich Painting
3 Wheels Painting
4 Shelter with Kudu, Crab, Chevrons & Numerous Stylised Paintings
5 Origin of Sex Painting
6 Horned Serpent Natural Cistern; Antelope & Cattle Paintings
8 Shields (Ladders), Half-Giraffe & Rainmaking Scene
9 Brightly Coloured 'Test Pattern' Panel
10 Hippo & Dancers Paintings
11 Laurens van der Post's Panel (Elands & Giraffe)
12 Giraffe Paintings
13 Divuyu
14 Giraffe, Antelope & Chequerboard Lion (#8)
15 Tree of True Knowledge Water Pit (#4)
16 Nqoma site (#7)
18 Wheels Painting (#16)
21 Rhino & Giraffe Painting (#15) & Numerous Eland Paintings (#14)
22 Rhinos, Buffalo Forgery & Faint Zebra Paintings (#10)
23 Dancing Penises & Eland Paintings (#17)
24 Whale, Penguin, Wildebeest, Hippo & Reclining Giraffe Paintings (#11)
25 Signpost & Cave (#12)
26 Elephant Shelter
27 Lion Painting

Note: Numbers in brackets are marked sites on the Rhino Trail

All roads on this map are in very poor condition and still require a 4WD

····· Cliff Trail
····· Divuyu Trail
+—+— Rhino Trail
— — Lion Trail
------ Male Hill Trail

North Hill

Child Hill

Cliff Trail Bypass

Female Hill

Sand Ridge

To Samuchina (30km)

new road to Nxamaseri (40km)

Pipeline

Bore Hole #1

Fields

Air Strip

Male Hill (420m)

Bore Hole

Fields

Buffalo Fence

To Tshukumutshu (39km)

!Kung Village

Bore Hole #2

Mbukushu Village

To Sepupa (44km)

0   1   2km
0 0.5 1mi

the base of the hills, but there are no shops or services. Water is sometimes available at the Main Camp and at the bore hole several hundred metres from the airstrip (this water is intended for cattle, so it's wise to purify it).

Getting There & Away

Most Maun safari companies and agencies can organise one-day air charters starting at US$450 for five people, but they'll allow only three hours of sightseeing, with little time to climb or explore in this remarkable area. Safari companies also run custom safaris, but they need advance notice and enough paying clients to make it worthwhile.

Thanks to three notorious access routes, Tsodilo was once one of Botswana's most inaccessible wonders. The good news (or bad news, depending on your perspective) is that the middle (Nxamaseri) road is currently being upgraded and by the time you read this, will have turned a four-hour grind through deep sand in low 4WD to a 30-minute 2WD jaunt through the bush. Note, however, that you'll still need 4WD to explore the hills area.

The Kalahari

The Kalahari sands stretch across parts of seven countries: Congo (Zaïre), Angola, Zambia, Namibia, Botswana, Zimbabwe and South Africa, and form one of Africa's most prominent geographical features. While a small portion is classic desert, most of the Kalahari is a vast deposit of sandy sediments that receive too much rainfall to be officially classified as an arid zone.

In Botswana, the Kalahari (*Kgalakgadi* in Setswana) offers a solitude all its own. Distances are vast, transport is rare and facilities are few and far between, and off main routes, the scant villages huddle around feeble boreholes. The most notable human inhabitants of the Kalahari are the San, who have inhabited the region from time immemorial (see the boxed text 'The San' under Population & People earlier in this chapter).

KHUTSE GAME RESERVE

The 2600-sq-km Khutse Game Reserve makes a popular weekend excursion for adventurous Gaborone dwellers. Expect to see a variety of antelopes, as well as such predators as lions, leopards, brown and spotted hyenas, jackals, caracals (which the San people believe to be the incarnation of the morning star) and even hunting dogs.

Khutse has eight **camp sites** but only Wildlife Camp, near the entry gate, has (brackish) running water and showers. Khutse II Pan, with a rudimentary camp site, is 14km west of the entry gate. The most distant site is the very pleasant Moreswa Pan, 67km from the gate, which has a natural water source that attracts wildlife. All sites must be pre-booked through DWNP in Gaborone and visitors must be self-sufficient in food, water and fuel.

The entrance gate is 226km from Gaborone; at Letlhakeng the sealed road becomes a rough 103km sandy 4WD track. From Letlhakeng, you may be able to hitch to the gate, but not inside the reserve itself.

CENTRAL KALAHARI GAME RESERVE

The Central Kalahari Game Reserve covers 52,000 sq km and is Africa's largest protected area, sprawling across the nearly featureless heart of Botswana. It's perhaps best known for Deception (or Letiahau) Valley, the site of Mark and Delia Owens' 1974 to 1981 brown hyena study, which is described in their book *Cry of the Kalahari*. At Deception Pan brown hyenas emerge just after dark and you may also see lions. Three similar fossil valleys: the Okwa, the Quoxo (or Meratswe) and the Passarge also bring topographical relief to the virtually featureless expanses, although the rivers ceased flowing more than 16,000 years ago. Other pans in the northern area of the reserve – Letiahau, Piper's, Sunday and Passarge – are artificially pumped to provide water for wildlife.

The only reasonably convenient public access is via the Matswere gate in the northeastern corner of the reserve.

Places to Stay

There are basic **camp sites** at Deception Pan, Lekhubu, Letiahau, Sunday Pan and Piper's Pan, but all lack facilities. The well-known Deception Pan enjoys a few rare, shady acacia trees, while Piper's Pan is known for its bizarre ghost trees *(Commiphora pyracanthoides)*. Other remote

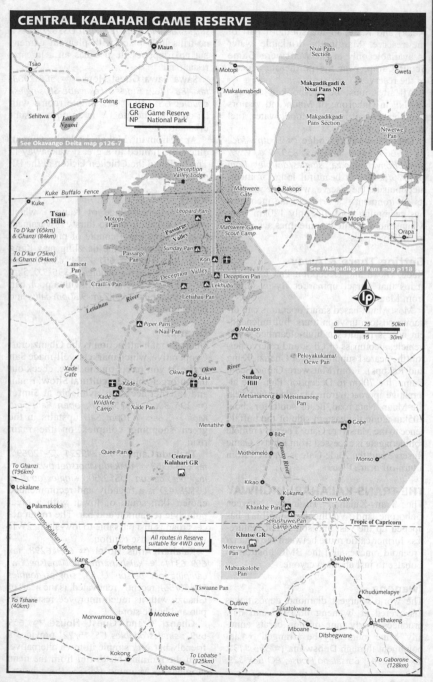

CENTRAL KALAHARI GAME RESERVE

BOTSWANA

LEGEND
GR Game Reserve
NP National Park

See Okavango Delta map p126-7

See Makgadikgadi Pans map p118

All routes in Reserve
suitable for 4WD only

Tropic of Capricorn

camp sites include **Okwa** (also known as Xaka) and **Xade**, in the southern part of the reserve. Marginally drinkable water is available only at the **Matswere Game Scout Camp**, near the northeastern gates of the reserve.

All sites must be pre-booked through DWNP in Gaborone or Maun and visitors must be self-sufficient in food, water, fuel and firewood.

Deception Valley Lodge (*☎ South Africa 27-12-665 8554, fax 665 8597;* **w** *www .deceptionvalley.co.za; singles/doubles from US$375/500*) is a beautiful lodge immediately outside the reserve, which blends with its environment – apart from the incongruous swimming pool. It's only 120km from Maun, and the route is sometimes accessible to 2WD vehicles.

Getting There & Away

Xade, Okwa and Deception Pan have airstrips that attract upmarket fly-in safaris from Maun.

Most Maun-based safari operators can organise custom drive-in tours, but independent access requires a high-clearance 4WD vehicle, a compass or GPS, and reserve petrol (the nearest supplies are at Ghanzi, Kang and Rakops). From Matswere Game Scout Camp, it's 70km to Deception Pan. The alternative approach, from Makalamabedi near the Maun–Nata road, heads south for about 105km along the eastern side of the buffalo fence to the Matswere Gate. The very remote southern gate is accessed from Khutse Game Reserve and the Xade Gate is reached from a turn-off near D'kar.

THE TRANS-KALAHARI HIGHWAY

The Trans-Kalahari Highway between Gaborone and Windhoek (Namibia) has opened up the vast and somewhat featureless former cattle route between the Ghanzi Freehold ranches and the BMC abattoir in Lobatse to just about everyone.

Jwaneng

The world's largest diamond deposit was discovered at Jwaneng in 1978 and now produces nearly nine million carats annually. Mine tours may be arranged by appointment through **Debswana** (*☎ 395 1131, fax 395 2941; Botsalano House, PO Box 329, Gaborone*).

Mokala Lodge (*☎ 588 0835, fax 588 0839; singles/doubles with breakfast US$82/97*) is a no-frills little place with pleasant gardens but no fripperies. It also has an à la carte restaurant.

Sawa Sawa Guest House (*☎ 588 2903, fax 488 1362; Block 3 Lekagabe St; singles/ doubles US$47/64*) has simple rooms with air con and satellite TV in an obscure suburban area.

Apart from the Mokala Lodge restaurant, diners are limited to a greasy **takeaway** in The Mall and the **Chicken Licken** at the BP petrol station.

Kang

The desultory village of Kang – which was once useful only to thirsty government trucks – now has a couple of public petrol stations, as well as the dazzling new **Kang Exel Ultra Stop** (*☎ 651 7294; camping per person US$2, singles/doubles US$35/37*), 5km west of the village turn-off, with a pool, bar, shop, restaurant (*open 7am-9.30pm daily*) and petrol pumps.

Ghanzi

Ghanzi's main attraction is the Ghanzicraft Cooperative, which markets well-made **San crafts**. If you're visiting in June, check out the unforgettable **Agricultural Show**. Email and Internet access is available at **Simtet** (*☎ 395 3000; US$5/hour; open 8am-5pm Mon-Fri, 8am-1.30pm Sat*) upstairs in the green shopping complex on the main road.

Thakadu Camp (*☎ 72-249221, 72-120695, fax 659 6959;* **e** *thakadu@botsnet.bw; camping per person US$3.50, singles/doubles US$28/42*) is a friendly and recommended choice 4km south of town, with a great pub-style restaurant and bar. The rough access road is just passable to low-slung 2WD vehicles, but use caution.

Kalahari Arms Hotel (*☎ 659 6298, fax 659 6311;* **e** *kalahariarmshotel@botsnet.bw; camping per person US$3, singles/doubles US$50/56*), recently renovated, is the heart of Ghanzi, with its much-improved restaurant, pub and bottle store.

Ghanzi Grand Guest House (*☎ 659 6992; singles/doubles US$15/22*) provides a friendly but very simple in-town alternative.

In the morning buses run from the main terminal to Mamuno (US$3, three hours)

and Gaborone (US$10, 11 hours); the daily bus to Maun (US$4.50, five hours) leaves at 2.30pm.

D'kar

The Ncoakhoe San people at the 7500 hectare game ranch **Dqãe Qare** (☎ 659 6285; W www.kuru.co.bw; PO Box 219, Ghanzi; admission US$1.80, camping per person US$5, San huts per person US$33, rooms with half-board per person US$40) offer guided hunting and gathering bushwalks (US$4 per hour), wildlife drives (US$6 per hour), and other activities providing insight into the lifestyles of the traditional Kalahari San. Transfers from Ghanzi cost US$22.

KGALAGADI TRANSFRONTIER PARK

The former Mabuasehube–Gemsbok National Park has now been combined with South Africa's former Kalahari–Gemsbok National Park into the new Kgalagadi Transfrontier Park. The result is one of the world's largest (28,400 sq km) and most pristine wilderness areas (see Northern Cape Province in the South Africa chapter for a map and information on the South African side).

Direct road access from Botswana is limited to the Mabuasehube and Kaa gates, both via Kang and Hukuntsi, while the Nossob River section is best accessed from South Africa.

The Mabuasehube Section

The Mabuasehube section of the park (the name means 'Red Earth'), covers 1800 sq km and focuses on the low red dunes around three major pans and several minor ones. Mabuasehube (open to day visitors 6.30am-6.30pm daily Mar-Sept, 5.30am-7.30pm daily Oct-Feb) is best in late winter and early spring when herds of eland and gemsbok migrate from the rest of the park. This section has eight rudimentary **camp sites**, for up to two groups of up to 12 people each, at the Entrance Gate, Lesholoago Pan, Monamodi, Mpaathutlwa Pan, Bosobogolo Pan and Khiding Pan, as well as two sites at Mabuasehube Pan. Facilities are limited to pit toilets, but all but Khiding Pan and

Bosobogolo Pan have water (it's still wise to carry a good supply of drinking water).

Two Rivers Section

Although you can now reach the Two Rivers section from either Kaa or Mabuasehube, access is still best from South Africa. The **Two Rivers Camp**, over the Nossob River from South Africa's Twee Rivieren Camp, has cold showers and toilets. There are also two basic sites further north on the Botswanan side: **Rooiputs**, 30km northeast of Two Rivers and **Polentswe Pan**, at Grootbrak, 223km north of Two Rivers and 60km north of South Africa's Nossob Camp.

Wilderness Trails

There are now two challenging wilderness 4WD tracks through this remote corner of Botswana. The Kgalakgadi Wilderness Trail, with two obligatory camp sites along the way, is a bone-shaped 285km loop beginning at Polentswe Pan, at Grootbak on the Nassob River, and winding north to Kaa (where there's water) before looping back toward the Nossob. The other is a two-day 150km route between the Nossob and Mabuasehube (there's also a parallel transit track to the south), which can be done only from east to west. Only one group is permitted per day, and must include two to five 4WD vehicles. Either route (US$37 per person per night) must be pre-booked through DWNP in Gaborone.

For fees and booking information, see National Parks & Reserves in the Facts about Botswana section earlier in this chapter.

Getting There & Away

All tracks into the park require 4WD, reserve petrol and self-sufficiency. The Mabuasehube section has only one entrance gate, which is accessed from Tshabong in the south, Hukuntsi in the north or along the cut line from Kokotsha (useful if you're coming from Gaborone). For the Two Rivers section, you can enter only at Kaa, which is accessed via Kang, Hukuntsi and Tshatswa (Zutshwa), or via South Africa.

Lesotho

The kingdom of Lesotho (Le-**soo**-too) is a mountainous island about the size of Belgium, in the middle of South Africa. Its forbidding terrain and the defensive Drakensberg and Maluti Ranges gave both sanctuary and strategic advantage to the Basotho (the people of Lesotho), who forged a nation while playing a key role in the manoeuvres of the white invaders on the plains below.

Facts about Lesotho

HISTORY

Lesotho was settled by Sotho peoples comparatively recently, possibly as late as the 16th century. The Khoisan, and possibly some Nguni people, lived among them, intermarrying and mingling their language.

The early society was made up of small chiefdoms. Cattle and cultivation were the economy's mainstays and were traded for iron from the northeast of South Africa.

By the early 19th century white traders were on the scene, exchanging beads for cattle. They were soon followed by the Voortrekkers (Boer pioneers) and pressure on Sotho grazing lands grew. Even without white encroachment, Sotho society had to face that it had expanded as far as it could and would have to adapt to living in a finite territory. On top of this came the disaster of the *difaqane* (forced migration). See History in the Facts for the Visitor chapter earlier in this book.

The rapid consolidation and expansion of the Zulu state under the leadership of Shaka, and later Dingaan, resulted in a chain reaction of turmoil throughout the whole of Southern Africa. That the loosely organised southern Sotho society survived this period was largely due to the abilities of Moshoeshoe (pronounced as Mo-shesh) the Great .

Moshoeshoe the Great

Moshoeshoe began as a leader of a small village and in around 1820 he led his villagers to Butha-Buthe (Place of Lying Down). From this mountain stronghold his people survived the first battles of the *difaqane* and in 1824

Highlights

Moshoeshoe began his policy of assisting refugees who helped in his defence. Later in the same year he moved his people to Thaba-Bosiu (Mountain at Night), a mountain top that was even easier to defend.

From Thaba-Bosiu, Moshoeshoe played a patient game of placating the stronger local rulers and granting protection – as well as land and cattle – to refugees. These people were to form Basotholand which, by the time of Moshoeshoe's death in 1870, had a population of more than 150,000.

The welcome Moshoeshoe gave to missionaries, and his ability to take their advice without being dominated by them, was another factor in Basotholand's emergence and survival. The first missionaries arrived in 1833 from the Paris Evangelical Missionary Society. In return for a degree of Christianisation of Sotho customs, the missionaries were disposed to defend the rights of 'their' Basotho against the new threat – British and Boer expansion.

The Boers had crossed the Orange River in the 1830s, and by 1843 Moshoeshoe was sufficiently concerned by their numbers to ally himself with the British Cape government. The British Resident, installed in Basotholand as a condition of the treaties, decided Moshoeshoe was too powerful and engineered an unsuccessful attack on his kingdom.

In 1854 the British withdrew from the area, having fixed the boundaries of Basotholand. The Boers pressed their claims on the land and increasing tension led to the Free State–Basotho Wars of 1858 and 1865. After success in the first war, Moshoeshoe was forced in the second to sign away much of his western lowlands.

Moshoeshoe again called on British assistance in 1868, this time on the imperial government in London. A high commission adjudicated the dispute and the result was the loss of more Basotho land. It was obvious that no treaty between Boers and Basotho would hold for long. Continual war between the Free State and Basotholand was not good for British interests, so the British annexed Basotholand and handed it to the Cape Colony to run in 1871.

After Moshoeshoe the Great

Moshoeshoe the Great had died the year before and squabbles over succession were dividing the country. The Cape government exploited this and reduced the powers of chiefs, limiting them to their individual areas.

The Gun War of 1880 began as a protest against the Cape government's refusal to allow the Basotho to own firearms, but it quickly became a battle between the rebel chiefs on one side and the government and collaborating chiefs on the other. The war ended in a stalemate with the Cape government being discredited.

A shaky peace followed until another war appeared imminent, and in 1884 the British government again took direct control of Basotholand. The imperial government decided to back strong local leaders rather than rule through its own officers, which helped to stabilise the country. One unexpected benefit of direct British rule was that when the Union of South Africa was created, Basotholand was classified as a British Protectorate and was not included in the Union.

Home Rule & Independence

In 1910 the advisory Basotholand National Council was formed from members nominated by the chiefs. After decades of allegations of corruption and favouritism, reforms in the 1940s introduced some democratic processes into council appointments.

In the mid-1950s the council requested internal self-government from the British and in 1960 a new constitution was in place and elections were held for a Legislative Council.

Meanwhile, political parties had formed. The main contenders were the Basotholand Congress Party (BCP), similar to South Africa's African National Congress (ANC), and the Basotholand National Party (BNP), a conservative party headed by Chief Leabua Jonathan.

The BCP won the 1960 elections then demanded, and won, full independence from Britain in 1966. However, after the 1965 elections the BCP lost power to the BNP and Chief Jonathan became the first prime minister of the new Kingdom of Lesotho. During the election campaign the BNP promised cooperation with the South African apartheid regime and in turn received massive support from it.

As most of the civil service was still loyal to the BCP, Jonathan did not have an easy time. Stripping King Moshoeshoe II of the few powers that the new constitution had left him did not endear Jonathan's government to the people and the BCP won the 1970 election.

Jonathan responded by suspending the constitution, arresting and expelling the king, and banning opposition parties. The king was eventually allowed to return from exile in Holland, and Jonathan attempted to form a government of national reconciliation. This ploy was partly successful, but some

BCP members, including the leader Ntsu Mokhehle, resisted and attempted to stage a coup in 1974. The coup failed miserably and resulted in the death of many BCP supporters and the jailing or exile of the BCP leadership.

Trouble continued and repressive measures were applied. Jonathan changed tack in his attitude to South Africa, calling for the return of land in the Orange Free State that had been stolen from the original Basotholand, and, more seriously from the South African point of view, began criticising apartheid, allegedly offering refuge to ANC guerrillas, and flirting with Cuba. Relations soured to the point where South Africa closed Lesotho's borders, strangling the country.

The Lesotho military took action. Jonathan was deposed in 1986 and the king was restored as head of state. This was a popular move, but eventually agitation for democratic reform rose again. In 1990 King Moshoeshoe II was deposed by the army in favour of his son, Prince Mohato Bereng Seeisa (Letsie III). Elections in 1993 resulted in the return of the BCP.

The BCP was split between those who wanted Prime Minister Ntsu Mokhehle to remain as leader and those who didn't. Mokhehle formed the breakaway Lesotho Congress for Democracy (LCD) party and continued to govern.

In 1995 Letsie III abdicated in favour of his father and, five years after being deposed, Moshoeshoe II was reinstated. He restored

Dancing in traditional dress, Johannesburg, South Africa

Tribal dance, Gaborone, Botswana

Swazi warrior dance, Mbabane, Swaziland

Carved wooden giraffes for sale near Kafue town, Zambia

Clay storage pots, Mochudi, Botswana

Beadwork souvenirs, Johannesburg, South Africa

calm to Lesotho after a year of unrest. Tragically, less than a year later he was killed when his 4WD plunged over a cliff in the Maluti Mountains. Letsie III was again made the king.

Elections & Invasion
Elections were held in 1998 amid accusations of widespread cheating by the LCD, which won with a landslide. Tensions between the public service and the government became acute, and the military was also divided. Meanwhile, Mokhehle handed over to his successor Pakalitha Mosisili.

Following months of protests, the government was losing control. In late September 1998 it called on the Southern African Development Community (SADC) treaty partners, Botswana, South Africa and Zimbabwe, to help restore order. Troops, mainly South African, invaded the kingdom.

Rebel elements of the Lesotho army put up a strong resistance and there was heavy fighting in Maseru. The fighting was soon over, but not before many shops and other businesses in Maseru were looted and torched.

The government agreed to call new elections, but the political situation remained tense and political wrangling delayed the elections until May 2002. The LCD won again and Prime Minister Pakalitha Mosisili began a second five-year term.

GEOGRAPHY
From Lesotho's northern tip to its western side where it juts out almost to the town of Wepener in South Africa, the border is formed by the Mohokare (Caledon) River. The eastern border is defined by the rugged escarpment of the Drakensberg, and high country forms much of the southern border.

All of Lesotho exceeds 1000m in altitude, with peaks in the central ranges and near the Drakensberg Range reaching to more than 3000m. Lesotho has the highest lowest point of any country. The tallest mountain in Southern Africa (the highest point south of Mt Kilimanjaro) is the 3482m Thabana-Ntlenyana, near Sani Pass in eastern Lesotho.

CLIMATE
Lesotho winters are cold and clear. Frosts are common and there are snowfalls in the high country and sometimes at lower altitudes. At

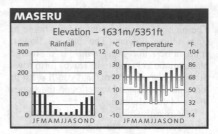

MASERU
Elevation – 1631m/5351ft

other times of the year, snow has been known to fall (especially on the high peaks where the weather is dangerously changeable) but rain and mist are more common bugbears for drivers and hikers. Nearly all of Lesotho's rain falls between October and April, with spectacular thunderstorms in summer. Down in the valleys, summer days can be hot with temperatures exceeding 30°C.

ECOLOGY & ENVIRONMENT
This high, corrugated and often freezing kingdom is a tough environment at the best of times. Overgrazing and slow but inexorable soil erosion do not bode well for Lesotho's fragile ecology. About 18 to 20 tonnes of topsoil per hectare are lost each year and it has been estimated that there will be no cultivable land left in Lesotho by 2040. Limited action is being taken to tackle erosion but it remains a huge problem.

There are also serious environmental concerns about the controversial Highlands Water Project, which provides water and electricity to South Africa. Traditional Basotho communities have been disrupted by the project (though compensation is promised) and the proposed Mohale Dam (about 35km southwest of Katse Dam) will flood some of the most fertile land in the country. There is also concern about the potential effect on the ecology of the Senqu and Orange Rivers and the impact on Namibia, a downstream user with its own water shortage problems; these are all troubling unknowns.

On a brighter note Lesotho and South Africa have combined in a multimillion dollar conservation project, beginning in 2000. The Maluti–Drakensberg Transfrontier Conservation and Development Project aims to protect and develop the eastern-alpine ecosystem of the Maluti–Drakensberg Mountains, which includes the spiral aloe flower and the rare bearded vulture.

LESOTHO

FLORA & FAUNA

The high plains and mountains are home to Cape alpine flowers. The national flower, spiral aloe *(Aloe polyphylla)*, is a strange plant unique to Lesotho. Its leaves form rows of striking, spiral patterns and you'll see it in left- and right-handed varieties on the slopes of the Maluti Mountains.

Due mainly to its altitude, Lesotho is home to fewer animals than many southern African countries. You may come across rheboks and reedbucks, and in the Drakensberg, elands are still present. Baboons and jackals are reasonably common and there are also mongooses and meerkats.

The birdlife is rich, with just under 300 species recorded. The Drakensberg is an excellent place for birdwatching and bearded vultures and black eagles are both found here. Lesotho is one of the few places you may spot the extremely rare bald ibis.

GOVERNMENT & POLITICS

The head of state is King Letsie III, and the prime minister is Pakalitha Mosisili of the LCD party. Under traditional law, the king can be deposed by a majority vote of the College of Chiefs.

ECONOMY

Lesotho is one of the world's poorest countries. Much of its food is imported. The main export is now labour; many Basotho work in South Africa.

It is hoped that sales of water and hydroelectricity to South Africa from the Highlands Water Project (see Ecology & Environment

earlier in this section) might make Lesotho more economically independent. Some manufacturing occurs in the kingdom but most goods are imported from South Africa.

Foreign aid is still a major source of income. Lately much of this has flowed in merely to feed the people in the face of severe food shortages caused by poor harvests. World Bank–funded poverty reduction schemes have been successful by many measures but compared to Lesotho's massive problems of AIDS and low agricultural productivity they are a drop in the ocean.

POPULATION & PEOPLE

The citizens of Lesotho are known as the Basotho people. Most are southern Sotho and most speak South Sotho. The melding of the Basotho nation was largely the result of Moshoeshoe the Great's 19th-century military and diplomatic triumphs; many diverse subgroups and peoples have somehow merged into a homogeneous society. Maseru, with 110,000 people, is the only large town.

Traditional culture, which is still strong, consists largely of the customs, rites and superstitions with which the Basotho explain and enrich their lives.

Music and dance play their part, mainly as important components of ceremony and everyday life. There are various musical instruments, from the *lekolulo* (a flutelike instrument played by herd boys), to the *thomo* (a stringed instrument played by women) and the *setolo-tolo* (a stringed instrument played with the mouth, by men).

Lesotho's White Gold

It might not seem like a valuable commodity, but for Lesotho water is a big money spinner. For more than 15 years huge construction projects have created dams and conduits for the water in Lesotho's highlands.

The scheme pipes water to rand-rich but water-poor Johannesburg. The first stages – the Katse Dam and associated waterworks – are complete, and by 2020 five dams and more than 200km of piping will supply water to South Africa.

In many ways the project has been a positive for the country – new roads and many jobs have been created – but it has not been without controversy.

Bribery scandals overshadowed the 1999 inauguration and hundreds of people moved from their homes to make way for the project never received their promised compensation. Environmental concerns over the loss of habitat and fears that the dam would silt up over the long term have also been raised.

There's no stopping the US$8 billion project now however, Lesotho's white gold – which will bring a quarter of the country's export earnings – is too valuable.

The Basotho

The Basotho, sometimes also referred to as the Southern Sotho, are a diverse group that includes the two million residents of Lesotho and almost two million South Africans, many of whom live in the area surrounding Lesotho. They were unified in the 1830s during the reign of the remarkable King Moshoeshoe I, who established control over several small groups of Sotho and Nguni speakers, many of them displaced by the *mfeqane* (forced migration), a chaotic time of upheaval and migration in Southern Africa caused by the Zulu nation's aggressive expansion.

Most Sotho were, and many still are, traditionally herders of cattle, goats, and sheep, as well as small-scale farmers. By the early 20th century, however, many Sotho villages were losing their claims to land, largely because of pressure from whites. As Western economic pressures intensified, many Sotho people increasingly turned to the mines for work.

By the early 1990s, an estimated 100,000 Basotho worked in South Africa's mines, and many others were part of South Africa's urban workforce throughout the country. During the apartheid era, Southern Sotho peoples outside Lesotho were assigned the tiny homeland of QwaQwa, which borders Lesotho.

The Basotho Cultural Village, in the former homeland near Golden Gate National Park, is one place where tourists and young Basotho are encouraged to learn more about Basotho culture. Perhaps a better way to get closer to Basotho culture, however, is simply to hike, or better still pony trek with a guide (see Malealea later in this chapter for details of lodges offering tours) through Lesotho's countless villages.

LESOTHO

Traditional medicine mixes rites and customs with a *sangoma* (witchdoctor), developing their own charms and rituals. The Basotho are traditionally buried in a sitting position, facing the rising sun – ready to leap up when called.

Death is ever-present in Lesotho. Food shortages – which in 2002 put 500,000 in danger of starvation – have made the appalling AIDS problem here much worse. It's a vicious circle as illness reduces the numbers of those able to produce food. More than 31% of the population is thought to be infected – one of the highest rates in the world.

LANGUAGE

The official languages are South Sotho and English. For some useful words and phrases in South Sotho, see the Language chapter at the end of this book.

Facts for the Visitor

SUGGESTED ITINERARIES

If you're here for a week, there's no need to stop long in Maseru – head south first to Morija where you'll find a great museum with displays of Basotho culture. Then continue to Malealea – the 'gem' of Lesotho – to go pony trekking. Depending on time, you could then pop down to Quthing (Moyeni)

and check out the 180 million-year-old dinosaur footprints.

With two weeks first make a visit to Teyateyaneng, north of Maseru, the craft centre of Lesotho. Then, after visiting Morija, Malealea and Quthing, head northeast to Lesotho's only national park, the remote Sehlabathebe National Park, where you can really get away from it all for a few days.

Even on an extended tour of Southern Africa, it's worth diverting into Lesotho, at least briefly, for its startlingly severe and rugged landscapes and the unfenced freedom it offers, especially to hikers or pony trekkers.

PLANNING

Lesotho is good to visit year-round but the weather can determine what you do. In winter be prepared for cold conditions and snow, in summer for rain and mist. In remote areas (which make up a large proportion of the country) roads are often overrun by flooding rivers in summer.

The **Department of Land Surveys & Physical Planning** (☎ 2232 2376; *Lerotholi Rd, Maseru; open 8am-12.45pm & 2pm-4.30pm Mon-Fri*) sells some excellent maps of Lesotho. The 1:250,000 scale map (1994), which covers the entire country, is best for driving and costs US$3.40. For trekking or driving in very rugged areas you might want the 1:50,000 series, costing about US$1 each.

TOURIST OFFICES

There is only one **tourist office** (☎ 2231 2896, fax 2231 0108; e ltbhq@ltb.org.ls; Kingsway, Maseru; open 8am-5pm Mon-Fri, 8.30am-1pm Sat) in Lesotho.

VISAS & DOCUMENTS

Citizens of most Western European countries, the USA and most Commonwealth countries are granted an entry permit (free) at the border. The standard stay permitted is two weeks (although you might get longer) and is renewable by leaving and re-entering the country or by application to the Department of Immigration. For a longer stay, apply in advance to the **Director of Home Affairs** (PO Box 174, Maseru 100, Lesotho).

For citizens of other countries, if you arrive at the Maseru Bridge border without a visa you might be given a temporary entry permit which allows you to go into Maseru and apply for a visa at the office of the **Department of Immigration** (☎ 2231 7339; Kingsway, Maseru; PO Box 174). Don't count on this though, as it depends on the whim of the border officials.

A single-entry visa costs US$3.40 and a multiple-entry visa is US$5.70. No vaccination certificates are necessary unless you have recently been in a yellow fever area.

EMBASSIES & CONSULATES
Lesotho Embassies

Lesotho has an embassy in South Africa (see Embassies & Consulates in the South Africa chapter). Elsewhere in the world, countries with a Lesotho embassy include

Belgium (☎ 02-705 3976) Boulevard General Wahis 45, 1030 Brussels
Germany (☎ 30 257 5720) Dessaur Strasse 28/29, 10963 Berlin
UK (☎ 020-7235 5686) 7 Chesham Place, Belgravia, London SW1 8HN
USA (☎ 202-797 5533/4) 2511 Massachusetts Ave NW, Washington DC 20008

Embassies & Consulates in Lesotho

A number of countries have representation in Maseru, including

Canada (☎ 2231 6435) Block D, 5th floor, LNDC Development House, Kingsway, Maseru
France (☎ 2232 7522) Kingsway, Maseru. Inquiries handled by Alliance Française, but all visas are issued in Johannesburg.

Ireland (☎ 2231 4068) Tonakholo Rd, Maseru West. Open from 8am to 12.45pm and 2pm to 4.30pm weekdays.
Netherlands (☎ 2231 2114) Lancer's Inn, Pioneer Rd, Maseru
South Africa (☎ 2231 5758) 10th floor, Lesotho Bank Towers, Kingsway, Maseru. Open from 8.30am to 12.30pm weekdays.
UK (☎ 2231 3961, e hcmaseru@lesoff.co.za) Linare Rd (opposite the police headquarters), Maseru. Open from 8am to 1pm weekdays.
USA (☎ 2231 2666) 254 Kingsway, Maseru. Open from 9am to noon and 2pm to 4pm Monday and Wednesday.

CUSTOMS

Customs regulations are broadly the same as those for South Africa (see Customs under Facts for the Visitor in the South Africa chapter later in this book). You can't bring in alcohol unless you're arriving from a country other than Botswana, Swaziland and South Africa – and that isn't likely.

MONEY
Currency

The unit of currency is the maloti (M), which is divided into 100 liesente.

Exchange Rates

The maloti is fixed at a value equal to the South African rand, and rands are accepted everywhere – there is no real need to convert your money into maloti. When changing travellers cheques you can usually get rand which saves having to convert unused maloti. (For exchange rates, see Money under Facts for the Visitor in the South Africa chapter.)

Exchanging Money

The only banks where you can change foreign currency, including travellers cheques, are in Maseru. The banks are the Bank of Lesotho and Standard Bank (see Money under Maseru later in this chapter for details). Banks are open from 8.30am to 3pm weekdays (until 1pm on Thursday) and 8.30am to 11am Saturday.

Costs

Lesotho is a cheaper country to travel in than South Africa if you take advantage of the opportunities to stay with local people and to camp in remote areas. Otherwise, hotel prices are about the same as South Africa. A goods and services tax (GST) of 10% is added to

most transactions. Note that hotels don't usually include the GST when quoting rates.

POST & COMMUNICATIONS

Post offices are open from 8am to 4.30pm weekdays and 8am to noon Saturday.

The telephone system works reasonably well. There are no area codes within Lesotho. Lesotho's country code is ☎ 266; to call Lesotho from South Africa dial the prefix ☎ 09-266. To call South Africa from anywhere in Lesotho, dial ☎ 00-27 and then the South African area code and phone number.

DIGITAL RESOURCES

Websites that are worth a look before you go to Lesotho are:

African Studies – Lesotho Page (W www.sas .upenn.edu/African_Studies/Country_Specific /Lesotho.html) Reliable links to a number of other Lesotho websites
All Africa (W http://allafrica.com/lesotho) Useful current news links for Lesotho
Kingdom in the Sky (W www.seelesotho.com) An excellent resource with all kinds of tourist information for planning a trip to Lesotho

BOOKS

Two good guides to look for in South Africa, and available in Maseru if you're lucky are *A Backpackers Guide to Lesotho* by Russell Suchet, which outlines several walks in the country and costs US$2, plus *Guide to Lesotho* by David Ambrose, on hiking in Lesotho.

NEWSPAPERS

Several thin newspapers such as *Southern Star* are available in the morning in Maseru and elsewhere later. Day-old South African newspapers are also available in Maseru.

RADIO

If you're a fan of the BBC World Service, Lesotho is a mecca as there's a transmitter here and you can pick up 'the Beeb' on short wave, medium wave (1197 kHz) and FM.

HEALTH

There is neither malaria nor bilharzia in Lesotho, but avoid drinking untreated water taken downstream from a village. The cold and changeable weather is the greatest threat to your health here, and the consequences could be a lot more serious than catching a cold if you're trapped on a mountain without proper clothing. For more information, see Health in the Regional Facts for the Visitor chapter.

DANGERS & ANNOYANCES

You may well get asked for money inside and outside the capital and especially if hiking in the countryside without a guide. Such requests are not usually made with any menace however. Outside Maseru, you'd better get used to hearing incessant requests for 'sweets! sweets!' from school children even if you're rolling past in a car.

Several lives are lost each year from lightning strikes. Keep off high ground during electrical storms and avoid camping in the open. The sheer ferocity of an electrical storm in Lesotho has to be seen to be believed.

Never go out into the mountains, even for an afternoon, without a sleeping bag, tent and sufficient food for a couple of days in case you get fogged in. Even in summer it can be freezing.

On the last Friday of the month, when many people are paid and some of them get drunk, things can get boisterous. It can be fun but as the day wears on some drinkers can become over-friendly or aggressive. There's a very slight risk of being robbed in Lesotho.

EMERGENCIES

The contact numbers for emergency services are: **police** *(☎ 123)*; and **ambulance** *(☎ 121)* – available in Maseru and nearby only. The main hospital is the **Queen Elizabeth II Hospital** *(Kingsway)* in Maseru.

BUSINESS HOURS

Most businesses are open from 8am to 5pm weekdays and 8am to noon Saturday. The civil service works between 8am and 4.30pm weekdays with a break for lunch from 12.45pm to 2pm.

PUBLIC HOLIDAYS

Lesotho's public holidays include:

New Year's Day January 1
Moshoeshoe Day 11 March
Good Friday, Easter Monday March/April
Independence Day 4 October
Christmas Day December 25
Boxing Day December 26

ACTIVITIES
Hiking
Lesotho offers great remote-area trekking in a landscape reminiscent of the Tibetan plateau. The eastern highlands and the Drakensberg's crown attract serious hikers, with the walk between Qacha's Nek and Butha-Buthe offering the best challenge.

As well as the appropriate hiking gear, you will need a compass and the relevant 1:50,000 maps from the **Department of Land, Surveys & Physical Planning** (Lerotholi Rd, Maseru).

Walking is dangerous if you aren't prepared. Temperatures can plummet to near zero even in summer, and thunderstorms are common. In summer many of the rivers flood, and fords can become dangerous: be prepared to change your route. Thick fog can also cause delays. By the end of the dry season clean water can be scarce.

Town stores often only stock the basics. It's best to bring all your own supplies especially specialist hiking supplies.

Hikers should respect the mounds of stones (cairns) marking graves. However, a cairn near a path, especially between two hills, can be added to by passing travellers; ensure your good luck by spitting on a stone and throwing it onto the pile.

Note that a white flag waving from a village means that *joala* (sorghum beer) has just been brewed; a yellow flag indicates maize beer; red is for fresh meat and green is for vegetables.

Pony Trekking
This is an excellent and popular way of seeing the Lesotho highlands, and is offered by Malealea Lodge, Trading Post Guest House and isolated Semonkong Lodge (see under Malealea, Roma, and Semonkong later in this chapter).

You will usually need to bring food, a sleeping bag, rainwear, sunscreen, warm clothing, a torch (flashlight) and water purification tablets. A long ride can be hard on the legs and backside if you're not used to it, but if you're fit enough to mix it with some walking, you don't *have* to ride all day.

Bird-watching
About 280 species of bird have been recorded in Lesotho – surprising for a landlocked country. The mountainous terrain provides habitats for many species of raptor (birds of prey). You might see the Cape vulture (*Gyps coprotheres*) or the rare bearded vulture or lammergeyer (*Gypaetus barbatus*).

Good bird-watching places include eyries in the Maluti Mountains and near the eastern Drakensberg escarpment.

Fishing
Trout fishing is very popular in Lesotho. The trout season runs from September to the end of May. There is a minimal licence fee, a bag limit of 12 fish, and a size limit; only rod and line and artificial nonspinning flies may be used. For more information contact the **Livestock Division of the Ministry of Agriculture** (☎ 2232 3986; Private Bag A82, Maseru 100).

The closest fishing area to Maseru is the Makhalaneng River (a two-hour drive from Maseru). Other places where you can cast a line are in the Malibamat'so near Butha-Buthe, 2km below the New Oxbow Lodge; in the De Beers' Dam, Khubelu and Mokhotlong Rivers near Mokhotlong; the Tsoelikana River, Park Ponds and Leqooa River near Qacha's Nek; and the Thaba-Tseka main dam.

Indigenous fish include barbel in lowland rivers, yellowfish in the mountains and the Maloti minnow in the upper Tsoelikana.

ACCOMMODATION
Maseru has a reasonable range of hotel accommodation. Most towns have small hotels that have survived from protectorate days. There are a few good ones, although many are run-down bars and liquor stores that also provide accommodation.

Camping isn't really feasible close to towns, but away from population centres you can camp, with the permission of the local landowners. (You might be offered a hut for the night instead; expect to pay about US$2.90 per person for this.) Camping is also possible in highland parks. See the boxed text 'Highland Parks & Reserves' later in this chapter for details.

There's one hostel in Maseru and one near Butha-Buthe. There are missions scattered around the country (the 1:250,000 Lesotho map shows them) where you can often get a bed. Agricultural Training Centres in several places such as Leribe and Qacha's Nek can also provide a bed for a small fee.

FOOD

You won't be writing home about the food in Lesotho. It's not notably bad, but nothing special either. The staples here are much the same as in South Africa. There's a rather bland range of fast food options in Maseru and you'll usually have to take what you're given outside the capital.

SHOPPING

Unfortunately, Lesotho's all-purpose garment, the blanket, is usually made elsewhere. There are plenty of other handicrafts to buy, including mohair tapestries, mohair ponchos and woven grass products such as mats, baskets and, of course, the Basotho hat. If you're going trekking you might want a sturdy stick; prices start at about US$4.50, but bargaining is expected.

In and around the town of Teyateyaneng, north of Maseru, there are many craft shops and cottage industries.

Getting There & Away

This section covers access into Lesotho from neighbouring countries only. Information about reaching Southern Africa from elsewhere on the African continent and from other continents is outlined in the regional Getting There & Away chapter earlier in this book.

AIR

Lesotho's Moshoeshoe International Airport is 18km from Maseru.

South African Airways (SAA) (☎ 27 11 978 5313) flies daily between Moshoeshoe International Airport and Johannesburg (Jo'burg) for around US$110, one way. The airport departure tax is US$4.50.

LAND

All Lesotho's land borders are with South Africa. Most people enter via Maseru Bridge. The main border crossings include: **Maseru Bridge** and **Ficksburg** further north (both open 24 hours); **Makhaleng Bridge** (open 8am to 6pm Mon to Fri, 8am to 4pm Sat, Sun); and **Sani Pass** (open 8am ro 4pm daily).

Most of the other entry points in the south and the east of the country involve very rough roads. The easiest entry points are on the north and west sides.

Bus & Minibus Taxi

There are no longer any direct buses between major South African cities and Maseru. It is best to take a bus to Bloemfontein or Ladybrand and then catch a minibus taxi into Lesotho from there.

Minibus taxis do run between Maseru and Jo'burg (US$10) and Bloemfontein (US$5.70). Buses from Maseru for places in South Africa leave from Maseru Bridge on the South African side of the border.

Car & Motorcycle

You can't enter Lesotho via Sani Pass unless your vehicle is 4WD, but you can leave in a conventional vehicle; although most 2WDs won't have the necessary ground clearance to get to Sani Pass.

Avis (☎ 2235 0328) and **Budget** (☎ 2231 6344) have offices in Maseru (see Getting There & Away under Maseru later in this chapter). In Lesotho it is far more economical to use a car hired in South Africa; just ensure that you have the written agreement from the hirer. There is a road tax of US$0.40, payable on leaving Lesotho.

Getting Around

BUS & MINIBUS TAXI

There is a good network of slow buses running to many towns. Minibus taxis are quicker but tend not to run long distances. In more remote areas you might have to arrange a ride with a truck, for which you'll have to negotiate a fare. Be prepared for long delays once you're off the main routes.

You'll be quoted long-distance fares on the buses but it's best to just buy a ticket to the next major town, as most of the passengers will get off there and you might be stuck waiting for the bus to fill up again, while other buses leave before yours. Buying tickets in stages is only slightly more expensive than buying a direct ticket.

CAR & MOTORCYCLE

Driving in Lesotho is getting easier as new roads are built in conjunction with the massive Highlands Water Project, but once you get off sealed roads there are still plenty of

places where even a 4WD will get into trouble. Apart from rough roads, rivers flooding after summer storms present the biggest problems, and you can be stuck somewhere for days. People and animals on the roads are another hazard.

There are sometimes army roadblocks, usually searching for stolen cars. The national speed limit is 80km/h and the speed limit in villages is 50km/h. Petrol is about the same price as in South Africa. There's a US$6 fine for not wearing a seat belt.

Before attempting a difficult drive, try to get some local information on current conditions: ask at a police station.

ORGANISED TOURS

Good tour operators in Lesotho are hard to find. The tourist information office in Maseru publishes a list of local operators, although they seem to come and go.

Malealea Lodge (☎ South Africa 051-447 3200; W www.malealea.co.ls; PO Box 12118, Brandhof, 9324, Bloemfontein, South Africa) probably offers the best range of tours from cross-country horse treks to 4WD excursions and can arrange pick-ups from Bloemfontein in South Africa; however, it doesn't offer a comprehensive overland tour of the entire country.

Maseru

Maseru has been a quiet backwater for much of its history. Kingsway was paved for the 1947 visit by the British royal family, and for some time remained the capital's only sealed road. Most of Maseru's 110,000 people have arrived since the 1970s, yet despite its rapid expansion, and its status as capital city, it remains fairly easy-going.

The 1998 invasion left many buildings scarred by torching and rampant looting. The city is still undergoing a major rebuilding programme.

Orientation

Most places to stay, eat and shop are on or near Maseru's main street, Kingsway. It runs from the border crossing at Maseru Bridge right through town to the Circle, a traffic roundabout and landmark. At the Circle the street splits to become two important highways: Main North Rd and Main South Rd.

Information

Tourist Offices The tourist office (☎ 2231 2896, fax 2231 0108; e ltbhq@ltb.org.ls; Kingsway; open 8am-5pm Mon-Fri, 8.30am-1pm Sat) is opposite the Basotho Hat. The staff are helpful, although they lack resources. The Lesotho accommodation price guide and the cheap map of Maseru are handy.

For bookings at Sehlabathebe National Park, contact the **Conservation Division of the Ministry of Agriculture** (☎ 2232 3600, ext 30; Raboshabane Rd), located on Raboshabane Rd, which is off Moshoeshoe Rd, near the train station.

Maps The **Department of Land Surveys & Physical Planning** (☎ 2232 2376; Lerotholi Rd; open 8am-12.45pm & 2pm-4.30pm Mon-Fri) sells good topographic maps. It's near the corner of Constitution Rd.

Money Changing money is no hassle but for the banking hours: 8.30am to 3pm weekdays (1pm on Thursday) and 8.30am to 11am Saturday. The last Friday of the month is pay day so there are long queues.

The main banks – Bank of Lesotho and Standard Bank – are on Kingsway. These are the only places in the country where you can change money. The only – often unreliable – automated teller machine (ATM) for international cards is at the Standard Bank.

Post & Communications The **main post office** is on Kingsway next to the Standard Bank. If you can help it don't use Maseru as a poste restante address, or you'll join the permanent group of people waiting to complain about missing mail. Your embassy (the UK one for example) may offer poste restante. There are a couple of places where you can make international calls on Kingsway.

Cultural Centres In Maseru there's an **Alliance Française** (☎ 2232 7522; Kingsway) at the French Consulate and an **American Cultural Center** (☎ 2231 2666; 254 Kingsway) in the US embassy.

Medical Services The **Queen Elizabeth II Hospital** (Kingsway) is near the Lesotho Sun hotel. Call ☎ 121 for an ambulance.

Dangers & Annoyances Maseru is fairly safe but be on your guard at night, especially

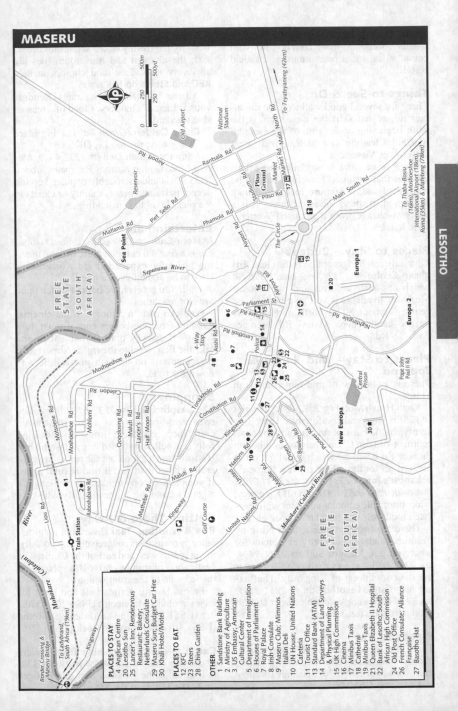

MASERU

To Ladybrand,
South Africa (19km)

Border Crossing &
Maseru Bridge

To Teyateyaneng (42km)

To Thaba-Bosiu
(16km), Moshoeshoe
International Airport (18km),
Roma (35km) & Mafeteng (78km)

PLACES TO STAY
4 Anglican Centre
20 Lesotho Sun
25 Lancer's Inn; Rendezvous
   Restaurant; Bakery;
   Netherlands Consulate
29 Maseru Sun; Budget Car Hire
30 Khali Hotel/Motel

PLACES TO EAT
12 KFC
23 Steers
28 China Garden

OTHER
1 Sandstone Bank Building
2 Ministry of Agriculture
3 US Embassy; American
   Cultural Center
5 Department of Immigration
6 Houses of Parliament
7 Royal Palace
8 Irish Consulate
9 Maseru Club; Mimmos
   Italian Deli
10 UN House; United Nations
   Cafeteria
11 Tourist Office
13 Standard Bank (ATM)
14 Department of Land Surveys
   & Physical Planning
15 UK High Commission
16 Cinema
17 Minibus Taxis
18 Cathedral
19 Queen Elizabeth II Hospital
21 Bank of Lesotho; South
   African High Commission
22 Standard Bank (ATM)
24 Old Post Office
26 French Consulate; Alliance
   Française
27 Basotho Hat

off the main street. Violent crime is unfortunately becoming more common but with common sense and precautions, you should be OK.

Things to See & Do

There are several good **walks** on the mountain ridges that skirt the city, such as the walk beginning at the gate of the Lesotho Sun hotel leading to a plateau with great views over Maseru.

Take some time to go into the **urban villages** that surround Maseru. You will be welcomed and, if you are lucky, you may be invited to spend the night there. It is a pleasant change from a sanitised Western-style hotel.

Places to Stay – Budget

Your only real budget option is the clean **Anglican Centre** (☎ 2232 2046; beds US$5.70) which has austere dorms and twin rooms. Meals are available if you give notice. The centre is about 500m north of Kingsway on the bend where Assissi Rd becomes Lancer's Rd.

Places to Stay – Mid-Range & Top End

There is a shortage of mid-range hotels in Maseru.

Khali Hotel/Motel (☎ 2232 2822; doubles US$28) is large and comfortable. There's an hourly shuttle bus that runs from/to the town centre or you can take a Thetsane minibus on Pioneer Rd near Lancer's Inn and get off at the turn-off for the suburb of New Europa.

Lancer's Inn (☎ 2231 2114, fax 2231 0223; singles/doubles US$30/52), just off Kingsway, is a comfortable colonial-era hotel with renovated rondavels. It's popular so book ahead.

There are two Sun hotels, both plush by Lesotho standards but pretty exorbitant for what you get. **Maseru Sun** (☎ 2231 2434, fax 2231 0158; rooms from US$68) is near the river southwest of Kingsway. The luxury resort-style **Lesotho Sun** (☎ 2231 3111, fax 2231 0104; singles/doubles from US$79) is on a hillside further east.

Places to Eat

There are plenty of central **street stalls**, mainly open during the day, selling grilled meat for about US$0.70. Servings of curry and rice cost US$0.60.

There is a good **bakery** next to Lancer's Inn – try the freshly baked scones for breakfast; the chicken and mushroom pies are also very tasty. Fast-food choices include **KFC** and **Steers** on Kingsway.

All the hotels have restaurants. **Rendez-vous** at Lancer's Inn serves food of a reasonable standard.

China Garden (Orpen Rd) is a big place off Kingsway; the food is OK.

Mimmos Italian Deli (☎ 2232 4979; Maseru Club, United Nations Rd; mains around US$3.40) is understandably popular, serving decent pasta and pizzas mainly to expats in the pleasant club surroundings.

Entertainment

Maseru Club (☎ 2232 6008; United Nations Rd) is a fine old colonial club, bar and meeting place for expats and aid workers. It's easy to be signed in as a guest.

Both Sun hotels have **bars** in which there are slot machines.

You can take in a movie at the **cinema**. Coming from the border end of town, turn left off Kingsway onto Parliament St and take the first street to the right (Airport Rd); the cinema is on the left, just a little way down the road.

Shopping

The **Basotho Hat** (☎ 2232 5102; Kingsway; open 9am-5pm daily) is a government-run craft shop, operating from an endearing folly of a building shaped like a Basotho hat. It's well worth a look but the prices are generally higher than you'll find in rural areas. If you plan on pony trekking or walking it's a good idea to buy a horsehair fly-whisk.

Getting There & Away

Bus & Minibus Taxi Buses and long-distance minibus taxis congregate, haphazardly, in the streets west and east of the Circle. The destination of minibus taxis is displayed on the left side of the front window.

From Maseru, destinations and fares for buses include Mafeteng (US$1.20), Quthing (US$1.70; change at Mafeteng), Roma (US$1.40) and Mohale's Hoek (US$1.90).

Car Hire cars are available from outlets at the two Sun hotels. **Avis** (☎ 2235 0328) is located at the Lesotho Sun and **Budget** (☎ 2231 6344) is at the Maseru Sun.

Getting Around

To/From the Airport Moshoeshoe International Airport is 18km from town, off Main South Rd. The Khali Hotel/Motel's shuttle bus runs to the airport. Minibus taxis cost about US$6.90.

Taxi & Minibus Taxi The standard minibus taxi fare around town is US$0.30. There are a few conventional taxi services – try **Moonlite Telephone Taxis** (☎ 2231 2695) or **Planet** (☎ 2231 7777).

Around Maseru

Most towns in Lesotho have risen around trading posts or protectorate-era administration centres, but none of these towns approach Maseru in size or facilities.

THABA-BOSIU

Moshoeshoe the Great's mountain stronghold, first occupied in July 1824, is east of Maseru. Thaba-Bosiu (Mountain at Night) played a pivotal role in the consolidation of the Basotho nation. The name may be a legacy of the site being first occupied at night, but another legend suggests that Thaba-Bosiu, a hill in daylight, grows into a mountain at night.

There's an **information centre** at the base of Thaba-Bosiu. Admission to the mountain itself costs US$0.50, and an official guide will take you to the summit. Good views from here include those of the Qiloane pinnacle (inspiration for the Basotho hat), along with the remains of fortifications, Moshoeshoe's grave, and parts of the original settlement.

Places to Stay & Eat

Melesi Lodge (☎ 2285 2116; singles/doubles US$24/33) is a neatly kept place about 2km before the Thaba-Bosiu visitors centre. The lodge has a terrific restaurant.

Getting There & Away

To get here from Maseru, look for a minibus taxi near the Circle; these go as far as the visitors centre (US$0.70). If you're driving, head out on Main South Rd, take the turn-off to Roma and after about 6km turn off to the left. Thaba-Bosiu is about 10km further along.

ROMA

Roma, only 35km from Maseru, is a university town and a good place to meet students. There are some attractive sandstone buildings dotted around the town, and the entry to town by the southern gorge is spectacular.

The important **Ha Baroana** rock paintings are just north of Roma. Although suffering from neglect and vandalism (including damage done by tourists who spray water on the paintings to produce brighter photos) they're worth seeing.

To get to the paintings from Roma head back to the Maseru road and turn right onto the road to Thaba-Tseka. After about 12km turn off to the left, just after the Ha Ntsi settlement on the Mohlsks-oa-Tuka River. To get to the site by minibus taxi from Maseru, head for Nazareth and get off about 1.5km before Nazareth. A signpost indicates the way to the paintings off to the left. Follow the gravel track 3km to the village of Ha Khotso then turn right at a football field. Follow this track a further 2.5km to a hilltop overlooking a gorge. A footpath zigzags down the hillside to the paintings inside a rock shelter.

Places to Stay & Eat

Trading Post Guest House (☎ 2234 0267; e tradingpost@leo.co.ls; camp sites per person US$3.50, rooms with bathroom US$17.50) is a lovely, relaxing place 2km west of Roma off the Maseru road. The trading post has been here since 1903, as has the Thorn family, which own the store and guesthouse. There's a 20-minute walk from the guesthouse to dinosaur footprints. Room rates include a continental breakfast. The Trading Post also runs **Trading Post Adventures** a few kilometres away, offering more accommodation, tours, hiking trails and horse rides. There is no restaurant (try the **Speakeasy Restaurant** in Roma) but you can use the kitchen. Everything is provided except towels.

Getting There & Away

A minibus taxi from Maseru to Roma costs US$1.70.

Northern Lesotho

TEYATEYANENG

Teyateyaneng (Place of Quick Sands) is usually known as TY. The town has been

Highland Parks & Reserves

While the building of a series of dams on the Orange River has created controversy, not least over environmental concerns, it has also led to the creation of the following nature reserves. For bookings and inquiries contact **LHDA Nature Reserves** (☎ 2246 0723; fax 2246 1226; **e** nature@lhda.org.ls; PO Box 333 Butha-Buthe 400, Lesotho). The website **W** www.lesothoparks.com features these new areas in greater detail.

Bokong Nature Reserve

The bearded vulture, the ice rat and the Vaal rhebok are just some of the denizens of this reserve (admission US$0.40, overnight hiking US$1.90, overnight huts US$18.50), at the top of the 3090m Mafika-Liseu Pass, near the Bokong River. The park is also home to Afro-alpine wetland sponges. There are a number of day walks, a visitors centre and an overnight camping ground. There are also horse trails from US$2.90.

Ts'ehlanyane National Park

Deep in the rugged Maluti Mountains this 5600-hectare national park (admission US$1.20, overnight hiking US$1.80, camping US$1.20, rondavels US$18.50) protects some interesting fauna – woodland and berg bamboo – but little in the way of big flora. There are walks, horse trails and a camping ground and rondavels.

Liphofung Cave

San rock art and historical links that go back as far as the Stone Age are the attractions of this small 4-hectare reserve (admission US$1.20, camping US$1.20, rondavels US$11.50) just off the main Butha-Buthe–Oxbow road. There are also horse trails, a small museum and a craft centre.

---

developed as the craft centre of Lesotho and has several places worth visiting.

Some of the best tapestries come from Helang Basali Crafts in the St Agnes Mission, 2km before TY on the Maseru road. More tapestries are available from Hatooa-Mose-Mosali. Wool products can be bought from Setsoto Design, Tebetebeng and Letlotlo Handcrafts.

The **Blue Mountain Inn** (☎ 2250 0362; singles/doubles US$22/25) has comfortable, cosy cottages. There's also a restaurant.

MAPUTSOE

This border town, 86km northeast of Maseru, across the Mohokare (Caledon) River from Ficksburg in South Africa, has a shopping centre and a few other civic amenities. It's effectively a black dormitory suburb of Ficksburg and is very impoverished. If you're stopping in the area overnight, the best bet is to head across the border to Ficksburg (see Free State in the South Africa chapter).

LERIBE

A large town by Lesotho's standards, Leribe (Hlotse) is a quiet village serving as a re-

gional shopping and market centre. It was an administrative centre under the British and there are some old buildings slowly decaying in the leafy streets. **Major Bell's Tower**, on the main street near the market, was built in 1879.

There is a set of **dinosaur footprints** a few kilometres south of Leribe at Tsikoane village. Going north towards Leribe, take the small dirt road going off to the right towards some rocky outcrops. Follow it up to the church and ask someone to direct you to the minwane. It's a 15- to 20-minute slog up the mountainside to a series of caves. The prints are clearly visible on the ceiling of the rock.

About 10km north of Leribe are the **Subeng River dinosaur footprints**. There is a signpost indicating the river but not the footprints. Walk down to the river from the road to a concrete causeway (about 250m). The footprints of at least three species of dinosaur are about 15m downstream on the right bank.

Agricultural Training Centre (☎ 2240 0226; dorm beds US$2.90) is on the main road just north of town.

Leribe Hotel (☎ 2240 0559; Main St; singles/doubles US$18.50/24) is an old-style place. It has a tea garden surrounded by well-established trees.

KATSE & THE HIGHLANDS WATER PROJECT

One of the benefits of the Lesotho Highlands Water Project is better accessibility for travellers into this remote part of Lesotho.

From Leribe you can take a sealed road all the way to the project headquarters at Katse. When you near the dam, ignore the two turn-offs signposted 'Katse Dam' and keep going until you see signs directing you to Katse village. Here you'll find the information centre in some blue buildings by the workers' compound, and a viewpoint overlooking the dam wall.

The Katse Lodge (☎ 2291 0202; singles/ doubles US$24/43) is modern and of a reasonable standard, but it can fill up with sightseers on weekends. The food in the restaurant is pretty good by Lesotho standards.

The spectacular road from Leribe to Katse passes the lowland village of Pitseng and climbs over the Maluti Mountains to drop to Ha Lejone, which one day will be at the edge of the dam's lake. It continues south past Mamohau Mission, crosses the impressive Malibamat'so Bridge, climbs over another series of hills to the Matsoku Valley, recrosses the Malibamat'so River and ends in Katse.

There are taxis from Leribe to Katse (US$3.50), and plenty of traffic if you want to hitch.

BUTHA-BUTHE

Moshoeshoe the Great named this town Butha-Buthe (Place of Lying Down) because it was here that his people first retreated during the difaqane. The Maluti Mountains form a beautiful backdrop to this small town.

There are signs on the road to **Ha Thabo Ramakatane Youth Hostel** (dorm beds US$3.50) though you may have to ask for directions. It's about 4km from the village. The hostel is very basic and there are no supplies, so buy food in the village before arriving. There's no electricity; you cook using gas and you fetch your own water just as the villagers do.

Crocodile Inn (☎ 2246 0223; Reserve Rd; singles/doubles from US$15/18) is simple and clean. The **restaurant** here is OK. There's also a fast-food place at the petrol station nearby.

OXBOW

South African skiers used to come to Oxbow in winter but the place has slowly died as a ski resort. The large **New Oxbow Lodge** (for bookings, ☎ South Africa 051-933 2247; ⓦ www.oxbow.co.za; room-only singles/doubles from US$21.50/37, half-board singles/doubles US$33/66) on the banks of the Malibamat'so River has a cosy bar and filling set meals. A few kilometres further north is a private chalet, **Club Maluti** (ⓦ www.clubmaluti.co.za; dorm beds US$2.90) belonging jointly to the Maluti and Witwatersrand University ski clubs. It's possible to sleep here although winter weekends are crowded. The website allows readers to book by email.

Eastern Lesotho

THABA-TSEKA

This remote town is on the eastern edge of the Central Range, over the badly potholed Mokhoabong Pass. It was established in 1980 as a centre for the mountain district.

You can usually get a bed at the **Farmer Training Centre** (☎ 2290 0201; dorm beds about US$2.30) which is on the street behind the Post Office, and there's also the basic but adequate **Maluti Guesthouse** (☎ 2290 0201; per person US$9.80), 2km from the main road.

About four buses a day run from Maseru to Thaba-Tseka (US$3.40), but heading south from Thaba-Tseka to Sehonghong and Qacha's Nek is more difficult – you'll probably have to negotiate with a truck driver. The roads around here can be tackled in a 2WD but are pretty shocking.

MOKHOTLONG

The first major town north of Sani Pass and Sehlabathebe National Park, Mokhotlong has basic shops and transport to Oxbow and Butha-Buthe. The town, about 270km from Maseru and 200km from Butha-Buthe, has a reputation as the coldest, driest and most remote place in Lesotho. The horses 'parked' outside the shops give the town a wild west feel.

The **Farmer Training Centre** (beds about US$1.80) has cold-water washing facilities and a kitchen. The **Lefu Senqu Hotel** (☎ 2292 0330; singles/doubles US$15/19.50) is 5km from the airport.

About 15km southwest of Mokhotlong in Upper Rafolatsane village is the **Molumong Guesthouse & Backpackers** (rooms US$7.50 per person). It's very basic (bring your own sleeping bag) and takes forever to reach along awful roads. There's no electricity or TV, just the stars. You should be able to arrange pony treks with the locals. There are three buses a day to the lodge from Mokhotlong.

SANI PASS

This steep pass is the only dependable road between Lesotho and KwaZulu-Natal but it's pretty appalling even so. On the South African side the nearest towns are Underberg and Himeville.

From the Sani Top Chalet at the top of the pass there are several day walks, including a long and strenuous one to **Thabana-Ntlenyana** (3482m), the highest peak in Southern Africa. There is a path, but a guide would come in handy. Horses can do the trip so consider hiring one.

Another walk leads to **Hodgson's Peaks**, 6km south, from where you get the benefit of views to Sehlabathebe National Park and to KwaZulu-Natal.

One three-day walk in this area that you could try before attempting something more ambitious is from the Sani Top Chalet, south along the edge of the escarpment, to the Sehlabathebe National Park. From here there's a track leading down to Bushman's Nek in South Africa. As the crow flies, the distance from Sani Top to Nkonkoana Gate is about 45km but the walk is longer than that. The altitude of much of this area is more than 3000m and it's remote even by Lesotho's standards – there isn't a horse trail much less a road or a settlement. Don't try this unless you are well prepared, experienced and in a party of at least three people.

Places to Stay & Eat

Sani Top Chalet (w www.sanitopchalet.co.za; camping US$3.50, dorm beds US$6.90, rooms US$29 per person with meals) is a great place perched dramatically at the top of the pass.

There are self-catering facilities and a bar. Travellers coming from South Africa should note that alcohol is likely to be confiscated at the Lesotho border. In winter the snow is often deep enough to ski (there are a few pieces of antique equipment available at the chalet) and horse trekking is available by prior arrangement. Book accommodation and tours through **Southern Drakensberg Tours** (☎ South Africa 033-702 1158; e sanitop@futurenet.co.za).

The other places to stay are the hostels on the South African side of the pass (see The Natal Drakensberg in the KwaZulu-Natal section in the South Africa chapter).

Getting There & Away

The South African border guards won't let you drive up the pass unless you have a 4WD. You can come down from Lesotho without one, though it's not recommended. The South African border is open from 8am to 4pm daily; the Lesotho border stays open an hour later to let the last vehicles through. Hitching up or down the pass is best on weekends when there is a fair amount of traffic to and from the lodge.

South African hostels at the bottom of the pass arrange transport up the pass, and some agencies in Himeville and Underberg arrange tours. A minibus taxi from Underberg to Sani Top is about US$2.30. There are a few minibus taxis, which cost much less, running Basotho into South Africa for shopping. You might have to wait a day or so for one of these.

Public transport on the slow, bumpy route from Sani Top to the rest of Lesotho is very sparse, but you may find something if you're patient.

SEHLABATHEBE NATIONAL PARK

Lesotho's first and today its least accessible national park, Sehlabathebe was proclaimed in 1970. It's very remote and always an adventure to get to. The park's main attraction is its sense of separation from the rest of the world. There are few animals other than a rare Maloti minnow, thought to have been extinct but rediscovered in the Tsoelikana River, rare birds such as the bearded vulture, and the odd rhebok or baboon. As well as hikes and climbs, the park has horse riding (or 'equine rental'); guided horseback tours are US$5.80.

This is a summer rain area and thick mist that's potentially hazardous to hikers is common. Winters are clear but cold at night, and there are sometimes light falls of snow.

Near the village of Sehonghong, to the northwest of the park, is **Soai's Cave**. Soai, the last chief of the Maloti San people, was attacked and defeated here by Cape and Basotho forces in 1871.

For bookings at the park, contact the **Conservation Division of the Ministry of Agriculture** (☎ *2232 3600; Raboshabane Rd; PO Box 92, Maseru 100, Lesotho*).

Places to Stay & Eat

You can camp in the park but there are no facilities (other than water) except at the **Sehlabathebe Lodge** (*camp sites per person US$1.20, singles/doubles US$3.50/5.80, 4-bed family rooms US$7.80, entire lodge US$27*). The lodge has firewood and coal available for purchase, but for food and petrol or diesel you'll have to rely on a small store about 4km west of the park entrance and quite a way from the lodge. You have to book the lodge in Maseru at the Conservation Division of the Ministry of Agriculture (see earlier for contact details).

Range Management Education Centre (*dorm beds US$4*), in Sehlabathebe Village, is modern and well equipped and serves meals. It's 1.5km down the road to Sehonghong.

Getting There & Away

Driving into the park can be a problem in spring and summer, as the 4WD tracks become impassable after heavy rains. Bear in mind that at the park you could be stuck waiting for a river to go down. Road building accompanying the hydroelectric scheme should improve some of the routes. Check with the Conservation Division of the Ministry of Agriculture in Maseru when you book accommodation.

The longest route into the park is the southern route via Quthing and Qacha's Nek. There's another route via Thaba-Tseka then down the Senqu River valley past the hamlet of Sehonghong and over the difficult Matebeng Pass. The park can also be reached from Matatiele in the extreme west of Kwa-Zulu-Natal. This route doesn't have as many difficult sections as the other routes but it is not well maintained so it is sometimes closed; check in Matatiele before trying it.

There is a daily bus between Qacha's Nek and Sehlabathebe village. This relatively short distance takes 5½ hours and costs US$2.30; the bus departs from Sehlabathebe at 5.30am and returns at noon.

Probably the simplest way in is to hike the 10km up the escarpment from Bushman's Nek (South Africa). From Bushman's Nek to Nkonkoana Gate, the Lesotho border crossing, takes about six hours. You can also take a horse up or down for US$4.60.

QACHA'S NEK

This pleasant town, with a number of sandstone buildings, was founded in 1888 near the pass (1980m) of the same name. Oddly enough, several California redwoods grow nearby, some more than 25m high.

The **Nthatuoa Hotel** (☎ *2295 0260; singles/doubles from US$17/23*) offers adequate accommodation and serves meals.

There's also the **Farmer Training Centre** (☎ *2295 0231; dorm beds US$3*) just off the main road (turn at the 'Forestry Division' sign).

Weather permitting (this area can get snowed in during winter), a bus to Sehlabathebe leaves daily around noon and costs US$4.60. There is more transport between here and Quthing. A bus leaves from both towns at 9am, takes about six hours and costs US$3.50. It is a spectacular drive.

Southern Lesotho

SEMONKONG

The **Maletsunyane Falls**, also known as Lebehane Falls after the French missionary who saw them in 1881, are about a 1½-hour walk from Semonkong (Place of Smoke). The 192m falls are at their most spectacular in summer and are best appreciated from the pit of the gorge (where there are **camp sites**).

The remote 122m **Ketane Falls** are also worth seeing. These are a solid day's ride (30km) from Semonkong or a four-day return horse ride from Malealea Lodge.

You can usually find a bed at the **Roman Catholic Mission** in Semonkong for a small contribution.

The **Semonkong Lodge** (*for bookings, ☎ South Africa 051-933 3106; ⓦ www.placeo fsmoke.co.ls; camp sites US$2.30, dorm beds US$5.20, singles/doubles US$19/30*) offers

hiking and pony trekking, with rates and options similar to those at the Malealea Lodge. A day horse/pony trek costs around US$18.

Buses between Maseru and Semonkong (US$1.80) leave from both places in the morning and arrive late in the afternoon.

MORIJA

This small village, about 40km south of Maseru on the Main South Rd, is where you will find the **Morija Museum & Archives** (☎ 2236 0308; admission US$0.70; open 8am-5pm Mon-Sat, noon-5pm Sun). The collection includes archives from the first mission to Basotholand, and as the missionary was associated with Moshoeshoe the Great, the collection is of great importance. There are some good displays of Basotho culture, some finds from the Stone and Iron Ages, and dinosaur relics.

Near the museum is the **Mophato Oa Morija** (☎ 2236 0308; camp sites US$2.30 per person, dorm beds US$5.20), an ecumenical centre. There's also the pleasant **Ha Matela Guest Cottages** (☎ 2236 0306; cottages US$11.50 per person). For bookings, call the museum and ask for Stephen Gill. Breakfast/dinner costs US$2.30/4.70.

A minibus to/from Maseru costs US$0.90.

MALEALEA

The valleys around Malealea have been occupied for a very long time, as evidenced by the many **San paintings** in rock shelters. Malealea is now one of the gems of Lesotho and is appropriately advertised as 'Lesotho in a nutshell'. You can go on a well-organised pony trek from here or wander on foot freely through the hills and villages.

Pony Trekking

Malealea Lodge (see Places to Stay & Eat later in this section) is the best place in Lesotho to arrange pony trekking, which offers a good chance to meet with Basotho villagers and experience the awesome scenery of the mountains and deep valleys. The villagers act as guides and provide the ponies, and the business makes a significant contribution to the local village economy.

The pony treks are priced on a per-day basis. Pony trek prices start at US$18. Overnight rides start at US$23 per person, plus US$4.60 for each night spent in one of the Basotho village huts.

Walks

The owners of Malealea Lodge have put together a number of walking and hiking options, and also provide a map. Your packs can be carried on ponies if you wish to go for longer than one day.

The walks include a two-hour return walk to the Botso'ela Waterfall; a six-hour return walk to the Pitseng Gorge (take your swimwear); a short, easy one-hour walk along the Pitseng Plateau; a walk along the Makhaleng River; and a hike from the Gates of Paradise back to Malealea. The scenery along these walks is nothing short of stunning and all walks include the local villages which dot the landscape.

Drives

Although it is slow going on the dirt roads in this area, there are some very scenic drives. Perhaps the best is the road that forms part of the Roof of Africa Rally. Take a right turn at the first junction you come to when leaving Malealea, heading north. The road passes through some picturesque villages before crossing the top of the **Botso'ela Waterfall**. After a few kilometres it reaches an impressive lookout over the Makhaleng and Ribaneng Valleys.

If you continue north from the lookout to Sebelekoane, you can return to Maseru via Roma. This scenic (but rough) road leads to Basotho villages and missions tucked away in the valleys. Allow three hours from Sebelekoane to Maseru.

Places to Stay & Eat

The Malealea Lodge (for bookings, ☎ South Africa 051-447 3200; w www.malealea.co.ls; camp sites US$4.60, dorm beds US$6.90, rondavels per person US$9.20, rooms with bathroom per person US$14-19) is part of the original Malealea Trading Store established in 1905 by Mervyn Smith, a teacher, diamond miner and soldier. It is now run by the exceedingly friendly Mick and Di Jones. Breakfast (US$3.50), lunch (US$4.60) and dinner (US$6.90) are served if you give prior notice. There are also self-catering facilities and the nearby shop is fully stocked.

Getting There & Away

From Maseru, the fastest public transport option is to take a minibus to Motsekuoa, and from there another to Malealea (US$1.80).

The lodge operates pricey transfers from Maseru (from US$46 return) and can sometimes arrange transfers from Bloemfontein.

The distance from Maseru to Malealea is 83km. From Maseru, head south on the well-signposted Mafeteng road for 52km to the town of Motsekuoa. Look out for the Golden Rose restaurant, the proliferation of taxis and the huddles of potential passengers. Opposite the restaurant turn left (east) onto the dirt road and follow it for 24km. When you reach the signposted turn-off to Malealea, it is another 7km to the lodge. You'll know you are on the right track when you pass through the Gates of Paradise and are rewarded with a stunning view of your destination. The plaque here aptly reads 'Wayfarer – Pause and look upon a gateway of paradise'.

The road to Malealea from the south, via Mpharane and Masemouse, is much rougher. Most drivers take the Motsekuoa road.

MAFETENG
The name Mafeteng means 'Place of Lefeta's People'. An early magistrate, Emile Rolland, was called Lefeta (or 'The One Who Passes By') by local Basotho. To the east is the 3096m Thaba Putsoa (Blue Mountain), the highest feature in this part of Lesotho.

There is not much of interest in town, although it is important as a bus and minibus taxi interchange.

The **Mafeteng Hotel** (☎ 2270 0236; singles/doubles US$20/24) has a restaurant and pleasant garden cottages.

MOHALE'S HOEK
This comfortable town is 125km from Maseru by sealed road. The younger brother of Moshoeshoe the Great, Mohale, gave this land to the British for administrative purposes in 1884. It is a much nicer place than nearby Mafeteng.

Mohale's Hoek has the high quality **Hotel Mount Maluti** (☎ 2278 5224; singles/doubles from US$20/28). There's a large garden with a pool and tennis court. Breakfast/dinner costs US$4/5.20. There's also **Monateng**

Lodge (☎ 2278 5337; singles/doubles US$18/22), although the hotel is better.

QUTHING
Quthing, the southernmost town in Lesotho, is often known as Moyeni (a Sephuthi word meaning 'Place of the Wind'). The town was established in 1877, abandoned three years later during the 1880 Gun War and then rebuilt at the present site.

Most of the town is in Lower Quthing. Up on the hill overlooking the dramatic Orange River Gorge is Upper Quthing, where there is a good hotel, a mission and sundry colonial-era structures. A minibus taxi between the two costs US$0.20 – you can hitch but you should still pay.

Off the highway, about 5km west of Quthing, is the five-roomed **Masitise Cave House**. This mission building was built into a San rock shelter in 1866 by Reverend Ellenberger. Inquire at the school about access to the cave house and someone will unlock it for you. There are San paintings nearby.

Probably the most easily located of the **dinosaur footprints** in Lesotho are close to Quthing. To get to them, go up the Mt Moorosi road from Quthing until you reach a thatch-roofed orange building. The footprints, a short walk away, are believed to be 180 million years old.

Between Quthing and Masitise there is a striking twin-spired **sandstone church**, part of the Villa Maria Mission.

At Qomoqomong, 10km from Quthing, there's a good gallery of **San paintings**; ask at the General Dealers store about a guide for the 20-minute walk to the paintings.

Places to Stay & Eat
Mountain Side Hotel (☎ 2275 0257; singles/doubles US$20/28.50), in Lower Quthing, is a basic pub with a restaurant and rooms. Breakfast/dinner is US$4/5.20.

Getting There & Away
Minibus taxis run daily between Quthing and Maseru (US$3.50), stopping at Mafetekeng (US$1.80) and Mohale's Hoek (US$1.20).

LESOTHO

Malawi

The tourist brochures bill Malawi as 'the warm heart of Africa' and, for once, the hype is true: Malawi's scenery is beautiful and (although we hate to generalise) Malawians really do seem to be among the friendliest people you could meet anywhere.

Most travellers come to experience Lake Malawi – a magnificent shard of crystal water stretching some 500km along Malawi's eastern border, separating it from the wild and mountainous coast of Mozambique and Tanzania. Isolated villages pepper the northern lakeshore and the highly regarded Liwonde National Park rests at its southern tip. Around 500 species of fish inhabit the lake and the freshwater diving and snorkelling here are excellent.

Malawi's terra firma is also visually rewarding, accented by diverse landscapes, more parks and reserves, and the highland wilderness areas of Mt Mulanje and the Nyika Plateau, where you find sheer escarpments, dramatic peaks, endless rolling grassland and some of the most enjoyable hiking routes in the whole of Africa.

Facts about Malawi

HISTORY
The pre-colonial history of Malawi is linked to the history of Southern Africa as a whole. For more detail see the History section of the Facts about the Region chapter.

Bantu Migrations
The Bantu people had been migrating from Central Africa into the area now called Malawi since the first millennium, but significant groups called Tumbuka and Phoka first settled around the highlands of Nyika and Viphya sometime during the 17th century. Meanwhile, in the south, the Maravi people (of whom the Chewa became the dominant group) established a large and powerful kingdom that spread all over southern Malawi and parts of present-day Mozambique and Zambia.

The early 19th century brought with it two more significant migrations. The Yao invaded southern Malawi from western Mozambique, displacing the Maravi, while

Malawi at a Glance

Area: 118,484 sq km (land area 94,080 sq km)

Population: 11.6 million

Capital: Lilongwe

Head of State: President Bakili Muluzi

Official Languages: English, Chichewa

Currency: Malawi kwacha (MK)

Exchange Rate: US$1 = k92.78

Highlights

- Lake Malawi – snorkelling, diving, kayaking and swimming in divine waters, then dossing in reed huts or reclining in five-star resorts

- Likoma Island – escaping to the heavenly beaches, traditional fishing villages, enjoying panoramic walks and the magnificent cathedral

- Liwonde National Park – spotting elephants, hippos, kingfishers, rhinos and antelopes

- Mt Mulanje – hiking the spectacular contours and absorbing the breathtaking views

- Nyika Plateau & Vwaza Marsh – horse riding, mountain biking and trekking alongside zebras and antelopes or dining with elephants and hippos in these sharply contrasting areas

- Malawi's colonial heritage – marvelling at Blantyre's magnificent cathedral, Zomba's government buildings and the missionary centre of Livingstonia

groups of Zulu migrated northward to settle in central and northern Malawi (where they became known as the Ngoni).

The Rise of Slavery

Slavery, and a slave trade, had existed in Africa for many centuries, but in the early 19th century demand from outside Africa increased considerably. Swahili-Arabs, who dominated the trade on the east coast of Africa, pushed into the interior, often using the services of powerful local tribes such as the Yao to raid and capture their unfortunate neighbours. Several trading centres were established in Malawi, including Karonga and Nkhotakota – towns that still bear a strong Swahili-Arab influence today.

Early Europeans

The first Europeans to arrive in Malawi were Portuguese explorers who reached the interior from Mozambique. One of these was Gaspar Bocarro who, in 1616, journeyed from Tete (on the Zambezi River) through the Shire Valley to Lake Chilwa (to the south of Lake Malawi), then through the south of what is now Tanzania and back into Mozambique.

The most famous explorer to reach this area was David Livingstone from Scotland, even though his claim to have been the first European to see Lake Malawi is refuted by the records of another Portuguese called Candido da Costa Cardoso, who came here in 1846. However, Livingstone's exploration heralded the arrival of Europeans in a way that was to change the nature of the region forever.

Livingstone & the First Missionaries

Between 1842 and 1856, Livingstone had been busy further south exploring the Kalahari Desert and the upper Zambezi. On his return to Britain, a speech in 1857 led to the founding of the Universities Mission in Central Africa (UMCA), which hoped to combat the slave trade by encouraging alternative commerce, and by establishing missions to promote Christianity.

Livingstone returned to Africa in 1858. His route up the Zambezi was blocked by the gorge and rapids at Cahora Bassa, so he followed a major Zambezi tributary called the Shire into southern Malawi. Blocked by more rapids at Kapichira, he continued on foot and

in September 1859 finally reached Lake Malawi, which he named Lake Nyassa. He returned in 1861 with seven UMCA missionaries. They established a mission in the Shire Highlands, and later on the Lower Shire, but suffered terribly from malaria and other illnesses, and were in conflict with slave-traders and local people. In 1864 the surviving missionaries withdrew to Zanzibar.

In 1866 Livingstone returned to Malawi again, on his quest to find the source of the Nile. In July 1869 he pushed north, to be eventually found by Henry Stanley at Lake Tanganyika in 1871, when Stanley uttered the immortal phrase 'Dr Livingstone, I presume'. Refusing to return with Stanley, Livingstone doggedly continued on his quest, finally dying near the village of Chief Chitambo, southeast of Lake Bangweulu in Zambia, in 1873.

Livingstone's death rekindled missionary zeal; in 1875, a group from the Free Church of Scotland built a new mission at Cape Maclear, which they named Livingstonia. In 1876 the Established Church of Scotland built a mission in the Shire Highlands, which they called Blantyre. Cape Maclear proved to be malarial, so the mission moved to Bandawe, then finally in 1894 to the high ground of the eastern escarpment. This site was successful; the Livingstonia mission flourished and is still there today (see Livingstonia under Northern Malawi later).

The Colonial Period

The early missionaries blazed the way for various adventurers and pioneer traders. In 1878 the Livingstonia Central African Mission Company (later renamed the African Lakes Corporation) was formed and built a trading centre in Blantyre. The company then established a commercial network along the Shire River and the shores of Lake Nyassa. As intended, this had a serious effect on the slave trade in the area, and after several clashes (the most notable being at Karonga) many slave-traders were forced to leave the area.

By the 1880s the competition among European powers in the area (known as the 'Scramble for Africa') was fierce. In 1889 Britain allowed Cecil Rhodes' British South Africa Company to administer the Shire Highlands, and in 1891 the British Central Africa (BCA) Protectorate was extended to

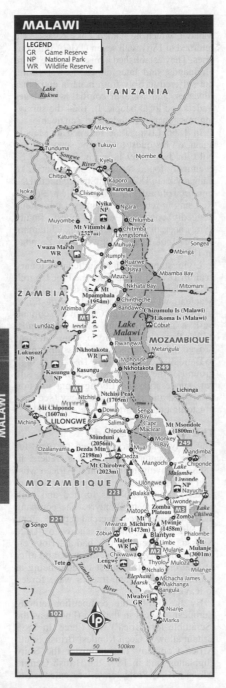

MALAWI

LEGEND
GR   Game Reserve
NP   National Park
WR   Wildlife Reserve

include land along the western side of the lake. Sir Harry Johnston was appointed first commissioner. In 1907 the BCA Protectorate became the colony of Nyasaland, and the number of settlers increased further from then on.

Initially colonial rule had some positive effects on the Africans in the region. Firstly, the colonialists got rid of the slave-traders. The intertribal conflicts that had plagued the area for so long also ceased, and other spin-offs included improvements in health care. However, as more European settlers arrived, the demand for land grew, and vast areas were bought from local chiefs. The hapless local inhabitants of the land found themselves labelled 'squatters' or tenants of a new landlord. A 'hut tax' was introduced and traditional methods of agriculture were discouraged. Hence, increasing numbers of Africans were forced to seek work on the white-settler plantations or to become migrant workers in Northern and Southern Rhodesia (present-day Zambia and Zimbabwe) and South Africa. By the turn of the 18th and 19th centuries some 6000 Africans were leaving the country every year. (The trend continued through the colonial period: by the 1950s this number had grown to 150,000.)

Early Protest
The first serious effort to oppose the Nyasaland colonial government was led by Reverend John Chilembwe, who protested in his preaching about white domination, and later about the forced conscription of African men into the British army at the outbreak of WWI.

In January 1915 Chilembwe and his followers attacked and killed the manager of a large estate. His plan had been to trigger a mass of uprisings, but these failed or didn't materialise, and the rebellion was swiftly crushed by the colonial authorities. Chilembwe was executed, his church was destroyed, and many supporters were imprisoned. Today Chilembwe is remembered as a national hero, with many streets named in his honour.

Transition & Independence
After WWI the British began allowing the African population a part in administrating the country. Things happened slowly, however, and it wasn't until the 1950s that

Africans were actually allowed to enter the government. The economic front was similarly sluggish; Nyasaland proved to be a relatively unproductive colony with no mineral wealth and only limited plantations.

In 1953, in an attempt to boost development, Nyasaland was linked with Northern and Southern Rhodesia in the Federation of Rhodesia and Nyasaland. But African disenchantment with colonial rule continued, and the federation was opposed by the pro-independence Nyasaland African Congress (NAC) party, led by Dr Hastings Banda. The colonial authorities declared a state of emergency and Banda was jailed.

By mid-1960 Britain was losing interest in its African colonies. Banda was released, and returned to head the now renamed Malawi Congress Party (MCP), which won elections held in 1962. The federation was dissolved, and Nyasaland became the independent country of Malawi in 1964. Two years later, Malawi became a republic and Banda was made president.

The Banda Years

President Banda began consolidating his position and demanded that several ministers declare their allegiance to him. Rather than do this, many resigned and took to opposition. Banda forced them into exile and banned other political parties. He continued to increase his power by becoming 'President for Life' in 1971, banning the foreign press, and waging vendettas against any group

regarded as a threat. He established Press Holdings, effectively his personal conglomerate, and the Agricultural Development and Marketing Corporation, to which all agricultural produce was sold at fixed rates, and thus gained total economic control.

Alongside this move towards dictatorship, Banda remained politically conservative. South Africa, concerned about the regional rise of African-governed socialist states elsewhere in the region, was delighted to have an ally, and rewarded Malawi with aid and trade. The Organisation of African Unity (OAU) was furious at Banda's refusal to ostracise the South African apartheid regime, although some commentators argued that at least his approach was honest and avoided the hypocrisy of countries that outwardly condemned South Africa while secretly maintaining links.

In 1978 in the first general election since independence, Banda personally vetted every candidate, and demanded that each pass an English examination (thereby precluding 90% of the population). Even with these advantages, one Banda supporter lost his seat. He was simply reinstated.

Banda retained his grip on the country through the 1980s. The distinctions between the president, the MCP, the country, the government and Press Holdings became increasingly blurred. Quite simply, Banda *was* Malawi.

The end of the East–West 'cold war' in the 1990s meant South Africa and the West no

The Naming of Malawi

The derivation of the name Malawi is disputed. When the explorer David Livingstone first reached Lake Malawi he called it Lake Nyassa (derived from the word nyanja, which simply means 'lake' in the language of the indigenous Chewa people) and recorded in his journal that Maravi people inhabited the area. Chewa and Nyanja may be two names for the same people, although some authorities refer to them as separate but part of the larger Maravi group. During colonial times, when the country was known as Nyasaland, the language of the Chewa was called Chi-Nyanja (or Chinyanja). (It was renamed Chichewa in 1968 and became the national language.)

At independence in 1964 a commission was established to find a new name for the new country. Malaŵi was chosen – inspired by the word *malavi*, which means 'reflected light', 'haze', 'flames' or 'rays' in Chichewa. (The word is also spelt *maravi* – 'l' and 'r' seem interchangeable in Chichewa.) This new name was seen as reference to the sun rising over the lake, bringing a fresh light to the country. It may also be connected to the Maravi people.

The 'ŵ' in Malawi was originally pronounced as a soft 'v'; English speakers should pronounce a sound somewhere between 'w', 'v' and 'f'. Nowadays the name of the country is generally pronounced with the 'w' sound, and the circumflex is often dropped.

MALAWI

longer needed to support Banda, and inside the country there was increasing opposition to him. In 1992 the Catholic bishops of Malawi condemned the regime and called for change. This was a brave action, for even bishops were not immune from Banda's iron grip. Demonstrations, both peaceful and violent, added their weight to the bishops' move. As a final blow, donor countries restricted aid until Banda agreed to relinquish total control.

In June 1993 a referendum was held for the people to choose between a multiparty political system and Banda's autocratic rule. Over 80% of eligible voters took part; those voting for a new system won easily, and Banda accepted the result.

Multiparty Democracy

Malawi's first full multiparty election (in May 1994) was a three-horse race between the United Democratic Front (UDF), led by Bakili Muluzi; the Alliance for Democracy (AFORD), led by trade unionist Chakufwa Chihana; and the MCP. Voting was largely along ethnic and regional lines: the MCP held the centre of the country, and AFORD dominated the north, but support in the more heavily populated south gave the UDF victory, although not an overall majority.

Once again, Banda accepted the result and Bakili Muluzi became Malawi's second president. He moved quickly – the political prisons were closed, freedom of speech and print was permitted, and free primary school education was to be provided. The unofficial night curfew that had existed during Banda's time was lifted. For travellers, the most tangible change was the repeal of Banda's notorious dress code that forbade women to wear trousers and men to have long hair.

The Muluzi Government also made several economic reforms with the help of the World Bank and the IMF; these included the withdrawal of state subsidies and the liberalisation of foreign exchange laws. Further measures led to the closure of many state-owned businesses. The downside of this was a rise in unemployment. A rationalisation of the civil service was also planned, which would add to the job losses.

In April 1995 former president Banda was brought to trial (with five others, including his 'official hostess' Cecelia Kadzamira and her uncle John Tembo, former second-in-command of the MCP). They were accused of ordering the murder of three government ministers who died in a mysterious car accident in 1983. All were acquitted and the result was greeted with general approval, especially when Banda went on to apologise publicly. As the population warmed once more to Banda, it became clear that the UDF's honeymoon period was well and truly over. Running the country was proving a tough job. Civil servants had gone on strike in mid-1995, following pay and job cuts. A scandal involving ministerial funds surfaced briefly, but was weathered.

By 1996 the economic reforms were hitting the average Malawian citizen very hard. Food prices soared as subsidies were reduced or withdrawn. The price of bread doubled, and the price of maize flour (the country's staple) rose eight-fold between mid-1994 and mid-1996. Unemployment was officially recorded at 50%, but may have been higher. There were reports of increased malnutrition, especially among the young. Crime, particularly robbery, increased in urban areas. Matters were made worse by a slow resumption of international aid, after it had been frozen in the final years of Banda's rule.

Malawi Today

In November 1997 Dr Banda finally died. His age was unknown, but he was certainly over 90. His death revived support for the MCP (now led by Gwanda Chakuamba), which was also helped by the continued poor performance of the UDF government. Unemployment and inflation remained high, while opposition politicians complained of corruption and mismanagement at the highest government levels. A UN report concluded that at least 70% of the population is nutritionally at risk.

Presidential and parliamentary elections were held in May 1999. President Muluzi won the race for president, and his party, the UDF, retained its majority in parliament, despite the two main opposition parties (MPC and AFORD) forming an alliance. Before and during the election the opposition accused the UDF of vote-rigging, and afterwards took their complaints to an electoral commission and then to the high court, claiming that Muluzi holding the position of president was unconstitutional.

While the MPs' claims and counterclaims are bandied back and forth, the ordinary people of Malawi have unfortunately become increasingly cynical and mistrustful of their politicians, and apathetic about the entire democratic process. Resentment is hardly alleviated by regular press reports of millions of dollars being spent on 'ghost' public servants, not to mention increased salaries and travel expenses for well-fed politicians (President Muluzi and his personal entourage clocked up US$2.5 million in travel expenses over just four months during 2002). Claims in the press of massive corruption and mismanagement of funds only adds fuel to the fire.

In July 2002 Muluzi attempted to change the constitution by proposing an Open Terms Bill to parliament, which would have given him life presidency. When it was defeated, he aired the idea of proposing a Third Term Bill instead, which would of course at least extend his presidency for one more term. The next elections are due in 2004 and it's yet to be seen whether or not his advances on power will be successful. Either way, President Muluzi and the UDF will need to make a significant change to the country in order to satisfy the heightened expectations of the Malawian people.

GEOGRAPHY

Malawi is wedged between Zambia, Tanzania and Mozambique, measuring roughly 900km long and between 80km and 150km wide, with an area of 118,484 sq km.

Lake Malawi covers almost a fifth of Malawi's total area. A strip of low ground runs along the western lakeshore, sometimes 10km wide, sometimes so narrow there's only room for a precipitous footpath between the lake and the steep wall of the valley. Beyond the lake, escarpments rise to high rolling plateaus covering much of the country. Malawi's main highland areas are Nyika and Viphya in the north and Mt Mulanje in the south.

Malawi's main river is the Shire (pronounced **Shir**-ee); it flows out of the southern end of Lake Malawi, through Lake Malombe and then southward as the plateau gives way to low ground, to flow into the Zambezi River in Mozambique. In this area, the lowest point is a mere 37m above sea level.

CLIMATE

Malawi has a single wet season, from November to April, when daytime temperatures are warm and conditions humid. May to August is dry and cool. September and October can become extremely hot and humid, especially in low areas.

Average daytime maximums in the lower areas are about 21°C in July and 26°C in January. In highland areas, average daytime temperatures in July are between 10°C and 15°C, while in September they reach 20°C and above. Average night-time temperatures in the highlands are low, sometimes dropping below freezing on clear nights in July.

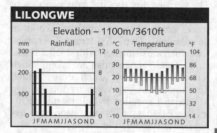

ECOLOGY & ENVIRONMENT

The main environmental challenges facing Malawi are deforestation and soil erosion, which result from a rapidly growing population and increasingly massive pressures on the land. Put starkly, Malawi's population is about the same as Mozambique's, but Malawi is one tenth of the size, giving it one of the highest population densities in Africa.

Deforestation

In the mid-1970s Malawi's forest cover was 4.4 million hectares. It's now under two million, with 50,000 hectares being cleared each year, mostly for fuel. Although some replanting is taking place, at this current unsustainable rate the woodlands and forests will eventually disappear.

Areas of grassland and scrubland (low bush) throughout Malawi are also being cleared and the land used to cultivate crops. Much of this is marginal land (ie, with poor soil or on steep hillsides), which would previously have been ignored by farmers. Because the soil is exposed for part of the year it is often washed away by rain, and the problem is compounded by unreliable rainfall; some years there's no rain, so the

MALAWI

crops fail and the bare soil is blown away by the wind. Even if the crops do grow, on the poor ground they tend to be stunted and low in nutrition. It's a grim scenario, and the end result is an increasing number of people living at starvation levels.

Overfishing

On Lake Malawi things are also at a difficult stage. Traditionally, people living by the lake have enjoyed a better standard of living than their cousins in the highlands. Fish supplies were plentiful and a good source of protein. But once again the population growth means things have changed. The demand for fish has grown, so more fish are caught every year, to an extent that stocks are now taken from the lake at an unsustainable level. As demand increases, fishermen are using nets with smaller holes, so even the youngest fish are taken, which reduces next year's catch even further. The amount of fish eaten by the average Malawian has fallen to half its mid-1970s level, a fall that means more people are living nearer starvation levels.

In an effort to minimise overfishing, the government imposes an 'off-season' moratorium, which prohibits the capture of certain fish for several months starting in November. The regulation is virtually impossible to police however, and most lakeshore inhabitants pay it scant regard.

Poaching

Poaching of wildlife from national parks was a major environmental problem in the 1980s and early 1990s (despite lip service paid to conservation by the former government), and wildlife was severely depleted. This hit tourism – a major money-earner in many parts of Malawi. The new government promised to combat poaching, but a lack of resources and commitment meant little changed. However, since the mid-1990s several parks and reserves have received funds from donor countries or organisations that should result in better antipoaching measures, plus improved access roads, management and staff morale. Part of the deal in most cases is that accommodation is leased out to private companies instead of being run by the Department of National Parks and Wildlife. This attracts tourists back and is better for Malawi in

the long run. One very positive step to reduce poaching in some parks has been the establishment of community-based Natural Resource Committees (see National Parks & Reserves later in this section).

FLORA & FAUNA

Malawi's vegetation zones include: miombo woodland in reliable rainfall areas (eg, Kasungu National Park); mopane woodland in hot lowland areas (eg, Shire Valley, lakeshore plains, Liwonde National Park); montane evergreen forest in highland areas (eg, Mulanje); semi-evergreen forest along river courses and on escarpment sides (eg, Zomba); montane grassland between 1800m and 2000m (eg, the Nyika Plateau); dense riverine woodland (eg, along the shores of Lake Malawi and along riverbanks); and wetland areas of reeds and grasses (all over the country – known locally as *dambos*).

Because Malawi lacks vast herds of easy-to-recognise animals such as rhinos and lions, it is not considered a major wildlife-viewing country. However, for those less concerned with simply ticking off the 'big five', the country has plenty to offer. The country's main park is Liwonde, noted for its herds of elephants, hippos and antelope species (including impalas, sables, kudus and elands) and its teeming birdlife. Kasungu National Park is also home to elephants, as is Nkhotakota Wildlife Reserve, where several antelope species, buffaloes and leopards also reside. Nyika National Park is renowned for roan antelopes and reedbucks, plus zebras, warthogs, elands, klipspringers, jackals, duikers and hartebeests. There's also a chance of seeing hyaenas and leopards. Nearby Vwaza Marsh has an abundance of hippos and elephants, but buffaloes, waterbucks, eland and roan antelopes, zebras, impalas and pukus are also present. In southern Malawi, Lengwe National Park supports a population of nyalas – at the northern limit of its distribution in Africa.

Malawi is a bird-watcher's dream because there's a good range of habitats in a relatively small area; over 600 species have been recorded, with several from the Central and East African regions. A visit to any of the parks or wildlife reserves will reward serious ornithologists, tourists and everyone in between with a diverse and colourful array of species.

Lake Malawi has more fish species than any other inland body of water in the world, with a total of over 500, of which more than 350 are endemic. (For more information see the boxed text 'Cichlid Fish' under Central Malawi later in this chapter.)

National Parks & Reserves

Malawi has five national parks: Liwonde, Lengwe, Kasungu, Nyika and Lake Malawi (around Cape Maclear). There are also four wildlife reserves: Vwaza Marsh, Nkhotakota, Mwabvi and Majete, which are less developed than the national parks, with fewer accommodation options and a more limited network of roads and tracks (if they exist at all). For more information on the facilities at each park and reserve see their individual listings later.

Malawi also has many forest reserves including Mt Mulanje and the Zomba Plateau. Some forest reserves have resthouses, and there's a series of huts on Mulanje for hikers.

In recent years, several of Malawi's national parks have benefited from successful relationships with community-based Natural Resource Committees. Each committee constitutes representatives from surrounding villages, and receives a percentage of the park's proceeds. The symbiotic result is reduced poaching and the capacity for local communities to take environmental issues such as overfishing and deforestation into their own hands

All parks and reserves cost US$5 per person per day (each 24-hour period), plus US$2 per car per day. Citizens and residents pay less. Other costs are for optional services: a fishing licence costs US$4 and the hire of a wildlife scout guide costs US$5 to US$10. All fees are payable in kwacha.

On top of these fees you pay for your accommodation; camping grounds and lodges

---

National Park Maps

The maps of national parks in this Malawi chapter show main routes only. It is not possible to show all roads: many original tracks have become overgrown or simply disappeared; some tracks are lost after heavy rains and rebuilt in other positions; and several new routes will be built as part of planned rehabilitation schemes.

---

are run by private safari companies in the most popular parks and reserves, but operated by the Department of National Parks and Wildlife elsewhere. Details of accommodation options in each park and reserve are given in the relevant sections.

GOVERNMENT & POLITICS

Malawi has a parliamentary system of government, with elections every five years. Separate presidential elections are held at the same time. The main parties are the Malawi Congress Party (MCP), the Alliance for Democracy (AFORD) and the United Democratic Front (UDF).

There are no major ideological differences between the various parties, except that the MCP is considered more traditional or conservative. Party following is based largely on regional or ethnic allegiances, and although various matters are hotly debated in parliament, there is very little genuine discussion on issues or policies. See the History section at the beginning of this chapter for more on government and politics.

ECONOMY

Malawi's economy is dominated by agriculture. Tobacco accounts for more than 60% of the country's export earnings. It is grown on large commercial plantations and on smaller farms cultivated by single families. Tea and sugar make up another 20% of export earnings. Tourism is seen as a great potential foreign currency generator, but has yet to be exploited fully.

For the average Malawian, economic conditions are not good. Malawi remains one of the world's 10 poorest countries, with a per capita gross national product (GNP) of US$170. Other socioeconomic indicators paint a grim picture: infant mortality is around 9% and although the population growth rate has dropped in recent years from around 4% to 1.4% per year, the fall is due largely to AIDS. Malawi has the second-highest disparity between rich and poor in the world.

In 2001 and 2002 unstable weather patterns caused a large percentage of Malawi's maize crops to fail. The government's reserve food stocks should have compensated for the disaster, except that they were sold in the following months (partly under instruction from the IMF) in order to repay

MALAWI

a commercial loan. Unfortunately private interests bought the grain, stored it and then sold it at augmented prices (at an increase of 400% between October 2001 and March 2002), effectively profiteering from starvation. The devaluation of the kwacha by almost half between 1999 and 2002 on top of a decrease in the price of tobacco (the country's main export) hasn't helped ordinary Malawians either; wages have remained the same, if not dropped and basic supplies have increased. Economic mismanagement and political uncertainty have further hindered domestic investment and the national debt is reported to be around US$2.8 billion, with very little prospect of it being reduced. Unemployment is also alarmingly high and it's estimated that less than 10% of young Malawians entering the job market each year will be employed.

POPULATION & PEOPLE

Estimates put Malawi's total population at approximately 11.6 million. About 85% of the people live in rural areas and are engaged in subsistence farming or fishing, or working on commercial farms and plantations.

The main ethnic groups are: Chewa, dominant in the central and southern parts of the country; Yao in the south; and Tumbuka in the north. Other groups are: Nguni, in parts of the central and northern provinces; Chipoka, also in the central area; and Tonga, mostly along the lakeshore. There are small populations of Asians and Europeans involved in commerce, plantations, aid or the diplomatic service. They are found mainly in the cities.

ARTS
Music

Home-grown contemporary music is becoming increasingly popular in Malawi, due largely to influential and popular musicians such as Lucius Banda, who plays soft 'Malawian-style' reggae with his band Zembani and the late Evison Matafale (see the boxed text 'The Martyr & the Music' following). Other reggae names to look out for are Billy Kaunda, Paul Banda and the Aleluya Band. Bubulezis play Jamaican-style reggae, while the Sapitwa Band tends towards Congo-style rhumba. Also popular is Ethel Kamwendo, one of Malawi's leading female singers. For more on other musical styles in the region, see the special colour section 'Beats of Southern Africa' earlier in this book.

Arts & Crafts

You'll see woodcarvings and stone carvings in craft shops and markets all over the country, but you won't find anything there by Nesto John Singano (see the boxed text

The Chewa

Although the Chewa constitute the largest ethnic group in Malawi, their ancestors actually originated in the Congo. Throughout the first millennium, they migrated first to Zambia and then down to central Malawi, conquering land from other Bantu people and establishing a vast kingdom in 1480 that encompassed southern Malawi and parts of Mozambique and Zambia. During the 17th century, Malawi experienced an influx of diverse cultures and dynasties, but the Chewa kept their ethnicity distinct through language, tattoos and secret societies.

The Chewa believe that God (Chiuta or Chautu) created all living things during a thunderstorm, at a mountain range bordering Malawi and Mozambique. They also believe that contact between spirits and the living is achieved through a dance called *gule wamkulu*, in which leading dancers dress in ragged costumes of cloth and animal skins, usually wearing a mask and occasionally standing on stilts. Today however, Chewa culture is an amalgamation of traditional beliefs and European influence; although Christianity is the dominant religion, it's common practise to seek resolution from a traditional witch doctor in times of illness or trouble. If you are interested in this process, you can arrange a consultation with the witch doctor on Likoma Island (for details see Likoma Island under Northern Malawi later in this chapter).

To really experience traditional Chewa culture, it's best to immerse yourself in a village. Njobvu Cultural Village (see Places to Stay under Liwonde National Park later in this chapter) hosts visitors for overnight stays, during which you can witness and participate in traditional dancing, rituals and village life.

The Martyr & the Music

In 2000 a young musician named Evison Matafale made his mark on Malawi's popular reggae scene, amassing huge domestic and growing international support with his charismatic melodies and outspoken social and political expression. His future was bright and he was soon declared Malawi's unofficial king of the genre.

Not all were charmed with his assessment of the government though and on 24 November 2001 he was arrested for allegedly writing a seditious letter criticising President Bakili Muluzi. Three days later, while still in police custody, Matafale was declared dead at Lilongwe Central Hospital.

The official post mortem, conducted by the hospital, indicated he died from acute pneumonia, and Matafale was certainly ill at the time of his incarceration (despite having performed in Blantyre a few days earlier). However, a second post mortem, conducted at the request of his brother – a UDF Regional Governor – suggested the cause of death was less clear, and that Matafale had sustained internal bleeding in the days leading to his death. An avalanche of public outrage ensued, prompting a joint commission of inquiry to probe the circumstances of the musician's death.

The official finding maintained the hospital's autopsy conclusion, but also found the police had exercised negligence by incarcerating Matafale when he was visibly ill. Of course, speculation regarding his final days continues to fuel public debate. What is without question is that the life of a talented and revered musician was tragically cut short, creating a martyr for all mediums of free expression in Malawi.

Matafale released two albums in his short-lived career – *Kuyimba 1* and *Kuyimba 2*; both can be bought on virtually any street corner in Malawi's larger towns and cities.

'Carving a Future' under Dedza later in this chapter), Kay Chirombo, Lemon Moses, Willie Nampeya, Berling Kaunda, Charley Bakari or Louis Dimpwa. These are some of Malawi's leading artists, producing sculpture, batiks and paintings, and many have exhibited outside Malawi. Possibly the best-known artist is Cuthy Mede – he is also actively involved in the development and promotion of Malawian art within the country and around the world. (See also Shopping under Facts for the Visitor later in this chapter.)

Literature

Like most countries in Africa, Malawi has a very rich tradition of oral literature. Since independence, a new school of writers has emerged, although thanks to the despotic President Banda's insensitivity to criticism, many were under threat of imprisonment and lived abroad until the mid-1990s. Not surprisingly, oppression, corruption, deceit and the abuse of power are common themes in their writing.

If you want a taste of current literature by well-known or new writers, try any of the short novels or poetry collections under the Malawi Writers Series imprint, available in good bookshops in Blantyre and Lilongwe. Most cost less than US$1.

Poetry is very popular: Steve Chimombo is a leading poet whose collections include *Napolo Poems*. His most highly acclaimed work is a complex poetic drama, *The Rainmaker*. To many Malawians he is better known for his popular short stories in newspapers and magazines, with their vivid combination of traditional themes and harsh urban settings.

Jack Mapanje's first poetry collection, *Of Chameleons and Gods,* was published in 1981, with much of its symbolism (chameleons play an important role in traditional Malawian beliefs) obscure for outsiders. Not too obscure for President Banda though – in 1987 Mapanje was arrested and imprisoned without charge. He was released in 1991, and two years later published *The Chattering Wagtails of Mikuyu Prison* – a reference to Malawi's notoriously harsh political jail.

Another significant literary figure is David Rubadi, who has compiled an anthology called *Poetry from East Africa* (which includes a section on Malawi) and also writes poetry himself. His novels include *No Bride Price*, which discusses the familiar themes of corruption and oppression.

Most critics agree that Malawi's leading novelist is Legson Kayira, whose semi-autobiographical *I Will Try* and *The Looming*

Banning the Press

It's worth noting that it wasn't only works of literature that incurred the wrath of President Banda. Several books on contemporary history were also banned, including, perhaps not surprisingly, *Malawi – the Politics of Despair*. Newspapers from other countries and from within Malawi were also frequently barred from circulation, especially if they were seen to be critical, but sometimes even if they weren't. Any form of pornography was also prohibited, but this included several medical textbooks, on the grounds that the diagrams were indecent. Even guidebooks didn't escape; an early Lonely Planet book called *Africa on the Cheap* (forerunner of *Africa on a shoestring*) was critical of the regime in the Malawi chapter, and was promptly banned as well. This meant travellers with a low-budget look were often searched for the scurrilous tome, and when I first visited Malawi in the early 1980s, getting across the Songwe border with the book intact was notoriously difficult.

David Else

Shadow earned him acclaim in the 1970s. A later work is *The Detainee*. Another novelist is Sam Mpasu. His *Nobody's Friend* was a comment on the secrecy of Malawian politics – it earned him a 2½-year prison sentence. After his release he wrote *Prisoner 3/75* and later became minister for education in the new UDF government. His comments on Banda's rule sum up the situation for all Malawian writers, and the people of Malawi too: 'We had peace, but it was the peace of a cemetery. Our lips were sealed by fear'.

LANGUAGE

English is the official language and very widely spoken. The different ethnic groups in Malawi also have their own languages or dialects.

The Chewa are the dominant group and Chichewa is the national language, widely used throughout the country as a common tongue. The 'Chi' prefix simply signifies 'language of'. Of all the other languages spoken, Tumbuka is dominant in the north and Yao in the south. See the Language chapter for some useful words and phrases in Chichewa, Tumbuka and Yao.

Facts for the Visitor

SUGGESTED ITINERARIES

Malawi is one of the smallest countries in the region and most of its attractions are relatively easy to reach, particularly with a combination of public transport and hire car. If you're tied completely to public transport (which is a cultural highlight in itself) and have limited time, you're best off focussing on either the north or south.

With a couple of weeks, you could head north from Lilongwe, via the Viphya Plateau to Mzuzu, from where you can reach the wilderness areas of Vwaza Marsh and Nyika Plateau and the historical sights of Livingstonia. You could then head to Nkhata Bay to enjoy Lake Malawi's sun, swimming and socialising, before catching the *Ilala* ferry over to Likoma and Chizumulu Islands. From here you could charter a flight or wait for the *Ilala* to take you back to the mainland and onto Lilongwe.

Alternatively, you could explore the south by heading straight to Senga Bay from Lilongwe, following Lake Malawi's southern curve to Mangochi and seeing the best of Malawi's wildlife in Liwonde National Park. Afterwards, you could wind past the Zomba Plateau to Blantyre, and then meander through Malawi's stunning tea plantations to get into some hiking on Mt Mulanje. If you've a day or two spare, you could take in a side trip to Majete Wildlife Reserve from Blantyre, before heading back to Lilongwe.

With a month or longer you could encompass all of these highlights and explore some of the lakeshore's remote retreats including Ruarwe and Usisya. Or maybe you could fill the days with bird-watching, scuba diving, snorkelling, horse riding, hiking or simply lazing on the beach.

The Big Trip

It's an easy route from Zambia's South Luangwa National Park to Lilongwe and many people access Malawi this way. The comfortable coaches between Harare and Blantyre are also popular. From either Lilongwe or Blantyre, you can take in some of Lake Malawi's scenery at Senga Bay or Cape Maclear and then head down, via Mangochi, to the Mozambican border town of Mandimba. From here you can head east to Cuamba, Nampula and ultimately, Mozambique Island.

Travel Tips

The road from Monkey Bay to Cape Maclear is only 12km or so, but allow plenty of time – it's a rough and slow ride. Before squeezing onto any matola (particularly those with 20 plus passengers) scan the tyres and clearance.

PLANNING
When to Go

The best time to visit Malawi is during the dry season from April/May to October. From May to July the landscape is attractive because the vegetation is green and lush. Malawi is coolest in July, increasingly warm towards September and when the landscape starts to dry out, positively hot in October and November before the rains break. Late in the dry season is the best time for wildlife viewing, but conditions can be sizzling.

Maps

Useful maps, available in local bookshops, include the government-produced *Malawi* (1:1,000,000), showing shaded relief features and most roads, and the *Malawi Road & Tourist Map* (same scale), showing all main roads, some minor roads and national parks (but no relief) plus street maps of the main towns.

For more detail, government survey maps (1:50,000 and 1:250,000) are available from the Department of Surveys Map Sales Offices in Blantyre and Lilongwe. Specific maps and guidebooks on national parks and hiking areas are detailed under the listings for these areas.

TOURIST OFFICES

There are tourist offices in Blantyre and Lilongwe, and a Department of Wildlife & Tourism office in Lilongwe (see that section for details). Outside Malawi, tourism promotion is handled by UK-based **Malawi Tourism** (☎ 0115-982 1903, fax 0115-981 9418; **w** www.malawitourism.com), which responds to inquiries from all over the world.

VISAS & DOCUMENTS
Visas

Visas are not needed by citizens of Commonwealth countries, the USA and most European nations (except Switzerland). Visas are limited to 30 days, although extensions are easy to get.

Visas for Onward Travel If you need visas for neighbouring countries while in Malawi, these are the conditions:

Mozambique Visas are available in Lilongwe and Limbe; both offices are open from 8am to noon weekdays. Transit visas cost US$12 and are issued within 24 hours. One-month single-entry visas cost US$18 and take four working days to issue, but you can pay an extra US$3.50 to have it issued in one day. It's also possible to get a one-month single-entry visa at the Zóbué border for US$22 (payable only in US currency).

South Africa Visas are free and take two days to issue. The high commission in Lilongwe is open from 8am to noon weekdays.

Tanzania There is no Tanzanian representation in Malawi, but visas are administered at the border, or on arrival at the airport and cost US$50.

Zambia The cost of a single-entry visa depends on your nationality: Brits pay US$42; all others pay US$24 (payable in kwacha). Applications can be made between 8am and 4.30pm (closed between 12.30pm and 2pm) on Monday and Tuesday, or Wednesday morning and passport collection is on Friday only, between 8am and noon.

Zimbabwe Single-entry visas for up to six months cost US$48 (payable in kwacha) and double-entry visas cost US$71. Both take a week to issue. The office in Lilongwe is open from 8am to noon weekdays. Visas are also available at the border, but you must pay in US dollars.

Visa Extensions You can get an extension on your visa at immigration offices in Blantyre or Lilongwe (see those sections for details) or at regional police stations. The process is straightforward and free.

EMBASSIES & CONSULATES
Malawian Embassies & High Commissions

Malawi has diplomatic missions in the following African countries: Kenya, Mozambique, South Africa, Tanzania, Zambia and Zimbabwe (embassies in the countries covered in this book are listed in the relevant country chapters). Elsewhere around the world, Malawian embassies include:

Canada (☎ 613-236 8931) 7 Clemow Ave, Ottawa, Ontario KIS 2A9
France (☎ 01 4070 1846) 20 Rue Euler, 75008 Paris
Germany (☎ 49 228 343 016) Mainzerstrasse 124, 53179 Bonn
Tanzania (☎ 255 22 113 239) 6th Floor Nic Life House, Dar es Salaam

UK (☎ 020-7491 4172) 33 Grosvenor St, London W1X 0DE
USA (☎ 202-797 1007) 2408 Massachusetts Ave NW, Washington DC 20008

Although Malawi has no high commission in Australia, it is represented by the **Consular Office, Australian Department of Foreign Affairs and Trade** (☎ 02-6261 3305; *John McEwen Crescent, Barton, ACT 2600*).

Embassies & Consulates in Malawi

The following countries have diplomatic representation in Malawi:

Canada (☎ 01 645441) Accord Centre, Limbe
Germany (☎ 772555) Convention Dr, City Centre, Lilongwe
Mozambique *Embassy:* (☎ 774100) Convention Dr, City Centre, Lilongwe
   Consulate: (☎ 643189) First floor Celtel Building, Rayner Ave, Limbe
South Africa (☎ 773722, e sahe@malawi.net) Kang'ombe Bldg, City Centre, Lilongwe
UK *High Commission:* (☎ 772400) off Kenyatta Rd, City Centre, Lilongwe
   Consulate: Hanover Ave, Blantyre
USA (☎ 773166) Convention Dr, City Centre, Lilongwe
Zambia (☎ 772590) Convention Dr, City Centre, Lilongwe
Zimbabwe (☎ 774997) off Independence Dr, City Centre, Lilongwe

CUSTOMS

There are no restrictions on the amount of foreign currency that travellers can bring into or take out of Malawi. Technically, import or export of more than MK200 is forbidden, but a bit more than this is unlikely to be a problem.

MONEY
Currency

Malawi's unit of currency is the Malawi kwacha (MK). This is divided into 100 tambala (t).

Bank notes include MK200, MK100, MK50, MK20, MK10 and MK5. Coins include MK1, 50t, 20t, 10t, 5t and 1t, although the small tambala coins are virtually worthless.

Inflation is high in Malawi, so quoting costs in MK is not helpful, as prices may

have changed significantly by the time you arrive. Therefore we have used US dollars (US$) throughout this chapter. Although the actual exchange rate will have changed by the time you reach Malawi, the cost of things in US dollars (or any other hard currency) should not have altered as much. At big hotels and other places that actually quote in US dollars you can pay in hard currency or kwacha at the prevailing exchange rate.

Exchange Rates

The following rates were correct at the time of print:

country	unit		kwacha
Australia	A$1	=	k61.51
Botswana	P1	=	k17.92
Canada	C$1	=	k68.69
euro zone	€1	–	k109.10
Japan	¥100	=	k78.80
Mozambique	Mtc100	=	k0.40
New Zealand	NZ$1	=	k53.57
South Africa	R1	=	k11.70
Tanzania	Tsh100	=	k9.25
UK	UK£1	=	k154.67
USA	US$1	=	k92.78
Zambia	ZK100	=	k1.93
Zimbabwe	ZW$100	=	k11.45

Exchanging Money

You can exchange your cash and travellers cheques at the National Bank of Malawi and the Commercial Bank of Malawi (for general opening hours, see Business Hours later). The charge is usually 1% of the transaction amount; for travellers cheques the bank also checks the original purchase receipt.

There are foreign exchange bureaus in the cities and large towns. These usually offer a slightly better rate than the banks, and have lower charges (or none at all), so they are always worth checking.

There's no real black market in Malawi. You may get one or two kwacha more for your dollar on the street, but the chances of robberies or cons (or fake US$50 and US$100 bills) means that the risk is not really worth taking compared to going to a bank or exhange bureau. Alternatively, shops that sell imported items sometimes need dollars and buy at around 5% to 10% more than bank or foreign exchange bureau rates.

'Sorry, No Change'

The lack of small coins and notes in shops and markets constantly frustrates travellers, who inevitably get large denomination notes when they change money in the banks and bureaus. Get and keep as much small change as you can, especially if you're going to Lake Malawi. Otherwise you'll end up with a pocket full of 'Cape Maclear currency' – little bits of cardboard saying 'I owe you 3 kwacha'.

Credit & Debit Cards You can get cash with a Visa card at the Commercial Bank of Malawi in Blantyre. The charge is US$3.80; the process sometimes takes several hours, but if you go in the morning before 9am it can be quicker. Otherwise, leave your card and details, and come back later to pick up your cash. No card transactions are started after 1pm. Alternatively, some foreign exchange bureaus provide the same service for around US$2.50 and transactions are completed on the spot.

You can use Visa cards at some but not all of the large hotels and top-end restaurants (be warned that this may add a 5% to 10% surcharge to your bill). It seems even harder to use a MasterCard, although Diners Club cards are accepted at a few places in Blantyre and Lilongwe that won't take Visa. If you usually rely on plastic, you're better off using it to draw out cash and paying with that.

Costs

Generally, costs in Malawi are low compared to costs in most other countries in the region, although some national park accommodation is relatively expensive. Budget travellers who camp or stay in hostel dorms, catch the cheapest (slowest!) forms of public transport and self-cater or eat at food stalls can manage on US$10 per day.

A little more comfort and quality in hotel rooms or double rooms in hostels, restaurants (including the odd drink) and quicker transport notches a daily budget up to US$30. Big spenders are also catered for in Malawi, with top-shelf hotels, domestic flights and transfers, and fine dining, all of which will cost around US$250 per day.

POST & COMMUNICATIONS
Post

Post in and out of Malawi is a bit of a lottery. Some letters get from Lilongwe to London in three days, others take three weeks. Mail from Lilongwe or Blantyre to Cape Town often takes a month. In rural areas, the post can be very slow. Post offices in Blantyre and Lilongwe have poste restante services.

To African destinations, letters less then 10g and postcards cost US$0.45. To Europe, India, Pakistan and the Middle East it's US$0.50 and to the Americas, Japan or Australasia postage is US$0.55. It's quicker (and probably more reliable) to use the EMS Speedpost service at post offices. Letters up to 500g cost US$5 to Europe and US$7 to Australia and the USA.

Airmail parcel rates used to be famously cheap, allowing you to send home large woodcarvings at a low price. It now costs about US$10 plus US$3 per kilo to send items outside Africa. Surface mail is cheaper.

Telephone

International calls (to destinations outside Africa) from public phone offices cost around US$8.50 for a three-minute minimum. Cheaper rates are technically available from 6pm Friday to 7am Monday but this often doesn't translate at phone bureaus. At hotels the service may be quicker, but charges are often US$25 for three minutes to anywhere outside Africa. To make an international call from Malawi, the code is ☎ 00. The international code for Malawi if you're dialling from abroad is ☎ 265.

Telephone calls within Malawi are inexpensive; around US$0.30 per minute depending on the distance, and the network between main cities is reliable, although the lines to outlying areas are often not working. Calls to mobiles within Malawi cost around US$0.65 per minute. Public phones (called 'booths') take new MK1 coins only.

Malawi does not have area codes, but all landline numbers begin with ☎ 01, so whatever number you dial within the country will have eight digits. Numbers starting with 7 are on the Lilongwe exchange; those starting with 6 are in Blantyre; 5 is around Zomba; 4 is the south; 3 is the north; and 2 is the Salima area. Numbers starting with 8 or 9 are for mobile phones and are prefixed with ☎ 08 and ☎ 09 respectively.

MALAWI

Email & Internet Access

Internet access is available in Lilongwe, Blantyre and Mzuzu (see those sections later for details). Internet bureaus are also making an appearance elsewhere in the country but tend to be more expensive. Some hotels and lodges will let guests send or receive email for a nominal fee.

DIGITAL RESOURCES

The following websites are worth a look (see Digital Resources in the Regional Facts for the Visitor chapter for a more comprehensive listing).

Africa News (**W** www.africanews.org) Use to follow the links for Malawi News online.
Malawi/Cities.Com (**W** www.malawi.com) A glossy and informative site with some useful links.
Malawi.Net (**W** www.malawi.net) This has links to sites of local newspapers and political parties.
Official Website of the Malawi Ministry of Tourism, Parks and Wildlife (**W** www.tourismmalawi.com) A comprehensive resource for all things tourism in Malawi.
Omni Resources (**W** www.omnimap.com) Topographic maps of Malawi can be ordered online.

BOOKS

This section covers books specific to Malawi; titles on the whole Southern Africa region are covered under Books in the Regional Facts for the Visitor chapter. Literature by Malawian writers is covered under Arts in the Facts about Malawi section.

Lonely Planet

Malawi, Lonely Planet's specific guide, gives more in-depth coverage of Malawi. *Trekking in East Africa* includes a good section on Malawi and is recommended for trekkers and hikers.

Guidebooks

Day Outings from Lilongwe and *Day Outings from Blantyre*, both published by the Wildlife Society of Malawi, are highly recommended. They are well written and researched, and include suggestions on places to visit, things to see and local walks in the region. They have an emphasis on wildlife and cover a surprisingly wide area. The only problem is that they're aimed mostly at people with cars – thereby precluding many travellers and about 99% of Malawi's population.

Malawi's National Parks & Game Reserves, by John Hough, covers all parks and reserves in the country, with full details of flora and fauna occurring in each.

Lake Malawi's Resorts, by Ted Sneed, covers in detail every place to stay (more than 70) on the lakeshore. It took so long to research that by the time Ted got to the southern end, some new places had opened in the north!

Field Guides

Birds of Malawi: A Supplement to Newman's Birds of Southern Africa, by KB Newman, 'bridges the bird gap' between species covered in Southern Africa and East African guides. (For more titles on bird-watching, see the Field Guides under Books in the Regional Facts for the Visitor chapter.)

Cichlids & Other Fishes of Lake Malawi, by A Koning, is encyclopaedic – in both size and coverage.

Guide to the Fishes of Lake Malawi, by L Digby, is sometimes called the 'WWF guide' as this organisation was the publisher. In contrast to Koning's tome, this guide is small, portable and perfect for amateurs, although not easy to find as it was published in 1986.

Trees of Malawi, by JS Pullinger & AM Kitchen, is a large-format book with detailed colour illustrations.

Travel

Venture to the Interior, by Laurens van der Post, describes the author's 'exploration' of Mt Mulanje and the Nyika Plateau in the 1940s, although in reality this was hardly trailblazing stuff.

History

A Lady's Letters from Central Africa, by Jane Moir, was written in the 1890s by 'the first woman traveller in Central Africa'.

Livingstone's Lake, by Oliver Ransford, a classic book on Lake Malawi and the surrounding countries, was published in the 1960s and is now quite rare.

Nyasa – A Journal of Adventures, by ED Young is a local history book written in the 1870s (reprinted in 1984); it's a missionary's account of the original Livingstonia mission at Cape Maclear.

A Short History of Malawi, by BR Rafael, is hard to find, but the writing is quite accessible.

Bungee jumping, Victoria Falls, Zimbabwe

Surfing, near Cape Town, South Africa

Palm trees, Makgadikgadi Pans, Botswana

Mokoro (canoe), Okavango Delta, Botswana

Lion, Moremi Wildlife Reserve, Botswana

General

Between the Cape and Cairo, by artist Tony Grogan, is a splendid coffee-table book, with a collection of sketches and paintings from all parts of Malawi.

Jungle Lovers, by Paul Theroux, is a light humorous novel, set in a mythical country immediately recognisable to many as Banda-era Malawi. It neatly captures life in Africa for locals and foreigners.

Malawi – Lake of Stars, by Frank Johnston, features a collection of beautiful photographs with evocative text by Vera Garland.

Malawi – The Warm Heart of Africa, by Frank Johnston and Sandy Ferrar, is a coffee-table book with excellent photography, but meatier text, focussing largely on Malawi's grave environmental issues.

NEWSPAPERS

Malawi's main newspapers are *the Daily Times* and *Malawi News,* both supportive of the MCP – and *The Nation,* which is more objective. *The Chronicle* is a smaller publication but with a stronger independent voice (read relentless criticism of the government).

RADIO & TV

Malawi's national radio station, the Malawi Broadcasting Corporation, combines music, news and chat shows in English, Chichewa and some other local languages. International news is brief but wide-ranging. There are also commercial music stations in the large cities.

Malawi's national TV station was launched in 1999 and consists mostly of imported programmes, news, regional music videos and religious programmes. International satellite channels are available in most mid-range and top-end hotels.

PHOTOGRAPHY & VIDEO

General aspects of photography in the region are covered in the Regional Facts for the Visitor chapter. In Malawi film and camera parts are generally only available in Blantyre and Lilongwe.

In the cities, Fuji or Konika 100 ASA 36-exposure print film costs about US$3.50 and developing and printing costs about US$6 for 24 exposures or US$8 to US$10 for 36. Two passport pictures will cost you around US$3.

HEALTH

General aspects are covered under Health in the Regional Facts for the Visitor chapter. The most important health concern specific to Malawi is the presence of bilharzia in Lake Malawi (see the boxed text 'The Great Bilharzia Story' later in this chapter).

Most large towns have a hospital and pharmacy that are reasonably well stocked. Malawi's main hospitals are at Blantyre and Lilongwe (see Information in those sections for more details).

DANGERS & ANNOYANCES
Crime

Unfortunately, reports of travellers being robbed in Lilongwe and Blantyre have increased. However, incidents are still rare compared with other countries, and violence is not the norm. Some safety advice is given in the Lilongwe and Blantyre sections. There have also been robberies at popular lakeshore areas such as Cape Maclear and Nkhata Bay, but here violence is very rare. While robbery can never be condoned, this problem shouldn't be blamed entirely on Malawians. It's also due partly to the increased number of tourists, some of whom are incredibly insensitive when it comes to displays of wealth and possessions, or downright irresponsible when it comes to walking in unlit areas late at night. Whatever the reason, the situation should be put into perspective: Malawi is still safer than many other parts of Southern Africa.

Scams to be aware of if you're buying curios are the eager young men who offer to wrap your purchase in paper and cardboard, then want more for this job than you paid for the carving. Also on the economic front, beware of locals asking you to break a US$100 bill into US$10 bills and US$20 bills. Naturally, the US$100 bill is a fake.

Wildlife

Potential dangers at Lake Malawi include encountering a hippo or crocodile, but for travellers the chances of being attacked are extremely remote. Crocodiles tend to be very wary of humans and are generally only found in quiet vegetated areas around river mouths (although they may sometimes be washed into the lake by floodwater). Therefore you should be careful if you're walking along the lakeshore and have to

MALAWI

wade a river. Popular tourist beaches are safe, although, just to be sure, you should seek local advice before diving in. The most dangerous animals in Malawi are the mosquitoes that transmit malaria (see Health in the Regional Facts for the Visitor chapter).

LEGAL MATTERS
Drugs
Cannabis is widely available in Malawi but be warned that buying, selling, possessing and using are all serious offences. The maximum penalty is life imprisonment or a fine of US$35,000. Travellers caught are likely to spend a few days in jail, be fined a lesser amount and then deported. Some dealers are police informers, and the police have been known to raid camp sites, arrest offenders and then let them go free on payment of a large unofficial 'fine'. Either way it can be scary and very expensive.

BUSINESS HOURS
Offices and shops in the main towns are usually open from 7.30am or 8am to 5pm weekdays, with an hour for lunch between noon and 1pm. Many shops are also open Saturday

morning. In smaller towns, shops and stalls are open most days, but keep informal hours. Bank hours are usually from 8am to 1pm or 2pm weekdays. Post and telephone offices are usually open from 7.30am to 4.30pm weekdays. In Blantyre and Lilongwe, they also open Saturday morning.

PUBLIC HOLIDAYS & SPECIAL EVENTS
Public holidays in Malawi are:

New Year's Day 1 January
John Chilembwe Day 15 January
Martyrs' Day 3 March
Easter March/April – Good Friday, Holy Saturday and Easter Monday
Labour Day 1 May
Freedom Day 14 June
Republic Day 6 July
Mother's Day October – second Monday
National Tree Planting Day December – second Monday
Christmas Day 25 December
Boxing Day 26 December

When one of these dates falls on a weekend, normally the following Monday is a

The Great Bilharzia Story

Bilharzia (or schistosomiasis) is a disease that occurs all over Africa. It is transmitted by minute worms carried by infected humans and water snails. Both 'hosts' need to be present for the worms to transmit the disease. Bilharzia can be contracted if you swim or paddle in lakes, ponds or any shallow water, especially near villages or where reeds grow.

For many years Malawi's health and tourism departments stated that Lake Malawi was bilharzia-free. Only since the mid-1990s has it emerged that this claim was simply untrue – bilharzia is definitely present. A lot of people fell for it, including, it has to be said, Lonely Planet. Early editions of our *Africa on a shoestring* duly reported that Lake Malawi was free of bilharzia. Local tour companies were hoodwinked also, or went along with the pretence. A hotel on the shore of Lake Malawi sent its staff out early every morning to clear surrounding reeds of snails, without warning guests that the worms might still be present.

Although parts of the lake may be very low risk, in other areas – including some popular tourist destinations – you undoubtedly have a high chance of contracting bilharzia. There's no need to panic, and absolutely no reason to avoid coming to Lake Malawi – and once there, who could resist swimming in those beautiful waters?! But you must be aware of the risk.

If you do decide to swim, and you do contract bilharzia, you might suffer from some symptoms almost immediately, in which case you should seek treatment fast. But usually symptoms do not show until the disease is well established – and this can be weeks or months after exposure. Long-term effects can be very harmful, so it is *absolutely essential* that you have a check-up for the disease when you get back home or reach a place with good medical services. Be sure your doctor is familiar with bilharzia, and be aware that the disease may have a long incubation period and may not be initially apparent, so you might need more than one test. For more information see Health in the Regional Facts for the Visitor chapter.

public holiday. Islamic holidays are also observed throughout Malawi by the Muslim population.

ACTIVITIES

This section provides only a brief overview of what's available throughout Malawi; for more information see the relevant sections (eg, for hiking see the Mulanje section later in this chapter).

Lake Malawi's population of colourful fish (see the boxed text 'Cichlid Fish' under Central Malawi later in this chapter) attracts travellers to **scuba diving**. The lake is reckoned by experts to be among the best freshwater diving areas in the world – and one of the cheapest places to learn how to dive. Places where you can hire scuba gear and learn to dive include Nkhata Bay, Cape Maclear, Likoma Island and Senga Bay, plus Club Makokola and some of the other hotels and camping grounds on the southern lakeshore. Most hotels and camps also rent **snorkelling** equipment.

Many of the more upmarket places along the lake have facilities for **water-skiing** or **windsurfing**. You can also go **sailing**, or join luxurious 'sail safaris' where everything is done for you. **Canoeing** is available at Cape Maclear and Nkhata Bay.

You can go **fishing** in Lake Malawi for *mpasa* (also called lake salmon), *ncheni* (lake tiger), *sungwa* (a type of perch), *kampango* or *vundu* (both catfish). There are trout in streams on Nyika, Zomba and Mulanje Plateaus, and tigerfish can be hooked in the Lower Shire.

The main areas for **hiking** are Nyika and Mulanje. Other areas include Zomba, and various smaller peaks around Blantyre. Mulanje is Malawi's main **rock climbing** area, with some spectacular routes (including the longest in Africa), although local climbers also visit smaller crags and outcrops.

The main area for **horse riding** is the Nyika Plateau, which lends itself perfectly to travel on horseback. You can go on short rides or longer multiday safaris. If you prefer non-animated transport, Nyika's hilly landscape and good network of dirt tracks are also great for **mountain biking**.

ACCOMMODATION

Malawi's range of places to stay has expanded rapidly in the last few years. Several smart new hotels and lodges have been built along the lake and in the national parks. Backpackers are well-catered for in lakeshore lodges and cheap resthouses in towns and villages. Mosquito nets are fairly important as malaria is a real problem, fortunately most places to stay provide nets in their rooms.

Budget

At the budget end of the price range, in almost every town there is a council or government resthouse. Prices vary from as little as US$1 up to around US$5 a double, but conditions are generally spartan to say the least and downright disgusting at worst. In national parks and along the lakeshore, many places offer camping and self-catering chalets or cabins. Some camping grounds are pretty basic, while others have good facilities.

Backpacker hostels are present in the main cities, and numerous in popular lakeshore destinations such as Cape Maclear and Nkhata Bay. Prices range from US$3 for a dorm up to about US$8 per person for a double or triple. Camping is usually about US$1 to US$3.

Mid-Range & Top End

Mid-range hotels range from about US$30 to US$80 per double, including taxes, usually with private bathroom and breakfast. The quality of service at a smaller place can be just as good as or even better than at the pricey establishments, though.

Top-end hotels or lodges generally range from US$150 to US$250 for a double room, with facilities such as private bathroom, TV, air-con and telephone, and including taxes and breakfast. At the very top of the scale in Malawi you may pay US$240 per person per night, although in such places (eg, Mvuu Wilderness Lodge in Liwonde National Park or Chelinda Lodge in Nyika National Park) this includes all meals and activities such as wildlife drives.

FOOD
Budget

If you're self-catering, **PTC** supermarkets are found all over Malawi and **Shoprite** has made an entrance in larger cities. Both stock locally produced and imported goods, many of them from South Africa or Europe and sold at similar prices.

MALAWI

Markets and bus stations usually harbour a collection of food stalls, where, for breakfast, you can get tea with milk for US$0.20 and a bread cake or deep fried cassava for US$0.10. At lunchtime, these may serve simple meals of beans or meat and *nshima* (maize meal) for about US$0.50. Fried potato is usually on offer all day for around US$0.20.

Up a grade from here are the local restaurants in small towns where the surroundings are slightly better and simple meals cost around US$1.50.

In cities and larger towns, cheap restaurants serve traditional Malawian food as well as chicken or fish (the most popular being *chambo*) with rice or chips for around US$2.50. Slightly fancier restaurants also do European- or American-style food such as burgers, fried chicken or simple curries. Prices are normally around US$3 to US$5, depending on the surroundings as much as the food itself, and whether you eat in or takeaway. Most also serve cheaper snacks such as sandwiches or sausage rolls for US$1 to US$2.

Mid-Range & Top-End

Most mid-range hotels and restaurants serve European-style food such as steak, chicken or fish, which is served with vegetables and chips or rice – usually around the US$5 mark.

At top-end hotels and restaurants in cities and along the lakeshore, you can find the straightforward international standards mentioned previously, plus more elaborate French, British or Italian cuisine. If you're hankering for something different, in Blantyre and Lilongwe you can find restaurants serving Ethiopian, Indian, Korean, Chinese and Portuguese food. Main courses range from around US$5 to US$10.

DRINKS

Tea, coffee and soft drinks are widely available in many places, from top-end hotels and restaurants to the lowliest local eateries.

Traditional beer of the region is made from maize; in Malawi this is commercially brewed as Chibuku, and sold all over the country in large red-and-blue cartons, with the tantalising slogan 'It's Hygienic'. For most travellers, the thick texture and bittersweet taste are not appealing.

Most travellers (and many Malawians) prefer the beer produced by Carlsberg at its Blantyre brewery (the only one in Africa). There are three main types of beer: 'greens' (lager), 'browns' (like a British ale) and 'golds' (a stronger brew). If you're a beer fan, you can visit the brewery (see Things to See & Do under Blantyre & Limbe later in this chapter).

SHOPPING

For shoppers, Malawi offers a wide range of curios and souvenirs, including animals and figures carved from wood; ornaments such as bowls and chess sets; and the popular chief's chair, a two-piece three-legged stool with a high and intricately-carved back.

You can also find plenty of objects made from grass and palm leaves, such as baskets and boxes, or intricate models of cars and lorries, and even overland trucks! (See the boxed text 'Carving a Future' later in this chapter.) Contemporary soapstone carvings, paintings, pottery, clay figures and malachite jewellery are also available.

You can buy at roadside craft stalls or curio shops – in among the stuff that's hammered out in a hurry you will also find works in wood and stone (and occasionally paintings) that have been created by artists of better-than-average talent. Salespeople often seem

---

Food & Accommodation Taxes

All mid-range and top-end restaurants and hotels charge 10% service charge, 10% tourist tax and 10% VAT. You should therefore add 30% to the costs shown on menus and tariff sheets. If in doubt, ask if the price is inclusive or not, as it can make quite a difference. Wherever possible in this book we have given prices inclusive of these taxes.

The 10% service charge officially means that tipping is not necessary, but this is not all it seems as hotels and restaurants who make the 10% service charge have to pass on 60% of this to the Ministry of Tourism, for use in a general marketing fund, so that the staff actually receive only 4% of the total you pay for your room and meal.

to make no distinction between good and mediocre work, so it's always worth spending time to search the better pieces out. Prices are usually not fixed, so you have to bargain. However, if you prefer not to haggle, there are some shops in Blantyre and Lilongwe that use price-tags. (See also Arts under Facts about Malawi earlier in this chapter.)

In markets all over Malawi you can buy *chitenjas*, sheets of brightly coloured cloth that local women use as wraps, cloaks, scarves and baby carriers. They're also available at several shops along Haile Selassie Rd in Blantyre. They make nice souvenirs and are practical items for women travellers, especially if you're heading for the beach or rural areas where shorts are frowned on.

Getting There & Away

This section covers access into Malawi from neighbouring countries only. Information about reaching Southern Africa from elsewhere on the African continent and from other continents is outlined in the regional Getting There & Away chapter.

AIR

Malawi's main airport for international flights is at Lilongwe. It has a pharmacy, a post office, a bookshop, banks and car hire desks, plus a restaurant and bar overlooking the runway where you can use up the last of your kwacha before flying out (although beware of waiters overcharging).

There is also an airport at Blantyre, which is mostly served by regional and domestic flights. It has a small cafeteria, a bookshop and an Avis desk.

Departure Tax

For travellers flying out, the airport departure tax for international flights is US$20, payable in US dollars in cash. No other currency is accepted.

Southern Africa

Most regional flights go to and from Lilongwe, but some flights serve Blantyre. All of the following fares are one way; returns are double, but 'excursion fares' or specials can be cheaper.

Air Malawi (W *www.airmalawi.net)* has a pretty good regional network, with three flights a week to Harare (US$213) and two flights a week to both Lusaka (US$189) and Johannesburg (Jo'burg) (US$477). The following regional airlines also serve Malawi, usually flying on the days Air Malawi doesn't (so you get a wider choice of flights), with fares mostly on a par: **Air Zimbabwe** (W *www.airzimbabwe.com)* flies three times per week to/from Harare (with connections to Victoria Falls and other parts of Southern Africa); **South African Airways** (W *www.flysaa.com)* flies twice per week to/from Jo'burg (with connections to Durban, Cape Town etc); and **Kenya Airways** (W *www.kenya-airways.com)* flies four times per week to/from Nairobi (US$475).

The **Nyika Safari Company** (☎ 330180; e *reservations@nyika.com)* operates charter flights out of Nyika National Park (see that section under Northern Malawi later in this chapter) and can arrange a five-seater plane between Chelinda Camp and Mbeya in Tanzania (US$850) or Mfuwe in Zambia (US$1250).

LAND
Border Crossings

Malawi shares borders with Tanzania, Zambia and Mozambique. The only land crossing to/from Tanzania is at Songwe, north of Kaporo, where a bridge crosses the Songwe River. (A new bridge is planned further upstream). The main border crossing with Zambia is about 100km northwest of Lilongwe, on the main road to Lusaka. Malawi does not directly border Zimbabwe, but a lot of traffic between these two countries passes through a neck of Mozambican territory called the Tete Corridor.

All Malawi's border crossings are officially open from 6am to 6pm (possibly open later and shut earlier, but never the other way around).

If you're bringing a car into Malawi from any other country without a carnet, a temporary import permit costs US$2.50 (payable in kwacha) and compulsory third-party insurance is US$19 for one month. There's also a US$20 road tax fee – you must produce the documentation for this if you are driving the car out. When you leave Malawi, a permit handling fee of US$3 is payable. Receipts are issued.

Mozambique

Road Travelling by road is a good idea because train services between Malawi and Mozambique can be very slow and unreliable.

South The quickest method to reach Mozambique south of the Zambezi is to take a minibus to the Mozambique border crossing at Zóbuè (**zob**-way) (US$2.30) and then a minibus to Tete (US$1.30), from where buses go to Beira and Maputo. A cheaper but more time consuming option is to take a local bus from Blantyre to the Malawi border crossing at Mwanza (US$1.30), and then to walk or hitch the 6km to Zóbuè.

Central If you are heading for central Mozambique, there are several buses per day from Blantyre to Nsanje (US$2.80), or all the way to the Malawi border at Marka (**ma**-ra-ka) (US$3.30). It's a few kilometres between the border crossings – you can walk or take a bicycle taxi – and you can change money on the Mozambique side. From here minibuses and pick-ups go to Mutarara, Nhamilabue and Vila de Sena, from where you can reach Caia.

North There are three border crossings from Malawi into northern Mozambique: Muloza, from where you can access Mocuba in Mozambique; and Nayuchi and Chiponde, both of which lead to Cuamba in Mozambique.

Regular buses run from Blantyre, via Mulanje, to Muloza (US$2). From here, you walk 1km to the Mozambique border crossing at Milange, from where it's another few kilometres into Milange *vila* (town) itself. There's a *pensão* (cheap hotel) and bank here if you need them. From Milange there's usually a *chapa* (pick-up or converted minibus) or truck about every other day in the dry season to Mocuba (US$4), where you can find transport on to Quelimane or Nampula.

Further north, minibuses and matolas run a few times per day between Mangochi and Namwera (US$2), where there are resthouses, or the remaining 10km to the border crossing at Chiponde (US$3). If you get stuck at Namwera, you can take a bicycle taxi to Chiponde (US$3). It's 7km to the Mozambique border crossing at Mandimba and the best way to get there is by bicycle taxi (US$2). Mandimba has a couple of pensãos, and there's at least one

vehicle daily, usually a truck, between here and Cuamba (US$4).

The third option is to go by minibus from Liwonde to the border at Nayuchi (US$3). You can walk to the Mozambique border post at Entre Lagos and possibly to hitch to Cuamba. Be warned though, there's very little transport of any sort on this route so you could be waiting a long time; the Mandimba crossing is a better option.

Train If you're heading to northern Mozambique, a passenger train departs Limbe on Wednesdays at 7am, travelling via Balaka and Liwonde to Nayuchi. The fare from Limbe to Nayuchi is US$3.30 but it's more popular to get on at Liwonde, from where it costs US$2. From Nayuchi (where there are moneychangers) you can walk to Entre Lagos, but transport from here into Mozambique is limited (see earlier).

South Africa

If you need to get to South Africa quickly and cheaply, **City to City** and **Translux** (☎ 09 937499 for both) run direct luxury coaches from Blantyre to Jo'burg every day between them, for US$40/50. **Vaal Africa** (☎ 621265) also operates a service between Blantyre and Jo'burg on Saturday and Sunday for US$49. All companies depart at 9am, arriving in Jo'burg around mid-afternoon the next day.

Tanzania

If you want to go the whole way between Lilongwe and Dar es Salaam, two buses a week (Tuesday and Saturday) depart from Devil St in Lilongwe. There's a ticket office where you can book; fares are US$33, and if you're travelling from the south, your first sight of a Tanzanian bus – like something from the movie *Mad Max* or the worst carnival ride you've ever had – may be quite a shock. These buses also pick up and drop off in Mzuzu and Mbeya (Tanzania) and are handy for going between northern Malawi and southern Tanzania.

If you're going in stages, buses and minibuses run between Mzuzu and Karonga (US$4), from where minibuses and matolas travel to the Songwe border crossing (US$1.30). It's 200m across the bridge to the Tanzanian border crossing.

Once you're on the Tanzanian side of the border, minibuses and bicycle taxis travel

the 5km distance to Kyela, from where you can get a bus to Dar es Salaam. You can change money with the bicycle taxi boys but beware of scams.

Zambia

There are three direct buses per week between Lilongwe and Lusaka (US$14), also departing from Devil St, but it's a long haul and you're better off doing the trip in stages. There is no specific office so ask at the Tanzanian bus ticket office for information. Regular minibuses run between Lilongwe and the Malawi border crossing, 2km west of the town of Mchinji (US$2). From here, it's 12km to the Zambian border. Local shared taxis shuttle between them for US$1.20 per person, or US$7 for the whole car.

From the Zambian border crossing minibuses run to Chipata (US$1), which is about 30km west of the border, from where you can reach Lusaka or South Luangwa National Park (for more details see the Eastern Zambia section of the Zambia chapter).

Zimbabwe

Although Zimbabwe doesn't border Malawi, many travellers go directly between the two countries. The cheapest option is the daily **Munorurama Bus** (☎ 6248735), between Blantyre and Harare (US$15). The bus departs from opposite the Chileka Rd bus station at 7.30am and arrives in Harare by late afternoon. The service in this direction is good and on Wednesday and Saturday it continues all the way to Jo'burg (US$38). Travelling from Harare to Blantyre costs the same, but is a much slower trip because local people bring in loads of Zimbabwean goods and there are big searches at the border. Some travellers have been on the northbound bus for over two days! If you do get interminably stuck at the Mwanza border crossing, you're better off abandoning the big bus, and getting a local minibus to Blantyre (US$2.50).

LAKE
Mozambique

The Lake Malawi steamboat *Ilala* (see the main Getting Around section later in this chapter) stops at both Cóbuè (kob-way) and Metangula on the Mozambican mainland. If you're planning a visit you must get your passport stamped at the immigration post in Chipyela (the main village) on Likoma

Island. For short visits, you can pay US$1.30 for a lakeshore pass, which enables you to spend 10 days on the Mozambican lakeshore only (you must return to Malawi).

Another way to get to the Mozambican lakeshore is to take a dhow (local sailing boat) from Likoma Island to Cóbuè (US$0.80). A road connecting Cóbuè and Metangula was being upgraded at the time of writing so you may be able to hitch a ride. Alternatively, you could do this section by boat (often on the same boat that brought you over from Likoma). A motorboat (US$5) takes six hours and a dhow (US$2.50) can take one or two days, so bring your own food and water.

For more information on the Mozambique side of Lake Malawi, see Lake Niassa under Northern Mozambique in the Mozambique chapter.

Tanzania

The *Songeya* ferry sails between Mbamba Bay in Tanzania and Nkhata Bay on Malawi's northern lakeshore every Saturday. The journey takes 3½ hours and fares for first/economy class deck are US$11/6.50. Cabins are also available and children travel for US$3.

Getting Around

You can travel around Malawi by air, road, rail or boat. Compared to other countries in the region, distances between major centres are quite short, and generally roads and public transport systems are quite good, making independent travel fairly straightforward.

AIR

Air Malawi (☎ 620811, 700811; e *it@air malawi.malawi.net*) has daily flights between Lilongwe and Blantyre, and four flights a week between Lilongwe and Mzuzu, both for US$77 one way. You can also fly from Lilongwe or Blantyre to Lake Malawi's Club Makokola for US$75 (you don't have to be a guest), from where you can reach other points on the lake. Domestic flights can be paid for in kwacha. Air Malawi's booking system is not always reliable, so be prepared for lost reservations or double bookings.

There are several air charter companies linking major towns and tourist centres around the country; these include **Proflight Air Services** (☎ *754717;* **e** *proflight@malawi.net)* and **Franco's Air Charters** (☎ *794281;* **e** *franco@malawi.net).* The **Nyika Safari Company** (see the entry under Air in the main Getting There & Away section earlier in this chapter) mainly services Nyika National Park, but often has promotional offers to other Malawian destinations. Fares for all vary according to the number of people in your group, so contact these companies direct for more details. For domestic flights, departure tax is US$2.

BUS & MINIBUS

There are three options for bus travel in Malawi. Top of the range is Coachline, operated by **Stagecoach** (☎ *743927).* This luxury nonstop service with air-con, toilet, snacks, steward service and good drivers travels daily between Blantyre and Lilongwe and three times a week between Lilongwe and Mzuzu (see Getting There & Away under Lilongwe, Mzuzu and Blantyre later for details). You can buy a ticket in advance and have a reserved seat; a week's notice is sometimes needed, particularly for Friday and Sunday services. **Shire Bus Lines** operate all other buses, which fall under the category of express – fast buses between the main towns with limited stops and no standing passengers allowed – and ordinary, which cover long-distance routes but stop everywhere, so are very slow. All journey durations for ordinary buses in this chapter are best estimates of the real length, which is usually double the official length. As a rule of thumb, express buses charge between US$1.50 and US$2 per 100km, and ordinary buses slightly less. In rural areas there are also local services that cover the quieter routes and tend to be slow and crowded.

There are also many private buses and minibuses on the roads, either slotting in between Shire bus services, or serving the routes they don't. Fares are about the same as express buses, or slightly more, depending on the route. There are also local minibus services around towns and to outlying villages, or along the roads that the big buses can't manage. (In Malawi vehicles with about 30 seats are called 'half-buses' to distinguish them from big buses and minibuses.)

In rural areas, the frequency of buses and minibuses drops dramatically – sometimes to nothing. In cases like this, the 'bus' is often a truck or pick-up, with people just piled in the back. In Malawi this is called a *matola.* Everyone pays a fare to the driver – normally a bit more than a bus would charge (ie, around US$2.50 per 100km).

If you get an overnight bus, when it arrives at its destination you're normally allowed to stay onboard until dawn.

TRAIN

Trains run every Wednesday between Blantyre and Balaka (US$1.50), but passengers rarely use them as road transport on this route is quicker and cheaper. The service of most use to travellers is the continuation of this line from Liwonde to the Malawi/Mozambique border crossing at Nayuchi (US$2). For details, see Train under Mozambique in the main Getting There & Away section earlier in this chapter.

The twice-weekly train service between Limbe and Nsanje (US$2), in the far south of Malawi, is popular as the line reaches areas where road transport is limited. Since a bridge washed away in 1998, trains terminate at Makhanga.

CAR & MOTORCYCLE

The majority of main routes are mostly good-quality sealed roads, but in recent years several stretches of road have not been repaired and potholes are opening up. In some areas these have made driving slow, difficult and dangerous. Secondary roads are usually graded dirt and also vary. Some are well-maintained and easy to drive on in a normal car; others are very bad, especially after rain, and slow even with 4WD. Rural routes are not so good, and after heavy rain they are often impassable, sometimes for weeks.

Fuel costs around US$0.70 per litre for petrol and US$0.50 per litre for diesel. Supplies are usually reliable and distances between towns with filling stations are not long in Malawi, so you rarely need to worry about running dry.

Rental

Most car hire companies are based in Blantyre and Lilongwe. Those with offices in more than one city can arrange pick-up-drop-off deals. International names include

Avis, and there are several independent outfits. You should shop around as companies often have special deals and some will negotiate. You can also hire a car through a travel agent – they may have access to special deals. Whoever you hire from, be prepared for a car that is not up to Western standards. Check the tyres and as much else as you can. If anything is worn or broken, demand repairs or a discount.

Self-drive rates for a small car start at US$40 per day, plus around US$0.10 per kilometre. Unlimited mileage (minimum seven days) costs from US$50 per day. To this add 20% government tax, plus another US$3 to US$7 a day for insurance.

Rental companies in Malawi include:

Avis (☎ 756103, 756105) Lilongwe; (☎ 692368) Blantyre; plus offices at Lilongwe and Blantyre airports and at some large hotels
Ceciliana Car Hire (☎ 643206, 641219) Blantyre
Sputnik Car Hire (☎ 761563, 08 823139) Lilongwe
Silver Car Hire (☎ 775573, 773388) Lilongwe

HITCHING

On the main routes, especially between Mzuzu, Lilongwe, Zomba, Blantyre and Lake Malawi, hitching free lifts, in the Western fashion, is fairly easy. At weekends well-off residents and expats living in Blantyre and Lilongwe head for Salima, Cape Maclear and the southern lakeshore, so it's easy to get a lift there on Friday (and Sunday in the opposite direction). Note, however, that just because we say hitching is possible doesn't necessarily mean we recommend it. See the general warning under Hitching in the Getting Around the Region chapter.

All over the country you will see Malawi government cars (with 'MG' numberplates). These are, of course, always on important official business, although drivers frequently assist stranded travellers and normally expect a payment.

BOAT

The *Ilala* ferry (☎ 587311; e ilala@malawi.net) chugs passengers and cargo up and down Lake Malawi, once per week in each direction. Travelling between Monkey Bay in the south and Chilumba in the north, it makes 13 stops at lakeside villages and towns in between. (You can get to the Mo-

zambique mainland via the *Ilala*; see Lake, Mozambique, in the main Getting There & Away section earlier in this chapter.) Many travellers rate this journey as a highlight of the country, although there are occasionally nasty storms. If you're unlucky, be prepared for some pitching and rolling.

The whole trip, from one end of the line to the other, takes about three days. Privatisation of the service in early 2002 also means that those notoriously long delays (sometimes the ferry was a day late!) are generally a thing of the past. Even so, keep in mind that the *Ilala* is a lifeline for many villages and the loading and unloading of goods, people, goats, chickens etc can put the official schedule back an hour or two. The official schedules are as follows (only selected ports are shown):

Northbound

port	arrival	departure
Monkey Bay	–	10am (Fri)
Chipoka	8.15pm	10pm (Fri)
Nkhotakota	5.30am	7am (Sat)
Metangula	10.30am	12pm (Sat)
Likoma Island	5.30pm	7.30pm (Sat)
Nkhata Bay	5am	7am (Sun)
Ruarwe	11.50am	12.50pm (Sun)
Chilumba	6.30pm (Sun)	–

Southbound

port	arrival	departure
Chilumba	–	2am (Mon)
Ruarwe	8.50am	10am (Mon)
Nkhata Bay	2.45pm	8pm (Mon)
Likoma Island	3.15am	6.15am (Tues)
Metangula	12.15pm	2.15pm (Tues)
Nkhotakota	5.45pm	7.20pm (Tues)
Chipoka	2.50am	4am (Wed)
Monkey Bay	2pm (Wed)	–

The *Ilala* has three classes. Cabin Class was once luxurious and the cabins are still in reasonable condition. The spacious First Class Deck is most popular with travellers, due largely to the sociable bar, around which you are likely to meet a new soul mate or two. There are also seats, a shaded area and mattresses for hire (US$0.70) in case you're doing the long-haul journey. Economy covers the entire lower deck and is dark and crowded with engine fumes permeating from below.

Cabin and First Class Deck passengers can dine in the ship's restaurant, where

a beef curry, chicken peri peri or meal of similar standard costs US$5. Food is also served from a galley on the Economy Deck; a meal of beans, rice and vegetables costs under US$1.

Reservations are usually required for Cabin Class. For other classes, tickets are sold only when the boat is sighted, so queuing tends to start about a day before it's due to arrive. However, there's no question of anyone being refused it just keeps filling up! If you travel Economy Class, you can visit the First Class Deck to buy a beer, but you'll have to pay extra for the privilege.

Ilala Sample Routes & Fares

All of the following sample fares are from Nkhata Bay.

destination	cabin (US$)	1st class (US$)	economy (US$)
Likoma Island	17.50	7.50	3
Metangula	30	18	5.50
Ruarwe	16	7	2.50
Chilumba	29	13	3.30
Monkey Bay	47.50	30.50	6.50

When the *Ilala* stops at lakeside towns or villages, the water is too shallow for it to come close; the lifeboat is used to ferry passengers ashore. On its southbound journey, the *Ilala* docks at Nkhata Bay for seven hours and traders come aboard, selling food, drinks and newspapers.

LOCAL TRANSPORT

In the cities and large towns, minibuses travel local routes. Private hire taxis also operate in cities and large towns, and can be found outside bus stations, airports or large hotels. There are no meters, so rates are negotiable, particularly on airport runs – check the price at the start of the journey. For more information see Getting Around under the city and town listings.

ORGANISED TOURS

Several companies organise tours around the country, ranging from a few days to three weeks. Trips into Zambia or Mozambique are also available, although Malawi's safari scene is much smaller than, say, South Africa's or Zimbabwe's. Tours may be 'mobile' (ie, moving from camp to camp every few days) or based in one place, with excursions each day. Most are vehicle-based although some outfits also organise walking trips, horseback safaris, or boating on the lake. Tours normally include transport, accommodation and food, but prices vary considerably according to standards – from budget to luxury. There are only a few budget companies that can arrange tours on the spot – most prefer advance bookings, although sometimes a couple of days is enough. Budget tours usually cost between US$30 and US$50 per day. Most mid-range and top-end companies also need advance bookings, and charge from US$80 per person per day, easily climbing to US$200 per day or more.

The following is a list of major tour operators in Malawi, with a variety of budgets to suit most wallets.

Barefoot Safaris (☎ 707346, e barefoot@malawi .net) offers budget and mid-range tours, mostly geared towards wildlife watching in Malawi, Zambia and Tanzania. It also arranges good walking tours, encompassing Lengwe National Park, Mount Mulanje, Liwonde National Park and Lake Malawi. Whether you're walking or viewing, tours cost from US$85 per person per day and include all meals and accommodation.

Central African Wilderness Safaris (☎ 771393, e info@wilderness.malawi.net, Bisnowaty Service Centre, Kenyatta Rd, Lilongwe) operates all accommodation and facilities in Liwonde National Park. It can also arrange flights, air charters, car hire and mid- to top-end safaris to South Luangwa National Park in Zambia, starting from US$500 per person all inclusive.

Kayak Africa (☎ 584456, e letsgo@kayakafrica .co.za,), based in Cape Maclear, offers guided two- or three-night island-hopping kayak tours for US$270/405 per person. The charge includes tented accommodation, meals, hot showers, snorkel gear and park fees. It also operates PADI open water courses for US$195.

Kiboko Safaris (☎ 751226, e kiboko@malawi.net, Livingstone Rd, Lilongwe) specialises in budget tours; fully inclusive three-day beach trips costing US$90 and four-day trips to South Luangwa costing US$275

Makomo Safaris (☎ 754695, e makomo@malawi .net, Mandala Rd, Lilongwe), offers mid-range tours and budget camping trips, which you can design yourself from US$50 per person per day

Monkey Business (☎ 252365, e njayalodge@ malawi.net) in Nkhata Bay, offers excellent kayak excursions along the northern lakeshore. Typical itineraries include idyllic spots such as Usisya

and Ruarwe, or spectacular trips to Likoma and Chizumulu Islands, sailing aboard the *Ilala* ferry, then paddling around the Mozambique shore. Journeys are broken by stopovers at fishing villages and empty beaches and these trips are a great way to explore the area. Tours cost US$30 per person per day (you can design you own itinerary ranging from two to seven days), which includes meals, kayaks, guides and tents. It also arranges one-day Kayak-Bushwalk-Dive tours for US$35 per person.

Red Zebra Tours (☎ 263165, W www.lakemalawi .com), based in Senga Bay specialises in diving and lake safaris with an experienced guide, from US$25/30 per person for a half/full day.

The Nyika Safari Company (☎ 330180, W www .nyika.com) operates purely indulgent horse-back safaris on the Nyika Plateau from US$250 per person per day, which includes all meals, rides and accommodation in luxury safari tents (hot showers and all!) or at the luxurious Chelinda Lodge. These tours only operate between May and October and last anywhere from two to 10 days.

Lilongwe

Lilongwe is the political capital of Malawi, while Blantyre is the commercial capital. Although fairly sleepy as capital cities go, Lilongwe's facilities are good and it's a pleasant spot to acclimatise to Malawi's pace. The city's soul is ensconced within the quiet buzz of the Old Town, where good eateries, craft stalls, the bustling market and some popular drinking holes will keep most visitors occupied for a couple of days. On the weekends movement is reduced to a trickle, particularly on Sunday, when sleeping and church-attendance seem to be the main activities.

Originally a small village on the banks of the Lilongwe River, Lilongwe became a British colonial administrative centre around the turn of the 20th century, after its chief requested protection from warlike neighbours. Due to its central location on the main north–south route and the road to Northern Rhodesia (later Zambia), Lilongwe soon became Malawi's second-largest urban centre. Plans announced in 1968 to relocate the country's administration from Blantyre were fully realised in 1975, when Lilongwe was officially declared the capital.

Orientation

Lilongwe is unusually spread out and rather than one CBD, has two centres: City Centre and Old Town. City Centre is a loose and rather sterile collection of ministries, embassies, some smart hotels, a shopping centre, airline offices and travel agents. Three kilometres south, Old Town has a good range of places to stay, the bus station, the market and several restaurants, all in a condensed area easily covered on foot.

Maps Survey maps of Malawi and some of its cities are available from the **Department of Surveys Map Sales Office**, about 500m south of the roundabout where Glyn Jones Rd meets Kamuzu Procession Rd. See also Maps under Planning in the Facts for the Visitor section earlier in this chapter.

Information

Tourist Offices The tourist office is at the **Department of Wildlife & Tourism** (☎ 757584; Murray Rd, Old Town; open 7.30am-5pm Mon-Fri & 8am-10am Sat), but information and advice is minimal. The Capital City Baptist Church produces an excellent booklet called *Lilongwe Lowdown* at a cost of US$6, full of useful details and contacts for Lilongwe. You can buy it at bookshops around Lilongwe (see Bookshops later). For details on tours, flights and hotels you're better off at a travel agency; several are listed in the Travel Agencies & Tour Operators section later.

Immigration Office Lilongwe's **immigration office** (☎ 754297; Murray Rd, Old Town) is next to the Department of Wildlife & Tourism office.

Money There are branches of the **National Bank of Malawi** (Kamuzu Procession Rd) and **Commercial Bank of Malawi** (Kamuzu Procession Rd) in Old Town. In the same area are several foreign exchange bureaus, generally offering better rates, no commission and quicker service. Two good ones are **The Money Bureau** (☎ 755934; Nico Shopping Centre, Kamuzu Procession Rd, Old Town) and **Dini Forex** (☎ 08 828528; Riverside Arcade, Glyn Jones Rd). There's another branch of **The Money Bureau** (☎ 772239; Centre House Arcade, City Centre Shopping Centre, City Centre) at the other end of town.

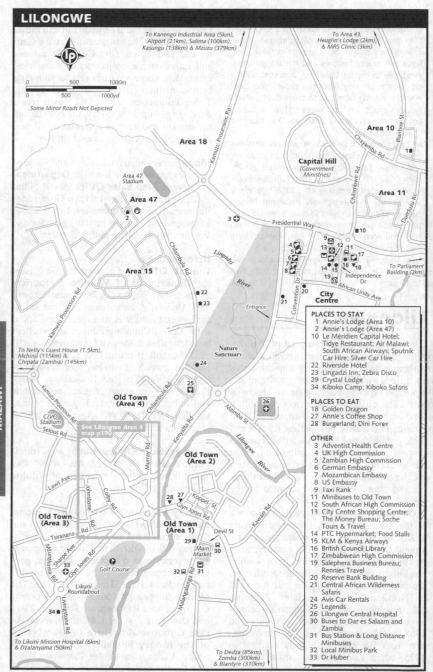

LILONGWE

To Kanengo Industrial Area (5km),
Airport (21km), Salima (100km),
Kasungu (138km) & Mzuzu (379km)

To Area 43,
Heuglin's Lodge (2km),
& MRS Clinic (3km)

0   500   1000m
0   500   1000yd

Some Minor Roads Not Depicted

Area 18

Area 10

Capital Hill
(Government
Ministries)

Area 47
Stadium

Area 47

Area 11

Presidential Way

Area 15

To Parliament
Building (2km)

Independence
Dr

African Unity Ave

City
Centre

Lingadzi River

Entrance

To Nelly's Guest House (1.5km),
Mchinji (115km) &
Chipata (Zambia) (145km)

Nature
Sanctuary

Old Town
(Area 4)

See Lilongwe Area 4
map p190

CIVO
Stadium

Old Town
(Area 2)

Old Town
(Area 3)

Old Town
(Area 1)

Koppel St

Glyn Jones Rd

Devil St

Main
Market

Golf Course

Likuni
Roundabout

To Likuni Mission Hospital (6km)
& Dzalanyama (50km)

To Dedza (85km),
Zomba (300km)
& Blantyre (310km)

PLACES TO STAY
1   Annie's Lodge (Area 10)
2   Annie's Lodge (Area 47)
10 Le Méridien Capital Hotel;
    Tidye Restaurant; Air Malawi;
    South African Airways; Sputnik
    Car Hire; Silver Car Hire
22 Riverside Hotel
23 Lingadzi Inn; Zebra Disco
29 Crystal Lodge
34 Kiboko Camp; Kiboko Safaris

PLACES TO EAT
18 Golden Dragon
27 Annie's Coffee Shop
28 Burgerland; Dini Forex

OTHER
3   Adventist Health Centre
4   UK High Commission
5   Zambian High Commission
6   German Embassy
7   Mozambican Embassy
8   US Embassy
9   Taxi Rank
11 Minibuses to Old Town
12 South African High Commission
13 City Centre Shopping Centre;
    The Money Bureau; Soche
    Tours & Travel
14 PTC Hypermarket; Food Stalls
15 KLM & Kenya Airways
16 British Council Library
17 Zimbabwean High Commission
19 Salephera Business Bureau;
    Rennies Travel
20 Reserve Bank Building
21 Central African Wilderness
    Safaris
24 Avis Car Rentals
25 Legends
26 Lilongwe Central Hospital
30 Buses to Dar es Salaam and
    Zambia
31 Bus Station & Long Distance
    Minibuses
32 Local Minibus Park
33 Dr Huber

MALAWI

Post & Communications Lilongwe has two main post offices: on Kamuzu Procession Rd, Old Town and next to City Centre Shopping Centre. For details of rates, see Post & Communications under Facts for the Visitor earlier. If you're receiving post restante mail addressed to GPO Lilongwe, most goes to Old Town, but some mysteriously lands at City Centre, the only way to avoid this is to have your letters addressed specifically Old Town or City Centre.

International telephone calls and faxes can be made at both **Salephera Business Bureau** (☎ 774834; ADL House, City Centre) and **Posts and Telecomms Executive Business Bureau** (Kandodo Plaza, City Centre Shopping Centre, City Centre). Calls cost US$8.50 for three minutes anywhere outside Africa, any time.

Email & Internet Access Internet access is readily available in Lilongwe. In City Centre both the **British Council Library** and the **US Information Service Library** (see Libraries & Cultural Centres later) offer comparatively cheap access at US$5 and US$2 per hour respectively. Unfortunately there are only a few terminals at each so queues tend to be long. Nearby, **Salephera Business Bureau** (see Post & Communications earlier) charges US$7.50 per hour.

Celtelplus Cyber Cafe (Nico Shopping Centre, Kamuzu Procession Rd, Old Town) offers quick access for US$3 per hour, while the nearby **Gigatech Internet** (☎ 759135; Mandala Rd, Old Town) charges US$9 per hour.

Travel Agencies & Tour Operators In Old Town, travel agencies selling flights include **Midland Travel** (☎ 756310; e midland@malawi.net; Kamuzu Procession Rd) and **Airco** (☎ 741442; Mandala Rd).

Ulendo Safaris (☎ 754950; e reservations@ulendo.net; Old Town Mall) sells air tickets and tours, and often has deals on trips to South Luangwa National Park (Zambia), including flights and accommodation. It's also the booking agent for the Ilala ferry.

Land & Lake Safaris (☎ 757120; e landlake@africa-online.net; Mandala Rd) offers budget and mid-range safaris to South Luangwa and various parts of Malawi. It also arranges car hire, sells hiking equipment and runs the Dzalanyama and Zomba forest resthouses. Nearby **Makomo Safaris** (☎ 754695;

e makomo@malawi.net; Mandala Rd), offers mid-range tours and budget camping trips.

Kiboko Safaris (☎ 751226), based at Kiboko Camp (see Places to Stay later), specialises in budget tours; three-day beach trips cost US$90 and or four-day trips to South Luangwa cost US$275.

In the City Centre, **Soche Tours & Travel** (☎ 772377; e sochetours@malawi.net; City Centre Shopping Centre) sells flights and can make hotel reservations, as can **Rennies Travel** (☎ 774144; e renniestravel@mw .celtelplus.com; ADL House). Also in this end of town is **Central African Wilderness Safaris** (☎ 771393; e info@wilderness.malawi .net; Bisnowaty Service Centre, Kenyatta Rd), a mid-range to top-end safari operator and travel agent dealing with hotels, flights, air charters, tours, car hire and so on. It also operates accommodation and facilities in Liwonde National Park.

Barefoot Safaris (☎ 707346; e barefoot@ malawi.net) offers budget and mid-range tours encompassing Malawi, Zambia and Tanzania. It's recommended to organise a tour in advance, but you can also ask about on-the-spot arrangements.

Bookshops In Old Town, **TBS bookshop** (Nico Shopping Centre, Kamuzu Procession Rd) sells international and local newspapers and magazines, and some paperback novels. **Maneno Bookshop** (Mandala Rd) sells mostly academic texts, but also stocks magazines and the invaluable Lilongwe Lowdown booklet (see Information earlier for details). **Central Bookshop** (Nico Shopping Centre, Kamuzu Procession Rd) sells a surprisingly good stock of African literature, local guidebooks and other books on Malawian subjects.

Photography Print film, developing, printing and instant passport photos are available at **Kolor Lab** (☎ 774292; City Centre Shopping Centre, City Centre). Note that photos printed in Lilongwe sometimes come out overexposed. If you're particular, save them for Zimbabwe or South Africa.

Libraries & Cultural Centres The British Council library (☎ 773244; off Independence Dr, City Centre; open 7.30am-12am & 1pm-4.30pm Mon-Thur, 7.30am-12.30pm Fri) and the **US Information Service Library** (USIS) (☎ 772222; Old Mutual Building, City

MALAWI

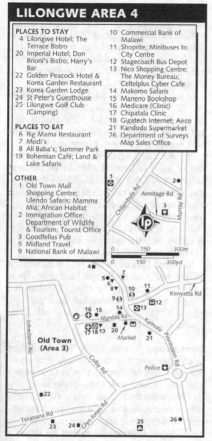

LILONGWE AREA 4

PLACES TO STAY
4 Lilongwe Hotel; The Terrace Bistro
20 Imperial Hotel; Don Brioni's Bistro; Harry's Bar
22 Golden Peacock Hotel & Korea Garden Restaurant
23 Korea Garden Lodge
24 St Peter's Guesthouse
25 Lilongwe Golf Club (Camping)

PLACES TO EAT
6 Big Mama Restaurant
7 Modi's
8 Ali Baba's; Summer Park
19 Bohemian Café; Land & Lake Safaris

OTHER
1 Old Town Mall Shopping Centre; Ulendo Safaris; Mamma Mia; African Habitat
2 Immigration Office; Department of Wildlife & Tourism; Tourist Office
3 Goodfellas Pub
5 Midland Travel
9 National Bank of Malawi
10 Commercial Bank of Malawi
11 Shoprite; Minibuses to City Centre
12 Stagecoach Bus Depot
13 Nico Shopping Centre; The Money Bureau; Celtelplus Cyber Cafe
14 Makomo Safaris
15 Maneno Bookshop
16 Medicare (Clinic)
17 Chipatala Clinic
18 Gigatech Internet; Airco
21 Kandodo Supermarket
26 Department of Surveys Map Sales Office

Old Town (Area 3)

Armitage Rd
Murray Rd
Chilambula Rd
Kenyatta Rd
Mandala Rd
Kamuzu Procession Rd
Johnstone Rd
Market
Colby Rd
Police
Glyn Jones Rd
Tsiranana Rd

Centre Shopping Centre, City Centre; open 8.30am-4.30pm Mon-Wed, 8.30am-12.30pm Thur) allow nonmembers to read books and magazines in the library, but not to take them away. The USIS shows the previous day's CBS evening news at lunchtime. Both places also show films on some afternoons and evenings. Check their noticeboards for details.

Medical Services For malaria blood tests, **Medicare** (☎ 750152; Mandala Rd, Old Town) charges US$2. Across the road, the **Chipatala Clinic** (☎ 758089) also provides blood tests and private consultations. **Dr Huber** (☎ 750404, 09 919548; Glyn Jones Rd, Old Town) has been highly recommended to us for private consultations. The **Adventist Health Centre** (☎ 775456; Presidential Way,

City Centre) is also good for consultations, plus eye and dental problems.

At **Lilongwe Central Hospital** (☎ 753555; off Mzimba St) conditions and facilities are not good, but an 'expat bed' (a private ward) costs about US$50 per night. A better option is **Likuni Mission Hospital** (☎ 766602; Glyn Jones Rd), 7km southwest of Old Town, with public wards, private rooms, and some expat European doctors on staff. Fees for those who can afford them start at US$100 per day.

The best place for major matters is the **Medical Air Rescue Service Clinic** (☎ 794036, 08 823590; **e** marsintl@malawi.net; Ufulu Rd, Area 43). Fees are US$60 per consultation, US$120 after hours and US$100 for an overnight stay. MRS also has ambulances with staff highly trained in emergency treatment. They will rescue you anywhere within 50km of Lilongwe for US$50 per half-hour, but need proof that you are insured or can pay. MRS is linked to Health International and MARS (Medical Air Rescue Service) and can arrange evacuation to Harare or Jo'burg if things get really serious.

There are **MPL pharmacies** at the Nico Shopping Centre in Old Town and in City Centre Shopping Centre.

Emergency The emergency number for police and ambulance is ☎ 199 (Lilongwe and Blantyre only), but there are never enough vehicles, so if you need assistance you'll probably have to go to the police station by taxi and bring an officer back to the scene of the crime. Once you've contacted the police, put aside several hours while they laboriously take a statement, which will then cost you US$20. If you are seriously injured, don't waste time phoning an ambulance – get a taxi straight to hospital.

Dangers & Annoyances We've had several reports from travellers who've had pockets picked or bags slashed as they pushed through the busy crowds around the market and bus station. Be on your guard here. During the day, once you leave Malangalanga Rd, things are OK and you can walk to Area 3. At night, Malangalanga Rd can be dangerous, and walking to Area 3 is not recommended. The bridge between Area 2 and Area 3 is a favourite haunt for muggers. If you arrive on a bus after dark, take a minibus or taxi to your accommodation.

MALAWI

Recent muggings and stabbings around the Nature Sanctuary have become a serious problem and if you plan to visit (see Things To See & Do later) get a taxi to inside the gate. Even minibuses can be unsafe, as the bus stop itself has become a target. Walking there is extremely risky. Ask at your lodge, hostel or hotel for up-to-date information regarding security around this area.

Bus tickets should only be bought at the bus station or the Stagecoach depot near Shoprite; some travellers have been conned out of money by buying tickets on the street but there is no such service.

Things to See & Do

Despite rumours to the contrary, Lilongwe has enough to keep you occupied for a couple of days. The **main market** *(Malangalanga Rd, Old Town)* is a pocket of frenetic activity, with traders, market stalls and food vendors packed into a swarming, small area (see Shopping later). For a total change of pace however, head for the **Nature Sanctuary** *(Kenyatta Rd; admission US$0.50; open 8.30am-4pm Mon-Fri, 8.30am-noon Sat)* – an incredibly peaceful wilderness area by the Lingadzi River. There is a signposted network of walking trails, and the information centre lists the birds and animals that may be seen. Less pleasing are the caged hyenas and leopards, but despite this the sanctuary is well worth a visit. The open-air café by the entrance is a good place to relax after your stroll.

For a view of Malawi's economic heart, go to the public gallery overlooking the

Tobacco

Tobacco is Malawi's most important cash crop, accounting for more than 60% of the country's export earnings, and Lilongwe is the selling, buying and processing centre of this vital industry. Most activity takes place in the Kenango industrial area on the northern side of Lilongwe, the site of several tobacco processing factories and the huge and impressive tobacco auction rooms.

Tobacco was first grown in Malawi by a settler called John Buchanan, who planted the crop on his farm near Blantyre in the 1880s. Large-scale tobacco farming started in the area around Lilongwe in the 1920s and has grown steadily in importance ever since. Two types of tobacco are produced in Malawi: 'flue', which is a standard-quality leaf, and 'burley', which is a higher-quality leaf much in demand by cigarette manufacturers around the world. Malawi is the world's largest producer of burley.

Tobacco is grown on large plantations or by individual farmers on small farms. The leaves are harvested and dried, either naturally in the sun or in a heated drying room, and then brought to Lilongwe for sale. (In southern Malawi the crops go to auction in Limbe.)

In the auction room (called auction 'floors'), auctioneers sell tobacco on behalf of the growers. It's purchased by dealers who resell to the tobacco processors. The tobacco comes onto the auction floors (the size of several large aircraft hangars) in large bales weighing between 80kg and 100kg and is displayed in long lines. Moisture content determines the value of the leaves: if the tobacco is too dry, the flavour is impaired; if it's too wet, mould will set in and the bale is worthless.

Dealers will have inspected the tobacco leaves in advance – employing a skilled eye, nose and 'feel' – then move down the line in a small group with an auctioneer, pausing briefly at each bale to put in their bids, recorded by the auctioneer in a rapid-fire language completely unintelligible to outsiders. It takes an average of just six seconds to sell a bale, and the auctioneer and buyers hardly miss a step as they move swiftly down the line.

As soon as the dealers reach the end of the line, they move straight onto the next (there may be as many as 100 lines, each containing 100 bales) and the sale continues. Barrow boys whisk the sold tobacco off the floor, and within an hour a new line of bales is in place ready for the next group of auctioneers and dealers. The sold tobacco is taken to one of the nearby processing plants; some goes by truck but a few processors are so close to the auction floors that it simply goes on a conveyor belt.

A small proportion of tobacco is made into cigarettes for the local market, but more than 90% gets processed in Malawi (the leaves are stripped of their 'core' and shredded into small pieces) before being exported to be made into cigarettes abroad. Most processed tobacco goes by road to Durban in South Africa, to be shipped around the world, but an increasingly large amount goes by rail to the port of Nacala in Mozambique, and is shipped out from there.

MALAWI

tobacco auction floors (☎ 710377; Kenango Industrial Area; admission free) at the vast Auction Holdings warehouse about 7km north of the city centre, east of the main road towards Kasungu. This is best reached by taxi, but local minibuses serve the industrial area. The auction season is May to September. See the boxed text 'Tobacco' earlier for more information on this vital commodity.

If you'd prefer a political view, head to the **Parliament Building** (Presidential Way), which moved from Zomba in the mid-1990s to the palace of former president Banda on the outskirts of Lilongwe. At least this obscenely grandiose monstrosity is being used now – during Banda's rule he stayed here only one night. Kiboko Safaris (see Travel Agencies & Tour Operators earlier) operates Lilongwe city tours, which incorporate both the tobacco auction floors and the Parliament Building for US$7.50.

If you're the sporting type, **Lilongwe Golf Club** (see Places to Stay later) offers daily membership for US$7. This allows you to enter the club, and use the bar or restaurant. To use the sports facilities there's a small extra charge: swimming pool, squash or tennis, about US$1; 18 holes of golf with hired clubs, US$7.

Places to Stay – Budget

All the budget places to stay are in Old Town.

Lilongwe Golf Club (☎ 753598; off Glyn Jones Rd; camp sites per person US$5) is a clean, safe and comfortable (hot showers!) option for campers. Discounts are common for two or more people and rates include access to the members bar, restaurant and swimming pool.

Kiboko Camp (☎ 08 828384; e kiboko@ malawi.net, Livingstone Rd; camp sites per person US$3, dorm beds US$5, doubles US$12) is a backpackers' favourite, with shaded, grassy camping areas, cool, double A-frame chalets and a wealth of information on Malawi. There's also a good bar (it closes at 10.30pm) and evening meals can be ordered. If arriving at the bus station at night grab a taxi here for around US$5.

St Peter's Guesthouse (☎ 08 857227; Glyn Jones Rd; rooms without bath US$8-10) offers excellent, clean and safe rooms with nets. It's quiet and part of the parish so guests should be respectful.

Crystal Lodge (☎ 724867; Malangalanga Rd; singles/doubles without bath US$5/6.50, doubles with bath US$9.50) is upstairs in the large building across the road from the bus station. Despite a seedy exterior, the spartan rooms are clean and the bathrooms are decent.

Annie's Coffee Shop (dorm beds US$3) (see Places to Eat later) is another cheapie, with small and basic two- or four-bed dorms in a courtyard out the back. There's a transient flow of visitors through here and Crystal Lodge so you should secure your gear.

Golden Peacock Hotel (☎ 756632; Johnstone Rd; rooms with/without bath US$15/9) has large but shabby rooms, which vary considerably in size and condition so check a few out.

Korea Garden Lodge (☎ 753467; Isiranana Rd; singles/doubles without bath US$16/19, with bath from US$32/39) has a variety of rooms for most budgets, a bar, restaurant and pool set in a grassy back yard. All rooms have nets and fans but the more expensive rooms are better value. It also offers business facilities including Internet.

Places to Stay – Mid-Range

The following all have restaurants for residents and rates include breakfast, unless otherwise specified.

Nelly's Guest House (☎ 759514; e nellys@ liccom.net; Area 9/156, Old Town; singles/ doubles US$32/42) is cosy and popular, with conservatively decorated rooms, although some feature highly alluring hot-pink velour bed sheets.

Heuglin's Lodge (☎ 795364; e info@wilderness.malawi.net; Area 43; singles/doubles from US$40/60) is a lovely guesthouse with tasteful rooms, pleasant gardens and a pool. There's also a great wildlife library here.

Annie's Lodge Area 47 (☎ 762163; Area 47/3; singles/doubles US$25/28) is all jungle prints and wooden decor with a small bar and a pleasant veranda, although the staff's obsession with Western pop music may interrupt any plans for relaxation. Its classier and more sedate cousin **Annie's Lodge Area 10** (☎ 794572; Area 10/285; rooms US$38-45) has a variety of tranquil rooms, some with private bathroom. There's also an inviting TV lounge, and the restaurant (dishes US$5-11) serves not-the-norm dishes like lamb paprika, inventive pastas and fish.

Breakfast at both is included for one guest only, regardless of occupancy.

Imperial Hotel (☎ 752201; e imperial@ eomw.net; Mandala Rd, Old Town; singles/ doubles without bath US$30/40, with bath US$55/80) is well positioned and popular. Spick and span rooms have nets, fans and comfy beds. The adjusted exchange rate makes it best to pay in US$ cash here.

Lingadzi Inn (☎ 754166; e lingadzi@sdnp .org.mw; Chilambula Rd; rooms US$78) is a little faded and the bar and restaurant are a tad poky, but the rooms are comfortable and there's a picturesque, sprawling garden out the back. Rates don't include breakfast.

Riverside Hotel (☎ 750511; Chilambula Rd; singles/doubles US$38/47) is a good mid-range choice, with spotless, compact and new rooms.

Places to Stay – Top End
Facilities at the following include travel and car hire agents, business centres, swimming pools, restaurants and bars.

Lilongwe Hotel (☎ 756333; Kamuzu Procession Rd, Old Town; rooms from US$159), set amid sprawling, manicured gardens, looks like a colonial palace from the outside, but its glory days are behind it and its rooms are now charmless.

Le Meridien Capital Hotel (☎ 773388; e capital@lemeridienmalawi.co.mw; Chilembwe Rd, City Centre; singles/doubles from US$137/155) is the smartest place to stay in Lilongwe, and its leafy compound and good facilities attract top-end tourists, business travellers and diplomats.

Places to Eat
Hotel Restaurants Most of the mid-range and top-end hotels listed have restaurants open to nonresidents, where standards and prices are on a par with the hotel.

Imperial Hotel (dishes US$4-6; open lunch and dinner daily) has a terrace restaurant serving tasty kebabs and chicken, steak and fish grills.

The Terrace Bistro (☎ 773388; Lilongwe Hotel; light dishes from US$3; open lunch daily) is open-air and a popular lunch spot and meeting place for business travellers and well-heeled tourists.

Tidye Restaurant (☎ 773388; Le Meridien Capital Hotel; starters US$4-6; mains US$7-11; open dinner daily) is suitably stylish with

exquisite dishes to match – it's all roast salmon and spiced guinea fowl here with not a chambo or chip to be seen.

Restaurants Usually buzzing with a lively infusion of locals and tourists, **Don Brioni's Bistro** (☎ 08 826756; Mandala Rd, Old Town; mains US$4-8; open nightly from 6pm), under the Imperial Hotel, is suitably Italian in decor and flavour. Excellent steak, fish, chicken and even Chinese dishes accompany pizzas and pastas on the menu.

Modi's (☎ 751489; Kamuzu Procession Rd, Old Town; starters US$1.50, mains US$3-4; open 11am-2pm & 6pm-late daily) has delicious Indian fare; you can get your tikka, masala or makhni fix here, but the real speciality is tandoori.

Mamma Mia (☎ 758362; Old Town Mall, Old Town; mains US$5-7; open noon-3pm & 6pm-9.30pm daily) is a light and airy restaurant away from the maddening crowds, serving plenty of pizzas and pasta dishes as wells as tasty Lake Malawi chambo and steaks.

Korea Garden Restaurant (☎ 751941; starters US$1-3, mains US$5-8; open 8am-late daily), within the Golden Peacock Hotel (see Places to Stay earlier) serves a large selection of Korean meals including vegetarian options and excellent bugolgi dishes. The only gripe is that portions are small.

Golden Dragon (☎ 773101; off Independence Dr, City Centre; mains US$2-3, specials US$7; open 11am-2pm & 6pm-11pm Tues-Sun) serves large helpings of straightforward Chinese food. Takeaways are the same price (but not taxed).

Restaurant Koreana (☎ 771004; Gemini House, City Centre Shopping Centre, City Centre; starters US$1-2, mains US$4-7; open noon-2pm & 7pm-10pm Mon-Sat) has very good east Asian food.

Food Stalls & Cafés Around the market in Old Town and near the **PTC Hypermarket** in City Centre, **food stalls** sell cheap eats, mostly in the fried cassava, meat and potato vein, but you can fuel up for around US$1.

Burgerland (☎ 727294; Riverside Arcade, Glyn Jones Rd, Old Town; dishes US$3-6; open 9.30am-9.30pm Tue-Thur, 9.30am-10.30pm Fri-Sun) belies its title by serving great Indian, peri-peri and grilled dishes alongside an exhaustive variety of burgers (including prawn).

MALAWI

Annie's Coffee Shop (☎ 09 930267; Conforzi Rd, Old Town; dishes US$2-3; open 8am-late daily), nearby, dishes up tasty breakfasts, curries, burgers and sandwiches in a cosy bistro-style restaurant.

Ali Baba's (☎ 751523; Kamuzu Procession Rd, Old Town; light dishes US$2, mains US$3-7; open 9am-8pm daily) is a sprawling food-hall serving good fast food, mostly in the way of pizzas and calzones, but with a smattering of chicken, steak and fish dishes. Behind here, **The Summer Park** (dishes US$1-3; open 10am-8pm daily) is like a mini theme park set in pleasant garden surrounds – perfect atmosphere to munch on a burger, sandwich or, of course, ice cream.

Big Mama Restaurant (☎ 08 841827; Kamuzu Procession Rd, Old Town; dishes US$2.50-5; open 9am-5pm Mon-Sat) serves up simple but tasty chicken dishes and snacks in a cool and nooky hole in the wall.

Bohemian Cafe (☎ 757120; Mandala Rd, Old Town; dishes US$2.50; open 8am-4pm Mon-Fri; 9am-1.30pm Sat) serves excellent breakfasts, sandwiches, snacks and cakes in a sheltered and breezy outdoor setting.

Tasty Take Aways (Centre House Arcade, City Centre Shopping Centre, City Centre; dishes US$1-2.50) is a good lunch spot, serving a combo of Malawian dishes, burgers and curries. Nearby, **Kuusa Cafe** (☎ 774503; Chief M'mbelwa House, City Centre Shopping Centre, City Centre; starters US$2, mains US$3-6; open 7.30am-9pm Mon-Sat, 12.30pm-8pm Sun) is a cut above with great snacks, large steaks and curries and plenty of vegetarian options. Its non-alcoholic cocktails are heaven on a hot day.

Entertainment

In Old Town the streets near the market have several **bottle stores**, which are basic bars that play music loud and late. This area has a very hard edge, so go here only with a streetwise friend, enough money for an evening's supply of beer and nothing that you can't afford to lose.

Lilongwe Hotel has a smart residents' bar open to nonguests, while the nonresidents' bar is livelier. There's a disco or live band on some evenings, when a US$2 cover charge is applied.

Harry's Bar, downstairs at the Imperial Hotel, has a relaxed atmosphere with a happy, mixed crowd of expats and locals.

It's a popular meeting place and on Friday night Harry can be found at the decks.

Goodfellas Pub (☎ 752545; Armitage Rd, Old Town; open 11.30am-late Mon-Sat) is another lively spot and an expat haven. You can socialise at the pool tables, find a cosy corner, or plant a stool at the impressive wooden bar.

Legends (☎ 753612; Onions Rd, Old Town; admission US$1.30; open 5pm-late) is a bar most evenings and a nightclub at weekends, where young expats and well-to-do Malawians mix it up in a happy and energetic atmosphere. The music is a fair blend of Western and African.

Zebra Disco (Lingadzi Inn; cover charge US$1.50; open Fri & Sat night) is the place to go for a more local feel. It plays mostly African music to a mostly Malawian clientele.

Spectator Sports

Football matches are played at the **CIVO stadium** (off Kamuzu Procession Rd, Area 9, Old Town) on Sunday, and at the **stadium** (Area 47). Look out for posters, or ask local fans for information.

Shopping

In Old Town the **Nico Shopping Centre** (Kamuzu Procession Rd) has a bookshop, travel agency, pharmacy and several other shops. The large **Shoprite** (Kenyatta Rd) opposite, is good for groceries, while the **Kandodo Supermarket** (Kamuzu Procession Rd) has more limited and cheaper stock.

Also in Old Town, **Old Town Mall** houses a small corridor of shops including **African Habitat**, selling a variety of African arts and crafts and **Central Africana** with an impressive selection of decorative and antique maps well-worth framing.

There's a large **craft market** near the Imperial Hotel for a more local focus, where vendors sell everything from trinket woodcarvings, basketware and jewellery to traditional Malawi chairs. If you go late in the day you're likely to get a better deal.

City Centre Shopping Centre (off Independence Dr) is a collection of buildings containing shops, travel agents, restaurants, a bank and a post office. Nearby is the large PTC Hypermarket.

To see what Malawians buy, go to the city's **main market**. It's always lively and colourful, and is a great place to buy second-hand

clothes, although photography is not appreciated. Note also that pickpockets operate in the crowds and that some visitors with large bags have been violently robbed, so travel lightly here.

Getting There & Away

Air For details on flights, see the main Getting There & Away and Getting Around sections earlier in this chapter. If you're buying a ticket, it's worth trying an agent first (see Travel Agencies & Tour Operators earlier) as they offer a wider range of options, charge the same rates as the airlines and sometimes have special deals. Airlines with offices in Lilongwe include:

Air Malawi (☎ 772132, 753181) Le Meridien Capital Hotel, City Centre

KLM & Kenya Airways (☎ 774227) Casa de Chez House, City Centre

South African Airways (☎ 772242) Le Meridien Capital Hotel, City Centre

Bus Coachline buses run between Lilongwe and Blantyre (US$18, four hours, three daily) and Mzuzu (US$13, five hours, Tuesday, Friday, Sunday). Book tickets at the **Stagecoach Bus Depot** (☎ 743927; Kenyatta Rd, Old Town), from where the buses depart.

Express and ordinary buses operate out of the bus station near the market in Old Town. Express buses run to: Blantyre via Zalewa (US$5, five hours, one daily), Zomba (US$3.50, six hours, one daily), Mzuzu (US$6, 6½ hours, two daily) and Kasungu (US$2.50, three hours, two daily). For information on any route, go to the back of one of the booths (you may have to look for one that's open) and speak to the supervisors inside. You can buy tickets once the buses have pulled into the station.

All other buses are ordinary (ie, slow) and travel between Lilongwe and Mchinji (US$1.50, two hours, three daily), Salima (US$1.50, 1½ hours, two daily) and Nkhotakota (US$2.50, 4½ hours, two daily). Getting to Monkey Bay can be a nightmare (see that section under Central Malawi later in this chapter).

Long distance minibuses depart from behind the bus station to nearby destinations such as Salima, Mchinji and Dedza (all around US$1.50).

Getting Around

To/From the Airport Lilongwe international airport is 24km north of the city. A taxi from the airport into town costs US$15.

The **Airport Shuttle** (☎ 08 897460) collects passengers from most of the hotels and lodges in town around three hours before a flight departure. The cost is US$6.50 and your hotel should be able to make a booking. It usually leaves the airport roughly every half-hour.

Local buses and minibuses run between Old Town and the commercial part of the airport (about 200m from the passenger terminal) for just US$1, or you can catch any minibus running along the main road towards Kasungu and get off at the airport junction, from where it's 3km to the airport. From the airport, you can hoof it to the main road, where minibuses run to Lilongwe, or hitch.

Bus The most useful local minibus service for visitors is between Old Town and City Centre. From Old Town, local minibuses leave from either the bus park near the market, or outside Shoprite. They then head north up Kenyatta Rd, via Youth and Convention Drs or via Independence Dr, to reach City Centre. From City Centre back to Old Town, the bus stop for the return journey is at the northern end of Independence Dr. The fare between the two centres is US$0.25.

Taxi The best places to find taxis are the main hotels. There's also a rank on Presidential Way, just north of City Centre Shopping Centre. The fare between Old Town and City Centre is about US$5. Short journeys within either City Centre or Old Town cost US$2.50 to US$4. It's always best to negotiate a price with the driver first.

AROUND LILONGWE
Dzalanyama

Dzalanyama is a beautiful forest reserve in a range of hills about 50km by road southwest of Lilongwe. The log-cabin-style **Forest Resthouse** (singles/doubles without bath US$18/24) is run by Land & Lake Safaris (see Travel Agencies & Tour Operators under Lilongwe earlier) and offers walking trails, mountain biking (at US$5 per day), bird-watching – or simply relaxing. It also arranges transfers to the forest for US$22, as there's no public transport here.

MALAWI

Dedza

Dedza is a small town 85km southeast of Lilongwe, just off the main road between Lilongwe and Blantyre. It's surrounded by forested hills, and the opportunity for good walks and spectacular views in the nearby **Dedza Mountain Forest Reserve**, as described in *Day Outings from Lilongwe* (see Books under Facts for the Visitor earlier in this chapter), are the main attraction. The road south of Dedza skirts the border of Mozambique, revealing on both sides vast plains broken by conical granite peaks and a quilt of farmland, trees, rust-red earth and grass.

For camping, the **Golf Club** (☎ 223322; camp sites US$2.50, singles/doubles without bath US$4.50/9) is close to the wooded backdrop, but its camping terrain is dry and the rooms are fairly uninspiring. You're better off at one of the cheapie resthouses on the main street. **Rainbow Resthouse & Restaurant** (☎ 223403; singles/doubles with bath US$2.50/3.80) is clean, friendly and good value.

On the northern outskirts of town is **Dedza Pottery** (☎ 223069; open 7am-5.30pm daily), with garishly kitsch ceramic products aimed squarely at the expat and tourist market. The **coffee shop** (lunches US$2-3), however, makes for a pleasant stopover, dishing out good moussaka, lasagne and quiche, as well as excellent filter coffee, cakes, tarts and scones. If you're a serious hiker, the **Forest Resthouse**, 8km north of town in the forest reserve, makes a good base.

Northern Malawi

This section covers most parts of Northern Province, from the northern tip of the country down to the Mzuzu and Nkhata Bay areas. Places are described roughly north to south.

KARONGA

In the surrounding dry and dusty country, Karonga is a surprising little oasis. It's the first and last town on the road between Malawi and Tanzania and has some good facilities, including the only bank north of Mzuzu, although it doesn't accept Tanzanian shillings – both Mufwa Lakeshore Lodge & Camping and Club Marina (see later) can advise where to change these.

The pretty, green town is strung out for about 2km along the main street between a roundabout on the north–south road and the lakeshore.

Zgambota Resthouse (singles/doubles US$2.50/3), opposite the Mobil petrol station at the roundabout, has clean and basic rooms with nets.

Safari Lodge (☎ 362340; singles/doubles US$6/7.50), on the road to the lake, is a friendly place, with good-size rooms and a restaurant.

Mufwa Lakeshore Lodge & Camping (☎ 362390; camp sites US$1, singles/doubles without bath US$3.30/5, with bath US$6.50/10) is a large, quiet property that can be difficult to find – it's set back from the road with the turn-off between Club Marina and the National Bank of Malawi. The simple,

---

Carving a Future

The rough S127 that links the M1 to the southern lakeshore is renowned largely for its spectacular scenery, but it's also home to some of Malawi's finest craftspeople.

The road was constructed in 1964, exposing many villagers en route to road graders and 4WDs for the first time. One young boy, Nesto John Singano, manifested his fascination with these huge and incongruous vehicles through carving wooden replicas, in an effort to alleviate poverty. By the 1980s, his talent was widely recognised and the British High Commission provided him with a small grant and the community with a tree-planting project; creating a sustainable industry for Nesto and other carvers in the area. Nesto's work now attracts a diverse clientele, including diplomats, hotels, car companies and of course tourists.

Working out of his workshop, about 10km from the M1 turn-off, Nesto produces meticulous reproductions of earthmovers, 4WDs, motorbikes, caterpillar trucks and any other vehicle he may be commissioned to carve. He uses local soft and hardwoods and devotes weeks to each piece. The result is certainly impressive, with even the finest details being duplicated. You can visit Nesto to see for yourself. His pieces range from US$18 to US$30.

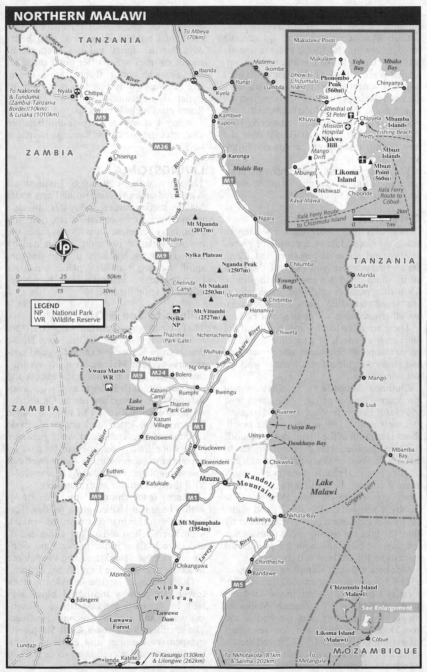

NORTHERN MALAWI

LEGEND
NP National Park
WR Wildlife Reserve

MALAWI

airy rooms have nets and fans and the grassy camping ground has plenty of trees.

Club Marina (☎ *362302; single/double standard chalets US$12/16, superior chalets US$19/22*), near Mufwa, is an excellent, up-market place. Classy chalets (superior ones have hot water) are set in a beautiful, leafy area and the large outdoor bar is perfect for a cold drink. Rates include breakfast.

Chefs Pride Restaurant (*mains US$0.80-1.50*) is a small, pleasant eatery near the roundabout, dishing up cheap and filling Malawian meals.

For transport details, see Tanzania under Land in the main Getting There & Away section earlier in this chapter.

CHITIMBA

Chitimba is little more than a stretch of beach on Lake Malawi, a couple of places to stay and some shops straggled along the highway where you turn off the main north–south road to reach Livingstonia. It's a nice place to chill out, especially if you've just travelled down from Tanzania, but otherwise there's little to see or do.

There are three local places to stay at the junction – all much of a muchness, and all very reasonable. They can store your gear and arrange a guide if you want to walk up to Livingstonia.

Chitimba Campsite (e *kaya01@bushmail .net; camp sites per person US$2, dorm beds US$4, stilt chalets without bath US$10, doubles with bath US$15*) is right on the beach, about 1km north of the Livingstonia turn-off, and very popular with overland trucks. In fact, it's the business they pitch for so it can be quite groupy. Frankly it's a bit of a shock to see a constant herd of bikinis and board-shorts converging on Lake Malawi. The shabby rooms and chalets aren't good value, but food is available all day (order dinner by 4pm!) and the bar usually rocks until late. A new bar is being built with the promise of more room for drinking and partying.

Mdokera's Beach Campsite (*camp sites US$1.50, bed in tree or tent US$2*), about 5km north of Chitimba, is close to the road and the beach and run by a friendly Malawian couple. Our favourite was the bed in the tree! Meals in the simple and clean restaurant range from US$0.50 to US$2.50, and there's a visitors book of hints and comments, which your host will proudly show you.

Namiashi Resort (*camp sites US$2, singles/doubles US$10/15, chalet US$20*), about 5km south of Chitimba, may have seen better days, but it's quiet and has a couple of enormous trees which offer good shade for lazing on the beach. Rooms are a decent size (although only one has nets) and the chalet is particularly good for families. Room rates include breakfast.

A minibus or *matola* (pick-up) between Chitimba and Mzuzu or Karonga is around US$2.

LIVINGSTONIA

The story of the founding of Livingstonia is covered under History in the Facts about Malawi section earlier. Today this town is a unique pocket of colonial Africa, rich with missionary remnants in both physique and psyche. Relative isolation, maintained by arduous access, has kept it quiet and un-spoilt, making it an ideal place to recover from hard travel in Tanzania or the rigours of beachlife on the lake.

Things to See & Do

The fascinating **museum** (*admission US$0.80; open 7.30am-5pm daily*) in the Stone House details early European exploration and missionary work in Malawi. In many regards, the exhibits are a tribute to the efforts and achievements of Dr Robert Laws, who established the Livingstonia mission. On display is an excellent collection of original magic lantern slides, letters and photos. Outside the Stone House, embedded in the grass, are huge stone letters, designed to be read by anyone who happens to be flying overhead in a small plane. They read *Ephesians 2-14*. Visit the museum for an explanation.

Nearby is the **church**, dating from 1894, with a beautiful stained-glass window featuring David Livingstone with his sextant, his medicine chest and his two companions, and Lake Malawi in the background. Sunday services are conducted and visitors are welcome to attend the English one at 8am.

Other places of interest include the **clock tower**. The nearby **industrial block** was built by the early missionaries as a training centre and is now a technical college. The excellent **Khondowe Craft Shop** sells inexpensive carvings and crafts made by local people; all proceeds go to directly to the hospital and mission.

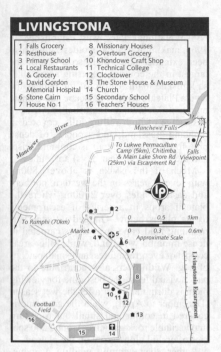

LIVINGSTONIA

1 Falls Grocery
2 Resthouse
3 Primary School
4 Local Restaurants & Grocery
5 David Gordon Memorial Hospital
6 Stone Cairn
7 House No 1
8 Missionary Houses
9 Overtoun Grocery
10 Khondowe Craft Shop
11 Technical College
12 Clocktower
13 The Stone House & Museum
14 Church
15 Secondary School
16 Teachers' Houses

Manchewe River
Manchewe Falls
To Lukwe Permaculture Camp (5km), Chitimba & Main Lake Shore Rd (25km) via Escarpment Rd
Falls Viewpoint
To Rumphi (70km)
Market
Football Field
Livingstonia Escarpment

0   0.5   1km
0   0.3   0.6mi
Approximate Scale

Down the road from here is the **David Gordon Memorial Hospital**, once the biggest hospital in Central Africa, and the **stone cairn** marking the place where missionary Dr Robert Laws and his African companion Uriah Chirwa camped in 1894 when they decided to build the mission here. Also nearby is **House No 1**, the original home of Dr Laws before he moved into the Stone House.

Manchewe Falls, about 4km from the town, is a spectacular 50m-high waterfall with a cave behind it where local people hid from slave-traders some 100 years ago. Allow an hour going down and 1½ hours back up. Alternatively, if you're walking to/from Chitimba, you can visit on the way.

The slightly more adventurous can also arrange abseiling trips for half a day or longer. For more details on either abseiling or hiking contact the friendly people at Lukwe Permaculture Camp (see Places to Stay & Eat following).

Places to Stay & Eat
Stone House (☎ 368223; camp sites per person US$1.50, dorm beds US$2.50, rooms without bath US$10) was built by missionaries in

the early 20th century and still has original Victorian furniture, along with a friendly caretaker, clean bathrooms and occasional hot water. There's an air of reverence about this place and the views from the veranda are superb. Meals are around US$2. Breakfast of tea and pancakes (US$0.50) is also available. You can provide your own food for the cook to prepare, or simply use the kitchen yourself. Campers can use the kitchen for another US$0.50.

There's another **resthouse** (camp sites per person US$1.25, dorm beds US$2, doubles without bath US$3.80) which you reach about 15 minutes before the Stone House if you come up the escarpment road. It's also in a large old colonial house with spectacular views, although maintenance hasn't been great and facilities are more basic. From the garden you can see down to Lake Malawi and the beautiful curved spit of land on the northern side of the bay that appears in the picture in the church window. Meals are served here for US$1, or there's a market and some shops on the road near the hospital if you're self-catering.

Falls Grocery (camp sites US$0.80) is opposite the path to Manchewe Falls, on the escarpment road and has a few dry and dusty places to pitch a tent.

Lukwe Permaculture Camp (e ecologiq ue2000@hotmail.com; camp sites per person US$2.50, 2-bed cabins per person US$7.50) is on the northern side of the escarpment road, above the steep zigzags, an hour's walk east (downhill) from Livingstonia, or about 20km from Chitimba if you're coming up. It's a beautiful, shady, restful place, with stunning views and a friendly atmosphere. Hot showers and clean compost toilets complete this sustainable paradise. All food comes from the garden, with meals around US$1.50 to US$3. Hikes, with or without local guides, can be arranged to surrounding hills and peaks, or down to Chitimba.

Getting There & Away
From the main north–south road between Karonga and Mzuzu, the road to Livingstonia turns off at Chitimba, forcing its way up the escarpment in a series of acute hairpin bends. Drivers should attempt this only in a 4WD, and only if there's been no rain. The road starts off well but the wide dirt road soon becomes a steep rutted track, only just

MALAWI

passable. There's no bus, and you'll wait a very long time if you're hitching.

The alternative is to walk up – it's about 25km, and steep, so it takes five hours from Chitimba if you follow the road. There are short cuts that can cut it to three or four hours, but these are even steeper. Local children will offer to carry your pack for about US$2. Take care on this road, isolated incidences of muggings have occurred so it's best to check the latest situation before you set off, or take a local guide.

The other way to reach Livingstonia, especially if you're coming from the south, is to go to Rumphi (see the following section), and catch a minibus or matola up the scenic 'old road' (west of the main north–south road) to Livingstonia (US$3.80). Sometimes these only go as far as Nchenachena (17km from Livingstonia) or Hananiya (7km from Livingstonia), from where you'll have to walk the remaining distance. If you're driving this route, a 2WD is adequate in dry conditions.

A third option is to walk to Livingstonia from the Nyika Plateau. See the boxed text 'Hiking & Trekking on the Nyika Plateau' under Nyika National Park later in this chapter for details.

RUMPHI

Rumphi (**rum**-pee) is a small town west of the main road between Mzuzu and Karonga, which you'll probably visit if you're heading for Nyika National Park, Vwaza Marsh or Livingstonia. The **Lunyina Motel** (☎ 372248; rooms with bath US$4), behind the Lunyina Savings and Credit Co-operative on the main road, has clean and tidy rooms with nets, although no hot water or electricity. Also on the main road and a better option is **Chimweno Side Lodge** (☎ 372395; singles/doubles with bath US$3.80/5.50, with breakfast US$6.50/9.50), where clean and spacious rooms come with electricity, nets and fans. Next door **Chef's Pride Restaurant** (snacks US$0.50, mains US$1-2.50) serves a variety of meals all day, including toasted sandwiches, chicken and beef stews, vegie dishes and curries.

Matolas to Nyika (US$6.30) and Vwaza (US$3) go from opposite the PTC supermarket. You can ask here about matolas to Livingstonia (US$3.80). Minibuses also run to Mzuzu (US$1.30).

NYIKA NATIONAL PARK

Nyika National Park was established in 1965, making it Malawi's oldest; it has also been extended since then, so it is now the largest in the country, covering some 3000 sq km. The main feature of the park is the Nyika Plateau, with a landscape and climate unique in Malawi, and unusual in Africa: a vast range of high rolling hills, covered in montane grassland, and a pocket of dense pine forest, where the air is cool and crisp, and the views (on clear days) are endless.

Much of the Nyika is above 1800m, with several peaks on the western, northern and eastern sides over 2000m, where the plateau drops in a series of escarpments to the plains below. Gouged into the surrounding landscape are valleys carpeted in dense miombo woodland, while other areas consist of evergreen forest and small patches of bog. Wildflowers also contribute to the park's visual feast; the best time for viewing them is during and just after the wet season (December to April), when the grassland is covered in colour and small outcrops turn into veritable rock gardens. Around 200 species of orchid alone grow on the plateau.

Rather than simply wildlife viewing, Nyika's allure is more of an opportunity to explore a unique and preserved patch of African wilderness by a variety of means. Common animals here include zebras, bushbucks, reedbucks and roan antelopes, (rare elsewhere), and you may also spot elands, warthogs, klipspringers, jackals, duikers and possibly hyaenas and leopards. In the grassland, spotting is easy – in fact the Nyika zebra seem to delight in posing for photos on the skyline. More than 400 species of bird have been recorded here.

Entry fees are payable (see National Parks & Reserves under Facts about Malawi earlier). All accommodation, tourist activities and charter flights are operated by the **Nyika Safari Company** (☎ 330180; e reservations@nyika.com), a small professional outfit based at Chelinda Camp, at the heart of the plateau.

It can get surprisingly cold on the Nyika Plateau, especially at night from June to August, when frost is not uncommon. Log fires are provided in the chalets and rooms, but bring a warm sleeping bag if you're camping. During dry periods, sectors of the park are burnt to prevent larger fires later in

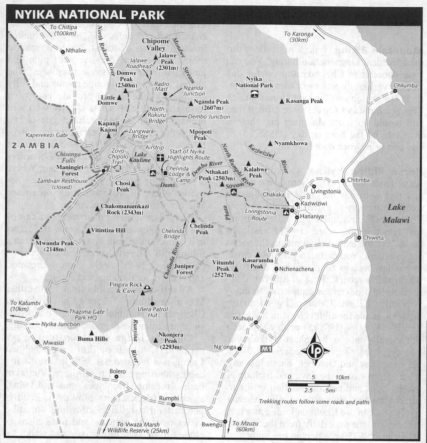

NYIKA NATIONAL PARK

Trekking routes follow some roads and paths

the season. Before setting off for drives or walks, inquire at the park headquarters and avoid areas that are being burnt.

Activities

Wildlife Viewing To appreciate the animals and flowers of Nyika, you can tour the park tracks in your own car (but you'll need a 4WD to access most areas), or arrange a guided wildlife-viewing drive at Chelinda Camp. Morning or night drives last around two hours (US$20 per person), but you can also go all day (US$50). Wildlife viewing is good all year, although in July and August the cold weather means the animals move to lower areas. Bird-watching is particularly good between October and April when migratory birds are on the move.

Day Hiking Although you can't enter the park on foot, hiking is allowed once you've checked into camp. There are several spots where you can leave your car and walk for an hour or all day; staff can advise you on routes. One of the most popular options is to park at the Jalawe roadhead, north of Chelinda Camp, then follow the path for 5km to Jalawe Peak. Beyond the summit is a rocky outcrop overlooking the Chipome Valley, some 1000m below. You can sometimes spot elephants here.

You can hire a guide for walks lasting 2½ hours (US$10 per person) or all day (US$25). Various paths and tracks wind through the plantation woodland, or across the grassland to nearby dams. For longer walks of more than a day, see the boxed text

'Hiking & Trekking on the Nyika Plateau' later.

Mountain Biking Nyika's network of dirt roads is ideal for mountain biking. You can base yourself at Chelinda and go for day rides in various directions or camp out overnight (for which you'll need to hire a guide). This is a fun way to cover more ground than you would on foot. Mountain bike hire is available by the hour or day (US$5/25) or you can bring your own bike in.

Horse Riding Nyika's wide open landscape lends itself perfectly to horse riding, and this is by far the most enjoyable and exhilarating way to experience the plateau. The tussock grass and boggy valley bottoms that can tire hikers are crossed easily by horse, and the extra height means the views are excellent. You can also get much closer to animals such as zebras, elands and roans when on horseback. Best of all, you don't need to be a dexterous equestrian to enjoy yourself; Chelinda Camp has good-quality horses suitable for all levels, which you can hire by the hour (US$15) or day (US$60). For a really thorough look at Nyika's vast beauty, there are horse safaris available between May and October. These last anywhere from two to 10 days and include all meals, rides and accommodation in luxury safari tents (hot showers and all!). Alternatively you can use Chelinda Lodge as a base and explore the park daily from there. Rates are from US$250 per person per night.

Fishing Some anglers reckon Nyika offers some of the best rainbow trout fishing in Malawi. The best time of year to fish is October and November. Fishing is allowed in the dams near Chelinda Camp and in nearby streams (Dam One has the lion's share). You'll need a daily licence (US$4) and rods can be hired by the day (US$5). Only fly fishing is permitted and there's a limit of six fish per rod per day to maintain numbers.

Scenic Flights A great way to see an overview of Nyika's spectacular scenery, particularly the dramatic and largely inaccessible northern section, is to take a scenic flight. Flights last 30 minutes (US$150 for up to five people) or one hour (US$250).

Places to Stay
Chelinda Camp *(4-bed chalets US$120, full-board singles/doubles US$180/280)*, tucked inside a pocket of forest, has atmospheric rooms and chalets dressed with pine and juniper furniture and stone fireplaces. The chalets also contain lounge rooms and fully equipped kitchens; you provide your own food and each chalet has a cook who will prepare meals for you. Chalet guests can also order meals in the restaurant *(continental breakfast US$5, buffet breakfast or lunch US$10, dinner US$15)*, where full-boarders are catered for. There's a cosy bar, where a beer by the roaring fire after a day's activities is one of Malawi's great pleasures. There's also a shop at reception.

About 2km from the main camp is a **camping ground** *(camp sites per person US$5)*, set in a secluded site with vistas of the plateau's rolling hills. The site has permanent security, clean toilets, hot showers, endless firewood and shelters for cooking and eating.

All self-caterers should stock up in either Mzuzu or Rhumpi. There's a small shop at Chelinda for National Parks staff but provisions are often basic and supplies sporadic.

Chelinda Lodge *(full-board cabins per person US$240)*, about 1km from Chelinda Camp, is a forest oasis with luxurious log cabins housing tasteful furniture, Victorian baths, roaring fireplaces and individual balconies (deck chairs provided). Each is perched on a hillside affording stunning views over the plateau, and rates also include full bar, wildlife drives and walks.

Getting There & Away
Despite most maps showing otherwise, there is *no road of any sort* between Chelinda and Livingstonia or any other town on the eastern side of the plateau.

Air The quickest way to reach Chelinda Camp is on a flight operated by the Nyika Safari Company. Flights for up to five people can be chartered from Chilumba (US$180) and Lilongwe (US$1040), while rates from Mzuzu are US$115 per person. It also flies to other Malawian destinations as well as Tanzania and Zambia (see the main Getting There & Away section earlier in this chapter for details) and it has regular promotional offers; contact the company for more information.

Hiking & Trekking on the Nyika Plateau

A good range of long-distance routes (sometimes called 'wilderness trails') are available on Nyika, and all hiking is efficiently organised by the Nyika Safari Company at Chelinda Camp. The company provides the obligatory guide and porters, who have their own sleeping bags, tents, cooking pots and food. You must provide all the equipment and food you need.

There is only one set route in the park; generally you either follow the park tracks, paths and wildlife trails or simply walk across the trackless grassland, but some paths are more popular than others – those to the peaks and viewpoints on the western and northern escarpments are especially popular. There are no set camp sites either. The wilderness trails are not designed so you can stalk wildlife to get better photos, but rather to show you the animals as part of the wider environment, and help you enjoy the splendid feeling of space that walking on Nyika provides. If you discuss your interests with the staff at Chelinda Camp, they can advise on a suitable route.

The only set route on Nyika – and by far the most popular – goes from Chelinda to Livingstonia, a spectacular and hugely rewarding walk, crossing east through the high grassland, then dropping steeply through the wooded escarpment and passing through villages and farmland to reach the old mission station at Livingstonia. This route takes three days. The third night is spent in Livingstonia, and you can walk down to the lakeshore at Chitimba on the fourth day. For more ideas, a chapter on trekking in Malawi is included in Lonely Planet's *Trekking in East Africa*.

Organised hikes can usually run with a day or two's notice, but advance warning is preferred.

Two-day (one-night) hikes cost US$30 per person for two hikers (US$50/70/110 for three/four/six days); add US$10 for each extra hiker. The Livingstonia Trail (three days, two nights) costs US$80 per person for two hikers; add US$10 for each extra hiker. Fees cover the guide and all his costs; porters are also available.

Bus There are no public buses into the park; the nearest you can get is the service from Mzuzu to Rhumpi (US$1). From there, you can get a matola or minibus to Chelinda Camp (US$6.50). To get from Chelinda Camp to either Nthalire in the north or Rhumpi, contact the radio operator at Chelinda Camp, who will advise matolas or minibuses heading through the park to divert to Chelinda for you.

Taxi You can hire a taxi (or a matola) in Mzuzu or Rumphi to take you all the way to Chelinda Camp. This costs around US$100 (less from Rumphi), which is not too bad if you get a few people together. Of course, if the taxi has to wait around for a few days to take you out again this will be more expensive, but we've heard from several travellers who used this method to reach Chelinda and then hitched out a few days later, or walked off via the Livingstonia route. If you take the taxi option, it's essential to leave early in the morning so your driver has time to get back.

Car The main Thazima gate (pronounced and sometimes spelt Tazima) is in the southwest of the park, 54km from Rumphi; to Chelinda Camp it's another 55km. The road is dirt after Rumphi and in fair condition as far as Thazima gate. In the park the tracks are rough and really only suitable for 4WD vehicles or 2WD vehicles with high clearance, although at the time of writing the road to Chelinda Camp was about to be upgraded to a full-gravel standard, making it accessible to all cars. Kaperekezi gate, in the west of the park, is rarely used by travellers. Fuel is available at Chelinda, but in limited supply so it's best to fill up before you enter the park.

Bicycle It's possible to bring a mountain bike into Nyika and you can cycle from Thazima gate to Chelinda, but an early start is recommended due to the distance.

VWAZA MARSH WILDLIFE RESERVE

For one reason or another this reserve seems to be one of Malawi's best-kept secrets, but it's possibly your best chance to get up close and personal with elephants and well worth a visit. Vwaza is an ideal destination for any budget; it's compact and accessible, the accommodation is close to the main gate,

MALAWI

and public transport here is straightforward. Entry fees are payable (see National Parks & Reserves under Facts about Malawi earlier). All tourist activities, places to stay and charter flights are operated by the **Nyika Safari Company** (see its entry under Nyika National Park earlier for details).

The main camp is conveniently located a safe but rewarding distance from the hippo-heavy Lake Kazuni, which also lures impalas, buffaloes (rumoured to be particularly aggressive here), waterbucks, elands, roans, sables, zebras, hartebeests and pukus. The big attraction however, is the 160 plus elephants within the park. There are regular parades in front of the camps and between July and September, diners at Kazuni Safari Camp often have to share their personal space with bulls munching on nuts around the restaurant. Vwaza's **bird-watching** is also excellent – this is one of the best places in Malawi to see waders.

There's a range of vegetation and habitats in the reserve. In the north is Vwaza Marsh itself and a large area of swamp surrounded by miombo woodland. There are also smaller areas of mopane and acacia woodland. The Luwewe River runs through the reserve (draining the marshland) and joins the South Rukuru River (the reserve's southern border), which flows into Lake Kazuni.

A good network of driveable tracks in the reserve is easily explored in a 4WD or high-clearance vehicle; if you're in a 2WD, ask at Kazuni Camp for advice on the condition of the tracks. The best driving route is along the southern edge of the reserve, parallel to the river, heading to Zoro Pools. A better way to witness wildlife is on foot – either around Lake Kazuni or on a longer wilderness trail, but you must be accompanied by a guide (US$5 per person).

It's also possible to arrange a **cultural tour** at Kazuni Safari Camp. The local Natural Resources Committee (see National Parks & Reserves under Facts about Malawi earlier) has established cultural centres in three of the surrounding villages, where visitors can witness traditional dancing, singing (participation is encouraged!) and day-to-day activities including blacksmithing, agricultural activities and cooking. It's a rewarding experience and an excellent opportunity to meet Malawian people in a genuine setting. Tours (US$8 per person)

can be done by car or bicycle and all proceeds go to education, health and welfare programmes within the villages. An additional donation after the tour is appreciated and can be as small or large as you like.

Places to Stay
Kazuni Camp *(camp sites per person US$5, single/double chalets without bath US$13/20)* has simple, rustic chalets with beds, clean sheets and mosquito nets. They are separated by a decent stretch of bush, so you still get a sense of privacy and wilderness while being within a camp. You must bring food, and the very friendly staff will cook for you if required. Alternatively, you can borrow the use of the kitchen and its utensils for an extra US$3 or make use of one of the barbecues. It's best to stock up in Rhumpi or Mzuzu.

Kazuni Safari Camp *(full-board singles/doubles US$195/300)* accommodates guests in smart and stylish chalets with thatched roofs and verandas in a prime position overlooking the lake. Rates also include game drives and walks, but if you don't want the whole package, cheaper rates may be available.

Getting There & Away
The Nyika Safari Company operates flights for a minimum of two people between Vwaza Marsh and Mzuzu (US$115 per person) or Chelinda Camp in Nyika National Park (US$80 per person). If you're travelling by public transport, first get to Rumphi (reached from Mzuzu by minibus for US$1.30). From there fairly frequent matolas and minibuses run to the main gate (US$3). By car, head west from Rumphi. Turn left after 10km (Vwaza Marsh Wildlife Reserve is signposted), and continue for about 20km. Where the road swings left over a bridge, go straight on to reach the park gate and camp after 1km.

MZUZU
Mzuzu (known as 'the capital of the north') is a large town established around a grand tree-lined avenue. It has banks, shops, a post office, supermarkets, pharmacies, petrol stations and other facilities, which are especially useful if you've come into Malawi from the north. Most travellers find themselves staying for at least one night, as a stopover on the north–south route, or

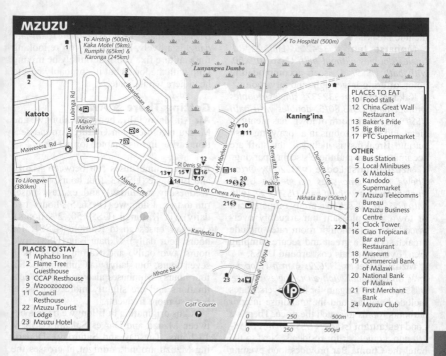

MZUZU

To Airstrip (500m),
Kaka Motel (5km),
Rumphi (65km) &
Karonga (245km)

To Hospital (500m)

Lunyangwa Dambo

Katoto

Kaning'ina

Lubinga Rd

Boardman Rd

M'Mbelwa Rd

Jomo Kenyatta Rd

Dunduzu Cres

Main
Market

Mawerera Rd

St Denis St

Mapale Cres

Orton Chewa Ave

Nkhata Bay (50km)

Police

Kanjedza Dr

Kabunduli Viphya Dr

Mhone Rd

Golf Course

To Lilongwe
(380km)

PLACES TO EAT
10 Food stalls
12 China Great Wall
    Restaurant
13 Baker's Pride
15 Big Bite
17 PTC Supermarket

OTHER
4 Bus Station
5 Local Minibuses
  & Matolas
6 Kandodo
  Supermarket
7 Mzuzu Telecomms
  Bureau
8 Mzuzu Business
  Centre
14 Clock Tower
16 Ciao Tropicana
   Bar and
   Restaurant
18 Museum
19 Commercial Bank
   of Malawi
20 National Bank
   of Malawi
21 First Merchant
   Bank
24 Mzuzu Club

PLACES TO STAY
1 Mphatso Inn
2 Flame Tree
  Guesthouse
3 CCAP Resthouse
9 Mzoozoozoo
11 Council
   Resthouse
22 Mzuzu Tourist
   Lodge
23 Mzuzu Hotel

0   250   500m
0   250   500yd

as a jumping-off point for Vwaza, Viphya, Nyika or Nkhata Bay.

Information

The **National Bank of Malawi**, **Commercial Bank of Malawi** and **First Merchant Bank**, all on Orton Chewa Ave, exchange travellers cheques and money, and offer credit card withdrawals. If you're heading to the lake cash up here as there is no foreign exchange facility in Nkhata Bay.

Internet access is available at the **Mzuzu Telecomms Bureau** (US$13.50/hr), or directly opposite at the **Mzuzu Business Centre** (☎ 334588; US$15/hr). The latter serves snacks and very good filter coffee.

Things to See

The **museum** (e museums@malawi.net; M'Mbelwa Rd; admission US$0.80; open 7am-noon & 1pm-5pm daily) has interesting displays on the history of African and European peoples in northern Malawi and a section on indigenous plants and wildlife. The best feature, however, is the cultural dancing, which staff can organise if they know visitors are coming.

Places to Stay

Council Resthouse (off M'Mbelwa Rd; singles/doubles US$1.50/3), near the small market, has basic rooms that will suffice if you're really short of cash.

CCAP Resthouse (also known as the William Koyi Guest House; ☎ 333050; Boardman Rd; camp sites per person US$0.80, dorm beds US$2.50, rooms with/without bath US$9.50/6), northeast of the bus station, is spotless and well organised. It's operated by the church so a respectful code of conduct is appropriate.

Mzoozoozoo (☎ 08 864493; camp sites US$1, dorm beds US$2.50, doubles US$5) is Mzuzu's only hostel and the very friendly owners make it a good one at that. Dorms are in a big timber bungalow and a constant stream of happy activity buzzes around the bar inside (there's another being built out the back). They also run **Tropicana Restaurant** (dishes US$1-4) here, which serves tasty steaks and perfect omelettes. Look for the Rasta colours on the gate or call to arrange collection from the bus station.

Flame Tree Guesthouse (☎ 333053; rooms with/without bath US$12/10) is a relaxed option, with clean, cool and homely rooms, a

MALAWI

pleasant veranda and a leafy garden. Rates include breakfast.

Mphatso Inn (☎ 334205; Lubinga Rd; singles/doubles without bath US$6.50/9.50, with bath US$9/14) is an accommodating hotel, offering large, light and airy rooms.

Kaka Motel (☎ 332337; singles/doubles without bath US$3.80/5, doubles with bath US$13-15), 6km north of town, has plenty of clean and simple rooms in a sprawling bush setting. Breakfast is included, the staff are accommodating and there's secure parking.

Mzuzu Tourist Lodge (☎ 332097; Orton Chewa Ave; camp sites per person US$5, singles/doubles without bath US$20/27, with bath US$29/36), set on a pretty property east of town, has pleasant but arguably overpriced rooms (although room rates include breakfast) and a green and secure camping area. Evening meals cost around US$3.

Mzuzu Hotel (☎ 332622; e mzh@sdnp.org .mw; off Kabunduli Viphya Dr; singles/doubles US$50/64) is a bargain for high-flyers. Rates include breakfast and the grandiose interior harbours rooms to match the price. There's a good **restaurant** (starters US$3, mains US$5-10) and a quiet bar for residents. Next to the hotel the **Choma Bar** provides loud evening entertainment with a local flavour.

Places to Eat

For cheap eats, there are **food stalls** around the market and Council Resthouse and the excellent **Baker's Pride** (Orton Chewa Ave), which sells delicious pies, sausage rolls, samosas and cakes. Self-caterers can stock up at the **PTC** supermarket (Orton Chewa Ave).

Big Bite (dishes US$0.60-2; open 8am-8pm Mon-Sat), near the PTC supermarket, is a good local joint serving hearty Malawian dishes. If you're really hungry a whole chicken with chips costs US$6.

China Great Wall Restaurant (☎ 333609; St Denis St; starters US$1.30, mains US$1.50-3; open lunch and dinner daily) serves a huge assortment of tasty Chinese dishes in virtually any variation, including seafood and vegetarian.

Mzuzu Club (off Kabunduli Viphya Dr; starters US$1, mains US$2.50; open dinner daily), next to the Mzuzu Hotel, has a small, sterile restaurant open to nonmembers, with a no-nonsense menu including steaks, chicken dishes and curries. Portions are decent and beers are cheap.

Ciao Tropicana Bar & Restaurant (St Denise St; snacks from US$2; open 10am-late daily) is a lively, local bar if you're looking for a culture fix. You'll definitely be mixing it up with the locals but it's probably best to head here with a mate.

Getting There & Away

Air Air Malawi flies between Lilongwe and Mzuzu (see the main Getting Around section earlier in this chapter for details).

Bus Coachline buses run between Mzuzu and Lilongwe (US$13, four hours, Monday, Wednesday, Saturday) and express buses run to/from Lilongwe (US$6, 5½ hours, two daily) via Kasungu (US$2.50, 2½ hours). Ordinary buses go to Rumphi (US$1, 1½ hours, four daily), Nkhata Bay (US$1, two hours, two daily) and Karonga (US$3.80, seven hours, four daily) via Chitimba (US$2, four hours). Minibuses also go to these destinations and are slightly more expensive, but also more frequent.

A bus originating in Lilongwe travels between Mzuzu and Dar es Salaam (US$28, 17 hours, Tuesday and Saturday). Departing Mzuzu around midnight, it crosses the border at first light, goes through Mbeya in the morning and gets to Dar es Salaam late in the afternoon.

NKHATA BAY

Nkhata Bay is a lush tropical indent on the northern lakeshore that lures a constant stream of travellers with its Caribbeanesque milieu. This may be a touch fanciful, but the bay is quite picturesque at sunrise and sunset, and most recreation certainly involves a good deal of lounging by the water. 'Town', nestled into a gully with the bay to the west and a gentle rise of dense forest to the east, is a bustling clutch of markets, craft stalls, local activity and visitors. The good cross section of 'lodges' here are all fully equipped to entertain you from dawn to well past bedtime, and it's easy to get lulled into eating, sleeping and drinking within their confines. However, patronising local eateries, mixing with the locals and general meandering is good fun and well worth the extra energy.

Information

There's nowhere to change money so make sure you cash up in Mzuzu, Nkhotakota

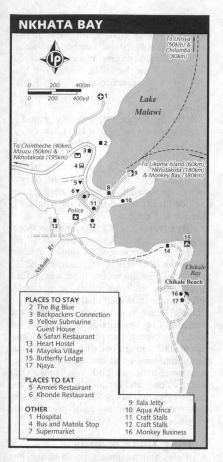

NKHATA BAY

Lake Malawi

To Usisya
(50km) &
Chilumba
(80km)

To Chintheche (40km),
Mzuzu (50km) &
Nkhotakota (195km)

To Likoma Island (60km),
Nkhotakota (180km)
& Monkey Bay (380km)

Police

Chikale
Bay
Chikale Beach

0   200   400m
0   200   400yd

PLACES TO STAY
2 The Big Blue
3 Backpackers Connection
8 Yellow Submarine
   Guest House
   & Safari Restaurant
13 Heart Hostel
14 Mayoka Village
15 Butterfly Lodge
17 Njaya

PLACES TO EAT
5 Annies Restaurant
6 Khonde Restaurant

OTHER
1 Hospital
4 Bus and Matola Stop
7 Supermarket
9 Ilala Jetty
10 Aqua Africa
11 Craft Stalls
12 Craft Stalls
16 Monkey Business

Activities

Swimming On the southern side of Nkhata Bay, **Chikale Beach** is a popular spot for swimming and lazing on the sand, especially at weekends. Snorkelling equipment is free for guests at most of the lodges.

Kayaking For something more active, **Monkey Business** (☎ 252365; e njayalodge@ malawi.net) operates fully inclusive (meals, kayaks, guides and tents) kayak excursions from anything between two to seven days for US$30 per person per day. Typical itineraries include idyllic spots along the northern lakeshore such as Usisya and Ruarwe, or spectacular trips to Likoma and Chizumulu Islands, sailing aboard the *Ilala* ferry, then paddling around the Mozambique shore. Journeys are broken by stopovers at fishing villages and empty beaches and these trips are a great way to explore the area. It also arranges one-day kayak–bushwalk–dive tours for US$35 per person.

Diving If you want to learn scuba diving, **Aqua Africa** (☎/fax 352284; e andy@aqua -africa.com) runs five-day courses with six dives for US$150, starting on Sunday, or day courses on Monday or Thursday for US$35. Travellers rave about these guys, particularly the company's attention to safety; groups are a maximum of six people. You should try to book in advance, but if they're full you only have to wait a few days for the next course to start.

Organised Tours

Baby Butterfly, based at Butterfly Lodge (see Places to Stay & Eat later) organises tours on request to Likoma and Chizumulu Islands, Mozambique, Usisya and Ruarwe on a speed boat for US$300 per day (maximum four people). It can also arrange tours by car to Nyika National Park, Vwaza Marsh Reserve and Livingstonia for US$50 per person per day, including all meals and camping.

Places to Stay & Eat

Nkhata Bay has several places to stay and eat, all strung out in a line along the road into town and along the lakeshore. Places are described roughly north to south. All beds at the following have mosquito nets.

The Big Blue (☎ 352370; e bigblue@sdnp .org.mw; camp sites per person US$1.30, dorm

*or Lilongwe. Alternatively, several of the lodges accept credit cards, US currency and travellers cheques for payment. Internet access is available at **The Big Blue** (see Places to Stay & Eat later).*

Unfortunately, security has become a bit of a problem here. Travellers have been attacked and robbed when walking outside the town centre (especially to/from Chikale Bay), and a few people have had bags snatched near the bus station while looking for a place to stay (thieves love new arrivals). These have been isolated incidents, but to combat the problem, the hotels, lodges, restaurants and Aqua Africa have got together and will 'lend' their watchman free of charge to anyone walking outside the town centre. Use this service and you'll have no worries.

MALAWI

beds/singles/doubles without bath US$2.50/ 3.80/7.50) is a friendly and serene haven, with five-bed dorms and small and comfortable bamboo chalets set over the water. The spacious bar and outdoor dining area have unlimited lake views, security is good, and there's an email service.

Backpackers Connection (e bigblue@sdnp .org.mw; camp sites US$2, dorm beds/singles/ doubles without bath US$2.50/3.80/6) is set back from the main road as you head into town. The accommodation is a little cramped and competition for the limited bathrooms may be fierce, but this is a genuine backpackers, complete with animated bar and traveller's graffiti adorning the walls. Party animals will enjoy this place.

Annies Restaurant (dishes US$0.80-2), on the corner of the main road and a small side road leading west past the bus stop, is a small local joint offering tasty chicken and fish dishes with rice. The nearby **Khonde Restaurant** is similar. Both have limited menus in low season.

Yellow Submarine Guest House (☎ 352371; singles/doubles/triples without bath US$2/2.50/3) has small, clean, safe rooms with fans and a secluded garden laden with brilliant bougainvillea. Next door, the **Safari Restaurant** (dishes US$0.90-2) serves light meals and good toasted sandwiches, which taste even better with a cold beer in the courtyard or around the pool table.

Aqua Africa (single/doubles with bath US$10/20) has a few secluded and comfortable rooms with balconies overlooking the private beach (see Diving under Activities earlier for contact details).

Heart Hostel (floor space US$0.60, singles/ doubles without bath US$1.20/2.50) is wedged into the village behind the main road. It's pretty rudimentary (no fans, basic bathrooms and a scarcity of nets) but an excellent way to pump funds straight into the local community because it's Malawian-owned. There's a constant stream of human traffic here so be discreet with your valuables.

The other accommodation options in town are scattered around Chikale beach further south. To get here stay on the dirt road, cross the bridge and head up hill and down dale (always seems harder with a backpack). It's about 30 minutes walk.

Mayoka Village (☎ 352421; e catedot com@sdnp.org.mw; single/double chalets without bathroom US$3.80/7.60) has neat and picturesque chalets, all meticulously constructed out of stone, bamboo and wood, with fans and private chairs and tables overlooking the bay. The restaurant here cooks up a great barbecue buffet on Friday night (US$4), to which nonresidents are welcome.

Butterfly Lodge (w www.lake-paradise .com; camp sites per person US$1, dorm beds US$3, single/double huts without bathroom US$5/10, cottages per person US$17) has comfortable rooms, a good restaurant and an atmospheric bar, all scattered over a rocky, tree-coated incline. Cottage rates include breakfast and use of the kitchen is free for self-caterers.

Njaya (☎/fax 352342; e njayalodge@com puserve.com; camp sites per person US$1.30, bandas per person US$3, singles/doubles with bath US$15/30, cottages from US$20) is a sprawling and secure hideaway, which is legendary on the travellers' grapevine. It offers Asian-style reed chalets (bandas) on Chikale Beach and a range of cabins and bungalows on the hillside overlooking the lake. The breezy bar (complete with animated staff you are bound to befriend) has panoramic views and the excellent restaurant serves delicious food. You can get your laundry done, and for all you city slickers, credit cards are accepted. A transfer van runs sporadic trips between Njaya and the town centre and also meets the Ilala.

Getting There & Away

All buses and minibuses go from the bus stand on the main road. Ordinary buses run to Mzuzu (US$1, two hours, two daily) and minibuses and matolas run to Nkhotakota (US$3.80, six hours), Chintheche (US$1, one hour) and Mzuzu (US$1.50, 1½ hours). To reach Lilongwe, go to Mzuzu and transfer. Many travellers also come or go on the Songeya and Ilala ferries (see the main Getting There & Away and Getting Around sections earlier in this chapter).

AROUND NKHATA BAY

North of Nkhata Bay, the steep slopes of the Rift Valley escarpment plunge straight down to the lake and there's no room for a road alongside the shore. The isolated villages along this stretch provide a remote experience that is well worth the trek.

Village life, Malealea, Lesotho

Mural on shop wall, Tishweshwe Crafts, Malkerns Valley, Swaziland

White-breasted cormorants, Liwonde National Park, Malawi

Horse riding, Nyika Plateau, Malawi

Sunset, Lake Malawi, Malawi

ANDREW VAN SMEERDIJK

DAVID ELSE

ANDREW MACCOLL

Usisya Lodge *(e bigblue@sdnp.org.mw; hammocks per person US$1.30, camp sites per person US$2, dorm beds US$2.50, single/ double reed huts without bath US$5/10)*, approximately 50km north of Nkhata Bay, is a small, Robinson Crusoesque beach lodge, sheltered by dense vegetation and spectacular mountains. An open bar furnished with cushioned benches, planted firmly near the water's edge, makes for some healthy lazing and free-flowing conversation, as do the communal meals (the local chefs were perfecting Delia Smith's cookbook at the time of research).

Fifteen kilometres further north and barely perceptible from the water is **Wherearewe** *(w www.lake-paradise.com; camp sites per person US$1.30, dorm beds US$2, single/ double chalets without bathroom from US$5/ 10)*. This hidden retreat, near the village of Ruarwe, has stone and thatch chalets and an impressive bar sculptured around natural rock formations, with rock art and pillars carved by Nkhata Bay artists. A troop of fish eagles, kingfishers and otters regularly entertain guests and on a clear day it's possible to spot tin roofs shimmering in the distance on the Tanzanian mountain ranges. This is also a great base to walk for an hour, or three days, on paths well trodden by local feet.

The *Ilala* ferry (see the main Getting Around section earlier in this chapter) stops at both Usisya and Ruarwe villages, which are a 20-minute walk north and south respectively of the lodges. Both lodges also transfer guests from Nkhata Bay by speed boat; it takes around 4½ hours to get to Usisya Lodge and six to Wherearewe and both destinations cost US$4.50. Book at **The Big Blue** for Usisya Lodge or at **Butterfly Lodge** for Wherearewe (see Places to Stay under Nkhata Bay earlier).

It's also possible to walk south from Chitimba Bay. This journey takes two to three days and you should be well prepared with water, food and a tent. The tracks are clear and it's an excellent way to explore the untouched northern shore and visit the many villages along the way. Speak to the lodges at either end before you set out for an update on track conditions.

THE CHINTHECHE STRIP

Chintheche is an unremarkable village about 40km south of Nkhata Bay. Nearby is a long and beautiful stretch of lakeshore known as the 'Chintheche Strip'. It's lined with hotels, lodges and camping grounds, each catering for different types of traveller. They all lie between 2km and 5km east of the main road that runs between Nkhata Bay and Nkhotakota, and usually involve a drive or walk along a dirt track through forest or farmland. If you're travelling by bus, the express services may not stop at every turn-off, but minibuses stop almost anywhere on request.

Places to Stay

The following places are described north to south.

Kawiya Kottages *(e sosmalawi@globemw .net; camp sites per person US$5, chalets US$10)*, about 3km north of Chintheche village, has two simple cabins in a shady site on a private bit of beach. Each is fully self-contained, including an equipped kitchen.

Forest Resthouse *(rooms with bath US$5)* is nearer to town, down the track running west from the PTC supermarket. It has clean, two-bed rooms and although you need to bring your own food the friendly caretaker will cook it for you. A second track leading west culminates at **London Cottages** *(☎ 357291; camp sites US$2.50, chalets US$6.50)*, with slightly neglected two-bed chalets, set on a sprawling, green site by the beach. There's also a bar and restaurant (dishes US$2) serving the usual chicken or chambo and chips fare.

Flame Tree Lodge *(camp sites per person US$2.50, chalets with bath US$19)*, about 2km down the main road, and another 2km along a track, is a peaceful place with smart and pleasant two-bed chalets set on a beautiful promontory jutting into the lake. The showers are hot and there's an open-air bar and restaurant (dishes US$5). This is a suitable place for families, couples or small groups.

Chintheche Inn *(☎/fax 357211; e chininn@ malawi.net; camp sites per person US$5.50, singles/doubles US$59/88)* is a grand and beautiful property, with cabanas on the beach and cane furniture under shady trees on the expansive lawns. Tasteful and elegant rooms each have their own veranda and path leading to the beach and rates include full buffet breakfast. The restaurant (dishes US$5 to US$10) serves very good food. Activities on offer include windsurfing (US$2 per hour),

village visits and birding walks. If you want to reserve a room and can't get through, call Central African Wilderness Safaris in Lilongwe (see Travel Agencies & Tour Operators under Lilongwe earlier).

Nkhwazi Lodge *(camp sites US$1)* is a good place overlooking a small sandy cove. It can be found by travelling another 1km south down the main road where you'll reach a signpost to the 'CCAP School' (also called New Bandawe); go through here to reach this South African-run place. There are basic but clean ablution blocks, and a 'pub' with home-cooked meals from US$3 to US$5. Scuba gear and motorboats for anglers can be hired.

Makuzi Beach *(☎ 357296; e makuzi beach@sdnp.org.mw; camp sites per person US$3, singles/doubles without bath US$23/35, single/double chalets US$45/70)* can be found by continuing south down the main road where you'll reach the turn-off to Bandawe (also called Old Bandawe); it's another 3.5km down the track. The accommodation and facilities here are a step up in quality, and the restaurant (dishes US$1 to US$4) serves the best food on the strip. If you're feeling active you can hire a windglider, power boat, mountain bike or even a yacht.

Kande Beach Camp *(☎ 357376; e kande ach@licom.net; camp sites US$2, dorm beds US$4, chalets with bath US$20)* is about 7km from the Makuzi turn-off (55km south of Nkhata Bay). It's a legendary stop for overland trucks, where beachlife, good times and late night partying is the name of the game. All accommodation is excellent and the smorgasbord of facilities include a large bar, a games room, a book exchange and the **Soft Sand Cafe** *(dishes US$4)*, which serves great pizzas. For activities, there's **Aquanuts**, a professional dive centre offering PADI courses for US$180 and casual dives from US$25, and **Kande Horse Trails** offering three-hour rides. If that doesn't float your boat you can hire mountain bikes, canoes, kayaks, sailboards, windsurfers or snorkelling equipment.

Mwaya Beach Lodge *(camp sites per person US$2, singles/doubles without bath US$5/10)*, another 7km further south, is a quiet, restful and friendly place, with simple and comfortable chalets. It's the complete opposite to Kande Beach and designed for relaxation rather than wild partying – the

entrance track even crosses weak bridges to keep the overland trucks out! There's no restaurant so you need to bring your own drinks and food, but the staff will cook it all up for you. You can stay here and learn to dive at Kande Beach for US$255, which includes the course, all food and accommodation.

LIKOMA ISLAND

Likoma and Chizumulu Islands are on the Mozambican side of Lake Malawi, but are part of Malawi.

The blissful island of Likoma measures 17 sq km and is home to around 6000 people. Isolation from the mainland has enabled the locals here to maintain their reserved culture, shaped partly by the religious legacy of missionaries, but also by the lack of any transient population – international or domestic. These are possibly the friendliest people in Malawi and there is no crime on the island.

Likoma's flat and sandy south is littered with stately baobabs, and has a constant panorama of Mozambique's wild coast only 40km away. In the hilly north, prolific eucalypts and mango trees compete for views over the vast enormity of the lake. The main drawcard is an abundance of pristine beaches and the activities revolving around them, but there's a healthy dose of other activities, both cultural and physical to fill several days here. Those looking for wild parties or another beach to conquer will be disappointed however; Likoma's beauty is it's preservation and both the lodges and locals are happy to keep it that way.

Things to See & Do

Most people use the *Ilala* ferry to get to and from Likoma, which yields a good five days to relax, wear yourself out or both. In Chipyela, the impressive Anglican **Cathedral of St Peter** should not be missed (see the boxed text 'Likoma Missionaries & The Cathedral of St Peter' later). You can climb the tower for spectacular views. Nearby, the neat **market place** contains a few shops and stalls, and an old baobab overtaken by a strangler fig, now rotted away from underneath and used by the locals as a storeroom. Down on the lakeshore is a beach where local boats come and go, and the people wash and sell fish. Don't be surprised if some people greet you in Portuguese; traders come here from nearby

Where to on the Lake?

Irresistible Lake Malawi dominates the country's landscape and lures visitors with the promise of pristine water, sandy beaches and stunning marine life. It has often been described as an inland sea and when trying to spot Mozambique's hazy silhouette on the horizon you can understand why. The lake's enigmatic weather often entertains storms thick enough to rouse five-metre waves and intimidating swells, shifting within an hour to flawless blue skies reflected in the water's glassy veneer.

The lakeshore's environment changes starkly from dramatic escarpments pressing against the water's edge in the north, to flat sandy bays in the south. It can be tough figuring out where to go, so the following should help you decide which destination (if not all!) appeals to you most.

The North

This is the least developed section of the lake, and travel between Chitimba and Nkhata Bay must be by foot or the *Ilala*. Chitimba is usually brimming with partying overlanders and travellers, unwinding after the trek from Tanzania. But the heady atmosphere is absent in the remote and tranquil villages of Ruarwe and Usisya.

Nkhata Bay

This scenic town is the backpackers' mecca and a great base to explore the rest of the lake. The glut of accommodation suits most tastes and wallets and many turn an intended stopover into a few weeks, seduced by the excellent diving, kayaking, walking, socialising and laid back atmosphere.

Likoma and Chizumulu Islands

Sublime beaches, unparalleled diving, breathtaking walks, preserved cultures and one of the country's finest cathedrals inhabit these small and unique islands. There's excellent accommodation and a rare opportunity to immerse yourself in untainted village life.

Chintheche Strip

A secluded collection of camping grounds, lodges and resorts pepper this picturesque stretch of the lake, a hop skip and jump from the wooded hills of the Viphya Plateau.

Senga Bay

Snorkelling and bush walking around this sleepy cove are popular, but it's the sunbaking fatigue that traps most visitors. It's reached easily and quickly from Lilongwe and offers a decent selection of places to stay.

Cape Maclear

Although the crowds that once swarmed this classic backpackers haunt have moved on, it's still a beautiful spot to swim, sail, kayak and dive, not to mention explore Lake Malawi National Park.

Monkey Bay to Mangochi

A smattering of top-end hotels, mid-range resorts and budget lodges here all have a few kilometres of private beach and the facilities to keep you from moving far.

Mozambique to sell firewood, vegetables and – bizarrely – fish. The *Ilala* stops at another beach about 1km to the south.

Swimming is a must on Likoma and best on the long stretches of beach in the south, although Yofu Bay in the north is also good. The tropical fish population has been undented by the mainland's overfishing and the **snorkelling** is excellent. For a closer look, Mango Drift (see Places to Stay & Eat later) arranges four-day open water PADI **scuba diving** courses for US$150, including accommodation. Casual dives cost US$20. If you want to explore the water's surface, Kaya Mawa (see Places to Stay & Eat later) offers **water skiing** for US$20. It's also worthwhile to drag yourself away from the beach to explore Likoma's network

MALAWI

of tracks, roads and small villages. The island's compact but diverse area is perfect for **walking** or **mountain biking** – you can bring these across on the ferry or hire them from Mango Drift for US$10 per day. Akuzike Guesthouse (see Places to Stay & Eat later) has produced a map of the island, showing the best beaches and areas of interest and suggesting a number of walks. When exploring, remember that this isn't the Costa del Sol – the people here live a very traditional way of life, so keep your clothing and behaviour suitably modest.

A greater understanding of Chewa culture can be experienced by a consultation with Likoma's witch doctor. His clinic is near Khuyu Village and you will need to make an appointment.

Places to Stay & Eat

Akuzike Guesthouse *(singles/doubles without bathroom US$2/3.80)*, in Chipyela, offers basic rooms with nets around a central courtyard. It has a small restaurant (dishes US$3) and is a nice place to immerse yourself in the village atmosphere.

Chikondano Restaurant *(mains US$0.50-1)* near the market, serves simple, tasty fare. Ordering meals in advance may prove rewarding, and don't expect a huge menu – the staples here are fish, nsima and rice; fruit and veg are more limited.

Mango Drift *(☎ 871 761, 684 670; e Kaya 01@bushmail.net; camp sites per person US$1, dorm beds US$3, single/double chalets without bath US$4/8)* is a series of simple stone and thatched chalets spread across a beautiful beach on the western side of the island. Each has its own patch of sand leading to the water amid a healthy smattering of trees for shade. The breezy, spacious bar and restaurant (dishes US$3 to US$4) hunkers beneath a stunning mango tree close to the water (order dinner by 4pm to allow for preparation). Guests can also dine at **Kaya Mawa** (see following) *(buffet lunch US$6, 4-course dinner US$13)*, which is highly recommended. Snorkelling is free and there are plans to add more comfortable chalets for US$20 per person.

Kaya Mawa *(full-board chalets per person US$85-160)* is run by the same friendly bunch as Mango Drift. This luxury lodge is one of Africa's finest paradise retreats, and its beauty lies in the ingenuity of its design. Each chalet has been meticulously constructed around the natural landscape, using rock faces as walls or screens for open-air showers and stone baths. The interiors are all teak, mahogany and thatch and all rooms have private access to the lake (the honeymoon suite even has its own islet). The bar, perched on the top of a huge rock buttress, offers seamless views of mango-hued sunsets and the meals are possibly the finest in Malawi. The owners have gone to painstaking length to be unobtrusive on both the landscape and local population and this aim is fully realised. Bookings made within Malawi and longer stays attract discounts.

Getting There & Away

Several charter companies fly to Likoma Island: these include **Proflight** *(☎ 754717; e proflight@malawi.net)*, the **Nyika Safari Company** *(☎ 330180; e reservations@nyika .com)* and **Franco's Air Charters** *(☎ 794281; e franco@malawi.net)*. The cost of a five-seater plane from Lilongwe is US$540, but you can purchase an empty seat in either direction for a discounted price; contact the companies directly for details.

The *Ilala* ferry (see the main Getting Around section earlier in this chapter) stops at Likoma Island twice a week, usually for three to four hours, so even if you're heading elsewhere, you might be able to nip ashore to have a quick look at the cathedral (see the boxed text 'Likoma Missionaries & the Cathedral of St Peter' later). Check with the captain before you leave the boat.

Heading south, the *Ilala* then sails to Cóbuè (**kob**-way) and Metangula on the Mozambican mainland. Local dhows also sail to Cóbuè for US$0.80. Alternatively, if you're planning to go to the exceptional **Mchenga Nkwichi** *(e mdw01@bushmail.net; Lake Niassa, Mozambique)* nearby on the opposite side of the lake, this lodge can organise a boat transfer, which costs US$40 plus US$5 per person (max 12 people). For more details, see Lake Niassa under Northern Mozambique in the Mozambique chapter.

CHIZUMULU ISLAND

'Chizzie' is smaller than Likoma (and just a few kilometres away), and even more detached from the mainland. Stretches of lucid azure water and white rocky outcrops give

Likoma Missionaries & The Cathedral of St Peter

European involvement on Likoma Island began in 1882 when members of UMCA (Universities Mission to Central Africa) established a base here. The leaders of the party, Will Johnson and Chauncey Maples, chose the island as protection from attacks from the warlike Ngoni and Yao peoples.

Chauncey Maples became the first bishop of Likoma, but he died only a few months after being appointed, drowning in the lake off Monkey Bay. Despite the setback, missionary work on the island continued. Between 1903 and 1905 the huge cathedral was built and dedicated to St Peter – appropriately a fisherman. Today it remains one of Malawi's most remarkable buildings.

The cathedral measures over 100m long by 25m wide (for British travellers, that's the size of Winchester Cathedral), and has stained-glass windows and elaborate choir stalls carved from soapstone. The crucifix above the altar was carved from wood from the tree where Livingstone's heart was buried in Zambia.

It was built at a part of the island called Chipyela, meaning 'Place of Burning', because the early UMCA arrivals had witnessed suspected witches being burnt alive here. The island's main settlement grew up around the cathedral and is still called Chipyela today.

The UMCA missionaries remained on Likoma until the 1940s. During that time they were hard at work – they claimed 100% literacy among the local population at one point. The cathedral fell into disrepair, but was restored in the 1970s and 1980s, and local people are understandably very proud of it.

---

this island a Mediterranean flavour, while the backdrop of dry scrub is positively antipodean. The slow and friendly village activity on the perimeter of idyllic beaches however, is unmistakably Malawian. If you want to visit both islands, transport links make it best to go to Chizumulu first.

Wakwenda Retreat *(camp sites US$2, dorm beds US$2.50, singles/doubles from US$3.80/6)*, smack bang on a postcard-perfect beach, is utter chill-out material. The sizeable bar is constructed around a massive, hollow baobab tree (which was being turned into a card room at the time of research) and the shaded lounge area is often the focus of lazy activity. The **restaurant** *(breakfasts US$1.50, dishes US$2.50)* serves good beachy fare, including sandwiches, omelettes and burgers. Snorkelling gear is free and you can hire diving equipment for US$15 to US$25 depending on where you dive. Every fourth night's accommodation is free.

About 4km south on Mocho Beach, there's a basic **resthouse** where rates are cheaper. The **Nzeru Za Atate Restaurant** here serves filling tea and buns, but little else.

The *Ilala* ferry (see the main Getting Around section earlier in this chapter) stops right outside Wakwenda Retreat, so even if you're not staying on the island you can pop over for a drink. A dhow ferry departs Mocho Beach daily between 10am and 1pm, and sails to Ulisa on Likoma Island

(US$1.30). The trip can take anything from one to three hours depending on the weather; it's an extremely choppy ride when the wind is blowing, and potentially dangerous if a storm comes up. If you're unsure ask Nick at Wakwenda for advice.

Central Malawi

This section covers most parts of Malawi's Central Province with the addition of the Viphya Plateau. Places are described north to south.

THE VIPHYA PLATEAU

The Viphya Plateau is a highland area, running like a broad backbone through north-central Malawi. Despite its name, this area is not flat but consists mostly of rolling hills, cut by river valleys and punctuated by occasional rocky peaks. The dense bush of the plateau's south gives way to pine plantations and colourful patches of jacaranda trees in the beautiful north. The journey along the main road between Kasungu and Mzuzu is stunning, particularly when a sunny day reveals distant mountains breaking through the western horizon (but don't be surprised if there's dense mist and rain). If you've got a few days to spare this is a good area to relax away from the hubbub of towns or cool down from the heat of the lakeshore.

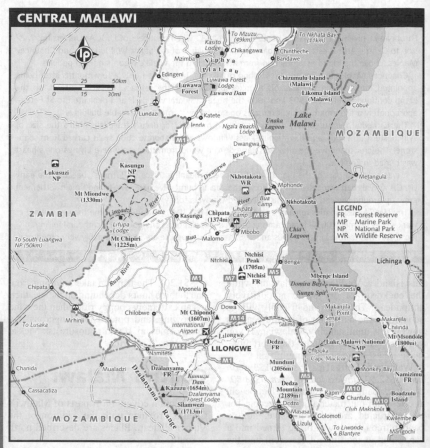

Places to Stay

Luwawa Forest Lodge (☎ 08 829725; e ward low@malawi.net; camp sites per person US$5, chalets with bath from US$30) lies 8km east of the main road between Kasungu and Mzuzu; take the signposted road marked Luwawa D37. The lodge used to belong to the forestry department, but it's managed now by the energetic George Wardlow. The comfortable chalets include a kitchen and sleep two to four people. Breakfast and lunch cost US$4, and a big three-course dinner is US$12. But you'll soon wear off the calories with the activities on offer: walking trails, mountain biking (US$5 per hour), sailing, boating (US$10 per hour), fishing and long-distance wilderness walks and rides to Chintheche on the lakeshore.

There's no public transport to Luwawa, so if you haven't got wheels you'll have to walk, although you may be lucky and get a ride from the main road on a logging truck.

Kasito Lodge (☎ 343219, camp sites per person US$1.30, rooms without bath per person US$6.50/13), less than 1km west of the main road between Kasungu and Mzuzu, is an absolute gem. There are five rooms in this colonial house, each varying in bed number and some still have their original furniture. The communal showers are hot, the toilets are clean and the large, stately lounge has a roaring wood fire. You can supply your own food and the friendly staff will cook (a tip is appropriate), or you can utilise the **restaurant** (dishes US$3.50), which serves simple chicken, fish or beef

dishes. Campers can also use the kitchen for an extra US$1.30. There are excellent views of the surrounding forests inside and out, with picnic tables and a barbecue on the lawn to really exploit the peace and quiet in fine weather. If the lodge is full, the nearby **Resthouse No 2** is cheaper but slightly less comfortable.

To reach Kasito by car from the south, you continue 27km beyond the Mzimba junction on the main sealed road towards Mzuzu; the lodge is signposted on your left. Coming from the north, you pass a large wood factory at Chikangawa village, and the turn-off to the lodge is a few kilometres beyond here on the right. If you're travelling by bus, ask the driver to drop you at the junction. Kasito Lodge is less than 1km from the junction.

KASUNGU

Kasungu is a fairly large town, just off the main north–south road, and about 130km northwest of Lilongwe. It has no major attractions, but you may find yourself changing transport here.

For a place to stay, the sorry-looking **KTC Resthouse** *(rooms without bath US$2)* on the main street has small and musty rooms with two beds and non-too-clean bathrooms. A better option is **Teja Resthouse** *(☎ 253387; singles/doubles US$2.50/3.50)*. It looks a little dilapidated outside but the clean rooms have nets and some have bathrooms (for the same price) so look at a few. It's east of the bus station, just as the sealed road becomes dirt. The **Kasungu Inn** *(☎ 253306; singles/doubles with bath US$36/48)*, at the western end of town on the main road, is set in pleasant and picturesque grounds and has neat and spacious rooms.

There are several cheap local restaurants on the main street and around the market. **Golden Dish** *(breakfasts US$1, mains US$1.30)* on the main road, is a clean and friendly joint serving the usual meat and nsima fare. Of similar quality and price is the nearby **Mr Spice**. The bar at the **Kasungu Inn** is a nice place to relax with a beer.

All buses and minibuses between Mzuzu and Lilongwe come through the town, and there are infrequent matolas along the road through Nkhotakota Wildlife Reserve to the lakeshore.

KASUNGU NATIONAL PARK

Kasungu National Park lies to the west of Kasungu town, and covers more than 2000 sq km. The gently rolling hills, with a few pointed rocky outcrops, are covered in miombo woodland, which is relatively dense because the park's elephant population (which would naturally act as 'gardeners') has been seriously reduced since the 1970s by poaching.

Optimistic estimates suggest about 300 elephants still remain, and the chances of seeing some is best in the dry season (May to October). Buffaloes, zebras, hippos and several antelope species, which were also drastically reduced due to poaching, have begun to reappear in recent years. The bird-life is excellent, with woodland and grass-land species, and waders.

Entry fees are payable (see National Parks & Wildlife under Facts about Malawi earlier in this chapter). The park has a network of driveable tracks that can be toured in your own vehicle or on a wildlife drive (US$40) organised at Lifupa Lodge (see Places to Stay following). Guided walks can also be arranged here (US$21).

Places to Stay

Lifupa Lodge *(☎ 770576; e tdic@sdnp.org.mw; singles/doubles with bath US$108/132)* has a tall thatched central bar and restaurant with a beautiful veranda overlooking the dam (where animals often come to drink). The simple, stylish twin-bedded chalets have private balconies, and rates include breakfast. Nearby is **Lifupa Camp** *(camp sites per person US$5)*. If you're taking this option you'll need to bring your own food (you can stock up at the PTC supermarket in Kasungu), which you can prepare in a communal kitchen.

Getting There & Away

The park entrance is 35km west of Kasungu town. From the entrance, it's 17km by the shortest route to Lifupa Lodge. There's no public transport, so without a car you'd have to hitch from Kasungu – the best place to wait is the turn-off to the park (signposted) near the petrol station on the main road.

NKHOTAKOTA

This was once the centre of slave trading in this region and is reputedly one of the oldest market towns in Africa. Today it's

MALAWI

strung out over 4km between the busy highway and the lake. Nkhotakota makes a good break in any journey along the lakeshore, but don't expect much action. So saying this, the sleepy and quiet pace in the village-like outskirts may be just what's needed after buses and tourist mayhem. There's a branch of the **Commercial Bank of Malawi** on the main north–south road, which offers foreign exchange facilities but no credit card withdrawals.

Things to see include the **mission**, with a spectacular tree in the grounds, under which Livingstone convinced Chief Jumbe to end the slave trade in the 19th century. In the part of town called Kombo is another **'Livingstone Tree'**, where an aspiring politician called Hastings Banda made political speeches in the 1960s. Next to the BP petrol station and set back from the highway, an aspiring group of artists headed by the affable Oster runs **Black History** out of a thatched shack, where you can pick up good wooden carvings, pottery and batiks.

Places to Stay & Eat

Nawo Guesthouse (☎ 292453; singles/doubles with bath US$3.80/5), on the north–south road, offers the most accommodating rooms in town and has safe parking.

Pick & Pay Resthouse (☎ 292459; camping US$2, rooms with/without bath US$5/3) is a clean and basic option off the highway. Follow the signpost from the main road and head towards the lake for 500m. There are nets and fans in the rooms and the restaurant (dishes US$2) serves filling portions of barbecued fish. Next door, **Kulinga Resthouse** (rooms without bath US$2.50) is more basic, and the shared bathrooms are best described as rustic.

Yamikani Restaurant & Bar (mains US$1-2.50) on the main road, serves simple, tasty meals, as does the **Prime Kitchen Restaurant**, a few doors down.

Getting There & Away

You can get to Nkhotakota by the *Ilala* ferry (see the main Getting Around section earlier in this chapter). To get here by bus from Lilongwe, take the 'Mzuzu via Lakeshore' ordinary bus (US$2.50, 4½ hours, two daily), which also stops in Salima. The bus will drop you off roughly outside Nkhotakota's BP petrol station on the highway.

Matolas leave 100m further north and go to Salima (US$1.80, three hours) and Nkhata Bay (US$4, 5½ hours).

SOUTH OF NKHOTAKOTA

About 11km south of Nkhotakota is **Sani Beach Resort** (☎ 292511; camp sites per person US$1.30, single/double huts US$10/19, single/double chalets US$13/24) a few kilometres off the main north–south road. Simple huts and larger brick and thatch chalets sit on a sandy beach, but aside from the great bar, which almost has 360-degree views, it's a little lacking in atmosphere.

About 2km further south, **Njobvu Safari Lodge** (☎ 292506; e njobvusafaris@eomw.net; camp sites per person US$2.30, singles/doubles with bath US$25/40) has appealing round chalets with thatched roofs and cane decor, all right on the lakeshore. Rates include breakfast, and meals in the stylish **restaurant** (snacks US$1.50, dishes US$2.50 to US$6) include roasted guinea fowl, vegetarian stir-fries, curries and of course fresh fish. The owners know a lot about wildlife in the area and arrange day safaris to Nkhotakota Wildlife Reserve (see that section following) for US$50, including meals, transport, entry fees, professional guide and a good chance of spotting elephants. They also arrange boat safaris to Chia Lagoon (see following), which are an excellent way to observe some of the 450 bird species spotted in the area. A half/full day for four people costs US$50/100 and the latter includes drinks and lunch.

About 24km south of Nkhotakota is the entrance to **Chia Lagoon**, a large bay linked to the main lake by a narrow channel, which is crossed by a bridge near the main road. Local people fish here using large triangular nets on poles, and seem resigned to having their photos taken by tourists on the bridge.

Nkhotakota Pottery (☎ 292444; singles/doubles US$12/24), signposted another 2.5km further south from the main road, has been recommended by readers. If you feel like resting here for a few days you could do a pottery course. The two/three day courses cost US$69/97 and include accommodation.

NKHOTAKOTA WILDLIFE RESERVE

Nkhotakota Wildlife Reserve lies west of the main lakeshore road, and covers around

1800 sq km of dense miombo forests with pockets of evergreens carpeting hills and escarpments. It's the largest reserve in Malawi, but was virtually abandoned during the 1980s and early 1990s. There's a healthy elephant population here, as well as roan and sable antelopes, waterbucks, buffaloes and even a few lions and leopards. Several large rivers cross the reserve, so the birdlife is also varied and rewarding. Walking is the best way to experience the area and at least a few hours is needed to spot wildlife.

Entry fees are payable (see National Parks & Reserves under Facts about Malawi earlier). You can hire a scout (ranger) here to be a guide or do a day safari from Njobvu Safari Lodge (see its listing under South of Nkhotakota earlier).

There are some dilapidated rondavels at **Chipata Camp**, the reserve headquarters, which is about 5km north of the end of the dirt road from Lilongwe, about 35km southwest of Nkhotakota town. The best place to aim for is **Bua Camp** (camp sites US$3), a beautiful clearing on the banks of a rocky river. The turn-off to Bua is 10km north of Nkhotakota town, then 15km on a dirt track; without your own wheels the only way to get here is on foot.

SALIMA

The town of Salima is spread out about 20km from the lake, where the road from Lilongwe meets the main lakeshore road. The **Mai Tsalani Motel** (☎ 262622; singles without bath US$3, doubles with bath US$5-13), about 10-minutes' walk from the bus station and close to the PTC supermarket, has a variety of rooms from small and basic singles with shared bathrooms to large doubles with sitting rooms and bathrooms. Bed and breakfast rates are also available. **Mwambiya Lodge** (☎ 262314; singles/doubles with bath US$10/12/50), across the train line from the bus station, is more of a hotel set-up, with bland but clean rooms. Rates include breakfast.

To reach Salima from Lilongwe, it's easiest to take a minibus (US$1.50). Minibuses and matolas also run frequently between Salima and Senga Bay (US$1.50) and less frequently to Nkhata Bay (US$6.50), Mzuzu (US$8.50) and Blantyre (US$4), via Mangochi. There are also ordinary buses to Mzuzu (US$6, seven hours, two daily) via Nkhata Bay (US$5.50, five hours).

SENGA BAY

Senga Bay is at the eastern end of a broad peninsula that juts into the lake from Salima. The water is remarkably clear here, and the beaches are also good. As a break from lazing on the beach, you can go windsurfing or snorkelling, take a boat ride or learn to dive. Alternatively, you can go hiking in the nearby **Senga Hills**. It's best to hire a local guide to show you the way (also because there have been isolated incidents of robbery and harassment here). Bird-watching in the area is excellent, with a good range of habitats in close proximity. If you're looking for souvenirs, there's a strip of craft stalls a few kilometres out of Senga Bay, on the Salima road.

About 10km south of Senga Bay is **Stewart Grant's Tropical Fish Farm** (☎/fax 263165 or 263407; e redzebra@lakemalawi.com), which breeds and exports cichlids. If you're genuinely interested you can do a half-hour tour of the farm (US$0.50). **Red Zebra Tours** (w www.lakemalawi.com), based here, offers lake safaris with an experienced guide from US$25/30 per person for a half/full day. For something less active, two-hour sundowner cruises are also available for US$15 per person (minimum charge for the boat US$50). Children are half price.

Dangers & Annoyances

Take great care when swimming near the large rocks at the end of the beach at Steps Campsite; you'll find there's a surprisingly strong undertow. Some of the beaches here are flat and reedy – perfect conditions for bilharzia, so get advice from your hotel or lodge to see if it's safe.

Many travellers have complained about persistent hassling from local youths, all wanting to sell souvenirs or arrange boat rides. Beware especially of the enthusiastic guys at the craft stalls who offer to wrap your purchase – they'll charge more for this than you paid for the carving, and swapping your souvenir for a lump of wood has been tried more than once. Be polite and firm in your dealings and you should be OK.

Places to Stay & Eat

There's a good choice of places to stay and a couple of eateries in Senga Bay. The following places are described roughly from south to north, following the lakeshore.

The Wheelhouse Marina (☎ 09 960266; camp sites per person US$2, 2-bed/10-bed house US$20/40), on the same road as the fish farm, is a bizarre marriage of grassy camp sites, trees and ruins of the old marina. The result is quite picturesque and the clean (if spartan) houses are excellent value for a group. If you've a yen to camp but no tent you can hire a huge one for US$5 per person. The round bar (dishes US$1 to US$4.50) is raised above the water on stilts and serves burgers, hot dogs, steaks and fish.

Red Zebra Lodge (singles/doubles US$15/20) based at Stewart Grant's Tropical Fish Farm (see Things to See & Do earlier) has several brick bungalows with spacious and comfortable interiors. More expensive bed and breakfast rates are also available and the restaurant (dishes US$4 to US$6) cooks up a good variety of dishes, including vegetarian options.

Carolina Holiday Resort (☎ 263220; e shelagh@malawi.net; camp sites per person US$1.50, dorm beds US$5, singles/doubles without bath US$18/30, chalets US$42) is 4km down a dirt road, at the western end of the main street. It's a friendly spot with accommodation to suit all budgets and a good restaurant (dishes US$3 to US$5). There's also a bar, outside terrace and shady gardens overlooking the lake. Boat hire is available from US$20 for fishing, snorkelling or day-trips. You can also hire kayaks for US$1 per hour, or mountain bikes, windsurfers and snorkelling gear, all US$5 per hour.

Baobab Chalets (☎ 263495; camp sites per person US$1.30, singles/doubles with bath US$14/15), near Carolina, has small brick chalets and a few grassy patches to pitch a tent. On weekends this is a popular spot for Malawians. Chimphango's (☎ 263350; camp sites US$2.50, rooms US$8), next door, is simple and low-key.

Riverside Hotel (☎ 263400; singles/doubles/family rooms US$40/50/70), also on this dirt road, is a tad sterile, but the commodious rooms come with TV, fridge, air-con and expansive verandas with lake views. There's also a garden and a large outdoor bar. The facilities and room to move in this hotel make it a good choice for families.

Le Meridien Livingstonia Beach (☎ 263222; e livingstonia@lemeridienmalawi.co.mw; singles/doubles US$64/72), all glistening white and opulent, sits at the end of the main street, past a set of imposing gates. Stylish rooms house a host of comforts including telephone, TV, tea and coffee making facilities and fans and each has a private veranda overlooking the cabana-dotted beach. On site is a tennis court, swimming pool (in case the lake at your doorstep is too far) bar and restaurant, all set amid lush gardens and made-for-a-brochure views.

Steps Campsite (camp sites per person US$3.80), next to Le Meridien Livingstonia Beach, is possibly Malawi's finest camping ground, with plenty of flat pitches, shady trees, electric hook-ups and spotless toilets and showers (but no hot water). Security is excellent and you can get tasty fast food at the bar (dishes US$3 to US$6) including burgers and chicken dishes.

Safari Beach Lodge (☎ 263143; e safwag@malawi.net; singles/doubles with bath US$35/55) is 1km off the main road, just before the gates to Le Meridien Livingstonia Beach. Accommodation is in commodious safari tents with spotless, attached bathrooms and wooden decks. The secure compound also has a bar and restaurant, where birds and small wildlife also come to feed regularly. Rates include breakfast.

Red Zebra Cafe (breakfast and snacks US$1-3, dishes US$2-4; open 7am-10pm daily), 500m towards town from Le Meridien Livingstonia Beach, is the best place to eat. Both the staff and decor are cheerful and good nosh in the form of fresh kampango (lake fish), steaks, omelettes, pastas and burgers can be devoured inside the restaurant or on the patio outside. If you've still got room, there's a decent selection of cakes to fill the gap. Tophill Restaurant (dishes US$1-2.50), just down the road, has simpler surrounds and fare and its speciality banana pancakes are excellent.

Getting There & Away

First get to Salima (for details see Salima earlier). From here, local pick-ups run to Senga Bay (US$1.50), dropping you in the main street. If you want a lift all the way to Steps Campsite, negotiate an extra fee with the driver. If you're travelling to/from Cape Maclear consider chartering a boat; it's not too expensive (US$140) if you get a group together, it's good fun and it saves one hell of a trip on the bus.

MUA

Mua is a small town between Salima and Balaka, and consists mostly of a large mission with a church, a school and a hospital, which has been here since the beginning of the 20th century. There is also a fabulous **craft shop**, full of paintings and wood sculptures by local people who have been encouraged in their work by one of the priests at the mission. Some is of very high quality, and quite unusual, covering religious and secular subjects. Prices are reasonable. Nearby is a workshop where you can see the carvers in action.

For a deeper understanding of the ideas behind the sculptures, a visit to the **museum** *(open 8am-5pm Mon-Sat)* is an absolute must. It concentrates on the three main cultural groups of the region (Chewa, Ngoni and Yao) and their approach to traditional beliefs, with exhibits from rituals and rites of passage. This is no dusty exhibition, but a journey deep into the very soul of Malawi. A guided tour is essential; it takes three hours and costs US$5.

See Getting There & Away under Monkey Bay (following) for transport connections to/from Mua.

MONKEY BAY

Monkey Bay is a port at the southern end of Lake Malawi, which most travellers pass through on the way to Cape Maclear. If you're here for a while, **Ziwadi Resthouse** *(☎ 587232; singles/doubles without bath US$1.50/2.50, doubles with bath US$4.40)* is just off the main road and offers tidy, simple rooms, as well as a basic restaurant. Monkey Bay also has a market and a **PTC** supermarket.

Just outside Monkey Bay, **Venice Beach** *(camp sites per person US$1.30, dorms US$2, doubles with shared bath US$2.50)* is a perennially-under-construction hostel and camping ground. It's been in the making for several years (although the bar is well established) and if completion ever eventuates it will be the perfect backpackers' lair to recuperate after an overnight on the *Ilala*.

Getting There & Away

From Lilongwe, ordinary buses go to Monkey Bay, either via Mua and the southern lakeshore (US$3.80, seven hours, two daily) or the long way round, via Balaka, Liwonde and Mangochi (US$4.50, 10 hours, two daily). From Lilongwe you're probably better off going by minibus to Salima (US$1.50), from where you might find a minibus or matola going direct to Monkey Bay. If not, take a minibus towards Balaka, get off at the Matakataka road junction near Mua (look out for the craft stalls), then take a matola (US$2) along the Matakataka road to the main road between Monkey Bay and Mangochi. Another option if you're in a group is to charter your own matola. We heard from a group of travellers who hired a matola in Salima to take them all the way to Cape Maclear for US$100.

It's much easier to reach Monkey Bay from Blantyre on the ordinary bus that travels via Liwonde and Mangochi (US$3.80, eight hours, one daily). A quicker option is to go by minibus (US$5, four hours), but you'll need to leave in the morning and you're likely to change at Limbe, Mangochi and sometimes Zomba.

To avoid the bus hassles, many travellers use the *Ilala* steamboat to travel up and down the country to or from Monkey Bay (see the main Getting Around section earlier in this chapter).

From Monkey Bay, a matola ride to Cape Maclear should cost US$1, although some travellers have reported paying US$15 and up so be assertive when negotiating.

CAPE MACLEAR

Cape Maclear sits on a scenic jut of land at the southern end of Lake Malawi, with the alluring Domwe and Thumbi Islands anchored off shore. It was once a travellers' byword for sun, sand, rest and recreation, but the massive influx of tourism has had the unfortunate effect of creating an interdependency within the local village of Chembe. This has lead to increasing amounts of hassle from local 'beach boys' and a change in the overall atmosphere to that of a tourist trap. However, in 2002 the government trained a group of youths to act as registered tour guides with the Chembe Village Tourist Association, and this has had some positive effect for travellers, most importantly in the reduction of crime. Possibly Cape Maclear has suffered the fate of many hotspots and the fad has moved elsewhere in Malawi, but it's still a picturesque and relaxing place to experience the beauty, lifestyle and activities of the lake.

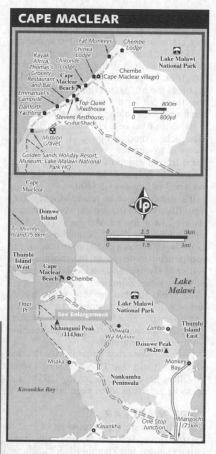

CAPE MACLEAR

There's also a **museum**, which is well worth a visit to learn about the formation of the lake and the evolution of the fish. The information is nontechnical and well presented.

Near the entrance gate to the Golden Sands, a path leads towards the hills overlooking the bay. A few hundred metres up here is a small group of **missionary graves**, marking the last resting place of the missionaries who attempted to establish the first Livingstonia Mission here in 1875 (see History under Facts about Malawi and also Livingstonia under Northern Malawi, both earlier in this chapter).

Activities

Snorkelling Guides registered with the Chembe Village Tourist Association can organise day trips to nearby islands for about US$10 to US$40 per boat, plus around US$15 per person, including snorkelling and lunch (fish and rice cooked on an open fire). If you want to stretch this out into a night or two on the islands, the cost is US$25/45 for one/two days, including tents. Your lodge can put you in contact with guides but before you arrange anything, get recommendations from other travellers and negotiate a price.

If you prefer to go snorkelling on your own, many places rent gear (rates start at about US$2 – but check the quality of your mask). Otter Point, less than 1km beyond Golden Sands, is a small rocky peninsula and nearby islet that is very popular with fish and snorkellers. You may even see otters here.

Scams to watch out for at Cape Maclear include the boys who take money in advance for a boat ride or barbecue and then disappear, or who take you on a boat then go through your day-pack while you're snorkelling. Real robberies do occasionally happen on the beach or surrounding hills; violence is very unlikely, but don't carry anything valuable.

Things to See

Much of the area around Cape Maclear, including several offshore islands, is part of **Lake Malawi National Park**, one of the few freshwater aquatic parks in Africa. The park headquarters are at Golden Sands Holiday Resort (see Places to Stay & Eat later).

Diving For diving, go to **Scuba Shack** (☎ 09 934220; e doogles@africa-online.net), based within Stevens Resthouse, or **Kayak Africa** (☎ 584456; e letsgo@kayakafrica.co .za) nearby. Both offer PADI open water courses for US$195, as well as casual dives for experienced divers at US$25. Scuba Shack also has an Instructor Development Centre (IDC) so you can become a qualified instructor here.

Kayaking If you prefer to stay on top of the water, **Kayak Africa** has top-of-the-range kayaks (single and double) suitable for experts or beginners, which can be hired from around US$12 for a few hours. A day trip with lunch costs US$35. The best option, if you've got the money, is to take a guided

two- or three-night island-hopping trip, using Kayak Africa's delightful camps on Domwe and Mumbo Islands. The charge is US$270/405 per person, and includes a roomy tent with mattress and duvet, good meals, hot showers, snorkel gear and park fees. Everyone who's done this trip raves about it.

Boat Cruises Yet another option is sailing on a yacht with an outfit called **Danforth Yachting** (☎ 09 960077; e danforth@malawi.net). A sunset cruise around Cape Maclear aboard the *Mufasa* costs US$20 per person (minimum six people required), a full-day island-hopping cruise costs US$60 per person (minimum four people), including lunch, and an overnight cruise including all meals as well as snorkelling and fishing equipment costs US$120 per person (minimum four people). The owners also have exquisite accommodation (see Places to Stay & Eat later).

Hiking There's a good range of hikes and walks in the hills that form a horseshoe around the plain behind the village and the beach. You can go alone (see Dangers & Annoyances earlier in this section) or arrange a guide, either from the village or at the national park headquarters at Golden Sands Holiday Resort; the park's rate for a guide is US$9 for a full-day trip. The main path starts by the missionary graves and leads up through woodland to a col below **Nkhunguni Peak**, the highest on the Nankumba Peninsula, with great views over Cape Maclear, the lake and surrounding islands. It's six hours return to the summit; plenty of water and a good sun hat are essential.

Another interesting place to visit on foot is **Mwala Wa Mphini** (Rock of the Tribal Face Scars), which is just off the main dirt road into Cape Maclear, about 5km from the park headquarters. This huge boulder is covered in lines and patterns that seem to have been gouged out by long-forgotten artists, but are simply a natural geological formation.

If you want a **longer walk**, a small lakeside path leads southwest from Otter Point, through woodland above the shore, for about 4km to a small fishing village called Msaka (which has a small bar/shop serving cold drinks). From here a track leads inland (west) to meet the main dirt road between Cape Maclear and Monkey Bay. Turn left and head back towards Cape Maclear, passing Mwala

Wa Mphini on the way. The whole circuit is about 16km and takes four to five hours.

Places to Stay & Eat
Places to stay in this section are described roughly from west to east.

Golden Sands Holiday Resort (camp sites per person US$0.50, 1/2/3-person rondavels with bath US$1/1.50/2) is at the far western end of the beach. This is also Lake Malawi National Park headquarters, and as it's inside the park you have to pay fees (see National Parks & Wildlife under Facts about Malawi earlier). It offers camping and basic, small rondavels. The beach here is cleaner and the atmosphere is generally much quieter than some other places in Cape Maclear, so it's ideal for families, drivers and people who don't want to drink and smoke all night. There's a small bar, but no restaurant, however, staff will prepare your food in the kitchen or you can cook yourself. If you camp, watch out for the monkeys – they'll run off with anything edible. If you're in a group it's worth renting a rondavel to store your gear – you also get your own bathroom, which will be in better condition than the communal ones. There's been talk for many years about Golden Sands being leased to a private investor (with the aim of building a resort) but this has yet to eventuate.

Danforth Yachting (full-board rooms with bath per person US$120), about 500m towards the village, is by far the swankiest place on the cape (see Boat Cruises under Activities earlier for contact details). Plush and pristine rooms sleep up to four people and rates include use of all equipment and activities (including cruises). There's also a bar, restaurant and outdoor lounge areas in front of a stretch of rich grass with prime views of the lake.

Emmanuel's Campsite (camp sites US$1.50, rooms US$3), within a fenced compound, is deservedly popular with campers, although the rooms are cramped and a tad shabby. There's also a bar and restaurant.

Top Quiet Resthouse (☎ 08 854211; camp sites per person US$0.80, rooms with bath US$1.50) has rudimentary rooms set around a sandy courtyard. The owners are relaxed and friendly, but its location away from the beach makes it hotter than the other lodges.

Stevens Resthouse *(☎ 587541, 09 927755; camp sites per person US$0.50, rooms with bath US$2.80)* straddles both sides of the track through town and is another favourite. Large, simple rooms with nets are good value and there are pleasant camping areas close to the water. The bar and restaurant are close to the beach, although both have seen kinder days and better maintenance.

Chikonde Lodge *(☎ 09 930488; camp sites per person US$1.30, singles/doubles without bath US$2.50/3.80)* is an excellent budget option, with welcoming staff and clean and accommodating rooms arranged around a pleasant courtyard. The restaurant (dishes US$1 to US$2.50) serves good curries, peri-peri dishes and fish. All profits from this lodge go towards the Chembe Aids Project, which promotes HIV/AIDS education and operates a food-for-work programme within the village.

Chirwa Lodge *(☎ 09 917181; camp sites US$1.30, rooms with shared bath US$3)* is a small, locally-run operation, offering simple rooms with nets, limited camping space out the back and a restaurant. This is probably your best option to hang with locals.

Fat Monkeys *(☎ 09 948501; camp sites per person US$1, rooms with shared bath US$5)*, almost 1km east of the village centre and away from the crowds, is a huge camping ground aimed primarily at overland trucks and car-campers. It also has small and comfortable rooms, good security, showers, and the ubiquitous bar and restaurant by the water.

Chembe Lodge *(☎ 635356, 08 828953; walk-in tents per person from US$25)*, at the far eastern end of Cape Maclear beach, is about as far from the tourist trap as you can get. Large safari tents facing the water (and sunrise) are idyllic, although the facilities are mediocre. The spacious restaurant (dishes US$4.50) serves a set menu, usually of fish or steak (the kampango is excellent), and you can lounge in the comfy chairs with a sundowner to wind the day down.

Thomas's Grocery Restaurant and Bar *(dishes US$1-2.30)* is a great local eatery if you want to leave the confines of your lodge. Meals are filling, tasty and predictable (although they do serve Indian chapatis) and the outdoor bench seating is the perfect spot to watch the village operate around you.

Getting There & Away

By public transport, first get to Monkey Bay, from where a matola should cost US$1 (see Getting There & Away under Monkey Bay earlier for more details). If you're driving from Mangochi, the dirt road to Cape Maclear (signposted) turns west off the main road, about 5km before Monkey Bay. Be warned however, it's a bumpy ride and unless you're in a 4WD or high-clearance vehicle, it'll be slow going.

From Cape Maclear, if you're heading for Senga Bay, ask at the dive schools about chartering a boat. It will cost around US$140, but it's not bad when split between four to six people and much better than the long, hard bus ride.

MONKEY BAY TO MANGOCHI

From Monkey Bay the main road runs south to Mangochi. Along this stretch of lake are several places to stay, catering for all tastes and budgets. A selection is described here, arranged north to south.

The K Lodge *(☎ 09 911723; camp sites per person US$1.30, singles/doubles without bath US$9.50/19)*, about 23km south of Monkey Bay, has small and poky rooms but an excellent camping area; lots of flat, grassy space and towering trees. It's in a relaxed and private spot with a restaurant and open-air bar, as well as satellite TV so you can get your couch potato fix if you need it.

OK Lake Shore Hotel *(rooms with bath US$7)*, a few kilometres further south, and 1.5km off the main road, is Malawian-run and a good, quiet, budget option. Basic rooms have nets and although meals aren't available, you can make use of the kitchen and the chef.

Boadzulu Lakeshore Resort *(☎ 594725; camp sites US$2.50, single/double walk in tents US$5/7.50, singles/doubles with bath from US$36/54, family chalets US$68)*, about 10km further south again, is a smart, spacious resort and great value for all budgets. The comfortable rooms here come with fans and nets and for a little extra you can go up in standard to include a TV, lounge and fridge. The restaurant is good, the bar is on the beach and if you're feeling adventurous, a boat accommodating up to 45 people can be hired to go to nearby Boadzulu Island for around US$100.

Cichlid Fish

There are around 500 species of fish in Lake Malawi. Most of these are of the family Cichlidae – the largest family of fish in Africa – and 99% of these cichlids are endemic to the lake. *Chambo*, familiar to anyone who has eaten in a restaurant in Malawi, are one type of cichlid. Others include the small *utaka*, which move in big shoals and are caught by fishermen at night. But Lake Malawi is most famous for the small, brightly coloured cichlids known as *mbuna*, of which there are many species. As well as being attractive to snorkellers and divers, mbuna are popular with aquariums, and for scientists they provide a fascinating insight into the process of evolution. Mbuna identification and classification is an ongoing process, and it is thought that many species of mbuna remain undiscovered, particularly around the northeastern shore of the lake.

Cichlids have evolved over the millennia from one common species into many hundreds, yet they have continued to coexist. This has been achieved by different species developing different ways of feeding. Chambo eat phytoplankton, which they filter out of the water through their mouths, but the different mbuna have developed a whole range of feeding mechanisms. Some mbuna have specialised teeth to scrape algae off the rocks; others specialise in scraping the algae off aquatic plants. There are also 'snail eaters', with strong flat teeth for crushing shells; 'sand diggers', which filter insects and small animals out of the sand; and 'zooplankton eaters', which have tube-like mouths for picking up minute creatures. Other species include plant-eaters and fish-eaters.

Equally fascinating is the cichlid breeding process. The male attracts the female with his bright colours, and if suitably impressed she lays eggs, which she immediately takes into her mouth for protection. The male has a pattern near his tail resembling the eggs, which the female tries to pick up, at which point the male releases sperm into the water, which the female inevitably inhales. This process is repeated until all or most of the eggs are fertilised. The female keeps the eggs in her mouth, and even when they become baby fish they stay there for protection. They emerge only to feed, but at the slightest sign of danger, the mother opens her mouth and the young swim straight back in.

Club Makokola (☎ 594244; e clubmak@ malawi.net; singles/doubles from US$103/ 165), about 50km from Monkey Bay, is a luxury holiday resort, with nicely decorated chalets and rooms (the newer bush-style ones are better than the original ones), two swimming pools, restaurants, bars, water sports, floodlit football fields, squash, tennis and volleyball courts and a long strip of private beachfront. Rates include full buffet breakfast, and a three-course meal costs US$10. Club Mak (as it's known) has its own airport, which is served by Air Malawi flights to/from Blantyre and Lilongwe (see the main Getting Around section earlier in this chapter). Based at the club, **Scuba Blue** offers day dives from US$25 and beginner courses for US$180. **Paradise Watersports** offers fishing, boat trips to the islands, and water-ski and wakeboard hire from US$10.

Nkopola Lodge (☎ 595619; e nkopola@ sdnp.org.mw; camp sites US$12, walk-in tents US$18, rooms from US$60, chalets US$72), just 1km down the road, is another top-end establishment. Cool and unfussy rooms in well-kept gardens overlook a beach, while the camping area, set further back, has spotless ablution blocks. Room rates include breakfast and the restaurant (dishes US$5 to US$8, weekend buffet US$12) serves suitably delectable fare. Sailboards, canoes and small sailing boats are free for guests' use, motorboats cost US$7.50 per person per hour and paddle boats US$2.50. More-questionable attractions include a bird sanctuary, petting zoo and casino.

Palm Beach Leisure Resort (☎ 594564; camp sites per person US$1.50, singles/doubles with bath from US$28/34), north of Mangochi, was once a smart resort on a beautiful beach surrounded by (not surprisingly) a grove of palm trees. Its large thatched chalets with nets and fans could now do with a lick of paint but it's a friendly and pleasant spot with loads of space and lush green lawns for camping. The restaurant (breakfasts US$1.50, dishes US$1.25 to US$4.50), which never closes, serves fish, steaks, burgers, curries, pastas and good vegetarian dishes. This place is quiet during the week, but livelier at weekends when people come from Blantyre and Lilongwe for boating and fishing.

MALAWI

MANGOCHI

Mangochi lies near the southern end of Lake Malawi, strung out between the main lakeshore road and the Shire River. This place was once an important slave market, and then an administrative centre in colonial days, when it was known as Fort Johnston. Relics of these times within the wide, tree-lined streets include a large mosque and the Queen Victoria clock tower. Even today the town has a vaguely Swahili feel, with palm trees, Arab-looking people and coconuts for sale in the street. The Shire Bridge is scenic, and the excellent **Lake Malawi Museum** (admission US$0.80; open 7.30am-5pm daily) houses ethnographic, environmental and historical exhibits. There's also a replica of the foredeck and bridge of the HMS *Guendolin* (see the boxed text 'The HMS *Guendolin*' following). Facilities include several shops, supermarkets, a post office and banks.

Places to Stay & Eat

The hospitality industry hasn't really taken off in Mangochi but there's a few cheap options. **Mangochi Icecream Den & Restaurant** (dishes US$1.25-6), on the highway, has tranquil outdoor tables amid leafy gardens. Its eclectic menu includes Malawian dishes, steaks, curries, burgers, fish and, of course, ice cream.

OK Restaurant & Resthouse (☎ 08 898451; single rooms without bath US$2.50), near the main minibus station and market, off the main road through town, only has single rooms but they're clean and cosy and have fans or air-con. The attached restaurant serves cheap and filling meals.

Mangochi Lodge (rooms without bath US$4.50), near the clock tower, is friendly and offers a few comfortable bedrooms with nets and fans. The nearby **Mangochi Holiday Motel** (☎ 594789; singles/doubles without bath US$5/7, with bath US$7.50/10) is larger, with simple, clean rooms, a cheap restaurant, big bar and good bakery.

Getting There & Away

All buses between Blantyre and Monkey Bay stop in Mangochi. There are minibuses to/from Liwonde (US$1.20), Zomba (US$2) and Blantyre (US$2.50). To get to Liwonde National Park take a matola to Ulongwe (US$1). You can get a matola to the border town of Chiponde (US$3) if you're heading to Mozambique (for border crossing information see Mozambique under Land in the main Getting There & Away section earlier in this chapter).

The HMS *Guendolin*

The HMS *Guendolin* was a military boat, made in Britain and assembled in Mangochi in 1899. For many years it was the largest boat on the lake (340 tonnes), with a top speed of 12 knots. It was also equipped with two powerful guns. The colonial authorities regarded such a show of strength necessary firstly to deter slave-traders, who crossed the lake in dhows with their human cargo, and secondly because both rival colonial powers, Germany and Portugal, had territory facing Lake Malawi (then Lake Nyassa) and were believed to want to increase their influence in the region.

The Germans also had a gunboat, called *Herman von Wissemann*, but despite the territorial disputes of their governments the captains of the two ships were reported to be great friends and drinking partners, often meeting at various points around the lake for a chat and a few beers.

When WWI was declared in 1914, the *Guendolin* was ordered to destroy the German boat. The British captain knew where the *von Wissemann* would be, as he and the German captain had previously arranged one of their regular get-togethers.

But the German captain was unaware that war had broken out, and his ship was completely unprepared. The *Guendolin* steamed in close, then bombed the *von Wissemann* and rendered it unusable. The German captain and crew were then informed of the commencement of hostilities and taken prisoner. This rather unsporting event happened to be the first British naval victory of WWI, and Lake Malawi's only recorded battle at sea.

In 1940 the *Guendolin* was converted to a passenger ship, and one of the guns was set up as a memorial in Mangochi, near the clock tower. Some years later the ship was scrapped. All that remains today is the gun, while the compass and the ship's bell are on display at the museum.

Southern Malawi

Malawi's Southern Province, with Blantyre roughly at its centre, lies between the southern end of Lake Malawi and the far southern tip of the country. Places are described roughly north to south.

LIWONDE

You may visit Liwonde town if you're heading for Liwonde National Park or for Mozambique by train. The Shire River divides the town; on the more pleasant eastern side are the train station, the market, a supermarket and several shops.

If you're here for a night, the **Liwonde Park Motel** (☎ 542338; singles/doubles with bath US$7/8) has neat and well-presented rooms, which are decent value. Down by the river **Manpower Shireside Lodge** (☎ 542421; single/double rondavels with bath US$5/10) has dilapidated but acceptable rondavels, some with mosquito nets. There's also a bar and restaurant (dishes US$2 to US$5), which serves mediocre fare aside from the excellent chambo. Next door, **Warthogs Wallow** (☎ 542426; singles/doubles with bath US$10.50/15) is the best option in town, with accommodating rooms and great views of hippos cavorting in the river. The restaurant (dishes US$3.80 to US$4.50) serves delicious food and the bar has satellite TV.

On the western side of the river, the **Liwonde Holiday Resort** (singles/doubles without bath US$1.80/2.50), just off the main road, is anything but. It's cheap, but that's about the only thing going for it and the bathrooms aren't pretty. There have been several reports of thefts here so secure your gear. Next door, **Waterline River Safaris** (☎ 542552, 542832; e colin_sue@malawi.net) operates wildlife-viewing boat trips for around US$14 per person per hour (the price decreases with more passengers). This is also a viable way to access Mvuu camp in Liwonde National Park, with one-way/return transfers costing from US$32/42.

LIWONDE NATIONAL PARK

Liwonde National Park is the best in Malawi. Dominating the west, the Shire River overflows with hippos and crocodiles and is a favourite stomping ground for the abundant elephants. Waterbucks are also common near the water, while beautiful

Malawi's Cup of Tea

South and east of Blantyre, on the rolling hills of the Shire Highlands, the climate is ideal for growing tea, and the area is covered with plantations (or 'estates'). The first tea bushes were imported from India during the early days of the Nyasaland colony, and tea production quickly became a major industry. It's now a major export crop (along with tobacco and sugar), providing thousands of people with jobs.

Travelling on the main road between Limbe and Mulanje the seemingly endless fields of tea appear as vivid green grids carpeting the hillsides. The tea-pickers (men and women) work their way slowly down the lines, picking just a few leaves and a bud from the top of each bush and throwing them into large baskets on their backs. At the end of each shift, the baskets are taken to a collection area, where they are weighed and each worker's wages are calculated. The leaves are then transported to a tea factory, where they are trimmed and dried before being packed in bags and boxes ready for export. A small proportion of low quality tea stays within the country to be sold locally.

If you have a genuine interest in tea production it may be possible to arrange a tour of an estate and factory. There is no established set-up; you simply call an estate and ask a senior manager if it's possible to visit. You'll probably need your own vehicle, or have to take a taxi, as most estate offices are off the main road and difficult to reach by public transport.

The best place to start with is **Satemwa Estate** (☎ 473356; e 113213.233@compuserve.com), near the small town of Thyolo (**cho**-low) on the main road between Limbe and Mulanje. Highly recommended is a night in their **Chawani Bungalow** (per night US$70), which sleeps up to eight guests and includes the services of a caretaker/cook. From the bungalow you can walk through the tea estates or go through the evergreen forest remnants on nearby Thyolo Mountain, which is a popular bird-watching spot.

Another estate that sometimes allows visits is **British African Estates** (☎ 472266). The tourist office in Blantyre may have more suggestions.

MALAWI

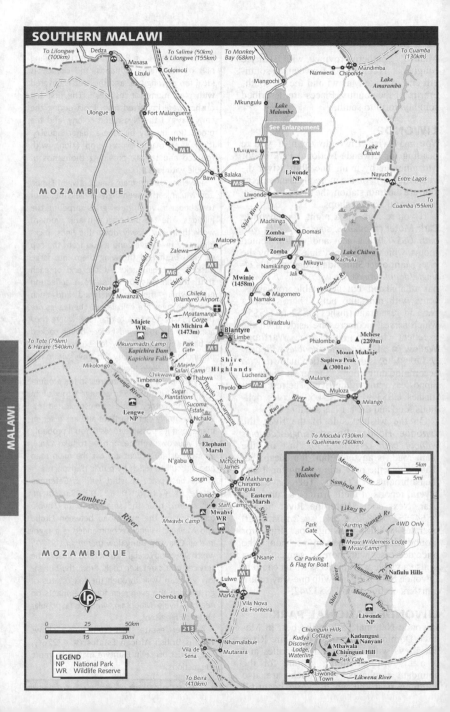

SOUTHERN MALAWI

To Lilongwe (100km)

To Salima (50km) & Lilongwe (155km)

To Monkey Bay (68km)

To Cuamba (130km)

Dedza

Masasa

Lizulu

Golomoti

Mangochi

Namwera

Chiponde

Mandimba

Lake Amaramba

Mkungulu

Lake Malombe

See Enlargement

Ulongue

Fort Malanguene

Ntcheu

M1

M2

Ulongwe

Liwonde NP

Lake Chiuta

Balaka

M8

Nayuchi

Entre Lagos

Bawi

Liwonde

To Cuamba (55km)

MOZAMBIQUE

Machinga

Shire River

Matope

Zomba Plateau

Domasi

Zalewa

Zomba

M3

Lake Chilwa

M6

M1

Namikango

Mikuyu

Kachulu

Zóbuè

Mwinje (1458m)

Jali

Mwanza

Chileka (Blantyre) Airport

Namaka

Magornero

Phalombe Rv

Mpatamanga Gorge

Chiradzulu

Majete WR

Mt Michiru (1473m)

Blantyre

Limbe

Mchese (2289m)

Mkurumadzi Camp

Kapichira Dam

Kapichira Falls

Park Gate

Phalombe

Mount Mulanje

Sapitwa Peak (3001m)

To Tete (75km) & Harare (540km)

Majete Safari Camp

Shire Highlands

Mikolongo

Chikwawa

Timbenao

Thabwa

Thyolo

Luchenza

M2

Mulanje

Muloza

Milange

Mwanja River

Thyolo Escarpment

Ruo River

Sugar Plantations

Lengwe NP

Sucoma Estate

Nchalo

Elephant Marsh

To Mocuba (130km) & Quelimane (260km)

N'gabu

Mchacha James

Zambezi River

Sorgin

Makhanga

Chiromo

Bangula

Eastern Marsh

Dande

Staff Camp

Mwabvi WR

Shire River

Mwavbi Camp

MOZAMBIQUE

Nsanje

M1

Lulwe

Marka

Chemba

Vila Nova da Fronteira

213

Nhamalabue

Vila de Sena

Mutarara

To Beira (410km)

Enlargement

Lake Malombe

Masange River

0   5km
0   5mi

Nambola Rv

Likuzi Rv

Nyangi Rv

Airstrip

4WD Only

Park Gate

Mvuu Wilderness Lodge

Mvuu Camp

Nafiulu Hills

Nanandwe Rv

Car Parking & Flag for Boat

Shire River

Mwalasi River

Liwonde NP

Chiunguni Hills Cottage

Kadungusi

Nanyani

Kudya Discovery Lodge; Waterline

Mbawala

Chiunguni Hill

Park Gate

Liwonde Town

Likwena River

0   25   50km
0   15   30mi

LEGEND
NP   National Park
WR   Wildlife Reserve

sable and roan antelopes, zebras and elands populate the surreal flood plains in the east. Night drives can reveal spotted genets, bushbabies, scrub hares, side-striped jackals and even spotted hyaenas. Seven (shy!) black rhinos are protected within a separate enclosure and the real attraction is the rich and colourful array of birdlife. Over 400 species of Malawi's 650 total have been recorded in the rich riverine, mopane and grassland habitats here. From October to January is particularly good for bird-watching, as migratory birds, including Bohms bee-eaters, set up summer camp.

Entry fees are payable (see National Parks & Reserves under Facts about Malawi earlier).

Tourism in the park revolves around Mvuu Camp (see Places to Stay later). If you have your own 4WD or high-clearance vehicle you can tour the park's network of tracks (although they close in the wet season and vary from year to year, so check the situation with the camp). Alternatively, game drives (US$18 per person) or guided wildlife walks (US$10) can be arranged at Mvuu Camp. To enter the rhino sanctuary costs an extra US$2 (the money goes directly to this project). Most rewarding and enjoyable are boat rides on the river (US$18), morning or evening, when you're virtually guaranteed to see elephants, hippos, crocodiles, fish eagles, a plethora of kingfishers and a whole host of other water birds.

If you can't stay in the park **Waterline River Safaris**, based in Liwonde, operates wildlife-viewing boat trips along the Shire River (for details see its listing under Liwonde earlier).

Places to Stay

Places to stay in Liwonde remain open all year – you can reach them by boat even if rain closes some of the park tracks.

Mvuu Camp *(camp sites per person US$5, accommodation only/full-board chalets per person US$35/140)*, managed by **Central African Wilderness Safaris** *(☎ 771393;* e *info@ wilderness.malawi.net)* in Lilongwe, is deep in the northern part of the park on the banks of the river. Stone chalets have tented roofs, lavish interiors and verandas overlooking the river, and the small but accommodating camp site has spotless ablution blocks and self-catering facilities, including utensils.

Alternatively, you can eat at the open-plan thatched restaurant (breakfast US$8, lunch US$13, dinner US$15); the food is excellent. There's also a bar and lounge area with wide lake views. Full-board rates include two wildlife activities and children between four and 12 are charged half price, but those under six are not allowed on wildlife-viewing trips.

Mvuu Wilderness Lodge *(full-board chalets per person US$240)*, a short distance upriver (also managed by Central African Wilderness Safaris), has large luxury double tents with private balconies overlooking a water hole where wildlife and birds are active. There's a maximum of only 10 guests, so this place is relaxed and intimate, with attentive staff and excellent food. There's also a small swimming pool. Rates includes park fees and all wildlife drives, boat rides, bird walks etc.

Chinguni Hills Cottage *(☎/fax 635356, 08 838159;* e *chinguni@africa-online.net; full-board singles/doubles without bath US$35/60, with bath US$45/80)*, in the south of the park, has five very accommodating rooms and the friendly host is a walking wealth of information on the park's flora and fauna. Walking and canoeing safaris are US$12.50 per person and night drives are US$15. Between January and May, cheaper 'Green Season' rates apply to accommodation.

Njobvu Cultural Village *(full-board hut per person US$50)* is actually 6km from the western boundary of Liwonde National Park and offers visitors a rare opportunity to stay in a traditional Malawian village. The experience includes dancing and crafts displays and allows you to participate in the daily activities of village life. All proceeds go directly to the community; you can book at Mvuu Camp or through Central African Wilderness Safaris.

Getting There & Away

The main park gate is 6km east of Liwonde town. There's no public transport beyond here, but hitching is possible. From the gate to Mvuu Camp is 28km along the park track (closed in the wet season), and a 4WD or high-clearance vehicle is recommended for this route.

Another way in for vehicles is via the dirt road (open all year) from Ulongwe, a village between Liwonde town and Mangochi. This leads for 14km through local villages to the western boundary. A few kilometres inside

the park is a car park and boat jetty, where a watchman hoists a flag to arrange a boat from Mvuu Camp to come and collect you. This service is free if you're staying at the camp.

Alternatively, if you make a booking in advance for Mvuu Camp through its Lilongwe office (for details see Places to Stay), the camp can arrange a boat transfer from Liwonde town for US$20 per person (it's half price if you're paying full-board at the camp).

For those without wheels, the best option is to get any bus or minibus between Liwonde town and Mangochi and get off at Ulongwe (make sure you say this clearly, otherwise the driver will think you want to go to Lilongwe). In Ulongwe local boys wait by the bus stop and will take you by bicycle to the park gate (US$2) or all the way to the boat jetty (US$3). If you've got a big pack there may be an extra charge or you may need two bikes. The ride takes about an hour and you should leave with plenty of time before dusk, otherwise you may encounter elephants and either way your cyclist will demand extra money for the trouble.

Another option is the boat transfer service along the Shire River offered by **Waterline River Safaris** (see its listing under Liwonde earlier). Approaching Mvuu by river is very enjoyable; along the way you're likely to see elephants and certain to see hippos.

ZOMBA

Zomba was the capital of Malawi until the mid-1970s and it's still a large, busy place, with all the attractions of a town and none of the downsides of a city. At its heart is the vibrant market (the largest in the country), a great place to do your shopping, or simply to wander around and watch Africa at work.

Overshadowing the town is the Zomba Plateau, and a walk through the suburbs on the lush and peaceful foothills reveals the faded but still impressive old Parliament Building – a reminder of Zomba's historical importance.

Zomba is not a place for wild parties, and you won't see many other tourists, but it somehow encapsulates what Malawi is all about; a visit here is highly recommended. Internet access is available at the **Photocopying and Typing Bureau** (open 8am-5pm Mon-Sat; US$12/hr), near the PTC supermarket.

Places to Stay & Eat

Council Resthouse (dorm beds US$0.80; singles/doubles without bath US$2/2.30, doubles with bath US$3.50) opposite the bus station has dorms and private rooms, but the toilet block is disgusting.

Ndindeya Motel (☎ 524068; rooms without bath US$7, singles/doubles with bath US$9.50/11) is a good budget option. The rooms are large, the shared bathrooms are clean and all rates include breakfast. The restaurant (dishes US$1 to US$2) serves tasty and substantial food.

Annie's Lodge (☎ 527002; Livingstone Rd; rooms with bath US$32), north of the town centre, has great value, spacious rooms, with fans and satellite TV. Rates include breakfast and there's also a popular bar.

Hotel Masongola (☎ 524688; Livingstone Rd; e hotelmasongola@clcom.net; singles/doubles with bath from US$37/48) is at the top of the hill and price scale. This was the house of the first colonial governor. Rates include breakfast. The older rooms are in the brick bungalows out the back, and rooms in the garden are more expensive and modern. The real attraction here is the pleasant beer garden on the private lawns and the restaurant (dishes US$3 to US$10), which serves rare treats including tiger prawns, guinea fowl, steak medallions and tandoori chicken.

Janet's House (☎ 542708; Mulunguzi Rd; singles/doubles with shared bath from US$20/25, doubles with bath US$38) is a friendly Malawian B&B with a healthy resident dog and cat population. There's only three rooms and the largest is absolutely charming.

Several **chip stalls** around the market area serve deep-fried potato chips, and one or two offer grilled meat and other street food. There's a **PTC** supermarket in town and plenty of cheap restaurants; **Angie's Takeaway** (dishes US$2), on the main street, is by far the most popular, serving good Malawian dishes.

Caboodles (☎ 542138; dishes US$1.50-4; open 8am-4pm Mon-Fri, 8am-2pm Sat) fixes all your Western-style cravings, with good sandwiches, burgers, pastas and pizzas in a café setting… and then there's coffee and cakes to polish it all off.

Zomba Gymkhana Club (☎ 527818; Mkulichi Rd; dishes US$1.50-3, 2/3-course buffet lunch US$3.80/6.50; open lunch & dinner daily), another colonial relic, offers

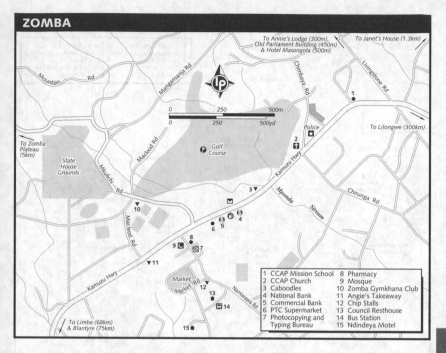

ZOMBA

To Annie's Lodge (300m),
Old Parliament Building (450m)
& Hotel Masongola (500m)

To Janet's House (1.3km)

To Lilongwe (300km)

To Zomba
Plateau
(5km)

State
House
Grounds

Golf
Course

To Limbe (68km)
& Blantyre (75km)

1	CCAP Mission School	8	Pharmacy
2	CCAP Church	9	Mosque
3	Caboodles	10	Zomba Gymkhana Club
4	National Bank	11	Angie's Takeaway
5	Commercial Bank	12	Chip Stalls
6	PTC Supermarket	13	Council Resthouse
7	Photocopying and	14	Bus Station
	Typing Bureau	15	Ndindeya Motel

good curries, stews, fish and chicken dishes in pleasant surroundings. Nonmembers need to pay US$0.70 entry.

Getting There & Away
Zomba is on a main route between Lilongwe and Blantyre. Express buses run to/from Zomba and Lilongwe (US$3.50, six hours, one daily), Blantyre (US$1.80, one hour, one daily), and Liwonde (US$1, 45 minutes, three daily). Minibuses go every hour or so to Limbe (US$1).

THE ZOMBA PLATEAU
The Zomba Plateau is divided into two halves by the Domasi Valley. The southern half has a road to the top, a hotel (the landmark Le Meridien Ku Chawe Inn), a camping ground, several picnic places and a network of driveable tracks and hiking paths that wind through pine forest or patches of indigenous woodland. There are several narrow ridges along the edge of the escarpment, with viewpoints overlooking the plains below. The plateau also has streams, waterfalls and a couple of lakes, where fishing is allowed. Some

people prefer to drive around, but Zomba is a good place for hiking. The cool air makes a welcome change from the heat of the lowland areas.

Note that some travellers have reported being hassled by 'ruffians' when hiking on the plateau. Locals say these are outsiders rather than people from Zomba. To avoid trouble, arrange a guide with the forest officer stationed at the Model Hut.

Things to See & Do
A few kilometres from Le Meridien Ku Chawe Inn are **Mandala Falls**, not as impressive as they used to be since **Mlunguzi Dam** was significantly enlarged in 1999. A nature trail leads upstream from Mandala Falls, through some beautiful indigenous forest and a trout farm, to **Williams Falls**, another fairly impressive cascade.

A popular place to visit is **Chingwe's Hole**, on the western side of the plateau, supposedly bottomless and the basis of various local legends, although now overgrown and not especially impressive. Nearby, however, is a splendid viewpoint, looking westward over the Shire Valley.

MALAWI

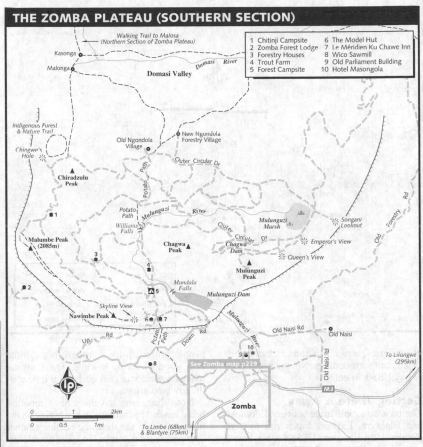

THE ZOMBA PLATEAU (SOUTHERN SECTION)

1 Chitinji Campsite	6 The Model Hut
2 Zomba Forest Lodge	7 Le Méridien Ku Chawe Inn
3 Forestry Houses	8 Wico Sawmill
4 Trout Farm	9 Old Parliament Building
5 Forest Campsite	10 Hotel Masongola

For even more impressive views, head for the eastern side of the plateau, where **Queen's View** (named after Queen Elizabeth, wife of King George VI, who visited Zomba in 1957) and **Emperor's View** (after Emperor Haile Selassie of Ethiopia, who visited in 1964) overlook Zomba town and out towards Mulanje.

Hiking

The southern half of the plateau is ideal for hiking. The network of tracks and paths can be confusing though, so for more help with orientation, there's a 3-D map of the plateau in the **Model Hut** (☎ 514258).

For detailed information on hiking routes on the southern half of the plateau, *A Guide to Zomba Plateau* (US$1.50) is a single sheet map with information on the back, including several suggested hiking routes, produced by the Wildlife Society, available in Blantyre and at Le Meridien Ku Chawe Inn. For more information still, the Zomba Plateau is covered in Lonely Planet's *Trekking in East Africa*.

Keen hikers may find the northern half of the plateau more interesting. There are few tracks here, and no pine plantation – the landscape is similar to that of Mt Mulanje and Nyika Plateau. For advice on hiking on the northern plateau, contact Chitinji Campsite (see Places to Stay & Eat later).

It's recommended to either walk in a group or to use a guide when hiking as there have been several robberies on the plateau in recent years. There are guides registered with

the Ministry of Forestry, Fisheries and Environmental Affairs based at the Model Hut, who charge around US$15 per day, although the rate is open to negotiation as there's no set price. More expensive guides are also available from Le Meridien Ku Chawe Inn.

The Potato Path You can hike all the way from Zomba town to the plateau via a direct route called the Potato Path, signposted at a sharp bend on the road up to the plateau about 2km from Zomba town. The path climbs steeply through woodland to reach the plateau near Le Meridien Ku Chawe Inn.

From near Le Meridien Ku Chawe Inn, the Potato Path then goes straight across the southern half of the plateau, sometimes using the park tracks, sometimes using narrow short cuts, and leads eventually to Old Ngondola Village, from where it descends quite steeply into the Domasi Valley.

The Domasi Valley is well known for its fertile soil, plentiful water and good farming conditions, so here the local people grow vegetables (especially potatoes) and take them along the Potato Path (hence the name) down to Zomba town to sell in the market.

Allow two to three hours for the ascent, and about 1½ hours coming down.

Places to Stay & Eat
Forest Campsite *(camp sites per person US$0.80)* is an aptly named spot with toilets and wood-fired hot showers all among large pine trees. It's one of those places that is beautiful in sunlight and a bit miserable in mist (you've got a 50:50 chance).

Chitinji Campsite *(e njussab_2000@yahoo .com; admission US$0.80; camp sites per person US$2.50, basic rooms per person US$5)*, near Malumbe Peak in the west, is run by an enterprising local called Nasiv Jussab, and is an excellent place to stay, although even more likely to be shrouded in mist. Nasiv has also taken over the running of the **Trout Farm** *(rooms per person US$6.50)*. He can advise on hikes in the surrounding area, and is especially keen to help people who want to explore the wilderness zone on the northern section of the plateau.

If you're camping, you should bring most of what you need from Zomba town, as there's no shop on the plateau, although there's a local-style tearoom and some stalls selling fruit, vegetables and (sometimes)

bread between Le Meridien Ku Chawe Inn and the Forest Campsite.

Le Meridien Ku Chawe Inn *(☎ 514237; e kuchawe@lemeridienmalawi.co.mw; superior/deluxe rooms US$72/90)* is like a small palace, built right on the edge of the escarpment with excellent views and very comfortable rooms. There's a good restaurant (buffet breakfast US$6.50, dishes US$9) and bar where they keep a fire going on cold nights, and the terraced gardens are particularly pleasant. Nonresidents can drink in the bar or dine here.

Zomba Forest Lodge *(☎ 09 926122; e landlake@africa-online.net; singles/doubles US$30/50, full-board singles/doubles US$40/65)* is on the western slopes of the plateau, 6km by winding dirt road past the entrance gate to the plateau. This is the former Kachere Forest Resthouse, which has now been renovated with a kitchen for self-catering. It has comfortable rooms and rates include breakfast. You can get more information from Land & Lake Safaris (see Travel Agencies & Tour Operators under Lilongwe earlier in this chapter).

Getting There & Away
A sealed road leads steeply up the escarpment from Zomba town to the top of the plateau (about 8km). After the entrance gate, a two-way sealed road, known as the Down Road, veers east and continues for another 2km, before turning to a dirt track. There is also an Up Road, but this is now only open to walkers.

There's no bus up to the plateau, but local people hitch by the junction on the main street in Zomba town near the PTC supermarket. Alternatively, you can take a taxi (negotiable from around US$8). If this is beyond your means, get a taxi part way through the suburbs, say as far as Wico Sawmill or the Zomba Forest Lodge turnoff, then simply walk up the Up Road. The views are excellent!

Alternatively, you can walk all the way from Zomba town to the plateau via the road or on the Potato Path (see Hiking earlier).

BLANTYRE & LIMBE
Blantyre is the commercial and industrial capital of Malawi. It stretches for about 20km, merging into Limbe – its 'sister city'. Blantyre buzzes a bit more than Lilongwe (if

MALAWI

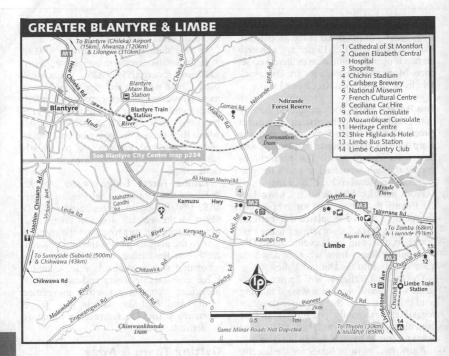

GREATER BLANTYRE & LIMBE

1 Cathedral of St Montfort
2 Queen Elizabeth Central Hospital
3 Shoprite
4 Chichiri Stadium
5 Carlsberg Brewery
6 National Museum
7 French Cultural Centre
8 Ceciliana Car Hire
9 Canadian Consulate
10 Mozambique Consulate
11 Heritage Centre
12 Shire Highlands Hotel
13 Limbe Bus Station
14 Limbe Country Club

any of Malawi's sleepy cities can be said to buzz at all) and during the week the city centre is a hive of energy. Despite the dense activity, you'll find relatively little hassle here. Most travellers stop only for a few days to send or receive mail, buy maps and books or pick up a visa for Mozambique. This is probably long enough to exploit some interesting sights, the most global selection of cuisine in Malawi, several enjoyable bars, and a fair selection of places to stay. (Unless stated otherwise, every address in this section is in Blantyre, rather than Limbe.)

Orientation

Despite the sprawling suburbs and townships surrounding Blantyre, the city centre is very compact, with most places of importance to travellers within easy walking distance. Central Blantyre's main street is Victoria Ave; along here are several large shops, the tourist office, the map sales office, banks, foreign exchange bureaus and travel agents. To the east is Haile Selassie Rd, which contains many smaller shops. At the northern end of Victoria Ave is the landmark Le Meridien Mount Soche Hotel.

East of Le Meridien Mount Soche Hotel is a major traffic roundabout, from where the main road north leads to the airport, Mwanza and Lilongwe. This road has no official name but is known as New Chileka Rd. About 500m further east is another roundabout, with a small clock on a concrete pedestal in the middle: from here Chileka Rd leads north to the bus station and outer suburbs; and Chipembere Highway, heading south, turns into the Kamuzu Highway, which veers east towards Limbe, and ultimately Zomba, Mulanje and Liwonde.

Maps Survey maps of Blantyre and the surrounding area are available from the **Department of Surveys Map Sales Office** *(Victoria Ave)*. See also Maps under Planning in the Facts for the Visitor section earlier in this chapter.

Information

Tourist Office The central **Tourist Office** *(☎ 620300; Victoria Ave; open 7.30am-noon & 1pm-5pm Mon-Fri)* has a few leaflets, and the people here make quite an effort to provide information and assistance.

Immigration Office If you need to extend your visa, Blantyre has an **immigration office** *(Building Society House, Victoria Ave)*.

Money All of the following banks are on Victoria Ave. There are branches of the **National Bank of Malawi** and **Commercial Bank of Malawi** in the centre of town, as well as **Rennies Travel** (☎ 624533) and **Finance Bank** (☎ 624799), which both have foreign exchange bureaus. **Victoria Forex** (☎ 621026) usually has more competitive rates and charges no commission. If you've got the time, shop around, as rates and commissions can vary considerably.

Post & Communications The main post office *(Glyn Jones Rd)* in Blantyre has poste restante.

There are several small phone bureaus around the main bus station, from which you can make national calls. Both Doogles and Tumbuka Lodge have international telephone facilities for guests (for details see Places to Stay later in this section).

Email & Internet Access There are plenty of Internet bureaus in Blantyre. **Malawi.Net Internet Bureau** (☎ 622436; *St George's St*) charges US$1.30 for 30 minutes and **Celtel Cyber Cafe** *(Victoria Ave)* charges US$1.90. The best deal is at **Business Machines Limited** *(Fatima Arcade, Haile Selassie Rd)*, charging US$0.80 for 30 minutes.

Travel Agencies & Tour Operators In the centre, there are several travel agencies including **AMI Travel** (☎ 620988; e amitravel@sndp.org.mw; *cnr Victoria Ave & Henderson St)* and **Rennies Travel** (see Money earlier). **Galaxy Travel** (☎ 621590; *St George's St)* is switched on. Most of these agencies deal mainly in outbound flights.

Two agencies dealing with tours, flights, safaris, car hire and hotel reservations within Malawi are **Soche Tours & Travel** (☎ 620777; e sochetours@malawi.net; *Hordelec House, 3 Victoria Ave)* and **Central African Wilderness Safaris** (☎ 636961; e wildblz@sdnp.org.mw; *Ryalls Protea Hotel)*. The latter also operates accommodation and facilities in Liwonde National Park.

Bookshops There's a **TBS** bookshop *(Victoria Ave)* in town and a smaller one at Le Meridien Mount Soche Hotel. For a much wider selection, visit the **Central Bookshop** *(Livingstone Rd)*. It stocks stationery, books and guides about Malawi, local language dictionaries and a good range of novels by local writers. There's also a pleasant coffee shop. The **Central Africana** bookshop *(Victoria Ave)*, next to the PTC supermarket, specialises in antiquarian and specialist African titles, plus old prints and maps.

The **Wildlife Society of Malawi giftshop** *(Churchill Rd, Limbe)* at the Heritage Centre, next to the Shire Highlands Hotel, specialises in books about natural history and national parks; its prices are very reasonable.

Medical Services The Malaria Test Centre at the government-run **Queen Elizabeth Central Hospital** (☎ 674333; *off Chipembere Highway; open 24hr)* charges US$1 for a malaria test. Ask for directions as the Test Centre is hard to find.

For private medical consultations or blood tests, **Mwaiwathu Private Hospital** (☎ 622999; *Chileka Rd; open 24hr)*, east of the city centre, is good. A consultation is US$10; all drugs and treatment are extra. An overnight stay in a private ward is US$80 – before any treatment, you must put down a US$220 deposit.

For medical or dental problems, the **Seventh Day Adventist Clinic** (☎ 620006; *Robins Rd)* charges US$6 for a doctor's consultation and US$10 for a malaria test.

There's a large **MPL pharmacy** *(Victoria Ave)*, and several smaller ones elsewhere around the city centre.

Emergency The advice in Blantyre is the same as for Lilongwe; see that section earlier.

Dangers & Annoyances Don't wander around alone at night. Some travellers walking between the city centre and Doogles, east of the city (see Places to Stay later), have been attacked at night under the railway bridge on Chileka Rd. During daylight this route is fine but after dark a taxi is recommended (from the centre to Doogles is US$4). At night taxi drivers will take you from the bus station to Doogles – all of 300m – but still charge US$1! As always, watch your back in busy bus stations. Limbe is particularly crowded, so stay alert there.

MALAWI

BLANTYRE CITY CENTRE

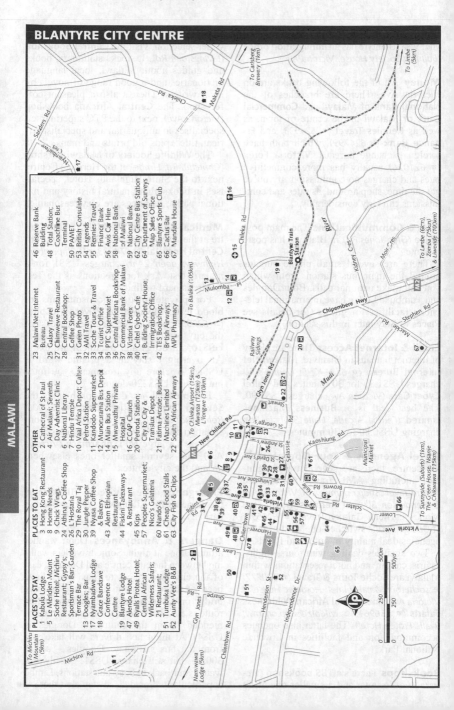

PLACES TO STAY
1 Kabula Lodge
5 Le Méridien Mount
　Soche Hotel; Michiru
　Restaurant; Gypsy's;
　Sportsman's Bar; Garden
　Terrace Bar
13 Doogles; Bar
17 Nyambadwe Lodge
18 Grace Bandawe
　Conference
　Centre
19 Blantyre Lodge
47 Alendo Hotel
49 Ryalls Protea Hotel;
　Central African
　Wilderness Safaris;
　21 Restaurant;
51 Tumbuka Lodge
52 Aunty Vee's B&B

PLACES TO EAT
3 Hong Kong Restaurant
8 Home Needs
9 Chick Wings
24 Athina's Coffee Shop
26 L'Hostaria
29 The Royal Taj
30 Jungle Pepper
39 Nyasa Coffee Shop
　& Bakery
43 Alem Ethiopian
　Restaurant
44 Fiskini Takeaways
　& Restaurant
45 Kips
57 Peoples Supermarket;
　Nico's Gelateria
60 Nando's
61 Cheap Food Stalls
63 City Hide & Chips

OTHER
2 Cathedral of St Paul
4 Air Malawi; Seventh
　Day Adventist Clinic
6 Hindu Temple
10 Vaal Africa Depot; Caltex
　Petrol Station
11 Kandodo Supermarket
12 Munorurama Bus Depot
14 Main Bus Station
15 Mwaiwathu Private
　Hospital
16 CCAP Church
20 Petroda Station;
　City to City &
　Translux Depot
21 Fatima Arcade; Business
　Machines Limited
22 South African Airways
23 Malawi.Net Internet
　Bureau
25 Galaxy Travel
27 Chimwewe Restaurant
28 Central Bookshop;
　Coffee Shop
31 Green Photo
32 AMI Travel
33 Scche Tours & Travel
34 Tcurist Office
35 PTC Supermarket
36 Central Africana Bookshop
37 Commercial Bank of Malawi
38 Victoria Forex
40 Celtel Cyber Cafe
41 Building Society House;
　Immigration Office
42 TES Bookshop;
　British Airways;
　MPL Pharmacy
46 Reserve Bank
　Building
48 Total Station;
　Coachline Bus
　Terminal
50 PAMET
53 British Consulate
54 Legends
55 Rennies Bank;
　Finance Bank
56 Avis Car Hire
58 National Bank
　of Malawi
59 National Bank
62 City Centre Bus Station
64 Department of Surveys
　Map Sales Office
65 Blantyre Sports Club
66 Cactus Bar
67 Mandaa House

Photography The large and busy **Green Photo** (cnr Livingstone Ave & Henderson St) sells print film, develops and can provide passport photos. (See Photography & Video under Facts for the Visitor earlier in this chapter for more photography details.)

Things to See & Do

The modern buildings of the **Municipal Market** (Kaoshiung Rd) give it a more formal feel than the hectic market in Lilongwe; it's still worth a visit even if you don't want to buy anything.

Probably the most impressive building in Blantyre is the **CCAP Church** (off Chileka Rd), officially called the Church of St Michael and All Angels. This magnificent church was built in 1891 by Scottish missionaries who had no construction training, using only local handmade bricks and wood. It has a basilica dome, towers, arches and bay windows. Although extensively renovated in the 1970s, what you see today is pretty much how it looked the day it was completed.

PAMET (Paper Making Education Trust; ☎ 623895; 10 Chilembwe Rd) is an inspiring project that was set up to teach people how to recycle paper. This is an important issue in Malawi, where some are too poor to buy exercise books for their children. They also make beautiful paper from materials such as banana leaves and baobab bark (even elephant dung!). You can visit their workshop to see how it's all done and they sell a lovely range of cards and other paper products.

The **National Museum** (Kasungu Cres; admission US$0.70, open 7.30am-5pm daily) is midway between Blantyre and Limbe. There's a small collection of traditional weapons and artefacts, and exhibits relating to traditional dance, European exploration and slavery.

Blantyre Sports Club (off Independence Dr) offers daily membership for US$5, which allows you to enter the club and use the bar and restaurant. To use the pool or to play squash or tennis costs another US$0.80. Nine holes of golf costs US$3; equipment can be hired.

If you're of a less active inclination, a visit to the **Carlsberg Brewery** (☎ 670022; Gomani Rd), east of the centre, may appeal. Free tours are conducted at 2.30pm every Wednesday; you must book. The tour ends with a free tasting session. Some places to stay in Blantyre arrange transport here. Alternatively, you can walk or get a taxi.

There are very good **craft stalls** (Victoria Ave) outside the PTC supermarket.

Places to Stay – Budget

Apart from the Limbe Country Club all of the following are in Blantyre:

Camping Backpackers can pitch their tents at **Doogles** (camp sites US$2.80, see Hostels & Guesthouses following for details) and there's also room for a few trucks and cars with tents. For camping in a quieter locale see the listing for Nyambadwe Lodge following.

Limbe Country Club (☎ 641145; Livingstone Ave, Limbe; camp sites per person US$7.50) is an alternative for those with wheels. Here you can park and camp on the edge of the playing fields. Rates include club membership, so you can use the showers and restaurant inside.

Hostels & Guesthouses Close to the main bus station is friendly **Doogles** (☎ 621128; e doogles@africa-online.net; Mulomba Place; dorm beds US$5.50, chalets without bath US$16, doubles with bath US$21), a large, secure property with teeming gardens, immaculate dorms and very comfortable rooms and chalets. The self-catering facilities are also good and the communal bathrooms spotless; these guys cater well to all budgets. The bar here is an attraction in itself (see Entertainment later) as is the restaurant (snacks US$1-2.50, dishes US$4), where you'll find excellent breakfasts, salads, enchiladas and gourmet burgers. The friendly staff provide a Mozambican visa service and know a lot about travel in Malawi and facilities in Blantyre. You can make international phone calls for US$3 per minute and send email for US$3.80 per hour. Some budget tour outfits run excursions from here.

Blantyre Lodge (☎ 634460; off Chileka Rd; singles/doubles without bath US$4/5.50, doubles with bath US$12.50) is also near the bus station if Doogles is full and you're on a tight budget, but the rooms are cramped and dingy and the toilets dirty. The rooms with a bathroom are slightly better. Security may also be questionable, as there's a market right outside the (unlocked) gates.

Grace Bandawe Conference Centre (☎ 634257; Chileka Rd; dorm beds US$9,

MALAWI

singles/doubles without bath US$19/24, doubles with bath US$30) is a large property, about 2km from the city centre, with neat, plain rooms (two rooms share a bathroom). Breakfast is US$1 and dinner (always chicken and rice) is US$3. Dorm beds are in the spartan annexe over the road behind Phoenix School.

Kabula Lodge *(☎ 621216; off Michiru Rd; dorm beds/singles/doubles US$5/19/25)*, northwest of the city centre, is highly recommended. Dorms have only three beds and rates for the commodious rooms (two rooms share a bathroom) include breakfast. A cool veranda wraps around the back of the building, offering great views of the city. The friendly Malawian lady who runs this place can prepare meals, or you can self-cater.

Nyambadwe Lodge *(☎ 633551; Nyambadwe Cres; camp sites per person US$5, singles/doubles with bath US$30/44)*, 3km by road north of the main bus station, has clean and tidy rooms, including TV, fan and fridge. A dinner of pork, chicken, chambo or beef here goes for US$5.50.

Aunty Vee's B&B *(☎ 09 937413; 19 Henderson St; singles/doubles with bath US$25/32)* is a small and welcoming guesthouse with accommodating rooms. Rates include breakfast.

Places to Stay – Mid-Range & Top End

Rooms at all of the following places include breakfast and a private bathroom.

Alendo Hotel *(☎ 621866; 15 Chilembwe Rd; singles/doubles from US$55/65)*, in the centre, is the Malawian Institute of Tourism training school and has super-eager staff but tight rooms. The facilities are good, however, and there's secure parking. The attached **Kachere Restaurant** *(3-course dinner US$7)* is good value.

Tumbuka Lodge *(☎/fax 633489; e jambo africa@africa-online.net; Sharpe Rd; rooms with/without bath US$90/70)* is deservedly popular. This old colonial bungalow has attractive gardens and tasteful rooms, which come with nets, fans, TV, and tea and coffee facilities. Drinks are served on the regal terrace, there's a TV lounge, dinner is around US$5 and you can make international phone calls or send email.

Ryalls Protea Hotel *(☎ 620955; e ryalls@ proteamalawi.com; 2 Hanover Ave; singles/*

doubles US$205/236) is all style and class, with executive facilities to match the rates.

Le Meridien Mount Soche Hotel *(☎ 620588; e mountsoche@lemeridienmalawi .co.mw; Glyn Jones Rd; rooms US$234)*, popular with business travellers, also has good facilities. Both Ryalls Hotel and Le Meridien Mount Soche Hotel have swimming pools and restaurants.

Places to Eat

Restaurants For some different African flavours, **Alem Ethiopian Restaurant** *(☎ 622529; Victoria Ave; dishes US$1-7.50; open 8am-7pm Mon-Sat)* serves *injera* (sour millet pancake) and *wot* (sauce), but you can also get 'normal' meals like chicken and chips or curry.

Home Needs *(Glyn Jones Rd; dishes US$1-2; open 11am-2pm weekdays except Thur, 4pm-8pm Fri & Wed)* is a South Indian snack bar and hardware shop. It serves *masala dosas* (spicy pancakes) and other tasty snacks at cheap prices.

The Royal Taj *(☎ 624030; Livingstone Ave; starters US$0.50-4, mains US$4-9; open lunch and dinner Mon-Sat)* is the best Indian restaurant in Blantyre, with excellent, traditional dishes, attentive service and exquisitely kitschy Taj decor.

Nico's Gelateria *(☎ 620624; Victoria Ave; dishes US$1.50-3; open 8am-10pm Sun-Thur, 8am-12am Fri & Sat)* has great Italian ice cream, good coffee and pizzas.

L'Hostaria *(☎ 625052; Chilembwe Rd; starters US$2.50, mains US$3.50-6; open noon-2pm & 6.30pm-9pm Tues-Sun)* has an Italian-flavoured atmosphere with meals to match. A wide variety of pizzas, pastas and chicken, fish and steak mains can be enjoyed inside or on the terrace outside.

Hong Kong Restaurant *(☎ 620859; Robins Rd; dishes US$2.50-4; open noon-1.30pm & 6-10pm Tues-Sun)* has an exhaustive Chinese menu, very good food and generous portions. It's highly recommended.

The Green House *(☎ 636375; Mbobe Close; starters US$3-5, mains US$6-8; open from 7pm Mon-Sat)* is in the posh suburb of Sunnyside. The menu is European and the food is fine.

21 Restaurant *(snacks US$3-7, buffet dinner US$12.50; open lunch and dinner daily)* at Ryalls Protea Hotel is a highly rated eatery, with five-star surrounds, food and service.

Michiru Restaurant *(mains US$12-17; open dinner Mon-Sat)*, is the smart, top-floor restaurant at Le Meridien Mount Soche Hotel. Excellent steak, fish, chicken and prawn dishes come with a hefty price tag but the views are pretty fine. Downstairs, the less formal Gypsy's *(mains US$6-7, buffet lunch or dinner US$15; open lunch and dinner daily)* has a discerning à-la-carte menu and extensive lunch and dinner buffet.

Food Stalls & Cafés For cheap eats, food stalls around the main bus station and the city centre bus station sell chips from US$0.30, grilled meat for US$0.40 and bowls of nsima and sauce for around US$0.50.

Several eateries offer filling meals for around US$1.50, including City Fish & Chips *(Lower Sclater Rd; open 8am-8pm daily)*, which serves large portions of chicken or fish with chips.

Another cheapie is Fiskini Takeaways and Restaurant *(cnr Henderson St & Hanover Ave; open 6am-8pm Sun-Thur, 24hr Fri & Sat)*. Athina's Coffee Shop *(Glyn Jones Rd; open 8am-6pm daily)* is a step up in decor and quality, serving good burgers, tasty Malawian dishes and a tempting selection of pastries for sweet tooths.

Western-style takeaways include: Nando's *(Haile Selassie Rd; dishes US$2-4; open 8am-9pm daily)*, with steak rolls, burgers and spicy chicken and chips; and the cheaper Chick Wings *(Glyn Jones Rd; open 9am-5pm Mon-Fri, 10am-4pm Sat)*.

Kips *(☎ 635247; Hanover Ave; breakfast US$1, dishes US$1.30-5; open 8am-10pm Sun-Thur, 8am-12am Fri & Sat)* dishes up a real mix of pizzas, burgers, fish, steak, Malawian and Indian meals. It's clean and deservedly popular with locals.

Jungle Pepper *(☎ 635135; off Livingstone Ave; pizzas US$3-4.50; open 10.30am-2.30pm & 4.30pm-9pm Thur-Tues)* teems with office workers over the lunch hour, due to a tasty and diverse selection of fresh pizzas.

Nyasa Coffee Shop and Bakery *(☎ 09 968200; Hanover Ave; dishes US$3-4; open 8am-7pm Mon-Fri, 9am-7pm Sat & Sun)* is a stylish, Mediterranean-style café with excellent fajitas, nachos, sandwiches, salads and a good selection of cakes.

Self-Catering The main PTC supermarket *(cnr Victoria Ave & Chilembwe Rd)* sells food and other goods, much of it imported from South Africa or Europe and sold at similar prices. The Peoples Supermarket *(Victoria Ave)* is similar. Cheaper but more limited supplies can be bought at Kandodo supermarket *(Glyn Jones Rd)*. There's also a huge Shoprite *(Kamuzu Highway)* a few kilometres out of town.

Entertainment
Chimwewe Restaurant *(cnr Henderson St & Haile Selassie Rd)*, despite its name, is more like a bar. Loud music and gaming machines mean it's low on charm but the congenial crowd and cheap drinks compensate.

The Garden Terrace Bar at Le Meridien Mount Soche Hotel caters to a more composed market and its tranquil surrounds are certainly appealing. Also at this hotel, the Sportsman's Bar is favoured by local businessmen and other movers and shakers.

Doogles bar *(open to 10.30pm)* is like a constant happy hour (see Places to Stay earlier), where a fluent stream of travellers chill out and socialise with devoted expats and well-to-do Malawians.

Cactus Bar *(Lower Sclater Rd)* is the late-night rendezvous point for the Doogles crowd. Things get pretty spirited here on Friday and Saturday nights and it's Blantyre's best spot for a boogie.

Legends *(Hanover Ave; admission US$1, live music US$3)* is a popular American-style bar and nightclub which gets hot and busy after 10pm.

Occasional live music is played at both Le Meridien Mount Soche Hotel and Ryalls Protea Hotel, where entry is also about US$3.

Blantyre Sports Club *(off Independence Dr)* features live music on the last Friday of every month.

A weekly run-down of live music and events is summed up in the small, pink and free *Friday!* flyers available at most venues.

Spectator Sports
Blantyre's main sports venue is the Chichiri Stadium *(off Makata Rd)* between the city centre and Limbe. This is also Malawi's national stadium; international football and other events are held here. There's no regular programme, but matches are advertised in the newspaper and on billboards around town.

Getting There & Away

Air Blantyre's Chileka airport is about 15km north of the city centre. For details on the airport and flights to/from Blantyre see the main Getting Around and Getting There & Away sections earlier in this chapter.

Airline offices in Blantyre include: **Air Malawi** (☎ 620811; Robins Rd); **KLM & Kenya Airways** (☎ 620106; Le Meridien Mount Soche Hotel); **British Airways** (☎ 624333; Victoria Ave); and **South African Airways** (☎ 620627; Haile Selassie Rd).

Bus & Minibus Coachline buses run between Blantyre and Lilongwe (US$18, four hours, three daily), stopping at the Total petrol station near Ryalls Protea Hotel on Hanover Street. The booking office is also here.

Blantyre's main bus station (for Shire Bus Lines long-distance express and ordinary services) is east of the centre on Mulomba Place. Express buses run between Blantyre and Lilongwe via Zalewa (the junction with the Mwanza road) (US$5, five hours, one daily); this route is also serviced by ordinary buses (US$3.80, seven hours, four daily). There's an express service to Zomba (US$1.80, one hour, one daily), which also continues to Lilongwe (US$5, seven hours). Ordinary buses travel between Blantyre and Zomba (US$1, 1½ hours, frequently), Mulanje (US$1.25, 1½ hours, seven daily), Mwanza (US$1.30, one hour, two daily) and Monkey Bay (US$3.80, eight hours, one daily), via Liwonde (US$2, three hours) and Mangochi (US$3, six hours).

Other buses (ie, not Shire Bus Lines) and long-distance minibuses go from the bus station in Limbe; most leave on a fill-up-and-go basis. It's often quicker to get a local minibus to Limbe bus station, and then a long-distance bus or 'half-bus' from there rather than wait for the Shire express or ordinary buses in Blantyre. Routes include: Zomba (US$1); Mulanje (US$1.50); and Mangochi (US$3).

Train For information on trains that stop at Blantyre and Limbe, see Train under the main Getting There & Away and Getting Around sections earlier in this chapter.

Getting Around

To/From the Airport A taxi from the airport to the city costs around US$8, but agree on a price with the driver first. The price can be negotiated down a bit if you're going from the city to the airport. If your budget doesn't include taxis, frequent local buses between the Blantyre city centre bus station and Chileka township pass the airport gate. The fare is US$0.30.

Bus Blantyre is a compact city, so it's unlikely you'll need to use public transport to get around, apart from the minibuses that shuttle along Chipembere Highway between Blantyre city centre bus station and Limbe bus station. The one-way fare is US$0.30.

Taxi You can find private hire taxis at the Le Meridien Mount Soche Hotel or at the bus stations. A taxi across the city centre is around US$2; between the centre and the main bus station costs from US$3 to US$4; and a taxi from Blantyre to Limbe costs around US$5.

AROUND BLANTYRE

Blantyre is surrounded by three 'mountains', Michiru, Soche and Ndirande, all actually large hills that can all be hiked to the summit. Some hikers have been attacked on **Mt Ndirande**, so you should only go here with a guide. These can be arranged from Doogles (see Places to Stay under Blantyre earlier) for around US$2 per day. The path up **Mt Soche** starts at Soche Secondary School.

The most rewarding is **Mt Michiru**, 8km northwest of the city, a conservation area with nature trails. Animals found here include monkeys, klipspringers and even leopards, but you're unlikely to see much of them. Bird-watching is much more rewarding – over 400 species have been recorded here. To reach the visitor centre (where the trails start), take Kabula Hill Rd from the city and Michiru Rd through a select suburb and then a township. At the end of the sealed road (3km from Blantyre), a dirt road leads along the eastern foot of the mountain. Take the left turn signposted 'nature trails', which takes you to the visitor centre, where you can buy a map. There's no public transport, but you can get a taxi as far as the driver is prepared to go along the dirt road, and walk the rest of the way. You may be able to get a lift back with other visitors.

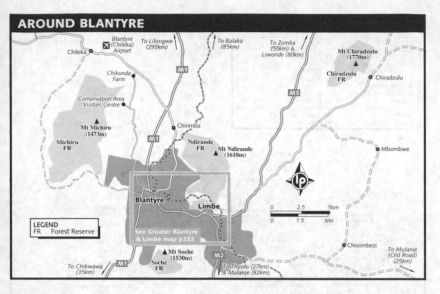

AROUND BLANTYRE

MULANJE

This small town is the centre of Malawi's tea-growing industry. You may stay overnight here if you're going to Mozambique, but most travellers come on the way to Mt Mulanje.

Mulanje Golf Club (☎ 466260; camp sites per person US$3.80), on the eastern side of town, is planted in a scenic spot below the mountain. The first night's rate includes membership, so you can use the showers and bar, and consecutive nights only cost US$2.

The **Council Resthouse** (rooms with/ without bath US$1/0.50), close to the bus station, is bargain basement in price and quality. Heading closer to Likhubula on the main road, **Mulanje Motel** (☎ 466245; rooms with/without bath US$6.50/3) is a much better budget option.

Limbani Lodge (☎ 466390; singles/doubles with bath US$5/7.50, VIP rooms US$13), near the School for the Blind, has the best beds in town. Standard rooms are comfy and the 'VIP' rooms contain TV and fully equipped kitchens.

Ordinary buses go to/from Blantyre and Limbe (US$1.30, 1½ hours, seven daily) as do minibuses (US$1.50, 40 minutes). If you're heading for the border of Mozambique, minibuses, matolas and buses all run to Muloza (US$0.50, 40 minutes). (For more border crossing information, see

Land under the main Getting There & Away section earlier in this chapter.)

MOUNT MULANJE

Mt Mulanje (also called the Mulanje Plateau) rises steeply from the undulating plain of the highlands, surrounded by near-vertical cliffs of bare rock, many over 1000m high. The cliffs are dissected by vegetated valleys, where rivers drop in spectacular waterfalls. It is often misty here and Mulanje's high peaks sometimes jut above the cloud, giving rise to the local name 'Island in the Sky'. Some people come to the base of the mountain just for a day visit, but the stunning scenery, easy access, clear paths and well-maintained huts make Mulanje a fine hiking area and many travellers spend at least a few days here.

Mulanje measures about 30km from west to east and 25km from north to south, with an area of at least 600 sq km. On its northeastern corner is the outlier Mchese Mountain, separated from the main massif by the Fort Lister Gap. The massif is composed of several bowl-shaped river basins, separated by rocky peaks and ridges. The highest peak is Sapitwa (3001m), the highest point in Malawi and in all Southern Africa north of the Drakensberg. There are other peaks on the massif above 2500m, and you can reach most of the summits without technical climbing.

MALAWI

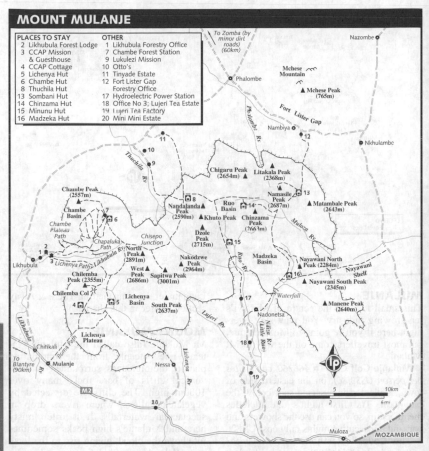

MOUNT MULANJE

PLACES TO STAY
2 Likhubula Forest Lodge
3 CCAP Mission & Guesthouse
4 CCAP Cottage
5 Lichenya Hut
6 Chambe Hut
8 Thuchila Hut
13 Sombani Hut
14 Chinzama Hut
15 Minunu Hut
16 Madzeka Hut

OTHER
1 Likhubula Forestry Office
7 Chambe Forest Station
9 Lukulezi Mission
10 Otto's
11 Tinyade Estate
12 Fort Lister Gap Forestry Office
17 Hydroelectric Power Station
18 Office No 3; Lujeri Tea Estate
19 Lujeri Tea Factory
20 Mini Mini Estate

For hikers, it's worth remembering that Mulanje is a big mountain with notoriously unpredictable weather. After periods of heavy rain, streams can become swollen and impassable – do not try to cross them! Wait until the flood subsides (sometimes after a few hours) or adjust your route to cross in safety further upstream. Even during the dry season, it's not uncommon to get rain, cold winds and thick mists, which make it easy to get lost. Between May and August, periods of low cloud and drizzle (called *chiperones*) can last several days, and temperatures drop below freezing. None of this is a problem as long as you've got warm, waterproof gear and don't get lost. Otherwise, you risk suffering from severe exposure. In 1999 an unfortunate traveller died up here.

Information

Hiking on Mt Mulanje is controlled by the **Likhubula Forestry Office** (☎ 467718; PO Box 50, Mulanje; open 7.30am-noon & 1pm-5pm daily), at the small village of Likhubula, about 15km from Mulanje town. The friendly and helpful staff can arrange guides and porters from an official list. You must register here and make reservations for the mountain huts (you can also call or write in advance). Camping is permitted only near huts and only when they're full. Open fires are not allowed – this is especially important during the latter part of the dry season, when there is a serious fire risk. The collecting of plants and animals is forbidden.

There is nowhere to buy food on Mt Mulanje, so you must carry all you need.

At Likhubula there's a small market, but you're better off getting supplies at Chitikali (where the dirt road to Likhubula turns off the main sealed Blantyre–Mulanje road), which has shops, stalls and a small supermarket, or in Blantyre.

Guidebooks & Maps

The *Guide to Mulanje Massif*, by Frank Eastwood, has information on ascent routes and main peaks plus a large section on rock climbing, but nothing on the routes between huts. There's more detail on Mulanje in Lonely Planet's *Trekking in East Africa*, which also covers Nyika and Zomba.

If you need detailed maps, the Department of Surveys prints a map of the mountain at 1:40,000, which shows most of the paths and huts. The 1:30,000 *Tourist Map of Mulanje* covers a similar area, overprinted with extra information for hikers. These maps are usually available from the public map sales offices in Blantyre and Lilongwe, but stocks occasionally run dry.

Guides & Porters

Porters are not obligatory, but they make the hiking easier, especially for the first day's steep hike from Likhubula Forestry Office. Guides are definitely recommended to help you through the maze of paths.

As you arrive in Likhubula (or Mulanje town) you'll be besieged by hopeful locals looking for work, but you should arrange guides and porters only at Likhubula, as the forest station keeps a registered list, which works on a rotation system. Some porters are not on the list but are 'cleared' by the office staff.

There is a standard charge of US$6.30 per day per porter and US$7.50 per guide (regardless of group size), payable in kwacha (you should avoid hiring porters who undercut this price in their eagerness to get work). The total fee for the whole trip should be agreed before departure and put in writing. Fees are paid at the end of the trip but porters are expected to provide their own food, so about 25% may be required in advance. Make sure guides and porters bring everything they need, and tell them no other food can be provided. Even if you do this, you'll still feel guilty when you stop for lunch and your escorts sit and watch you, so take a few extra packets of biscuits for them. You may

want to tip your porters and guides if the service has been good; a rule of thumb is to pay something around an extra day's wage for every three to five days. The maximum weight each porter can carry is 18kg.

Places to Stay

Below the Mountain At Likhubula, the stylish **Likhubula Forest Lodge** (☎ 467737; e *likhubula@cholemalawi.com; camping per person US$5, singles/doubles/triples without bath US$12/15/20, with bath US$15/19/25)* has a kitchen, comfortable lounge, several bedrooms and is spotless all over. A cook will prepare your food and wash up. You can camp in the grounds.

CCAP Guesthouse *(camp sites US$1, chalets per person US$6.50)* at the CCAP Mission has cosy rooms, self-catering chalets and camping.

On the Mountain On Mulanje are seven **forestry huts** *(camp sites per person US$0.80, huts per person US$1.30)*: Chambe, Lichenya, Thuchila (**chu**-chila), Chinzama, Minunu, Madzeka and Sombani. Each is equipped with benches, tables and open fires with plenty of wood. Some have sleeping platforms (no mattresses); in others you just sleep on the floor. You provide your own food, cooking gear, candles, sleeping bag and stove (although you can cook on the fire). A caretaker chops wood, lights fires and brings water, for which a small tip should be paid.

Payments must be made at Likhubula Forestry Office – show your receipt to the hut caretaker. The huts are an absolute bargain. Camping is permitted near the huts when there are no more beds. Some huts may be full at weekends, but you can normally adjust your route around this. As the reservation system doesn't require a deposit, some local residents book and then don't turn up – it's worth checking to see if this has happened.

CCAP Cottage *(beds US$1.30)* on the Lichenya Plateau is similar to the forestry huts, but there are utensils in the kitchen, plus mattresses and blankets. You can make reservations at the CCAP Mission in Likhubula.

Hiking Routes There are about six main routes up and down Mulanje. The three main ascent routes go from Likhubula: the Chambe Plateau Path (also called the Skyline Path), the Chapaluka Path and the Lichenya

MALAWI

Path. Other routes, more often used for the descent, are: Thuchila Hut to Lukulezi Mission; Sombani Hut to Fort Lister Gap; and Minunu Hut to Lujeri tea estate.

Once you're on the massif, a network of paths links the huts and peaks, and many different permutations are possible; we outline some choices here. Be warned that some of the routes are impassable or otherwise dangerous. The route from Madzeka Hut to Lujeri is very steep, and the wooden ladders required to cross the steepest sections have rotted away, making it effectively impassable. On the southwestern side of Mulanje, the Boma Path and the path from Lichenya to Nessa are both dangerously steep and very rarely used.

It normally takes about three to six hours to hike between one hut and the next, which means you can walk in the morning, dump your kit, then go out to explore a nearby peak or valley in the afternoon.

A Mulanje Traverse There are many ways to traverse the Mulanje massif. The route we describe briefly here, from Likhubula to Fort Lister, is one of several options, although it seems to be the most popular. It can be done in four days, but there are several variations that can extend this period, and plenty of opportunities for sidetracking, to take in a few peaks and ridges or explore small valleys.

Likhubula Forestry Office to Chambe Hut There are two options: the Chambe Plateau Path, which is short and steep (two to four hours); and the Chapaluka Path (3½ to five hours), which is less steep and more scenic. From the hut veranda, there are good views of the southeastern face of Chambe Peak (2557m), but if you fancy reaching the summit of this spectacular peak, from Chambe Hut it will take you five to seven hours to get to the top and back. The ascent is stiff and the paths are vague, so you may need a guide. About two to 2½ hours from the hut, you reach a large cairn on a broad level part of the ridge at the foot of the main face. You might be happy with reaching this point, which offers excellent views over the Chambe Basin to the escarpment edge and the plains far below.

Chambe Hut to Thuchila Hut (12km, five to six hours) About two hours from Chambe,

you reach Chisepo Junction, where a path leads up to the summit of Sapitwa Peak (3001m). You can hike to the summit of Sapitwa, but it's a toughie, and the upper section involves some tricky scrambling among large boulders and dense vegetation. From Chisepo Junction you should allow three to five hours for the ascent, plus two to four for the descent, plus the time it takes you to get from and back to either Chambe or Thuchila Hut. Perhaps not surprisingly, Sapitwa means 'Don't Go There' in the local language. If you're short of time, you can do a shorter loop by descending from Thuchila Hut to Lukulezi Mission, then hiking or catching a matola back to Likhubula.

Thuchila Hut to Sombani Hut (12km, four to five hours) This stage takes you across a small col and down into the Ruo Basin. About two hours from Thuchila Hut, you reach Chinzama Hut, where you can stop if you want an easy day. The large mountain directly opposite Sombani Hut is Namasile (2687m), which takes about three hours to ascend, plus two hours on the descent. The path is steep and strenuous in places, spiralling round the northern side of the mountain to approach the summit from the west. A guide is recommended unless you're competent on vague paths in bad weather.

Sombani Hut to Fort Lister Gap (5km, three hours) This is all downhill, with great views over the surrounding plains. There are a lot of forks, so a guide is useful to show you the way, but otherwise at every fork keep going down. For the last section you follow a dirt track, past Fort Lister Forest Station, from where it's another 8km along the dirt road to Phalombe village. There's little or no traffic, so you'll have to hike (about two hours), but it's pleasant enough. Most porters include this stretch in the fee you pay for the final day.

From Phalombe ordinary buses go back to Likhubula or Mulanje (US$0.50, one hour, three daily), as do matolas (US$1).

The Chambe–Lichenya Loop This short but beautiful route is not an officially named trail, but we give it this title and recommend it for a good taste of Mulanje if you haven't got time for a traverse of the whole massif. It starts and finishes at Likhubula Forestry

Pines on Mulanje

The pine plantations on Mulanje were first established by the colonial government in the early 1950s, mainly around Chambe. The sides of the massif are too steep for a road, so all the timber is cut by hand and then carried down on a cableway (called the 'skyline') or on the heads of forest labourers. As you're going up the Chambe Plateau Path you'll see these incredibly hardy guys walking downhill, sometimes running, with huge planks of wood balanced on their heads.

The plantations provide employment for local people and wood for the whole of southern Malawi. A bad side effect, apart from the ugliness of the plantations, is the tendency of pine trees to spread slowly across the natural grassland as seeds are blown by the wind. These introduced trees disturb the established vegetation balance – which is always precarious in highland areas.

Office, and takes three days and two nights, but could be shortened to two days.

Stage 1: Likhubula Forestry Office to Chambe Hut This stage is the same as stage 1 of the Mulanje traverse described earlier.

Stage 2: Chambe Hut to Lichenya Basin (four to five hours) Heading east from Chambe Hut (towards Thuchila), turn right at a junction about 1½ hours from Chambe Hut to reach the Lichenya Basin, and either the CCAP Cottage or Lichenya Hut.

Stage 3: Lichenya Basin to Likhubula Forestry Office (four to five hours) Go across a col to the east of Chilemba Peak (you could sidetrack up here for fine views – allow two hours return) then descend through beautiful forest to eventually reach Likhubula.

Getting There & Away

Buses between Blantyre and Mulanje town are detailed in those sections. The dirt road to Likhubula turns off the main sealed Blantyre–Mulanje road at Chitikali, about 2km west of the centre of Mulanje town – follow the signpost to Phalombe. If you're coming from Blantyre on the bus, ask to be dropped at Chitikali. From here, irregular matolas

run to Likhubula (US$0.50). If you're in a group, you can hire the whole matola to Likhubula for around US$10. Alternatively, you can walk (10km, two to three hours); it's a pleasant hike through tea estates, with good views of the southwestern face of Mulanje on your right.

THE LOWER SHIRE

The main road south from Blantyre plunges down the Thyolo Escarpment in a series of hairpin bends to reach the Lower Shire, a thin spine of Malawian territory jutting into Mozambique. From the escarpment road, there are excellent views across the Shire River floodplains and out towards the Zambezi on the hazy horizon. Even when it's cool in the highlands, it can be blisteringly hot down here. The sharp change of temperature and landscape, in less than 30km, is most striking.

This is one of the least visited areas of Malawi, very different from the rest of the country, and contains Lengwe National Park, the reserves of Majete and Mwabvi, and the Elephant Marsh, a vast area of seasonally flooded swampland. Lengwe, Majete and Mwabvi are often overlooked, but plans are afoot to improve their infrastructure and facilities, so this may change in the future.

Majete Wildlife Reserve

Majete Wildlife Reserve lies west of the Shire; it's mainly miombo woodland, with dense patches of forest along the river. Animals recorded here include elephants, sables, kudus and hartebeests. Poaching has taken a heavy toll on the mammal population, but numbers are returning. You'll still be able to appreciate the reserve as a beautiful wilderness area though, and you're almost certain to have the place to yourself. The bird-watching is good, and hiking is allowed (with a game scout). Entry fees are payable (see National Parks & Reserves under Facts about Malawi earlier in this chapter).

The only driveable track in the reserve runs parallel to the Shire River (although not near enough for you to see it from the track), to the Shire River's confluence with the Mkurumadzi River, where you can pitch a tent at the Mkurumadzi Camp ranger post (although there are no facilities). If you're in a car, this track crosses some steep gullies so high clearance is essential. If you're hiking you can go

MALAWI

from the gate to Mkurumadzi in a day, stay the night and hike back. Just past the gate, a track leads east to the spectacular Kapichira Falls, although the view is tarnished slightly by the vast dam and power station.

Places to Stay The friendly **Majete Safari Camp** *(camp sites US$3, chalets with bath per person US$5)* is outside the reserve, just a few kilometres from the gate, overlooking the Shire River and the Matitu Falls, the southernmost of the Shire cataracts. (This was one of the notorious barriers to Livingstone's exploration; he camped in this very spot in 1858 – for more details see History under Facts about Malawi earlier in this chapter.) The camp has seen better days but the chalets are fair value. The service is relaxed: there's a bar and a kitchen for self-catering, or you can buy meals (US$1.50 to US$3) if you order long in advance. Motorboat hire for fishing or birding costs US$1.50 per hour.

Getting There & Away Majete Safari Camp is 15km north of Chikwawa, on the road to Majete Wildlife Reserve. By bus, the nearest you can get is Chikwawa; there are several per day to/from Blantyre. From Chikwawa, matolas run to Kapichira village, which is on the eastern bank of the Mkurumadzi River (this place has recently grown to house staff from the dam and power station).

Lengwe National Park

Lengwe is Malawi's southernmost park. Much of the surrounding area has been turned into sugarcane plantations, but the natural vegetation – mixed woodlands and grassy *dambos* (wetlands) – is protected here. Mammals include nyalas (at the northern limit of their distribution in Africa), bushbucks, impalas, duikers, kudus and buffaloes. There's also a large and varied bird population.

Standard entry fees must be paid at the gate (see National Parks & Reserves under Facts about Malawi earlier). There's a network of vehicle tracks for driving (some are impassable), but it's more rewarding to walk in the park or spend some time at the hides overlooking water holes; there's one within walking distance of the Visitors Camp.

Places to Stay In a beautiful setting under big shady trees, the **Visitors Camp** *(camp sites per person US$3, double chalets US$20)* is the only place to stay inside the park. Shared bathrooms are basic and the kitchen for self-catering is virtually unusable. You must bring all your own food.

Sucoma Sports Club *(☎ 428200 ext 287; chalets per person US$5.50)*, 8km east of Nchalo, is an option if you've got a car and seek more comfortable accommodation. It has comfortable chalets overlooking the river. This club is for senior staff at the sugar estate; meals and drinks are also available.

Getting There & Away By car, take the main road from Blantyre south towards Nsanje. By public transport, take a bus from Blantyre to Nchalo or Nsanje. About 20km from the Shire Bridge a signpost indicates Lengwe National Park to the right. The park entrance is another 10km to the west through sugarcane plantations. If you're without wheels you may be able to hitch this last bit on a tractor.

To reach Sucoma Sports Club, enter the sugar estate at the main gates in Nchalo, then follow the signs to the 'Sports Club' (not the Shire Club).

Mwabvi Wildlife Reserve

In the southernmost tip of Malawi, Mwabvi is the country's smallest (under 350 sq km) and least-visited game reserve, with a genuine wilderness atmosphere. It consists of low hills covered by mixed woodland, with numerous streams in rocky gorges and spectacular views over the Shire and Zambezi Rivers. Mwabvi was virtually abandoned in the 1980s and early 1990s; rhinos and lions were once recorded here, but apart from a few buffaloes and nyalas it's unlikely that any large wildlife remains today.

Fees are payable (see National Parks & Reserves under Facts about Malawi earlier).

Access is possible only with a 4WD car or great determination. The reserve office is reached from the main road between Chikwawa and Nsanje, just east of the village of Sorgin, and about 10km west of Bangula. The Wildlife Society of Malawi is currently involved in projects to protect the reserve that encourage local people to benefit from its resources. These may also improve access for visitors, so it would be worth inquiring

about the latest situation at the Wildlife Society giftshop in Limbe (see Bookshops under Blantyre & Limbe earlier).

The Elephant Marsh

The Elephant Marsh is a large area of seasonally flooded plain on the Shire River about 30km downstream from Chikwawa, just south of the vast Sucoma sugar estates. Despite the name there are no elephants here any more, although vast herds inhabited the area less than 100 years ago. Some hippos and crocodiles occur in quiet areas, but the main draw is the spectacular selection of birds – predominantly water species. This is one of the best **bird-watching** areas in Malawi, but it's well worth considering a visit here if you simply want to sample this peaceful and very unusual landscape.

As mornings and evenings are the best times to see birds (it's also not so hot), travellers without wheels may find it convenient to stay overnight in the village of Makhanga, about 10km northeast of Bangula. The **Makhanga Leisure Centre** has cheap rooms, and the **New Makhanga Restaurant** offers cheap food. If you have a car, you could stay at Sucoma Sports Club (see Lengwe National Park earlier).

Getting There & Away The only way to see the marsh properly is by boat. The usual way of doing this is to hire a boatman and his dugout canoe from the Fisheries Depot at a small village called Mchacha James on the east side of the marsh, about 7km from Makhanga.

If you're driving, head southwest of Blantyre for 30km and turn left (east) at Thabwa (the bottom of the escarpment). Makhanga is another 65km or so further south, following the Thyolo Escarpment. From Makhanga, head north towards Muona village. After 2.5km a dirt track leads west for 4.5km through villages and small fields to Mchacha James. This route is not signposted, so ask for directions – it may be worth arranging a local guide in Makhanga.

If you're without wheels, take the bus from Blantyre that travels to Nchalo and Nsanje. You can get a matola from either of these towns to Makhanga. Alternatively, you can get off this bus at Bangula, then walk 3km to the point where the road is washed away, get a canoe across, and then take a matola through Chiromo to Makhanga. From Makhanga, you can walk, take a bicycle taxi, rent a bike or charter a matola to Mchacha James. Another option is to visit the Department of Fisheries office in Makhanga, on the Muona road, about 1km west of the train tracks – the staff here have motorcycles and may be able to help you with a lift to the jetty.

MALAWI

Mozambique

Mozambique is one of southern Africa's best kept secrets, with beautiful beaches, vibrant and fascinating cultures, and artistic and musical traditions that are among the best on the continent. Among its attractions are unforgettable Indian Ocean sunrises, seemingly endless stretches of coastline, the paradisiacal islands of Bazaruto National Park, quiet inlets and mangrove-lined channels in the Quirimbas Archipelago, and Ilha de Moçambique (Mozambique Island), an architectural and historical treasure-trove and Unesco World Heritage site.

It's true that things are less developed than elsewhere in the region, particularly in comparison with neighbouring South Africa. Yet, despite this – or more likely because of it – Mozambique invariably gets rave reviews from the small but steady band of travellers who venture this way. Since peace accords were signed over a decade ago ending the country's 17-year civil war, reconstruction has proceeded at a remarkable pace, the atmosphere is upbeat and tourism is off to an ambitious start.

Travel is easiest in the south, where roads are good and lodging options abound. Elsewhere, you'll need to allow time for getting around and be prepared to rough it. No matter what part of the country you visit, the rewards make it well worth the time and effort. It's likely to wind up being one of the highlights of your travels in Southern Africa.

Facts about Mozambique

HISTORY
To learn more about the early history of Mozambique (*Moçambique* in Portuguese), along with the history of Southern Africa, see the Facts about the Region chapter earlier in this book.

The Arrival of the Portuguese
The long and often torturous era of European involvement in Mozambique began over 500 years ago when Portuguese explorer Vasco da Gama landed at Ilha de Moçambique in 1498 en route to India. Over the next 200 years, the

Mozambique at a Glance

Area: 801,590 sq km

Population: 17 million

Capital: Maputo

Head of State: President Joaquim Chissano

Official Language: Portuguese

Currency: metical (Mtc)

Exchange Rate: US$1 = Mtc23,595

Highlights

- Maputo – soaking up the city's rhythms, with its energetic, pulsating nightlife, and enough diversions to keep you busy for days

- Bazaruto Archipelago – basking in the ultimate tropical paradise with azure waters, pristine sands and a languid ambience

- Inhambane Province – wandering through historical and charming Inhambane city, then head to beautiful Tofo or other idyllic beaches nearby

- Ilha de Moçambique – exploring one of Southern Africa's most exotic attractions, shrouded in centuries of history, with a time-warp atmosphere and fascinating architecture

- Cabo Delgado Province – discovering Mozambique's insiders' tip, with a spectacular coastline and the enticing islands of the Quirimbas Archipelago

- Lake Niassa - revelling in the remoteness of Mozambique's most far-flung province, and relax amidst the rugged beauty of the lake shore

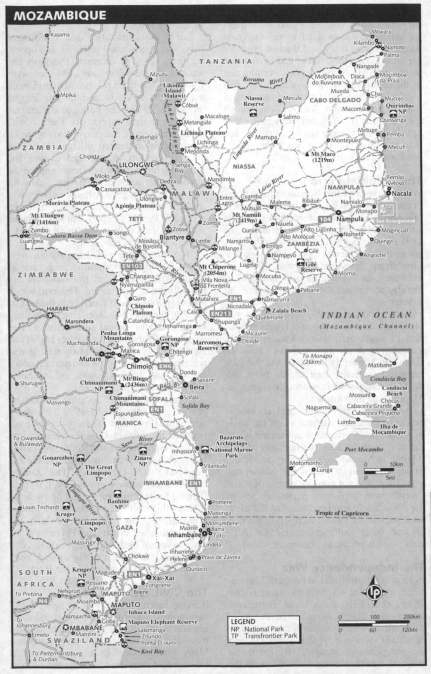

MOZAMBIQUE

Portuguese established trading enclaves along the coast, and several settlements in the interior along the Zambezi River valley. Trade focused first on ivory, and then on gold. By the late 18th century, slaves had been added to this list. Mozambican ports became one of the continent's main slave channels, with hundreds of thousands (some estimates say as high as one million) of Africans sold through them into slavery. Yet, there was little cohesion to the Portuguese slavery ventures, and their overall influence in Mozambique was weak and fragmented.

The Colonial Period

With the onset of the 'Scramble for Africa' in the 1880s, growing competition from the other colonial powers forced Portugal to strengthen its claims on its territories. In 1891 Portugal signed a treaty with the British giving the country its present shape and formalising Portuguese control. However, even then, the Portuguese were only able to directly administer the southern part of the vast territory.

Early 20th century Mozambique was characterised by large-scale labour migration to South Africa and Rhodesia (now Zimbabwe). A rail link was built between Beira and Mutare (Rhodesia), and the Portuguese transferred their capital from Ilha de Moçambique to Lourenço Marques, as Maputo was then known.

In the late 1920s António Salazar came to power in Portugal, and sealed off the colonies from non-Portuguese investment. Over the next three decades, the numbers of Portuguese in Mozambique steadily increased, as did repression by the colonial administration. There was not even a pretence of social investment in the African population, and of the few schools and hospitals that did exist, most were in the cities and reserved for Portuguese, other whites and *asimilados* (Africans who assimilated to European ways).

The Independence War

In June 1960, at Mueda in northern Mozambique, a meeting was held by villagers protesting peacefully about taxes. Portuguese troops opened fire, killing a large number of demonstrators. Resentment at this 'massacre of Mueda' was one of the sparks kindling the independence struggle. Resistance to colonial rule coalesced in 1962 with the formation of Frelimo, the Mozambique Liberation Front.

Led by the charismatic Eduardo Mondlane (who was assassinated in 1969), and operating from bases in Tanzania, Frelimo's aim was the complete liberation of Mozambique. By 1966 it had freed two northern provinces, but progress was slow and the war dragged on into the 1970s. The Portuguese attempted to eliminate rural support for Frelimo with a scorched earth campaign and by resettling people in fenced villages. However, struggles within its colonial empire and increasing international criticism sapped the government's resources. The final blow for Portugal came in 1974 with the overthrow of the Salazar regime. On 25 June 1975, the independent People's Republic of Mozambique was proclaimed with the wartime commander Samora Machel as president.

The Portuguese pulled out almost overnight, leaving Mozambique in a state of chaos, with few skilled professionals and virtually no infrastructure. Frelimo, which suddenly found itself faced with the task of running the country, threw itself headlong into a policy of radical social change. Ties were established with the former USSR and East Germany, private land ownership was replaced with state farms and peasant cooperatives, and schools, banks, and insurance companies were nationalised.

However, Frelimo's socialist programme proved unrealistic and by 1983 the country was almost bankrupt. The crisis was compounded by a disastrous three-year drought and by South African and Rhodesian moves to destabilise Mozambique because the African National Congress (ANC) and Zimbabwe African People's Union (ZAPU) – both fighting for majority rule – had bases there. Onto this scene came the Mozambique National Resistance (Renamo), which had been established in the mid-1970s by Rhodesia as part of its destabilisation policy, and which was later backed by the South African military and certain sectors in the West.

The Civil War

Renamo had no ideology of its own beyond the wholesale destruction of social and communications infrastructure within Mozambique and destabilisation of the government. Many commentators have pointed out that the war that went on to ravage the country

for the next 17 years was thus not a 'civil' war, but one between Mozambique's Frelimo government and Renamo's external backers.

Roads, bridges, railways, schools and clinics were destroyed. Villagers were rounded up, anyone with skills was shot, and atrocities were committed on a massive and horrific scale. Faced with this dire situation, Frelimo opened Mozambique to the West in return for Western aid. On 16 March 1984, South Africa and Mozambique signed the Nkomati Accord, under which South Africa undertook to withdraw its support for Renamo and Mozambique agreed to expel the ANC and open the country to South African investment. While Mozambique abided by the agreement, South Africa exploited the situation to the full and Renamo activity continued unabated.

Samora Machel died in a plane crash in 1986 under questionable circumstances, and was succeeded by the more moderate Joaquim Chissano. While the war between the Frelimo government and the Renamo rebels continued, by the late 1980s, political change was sweeping through the region. The collapse of the USSR altered the political balance, and the new president of South Africa, FW de Klerk, made it more difficult for right-wing factions to supply Renamo.

By the early 1990s, Frelimo had disavowed its Marxist ideology and announced that multiparty elections were to be scheduled. After protracted negotiations in Rome during 1990, a cease-fire was arranged, followed by a formal peace agreement in October 1992 and a successful UN-monitored disarmament and demobilisation campaign.

Modern Times

In October 1994, Mozambique held its first democratic elections, in which Renamo won a surprising 38% of the vote against 44% for Frelimo, and majorities in five provinces. The victory was attributable in part to ethnic considerations and in part to Frelimo's inability to overcome widespread grassroots antipathy. In the country's second national elections in 1999, Renamo made an even stronger showing. However, unlike the first elections, which earned Mozambique widespread acclaim as an African model of democracy and reconciliation, the 1999 balloting sparked protracted discord. Renamo protested its loss, accusing Frelimo of irregularities in tabulating the votes and boycotting

the presidential inauguration. In late 2000, Renamo demonstrations in northern Mozambique sparked a wave of rioting and violence, resulting in several dozen deaths. Following a government crackdown, 80 more people died in an overcrowded prison cell in Montepuez, west of Pemba.

Since then, things have settled down. Both Frelimo and Renamo have voiced renewed commitments to democracy, and as attention turns to the upcoming presidential elections, the overall atmosphere is optimistic. While the coming years will undoubtedly have their share of bumps, Mozambique has shown a remarkable ability to rebound in the face of adversity, and most observers continue to count the country among the continent's success stories.

GEOGRAPHY

Mozambique's vast area encompasses just over 800,000 sq km, including an enticing coastline that stretches for about 2500km. It's bordered to the east by a wide coastal plain that rises gradually to mountains and plateaus on the borders with Zimbabwe, Zambia and Malawi. The highest peak is Mt Binga (2436m) in the Chimanimani Mountains on the Zimbabwe border.

Two of Southern Africa's largest rivers – the Zambezi and the Limpopo – cut through the country on their way to the sea. Other major rivers are the Save (Savé) and the Rovuma, which forms the border with Tanzania.

CLIMATE

The dry season runs from April/May to October/November, during which daytime maximums are around 24° to 27°C on the coast, and cooler inland. In the rainy season from November to March, average temperatures range from 27° to 31°C, although in some areas it gets much hotter, with high

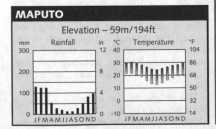

MOZAMBIQUE

humidity. The hottest areas are in the north around Pemba, and in the dry west around Tete and along the Zambezi valley. Rainfall averages 750mm annually in Maputo, and rainy season flooding is common in much of southern and central Mozambique.

ECOLOGY & ENVIRONMENT

Mozambique has an exceptional diversity of ecosystems. Along the southern coast are extensive wetlands, including numerous coastal barrier lakes. Inland there are lush and highly diverse montane habitats, most notably around the Chimanimani Mountains and the Gorongosa massif in the central part of the country. Offshore waters are rich with marine life.

Mozambique's environment has received a considerable amount of international attention in recent years, and several new national parks have been declared. However, a shortage of financial resources and personnel continues to thwart efforts to enforce conservation measures. As a result, many national parks are languishing, with only skeletal tourism facilities. In northern and central Mozambique, the tropical hardwood timber trade poses a significant environmental threat as large trees are felled with little or no regulation.

FLORA & FAUNA

Mozambique's abundant flora includes numerous endemic species. Two notable areas are the Chimanimani Mountains, with at least 45 endemic plant species, and the Maputaland area south of Maputo, which is considered a site of global botanical significance. For general information on local vegetation zones, see Flora in the Facts about the Region chapter.

Mozambique is home to a wide range of mammal species, although most large mammal populations were decimated during the war. Nevertheless, there are still enough elephants and lions around that attacks on villages are a frequent staple of local lore in the Cabo Delgado and Niassa provinces. There are also significant populations in the remote Niassa Reserve, including over 6000 elephants, 2000 buffaloes and close to 3000 zebras.

Marine species that make their home in Mozambique's offshore waters include dolphins, whales and the endangered dugong.

Loggerhead, leatherback, green, hawksbill and olive ridley turtles are found along the coast, although these populations have been reduced by the widespread use of turtles and their eggs as food, and by the sale of turtle shells as souvenirs.

Close to 600 bird species have been recorded in Mozambique, including several near endemics, and some rare or endangered species, such as the Cape vulture, the ogot oocot okalat and the wattled crane.

National Parks & Reserves

Mozambique has six national parks: Gorongosa, Zinave, Banhine and Limpopo in the interior; Bazaruto Archipelago National Marine Park offshore; and the recently gazetted Quirimbas National Park in Cabo Delgado province. Bazaruto is the most accessible, and the only one that attracts significant visitor numbers. Gorongosa can also be visited, although there's only limited infrastructure. Limpopo National Park forms part of the new Great Limpopo Transfrontier Park. Zinave and Banhine are currently closed, but will ultimately be incorporated into a Transfrontier Conservation Area surrounding Great Limpopo Transfrontier Park.

There are also several wildlife reserves including: Niassa, Marromeu, Pomene, Maputo and Gilé, and numerous controlled hunting areas and forest reserves. The only reserves where tourism is possible (quite limited in both) are Niassa Reserve and the Maputo Elephant Reserve.

In addition to these gazetted areas, the government has approved development of several Transboundary Natural Resources Management Areas, emphasising multiple resource use and community management across national boundaries. In an exciting recent development, a large section of one of these areas was designated to form part of the vast Great Limpopo Transfrontier Park, linking Mozambique's Limpopo National Park with South Africa's Kruger and Gonarezhou National Park in Zimbabwe. There's been no major tourism development on the Mozambique side as yet, but elephants from Kruger National Park have already been introduced into Limpopo National Park, and the fact that this foundation now exists represents a significant step forward.

GOVERNMENT & POLITICS

Representatives of political parties are elected to the National Assembly by universal suffrage using a system of proportional representation. The president is elected separately. Mozambican politics is dominated by Frelimo and Renamo. There are about a dozen minor parties, although most don't hold seats in parliament. Political allegiance tends to be on a regional basis, with Renamo enjoying considerable support in the centre while Frelimo is stronger in the north and south. The next presidential elections are scheduled for 2004. Incumbent president Chissano has announced that he will step down, so attention has turned to electing his successor.

Mozambique's Provinces

Mozambique is divided into 10 provinces, each with a governor and some autonomy. The provinces (and their capitals) are: Maputo (Maputo); Gaza (Xai-Xai); Inhambane (Inhambane); Sofala (Beira); Manica (Chimoio); Tete (Tete); Zambézia (Quelimane); Nampula (Nampula); Niassa (Lichinga); Cabo Delgado (Pemba).

ECONOMY

Thanks to a rigorous programme of market-oriented reforms, Mozambique has been ranked as one of sub-Saharan Africa's fastest growing economies for much of the past decade. Most of this growth has been concentrated in the south around Maputo, where proximity to South Africa and to the 'Maputo corridor' transport and development initiative linking Maputo with Johannesburg (Jo'burg) have pushed things along at a rapid pace. However, much of the north continues to be isolated, and the country overall remains one of the world's poorest, with an annual per capita income of about US$220.

Most Mozambicans (an estimated 80%) are involved in subsistence agriculture – tending small plots with cassava, maize and other basic crops. Along the coast, fishing is also an important source of subsistence and income. At the national level, the commercial fishing industry – especially the prawns for which Mozambique is famous – accounts for about 25% of merchandise exports.

POPULATION & PEOPLE

Mozambique's population is approximately 17 million. There are 16 main tribes. The Makua – who are the largest group, and who are often further divided into various sub-groups – live primarily in the provinces of Cabo Delgado, Niassa, Nampula and parts of Zambézia. Other major groups include the Makonde in Cabo Delgado; the Sena in Sofala, Manica and Tete; and the Shangaan, who dominate the southern provinces of Gaza and Maputo. Although Mozambique is relatively free of tribal rivalry, ethnic groups and geography are important factors in politics.

Native Portuguese comprise about 1% of the population. There are also small numbers of other Europeans and of Asians, particularly from the Indian subcontinent.

ARTS

Mozambique has rich artistic traditions that continue to thrive despite decades of colonial occupation and civil war.

Music

Traditional music is widely played in Mozambique. The Makonde in the north are noted for their *lupembe* (wind instruments), made from animal horn, or sometimes from wood or gourds. In the south, the renowned Chope musicians play the *timbila*, a form of *marimba* or xylophone, and are famous throughout the continent for their *timbila* orchestras.

Modern music flourishes in the cities, and Maputo's live music scene is excellent. *Marrabenta* is perhaps the most typical Mozambican music, its light style inspired by traditional rural *majika* rhythms. One of its most well-known proponents was Orchestra Marrabenta, formed in the 1980s by members of another well-known band, Grupo RM with dancers from the National Company of Song and Dance. When Orchestra Marrabenta split in 1989, several members formed Ghorwane, who perform frequently in Maputo. Kapa Dêch is one of the best known of the new generation groups.

Other well-known musicians include Chico António, who plays sophisticated, traditionally based melodies with congo drums, flute and bass, electric and acoustic guitars; Léman, a trumpeter and former member of Orchestra Marrabenta whose music combines traditional beats with contemporary

MOZAMBIQUE

The Makonde

The Makonde, known throughout Africa for their woodcarvings, are one of Mozambique's largest ethnic groups. Although many Makonde have migrated to Tanzania over the past three centuries, about 600,000 remain in Mozambique, where they make their home on the Makonde Plateau around Mueda.

Like many tribes in this part of the region, the Makonde are matrilineal. Children and inheritances normally belong to the woman, and it's common for husbands to move to the village of their wives after marriage. Settlements are widely scattered – possibly a remnant of the days when the Makonde sought to evade slave raids – and there is no tradition of a unified political system. Each village is governed by a hereditary chief and a council of elders.

Due to their isolated location, the Makonde have remained largely insulated from colonial and post-colonial influences. Even today, most Makonde still adhere to traditional religions, with the complex spirit world given its fullest expression in their carvings.

Traditionally, the Makonde practised body scarring and while it's seldom done today, you may see older people with markings on their face and bodies. It's also fairly common to see elderly Makonde women wearing a wooden plug in their upper lip, or to see this depicted in Makonde artwork.

The Makonde are renowned for their masked *mapiko* dancing, which is said to have grown out of male attempts to limit the power of women in matrilineal Makonde society, and to define the traditional relationship between the sexes. *Mapiko* masks are characterised by exaggerated features and by their use of etchings, dyes and human hair. Before *mapiko* begins, the dancer's body is covered with large pieces of cloth so that nothing can be seen except the fingers and toes. The idea is that the dancer and mask represent the spirit of a dead person who has come to do harm to the women and children, from which only the men of the village can protect them. According to tradition, young boys are told the secret of the dance during their initiation rites, while women are never supposed to learn it, and remain in fear of the *mapiko*. The dance itself is accompanied by distinctive rhythms played on special drums. It's usually performed on weekend afternoons and must be finished by sunset.

The best place to see *mapiko* dancing and visit Makonde carvers is in the villages around Mueda, though these are difficult to access. There are also many Makonde carvers in Pemba.

inspiration; Roberto Chidsondso; José Mucavele; and Elvira Viegas.

For more on other musical styles in the region, see the special colour section 'Beats of Southern Africa' earlier in this book.

Dance

Mozambicans are superb dancers, and experiencing the rhythms and moves – whether in a Maputo nightclub or at a traditional dance performance in the provinces – is a chance not to be missed.

One of the most common traditional dance styles on Ilha de Moçambique and along the northern coast is *tufo*. This is a slower-paced dance of Arabic origin, generally performed only by women, all usually wearing matching *capulanas* (sarongs) and scarves and accompanied by special drums. In the south, you'll likely come across the faster *makwaela*, characterised by *a cappella* singing and sophisticated foot percussion.

Literature

The development of Mozambican literature has closely paralleled the country's struggle for independence. During the colonial era, local literature generally focused on nationalist themes. Two of the most famous poets of this period were Rui de Noronha and Noémia de Sousa.

In the late 1940s José Craveirinha began to write poetry focusing on the social reality of the Mozambican people and calling for resistance and rebellion. This eventually led to his arrest. He is now recognised as one of Mozambique's most outstanding writers, and his work, including *Poem of the Future Citizen*, is regarded worldwide.

A contemporary of Craveirinha's was another nationalist called Luis Bernado Honwana, famous for short stories such as *We Killed Mangey Dog* and *Dina*.

As the armed struggle for independence gained strength, Frelimo freedom fighters began to write poems reflecting their life in

the forest, their marches and the ambushes. One of the finest of these guerrilla poets was Marcelino dos Santos. Others included Sergio Vieira and Jorge Rebelo.

With Mozambique's independence in 1975, writers and poets felt able to produce literature free of interference. The new-found freedom was soon shattered by Frelimo's war against the Renamo rebels, but new writers emerged, including Mia Couto, whose works include *Voices Made Night* and *The Tale of the Two Who Returned from the Dead*. Other writers from this period include: Ungulani Ba Ka Khossa (*Ualapi*), Lina Magaia, Heliodoro Baptista and Eduardo White. A more recently published book is *A Shattering of Silence* by Farida Karodia, which describes a young girl's journey through Mozambique following the death of her family.

Arts & Crafts

Mozambique is well known for its high quality woodcarvings, particularly for the sandalwood carvings found in the south and the ebony carvings of the Makonde in the north. The country's most famous sculptor is the late Alberto Chissano, whose work has received international acclaim and inspired many younger artists. The main centre of Makonde carving is in Cabo Delgado province, followed by Nampula. While some pieces have traditional themes, many Makonde artists have developed contemporary styles. One of the leading members of the new generation of sculptors is Nkatunga, whose work portrays different aspects of rural life. Others include Miguel Valingue and Makamo.

The most famous painter in the country is Malangatana, whose art is exhibited around the world. Other internationally famous artists include Bertina Lopes, whose work reflects her research into African images, colours, designs and themes, and Roberto Chichorro, known for his paintings which deal with childhood memories. Naguib, Victor Sousa and Idasse are among the best known artists in the newer generation. All of these painters and sculptors have exhibits in the National Art Museum in Maputo.

LANGUAGE

Portuguese, the official language of Mozambique, is widely spoken. All of Mozam-

bique's African languages belong to the Bantu language family and can be divided into three groups: Makua-Lomwe languages, spoken by more than one-third of the population, primarily in the north; Sena-Nyanja languages heard in the centre and near Lake Niassa (Lake Malawi); and Tsonga languages in the south. Except for the southern tourist destinations, and areas bordering Zimbabwe and Malawi, few people know English. Near the Tanzanian border, Swahili is just as useful as Portuguese.

See the Language chapter for some useful Portuguese words and phrases.

Facts for the Visitor

SUGGESTED ITINERARIES

Mozambique's best attractions are in the south and in the far north. To combine both areas, allow at least a month unless you take an internal flight or two. The following suggestions are based on land travel, which takes time in Mozambique – allow at least a month south to north with a private vehicle, and twice this travelling by public transport and including inland destinations. If you intend to fly, remember that flights frequently don't coordinate well, so build extra days into your itinerary.

Two Weeks

If you're coming from South Africa, spend a few days in Maputo relaxing and enjoying the good restaurants and the nightlife. Take the bus north to Inhambane town where you can spend a day wandering around before heading to Tofo or Barra beaches. Continue north to Vilankulo, and finish up with a few days snorkelling around the Bazaruto Archipelago before continuing on by bus, or flying back to Maputo or Jo'burg.

For travellers entering Mozambique from Zimbabwe via Machipanda, two weeks is just enough time to make your way to Beira and then south along the coast to Maputo, visiting the Bazaruto Archipelago and Tofo or other beaches along the way.

Two weeks in northern Mozambique could easily be spent entirely on the coast between Ilha de Moçambique and the Quirimbas Archipelago: after a day in Nampula head to Ilha de Moçambique. From there, take the bus to Pemba, where you can relax

MOZAMBIQUE

at the beach, and make a side trip to Ibo Island before flying to Maputo or continuing north to Tanzania.

One Month

Coming from South Africa, start at Ponta d'Ouro with a couple of days at the beach, before heading north to Maputo. Spend the remainder of the week in Maputo before taking the bus north to Inhambane, Tofo and Barra. Continue northwards to Vilankulo and Bazaruto. From here, if you have the budget, it's worth splurging on flights to get you to Beira and on to Nampula to bypass the long, rough public transport journey. Once in Nampula, go to Nacala for a day or two of diving, and then on to Ilha de Moçambique, where it's well worth spending at least two or three days. From here, continue north to Pemba and the Quirimbas Archipelago. Fly back to Maputo, or continue north into Tanzania. Ideally, budget at least five or six weeks for this itinerary.

An alternative route (though this will likely run over one month) is to head northwest from Beira towards Malawi via Tete, and then after re-entering Mozambique, continue to Cuamba, and from there on to Nampula and Ilha de Moçambique.

If you're entering Mozambique along the adventurous route from Malawi via Cóbuè, head south to Metangula, then on to Lichinga. Continue via Cuamba to Nampula, Ilha de Moçambique and (time permitting) Pemba.

The most popular route from Zimbabwe is via Chimoio and Beira towards Vilankulo, and then south from there. From Blantyre or southern Malawi, the main routes (both requiring lots of time on public transport and rough roads) are either via Cuamba and then east to Nampula and the coast, or via Quelimane and then north or south from there.

The Big Trip

Good Mozambique destinations to combine with a larger regional itinerary include Maputo, Pemba, Ilha de Moçambique, the Bazaruto Archipelago and Lake Niassa. Maputo is a great starter: for mid-range and top-end, there are excellent flight-and-accommodation packages available from Jo'burg through places like Hotel Polana. Hotel Rovuma Carlton offers deals that include Inhaca Island. For backpackers, there's a daily bus between Jo'burg and Maputo, and good connections from South Africa to Ponta d'Ouro.

Ilha de Moçambique can be reached by flight via Maputo to Lumbo, on the nearby mainland, or as a rewarding detour on an overland trip from Malawi: travel by road and rail from Blantyre to Nampula via Cuamba, and then by bus to Ilha de Moçambique. Once at Ilha de Moçambique, it's easy to extend your Mozambique travels north to Pemba by road or air. Pemba in turn is connected with South Africa via good fly-in packages to/from Jo'burg, some including a stop in Maputo. Alternatively, you can exit Mozambique overland or by air to Tanzania, or splurge on a flight south, exiting to South Africa via Maputo or Ponta d'Ouro.

For the Bazaruto Archipelago, there are daily flights between Jo'burg and Vilankulo (the mainland gateway to the archipelago) and easy bus connections to/from Maputo, opening the possibility for a good air-road circuit tour of southern Mozambique. Many visitors also reach Vilankulo by road from Zimbabwe via Beira, head south along the coast towards Maputo, and then exit to South Africa.

The Mozambican side of Lake Niassa (Lake Malawi) is an enticing off-beat adventure destination easily combined with travels in Malawi via the *Ilala* ferry.

Travel Tips

Allow plenty of time, and don't try to cover too much distance. Stick to the coast if your time is limited – Mozambique's beaches are some of the best on the continent. Focus on either the south or the north if you're short of time; to link them, consider an internal flight. Carry a mix of finances – credit cards, cash and travellers cheques – and always be prepared with some emergency cash. Be sure to enjoy the 'off-beatness' of this country. Don't be hunting for comparisons with elsewhere in the region, because Mozambique is in a class of its own. Learn a few words of Portuguese, or greetings in local languages. Don't insulate yourself from Mozambique or Mozambicans. Travel at least some of the time on public transport. Try to get away from the tourist resorts and learn about local life. Enjoy the delicious coastal cuisine.

PLANNING
When to Go
The best time to visit is during the cooler dry season from June to November. During the rainy season, many roads are impassable, flooding is common in the south and centre of the country, and chances are high you'll get stuck somewhere!

Maps
The best is the *Ravenstein* map (1:2,000,000), readily available outside Mozambique. In Maputo, look for the *Time Out Mozambique* map, with a Maputo city map on the reverse.

TOURIST OFFICES
The National Tourist Organisation (ENT) has an office in Maputo (see Information under Maputo later in this chapter for details), though it's not particularly useful for budget or independent travellers. In South Africa, ENT is represented by **Mozambique National Tourist Co** (*☎ 011-339 7275, fax 339 7295; Braamfontein, PO Box 31991, Johannesburg 2017*).

VISAS & DOCUMENTS
Visas
Visas are required by all visitors and are best arranged in advance, though they're also available at land borders. Fees vary according to where you buy your visa. Outside Africa, it costs about US$20 for a one-month single-entry tourist visa, and about US$40 for a three-month multiple-entry visa. Within the region, fees are generally slightly cheaper, although you'll need to pay at least double this for express service. Visas are currently being issued at airports, but regulations on this are notorious for changing frequently, so it's much better to get one before flying in.

Visas can be extended at immigration offices in provincial capitals provided you haven't exceeded the three-month maximum stay. Processing takes one to three days and is usually a hassle, so try to get a long enough visa at the outset.

Visas for Onward Travel If you need visas for other countries in the region, the conditions are as follows (prices are for one-month single entry visas). All embassies are in Maputo and open for applications from 8am or 8.30am to 11am, and in theory, all usually issue visas within 24 hours. For Botswana, Namibia and Lesotho, you'll need to apply for a visa in South Africa.

Malawi US$24 to US$40, depending on nationality, plus two photos
South Africa R250
Swaziland R100 plus one photo
Tanzania US$20 to US$50 depending on nationality, plus two photos
Zambia US$25 plus two photos
Zimbabwe US$32 to US$55, depending on nationality, plus two photos

Driving Licence & Permits
In addition to a passport, drivers need an international or South African driving licence, third-party insurance and a temporary import permit (both available at land borders) and vehicle registration papers.

International Health Card
It's required to carry proof of yellow fever and cholera vaccinations, although you'll rarely be asked to show it.

EMBASSIES & CONSULATES
Mozambican Embassies & Consulates
In Africa, Mozambique has diplomatic representation in Angola, Egypt, Ethiopia, Kenya, Malawi, South Africa, Swaziland, Tanzania, Zambia and Zimbabwe. Embassies for countries covered by this book are listed in the relevant country chapters. Mozambique representations elsewhere in the world include:

France (*☎ 01 47 64 91 32*) 82 Rue Laugier, Paris 75017
Germany (*☎ 0228-224024/5*) Adenauerallee 46A, 53113 Bonn
Portugal (*☎ 021-797 1747, 797 1994*) Avenida de Berna 7, 1000 Lisbon
Tanzania (*☎ 022-211 6502*) 25 Garden Ave, Dar es Salaam
UK (*☎ 020-7383 3800*) 21 Fitzroy Square, London W1P 5HJ
USA (*☎ 202-293 7146*) 1990 M St, NW, Suite 570, Washington, DC 20036

Embassies, High Commissions & Consulates in Mozambique
The following countries have diplomatic representation in Maputo. For a more complete listing, check the Maputo telephone directory, which is available at hotels throughout the city.

Australia (☎ 422780) 1st floor, 33 Storey Bldg, corner Avenidas Zedequias Manganhela and Vladimir Lenin
Canada (☎ 492623) 1128 Avenida Julius Nyerere
France (☎ 491603) 2361 Avenida Julius Nyerere
Germany (☎ 492714) 506 Rua Damião de Gois
Malawi (☎ 492676) 75 Avenida Kenneth Kaunda
Portugal (☎ 490316) 720 Avenida Julius Nyerere
South Africa (☎ 490059) 41 Avenida Eduardo Mondlane
Swaziland (☎ 492451) Avenida Kwame Nkrumah
Tanzania (☎ 490110) 852 Avenida Mártires de Machava
UK (☎ 420111) 310 Avenida Vladimir Lenin
USA (☎ 492797) 193 Avenida Kenneth Kaunda
Zambia (☎ 492452) 1286 Avenida Kenneth Kaunda
Zimbabwe (☎ 490404) 1657 Avenida Mártires de Machava

MONEY
Currency
Mozambique's currency is the metical (plural meticais, pronounced *meticaish*), abbreviated Mtc. Note denominations include Mtc1000, Mtc5000, Mtc10,000, Mtc20,000, Mtc50,000 and Mtc100,000. The most commonly used coins are Mtc500, 1000 and 5000. A unit of Mtc1000 is called a *conto* or, occasionally in street slang, a *pão* – thus a price of Mtc5000 will be quoted as '*cinco contos*', or sometimes '*cinco pão*'. Because of the weakness of the metical and the absence of large denomination notes, you'll always be carrying around large wads of cash. Especially upcountry, you'll need a lot of coins and small bills, as nobody ever has change.

Exchange Rates
Prices throughout this chapter are quoted in US dollars, as they're likely to remain more constant.

country	unit		metical
Australia	A$1	=	Mtc15,642
Botswana	P1	=	Mtc4558
Canada	C$1	=	Mtc17,468
euro zone	€1	=	Mtc27,743
Japan	Ÿ100	=	Mtc20,039
Malawi	MK1	=	Mtc264
New Zealand	NZ$1	=	Mtc13,624
South Africa	R1	=	Mtc2976
Tanzania	Tsh100	=	Mtc2354
UK	UK£1	=	Mtc39,333
USA	US$1	=	Mtc23,595
Zambia	ZK100	=	Mtc491
Zimbabwe	ZW$100	=	Mtc2911

Exchanging Money
Cash US dollars are easily exchanged anywhere in the country, though some places decline US$50 and US$100 notes because of forgeries. South African rand are widely accepted in the south, and many places accept direct payment in rand or dollars. Other major currencies can be changed in Maputo, but often with extra commissions.

Most banks don't charge commission for changing cash. In Maputo there are private exchange bureaus, which give a rate slightly higher than the banks. Shops selling imported goods will often change cash dollars or rand into meticais at a rate about 5% higher than the bank, and can be helpful outside banking hours. Changing money on the street isn't safe anywhere, and is illegal. If you do try, be discreet, and be wary of set-ups involving the police.

In a few places, banks will only let you change cash if you have an account; if you get stuck, ask shopkeepers if they can help you out before resorting to changing on the street.

Travellers Cheques Regulations on travellers cheques change frequently, but when this chapter was researched they could only be changed in Maputo and in one or two upcountry destinations – and only with high commissions, averaging US$30 or more per transaction. Hopefully this will change, but come prepared with another source of funds just in case. Where you can change cheques, you'll need to show the original purchase receipt. Ideally bring a mix of Thomas Cook and American Express, as some places only accept one or the other. Only a few hotels accept travellers cheques as direct payment.

ATMs There are automated teller machines (ATMs) in Maputo and most provincial capitals affiliated with Banco International de Moçambique (BIM), where you can get cash meticais on a Visa card up to US$125 per transaction. They're moderately reliable, and until it gets easier to change travellers cheques, these are the best way to access money. However, have enough dollars as a standby, especially outside of banking hours.

Credit Cards You can use credit cards at most top-end hotels and at car rental agencies, but otherwise they are not widely used.

MOZAMBIQUE

Visa and MasterCard are the most widely accepted.

It's possible to use credit cards for cash advances at a few banks in Maputo and major towns, including some branches of BIM (Visa card) and Banco Austral (MasterCard).

Costs

Mozambique is expensive in comparison with its neighbours, although there are an increasing number of places catering to backpackers in the south and the far north. While locally produced goods are cheap, most tourist-related items are costly. Budget travellers staying in basic lodging, and eating local food should plan on at least US$20 per day. Mid-range travel with some comforts will cost from US$40 per day. For top-end, plan on at least US$100 per day, more including rental car or flights.

POST & COMMUNICATIONS
Post

International mail takes about two weeks to Europe (about US$1 per letter) from Maputo, and often much longer when sent from elsewhere in the country.

The main post offices in Maputo and provincial capitals have poste restante. Letters are held about one month, and cost US$0.10 to receive.

Telephone & Fax

Mozambique's telephone system is surprisingly efficient, though there aren't enough lines to meet demand. For international calls, most towns have telecom offices open daily. In larger towns, there are also card phones that can be used for domestic and international calls.

Domestic calls cost about US$0.10 per impulse; most short calls (ie, of five minutes or less) won't use more than two or three impulses. Calls to Europe, the USA and Australia cost about US$6 for the first three minutes (minimum), plus US$2 for each additional minute. Regional calls cost about US$3 for the first three minutes. Rates are slightly cheaper on weekends and evenings.

Faxes can be sent and received from telecom offices in Maputo, Beira and a few larger towns (US$15 per page to Europe, Australia and the USA), and from upscale hotels.

Telephone Codes

These are listed under town entries. Where there's no code listed, you'll need to go through the operator. When calling Mozambique from abroad, dial the international access number, then the country code (☎ 258), and omit the zero of the town area code or mobile phone code. Local numbers are five or six digits.

Mobile Phones

Also called cell phones mobile phones are widely used; the numbers are six digits, preceded by ☎ 082 or ☎ 083 (though some ☎ 082 numbers are in South Africa). The mobile network covers most provincial capitals, but doesn't reach most rural areas. If you're bringing your own phone, check with your home company about using it in Mozambique, and watch out for local calls being routed internationally.

Email & Internet Access

There are public Internet services in most provincial capitals. Rates average US$2 per hour and connections are reasonably good.

DIGITAL RESOURCES

Websites to check on Mozambique include:

Kanimambo (W www.kanimambo.com) In Portuguese, but with English listings and information on other sites in English

Mozambique Home Page (W www.mozambique .mz) This is Mozambique's official website, with general information in Portuguese as well as news and links to other Mozambique-related sites

BOOKS

Literature by Mozambican writers is covered under Arts in the Facts about Mozambique section.

Lonely Planet

Lonely Planet's comprehensive *Mozambique* has in-depth coverage of the country. The *Portuguese phrasebook* is an indispensable travelling companion. Lonely Planet's *Swahili phrasebook* is useful if you'll be spending time in northern Mozambique.

History & Politics

And Still They Dance, by Stephanie Urdang, is a study of women's roles in the wars and struggles for change in Mozambique.

Apartheid's Contras, by William Minter, is an inquiry into the roots of the civil wars in Angola and Mozambique and the role of South Africa in the conflicts.

A Complicated War – The Harrowing of Mozambique, by William Finnegan, covers the same subject as *Apartheid's Contras,* earlier.

A History of Mozambique, by Malyn Newitt, is an excellent survey of the country's history since about 1500.

Kalashnikovs and Zombie Cucumbers: Travels in Mozambique, by Nick Middleton, is part travelogue, part historical overview. This entertaining book covers colonial times, the war, South African and superpower involvement and more.

General

For overviews of Mozambique's traditional cultures, look for *Artistas de Moçambique,* on the country's principal artists, and *Mascaras,* a study of traditional masks. Both are in English and Portuguese, and available at the Public Information Bureau (see Tourist Offices under Maputo later in this chapter), and in hotel bookshops.

NEWSPAPERS & MAGAZINES

Mozambique's national daily (in Portuguese) is *Notícias.*

The Mozambique News Agency (AIM) puts out the monthly *MozambiqueFile,* with English-language summaries of current affairs. It's available at bookshops and hotels in Maputo. The weekly Portuguese version is available on the Web (**w** www.sortmoz.com /aimnews).

Hotel Polana (see Places to Stay – Top End under Maputo later in this chapter) has a condensed version of *The New York Times* in its coffee shop.

Índico, LAM's bimonthly and bilingual inflight magazine, often has worthwhile articles on culture and other aspects of Mozambique.

RADIO & TV

Radio Maputo's English language service broadcasts at 1pm and 8pm (88 FM). Radio Moçambique, in Portuguese, is at 92.3FM. For TV channels, there's the state-run TVM and the commercial RTK; all top-end hotels subscribe to English-language cable news.

PHOTOGRAPHY & VIDEO

General photographic hints are given in the Regional Facts for the Visitor chapter. Print film is available in Maputo, Beira and larger towns (from US$5 for a roll of 100ASA 36-exposure film). Slide film is occasionally available in Maputo (about US$9 for 36-exposure 100ASA).

As it is elsewhere in the region, don't photograph government buildings, ports, airports, or anything connected with the police or military, and ask permission before photographing people.

HEALTH

For general information see Health in the Regional Facts for the Visitor chapter.

Malaria is widespread in Mozambique, and precautions are essential. If you'll be spending much time in the bush, consider carrying a self-test malaria kit (available at pharmacies in most Western countries) and malaria medication. While bilharzia infestation on the Mozambican side of Lake Niassa (Lake Malawi) isn't considered to be as bad as on the Malawi side, you should exercise caution, and avoid reedy areas and still water.

Maputo has good emergency medical service. Upcountry, facilities leave much to be desired, although all provincial capitals have hospitals that can test for malaria. If you become seriously ill, it's best to seek treatment in South Africa or return home.

WOMEN TRAVELLERS

Mozambique can be safely (and very enjoyably) travelled as a woman alone as long as you keep your wits about you. Heed the precautions under Dangers & Annoyances, following, and especially avoid isolating situations. This is more to minimise the risk of mugging or theft, than sexual assault, which is rare against travellers.

Tampons are available only in Maputo and Beira.

DANGERS & ANNOYANCES

Mozambique has calmed down considerably from the war days when going anywhere by road meant by convoy, and a high risk of attack. Today, it's a relatively safe country for travel, and most visitors don't have any difficulties. That said, there are a few areas where caution is warranted.

Road Accidents

Drunken driving and speeding are common. Travel in the mornings whenever possible, and when there's a choice, by bus rather than *chapa* (pick-up or converted minivan). Night travel should be avoided.

Crime

Thefts and robberies are the main risk: watch your pockets in markets and avoid carrying a bag; don't leave personal belongings unguarded on the beach or elsewhere. Especially don't wear things like jewellery, watches, headsets and external money pouches. Never hold your wallet or money in your hand while bargaining for prices. If you leave your vehicle unguarded, expect windscreen wipers and other accessories to be gone when you return. Don't leave anything inside a parked vehicle. When at stoplights or slowed in traffic, keep your windows up and doors locked, and don't leave anything on the seat next to you where it could be snatched.

In Maputo and southern Mozambique, due to the proximity to South African organised crime rings, car jackings and more violent robberies do occur, though the situation is nowhere near as bad as in Jo'burg, and most incidents can be avoided by taking the usual precautions – avoid driving at night, and don't wander around isolated or dark streets. If you're driving and your car is hijacked, hand over the keys straight away.

More likely are simple hassles such as underpaid authorities in search of bribes, though this isn't as common as it's made out to be. If you do get stopped you shouldn't have any problem as long as your papers are in order. Being friendly and respectful helps, as does trying to give the impression that you know what you're doing and aren't new in the country. Sometimes the opposite tack is also helpful – feigning complete ignorance if you're told that you've violated some regulation, and apologising profusely. If you are asked to pay a *multa* (fine) for a trumped-up charge, playing the game a bit (asking to speak to the supervisor or *chefe*, and requesting a receipt) helps to counteract some of the more blatant attempts.

BUSINESS HOURS

Banks are generally open from 8am to 3pm weekdays. Most shops and offices open from 8am to noon and 2pm to 6pm

Warning: Land Mines

Thanks to a massive demining effort, many of the unexploded land mines – the legacy of Mozambique's long war – have been eliminated. However, they are still a risk, which means that it's unsafe to free camp or go wandering off into the bush anywhere in Mozambique without first seeking local advice. Even then, stick to well-used paths. Areas which should always be avoided include the base of bridges, old schools or abandoned buildings, and antennas, water tanks or other structures. Also take special care on road verges in rural areas – if you need to relieve yourself, stay on the road or seek out a trodden path.

or 6.30pm weekdays, and on Saturday morning. In northern Cabo Delgado, many places open earlier – by 7.30am, closing about 5pm.

PUBLIC HOLIDAYS & SPECIAL EVENTS

Mozambique's public holidays include:

New Year's Day 1 January
Mozambican Heroes' Day 3 February
Women's Day 7 April
International Workers' Day 1 May
Independence Day 25 June
Lusaka Agreement/Victory Day 7 September
Revolution Day 25 September
Christmas/Family Day 25 December

Each city/town also has a 'city/town day' when businesses are closed; Maputo's is 10 November.

ACTIVITIES

The coast offers excellent opportunities for water sports. The main areas for **diving** are Ponta d'Ouro, Inhaca Island, Tofo, Barra, Bazaruto and Pemba. Conditions tend to be quite variable, with a string of mediocre days punctuated by a few days of superb diving. However, this is compensated for by highly diverse marine life and reefs that are in good to excellent condition. The other draws are the natural beauty of Mozambique's coast, the adventure of exploring relatively unknown sites, and the chance of spotting sharks, dugong and more.

The best part of the coast for **game fishing** is in the south between Ponta d'Ouro

MOZAMBIQUE

and Inhassoro. If you're bringing your own boat, you'll need a licence.

For **surfing**, the main places are Ponta d'Ouro and Tofinho (just south of Tofo).

Mozambique has diverse birdlife, and is especially notable for its wetland species. Good areas for **bird-watching** include the Bazaruto Archipelago and Gorongosa National Park.

There are highly enjoyable day or overnight **dhow safaris** around the Bazaruto Archipelago (see Dhow Safaris under Vilankulo), and from Ibo island in the Quirimbas Archipelago (see Places to Stay & Eat under Quirimbas Archipelago).

ACCOMMODATION

Accommodation in Mozambique is pricey for what you get. All backpackers hostels and most tourist-area hotels fill up around Christmas and during the South African school holidays, so book in advance if you'll be travelling then.

When quoting prices, many places distinguish between a *duplo* (room with two twin beds) and a *casal* (double bed). Many hotels offer mid-week and low-season discounts, and most tourist places have reductions for children under 12.

Budget

The cheapest options are pensões (cheap local hotels), which start at about US$6 per room and are usually quite basic. Expect shared bathrooms with cold water and poor ventilation, though sometimes you'll be pleasantly surprised.

Backpackers are much better value, and well worth checking out wherever you can find them. Most are along the southern coast in the main tourist areas.

Camping is also a possibility, although free camping isn't advisable due to security concerns and the possibility of landmines. Many camping grounds charge per site, which means it's cheaper in a group. In rural areas, ask the village *regulo* (chief) for permission to camp.

Mid-Range & Top End

For mid-range standards, expect to pay from about US$35 to US$75 per double. This should get you a room ranging from decent to quite nice, with bathroom and hot water, sometimes a television, and usually a restaurant on the premises. All provincial capitals and the main tourist areas have at least one mid-range place.

Top-end places are few and far between, but where they exist (Maputo, Pemba and a few places along the coast), expect all the usual amenities, sometimes at surprisingly reasonable prices, especially if you can take advantage of special weekend deals.

FOOD

Mozambique has some of the best cuisine in the region, blending African, Indian and Portuguese influences, with a dash of *piri-piri* (hot pepper) to top things off. It's especially noted for its seafood, including excellent *camarões* (prawns) and *lagosta* (crayfish). The local maize and cassava-based staples are *xima* and *upshwa*. One local speciality is *matapa*, cassava leaves cooked in peanut sauce, often with prawns.

Self-catering is easy in Maputo, where there's a wide selection of produce, and items imported from South Africa. There's also a good selection of imported items in other major towns. Elsewhere, you'll be limited to a few basic grocery items, whatever produce is in season, and the catch of the day, grilled up and prepared to order.

SHOPPING

Maputo, Nampula and Pemba have good selections of beautiful woodcarvings, including some of a high quality if you look around enough. In the north, the etched clay pots made by Makonde women make attractive, but heavy, souvenirs.

Inhambane province is known for its basketry, and in Cabo Delgado you'll find attractive and colourful woven mats. The best silver craftsmanship comes from Ibo Island in the far north. While the silver itself is often not of high quality, the craftsmanship is highly refined. *Capulanas*, the colourful cloths worn by women around their waist, can be found at markets everywhere.

Getting There & Away

This section covers access into Mozambique from neighbouring countries. Information about reaching Southern Africa from outside

the region is outlined in the regional Getting There & Away chapter.

AIR
Departure Tax
Departure tax is US$20/10 for intercontinental/regional flights, payable in meticais, dollars or rand.

Southern Africa
Linhas Aéreas de Moçambique (LAM), Mozambique's national carrier, flies between Maputo and Jo'burg (daily, US$130 one way), Dar es Salaam (three times weekly, via Pemba, US$325 one way) and Harare (twice weekly, US$225 one way).

Regional airlines serving Mozambique include: South African Airways, with daily flights between Jo'burg and Maputo for about US$130 return; SAAirlink, with flights five times weekly between Maputo and Durban (US$120); Serviço Aereo Regional (SAR), with weekly flights connecting Cuamba and Nampula with Blantyre (Malawi); and TTA flying six times weekly between Jo'burg and Vilankulo.

LAND
Mozambique has borders with Malawi, South Africa, Swaziland, Tanzania, Zambia and Zimbabwe. There's a US$5 immigration tax at all land borders, for which you should get a receipt or a stamp in your passport. Drivers need to pay about US$3 for a temporary import permit plus US$15 for one-month compulsory third-party insurance.

Most land borders are open from 6am to 6pm (7am to 7pm at Namaacha; 6am to 7pm at Ressano Garcia; 8am to 5pm at Ponta d'Ouro).

Malawi
The busiest crossing is Zóbuè, on the road linking Blantyre and Harare (Zimbabwe). From Tete to the border there are daily *chapas* and buses from Beira, Chimoio and Harare. At the border, walk about 300m for transport to Mwanza and Blantyre.

The crossing at Dedza (north of Zóbuè) is more convenient to Lilongwe, and scenic, passing through cool and hilly Angónia; however, there's only sporadic public transport.

For central Mozambique, there's a crossing at Vila Nova da Fronteira on the southern tip of Malawi, reached by daily minibuses from Blantyre to Nsanje and on to the border. Once at the border, there are frequent *chapas* along a good road to Mutarara and Sena (opposite Mutarara across a bridge over the Zambezi River). From Sena there are daily *chapas* towards Caia (the junction with the main north–south road), Inhaminga and then on to Beira. Some sections of the Caia to Beira stretch are quite rough.

Several vehicles run daily between Mocuba (north of Quelimane) and Milange, from where you walk or hitch 2km to the border, and another 1km for Malawian transport to Mulanje and on to Blantyre.

For northwestern Mozambique, there's no longer train service between Entre Lagos and Cuamba, which means that most travellers use the more northerly crossing by Mandimba. There's at least one truck daily in the dry season from both Cuamba and Lichinga to Mandimba. From Mandimba, it's 7km to the border (about US$1 and a rough ride on a bicycle-taxi), where you can find transport to Mangochi (Malawi).

South Africa
Road Daily minibuses (departing by 7am) connect Maputo with Ressano Garcia on the border (US$3), Nelspruit (US$8) and Jo'burg (US$16), though most travellers use one of the large 'luxury' buses which do the route daily (about US$20 one way, eight hours). The best option is **Translux** (☎ 01-300622, ☎ Jo'burg 011-774 3333; ⓦ www.translux.co.za), which departs Maputo daily from 1235 Avenida 24 de Julho diagonally opposite Pensão Martins (see Places to Stay under Maputo later in this chapter) at 7.45am. Departures from Jo'burg (corner of Walmarans & Rissik Sts) are at 9am. You can also embark/disembark in Pretoria.

Panthera Azul (☎ 01-494238, 01-498868, South Africa 011-337 7409; ℮ panthera@virconn.com) also does this route, departing Maputo daily at 8am from the Panthera Azul office on Avenida Zedequias Manganhela near the main post. Departures from Jo'burg (105 Kerk St, on the corner of Polly Ave) are at 7.30am.

You can also travel in each direction on these lines between Maputo and Nelspruit.

Panthera Azul also has buses between Maputo and Durban (US$21 one way, 8½ hours) via Big Bend (Swaziland). Departures

are at 7.30am Tuesday, Thursday and Saturday from Maputo, and at 7am Wednesday, Friday and Sunday from Durban.

With your own vehicle, there's now a good sealed toll road connecting Maputo with Jo'burg via Ressano Garcia, with tolls in Mozambique at Matola (US$3) and Moamba (US$5).

For travel to/from South Africa via the Kosi Bay border post south of Ponta d'Ouro, you'll need your own 4WD. Alternatively, most of the Ponta d'Ouro hotels do transfers for about US$10, and hitching between the border and Ponta d'Ouro is usually easy.

Train There's a train service between Maputo and Jo'burg via Komatipoort (opposite Ressano Garcia), Nelspruit and Pretoria, departing Maputo at 11am daily (US$25/20/10 for 1st/2nd/3rd class). However, service on the Mozambique side is very slow, and the best way is to take a minibus between Maputo and Komatipoort (US$3), and then get the train on the South African side between Komatipoort and Jo'burg. Departures from Komatipoort to Jo'burg are at 6pm; from Jo'burg, the train reaches Komatipoort about 6.45am.

Swaziland
Minibuses depart Maputo about 6am for Manzini (US$2.50) and Mbabane. Otherwise, change vehicles at the border at Namaacha.

Tanzania
Daily *chapas* connect Moçimboa da Praia, Palma and Namoto (the Mozambican immigration post). Except during the heaviest rains, they then continue 4km to the Rovuma River, which you cross by dugout canoe (US$2). When the river is low, you may need to walk and wade for up to 45 minutes through the riverbed on the Tanzanian side, from where minivans or beat-up Land Rovers will take you to Kilambo (the Tanzanian border post), and on to Mtwara (US$2, one hour). During the rainy season the river crossing can take over an hour, and can be dangerous because of fast-moving water.

There's also a vehicle ferry that runs at high tide and costs US$20 per vehicle. To avoid getting stuck waiting, check at Russell's Place in Pemba (see Places to Stay under Pemba later in this chapter) or at the Tamofa office on Tanu Rd in Mtwara (Tanzania) to be sure the ferry captain will be around when you get to the river.

We've heard that there's a border crossing upriver, north of Moçimboa do Rovuma (reached by *chapa* from Mueda), from where you reportedly can find transport further north to Newala (Tanzania).

Zambia
The main border crossing is between Cassacatiza and Chanida, northwest of Tete. The road is in decent shape, but infrequently used, with only sporadic public transport from Matema. Most travellers go through Malawi. Once at the border, there's occasional transport to Katete, and on to Lusaka or Chipata.

You can also cross into Zambia via Zumbo (at the western end of Lake Cahora Bassa), but the route is rarely used. The best way to Zumbo from Tete is via Zimbabwe.

Zimbabwe
The two main crossing points between Mozambique and Zimbabwe are Nyamapanda on the Tete Corridor, linking Harare with Lilongwe, and Machipanda on the Beira to Harare road. Both are heavily travelled, and hitching is easy. From Tete, there's frequent transport to Changara (US$2.50) and to the border, for onward transport to Harare.

From Chimoio, there's frequent transport to Machipanda and on to the border, from where you'll need to take a taxi (about US$5) or hitch the 12km to Mutare.

The other route via Espungabera further south is slow and scenic, and a good option for those with a 4WD. Public transport on the Mozambique side is scarce.

SEA & LAKE
Malawi
The Malawi ferry *Ilala* services several Mozambican ports on its way up and down Lake Niassa. The schedule is subject to constant change, but at the moment, it arrives in Metangula from Nkhotakota (Malawi) around midday on Saturday, then continues north, reaching Cóbuè Saturday evening. From Cóbuè, it continues on to Likoma Island and Nkhata Bay (both in Malawi), where it arrives Sunday morning. Going south, the *Ilala* departs Nkhata Bay on Monday evening, arriving in Cóbuè Tuesday morning and Metangula at midday, before continuing on to Nkhotakota. There

are immigration posts in Metangula and in Cóbuè. Nkwichi Lodge (see Cóbuè under Lake Niassa later in this chapter) also can arrange transfers to/from Nkhata Bay or Chintechi (Malawi) in its motorised dhow.

Local boats travel frequently between Meponda and Senga Bay (Malawi), but the crossing can be risky as lake squalls blow up quickly, and the journey isn't recommended. The closest immigration office is in Lichinga.

South Africa
Cargo ships from **Unicorn Lines** (☎ 031-301 1476; W www.unicorn.co.za) sail between Durban and Nacala, some with reasonably priced passenger accommodation. Also check **Navique** (W www.tallships.co.za), which has cargo ships between Durban, Maputo, Beira, Nacala and Pemba that may take passengers. **Starlight Lines** (W www.starlight.co.za) runs luxury liners between Durban, Inhaca Island and Bazaruto Archipelago.

Tanzania
It's possible to go between Mozambique and Tanzania by dhow, but the trip can be rough; see Boat in the Getting Around section, following. The best places to arrange dhou trips are Moçimboa da Praia and Palma, or in Tanzania.

Getting Around

AIR
LAM flights connect Maputo, Beira, Quelimane, Nampula, Tete, Lichinga and Pemba. Flights can be paid for in local currency, dollars or rand, and in Maputo, Beira and Nampula by Visa or MasterCard. Sample one-way fares and frequencies include: Maputo to Beira (US$150, daily); Beira to Nampula (US$145, three times weekly); Maputo to Vilankulo (US$145, three times weekly); Maputo to Pemba (S$260, five times weekly).

LAM has improved markedly in recent years and is one of the better regional airlines in Southern Africa. However, overbookings and cancellations happen, so reconfirm your ticket and get to the airport well in advance. Baggage handling has also improved, although you should carry anything that you don't want to lose with you.

It's also well worth checking with some of the small private carriers, as most charge lower fares than LAM and reach additional destinations. These include Serviço Aereo Regional (SAR), which services Nampula, Guruè, Quelimane, Cuamba, Lichinga, Nacala and Pemba; STA, which services Maputo, Chimoio, Tete, Songo, Beira, Quelimane, Nampula, Nacala and Pemba; and TransAirways, which flies between Maputo and Inhaca Island.

Domestic Departure Tax
There is a tax on domestic flights of US$5.

BUS
Good *machibombo* (bus) services connect major towns at least once daily. The main companies are Transportes Oliveiras, with an extensive route network in southern and central Mozambique; TSL (tay-sayel), which operates on the southern routes and to Tete, Quelimane and Nampula; and Grupo Mecula, which has a good network in Cabo Delgado and Nampula provinces. Many lines run both express and stopping services; it's usually worth paying the small difference between the two, as express is significantly faster. Some sample journey fares, times and distances: Chimoio to Tete (US$5, six hours, 385km); Maputo to Inhambane (US$5, six to seven hours, 455km); Nampula to Pemba (US$6, seven hours, 425km); and Maputo to Beira (US$19, 17 to 20 hours, 1190km).

Most places don't have central bus stations. Rather, transport usually leaves from the start of the road towards the destination, which frequently involves a hike of 1km to 2km from the centre of town. Long-distance transport in general, and all transport in the north, leaves early – between 3.30am and 7am – and outside of southern Mozambique and along the Beira corridor, it's often difficult to get a vehicle anywhere after mid-morning. And, unlike many countries, where you spend interminable periods waiting for vehicles to fill, Mozambican transport usually leaves quickly and close to the stated departure time. Outside resort areas (where hitching is usually easy with holidaymakers returning from the beach), Sundays generally aren't good travel days as there are fewer vehicles.

MOZAMBIQUE

TRAIN
The main passenger train is the line between Nampula and Cuamba. See Cuamba later in this chapter for details.

CAR & MOTORCYCLE
For driving, you'll need your documents (see Driving Licence & Permits under Visas & Documents, earlier in this chapter), plus two red hazard triangles. There's also a seatbelt requirement for the driver and front seat passenger. Speed limits (usually 80km/h, and 50km/h or less in towns) are enforced by radar. Another reason to avoid high speeds are the axle-shattering potholes that can appear out of nowhere. Except for the main highway (EN1) between Maputo and Vilankulo, along the Beira corridor, and along the Tete corridor between Harare (Zimbabwe) and Tete, you'll need 4WD with high clearance for most parts of the country. Especially in the north, petrol is scarce off main roads; diesel supplies are more reliable and cheaper. Whether you have a petrol or diesel vehicle, it's a good idea to carry an extra can or two and tank up whenever possible, as filling stations sometimes run out.

If you're travelling by motorcycle, many beach access roads have deep, soft sand, so you may wind up pushing your bike more than riding it.

Most of the main north–south highway is sealed and in reasonable shape except for the stretches between the Save River and Beira, from Beira to Caia, and from Palma north to the Rovuma River. A new road is under construction from Caia to Gorongosa town (on the western edge of Gorongosa National Park) and on to Inchope, where it joins the Beira–Chimoio road. Once it's open (within the lifetime of this book), north–south travel in Mozambique will be much easier.

Driving on the beach is illegal in Mozambique, and driving off-road anywhere isn't advisable because of the risk of land mines.

Rental
There are car rental agencies in Maputo, Nampula, Nacala and Pemba. Elsewhere, you can usually arrange something with an upscale hotel. Rates average from US$100 per day for 4WD. At the moment, only Europcar (see the Maputo section) offers unlimited kilometres with rentals.

For a list of car rental agencies in Mozambique see Getting Around under Maputo later in this chapter.

BICYCLE
Cycling is a seldom used but good way to see Mozambique, but you'll need plenty of time as distances are long. You'll also need to plan the legs of your trip fairly carefully and to carry almost everything with you, including all spares, as there are long stretches with little or nothing en route. Try to avoid main roads as there's often no shoulder, traffic moves fast, drivers have little respect for cyclists (assuming they see you at all) and it's not uncommon for trucks to be carrying long poles or similarly lethal objects *sideways* across their truck! Also, to avoid the heat and the worst of the traffic, try to plan your cycling between dawn and mid-morning. Because of land mines, wildlife and security, it's not a good idea to free camp (plus it's illegal in Mozambique). It's much better to arrange something with villagers in rural areas. Secondary and tertiary roads are the best, but you'll need a mountain bike, including for beach access roads.

TAXIS
Maputo, Beira, Nampula and Pemba have a taxi service, and there's the occasional vehicle in Quelimane. Apart from airport arrivals, taxis don't cruise for business, so you'll need to seek them out. In Nampula and Pemba, most taxis have meters, as do some in Maputo. Elsewhere, you'll need to negotiate a price. Depending on location, expect to pay from about US$2 for town trips.

HITCHING
Hitching is fairly easy, though it can be slow off main routes. To/from beaches, it's best on weekends. Usually there are no problems, but especially if you're a woman, try to avoid hitching alone. Also see Hitching in the Getting Around the Region chapter.

BOAT
There's no regular passenger service between major coastal towns. However, it's worth asking at ports, as there's frequent cargo traffic along the coast and captains are sometimes willing to take passengers. Chances improve the further north you go. On Lake Niassa, there are regular boats between Metangula

and Cóbuè (see those sections later in this chapter for details).

Dhows

In the far north, dhows can be arranged to most destinations; fees are negotiable, averaging US$15 per day. There are no luxuries on board, and journeys often take far longer than anticipated. Bring plenty of extra water, food and sun protection, and stay with the winds – south to north from April to September and north to south from November to February. We've heard several horror stories from readers who tried to sail against the winds, only to wind up stranded for days in the sun without adequate food and water. A better option to experience dhow life is to charter one for a short local trip. Good places to do this include Vilankulo and Ibo Island.

LOCAL TRANSPORT

The main form of local transport in Mozambique is the *chapa* – the name given to any public transport that isn't a bus or truck. They're usually a converted passenger truck or minivan, and are notorious for being packed to the bursting point and for their poor safety records – if you have a choice, buses are much better. On some routes, your only option will be a *camião* (truck). Many have open backs, and on long journeys the sun and dust can be brutal. There's great competition for the front seats next to the driver, so these usually cost slightly more.

ORGANISED TOURS

Most organised tours focus on southern Mozambique or on the far north. Companies to check include:

Mozaic (Zimbabwe ☎/fax 04-300981, ℮ mozaic@mweb.co.zw)
Mozambique Connection (South Africa ☎ 011-803 4185, fax 011-803 3861, ℮ bookings@mozcon.com, W www.mozambique connection.co.za)
Mozambique Tours (South Africa ☎ 031-303 2190, fax 031-303 2396, W www.mozambique travel.co.za)
Wildlife Adventures (South Africa ☎ 021-461 2235, fax 021-461 2068, ℮ sales@wildlife adventures.co.za, W www.wildlifeadventures.co .za) The main company focusing on northern Mozambique

A good source of information on package tours and cruises are the Mozambique pages at the end of each edition of the South African travel magazine *Getaway* (W www.geta waytoafrica.com).

Maputo

☎ 01

Maputo (formerly Lourenço Marques), is one of Africa's most attractive capitals. It's set on a small cliff overlooking Maputo Bay, with wide avenues lined by jacaranda and flame trees, a plethora of pleasant sidewalk cafés and a relaxed atmosphere. For decades, the city's charms and its economic potential were overshadowed, first by colonialism, then by war, and it's only recently that the city has come into its own. Today Maputo is a lively, bustling place with colourful markets, intriguing architecture, a wealth of cultural offerings, and great nightlife. It's well worth spending some time here before heading north.

Orientation

Maputo sits on a low hill, with the long avenues of its upper-lying residential sections running down to the busy port and *baixa* (commercial area). Major north–south roads paralleling the seaside Avenida Marginal are Avenidas Julius Nyerere and Vladimir Lenine. Main east–west thoroughfares parallel to the port are Avenidas 25 de Setembro, 24 de Julho and Eduardo Mondlane.

Many businesses, the train station, banks, post and telephone offices and some budget accommodation are located in the *baixa*, on or near Avenida 25 de Setembro, while embassies and most of the mid-range and top-end hotels are in the city's upper section. The tallest building and a good landmark is the 33 Storey building (*'trinta e trés andares'*) in the *baixa* on the corner of Avenidas 25 de Setembro and Rua da Impresa. At the northernmost end of the Marginal and about 7km from the centre is Bairro Triunfo and the Costa do Sol area, with a small beach and several places to stay and eat.

Maps There's an excellent city map put out by Conselho Municipal and Coopération Française, for sale at the Public Information Bureau (BIP; see Tourist Offices following).

MOZAMBIQUE

CENTRAL MAPUTO

PLACES TO STAY
3 Residencial Augustijn
10 Holiday Inn
11 Residencial Halima
18 Fatima's Backpackers
22 Hotel Polana
30 Villa Itália
32 Hotel Avenida
36 Hotel Terminus
38 Villa das Mangas
42 Hotel Cardoso
43 The Base Backpackers
44 Hotel Monte Carlo
46 Pensão Martins
50 Hotel Rovuma-Carlton; ATM
60 Residencial Taj Mahal
64 Hotel Central

PLACES TO EAT
1 Restaurante Micael
15 Vasilis Bakery, Nando's & Pizza Inn
17 Estoril
27 Pequim (Lulas); Portuguese Embassy; Xenon Cinema
31 Piri Piri
33 Bistro
35 Mundo's
45 Mimmo's
72 Café Continental
73 Café Scala
78 Feira Popular; O Escorpião; Coqueiro

OTHER
2 Zambia High Commission
4 South African Airways
5 Clínica de Sommerschield
6 German Embassy
7 US Embassy
8 Malawi High Commission
9 French Embassy
12 Swaziland High Commission
13 Transport to Costa do Sol & Bairro Triunfo
14 Farmácia Calêndula
16 Zimbabwe High Commission
19 Dana Travel
20 LAM Sales Office; Avis Car Rental; Complexo Sheik
21 Europcar Car Rental
23 Canadian High Commission
24 Tanzania High Commission
25 Public Information Bureau (BIP)
26 South African High Commission
28 Imperial Car Rental
29 Clube Naval
34 Connection Time Internet Cafe
37 Escola 3 de Fevereiro & Local Bus Stop
39 Geology Museum
40 Natural History Museum & Transport Stand
41 Transport to Airport
47 British High Commission & British General
48 Iron House (Casa de Ferro)
49 French-Mozambican Cultural Centre
51 City Hall (Conselho Municipal)
52 Cathedral of Nossa Senhora da Conceição
53 Teledata
54 Bar Africa; Ciné Africa
55 Ronil
56 Ponto Final
57 Transportes Oliveiras
58 Museum of the Revolution
59 Casa de Cultura
61 National Art Museum
62 Transport for Swaziland, South Africa, Namaacha, Boane & Goba; Laurentina Beer Factory
63 Transport to Xikelene; Costa do Sol & Ronil
65 LAM Office
66 Brazilian Cultural Centre
67 Banco Austral
68 Banco Internacional de Moçambique (BIM)
69 Banco Comercial de Moçambique (BCM)
70 Money Museum
71 Saturday Morning Craft Market
74 Teatro Avenida
75 33 Storey Building; Telephone Office; Australian Consulate
76 Mextur
77 National Tourism Organisation (ENT)
79 Ministry of Finance
80 Chapas to Ponta d'Ouro
81 Ferry to Catembe

To 'Junta' Transport Junction (4km), Marracuene (25km), Macaneta (35km) & Points North

To Mavalane Airport (3.5km)

To Mavalane Airport (3.5km)

Avenida Acordos de Luska

Avenida Milagre Mabote

Avenida de Angola

Avenida de Angola

Rua dos Irmãos Roby

Avenida Marien N'Gouabi

Avenida Emília Daússe

Avenida de Maguiguana

Avenida Romão Fernandes Fanhina

Avenida Mahomed Said Barre

Avenida Lucas Luali

Avenida Albert Luthuli

Avenida da Guerra Popular

Avenida Filipe Samuel Magaia

55

56

Avenida do Trabalho

Avenida do Rio Tembe

Avenida da Tanzania

Avenida do Rio Limpopo

Avenida da Zambia

Praça 16 de Junho

Rua Paiva Couceiro

57

To Benefica (8km), Matola (10km), Namaacha (70km) & Ressano Garcia/Komatipoort (75km)

58

59

60

61

Avenida Josina Machel

Avenida Organização das Nações Unidas

Avenida Fernão Magalhães

Avenida Zedequias Manganhela

62

Avenida 25 de Setembro

Train Station

63

Praça dos Trabalhadores

Rua do

68
Jardim Tunduru

Avenida Zedequias Manganhela

Municipal Market

66 67 69

Av. Samora Machel

73

75

76

Rua da Imprensa

Avenida 25 de Setembro

Old Mosque

65

72 74

77

Rua Consiglieri Pedroso

70

Rua de Timor Leste

64

Rua do Bagamoyo

71

Fort

Rua da Mesquita

Avenida Mártires de Inhaminga

Praça 25 de Junho

0   300m
0   300yd

MOZAMBIQUE

CENTRAL MAPUTO

To Praça dos
Combatentes
(Xikelene) &
TSL Depot (4km)

Eduardo Mondlane
University

Sommerschield

To Bairro Triunfo,
Shanty Craft (4.5km) &
Restaurante Costa
do Sol (5km)

Praça da
OMM

Avenida do Zimbabwe

Avenida Kenneth Kaunda

Rua Pereira Marinho

Avenida Fernão
Melo E Castro

Rua Pereira do Lago

Rua Duarte Galvão

MAPUTO
BAY

Presidential
Palace

Rua da Resistência

Avenida Vladimir Lenine

Rua da Base N'Tchinga

Avenida Kim II Sung

Avenida Julius Nyerere

Rua Malhangalene

Avenida Kwame Nkrumah

Avenida Mao Tse Tung

Parque dos
Continuadores

Janeta
Market

Avenida Paulo Samuel Kankhomba

Avenida Agostinho Neto

Avenida Olof Palme

Avenida Vladimir Lenine

Avenida Amílcar Cabral

Avenida Salvador Allende

Central Hospital

Avenida Tomás Nduda

Avenida Mártires de Machava

Avenida Francisco Magumbwe

Avenida Armando Tivane

Avenida Marginal

Avenida Friedrich Engels

Avenida Eduardo Mondlane

Avenida Ahmed Sekou Touré

Avenida Karl Marx

Avenida 24 de Julho

Avenida Ho Chi Min

Avenida Patrice – Lumumba

Avenida José Mateus

Rua da Argélia

Rua Muthemba

Rua de Nachingwea

Ponta
Vermelha

Rua da Rádio

Jardim Tunduru
(Botanical Gardens)

Campo do
Desportivo

Avenida Mártires de Mueda

Praça da
Independência

Rua da Imprensa

Praça Robert
Mugabe

Av Samora Machel

Avenida 25 de Setembro

Rua de Timor Leste

Bagamoyo

Avenida 10 de Novembro

Praça 25
do Junho

See Enlargement

Port

Some Minor Roads Not Depicted

0   250   500m
0   250   500yd

MOZAMBIQUE

Information

Tourist Offices The **National Tourism Organisation** (ENT; ☎ 421794, fax 421795; e entur@virconn.com; 1179 Avenida 25 de Setembro) has brochures featuring Mozambique's provinces, but otherwise isn't a particularly useful stop.

More worthwhile is the **Public Information Bureau** (BIP; ☎ 490200; cnr Avenidas Eduardo Mondlane & Francisco Magumbwe), with city maps and books about Mozambique.

Money Most banks have their head offices in the baixa, with branches in the upper part of town. Among the most useful are **Banco Internacional de Moçambique** (BIM; 247 Avenida Samora Machel) and **Banco Austral** (Avenida 25 de Setembro) where you can get cash advances on a MasterCard. Several BIM branches have ATMs that give cash against a Visa card, including at Polana Shopping Centre on Avenida Julius Nyerere and at Hotel Rovuma Carlton.

The most useful foreign exchange bureau and the best place to change travellers cheques is at Hotel Polana.

Post & Communications There's post restante at the **main post office** (CTT; Avenida 25 de Setembro). The **telephone office** (ground floor, 33 Storey Bldg, Avenida 25 de Setembro & Rua da Impressa; open 7.30am-10pm daily) is nearby. For email and Internet access, try **Connection Time** (Avenida Julius Nyerere), next to Mundo's restaurant (see Places to Eat later in this section), or **Teledata** (Avenida 24 de Julho), diagonally opposite Ciné Africa.

Travel Agencies About five blocks west of Avenida Julius Nyerere, **Dana Travel** (☎ 494060, fax 494042; e travel@dana.co.mz; 729 Avenida Mao Tse Tung) has English-speaking staff, and can assist with domestic and international flights and travel arrangements. Another one to try is **Mextur** (☎ 428427; e mextur@emilmoz.com; 1226 Avenida 25 de Setembro).

Bookshops & Music Stores For books on Mozambique try the **BIP** (see Tourist Offices earlier). **Sensações**, with branches on the corner of Avenidas Julius Nyerere and Eduardo Mondlane and at Shoprite, has books, cassettes and CDs.

Cultural Centres The **British Council** (Rua John Issa), near the British High Commission, the **French–Mozambican Cultural Centre** (Praça da Independência) and the **Brazilian Cultural Centre** (cnr Avenidas Karl Marx & 25 de Setembro) all have exhibitions and cultural offerings.

Medical Services The best place is **Clínica de Sommerschield** (☎ 493924; 52 Rua Pereira do Lago; open 24 hrs), just off Avenida Kim Il Sung, which has a good lab and a doctor always on call. Advance payment is required (credit cards accepted for amounts over US$500).

Farmácia Calêndula (☎ 497606; 222 Avenida Mao Tse Tung; open 8am-8pm Mon-Sat, 9am-1pm Sun), near Avenida Julius Nyerere, is well stocked.

Dangers & Annoyances While Maputo is considerably safer than nearby Jo'burg, crime does occur – and it can be violent. Although most tourists visit the city without mishap, you should be vigilant when out and about both during the day and night, and take the precautions discussed in Dangers & Annoyances under Facts for the Visitor, earlier in this chapter. In particular, try to avoid carrying a bag or having any external trappings of 'wealth' when walking around town – don't give a potential thief any reason to think that you might have something of value. At night, always take a taxi and, day or night, avoid putting yourself in isolated situations. Areas to avoid during the day include the isolated stretches of the Marginal between Praça Robert Mugabe and the Holiday Inn, and the two access roads leading down to the Marginal from Avenida Friedrich Engels. Also avoid the area below the escarpment just south of Avenida Patrice Lumumba.

Carry your passport or (better) a copy of the front and visa pages with you when out and about. It's rarely checked, but when it is, it's usually by underpaid policemen looking to top up their meagre salaries with bribes.

There are several restricted areas that are off-limits to pedestrians (no photos). These include the eastern footpath on Avenida Julius Nyerere in front of the president's residence and the Ponta Vermelha zone in the city's southeastern corner.

Things to See & Do

The **fort** (Praça 25 de Junho) was built by the Portuguese in the mid-19th century on the site of an earlier fort. At present it is closed to the public. Several blocks west is the impressive **train station** dating from 1910, with a dome designed by Gustav Eiffel of Eiffel Tower fame. Between the fort and the train station is the oldest part of town, centred around **Rua de Bagamoyo**, with some interesting architecture and the city's oldest **mosque**. Near the train station is the **Municipal Market** (Mercado Municipal; Avenida 25 de Setembro) with everything from fruit, vegetables, spices and basketware.

Several blocks northeast of the market is the modern **cathedral** (Praça da Independência). Nearby are the neo-classical **City Hall** building; the bedraggled **Botanical Gardens** (Jardim Tunduru); and the **Iron House** (Casa de Ferro). This house was designed (also by Eiffel) in the late 19th century as the governor's residence, but its metal-plated exterior proved unsuitable for tropical conditions.

The **National Art Museum** (Museu Nacional de Arte; Avenida Ho Chi Min; admission free; open 3pm-7pm Tues-Sun) has an excellent collection of works by Mozambique's finest contemporary artists.

The **Museum of the Revolution** (Museu da Revolução; Avenida 24 de Julho; admission $0.50; open 9am-noon Mon-Fri & Sun, 2pm-6pm Mon-Sat, 3pm-6pm Sun) documents Mozambique's independence struggle (in Portuguese, but with good photos). The **Money Museum** (Museu da Moeda; Praça 25 do Junho; open 9am-noon & 2pm-4.30pm Tues-Sat, 2pm-5pm Sun), in one of the city's oldest buildings, has exhibits of local currency from early barter tokens to modern-day bills.

The **Natural History Museum** (Museu da História Natural; admission US$2, US$0.50 on Sunday; open 9am-11.30pm & 2pm-4pm Tues-Sun) near Hotel Cardoso is worth visiting to see its Manueline architecture, and its garden with a mural by Mozambique's premier painter, Malangatana. Inside are some moderately interesting taxidermy specimens, and probably the region's only collection of elephant foetuses. The **Geology Museum** (Museu da Geologia; Avenida 24 de Julho; open 3pm-6pm Tues-Sat, also Sat morning) has mineral exhibits and a geological relief map of the country.

Places to Stay – Budget

For camping, the best bets are well south of Maputo in Ponta d'Ouro, or north around Marracuene and Macaneta.

There are two good backpackers, both with English-speaking staff and information about what to do in and around Maputo. Both can also help with airport pick-ups and transfers to the bus depots.

The long-standing **Fatima's Backpackers** (☎ 302994; e fatima@virconn.com; 1317 Avenida Mao Tse Tung; dorm beds from US$4, doubles US$12-15) has a very helpful owner, tiny rooms around a small garden, and larger rooms in a nice house next door. There's also an outdoor kitchen and eating area, and lots of information on the local scene.

The **Base Backpackers** (☎ 302723; e the base@yahoo.uk.com; 545 Avenida Patrice Lumumba; dorm beds US$5; doubles US$16) has a mixture of dorm rooms and doubles, a kitchen, helpful staff, and a backyard and braai area with views over the port in the distance.

Other than the backpackers hostels, good, safe budget accommodation in Maputo is scarce, and most people opt to pay a bit more for one of the mid-range places. Other budget places that see a small trickle of visitors, most of whom head elsewhere after a day or two, include **Residencial Taj Mahal** (☎ 732122; Avenida Ho Chi Min near Casa de Cultura; singles/doubles from US$15/20), where rooms are clean but the area is unsafe at night, and **Hotel Central** (☎ 431652; Rua Consiglieri Pedroso; singles/doubles from US$15/20), near the train station, with basic rooms. Solo women travellers likely won't feel comfortable at either of these places. **Restaurante Costa do Sol** (☎ 450038, 450115; e rcs@teledata.mz; singles/doubles US$25/46) is another option if you have your own transport. It's 5km north of the centre at the northern end of the Marginal. Rooms are clean, with bathroom and fan, and there's a popular **restaurant** downstairs.

Places to Stay – Mid-Range

Hotel Terminus (☎ 491333; e termhot@ter minus-hotel.com; cnr Avenidas Francisco Magumbwe & Ahmed Sekou Touré; rooms from US$60) has a restaurant, small pool and small but spotless rooms with TV and air-con. It's popular with business travellers and often fully booked.

Pensão Martins (☎ 324926, 324930, fax 429645; e morest@isl.co.mz; 1098 Avenida 24 de Julho; singles/doubles US$47/53) is an older, low-key place with a convenient location and no-frills rooms that are good value for the doubles. There's an outdoor restaurant and a tiny pool.

Villa das Mangas (☎/fax 497507, 497078; e villadasmangas@tvcabo.co.mz, villadasman gas@hotmail.com; 401 Avenida 24 de Julho; singles/doubles from US$60/75), in the same area, is new, with small, clean rooms with TV and air-con. There's a small garden area with a tiny pool in the centre, and a restaurant.

Hotel Monte Carlo (☎ 304048; e res@ montecarlo-hotel.net; 620 Avenida Patrice Lumumba; rooms from US$45), diagonally opposite The Base Backpackers, has nice, good value rooms, a restaurant and an Internet connection.

Villa Itália (☎ 497298, fax 496190; e vit alia@virconn.com; 635 Avenida Friedrich Engels; singles/doubles US$65/75, suite US$85) is a large colonial-era house with a popular **restaurant** downstairs and a few large, spotless rooms on the upper level.

There are several private houses in the Sommerschield area offering B&B-style accommodation. All are of similar standard, with nicely furnished, comfortable rooms, usually with TV and telephone. They include **Residencial Halima** (☎ 491127; e dr .svee@tvcabo.co.mz; 113 Rua Duarte Galvão), and **Residencial Augustijn** (☎ 493693; e t .theunissen@tvcabo.co.mz; 204 Rua Pereira Marinho; singles/doubles US$50/55).

Places to Stay – Top End

Except as noted, rates at these places include a buffet breakfast.

Hotel Polana (☎ 491001, fax 491480; e res@polana-hotel.com; w www.polana -hotel.com; 1380 Avenida Julius Nyerere; 'Polana Mar' rooms from US$165, main building rooms from US$130; full breakfast buffet US$15), in a superb location overlooking the sea, is Mozambique's best, and one of the best hotels in the region. It has rooms in the elegant main building or in the luxurious 'Polana Mar' section closer to the water. There's a beautiful pool, several restaurants, and good-value breakfast, lunch and dinner buffets. They offer attractively priced package deals from Jo'burg including flights, accommodation and meals. If you're nervous about experiencing Mozambique, this is a great way to get an introduction to the country and well worth a splurge.

Hotel Cardoso (☎ 491071, fax 491804; e hcardoso@zebra.mz; 707 Avenida Mártires de Mueda; singles/doubles from US$115/ 145) opposite the Natural History Museum has views over the bay, comfortable, well-appointed rooms, a pool and restaurant.

Hotel Rovuma-Carlton (☎ 305000, fax 305305; singles/doubles from US$115/144) opposite the cathedral is similar, with a restaurant, a fast Internet connection, and good package deals to Inhaca Island.

Two others to check are **Hotel Avenida** (☎ 492000, fax 499600; e h.avenida@tele data.mz; 627 Avenida Julius Nyerere; singles/ doubles US$105/125), and **Holiday Inn** (☎ 495050; e himaputo@southernsun.com.mz; Avenida Marginal; rooms from $99).

Places to Eat

Cafés & Fast Food There are dozens of sidewalk cafés where you can get pastries and light meals, and watch the passing street life. Some to try include **Café Continental** and **Café Scala** on Avenida 25 de Setembro – both around since colonial days – or **Estoril** (Avenida Mao Tse Tung).

Vasilis Bakery, Nando's, Pizza Inn, together on Avenida Mao Tse Tung, have pastries, chicken and pizza from US$2.50.

Piri Piri (cnr Avenidas 24 de Julho & Julius Nyerere) serves spicy chicken from US$4.

Restaurants Maputo has dozens of good restaurants, enough to keep you busy sampling new places for weeks. Main dishes at most range from US$5 to US$12.

Popular ones include: **Restaurante Micael** (Rua da Resistência) for Brazilian cuisine; **Mundo's** (☎ 494080; cnr Avenidas Julius Nyerere & 24 de Julho), with large portions of everything, including burritos and burgers; the cosy **Bistro** (☎ 497644; 657 Avenida Julius Nyerere; closed Sunday), next to Mundo's, serving delectable French cuisine; **Pequim (Lulas)** (☎ 493899; Avenida Julius Nyerere; closed Sunday), a long-standing establishment with reliable seafood and steaks; and **Mimmo's** (cnr Avenidas 24 de Julho & Salvador Allende), a casual, bustling place serving pizzas and other dishes.

The **Feira Popular complex** (Avenida 25 de Setembro; admission US$0.50) has dozens of

small bars and restaurants and is popular in the evenings. **O Escorpião** and **Coqueiro** are two of the best known. Parking is available, and taxis wait outside.

Restaurante Costa do Sol (see Places to Stay – Budget) has a good selection of seafood, and is packed on weekend afternoons.

Entertainment

Casa de Cultura (House of Culture; cnr Avenidas Albert Luthuli & Ho Chi Minh) is the home of Mozambique's excellent **National Company of Song and Dance**. Rehearsals are often open to the public.

Teatro Avenida (☎ 424411; 1179 Avenida 25 de Setembro) has good performances in Portuguese by local theatre groups.

Maputo has a thriving nightlife with many pubs, clubs, bars and discos. Things get going on Friday and Saturday after 11pm. Cover charges at most places range from US$3 to US$7.

Bar Africa (2182 Avenida 24 de Julho) next to Ciné Africa is a great spot, especially on Thursday (jazz night), when it's the main place to be in town.

For dancing, try **Complexo Sheik**, a pricey and popular disco near the intersection of Avenidas Julius Nyerere and Mao Tse Tung.

Shopping

For crafts, try the **Saturday Morning Craft Market** (Praça 25 de Junho) or the **vendors** in front of Hotel Polana or opposite Piri Piri restaurant.

Shanty Craft (☎ 450111, 450305; Bairro Triunfo; open 10am-5pm Tues-Sun) has an excellent assortment of high-quality crafts from around the country.

Getting There & Away

Air Details for domestic and international flights to/from Maputo are given in the main Getting There & Away and Getting Around sections earlier in this chapter.

Airlines with offices in Maputo include:

LAM (☎ 426001, 465810, central reservations, W www.lam.co.mz) corner of Avenidas 25 de Setembro and Karl Marx; (☎ 490590, sales office) corner of Avenidas Julius Nyerere and Mao Tse Tung
SAAirlink (W www.saairlink.co.za) Maputo airport
South African Airways (☎ 495483, 495484, 498097) Avenida Fernào Melo e Castro, Sommerschield

STA (☎ 491765, W www.sta.co.mz) Maputo airport
TAP Air Portugal (☎ 431006/7) Hotel Rovuma-Carlton
TransAirways (☎ 465108, e sabinair@virconn .com) Maputo airport

Bus Most long-distance depots are well outside the city centre. They include:

Benefica On the northwestern edge of the city along Avenida de Moçambique. Chapas for Marracuene and other points close to Maputo depart from here.
'Junta' Avenida de Moçambique just past Lhanguene cemetery. All northbound long-haul transport stops here, although for a good seat it's better to go to the bus depots.
Transport for Swaziland, South Africa, Namaacha, Boane and Goba Fábrica de Cerveja Laurentina (Laurentina Beer Factory), corner of Avenidas 25 de Setembro and Albert Luthuli.
Transportes Oliveiras (☎ 405108, 400475) Avenida 24 de Julho, just beyond Praça 16 de Junho (US$6 in a taxi from the centre). Coming into Maputo, many Oliveiras buses conveniently continue past the Oliveiras depot along Avenida 24 de Julho, stopping near the Museum of Natural History.
TSL (☎ 460502, 460119) Praça dos Combatentes at the northeastern end of Avenida Vladimir Lenine (about US$8 in a taxi). Coming into Maputo, some TSL buses continue to Ponto Final (see Getting Around, following).

Oliveiras has express buses to Xai-Xai, Maxixe and Vilankulo departing at 6.30am daily. Most TSL northbound buses depart between 6am and 8am.

Train There's no train service from Maputo to destinations within Mozambique. For international services to Komatipoort and Jo'burg, see the Getting There & Away section earlier in this chapter.

Getting Around

To/From the Airport Mavalane international airport is 6km northwest of the centre (US$6 in a taxi).

Bus & Chapa Buses are numbered, and have nameboards with their destination. City rides cost US$0.10.

Chapas go everywhere (US$0.15). Some have nameboards, otherwise listen to the destination called out by the conductor. Major transport stands include:

MOZAMBIQUE

Hospital Central/Escola 3 de Fevereiro Avenida Eduardo Mondlane, four blocks down from Avenida Julius Nyerere; transport to Ronil and various city destinations

Museu (Natural History Museum) transport to the airport and numerous city destinations

Ponto Final intersection of Avenidas Eduardo Mondlane and Guerra Popular; terminus for many bus and *chapa* routes; transport along Avenida Eduardo Mondlane

Praça dos Trabalhadores the train station; transport to Xikelene, Costa do Sol, Ronil and elsewhere

Ronil Intersection of Avenidas Eduardo Mondlane and Karl Marx; transport to 'junta', Benefica and Matola

For Costa do Sol and Bairro Triunfo, you can also take bus No 17 or a *chapa* from the intersection of Avenidas Mao Tse Tung and Julius Nyerere.

Car There are numerous car rental agencies in Maputo. When this book was researched, Europcar was offering the best rates, and was the only company offering unlimited kilometres.

Avis (☎ 465498, 494473, fax 465193) intersection of Avenidas Julius Nyerere and Mao Tse Tung; also at the airport

Europcar (☎ 497338, 466172, 082 302833, fax 466163, e europcar@virconn.com) 1418 Avenida Julius Nyerere, next to the Hotel Polana

Imperial (☎ 493545, fax 493540) corner of Avenidas Julius Nyerere and Eduardo Mondlane

Taxi There are taxi ranks at Hotel Polana (☎ 493255 to call a cab), Hotel Rovuma-Carlton and Hotel Cardoso; and sometimes near the train station and Municipal Market.

AROUND MAPUTO
Catembe
☎ 01

Across the bay from Maputo is the quiet town of Catembe, which offers views of Maputo's skyline and a taste of upcountry life for those who won't have a chance to leave the capital.

Catembe Gallery Hotel (☎ 380003, 380050; e office@catembe.net; w www.catembe.net; rooms with/without Jacuzzi US$95/50), on a hill overlooking the water and about 2km north of the ferry dock, is well worth a visit. The hotel was designed to provide a forum for local art. Each room has its own unique decor, all featuring artwork by Mozambican artists, and one has a Jacuzzi. There's a small beach, a pool, and a popular and very reasonably priced **restaurant** with good Mozambican cuisine as well as home-made pasta and Italian cheeses. Staff can help you organise trips to Inhaca Island and elsewhere.

Changada Restaurant, just north of the ferry dock, makes a good lunch stop.

Getting There & Away A ferry runs daily from the dock near the Ministry of Finance (US$0.15/0.60 per person/vehicle, 20 minutes). Departures are hourly between 6am and 8am, and 4pm to 6pm, and every two hours otherwise. The last departure from Catembe to Maputo is scheduled for 9.30pm, but depends on the whim of the captain.

Xefina Grande

This island just offshore from Costa do Sol has a long history as a trading base, prison and war garrison. Now, there's nothing but a few old cannons, and beaches. You can arrange motorboat charters through Maputo travel agencies (about US$35 per person, minimum of four) or by asking around at **Clube Naval**.

Marracuene & Macaneta Beach
☎ 01

Macaneta is the closest open-ocean beach to Maputo and a popular weekend trip from the capital. It's on a narrow peninsula divided from the mainland by the Nkomati River, and reached via the town of Marracuene, which lies 35km north of Maputo along the EN1.

Parque do Campismo (camping about US$3), along the river a few kilometres south of Marracuene, has good camping and some chalets.

The restaurant at the beachside **Complexo Turístico Macaneta** (☎ 309073) is the main place for day-trippers.

Jay's Beach Lodge (☎ 082 300143 from 8am-9am & 5pm-6pm; campsites US$20, 2-/4-/6-person chalets US$40/60/70) has good camping amid the sand dunes, comfortable self-catering chalets, a *braai* area and a restaurant. Day guests are charged US$5 per vehicle. It's 12km from the ferry and signposted (4WD only); there's no public transport.

Incomati River Camp (☎ 082 311916; e sencormoz@emilmoz.com; campsites US$4.50; chalets without/with bathroom

MOZAMBIQUE

US$15/20 per person) is a quiet, rustic place on the river near the tip of the peninsula, well-suited to sitting back and watching the water flow by. There are hot showers, a cooking area and a restaurant. You'll need to reserve in advance for midweek stays. The camp will pick you up from the ferry (US$8). Otherwise, you'll need your own vehicle; follow the road towards Jay's Lodge for about 5km, where the turnoff for the camp is signposted.

Casa Lisa *(☎ 082 304199;* e *buckland@ teledata.mz; campsites US$5 per person, chalets from US$15)* is signposted just west of the EN1 about 18km north of Marracuene. It's a popular overnight spot for people driving between South Africa and points north who want to avoid staying overnight in Maputo. There are no-frills chalets, camping and a restaurant serving dinner and breakfast.

Getting There & Away Via public transport, take any northbound *chapa* from Benefica (see Getting There & Away under Maputo, earlier in this chapter) to Marracuene. It's a 10-minute walk through town to the Nkomati River, which you'll need to cross by ferry (US$1/7 per person/vehicle, five minutes). On the other side you'll need to walk or hitch. Hitching is easy on weekends, otherwise very slow. The ferry stops running around 6pm.

Inhaca Island
☎ 01

Inhaca, about 40km east of Maputo, is an important marine research centre and a popular weekend getaway. Its offshore coral reefs are among the most southerly in the world, and parts of the island and surrounding waters have been designated a protected reserve. About 3km northwest of Inhaca is tiny Portuguese Island *(Ilha dos Portuguêses),* formerly a leper colony and now part of the Inhaca marine reserve system.

Things to See & Do There are good **beaches** on Inhaca's northeastern edge, and on Portuguese Island. On Inhaca's southwestern corner is a marine research station and a tiny **museum** *(admission free)* containing some specimens of the island's fauna. Transport to the research station (US$5) and the

lighthouse at Inhaca's northern tip (US$10) can be arranged through Inhaca Island Lodge. Otherwise, it's a 50-minute walk from the lodge to the biology station, and about double that to the lighthouse.

Diving & Water Sports At Inhaca Island Lodge, **Dive Africa Watersports** *(☎ 760005/6;* e *mozambique@diveafrica.com;* w *www.diveafrica.com)* offers diving, windsurfing, sea kayaking and snorkelling. Dives are tide dependent and conditions vary, though with luck you may see sharks, manta rays, potato bass and more. The best months are November to April, and the least favourable are August and September, when it's often too windy.

Places to Stay & Eat Camping is permitted at **Ponta Torres** (Inhaca's southeastern tip), and on **Portuguese Island** *(camp sites US$2.50 per person).* There's a guard at both sites, and brackish water sources; bring all supplies from the mainland.

It's also possible to camp or stay in basic thatched huts in Inhaca village, next to Inhaca Island Lodge. Check with Lucas Restaurant for information.

Marine Biology Research Station *(☎ 760009, 490009, fax 492176; rooms without bathroom US$15 per person)* offers basic rooms with shared facilities and is open to the public on a space-available basis. You'll need to bring your own food.

Inhaca Island Lodge *(☎ 305000, fax 305305; singles/doubles with half-board US$126/194, mid-week US$106/152)* on the island's western side is under the same management as the Rovuma-Carlton in Maputo and of similar standard. It has comfortable chalet-style accommodation, a pool, and offers various attractive package deals from Jo'burg.

Apart from the **restaurant** *(meals US$18)* at Inhaca Island Lodge, the main place to get a meal is the local-style **Lucas Restaurant** just past the market.

Getting There & Away TransAirways has daily flights to/from Maputo for US$35/ 50 one way/return.

Speedboat charters (arrange with any Maputo travel agency) cost US$50 return, minimum four, and take about an hour. All boats drop you at Inhaca Island Lodge.

For Portuguese Island, arrange a boat from the beach in front of Inhaca Island Lodge. At very low tide you can walk.

Southern Mozambique

This section covers the area between Ponta d'Ouro and the Save River, encompassing Maputo, Gaza and Inhambane provinces. It's the most developed part of the country for tourism, although this is almost completely concentrated along the coast, where the main attractions are stunning, seemingly endless stretches of white-sand beach fringed by clear, blue waters. Places are described roughly from south to north.

PONTA D'OURO & PONTA MALONGANE
☎ 01

Ponta d'Ouro has boomed in popularity over the past few years, and is the first stop for many travellers doing Mozambique as part of a larger Southern Africa loop. Its main attraction is the excellent beach – long, wide and usually deserted, once you get away from the town area. The offshore waters host abundant sea life, including dolphins, whale sharks and more. From July to November, you may see whales. Thanks to the area's proximity to South Africa, it fills up completely on holiday weekends.

About 5km north of Ponta d'Ouro is the quieter Ponta Malongane, with a beautiful and seemingly endless windswept coastline fringed by high, vegetated dunes.

Diving
There are some good diving spots along this stretch of coast, and numerous operators have set up shop. In addition to the ones based at Parque de Campismo (see Places to Stay & Eat later in this section for more details) these include the good **Devocean Diving**; **Africa Scuba Travel** (e scubatravel@iafrica.com; w www.scuba diver.co.za), based at Fishmonger Barracas; and the long-established **Ponta Malongane**. Rates average US$15 for a single dive, plus around US$15 per day for full equipment hire. Four-day open-water certification courses cost about US$220. Diving is

possible year round, and is best from November to April/May.

Dolphin Tours
Dolphins frequent the waters offshore from Ponta d'Ouro, and catching a glimpse of them can be a beautiful experience. However, remember that they're wild creatures, and sightings can't be guaranteed – let them come to you, if they wish, and don't go off in wild pursuit, or try to touch them. **Dolphin Encounters** (☎ 082 3303859, Jo'burg 011-462 4551; e dca1@mweb.co.za; w www.dolphin -encountours.co.za), based at the Parque de Campismo, runs the best tours. Most are done as part of a package from Jo'burg (from US$170 per person) and include a short marine ecology course where you can learn about the dolphins, three nights accommodation with half-board, transfers to/from the Kosi Bay border post and – weather permitting – daily excursions to snorkel with the dolphins. The packages run from Thursday to Sunday, and can accommodate walk-ins on a space-available basis (US$13 per person per launch). Between June and August, bring a Windbreaker.

Places to Stay & Eat
Ponta d'Ouro Most backpackers stay at one of the dive operators based at the entrance to the Parque de Campismo at the southern end of town. All offer simple tented accommodation and catered or self-catering options, as well as the full range of diving options. They include **Dolphin Encounters** (see under Dolphin Tours earlier; US$29 per person with half-board), with a nice setup and good accommodation; **The Whaler** (w www.divesouthafrica.com; 2 people US$26) next door; **Simply Scuba** (☎ 011-678 0972; w www.simplyscuba.co.za; 2 people US$26), next up, with good tents and ablution blocks with hot water; and **Aqua Sports** (☎ 072 4465693; 2 people US$26).

The new and recommended **Café del Mar** (☎ 082 3303859, Jo'burg 011-462 4551; e dca1@mweb.co.za; US$38 per person with half-board) is another place catering to divers, with simple, clean double rooms sharing facilities. It has a prime setting on a hilltop about 200m in from the beach, with views over the sea. There's also a good restaurant overlooking the water and secure parking. It's the base for Dolphin Encounters' marine

ecology courses, and dive-accommodation packages are offered.

Devocean Diving (☎ *South Africa 082 332 9029, from 9am-4pm Mon-Fri only, fax 01-650028;* e *devoceandiving@absamail .co.za; tented accommodation/rooms from per person US$20/24; 8-person self-catering house US$220),* about 700m up the road to the north, is equally good. It has comfortable doubles, and two self-catering houses nearby, plus delicious meals and dive-accommodation packages.

Motel do Mar (☎/fax 650000; 4-person chalets with/without sea view US$65/54), on the beach below Café del Mar, is a throwback to colonial days, with a pleasant **restaurant** and faded but quite decent self-catering chalets lined up near the beach.

For food, try **Fishmonger Barracas** in the centre of town, or **A Florestinha do Indico** nearby. There's also an expensive and poorly stocked grocery store.

Ponta Malongane Based at the sprawling Parque de Malongane, **Ponta Malongane** (☎ *South Africa 013-741 1975;* w *www .malongane.co.za; camp sites per person US$6.50, 2-bed rondavels from US$17, 2-bed log huts US$28)* has shaded camping, simple rondavels and twin-bedded log cabins. There's a restaurant and self-catering facilities, and various good deals on dive-accommodation packages.

Tartaruga Maritima Luxury Camp (☎ *South Africa 083 309 3469, 083 797 6433;* e *tartaruga@mweb.co.za;* w *www .tartaruga.co.za; doubles US$70),* about 2km further north, is a quiet, beautiful place. Accommodation is in comfortable, good value safari-style luxury tents tucked away in the coastal forest just behind the dunes and close to the sea. There's no food available, but there's a raised self-catering area with views over the water.

Ponta Mamoli (e *bookings@pontamam oli.com;* w *www.pontamamoli.com),* under the same management as Tartaruga and of similar standards, has accommodation in log cabins, a small pool and a large deck overlooking the sea. It's 11km north of Ponta Malongane at Ponta Mamoli.

Getting There & Away

Ponta d'Ouro is 120km south of Maputo. The road is in good shape for the first 60km,

but has soft, deep sand and is slow going thereafter. Allow about 3½ hours in a private vehicle (4WD only).

A direct *chapa* departs from Maputo's Catembe ferry pier at 8am on Tuesday and Friday (US$5.50, five hours). Departures from Ponta d'Ouro are Wednesday and Saturday at 8am. Otherwise, take the ferry to Catembe, where you can find transport to Salamanga (US$2.50, 1½ hours) or Zitundo (US$4, 4½ hours). From Zitundo, there's sporadic transport to Ponta d'Ouro (US$1.60), 20km further south, and on weekends hitching is possible.

Kosi Bay border post is just 11km south of Ponta d'Ouro (4WD), but there's no public transport. Coming from South Africa, there's a guarded lot at the border where you can leave your vehicle (about US$2.50 per day). All the hotels do pick-ups from the border, and it's easy hitching on weekends.

MAPUTO ELEPHANT RESERVE

En route to Ponta d'Ouro and two hours from Maputo is the **Maputo Elephant Reserve** (admission adult/child US$4/3 per visit; camping adult/child US$5/3 per night), which was gazetted in 1969 to protect the local elephant population and several turtle species. Due to the war and poaching, it's estimated that only about 100 to 150 elephants remain, most of which are quite skittish and seldom seen. However, the reserve's birdlife is good – including fish eagles and many wetland species – and as there are few visitors, a journey here offers the chance for a bush adventure close to the capital.

Kutlhanga Tours (☎ *01-490845, 082 308031;* e *kutlhanga@hotmail.com)* in Maputo can help you arrange things. Expect to pay from about US$105/85 per person for groups of two/four people for an overnight stay.

To visit the reserve on your own, you'll need a 4WD, tent, food and water. There's an area at the main entrance where you can pitch a tent and (usually) get some water, though almost everyone goes further into the reserve to camp along the beach.

Getting There & Away

You'll need your own transport to visit the reserve. The *campeamento principal* (main entrance) is marked with a rusty signboard about 65km from Catembe off the road to Ponta d'Ouro. From the turnoff, it's 3km to

the park gate, and from the gate, about 35km further through the reserve to the coast. There's a second entrance further along the Ponta d'Ouro road and marked with a barely legible signpost, from where you'll need to drive about 22km to the reserve.

NAMAACHA
☎ 01

Namaacha is a cool, pleasant town on the Swaziland border with an ornate colonial-era church and lots of flowering trees. East of town is a rusty sign marking the way down to a small but scenic **cascata** (waterfall), 3.6km north of the main road.

Libombos Hotel (☎ 960102, 960218; singles/doubles from US$45/65) on the main road has comfortable rooms and a pricey restaurant. Otherwise there are a few local food places in town.

Chapas run frequently to and from Maputo (US$1.60).

BILENE
☎ 022

This small resort town (known locally as Praia do Bilene) sits on a large lagoon separated from the open sea by a sandy spit. Its calm waters are good for swimming, although conditions vary markedly with the seasons. If you're based in Maputo and have a car at your disposal, it's an enjoyable week-end excursion, but if you're backpacking and want some beach, it's better to head further north to Tofo or south to Ponta d'Ouro.

Complexo Palmeiras (☎ 59019; e palmeira@bilene.virconn.com; w www.palmeiras.itgo.com; camping sites US$10 plus US$5 per person, 4-person chalets about US$40) has camping, no-frills chalets and a restaurant. Follow the main road into town to the final T-junction, then go left for about 1km.

Pousada de São Martinho (☎ 59002; doubles without bathroom about US$20, 4-person chalets about US$60), 200m inland from the beach past the market, is also worth a look. There are double rooms with clean common bath, as well as self-catering chalets.

Praia do Sol (☎ 082 319304; w www.pdsol.co.za; 2/4-person chalets with half-board per person US$35), 4km south of town along the beach, has rustic chalets, diving and water sports. Follow the main road into town to the T-junction, turn right and continue straight for 3km.

Complexo Humula (☎ 59020, 59022; 2-/5-/6-person chalets about US$65/130/150) is set amidst manicured lawns in the town centre, and signposted from the main road. Accommodation is in comfortable self-catering chalets.

For meals, try **Estrela do Mar** on the beach road, or **Pavilhão Tamar** nearby.

Getting There & Away
Bilene is 140km north of Maputo and 40km off the main road. Via public transport, have any north or southbound bus drop you at the junction town of Macia, from where pick-ups run to/from Bilene (US$0.50).

Leaving Bilene, there's a direct bus to Maputo from Pousada do Paraiso in the town centre, departing daily at 6am. However, it's faster to take a chapa to Macia and get a southbound or northbound express bus from there. Chapas depart from the roundabout at the entrance to Bilene, about 2km from the beach.

XAI-XAI
☎ 022

Xai-Xai ('shy-shy'), the capital of Gaza province, is a long town stretched out along the EN1. Most visitors head for the beach at **Praia do Xai-Xai**, 8km off the main road and 10km from the town centre. Relatively few tourists come here, most preferring the beaches further north. However, the salty air and ocean breezes are invigorating, and make a good break if you find yourself in the area.

Places to Stay & Eat
Complexo Halley (☎ 35003; doubles from US$30, air-con suite US$50), a long-standing place on the beach, is the first hotel you reach heading north from the main access road. It has large, no-frills rooms, a restaurant and a popular disco.

Xai-Xai Camping & Caravan Park (☎ 35022; camp sites US$6, 2-person bungalows from US$20, 4-bed self-catering house US$55), just to the north, is shaded and well located, but everything's a bit rundown and we've had reports of security problems here.

Xai-Xai Beach Lodge (☎ South Africa 031-304 8817; doubles about US$70) is a new place about 2km further north along the beach, with comfortable rooms and a restaurant.

For food, try **Golfinho Azul** on the beach south of Complexo Halley. In town, you can

get inexpensive meals at **McMozzy's** in the Pôr do Sol complex on the main road at the southern end of town next to the transport stand.

Getting There & Away

Oliveiras runs twice daily express buses between Xai-Xai and Maputo, departing in each direction about 6am and 1.30pm (US$3, four hours). There are also frequent ordinary buses to Maputo (US$2.50, five hours) from the Oliveiras depot on the main road in the town centre.

Otherwise, all north–south express buses stop in Xai-Xai. Wait by the Pôr do Sol complex on the main road at the southern end of town.

Chapas to Praia do Xai-Xai (US$0.15) depart from the transport stand in the town centre and drop you at the roundabout about 700m uphill from the beach.

QUISSICO

Quissico (known locally as Zavala) is on the EN1 overlooking some beautiful lagoons. It's the capital of Zavala district, which is famed for its Chope *timbila* (marimba) players. One of the best known is Venancio Mbande, whose internationally acclaimed orchestra rehearses some Sunday afternoons at his house about 20km north of Quissico in Helene. There's also an annual *timbila* festival here, usually in late August.

Pousada de Zavala 'Quissico' (*rooms about US$8*) on the main road in the town centre has basic rooms and a restaurant.

About 55km north of Quissico and 17km off the main road (4WD only) is **Praia de Závora** and **Závora Beach Camp** (☎ *South Africa 013-706 4926; camp sites about US$6*) with camping behind the sand dunes, and some simple chalets. Meals and snorkelling gear are available.

Most transport between Maputo and Maxixe stops at Quissico. For Závora, you'll need your own vehicle.

MAXIXE

☎ 023

Maxixe (ma-sheesh), about 450km northeast of Maputo on the EN1, doesn't have much to offer, although it's a convenient stopping point for traffic up and down the coast. It's also the place to get off the bus if you want to visit Inhambane, across the bay.

Maxixe Camping (☎ *30351; camp sites US$2 per person, 2-person beach bungalows from US$15*) next to the jetty has good security, hot showers, self-catering facilities and a good **restaurant**. There are also a few simple, clean bungalows with bathroom. You can leave your vehicle here (US$1.50 per day) while visiting Inhambane.

Across the road are **Hotel Golfinho Azul** (☎ *30071; singles/doubles US$12/15*) and **Pousada de Maxixe** (☎ *30199; doubles US$15*), both with adequate, no-frills rooms.

For meals, other than the restaurant at Maxixe Camping, the best bet is **Stop** (☎ *30025*), on the northern edge of the jetty.

Getting There & Away

Several buses daily run to/from Vilankulo (US$2.50, 3½ hours) and Maputo (US$6, six to seven hours). The 4.30am Oliveiras bus from Vilankulo to Maputo passes Maxixe about 7.30am. For information on getting to Inhambane, see the following section.

INHAMBANE

☎ 023

Inhambane is one of Mozambique's oldest towns and one of its most charming. Well before the Portuguese arrived, it was a stop for Muslim dhows plying the coast. From the 18th century, Inhambane was an important trading port for ivory and slaves, with commerce controlled primarily by Indians. In 1834, the settlement was ravaged by the warriors of chief Soshangane, but soon recovered to again become one of the largest towns in the country. During the 20th century, focus shifted elsewhere and Inhambane declined. Today, you can see many old houses and buildings. Among the most interesting are the old **cathedral**, near the water, and some of the houses nearby, as well as the old and new **mosques**.

Information

Banco Austral on Avenida da Independência (the main road leading up from the ferry) gives cash against a MasterCard. The BIM branch nearby gives cash advances against Visa, and also has an ATM.

International telephone calls can be made from the Telecom Building just south of the jetty on the road paralleling the water. There's Internet access at **Centro de Pesquisa e Informática** 500m further

MOZAMBIQUE

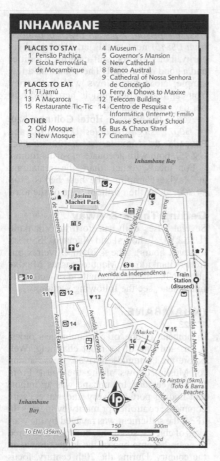

INHAMBANE

PLACES TO STAY
1 Pensão Pachiça
7 Escola Ferroviária de Moçambique

PLACES TO EAT
11 Ti Jamú
13 Á Maçaroca
15 Restaurante Tic-Tic

OTHER
2 Old Mosque
3 New Mosque
4 Museum
5 Governor's Mansion
6 New Cathedral
8 Banco Austral
9 Cathedral of Nossa Senhora de Conceição
10 Ferry & Dhows to Maxixe
12 Telecom Building
14 Centro de Pesquisa e Informática (Internet); Emilio Dausse Secondary School
16 Bus & Chapa Stand
17 Cinema

Inhambane Bay

Rua 3 de Fevereiro
Josina Machel Park
Rua da Vigilância
Rua dos Combatentes
Avenida da Independência
Train Station (disused)
Avenida de Moçambique
Avenida Eduardo Mondlane
Avenida Acordos de Lusaka
Avenida da Revolução
Market
To Airstrip (5km), Tofo & Barra Beaches
Inhambane Bay
Avenida Samora Machel
To ENI (35km)
0   150   300m
0   150   300yd

down the same road next to Emilio Dausse secondary school.

Places to Stay

Pensão Pachiça *(☎ 20565; dorm beds US$6; double rooms from US$16)* is a popular backpackers on the waterfront near the cathedral. In addition to dorm beds, it has a few no-frills private rooms, an outdoor restaurant/bar area, and a rooftop with sunset views. The owner is very helpful, and can assist with changing money, sightseeing, excursions etc. Coming off the ferry, Pensão Pachiça is about 300m down to the left.

Escola Ferroviária de Moçambique *(☎ 20781; rooms with/without fan US$12/ 10)*, by the train station at the eastern edge of town, is the only other option. It

has functional, reasonably clean attached doubles without nets, with a shared bathroom. From the ferry dock, continue straight through town to the end of the main road (Avenida da Independência).

Places to Eat

Á Maçaroca *(☎ 20489; mains around US$7)*, one block south of Avenida da Independência, is Inhambane's best, with prompt service, pleasant atmosphere and very good food.

For cheap meals, try **Restaurant Tic-Tic** near the market or **Ti Jamú** *(mains with bread & salad US$4)* near the pier.

Getting There & Away

Bus The bus station is behind the market. To Maputo, the best option is the Oliveiras' express (US$5, six to seven hours), departing daily at 6am. There's a second express at 11am, and a much slower ordinary bus at 7am (US$3). TSL also has daily departures at 6am. For other southbound buses, and for all northbound transport, take the ferry to Maxixe, and catch a bus there.

There's a local bus called TUCI that runs several times daily between Inhambane and Tofo (US$0.15, one hour), also stopping at Conguiana (for Barra).

Boat An old and precipitously overloaded ferry runs throughout the day between Inhambane and Maxixe (US$0.25, 25 minutes). Dhows do the trip for US$0.15. The first boats to Maxixe start leaving at dawn.

AROUND INHAMBANE

There are many good beaches nearby. Tofo and Barra – the most popular – are covered later in this chapter. About 30km south of Inhambane is Pandane beach, where **Paindane Beach Resort** *(Ⓦ www.paindane.com; camping per person US$6; 4-person chalets US$50)* offers snorkelling, camping and basic self-catering chalets. North of here is Guinjata Bay, where **Guinjata Bay** *(Ⓦ www.guinjata.com; camping per person US$6, 4-person self-catering chalets US$85)* has camping and chalets, and can arrange fishing charters. Further north is Jangamo, where **Jangamo Beach Resort** *(Ⓦ www.jangamo.co.za; 4-person bungalows about US$50)* has simple bungalows, plus rooms in a main house that can be rented in its entirety. All places require a 4WD

MOZAMBIQUE

for access. Most can also organise transfers to/from Inhambane.

Linga Linga

Ponta Linga Linga, with the no-frills **Linga Linga (Funky Monkey)** *(camp sites US$5, dorm beds US$5)*, is a popular stop on the southern Mozambique backpackers' trail. It's about 15km north of Inhambane, and accessible only by boat.

To get here, take a *chapa* to Morrumbene (US$0.50 from Maxixe, US$2 from Vilankulo), then walk about 20 minutes to the water (ask for the 'ponta' if you need directions from a local) to catch a dhow to Linga Linga (US$0.50). The dhows depart about 11am daily except Sunday. You can also hire your own dhow (US$4, best arranged before 3pm due to tides and winds). Once in Linga Linga, you'll need to walk another couple of kilometres to the campsites. It is usually possible to hire a dhow in Inhambane to take you to Linga Linga (about US$5). Ask at Pensão Pachiça or at the port.

If you do get stuck in Morrumbene, **Pousada do Litoral** *(rooms around US$8)* on the main road has basic rooms.

TOFO
☎ 023

Tofo has long been legendary on the southern Africa holiday makers' scene, with its azure waters, long stretches of sand and easy access. The town has a bustling vacation-time atmosphere, with a good selection of places to stay. Just to the south and easily accessed from Tofo is **Tofinho**, known for its surfing.

Diving

The best place to arrange diving is at the friendly and efficient **Diversity Scuba** *(☎ 29002; e info@diversityscuba.com; w www.diversityscuba.com)* in the town centre. Staff are experienced and helpful, and they offer PADI certification courses. Other dive shops in the area include **Tofo Scuba** *(☎ 082 826014; e tofo.scuba@mantascuba .com)* at Casa Barry (see Places to Stay & Eat following), and **Manta Divers** at Bamboozi's (also see Places to Stay & Eat). Prices at all of these places average US$30/ 125 for a single dive/five-dive package, and US$180 for an open-water course.

Places to Stay & Eat

Bamboozi *(☎/fax 29004; e bamboozi@tele data.mz; w www.bamboozi.com; camping US$4, dorm beds US$6, 'honeymoon hut' US$13)* is one of the best backpackers' in the region, with great dorm facilities, hot water ablutions, a self-catering area, and a dune-top bar/restaurant with superb views over the sea. There's also a 'honeymoon hut', and some self-contained bungalows are planned. It's about 3km north of town and signposted.

Just south of here on the beach is the low-key **Fatima's Backpackers** *(e fatima@ virconn.com; camping with your/their tent US$3/4, dorm bed US$6, 2-person bungalow US$25)*, under the same management as Fatima's Backpackers in Maputo, and just getting started as we passed through. They have camping, simple bungalows and a kitchen, and can help with pick-ups from Inhambane and excursions.

Nordin's Lodge *(☎ 29009; chalets US$21)* is a quiet place south of here, and at the far northern end of town, with a good beachfront location, and accommodation in several pleasant, thatched four-person chalets with bathroom and fridge. Self-catering facilities are available for an extra US$1.

Hotel Marinhos *(☎ 29015, fax 29002; singles/doubles with sea view US$35/60)*, on the beach in the town centre, is the main midrange place and the only hotel (ie, non-chalet style place). It has pleasant rooms – some overlooking the sea – and a restaurant.

Casa Barry *(☎ 29007, ☎/fax South Africa 031-207 8422; camp sites US$5, dorm beds US$7, 4-person chalets US$56)*, on a hill at the southern end of town, is popular and often full. In the back of the compound are simple dorms and a camping area, and to the front on a low hill overlooking the water are pleasant thatched self-catering chalets.

For meals, try **Restaurante Ferroviário** *(☎ 29018; open Tues-Sun)* found at the main junction.

Bar Babalaza, 15km from Inhambane where the roads to Tofo and Barra diverge, is a local institution, with a very helpful owner, good meals, drinks, air for your tyres, and lots of information on the area.

Getting There & Away

There are *chapas* throughout the day along the 22km sealed road between Tofo and Inhambane, with the first departure from

Tofo about 6am. The TUCI bus also does the route several times daily (US$0.15). There's no direct transport to Maputo or points north; you'll need to go via Inhambane or Maxixe, which means that to catch a north or southbound express bus, you'll need to stay in Inhambane the night before.

BARRA
☎ 023

Barra is quieter than Tofo and not as well connected via public transport, but its good beaches draw a steady stream of visitors.

Palm Grove Lodge (*☎ 082 45997, South Africa 013-744 9110; camp sites per person US$5; 4/8-person chalets per day US$40/80*) is the first place you come to, with no-frills thatched chalets set behind some sand dunes, ablution blocks and power points, and prices that are often negotiable.

Barra Lodge (*☎ 20561, South Africa 011-314 3355; e barralodge@teledata.mz; camp sites US$6, dorm beds US$7, 2-/3-/4-person chalets US$35/25/22 per person with half-board*) is next up and the largest and most developed of the places. It offers a full range of activities, including diving, water sports and horseback riding, plus fly-in packages from Jo'burg.

Barra Reef (*☎ 20864, 082 307849; e moz barrareef@hotmail.com; camp sites US$7, 5- or 6-person chalets about US$70*), about 1km further on, has the nicest setting directly on the beach, with no dunes in between as at the other places. Accommodation is in pleasant self-catering chalets, and there's a beachside restaurant.

Apart from the restaurants at Barra Lodge and Barra Reef, there are no shops or restaurants, but you can buy fish from the local fishermen.

Getting There & Away
The turn-off for Barra is about 15km from Inhambane on the road to Tofo. The TUCI bus between Inhambane and Tofo stops at Conguiana village, from where it's about 4km on foot to Barra unless you've arranged a pick-up. Hitching is easy on weekends from Bar Babalaza.

MASSINGA
☎ 023

Massinga, a bustling district capital, has mid-range accommodation and meals at

Dalilo's Hotel along the main road at the northern end of town.

Several kilometres further north is the signposted turn-off for **Morrungulo Beach Resort** (*☎ South Africa 011-783 7116; e bookings@divetheworld.co.za; camp sites US$9, self-catering 4-person chalets US$120*), a large complex on a beautiful stretch of beach. Fishing and diving can be arranged. It's 13km from the main road; sporadic *chapas* will take you to within about 5km.

VILANKULO
☎ 023

Vilankulo is the finishing (or starting) point of Mozambique's popular southern tourist circuit, and the gateway for visiting the nearby Bazaruto Archipelago. During holidays, it's overrun with 4WDs, but otherwise it is very quiet.

There's an ATM at the **Banco Internacional de Moçambique (BIM)** bank at the northern end of town, and Internet access at **Casa de Cultura** near the market. The helpful **Tourist Services** near Baobab Beach backpackers sells maps of town and can assist with information and arranging excursions.

Vilankulo is very spread out and there are no taxis, though finding a lift is usually easy.

Diving & Snorkelling
Vilankulo offers some highly rewarding diving and snorkelling around the reefs and islands of the Bazaruto Archipelago. **Vilanculos Dive Charters** (*contact through Aguia Negra Lodge, see Places to Stay – Mid-Range & Top End*) is the main operator. Single/double dives including equipment and time relaxing on Benguera Island cost US$45/75 per person, and various package deals are available, as is PADI open water instruction. It also arranges day snorkelling trips to Santa Carolina Island (US$40 per person, minimum five), and island transfers elsewhere in the archipelago. March to June, and November are the best months, and February (due to rain) is the worst.

Dhow Safaris
Sail Away (*☎ 82385; w www.dhowsafari.com*) is an excellent contact for budget travellers, offering day and overnight dhow safaris among the islands of the Bazaruto Archipelago. Prices are very reasonable: a day trip including snorkelling around Magaruque

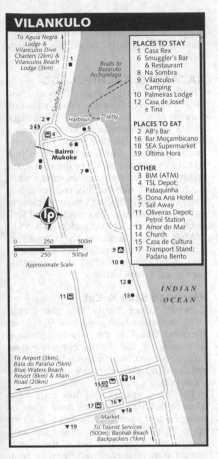

VILANKULO

To Aguia Negra
Lodge &
Vilanculos Dive
Charters (2km) &
Vilanculos Beach
Lodge (3km)

Sandy Track

Boats to
Bazaruto
Archipelago

Harbour — Jetty

Bairro
Mukoke

PLACES TO STAY
1 Casa Rex
6 Smuggler's Bar
& Restaurant
8 Na Sombra
9 Vilanculos
Camping
10 Palmeiras Lodge
12 Casa de Josef
e Tina

PLACES TO EAT
2 AB's Bar
16 Bar Moçambicano
18 SEA Supermarket
19 Última Hora

OTHER
3 BIM (ATM)
4 TSL Depot;
Pataquinha
5 Dona Ana Hotel
7 Sail Away
11 Oliveiras Depot;
Petrol Station
13 Amor do Mar
14 Church
15 Casa de Cultura
17 Transport Stand;
Padaria Bento

0   250   500m
0   250   500yd
Approximate Scale

INDIAN OCEAN

To Airport (3km),
Baía do Paraíso (5km)
Blue Waters Beach
Resort (8km) & Main
Road (20km)

Market

To Tourist Services
(500m); Baobab Beach
Backpackers (1km)

or Benguera island, a seafood lunch buffet, park entry fees and snorkelling equipment costs US$35, with discounts available for walk-ins. Overnight safaris range from two to four days and cost US$60 per person per day (discounts for walk-ins), including everything that the day trip includes, plus full board, and camping at Gabriel's Lodge on Benguera Island or staying overnight in one of the dhow's cabins. Sail Away's Vilankulo base is on the road parallel to the beach road, and about 400m south of the Dona Ana Hotel (ask for Dave and Emma). Diving can also be arranged.

Places to Stay – Budget

Vilanculos Camping (☎ 82043; *camp sites US$7; bungalows from US$15 per person,*

double rooms US$25) is a large, shaded and very nice camping area directly on the beach. There are ablution blocks, and some straightforward rooms and bungalows with bedding.

Baobab Beach (☎ 82202; ⓔ *2baker@bush mail.net; camping US$3, dorm beds US$4, chalets US$12)* is a popular backpackers with a good beachside setting, plenty of space to pitch a tent, a self-catering area, and a few chalets. If they're full, ask around as another backpackers is planned nearby.

Casa de Josef e Tina (☎ 82146; *rooms US$13)* is a friendly local-style place on the beach road offering camping, a self-catering area, and some basic, clean rooms.

Na Sombra (☎ 023-82090; *singles/doubles US$9/12),* near BIM at the northern end of town, has tiny, no-frills rooms with fan and shared bath, and a good **restaurant**.

Smuggler's Bar & Restaurant (☎ 82118; ⓔ *smugglers@teledata.mz; per person US$14),* near the Dona Ana Hotel, has nice, clean, well-ventilated rooms around a small yard. All have a fan and shared bathroom, there's secure parking, and family rooms are planned. The popular **restaurant** *(meals from US$2.50)* serves a good selection of pub food and full breakfasts.

Blue Waters Beach Resort (*camp sites US$5 per person, chalets from US$25),* about 8km out of town past the airport, has good camping and a restaurant, and is popular with holiday makers from Zimbabwe and South Africa. You'll need your own transport.

Places to Stay – Mid-Range & Top End

Palmeiras Lodge (☎ 82257, *or through Vilanculos Beach Lodge; dorm beds US$25, singles/doubles US$35/70)* is a new place with accommodation in nice white stone and thatch cottages set in attractive, grassy grounds bordering the beach.

Casa Rex (☎ 82048; ⓔ *casarex@teledata.mz; singles/doubles from US$45/90)* is a small, upmarket getaway with peaceful, manicured grounds, comfortable good-value rooms and delicious cuisine. It's at the northeastern edge of town, about 500m north of the Dona Ana Hotel. Rates include breakfast.

Aguia Negra Lodge (☎ 82387; ⓔ *aguian egra@teledata.mz;* Ⓦ *www.aguianegra.co.za; 6-person chalets US$150, singles/doubles US$45/70),* about 2km further along, is

MOZAMBIQUE

popular and good value. Accommodation is in breezy A-frame chalets set around a large, grassy compound overlooking the sea. Each has an open loft area and room to sleep six, plus a bathroom with hot water. Rates include breakfast, and there's a restaurant, a small pool and a resident dive operator.

Vilanculos Beach Lodge (☎ *South Africa 021-715 7011;* e *beachlodge@vilanclos.co.za;* w *www.vilanculos.co.za; singles/doubles US$92/140),* a large, resort-style place 1km further north, is similar, though not as good value. There's chalet-style accommodation, a restaurant and a range of water sports.

There's no public transport to any of these places, but lifts are easy to find. All can help you arrange trips to the islands.

Outside town to the east is **Baià do Paraiso**, a large resort run by Zimbabwe Sun hotels.

Places to Eat

Última Hora, 200m west of the market, has good, reasonably priced meals, as does **AB's Bar** at the northern edge of town.

SEA Supermarket, near the market, is the best supermarket. **Bar Moçambicano** nearby has cheap snacks.

Getting There & Away

Air LAM flies three times weekly to/from Maputo (US$145 one way), and **TTA** (☎ *82348, 82149, South Africa 011 973 6349;* e *tta@icon.co.za)* has flights six times weekly between Jo'burg and Vilankulo (about US$350 return). The airport is about 3km from town. There are no taxis, so you'll need to arrange a lift with a hotel, or hitch (which usually easy).

Bus & Chapa Vilankulo lies 20km east of the main road. Some buses come into town, while others drop you at the intersection, from where you'll need to take a *chapa* to the centre (US$0.50).

Oliveiras has daily buses to Maputo (US$7.50, nine to 10 hours, departing 4.30am) and Chimoio (US$7, 10 hours, departing 5.30am), departing from their depot on the main road about 1km north of the roundabout. For Beira, you'll need to get out at Inchope and catch a *chapa* from there. TSL also has daily buses to Maputo departing around 5am from their depot at the northern end of town near Pataquinha's bar.

All buses stop at Padaria Bento (bakery) near the market to collect passengers before leaving town. *Chapas* depart from Padaria Bento.

BAZARUTO ARCHIPELAGO

The Bazaruto Archipelago, 10km to 25km offshore between Vilankulo and Inhassoro, consists of five main islands – Magaruque (Santa Isabel), Benguera (Santo António), Santa Carolina ('Paradise Island'), Bazaruto and tiny Bangué. Much of the area is protected as a national park. For the visitor, the archipelago offers stunning turquoise waters, sandy beaches, rich birdlife, and rewarding diving and snorkelling. It's about as close to a tropical paradise as you can get, and well worth a visit. Entry to the park costs US$4.

Most visitors come on fly-in packages from South Africa, arranged through one of the top-end lodges, all of which also arrange diving and fishing charters.

Places to Stay & Eat

Gabriel's Lodge (*camp sites per person US$8; bungalows from per person US$15)* on Benguera Island, is the only backpackers, with camping and simple bungalow-style accommodation, an ablutions block and a restaurant (no self-catering) with meals from about US$5.

The other options (all top end) need advance bookings with their head office or through a tour operator, although if you turn up at Vilanculo or Inhassoro and talk to a boat owner with a radio link to the islands you can often arrange something on the spot. Rates are between US$130 and US$300 per person per night sharing, with full board.

On Benguera Island, there's **Benguerra Lodge** (☎ *South Africa 011-483 2734, fax 011-728 3767;* e *benguela@icon.co.za)* and **Marlin Lodge** (☎ *South Africa 012-543 2134;* w *www.marlinlodge.co.za).*

Bazaruto Island has **Bazaruto Lodge** (☎ *01-305000, fax 305305)* and **Indigo Bay** (☎ *South Africa 011-465 6904;* e *reservations@raniafrica.co.za).*

The **hotels** on Magaruque and Santa Carolina islands are slated for renovation.

Getting There & Away

Air For flights to/from Maputo, see Getting There & Away under Vilankulo earlier in this chapter.

Boat The top-end lodges provide speedboat transfers for guests, often included in the quote; otherwise it's about US$100 return. For day visitors, a speedboat from Vilankulo costs between US$80 and US$200 return, depending on the island.

Alternatively, you can go by dhow from Vilankulo or Inhassoro. In Vilankulo, places to arrange this include Sail Away (see Dhow Safaris under Vilankulo earlier in this chapter), and **Amor do Mar** (☎ 82067), on the beach road near Casa de Josef e Tina in Vilankulo. Expect to pay from about US$15 per person for a one-way transfer to Gabriel's Lodge, and from about US$65 per boat for a day sail. Vilankulo Dive Charters (see Diving & Snorkelling in the Vilankulo section, earlier) also arranges boat transfers.

For nonmotorised dhows, allow plenty of extra time to account for wind and water conditions; from Vilankulo to Benguera or Magaruque takes two to six hours.

INHASSORO

Inhassoro is a jumping-off point for Bazaruto and Santa Carolina Islands, and a popular destination for South African anglers. The best place to stay is **Hotel Seta** (☎ 082 302099; *camp sites US$5, chalets about US$30*), which has camping, and accommodation in white stone cottages with some thatching. There's a restaurant and the hotel can assist with motorboat transfers to the archipelago.

Inhassoro is about 15km east of the main road. Oliveiras has a daily bus to Maputo (US$11). There's also at least one bus daily northwards.

Central Mozambique

Central Mozambique – here, the provinces of Sofala, Manica, Tete and Zambézia – is seldom visited in comparison with the southern beaches. However, it's an important transit zone for travel to/from Malawi and Zimbabwe, and chances are good you'll at least pass through.

Among the attractions are the beautiful hill landscapes of western Manica and northwestern Zambézia, with vast, parched baobab-studded tracts around Tete, and their intriguing cultures. Thanks to the proximity of Zimbabwe, and Malawi, you'll encounter more English speakers here than elsewhere in the country. Places are described roughly south to north.

BEIRA
☎ 03

Beira, Mozambique's second-largest city, owes its existence to development of its port (the country's busiest) and construction of the railway from Zimbabwe. Although it has long suffered under a somewhat tarnished image, it's not a bad place, with a faded colonial-era ambience and a short stretch of coastline.

About 40km south was the ancient gold-trading port of **Sofala**, dating from at least the 9th century. In its heyday, Sofala was one of East Africa's most influential centres, with links to Kilwa (Tanzania), Madagascar, India and even Indonesia. San Caetano, the first Portuguese fort in Mozambique (1505), was built here with stones shipped from Portugal. Today, nothing remains of Sofala's former glory, and the ruins of the fort have been taken over by the sea.

Orientation

The heart of the city are the adjacent squares of Praça do Município and Praça do Metical, with shops, banks and telecom facilities nearby. North of here is the old commercial area with the LAM office, BIM and the port. Various streets lead south and east from Praça do Município to Avenida das FPLM, which runs for several kilometres along the ocean past the hospital, to Makuti Beach and the lighthouse.

Information

Banco Internacional de Moçambique (BIM) has ATMs (Visa) at the airport, at BIM's headquarters near the port (look for the pink building between Praça do Metical and the LAM office), and in Makuti, signposted from the main road near Biques (see Places to Stay).

Banco Standard Totta on Praça do Metical sometimes is willing to change Thomas Cook travellers cheques.

For Internet access try **Teledata**, opposite the Telecom Building.

For medical emergencies, try the **health clinic** on Avenida Poder Popular, just north of Praça do Metical.

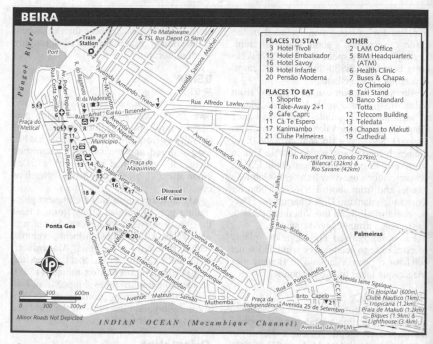

BEIRA

PLACES TO STAY	OTHER
3 Hotel Tivoli	2 LAM Office
15 Hotel Embaixador	5 BIM Headquarters;
16 Hotel Savoy	(ATM)
18 Hotel Infante	6 Health Clinic
20 Pensão Moderna	7 Buses & Chapas
	to Chimoio
PLACES TO EAT	8 Taxi Stand
1 Shoprite	10 Banco Standard
4 Take-Away 2+1	Totta
9 Cafe Capri;	12 Telecom Building
11 Cà Te Espero	13 Teledata
17 Kanimambo	14 Chapas to Makuti
21 Clube Palmeiras	19 Cathedral

Things to See & Do

The **cathedral** (*Avenida Eduardo Mondlane*), southeast of the centre, was built in the early 20th century with stones from the fort at San Caetano in Sofala. Near the **port** are many colonial era buildings. East of the centre is **Praia de Makuti** (Makuti Beach), an attractive beach with a few places to stay and eat.

Clube Náutico on Avenida das FPLM has a **swimming pool** (*US$2 per day*). For **crafts**, try the vendors near Clube Náutico or Tropicana restaurant.

Places to Stay – Budget

Biques (☎ *313051;* e *biques@teledata.mz; camp sites per person US$3*) on Makuti Beach has seaside camping with hot showers, a popular bar and a good **restaurant**. Take any *chapa* heading to Makuti and ask them to drop you at the turnoff, from where it's about 400m further on foot. A hire taxi costs about US$3.

Pensão Moderna (☎ *324537, 329901; Rua Alferes da Silva; doubles/triples US$12/18*) is one of the better budget choices. Rooms are basic but adequate, with a fan and shared

bathroom, and there's a **restaurant**. It's two blocks south of the cathedral, and opposite the park with an old aeroplane in the centre; all the taxi drivers know it.

Hotel Savoy (*Rua Major Sepia Pinto, rooms about US$10*), near Hotel Embaixador, is also worth a look, with no-frills rooms and a convenient central location.

Rio Savane (☎ *Zimbabwe 04-495470; camp sites per person US$7, 4-person bungalows US$100*) is a rustic place about 40km north of town in a relaxing setting on the Savane River. It offers camping with ablutions, a few self-catering chalets (bring your own linen) and a restaurant. You'll need your own vehicle (4WD). Take the Dondo road past the airport to the right-hand turn-off for Savane. Continue 35km to the estuary, where there's secure parking and a boat (until 5pm) to take you to the camp site.

Places to Stay – Mid-Range & Top End

Hotel Infante (☎ *326603, 323041; just off the southern extension singles/doubles with fan US$21/23, with air-con US$23/25*), in a high-rise building near Hotel Embaixador, is

a friendly place with small, clean rooms with bathroom, and a restaurant.

Hotel Embaixador (☎ 323121; just off Rua Major Serpa Pinto; singles/doubles US$36/48, with air-con, TV & hot water US$52/60), a few blocks southeast of Praça do Município, used to be Beira's top hotel. These days, most business travellers prefer the new Hotel Tivoli, so the Embaixador is usually empty, with a down-at-the-heel feel. The location is convenient, though, rooms are spacious, and it's worth a look.

Hotel Tivoli (☎ 320300, fax 320301; e h.tivoli-beira@teledata.mz; cnr Avenida de Bagamoio & Rua da Madeira; singles/doubles US$77/94) is Beira's best, and frequented by business travellers. Rooms are small but clean and well-appointed, with TV and air-con. There's a restaurant and a guarded parking area, and breakfast is included in the prices.

Places to Eat

Café Capri (Praça do Município) has pastries and light meals, and is a good place to watch the passing scene.

Take-Away 2 + 1 (Praça do Maquinino; open daily from 7am; meals about US$3) has a takeaway counter, and a better air-con restaurant inside serving local dishes and standard fare.

Kanimambo (open lunch & dinner Sun-Fri; main dishes about US$4) behind Hotel Embaixador is pricier but well worth the splurge, with good Chinese food and a friendly proprietor.

Cà Te Espero (☎ 082-447886; meals from US$4), opposite the Telecom Building, features meat and seafood dishes in a pub-style atmosphere.

The main expat hangouts are along Avenida das FPLM towards Makuti, including **Tropicana**, overlooking the beach, with a good seafood selection; **Clube Palmeiras** (☎ 312947), known for its bife pedra (steak on a rock); and the restaurant at **Biques** (see Places to Stay – Budget earlier in this section). Meals at all cost from about US$5.

The best-stocked supermarket is **Shoprite** (cnr Avenidas Armando Tivane & Samora Machel).

Getting There & Away

Air As well as flying between Beira and Maputo daily, **LAM** (☎ 324141; 85 Rua Costa Serrão) also goes to Tete, Nampula, Quelimane, Pemba and Lichinga several times weekly. There are flights twice weekly to Harare, and several times weekly to Jo'burg. **STA** (☎ 302170) at the airport has flights to Maputo and Quelimane.

Bus & Chapa There's at least one bus most days to Maputo (about US$19, 17 hours). TSL is probably the best, with departures from its depot in Matakwane, 2km northeast of town, and reached by chapa from Praça do Maquinino in the town centre. Other lines depart from Praça do Maquinino. All departures are around 4.30am.

To Vilankulo (US$7; 10 to 12 hours), TSL sometimes has a direct bus. Otherwise, you'll need to take any southbound bus, and have them drop you at the junction, and take a chapa for the remaining 20km.

To Chimoio (US$2.50) and Machipanda (US$3.50) there are minibuses throughout the day from Praça do Maquinino.

To Tete (US$6), it's best to go to Chimoio and get transport there. This will mean staying overnight in Chimoio since transport to Tete leaves in the morning.

Most transport to Quelimane leaves from 'Bilança', about 30km from Beira past Dondo. Take any chapa from Praça do Maquinino towards Mafumbisse and have them drop you Bilança. As the stretch between Beira and Caia (US$6) is rough, many people splurge on a flight to Quelimane, or go via Tete and Malawi. If you take the direct route via Caia, you'll need to travel by truck and in stages; allow two days for the whole journey by public transport, or six to eight hours between Beira and Caia in a private vehicle. At Caia there's a vehicle ferry (about US$5 per vehicle) which – as well as having frequent mechanical problems – can only run when the water levels are right. Backpackers can cross by dugout canoe, but if you're driving, you'll need to inquire locally about whether the ferry is operating. Once over the Zambezi, there's regular transport on to Quelimane (US$3.50). A new road that runs from Beira via Inchope along the western edge of Gorongosa National Park to Caia should be opening soon that will make all this much easier. Chapas between Beira and Inchope (US$1.50) run throughout the day.

Getting Around

To/From the Airport The airport is about 7km northwest of town (about US$6 in a taxi).

Bus & Chapa *Chapas* to Makuti (US$0.15) leave from Rua Major Serpa Pinto near Hotel Embaixador. Most other transport, including to Chimoio, leaves from Praça do Maquinino.

The main taxi stand (☎ 322921 to call a cab) is just west of Praça do Maquinino. A trip from the centre to Makuti costs US$3.

Car Based at the airport are **Imperial** (☎ 302650, fax 302651) and **Avis** (☎ 301263).

CHIMOIO
☎ 051

Chimoio, capital of Manica Province, is a low-key place with an agreeable climate. About 5km northeast of town is **Cabeça do Velho**, a large rock resembling the face of an old man at rest. To get here, head past the market on Rua do Bárue. From the base, you can reach the top in about 10 minutes for some views.

About 35km west of Chimoio is the signposted turn-off for **Chicamba Real Dam**, a popular weekend getaway. To the southwest on the Zimbabwe border is **Mt Binga** (2436m), Mozambique's highest peak. It's best climbed from Zimbabwe (see Chimanimani National Park in the Zimbabwe chapter for more details).

You can change cash at **BCM** (*Avenida 25 de Setembro*) and at Banco Standard Totta across the street.

Places to Stay & Eat

It's usually possible to arrange camping with **Chicoteca** restaurant, 5km out of town. Follow the main road west to the signposted turnoff. Go south from here for about 500m, then left for 250m, then left again to the restaurant. *Chapas* heading to Machipanda will drop you at the turnoff.

Pensão Flor de Vouga (☎ 22027, 22169; *Rua do Barue; rooms US$10*), near the post office, and the nicer **Residencial Flor de Vouga** (☎ 22469; *Avenida 25 de Setembro; doubles with shared bathroom US$20*), one block south, have basic no-frills rooms.

Motel Moinho (☎ 23130; *rooms from US$15*), about 2.5km outside town off the Beira road, is a better bet. Rooms are simple but acceptable, and there's a restaurant.

Executive Manica Hotel (☎ 23135; *singles/doubles US$40/60*) is a big step up. We've also heard about **Castel Blanco** (*Rua Sussendenga; rooms US$42*), which is used by many business travellers.

Casa Msika (☎ 22675, or Zimbabwe 011-603719; *camp sites per person US$2, doubles US$15, 3-bed rondavels US$25*) at Chicamba Real Dam is popular with Zimbabwean anglers. It's 4km south of the main road; the signposted turn-off is 45km west of Chimoio. There's no public transport from the turnoff, but hitching is easy on weekends.

Feira Popular, at the southern edge of town, has several good local food restaurants, including the long-standing **Maua**. For Western fare, try **Elo 4** (*Avenida 25 de Setembro; dishes from US$7*), opposite the government building, with Italian dishes, and **O Quintal** (*Avenida 25 de Setembro*) nearby, with good pizzas.

Getting There & Away

All transport leaves from near the train station. TSL buses depart at 5am daily for Tete (US$5, six hours), and Oliveiras departs about 5am for Vilankulo. There are frequent *chapas* to/from Manica (US$1) and the border, and frequent minibuses and *chapas* to/from Beira (US$2.50, three hours).

GORONGOSA NATIONAL PARK

About 65km east of Chimoio is the turn-off for Gorongosa National Park (*admission US$20*), once one of Southern Africa's best wildlife parks before it was destroyed by poaching and the war. Rehabilitation work has begun, but only basic infrastructure is in place. Little remains of the park's earlier wildlife, including lions for which it was renowned, and those animals that are there are very skittish. The beautiful, dense foliage also complicates viewing. However, with luck, you may still see impalas, hippos and the occasional elephant. More accessible is the park's rich birdlife, including several endemic species.

Entry includes use of the park's camp site. You'll need to bring everything in with you, and have your own 4WD.

In Gorongosa village on the western edge of the park, and along the new road between

Caia and Inchope, is a basic **pensão** (rooms US$4) with a restaurant.

MANICA
☎ 051

Tiny Manica, 70km west of Chimoio, lies in what was once the heart of the kingdom of Manica and an important gold-trading area. Most people who pass through stop to visit the **Chinamapere rock paintings**, about 5km from town and signposted from the centre. The site is considered sacred, and before you can visit, there's an elderly woman who will conduct a brief prayer ceremony. According to tradition, no pregnant or menstruating women can visit.

About 20km north of Manica are the **Penha Longa Mountains**, which straddle the border with Zimbabwe. The area – home to the Shona people – offers pleasant scenery and good walking (stick to the beaten path).

Flamingo just west of the market and **São Cristovão** next door have basic rooms for US$8. Signposted about 1.5km further west and 500m south of the main road is **Manica Lodge** (rooms about US$20), with reasonable rooms and a **restaurant**.

Chapas run frequently to/from Chimoio (US$1) and to the border, and several times daily from Manica market to Penha Longa (US$1). To get to the rock paintings, go west from Manica along the main road about 3km, and then south along a dirt road, following signs for *pinturas rupestres*.

TETE
☎ 052

Tete was an important trading outpost well before the arrival of the Portuguese and today continues to be a major transport junction. There are few tourist attractions and Tete's reputation as one of the hottest places in Mozambique often discourages visitors. Yet, the dusty, brown landscape dotted with baobab trees and cut by the wide swathe of the Zambezi River gives it a unique charm and an atmosphere quite unlike that of Mozambique's other provincial capitals.

BCM changes cash. The immigration office is a few blocks uphill from Hotel Zambeze.

Places to Stay & Eat

Hotel Zambeze (singles/doubles US$8/10, with air-con US$16/20), opposite BCM, offers cheap lodging, with undistinguished rooms. **Piscina** (rooms around US$25) on the riverbank is several notches up, and there's a **restaurant**.

Motel Tete (☎ 23467, 23498; rooms around US$50), just past Piscina, is the most upscale place and Tete's only real hotel, with self-contained air-con rooms and a **restaurant**.

Getting There & Away

Air With flights (three weekly) connecting Tete with Maputo, **LAM** (☎ 2055; Avenida 24 de Julho) also flys to Beira, Lichinga, Nampula and Quelimane (once or twice weekly). **STA** (☎ 22670) at the airport has twice weekly flights linking Tete with Chimoio and Songo. The airport is 6km out of town on the Moatize road.

Bus & Chapa *Chapas* to Moatize leave frequently from the bus stand near immigration (US$0.15).

Chapas to Chimoio (US$5) depart from Mercado 1 de Maio. Once in Chimoio, there's a daily Oliveiras bus on to Vilankulo, departing at 5am.

For Malawi, *chapas* run frequently to Zóbuè and sporadically to Dedza from Mercado da OUA on the western side of town. At the border you'll need to change to Malawian transport. The daily TSL bus from Chimoio departs Hotel Kassuende in Tete about 10.30am, continuing to Zóbuè. Alternatively, catch the bus that runs near Tete on its route between Harare and Blantyre.

For Harare, a few vehicles go direct to the border – otherwise take a *chapa* to Changara (US$2.50) and get transport from there. Departures are from Mercado 1 de Maio, 300m south of Hotel Kassuende. Alternatively, wait at the intersection of the bridge road and the road to Harare and try to catch one of the buses running between Blantyre and Harare, though this will be more expensive.

For Zambia, take a Moatize *chapa* over the bridge past the SOS compound to the petrol station, where you'll find *chapas* to Matema. From Matema, there's infrequent transport to Cassacatiza (on the border). There's no direct transport from Tete to the border town of Zumbo.

CAHORA BASSA DAM & SONGO
☎ 052

About 150km northwest of Tete near the town of Songo is Cahora Bassa Dam, one

of the world's largest dams. It harnesses the waters of the Zambezi River, creating the massive Cahora Bassa Lake to the west. The dam is at the head of a magnificent gorge in the mountains and makes a good excursion from Tete. Tours are possible only on certain days. For information, inquire at the Tete offices of Hidreléctrica de Cahora Bassa (HCB, pronounced ach-seh-beh) near the immigration office, a few blocks uphill from Hotel Zambeze.

In Songo, **Pousada Sete Montes** *(rooms around US$12)* has basic rooms with hot running water, and a restaurant.

STA (☎ 82592) flies three times weekly between Tete and Songo.

Chapas from Tete to Songo (US$3) depart several times daily from Mercado 1 de Maio. From Songo, it's another 6km down to the dam; you'll have to walk or hitch.

QUELIMANE
☎ 04
Quelimane is the capital of Mozambique's densely populated Zambézia province and heartland of the Chuabo people. It stands on the site of an old Muslim trading settlement built on the banks of the Bons Sinais (Qua Qua) River in the days when it was linked to the River Zambezi. At one time it was the main entry port to the interior. Few traces of Quelimane's long history are evident today, and almost no old buildings remain, but the town's compact size and energetic atmosphere make it an agreeable stop. The main sights are the abandoned Portuguese **cathedral** on the waterfront, and the nearby **mosque**. Well outside town are several attractive **beaches**.

Places to Stay
Pensão Ideal *(Avenida Filipe Samuel Magaia; rooms from US$8)* and **Hotel 1 de Julho** (☎ 213067; doubles US$14), several blocks away on the same street near the old cathedral, are the main budget places. Both see a fair amount of business by the hour, and the rooms could all use a good scrub, but they're worth a look if your budget is tight.

Hotel Zambeze *(☎ 215490; Avenida Acordos de Lusaka; singles/doubles without bathroom US$15/20, with bathroom US$25/ 27)* is a step up, with tolerable rooms and a restaurant.

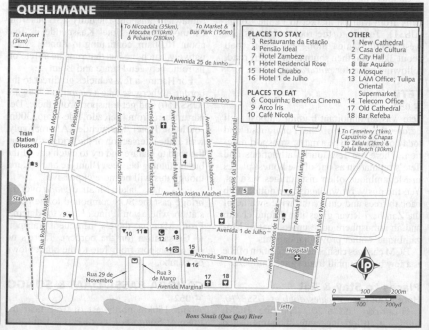

QUELIMANE

To Airport (3km)

To Nicoadala (35km), Mocuba (110km) & Pebane (280km)

To Market & Bus Park (150m)

Avenida 25 de Junho

Avenida 7 de Setembro

Rua de Moçambique

Rua Ga Resistência

Avenida Eduardo Mondlane

Avenida Paulo Samuel Kankhomba

Avenida Filipe Samuel Magaia

Avenida dos Trabalhadores

Avenida Heróis da Liberdade Nacional

Train Station (Disused)

Stadium

Rua Roberto Mugabe

Avenida Josina Machel

Avenida Francisco Manyanga

Avenida Acordos de Lusaka

Avenida Július Nyerere

To Cemetery (1km), Capuzinio & Chapas to Zalala (2km) & Zalala Beach (30km)

Avenida 1 de Julho

Hospital

Avenida Samora Machel

Rua 29 de Novembro

Rua 3 de Março

Avenida Marginal

Bons Sinais (Qua Qua) River

Jetty

PLACES TO STAY
3 Restaurante da Estação
4 Pensão Ideal
7 Hotel Zambeze
11 Hotel Residencial Rose
15 Hotel Chuabo
16 Hotel 1 de Julho

PLACES TO EAT
6 Coquinha; Benefica Cinema
9 Arco Íris
10 Café Nícola

OTHER
1 New Cathedral
2 Casa de Cultura
5 City Hall
8 Bar Aquário
12 Mosque
13 LAM Office; Tulipa Oriental Supermarket
14 Telecom Office
17 Old Cathedral
18 Bar Refeba

0   100   200m
0   100   200yd

MOZAMBIQUE

Hotel-Residencial Rose (☎ 214969; Avenida 1 de Julho; rooms US$25) near the central mosque has air-con rooms with TV, a fan and bathroom (water supplies are erratic), and there's a small restaurant.

Restaurante da Estação (rooms about US$40), near the train station, has a few rooms and is the most comfortable place. It's popular with aid workers and expats and usually full. The good **restaurant** (open Tues-Sun) serves pizza and Italian meals.

Hotel Chuabo (☎ 213181, fax 213812; Avenida Samora Machel; singles/doubles US$85/115) is a Quelimane institution, with large, faded rooms with TV, fridge and air-con. They're overpriced at the regular rates, but if you can negotiate reduced residents' rates, they're decent value.

Places to Eat
For snacks and light meals from about US$3, try **Café Nícola** (Avenida 1 de Julho). **Arco Íris** near the train station has air-con and a wider menu selection.

Coquinha (just off Avenida Josina Machel) has good Zambézian dishes. It's about 100m east of the Benefica cinema. We've also heard good things about **El Cubanito** in the town centre.

Tulipa Oriental supermarket next to the LAM office is well stocked.

Entertainment
Check with **Casa de Cultura** near the new cathedral for information about performances of Montes Namúli, Zambézia province's traditional dance group.

The most popular bars are **Bar Refeba** on the waterfront, and **Bar Aquário** in the gardens near City Hall.

Getting There & Away
Air There are flights several times weekly to/from Maputo, Beira, Lichinga and Nampula and weekly to/from Tete on **LAM** (☎ 04-212801; Avenida 1 de Julho), near Hotel Chuabo. **SAR** (☎ 082 841316; airport) flies twice weekly between Quelimane and Gurue, and **STA** (☎ 212686; airport) stops at Quelimane three times weekly on its route between Maputo and Nacala.

The airport is about 3km northwest of town – start walking and you'll find a lift, or call Quelimane's **taxi service** (☎ 212704, 212660).

Bus & Chapa The bus park is near the market at the northern edge of town. Chapas run frequently to/from Nicoadala on the main highway (US$1). The Grupo Mecula bus to Nampula (US$10, 10 to 12 hours) departs daily about 4.30am. Several vehicles run daily to Mocuba (US$2.50, two hours), for onward transport to Nampula via Alto Molócuè, or to Milange.

For information on travelling between Quelimane and Beira, see Getting There & Away under Beira, earlier in this chapter.

AROUND QUELIMANE
About 30km northeast of Quelimane is **Zalala**, a village on an attractive beach that fills up on weekends. The only lodging is **Complexo Kass-Kass** (☎ 04-212302; bungalows US$28) with unappealing four-person bungalows, and a mediocre restaurant. Chapas to Zalala (US$1) depart Quelimane from the Capuchin capuzinio (mission), about 1km from the cemetery on the Zalala road.

About 280km by road northeast of Quelimane is **Pebane**, once an important fishing port, and a favoured holiday destination during colonial times. For accommodation there's a basic **pensão** in town, and further developments planned for the nearby beach.

Pebane can be reached by public transport in slow stages via Namacurra, Olinga (Maganja) and Mucubela, or by 4WD.

MOCUBA
Mocuba is the junction town for travel from Quelimane to Nampula or Malawi. **Pensão Cruzeiro** (rooms US$10) on the main street has meals from US$3.

Transport to Quelimane (US$2, two hours) leaves from the market. Transport to Nampula (US$8) leaves from the northern end of the main street. There are several vehicles daily between Mocuba and Milange (US$4) departing from the market, though you'll maximise your chances of a lift by walking west past the airstrip to the Milange road junction.

MILANGE
Milange is on the border with southeastern Malawi. **Pensão Esplanade** (singles/doubles US$7/14) has no-frills rooms, and meals. The bank changes dollars and rand (cash only); moneychangers can help with Malawi kwacha. The road between Milange and

MOZAMBIQUE

Climbing Mt Namúli

Rising over Gurúè in the distance are the mist-shrouded slopes of Mt Namúli (2419m), from which flow the Licungo (Lugela) and Malema Rivers. The mountain is considered sacred by the local Makua people, so while climbing is permitted, you'll need to observe the local traditions. Before setting out buy some *farinha de mapira* (sorghum flour) and some rice at the market in Gurúè. (It shouldn't cost more than about US$0.50 for everything.) The climb begins about 6km outside Gurúè near UP5 (pronounced oo-pay-cinco), an old tea factory. To reach here, head south out of Gurúè along the Quelimane road. Go left after about 2km and continue several kilometres further to UP5. With a vehicle, you can drive to the factory and park there. With a 4WD it's also possible in the dry season to drive further up the mountain's slopes to Mugunha Sede, about 40km from Gurúè and the last village below the summit.

Shortly before reaching UP5 you'll see a narrow but obvious track branching left. Follow this as it winds through unrehabilitated tea plantations and stands of bamboo and forest, until it ends in a high, almost alpine, valley about 800m below the summit of Mt Namúli. The views en route are superb. On the edge of this valley is Mugunha Sede, where you should seek out the *régulo* (chief) and request permission to climb the mountain. If you don't speak Portuguese, bring someone along with you who knows either Portuguese or the local language, Makua. If you've come this far with a 4WD, you'll need to arrange to leave it here. The sorghum flour that you bought in Gurúè should be presented to the chief as a gift, who may save some to make traditional beer, and scatter the remainder on the ground to appease the ancestors who inhabit the area. The chief will then assign someone to accompany you to the top of the mountain, where another short ceremony may be performed for the ancestors.

About two-thirds of the way from the village is a spring where you can refill your water bottle, although it's considered a sacred spot and it may take some convincing to persuade your guide to show you where it is. Just after the spring, the climb becomes steeper, with some crumbling rock and places where you'll need to use your hands to clamber up. Once near the summit, the path evens out and then gradually ascends for another 1.5km to the mountain's highest point. The top of Namúli is often shrouded in clouds, so it's likely you will have better views during the climb than from the summit itself. After descending the mountain, present the rice that you bought at the Gurúè market to the chief as thanks.

There's no public transport on the mountain's lower slopes. If you want to walk to Mt Namúli from either Gurúè or the UP5 warehouse, you'll need to set out early and come equipped to camp. The best camping spot is in the high valley near Mugunha Sede. It's also possible to pitch a tent in the level area on the summit just below Namúli's highest point, although you may have to scratch around for a bit of earth. If you do this, the closest water source is the spring mentioned earlier, about a one-hour walk from the summit.

It's possible to do the climb in a long day from Gurúè if you drive as far as Mugunha Sede (allow about four hours), from where it's another three hours on foot to the summit. The road to Mugunha Sede has been rehabilitated and is in rough but decent condition, but a few of the bridges are rickety and difficult to drive over. En route, about 20km from Gurúè, is a bridge which isn't passable by 4WD (although a motorbike could make it over). During the dry season, you can negotiate this spot by going down through the riverbed.

Mocuba is fairly well travelled and finding a lift usually isn't a problem. For information on crossing the border, see Land under Getting There & Away, earlier in this chapter.

GURÚÈ

Gurúè has a beautiful setting in the hills amid lush vegetation and tea plantations in one of the coolest, highest and rainiest parts of the country. There are some good walks in the surrounding area, starting with a stroll through the jacarandas on the northern edge of town. Gurúè is also the starting point for climbing Mt Namúli (2419m), Mozambique's second highest peak (see the boxed text 'Climbing Mt Namúli' for details). Banks change cash only.

Pensão Gurúè (*rooms US$14*) on the main street has no-frills rooms with bathroom but no running water, and a **restaurant**.

Getting There & Away

SAR flies twice weekly between Gurué and Quelimane.

A few vehicles daily go to Quelimane, departing between 3am and 5am from near the market (US$5). Otherwise go to Mocuba (US$3), where you'll find transport to Quelimane. There's at least one vehicle daily to Alto Molócuè, for onward transport to Nampula.

Most private vehicles to/from Alto Molócuè go via Nauela or a parallel shortcut road, while most public transport goes via Errego and the Nampevo junction, where you'll most likely need to change vehicles.

The road to Cuamba is in decent shape, though there's little traffic. The best option to Cuamba is to go by road as far as Mutuáli, and then continue from there by train. There's usually at least one *chapa* daily from Gurué to Mutuáli, leaving in the morning. In Mutuali, you'll have to wait at least several hours for the Nampula–Cuamba train to arrive. To Milange, it's fastest to go via Mocuba.

ALTO MOLÓCUÈ

This pleasant town is a refuelling point between Mocuba and Nampula.

Pensão Santo António *(doubles US$12)* on the main square, has clean rooms and meals.

Several vehicles daily go to/from Mocuba (US$3, five hours) and Nampula (US$3, five hours).

Northern Mozambique

This section covers Mozambique's far north, including the provinces of Nampula, Niassa and Cabo Delgado. It's a scenic, topographically varied area, with Lake Niassa and the cool Lichinga Plateau to the west, dozens of massive and striking inselbergs between Cuamba and Nampula, and some idyllic beaches and islands along the coast. It's also fascinating culturally and historically – home to the large Makonde (see the boxed text 'The Makonde' earlier in this chapter for more on the Makonde) and Makua tribes, birthplace of the Mozambican independence struggle, and site of Ilha de Moçambique, one of the country's top tourist drawcards.

There's been considerable tourism development in recent years along the coast, and you should find something to suit, no matter what your tastes and budget. The far west along the shores of Lake Niassa is also opening up, though it's still very much a true bush experience.

NAMPULA
☎ 06

Nampula is Mozambique's third-largest city and the commercial centre of the north. While there aren't many tourist attractions here, the town has a pleasant, bustling feel, long wide avenues and a temperate climate, and isn't a bad place to spend a night or two. It's also a convenient transport hub en route to Ilha de Moçambique or other points north.

Information

There's an ATM at **Banco Internacional de Moçambique (BIM)** *(Avenida da Independência)*, and the bank may be able to help you out with cash advances on a credit card. For Internet access, try **Teledata** opposite the Telecom Building on Rua Monomatapa.

Things to See & Do

The **National Ethnography Museum** *(Avenida Eduardo Mondlane; open 2pm-4.30pm Tues-Thur & Sat, 2pm-6pm Fri, 10am-noon & 2pm-4pm Sun)* has explanations in English and Portuguese and is well worth a visit. Entrance is free, but donations are welcome.

There's a lively **Sunday Craft Market** near Hotel Tropical, a craft shop next to Café Carlos (see Places to Eat, following), and Makonde carvers behind the museum. The large **cathedral** is a major landmark.

Places to Stay

Pensão Estrela *(☎ 214902; Avenida Paulo Samuel Kankhomba; singles/doubles US$12/24, doubles with bathroom from US$16)* is the best budget place, with a central location and no-frills rooms with a fan. It's one block down from the post office.

Otherwise the budget pickings are slim. **Pensão Marques** *(☎ 212527; Avenida Paulo Samuel Kankhomba; rooms from US$19)* is probably the next best bet, though it's dingy and unappealing.

The better **Hotel Brasília** *(☎ 217531; singles/doubles US$27/31; Rua dos Continuadores)* has decent rooms with bathroom,

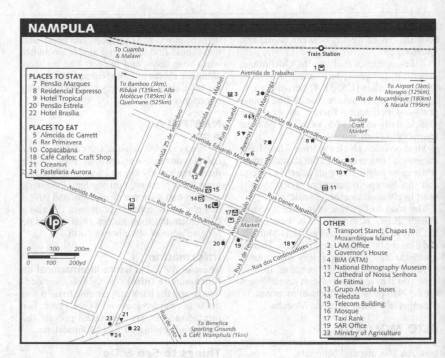

NAMPULA

PLACES TO STAY
7 Pensão Marques
8 Residencial Expresso
9 Hotel Tropical
20 Pensão Estrela
22 Hotel Brasilia

PLACES TO EAT
5 Almeida de Garrett
6 Bar Primavera
10 Copacabana
18 Café Carlos; Craft Shop
21 Oceanus
24 Pastelaria Aurora

To Cuamba & Malawi
Train Station
Avenida de Trabalho
To Bamboo (3km), Ribáuè (135km), Alto Molócue (185km) & Quelimane (525km)
To Airport (3km), Monapo (125km), Ilha de Moçambique (180km) & Nacala (195km)
Sunday Craft Market

Avenida Josina Machel
Rua da Mueda
Avenida Francisco Manyanga
Avenida da Independência
Avenida 25 de Setembro
Avenida Eduardo Mondlane
Avenida Paulo samuel kankhomba
Rua Macombe
Rua Monomatapa
Rua Cidade de Moçambique
Rua Daniel Napatima
Avenida Moma
Rua 3 de Fevereiro
Market
Rua dos Continuadores
Rua de Tete
To Benefica Sporting Grounds & Café Wamphula (1km)

0 100 200m
0 100 200yd

OTHER
1 Transport Stand; Chapas to Mozambique Island
2 LAM Office
3 Governor's House
4 BIM (ATM)
11 National Ethnography Museum
12 Cathedral of Nossa Senhora de Fátima
13 Grupo Mecula buses
14 Teledata
15 Telecom Building
16 Mosque
17 Taxi Rank
19 SAR Office
23 Ministry of Agriculture

though they're pricey for what you get. Downstairs is a small restaurant.

The situation picks up for mid-range accommodation.

Residencial Expresso (☎ 218808/9, fax 218806; Avenida da Independência; singles/doubles US$50/70) is the best place in town, with six large, spotless rooms with air-con, fridge and TV. Book in advance as it's often full.

Hotel Tropical (☎ 212232; Rua Macombe; singles/doubles with air-con US$55/80), behind the museum, does a steady business, though it's seen better days and isn't good value in comparison with Residencial Expresso. Rooms have air-con, TV and bathroom, and there's a popular **restaurant** downstairs.

Places to Eat
Oceanus (Avenida Josina Machel), opposite the Ministry of Agriculture in the southwestern end of town, is the best place for pizzas.

Other popular spots include **Café Carlos** (☎ 217960; closed Sunday), just off Rua dos Continuadores, with Italian and seafood

meals in a tiny walled courtyard; **Copacabana** (☎ 218121; closed Sunday), opposite Hotel Tropical, with fresh pasta and a large menu selection; and **Almeida de Garrett** (Avenida Francisco Manyanga) with Indian food.

For light meals and snacks, try **Pastelaria Aurora** (☎ 214279; Rua dos Continuadores), near Hotel Brasilia, or **Bar Primavera** (Avenida Eduardo Mondlane), just down from the BIM, and a good place to meet people.

Bamboo (☎ 216595), about 3km from town off the Ribáuè road, is worth a look if you have your own transport. Besides their popular restaurant, they also have **rooms** (about US$45).

Entertainment
The open-air **Café Wamphula** has a Friday evening discotheque. It's about 20 minutes on foot from the town centre: follow Rua dos Continuadores towards Hotel Brasilia, turning left just before the hotel onto Rua de Tete. Follow this to the end, turn left and continue about 400m to Benefica sporting grounds. Café Wamphula is inside this compound, near the radio antenna.

MOZAMBIQUE

Getting There & Away

Air LAM *(☎ 212801; Avenida Francisco Manyanga)* flies from Nampula to Maputo (daily), Beira, Lichinga, Quelimane, Tete and Pemba (all several times weekly). **SAR** *(☎ 212401)*, opposite the market, has flights to Blantyre (weekly, US$100 one way), Nacala, Cuamba, Lichinga (US$85 one way) and Guruè (US$45 one way), and **STA** *(☎ 214652)* at the airport has flights to Beira, Maputo, Quelimane, Nacala and Lumbo (for Ilha de Moçambique). The airport is about 4km northeast of town (US$4 in a taxi).

Bus & Chapa Grupo Mecula has daily buses to Nacala (US$2, four hours); Pemba (US$6, seven hours); Quelimane (US$10, 10 to 12 hours) and Montepuez (US$6, four to five hours). All depart at 5am except the bus to Nacala, which departs at 1pm. Departures are from the Grupo Mecula garage (known as 'Roman') on Avenida Moma, just off Avenida 25 de Setembro one block south of Rua Cidade de Moçambique.

To Ilha de Moçambique (US$2), there are *chapas* throughout the day from the train station. Look for one that's going direct – many that say they're going to the island go only as far as Monapo, where you'll need to wait for another vehicle. The best connection is on the *chapa* known as the *Tanzaniano*. There are usually two daily, passing the train station on their way back to Ilha de Moçambique between around 7am and 9am.

Chapas to Ribáuè, Mocuba (US$8) and Quelimane (US$10) leave from the same road, but about 2km west of the train station near the Ribáuè road junction. Transport to Angoche (US$2.50) leaves from the base of Avenida Eduardo Mondlane, 300m downhill from the museum opposite Predio Lopes, though this may change so ask in town.

Train A daily passenger train connects Nampula and Cuamba (see Getting There & Away under Cuamba, later in this chapter).

Getting Around

Moti Rent-A-Car *(☎ 218687, fax 218688)* has an office at Nampula airport. There's a **taxi rank** *(☎ 218866)* on Avenida Paulo Samuel Kankhomba.

MOGINCUAL
☎ 06

Mogincual, an old trading settlement 175km southeast of Nampula, sits near an estuary divided by a narrow finger of land from the sea. Fim do Mundo Safaris (see Places to Stay & Eat under Nacala later in this chapter) runs the private **Fim do Mundo Camp** *(full board per person US$35; advance reservations only)*, in a good setting on the estuary 3km from town. It has rustic chalet-style accommodation, and diving and excursions can be arranged.

Fim do Mundo can help you with transport from Nacala. *Chapas* run to Mogincual once or twice daily from the market in Monapo (US$3).

ANGOCHE

Angoche, an old Muslim trading centre dating from at least the 15th century, was one of the earliest settlements in Mozambique and an important gold- and ivory-trading post. Although it later declined, the town continued to play a significant role in coastal trade and in the 18th century was one of the major economic and political centres along the northern coast. Little remains from those days, although there are some attractive islands offshore. About 7km north of town is Praia Nova, a good beach. There are no facilities here, and you'll need to walk or have 4WD. Hitching is easiest on weekends.

In town, there's a basic **pensão** *(rooms around US$8)*.

Daily *chapas* connect Nampula and Angoche during the dry season, departing Nampula about 5am.

ILHA DE MOÇAMBIQUE
☎ 06

Ilha de Moçambique (Mozambique Island), about 3km off the mainland, is one of Mozambique's most fascinating destinations.

As early as the 15th century it was an important boat-building centre, and its history as a trading settlement – with ties to Madagascar, Persia, Arabia and elsewhere – dates back well before that. Vasco da Gama landed here in 1498, and in 1507 a permanent Portuguese settlement was established on the island. Unlike Sofala to the south, where the Portuguese established a settlement at about the same time, Ilha de Moçambique prospered as both a trading station and a naval

MOZAMBIQUE

ILHA DE MOÇAMBIQUE (MOZAMBIQUE ISLAND)

PLACES TO STAY
3 Omuhi'piti
1 Casa d'Thmo (Muslim)
5 Casa de Cakú &
   Dugong Dive Centre
13 Casa Branca
19 Residencial Amy
20 O Escondidinho
22 Casa de Najú
24 Patio dos Quintalinhos
   (Casa de Gabriele)
25 Private Gardens
   (Casa de Luís)
28 Residencial Meia-Lua

PLACES TO EAT
11 Âncora d'Ouro
12 Relíquias
17 Complexo Índico
18 O Paladar; Old Market
26 Night Market

OTHER
1 Chapel of Nossa Senhora
  de Baluarte
2 Fort of São Sebastião
6 Dhows to Cabaceira Pequena
7 Telecom Building; Internet
8 Tourist Information Office
9 Palace & Chapel of
  São Paulo (Museum)
10 Church of the Misericórdia;
   Museum of Sacred Art
14 Camões statue
15 Banco Comercial de
   Moçambique
16 Hindu Temple
21 Colonial Administration
   Offices
23 Mosque
27 16 de Junho Primary School
29 Church of Santo António
30 Transport Stand

base. In the late 16th century, the sprawling fort of São Sebastião was constructed. The island soon became capital of Portuguese East Africa – a status that it held until the end of the 19th century when the capital was transferred to Lourenço Marques (now Maputo).

Apart from its strategic and economic importance, Ilha de Moçambique also developed as a missionary centre. Numerous orders established churches here and Christians intermixed with the island's traditional Muslim population and its Hindu community. Various small waves of immigration over the years – from places as diverse as East Africa, Goa, Macau and elsewhere – contributed to the ethnic mix on the island. Today, this heterogeneity continues to be one of its most marked characteristics, although Muslim influence, together with local Makua culture, dominates.

Today, Ilha de Moçambique is an intriguing anomaly – part ghost town and part active community. It's also a picturesque and exceptionally pleasant place to wander around. While many of its buildings are sadly dilapidated, quite a few have been restored in recent years, and there's lots of rehabilitation work ongoing. In 1991, the island was declared a World Heritage Site by Unesco.

Most of Ilha de Moçambique's historic buildings – many of which date from between the 16th and 19th centuries – are located at its northern end (Stone Town), while the majority of residents live in reed houses in the southern end (Makuti Town).

Information

There's an excellent **tourist information office** (☎ *610081; open 8.30am-noon & 2pm-5pm daily*) next to the museum, with information on things to do and see on and around the island, as well as some crafts for sale. Staff are very helpful and can assist you with finding accommodation, and arranging excursions to nearby destinations. They also offer guided tours of the fort, and bike rental for about US$4 per half day, and can arrange car hire for visiting Chocas and other places on the mainland.

You can change cash dollars, euro and rand at **Banco Comercial de Moçambique** (*open 8am-3pm Mon-Fri*) on the western side of the island. The closest ATMs are in Nampula and Nacala.

There's **Internet** access next to the Telecom Building.

Diving

Dugong Dive Centre (☎ *610156;* **W** *www.du gongadventures.com*) arranges diving around Goa and Sena, two tiny islands off Ilha de Moçambique. They also can help organise dhow safaris and boat transfers to Chocas.

Things to See & Do

The main attraction is the **Palace and Chapel of São Paulo** – formerly the governor's residence – dating from 1610 and now a **museum** (☎ *610081, fax 610082;* **e** *ilha@teledata.mz*). Many rooms have been renovated to give a remarkable glimpse into what upper-class life must have been like during the island's heyday in the 18th century. In addition to a variety of ornaments from Portugal, Arabia, Goa, India and China, the museum contains many pieces of original furniture, including an important collection of heavily ornamented Indo-Portuguese pieces. In the chapel, note the altar and the pulpit, which was made in the 17th century by Chinese artists in Goa. On the ground floor of the building a maritime museum is planned. Behind the palace are the **Church of the Misericórdia** and the **Museum of Sacred Art** (currently closed), containing religious ornaments, paintings and carvings. The museum is housed in the former hospital of the Holy House of Mercy, a religious guild which operated in several Portuguese colonies from the early 1500s, providing charitable assistance to the poor and sick. The museums are open from 8am to 2pm daily. Entry is free, but a small donation (in the box by the entrance) is appreciated.

At the northern end of the island is the **Fort of São Sebastião** (*admission free; open to around 5pm daily*), the oldest complete fort still standing in sub-Saharan Africa. Immediately beyond the fort, on the tip of the island, is the rehabilitated **Chapel of Nossa Senhora de Baluarte**, built in 1522 and considered to be the oldest European building in the southern hemisphere. At the southern end of the island is the **Church of Santo António**.

In the main town are several more recent buildings including the restored **bank** (*Avenida Amilcar Cabral*), and the ornate **colonial administration offices** overlooking the gardens east of the hospital. In the centre of the island is a **Hindu temple**, and on its western edge a fairly modern **mosque**. To the south is a **cemetery** with Christian, Muslim and Hindu graves.

The island has several small beaches, though if it's beach you're after it's better to head across Mossuril Bay to Chocas, or up to the beaches near Nacala.

Places to Stay – Budget

Casuarina Camping (*camping US$3, singles/doubles US$6/10*) is on the mainland opposite Ilha de Moçambique in Lumbo, just a two minute walk from the bridge. It has camping on a small beach (where you can also swim), as well as some basic bungalow-style rooms and simple but spotless ablution blocks. Food is available.

There are numerous backpackers options; most are in homes with local families.

Private Gardens (Casa de Luis) (☎ *082 436757; Travessa dos Fornos, Makuti Town; camping US$2.50, singles/doubles US$6/10*) is one of the most popular, with a few bungalows around a tiny garden, where you can also pitch a tent. There's also a room in the main house, though it's not as good, as well as a fridge and area where you can cook. The turn-off to the house is near the mosque, but it's hard to find so ask one of the small boys who will inevitably attach themselves to you to show you the way.

Most of the other places are in the Stone Town, and it's worth stopping by the tourist information office to get the full listing. They include **Residencial Amy** (*US$8 per person*) a family-style place near the park, with several rooms and a common area with

TV; the quieter **Casa de Najù** (☎ *610008; per person US$8)* about 300m from the mosque, with rooms around a tiny inner courtyard; **Casa de Himo (Yasmin)** (☎ *610073; doubles from US$13),* at the northern end of the island near the renovated school, with three small rooms in an annexe next to the family house; the nice **Casa de Cakù** (☎ *610156; singles/ doubles US$35/50)* nearby; and **Residencial Mela-Lua** (☎ *610163; singles/doubles from US$8/16)* on the edge of Makuti Town opposite 16 de Junho primary school on the island's eastern edge, which is signposted.

O Escondidinho (e *ilhatur@teledata.mz; dorm beds US$7; rooms US$14-25)* is another place to check. It will be opening soon near the public gardens, with dorm beds and a variety of rooms, some with private bathroom, as well as some family rooms.

Places to Stay – Mid-Range & Top End

Casa Branca (☎ *610076;* e *flora204@hotmail .com; singles/doubles US$21/25),* on the island's eastern side near the Camões statue, has three simple but spotless rooms with views of the sea, and a kitchen. One of the rooms has its own bathroom, and the other two share. Rates include breakfast.

Patio dos Quintalinhos (Casa de Gabriele) (☎ *610090;* e *gabriele@patiodosquintalin hos.com; singles/doubles US$12/16, double/ quad with bathroom US$25/33; suite US$30),* opposite the mosque, is worth stopping by just to see the appealing design. The suite has its own starview skylight and private rooftop balcony with views over town to the sea. The other rooms are just as good, and one has a loft. All are self-contained except for two smaller rooms sharing a bathroom. There's a central courtyard area for relaxing, a rooftop terrace and a restaurant, and a pool is planned. There's also secure parking.

Omuhi'piti (☎ *610101, fax 610105; singles/ doubles from US$65/75),* in a good setting at the island's northern tip, has modern air-con rooms. There's a restaurant and the hotel can arrange diving and excursions.

Places to Eat

O Paladar *(meals from US$2),* at the eastern corner of the old market and unmarked, is the best place for local dishes. **Âncora d'Ouro** opposite the Church of the Misericordia has inexpensive fish, chicken and rice dishes. For street food, there's a good **night market** near Private Gardens (Casa de Luis).

Relíquias (☎ *610092; dishes from around US$4; open Tues-Sun)* is the island's upscale dining option, with a pleasant ambience and good food. It's on the western side, not far from the museum.

Complexo Índico, overlooking the water on the island's eastern side, has grilled fish and other dishes.

Getting There & Away

Air The small **STA** (☎ *Nampula 214652)* stops three times weekly at Lumbo, on the mainland opposite Ilha de Moçambique, on its run between Maputo and Nampula.

Minibus & Chapa Ilha de Moçambique is joined by a 3km bridge to the mainland. All minibuses to the island stop about 1km before the bridge in Lumbo, where you'll need to get into a smaller minivan to cross over Mossuril Bay (due to vehicle weight restrictions on the bridge).

The only direct buses to Nampula (US$2, three hours) are the *Tanzaniano* minibuses, departing daily at 4am and again around 5am. If you want to take one of these, the best thing is to go the day before to the minibus stop in Lumbo and arrange with the driver to pick you up at your hotel. Most of the hotels can also help you get a message to the drivers. Otherwise, there are *chapas* throughout the day to Monapo, where you can get transport on to Nampula or Nacala. All transport departs from the bridge. Once in Nampula, there are daily buses north to Pemba and south to Quelimane, though both leave early so you'll need to stay overnight in Nampula. There are also good flight connections to Maputo and most provincial capitals, and a daily train to Cuamba.

If you're driving, be aware that wide vehicles won't pass over the bridge and maximum weight is 1.5 tonnes.

Boat For details of boat connections between Ilha de Moçambique and Chocas, see Chocas, following.

CHOCAS
☎ 06
Chocas, opposite Ilha de Moçambique near Mossuril, has an attractive beach and makes

a possible day or overnight excursion from the island.

Nearby are two villages formerly used as summer holiday spots by wealthy residents of Ilha de Moçambique. **Cabaceira Grande**, the more interesting of the two, has a well-preserved church dating from the late 16th century and ruins of the mid-19th century former governor general's palace. **Cabaceira Pequena**, a few kilometres southeast, has an old Swahili-style mosque and the ruins of a cistern used as a watering spot by Portuguese sailors.

Complexo Chocas-Mar (☎ 212798; 4-person bungalows with bathroom midweek/weekends US$27/31) has straightforward bungalows on the beach. Meals can be arranged.

To reach Chocas by road, take any transport between Monapo and Ilha de Moçambique, and get off at the signposted Mossuril junction 25km from Monapo. *Chapas* go from here to Mossuril (20km), from where it's another 12km or so (traversed sporadically by *chapas*) to Chocas. Hitching is fairly easy on weekends, otherwise very slow.

From Chocas, it's about a 30-minute walk at low tide to Cabaceira Pequena, and an hour to 1½ hours to Cabaceira Grande. Alternatively, dhows depart daily for Cabaceira Pequena from the pier in front of the tourist information office on Ilha de Moçambique between about 11am and 1pm (US$0.20). If you want to return the same day, you'll need to charter a return (US$2). If there's no wind, the trip across the bay can take up to six hours or more. Dugong Dive Centre (see Diving under Ilha de Moçambique, earlier in this chapter) also organises boat trips to Chocas for about US$30 return.

NACALA
☎ 06
Nacala is northern Mozambique's busiest port, and gateway to some attractive beaches, including the relaxing **Fernão Veloso**, about 10km from town.

The main street runs from Nacala Porto (the area near the harbour) to Nacala Alta (the higher town). BIM on the main street has an ATM (Visa cards); Banco Austral, also in the centre, gives cash against a MasterCard.

Places to Stay & Eat
Most travellers head for **Bay Diving** (☎/fax 520017; e fimdomundo@teledata.mz; w www.fimdomundosafaris.com; camping US$2.50 per person, dorm beds US$5, doubles without/with bathroom US$20/25), a popular and recommended dive lodge at Fernão Veloso beach run by Fim do Mundo Safaris. It has accommodation in either thatched A-frame chalets, dorm beds or camping, plus a restaurant, sauna and massage room. They also offer fully-equipped diving, including PADI instruction, at very reasonable prices; kayaking; and excursions to Ilha de Moçambique.

Staff can help you with transport from Nacala and Nampula. To get here on your own, take the turn-off for the airport and military base at the entrance to Nacala, and after about 5km watch for the signposted turn-off opposite the base, from where it's another 1.5km. There's no public transport, but hitching is easy on weekends.

Hotel Maiaia (☎ 526827; singles/doubles about US$55/70), in the town centre, with clean modern rooms and a restaurant, is where most business travellers stay.

Getting There & Away
Grupo Mecula buses to Nampula and Pemba depart Nacala daily at 5am. There are also several *chapas* each morning to Nampula departing from near the market, as well as to Monapo (US$1.50, one hour), where you can get transport to Ilha de Moçambique or Namialo (the junction town for Pemba).

CUAMBA
☎ 071
Cuamba is an important rail and road junction, the economic centre of Niassa province and a convenient stopping point if you're travelling to/from Malawi. Although the town itself is fairly non-descript, it's lively and bustling thanks to its large student population and location near the border.

For inexpensive lodging, try **Pensão São Miguel** (rooms without/with bathroom US$14/16) or **Namaacha**, both in the town centre, and both with basic rooms and meals.

Vision 2000 (☎ 62632; e h-vision2000@teledata.mz; rooms about US$25) is the only mid-range place, with faded but decent rooms with TV and fridge, and a slow restaurant.

MOZAMBIQUE

Getting There & Away

Bus & Chapa To/from Nampula, it's cheaper and more comfortable to travel by train. By road, there are two possibilities, with the longer route via Gurúè in better shape than the direct route via Malema and Ribáuè. Public transport is scarce on both.

To Gurúè, the best way is to take the train from Cuamba to Mutuáli, where you can get a *chapa* for the remainder, although you may have to wait several hours as *chapas* don't coordinate with the train.

To Lichinga, a truck departs daily about 6am from Maçaniqueira market behind the rail yard.

To Entre Lagos at the Malawi border, there are several vehicles weekly during the dry season (US$2.50, three hours). Once at Entre Lagos, you'll need to walk across the border, where you can catch a train on the Malawi side to Liwonde. For more information see Land under Getting There & Away in the Malawi chapter.

Train The Cuamba–Nampula train departs daily at 5am from Cuamba and at 6am from Nampula (US$26/7/4 for 1st/2nd/3rd class, eight to 10 hours). First and 2nd-class service alternate days (and some days there's neither 1st- or 2nd-class); 3rd-class is available daily. Second class is better than 1st-class in some respects, as you can open the windows, whereas 1st-class has nonfunctional air-con. Third-class is hot and crowded. If you're travelling on a day when there's 3rd-class only, try heading to the more comfortable dining car and ingratiating yourself with staff – though we heard from some travellers that they had to buy something every hour or so for the privilege of sitting there. Women travelling alone in 1st or 2nd-class will be given seats in a females-only cabin.

To transport your vehicle (about US$100), you'll need to load it on the train the night before and arrange a guard to be sure it's not tampered with. During the journey you can ride with your vehicle.

MANDIMBA

The best place to stay in this border town with Malawi is the no-frills **Restaurante-Bar Ngame** *(rooms per person US$8)*, about 200m from the bus stand. There's at least one truck daily from both Lichinga and Cuamba to Mandimba in the dry season, departing both places at 5am. For information on the border, see Malawi under Land in the main Getting There & Away section, earlier in this chapter.

LICHINGA
☎ 071

Lichinga (formerly Vila Cabral) is the capital of Niassa province, which is the most remote and least visited part of Mozambique. Not only do tourists seldom make their way here; it's the least populated of Mozambique's provinces, and many Mozambicans seem to forget about its existence. Yet, if you're after adventure and time in the bush well off the tourist circuits, it's a rewarding destination. Apart from its scenic rugged terrain, the main attraction is the Lake Niassa (Lake Malawi) coastline.

Lichinga itself is a low-key town at about 1400m altitude, dotted with jacarandas and pine groves. It's also home to Niassa province's well-known song and dance group, Massukos.

There's an ATM that gives cash on a Visa card as long as the power in town is on. The bank only lets you change cash if you have an account there. If you resort to changing on the street, do so with lots of caution; it's better to ask a shop owner if they can help you out. The immigration office is just off the airport road, diagonally opposite Escola Industrial e Comercial Ngungunhane.

Places to Stay

Hotel Chiwindi *(☎ 20345; singles/doubles about US$8/16)*, near the market, has no-frills rooms and is one of the cheapest places.

Pousada Lichinga *(☎ 20288, 20227; doubles about US$20)* in the town centre is better, with straightforward rooms and a **restaurant**.

Hotel Lichinga behind Pousada is scheduled to open imminently as Lichinga's only upscale accommodation. Rooms have air-con and TV, and there's a restaurant.

Most budget travellers head to **Quinta Capricórnio** *(☎ 20160; camp sites per person US$4, cottages from per person US$10)* about 2km outside town in the forest. There's camping as well as several cottages, and a restaurant using produce from the large garden on the premises. To get here, take the road heading west past the government building until the tarmac ends. Continue southwest

through the forest for about 1.5km, staying left at the forks.

Places to Eat

O Chambo (☎ 203354; mains from US$3), in the Feira Exposição Niassa (FEN) compound next to the market, has great soups and well-prepared main dishes.

Comércio Geral (Nurbay's) on the main street is the best-stocked supermarket; they also have some rooms to let.

Getting There & Away

Air There are flights several times weekly to/from Maputo, Tete, Nampula, Beira and Quelimane on LAM (Rua da LAM), off the airport road. SAR (☎ 20659) at the airport flies twice weekly to Lichinga from Cuamba and Nampula.

Bus & Chapa All transport departs from next to the market, and buses/chapas to most destinations leave early, by around 5am. There's usually one minibus and one or two trucks daily along the unpaved road to Cuamba (US$8, eight to 11 hours), several pick-ups to Metangula (US$4, three hours), and a couple daily to Meponda (US$2, two hours). To Mandimba, there's a daily truck in the dry season (US$4, 4½ hours). Otherwise, take any transport heading to Cuamba.

It's also possible to reach Lichinga from Malawi, via Likoma Island and Cóbuè (see Sea & Lake, Malawi, under Getting There & Away, earlier in this chapter).

AROUND LICHINGA
Meponda

This tiny town about 60km southwest of Lichinga doesn't have much allure, but the shoreline is pretty, and it offers a taste of lakeshore life if you don't have time to explore further north. O Pomar das Laranjeiras (rooms US$4 per person) on the beach has one brick rondavel, and food is available with lots of advance notice.

It's possible to get a boat to Malawi (US$5.50) from the tiny harbour in the centre of town, though most are ill-suited to weather the lake's sudden squalls and the journey isn't recommended.

LAKE NIASSA

The beautiful Mozambican side of Lake Niassa (the Mozambican name for Lake Malawi) is much less developed than the Malawian side, and sees a small but steady stream of adventure travellers. The main area for exploring is between Metangula and Cóbuè.

Metangula

Metangula is a district capital and the main town on the Mozambican lakeshore.

Complexo Cetuka (camp sites US$4, single/double bungalows US$7/8, 4-person chalet US$16) on the beach at Chuwanga, 8km north of Metangula, is the main place to stay. There's camping, simple bungalows on the sand and a chalet. Meals are available from US$3.

Several chapas daily go between Metangula and Lichinga, usually in the mornings. Departures in Metangula are from the fork in the road just up from the market. There's no regular public transport between Metangula and Chuwanga, but hitching is usually easy, especially on weekends.

You can hire boats to go up and down the coast from the small dhow port down from the market. For information on the *Ilala* ferry between Metangula and Cóbuè (US$8/3 1st/3rd class), see Sea & Lake, Malawi, under Getting There & Away, earlier in this chapter.

Cóbuè

Tiny Cóbuè is the immigration post for travellers heading to/from Malawi via Likoma Island (for details, see Sea & Lake under Getting There & Away earlier in this chapter). Pensão San Miguel (rooms US$3) has accommodation, and meals with plenty of advance notice.

About 15km south of Cóbuè in a beautiful setting on the shores of Lake Niassa is the highly recommended Mchenga Nkwichi Lodge (satellite ☎ 0088-163-152-9151 mornings only; e mdw01@bushmail.net; singles/doubles with full board US$120/200), which is part of the Manda Wilderness Area – a project promoting nature conservation and sustainable community development. The lodge offers the chance to explore an area of Southern Africa that's about as remote as it gets while enjoying all the comforts in rustic private chalets that blend in with the surrounding bush. In addition to the beauty of the lakeshore, there's excellent bird life here, and with luck, you may even

MOZAMBIQUE

see the occasional elephant or antelope. No free camping is permitted. Check out **w** www.niassatourism.com for some photos.

The lodge can also help you arrange sailing, canoeing or walking safaris of up to 12 nights in the wilderness – an excellent opportunity if you have the time. Bookings can be made in Malawi through **Ulendo Safaris** (☎ *Lilongwe 743501, 743507*).

The road between Cóbuè and Metangula is being renovated, and once it's finished, there should be regular public transport. Meanwhile, the best way to get around is via the weekly *Ilala* ferry (see Sea & Lake, Malawi, under Getting There & Away earlier in this chapter). There are also several slow, local boats weekly between Cóbuè and Metangula (US$4), though some take up to three days for the trip. With luck, you can also find a ride with one of the occasional speedboats doing business along the lakeshore. These take between six and eight hours, and are more easily arranged in Metangula than in Cóbuè. Mchenga Nkwichi Lodge does transfers in its motorised dhow (US$130 plus US$10 per person, five hours). There are also occasional flights into Cóbuè; check with Mchenga Nkwichi Lodge for an updated schedule.

NIASSA RESERVE
About 160km northeast of Lichinga on the Tanzanian border is the 42,000-sq-km Niassa Reserve, a vast tract of wilderness with the largest wildlife populations in Mozambique. It's particularly notable for its elephants and buffaloes; there are also populations of duikers, zebras, elands, leopards and more. For the moment, most facilities in the reserve belong to hunting concessions. There are few roads, and tourism to date has been exclusively top-end, with private charter planes, although this is likely to change soon. For information, contact **e** rdn01@bushmail.net.

PEMBA
☎ 072
Pemba (formerly Porto Amelia) has a beautiful setting on a peninsula jutting into the enormous and stunning Pemba Bay. It was established in 1904 as administrative headquarters for the Niassa Company. Today, it's capital of Cabo Delgado province and northern Mozambique's main town outside Nampula.

Pemba is the gateway for visiting Ibo and the other islands of the Quirimbas Archipelago, as well as a relaxing and enjoyable stop in its own right, and it's well worth planning at least several days here.

Orientation
At the southwestern tip of the peninsula is the low-lying *baixa* area around the port and old town, with traders and several banks along Rua do Comércio, the main street. East of here and up the hill is the town centre where there are a few hotels and restaurants, more shops, and offices.

Information
There's an ATM at **Banco Internacional de Moçambique (BIM)** (*Avenida Eduardo Mondlane*), and **Banco Standard Totta** changes travellers cheques for a commission per transaction.

For Internet access, try the Internet café next to **Super Wimbe** restaurant at Wimbe beach, or the **Artes Maconde** shop about 1km from town on the road going to the airport.

For assistance with car rentals and airline bookings, contact **Viatur** (☎ *21431;* **e** *viatur@ teledata.mz*), on the main road just up from Banco Standard Totta.

Things to See & Do
Most visitors head straight for the attractive **Wimbi Beach**, 5km east of town.

On the outskirts of Pemba are several lively and interesting bairros worth visiting, including the Muslim area of **Paquitequete** on the southwestern edge of the peninsula, and **Cariacó**, east of town, which has a good market.

Diving There's good diving around Pemba, starting about 300m offshore from Wimbi Beach, where the coastal shelf drops off steeply. The two main operators are:

CI Divers (☎ 20102, **e** cidivers@teledata.mz) at Complexo Nautilus
Pemba Dive (☎ 20820) on Wimbi Beach opposite Complexo Caraçol

Both offer a variety of excursions as well as full equipment rental and instruction. Jet skis, fishing boats, sailboards, windsurfing equipment and bicycles can also be hired.

PEMBA

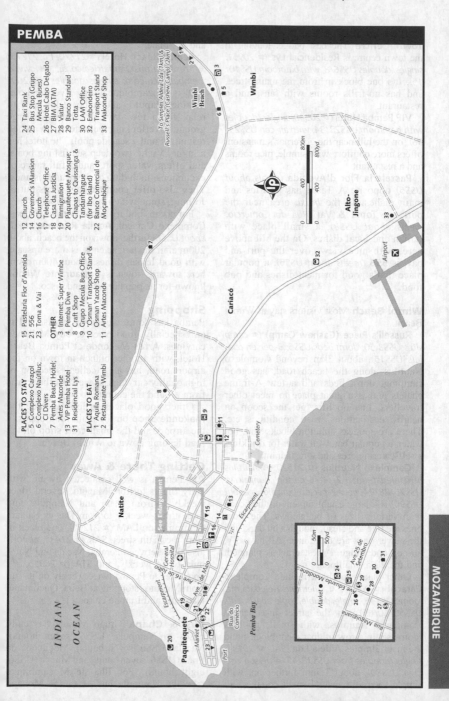

PLACES TO STAY
5 Complexo Caraçol
6 Complexo Náutilus;
   CI Divers
7 Pemba Beach Hotel;
   Artes Maconde
13 VIP Pemba Hotel
31 Residencial Lys

PLACES TO EAT
1 Aquila Romana
2 Restaurante Wimbi

15 Pastelaria Flor d'Avenida
21 556
23 Toma & Vai

OTHER
3 Internet; Super Wimbe
4 Pemba Dive
8 Craft Shop
9 Grupo Mecula Bus Office
10 'Osman' Transport Stand &
   Osman Yacob Shop
11 Artes Maconde

12 Church
14 Governor's Mansion
16 Church
17 Telephone Office
18 Casa da Justiça
19 Immigration
20 Paquitequete Mosque;
   Chapas to Quissanga &
   Tandanhangue
   (for Ibo Island)
22 Banco Comercial de
   Moçambique

24 Taxi Rank
25 Bus Stop (Grupo
   Mecula Buses)
26 Hotel Cabo Delgado
27 BIM (ATM)
28 Viatur
29 Banco Standard
   Totta
30 LAM Office
32 Embondeiro
33 Makonde Shop

Places to Stay & Eat

Town Centre The best budget lodging in the town centre is **Residencial Lys** *(☎ 20951; singles/doubles US$6/8, with bathroom US$10/15)*. It's one block in from the main street, and has no-frills rooms with fans, and a restaurant.

VIP Pemba Hotel *(☎ 20548; singles/doubles with bathroom US$23/34, with air-con US$25/36)*, on the hill near the governor's mansion, offers more comfort, with simple, nice rooms and a restaurant.

Pastelaria Flor d'Avenida *(meals about US$5)* opposite Á Tasca has pastries and main dishes. In the *baixa* area near the port, try **Toma & Vai** *(Rua do Comercio; meals about US$3)*, a small place with Italian and local dishes. On the hill above here, with nice views over the port and bay, is **556** *(meals about US$5)*, a popular place that's good for meat dishes and pub food.

Wimbi Beach Most visitors stay at Wimbi Beach.

Russell's Place (Cashew Camp) *(☎ camp sites US$3.50; dorm beds US$5; 3-person chalets US$15)*, about 3km beyond Complexo Nautilus along the beach road, has good camping, dorm beds and a few A-frame chalets and is a great place to meet other travellers, line up lifts, get the scoop on nearby destinations, road conditions etc. There are spotless ablution blocks with hot water, a popular bar, well water for drinking, a self-catering area and a restaurant.

Complexo Nautilus *(☎ 21520; e nautilus htl@teledata.mz; 2-/4-/6-person bungalows US$75/88/94, new 2-person bungalows about US$90)* is a large establishment on the beach with various sizes of bungalows. The older ones are fine and clean, though a bit dark, and the newer ones are quite nice. All have TV, air-con and fridge. A restaurant is planned, and there's a small pool.

Other places to check include **Complexo Caraçol** *(☎ 20147; e sulemane@teledata.mz; rooms US$45, single/double/triple apartments US$50/60/65)*, on the street just behind Complexo Nautilus, with small, no-frills rooms set in a row of apartment blocks; and the nicer **Simples Aldeia Lda** *(SAL; ☎ 20134; singles/doubles from US$38/43; 4-person cottage US$80)*, about 1.5km further on, with simple rooms in several small cottages, all with twin beds, TV, screens, air-con, fridge and hot-plate.

Pemba Beach Hotel *(☎ 21770, fax 21779; e reservations@raniafrica.co.za; w www.pembabeach.com; singles/doubles US$260/390)* is Mozambique's only five-star hotel outside Maputo, and a beautiful spot to relax for a few days. It's built on large grounds overlooking the water, with a good restaurant and a seaside pool. The hotel has a luxury yacht, two deep sea fishing boats, and offers water sports and a full range of excursions, including to the nearby islands. They also offer good package deals out of Jo'burg, some with a stop in Maputo.

For cheap food try **Super Wimbe** just past Complexo Caraçol. **Aquila Romana** *(meals about US$6)* further down on the beach, about 200m after the tarmac ends, is more upscale, with good Italian dishes. About 400m from here towards town is **Restaurante Wimbi**, known for its popular weekend disco.

Shopping

Pemba has some wonderful crafts, and is an especially good place to buy Makonde carvings. **Artes Maconde** at Pemba Beach Hotel, with another branch in town on the airport road, has an excellent selection of high quality carvings, as well as other crafts from around the country.

Other good places to look include the **Makonde Shop** on the main road opposite the airport, and the small **craft shop** on the road leading down to Wimbi Beach.

Getting There & Away

Air Pemba is well connected by air, with daily flights to/from Maputo, several times weekly to/from Beira and Nampula, and three times weekly to/from Dar es Salaam (Tanzania) on **LAM** *(☎ 21251)*, one block in from the main street. **SAR** *(☎ 21431; airport)* also flies between Pemba, Nacala and Nampula twice weekly, and **STA** *(☎ 20915; airport)* flies to Pemba twice weekly on its run from Maputo (stopping at Beira, Quelimane, Nampula and Lumbo en route).

Bus & Chapa Grupo Mecula has daily buses to Nampula (US$6, seven hours), Nacala (US$6, seven hours), Moçimboa da Praia (US$6, seven hours) and Mueda (US$6, eight hours). For Ilha de Moçambique, take the Nampula bus as far as Monapo

(US$5.50), where you'll need to get out and catch a *chapa* for the remaining 55km (US$1). Departures are at about 4.45am from Grupo Mecula office, on a small side street behind the Osman Yacob shop ('Osman') on the main road, and about 1.5km from the centre. The buses then all pass by the corner of Avenidas 25 de Setembro and Eduardo Mondlane, diagonally opposite Hotel Cabo Delgado, to pick up passengers, departing by 5am.

If you miss the bus and want to try your luck with *chapas* and other transport, head to Embondeiro, Pemba's long-distance bus station on the Nampula road about 3km from the centre.

Transport to Metuge and other nearby villages, and some northbound transport, leaves from the Osman Yacob shop.

Getting Around
Pemba's **taxi rank** (☎ 20187) is on Avenida Eduardo Mondlane, just down from Hotel Cabo Delgado.

For car rental, try **Moti Rent-A-Car** (☎ 21687; e *motimoz@teledata.mz*), based at the airport.

QUIRIMBAS ARCHIPELAGO
☎ 072
The Quirimbas Archipelago is a chain of about a dozen islands and islets along the coastline between Pemba and the Rovuma River. Some, including Ibo and Quirimba, have been settled for centuries and were already important Muslim trading posts when the Portuguese arrived in the 15th century.

The best-known of the islands is **Ibo**, which was fortified as early as 1609, and which had become the second-most important town in Mozambique by the late 18th century, after Ilha de Moçambique. It was a major slave trading post during this era, with demand spurred by French sugar plantation owners on Mauritius and elsewhere. Today, Ibo is a fascinating, almost surreal place with wide streets lined with dilapidated villas, and crumbling, moss-covered buildings. At its northern end is the star-shaped fort of São João dating from the late 18th century, known now for its silversmiths.

Other islands include **Quirimba**, which in the 16th century served as a centre for missionary work, and later was the site of a large coconut plantation; and **Matemo**

and **Quisiva**, both sites of large Portuguese plantation houses. Tiny **Rolas Island** (Ilha das Rolas), between Matemo Island and Pangane, is uninhabited except for some seasonal fishing settlements. The privately owned **Quilaluia** is also uninhabited, and part of a protected sanctuary due to the richness of its offshore marine life.

All the islands can be visited, although many don't have fresh water and several are privately owned. Some of the islands, including Ibo, Quirimba, Matemo and Rolas are part of the recently gazetted Quirimbas National Park, which also includes large inland areas on the coastline opposite. There's no infrastructure and entry fees aren't yet established, but once they are, you'll need to pay these to visit the islands belonging to the park.

When travelling among the islands, remember that access and exit are tide dependent and plan accordingly to avoid being stranded. Dense mangrove swamps connect some of the islands. Although channels were cut during Portuguese times, you'll need to take a guide along to navigate among them.

Places to Stay & Eat
Karibuni (Casa de Janine) (e *ibo_pemba@ yahoo.fr; camp sites US$1.50, rooms US$10*), on Ibo, is cheap and friendly. There are two houses – one along the water just northwest of the tiny port, and the other in town near the Telecom Building. Both have a few basic rooms with shared bathroom and bucket bath, and meals can be arranged.

Telecomunicações de Moçambique Guesthouse (☎ *43001, 43000; rooms US$10*) is on Ibo, about 500m east of the port. Rooms are spacious and clean, with electricity and a TV in the common area, clean bucket showers, and meals can be arranged. It's a good deal – the only problem is that there's not always someone around to open it up for you, and travellers rarely stay here. **Bar São Joaõ**, diagonally opposite, has cheap meals and drinks.

Bela Vista Lodge (e *sales@wildlifeadven tures.co.za; camping per person US$5, rooms per person US$10-50*), on Ibo just northwest of the port, is run by Ibo Island Safaris (contact through Wildlife Adventures, see Organised Tours under Getting There & Away earlier in this chapter). It has spacious high-ceilinged rooms with

MOZAMBIQUE

nets in a restored house overlooking the water, running hot and cold water and spotless ablution blocks, and good meals (breakfast/dinner US$4/5). It's also the most organised place if you want to do **dhow safaris** among the other islands of the archipelago. There's a yard out back where you can pitch a tent, and a rooftop terrace for watching the sunset.

On Quirimba, there's **Quirimba Island Villa Resort** (W www.quirimbaislandlodge .co.za; US$90 per person), an upscale self-catering place (no camping). Meat, produce and purified water are available on the island, but otherwise you'll need to bring supplies with you.

If you're looking for an idyllic tropical island retreat, the place to come is the beautiful **Quilalea** (☎ 21808; e quirimbas@teledata.mz; W www.quilalea.com; US$450 per person all-inclusive with full board plus US$10 per day sanctuary fee) on tiny Quilaluia Island. Accommodation is in nine luxurious private chalets, with excellent cuisine and the sea stretching out before you to the horizon.

Several new places are planned, including on Quipaco, a tiny island between Pemba and Quissanga, notable for its birdlife, and an exclusive private conservation project on the northern islands of Vamizi and Rongui.

Getting There & Away

To reach Ibo or Quirimba, you'll need to go first to Quissanga, on the coast north of Pemba. There's a direct *chapa* daily from the fish market behind the mosque in Paquitequete in Pemba (US$3.50, five hours, departing about 4am). Otherwise, there's usually another vehicle or two leaving Pemba in the morning from Embondeiro (Pemba's long-distance bus station on the Nampula road), or you can try looking for a lift at Russell's Place (see Places to Stay & Eat under Pemba earlier in this chapter). From Quissanga, most vehicles continue on to the village of Tandanhangue (US$2 from Pemba), which is the departure point for dhows to Ibo (US$1), as well as to Quirimba island.

If you're driving to Tandanhangue, take the dirt track to the left about 2km before Quissanga town. You'll need 4WD for the road from Pemba. There's secure parking at Casa de Isufo (signposted 2km before the Tandanhangue port – you'll need to walk back to the port) for about US$2 per day. There's a less reliable parking area at the port itself for the same price.

Dhows leave only at high tide, and take from one to six hours. If you get stuck waiting, Isufo (at Casa de Isufo) can help you find a meal, and has an enclosed area where you can sleep.

An alternative to a dhow is to charter the local **Administrator's boat** (☎ 43000; US$21 one way). For those with larger budgets, it's easy to arrange speedboat charters from Pemba direct to the islands. Ask at Pemba Beach Hotel, Complexo Naútilus or Russell's Place (for more information on these see Places to Stay under Pemba earlier in this chapter).

Island-hopping along the coast sounds good, but in reality, logistics such as wind and tide mean it's not that practical. The better thing to do is to base yourself either on Ibo or in Pemba and arrange a dhow safari from there. Bela Vista Lodge (see Places to Stay & Eat earlier in this section) on Ibo arranges dhow safaris. Another good contact is Russell's Place in Pemba. Pemba Beach Hotel can organise upscale cruises.

MACOMIA

Macomia is the turn-off point for the beach at Pangane. **Pensão Kwetu Kumo**, about 1.5km from the main road, has basic rooms for US$6. There's at least one vehicle daily between Macomia and Mucojo, a few kilometres before Pangane; hitching is possible, but slow.

About 40km north of Macomia is **Chai**, where Frelimo's military campaign against colonial rule began in 1964 with an attack on a Portuguese base.

PANGANE

Pangane is a long, beautiful palm-fringed beach just north of Mucojo, and about 50km off the main north–south road.

There's a **camp site** (per person US$2.50) here, but you'll need to be self-sufficient, and **Suki's Guesthouse** (rooms around US$6). It's easy to arrange fish meals with locals, but otherwise you'll have to bring whatever you'll need with you.

There's at least one vehicle daily to/from Macomia.

MUEDA

Mueda, the main town on the Makonde Plateau, was built as an army barracks during the colonial era. In 1960, the town was the site of the infamous 'massacre of Mueda' (see The Independence War under History earlier in this chapter). There's a statue commemorating Mueda's role in Mozambican independence, and a mass grave for the 'martyrs of Mueda', at the western end of town. Just behind this monument is a ravine over which countless more Mozambicans were hurled to their deaths.

While Mueda itself is lacking in charm, its setting is attractive and there are views from the escarpment along the southern and western edges of town. Many Makonde carvers live in the outlying villages.

Pensão Takatuka *(rooms US$12, annexe rooms US$16)* on the sealed road has basic rooms with shared bucket bath. Meals are available with lots of advance notice.

Grupo Mecula has daily buses to Pemba (about US$8) and Nampula (US$10), both departing at 5am, and there are several vehicles each morning to Mocda Praia (US$2.50). There's usually one *chapa* daily to either Moçimboa da Praia or to Nangade (both about US$4), from where you can cross the border into Tanzania; see Land under Getting There & Away earlier in this chapter. All transport leaves from the main road opposite the market.

MOÇIMBOA DA PRAIA

Moçimboa da Praia is an important dhow port and the last major town before the Rovuma River. If you're travelling by dhow and enter or leave Mozambique here, have your passport stamped at the immigration office near Complexo Miramar. Tanzanian shillings are accepted at some places and a few words of Swahili will often get you further than Portuguese. To change cash, try Banco Austral or some of the Indian shop owners.

Pensão Leeta *(☎ 072-2515 or 2326, ext 130 or 166; rooms US$5)* near the transport stand has basic rooms with shared bathroom.

Complexo Miramar *(singles/doubles US$14/ 16)* is better, and the only other choice. Rooms are in three no-frills rondavels, with just a trickle of running water, but the setting is good – directly on the beach. The **restaurant** here is Moçimboa's main spot for dining and socialising.

Getting There & Away

Two pick-ups daily go to/from the Rovuma River (US$8, four hours) via Palma, leaving Moçimboa da Praia between 3.30am and 5am. The transport stand is near the market at the entrance to town. Coming from Tanzania, be at the Rovuma early, as the last vehicle to Moçimboa da Praia leaves by about 1pm, sometimes earlier.

To Pemba, a Grupo Mecula bus departs daily at 5am sharp (US$6, seven hours) from their garage mid-way between Complexo Miramar and the bus stand in the upper part of town. If you miss this, there are usually one or two chapas or pickups that do the journey as well, departing by 7am from the main road in front of the market.

PALMA

Palma is a large village nestled among coconut groves about 45km south of the Tanzania border. It's a centre for basketry and mat weaving, though most of this is done in the outlying villages.

The immigration office and the post office are in the upper part of town. Offshore are a few idyllic islands, some of which are slated for private development.

The friendly but very basic **Hotel Palma** *(rooms around US$5)*, about 2km downhill from the immigration office, is the only place to stay. Meals can be arranged with advance notice.

All transport leaves from the Boa Viagem roundabout at the entrance to town, about 3km from Hotel Palma. Travelling between Palma and Tanzania is described in the Getting There & Away section earlier in this chapter. From Palma to the Rovuma River, *chapas* charge US$4. Transport from the Rovuma, south to Moçimboa da Praia, passes through Palma between 11am and 2pm. From Palma to Moçimboa da Praia costs US$4.

Dhow transport to offshore islands can be arranged from the harbour near Hotel Palma; take everything with you, including water.

Namibia

Wedged between the Kalahari and the chilly South Atlantic, Namibia enjoys both vast potential and promise. Rich in resources and spectacular natural beauty, it has also inherited from its colonial and African roots a solid modern infrastructure and a diversity of cultures and national origins: Herero, San, Nama, Damara, Owambo, Afrikaner, German, Asian and others. Its attractions are unparalleled in Africa and include fine bushwalking opportunities, wild seascapes, rugged mountains, lonely deserts, appealing African and European cities and villages, and nearly unlimited elbow room.

Facts about Namibia

HISTORY

For information on the general history of Southern Africa, see the Facts About Southern Africa chapter at the beginning of this book.

Early Human History

It's generally accepted that Southern Africa's earliest inhabitants were San, nomadic people organised in extended family groups who had adapted to the severe terrain. Population densities were low and small family or community groups typically migrated in search of resources. San communities came under pressure from Khoikhoi (Hottentot) groups (due to competition for territory, water and hunting grounds), the ancestors of the modern Nama, with whom they share a language group. The descendants of these Khoisan (the modern group comprising the San and Khoikhoi peoples) still live in Namibia, but few have retained their traditional lifestyles.

Between 400 and 300 BC, the first Bantu people appeared on the plateaus of southcentral Africa. Their arrival marked the appearance of the first tribal structures in Southern African societies. Most of the San gradually disappeared from the scene – retreating to the desert or the swamps of the Okavango Delta to avoid enslavement by the dominant Bantu society.

Namibia at a Glance

Area: 825,000 sq km

Population: 1.83 million

Capital: Windhoek

Head of State: President Sam Nujoma

Official Language: English

Currency: Namibian dollar (N$)

Exchange Rate: US$1= N$8.05

Highlights

- Etosha National Park – seeing the incredible variety of African animals at one of the world's greatest wildlife-viewing venues
- Skeleton Coast Park – exploring this lonely, ethereal coastline, studded with rusting shipwrecks
- Damaraland – visiting rock engravings, the spectacular Spitzkoppe and the Brandberg, Namibia's highest massif
- Fish River Canyon – marveling at the spectacular vistas while hiking through this enormous canyon
- Diverse cultures – learning about Namibia's rich cultural heritage
- Namib Desert – wandering amid this vast, dune-studded desert and discover a variety of desert wildlife

Around AD 1600 the Herero people, who were Bantu-speaking pastoralists, arrived in Namibia from the Zambezi area and occupied the north and west of the country.

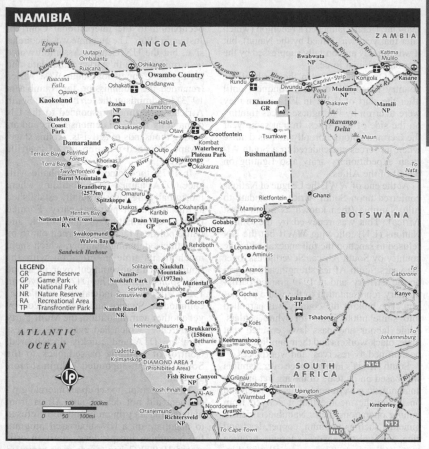

NAMIBIA

LEGEND	
GR	Game Reserve
GP	Game Park
NP	National Park
NR	Nature Reserve
RA	Recreational Area
TP	Transfrontier Park

This caused conflicts with the Khoikhoi, with whom they were competing for the best grazing lands and water holes. In what is now called Kaokoland, the more aggressive Herero displaced not only the Khoikhoi but also the few remaining San and Damara people (whose origin is unclear).

It's thought that the Nama people of present-day Namibia are descended from South African Oorlam Khoikhoi groups (bands of Khoisan people displaced from the Cape region by European encroachment) who held out against the Herero through violent clashes in the 1840s to 1880s. The Bantu group known as the Owambo settled in the north along the Okavango and Kunene Rivers, and was probably descended from people who had migrated from eastern Africa over

500 years earlier. Their language is similar enough to that of the Herero that it's thought they were part of the same migration.

European Colonisation

Because Namibia has one of the world's most inhospitable coastlines, it was largely ignored by the European maritime nations until relatively recently. The first European visitors were Portuguese mariners seeking a route to the Indies in the late 15th century, but they confined their activities to erecting stone crosses along the shoreline as votive monuments and coastal navigational aids. It wasn't until the last-minute scramble for colonies in the late 19th century that Namibia was annexed by Germany, except for the port of Walvis Bay, which was taken in

1878 by the British for the Cape colony. In 1904 the Herero launched a rebellion (which later that year was joined by the Nama), but it was quickly and brutally suppressed by the German colonial forces.

The Owambo living in the north of the country managed to avoid conquest until after the start of WWI in 1914, when they were overrun by Portuguese forces fighting on the side of the Allies. In that same year the German colony abruptly met its demise when its forces surrendered to a South African expeditionary army also fighting on behalf of the Allies.

At the end of WWI, the League of Nations conferred upon South Africa a mandate to rule Namibia (then known as South West Africa). This was renewed by the United Nations (UN) following WWII but the UN refused to sanction the full annexation of the country by South Africa. Nevertheless, over the years South Africa strengthened its grip on the territory, and in 1949 granted parliamentary representation to the white population. The bulk of the country was parcelled into some 6000 farms for white settlers, while labour and pass laws ensured that male, black workers and their families would be confined to 'reserves' and workplaces.

South Africa's intransigence over Namibia was based on its fears of having yet another antagonistic government on its doorstep and on losing the income that it derived from mining operations there. Namibia is rich in minerals such as uranium, copper, lead and zinc, and is also the world's foremost source of gem diamonds. These were all mined by South African and Western multinational companies under a generous taxation scheme that enabled them to export up to a third of their profits every year.

Nationalism Emerges

Forced labour had been the lot of most Namibians since the German annexation, and was one of the main factors that led to mass demonstrations and the development of nationalism in the late 1950s. Around this time, a number of political parties were formed and strikes organised, not only among Namibian workers but also among contract labourers who had left to work in South Africa. Support was sought from the UN and by 1960 most of these parties had merged to form the South-West African People's Organisation (Swapo).

Swapo took the issue of South African occupation to the International Court of Justice in 1966. The outcome was inconclusive, but the UN General Assembly voted to terminate South Africa's mandate and set up the Council for South West Africa (renamed the Commission for Namibia in 1973) to administer the territory. The South African government responded to the UN demand by firing on demonstrators and arresting thousands of activists. At this stage Swapo launched its campaign of guerrilla warfare.

In 1975, the Democratic Turnhalle Alliance (DTA, named for the building where it originally met) was officially established as the dominant political party. Formed from a combination of both black and while political factions, it turned out to be a toothless debating chamber, which spent much of its time in litigation with the South African government over its scope of responsibilities. The DTA dissolved in 1983, after it had indicated it would accommodate Swapo, and was replaced by yet another administration, the Multi-Party Conference, which had even less success than the DTA and quickly disappeared. Control of Namibia passed back to the South African-appointed administrator-general.

These attempts to set up an internal government did not deter South Africa from maintaining its grip on Namibia. It refused to negotiate on a UN-supervised program for Namibian independence until an estimated 19,000 Cuban troops were removed from neighbouring Angola. In response, Swapo intensified its guerrilla campaign, which severely restricted movement in the north of the country.

The Road to Independence

In the end, it may not have been the activities of Swapo or the pressure of international sanctions which forced the South Africans to the negotiating table. The white Namibian population was growing tired of the war and the economy was suffering badly. South Africa was also facing crippling internal problems; by 1985, the war was costing it some R480 million per year and conscription was widespread. Mineral exports, which once provided around 88% of the country's GDP, had plummeted to just 27%, due mainly to

falling world demand and depressed prices, but also to fraud and corruption.

Thus, the stage was finally set for negotiations on Namibia's future. Under the auspices of the UN, the USA and the former USSR, a deal was struck between Cuba, Angola, South Africa and Swapo, in which Cuban troops would be removed from Angola and South African troops removed from Namibia. UN-monitored elections were held in late 1989 on the basis of universal suffrage. Swapo collected a clear majority of the votes, but its support was insufficient to give it the sole mandate to write the new constitution.

Following negotiations between the various parties, a constitution was adopted in February 1990 and independence was granted the following month under the presidency of Swapo leader, Sam Nujoma. Namibia's constitution is one of the few in Africa that provides for a democratically elected government and incorporates a series of checks and balances.

Recent Developments

Initially, President Sam Nujoma's policies focused on programmes of reconstruction and national reconciliation to heal the wounds left by 25 years of armed struggle. In 1999, however, Nujoma had nearly served out his second (and constitutionally, his last) five-year term; alarm bells went off among watchdog groups when he changed the constitution to allow himself a third five-year term, which he won with nearly 77% of the vote. On 2 August 1999, a separatist Lozi faction in the Caprivi Strip launched a coup attempt – which was summarily put down by the Namibian Defence Force. In December 1999, the Caprivi Strip also suffered a spate of violent attacks on civilians and tourists, which were rightly or wrongly blamed on the National Union for the Total Independence of Angola (Unita) sympathizers from Angola.

Despite President Sam Nujoma's recent attacks on homosexuality and Christianity, his desire for a fourth presidential term, and his open support of Robert Mugabe's disastrous policies in Zimbabwe (see the Zimbabwe chapter), Namibia's economy remains relatively stable, corruption remains somewhat under control and most Namibians harbour guarded hopes for the future of their fabulous country.

GEOGRAPHY

A predominantly arid country, Namibia can be divided into four main topographical regions: the Namib Desert and coastal plains in the west; the eastward-sloping Central Plateau; the Kalahari (often mistakenly called the 'Kalahari Desert') along the Botswanan and South African borders; and the densely wooded bushveld of the Kavango and Caprivi regions.

CLIMATE

Namibia's climatic variations correspond roughly to its geographical subdivisions. In the arid Central Namib, summer daytime temperatures may climb to over 40°C, but can fall to below freezing during the night. Rainfall is heaviest in the northeast, which enjoys a subtropical climate, and along the Okavango River, rainfall reaches over 600mm annually. The northern and interior regions experience the 'little rains' between October and December, while the main stormy period occurs from January to April.

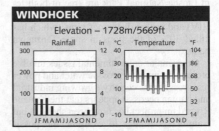

ECOLOGY & ENVIRONMENT

With a small human population spread over a large land area, Namibia is in better environmental shape than most African countries, but challenges remain. The Ministry of Environment & Tourism (MET) is largely a holdover from pre-independence days and its policies strongly reflect those of its South African counterpart. Although changes are afoot, at the time of research the country still lacked coherent environmental guidelines.

While local people are increasingly seeing more benefits from wildlife-oriented tourism, their activities in and near protected areas continue to affect local ecosystems. Many ranchers in the south view wildlife as a nuisance, while people in the more densely populated north see wildlife reserves as potential settlement areas and

wildlife itself as a food resource, and a threat to crops and human life.

In the wild areas of Damaraland and Kaokoland, which aren't officially protected, the desert lion is now extinct, but small numbers of desert elephants and black rhinos still roam freely. Although the white rhino was wiped out in Namibia prior to 1900, some have now been reintroduced into Waterberg and Etosha parks and are doing relatively well. Namibia was a pioneer in using dehorning to protect its rhino, but happily, recent declines in the international market for rhino horn have made such measures less relevant than in the past. The non-governmental **Save the Rhino Trust** (☎/fax 064-403829, e srt@rhino-trust.org.na; w www.rhino-trust.org.na; PO Box 224, Swakopmund) and the **Desert Research Foundation of Namibia** (☎ 061-229855, fax 230272; e drfn@drfn.org.na; PO Box 20232, Windhoek) both promote conservation education.

Although Namibia's lion population fluctuates greatly from season to season, the lions in Etosha National Park are free of both feline immunodeficiency virus (a feline form of HIV) and canine distemper virus (which has killed 30% of the lions in some Tanzanian parks).

Other major environmental issues involve projects designed to provide water and power resources for the country's growing industrial and human needs. It appears that the Kunene River dam project has now been shelved, but Namibia continues to examine the possibilities of bringing water to populated areas from the country's five perennial rivers.

FLORA & FAUNA

As Namibia is mostly arid, its typical vegetation features mainly scrubby bushveld and succulents, such as *Euphorbia*. Some unique floral oddities include the *kokerboom* (quiver tree; see the boxed text 'Kokerbooms' in the Southern Namibia section later in this chapter), which is a species of aloe, and the bizarre *Welwitschia mirabilis* (the welwitschia plant). Along the coastal plain around Swakopmund lie the world's most extensive and diverse lichen fields; in dry weather, they appear to be merely plant skeletons, but with the addition of water they burst into colourful bloom.

Etosha, Namibia's greatest wildlife park, contains a variety of antelope species, as well as other African ungulates, carnivores and pachyderms. Damaraland, in the northwest, is home to antelopes and other ungulates, and also harbours desert rhinos, elephants and other species that have specially adapted to the arid climate. Hikers in the Naukluft Massif may catch sight of the elusive Hartmann's mountain zebra, and along the desert coast live jackass penguins, flamingoes, Cape fur seals and the rare *strandwulf* (brown hyena). For more on flora and fauna, see 'The Dune Community' in the Central Namib Desert section, later in this chapter.

National Parks & Reserves

Despite its harsh climate, Namibia has some of the world's grandest national parks, ranging from the world-famous wildlife-oriented Etosha National Park to the immense Namib-Naukluft Park, which protects vast dunefields, desert plains, wild mountains and unique flora. There are also the smaller reserves of the Caprivi region, the renowned Skeleton Coast parks and the awe-inspiring Fish River Canyon, which ranks among Africa's most spectacular sights.

In addition to the national parks, Namibia has a network of conservancies, which are usually amalgamations of private farms, and private game reserves, which are individual farms supporting either tourist lodges or hunting opportunities. The latter designation, however, includes both the 200,000 hectare Namib–Rand Nature Reserve and the 102,000 hectare Gondwana Cañon Park.

Access to most wildlife-oriented parks is limited to enclosed vehicles only; no bicycles or motorcycles are allowed. For some parks, such as Etosha and Namib-Naukluft, 2WD is sufficient, but you need 4WD in Mamili National Park and the Khaudom Game Reserve.

Facilities in Namibian national parks are operated by the semi-official **Namibia Wildlife Resorts** (☎ 061-236975, fax 224900; e reservations@mweb.com.na; w www.namibia wildliferesorts.com; Independence Ave; Private Bag 13267, Windhoek; office open 8am-3pm Mon-Fri). When booking park camp sites or accommodation by post, phone, fax or email, include your passport number; the number of people in your group (including the ages of any children); your full address, telephone/fax number or email address; the type of accommodation required; and dates of arrival and departure (including alternative dates).

Bookings may be made up to 12 months in advance. Fees must be paid by bank transfer or credit card before the bookings will be confirmed. Note that camping fees are good for up to four people; each additional person up to eight people will be charged extra. In addition, parks charge a daily admission fee per person and per vehicle, payable when you enter the park.

Pre-booking is always advised. While you may be able to pick up accommodation at the last minute by just turning up at the park gates, it isn't recommended (especially for Etosha and Sesriem), as you may be caught out. Note that pets aren't permitted in any wildlife-oriented park.

Hiking is limited and highly regulated in Namibian national parks, advance booking is essential. Several long-distance routes are available: Waterberg Plateau four-day hike (US$12/24 unguided/guided routes); Naukluft eight-day hike (US$12); Ugab River four-day hike (US$24), Daan Viljoen two-day hike (US$8.50); and the five-day Fish River Canyon hike (US$12). The Naukluft and Daan Viljoen hikes are limited to groups of three to 12 people; the Waterberg unguided hike is open to three to 10 people; the Ugab and Waterberg guided hikes accommodate groups of three to eight people; and the Fish River hike allows groups of three to 40 people.

GOVERNMENT & POLITICS

Namibia is an independent republic, divided into 13 regions, each with its own regional government. The national president is elected by popular ballot for a maximum of three five-year terms; the legislative body, the National Assembly, is comprised of 72 members, who are elected by the people; and the independent judiciary is presided over by a chief justice.

Since independence on 21 March 1990 Namibia has been governed by a Swapo-dominated National Assembly, led by three-term President Sam Nujoma, which took 57% of the vote in the first national election. The main opposition is the moderate Democratic Turnhalle Alliance (DTA), a coalition of 11 parties with little in common but an opposition to Swapo's Owambo-centred position.

ECONOMY

The relatively prosperous Namibian economy is dominated by mining (diamonds and

---

Firewood

Firewood – normally split camelthorn acacia – is available for around US$2 per bundle at national park rest camps, most private camping grounds and general stores. Firewood gathering and open fires are prohibited in national parks, but even outside the parks wilderness hikers are advised to carry a fuel stove and avoid lighting open fires, which can scar the landscape and may get out of control in the typically dry conditions. If you must gather your own firewood, note that it's technically illegal in Namibia to use anything but mopane or acacia; burning or even carrying any other sort of wood will incur a fine, even outside national parks.

Warning: DO NOT burn dried branches of *Euphorbia*, as the plant contains a deadly toxin and it can be fatal to inhale the smoke or eat food cooked on a fire containing it. If you're in doubt about any wood you've collected, leave it out of the fire.

---

uranium), cattle and sheep herding, tourism and fishing, as well as subsistence agriculture. The economy faces some challenges such as water shortages, lack of local fuel sources, vast distances and a widely scattered population – but the country's GDP is twice the African average and its population remains small and diverse. Over 80% of the food and manufactured goods are imported from South Africa.

POPULATION & PEOPLE

Namibia has an estimated 1,826,854 people, which represents one of Africa's lowest population densities at approximately two people per sq km. This number comprises 11 major tribal groups, including Owambo (1 million people), Kavango (160,000), Herero/Himba (180,000), Damara (120,000), Caprivian (100,000), Nama (65,000), Afrikaner (65,000), Baster (35,000), German (20,000), San (19,000) and Tswana (8000). The remainder includes mainly Asians, non-German or non-Afrikaner Europeans (especially Portuguese), and refugees from other African countries. About 75% of the people inhabit rural areas, but urban drift in search of work or higher wages has resulted in increased homelessness, unemployment and crime in the capital and other towns.

NAMIBIA

ARTS

Although Namibia is still developing a literary tradition, its musical, visual and architectural arts are fairly well established. The country also enjoys a wealth of amateur talent in the production of material arts, including carvings, basketware and tapestry, along with simple but resourcefully designed and produced toys, clothing and household implements.

Dance

Each Namibian group has its own dances, but common threads run through most of them. San dancing tends to mimic the animals they hunt. The Himba dance *ondjongo* is performed only by cattle owners, who dance to demonstrate the care and ownership of their animals. Herero dances feature the *outjina* for women and *otjipirangi* for men, in which dancers strap planks to one foot in order to deliver a hollow, rhythmic percussion. In the Kavango and Caprivi regions, traditional dancing involves rhythmic and exaggerated stamping and gyrating, accompanied by repetitive chanting and a pervasive drumbeat.

Music

Namibia's earliest musicians were the San, whose music probably emulated the sounds made by their animal neighbours and was sung to accompany dances and storytelling. The early Nama, who had a more developed musical technique, used drums, flutes and basic stringed instruments, also to accompany dances. Some of these techniques were later adapted by Bantu peoples, who added marimbas, gourd rattles and animal-horn trumpets to the range. A prominent European contribution to Namibian music is the choir; the German colonists also introduced their traditional 'oom-pah-pah' bands, which feature mainly at German festivals.

Architecture

The most obvious architectural contribution in Namibia was made by the German colonists, who attempted to re-create late 19th-century Germany along the desert coast. In deference to the warmer climate, however, they added such features as shaded verandas, to provide cool outdoor living space. The best examples can be seen in Lüderitz,

---

The Himba

The distinctive Himba (or Ovahimba – 'those who ask for things') of Kaokoland are actually descended from a group of Herero herders who were displaced by Nama warriors in the 19th century. They fled to the remote northwest and continued their semi-nomadic lifestyle, raising sheep, goats and some cattle.

The Himba still largely eschew the modern world, and the missionary 'modesty police' never managed to persuade Himba women not to go topless. As a result, they maintain their lovely and distinctive traditional dress of multilayered goat-leather miniskirts and ochre-and-mud-encrusted iron, leather and shell jewellery. The use of a natural herbal perfume known as *otjizumba*, and their skin is smeared with a mixture of butter, ash and ochre, known locally as *otjize*. This is ostensibly to keep it youthful-looking and it must work, as even elderly Himba women have beautifully smooth skin. They also plaster their plaited hair with the same mixture, and the effect is truly stunning.

Visiting the Himba areas of Kaokoland requires awareness of the environment and people. Ask permission before entering or camping near a settlement, particularly as you may inadvertently violate a sacred fire or cross a ritual burial line. Also, ask permission before taking photos. Most rural Himba people, especially those who've had little contact with tourists, will be willing models. Some, however, may ask for payment, generally in the form of sweets, tobacco, sugar, mielies or soft drinks. In the interest of protecting teeth that may never meet a dentist, it's probably best to stick with fruit or mielies.

Because natural water sources are vital to local people, stock and wildlife, please don't use clear streams, springs or water holes for washing yourself or your gear. Similarly, avoid camping near springs or water holes lest you frighten the animals and inadvertently prevent them drinking.

Although the Himba remain one of Africa's most traditional societies, as tourism increases and Western values encroach on the region, things will change. Along main routes, visitors may encounter traditionally dressed Himba people who wave down vehicles and offer to model for photos in exchange for payment. Whether you accept is naturally up to you, but bear in mind that encouraging this trade draws people away from their herds and their semi-nomadic lifestyle and towards a cash economy.

Swakopmund and Windhoek. The most memorable structures were done in Wilhelminischer Stil and Jugendstil (Art Nouveau).

Art

Most of Namibia's renowned modern painters and photographers are of European origin; they mainly interpret the country's colourful landscapes, bewitching light, native wildlife and diverse peoples. Names include François de Mecker, Axel Eriksson, Fritz Krampe and Adolph Jentsch, as well as colonial landscape artists Carl Ossman and Ernst Vollbehr. Non-European rural Namibians, on the other hand, have generally concentrated on wood and stone sculpture. Township art, which develops sober themes in an expressive, colourful and generally light-hearted manner, first appeared in the townships of South Africa during the apartheid years. Names to watch out for include Tembo Masala and Joseph Madisia, among others.

LANGUAGE

At independence in 1990, the official language of Namibia was designated as English, but the first language of most Namibians is either a Bantu language, which would include Owambo, Kavango, Herero and Caprivian languages; or a Khoisan language, including Khoikhoi (Nama/Damara) and San dialects. In addition, Afrikaans is used as a lingua franca, and is the first language of over 100,000 Namibians of diverse ethnic backgrounds. German is also widely spoken but is the first language of only about 2% of the population. In the far north, Portuguese is the first language of an increasing number of Angolan immigrants. (See the Language chapter at the back of this book for some useful words and phrases.)

Facts for the Visitor

SUGGESTED ITINERARIES

Those with limited time may well want to stick to the highlights, but also to include a lesser-known area or two, to provide a taste of the 'best of Namibia'. Those with two weeks may want to begin in Windhoek and either hire a car or take an inexpensive organised tour to visit Etosha, Swakopmund, Sossusvlei and the Namib Desert Park, plus the Skeleton Coast, Twyfelfontein and other

Damaraland sites. If you have a month, cover those sites then either head south and add the Naukluft Mountains, Lüderitz and Fish River Canyon or thoroughly explore the north, taking in the Kaokoland, Kavango and Caprivi regions.

The Big Trip

For those on an extended trip in Southern Africa, your trip through Namibia will probably involve a journey in either direction between Ngoma Bridge (the nearest point to Victoria Falls) and either Noordoewer (for access to Cape Town) or Buitepos (en route to or from Botswana). These access points are relatively well-connected with Windhoek by the Intercape Mainliner and local minibuses. Once in the capital, you can most economically launch your circuit through Namibia's highlights either by hiring a vehicle or joining a local safari.

Travel Tips

In Namibia, where public transport is far from convenient, camping safaris are the way to go. They'll take you to the scenic highlights and still provide a measure of adventure, and you won't need to worry about driving, hitching – or hiking – along little-travelled gravel roads. If you are driving around the Central Namib, be sure to have a good map, as route numbers change on occasion and many turnoffs are poorly marked.

PLANNING
When to Go

Most of Namibia enjoys at least 300 days of sunshine a year, but generally, winter is the most pleasant season, while November to March can be very hot. Owamboland, Kavango and Caprivi are generally more humid and receive more summer rainfall than the Central Plateau.

Note that accommodation is frequently booked out in national parks and other tourist areas, especially during public holidays. The busiest times are consistently during Namibian, South African (see Public Holidays in the South Africa chapter) and European school holidays.

Maps

The Shell *Roadmap – Namibia* is probably the best reference for remote routes; it also has an excellent Windhoek map. Shell also

publishes the *Kaokoland-Kunene Region Tourist Map*, which depicts all routes and tracks through this remote area. It's available at bookshops and tourist offices for US$3.

The Macmillan *Namibia Travellers' Map*, at a scale of 1:2,400,000, has clear print and colour-graded altitude representation, but minor routes aren't depicted.

Beautiful but generally outdated government survey topographic sheets and aerial photos are available from the **Office of the Surveyor General** (☎ 061-245055, fax 249802; *Ministry of Justice, Robert Mugabe Ave, Private Bag 13267, Windhoek*). The 1: 250,000 series maps cost US$4 each and the 1:50,000 maps are US$3.

TOURIST OFFICES
Local Tourist Offices
Windhoek has both city and national tourist offices, and Karibib, Usakos, Omaruru, Okahandja, Gobabis, Keetmanshoop, Lüderitz, Swakopmund, Grootfontein and Tsumeb all have private or municipal tourist information offices. Look for the free publication *Welcome to Namibia – Tourist Accommodation & Info Guide*, which is distributed by **Namibia Tourism** (☎ 061-284 2360, fax 284 2364; e tourism@mweb.com.na; w www.tourism.com.na; *Continental building, ground floor, 272 Independence Ave, Private Bag 13346, Windhoek*). Also very useful is the glossy *Namibia Holiday & Travel* (☎ 061-225665, fax 220410; e nht@mac.com.na; w www.holidaytravel.com.na; PO Box 21593, Windhoek), which provides background information and listings. Those with a long-term interest in the country may want to subscribe to *Travel News Namibia* (☎ 061-225665, fax 220410; e tnn@iafrica.com.na; w www.travelnews.com.na; PO Box 21593, Windhoek).

Namibia Community Based Tourism Association (*Nacobta;* ☎ 061-250558, fax 222647; e nacobta@iafrica.com.na; w www.nacobta.com.na/en; *3 Weber St, PO Box 86099, Windhoek*) provides information on its network of community camping grounds and craft outlets around the country.

Tourist Offices Abroad
Germany *Namibia Verkehrsbüro:* (☎ 069-1337 3620, fax 1337 3615, e info@namibia-tour .com, w www.namibia-tourism.com) Schillerstrasse 42-44, D-60313 Frankfurt-am-Main

South Africa *Namibia Tourism:* (☎ 021-419 3190, fax 421 5840, e namibia@saol.com) Main Tower, Standard Bank Centre, Ground floor, Adderley St, PO Box 739, Cape Town 8000
Namibia Tourism: (☎ 011-784 8024, fax 784 8340, e namtour@netdail.co.za) 11 Alice Lane, 3rd floor, East Wing, Standard Bank Bldg, PO Box 78946, Sandton 2146
UK *Namibia Tourism:* (☎ 020-7636 2924, fax 7636 2969, e info@namibiatourism.co.uk, w www.namibiatourism.co.uk) 6 Chandos St, London W1G 9LU
USA *Kartagener Associates Inc:* (☎ 516-858 1270, e kainyc@att.net) 631 Commack Rd, Suite 1A, Commack, NY 11725

VISAS & DOCUMENTS
All visitors require a passport that is valid for at least six months after their intended departure date from Namibia, as well as a means of leaving the region (a vehicle or an onward plane or bus ticket). No visas are required for visitors from Australia, New Zealand, France, Germany, the UK, Ireland, Canada or the US. Tourists receive entry for an initial 90 days, but extensions are available from Immigration offices. Windhoek is useful for picking up visas for Mozambique, Malawi, Zambia, Kenya and Tanzania; for Angolan visas, your best bet is the Angolan Consulate in Oshakati (see the Northern Namibia section).

Hostel cards, student cards and senior cards are of little use in Namibia.

Visas for Onward Travel
Windhoek is a good place to pick up visas for several countries; for contact details, see Embassies & Consulates in Namibia.

Angola Visas are readily available only to Namibian citizens and residents; others must apply in their home country (usually limited to fly-in visas for arrival in Luanda) or attempt to secure an overland visa in Oshakati.
Kenya UK citizens need a visa, which costs US$50 and takes two days to process. A multiple-entry visa costs US$100 and can take up to six weeks to issue. Citizens of the US and Australia can enter Kenya for 30 days without a visa; longer stays require a visa which is issued in two days and costs US$53.
Zambia Visas are required by US, Australian and UK citizens. In Windhoek, they take one day to process and cost US$59/94 for a single/double-entry visa, and US$188 for a multiple-entry visa. Note that they're available at the border

for considerably less (normally US$25 for US citizens and £45 for UK citizens). However, they're free if you're 'introduced' to Zambia by a Zambian company (such as a hotel, backpackers' hostel or tour company).

Zimbabwe Australia, New Zealand and US citizens need a visa, which can be processed at the border (US$30/45 for single/double entry). However, you can also secure a visa in advance for the same rates; multiple-entry visas cost US$55 and aren't available at the border.

EMBASSIES & CONSULATES
Namibian Embassies
Namibia has embassies and high commissions in South Africa, Zambia and Zimbabwe (see the relevant country chapters). If you need a visa and your home country lacks a Namibian diplomatic mission, fax or post your passport details and desired length of stay to the **Ministry of Home Affairs** (☎ *061-292 2111, fax 292 2185;* e *mlusepani@mha.gov.na; Private Bag 13200, Windhoek)* and hope for the best.

Namibian diplomatic representatives elsewhere include:

Angola (☎ 02-395483, fax 333923) 95 Rua Dos Coqueiros, PO Box 953, Luanda
France (☎ 01-44 17 32 65, fax 44 17 32 73) 80 avenue Foch, Square de l'Avenue Foch, F-75116 Paris
Germany (☎ 0228-346021, fax 346025) Mainzerstr 47, D-53179 Bonn
UK (☎ 020-7636 6244, fax 7637 5694, e namibia-highcomm@btconnect.com) 6 Chandos St, London W1G 9LU
USA (☎ 202-986 0540, fax 986 0443, e emb namibia@aol.com, w www.grnnet .gov.na) 1605 New Hampshire Ave NW, Washington DC 20009

Embassies & Consulates in Namibia
All of the following are in Windhoek (area code ☎ 061); opening hours are weekdays only:

Angola (☎ 227535, fax 221498) Angola House, 3 Ausspann St, Ausspannplatz, Private Bag 12020. Open 9am to 1pm.
Botswana (☎ 221941, fax 236034) 101 Nelson Mandela Dr, PO Box 20359. Open 8am to 12.30pm.
European Union (☎ 220099) 4th Floor, Sanlam Centre, 154 Independence Ave, PO Box 231. Open 9am to 12.30pm.

France (☎ 229022, fax 231436) 1 Goethe St, PO Box 20484. Open 9am to 12.30pm and 1.30pm to 5pm.
Germany (☎ 223100, fax 222981) 6th floor, Sanlam Centre, 154 Independence Ave, PO Box 231. Open 9am to 12.30pm.
Kenya (☎ 226836, fax 221409) Kenya House, Robert Mugabe Ave, PO Box 2889. Open 9am to 12.30pm and 2pm to 5pm.
Malawi (☎ 221391, fax 227056) 56 Bismarck St, Windhoek West, PO Box 23547. Open 9am to noon and 2pm to 5pm.
South Africa (☎ 205 7111, fax 224140) RSA House, cnr Jan Jonker St and Nelson Mandela Dr, Klein Windhoek, PO Box 23100. Open 8.15am to 12.15pm.
UK (☎ 223022, fax 228895, e bhc@mweb .com.na) 116A Robert Mugabe Ave, PO Box 22202. Open 9am to noon.
USA (☎ 221601, fax 229792, w www.us embassy.namibnet.com) 14 Lossen St, Ausspannplatz, Private Bag 12029. Open 8am to noon Monday, Wednesday and Friday.
Zambia (☎ 237610, fax 228162) cnr Sam Nujoma Dr and Mandume Ndemufayo Ave, PO Box 22882. Open 8am to 1pm and 2pm to 4pm.
Zimbabwe (☎ 228134, fax 226859) Gamsberg Bldg, cnr Independence Ave & Grimm St, PO Box 23056. Open 9am to 12.30pm and 2pm to 3pm.

CUSTOMS
Any item (except vehicles) from elsewhere in the Southern African Customs Union – Botswana, South Africa, Lesotho and Swaziland – may be imported duty free. From elsewhere, visitors can import duty free 400 cigarettes or 250g of tobacco, 2L of wine, 1L of spirits and 250ml of eau de Cologne.

MONEY
Currency
The Namibian dollar (N$) equals 100 cents, and in Namibia it's pegged to the South African rand (in South Africa, it fetches only about R0.70), which is also legal tender at a rate of 1:1. This can be confusing, given that there are three sets of coins and notes in use, all with different sizes: old South African, new South African and Namibian. Namibian dollar notes come in denominations of N$10, N$20, N$50, N$100 and N$200, and coins in values of 5, 10, 20 and 50 cents, and N$1 and N$5.

Exchange Rates
At the time of publication, the Namibian dollar had the following values against other currencies:

country	unit		N$
Australia	A$1	=	N$5.33
Botswana	P1	=	N$1.55
Canada	C$1	=	N$5.95
euro zone	€1	=	N$9.46
Japan	¥100	=	N$6.83
Malawi	MK1	=	N$0.09
Mozambique	Mtc100	=	N$0.03
New Zealand	NZ$1	=	N$4.63
South Africa	R1	=	N$1.02
Tanzania	Tsh100	=	N$0.80
UK	UK£1	=	N$13.41
USA	US$1	=	N$8.05
Zambia	ZK100	=	N$0.16
Zimbabwe	ZW$100	=	N$0.99

Exchanging Money
Visitors can bring unlimited currency or travellers cheques into Namibia. Major foreign currencies and travellers cheques may be exchanged at any bank (for up to 7% commission). In Windhoek, both AmEx and Thomas Cook have outlets where you can exchange their travellers cheques without commission. When changing money, you can opt for either South African rand or Namibian dollars; to change leftover currency outside the country, you'll need rand.

Credit cards are widely accepted in shops, restaurants and hotels, and credit-card cash advances are available at banks and from ATMs.

Costs
If you're camping or staying in backpackers hostels, cooking your own meals and hitching or using local minibuses, you'll get by on as little as US$15 per day. A plausible mid-range budget, which would include B&B or doubles in backpackers accommodation, public transport and at least one restaurant meal daily, would be around US$50 to US$80 per person (if accommodation costs are shared between two people). In the upper range, accommodation at hotels, meals in restaurants and escorted tours will cost upwards of US$300 per person per day.

To reach Namibia's most popular tourist sites, you'll have to take an organised tour or hire a vehicle (see the Getting Around section). Car hire may be expensive for budget travellers, but if you can muster a group of four people and share costs, you can squeak by on an additional US$20/50 per day for a 2WD/4WD vehicle, including petrol, tax, insurance and 200 free km per day.

Tipping & Bargaining
Tipping is expected only in upmarket tourist establishments, but many places add a service charge as a matter of course. Tipping is officially prohibited in national parks and reserves, and bargaining is only acceptable when purchasing handicrafts and arts directly from the artist or artisan.

POST & COMMUNICATIONS
Post
Domestic post generally moves slowly; for example, it can take several weeks for a letter to travel from Windhoek to Lüderitz or Katima Mulilo. Overseas airmail post is normally more efficient, and is limited only by the time it takes the letter to get from where you post it to Windhoek. Poste restante works best in Windhoek (Poste Restante, GPO, Windhoek, Namibia). Photo identification is required to collect mail.

Telephone
Namibian trunk dialling codes all have three digits and begin with ☎ 06. When phoning Namibia from abroad, dial the international access code (☎ 09 from South Africa, ☎ 011 from the US and ☎ 00 from most other places), then the country code (☎ 264), followed by the trunk dialling code (without the leading zero) and the desired number. To phone out of Namibia, dial ☎ 00 followed by the country code, area code and number. Telecom Namibia Flexicards (you buy only as much time as you want) are sold at post offices and some retail shops, and most Internet cafés also have fax services. Some remote bush locations subscribe to a message service operated by **Walvis Bay Radio** (☎ 064-203581), which relays messages.

Mobile phones are widely used, but won't function more than 20km or so out of a major city or town. Mobile telephone numbers typically begin with the prefixes ☎ 0811 and ☎ 0812, followed by a six-digit number.

Email & Internet Access
Both email and Internet access are available at backpackers hostels, Internet cafés and

hotels in larger towns, and also at several tourist offices and remote lodges.

DIGITAL RESOURCES

Cardboard Box Travel Shop (W www.namibian .org) Namibia's best budget and adventure travel agency is the place for a range of travel options, excellent background information, and efficient bookings.

Gorp Travel (W www.gorp.com) This is another useful trip-planning site, with links to adventure outfits featuring Namibia.

The Namibian (W www.namibian.com.na) For up-to-date news from Namibia, try the *Namibian* newspaper site.

Namibia Tourism (W www.tourism.com.na) The national tourist office site provides a wide range of local travel information.

Namibia Wildlife Resorts (W www.namibiawild liferesorts.com) Includes guidelines on booking national parks, permits, and accommodation.

Namibia Holiday & Travel (W www.holidaytravel .com.na) This site provides information from the glossy publication of the same name.

Natron.Net (W www.natron.net/etour.htm) This is a good tourism site, with useful links.

For more information, see the Digital Resources section in the Regional Facts for the Visitor chapter.

BOOKS
Guidebooks

Guide to Namibian Game Parks, by Willie and Sandra Olivier, has the lowdown on national parks, wildlife reserves and other conservation areas, with useful maps and advice on wildlife viewing. It's available locally.

Travel

Horns of Darkness – Rhinos on the Edge, by conservationists Carol Cunningham and Joel Berger, describes a journey through the Namibian wilds to find and protect the country's remaining desert rhinos.

The Sheltering Desert, by Henno Martin, is a Namibian classic recounting the adventures of German geologists Henno Martin and Hermann Korn, who spent two years in the Namib Desert avoiding Allied forces during WWII.

History & Politics

The Colonising Camera, by Wolfram Hartmann (ed) et al, is part of the new historical writings. This book is an illustrated history of the country.

To Free Namibia: The Life of the First President of Namibia, by Sam Nujoma, is an autobiography of the president.

Herero Heroes, by JB Gewald, blends oral and written accounts to provide a fascinating history of Namibia's Herero people.

Namibia – the Struggle for Liberation, by Alfred T Moleah, is an account of Swapo's independence struggle and describes the situation before success was certain.

General

The Burning Shore, by Wilbur Smith, is highly entertaining and is probably the best novel set in Namibia.

Kaokoveld - the Last Wilderness, by Anthony Hall-Martin, J du P Bothma and Clive Walker, is a breathtaking compilation of beguiling photos and will have you heading for Northwestern Namibia.

NEWSPAPERS & MAGAZINES

Most of Namibia's English-language newspapers are based in Windhoek: the *Namibian*, published weekdays; the *Windhoek Observer*, published on Saturday; and the government-owned *New Era*. The *Namib Times*, from Walvis Bay, is issued twice weekly. The two main German-language newspapers are the *Allgemeine Zeitung* and the *Namibia Nachrichten*. The monthly English-language *Namibia Review* is good for national political, cultural and economic issues; contact **Namibia Review** (☎ 061-222246, fax 224937; Ministry of Information & Broadcasting, Private Bag 11334, Windhoek).

RADIO & TV

The Namibian Broadcasting Corporation (NBC) operates nine radio stations broadcasting on different wavebands in 12 languages; the best pop station is Radio Wave, at 96.7FM in Windhoek.

NBC television broadcasts government-vetted programming in English and Afrikaans from 4pm to 11pm weekdays and later on Friday and Saturday. On Sunday, Christian programming is broadcast from 11am to 1pm and other programming from 3pm. News is broadcast at 10pm nightly. Most hotels also offer DSTV, a satellite service with a cocktail of cable channels.

HEALTH

Malaria is currently endemic in northern Namibia. For further information, see Dangers & Annoyances following, as well as the Health section in the Regional Facts for the Visitor chapter.

DANGERS & ANNOYANCES

Theft isn't particularly rife in Namibia, but in Windhoek and Swakopmund, avoid walking alone at night and conceal your valuables. Similarly, don't leave anything in sight inside a vehicle or at camp sites, and keep valuables inside your sleeping bag at night.

Kavango and Caprivi both have malarial mosquito problems, and bilharzia is present all over northern Namibia; in the eastern Caprivi, the tsetse fly is especially active at dusk, and all of northern Namibia's rivers harbour very large crocodiles.

East of Lüderitz, keep well clear of the Sperrgebiet, the prohibited diamond area, as well-armed patrols can be overly zealous. The area begins immediately south of the Lüderitz–Keetmanshoop road and continues to just west of Aus, where the off-limits boundary turns south towards the Orange River.

LEGAL MATTERS

Police and military officials are generally polite and well-behaved, but visitors would be wise to treat them with utmost deference, especially in areas which may be experiencing tension.

BUSINESS HOURS

Normal business hours are from 8am to 1pm and 2.30pm to 5pm weekdays. In the winter, when it gets dark early, some shops open at 7.30am and close at around 4pm. Lunchtime closing is almost universal. On Saturdays, most city and town shops open from 8am to 1pm. Banks, government departments and tourist offices also keep these hours, but some petrol stations, especially along highways, are open 24 hours.

PUBLIC HOLIDAYS & SPECIAL EVENTS

Resort areas are busiest over both Namibian and South African school holidays, which normally occur from mid-December to mid-January, around Easter, from late July to early August, and for two weeks in mid-October.

New Year's Day 1 January
Good Friday March or April
Easter Sunday March or April
Easter Monday March or April
Independence Day 21 March
Ascension Day April or May – 40 days after Easter
Workers' Day 1 May
Cassinga Day 4 May
Africa Day 25 May
Heroes' Day 26 August
Human Rights Day 10 December
Christmas 25 December
Family/Boxing Day 26 December

A major local event is Maherero Day, on the weekend nearest 26 August, when the Red Flag Herero people gather in traditional dress at Okahandja for a memorial service to the chiefs killed in the German Nama wars. A similar event, also at Okahandja, is staged by the Mbanderu or Green Flag Herero on the weekend nearest 11 June. On the weekend nearest 10 October, the White Flag Herero gather in Omaruru to honour their chief Zeraua.

Among the ethnic European community, events include the Windhoek Karnival (WIKA) in late April/early May; the Küska (Küste Karnival) at Swakopmund in late August/early September; the Windhoek Agricultural Show in late September; and the Windhoek Oktoberfest in late October.

ACTIVITIES

Hiking is a highlight in Namibia, and a growing number of private ranches have established wonderful hiking routes for their guests; the finest ones include Klein-Aus Vista, near Aus; Namibgrens Rest Camp, in the Khomas Hochland near the Namib-Naukluft Park; and Canyon Adventures, south of Keetmanshoop. You'll also find superb routes in the national parks: Daan Viljoen, Namib-Naukluft, Fish River Canyon, Waterberg Plateau and the Ugab River area of the Skeleton Coast. For more about the latter, see Hiking under National Parks, earlier in this chapter.

A growing craze is **sandboarding**, which is commercially available in Swakopmund. In the same area, operators offer **horse** and **camel riding, quad-biking, deep-sea fishing, sea kayaking, bird-watching** and **skydiving**. A growing number of **4WD** routes are opening up for a largely South African market, including several popular routes along remote sections of the Namib Desert.

White-water rafting is available on the Kunene River, but it's extremely expensive; more down-to-earth is the white-water canoeing along the Orange River, on the South African border.

WORK

The chances of a foreigner scoring a long-term Namibian work or residence permit are remote, but some are successful. Namibia's current policy is to accept only wealthy overseas investors starting up a business in the country or those who can provide skills and expertise that's not locally available. If you are offered a job, you (or better, your prospective employer) must secure a temporary residence permit from the Ministry of Home Affairs (☎ 061-292 2111, fax 292 2185; e mlusepani@mha.gov.na; Private Bag 13200, Windhoek). While it may be relatively easy to get a three-month work permit, to extend it or secure a one-year permit is usually quite difficult. Getting a permanent residence permit may well subject you to more insanity-inspiring bureaucracy than you're prepared to face. Note that even marrying a Namibian citizen won't guarantee a permanent residence permit.

ACCOMMODATION

Namibia has an exhaustive (and growing) array of hotels, rest camps, camping grounds, caravan parks, guest farms, backpackers hostels, B&Bs, guesthouses and safari lodges. It would take an enormous volume to mention everything that's available, so those included in this book are recommended and/or provide accommodation in areas with few options. Note, however, that the lack of a mention here doesn't mean that an establishment isn't recommended.

For further information, see the following annual publications, which are distributed at tourist offices: Where to Stay – Namibia, Welcome to Namibia – Tourist Accommodation & Info Guide, Namibia Holiday & Travel and the listings and accompanying map produced by the Hospitality Association of Namibia (HAN).

Hotels and most other establishments are graded using a star system; awards are based on guidelines from the Ministry of Environment & Tourism. The accommodation rates listed in this chapter are rack rates for overseas bookings, and include 15% VAT. In most cases, you'll get the best rates when booking from within Namibia.

Camping

Most towns have caravan parks with bungalows or rondavels (round African-style huts) where you can stay for very reasonable rates. For information on camping in national parks, see National Parks Accommodation, later in this section. Anyone is welcome to camp on communal lands, but if you can't get out of sight, it's polite to ask locals to direct you to an unobtrusive place to set up. On private land, you must secure permission from the landowner.

Hostels & B&Bs

Backpackers hostels now operate in Windhoek, Swakopmund, Walvis Bay, Outjo, Keetmanshoop, and Lüderitz, and more are planned. They provide dorm accommodation and cooking facilities, and range from US$5.50 to US$8 per person. B&B establishments are also emerging around the country; for listings, contact the Budget & Home Association of Namibia (☎ 061-222899, fax 239382; e info@bed-breakfast-namibia.com; w www.bed-breakfast-namibia.com; PO Box 90270, Klein Windhoek).

Hotels

The Namibian hotel-classification system rates everything from small guesthouses to four-star hotels. Most are locally owned and managed, and most have at least a breakfast room, if not a dining room and a bar. Any hotel with a name that includes the word garni lacks a full dining room, but does offer a simple breakfast. The most luxurious hotels include the Kalahari Sands and Windhoek Country Club, both in Windhoek, and the Swakopmund Hotel & Entertainment Centre.

National Parks Accommodation

Namibia Wildlife Resorts (NWR) oversees accommodation in the national parks and offers a range of camp sites, bungalows, chalets and 'bus quarters' (for bus tours). Most sites include access to a swimming pool, shop, kiosk, restaurant, braai (barbecue) facilities and well-maintained ablutions (amenities) blocks. During school holidays, visitors may be limited to three nights at each

of the three Etosha National Park camps and 10 nights at other camps. Pets aren't permitted in any camp, but kennels are available at the gates of Daan Viljoen, Von Bach Dam, Gross-Barmen, Ai-Ais and Hardap Dam. For booking information, see the National Parks section, under Facts About Namibia, earlier in this chapter.

Guest Farms

A growing number of mainly German-Namibian private farms welcome guests, and provide insight into the white rural lifestyle. Many of these farms have also established hiking routes and set aside areas as wildlife and hunting reserves. In all cases, advance bookings are essential.

Safari Lodges

Most of Namibia's lodges offer luxury accommodation and superb international cuisine. Rates are very reasonable when compared to similar places in other countries in the region and there's little multi-tier pricing. Even around the popular Etosha National Park, you'll pay a third of what you'd pay for similar lodges in the Okavango Delta. Other areas are even more reasonably priced.

FOOD

Outside Windhoek and Swakopmund, you'll find few gourmet pretences. Most hotels serve three meals, but menus are usually meat-orientated and are rarely very creative. For a treat, try one of the German-style *konditorei* (pastry shops) in Windhoek or Swakopmund, or try one of the pleasant cafés that exist in most towns.

Small hotels normally provide a cooked breakfast with cereal and toast, and big hotels may include a buffet breakfast. In addition to bread, cereals, fruit, yogurt and cold meat, they may offer kippers (smoked kingclip) and mielie meal (porridge, also called *pap*). Cooked breakfasts always include eggs, bacon and *boerewors* (farmer's sausages), as well as steaks and often even curried kidneys.

For lunch, many people go for takeaway snacks, which may include fish and chips, meat pies and sandwiches in *brötchen* ('little bread' rolls). Evening meals normally feature meat, and restaurants serve typically high-quality cuts. Fish (normally kingclip) is best eaten in Swakopmund or Lüderitz,

where it's probably fresh. Chicken is often prepared with a fiery *peri-peri* sauce.

DRINKS
Nonalcoholic Drinks

Tap water is generally safe to drink, but in some places it may emerge salty or otherwise unappealing, especially in desert areas and around Windhoek and Etosha. Packaged fruit juices provide an alternative. Every café and takeaway serves coffee and tea – as well as the strong herbal tea known as rooibos (red bush).

Alcoholic Drinks

Namibia's dry heat means big sales for Namibia Breweries. The most popular drop is Windhoek Lager, a light and refreshing lager-style beer, but the brewery also produces Tafel Lager, the stronger and more bitter Windhoek Export and the slightly rough Windhoek Special. Windhoek Light (a tasty beer with just 2% alcohol) and the similarly light Das Pilsner are both drunk as soft drinks. The same brewery also produces a 7% stout known as Urbock.

Namibia Breweries' main competitor is Hansa, in Swakopmund, which produces both standard and export-strength beer. South African beers like Lion, Castle and Black Label are widely available and you'll also find a range of refreshing spirit coolers and typically excellent and great-value South African wines. The best place to buy beer, wine or spirits is a *drankwinkel* (bottle store), but small convenience shops may also sell beer and coolers.

In the rural areas – especially the Owambo regions – people socialise in tiny makeshift bars, enjoying such traditional local brews as *oshikundu* (millet beer), *mataku* (watermelon wine), *tambo* (fermented millet and sugar), *mushokolo*, (a beer made from small seeds) and *walende*, which is distilled from the makalani palm and tastes similar to vodka. Apart from *walende*, all of these rural confections are brewed in the morning and drunk the same day, and they're all dirt cheap – around US$0.20 per glass.

SHOPPING

Potential souvenirs range from kitsch African curios and airport art to superb Owambo basketry and Kavango woodcarvings. Along the highway between Rundu and Grootfontein,

roadside stalls sell locally produced items, from woven mats and baskets to appealing wooden aeroplanes and helicopters, which are a Kavango speciality. In Bushmanland, Rundu and the northeast, you'll find distinctive San material arts – bows and arrows, ostrich-egg beads, leather pouches and jewellery made from seeds and nuts.

The Namib Desert's pastel colours inspire artists, and galleries in Windhoek and Swakopmund specialise in local paintings, weavings and sculpture. Also, some lovely items are produced in conjunction with the karakul wool industry, such as rugs, wall hangings and textiles that can be made to order.

Minerals and gemstones also make popular purchases, either in the raw form or cut and polished as jewellery, sculptures or carvings. For fine work, see the Kristall Gallerie in Swakopmund, Henckert Tourist Centre in Karibib or the House of Gems near the corner of Stübel and John Meinert Streets in Windhoek.

Namibian stamps are also quite collectable; contact **Namibia Post Philatelic Services** (☎ 061-201 3107, fax 259467; ℮ philately@ nampost.com.na; W www.nampost.com.na; Private Bag 13336, Windhoek).

Getting There & Away

This section covers access into Namibia from neighbouring countries only. You'll find information about reaching Southern Africa from elsewhere in Africa and other continents in the Regional Getting There & Away chapter.

AIR
Airports & Airlines
South African Airways and **Air Namibia** (☎ 061-298 2531; W www.airnamibia.com.na) operate daily flights between Johannesburg, Cape Town and Windhoek. A one-way fare from Windhoek to Jo'burg/Cape Town starts at around US$200. Air Namibia has daily flights between Windhoek's in-town Eros airport and Alexander Bay (South Africa), which is the airport for Oranjemund. It also flies twice weekly between Windhoek and Harare (Zimbabwe) for US$385 return, Victoria Falls (Zimbabwe) for US$475, Lusaka

(Zambia) for US$380, Maun (Botswana) for US$250 and Gaborone (Botswana) for US$247.

LAND
Namibia's public transport system is very limited, and there are very few cross-border services. Note that if you're taking a Namibian registered vehicle out of the country, you must first secure police clearance from any Namibian police station; you'll also need a 'Blue Book' sheet with the vehicle's engine and chassis number. To enter Namibia with a foreign-registered vehicle, at the border you must purchase a US$10 road-use tax certificate.

Angola
There are three border crossings between Namibia and Angola, at Ruacana/Calueque (6pm to 10pm), Oshikango/Namacunda (8am to 6pm) and Nkurenkuru/Cuangar (7am to 5pm), but travellers need an Angolan visa permitting overland entry. These are best obtained at the Angolan consulate in Oshakati, as the embassy in Windhoek tends to only give visas for air travel into Luanda. At Ruacana Falls, you can briefly enter the border area without a visa; just sign in at the border post.

Botswana
The Trans-Kalahari Highway crosses the border between Buitepos and Mamuno (8am to 1am). From the Rhino Park terminus in Windhoek, minibuses run to Buitepos (US$7, five hours), on the Botswanan border. From there, buses leave for Ghanzi when full, but note that you may wait awhile at the border. At 7.30am on Wednesday, Audi Camp in Maun, Botswana, runs a useful shuttle service (Windhoek ☎ 0811- 272870, Maun ☎ 686 0599) from Windhoek to Maun (US$55, 10 hours); from Maun, it returns on Monday at 7.30am. Pre-booking is essential.

In the Caprivi, you can cross the border at Ngoma Bridge (8am to 6pm) or between Mahango and Mohembo (6am to 7pm). The border crossing between Mpalila Island and Kasane (7am to 12.30pm and 1.45pm to 4pm) is served by boat transfer from Kasane for guests of safari lodges on the island. There's also a 4WD border crossing at Dobe in Bushmanland, but to cross here you'll need to carry extra fuel.

Although the Intercape Mainliner between Windhoek and Victoria Falls passes briefly through Botswana, passengers may not embark or disembark there.

South Africa

The **Intercape Mainliner** (☎ 061-227847; e info@intercape.co.za; w www.intercape.co .za) coach service from Windhoek to Cape Town (US$45, 19½ hours) and Johannesburg (US$58, with a change at Upington, 24½ hours) leaves on Monday, Wednesday, Friday and Sunday at 6pm. In Windhoek, visit the office on Gallilei Street or book through their agent, the **Cardboard Box Travel Shop** (☎ 061-256580, fax 256581; e namibia@bigfoot.com). Students, seniors and backpackers receive a 15% to 20% discount.

Most highway traffic between Namibia and South Africa passes through the crossing between Noordoewer and Vioolsdrif (24 hours); secondary routes include the crossings at Ariamsvlei (24 hours), and between Aroab and Rietfontein (6am to 10pm). Namdeb (formerly Consolidated Diamond Mines or CDM) allows no public access between Alexander Bay and Oranjemund without permission (this is normally only granted to individuals on official business).

By rail, Trans-Namib runs trains between Windhoek and Upington on Tuesday and Friday southbound and Sunday and Thursday northbound.

Zambia

The only crossing between Namibia and Zambia is via the Zambezi pontoon ferry at Wenela/Sesheke. From Sesheke, at least one daily bus chugs down the horribly potholed road to Livingstone (US$8.50, 5 to 6 hours). From Livingstone, buses to Sesheke leave anytime after 6am from the Muramba bus station, 1km from the centre. If you're heading for Namibia, check whether your bus continues to the border; if not, you'll have to walk or hitch the last 5km from Sesheke to the border crossing.

The pontoon ferry over the Zambezi between Wenela (4km from Katima Mulilo) and the Zambian riverfront 5km from Sesheke costs US$10 per vehicle; pedestrians ride free. Alternatively, passengers can opt for the small private boats which carry passengers across the river for a negotiable fee –

usually between US$0.50 and US$1.50. Zambian Immigration is 500m from the ferry crossing and Namibian Immigration is 1km away.

A bridge is now being built over the river, but its opening remains several years off. For those with a vehicle, more convenient access to Livingstone and the rest of Zambia (apart from the extreme southwest) involves crossing into Botswana at Ngoma Bridge, transiting Chobe National Park, and then using the Kazungula ferry (US$12 to US$20 per vehicle, passengers US$0.50) across the Zambezi to Kazungula, Zambia. Alternatively, it's easy to take the Intercape Mainliner bus to Victoria Falls, Zimbabwe, from where it's an easy border crossing into Zambia (but most travellers need a visa to transit Zimbabwe; see the Zimbabwe chapter for further details).

Zimbabwe

There's no direct border crossing between Namibia and Zimbabwe; the easiest access is via the Chobe National Park transit route from Ngoma Bridge through northern Botswana to Kasane and Kazungula, and from there to Victoria Falls. On Monday and Friday at 8pm, Intercape Mainliner (see under South Africa, earlier in this section) connects Windhoek with Victoria Falls (US$52, 19¾ hours), via Grootfontein, Rundu and Katima Mulilo.

Getting Around

AIR

Air Namibia (☎ 061-298 2531; w www.air namibia.com.na) serves domestic routes out of Eros airport in Windhoek, including flights to and from Tsumeb; Katima Mulilo (Mpacha); Keetmanshoop; Etosha (Mokuti Lodge); Lüderitz, Alexander Bay (South Africa); Swakopmund and Ondangwa/ Oshakati. There is no domestic departure tax.

BUS

From Windhoek, **Intercape Mainliner** (☎ 061-227847; e info@intercape.co.za; main offices Gallilei St) serves Swakopmund, Walvis Bay, Grootfontein, Rundu and Katima Mulilo. (For international services, see Getting There & Away, earlier in this chapter.) The main

terminal in Windhoek is near the corner of Fidel Castro and Rev Michael Scott Streets, uphill from the large car park along the main street, Independence Avenue.

Trans-Namib runs its **Star Line buses** (☎ 061-298 2030, fax 298 2383), which combine with Trans-Namib's rail services to access Lüderitz, Maltahöhe, Mariental, Helmeringhausen, Keetmanshoop, Koes, Gochas, Gobabis, Khorixas, Uis, Henties Bay, Tsumkwe, Walvis Bay and other destinations.

Mass public transport in Namibia is provided by long-distance minibuses, which operate according to no set schedule, and simply depart when full from designated stops in major towns. Fares work out to US$0.03 per km, but there may be an additional charge of US$1 or so if you have a large piece of luggage to stow in the trailer. From Windhoek, the minibus terminal is at the Rhino Park petrol station; services from the capital are most frequent on Friday afternoons, with return trips on Sunday afternoons.

TRAIN

Windhoek is the hub for the Trans-Namib rail lines, with four services: south to Rehoboth, Mariental and Keetmanshoop; north to Omaruru and Tsumeb; west to Swakopmund and Walvis Bay; and east to Gobabis. Note that on weekends (Friday to Monday), seats are normally double what they are during the week. Book through the **Windhoek Booking Office** (☎ 061-298 2030, fax 298 2495) in the main Windhoek train station. Bookings cost US$0.60 and tickets must be collected by 4pm on the day of departure.

The plush 'rail cruise' aboard the **Desert Express** (☎ 061-298 2600, fax 298 2601; e dx@transnamib.com.na; w www.desert express.com.na) runs overnight trips between Windhoek and Swakopmund (US$245/360 single/double) twice weekly in either direction. It also does four-day return trips between Windhoek and Tsumeb for US$325/ 550 for single/double sleepers and meals, with visits to Omaruru, Tsumeb and Etosha.

The tourist-oriented **Shongololo Dune Express** (☎ South Africa 27-21-556 0372, fax 557 1034; e info@shongololo.com; w www .shongololo.com) starts in Windhoek and spends 15 days covering Namibia's major sites of interest. The all-inclusive one-way fare is US$2500/4625 for a single/double.

CAR & MOTORCYCLE

An excellent system of sealed roads runs from Noordoewer in the south to Ngoma Bridge in the northeast. Similarly, sealed spur roads connect the main north–south arteries to Buitepos (on the Trans-Kalahari Highway to Lobatse and Gaborone, in Botswana), Lüderitz, Outjo, Kamanjab, Swakopmund and Walvis Bay. Most other towns and sites of interest are accessible on good gravel roads.

Vehicles keep to the left, with a general speed limit of 120km/h on open roads and 60km/h in built-up areas. Drivers and passengers in the front seat must use seat belts. Most car hire companies will accept a valid driving licence from your home country. Note that motorcycles aren't permitted in the national parks, except along main transit routes.

Car & 4WD Rental

Due to a shortage of reliable public transport to sites of visitor interest, car hire is the best way of seeing Namibia. For those on a tight budget, it can be quite expensive, but if you muster a group of four people, it's a reasonable option. Be warned there's a chronic shortage of rental cars, so book well in advance. The least expensive companies charge US$45 to US$55 per day with unlimited kilometres (some have a minimum rental period) for a compact car. Most require a deposit of N$1000 (about US$120) and minimum ages range between 21 and 25. It's generally less expensive to hire a car in South Africa and drive it into Namibia, but you need permission from the rental company, as well as proof of insurance and a 'Blue Book' sheet detailing both the chassis and engine serial numbers. Be sure to verify what sort of repairs will be your responsibility; under normal circumstances, your liability should be limited to tyres and windows. Note that not all petrol stations in Namibia sell unleaded petrol, so take this into consideration when hiring a vehicle.

The following agencies offer car and/or 4WD hire:

Avis Car Hire *Windhoek:* (☎ 061-233166, fax 223072, w www.avis.co.za) Hotel Safari, PO Box 2057, Aviation Rd
Swakopmund: (☎ 064-402527, fax 405881) Swakopmund Hotel & Entertainment Centre
Tsumeb: (☎ 067-220520, fax 220821) Safari Centre, Jordaan St

NAMIBIA

Gravel Roads

Many of Namibia's roads – even major routes – are surfaced with unsealed gravel, and while some are well-maintained, others are rutted, potholed, corrugated and unevenly surfaced. For drivers, this can be at best tricky and at worst, treacherous. In fact, the price of car hire relates directly to the number of cars rolled by foreigners who are inexperienced at driving on gravel roads. The following points may help.

- Keep your tyre pressure slightly lower than you would when driving on sealed roads.
- Try to avoid travelling at night when dust and distance may create confusing mirages.
- Keep your speed down to a maximum of 100km/h.
- Maximise your control by keeping both hands on the steering wheel.
- Follow ruts made by other vehicles.
- If the road is corrugated, gradually increase your speed until you find the correct speed – it'll be obvious when the rattling stops.
- Be especially careful on bends; slow right down before attempting the turn.
- If you have a tyre blowout, DO NOT hit the brakes or you'll lose control and the car will roll. Instead, steer straight ahead as best you can and let the car slow itself down before you attempt to bring it to a complete stop.
- You don't meet other cars very often, but when you do, it's like dust clouds passing in the night. When a vehicle approaches from the opposite direction, reduce your speed and keep as far left as possible. On remote roads, it's customary to wave at the other driver as you pass.
- In rainy weather, gravel roads can turn to quagmires and desert washes may fill with water. If you're uncertain about the water depth in a wash, get out to check the depth (unless it's a raging torrent, of course!) and only cross when it's safe for the type of vehicle you're driving.
- Be on the lookout for animals. Kudu, in particular, often bound onto the road unexpectedly, resulting in an unpleasant meeting.
- Avoid swerving sharply or braking suddenly on a gravel road or you risk losing control of the vehicle. If the rear wheels begin to skid, steer gently into the direction of the skid until you regain control. If the front wheels skid, take a firm hand on the wheel and steer in the opposite direction of the skid.
- Dust permeates everything on gravel roads; wrap your food, clothing and camera equipment in dust-proof plastic or keep them in sealed containers. To minimise dust inside the vehicle, pressurise the interior by closing the windows and turning on the blower.
- In dusty conditions, switch on your headlights so you can be more easily seen
- Overtaking (passing) can be extremely dangerous because your view may be obscured by flying dust kicked up by the car ahead. Try to gain the attention of the driver in front by flashing your high beams, which will indicate that you want to overtake (this isn't considered obnoxious in Namibia). If someone behind you flashes their lights, move as far to the left as possible.

Walvis Bay: (☎ 064-207527, fax 209150) Rooikop airport

Budget Car Hire *Windhoek*: (☎ 061-228720, fax 227665, 081 128 7200, W www.budget.co.za) 72 Mandume Ndemufayo

Walvis Bay: (☎ 064-204128, fax 202931) Protea Lodge, cnr 10th Rd & Sam Nujoma Drive

Camel Car Hire (☎ 061-248818, fax 248819, 0811 286353, e info@camelcarhire.com.na, W www.camelcarhire.com.na) 8 Edison St, PO Box 6200, Windhoek

Camping Car Hire (☎ 061-237756, fax 237757, e carhire@mweb.com.na, W www.camping carhire.com.na) 36 Joule St, Southern Industrial Area, Windhoek, PO Box 5526

Classic Car Hire (☎ 061-246708, fax 246709, e info@carhireandtours.com, W www.carhire andtours.com) PO Box 40222, Windhoek

Elena Travel Services & Car Hire (☎ 061-244443, fax 244558, 0811 246286, e elena@ namibweb.com, W www.namibweb.com)

Imperial Car Rental (☎ 061-220728, fax 220916, e tnn@iafrica.com.na) Travel North Namibia, 1551 Omeg Allee, Tsumeb

Maui RV Rentals (☎ 061-219590, fax 250653, e britznam@britz.com.na or maui@iafrica.com, W www.maui.co.za) 19 Newcastle St, Northern Industrial Area, PO Box 23800, Windhoek

HITCHING

Hitching is possible in Namibia, but it's illegal in national parks, and even main highways see relatively little traffic. Truck drivers generally expect to be paid around US$1.50 per 100km, so agree on a price

before climbing in. Your best options for lifts are Windhoek backpackers lodges, where you can post notices about rides wanted or offered. (For warnings about hitching, see the Getting Around the Region chapter.)

LOCAL TRANSPORT
Local transport in Namibia is limited to minibuses, which connect the Windhoek and Swakopmund city centres with outlying suburbs, and both radio dispatch and shared taxis in larger towns.

ORGANISED TOURS
Namibia's public transport system will get you to population centres, but not the sites most visitors want to see: the Skeleton Coast, Damaraland, the Kaokoland, the Kunene River, Fish River Canyon, Sossusvlei, the Naukluft, and so on. Therefore, even those who'd normally spurn organised tours may want to consider joining an inexpensive participation safari or a more luxurious option:

Afro Ventures (☎ 064-463812, fax 400216, e swp@ afroventures.com, w www.afroventures .com) PO Box 1772, Swakopmund. Afro Ventures offers several Namibian highlights tours, focusing on fine lodges and 4WD tours. Their five- and seven-day Namib Desert tours explore the desert coast and dunes. They also run the beautiful Sossusvlei Mountain Lodge.

Campfire Safaris (☎ 062-523946, 081 242 6116, e namibia@bigfoot.com) PO Box 4500, Rehoboth. This economically priced company offers combi tours through a range of Namibian highlights. The booking agent is the Cardboard Box Travel Shop (see following).

Cardboard Box Travel Shop (☎ 061-256580, fax 256581, e namibia@bigfoot.com, w www.na mibian.org) PO Box 5142, Windhoek. This friendly, recommended agency offers bookings (including last-minute options) for all budget safaris; lodge, safari, car hire and transport bookings; national parks bookings; good advice; and other travel services.

Chameleon Safaris (☎/fax 247668, e info@cha meleon.com.na or chamnam@mweb.com.na, w www.chameleonsafaris.com) 8 Voight St, PO Box 6017, Windhoek. This budget safari company is geared to backpackers and does a range of good-value safaris: six-day Damaraland/Skeleton Coast (US$400); three-day Sossusvlei (US$150); 18-day 4WD tour (US$950); 14-day Northern & Southern Highlights (US$600); and seven-day Northern/Southern Highlights (US$350 each).

Crazy Kudu Safaris (☎ 222636, fax 255074, e namibia.safaris@crazykudu.com, w www.crazy kudu.com) PO Box 99031, Windhoek. One of Namibia's friendliest and most economical safari companies, Crazy Kudu does 10-day all-inclusive 'Namibia Explorer' adventures through northern and central highlights (US$440); a six-day northern highlights tour (US$275); and a three-day Sossusvlei Express tour (US$130), which may also be joined in Swakopmund; all departures are guaranteed. They'll also organise custom safaris; an Okavango Delta and Victoria Falls excursion; and Fish River or Kaokoland extensions for the best possible price.

Enyandi Safaris (☎ 061-255103, fax 255477, 0811 243426, e enyandi@iafrica.com.na) This recommended company runs budget tours mainly in northwestern Namibia, starting at US$245 per person for a seven-day trip.

Felix Unite (☎ 061-255488, fax 251400, e rvanroo yen@africansolutions.org, w www.felix unite.com) This water-oriented company runs river-rafting and canoeing adventures on the Kunene (US$700 for 10 days) and Orange rivers (US$160/180 for four/six days).

Itenge Safaris (☎ 067-221777, fax 221778; e info@itenge-safaris.com, w www.itenge -safaris.com) Based in Tsumeb, this company does short tours to Etosha and Bushmanland, transfers between Windhoek and Tsumeb, and seven-day tours between Windhoek and Livingstone, Zambia (US$410), via a cheetah farm near Otjiwarongo, Bushmanland, Grootfontein, Rundu, Bwabwata National Park, the Okavango Panhandle (Botswana), Mudumu National Park, Lizauli Traditional Village and Katima Mulilo

Kaokohimba Safaris (☎/fax 061-222378, e kaoko himba@natron.net, w www.natron.net/tour /kaoko/himbae.htm) PO Box 11580, Windhoek. Kaokohimba organises cultural tours through Kaokoland and Damaraland and wildlife-viewing trips in Etosha National Park. A highlight is Camp Syncro, in remote Marienflüss.

Magic Bus Safaris (☎ 061-259485, 0811 298093, e magicbus@iafrica.com.na) 5 Grieg St, Windhoek. This small company runs budget trips from Windhoek to Sossusvlei (US$160 to US$190), Etosha (US$170), a seven-day combination (US$360) and other options.

Muramba Bushman Trails (☎ 067-220659, e bush man@natron.net) PO Box 689, Tsumeb. This recommended company, owned by Reinhard Friedrich, provides a unique introduction to the Heikum San people.

Namib Sky (☎ 293233, fax 293241, e namib sky@mweb.com.na) PO Box 5197, Windhoek. For those who dream of looming over the dunes in a balloon, this company offers Namib desert balloon flights for US$246 per person. The early morning flight departs before sunrise, when not a breath of wind is stirring.

Okakambe Trails (☎ 064-402799/405258, 0811 246626) D1901, PO Box 1668, Swakopmund. With Okakambe, you can ride on horseback

along the Swakop River to a moon landscape; they also organise longer trips.

Outside Adventures (☎ 061-245595, 0812 2470329, e info@namibia-adventures.com, w www.namibia-adventures.com) These folks run excellent day tours from Windhoek: brewery tours (US$17), mountain biking in Daan Viljoen (US$28), Arnhem Caves (US$45 to US$85), Katutura township (US$17), and tours to see cheetahs, leopards and rhinos (US$45 to US$70).

Pack Safaris (☎ 061-275802, fax 247755, 0811 284006, e peter.pack@packsafari.com, w www.packsafari.com) PO Box 29, Windhoek. This company does general German-oriented tours around Namibian highlights, including several day tours from Windhoek (including tours of the city, Khomas Hochland and Daan Viljoen), as well as Sossusvlei and Etosha tours. Rates are dependent on the number of participants.

Pleasure Flights (☎/fax 064-404500, e red baron@iml-net.ocrn.na, w www.pleasureflights .com.na) PO Box 537, Swakopmund. Pleasure Flights runs 'flightseeing' tours from the Skeleton Coast right down to Fish River Canyon. For an economical price, you need a group of five people.

Skeleton Coast Fly-In Safaris (☎ 061-224248, fax 225178, e sksafari@mweb.com.na, w www .orosovo.com/sksafari) PO Box 2195, Windhoek. This highly recommended operator runs all-inclusive four-day tours of the Skeleton Coast and Kunene River region for US$2585 per person; add Sossusvlei and it's US$2770. Five-day trips to the Skeleton Coast, the Kunene River, Etosha and Sossusvlei are US$3040. Add the Namib Rand Nature Reserve and Lüderitz and the six-day trip is US$3575.

Turnstone Tours (☎ 064-403123, fax 403290, e turn@iafrica.com.na, w www.turnstone-tours .com) PO Box 307, Swakopmund. Turnstone runs 4WD camping tours around Swakopmund, including Sandwich Harbour and Damaraland. Day tours are US$75 and all-inclusive longer trips cost US$300 per person per day.

West Coast Safaris (☎/fax 061-256770, e wes coast@iafrica.com.na, w www.westcoast.demon .nl) The company runs camping participation safaris, including the following: seven-day tours through Kaokoland (US$460); eight days in Kaokoland and Etosha (US$447); seven-day wildlife tours to Etosha; Damaraland and Waterberg (US$442); seven-day Bushmanland tours (US$442); and Damaraland tours (US$460).

Wild Dog Safaris (☎ 061-257642, fax 240802, e lp@wilddog-safaris.com, w www.wilddog -safaris.com) 19 Johann Albrecht St, PO Box 26188, Windhoek. This friendly operation runs seven-day Northern Namibia Adventures and Southern Swings (US$340 each); three-day Etosha or Sossusvlei circuits (US$160 each, or US$350 for both); as well as longer participation safaris and accommodated excursions.

Wilderness Safaris Namibia (☎ 061-274500, fax 239455, e info@nts.com.na, w www.wilderness -safaris.com) 8 Bismarck St, PO Box 6850, Windhoek. This company does camping safaris, rock-hounding/geology tours, Namib Desert tours and Etosha wildlife drives, as well as rafting trips on the Kunene River. They also own and operate several unique upmarket lodges in wild spots around the country: Skeleton Coast Wilderness Lodge, Sossusvlei Wilderness Lodge, Damaraland Camp, Kulala/Little Kulala Lodges and Ongava Lodge.

Windhoek

☎ 061 • pop 240,000

Namibia's central highlands are dominated by its small and colourful capital, Windhoek. Set in the geographical heart of Namibia, it serves as the road and rail crossroads and the country's commercial nerve centre. At an elevation of 1660m and surrounded by low hills, it enjoys dry, clean air and a healthy highland climate, and its people reflect the country's ethnic mix; on the streets, you'll see Owambo, Kavango, Herero, Damara, Caprivians, Namas, San, 'coloureds' and Europeans, all bustling along together.

Windhoek has only existed for just over a century. The modern name Windhoek, or 'windy corner', was corrupted from the original 'Winterhoek' during the German colonial occupation. At that time, it became the headquarters for the German Schutztruppe, which was ostensibly charged with brokering peace between the warring Herero and Nama. For over 10 years around the turn of the 20th century, Windhoek served as the administrative capital of German South-West Africa.

Orientation

Maps Free city maps are available from the tourist office on Post Street Mall. You can buy topographic sheets (US$3 for maps and US$2.50 for photocopies) for much of Namibia from the office of the **Surveyor General** (☎ 245055, fax 290 2050), at the corner of Robert Mugabe Avenue and Lazarett St.

Information

Tourist Offices The friendly **Windhoek Information & Publicity Office** (☎ 391 2050, fax 391 2091; Post St Mall; open 7.30am-1pm & 2pm-4.30pm Mon-Fri) answers questions and distributes local advertising. **Namibia Wildlife Resorts** (☎ 256443, fax 256715;

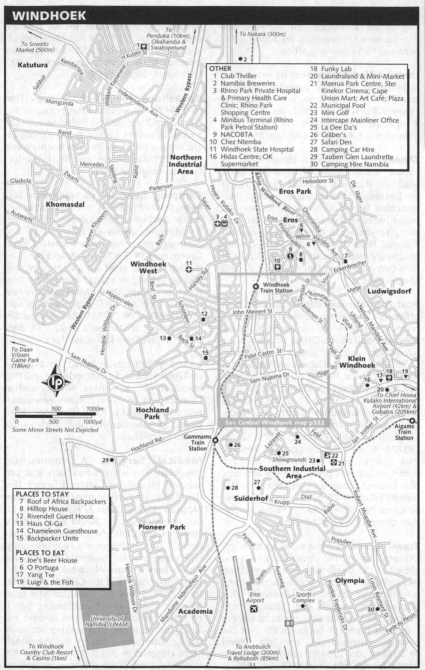

WINDHOEK

OTHER
1 Club Thriller
2 Namibia Breweries
3 Rhino Park Private Hospital & Primary Health Care Clinic; Rhino Park Shopping Centre
4 Minibus Terminal (Rhino Park Petrol Station)
9 NACOBTA
10 Chez Ntemba
11 Windhoek State Hospital
16 Hidas Centre; OK Supermarket

18 Funky Lab
20 Laundraland & Mini-Market
21 Maerua Park Centre; Ster Kinekor Cinema; Cape Union Mart; Art Café; Plaza
22 Municipal Pool
23 Mini Golf
24 Intercape Mainliner Office
25 La Dee Da's
26 Gräber's
27 Safari Den
28 Camping Car Hire
29 Tauben Glen Laundrette
30 Camping Hire Namibia

PLACES TO STAY
7 Roof of Africa Backpackers
8 Hilltop House
12 Rivendell Guest House
13 Haus Ol-Ga
14 Chameleon Guesthouse
15 Backpacker Unite

PLACES TO EAT
5 Joe's Beer House
6 O Portuga
17 Yang Tse
19 Luigi & the Fish

See Central Windhoek map p332

0   500   1000m
0   500   1000yd
Some Minor Streets Not Depicted

W *www.namibiawild liferesorts.com; Private Bag 13378, Windhoek)*, on Independence Avenue near Gathemann's restaurant is the National Parks booking office.

Immigration Office For visa extensions, information on work permits and other Immigration matters, see the **Ministry of Home Affairs** (☎ *292 2111, fax 292 2185;* e *mlusepani@mha.gov.na; cnr Kasino St & Independence Ave; open 8am-1pm Mon-Fri)*.

Money The best places to change travellers cheques are the AmEx office on Post Street Mall and Rennie's (Thomas Cook) Travel on Levinson Arcade, which change their respective brands without commission. All major banks change currency, and can usually give you South African rand. The First National Bank ATM system, BOB, handles credit-card cash advances, but note that BOB (like everyone else) often runs short of cash at weekends.

Post & Communications The main post office *(GPO; Independence Ave)* has telephone boxes in the lobby and just up the hill at the **Telecommunications Office** you can make international calls and send or receive faxes.

Email and Internet access are available at the **Web Cafe** (☎ *250540; cnr Robert Mugabe Ave & John Meinert St)*, which charges US$4 per hour. In Gutenberg Platz, the **Namibia Information & Tourism Centre** (☎ *276600, fax 276611)* offers Internet access for US$2.50 per hour. **Postnet** (☎ *271193, fax 271774;* e *postnet@iafrica.com.na; Wernhill Park Centre; open 8.30am-6pm Mon-Fri, 9am-1pm Sat)* has phone and fax services, plus Internet access for US$3 per hour. **Namibnet I-Café** (☎ *255570; Daniel Munamava St; open 8am-9pm Mon-Fri, 9am-9pm Sat-Sun)* charges US$2.50 per hour.

Travel Agencies Most travel agencies are clustered around the central area. A good choice is the **Cardboard Box Travel Shop** (☎ *256580, fax 256581;* W *www.namibian.org; John Meinert St)*, at the Cardboard Box Backpackers, which can arrange both budget and upmarket accommodation, tours and transport bookings all over the country. Alternatively, try **Trip Travel** (☎ *236880, fax 225430; Levinson Arcade)*; **Africa Tourist Info** (☎ *228717, fax 247668;*

W *www.infotour-africa.com; Chameleon City Backpackers, 5 Voight St)*; **Tourist Junction** (☎ *231246, fax 231703;* e *info.ritztours@galil eosa.co.za; 40 Fidel Castro St)*; or the **Namibia Information & Tourism Centre** (☎ *276600, fax 276611; Gutenberg Platz)*.

Bookshops The **Windhoek Book Den** (☎ *239976;* e *wbd@iwwn.com.na)*, in the Gutenberg Platz mall on Stübel Street, sells a range of novels, European and African literature and travel books. **Zum Bucherwurm** (☎ *255885; Kaiserkrone, Post St Mall)* offers German-language titles.

Camping Gear Try **Camping Hire Namibia** (☎/fax *252995;* e *camping@natron.net;* W *http://natron.net/tour/camping/hiree.html; 78 Malcolm Spence St, Olympia)* to hire camping gear, but phone first. **Cymot Greensport** (☎ *234131; 60 Mandume Ndemufayo Ave)* is good for quality camping, hiking, cycling or vehicle outfitting equipment, as is **Cape Union Mart** *(Maerua Park Centre)*. Gear for 4WD expeditions is sold at **Safari Den** (☎ *231931; 20 Bessemer St)*; alternatively, try **Gräber's** (☎ *222732; Bohr St)* in the Southern Industrial Area.

Laundry Self-service laundry is available at **Tauben Glen Launderette** (☎ *252115; Hochland Pk)*, at Village Square, and at **Laundraland** (☎ *224912; Klein Windhoek)*, near Mini-Market in Klein Windhoek. Most hotels, guesthouses and hostels also offer laundry services.

Medical Services A recommended physician who accepts travellers and can provide hikers' medical certificates (for the Fish River Canyon route) is **Dr Algene Mouton** (☎ *229628, fax 229634; M&Z Building, John Meinert St)*. **Rhino Park Primary Health Care Clinic** (☎ *230926; Windhoek North)* also does private consultations, and recommended hospitals include the **Rhino Park Private Hospital** (☎ *225434; Windhoek North)* and the **Catholic Hospital** (☎ *237237; Stübel St)*. Note that you must produce a valid credit card before you'll be seen. Those who are short of cash but have time to wait – and nothing seriously wrong with them – can try the **Windhoek State Hospital** (☎ *303 9111; off Harvey Rd, Windhoek West)* or the government clinic on

Robert Mugabe Avenue, near John Meinert Street.

For prescriptions and other remedies, try the **Medi-Sun Pharmacy** (☎ 235254; Wernhill Park Centre; open 8:30am-6.30pm Mon-Fri, 8.30am-1.30pm Sat & 10am-1pm Sun).

Emergency Windhoek's all-purpose emergency number (ironically known as 'Rescue 911' after the TV programme) is in fact ☎ 10111.

Dangers & Annoyances Windhoek is generally safe by day, but avoid going out alone at night, and be wary of newspaper sellers, who may shove the paper in your face as a distracting ruse. Don't use bum bags or carry swanky camera or video totes, and never leave anything of value visible in a vehicle. Parts of Katutura and other northwestern suburbs, where boredom and unemployment are rife, should be avoided unless you have a local contact and/or a specific reason to go there.

THINGS TO SEE & DO
Hofmeyer Walk
The Hofmeyer Walk walking track through Klein Windhoek Valley starts from either Sinclair Street or Uhland Street and heads south through the bushland to finish at the point where Orban Street becomes Anderson Street. It takes about an hour and affords a panoramic view over the city, as well as a look at the *Aloe littoralis* aloes, which characterise the hillside vegetation. Hikers have recently been robbed along this route, so don't go alone and avoid carrying valuables.

Christuskirche
One of Windhoek's most recognisable landmarks, the 1907 Christuskirche stands at the top of Fidel Castro Street. This unusual building, constructed of local sandstone, was designed by Gottlieb Redecker in neogothic and Art Nouveau styles. To see the interior, pick up the key during business hours from the church office on Fidel Castro Street.

Alte Feste & the Owela Museum
The whitewashed ramparts of Alte Feste (National Museum of Namibia), Windhoek's oldest surviving building, date from 1890 to 1892. It originally served as the headquarters of the Schutztruppe, which arrived in 1889, but now houses the Historical Section of the **State Museum** (☎ 293 4437; Robert Mugabe Ave; admission by donation; open 9am-6pm Mon-Fri, 3pm-6pm Sat-Sun). The other half of the State Museum, known as the **Owela Museum** (☎ 293 4358; 4 Lüderitz St; admission US$1.20; open 9am-6pm Mon-Fri, 3pm-6pm Sat-Sun), features exhibits that focus on Namibia's natural and anthropological history.

National Art Gallery
The National Art Gallery (☎/fax 240930; cnr Robert Mugabe Ave & John Meinert St; admission free; open 9am-5pm Mon-Fri, 9am-11am Sat) contains a permanent collection of works reflecting Namibia's historical and natural scene. It also hosts visiting exhibitions.

Tintenpalast
The Tintenpalast, now the Parliament building, was designed by architect Gottlieb Redecker and built in 1912 to 1913 as the administrative headquarters for German South-West Africa. The name, 'ink palace', honours the ink spent on the typically bureaucratic paperwork it generated. It has also served as the nerve centre for all subsequent governments, including the present one. On the lawn sits Windhoek's first **post-Independence monument**, which depicts Herero chief Hosea Kutako, known for his vociferous opposition to South African rule. On weekdays – except when the assembly is in session – you can reserve a place on a 45-minute tour by phoning ☎ 288 5111.

Other Historic Buildings
Near the corner of Lüderitz and Park Streets, take a look at the **Old Magistrates' Court**. It was built in 1897 to 1898 as quarters for Carl Ludwig, the state architect, and now houses the **Namibia Conservatorium**. Down Park Street towards Robert Mugabe Avenue lies South-West Africa House, now called the **State House**. The site was once graced by the residence of the German colonial governor, but it was razed in 1958 and replaced by the present building. After independence, it became the official residence of the Namibian president.

Robert Mugabe Avenue affords good city views and colonial architecture. The **Kaiserliche Realschule**, Windhoek's first German primary school, dates from 1907 to 1908. The curious turret with wooden slats, which was

part of the original building, was designed to provide ventilation. The **Old Supreme Court** (Obergericht; cnr Korner St & Robert Mugabe Ave) is a gabled brick structure which dates from 1908.

Further south is the **Turnhalle** (cnr Bahnhof St & Robert Mugabe Ave), designed by Otto Busch and built in 1909 as a gymnasium. On 1 September 1975, however, the first Constitutional Conference on Independence for Southwest Africa (subsequently known as the Turnhalle Conference) was held here. In the 1980s, it hosted political summits and debates which later resulted in Namibian Independence.

The classic 1902 **Oode Voorpost** (cnr John Meinert & Moltke St) originally held the colonial surveyors' offices, where government maps were stored in fireproof archives. It was restored in 1988 and now houses a portion of the Ministry of Finance.

Southward along Independence Avenue are three colonial buildings designed by architect Willi Sander. The southernmost building was built in 1902 as the **Kronprinz Hotel**. In 1920, Heinrich Gathemann bought it and converted it into a private business, to adjoin **Gathemann House** next door, which he had built in 1913. The northernmost building is the **Erkrath building**, which dates from 1910.

Train Station & Trans-Namib Transport Museum

Windhoek's Cape Dutch-style train station dates from 1912, and near the entrance sits the German steam locomotive *Poor Old Joe*, shipped to Swakopmund in 1899 and reassembled for the run to Windhoek. The small but worthwhile Trans-Namib Transport Museum (☎ 298 2186; admission US$0.70; open 8am 1pm & 2pm-5pm Mon-Fri), upstairs in the station, outlines the history of Namibian transport, particularly the railroads.

Post Street Mall & Meteorite Exhibit

The throbbing heart of the Windhoek shopping district is the bizarrely colourful Post Street Mall, and its odd architecture could have provided a set for the film *Dick Tracy*. It's lined with vendors selling curios, artwork, clothing and other tourist items, and in the centre is a prominent display of 33 meteorites from the Gibeon meteor shower,

which deposited at least 21 tonnes of mostly ferrous extraterrestrial boulders around Gibeon in southern Namibia.

Katutura

The lively black township of Katutura is relatively safe by day if you stick to the northern areas or find a local who can act as a guide. If you want to visit, Outside Adventures (see Organised Tours in the Getting Around section earlier) runs day trips, guided by a Katutura resident. A taxi from Windhoek centre to Katutura costs US$1.

Organised Tours

Day tours are available from Outside Adventures and Pack Safaris. If you're looking for a budget safari around Namibia, contact Crazy Kudu Safaris, Chameleon Safaris, Wild Dog Safaris or Campfire Safaris (see contact details under Organised Tours in the Getting Around section, earlier in this chapter).

Special Events

Windhoek's annual cultural bash is the September /Ae//Gams street festival, which replaces the former Enyando Street Festival; it features colourful gatherings of dancers, musicians and people in ethnic dress. True to its partially Teutonic background, Windhoek also stages its own Oktoberfest in late October. Similarly, the German-style Windhoek Karnival (or WIKA) is held in late April and features a week of events.

Places to Stay – Budget

Camping The **Arebbusch Travel Lodge** (☎ 252255, fax 251670; e atl@iwwn.com.na; Auasweg, PO Box 80160, Olympia; tent or caravan sites US$7 per person, 2 to 3-bed rooms US$42, 2-bed/4-bed chalets with bathroom US$37/52) is just south of town.

Some of the following budget options also offer camping; see also Daan Viljoen Game Reserve, under Around Windhoek.

Hostels & Guesthouses The **Cardboard Box Backpackers** (☎ 228994, fax 245587; e cardboardbox@bigfoot.com; w www.namibian.org; 15 Johann Albrecht St, PO Box 5142; camping US$3, dorm beds US$6, tents US$12, doubles US$17), 15 minutes' walk from the city centre, is the favourite backpackers hostel. Rates include use of the cooking facilities and access to the swimming pool and

Katutura – A Permanent Place?

In 1912, during the days of the South African mandate – and apartheid – the Windhoek Town Council set aside two 'locations', which were open to settlement by black Africans who were working in the city: the Main Location, which was west of the centre, and Klein Windhoek, to the east. The following year, people were forcibly relocated to these areas, which effectively became communal areas of haphazard settlement. In the early 1930s, however, streets were laid out in the Main Location and the area was divided into regions set aside for each ethnic group. Each subdivision within these regions was referred to by the name of its assigned ethnic group (eg Herero, Nama, Owambo, Damara), followed by a soul-less numerical reference.

In the 1950s, the Windhoek municipal council – with encouragement from the South African government (which regarded Namibia as a province of South Africa) – decided to 'take back' Klein Windhoek and consolidate all 'location' residents into a single settlement northwest of the main city. However, there was strong opposition to the move, and in early December 1959, a group of Herero women launched a protest march and boycott against the city government. On 10 December, unrest escalated into a confrontation with the police, resulting in 11 deaths and 44 serious injuries. Frightened, the roughly 4000 residents of the Main Location submitted and moved to the new settlement, ultimately named 'Katutura', which is Herero for 'we have no permanent place' – but it can also be translated as 'the place we do not want to settle'.

In modern, independent Namibia, Katutura is a vibrant Windhoek suburb – Namibia's Soweto – where poverty and affluence brush elbows. Sadly and inexplicably, Katutura's once-lovely Independence murals along Independence Avenue have been removed, but the town council has now extended municipal water, power and telephone services to most areas of Katutura and has also established the colourful and perpetually busy Soweto Market.

the lively bar and restaurant. There's also a noticeboard for lifts and three daily shuttles to the bus terminals, and it's a great place to join a group for car hire. Email and Internet access are available.

Chameleon Guesthouse (☎/fax 247668; e info@chameleon.com.na; w www.chameleonbackpackers.com; 22 Wagner St, PO Box 6107, Windhoek West; dorm beds US$7, doubles without/with bathroom US$13/17) is a friendly place that's ideal for backpackers in search of a quiet atmosphere. Rates include linen and a basic self-service breakfast, and guests have access to the pool, dart board, kitchen, video lounge, city shuttles, laundry, secure parking, bar and phone, fax and email facilities (US$0.12/min).

Chameleon City Backpackers (☎/fax 244347, fax 247668; e info@chameleon.com.na; w www.chameleonbackpackers.com; 5 Voight St, PO Box 6107; dorm beds US$6, doubles without/with bathroom US$15/22) is a well-located option, which is affiliated with the Chameleon Guesthouse. It offers secure parking, cooking facilities, a pool, satellite TV, a video library and easy access to the city centre; it also features a popular thatched 'honeymoon suite'.

Roof of Africa Backpackers (☎ 254708, 0811 244930, fax 248048; e roofofaf@mweb.com.na or info@roofofafrica.com; 124 Nelson Mandela Ave, PO Box 11745; camping US$5, dorm beds US$6, singles/doubles US$27, doubles with self-catering & air-con US$48) is a pleasant haven just a 30-minute walk from the centre. Email and Internet access is available, and there's a frog pond, a great bar and a dinner buffet (US$5).

Puccini House (☎/fax 236355; e puccinis@mweb.com.na; 4 Puccini St, PO Box 31396; camping US$3, dorm beds US$5-6, singles/doubles US$9.50/17) is another option. Use of the sauna is US$4 per hour. If you're walking from the Wernhill Park Centre, watch your luggage, especially on the Mozart Street bridge over the rail line.

Backpacker Unite (☎ 259485, 0811 298093; e magicbus@iafrica.com.na; 5 Grieg St, PO Box 23658, Windhoek West; camping US$3.50, dorm beds US$5, doubles without/with bathroom US$12/14) is probably Windhoek's quietest and most relaxed backpackers; rates include use of the communal kitchen.

Tramper's Haven (☎ 223669; 78 Bülow St, PO Box 20222; dorm beds US$13, singles/

NAMIBIA

CENTRAL WINDHOEK

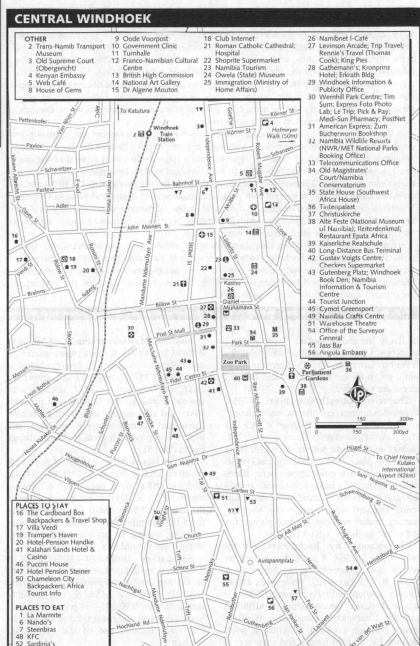

OTHER
2 Trans-Namib Transport Museum
3 Old Supreme Court (Obergericht)
4 Kenyan Embassy
5 Web Café
8 House of Gems
9 Oode Voorpost
10 Government Clinic
11 Turnhalle
12 Franco-Namibian Cultural Centre
13 British High Commission
14 National Art Gallery
15 Dr Algene Mouton
18 Club Internet
21 Roman Catholic Cathedral; Hospital
22 Shoprite Supermarket
23 Namibia Tourism
24 Owela (State) Museum
25 Immigration (Ministry of Home Affairs)
26 Namibnet I-Café
27 Levinson Arcade; Trip Travel; Rennie's Travel (Thomas Cook); King Pies
28 Gathemann's; Kronprinz Hotel; Erkrath Bldg
29 Windhoek Information & Publicity Office
30 Wernhill Park Centre; Tim Sum; Express Foto Photo Lab; Le Trip; Pick & Pay; Medi-Sun Pharmacy; PostNet
31 American Express; Zum Bucherworm Bookshop
32 Namibia Wildlife Resorts (NWR/MET National Parks Booking Office)
33 Telecommunications Office
34 Old Magistrates' Court/Namibia Conservatorium
35 State House (Southwest Africa House)
36 Tintenpalast
37 Christuskirche
38 Alte Feste (National Museum of Namibia); Reiterdenkmal; Restaurant Epata Africa
39 Kaiserliche Realschule
40 Long-Distance Bus Terminal
42 Gustav Voigts Centre; Checkers Supermarket
43 Gutenberg Platz; Windhoek Book Den; Namibia Information & Tourism Centre
44 Tourist Junction
45 Cymot Greensport
49 Namibia Crafts Centre
51 Warehouse Theatre
54 Office of the Surveyor General
55 Jass Bar
56 Angola Embassy

PLACES TO STAY
16 The Cardboard Box Backpackers & Travel Shop
17 Villa Verdi
19 Tramper's Haven
20 Hotel-Pension Handke
41 Kalahari Sands Hotel & Casino
46 Puccini House
47 Hotel Pension Steiner
50 Chameleon City Backpackers; Africa Tourist Info

PLACES TO EAT
1 La Marmite
6 Nando's
7 Steenbras
48 KFC
52 Sardinia's
53 King Pies
57 Homestead

doubles US$14/17) is a sparkling, Christian-oriented backpackers' lodge that has kitchen facilities and plenty of showers. There's no bar, but you can buy soft drinks and light beer; only married couples may use the doubles and smoking is allowed only in the garden.

Places to Stay – Mid-Range

Rivendell Guest House (☎ 250006, fax 250010; e rivendell@toothfairy.com; w www.rivendell-namibia.com; PO Box 5142, 40 Beethoven St, Windhoek West; doubles US$17-25, self-catering flat US$45) provides quiet, comfortable accommodation within easy walking distance of the centre. You can choose between doubles with or without a bathroom – but all have use of the swimming pool and communal kitchen. A continental breakfast costs an additional US$2.50. While you're there, don't miss the unique wall paintings at the corner of Beethoven and Simpson Streets.

Haus Ol-Ga (☎ 235853, fax 255184; e metzger@mweb.com.na; w www.olga-namibia.de; 91 Bach St, PO Box 20926; singles/doubles from US$22/27, rates include breakfast) is a friendly choice, with a nice, quiet garden atmosphere. Add 10% for a one-night stay).

Hotel-Pension Handke (☎ 234904, fax 225660; e pensionhandke@iafrica.com.na; 3 Rossini St, PO Box 20881; singles/doubles US$36/50, family rooms US$22 per person) is one of the best-value mid-range options, with a nice, quiet garden atmosphere in Windhoek West.

Hotel-Pension Steiner (☎ 222898, fax 224234; e steiner@iafrica.com.na; w www.steiner.com.na; 11 Wecke St, PO Box 20481; singles/doubles from US$34/52, family rooms US$63) is a comfortable, convenient and spotless B&B, where guests have access to the swimming pool, braai and lounge.

Places to Stay – Top End

Villa Verdi (☎ 221994, fax 222574; e villav@mweb.com.na; w www.villa-verdi.com; 4 Verdi St, PO Box 6784; singles/doubles US$58/94) is a recommended Mediterranean-African hybrid. Rates include telephone, TV and private bathroom, with access to a pool, bar and dining room.

Hilltop House (☎ 249116, fax 247818; e hilltop@iafrica.com.na; 12 Lessing St, PO Box 4327, Eros; singles/doubles US$58/88) featuring unique rooms and décor, is a very atmospheric six-room place with verandas and great views over the Klein Windhoek valley. Breakfast and light meals are available for US$3 to US$4.50.

Kalahari Sands Hotel & Casino (☎ 222300, fax 222260; Gustav Voigts Centre, 129 Independence Ave, PO Box 2254; singles/doubles from US$90/100) provides four-star international-standard rooms in the heart of the city.

Windhoek Country Club Resort & Casino (☎ 205 5911, fax 205 2797; e hrwccr@legacyhotels.co.za; PO Box 307777; standard singles/doubles US$116/140, with specials at weekends), a posh place built to host the 1995 Miss Universe pageant, is a Las Vegas-style hotel with several restaurants, a casino and 18-hole golf course. It's located on the Western Bypass, 1km southeast of the University of Namibia.

Places to Eat

Steenbras (☎ 231445; Bahnhof St; light meals US$2-3.50), near Independence Avenue, is one of Windhoek's best takeaways, serving memorable fish, chicken burgers and spicy chips.

King Pies (☎ 248978, Levinson Arcade & 46 Independence Ave; pies US$0.75-1.50), with two outlets, serves up a variety of filled meat and vegetable pies.

Nando's (☎ 231792; 43 Bahnhof St; mains US$3-4) sizzles up fiery peri-peri chicken, plus spicy rice, chips and other goodies. There are also two **KFC** outlets (Independence Ave & 67 Tal St).

Sardinia's (☎ 225600, 39 Independence Ave; pizza & pasta dishes US$3.50-5; open lunch & dinner Wed-Mon) is a rather loud and boisterous place that is good for pizza and standard Italian fare, as well as great coffee and ice cream.

Art Café (☎ 255020; Maerua Park Centre; breakfast US$1.75-2.50, lunch US$2.50-3.50) is a fashionable place that specialises in breakfast, sweet and savoury crêpes and light lunches – with excellent results. It also sells Namibian art.

Gathemann's (☎ 223853; 179 Independence Ave; mains US$4.50-9), in a prominent colonial building (see Other Historic Buildings earlier in this section) with a sunny terrace, is a great splash-out. In the

morning and afternoon, it serves meals, plus rich European-style gateaux and pastries. Downstairs there's a good sandwich takeaway.

Homestead *(☎ 221958, 53 Feld St; starters US$1.50-4, salads US$3-6.50, mains US$4-8.50; open dinner Mon-Sat)*, arguably Windhoek's best restaurant, features a range of starters, salads, pasta, vegetarian dishes, fresh fish, beef and chicken dishes, as well as oryx, crocodile, fondues and a hunters' grill featuring zebra. The herbs and vegetables come from their own garden and it's all served up in a pleasant outdoor setting. There's also an extensive selection of wines, liqueurs and cigars.

O Portuga *(☎ 272900, 151 Nelson Mandela Ave; starters US$3-4, mains US$4-8; open dinner daily)* is the best place in town for genuine Portuguese and Angolan dishes, including numerous seafood options. There is also a good selection of wines.

Joe's Beer House *(☎ 232457, Green Market Square, 160 Nelson Mandela Ave; mains US$4-7; open 5pm-late Mon-Thu, 11am-late Fri-Sun)* is an extremely popular spot north of the centre for a large, meat-oriented evening meal in a crowded and very hectic atmosphere – with prolonged drinking until late. Reservations are requisite.

Yang Tse *(☎ 234779, /Ae//Gams Shopping Centre, 351 Sam Nujoma Dr, Klein Windhoek; mains US$3.50-6)* is a long-standing Chinese option.

Luigi & the Fish *(☎ 256399, 320 Sam Nujoma Dr, Klein Windhoek; starters US$3-4.50, mains US$3.50-12; open noon-3pm & 6pm-late daily)* features seafood (fish, shellfish, seafood paella, calamari etc) as well as steaks, pasta, chicken, cajun dishes and vegetarian cuisine. The attached **Explorers Pub** is known for its extensive list of shooters, and the deck wobbles even before your first drink. Both the restaurant and bar offer great outdoor seating.

La Marmite *(☎ 248022, Independence Ave; mains US$4.50-8; open 6pm-10pm daily)* lets you sample wonderful North and West African cuisine, and its popularity is well-deserved. Bookings are advisable.

Dial-a-Meal *(☎ 220111; delivery charges US$2-3)*, for those who are feeling lazy, delivers orders from a wide range of local restaurants, as well as the Pioneerspark Drankwinkel!

Self-Catering The big names are **Pick & Pay** in the Wernhill Park Centre and **Checkers** in the Gustav Voigts Centre. The cheapest supermarket is the crowded **Shoprite** on lower Independence Avenue. The **Mini-Markt** in Klein Windhoek is larger than it sounds and is open 7am-midnight daily. The well-stocked **OK** at Hidas Centre is the best place for foreign and ethnic ingredients. On weekdays, a small market on Mandume Ndemufayo Ave sells fruit and vegetables.

Entertainment

The **Warehouse Theatre** *(☎ 225059, old South-West Brewery Bldg, 48 Tal St; admission US$3.50)* is a delightfully integrated club staging live African and European music and theatre productions.

Funky Lab *(☎ 271964, fax 271946; /Ae//Gams Centre, Klein Windhoek; open 4pm-late Sun-Thu, 2pm-late Fri-Sat)*, both very popular and very blue, is currently one of Windhoek's hottest night-time disco dancing spots.

Jass Bar *(☎ 256776; Shinz St 4; open 6pm-late Tue-Sat)*, a quiet club and cigar bar, provides a leisurely respite for the over 21 crowd.

Chez Ntemba *(☎ 253548; 154 Uhland St; admission US$1.25 Thu & Sun, US$3.50 Wed, Fri-Sat; open 9pm-5am Wed-Sun)* features drinking and dancing to the strains of Zambian, Congolese, South African and Angolan music.

Plaza *(☎ 0812 560780; Maerua Park Centre, open 5pm-late daily)* is a pleasant and quiet gay-friendly venue where you'll hear a range of music at conversational levels.

Club Thriller *(Samuel Shikongo St, Katutura; admission US$3)* lies in a rough area, but beyond the weapons search at the door, the music is Western and African and the atmosphere upbeat and relatively secure. However, avoid carrying valuables or wearing jewellery; foreigners may also have to fend off strangers hitting them up for beers and cash.

La Dee Da's *(☎ 081 243 4432, Ferry Street near Patterson, Southern Industrial Area; admission US$2.50/3.50 before/after midnight; open 10.30pm-4am Thur-Sat)* boasts Namibia's largest national flag and here you can dance to Angolan *kizomba*, hip-hop, rave, traditional African, rock and commercial pop accompanied by special effects.

For films, try the five-screen **Ster Kinekor Cinema** (☎ 249267; admission US$2.50; half price on Wednesday) in Maerua Park Centre. The **Franco-Namibian Cultural Centre** (☎ 222122; e secretary@fncc.org.na; w www.fncc.org; 118 Robert Mugabe Ave) screens popular films in English and French on Wednesdays at 7.15pm.

Shopping

The plethora of handicrafts sold in Post Street Mall are mostly imported from Zimbabwe, but you can buy local Herero dolls from outside the Kalahari Sands Hotel, or baskets and woodcarvings around Zoo Park. The **Namibia Crafts Centre** (☎ 222236; 40 Tal St; open 9am-5.30pm Mon-Fri, 9am-1pm Sat) sells a variety of souvenirs. For raw minerals and gemstones, check out the **House of Gems** (e scrap@iafrica.com.na; 131 Stübel St).

Getting There & Away

Air Flying daily between Chief Hosea Kutako International Airport (42km east of the city centre), Cape Town and Jo'burg is **Air Namibia** (☎ 298 2552, fax 221382; w www.airnamibia.com.na). There is also a twice-weekly service to and from London and Frankfurt; and several airlines fly to and from Gaborone and Maun (Botswana), Harare and Victoria Falls (Zimbabwe) and Lusaka (Zambia).

Domestic Air Namibia flights connect Eros airport, 2km south of the city centre, with Katima Mulilo (US$140), Lüderitz (US$115), Ondangwa (US$95), Rundu (US$137), Walvis Bay (US$88) and Etosha (US$90).

Bus From the main bus terminal, at the corner of Fidel Castro Street and Rev Michael Scott Street, the Intercape Mainliner runs on Monday, Wednesday, Friday and Sunday to and from Cape Town (US$45, 19½ hours) and Johannesburg (US$58, 24½ hours, with a change in Upington). There are also daily services to Swakopmund (US$13, 4½ hours); and Monday and Friday departures to Victoria Falls, Zimbabwe (US$52, 19¾ hours), via Okahandja, Otjiwarongo, Grootfontein, Rundu and Katima Mulilo.

Local minibuses leave when full from the Rhino Park petrol station and can get you to most urban centres in Namibia: Gobabis (US$4.50, 2½ hours), Buitepos (US$7, five hours), Swakopmund (US$7, four hours),

Walvis Bay (US$7.50, 4½ hours), Rehoboth (US$2.50, 1½ hours), Mariental (US$6, three hours), Keetmanshoop (US$8, six hours), Lüderitz (US$13, 10 hours), Otjiwarongo (US$7, three hours), Outjo (US$7.50, four hours), Grootfontein (US$8, seven hours), Tsumeb (US$8, seven hours), Oshakati (US$9, 11 hours), Ruacana (US$15, 15 hours), Rundu (US$10.50, 10 hours), Divundu (US$12, 12 hours) and Katima Mulilo (US$14, 15½ hours).

Train The station has a **booking office** (open 7.30am-4pm Mon-Fri); note that on Monday to Thursday, fares are about 60% of those quoted here, and that economy-class fares are around 10% lower. Overnight trains run daily except on Saturday between Windhoek and Keetmanshoop, leaving at 7.10pm/6.30pm southbound/northbound. Times and Friday to Sunday business class fares from Windhoek are: Rehoboth (US$4.30, 2¾ hours), Mariental (US$6, six hours) and Keetmanshoop (US$7.50, 9½ hours). The Keetmanshoop run now offers sleepers on Monday, Wednesday and Friday.

On Sunday, Tuesday and Thursday, the northern-sector line connects Windhoek with Tsumeb (US$7, 16 hours) via Okahandja (US$3, 2½ hours) and Otjiwarongo (US$5.25, 10½ hours). Other lines connect Windhoek with Swakopmund (US$8, 9½ hours) and Walvis Bay (US$8, 11 hours) daily except Saturday; and Windhoek with Gobabis (US$4.25, 7½ hours) on Tuesday, Thursday and Sunday.

Getting Around

To the Chief Hosea Kutako International Airport, the **Elena Airport Shuttle** (☎ 244443, 0811 246286; e elena@namibweb.com) provides 24-hour door-to-door airport transport for US$17 per bus; they also meet international flights. Alternatively, try the **Marenko Shuttle** (☎ 226331) or **VIP Shuttle** (☎ 0812 563657), which charges US$12 per person for the trip; coming from the airport, you'll be able to choose between several shuttle services. Airport taxis on the same trip cost a maximum of US$27.

City buses have been phased out in favour of inexpensive shared taxis and minibuses. Collective taxis from the main ranks at Wernhill Park Centre follow set routes to Khomasdal and Katutura, and if your destination is

NAMIBIA

along the way, you'll pay less than US$1. With taxis from the main bus terminals or by radio dispatch, fares are either metered or are calculated on a per km basis, but you may be able to negotiate a set fare per journey. Plan on US$3 to US$3.50 to anywhere around the city centre. Try **Crown Radio Taxis** (☎ 211115, 0811 299116), **Express Radio Taxis** (☎ 239739) or **Sunshine Radio Taxis** (☎ 221029).

AROUND WINDHOEK
Daan Viljoen Game Park

The beautiful Daan Viljoen Game Park (admission US$2.50 per person & US$2.50 per vehicle; open to day visitors sunrise-6pm) sits in the Khomas Hochland about 18km west of Windhoek. Because there are no dangerous animals, hikers can wander freely through lovely desert-like hills and valleys. You'll almost certainly see gemsboks, kudus, mountain zebras, springboks, hartebeests, elands and up to 200 bird species.

The 3km **Wag-'n-Bietjie Trail** follows a dry riverbed from near the park office to Stengel Dam. A 9km circuit, the **Rooibos Trail**, crosses hills and ridges and affords great views back to Windhoek in the distance. The 34km **Sweet-Thorn Trail** circuits the empty eastern reaches of the reserve. One group of three to 12 people is permitted on this trail each day for US$8 per person, including accommodation in a shelter halfway along. Advance bookings through Namibia Wildlife Resorts (NWR) are required.

Daan Viljoen Rest Camp (camping US$15 for up to four people, single/double bungalows US$25/31, four-bed self-catering unit US$65) sits on the shores of Augeigas Dam; there's also a **restaurant** (open 7.30am-9am & noon-2pm & 7pm-10pm daily) further along the road. Pre-book at NWR in Windhoek.

There's no public transport to Daan Viljoen, but taxis charge around US$17 each way and persistent hitchers will eventually get a lift. No motorcycles are permitted.

Gobabis
☎ 062

Gobabis, 120km from the Botswana border, serves as a logical stopover along the Trans-Kalahari Highway. The name is Nama for 'the place of strife', although a slight

misspelling ('Goabbis') would render it 'place of elephants', which most locals prefer (despite its lack of elephants). The town isn't much to look at; the only historic building is the old military hospital, the **Lazarett**, which once served as a town museum (pick up a key at the library).

Places to Stay & Eat 20kms west of town, **Xain Quaz** (☎ 562688, fax 562824; camping US$4 per person, double tents US$12, six-bed bungalows US$37) is a pleasant family-oriented camp with a pool and a friendly ambience.

Onze Rust Guest House (☎ 562214, fax 565060; e onzerust@iafrica.com.na; 95 Rugby St; singles/doubles US$22/32) is a small and homely option in a quiet neighbourhood. Meals are available.

Goba-Goba Lodge (☎ 564499, fax 464466; e goba-goba@iafrica.com.na; PO Box 599, Gobabis; singles/doubles US$36/50) is a friendly, well-appointed and highly recommended lodge 2km from town, with a pool, tennis court and inspiring landscaping.

Harnas Wildlife Foundation & Guest Farm (☎ 568788, fax 568887; e harnas@ mweb.com.na, e harnas@iway.na; w www .harnas.de; PO Box 548; camping US$16, Wendy house US$50, Igloo hut US$65, cottage US$70), a popular rural development project which likens itself to Noah's Ark, lets you see wildlife close-up, and provides a chance to cuddle baby cheetahs, leopards and lions, if they haven't already grown

Gobabis Green

It's said Gobabis once had a traffic light, but when it turned green, the cows ate it. That's not just any cows, but rather the purebred stock that makes up the Omaheke region's best: Red Poll, South Devon, Hereford, Sussex, Brown Swiss, Angus, Shorthorn, Simmenthaler, Santa Gertrudis and Brahman. While drought is definitely the norm in this semi-desert country, the average rainfall of 200mm to 300mm per year belies the fact that in a good rainy season, the vast landscapes of the Namibian Kalahari turn beautifully lush, green and cattle-friendly. And incidentally, the traffic light has somehow resurfaced...

too big for that sort of thing. The idea is to return orphaned animals to the wild, but those who are sensitive to ecological issues may suspect conflicts of interest. To get there, turn north on the C22 past Gobabis and continue for 50km, then turn east on the D1668. After 42km, turn left at the Harnas gate and continue 8km to the farm. Transfers are available from Windhoek on request. Day admission costs US$7, wildlife drives/animal feedings are US$7/21 and lunches/dinners cost US$7/12.

Getting There & Away Slow overnight rail services connect Windhoek with Gobabis (US$4.25, 7½ hours) on Tuesday, Thursday and Sunday. From the town centre bus terminal, you can travel between Gobabis and Windhoek (US$4.50, 2½ hours) or Buitepos (US$3.50, three hours), where you can connect with Botswanan buses to Ghanzi and Gaborone.

Dordabis
☎ 062
In Dordabis, the heart of Namibia's Karakul country, it's worth visiting the renowned weavery at **Farm Ibenstein** (☎ 573524; e gebhardt@ibenstein-weavers.com.na; w www.ibenstein-weavers.com.na; open 9am-4pm Mon-Fri & Sat morning), 4km down the C15 from the village.

Arnhem Cave, the longest cave system in Namibia (2800m), was discovered by farmer DN Bekker in 1930 and was originally used as a source of bat guano fertiliser. This dry cave lacks large stalagmites or stalactites, but it is home to five species of bat and words can't describe the first view of the blue-cast natural light as you emerge from its depths. It gets extremely dusty, so wear old clothing and avoid wearing contact lenses. Cave tours cost US$11.50; alternatively, guided day tours from Windhoek are available from Outside Adventures (see Organised Tours in the Getting Around section earlier).

Arnhem Cave Guesthouse (☎ 581885; e arnhem@mweb.com.na; camping US$7 per person, double self-catering chalets US$32, singles/doubles with half board US$37/63) offers both meals and comfortable digs. To get there, turn south just east of the international airport on the D1458, towards Nina. After 66km, turn northeast on the D1506 and

continue for 11km to the T-junction, where you turn south onto the D1808. The farm is 6km down this road.

Eningu Clay House Lodge (☎ 581880, fax 581577; e logufa@mweb.com.na; w www.natron.net/tour/eningu/eningu.htm; singles/doubles US$66/111 with half-board), constructed of sun-dried adobe, presents an appealing African-American Indian architectural cross. With a 19km hiking trail, rewarding wildlife viewing and a remarkable wine cellar, it's one of Namibia's most original lodges. At the nearby **Dorka Teppiche Weavery** you'll find superb original weavings. Follow the D1458 for 64km south of the Hosea Kutako International Airport and turn west on the D1471 for 1km to the Eningu gate.

Buitepos
☎ 062
At Buitepos, a wide spot in the desert with a border crossing, you can stay at the oasis-like **East Gate Service Station & Rest Camp** (☎ 560405, fax 560406; e eastgate@namibnet.com; PO Box 422, Gobabis; camping US$3 per person, cabins US$7 per person, doubles US$18).

Guest Farm Zelda (☎ 560427, fax 560431; e zelda.guestfarm@iafrica.com.na; w www.zelda-game-and-guestfarm.com; 20km west of Buitepos; PO Box 75, Gobabis; camping US$5 per person, singles/doubles US$55/88) has beautiful gardens, a cattle ranch and a variety of captive animals. They also offer walking tracks and wildlife drives, and workers on the farm are local San people, who happily provide cultural information and experiences.

North-Central Namibia

Almost everything along the tourist trail in North-Central Namibia is aimed at ushering visitors into Namibia's most popular destination, Etosha National Park, which is one of the world's pre-eminent wildlife areas.

OKAHANDJA
☎ 062
Okahandja, the Herero administrative centre, is best-known for its two immense **craft**

markets – one near the junction of the B1 and B2, the other about 1km out on the B1 towards Windhoek. At the southern end of Church Street is **Friedenskirche**, the Rhenish mission church, which was consecrated in 1876. Both in the churchyard and over the road are the **graves** of several historical figures, including those of Herero leader Willem Maherero, Nama leader Jan Jonker Afrikaner, and Hosea Kutako, the 'father of Namibian Independence'. Okahandja's big events are **Maherero Day** in August and the **gathering** of the Green Flag Herero people in June.

Okahandja Rest Camp (*☎/fax 504086; camping US$9, double bungalows without/ with bathroom US$11.50/22*) is a secure camp just outside of town that offers communal kitchens and *braai* facilities.

Sylvanette B&B (*☎ 501213, 0811 273759; e sylvanet@iafrica.com.na; singles/doubles with breakfast US$22/33*) is a pleasant B&B in a quiet and garden-like suburban setting.

Okahandja lies on the Intercape Mainliner, minibus and train routes between Windhoek and points north. For train information, phone **Trans-Namib** (*☎ 503315*).

GROSS BARMEN

The former mission station of Gross Barmen (*☎ 501091; admission US$2.50 per person, US$1.50 per vehicle; camping US$12 for up to four people, doubles US$24, five bed bungalows US$38-65*), 26km southwest of Okahandja, has hot springs, short hikes and fine bird-watching around the adjacent dam. Book through Namibia Wildlife Resorts (NWR) in Windhoek.

KARIBIB
☎ 064

The rustic ranching town of Karibib began as a station on the narrow-gauge rail line between Windhoek and Swakopmund. It's now dominated by the Palisandro marble quarries, which annually yield over 1200 tonnes of aragonite, the world's hardest and highest-quality marble. For tourist information, contact **Henckert Tourist Centre** (*☎ 550028, fax 550720; e tourist@henckert .com; w www.henckert.com; 38 Main St; open 8am-5.30pm daily*), which also sells mineral specimens and local weavings.

Hotel Erongoblick (*☎/fax 550009; dorm beds US$6, singles/doubles without bathroom*

US$12/22, with bathroom US$18/30*) offers nice digs and a swimming pool. The best place to eat is the **Western Restaurant**, on the main road. **Karibib Bakery**, which dates from 1913, does great breakfasts and brewed coffee.

All bus and rail services between Windhoek and Swakopmund pass through Karibib.

OMARURU
☎ 064

Dusty Omaruru, beside the shady Omaruru Riverbed, has a real outback feel to it. For a view over the town, you can climb **Captain Franke's tower**, which was erected in honour of German Captain Victor Franke, who defended the Colonial town in 1904 against a Herero attack. The **Rhenish mission station** (*admission free*), constructed in 1872 by missionary Gottlieb Viehe, now houses a small **town museum**. Pick up keys to either place at the Central Hotel in the town centre.

A highlight is the **Kristall Kellerei** (*☎ 570083; e winery@omaruru.na; open 9am-6pm Mon-Fri, 9am-1pm Sat; dinner by appointment only*). This, Namibia's only winery, produces colombard and ruby cabernet, and offers wine-tasting and great meals just 4km from town on the D2328. Don't miss its wonderful mineral water, Oasis, which is sold only in Omaruru.

Each year on the weekend nearest 10 October, the White Flag Herero people hold a **festive procession** in Omaruru.

A worthwhile day trip from Omaruru would be to the **Otjihaenamparero dinosaur footprints**, 23km east of Kalkfeld, which features the 170-million-year-old tracks of a three-toed dinosaur.

Places to Stay & Eat

Omaruru Rest Camp (*☎/fax 570516; e jdg@ iway.na; camping US$4 per person, single/ double bungalows US$19-27/24-40; breakfast US$3, lunch US$3, mains US$4.50-7*), a leafy site at the edge of town, attracts lots of locals with its popular restaurant and sports bar. Email and Internet access are available for US$4.50 per hour.

Hotel Staebe (*☎ 570035, fax 570450; e staebe@iafrica.com.na; camping US$4.50 per person, singles/doubles US$30/43*) is a quiet German-run place with a pool and

NORTH-CENTRAL NAMIBIA

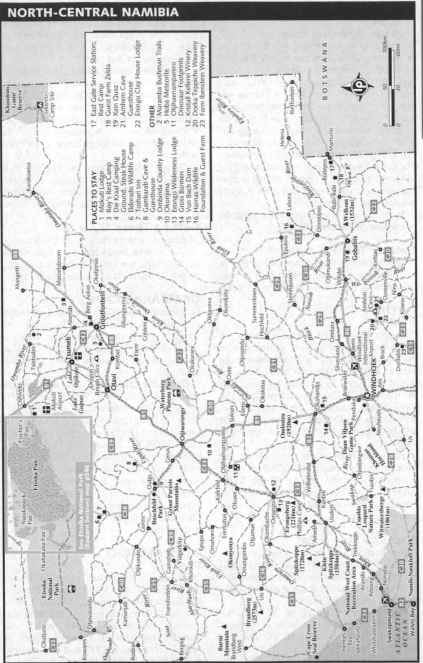

PLACES TO STAY
1 Mokuti Lodge
3 Roy's Rest Camp
4 Die Kraal Camping
  Ground; Steak House
6 Eldorado Wildlife Camp
7 Toshari Inn
8 Gamkarab Cave &
  Guesthouse
9 Ombinda Country Lodge
10 Okonjima
13 Erongo Wilderness Lodge
14 Gross Barmen
15 Von Bach Dam
16 Harnas Wildlife
  Foundation & Guest Farm

17 East Gate Service Station;
   Rest Camp
18 Guest Farm Zelda
19 Xain Quaz
21 Arnhem Cave
   Guesthouse
22 Eningu Clay House Lodge

OTHER
2 Muramba Bushman Trails
5 Hoba Meteorite
11 Otjihaenamparero
12 Kristall Kellerei Winery
20 Dorka Teppiche Weavery
23 Farm Ibenstein Weavery

a green riverside setting. Rates include breakfast.

Erongo Wilderness Lodge (☎ 570537, fax 570536; e info@erongowilderness.com, w www.erongowilderness.com; PO Box 581, km10 D2513; singles/doubles with half-board US$105/170), 10km west of town, is surely one of Namibia's finest lodges. Guests will enjoy the well-appointed tents, set amid stunning boulder formations, as well as the excellent meals and a range of hiking and wildlife-viewing activities on the surrounding Erongo Mountain Nature Conservancy. For something different – if you're willing to forego a shower – request the basic treehouse, where you'll sleep 5m high in a tree overlooking a waterhole.

For meals and snacks, try the **Kaffeestube** or the **Dampf Backerei/Café**.

Getting There & Away

Trains to Tsumeb from either Walvis Bay or Windhoek pass through Omaruru. For train information, call **Trans-Namib** (☎ 570006).

OUTJO
☎ 067

Bougainvillea-decked Outjo, settled in 1880, was never a mission station, but in the mid-1890s it did a short, uneventful stint as a German garrison town. For visitors, it best serves as a staging point for trips to Okaukuejo, in Etosha National Park. The 1899 military residence, the Franke House, now houses the **Outjo Museum** (admission US$0.60; open 10am-12.30pm & 3pm-5pm Mon-Fri).

Tourist information is available at the **African Curios Shop** (☎ 313513; e corne delange@yahoo.com), and the **Outjo Café-Backerei** next door provides email and Internet access for US$4 per hour. It's open 7am to 7pm daily.

Places to Stay & Eat

Outjo Backpackers (☎/fax 313470; camping US$3, dorm beds US$6, doubles US$13), behind the African Curios Shop, provides comfortable, centrally located accommodation with kitchen facilities.

Etosha Garten Hotel (☎ 313130, fax 313419; e egh@mweb.com.na; w www.etosha -garden-hotl.com; 6 Otavi St, PO Box 31; singles/doubles US$24/43) offers shady accommodation just a short walk from the

centre. Its Austrian-run dining room serves up a varied menu of imaginative dishes; so how about zebra steak with blueberry red wine sauce or roast kudu with red apple, cabbage, croquettes and pears?

Ombinda Country Lodge (☎ 313181, fax 313478; e ombinda@ovt.namib.com; camping US$4 per person, singles/doubles US$33/49 with breakfast), a jacaranda-studded place 1km south of town, has reed-and-thatch chalets with satellite TV. Non-guests can use the swimming pool for the price of a few beers at the bar.

Outjo Cafe-Bäckerei (☎ 313055; light meals US$2-3.50) serves chicken, schnitzels and burgers, and its bread and sweet treats are famous throughout the area.

Getting There & Away

Minibuses connect Outjo with Otjiwarongo (US$2.50, one hour) from the bakery and the OK supermarket, but there's currently no public transport to Etosha or Khorixas.

GAMKARAB CAVE

Gamkarab Cave, 50km northeast of Outjo, is replete with lovely stalagmites and stalactites, and the surrounding area has an abundance of hiking trails, unusual vegetation and the world's only source of *pietersite*.

Gamkarab Cave Guesthouse & Adventure Trails (☎ 313827, 0811 291631, fax 313318; e evg@agrinamibia.com.na; PO Box 197, Outjo; camping US$4.50 per person, basic accommodation US$11 per person) offers cave tours (US$4.50), horse riding (US$6/hour), three-day horse tours (US$110) and hiking trails (US$6/day). With your own equipment, on the same farm you can also go cave diving in the underground lake (US$7) or participate in camping tours to Mooeihoek Cave and the upper Ugab Canyon (US$83, with meals).

OTJIWARONGO
☎ 067

Otjiwarongo ('the pleasant place' in Herero) lies at the junction of the roads between Windhoek, Swakopmund, Outjo, Etosha and the Golden Triangle. At the train station sits **Locomotive No 41**, which was manufactured by the Henschel company of Kassel, Germany, in 1912 and was brought to Namibia to haul ore between the Tsumeb

mines and the port at Swakopmund. The **Otjiwarongo Crocodile Ranch** *(☎ 302121; admission US$2; open 9am-4pm Mon-Fri, 11am-2pm Sat-Sun)*, beside the caravan park, provides a marginally interesting attraction.

The very basic **tourist office** *(☎ 303830; e otjtc@iafrica.com.na)* is in the mineral shop opposite the Hamburger Hof Hotel.

Places to Stay & Eat

Acacia Caravan Park *(☎ 302121, fax 302926; Hindenburg St; camping US$6/8 per tent/ caravan plus US$2 per person)* is conveniently located beside the crocodile ranch, but security is poor.

C'est Si Bon *(☎ 301240, fax 303208; e sibon@iafrica.com.na; Schwimbadweg, PO Box 2060; singles/doubles US$37/63)*, Otjiwarongo's best option, provides a continental atmosphere, a pool and a great restaurant with an especially varied menu.

Falkennest B&B *(☎/fax 302616; e otjbb@ iafrica.com.na; 21 Industria Ave; singles/ doubles with breakfast US$16/26)* is a welcome mid-range option, and bird lovers will appreciate the colourful aviary. Rates include the use of the self-catering facilities, pool and *braais.*

Out of Africa Guesthouse & Town Lodge *(☎ 303397, 304383; e luaneck@iway.na; 94 Tuinweg; singles/doubles US$20/28 in the B&B & guesthouse, US$37/53 in the town lodge)* is a three-part establishment with a homely B&B, a guesthouse and a large, opulent lodge, bar and bistro.

Okonjima *(☎ 304563, fax 304565; e okon jima@mweb.com.na; w www.okonjima.com; PO Box 793, Otjiwarongo; singles/doubles US$84/170, US$255/420 with full board & activities)*, the 'Place of Baboons', offers nature trails, a Bushman walk, hiking trails up to 10km, and the possibility of seeing over 300 bird species – but the big attraction is the cats. The owners' Africat Foundation sponsors a cheetah and leopard rehabilitation centre, where problem cats are taught not to ravage cattle, and also keeps orphaned or problem lions, cheetahs and other cats. Note that it's closed from 20 December to late January and children under 12 aren't allowed. To get there, turn west onto the D2515, 49km south of Otjiwarongo; follow this road for 15km and turn left onto the farm road for the last 10km.

On the main street are several takeaways and the excellent **Carstensen's** *(☎ 302326;*

St George's St), which does light meals and coffee. Alternatively, there's **Tony's Tea Room** *(light meals US$1.50-3.50)*, in the Spar Supermarket.

Getting There & Away

The Intercape Mainliner service between Windhoek and Victoria Falls passes through Otjiwarongo and minibuses between Windhoek and the north stop at the Engen petrol station. All train services between Tsumeb and Windhoek or Walvis Bay (via Swakopmund) also pass through.

WATERBERG PLATEAU PARK

Waterberg Plateau Park *(daily admission US$2.50 per person plus US$2.50 per vehicle; open 8am-1pm & 2pm-sunset year-round)* takes in a 50km-long and 16km-wide Etjo sandstone plateau, which looms 150m above the plain. Around this sheer-sided 'Lost World' are numerous freshwater springs, which support a lush mosaic of trees and an abundance of wildlife. The park is also known as a repository for rare and threatened species, including sables, roans and white rhinos.

Visitors may not explore the plateau in their own vehicles, but twice daily, NWR conducts three-hour wildlife drives (US$12/5 per adult/child).

Hiking

There are nine short walking tracks around Bernabé de la Bat Rest Camp, including one up to the plateau rim at Mountain View. A four-day, 42km unguided hike around a figure-eight track (US$12 per person) starts at 9am every Wednesday from April to November. Groups are limited to between three and 10 people. Hikers stay in basic shelters and don't need a tent, but must otherwise be self-sufficient.

Also from April to November, the four-day guided Waterberg Wilderness Trail (US$24 per person) operates every second, third and fourth Thursday of the month and is open to groups of six to eight people. Accommodation is in huts, but participants must carry their own food and sleeping bags. All hikes must be pre-booked through NWR in Windhoek.

Places to Stay & Eat

Bernabé de la Bat Rest Camp *(camping US$12 for up to 4 people, double/triple*

bungalows US$39/43, 5-bed bungalows/ suites US$48/60) offers a range of accommodation with fans, *braais* and outdoor seating areas. The camp **restaurant** serves meals during limited hours and a shop sells staple foods in the morning and afternoon.

Getting There & Away
There's no public transport, but taxis from Otjiwarongo will get you there for around US$25 each way and quite a few budget safaris include it in their itineraries. Note that bicycles and motorcycles aren't permitted.

GROOTFONTEIN
☎ 067

With a pronounced colonial feel, Grootfontein (Big Spring) has an air of uprightness and respectability, with local limestone construction and avenues of jacaranda trees that bloom in September. It was the water that attracted the earliest travellers, and in 1885, the Dorsland (Thirst Land) trekkers set up the short-lived Republic of Upingtonia. By 1887, the settlement was gone, but six years later Grootfontein was selected as the headquarters for the German South-West Africa Company, thanks to the area's agricultural potential and mineral wealth. In 1896, the German Schutztruppe (the Imperial Army) constructed a fort and it became a garrison town.

You'll find the most useful tourist information at **Meteor Tours** (☎/fax 240086; e dirkv@namibnet.com; open 8am-1pm & 2pm-5pm Mon-Fri), which also provides email and Internet access.

Dangers & Annoyances
Grootfontein has more of a security problem than most other Namibian towns, and women are especially vulnerable. Don't walk around at night (just about everything is closed, anyway), and if you're jostled in the street, you can be fairly sure that it's a pickpocketing or robbery attempt. Be on your guard.

German Fort & Museum
In 1968 it was only a last-minute public appeal that saved the old German fort from demolition, and in 1974 it was restored to house the **municipal museum** (☎ 242478; open 4pm-6pm Tues & Fri, 9am-11am Wed). To visit at other times, phone Mrs Pricket or Mrs Blumer (☎ 242479).

Hoba Meteorite
Near the Hoba Farm, 25km west of Grootfontein, the world's largest meteorite (admission US$1.30) was discovered in 1920 by hunter Jacobus Brits. This cuboid blot of space debris is composed of 82% iron, 16% nickel and 0.8% cobalt, along with traces of other metals. No one knows when it fell

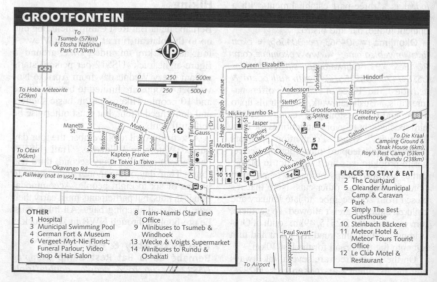

GROOTFONTEIN

To Tsumeb (57km) & Etosha National Park (170km)

To Hoba Meteorite (25km)

To Otavi (96km)

Railway (not in use)

Queen Elizabeth

Hindorf

Andersson

Steffen

Grootfontein Spring

Historic Cemetery

To Die Kraal Camping Ground & Steak House (6km), Roy's Rest Camp (6km) & Rundu (238km)

To Airport

Paul Swart

PLACES TO STAY & EAT
2 The Courtyard
5 Oleander Municipal Camp & Caravan Park
7 Simply The Best Guesthouse
10 Steinbach Bäckerei
11 Meteor Hotel & Meteor Tours Tourist Office
12 Le Club Motel & Restaurant

OTHER
1 Hospital
3 Municipal Swimming Pool
4 German Fort & Museum
6 Vergeet-Myt-Nie Florist; Funeral Parlour; Video Shop & Hair Salon
8 Trans-Namib (Star Line) Office
9 Minibuses to Tsumeb & Windhoek
13 Wecke & Voigts Supermarket
14 Minibuses to Rundu & Oshakati

The Red Line

Between Grootfontein and Rundu, and between Tsumeb and Ondangwa, the B8 and B1 cross the Red Line, the Animal Disease Control (veterinary control fence) Checkpoint separating the commercial cattle ranches of the south from the communal subsistence lands to the north. This fence bars the north–south movement of animals as a precaution against foot-and-mouth disease and rinderpest, and animals bred north of this line may not be sold to the south or exported to overseas markets.

As a result, the Red Line also marks the effective boundary between the First and Third Worlds. The landscape south of the line is characterised by a dry scrubby bushveld (open grassland) of vast ranches which are home only to cattle and a few scattered ranchers. However, north of the Animal Disease Control Checkpoint, travellers enter a landscape of dense bush, baobab trees, mopane scrub and small kraals, where people and animals wander along the road and the air is filled with smoke from cooking fires and bush-clearing operations.

to earth (it's thought to have been around 80,000 years ago), but since it weighs in at 54,000 kg it must have made a hell of a thump. There's no public transport, but taxis from town charge about US$15 each way.

Places to Stay & Eat

Oleander Municipal Camp & Caravan Park (☎ 243101; camping US$5 plus US$1.75/1.25 per vehicle/person, singles/doubles US$42/53) provides inexpensive accommodation, but security is a problem. Don't leave anything of value in your car or tent.

Die Kraal Camping & Steak House (☎ 240300; camping US$3 per person), 6km north of town (phone for a lift), is a better choice for camping, and the attached steakhouse sizzles up some of Namibia's best – and most enormous – steaks. Meal bookings are essential.

Simply the Best Guesthouse (☎ 243315; 6 Weigel St; singles/doubles US$17/27) is a friendly and pleasant little place. Before 6pm, check in at the **Vergeet-Myt-Nie** (☎ 242431) florist, funeral parlour, video shop and hair salon.

Meteor Hotel (☎ 242078, fax 243072; Okavango Rd; singles/doubles from US$27/41) is an old stand-by, with ho-hum rooms and a nice restaurant. On Sundays, it does a buffet lunch (US$7) from noon to 2pm and on Fridays, a US$7 pizza bake.

The Courtyard (☎/fax 240027; e plat inum@iway.na; 2 Gauss St, PO Box 1425; singles/doubles US$37/53) provides a quiet retreat within easy walking distance of the centre. Regional travellers receive a 30% discount on the enormous and, notably,

disabled-accessible rooms. Email and Internet access is available for US$3 per hour.

Roy's Rest Camp (☎/fax 240302; e roys camp@iway.na; w www.swiftcentre.com; PO Box 755, Grootfontein; camping US$4.50 per person, single/double bungalows from US$27/40), 53km out on the Rundu road, is a wonderfully rustic option, from the fairy-tale bungalows to the handmade furniture in the bar and dining area. On the farm, they run three-day camping trips (US$68 per person) featuring San guides who demonstrate their traditional culture; participants need their own camping gear. Half-day hunting and gathering trips with a San guide cost US$17.

Le Club Motel & Restaurant (☎ 242414; Hidipo Hamutenya St; singles/doubles US$21/30; breakfast US$2.50-3.50, mains US$3.50-7) is a small and rather noisy town motel and restaurant that's well-located for the transport terminals.

Steinbach Bäckerei (☎ 242348; snacks US$2-3.50) serves as the best place in town to pick up a quick snack or light meal, although both supermarkets also serve light meals and takeaways.

Getting There & Away

Minibuses run frequently between Grootfontein and Tsumeb, Rundu, Katima Mulilo and Windhoek, departing when full from informal bus stops along Okavango Road at the appropriate ends of town. The Intercape Mainliner bus between Windhoek and Victoria Falls also passes through. On Thursdays at 11.30am, Star Line runs buses from the train station to Tsumkwe (US$8, 6½ hours); it returns the next day, leaving Tsumkwe at 10.15am.

NAMIBIA

TSUMEB
☎ 067

Tsumeb, which is perhaps Namibia's loveliest town, enjoys quiet streets lined with flame trees and jacarandas and surroundings that have geologists salivating. Of the 184 minerals that have been discovered here, 10 are found nowhere else in the world, and mineral collectors justifiably rank the area as one of the world's great natural wonders.

The town's name is derived from a melding of the San word *tsoumsoub* ('to dig in loose ground') and the Herero *otjisume* ('place of frogs'). Tsumeb isn't really known for little croakers, but the red, brown, green and grey streaks created by minerals of the area resemble dried frog spawn, and both the frogs and digging equipment appear on the town's crest.

Information
The friendly **Travel North Namibia Tourist Office** (☎ 220728, 0811 246722, fax 220916; e travelnn@tsu.namib.com; 1551 Omeg Alee, PO Box 799) provides nationwide information, accommodation and transport bookings, as well as car hire anywhere in northern Namibia (with special rates for Etosha trips); Etosha bookings; fax, email and Internet services; and laundry (US$2 to wash and dry; US$3 for a service wash).

At **Dotcom Internet** (☎ 221628; open 8am-6pm Mon-Fri, 9am-6pm Sat, 11am-6pm Sun), email and Internet access costs US$2.50 per hour.

Things to See & Do
Tsumeb's history and mineralogical heritage is recounted in the worthwhile **Tsumeb Museum** (☎ 220447; Main St; admission US$1; open 9am-noon & 2pm-5pm Mon-Fri, 9am-noon Sat), in the 1915 Old German Private School.

The **Tsumeb Cultural Village** (☎ 220787; admission US$1.30), on the Grootfontein road, presents Namibia's many cultures with artefacts, demonstrations and buildings from around the country.

Lake Otjikoto (admission US$1.30), meaning 'deep hole' in Herero, lies on the B1 about 24km northwest of Tsumeb. It was created when the roof of a 150m by 100m limestone sinkhole collapsed; the resulting 55m-deep lake and nearby Lake Guinas are the only natural lakes in Namibia. In 1915, during WWI, the retreating Germans dumped weaponry and ammunition into Lake Otjikoto – most of which is still there – to prevent the equipment falling into South African hands. If you'd like to dive in the lake, contact the **Windhoek Underwater Club** (☎ 061-238320, 0811 281945, fax 232201; e theo@schoemans.com.na).

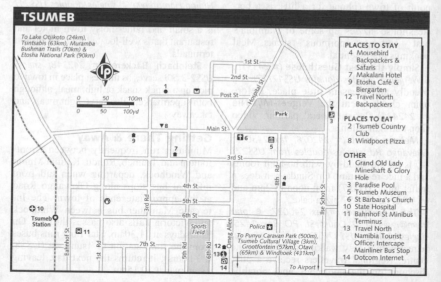

TSUMEB

To Lake Otjikoto (24km),
Tsintsabis (63km), Muramba
Bushman Trails (70km) &
Etosha National Park (90km)

0   50   100m
0   50   100yd

Tsumeb
Station

To Punyu Caravan Park (500m),
Tsumeb Cultural Village (3km),
Grootfontein (57km), Otavi
(65km) & Windhoek (431km)

To Airport

PLACES TO STAY
4 Mousebird Backpackers & Safaris
7 Makalani Hotel
9 Etosha Café & Biergarten
12 Travel North Backpackers

PLACES TO EAT
2 Tsumeb Country Club
8 Windpoort Pizza

OTHER
1 Grand Old Lady Mineshaft & Glory Hole
3 Paradise Pool
5 Tsumeb Museum
6 St Barbara's Church
10 State Hospital
11 Bahnhof St Minibus Terminus
13 Travel North Namibia Tourist Office; Intercape Mainliner Bus Stop
14 Dotcom Internet

Organised Tours

Itenge Safaris (☎ 221777, fax 221778; e info@itenge-safaris.com, w www.itenge-safaris.com) operates weekly three-day safaris to Etosha (US$160), two days in Bushmanland (US$125), Thursday/Friday transfers to/from Windhoek, and six-day one-way tours to Livingstone, Zambia (US$410).

The **Tsumeb Museum** (☎/fax 220447) runs excursions (US$6) through the Otavi Minen und Eisenbahn-Gesellschaft (OMEG) opencast mine (now run by the Ongopolo Corporation) on Tuesday and Thursday at 10am. Tours include a descent into the mine shaft and need a minimum of four participants.

Places to Stay & Eat

Punyu Caravan Park (☎ 221952; camping US$6/tent & US$2 per person) has an electrified fence, but it's wise to watch your belongings.

Mousebird Backpackers & Safaris (☎ 221777, fax 221778; e info@mousebird.com; w www.mousebird.com; 533 4th St, PO Box 1712; camping US$4 per person, dorm beds US$6-7.50, doubles US$16), Tsumeb's friendliest and most economical accommodation, offers comfortable rooms, excellent kitchen facilities and a nice little bar. Their company, Itenge Safaris, runs scheduled tours to Etosha and Bushmanland, among other places (see Organised Tours earlier in this section).

Travel North Backpackers (☎ 220728, or after hours 0811 246722; e travelnn@tsu.namib.com; Omeg Alee; camping US$3 per person, dorm beds US$6, singles/doubles from US$14/25), adjacent to the tourist office, makes a good choice for budget accommodation.

Etosha Café & Biergarten (☎ 221207; Main St; singles/doubles with shared bathroom US$13/22) is a friendly place offering clean, inexpensive accommodation. It's also great for breakfast (real brewed coffee!), lunch or a drink in the relaxed beer garden.

Makalani Hotel (☎ 221051, fax 221575; e makalani@mweb.com.na; w www.makalanihotel.com; 3rd St, PO Box 64; singles/doubles US$37/51), in the town centre, is Tsumeb's most comfortable mid-range choice. Rates include breakfast, and there's also a pub, a lively sports bar and a dining room serving lunch and dinner.

Windpoort Pizza (☎ 220243; Main St; medium pizzas US$2.50-4; open 7am-8pm Mon-Fri, 8am-2pm & 5pm-7.30pm Sat, 5pm-7.30pm Sun), housed in a video shop, does a range of excellent (and often bizarre) pizza concoctions.

Tsumeb Country Club (☎ 222192, 0812 401237; Ilse Schot St; open noon-2pm & 5pm-10pm Mon-Sat; meals US$3.50-5.50) has an a la carte restaurant and a **Sports Bar** (open 4pm-late Mon-Sat).

Getting There & Away

The Intercape Mainliner between Windhoek and Victoria Falls calls in at the Travel North Namibia office. Minibuses travel frequently from the Bahnhof Street terminus in Tsumeb to Grootfontein, Oshakati and Windhoek.

Trains run three times weekly to and from Windhoek (US$7, 16 hours) and Walvis Bay (US$7, 17½ hours). For train information, contact **Trans-Namib** (☎ 220358).

ETOSHA NATIONAL PARK

☎ 067

Etosha National Park, the 'Great White Place of Dry Water', takes in approximately 20,000 sq km surrounding its namesake, the vast white and greenish-coloured Etosha Pan. This vast park protects 114 mammal species, as well as 340 bird species, 16 reptiles and amphibians, one fish species and countless insects.

The first Europeans in Etosha were traders and explorers John Andersson and Francis Galton, who arrived by wagon at Namutoni in 1851, but Etosha didn't attract the interest of tourists or conservationists until after the turn of the 20th century, when the governor of German South-West Africa, Dr F von Lindequist, became concerned over diminishing animal numbers and founded a 99,526-sq-km reserve. In subsequent years, the park boundaries were altered several times, and by 1970 Etosha had been pared down to its present 23,175 sq km.

Orientation

Only the eastern two-thirds of Etosha is open to the general public. All roads are passable to 2WD vehicles and it's in this area that you'll find the rest camps. The western third is reserved exclusively for tour operators. Each of the three rest camps has an information centre, and the staff and shops at either of the main gates sell maps and provide basic information.

NAMIBIA

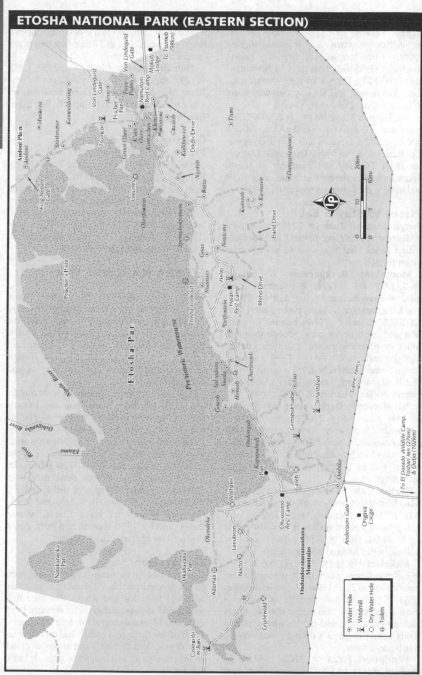

ETOSHA NATIONAL PARK (EASTERN SECTION)

Etosha Pan

Prehistoric Watercourse

Nsak River

Oshigambo River

Ekuma River

Natukanaoka Pan

Okatukana Pan

Ondundozonananandana Mountains

Andoni Plain

Andoni
Masaieva
Kameeldoring
Stinkwater
Tsuineor
King Nehale Gate
Poacher's Point
Grood Otavi
Leeuwes
Okerfontein
Tsuneor
Fischer's Pan
Von Lindequist Gate
Von Lindequist Gate
Twee Palms
Anne
K'vai
Okevi
Koinachas
Klein
Namutoni
Namutoni Rest Camp
Dikdik Drive
Claudob
Kalkheuwel
Njobib
Batia
Tsam
Dungariespoort
Springbokfontein
Goas
Nonciws
Koinseb
Kawaseb
Eland Drive
Etosha Lookout
Naumser
Rietfontein
Helio
Halali
Halali Rest Camp
Rhino Drive
Gnosb
Salvadora
Sueda
Homob
Charitsaub
Gemsbokwakte
Aus
Olifantsbad
Game Fence
Ondongub
Kapupuhedi
Pan
Kapupuhedi
Gaseb
Wolfsnes
Ombika
Andersson Gate
Ongava Lodge
To El Dorado Wildlife Camp,
Toshari Inn (27km)
& Outjo (102km)
Okondeka
Okaukuejo
Okaukuejo Res Camp
Leeubron
Nacto
Adamax
Grünewald
Leeubron
Czonsnulli
m Bari

20km
10mi
0 5 10

● Water Hole
✗ Windmill
◌ Dry Water Hole
⊚ Toilets

Information

Visitors must check in at Von Lindequist, Andersson or King Nehale Gates and purchase a daily permit, which costs US$3.50/0.30 per adult/child and US$2.50 per vehicle. The permits must then be presented at your reserved rest camp, where you pay any outstanding camping or accommodation fees, which must be pre-paid through a travel agency or NWR in Windhoek. For contact details, see under National Parks in the Facts About Namibia section.

Book well in advance for visits during Namibian or South African school holidays (normally mid-December to mid-January; around Easter; late July to early August; and for two weeks in mid-October). During this period, you may be limited to three nights in each of the three camps, although exceptions can sometimes be made.

Note that pets and firearms are prohibited in the park. Those booked into the rest camps must arrive before sunset and can only leave after sunrise; the daily times are posted on the gates.

Places to Stay

Etosha is open to day visitors, but it's impossible to see much of the park in less than three days. Most visitors spend a couple of nights at one of its three rest camps, Namutoni, Halali and Okaukuejo. Each camp has a restaurant *(open 7am-8.30am, noon-1.30pm & 6pm-9.30pm daily)*, bar, shop, swimming pool, picnic sites, petrol station and kiosk.

In the Park The site of the Etosha Research Station is **Okaukuejo Rest Camp** *(camping US$20 for four people, economy rooms or bungalows US$33, two-bed rooms US$41, three-bed bungalows US$41, four-bed chalets US$50, four-bed 'luxury' bungalows US$58, four-bed self-catering bungalows US$95)*, pronounced 'o-kau-**kui**-yo', and the visitors centre outlines ongoing park research (one display identifies examples of animal droppings with their perpetrators). The camping ground is a bit of a dust hole, but the self-catering accommodation may be the nicest in the park.

The floodlit water hole is probably Etosha's best rhino-viewing venue, particularly between 8pm and 10pm. Also popular is the sunset photo frenzy from Okaukuejo's landmark stone tower, which affords a view

The Wild World of Etosha

Etosha's most widespread vegetation is mopane woodland, which fringes the pan and covers about 80% of the park. There are also stretches of savanna, dominated by the umbrella-thorn acacia (*Acacia torilis*) and other trees favoured by browsing animals; from December to March, this sparse bush country bears a pleasant green hue.

Depending on the season, visitors may observe elephants, giraffes, Burchell's zebras, springboks, red hartebeests, blue wildebeests, gemsboks, elands, kudus, roans, ostriches, jackals, hyenas, lions, and even cheetahs and leopards. Among the endangered species are the black-faced impala, frequently observed around Namutoni, and the black rhino, often seen at Okaukuejo. Birdlife is also profuse.

In the winter dry season, wildlife clusters around water holes and is easily observed, while in the hot, wet summer months, animals disperse and spend the days sheltering in the bush and are difficult to see. On the other hand, this is the most rewarding time for bird-watching.

across the spaces to the distant Ondundozonananandana (Lost Shepherd Boy) Mountains; try saying that after three pints of Windhoek lager (or even before!).

Halali Rest Camp *(camping US$20 for four people, four-bed economy bungalow US$42, four-bed self-catering bungalows US$48-81, two-bed rooms US$37)* nestles between several incongruous dolomite outcrops, which you can reach on the short Tsumasa Kopje hiking track. It's currently the best wildlife-viewing camp in the park, and a floodlit water hole extends opportunities into the night.

Namutoni Rest Camp *(camping US$20 for four people; 2-bed room without/with bathroom US$18/41, 2-bed economy flats inside/outside the fort US$38/27, 4-bed chalets US$45, 4-bed flats US$42/50, 4-bed 'luxury' suites US$87)* is the best-kept of the camps, with its landmark whitewashed German fort. It originally served as an outpost for German troops, and in 1899 the German cavalry built a fort from which to control Owambo uprisings. In the battle of Namutoni, on 28 January 1904, seven German soldiers unsuccessfully defended it against 500 Owambo warriors. Two years later, the damaged structure was

renovated and pressed into service as a police station. In 1956, it was restored to its original specifications and two years later was opened as tourist accommodation.

The tower and ramparts provide a great view, and crowds gather every evening to watch the sunset. Beside the fort is a lovely freshwater limestone spring, full of vociferous frogs, and the floodlit King Nehale water hole.

Outside the Park Several options exist nearby, outside the park gates. Some of the most popular include:

Mokuti Lodge (☎ 229084, fax 229091; e mokuti@mweb.com.na; w www.namibsun hotels.com.na/mokutilodge; PO Box 403, Tsumeb; singles/doubles from US$77/110, family rooms US$120 with breakfast) is a very large and popular lodge 2km from Von Lindequist Gate. It doesn't pretend to be exclusive – it has over 100 rooms and offers pools, tennis courts, air-con and colour TV – but the low-profile buildings still create an illusion of intimacy. Don't miss the attached reptile park and its resident snake collection.

Ongava Lodge (☎ 061-274500, fax 239455; e info@nts.com.na; w www.wilderness safaris com; 8 Bismarck St, Windhoek, PO Box 6850, Windhoek; singles/doubles US$340/500 in the high season) occupies its own wildlife reserve just outside Etosha's Andersson Gate. Chalets afford wide vistas over the bush, and rates include meals and wildlife-viewing activities; fly-in options are available through Wilderness Safaris Namibia (see Organised Tours in the Getting Around section).

Toshari Inn (☎ 333440 fax 333444; e toshari@out.namib.com; 27km south of Andersson Gate, PO Box 164, Outjo; singles/doubles US$36/55 with breakfast) offers light hiking and bird-watching in a natural backdrop.

Eldorado Wildlife Camp (☎/fax 333421; e epienaar@mweb.com.na; w www.natron .net/eldorado; camping US$4 per person, double tents US$14; breakfast/dinner US$3.50/6), a convenient and low-key place along the road to Outjo, is an inexpensive alternative to the safari lodges or national parks accommodation.

Getting There & Away
Air Namibia flies daily between Windhoek's Eros airport and Mokuti airport (US$90/145 one way/return), immediately south of Von Lindequist Gate.

Etosha's three main entry gates are Von Lindequist (Namutoni), west of Tsumeb; King Nehale, southeast of Ondangwa; and Andersson (Okaukuejo), north of Outjo. There's no public transport into the park, but Tsumeb, the nearest bus and rail terminal, 110km away, has several car hire agencies. Otherwise, plenty of safari companies run Etosha tours including some extremely economical options (see the Getting Around section, earlier in this chapter).

Hitching is prohibited inside Etosha, but hitchers may be able to find lifts from Tsumeb to Namutoni or Outjo to Okaukuejo. Sort out entry permits when you enter the park or your driver may have problems when trying to exit the park (it will appear that some of their original party has vanished!) Your best bet is to explain when you enter the park that you need separate entry permits for your own records.

Getting Around
Pedestrians, bicycles, motorcycles and hitching are prohibited in Etosha, and open bakkies must be screened off. Outside the rest camps, visitors must stay in their vehicles (except at toilet stops).

Northern Namibia

The various regions of northeastern Namibia, along with Owamboland, form Namibia's cultural heartland. In the northeast, the gently rolling Kavango region is dominated by the Okavango River and its broad flood plains where people cultivate maize, sorghum and green vegetables and supplement their diet with fish caught in woven funnel-shaped fish traps. Thanks to their woodlands, Kavango people have also developed woodcarving skills and arguably produce Namibia's finest woodwork. Animal figures, masks, wooden beer mugs, walking sticks and boxes are carved in the light *dolfhout* (wild teak) hardwood and make excellent souvenirs.

East of Kavango, in the spindly Caprivi Strip, the flat, unexceptional landscape is characterised by expanses of forest. To the south lies Bushmanland, where a growing worldwide interest in Kalahari cultures has brought about significant changes.

What's Brewing in the Owambo Country?

Forget the Pig & Whistle, Hare & Hounds or King George & the Dragon. The Owambo have their own pub culture, and the bars, nightclubs and bottle shops – better known as 'cuca shops' – along the northern highways bear wonderfully colourful names. One bottle store is called Serious, another is the Fruit of Love and yet another is California BS. Perhaps the best is simply the unpretentious Botol Stor.

Then there are the bars: the Clinic Happy Bar, Hot Box, Daily Needs, Salon for Sure, Club Jet Style, Sorry to See, Bruce Lee Bar, Oversize Bar, Club Euro Frique, Let's Push, California City Style, Come Together Good Life, Happy Brothers & Sisters, Join Us, Hard Workers Bar, Every Day Bar, Bar We Like and USA No Money No Life. A few are more philosophical: The System, Just Another Life, The Agreement Centre, Take Time, Keep Trying No 1, Keep Trying No 2, Tenacity Centre and Try Again. There also seems to be a new hydrological theme emerging: Sea Point, Quay 4, Club LA Coast, Pelican, Friend Ship, Titanic, Titicaca, and Seven Seas Up & Down.

Some names, however, boggle the mind. Who, for example, came up with the Sign of Mr Hans, We Push & Pull, One Moo, No Wally Let's Support Bar, Far Well Mr Happy Bar, Let's Sweat for Tailor Bar, Club Say Father of Mustache, Let We Trust Uncle Simon, Three Sister in Beer Garden and Wet Come to Big Mama? And given the choice, would you prefer to down a drop in the Peace Full Bar or the Water is Life, or choke down a foul brew in the Oshakati establishment known as Vile Waters?

During Namibia's war for independence, Owamboland, the home of the Owambo people, served as a base for the Southwest African People's Organisation (Swapo), and the villages of Oshakati, Ondangwa and (Uutapi) Ombalantu were pressed into service as bases and supply centres for the occupying South African army. After the South Africans left, these new commercial centres attracted entrepreneurs, who set up small businesses, and government development projects: housing, electrical lines, roads, irrigation systems, healthcare and education.

Today, most Owambo follow subsistence agricultural lifestyles, growing staple crops and raising cattle and goats. For visitors, the region is especially known for its high-quality basketware, with its simple and graceful designs, usually incorporating a brown geometric pattern woven into the pale-yellow reed. Quality examples may be purchased at roadside stalls or artists' homes for favourable prices.

OSHAKATI
☎ 065

The Owambo capital, Oshakati, may be a friendly, bustling hive of activity, but the uninspiring commercial centre is little more than a strip of development along the highway. Most visitors will enjoy an hour at the large and odorous covered market, which proffers everything from clothing and baskets to *mopane* worms and glasses of freshly brewed *tambo*.

Information

There's no tourist office, but any petrol station or accommodation option can provide basic information. For changing money, major banks are represented along the bustling commercial centre. Lots of places offer mobile phone calls for a nominal charge. Email and Internet access are available at the **Iway I-café** (☎ 224070; open 8am-5pm Mon-Fri), which charges US$4.50 per hour. Alternatively, there's the **Pick-a-Phone** (☎ 221300; open 8am-6pm daily), in the Yetu Centre, charging US$3.50 per hour.

The **Angolan Consulate** (open 9am-4pm Mon-Fri) issues 30-day visas for an average of US$47. Drop off your passport in the morning and pick it up in the afternoon.

Fuji and Agfa slide and print film is available at the **Agfa Oshakati Photo Shop** on the main road. The **Oshakati Bookshop** offers used paperbacks, textbooks and a couple of reference titles.

There is a government hospital in town, but if you need medical attention and your health is important to you, opt for the **Onandjokwe Lutheran Hospital** (☎ 240111) in Ondangwa or the **Oshikuku Roman Catholic Hospital** in Oshikuku, 26km west of town.

NORTHERN NAMIBIA

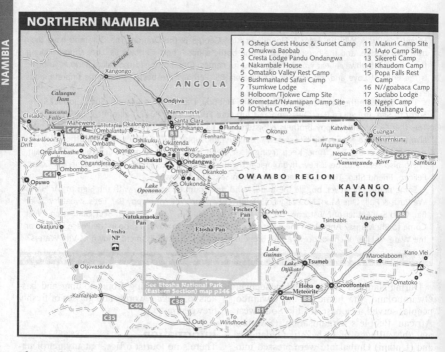

1 Osheja Guest House & Sunset Camp	11 Makuri Camp Site
2 Omukwa Baobab	12 !A≠o Camp Site
3 Cresta Lodge Pandu Ondangwa	13 Sikereti Camp
4 Nakambale House	14 Khaudom Camp
5 Omatako Valley Rest Camp	15 Popa Falls Rest Camp
6 Bushmanland Safari Camp	
7 Tsumkwe Lodge	16 N//goabaca Camp
8 Holboom/Tjokwe Camp Site	17 Suclabo Lodge
9 Kremetart/N≠amapan Camp Site	18 Ngepi Camp
10 IO'baha Camp Site	19 Mahangu Lodge

Places to Stay & Eat

Oshakati International Youth Hostel (☎ 224294; San Nujoma Rd; dorm beds US$3.50, rooms US$9 per person) serves mainly as accommodation for Namibian school groups and their supervisors; it's clean and friendly, but note that men and women are separated.

Santorini Inn (☎ 220457, fax 220506; e bookings@santorini-inn.com; Ondangwa Rd, PO Box 5569; singles/doubles from US$45/ 56 with breakfast) may inspire the sensation that you've died and gone to Florida. With a distinctly tropical feel, this motel features a pool, bar, DSTV, restaurant, and a refrigeration shop which ensures the air-con is functional.

Oshandira Lodge (☎ 220443, fax 221189; e oshandira@iway.na; Oshakati Airport, PO Box 958; singles/doubles US$32/47 with breakfast) recently had a kitchen fire, but should be renovated by the time you read this – and it'll be twice as good as before. Amenities include a pool, green lawns, a traditional restaurant, and a bar with sports TV.

Oshakati Country Lodge (☎ 222380, fax 222384; e countrylodge@mweb.com.a, Robert Mugabe, PO Box 15200; singles/ doubles US$56/75, family rooms US$112) provides posh but fairly heartless accommodation for business travellers and government officials.

Rocha's (☎ 222038; Ondangwa Rd; sandwiches US$1.50, mains US$4.50-8) specialises in Portuguese-style fare, including a range of fish dishes.

For fast food, try the **KFC** in the Yetu centre or the **Wimpy** in the Engen petrol station. Self-caterers have a growing number of supermarkets which are open business hours Monday to Friday and Saturday mornings. On Sundays, the hours are shared by the **Spar** (open 8.30am-2pm) and **Pick&Pay** (open 2pm-6pm). There's also a **Spar Supadupa** (open until 10pm daily).

Getting There & Away

From the bus terminal at the market, white minibuses leave frequently for Ondangwa (US$1.25, one hour) and Uutapi/Ombalantu (US$1.75, two hours). Minibuses for Windhoek (US$9, 11 hours), via Tsumeb (US$3, four hours) set out when full, with extra departures on Sunday afternoon.

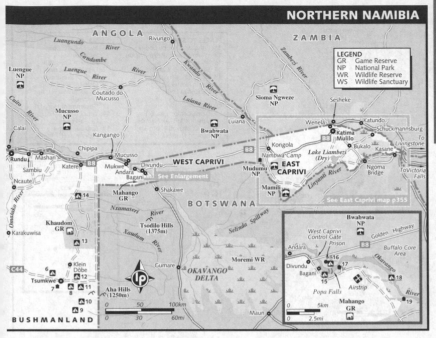

NORTHERN NAMIBIA

LEGEND
GR Game Reserve
NP National Park
WR Wildlife Reserve
WS Wildlife Sanctuary

Getting Around

Economical car hire is available from **Santorini Car Hire** (☎ 220504, 0811 240234), where you'll pay US$21 per day plus US$0.30 per km; there's no charge for pickup or drop-off at the airport in Ondangwa.

ONDANGWA
☎ 065

The second-largest Owambo town, Ondangwa boasts several colourful buildings, a booming market, and warehouses that provide stock to the 6000 tiny *cuca* shops (small bush shops named after the brand of Angolan beer they once sold) that serve the area's rural residents.

Lost in the maze of routes and tracks south of Ondangwa lies **Lake Oponono**, a large wetland fed by the Culevai *oshanas* (underground river channels). After rains, the region attracts a variety of birdlife, including saddlebill storks, crowned cranes, flamingoes and pelicans. The edge of the lake lies 27km south of Ondangwa.

Also worthwhile is **Nakambale House** (*admission US$0.75; open 8am-1pm & 2pm-5pm Mon-Fri, 8am-1pm Sat, noon-5pm Sun*)

which was built in the late 1870s by Finnish missionary Martti Rauttanen, and is the oldest building in northern Namibia. It now houses a museum. In 1889, Reverend Rauttanen also constructed the area's first church, which is open by request.

Places to Stay & Eat

Ondangwa Rest Camp (☎ 240351; **e** rest camp@osh.namib.com; *camping US$4 per person*) surrounds a rather fetid pond behind Ondangwa's very obviously pink shopping centre. The attached **Oasis Restaurant & Beer Garden** is probably the best place in town to hang out, but the camping sites could be more appealing.

Cresta Lodge Pandu Ondangwa (☎ 241900, fax 241919; **e** ondangwa@cresta namibia.com.na; **w** www.cresta-hospitality.com; *PO Box 2827; singles/doubles from US$53/68*), a plush new business travellers' option, features bright rooms and tasteful artwork, as well as the attached **Chatters** restaurant and a small **takeaway** in the lobby.

Olukonda National Monument (☎ 245668; **e** olukonda.museum@elcin.org.na; *camping US$4/tent plus US$1.50 per person, traditional*

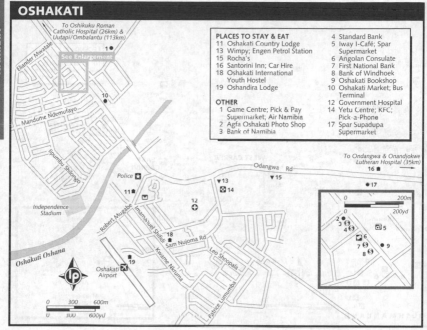

OSHAKATI

PLACES TO STAY & EAT
11 Oshakati Country Lodge
13 Wimpy; Engen Petrol Station
15 Rocha's
16 Santorini Inn; Car Hire
18 Oshakati International Youth Hostel
19 Oshandira Lodge

OTHER
1 Game Centre; Pick & Pay Supermarket; Air Namibia
2 Agfa Oshakati Photo Shop
3 Bank of Namibia
4 Standard Bank
5 Iway I-Café; Spar Supermarket
6 Angolan Consulate
7 First National Bank
8 Bank of Windhoek
9 Oshakati Bookshop
10 Oshakati Market; Bus Terminal
12 Government Hospital
14 Yetu Centre; KFC; Pick-a-Phone
17 Spar Supadupa Supermarket

---

huts per person without/with linen US$4.50/8, cottage US$9 per person with breakfast), at Olukonda village, 6km southeast of Ondangwa on the D3606, is a collection of historic Finnish mission buildings (including the previously mentioned Nakambale House) and a demonstration Owambo *kraal*.

Getting There & Away
All transport services between Oshakati and Tsumeb or Windhoek stop at Ondangwa's BP petrol station.

UUTAPI (OMBALANTU)
Dusty Uutapi (frequently spelled Outapi, or called Ombalantu, after a formerly adjacent village) is one of Namibia's most typically African commercial towns.

Its main attraction is its former South African army base, which is dominated by the enormous **Omukwa Baobab**. In the past, this amazing hollow tree was used to shelter cattle from invaders, and later used as a turret from which to ambush invading tribes. It didn't work against the South African army, however, which invaded and used the tree for everything from a chapel to a coffee shop (a

sign outside reads 'Die Koffiekamer Koelte', meaning 'The Coffee Chamber Cult'), a post office, a storage shed and an interrogation chamber for prisoners of war. The site is loosely described as the **Omusati Region Museum** *(1km off the D3612; admission free; open 24 hr)*, and includes a nearby bunker and watchtower from the South African days.

RUACANA
☎ 065
The tiny Kunene River town of Ruacana (from the Herero words *orua hakahana* – 'the rapids'), was built as a company town to serve the 320-megawatt underground Ruacana hydroelectric project, which now supplies over half of Namibia's power requirements.

The dramatic 85m-high **Ruacana Falls** was once a great natural wonder, but thanks to Angola's Calueque Dam, the water flows only during heavy rains, when the power station is satisfied and excess water is released over the dam. in 2001 and 2002, the falls roared to life in March and April, presenting a spectacle comparable to Victoria Falls – if you hear that it's flowing, you

certainly won't regret a side trip to see it. To enter the border area, visitors must sign the Namibian immigration register.

Osheja Guest House & Sunset Camp (☎ 0812 424916; camping US$3.50/2 per adult/child, Sunset bungalows US$8 per person, Osheja guest house US$16 per person) is a two-part lodge taking in the leafy camping and bungalow area and the nearby Osheja guest house. During business hours, you can register with Venessa at the BP petrol station. Meals are available with advance booking.

Minibuses connect Ruacana with Oshakati daily from the BP petrol station.

RUNDU
☎ 066

Rundu, a sultry tropical outpost on the bluffs above the Okavango River, has little of specific interest for tourists, but it's great to laze at one of its very nice lodges and take in the riverside scene. It's also a centre of activity for Namibia's growing Angolan and Portuguese communities. Every May at Rundu Beach, locals put on the *Anything that Floats* regatta, accompanied by the usual drinking, dining and socialising.

The **Tourism Centre** (☎/fax 256140, e ngandu@mweb.com; Kakakuru St; open 8am-5pm Mon-Fri, 8am-1pm Sat), run by the same folks as Ngandu Safari Lodge, can provide basic tourist information.

The well-stocked **Okavango Pharmacy** (Siwaronga St) is probably the best in northern Namibia.

Places to Stay & Eat

Ngandu Safari Lodge (☎ 256723, fax 256726; e ngandu@mweb.com.na; w www.resafrica.net/ngandu-safari-lodge, Sarasungu Rd, PO Box 519; camping per person US$3.50, singles/doubles from US$27/40) tries to be everything to everybody, with a range of accommodation. While it's convenient for the centre of town and boasts the very amenable **Croc Bites restaurant** (mains US$4-8, weekend specials US$5), it's still over 1km from the river.

N'Kwazi Lodge (☎/fax 255467; e nkwazi@iafrica.com.na; 4km off Okavango River road, PO Box 1623, Rundu; camping per person US$3.50, camping bungalows per person US$13, double bungalows with breakfast US$35) makes a great riverside retreat, with family-style meals and

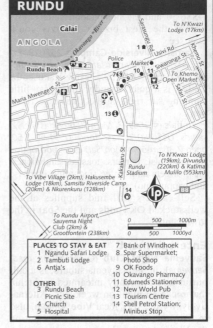

hospitality. Discounts are available during low periods. In the evening, you can take a sunset cruise on the Okavango; the lodge also organises cultural evenings with residents of adjacent Mayana village, and visits to Mayana School, which is supported by the lodge. Transfers from town cost US$29 per group.

Hakusembe Lodge (☎ 257010, fax 257011; e hakusemb@mweb.com.na; PO Box 1327; camping per person US$3.50, singles/doubles with half-board US$65/105, honeymoon suite US$155) is a secluded hideaway amid lush riverside gardens. Activities here focus on the river – sunset cruises, canoeing, fishing, water-skiing and wildlife-viewing trips to Mahango Game Reserve (US$42 per person). It lies 17km down the Nkurenkuru road, then 2km north to the riverbank

Tambuti Lodge (☎/fax 255711, 0812 494844; e tambuti@namibnet.com; w www.tambuti.lodge.na; PO Box 2343; singles/doubles with breakfast US$32/41, honeymoon suite US$78), a small Swiss-run lodge at Rundu Beach, combines in-town accommodation with a river setting. The menu

features a host of Swiss dishes for US$5 to US$6.50 and the honeymoon suite enjoys one of the most bizarre Jacuzzis you'll ever see.

Samsitu Riverside Camp (☎ 257023, fax 255602; e kavpharm@iafrica.com.na; camping per person US$3.50), beside Hakusembe Lodge, is a quiet, friendly and grassy little camping site right on the Okavango riverbank.

Antja's (☎ 256973, Main St; breakfast US$2, salads US$0.80-2, fast food US$1.50-2.50; open 7.30am-5pm Mon-Sat) is a good option for breakfast, burgers, toasted sandwiches, pies, sweets and coffee (including espresso and cappuccino).

Self-caterers will find supplies at the well-stocked **OK Foods** and the **Spar** in the town centre.

Entertainment

Sauyema Night Club (Grootfontein road, Sauyema), in the Sauyema suburb, is a colourful and pleasantly integrated nightclub that rocks all night on weekends. Alternatively, try the very local **Vibe Village**, also in Sauyema a couple of kilometres out on the Nkurenkuru road.

New World Pub (☎ 255003, behind Edumeds stationers) has dancing and a popular sports bar, which attracts a mixed crowd with its wide-screen TV, pizza, beer and billiards.

Getting There & Away

Intercape Mainliner's two weekly buses between Windhoek (US$36, 9¼ hours) and Victoria Falls (US$36, 10¾ hours) stop at the Engen petrol station on Kakakuru St. Minibuses to and from Windhoek, Grootfontein and Katima Mulilo stop at the Shell petrol station on the corner of Main Street and the Grootfontein road.

A car ferry and border crossing are expected soon between Rundu and Calai, across the river in Angola.

KHAUDOM GAME RESERVE

If you're looking for a truly wild and un-touristed wildlife venue in Namibia, head for the undeveloped Khaudom Game Reserve (day admission US$2.50 per person plus US$2.50 per vehicle) which takes in 384,000 hectares. Along its meandering sand tracks you'll see roans, wild dogs,

elephants, zebras and most other species you'd encounter at Etosha National Park, but in a much lonelier context.

NWR asks visitors to travel in a two-vehicle convoy and be self-sufficient in food, water and spares. Caravans, trailers and motorcycles are prohibited. The two camps **Khaudom** and **Sikereti** (camping for 4 people US$12, 4-bed huts US$14) won't disappoint. All visitors must pre-book through NWR in Windhoek.

BWABWATA NATIONAL PARK
☎ 066

Namibia's newest national park, gazetted in 1999 but not yet officially recognised, includes five main zones: the 20,500-hectare West Caprivi Triangle around Kongola, also known as the Kwando Core Area; the Mahango Game Reserve; the Popa Falls Rest Camp; the Buffalo Core Area, near Divundu; and the best of the now-defunct West Caprivi Game Reserve. While private concessions here handle their own bookings, the NWR site at Popa Falls must be pre-booked through the office in Windhoek.

Mahango Game Reserve

The 25,400-hectare Mahango Game Reserve (admission US$3.50 per person plus US$3.50 per vehicle) occupies a broad flood plain that's best known for its dry-season concentrations of thirsty elephants. This is the only national park unit in Namibia where visitors are permitted to walk at will; winter is the best time for observing the area's ample wildlife. The nearest NWR camp is Popa Falls, 15km north of Mahango.

Divundu

Non-descript Divundu, which serves as a commercial centre for the adjacent villages of Mukwe, Andara and Bagani, has a couple of supermarkets and three (ostensibly) 24-hour petrol stations.

Popa Falls

Near Bagani, the Okavango River tumbles down a broad series of cascades known as Popa Falls (day admission US$2.50 per person plus US$2.50 per vehicle). They're nothing to get steamed up about, but low water does expose a 4m drop. A kiosk sells the basics: tinned food, beer, candles and mosquito coils.

Places to Stay & Eat

Popa Falls Rest Camp *(camping US$11 for four people, four-bed huts US$26-28)*, operated by NWR, is getting a bit shabby but does afford great views of the cascades.

N//goabaca Camp *(camping US$2.50-3 per person)* is a quiet Nacobta community camping ground that sits beside the Okavango River opposite the Popa Falls Rest Camp.

Nambwa *(14km south of Kongola; camping US$3.50 per person & US$3.50 per vehicle)*, in the lovely West Caprivi Triangle, may be booked at the **Susuwe ranger station**, north of Kongola. Access is by 4WD only.

Ngepi Camp *(☎ 259903; e getalife@get alifeplanet.com; w www.getalifeplanet.com; PO Box 5140, Rundu; camping US$5 per person, double huts US$22)*, 4km off the road north of the Mahango gate, is a great, green riverside camp which invites serious relaxation. The camp can organise canoe trips (US$17), Mahango wildlife drives (US$17), houseboats (three days from US$155) and mokoro trips (three days from US$125) on the Okavango Delta Panhandle nearby in Botswana. Note that the sandy access road

may sometimes prove challenging for 2WD vehicles.

Suclabo Lodge *(☎ 259005, fax 259026; e suclabo@iway.na; w www.suclabo.iway.na; PO Box 66520, Windhoek; single/double bungalows US$73/105 with half-board & activities)* is an amenable German-run lodge overlooking the Okavango River 500m upstream from Popa Falls. Activities include booze cruises (US$8.50) and Mahango wildlife drives (US$18).

Mahangu Lodge *(☎ 259037, fax 259115; e eden@mweb.com.na; w www.mahangu.com .na; PO Box 20080, Windhoek; camping US$4.50 per person, small/luxury tents US$10/ 28 per person, singles/doubles US$63/105 with half-board, discounts for regional visitors)* lazes amongst jackalberry trees along the Okavango River, just outside the Mahango Game Reserve gate. Note that in rainy periods, the access road may be impassable to 2WD vehicles.

Getting There & Away

All buses and minibuses between Katima Mulilo and Rundu pass through Divundu. The gravel road between Divundu and Mohembo

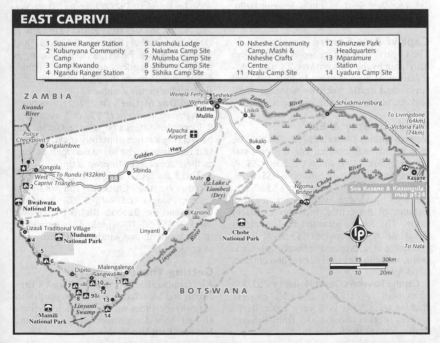

EAST CAPRIVI

1 Susuwe Ranger Station	5 Lianshulu Lodge
2 Kubunyana Community	6 Nakatwa Camp Site
Camp	7 Muumba Camp Site
3 Camp Kwando	8 Shibumu Camp Site
4 Ngandu Ranger Station	9 Sishika Camp Site
10 Nsheshe Community	12 Sinsinzwe Park
Camp, Mashi &	Headquarters
Nsheshe Crafts	13 Mparamure
Centre	Station
11 Nzalu Camp Site	14 Lyadura Camp Site

(on the Botswana border) is accessible by 2WD, and there's lots of traffic but no public transport; drivers may transit the park without charge, but incur national park entry fees to use the loop drive through the park.

KATIMA MULILO
☎ 066

Out on a limb at the eastern end of the Caprivi Strip lies remote Katima Mulilo, which is as far from Windhoek as you can get in Namibia. This very African town features lush vegetation and enormous trees, and was once known for the elephants that marched through. Nowadays little wildlife remains, but the ambience is still pleasant.

Information
Tourist information is dispensed at **Tutwa Tourism & Travel** (☎ 253048, fax 252238; e tutwa@mweb.com.na; PO Box 126), which also organises custom tours around the region. On weekdays, the **Bank of Windhoek**, beside the main square, changes cash and travellers cheques at an appropriately tropical pace. For fax, email and Internet access, see **IWAY** (US$2.50/hr; open 8am-9pm Mon-Sat, 1pm-9pm Sun), in a non-descript building beside the Caprivi Arts Centre.

Caprivi Arts Centre
The Caprivi Arts Centre (open 8am-5.30pm daily), run by the Caprivi Arts & Culture Association, is a good place to look for local curios and crafts, such as woodcarvings, baskets, bowls and traditional weapons.

Places to Stay & Eat
Mukusi Cabins (☎/fax 253255, fax 252359; e mukusi@mweb.com.na; Engen petrol station, PO Box 1194; budget cabins US$14, singles/doubles without bathroom US$20/28, singles/doubles with bathroom US$30/38), an oasis-like lodge within easy walking distance of the centre, provides excellent value. The lovely attached bar/restaurant (breakfast US$3.50, mains US$3.50-7) dishes up a range of unexpected options – calamari, snails, kingclip – as well as beef and chicken stand-bys.

Caprivi Travellers Guest House (☎ 252788; dorm beds or caravans US$4.50, singles/doubles US$12/14) is a very basic backpackers' option about 400m from the city centre, just off the Rundu road.

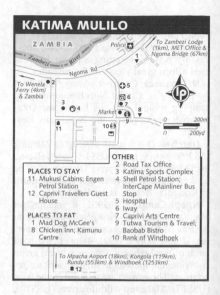

KATIMA MULILO

To Zambezi Lodge (1km), MET Office & Ngoma Bridge (67km)

ZAMBIA — Police

Zambezi River

Ngoma Rd

To Wenela Ferry (4km) & Zambia

Market

0   200m
0   200yd

OTHER
2 Road Tax Office
3 Katima Sports Complex
4 Shell Petrol Station; InterCape Mainliner Bus Stop
5 Hospital
6 Iway
7 Caprivi Arts Centre
9 Tutwa Tourism & Travel; Baobab Bistro
10 Bank of Windhoek

PLACES TO STAY
11 Mukusi Cabins; Engen Petrol Station
12 Caprivi Travellers Guest House

PLACES TO EAT
1 Mad Dog McGee's
8 Chicken Inn; Kamunu Centre

To Mpacha Airport (18km), Kongola (119km), Rundu (553km) & Windhoek (1253km)

Zambezi Lodge (☎ 253203, fax 253631; e katima@iafrica.com.na; Ngoma Rd, PO Box 98; camping per person US$3.50 plus US$2.50 per vehicle, single/double bungalows with breakfast US$52/73), more upmarket, does river cruises (from US$9 per person) and tours to Victoria Falls (Zimbabwe; US$125), Chobe (Botswana; US$83) and Mamili National Park (US$83). Camping is in the flowery garden and all guests, including campers, can use the pool, restaurant and floating bar on the Zambezi.

Mad Dog McGee's (☎ 252021; one block off Ngoma road; mains US$3.50-7; open 8am-9.30pm Mon-Sat) is a popular restaurant and bar serving a range of mainly meat, chicken and fish dishes. The bar stays open as long as there are patrons to prop it up.

There are also a couple of greasy-spoon takeaways; the **Chicken Inn** (Kamunu Centre; snacks US$1.75-3.50) fast-food outlet; and the **Baobab Bistro** (☎ 252047; snacks US$1.50-3), which does breakfast in the morning and sandwiches until mid-afternoon.

Getting There & Away
Air Namibia flies between Windhoek's Eros airport and Mpacha airport (18km southwest of town) five times weekly, stopping en route at Lianshulu Lodge (see under Mudumu National Park later in this chapter).

The Intercape Mainliner passes Katima Mulilo en route between Windhoek and Victoria Falls (Zimbabwe). Minibuses run when full to and from Windhoek (US$15, 15½ hours) and points in between.

Drivers of foreign-registered vehicles leaving Namibia at Ngoma Bridge or Wenela need a US$10 road tax certificate; if you didn't receive one on entry, purchase one at the road tax office in town. For information on the Wenela ferry, see Land in the Getting There & Away section of this chapter.

MPALILA ISLAND
☎ 066

Mpalila Island, wedged between Botswana and Zambia, sits at Namibia's easternmost limits. The Kakumba sandbank, at its eastern end, actually reaches out and touches the western point of Zimbabwe, at the one place in Africa where four countries meet. On a map, the area recalls Michelangelo's *Creation of Adam* on the ceiling of the Sistine Chapel (really – check it out!). In addition to that gratuitous distinction, it's within easy reach of Victoria Falls (Zimbabwe & Zambia) and Chobe National Park (Botswana).

The following places to stay appear on the 'Kasane & Kazungula' or 'Chobe National Park' maps in the Botswana chapter. They're accessed by boat from Kasane via the **Mpalila** or **Kasika border posts** *(open 7.30am-12.30pm & 1.45pm-4.30pm Botswana time)*.

Impalila Island Lodge *(☎/fax South Africa 11-706 7207, fax 463 8251; e info@ impalila.co.za; w www.impalila.co.za; PO Box 70378, Bryanston 2021, South Africa; singles/ doubles US$355/550)*, overlooks the lovely Mombova rapids, and its rates include full board, boat transfers from its Kasane office *(☎ 267-650795)* and all wildlife walks, drives and cruises.

King's Den/Zambezi Queen *(☎ 253203, fax 253631; e katima@iafrica.com.na; singles/ doubles US$140/250 with full-board & activities)* puts guests up in small bungalows and on the Zambezi Queen riverboat, which is moored opposite Kasikile/Sedudu Island on the Chobe River.

Ichingo Lodge *(☎ Botswana 650143, fax 650223; e ichingo@iafrica.com; PO Box 206, Kasane, Botswana; singles/doubles US$220/ 375)*, near the Mpalila immigration post, is simpler than its nearby counterparts. Its focus is on fishing, but river cruises and wildlife drives are also available.

Chobe Savanna Lodge *(☎ South Africa 11-706 0861, fax 706 0863; e reservations@ desertdelta.com; w www.desertdelta.com; PO Box 130555, Bryanston 2074, South Africa; singles/doubles US$500/780, with meals, activities & Chobe National Park fees)* overlooks the Chobe River, peering across the wildlife-rich Puku Flats into Botswana's Chobe National Park.

Getting There & Away
Access to Mpalila Island is by boat from Kasane, Botswana. Lodges organise transport for their booked guests.

MUDUMU NATIONAL PARK
☎ 066

Until the late 1980s, Mudumu was a hunting concession gone mad, and over the years the wildlife was depleted by both locals and trophy hunters. In 1989, Mudumu National Park and Mamili National Park were officially proclaimed in a last-ditch effort to rescue the area from environmental devastation.

In hopes of linking wildlife conservation and the sustainable use of natural resources and local economic development, the former managers of Lianshulu Lodge helped the local community establish **Lizauli Traditional Village** *(tours US$2.30 per person; open 8.30am-5pm daily)*, where visitors learn about rural Caprivian life. To get there, follow the D3511, south of the Kongola petrol station.

Places to Stay & Eat
Mudumu's official camping sites, at **Nakatwa** *(US$3.50 per person & US$3.50 per vehicle; Game Scout Camp 7km southeast of Lianshulu)*, enjoy lovely views over extensive riverine wetlands. Book through the **MET office** *(☎ 253027 or 253341; Katima Mulilo)* or take your chances and pay at the Game Scout Camp.

Kubunyana Community Camp *(Choyi village, 7km south of Kongola petrol station; camping US$3.50 per person, fixed tents US$8 per person)* is a lovely Nactoba unit beside the Kwando River; you can rent canoes (US$3 per hour) to paddle around the adjacent backwater, or take a guided walk (US$3.50 per hour). In dry weather – with some difficulty – it's accessible by 2WD.

Camp Kwando (☎ 061-270 4960, 0811 245177; e kwando@natron.net; w www.nat ron.net/camp-kwando; camping US$4.50 per person, bungalows per person with breakfast US$22) is outside the park between Kongola and Lianshulu. Meals (US$7), mountain bike hire, wildlife drives (US$10) and mokoro trips (US$3.50 per hour) are available. Transfers from Kongola cost US$6/trip.

Lianshulu Lodge (☎ 061-254317, fax 251900; e lianshul@mweb.com.na; w www .lianshulu.com.na; PO Box 90391, Windhoek; singles/doubles with half board US$110/170) overlooks a magical backwater along the Kwando River. Activities here include wildlife walks and drives in Mudumu, cruises in the pontoon *Jacana* and boat trips on the Kwando. Everywhere you're serenaded by an enchanting wetland chorus of insects, birds and frogs, and in the evening, hippos emerge to graze on the lawns. Accommodation is in reed bungalows or A-frame chalets; activities cost an additional US$12 per person. By private vehicle, follow the D3511 for about 40km south of Kongola and turn west onto the signposted track to Lianshulu, 5km from the turn-off. Alternatively, Air Namibia flies five times weekly to Lianshulu from Windhoek and Katima Mulilo. A new border crossing here allows access to Botswana's Kwando Camp, but may not be used for travel further into Botswana.

MAMILI NATIONAL PARK
☎ 066

Wild and little visited, 320-sq-km Mamili National Park is Namibia's equivalent of the Okavango Delta, and when there's water, the park combines river channels, delightful wetlands and wildlife-rich islands. The forested areas brim with stands of sycamore figs, jackalberry, leadwood and sausage trees, and are fringed by vleis and reed-choked marshes. Mamili's crowning glory is its birdlife and over 430 species have been recorded. The best time to visit is from September to early November.

Accommodation is limited to the **Lyadura** and **Nzalu** wilderness camping sites in the eastern part of the park and **Muumbu**, **Shibumu** and **Sishika** in the west, but no facilities are available and campers must be self-sufficient. Camping permits (US$3.50 per person and US$3.50 per vehicle) are available at Sinsinzwe Gate or from the MET

office (☎ 253027 or 253341; Katima Mulilo). Access is by 4WD only.

At Sangwali village, north of the park, Nactoba runs the **Mashi & Nsheshe Crafts centre**, which produces and markets Caprivian wood carvings, basketry and jewellery. It also runs the **Nsheshe Community Camp** (☎ 696999; 1km north of Sangwali, PO Box 1707, Ngweze; camping US$3.50 per person).

EASTERN BUSHMANLAND
☎ 067

The flat, scrubby expanses of Eastern Bushmanland are cut by numerous meandering *omiramba* (fossil river channels), which support a rich ecosystem, including stands of camelthorn, red umbrella thorn and blackthorn acacia. Elephants roam freely, and in the dry season, antelope herds congregate around the *panveld* (flat area containing many pans); when the rains come, they fan out to the west and northwest.

Forming an arc east of Tsumkwe is a remote landscape of phosphate-rich natural pans, which are transformed after rain into an ephemeral wetland that attracts not only itinerant water birds – including throngs of flamingos – but also provides a breeding habitat for ducks, spurwing geese, cranes, egrets and herons.

The dry hard-crust landscape also supports baobabs, including several giants. The imaginatively named **Grootboom** (Big Tree) has a circumference of over 30m, and the historic **Dorslandboom** (Thirst Land Tree) bears carvings made by the Dorsland trekkers who camped here on their 1891 trek to Angola. The immense **Holboom** (Hollow Tree) grows near the village of **Tjokwe** (also spelled Djokhoe).

The region's diminutive service centre, **Tsumkwe**, provides little more than basic groceries, snacks and a tourist lodge.

Information

Tourism in Eastern Bushmanland is regulated by the **Nyae Nyae Conservancy** (☎ 244011; e nndfn@iafrica.com.na; entry US$3.50 per person), which also collects fees and activities charges from visitors. You can arrange activities such as hunting with the San (US$8) and gathering wild foods (US$4); fees are per guide (up to three or four guides); there will also be a fee for the translator (US$15/group). In the evening, you can experience traditional

music and dancing by up to 15 performers for US$33. Book through the Nyae Nyae office during regular business hours.

Places to Stay & Eat

The conservancy has set up five very basic camp sites beneath notable baobab trees: **Makuri**, **Kremetart/N≠amapan**, **!O'baha**, **Holboom/Tjokwe** and **!A≠o**. Holboom/ Tjokwe costs US$4.50 per person and the others, US$2.30 per person. Water is normally available in adjacent villages, but otherwise, campers must be self-sufficient. Avoid building fires near the baobabs, as it damages the tree roots.

Bushmanland Safari Camp (☎ 061-246708, fax 246709; e bushmanland@mweb.com.na; camping US$6 per person) is a wilderness outpost offering meals, fuel, mechanical repairs and a small shop.

Omatako Valley Rest Camp (camping US$2.50/3 per person in tents/thatched shelters), outside the conservancy at the junction of the C44 and D3306, has solar power, a water pump, hot showers and a caretaker. It offers both hunting/gathering trips (US$1.30) and traditional music presentations US$17/ group).

Tsumkwe Lodge (☎ 244028, fax 244027; e tsumkwel@iway.na; w www.tsumkwel.iway .na; PO Box 1899, Tsumeb; camping US$7 per person, single/double bungalows US$40/ 63, full board US$58/105) offers comfortable accommodation and runs tours to local Ju/hoansi San communities (US$150 per person), baobab circuits (US$43), Nyae Nyae pan tours (US$43) and two-day trips through Khaudom Game Reserve (US$290). They also do a five-day regional tour (US$1800). From Tsumkwe, go 1.5km south of the crossroads, turn right at the Ministry of Housing and continue for 500m.

Getting There & Away

Remote Tsumkwe is surprisingly accessible on the Thursday Star Line bus from Grootfontein (US$7.50, 6½ hours), but beyond there, you'll need a private vehicle or a tour. There are no sealed roads and only the C44, with good gravel, is open to low-clearance vehicles. Petrol is available at the Bushmanland Safari Camp. The Dobe border crossing to Botswana requires 4WD and extra fuel to reach the petrol stations at Maun or Etsha 6 (both in Botswana), which are accessed by a difficult sand track through northwestern Botswana.

Northwestern Namibia

For many armchair travellers, the word Namibia conjures up images of the mysterious Skeleton Coast, a desert coastline dotted with the corpses of ships run aground in sinister fogs. Namibia's wildly desolate northwestern corner also takes in the regions of Damaraland and Kaokoland (or Kaokoveld), which dazzle their relatively few visitors with some of Namibia's most unusual natural features and fascinating cultures, including those of the Damara people and the enigmatic Himba people.

DAMARALAND

The territory between the Skeleton Coast and Namibia's Central Plateau has traditionally been known as Damaraland, after the people who make up much of its population. Although it's not an officially protected area, its wild open spaces are home to many desert-adapted species, including giraffe, zebra, lion, elephant and rhino. In addition to its sense of freedom, the region is rich in both natural and cultural attractions, including **Brandberg**, Namibia's highest massif, and the **rock engravings** of Twyfelfontein.

Spitzkoppe

☎ 064

The 1728m Spitzkoppe (D3716, Groot Spitzkoppe village; admission US$1.80 per person & US$1/car; open sunrise-sunset daily), one of Namibia's most recognisable landmarks, rises mirage-like above the dusty pro-Namib plains of southern Damaraland. Its dramatic shape has inspired its nickname, the Matterhorn of Africa, but similarities between this granite inselberg and the glaciated Swiss alp begin and end with its sharp peak. Beside the Spitzkoppe rise the equally impressive Pondoks, another inselberg formation that's comprised of enormous granite domes.

Around the massif are dotted a number of beautiful wild **camp sites** (☎ 530879; camping US$4 per person), which are maintained by the local community. Near the entrance, a small shop sells staples and a range of local

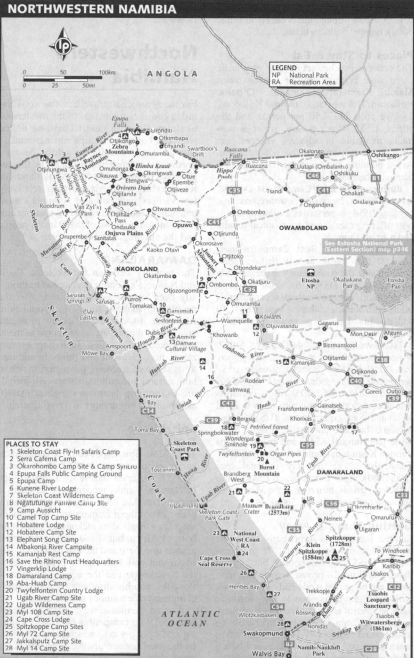

NORTHWESTERN NAMIBIA

LEGEND
NP   National Park
RA   Recreation Area

ANGOLA

0 ___ 50 ___ 100km
0 ___ 25 ___ 50mi

Epupa Falls
Kunene River
Zebra Mountains
Uronditi
Otjikongo
Otkimbapa
Enyandi
Omuramba
Swartbooi's Drift
Ruacana Falls
Okalongo
Oshikango
Uutapi (Ombalantu)
Oshikuku
Baynes Mountains
Otjinungwa
Omuhonga
Okaukwa
Himba Kraal
Okongwati
Otue
Epembe
Otjiveze
Ruacana
Hippo Pools
Tsandi
Oshakati
Ondangwa
Marienfluss
Hartmann's Valley
Etengwa
Orivero Dam
Otjitanda
Ongandjera
Etanga
Otjihaa Pass
Otwazumba
Ombombo
OWAMBOLAND
Rooidrum
Van Zyl's Pass
Ondauka
Onjuva Plains
Opuwo
Okorosave
Okaotavi
Otjitoko
See Estosha National Park (Eastern Section) map p346
Orupembe
Sanitatas
KAOKOLAND
Okatumba
Otjondeka
Etosha NP
Okahakana
Etosha Pan
Sarusas Springs
Sarusas
Purros
Tomakas
Otjozongombe
Ombombo
Okatjuru
Omuramba
Köwares
Gagarus
Mon Desir
Afguns
Clay Castles
Sesfontein
Ganumib
Warmquelle
Oljivasandu
Biermanskool
Otjitambi
Wilderness
Dubis
Anmire
Khowarib
Damara Cultural Village
Kamanjab
Otjikondo
Goreis
Outjo
Amspoort
Môwe Bay
Hunkab River
Palmwag
Rodean
Terrace Bay
Uniab River
Huab
Fransfontein
Gainatseb
Khorixas
Vingerklip
Torra Bay
Bergsig
Petrified Forest
Springbokwater
Wondergat Sinkhole
Twyfelfontein
Organ Pipes
Ugab River
DAMARALAND
Skeleton Coast Park
Toscanini
Burnt Mountain
Brandberg West
Messum Crater
Brandberg (2573m)
Uis
Okombahe
Omaruru
Ogabmund
Skeleton Coast Park Gate
National West Coast RA
Neineis
Uigaran
Spitzkoppe (1728m)
Klein Spitzkoppe (1584m)
To Windhoek
Cape Cross Seal Reserve
Karibib
Henties Bay
Trekkopje
Usakos
Tsaobis Leopard Sanctuary
ATLANTIC OCEAN
Wlotzkasbaken
Arandis
Rössing
Tsaobis
Witwatersberge (1861m)
Nonidas
Swakopmund
Namib-Naukluft Park
Walvis Bay

PLACES TO STAY
1 Skeleton Coast Fly-In Safaris Camp
2 Serra Cafema Camp
3 Okarohombo Camp Site & Camp Syncro
4 Epupa Falls Public Camping Ground
5 Epupa Camp
6 Kunene River Lodge
7 Skeleton Coast Wilderness Camp
8 Ngatutunge Pamwe Camp Site
9 Camp Aussicht
10 Camel Top Camp Site
11 Hobatere Lodge
12 Hobatere Camp Site
13 Elephant Song Camp
14 Mbakonja River Campsite
15 Kamanjab Rest Camp
16 Save the Rhino Trust Headquarters
17 Vingerklip Lodge
18 Damaraland Camp
19 Aba-Huab Camp
20 Twyfelfontein Country Lodge
21 Ugab River Camp Site
22 Ugab Wilderness Camp
23 Myl 108 Camp Site
24 Cape Cross Lodge
25 Spitzkoppe Camp Sites
26 Myl 72 Camp Site
27 Jakkalsputz Camp Site
28 Myl 14 Camp Site

rocks and minerals. Water (US$0.05/litre) is scarce, it's wise to bring all you'll need.

There's no public transport, and although Swakopmund agencies offer day tours, you'd probably regret not allowing more time to explore this incredible place.

Brandberg
☎ 064

The Brandberg (Fire Mountain) is named for the effect created by the setting sun on its western face, which causes the granite massif to resemble a burning slag heap. Its summit, Königstein, is Namibia's highest peak at 2573m. Its best-known attraction, the gallery of rock art in **Tsisab Ravine**, features the famous *White Lady of the Brandberg*. The figure, which isn't necessarily a lady, stands about 40cm high and has straight, light hair. It's a 45-minute walk from the car park; guides charge US$3 per person.

Ugab Wilderness Camp (*camping US$4 per person & US$2.50 per vehicle, single/double tents US$18/26*), a Nacobta camp 10km from Tsisab Ravine, organises guided Brandberg hikes or climbs for US$33 per person per day. The turnoff is signposted from the D2359.

Uis
☎ 064

Near the Brandberg, the former mining town of Uis has a petrol station, as well as Internet access (US$3.50/hour plus phone charges) at the One Stop Super Shop. There are also several accommodation and meal options.

Brandberg Rest Camp (*☎ 504038, fax 504037; e brandbrg@iml-net.com.na; camping US$3.50 per person, singles/doubles US$27/50 with breakfast*) is the old stand-by. Lunch and dinner are also available.

Haus Lizenstein (*☎ 504052, fax 504005; e lizen@iway.na; w www.swakop.com/lizen stein; camping US$4.50, rooms US$33 per person with breakfast*) is an amenable family-run place at the edge of town.

White Lady B&B (*☎ 504102; e nicovdyk@iway.na; camping US$4.50 per person, rooms US$33 per person*), more a lodge than a guest house, occupies an incongruously green compound with a welcoming pool and bird-friendly waterhole. It also runs day tours to the Brandberg (US$48) and the Uis tin mine (US$12), plus an overnight camping tour

in the Ugab valley (US$53); rates require a minimum of three people.

White Lady Restaurant (*☎/fax 504120; breakfast US$2.50, mains US$5-6; open 7.30am-late Mon-Sat, 10.30am-late Sun*), a block from the petrol station, does breakfast, light meals and full meat-oriented dinners.

Khorixas
☎ 067

As the administrative capital of Damaraland, Khorixas serves mainly as a refuelling spot. You may want to visit **Khorixas Community Craft Centre** (*☎ 232154*), a self-help cooperative, which provides an outlet for local artists. The town holds an annual arts festival in May.

iGowati Lodge (*☎ 331592, fax 331594; e igowati@mweb.com.na; PO Box 104; camping US$4 per person, bungalows US$35 per person with breakfast*), in the flooding zone opposite the petrol station, provides a splash of colour and the best meals in town.

Star Line has a Sunday bus from Khorixas to Henties Bay (US$6, 4½ hours), Swakopmund (US$8, six hours) and Walvis Bay (US$9.50, 6½ hours); it returns on Fridays. Minibuses do the same route several times daily, and also provide transport to and from Outjo.

Petrified Forest

In an open area of veld 40km west of Khorixas lies a garden of scattered petrified tree trunks up to 34m long and six metres around, which are estimated to be around 260 million years old. The original trees belonged to an ancient group of cone-bearing plants known as *gymnospermae*, which includes such modern plants as conifers, cycads and welwitschias. There's no entry charge, but the compulsory guides live only from tips; plan on US$0.80 per person for the 500m walking tour. Note that it's strictly forbidden to carry off even the smallest scrap of petrified wood.

Twyfelfontein
☎ 067

Twyfelfontein (*admission US$0.80 per person & US$0.80 per vehicle*), at the head of a grassy valley, is one of the most extensive galleries of rock art in Africa. The original name of this water source in the Aba-Huab Valley was /Ui-//Ais (Surrounded by Rocks), but in 1947 it was renamed Twyfelfontein,

or 'doubtful spring', by European settler D
Levin, who deemed its daily output of one
cubic metre of water insufficient for life in
the harsh environment. The 6000-year-old
petroglyphs here were executed by cutting
through the hard patina covering the local
sandstone. Guides are available (plan on
US$1 as a tip), but the route is easy and you
can usually walk alone.

Nearby sites of interest include the **Wondergat sinkhole**, the volcanic **Burnt Mountain** and the very worthwhile **Organ Pipes**
dolerite (basalt) columns. There's no public
transport here; access is only by private
vehicle or organised tour.

Places to Stay Often described as 'simple, rustic and natural', **Aba-Huab Camp**
(☎ 697981, fax 331749; PO Box 131, Khorixas;
camping US$4 per person, exclusive camp sites
US$6 per person, double tents US$7, single/
double chalets US$27/42) serves as a popular
stopover for participation safaris and overland trucks. Those who don't want to pitch
a tent can opt for the open-sided A-frame
shelters. A new bar has injected more life
into the place, and dinner (US$6) is available
if pre-booked.

Twyfelfontein Country Lodge (☎ 697
021, fax 697023; e afrideca@com.na;
w www.schoemans.com.na/namibialodges/
wyfelfontein.htm; singles/doubles US$78/
130), over the hill from Twyfelfontein, is
an architectural wonder – a huge thatched
complex flanked by its own desert waterfall
and several original petroglyphs. Petrol is
sold and meals and activities are available
for an additional charge.

Kamanjab
☎ 067

Flanked by lovely low rock formations,
tiny Kamanjab functions as a minor service
centre for northern Damaraland. However,
several nearby lodges make it an appealing
stopover en route between Damaraland and
Kaokoland.

Oase Guesthouse (☎/fax 330032; PO Box
66; singles/doubles US$29/45 with breakfast),
offers clean, friendly accommodation, as well
as tours to Kaokoland (US$120/day) and a
nearby Himba community (US$17). It's also
your best choice for meals in Kamanjab.

Kamanjab Rest Camp (☎ 330274, 0811
287761; PO Box 88; camping US$5 per per-

son, singles/doubles US$25/43) is 3km from
town in a beautifully rocky spot along the
Torra Bay road; it also offers a vehicle repair
service.

Hobatere Lodge (☎ 330261, fax 330268;
e hobatere@mweb.com.na; w http://www
.resafrica.net/hobatere-lodge/; PO Box 110;
camping US$6 per person, singles/doubles
US$68/125 with half board) has a fabulous
camp site on the main Kamanjab–Opuwo
road and a wildlife-studded main camp to
the north, about 11km west of the road. Book
through **Nabozazi Collection** (☎ 061-253992,
fax 221919; e res@discover-africa.com.na) in
Windhoek.

Vingerklip

The unusual Vingerklip lies on the Bertram
farm, 54km east of Khorixas on the C39, then
21km south on the D2743. This towering
35m-high pillar of limestone is an erosional
remnant of a plateau formed over 15 million
years ago.

Vingerklip Lodge (☎/fax 061-255344;
e vingerkl@mweb.com.na; PO Box 11550,
Windhoek; singles/doubles US$85/130) af-
fords spectacular views that include the
Vingerklip itself, and the panorama from the
bar recalls the famous scenes of Monument
Valley in old John Ford westerns.

Palmwag

The Palmwag oasis lies amid stark red
hills and plains in a rich wildlife area, and
the enormous concession around it sprawls
across some fabulous natural landscapes, including the **Van Zylsgat gorge** on the Uniab
River. Palmwag currently serves as a study
centre for the **Save the Rhino Trust** and at
the time of writing, the Palmwag Concession
was up for tender.

Mbakonja River Campsite (50km north
of Palmwag, PO Box 137, Kamanjab; camping US$3.50 per person) will give you a truly
local perspective on rural life in Damaraland.
Wildlife drives (US$6 for up to five people)
are in a donkey cart. It's remarkably friendly,
and the signs alone are worth the trip off the
main road.

Damaraland Camp (☎ 061-274500, fax
239455; w www.wilderness-safaris.com; PO
Box 6850, Windhoek; singles/doubles US$330/
500 in the high season) is a lonely desert
camp, 11km off the main road between
Twyfelfontein and Sesfontein. Rates include

nature walks and wildlife drives through its surrounding other-worldly landscapes.

Sesfontein
☎ 067

Sesfontein (Six Springs), which seems reminiscent of the Algerian Sahara, is built around a petrol station and a 1901 German fort. You'll find food staples at a small shop featuring a painting of a Score *mielie* meal.

Fort Sesfontein *(☎ 065-275534, fax 275533; e fort.sesfontein@mweb.com.na; camping US$6 per person, singles/doubles US$73/125)* occupies the enigmatic old German fort. While the camping ground is clean and the meals are pretty good, this place clearly realises it's the only place to stay in town.

Camel Top Camp Site *(camping US$3.50 per person)* is a well-run community camping ground with hot showers and large shade trees. It's 2km west of town, then 1km north of the road.

Camp Aussicht *(☎ 064-203581 ask for radio 217; e nomad@namibnet.com; camping US$4.50 per person, doubles US$22)*, flanked by a dioptase (crystal copper) mine (tours US$3), is a rockhound's dream. Although the accommodation is quite simple, the friendliness, the views and the geology are sure to inspire. Turn east off the D3704 at the Camp Aussicht signpost, 55km north of Sesfontein; the final 5km requires a high-clearance vehicle.

KAOKOLAND
☎ 065

You'll often hear Kaokoland described as 'Africa's last great wilderness', and even if that isn't exactly accurate, this faraway corner of Namibia is certainly a beguiling and primeval repository of desert mountains and fascinating indigenous cultures. Being so isolated, even the wildlife of the Kaokoveld has specially adapted to local conditions, the most renowned of which is the desert elephant. In addition, small numbers of black rhinos survive here, alongside gemsboks, kudus, springboks, ostriches, giraffes and mountain zebras.

There's no public transport anywhere in the region and hitching is practically impossible, so the best way to explore Kaokoland is with a well-outfitted 4WD vehicle or an organised camping safari (see Organised Tours in the Getting Around section). In the dry season, the routes from Opuwo to Epupa Falls, Ruacana to Okongwati (via Swartbooi's Drift) and Sesfontein to Purros may be passable to high-clearance 2WD vehicles, but otherwise, you'll need 4WD. The best map to use is the *Kaokoland-Kunene Region Tourist Map*, produced by Shell. For serious trips, check out Jan Joubert's 4WD guide (available from Cymot Greensport in Windhoek), which shows all main routes, including GPS coordinates.

Opuwo
☎ 065

Although it's the regional 'capital', Opuwo is little more than a dusty collection of commercial buildings ringed by traditional rondavels. You'll see lots of Himba and Herero people here; the going rate for a 'people photo' is about US$1, but many people will ask for US$2. Please either respect local wishes or put the camera away. To meet local artisans and purchase arts and crafts, see the **Kunene Crafts Centre** *(☎ 273209; open 8am-5pm Mon-Fri, 9am-1pm Sat)*.

KK and Kemuu, the friendly guys at the **Kaoko Information Centre** *(☎ 273420; e gnn@iway.na; PO Box 217; open 8am-6pm daily)*, provide direction and guides for your trip through the Kaokoland region. Ohakane Lodge runs half-day visits to Himba villages (from US$22) and camping trips around Kaokoland, including Epupa Falls (from US$105/day). Book tours at least a week in advance.

Places to Stay & Eat For rooms with air-con and nice comfy furniture try **Ohakane Lodge** *(☎ 273031, fax 273025; e ohakane@iafrica.com.na; PO Box 8; singles/ doubles with bathroom US$39/55)*. There's also a swimming pool, bar, restaurant (guests only) and café serving breakfasts, snacks and light lunches.

Opuwo (Power Safe) Guesthouse *(☎ 273036, 0812 555088; camping US$4 per person, dorm beds US$8.50)* offers camping on the green lawn, pleasantly cool dorms and kitchen facilities. Coming from the south, turn left at the BP petrol station then take the next right; turn left after the hospital and it's several houses down on the right; look for the large reeds and fence.

Uniting Guest House *(☎ 273400; doubles without/with bathroom US$12/14)* is a small

OPUWO

PLACES TO STAY
1 Kunene Village Rest Camp
3 Uniting Guest House
4 Opuwo (Power Safe) Guesthouse
9 Ohakane Lodge
11 Oreness Camp Site

PLACES TO EAT
10 Bakery
12 Oreness Restaurant; Kaoko Information Centre

OTHER
2 Church
5 Hospital
6 Opuwo Supermarket
7 Power Safe Supermarket
8 Drankwinkel
13 Kunene Crafts Centre
14 School
15 Government Housing Project

and simple place one block east of the church on the hill. Rates include breakfast and meals are available.

Kunene Village Rest Camp (☎ 273043; camping US$4.50 per person, single/double huts US$16/19) is an amenable camping site with *braais*; follow the signposted turn-off from the government housing project at the edge of town, en route to Sesfontein.

Oreness Campsite (☎ 273572; camping US$4 per person, bungalows US$14 per person), French-owned, occupies a compound immediately east of the centre. Its non-detached **Oreness Restaurant** (burgers US$2.50, mains US$5.50, game dishes US$7), on the main road through town, shares Opuwo's restaurant responsibilities with the Ohakane Lodge.

You'll find the Opuwo equivalent of quick culinary delights at the **bakery** beside the petrol station on the main road, which sells doughnuts, yoghurt, beer, bread and renowned sausage rolls. For such local specialities as mahango pancakes, try the **Kunene Crafts Centre**. The best-stocked supermarket is the **Power Safe**, and the **Drankwinkel** next door sells soft drinks and alcohol.

Getting There & Away There's currently no public transport to Opuwo, but minibus taxis may be hired from Ruacana or Outjo for a negotiated rate. The most economical option for visiting Opuwo and the surrounding Himba villages would be a budget safari from Windhoek; a recommended company is Enyandi Safaris.

Epupa Falls
☎ 065

At this dynamic spot, whose name means 'falling waters' in Herero, the Kunene River fans out and is ushered through a 500m-wide series of parallel channels, dropping a total of 60m over 1.5km. The greatest single drop – 37m – is commonly identified as *the* Epupa Falls, where the river tumbles into a dark, narrow cleft. During periods of low water, the pools above the falls make fabulous natural Jacuzzis. Here you're safe from crocs in the eddies and rapids, but hang onto the rocks and keep away from the lip of the falls, where there's a real risk of being swept over; swimming here isn't suitable for young children.

There's excellent hiking along the river west of the falls, and plenty of mountains to climb for panoramic views along the river and far into Angola.

Places to Stay & Eat The enclosed **Epupa Falls public camping ground** (camping US$1 per person), right at the falls, can get very crowded, but it has hot showers and flush toilets which are maintained by the local community. There's a less-crowded overflow section east of its neighbour Omarunga Camp.

Epupa Camp (☎ 695102, reservations ☎ 061-232740, fax 249876; e epupa@mweb.com.na; PO Box 26078, Windhoek; singles/doubles US$135/205), 800m upstream from the falls, was originally used as an engineering camp for a now-shelved hydro project. It has now been converted into a beautifully situated camp where rates include tented accommodation with meals, drinks and activities (Himba visits, sundowner hikes, bird-watching walks, and trips to rock-art sites).

Epupa village now boasts a real **supermarket** where visitors and locals alike buy food staples or gather to socialise and drink a cold beer in the shade.

Getting There & Away From Opuwo or Swartbooi's Drift, it's possible to drive to Epupa Falls via Okongwati in a high-clearance 2WD, but the route remains very rough. Via the Kunene River road, it's 93km to Epupa Falls from Swartbooi's Drift. Even with a 4WD vehicle it takes at least 12 hours, but this lovely stretch – known as the Namibian Riviera – serves as an increasingly popular hiking route.

Swartbooi's Drift
☎ 065

From Ruacana, a rough track heads west along the Kunene to Swartbooi's Drift, where a monument commemorates the Dorsland trekkers who passed en route to their future homesteads in Angola.

Kunene River Lodge (☎ 274300, fax 274301; e info@kuneneriverlodge.com; w www.kuneneriverlodge.com; PO Box 643, Ondangwa; camping US$6 per person, single/double tents US$28/38, single/double huts US$37/53), 5km east of Swartbooi's Drift, makes a lovely, leafy riverside stop. You can hire canoes (US$12), fishing gear (US$8.50) and mountain bikes (US$12), and organise a range of quad-biking tours (from US$47) and white-water rafting trips on the Kunene (from US$47).

The Northwest Corner

West of Epupa Falls lies the Kaokoland of travellers' dreams: stark, rugged desert peaks, vast landscapes, sparse scrubby vegetation, drought-resistant wildlife and semi-permanent settlements of beehive-shaped Himba huts. This region, which is contiguous with the Skeleton Coast Wilderness, has been designated as the Kaokoland Conservation Area.

A large number of 4WD tracks cross the area, but some which appear on maps are now impassable, or may be used only during dry periods (mainly due to flooding of the potentially raging Hoarusib River).

Obvious destinations include the wild Otjinjange (also called Marienflüss) and Hartmann's Valleys, both of which end at the Kunene River. From Okongwati, follow the westward route through Etengwa to Otjitanda, where you can choose between the dramatic and treacherously steep Van Zyl's Pass (which may only be traversed from east to west) or head south over the equally

beautiful but much easier Otjihaa Pass towards the scenic desert country around Orupembe. About 9km north of Orupembe, a track turns north and follows a broad valley to a fork where you can choose between Hartmann's and Otjinjange Valleys; note that wild camping is prohibited in either valley.

An easier but equally spectacular route leads westward from Sesfontein through a series of desert valleys to the tiny settlement of Purros, on the Hoarusib River. A logical circuit heads south from Purros to the river junction known as Amspoort, then northeast back to Sesfontein via the Hoanib riverbed. Note that the Hoanib lies within the Palmwag Concession, and access costs US$7 per vehicle plus US$2.50 per person per day, payable at Elephant Song Camp. Wild camping is possible anywhere away from the Hoanib riverbed.

Places to Stay A community camp site, **Okarohombo Camp Site** (Otjinungwa; camping US$3.50 per person) is at the mouth of the Otjinjange Valley. Facilities are limited to long-drop toilets and a water tap. Otherwise, travellers must be self-sufficient.

Ngatutunge Pamwe Camp Site (camping US$3.50 per person, double bungalows US$18), along the Hoarusib River in Purros, is a real surprise, with hot showers, flush toilets, well-appointed bungalows, a communal kitchen and (believe it or not!) a swimming pool. Here campers may hire guides to Himba villages and to observe desert-adapted wildlife.

Elephant Song Camp (☎ 064-403829; Hoanib River track, PO Box 339, Swakopmund; camping US$4 per person, bungalow US$7 per person), in the Palmwag Concession a very rough 25km down the Hoanib River from Sesfontein, offers hot showers, great views, hiking, bird-watching and the chance to see rare desert elephants. There's a bar, but otherwise, you'll have to be self-sufficient. Access is by 4WD only. Private trips further into the Palmwag Concession (including camping in permitted areas) cost US$7 per vehicle plus US$2.50 per person.

Otjinjange Valley ends at Kaokohimba Safaris' **Camp Syncro** on the Kunene River, and the Hartmann's track ends at

the **Skeleton Coast Fly-In Safaris Camp** and Wilderness Safaris' beautiful **Serra Cafema Camp** *(four-day fly-in singles/ doubles US$3900/5900).* The last, sheltering beneath shady ana trees, features six comfortable tented chalets. These are open only to booked clients of those operators; see Organised Tours in the main Getting Around section earlier in this chapter.

SKELETON COAST

Although it has been extrapolated to take in the entire Namib Desert coastline, the term 'Skeleton Coast' properly refers to the coastal stretch between the mouths of the Swakop and Kunene Rivers The Skeleton Coast parks take in nearly two million hectares of gravel plains and sand dunes to form one of the world's most inhospitable waterless areas. The name is derived from the treacherous nature of the coast – a foggy region with rocky and sandy coastal shallows – that has long been a graveyard for unwary ships and their crews. Once sailors were washed ashore in this desert wilderness, survival was out of the question.

The salt road which begins in Swakopmund and ends 70km north of Terrace Bay provides access to the National West Coast Recreation Area and the southern half of the Skeleton Coast Park. The park is also accessible via the C39 gravel road which links Khorixas with Torra Bay. Note that motorcycles are not permitted in the Skeleton Coast Park.

National West Coast Recreation Area
☎ 064

The National West Coast Recreation Area, a 200km-long, 25km-wide strip from Swakopmund to the Ugab River, makes up the southern end of the Skeleton Coast. It's extremely popular with anglers, and no one needs a permit to visit.

Most visitors head for the **Cape Cross Seal Reserve** *(admission US$3 per person & US$3 per vehicle; open 10am-5pm daily),* a breeding reserve for thousands of Cape fur seals. There's a basic snack bar with public toilets. No pets or motorcycles are permitted and visitors may not cross the low barrier between the seal-viewing area and the rocks where the colony lounges.

For keen hikers, a new **40km trail** begins at the southern end of Henties Bay and follows the coast south to Jakkalsputz (jackals' well), then back north to the Omaruru River Mouth. Highlights include the sand dunes, freshwater springs and fields of desert lichen that flank the route.

Places to Stay & Eat Along the coastal salt-road north of Swakopmund, you'll find several bleak beach camping grounds set up mainly for sea anglers. **Myl 14, Jakkalsputz, Myl 72** and **Myl 108** sites cost US$14 for up to four people. Supplies are available only at Henties Bay.

Cape Cross Lodge *(☎ 694012, fax 694013;* e *capecrossnamibia@africaonline.com.na; singles/doubles US$88/106)* rises miragelike 4km from the Cape Cross Seal Reserve. The odd architecture is self-described as a cross between Cape Dutch and fishing village style, but it's quite amenable and well sheltered from the odiferous seal colony.

Hotel De Duine *(☎/fax 500001;* e *afri deca@mweb.com.na; PO Box 1, Henties Bay; singles/doubles with bathroom US$42/61)* is unfortunately very ordinary, despite its stunning coastal location.

Pirate's Cove Sports Bar & Pizza Bay *(Jak kalsputz Rd, Henties Bay; pizzas US$2.50-6)* is probably Henties Bay's best venue for light, tasty meals.

Spitzkoppe Restaurant & Beer Garden *(☎ 500394; Henties Bay; breakfast US$1.50- 5; mains US$4.50-6.50; open 9am-2.30pm & 6pm-midnight daily)* specialises in seafood (what else?) and boasts Namibia's longest bar and unusual billiards tables.

Skeleton Coast Park

At Ugabmund, 110km north of Cape Cross, the salt road crosses into the Skeleton Coast Park. Only the zone south of the Hoanib River is open to individual travellers, and everyone requires a permit (US$2.50 per person and US$2.50 per vehicle). To reach the accommodation options at Terrace Bay or Torra Bay, you must pass the Ugabmund gate before 3pm or the Springbokwater gate before 5pm.

Day visits are not allowed, but transit permits (US$2.50 per person and US$2.50 per vehicle) for the road between the Ugabmund and Springbokwater gates are available at the Springbokwater and Ugabmund

Skeletons on the Coast

Despite the many postcard images of rusting ships embedded in the hostile sands of the Skeleton Coast, the most famous wrecks have either long disappeared or remain remote and inaccessible to the average visitor. Little more than traces remain of the countless ships which were swept ashore on this barren coast during the sailing era. Of the more recent wrecks, few could be more remote than the *Dunedin Star* which was deliberately run aground just south of the Angolan border after hitting offshore rocks. She was en route from Britain around the Cape of Good Hope to the Middle East war zone, and was carrying more than 100 passengers and a military crew and cargo.

Fifty of the passengers and crew were ferried ashore through heavy surf in a lifeboat before a wave slammed the *Dunedin Star* onto the beach and stranded the rest of the people on board. When help arrived two days later, getting the castaways off the beach proved an almost impossible task. Some people were hauled back onto the wreck by a line through the surf and more were taken off the beach in another lifeboat (before it too was damaged by the surf). Meanwhile, one of the rescue ships had also been wrecked and a rescue aircraft had managed to land on the beach but became bogged down in the sand. They were evacuated by an overland truck convoy which took two weeks of hard slog to cross 1000km of desert, but eventually all the passengers were rescued. Today, the *Dunedin Star* is little but scattered wreckage.

Further south – and nearly as difficult to reach – are several more intact wrecks. The *Eduard Bohlen* ran aground south of Walvis Bay in 1909 while carrying equipment to the diamond fields in the far south. The shoreline has since changed so much that she now lies beached in a dune nearly 1km from the shore. On picturesque Spencer Bay, 200km further south and just north of the abandoned mining town of Saddle Hill, lies the dramatic wreck of the *Otavi*. This cargo ship was wrecked in 1945 and lies mainly intact on Dolphin's Head (the highest point on the coast between Cape Town's Table Mountain and the Angolan border), although the bow has broken off. In 1972, Spencer Bay also claimed the Korean ship *Tong Taw*.

checkpoints. You must enter through one gate before 1pm and exit through the other before 3pm the same day. Transit permits can't be used to visit Torra Bay or Terrace Bay, but in December and January, transit travellers may refuel in Torra Bay.

All park accommodation must be pre-booked through NWR in either Windhoek or Swakopmund.

Ugab River Hiking Trail The 50km Ugab River guided hiking trail crosses the coastal plain before climbing into hills and following a double loop through fields of lichen and past caves, natural springs and unusual geological formations. Groups of three to eight people can leave from Ugabmund at 9am on the second and fourth Tuesday of each month. It costs US$24 per person and must be pre-booked through the NWR in Windhoek. Hikers provide and carry their own food and camping gear.

Torra Bay The **camping ground** (*camping US$12 for four people; open Dec & Jan only*) here is open to coincide with Namibian school holidays. Petrol, water, firewood and basic supplies are available, and campers may use the **restaurant** at Terrace Bay.

Terrace Bay The more luxurious **Terrace Bay resort** (*singles/doubles US$59/84, self-catering suites US$265 for up to eight people*) attracts mainly surf anglers, but there's also a nice line of dunes to the north. Rates include three meals and, of course, freezer space for the day's catch. The site has a **restaurant**, shop and petrol station.

Ugab River SRT Camp The lovely Ugab River Camp Site (☎ 403829; ℮ ugab@rhino-trust.org.na; camping US$4 per person), operated by the Save the Rhino Trust (SRT), offers good chances of observing the elusive desert rhino. To get there, turn east onto the D2303, 67km north of Cape Cross; it's then 76km to this enigmatic wilderness camp, which has bucket showers and long-drop toilets. Guided hiking (US$2.50 per hour) and wildlife drives (US$12) are available, and four- to five-

day rhino tracking expeditions with the rangers costs US$88 per day; participants must book in advance and supply their own food, water and camping gear.

Skeleton Coast Wilderness

The Skeleton Coast Wilderness makes up the northern half of the Skeleton Coast Park. Here, seemingly endless stretches of foggy beach are punctuated by rusting shipwrecks and the cries of gulls and gannets. The most commonly visited sites lie around Sarusas Springs, near Wilderness Safaris' **Skeleton Coast Wilderness Camp**. Other sites of interest include the coastal dunes, the **Cabo Frio seal colony**, the Clay Castles in **Hoarusib Canyon** and the **Roaring Sands**.

A lone park ranger at **Möwe Bay** maintains a small museum of shipwreck detritus and newspaper clippings recounting the stories of shipwreck survivors.

Places to Stay Just near Sarusas Springs, **Skeleton Coast Wilderness Camp** (☎ 061-274500, fax 239455, ℮ info@nts.com.na; ⓦ www.wilderness-safaris .com, 8 Bismarck St, PO Box 6850, Windhoek; singles/doubles US$2586/4372 for four days, US$2966/4932 for five days) is accessible only to fly-in safaris operated by the concessionaire, Wilderness Safaris. If your budget stretches this far, it's most emphatically worth visiting. Rates include accommodation, meals, activities and flights from Windhoek (or from another Wilderness Safaris Camp).

The Roaring Dunes

The lonely barchan dunes of the northern Skeleton Coast hold a unique distinction – they roar – and if you don't believe it, sit down on a lee face, dig in your feet and slide slowly down. If you feel a jarring vibration and hear a roar akin to a four-engine cargo plane flying low, don't bother looking up – it's just the sand producing its marvellous acoustic effect. It's thought that the roar is created when air pockets between electrically-charged particles are forced to the surface. The effect is especially pronounced in the warmth of late afternoon, when spaces between the sand particles are at their greatest.

The Central Namib Desert

Unlike the relatively lush Kalahari, the Namib Desert creates an impression of utter barrenness. Stretching more than 2000km along the coast from the Oliphants River in South Africa to San Nicolau in southern Angola, it defines the lonely coastline of southwestern Africa. The Nama word 'Namib', which inspired the name of the country, rather prosaically means 'vast dry plain', but nowhere else on earth do such desolate landscapes reflect so many moods and characters. Around every bend lies another grand vista, and few visitors ever tire of its surprises.

Much of the surface between Lüderitz and Swakopmund is covered by enormous linear dunes, which roll back from the sea towards inland gravel plains. In the north, the dunes stop at the Swakop River, where they give way to flat, arid gravel plains interrupted by isolated ranges and inselbergs. The dunes may seem lifeless but in fact, they support a complex ecosystem capable of extracting moisture from the frequent fogs.

SWAKOPMUND
☎ 064 • population 25,000

With palm-lined streets, seaside promenades and fine accommodation for all budgets, Swakopmund is Namibia's most popular holiday destination, and its pleasant summer climate and decent beaches attract surfers, anglers and beach lovers from all over Southern Africa.

Thanks to its mild temperatures and negligible rainfall, Swakopmund generally enjoys a pleasantly cool climate, but there's a bit of grit in the oyster. When an easterly wind blows, the town gets a good sand-blasting, and in the winter, cold fogs produce a dreary, almost perpetual drizzle. This fog rolls up to 30km inland and provides moisture for desert-dwelling plants and animals, including 80 species of lichen.

For better or worse, Swakopmund feels overwhelmingly Teutonic – indeed, it has been described as more German than Germany – but for visitors, it's Namibia's adrenalin capital, and offers a wide range of gut-curdling activities, from sandboarding and quad-biking to skydiving and camel-riding. Note, however, that it gets especially

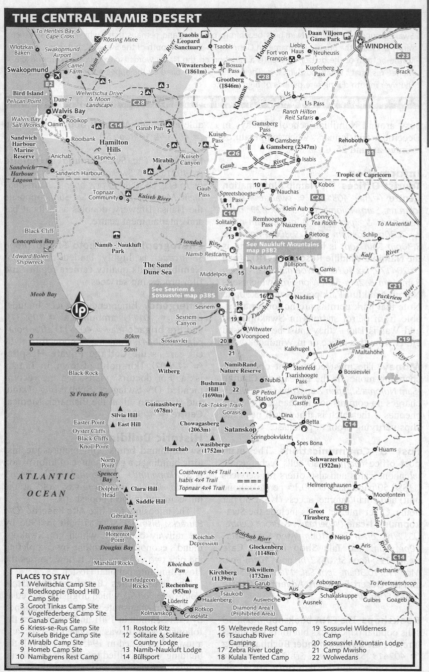

THE CENTRAL NAMIB DESERT

NAMIBIA

PLACES TO STAY
1 Welwitschia Camp Site
2 Bloedkoppie (Blood Hill) Camp Site
3 Groot Tinkas Camp Site
4 Vogelfederberg Camp Site
5 Ganab Camp Site
6 Kriess-se-Rus Camp Site
7 Kuiseb Bridge Camp Site
8 Mirabib Camp Site
9 Homeb Camp Site
10 Namibgrens Rest Camp
11 Rostock Ritz
12 Solitaire & Solitaire Country Lodge
13 Namib-Naukluft Lodge
14 Büllsport
15 Weltevrede Rest Camp
16 Tsauchab River Camping
17 Zebra River Lodge
18 Kulala Tented Camp
19 Sossusvlei Wilderness Camp
20 Sossusvlei Mountain Lodge
21 Camp Mwisho
22 Wolwedans

Coastways 4x4 Trail
Isabis 4x4 Trail
Topnaar 4x4 Trail

By Any Other Name Would it Smell as Sweet?

Swakopmund bills itself as Namibia's beachfront paradise, and perhaps that's why the tourist office rarely discloses the origin of its name. In German, it's simply 'mouth of the Swakop', but when you get to the bottom of the matter, *swakop* is a variation on the Nama words *tsoa xoub*, or 'bottom excrement'. Yes, that's what you think it is. The moniker was inspired by the appearance of the sea around the river mouth during rare periods of high water.

busy around Namibian school holidays in December and January, when temperatures average around 25°C.

Information

Tourist Offices The **Namib i Information Centre** (☎/fax 403129, e swakinfo@iafrica.com.na; Sam Nujoma St, PO Box 829; open 8am-1pm & 2pm-5pm Mon-Fri, 9am-noon & 3.30pm-5.30pm Sat, 9.30am-noon & 3.30pm-5pm Sun) is helpful. Also useful is the **Namibia Wildlife Resorts (NWR) office** (☎ 204172, fax 402697; Woermannhaus; open 8am-1pm & 2pm-5pm Mon-Fri), which sells Namib-Naukluft Park permits until 3.30pm. Note that park permits are no longer available from petrol stations in Swakopmund and Walvis Bay – they must be purchased either from this office or in Windhoek.

Money The most convenient option for changing money is the **Bureau de Change** (Sam Nujoma St; open 7am-7pm daily), which charges no commission to change travellers cheques – the catch is that you'll need the slips verifying proof of purchase.

Post & Communications The **main post office** (Garnison St) sells rechargeable telephone cards and also offers fax services (US$0.50/page plus US$0.15 per telephone unit) and email/Internet access (US$2.30 per hour). Other Internet cafés include the **Swakopmund I-café** (Woermann & Brock Centre; US$2/hr; open 7am-10pm Mon-Sat, 10am-10pm Sun) and **Talk Shop Internet Cafe** (☎ 461333; Roon St; US$2/hr; open 10am-6pm Mon-Fri, 10.30am-3pm Sat, 11am-3pm Sun); and the **Desert Explorers Adventure Centre** (US$3.50/hour).

Bookshops The **CNA bookshop** (Roon St) sells popular paperbacks but for better literature, see the **Swakopmunder Büchhandlung** (☎ 402613; Sam Nujoma St). More esoteric works on art and local history are avail-able at the **Die Muschel Book & Art Shop** (☎ 402874; 10 Roon St).

Laundry The **Swakopmund Laundrette** (☎ 402135; 15 Swakop St; US$1.30 to wash up to 6kg, US$0.80 to dry; open 7.30am-midnight Mon-Fri, 8am-8pm Sat-Sun), opposite the Hansa Brewery, doubles as a local bar and entertainment centre.

Photography The **Photo Studio** (Roon St arcade) is highly lauded throughout Namibia for its quality camera repairs and film processing services.

Emergency Emergency services include: **police** (☎ 10111); **ambulance** (☎ 405731); and **fire brigade** (day ☎ 402411, after hours pager 405544). Your best option for medical care is the **Cottage Private Hospital** (☎ 412201), 1km north of town, in Tamariskia. For doctors' visits, see the recommended Drs Swiegers, Schikerling, Dantu and Biermann, all at the **Bismarck Medical Centre** (☎ 405000).

Historic Buildings

Swakopmund brims with picturesque historic buildings; a good source of information is *Swakopmund – A Chronicle of the Town's People, Places and Progress*, sold at the museum and in local bookshops.

The imposing, fort-like **Alte Kaserne** (Old Barracks; Bismarck St) was built in 1906 by the railway company, which got Swakopmund's economic ball rolling by completing the pier two years earlier. It now houses the Hostelling International Hostel.

The **Kaiserliches Bezirksgericht** (State House; Am Zoll St), which originally served as the District Magistrate's Court, was designed by Carl Schmidt in 1901 and constructed the following year. It was extended in 1905 and a tower was added in 1945. After WWI, the building was modified to serve as an official holiday home of the territorial administrator.

SWAKOPMUND

PLACES TO STAY

4 Swakopmund Hotel & Entertainment Centre; Historic Train Station (Bahnhof); Captain's Tavern
18 Hansa Hotel
32 Cooke's House
33 Karen's Attic
35 Villa Wiese
38 Grüner Kranz
49 Prinzessin-Rupprecht Residenz
51 Desert Sky
52 Sam's Giardino Hotel
56 Gull's Cry
57 Alte Brücke
58 Swakopmund Rest Camp

PLACES TO EAT

7 Lighthouse Pub & Cafe
12 Cafe Anton
16 Oasis Bistro; Phumba's Sports Bar
20 Out of Africa Coffee Shop
20 Blue Whale Café; Fagin's Pub
23 Swakopmund Brauhaus
36 Papa's
39 Napolitana
44 Kücki's Pub
48 The Tug

OTHER

1 Karakulia Craft Centre
2 Alte Gefängnis (Old Prison)
3 African Café
5 Kristall Galerie
6 Altes Amtsgericht
8 Swakopmund Museum
9 Lighthouse
10 Marine Memorial
11 Kaiserliches Bezirksgericht (State House)
13 Bismarck Medical Centre
15 O'Kelley's
17 Atlanta Cinema
19 Photo Studio
21 Die Muschel Book & Art Shop
22 CNA Bookshop
24 Swakopmunder Büchhandlung; Commercial Bank
25 Bureau de Change
26 Namib I Information Centre
27 Pleasure Flights
28 Model/Pick & Pay Supermarket
29 Bank of Windhoek & former Hotel Kaiserhof
30 Swakopmund I-café & Woermann & Brock Supermarket
31 Historic Deutsche-Afrika Bank Building; First National Bank; American Express
34 German Evangelical Lutheran Church
37 OMEG House; Otavi Bahnhof; Living Desert Snake Park; Transport Museum; Sam Cohen Library; Save the Rhino Trust Office
40 Desert Explorers Adventure Centre & I-café
41 Rafter's Action Pub
42 Air Namibia & Charly's Desert Tours
43 Woermannhaus; NWR Office; Swakopmund Military Museum & Public Library
45 Peter's Antiques
46 Talk Shop Internet Cafe; Intercape Mainliner Bus Stop
47 Hohenzollern building
50 Alte Kaserne
53 Hansa Brewery
54 Swakopmund Laundrette
55 National Marine Aquarium

To Rossmund Golf Club (5km); Camel Farm (12km); Welwitschia Camp Site (27km), Rössing Uranium Mine (55km) & Windhoek (363km)

To Alternative Space & Bakoonie (750m)

Nonidas St

Südring

Windhoeker St

Train Station

Nordring

Schlachter St

Feld St

Schlosser St

Lüderitz St

Daniel Tjongarero St

Sam Nujoma St

Leutwein St

African Cemetery

Old German Cemetery

Otavi St

Libertine St

Lazarett St

Rhode Allee

Kraal St

Bahnhof St

Mittel St

Neser St

To Cottage Private Hospital (1km)

To Beach; Lodge B&B (1km) & Vineta Point (2km)

Garnison St

Ludwig B Koch St

Police

Nathaniel Maxuilili St

Roon St

Moltke St

Bismarck St

Woermann St

Swakop St

SFC Sports Club

To Langstrand (20km) & Walvis Bay (35km)

Am Zoll St

Strand St

Arnold Shad Promenade

The Mole

Palm Beach

The Jetty

To The Dunes (750m)

Roon St

Sam Nujoma St

Moltke St

0   125   250m
0   125   250yd

0   50m
0   50yd

In keeping with that tradition, it's now the official Swakopmund residence of the executive president.

Designed by Otto Ertl, the gabled **Altes Amtsgericht** (Garrison St) was constructed in 1908 as a private school. However, when the funds ran out, the government took over the project and requisitioned it as a magistrates' court. In the 1960s, it functioned as a school dormitory, and now houses municipal offices. Just so its identity isn't left to question, the words *Altes Amtsgericht* are painted across the building.

The ornate **train station** (Bahnhof) was built in 1901 and declared a national monument in 1972. It was originally constructed as the terminus for the Kaiserliche Eisenbahn Verwaltung (Imperial Railway Authority) railway, which connected Swakopmund with Windhoek. When this state railway was closed in 1910, the building assumed the role as the main station for the narrow-gauge mine railway between Swakopmund and Otavi. It now houses the Swakopmund Hotel & Entertainment Centre.

The 1906 Baroque-style **Hohenzollern building** (cnr Moltke & Libertine Sts) was originally intended to be a hotel. Its outlandish decor is crowned by a fibreglass cast of Atlas supporting the world, which replaced the precarious cement version that graced the roof prior to renovations in 1988.

Especially picturesque is the 1905 **Woermannhaus** (Bismarck St), which over the years has served as the main offices for the Damara & Namaqua Trading Company, a hostel for merchant sailors, a school dormitory, and now, the **public library**. The prominent Damara tower once served as a water tower and a landmark for ships at sea and traders arriving by ox-wagon from the interior. In the 1920s it fell into disrepair, but was declared a national monument and restored in 1976. It now contains the **Swakopmund Military Museum** (Bismarck St; admission US$1.30; open 10am-noon Mon-Tues & Thur-Sat, 3pm-6pm Mon-Thur) and a gallery of historic paintings, and the **tower** (US$1.30/0.80 adult/child) affords a splendid panorama over the town; stop by the library and pick up a key.

The impressive **Alte Gefängnis** (Old Prison; Nordring) was designed by architect Heinrich Bause and dates back to 1909. If you didn't know this building was a prison, you'd swear it was either an early German

train station or health-spa hotel. In fact, the main building was used only for staff housing, while the prisoners occupied less opulent quarters to one side. Note that it still serves as a prison and is considered a sensitive structure, so photography is not permitted.

The colonial company Otavi Minen und Eisenbahn-Gesellschaft (OMEG) oversaw the rich mines around Otavi and Tsumeb in northcentral Namibia. As there was a connection to the coast by a narrow-gauge railway in the early 1900s, the company also maintained an office in Swakopmund. Until 1910, the **OMEG House** (Sam Nujoma St) served as a warehouse. Next door is the **Otavi Bahnhof**, the old train station for the Tsumeb line, which is slated to house a **Transport Museum** (it wasn't open at the time of writing). The complex now houses the **Sam Cohen Library** (open 9am-1pm & 3pm-5pm Mon-Fri, 10am-12.30pm Sat), with 2000 titles on local history, as well as the **Save the Rhino Trust office** and the **Living Desert Snake Park** (☎ 0811 205100; admission US$2; open 9am-1pm & 2.30pm-5pm Mon-Fri, 9am-4pm Sat), which houses an array of serpentine sorts. Here you'll learn everything you'd want to know – or not know – about snakes, scorpions, spiders and other widely misunderstood creatures. Feeding times are 10am and 12.30pm.

National Marine Aquarium

The National Marine Aquarium (admission adult/child US$3.50/1.80; open 10am-4pm Tues-Sun), on the waterfront, provides an excellent introduction to the cold offshore world in the South Atlantic. Most impressive is the tunnel through the largest aquarium, which allows close-up views of graceful rays, toothy sharks (you can literally count the teeth!) and other marine beasties found on seafood platters around the country. The fish are fed daily at 3pm, which makes for an interesting spectacle.

Kristall Galerie

The architecturally fascinating Kristall Galerie (☎ 406080, fax 406084; e gems@kristall galerie.com; w www.kristallgalerie.com; Bahnhof St; admission US$2.50; open 9am-5pm Mon-Sat) presents some of the world's most incredible crystal formations, including the largest quartz crystal ever found. The adjacent shop features some lovely items,

including mineral samples, crystal jewellery, and intriguing plates, cups and wine glasses carved from local stone.

Swakopmund Museum

The superb Swakopmund Museum (☎ 402046; Strand St; e museum@mweb.com.na; adult/ student US$2/1; open 10am-1pm & 2pm-5pm daily), in an old harbour warehouse near the lighthouse, displays exhibits on Namibia's history, ethnology and flora and fauna. It also contains a well-executed reconstruction of early colonial home interiors and an informative display on the Rössing Mine.

Hansa Brewery

Aficionados of the amber nectar will want to visit the Hansa Brewery (☎ 405021; 9 Rhode Allee), which is the source of Swakopmund's favourite drop. Free brewery tours – with ample opportunity to sample the product – run on Tuesday and Thursday at 10am and 2pm if there are at least six participants; pre-book at the office on Rhode Allee near the corner of Bismarck Street.

Dunes

A short hike across the Swakop riverbed from town will take you into the dunes, where you can easily spend several hours exploring the sand formations and their unique vegetation. Alternative Space loans dune carts to its guests, and several tour companies offer sandboarding and quad-biking (see Activities, following).

Activities

Swakopmund fancies itself as the adrenalin capital of Namibia, and a growing number of companies are constantly adding new and exciting activities for visitors. Not to be missed is sandboarding on the dunes; participants get a sandboard, gloves, goggles, transport to the dunes and enough polish to ensure an adrenalin high. The highlight is a 60km/h *schuss* down a 120m mountain of sand. There are no lifts and slogging up the dunes can be taxing, so you need to be somewhat fit and healthy.

Your one-stop booking agent for just about every breathtaking activity you'd like to pursue is the **Desert Explorers Adventure Centre** (☎ 406096, fax 405038; Woermann St; e swkadven@iafrica.com.na; w www.swakop.com/adv/). Here you can organise sandboarding (US$22-33), ecologi-

cally sensitive quad-biking (US$53), tandem skydiving (US$160), dolphin cruising (US$36), deep-sea fishing (US$58), hot-air ballooning (US$130-180), descending on the flying-fox (foofie slide) at Rössing Mountain (US$53), dune parasailing (US$38), paragliding (US$53), horse-riding (US$33), and kayaking (US$13-28) in Walvis Bay. Check out their 10-minute introductory video, which describes what's on offer.

Swimming in the sea is best in the lee of the Mole (the seawall), although even in summer, the water is never warmer than 20°C. The best **surfing** is at Nordstrand or 'Thick Lip' near Vineta Point.

If you want to climb or abseil on a 15m climbing tower, contact **Walker's Rock & Rope Adventures** (☎/fax 403122; e walker@ iafrica.com.na; PO Box 2143). Note that it is currently in the process of moving, and will eventually wind up in the desert somewhere east of town.

Organised Tours

From Swakopmund, the only company to offer organised tours to Sossusvlei is Crazy Kudu Safaris (see Organised Tours in the Getting Around section of this chapter). Several other safari operators offer local day tours. Among the most popular budget operators are **Charly's Desert Tours** (☎ 404341, fax 404821; e charlydt@mweb.com.na; 11 Sam Nujoma St, PO Box 1400); **Namib Tours** (☎/fax 404072, 0811 286111; PO Box 1428) and **Swakop Tour Company** (☎ 404088, 405128, 0811 242906; e proverb@mweb.com.na; PO Box 1725). Half-day options include Rössing Mine gem tours (US$27); mineral tours (US$29), Welwitschia Drive (US$29), Cape Cross (US$39), Swakopmund and Walvis Bay town tours (US$30) and dune trips (US$12). Full-day trips run to the Spitzkoppe (US$48), Welwitschia Drive (US$38) and the Kuiseb Delta (US$53).

Hata-Angu Cultural Tours (☎ 081 251 5916, fax 462721; e hata-angu@hotmail.com; PO Box 2801) operates fascinating tours to Mondesa township, where you'll visit a shebeen, eat at a traditional restaurant, and meet local people and learn about their traditions and cultural pride.

Pleasure Flights (☎/fax 404500; e red baron@iml-net.ocm.na; w www.pleasureflights .com.na; Sam Nujoma St, PO Box 357) offers 'flightseeing' tours over the colourful salt

works, Sandwich Harbour, Welwitschia Drive, the Brandberg, the dunes, the Skeleton Coast and beyond; rates start at around US$78 per person for a one-hour circuit.

Places to Stay – Budget

Gull's Cry (☎/fax 461591, 0812 466774; e rdowning@iafrica.com.na; PO Box 1496; camping sites US$9 plus US$1.80 per person) sits right on the sand at the beach front, sheltered from the wind by lovely tamarisk trees. It's convenient to the centre, but facilities are basic and security can be a problem.

Alternative Space (☎ 402713; e nam 0352@mweb.com.na; 46 Dr Alfons Weber St; suggested donations; dorm beds US$6, doubles US$17), on the desert fringe, is the most delightfully alternative budget choice, run by Frenus and Sybille Rorich. The main attractions are the castle-like architecture, saturation artwork and an industrial-scrap-recycling theme. The catch is that only 'friends of Frenus' are welcome, but he's a great guy and makes friends easily. On Fridays there's a free fish barbecue and guests have access to cooking facilities, a free breakfast, email, free transfers to the centre and great sunset views from the dunes, just a 15-minute walk away. Dune carts (free to guests) are guaranteed to provide a thrilling experience.

Desert Sky (☎ 402339, 0812 487771; e dsbackpackers@swakop.com; w www.swa kop.com; 35 Lazarett St, PO Box 2830; camping US$4.50 per person, dorm beds US$6, doubles US$17) offers all the amenities backpackers come to expect: kitchen facilities, storage lockers, email access, laundry services and a consistently lively atmosphere. Free coffee is available all day and it's within easy stumbling distance of the pubs in the town centre.

Villa Wiese (☎/fax 407105; e villawiese@ compuscan.co.za; cnr Bahnhof & Windhoeker Sts, PO Box 2460; dorm beds US$6, doubles US$17) is a friendly and funky backpacker place with a nice woody smell, housed in a historic mansion. Kitchen facilities are available and the lounge features satellite TV.

Karen's Attic (☎/fax 402707; e kattic@ iafrica.com.na; 37 Daniel Tjongarero St, PO Box 24; dorm beds US$6, singles/doubles US$9/14) is a quiet and simple backpackers' choice with nice kitchen facilities and a TV lounge.

Grüner Kranz (☎ 402039, 0812 488688, fax 405016; e swakoplodge@yahoo.com or c2c@iway.na; Nathaniel Maxuilili St, PO Box 438; dorm beds US$6, singles/doubles US$27/ 30) caters especially to overlanders and travellers with its kitchen facilities, laundry services (US$4.50), an I-café (US$3.50 per hour), satellite TV, two bars, the attached Crazy Corner Café (with an all-day breakfast from 7am), the Cape to Cairo restaurant (which specialises in African cuisine), and nightly briefings plus video screenings for participants in adrenalin activities.

Places to Stay – Mid-Range

Swakopmund Rest Camp (☎ 410 4333, fax 410 4212; e swkmun@swk.namib.com; w www.swakopmund-restcamp.com; Private Bag 5017; 2-bed/4-bed 'fishermen's shacks' US$17/27, 4-bed flats US$30, 4-bed A-frame huts US$43, self-contained 6-bed bungalows/ flats US$53/58) has recently been renovated and now boasts very amenable – if rather high-density – accommodation. The units range from basic to fully self-contained and booking is essential, especially during holiday periods.

Beach Lodge B&B (☎ 400933, fax 400934; e vulkb@iafrica.com.na; w www.natron.nel/ tour/belo/main.html; Stint St, PO Box 79; singles/doubles US$38/53, family rooms US$53-84) is a remarkable boat-shaped lodge which sits right on the sand and offers some of the most unusual architecture and the best sea views in the area.

Cooke's House (☎ 462837, 0812 402088, fax 462839; e cooksb.b@mweb.com.na; 32 Daniel Tjongarero St, PO Box 2628; singles/ doubles US$22/33), housed in a 1910 historic home, is a warmly recommended B&B in a quiet corner of town.

Prinzessin-Rupprecht Residenz (☎ 412540, fax 412541; e reservation@prinzrupp.com.na; w www.prinzrupp.com.na; 15 Lazarett St, PO Box 124; singles/doubles US$22/38, family rooms US$38-80), housed in the former colonial hospital, has a lovely garden and features distinctly German-style hospitality. All rates include breakfast.

Alte Brücke (☎ 404918, fax 400153; e ac commod@iml-net.com.na; w www.geocities .com/alte_brucke; PO Box 3360, Vineta; camping US$17 for up to six people, single/double self-catering chalets US$43/53), a complex of self-catering flats at the mouth of the Swakop

River, restricts the noise to the sizzling *braais* and sounds of the nearby sea.

Places to Stay – Top End

Sam's Giardino Hotel *(☎ 403210, fax 403500; e samsart@iafrica.com.na; w www.giardino .com.na; 89 Lazarett St, PO Box 1401; singles/ doubles from US$60/74, suites US$78/90)* is a slice of central Europe in the desert, which mixes Swiss and Italian hospitality and architecture while emphasising fine wines, fine cigars and relaxing in the rose garden with a St Bernard called Mr Einstein. Room rates include a wonderful continental breakfast.

Hansa Hotel *(☎ 400311, fax 402732; e hansa@iafrica.com.na; PO Box 44; singles/ doubles from US$88/115)* is Swakopmund's most established upmarket stand-by, and bills itself as 'luxury in the desert'. Each room features unique décor.

Swakopmund Hotel & Entertainment Centre *(☎ 400800, fax 400801; e shec@ iafrica.com.na; 2 Bahnhof St, PO Box 616; singles/doubles from US$101/153)*, in the renovated historic train station, houses a posh four-star hotel, Platform One restaurant, Captain's Tavern Pub, Mermaid Casino, a large pool and a conference centre. Happily, much of the original train station has been left intact.

Places to Eat

Out of Africa Coffee Shop *(☎ 404752; 13 Daniel Tjongarero St; open 8am-4pm Mon-Sat)* has the motto 'Life is too short to drink bad coffee', and it does something about it! It welcomes you in the morning with Namibia's best coffee – espresso, cappuccino, latte and other specialities – served up in French-style cups, along with memorable breakfasts and delicious muffins. At lunchtime and in the afternoon, it serves light meals, snacks and more coffee.

Oasis Bistro *(☎ 402333; 5 Moltke St; lunches US$3-5.50, dinners US$3.50-8; open 8am-10pm daily)* does excellent and imaginative breakfasts, lunches and dinners, including a variety of salads, vegetarian specialities, crepes, gyros, steaks and seafood specials.

Blue Whale Café *(☎ 0811 294018; Atlanta Hotel, Roon St; salads US$3.50-4, mains US$4.50-5; open 7am-late Mon-Fri, except Tues eve, 7.30am-late Sat, 8am-late Sun)* is a popular lunch spot with sidewalk seating.

Don't miss the creative lunch menu, which features healthy crepes, seafood, vegetarian dishes, steak and tempting desserts.

Papa's *(☎ 404747; Shop-Rite Centre, Sam Nujoma St; large pizzas US$3.50-7; open 9am-9pm Tues-Fri, 9am-1pm & 6pm-9pm Sat-Sun)* has a reputation for the best pizzas in town; in the evening, deliveries are available for US$1. It also serves breakfast and a range of burgers.

Napolitana *(☎ 402773, 0812 688266; 33 Nathaniel Maxuilili St; large pizzas US$4-5, light meals US$2.50-4.50; mains US$4.50-8; open 11am-2pm & 5.30pm-10pm daily)* is an Italian-oriented place specialising in pizza, pasta, and meat and seafood dishes. Deliveries are available.

Swakopmund Brauhaus *(☎ 402214; Brauhaus Arcade, 22 Sam Nujoma St; mains US$4-9; open 10am-2.30pm & 5pm-9.30pm Mon-Sat)* is a boutique brewery producing one of Swakopmund's most sought-after commodities (German-style beer), as well as excellently prepared beef and seafood.

The Tug *(☎ 402356; mains US$5-12; open Mon-Sat for dinner only)*, housed in the beached tugboat *Danie Hugo*, is an atmospheric choice for fresh fish and seafood. Its extreme popularity means that advance bookings are essential.

Lighthouse Pub & Cafe *(☎ 400894; Palm Beach; mains US$3.50-7; open lunch & dinner daily)*, with a view of the beach and crashing surf, serves up good-value seafood, including kabeljou, calamari, kingclip, lobster and a large seafood platter. Other specialities include burgers, salads, pasta, steaks, ribs and pizzas.

Cafe Anton *(☎ 402419; Daniel Tjongarero St; snacks US$1.50-3, mains US$4-8; open afternoons and evenings daily)* is a rather pretentious eatery that does superb – albeit expensive and skimpy – coffee, *apfelstrüdel*, *linzertorte* and a host of other German delights. It's a popular spot for decadent snacks in the afternoon sunshine.

Kücki's Pub *(☎ 402407; Moltke St; lunches US$3-6, dinner US$3.50-9, seafood platter US$17; open lunch Mon-Fri & dinner Mon-Sat)* serves up some of the best pub meals in town; don't miss the excellent fresh seafood platter.

Self-caterers will find joy at the **Model/ Pick & Pay** and **Woermann & Brock** supermarkets on Sam Nujoma Street.

Entertainment

O'Kelley's (☎ 407100; Moltke St; open 9pm-late daily) emphasises local disco music, dancing and billiards; this is the place to go when you 'don't want to go home and you're too drunk to care'.

Phumba's Sports Bar (☎ 402333, 5 Moltke St; open 8pm-late daily), above the Oasis Bistro, is the local hang-out for rugger, footy and draught beer fanatics.

Rafter's Action Pub (☎ 400893; cnr Moltke & Woermann Sts) likes to bill itself as the hottest spot in town; currently, this is the hangout for the adrenalin crowd.

Fagin's Pub (☎ 402360; Roon St) is a popular and down-to-earth watering hole that's complete with a jocular staff and faithful clientele.

African Café (☎ 403160, 0812 400463; 3B Schlosser St; open 9pm-late Fri-Sat) has a jazz bar with live music, and an adjacent disco.

The **Atlanta Cinema** (US$2.50-3; open 10am-11.30pm Mon-Sat, 5.15pm-10pm Sun), in the Brauhaus Arcade, screens several popular films nightly and the attached café serves up breakfast (US$2-3.50), lunch (US$2-3), dinner (US$3.50-5) and snacks (US$0.80-2).

Shopping

For inexpensive Zimbabwean crafts, check out the street stalls on the steps below Cafe Anton.

Peter's Antiques (☎/fax 405624; 24 Moltke St) is an Ali Baba's cave of treasures, specialising in colonial relics, historic literature, West African art, politically incorrect German paraphernalia and genuine West African fetishes.

Karakulia Craft Centre (☎ 461415, fax 461041; e kararugs@iafrica.com.na; w www.karakulia.com.na; 3 Knobloch St, PO Box 1258) produces original and beautiful African rugs, carpets and wall-hangings in karakul wool, and offers tours of the spinning, dyeing and weaving processes.

Getting There & Away

Air Namibia (☎ 405123, fax 402196) flies between Windhoek's Eros Airport and Swakopmund (US$89) at least once daily.

From the Talk Shop I-café in Roon Street, the **Intercape Mainliner** bus travels to and from Walvis Bay (US$8, ½ hour) and Windhoek (US$14, 4¼ hours) on Monday, Wednesday, Friday and Sunday, with connections to and from South Africa. Minibuses between Swakopmund and Windhoek (US$7, three hours) stop at the Engen petrol station in Vineta; phone **Eddie** (☎ 0812 420077) and request a pick-up from your accommodation. The Friday Star Line bus between Khorixas (US$8, 6½ hours) and Walvis Bay (US$2, one hour) passes through Swakopmund (see Getting There & Away under Walvis Bay); it returns on Sundays.

Overnight trains connect Windhoek with Swakopmund (US$7, 9½ hours) and Walvis Bay (US$3.80, 1½ hours) daily except Saturday. The three-times-weekly trains between Walvis Bay and Tsumeb (US$7, 17½ hours) also pass through Swakopmund. For rail or Star Line information, phone **Trans-Namib** (☎ 463538). See the Getting Around section earlier in this chapter for information on the plush Desert Express 'rail cruise' to and from Windhoek.

Hitching generally isn't difficult between Swakopmund and Windhoek or Walvis Bay, but if you're heading for the Namib-Naukluft Park or Skeleton Coast, conditions can be rough and hitchers risk heat stroke, sandblasting and hypothermia – sometimes all in the same day. Plan for lots of time and lots of water.

Getting Around

Largely flat Swakopmund is excellent for sightseeing by bike; at the **Alternative Space** (see Places to Stay earlier in this section), the man called Bakoonie rents mountain bikes for US$1.30 per hour or US$6 per day.

AROUND SWAKOPMUND
The Martin Luther

In the desert east of Swakopmund sits a lonely and forlorn little steam locomotive. The 14,000kg machine was imported to Walvis Bay from Halberstadt, Germany in 1896 to replace the ox-wagons used to transport freight between Swakopmund and the interior. However, its inauguration into service was delayed by the outbreak of the Nama-Herero Wars, and in the interim, its locomotive engineer returned to Germany without having revealed the secret of its operation.

A US prospector eventually got it running, but it consumed enormous quantities of locally precious water. It took three months

to complete its initial trip from Walvis Bay to Swakopmund and subsequently survived just a couple of short trips before grinding to a halt just east of Swakopmund. Clearly, this particular technology wasn't making life easier for anyone, and it was abandoned and dubbed the *Martin Luther*, in reference to the great reformer's famous words to the Diet of Reichstag in 1521: 'Here I stand. May God help me, I cannot do otherwise'. It was restored in 1975 and declared a national monument.

Camel Farm

If you want to play Lawrence of Arabia in the Namib Desert, visit the Camel Farm (☎ 400363; open 2pm-5pm daily), 12km east of Swakopmund on the D1901. Camel rides cost US$12 for half an hour. To book or arrange transport from town, phone and ask for Ms Elke Elb.

Rössing Uranium Mine

Rössing Uranium Mine (☎ 402046), 55km east of Swakopmund, is the world's largest open-cast uranium mine and certainly merits a visit. The scale of operations is staggering and at full capacity the mine processes about one million tonnes of ore per week. Three-hour mine tours (US$2.50) leave from Cafe Anton at 10am on the 1st and 3rd Friday of each month; book the previous day at the museum.

Welwitschia Drive & Moon Landscape

A worthwhile excursion by vehicle or organised tour is to Welwitschia Drive, east of Swakopmund. The NWR office in Swakopmund issues entry permits and a leaflet describing the drive, with numbered references to 'beacons', or points of interest, along the route. The drive can be completed in two hours, but allow more time to experience this other-worldly landscape. The **Welwitschia camp site** (US$10 for up to four people) at the Swakop River must also be booked through NWR in Swakopmund or Windhoek.

WALVIS BAY
☎ 064
Architecturally uninspiring Walvis Bay, 30km south of Swakopmund, does have a sort of dusty, other-worldly charm that may elude some visitors. It thrives mainly because

the Pelican Point sandspit makes it the only feasible port between Lüderitz and Luanda.

During the UN-sanctioned South African mandate over Namibia, the port of Walvis Bay was appended to South Africa's Cape Province, but when Namibia gained independence in 1990, its new constitution included Walvis Bay as Namibian territory. Although South Africa stubbornly held its grip, the town's strategic and economic value made control of Walvis Bay a vital issue in Namibian politics. After much negotiation and deliberation, control finally passed to Namibia on 28 February 1994.

Orientation & Information

Although some streets have been renamed after Swapo luminaries, Walvis Bay streets, from 1st Street to 15th Street, run northeast to southwest. The roads, from 1st Road to 18th Road, run northwest to southeast. The helpful **Walvis i Tourist Bureau** (☎ 209170, fax 209171; Shop 6, Hickory Creek Spur Building, Theo-Ben Gurirab St; open 9am-5pm Mon-Fri, 9am-1pm Sat) provides visitor information.

Things to See & Do

The **Walvis Bay Museum** (Nangolo Mbumba Dr; admission free; open 9am-12.30pm & 3pm-4.30pm Mon-Fri), in the library, describes the town's maritime and natural history and archaeology.

About 10km north of town on the Swakopmund road, look out to sea and you'll see the huge wooden platform known as **Bird Island**, which was built to provide a roost and nesting site for sea birds and to annually provide 1000 tonnes of smelly bird guano.

Dune 7 rises above the bleak expanses just off the C14, 8km northeast of town; there's a picnic site, but water is available only sporadically.

Three diverse wetland areas – the **Walvis Bay Lagoon**, the **Bird Paradise** and the **salt works** – together form the single most important coastal wetland for migratory birds in Southern Africa, annually attracting up to 150,000 transient avian visitors. The 45,000-hectare Walvis Bay Lagoon, a shallow bay southwest of town, boasts half the flamingo population of Southern Africa, as well as pelicans, chestnut banded plovers, avocets, damara terns and curlew

NAMIBIA

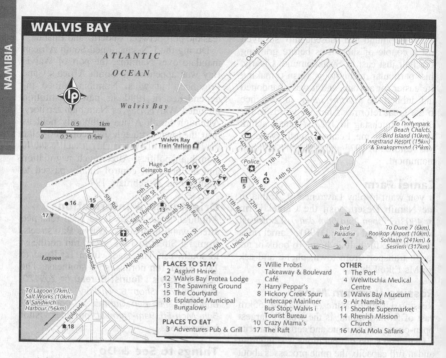

WALVIS BAY

ATLANTIC OCEAN

Walvis Bay

Walvis Bay Train Station

Hage Geingob Rd

Police

To Dolfynpark Beach Chalets, Bird Island (10km), Langstrand Resort (15km) & Swakopmund (35km)

Bird Paradise

To Dune 7 (6km), Rooikop Airport (10km), Solitaire (241km) & Sesriem (317km)

Lagoon

To Lagoon (7km), Salt Works (10km) & Sandwich Harbour (56km)

Esplanade

PLACES TO STAY	6	Willie Probst	OTHER
2 Asgard House		Takeaway & Boulevard	1 The Port
12 Walvis Bay Protea Lodge		Café	4 Welwitschia Medical
13 The Spawning Ground	7	Harry Peppar's	Centre
15 The Courtyard	8	Hickory Creek Spur;	5 Walvis Bay Museum
18 Esplanade Municipal		Intercape Mainliner	9 Air Namibia
Bungalows		Bus Stop; Walvis i	11 Shoprite Supermarket
		Tourist Bureau	14 Rhenish Mission
PLACES TO EAT	10	Crazy Mama's	Church
3 Adventures Pub & Grill	17	The Raft	16 Mola Mola Safaris

sandpipers, plus other migrants and waders. Southwest of the lagoon is the **Walvis Bay Salt Works** (☎ 202376), a 3500-hectare complex that supplies over 90% of South Africa's salt and also attracts flamingoes with its mineral content; tours are available with advance booking. At the municipal sewage works immediately east of town, an observation tower overlooks a series of shallow artificial pools, fringed by reeds, and provides rewarding bird-watching. The site is locally known as the **Bird Paradise**.

Organised Tours

Mola Mola Safaris (☎ 205511, fax 207593, e *mola-mola@iafrica.com.na*; w *www.mola-mola.com.na*); cnr Esplanade & Atlantic St, PO Box 980) runs a dolphin and seal cruise (US$38) and a **Sandwich Harbour tour** (US$74).

Eco-Marine Kayak Tours (☎/fax 203144, e *jeannem@iafrica.com.na*; w *www.gateway-africa.com/kayak/index.html*; PO Box 225), run by Jeanne Mientjes, offers wonderful sea kayaking trips around the beautiful Walvis Bay wetlands (US$17), as well as trips to Pelican Point (US$33).

Places to Stay

The Spawning Ground (☎ 204400, 0811 277636; e *spawning@iafrica.com.na*; 84 Hage Geingob Rd; camping US$5 per person, dorm beds US$7, doubles US$17) must be Namibia's most oddly named accommodation, and no, it's not a brothel, but a very agreeable backpackers lodge. Note the chunky beds, which are made of salvaged wood from the old jetty.

Langstrand Resort (☎ 203134; camping US$9/site plus US$1.30 per person, 2-/4-bed bungalows US$29/42), an other-worldly place 15km north of town, rises from the beach sand like a desert mirage, especially in a fog or sandstorm.

Asgard House (☎ 209595, fax 209596, e *asgard@iway.na*; w *www.gateway-africa.com/asgard*, 72 17th Rd, PO Box 1300; singles/doubles US$33/42) is a homely family-run guest house with a beautiful lounge, garden and frog pond (the frogs eat the mosquitoes). It's friendly and recommended.

The Courtyard (☎ 206252, fax 207271; e *courtyrd@iafrica.com.na*; 16 3rd Rd, PO Box 3493; doubles US$50) is a spotlessly clean

hotel with a pool, sauna, *braai* facilities and a bright spacious garden.

Between the dunes and near the sea wall, **Esplanade Municipal Bungalows** (☎ 206145, fax 209714; e gkruger@walvisbaycc.or.na; Esplanade, PO Box 86; 5-/7-bed self-catering bungalows US$36/43) features a quiet complex of large units.

Dolfynpark Beach Chalets (☎ 204343, fax 209714, e gkruger@walvisbaycc.org.na, Dolphin Park; 4-bed self-catering chalets US$34), on the beach 12km north of town, has a swimming pool and water park. You couldn't imagine a structure more alien to its setting than this. Kids will love the pool and 'hydro-slide'.

Walvis Bay Protea Lodge (☎ 209560, fax 209565; e bay@iafrica.com.na; w www.protea hotels.com; cnr Sam Nujoma Ave & 10th Rd, PO Box 30; singles/doubles from US$49/55) is a plush and centrally located business travellers' hotel.

Places to Eat

Crazy Mama's (☎ 207364; cnr Sam Nujoma Ave & 9th Rd; pizzas US$4-6, main dishes US$3.50-7; open daily except Mon lunch & dinner) features great service and atmosphere, the prices are right and it serves excellent pizzas, salads and vegetarian options, among other things.

The Raft (☎ 204877; Esplanade; main dishes US$6-11; open lunch & dinner daily) sits on stilts offshore and looks more like a porcupine than a raft, but serves excellent fare and affords a great front-row view of the ducks, pelicans and flamingoes that inhabit the lagoon.

Harry Peppar's (☎ 203131; 11th Rd; pizzas US$3-5.50; open 11am-11pm daily) comes up with all sorts of creative thick-crust pizzas. Delivery is free anywhere in town.

Hickory Creek Spur (☎ 207991; cnr 9th St & 12th Rd; mains US$3.50-7; open 11am-2am daily) belongs to the ubiquitous South African chain specialising in steak; the salad bar is recommended.

Adventures Pub & Grill (☎ 206803; 230 12th St; pub meals US$3.50-4.50; open 10am-very late daily) serves not only as a pub, but also dishes up traditional Namibian fare, as well as *potjies* (stew), *braais* and of course beer, booze, pool tables and travellers' advice. It's also a popular night spot.

Willie Probst Takeaway & Boulevard Café (☎ 202744; cnr 12th Rd & 9th St; lunches US$3-7, takeaways US$1.75-3.50; open lunch & dinner daily except Sunday) specialises in stodgy German fare: pork, meatballs, schnitzel and the like. It's always crowded at lunchtime.

The best self-catering option is the **Shop-rite Supermarket** on Sam Nujoma Avenue.

Getting There & Away

Air Namibia (☎ 203102) has five weekly flights between Windhoek's Eros Airport and Walvis Bay's **Rooikop airport** (☎ 200077), with direct 'milk-run' services to and from Lüderitz, Oranjemund and Cape Town.

Intercape Mainliner has Monday, Wednesday, Friday and Saturday services from Windhoek (US$13, five hours) to the Spur Restaurant bus terminal in Walvis Bay, via Swakopmund. Star Line has a Friday bus from Walvis Bay to Khorixas (US$9.50, 7½ hours); it returns on Sundays. Book at the train station. Minibuses run occasionally to Swakopmund and some continue to Windhoek.

The overnight rail service to Windhoek (US$8, 11 hours) runs daily except Saturday. On Tuesday, Thursday and Sunday northbound, it leaves for Tsumeb (US$7, 17½ hours) at 4.15 pm, meeting a train from Windhoek at Kranzberg, where they add/exchange cars. For rail information, phone **Trans-Namib** (☎ 208504).

NAMIB-NAUKLUFT PARK

The present boundaries of Namib-Naukluft Park, one of the world's largest national parks, were established in 1978 by merging the Namib Desert Park and the Naukluft Mountain Zebra Park with parts of Diamond Area 1 and bits of surrounding government land. Today, it takes in over 23,000 sq km of desert and semi-desert, including the diverse habitats of the Namib Desert Park between the Kuiseb and Swakop Rivers, the Naukluft, the dune fields around Sossusvlei and the bird lagoon at Sandwich Harbour.

The main park transit routes, the C28, C14, D1982 or D1998, are open to all traffic, but use of the minor roads (note that some minor routes require 4WD), picnic sites or sites of interest require park permits (US$3.50 per person plus US$2.50 per vehicle). They're

available at NWR offices in Windhoek, Swakopmund and Sesriem.

Camp sites in Namib Desert Park and Sesriem/Naukluft must be pre-booked through the NWR offices in Windhoek or Swakopmund. Permits for the Naukluft 4x4 Trail, the multiday Naukluft hikes and day entry to Sesriem/Sossusvlei are most successfully booked in Windhoek.

Sandwich Harbour

Sandwich Harbour *(open 6am-8pm daily)*, 50km south of Walvis Bay, historically served as a commercial fishing and trading port. Despite a period of silting in recent years, it seems to be recovering and the northern end of the lagoon continues to attract large numbers of migratory birds. There are no visitor facilities – not even a camp site – and it's accessible only with a sturdy 4WD high-clearance vehicle. The final 20km is tricky and, depending on dune conditions, may involve timing your arrival with low tide in order to run down to the sandy beach. The easiest access is with a tour; see Organised Tours under Walvis Bay earlier in this section.

Topnaar 4WD Trail The 4WD trail from Walvis Bay through the sand sea to Sandwich Harbour, Conception Bay and the renowned *Edward Bolen* shipwreck creates a challenge for 4WD enthusiasts. Only guided trips are available and while you can use a private vehicle, it's probably better to rent a Uri – a desert-adapted vehicle that is produced in Namibia. Currently, a six-day camping trip covering the entire route costs US$700 per person in your own vehicle and US$950 in a rented Uri. Other options which cover parts of the route start at US$350/570 in a private/rented vehicle. Book through **Tourist Junction** *(☎ 061-231246, fax 231703, ⓔ info.tjunction@galileosa.co.za; ⓦ www.touristjunction.com.na; PO Box 1591, Windhoek)*.

Namib Desert Park

The relatively accessible Namib Desert Park lies between the canyons of the Kuiseb River in the south and the Swakop River in the north. Although it has a small area of linear dunes, it's characterised mostly by broad gravel plains punctuated by abrupt and imposing ranges of hills.

Although this area doesn't support a lot of large mammals, you may see chacma baboons, as well as *dassies*, which like to bask on the *kopjes* (small rocky hills). The **Kuiseb Canyon**, on the Gamsberg Route between Windhoek and Walvis Bay, is also home to klipspringers and even leopards. Spotted hyenas are often heard at night and jackals make a good living from the springbok herds on the plains.

Places to Stay Namib Desert Park has nine basic **camp sites** *(US$10 for four people)*, several of which accommodate only one party. These sites also function as picnic areas which may be used with a day-use permit. Sites have tables, toilets and *braais*, but you'll have to bring all the drinking water you'll need (some sites have brackish water suitable for cooking). Prebook the following camp sites through NWR in Windhoek or Swakopmund; fees are payable when your park permit is issued.

Welwitschia has shady sites that lie beside the Swakop River, in the far northern reaches of the park. The southern area has five camp sites and is the better of the two locations, with lots of greenery – camelthorn, anaboom and tamarisk trees – while the northern one, which is beside a plain of welwitschias, is flat and treeless. The sites are accessible from Welwitschia Drive (see Around Swakopmund earlier in this chapter).

Bloedkoppie (Blood Hill) has among the most beautiful and popular sites in the park. If you're coming from Swakopmund, they lie 55km northeast of the C28, along a signposted track. The northern sites may be accessed with 2WD, but they tend to attract ne'er do wells who drink themselves silly and get obnoxious. The southern sites are quieter and more secluded, but can be reached only by 4WD. The surrounding area offers some pleasant walking, and at Klein Tinkas, 5km east of Bloedkoppie, you'll see the ruins of a colonial police station and the graves of two German police officers dating back to 1895.

Groot Tinkas must be accessed with 4WD and rarely sees much traffic. It enjoys a lovely setting beneath shady rocks and the surroundings are super for nature walks. During rainy periods, the brackish water in the nearby dam attracts a variety of birdlife.

Vogelfederberg, a small facility, 2km south of the C14, makes a convenient overnight camp just 51km from Walvis Bay, but it's more popular for picnics or short walks.

It's worth looking at the intermittent pools on the summit, which shelter a species of brine shrimp whose eggs hatch only when the pools are filled with rainwater. The only shade is provided by a small overhang where there are two picnic tables and *braai* pits.

Ganab, a dusty, exposed facility (the name is 'camelthorn acacia' in Nama) sits beside a shallow stream bed on the gravel plains. It's shaded by hardy acacia trees, and a nearby bore hole provides water for antelopes.

Kriess-se-Rus is a rather ordinary site in a dry stream bank on the gravel plains, 107km east of Walvis Bay on the Gamsberg Pass Route. It is shaded, but isn't terribly prepossessing and is best used simply as a convenient stop en route between Windhoek and Walvis Bay.

Kuiseb Bridge, a shady site at the Kuiseb River crossing along the C14, is also a convenient place to break up a trip between Windhoek and Walvis Bay. The location is scenic enough, but the dust and noise from passing vehicles makes it less appealing than other camp sites. There are pleasant short canyon walks, but during heavy rains in the mountains the site can be flooded; in the summer months, keep tabs on the weather.

Mirabib is a pleasant facility that accommodates two parties at separate sites and is comfortably placed beneath rock overhangs in a large granite inselberg. There's evidence these shelters were used by nomadic peoples as much as 9000 years ago, and also by nomadic shepherds in the 4th or 5th century.

Homeb, which accommodates several groups, is in a scenic spot upstream from the most accessible set of dunes in the Namib Desert Park. Residents of the nearby Topnaar Khoikhoi village dig wells in the riverbed to access water beneath the surface, and one of their dietary staples is the !nara melon, which obtains moisture from the water table through a long taproot. This hidden water also supports a good stand of trees, including camelthorn acacia and ebony.

Getting There & Away There's no public transport to any of these sites, but the rare minibuses between Mariental and Walvis Bay pass within walking distance of Kuiseb Bridge, Kriess-se-Rus and Vogelfederberg camp sites.

Naukluft Mountains
☎ 063

The Naukluft Massif, which rises steeply from the gravel plains of the central Namib, is mainly a high-plateau area cut around the edges by a complex of steep gorges, forming an ideal habitat for mountain zebras, kudus, leopards, springboks and klipspringers.

Most visitors to the Naukluft come to hike one of the area's two-day walks, the Waterkloof Trail or the Olive Trail. These day hikes need not be booked, but the amazing four-day and eight-day loops have more restrictions attached. Thanks to stifling summer temperatures and potentially heavy rains, the multiday hikes are only open from 1 March to the third Friday in October on Tuesday, Thursday and Saturday of the first three weeks of each month. The price (US$12 per person) includes accommodation at the **Hikers Haven Hut** on the night before and after the hike, as well as camping at trailside shelters and the **Ubusis Canyon Hut**. In addition, you'll have to pay US$3.50 per person per day and another US$2.50/day for each vehicle you leave parked. Groups must be three to 12 people.

Due to the typically hot, dry conditions and lack of reliable natural water sources, you must carry at least 3L to 4L of water per person per day – and use it sparingly.

Waterkloof Trail The lovely 17km Waterkloof Trail begins at the Koedoesrus Camp Site and follows a counter-clockwise loop which takes about seven hours to complete. It first crosses a weir on the Naukluft River and climbs past a series of pools offering refreshing swimming. After climbing out of the canyon, 6km later, the trail turns west and traverses more open country. After the half-way mark, it climbs to a broad 1910m ridge that affords fabulous desert views in all directions. It then descends steeply into several inviting pools filled with reeds and tadpoles before dropping past an impressive tufa waterfall and meeting up with the normally dry Naukluft River.

Olive Trail The 10km Olive Trail leaves from the car park about 4km northeast of the park headquarters and follows a four- to five-hour triangular route. The route begins with a steep climb onto the plateau, affording good views of the Naukluft Valley. It

NAUKLUFT MOUNTAINS

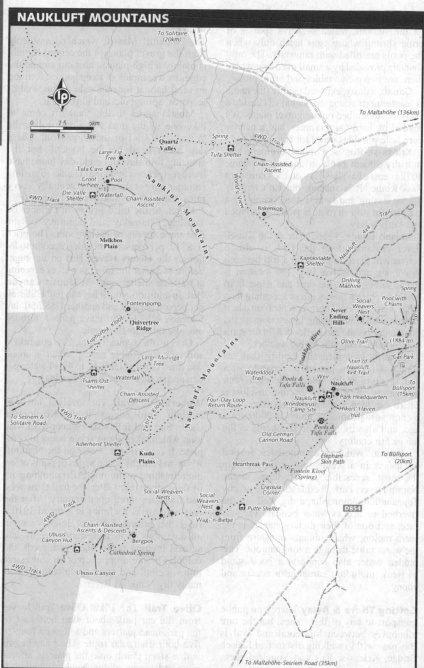

To Solitaire
(20km)

To Maltahöhe (136km)

Spring
4WD Track

Quartz Valley

Tufa Shelter

Large Fig Tree

Tufa Cave

Groot Hartseer
Pool

Die Valle Shelter
Waterfall

4WD Track

Chain-Assisted Ascent

Chain-Assisted Ascent

World's View

Bakenkop

Melkbos Plain

Naukluft Mountains

Kapokvlakte Shelter

Drilling Machine

Spring

Social Weavers' Nest

Pool with Chains

Fonteinpomp

Quivertree Ridge

Euphorbia Kloof

Never Ending Hills

Naukluft River

Olive Trail

(1884 m)

Naukluft 4x4 Trail

Large Muringa Tree

Waterfall

Tsams Ost Shelter

Chain-Assisted Descent

Zebra Kloof

Naukluft Mountains

Waterkloof Trail

Pools & Tufa Falls

Weir

Start of Naukluft 4x4 Trail

Car Park

Naukluft

Park Headquarters

To Büllsport
(15km)

Four-Day Loop Return Route

Naukluft (Koedoesrus) Camp Site

Hikers' Haven Hut

To Sesriem & Solitaire Road

4WD Track

Old German Cannon Road

Pools & Tufa Falls

Adlerhorst Shelter

Kudu Plains

Elephant Skin Path

Heartbreak Pass

Fontein Kloof (Spring)

To Büllsport
(20km)

Social Weavers' Nests

Social Weavers' Nest

Crassula Corner

Putte Shelter

D854

Wag-'n-Bietjie

Chain-Assisted Ascents & Descents

Bergpos

Ubusis Canyon Hut

Cathedral Spring

4WD Track

Ubusis Canyon

To Maltahöhe-Sesriem Road (35km)

0   2.5   5km
0   1.5   3mi

then turns sharply east and descends a kloof, which becomes deeper and steeper until it reaches a point where hikers must traverse a canyon wall – past a pool – using anchored chains. Near the end of the route, the trail strikes the Naukluft 4WD route and swings sharply south, where it makes a beeline back to the car park.

Four-Day & Eight-Day Loops The two big loops through the massif can be hiked in four and eight days. The four-day, 60km loop is actually just the first third of the eight-day 120km loop, combined with a 22km cross-country jaunt across the plateau back to park headquarters. It joins up with the Waterkloof Trail at its half-way point and follows it the rest of the way back to park headquarters. Alternatively, you can finish the four-day route at **Tsams-Ost Shelter**, mid-way through the eight-day loop, where a road leads out to the Sesriem–Solitaire road. However, you must pre-arrange to leave a vehicle there before setting off from park headquarters. Note that hikers may not begin from Tsams-Ost without special permission from the rangers at Naukluft.

Conditions are typically hot and dry, and water is reliably available only at overnight stops (at Putte, it's 400m from the shelter). Hikers must carry at least 4L of water per day (see the boxed text Desert Hiking in the Regional Facts for the Visitor chapter). Eight-day hikers can lighten their packs by dropping off a re-supply cache of food and stove fuel at Tsams-Ost Shelter prior to the hike. In four places – Ubusis Canyon, above Tsams Ost, Die Valle and just beyond Tufa Shelter – hikers must negotiate dry waterfalls, boulder-blocked kloofs and steep tufa formations with the aid of chains. Some people find this off-putting, so be sure you're up to it.

Naukluft 4WD Trail Off-road enthusiasts can now exercise their machines on the new National Parks 73km Naukluft 4WD Trail. The route costs US$24 per vehicle plus US$3.50 per person per day, including accommodation in one of the four stone-walled A-frames at the 28km point. Facilities include shared toilets, showers and *braais*. Up to four vehicles per 16 people are permitted at a time. Book through NWR in Windhoek.

Places to Stay The **Koedoesrus Camp Site** (*sites US$12 for four people*), pleasantly situated in a deep valley, has running water and ablutions blocks. The maximum stay is three nights.

Büllsport (*☎/fax 693371, fax 293365; e buellsport@natron.net; w www.natron.net /tour/buellspt/; Private Bag 1003, Maltahöhe; singles/doubles US$68/100 with half board*) occupies a lovely, austere setting below the Naukluft Massif. A highlight is the 4WD excursion up to the plateau (US$23) and the hike back down the gorge, past several idyllic natural swimming pools. There's also a shop and petrol station. Transfers from Windhoek or to Naukluft cost US$0.50 per km.

Zebra River Lodge (*☎ 693265, fax 693266; e marianne.rob@zebrariver.com; w www .zebrariver.com; km19 D850, PO Box 11742, Windhoek; singles/doubles US$60/95 with full board, self-catering cottage US$77*), in the Tsaris Mountains, is Rob and Marianne Field's private Grand Canyon. The surrounding wonderland of desert, mountains, plateaus, valleys and natural springs is accessible on a network of hiking trails and 4WD tracks (guided drives cost US$18). With caution, the 5km lodge road is accessible by 2WD.

Tsauchab River Camping (*☎ 293416, fax 245286; e tsauchab@triponline.net; w www.triponline.net/tsauchab; PO Box 221, Maltahöhe; camping US$6 per person; 4WD exclusive camp US$7 per person, rooms US$27 per person with breakfast*) has fabulous sites beside the Tsauchab riverbed, each with ablutions, a sink and *braai* area. From the main camp, the 11km Kudu hiking trail climbs to the summit of Aloekop. Beside a spring 11km from the main site is the 4WD exclusive site, where you can embark on the 21km Mountain Zebra Hiking Trail. Meals (US$4.50-11) are available on request and the farm shop sells bread, biscuits and home-made ginger beer.

Getting There & Away The Naukluft is accessible only with a private vehicle or an organised tour.

Sesriem & Sossusvlei
☎ 063

Welcome to Namibia's number one attraction, which seems to be every travellers' destination. If you visit Namibia and fail

The Namib Dunes

The magnificent Namib dunefields, which take on mythical proportions in tourist literature and nature specials, stretch from the Orange River to the Kuiseb River in the south (this area is known as 'the dune sea') and from Torra Bay in Skeleton Coast Park to Angola's Curoca River in the north. They're composed of colourful quartz sand, and come in varying hues – from cream to orange and red and violet.

Unlike the ancient Kalahari dunes, those of the Namib are dynamic, shifting with the wind, which sculpts them into a variety of distinctive shapes. The top portion of the dune, which faces the direction of migration is known as a slipface, where the sand spills from the crest and slips down. Various bits of plant and animal detritus also collect here and provide a meagre food source for dune-dwelling creatures, and it's here that most dune life is concentrated.

Parabolic Dunes
Along the eastern area of the dune sea – including around Sossusvlei – the dunes are classified as parabolic or multi-cyclic and are the result of variable wind patterns. These are the most stable dunes in the Namib and, therefore, are also the most vegetated.

Transverse Dunes
Near the coast south of Walvis Bay, the formations are known as transverse dunes, which are long narrow, linear dunes lying perpendicular to the prevailing southwesterly winds. Therefore, their slipfaces are oriented towards the north and northeast.

Seif Dunes
Around Homeb in the Namib Desert Park are the prominent linear or seif dunes, which are enormous northwest/southeast oriented sand ripples. With heights of up to 100m, they're spaced about 1km apart and show up plainly on satellite photographs. They're formed by seasonal winds; during the prevailing southerly winds of summer, the slipfaces lie on the northeastern face. In the winter, the wind blows in the opposite direction and slipfaces build up on the southwestern faces.

Star Dunes
In areas where individual dunes are exposed to winds from all directions, a formation known as a star dune appears. These dunes have multiple ridges and when seen from above may appear to have a star shape.

Barchan Dunes
Around the southern portion of the Skeleton Coast Wilderness and south of Lüderitz, barchan dunes prevail. These are the most highly mobile dunes of all, and are created by unidirectional winds. As they shift, these dunes take on a crescent shape, with the horns of the crescent aimed in the direction of migration. It is barchan dunes that are slowly devouring the ghost town of Kolmanskop near Lüderitz. These are also the so-called 'The Roaring Dunes' of the northern Skeleton Coast (see the boxed text in the Northwestern Namibia section).

Hump Dunes
Considerably smaller than other dune types are hump dunes, which typically form in clusters on flat expanses near water sources. Sand builds up around vegetation – usually a tuft of grass – and is held in place by the roots of the plant, forming a sandy tussock. They rarely rise more than 2m to 3m above the surface.

---

to reach Sossusvlei…well, it just wouldn't be normal!

The gateway to Sossusvlei is Sesriem; the name means 'six thongs', which was the number of joined leather ox-wagon thongs needed to draw water from the gorge. Both Sesriem Canyon and Sossusvlei are open year-round between sunrise and sunset. If you want to witness the sunrise over the dunes – as most people do – you must stay at

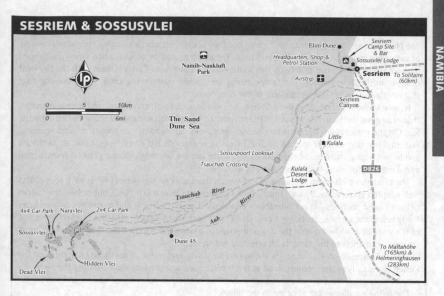

SESRIEM & SOSSUSVLEI

Sesriem (the camp site) or Sossusvlei Lodge or at one of the four nearby Wilderness Safaris' lodges. Otherwise, you can't pass the gate early enough to reach the dunes before sunrise.

Sesriem At Sesriem are the park headquarters, a small food shop, a petrol station, the camp site and the Sossusvlei Lodge. All visitors headed for Sossusvlei must check in at the park office and secure a park entry permit (US$3.50 per person plus US$2.50 per vehicle).

The 2km-long and 30m deep **Sesriem Canyon**, 4km south of the Sesriem headquarters, was carved by the Tsauchab River through the 15-million-year-old deposits of sand and gravel conglomerate. From the car park, you can hike upstream to the brackish pool at its head or downstream to the canyon mouth.

Dune 45 The most accessible of the red dunes along the Sossusvlei road is the 150m Dune 45, so called because it's 45km from Sesriem and 45 dunes from Sossusvlei. For tour groups, it's a popular sunrise and bush breakfast venue.

Sossusvlei & Around Sossusvlei, a large ephemeral pan, is set amid red sand dunes which tower up to 200m above the valley floor and over 300m over the underlying strata. This is the most accessible part of the 300km-long and 150km-wide sand sea that covers over 32,000 sq km of western Namibia and contains the world's highest, oldest and arguably most picturesque dunes. The pan rarely holds water, but when the Tsauchab River has gathered enough volume and momentum to push beyond the thirsty plains to the sand sea (as it did in 1997 and 2001), it's transformed into a verdant oasis.

A rugged 5km return walk from Sossusvlei takes you to **Dead Vlei** which, despite its name, is even more impressive than its popular neighbour. Alternatively, from the 2x4 Car Park, a rewarding 4km return hike, marked by white-painted posts, leads to **Hidden Vlei**, an unearthly dry vlei amid lonely dunes.

From Sesriem, take the 65km 2WD road to the 2x4 Car Park; the last 4km to Sossusvlei requires 4WD, so visitors with lesser vehicles park at the 2x4 Car Park and walk, hitch or take the Sossus 4WD Shuttle Service (US$3.50/6 one-way/return). If you're walking, carry enough water for a hot sandy slog in the sun.

Organised Tours Most Namib area lodges run day tours to Sossusvlei, and prices are generally proportional to the amount you're paying for accommodation. In addition, nearly every Namibian tour operator includes

The Dune Community

The Namib dunes may appear to be lifeless, but they actually support a complex ecosystem capable of extracting moisture from the frequent fogs. These are caused by condensation when cold, moist onshore winds, influenced mainly by the South Atlantic's Benguela Current, meet with the dry heat rising from the desert sands. The temperatures are coolest overnight, causing thick morning fogs that normally burn off during the heat of the afternoon.

Nowhere else on earth does such diverse life exist in such harsh conditions, and it only manages thanks to grass seed and bits of plant matter deposited by the wind and the moisture carried in by the fog. On the gravel plains live ostriches, zebras, gemsboks, springboks, mongooses, ground squirrels, and small numbers of other animals, such as black-backed jackals, bat-eared foxes, caracals, aardwolfs and brown hyenas. After good rains, seeds germinate and the seemingly barren gravel is transformed into a meadow of waist-high grass teeming with life.

The sand also shelters small creatures and even a short walk on the dunes will reveal traces of this well-adapted community. By day, the surface temperatures may reach 70°C, but below, the spaces between sand particles are considerable – especially if you're a bug – and therefore, air circulates freely below the surface, providing a cool shelter. In the chill of a desert night, the sand retains some of the warmth absorbed during the day and provides a warm place to burrow. When alarmed, most creatures can also use the sand as an effective hiding place.

The best places to observe dune life are around Sossusvlei and on the dunes south of Homeb, on the Kuiseb River. Early in the morning, look at the tracks to see what has transpired during the night; it's easy to distinguish the trails of various dune-dwelling beetles, lizards, snakes, spiders and scorpions.

The following species are at home in the dunes:

Tenebrionid Beetle (Onomachris unguicularis) This fog-basking beetle, which is locally known as a *toktokkie*, has a particularly interesting way of drinking. By day, these beetles scuttle over the dunes in search of plant detritus, but at night, they bury themselves in the sand. They derive moisture by condensing fog on their bodies; on foggy mornings, *toktokkies* line up on the dunes, lower their heads, raise their posteriors in the air, and slide the water droplets down the carapace into the mouth. They can consume up to 40% of their body weight in water in a single morning.

Dancing Spider (Orchestrella longpipes) This large spider, known as the 'White Lady of the Namib' (doesn't the Latin name sound like a character in a children's novel!) constructs tunnels beneath the dune surface, where it shelters from heat and predators. These tunnels are prevented from collapsing by a lining of spider silk, which is laid down as they're excavated. This enormous spider can easily make a meal of creatures as large as a palmato gecko.

Golden Mole (Eremitalpa granti) The dunes are also home to this loveable yellowish-coloured carnivore that spends most of its day buried in the sand. It was first discovered in 1837, but wasn't seen again until 1963. The golden mole, which lacks both eyes and ears, doesn't burrow like other moles, but simply swims through the sand. Although it's rarely spotted, look carefully around tufts of grass or hummocks for the large rounded snout, which may protrude above the surface. At night, it emerges and roams hundreds of metres over the dune faces foraging for beetle larvae and other insects.

---

it in their itineraries; see the Getting Around section earlier in this chapter.

Places to Stay & Eat The **Sesriem Camp Site** (camping US$20 for four people) must be booked in Windhoek, but arrive before sunset or the staff will re-assign your site on a stand-by basis; those who were unable to

book a site in Windhoek may get in on this nightly lottery. A small shop at the office here sells snacks and cold drinks, and the camp-site bar provides music and alcohol nightly.

Solitaire (☎ 693021, fax 693019; 65km north of Sesriem, Private Bag 1009, Maltahöhe; camping US$2.50 per person plus

The Dune Community

Shovel-Snouted Lizard (*Aporosaura anchitae*) This lizard uses a unique method of regulating its body temperature while tearing across the scorching sand. It can tolerate body temperatures of up to 44°C, but when surface temperatures on the dunes climb as high as 70°C, the lizard does a 'thermal dance', raising its tail and two legs at a time off the hot surface of the sand to prevent overheating. When threatened, the lizard submerges itself in the sand.

Palmato Gecko (*Palmatogecko rangei*) The unique and exceptionally cute palmato gecko is also known as the 'web-footed gecko', after its unusual feet, which act as scoops for burrowing in the sand. This translucent nocturnal lizard, which grows to 10cm in length is coloured pinkish-brown on its back and has a white belly. The enormous eyes aid with its nocturnal hunting habits, and the gecko is often photographed using its long tongue to clear its eyes of dust and sand, or to drink from condensed fog droplets from the head and snout. Other gecko species present in the dunes include the barking gecko (*Ptenopus garrulus*) and the large-headed gecko (*Chondrodactylus anguilifer*).

Namaqua Chameleon (*Chamaeleo namaquensis*) Another dune lizard, the bizarre and fearsome-looking Namaqua chameleon grows up to 25cm in length, and is identified by the unmistakable fringe of brownish bumps along its spine. When alarmed, it emits an ominous hiss and exposes its enormous yellow mouth and sticky tongue, which can spell the end for up to 200 large beetles every day. Like all chameleons, its cone-shaped eye sockets operate independently, allowing it to look in several directions at once.

Namib Sidewinding Adder (*Bitis peringueyi*) This small, buff-coloured snake is perfectly camouflaged on the dune surface. It grows to a length of just 25cm and navigates by gracefully moving sideways through the shifting sands. Because the eyes are on top of the head, the snake can bury itself almost completely in the sand and still see what's happening above the surface. When its unsuspecting prey happens along – normally a gecko or lizard – the adder uses its venom to immobilise the victim before devouring it. Although it is also poisonous to humans, the venom is so mild that it rarely causes more than an irritation.

Namib Sand Snakes (*Psammophis sp*) The Namib's three species of sand snake are longer, slinkier and faster-moving than the adders, but hunt the same prey. These 1m-long back-fanged snakes grab the prey and chew on it until it's immobilised by venom, then swallow it whole. As with the adders, they're well camouflaged for life in the sand, coloured from off-white to pale grey. The back is marked with pale stripes or a pattern of dots.

Namib Skinks (*Typhlosaurus sp*) Several varieties of skinks are commonly mistaken for snakes. Because they propel themselves by swimming in the sand, their limbs are either small and vestigial or missing altogether, and their eyes, ears and nostrils are tiny and therefore well-protected from sand particles. At the tip of their nose is a 'rostral scale', which acts as a bulldozer blade to clear the sand ahead and allow the skink to progress. Skinks spend most of their time burrowing beneath the surface, but at night, emerge on the dune slipfaces to forage. In the morning, you'll often see their telltale tracks.

US$3.50 per vehicle), named for the dead tree that's its renowned motif, might have provided the inspiration for the film *Baghdad Café*. This warm, friendly spot remains a favourite with travellers, and everyone stops for one reason or another (including petrol). At the shop, Moose continues to bake the best bread and *apfelstrüdel* in Africa (don't just take our word for it!), and the breakfasts are a great way to wake up. The attached **Solitaire Country Lodge** (☎ 061-256597, fax 256598; e *afrideca@mweb.com.na;* w *www .namibialodges.com; singles/doubles US$24/ 33 with breakfast*) has a pool and incongruously green lawn.

Rostock Ritz (☎ 064-403622, fax 403623, e kuecki@mweb.com.na; w www.desertlodge .web.na/index; PO Box 536, Swakopmund; singles/doubles US$69/105 with breakfast) is best known for its water garden and its cool and cave-like cement-domed architecture. Meals and activities are available for an extra charge.

Namibgrens Rest Camp (☎ 062-572021, fax 061-222893; e rabie@namibnet.com, D1275, PO Box 21587, Windhoek; camping US$6 per person, singles/doubles US$33/58), known for its several wonderful hiking trails, occupies a scenic position on Spreetshoogte Pass (Namibia's steepest road, with one hair-raising 1:4 slope!). The hiking routes (US$4.50/day), with boreholes along the way, form a ragged cloverleaf; hikers' accommodation is in the Granite Rock Hut (US$7.50) where the loops cross. Non-hikers can take the soft option and tour the farm by vehicle for US$12.

Weltevrede Rest Camp (☎ 293374, fax 293375; e aswarts@mweb.com.na; PO Box 4119, Walvis Bay; camping US$12 for 3 people, single/double tents US$33/43, single/ double bungalows US$48/84 with full board), 30km south of Solitaire, has shady camping, bungalow accommodation and a tented dune camp in a lonely desert setting. Guided trips run to the farm's rock paintings (US$2.50) and desert sundowners (US$9).

Sossusvlei Lodge (☎ 693223, fax 693231; e reservations@sosvlei.com; w www.sossusvlei lodge.com; PO Box 6900, Ausspannplatz, Windhoek; single/double bungalows US$138/185 with half board) bears a strong resemblance to what happens when squabbling children topple a stack of coloured blocks. People either love it or hate it, but it does make a statement and it's inside the Sesriem Gate and therefore allows pre-dawn access to Sossusvlei (US$40).

Wilderness Safaris' Camps (☎ 061-274500, fax 239455, e info@nts.com.na; w www.wilderness-safaris.com; 8 Bismarck St, PO Box 6850, Windhoek) include four diverse units, all of which have access to Wilderness Safaris' private entrance to Sossusvlei. **Kulala Desert Lodge** (singles/ doubles US$317/480) and **Little Kulala** (singles/doubles US$328/500) camps overlook ephemeral riverbeds with excellent dune views. **Sossusvlei Wilderness Camp** (singles/doubles US$328/500) perches above

a desert valley, 40km from Sesriem, with accommodation in beautiful stone, timber and thatched bungalows nestled between rock kopjes, as well as star-gazing classes at night. Neighbouring **Kulala Tented Camp** (singles/doubles US$302/448) offers simpler accommodation overlooking the same valley. All rates include half board, Sossusvlei trips and other activities. Bungalows at Little Kulala and Sossusvlei Wilderness Camp have private splash pools.

Namib-Naukluft Lodge (☎/fax 693381; w www.natron.net/nnl; C19, PO Box 22028, Windhoek; singles/doubles US$84/140 with half board, tents US$38 per person), on a 13,000 hectare farm, this beautiful lodge occupies a boulder-strewn landscape 20km south of Solitaire. Activities include a four-hour hiking trail, bird-watching, Sossusvlei excursions (US$33) and sundowners in the surrounding granite hills.

For more options, see Namib-Rand Nature Reserve and Maltahöhe, both later in this chapter.

Getting There & Away Sesriem is reached via a signposted turn-off from the C19. You'll find petrol at Solitaire, Namib Restcamp, Sesriem and a bush BP station 93km south of Sesriem on the D826.

Namib-Rand Nature Reserve

The large private Namib-Rand Nature Reserve, which abuts the Namib-Naukluft Park, was formed from a collection of private farms to eventually take in 200,000 hectares of dunes, desert grasslands and wild, isolated mountain ranges. It's currently the largest privately owned property in Southern Africa, but several concessionaires operate on the reserve, offering a range of experiences amid one of Namibia's most stunning and colourful landscapes.

On Die Duine Farm, within the reserve, **Tok-Tokkie Trails** (☎ 061-234342, fax 233872; e eden@mweb.com.na; Die Duine Farm, PO Box 162, Maltahöhe; US$112 per day) offers fully-inclusive one- to four-day desert hiking and camping trips.

Places to Stay The **Wolwedans** (☎ 061-230616, fax 220102; e info@wolwedans.com .na; w www.wolwedans .com; PO Box 5048, Windhoek; Dunes Lodge: singles/doubles

US$235/330, Dune Camp: US$140/200, Private Camp: US$160/225 self-catering, US$315/450 with full board) with raised wooden chalets amid brilliant red dunes is enhanced by long views and an elegant ambience. The Dune Camp is open only from 1 March to 30 November and the Private Camp from 15 April to 15 October.

Camp Mwisho *(☎ 293233, fax 293241; e namibsky@mweb.com.na; PO Box 5197, Windhoek; singles/doubles US$119/192 with full board)* is best-known for its company Namib Sky, which does dawn balloon trips (US$250 per person) over the dune sea.

Sossusvlei Mountain Lodge *(☎ South Africa 11-809 4300, 27-11-809 4514; e bookings@ ccafrica.com; w www.ccafrica.com; Private Bag X27, Benmore 2010, South Africa; doubles US$750 with half board & activities)* elegantly melds so well with its environment that it appears to belong in its landscape. Natural stone chalets feature fireplaces, marble baths and covered patios. Of special interest is the observatory, with a high-powered telescope and local star charts.

Southern Namibia

Southern Namibia takes in everything from Rehoboth in the north to the Orange River along the South African border, and westward from the Botswana border to the Diamond Coast. The Central Plateau is characterised by wide open country, and the area's widely spaced and largely uninspiring towns function mainly as commercial and market centres. This is rich cattle-ranching country, and around Mariental, citrus fruit and market vegetables are grown under irrigation. Further south, however, the landscape opens up into seemingly endless desert plains, ranges and far horizons – and the surprising Fish River Canyon forms a spectacular gash across the landscape.

REHOBOTH
☎ 062 ● pop 20,000

Rehoboth lies 85km south of Windhoek and just a stone's throw north of the Tropic of Capricorn. The original German mission was abandoned in 1864, but the town was revived in the early 1870s by the Basters, an ethnic group of mixed Khoikhoi/Afrikaner origin, who migrated north from the Cape under their leader Hermanus van Wyk. The **town museum** *(☎ 522954; beside the post office; admission US$1.30; open 10am-noon Mon-Sat, 2pm-4pm Mon-Fri)* is dedicated to Baster heritage. There's also an archaeological annexe at an Iron Age site, 10km from town, which can be visited by prior arrangement.

Reho Spa *(☎ 522774; admission US$2.50 per person plus US$1.25 per vehicle; camping US$12 per person, bungalows US$24-38)*, a hot-spring resort administered by NWR, was originally known by its Nama name *aris* (smoke), after the steam which rose from the hot spring. Note that security isn't optimum so watch your valuables. Book through NWR in Windhoek.

Lake Oanob Resort *(☎ 522370, fax 524112, e oanob@iafrica.com.na; km6 D1237, PO Box 3381; camping from US$14-22/site, 6-bed chalets US$78-100, 8-bed chalets US$125-160, singles/doubles US$43/53)*, on the 2.7-sq-km Oanob Dam, west of town, has a pleasant camp site, restaurant, bar and beautiful stone and thatch self-catering bungalows that overlook the water. Access is by private vehicle only.

HARDAP DAM
☎ 063

The 25-sq-km Hardap Dam *(US$2.50 per person plus US$2.50 per vehicle)*, 15km northwest of Mariental, offers good fishing and a 25,000-hectare wildlife park with 80km of gravel roads and a sadly fading 15km hiking loop. It's also home to over 260 bird species. Entry permits allow access to the pool and picnic sites. Walking is permitted anytime between sunrise and sunset but accommodation is available only at the rest camp.

Hardap Dam Rest Camp *(2-bed bungalow US$28-30, 4-bed bungalow US$48, 5-bed bungalow US$37-42, 4-bed luxury suite US$59, 12-bed dormitory US$48)* offers varied accommodation, plus a shop, restaurant, kiosk and swimming pool. The restaurant and cliff-top pool afford a great vista over the lake. Book through NWR in Windhoek.

To get there, take the signposted turning off the B1, 15km north of Mariental, and continue 6km to the entrance gate. For cruises on the lake, contact **Oasis Ferries** *(☎ 240805 or 243292)*.

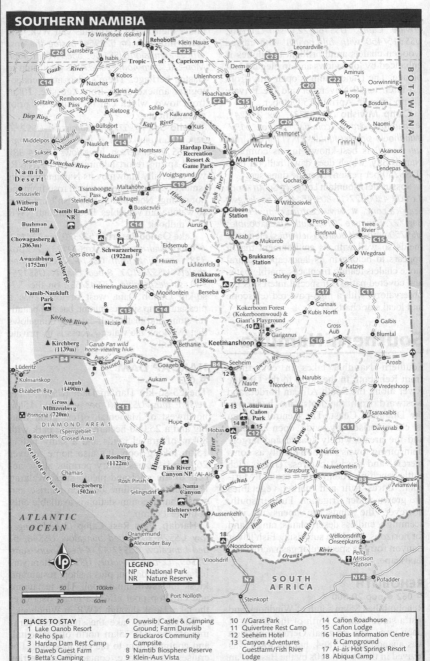

SOUTHERN NAMIBIA

LEGEND
NP National Park
NR Nature Reserve

ATLANTIC OCEAN

BOTSWANA

SOUTH AFRICA

PLACES TO STAY
1 Lake Oanob Resort
2 Reho Spa
3 Hardap Dam Rest Camp
4 Daweb Guest Farm
5 Betta's Camping
6 Duwisib Castle & Camping Ground; Farm Duwisib
7 Bruckaros Community Campsite
8 Namtib Biosphere Reserve
9 Klein-Aus Vista
10 //Garas Park
11 Quivertree Rest Camp
12 Seeheim Hotel
13 Canyon Adventures Guestfarm/Fish River Lodge
14 Cañon Roadhouse
15 Cañon Lodge
16 Hobas Information Centre & Campground
17 Ai-ais Hot Springs Resort
18 Abiqua Camp

MARIENTAL
☎ 063

The small administrative and commercial centre of Mariental sits on the bus and rail lines between Windhoek and Keetmanshoop, and serves as a popular petrol stop. It's also home to the large-scale Hardap irrigation scheme which allows citrus-growing and ostrich farming.

Guglhupf (☎ 240718, fax 242525; Park St, PO Box 671; singles/doubles US$22-37) has a swimming pool, and the attached café serves excellent steaks and beef dishes.

River Chalets (☎ 241295, 0811 282601; B1, PO Box 262; single/double self-catering chalets US$27/38) aren't anywhere near a river, but do offer bright and airy pastel-coloured accommodation. They're by far the nicest option in Mariental.

For quick meals, try **Bambi's Takeaways** (☎ 240767; Marie Brandt St; snacks US$1.30-2.50), beside the central Engen petrol station, or the **Wimpy** (☎ 242138; mains US$1.30-3.50) at the petrol station complex on the B1.

All trains, buses and minibuses between Windhoek and Keetmanshoop pass through Mariental.

DUWISIB CASTLE
☎ 063

Duwisib Castle (☎ 06638-5303; admission US$2.50; open 8am-1pm & 2pm-5pm daily), a curious Baroque structure 70km south of Maltahöhe, was built in 1909 by Baron Captain Hans-Heinrich von Wolf. After the German-Nama Wars, he commissioned architect Willie Sander to design a home that would reflect his commitment to the German military cause. It purposely resembles a Schutztruppe fort, and now houses an impressive collection of 18th- and 19th-century antiques and armour. Official guided tours are available.

The camping ground (camping US$13 for four people) is just down the hill from the castle, and there's a small **snack bar** beside the castle.

Farm Duwisib (☎/fax 223994; e duwisib@ iway.na; D826, PO Box 21, Maltahöhe; rooms US$35 per person with half board), 300m from the castle, has self-catering rooms for two or four people.

Betta's Camping (☎ 693003; junction of C27 & D826; camping US$4.50 per person),

with a small shop and petrol station, lies en route to Sossusvlei 20km west of Duwisib.

MALTAHÖHE
☎ 063

Maltahöhe, in the heart of a ranching area, has little to recommend it, but thanks to its convenient location along the back route between Namib-Naukluft Park and Lüderitz, the area supports a growing number of guest farms and private rest camps.

Hotel Maltahöhe (☎ 293013, fax 293133; PO Box 20; singles/doubles US$25/41) has won several national awards for its amenable accommodation. It also has a restaurant and bar, and organises good-value day trips to Sossusvlei.

Daweb Guest Farm (☎/fax 293088; e daweb@natron.net, w www.natron.net/ tour/daweb; C14, PO Box 18; camping US$3.50/person, singles/doubles US$28/38 with half board), on a working cattle ranch 2km south of Maltahöhe, is a lovely Cape Dutch-style farmhouse where you can participate in guided walking or 4WD expeditions in the surrounding countryside.

On Monday and Thursday, Star Line runs a return bus between Mariental (US$2.50, two hours) and Maltahöhe.

HELMERINGHAUSEN
☎ 063

Tiny Helmeringhausen is little more than a homestead, hotel and petrol station, and has been the property of the Hester family since 1919. The highlight is the idiosyncratic **Agricultural Museum** (☎ 283083; Main St; admission free; open on request), established in 1984 by the Helmeringhausen Farming Association. It displays all sorts of interesting old furniture and farming implements collected from local properties, as well as an antique fire engine from Lüderitz.

Helmeringhausen Hotel (☎ 233083, fax 283132; singles/doubles US$38/42 with breakfast) is a friendly and pleasant country hotel with a restaurant and bar. The food is excellent, the beer is always cold and they keep a well-stocked cellar.

BRUKKAROS
With a 2km-wide crater, this extinct volcano dominates the skyline between Mariental and Keetmanshoop. It was formed some 80 million years ago when a magma pipe

Kokerbooms

Kokerbooms (*Aloe dichotoma*), or quiver trees, are widespread throughout southern Namibia and northwestern South Africa. They are in fact aloes and can grow to heights of 8m. The name is derived from the lightweight branches, which were formerly used as quivers by San hunters; they removed the branches' fibrous heart, leaving a strong, hollow tube.

The slow-growing kokerbooms occur mainly on rocky plains or slopes – they need rocks to anchor their shallow root systems – storing water in their succulent leaves and fibrous trunk and branches. Water loss through transpiration is prevented by a waxy coating on the leaves and branches. In June and July, their yellow blooms appear, lending bright spots of colour to the desert.

encountered ground water about 1km below the earth's surface and caused a series of volcanic explosions. From the car park, it's a 3.5km hike to the crater's southern entrance; along the way, watch for the remarkable **quartz formations** embedded in the rock. From here, you can head for the other-worldly **crater floor** or turn left and follow the southern rim up to the abandoned **sunspot research centre**, which was established by the US Smithsonian Institute in the 1930s.

Brukkaros Community Campsite (*camping US$3 per person, day visits US$1.25*) offers camping with toilets and a bush shower, but campers must supply all their own water. To get there, follow the C98 west from Tses for 40km, then turn north on the D3904 and continue 18km to the site. The nearest public transport is Star Line's Monday and Friday bus between Keetmanshoop (US$3.80, 3¼ hours) and Beerseba (20km from Bruckkaros).

KEETMANSHOOP
☎ 063 ● pop 15,000
Keetmanshoop (pronounced 'kayt-mahns-hoo-up') sits at the main crossroads of southern Namibia and has more petrol stations per capita than any other town in Namibia, which may hint at its main function for travellers. The helpful **Southern Tourist Forum** (*☎ 221266, fax 223813; cnr 5th Ave & Fenschel St; open 7.30am-12.30pm & 1.30pm-4.30pm Mon-Fri*), in the municipal building, provides bookings, brochures and historical data.

For email and Internet access the **I-Zone** (*6th Ave*) charges US$3/hour.

Things to See
The most prominent example of colonial architecture is the 1910 **Kaiserliches Postampt** (*Imperial Post Office; cnr 5th Ave & Fenschel St*). The **town museum** (*☎ 221256; admission free; open 7.30am-12.30pm & 2.30pm-4.30pm Mon-Fri*), housed in the 1895 **Rhenish Mission Church**, outlines the history of Keetmanshoop with old photos, early farming implements, an old wagon and a model of a traditional Nama home.

For more sites of interest, see Quivertree Rest Camp, //Garas Park and Seeheim Hotel under Places to Stay, following.

Places to Stay
Municipal Camp & Caravan Park (*☎ 223316; 8th Ave; sites US$3 per person plus US$2 per vehicle*) is a bougainvillea-decked compound at the western end of town.

Burgersentrum Backpackers (*☎ 223454; 12 Schmeide St; dorm beds US$5*) offers bland, no-frills backpackers accommodation.

Quivertree Rest Camp (*☎/fax 222835; e quiver@iafrica.com.na; Gariganus Farm, PO Box 262; camping US$4 per person, single/double 'igloo' bungalows US$20/30, day admission US$2 per person plus US$2 per vehicle*), on Garaganus Farm 14km east of town, boasts Namibia's largest stand of kokerbooms or quiver trees (*Aloe dichotoma*). Rates include use of the picnic facilities and entry to the **Giant's Playground**, a bizarre natural rock garden 5km away.

//Garas Park (*☎/fax 223217; e morkel@namibnet.com; B1, PO Box 106; camping US$2.50 per person plus US$1 per vehicle, day admission US$1 per person plus US$1 per vehicle*), 25km north of town, also boasts stands of kokerbooms and lots of hiking tracks and drives through a fantasy landscape of stacked boulders. It's enhanced by a series of sculptures made from spare junk.

Pension Gessert (*☎/fax 223892; e gesserts@iafrica.com.na; 138 13th St, PO Box 690; singles/doubles US$25/35 with breakfast*), in the quiet Westdene neighbourhood, has a beautiful garden and swimming pool. It is especially proud of its breakfast, which may well be the best of any B&B in Namibia.

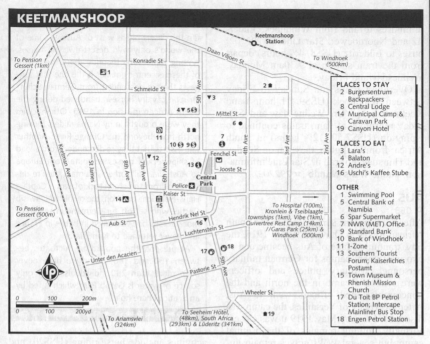

KEETMANSHOOP

PLACES TO STAY
2 Burgersentrum Backpackers
8 Central Lodge
14 Municipal Camp & Caravan Park
19 Canyon Hotel

PLACES TO EAT
3 Lara's
4 Balaton
12 Andre's
16 Uschi's Kaffee Stube

OTHER
1 Swimming Pool
5 Central Bank of Namibia
6 Spar Supermarket
7 NWR (MET) Office
9 Standard Bank
10 Bank of Windhoek
11 I-Zone
13 Southern Tourist Forum; Kaiserliches Postamt
15 Town Museum & Rhenish Mission Church
17 Du Toit BP Petrol Station; Intercape Mainliner Bus Stop
18 Engen Petrol Station

Central Lodge (☎ 225850, fax 224984; e clodge@iway.na; 5th Ave, PO Box 661; singles/doubles from US$20/35), right in the town centre, features a lovely dining room and comfortable rooms arranged around a pool and large courtyard.

Canyon Hotel (☎ 223361, fax 223714; e canyon@iafrica.com.na; 5th Ave, PO Box 950; singles/doubles US$42/65) is Keetmanshoop's standard mid-range option.

Seeheim Hotel (☎ 250503; B4, PO Box 1338; camping US$5 per person, singles/doubles US$20/38), at the Seeheim rail halt 48km west of Keetmanshoop, is a historic property featuring an atmospheric bar and several rooms full of period furniture. A range of meals (US$4-7) are available and the toasties are reputedly the best in Southern Africa.

Places to Eat

Andre's (☎ 222572; Fenchel St; snacks US$1-1.50, mains US$3-4) has declined a bit of late, but it's still a good solid option for breakfast, pizza, steaks and tasty desserts.

Lara's (☎ 222233; cnr 5th Ave & Schmeide St; breakfast US$3.50, lunch US$2-3, mains US$3-6; open 8am-9pm Mon-Sat) serves up

a range of choices, from steak, pork and chicken to seafood and ostrich.

Balaton (☎ 222539; Mittel St; breakfast US$1-2, takeaways US$1-1.50, mains US$2-3.50; open 9am-9pm daily) dishes up quick and tasty Hungarian-oriented fare, as well as breakfast, sandwiches and fruit shakes.

Uschi's Kaffee Stube (☎ 222445, 5th Ave; breakfast US$2-3, pizzas US$3.50-4, mains US$2.50-4; open 9am-7pm Mon-Sat) is primarily a pizza place that also does breakfast, lunch, snacks and afternoon tea.

Entertainment

Vibe (☎ 222861; admission US$0.80; open 10pm-late Fri-Sat), a night club in Kronlein township, is the place to go for a night of partying with the local crowd. Visitors are welcome, but don't carry valuables.

Getting There & Away

Intercape Mainliner buses between Windhoek (US$24, 5¾ hours) and Cape Town (US$32, 13¾ hours) stop at the Du Toit BP petrol station four times weekly in either direction; they also leave for Jo'burg (US$46, 17 hours) via Upington. The Engen station,

opposite, serves as the bus terminal for minibuses to and from Windhoek, Lüderitz and Noordoewer. **Star Line** (☎ 292202) buses to Lüderitz (US$8, 4¾ hours) depart from the train station at 7.30am Monday, Wednesday and Friday.

Overnight trains run Sunday to Friday between Windhoek (US$9, 11 hours) and Keetmanshoop. On Wednesday and Saturday mornings at 9am, trains continue to Upington (US$7.50, 12½ hours) in South Africa; from Upington, they run on Sunday and Thursday. For rail or Star Line information, phone **Trans-Namib** (☎ 292202).

AUS
☎ 063

After the Germans surrendered to the South African forces at Otavi on 9 July 1915, the tidy, tranquil village of Aus became one of two internment camps for German military personnel. Military police and officers were sent to a camp in the north and the noncommissioned officers went to Aus. After the Treaty of Versailles, the camp was dismantled and by May 1919 it was closed. Virtually nothing remains of the original camp, but several WWI graves remain immediately north of the village.

En route to Lüderitz, you may observe the feral **desert horses** of the Namib; for the best viewing, stop by the **hide** at Garub Pan, 20km west of Aus.

Places to Stay & Eat
Namib Garage (☎/fax 258029 or 258017; Bahnhof St, PO Box 29; camping US$2 per person, singles/doubles US$12/18) provides simple accommodation as well as snacks, burgers and grills.

Klein-Aus Vista (☎/fax 258021; e ausvist@ namibhorses.com, w www.namibhorses.com; PO Box 25; camping US$4 for six people, single/double chalets US$60/87, 10-bed hut from US$40) occupies a 10,000-hectare ranch along the Lüderitz road, 3km west of Aus. Hikers will love the magical four-day hiking route, which traverses fabulous wild landscapes. Meals are available at the main lodge and accommodation is in the main lodge or one of the two wonderful hikers' huts: the dormitory hut **Geister Schlucht**, in a Shangri-La-like valley, or the opulent **Eagle's Nest** complex, with several chalets built right into the boulders. Beyond the wonderful hiking,

Feral Desert Horses

On the desert plains west of Aus live some of the world's only wild desert-dwelling horses. Among the several theories about the origins of these eccentric equines is the one that suggests they're descended from German Schutztruppe cavalry horses abandoned during the South African invasion in 1915. Others claim they were brought in by Nama raiders moving north from beyond the Orange River. Another tale asserts that they're descended from a load of shipwrecked horses en route from Europe to Australia. Still, others maintain they're descended from the stud stock of Baron Captain Hans-Heinrich von Wolf, the owner of Duwisib Castle, who set off for Germany in search of more horses but was killed in battle in France and never returned to Namibia.

At present, the population fluctuates between 150 and 160, but there have never been more than 280 individuals. Their only source of water is Garub Pan, which is fed by an artificial bore hole.

activities include horse-riding (US$20) and 4WD tours through their vast desert concession (US$38/76 for a half/full day).

Namtib Biosphere Reserve (☎ 061-233597; e namtib@iafrica.com.na; bungalows US$45 per person with full board), in the beautiful Tirasberge, is run by ecologically conscious owners who've created a self-sustaining farm in a narrow valley, with distant views of the Namib plains and dunes. Take the C13 north of Aus for 55km, then turn west on the D707; after 48km turn east onto the 12km farm road to the lodge.

LÜDERITZ
☎ 063

Lüderitz is a surreal colonial relic – a 19th-century Bavarian village on the barren, windswept Namib Desert coast, seemingly untouched by the 20th century. It has everything you'd expect of a small German town – delicatessens, coffee shops and Lutheran churches. Here, the icy but clean South Atlantic is home to seals, penguins and other marine life and the desolate beaches support flamingoes and ostriches.

Lüderitz merits the 600km detour from Keetmanshoop, via the sealed B4, which

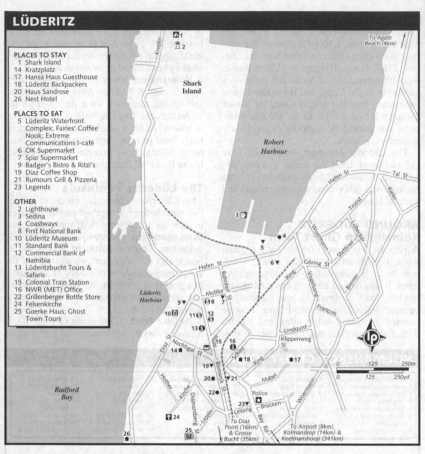

LÜDERITZ

PLACES TO STAY
1 Shark Island
14 Kratzplatz
17 Hansa Haus Guesthouse
18 Lüderitz Backpackers
20 Haus Sandrose
26 Nest Hotel

PLACES TO EAT
5 Lüderitz Waterfront
 Complex; Fairies' Coffee
 Nook; Extreme
 Communications I-café
6 OK Supermarket
7 Spar Supermarket
9 Badger's Bistro & Ritzi's
19 Diaz Coffee Shop
21 Rumours Grill & Pizzeria
23 Legends

OTHER
2 Lighthouse
3 Sedina
4 Coastways
8 First National Bank
10 Lüderitz Museum
11 Standard Bank
12 Commercial Bank of
 Namibia
13 Lüderitzbucht Tours &
 Safaris
15 Colonial Train Station
16 NWR (MET) Office
22 Grillenberger Bottle Store
24 Felsenkirche
25 Goerke Haus; Ghost
 Town Tours

features far vistas between the desolate southern Namib and the forbidden Diamond Area 1. When the wind blows – which is most of the time – the final 10km into Lüderitz may be blocked by the barchan dune field which seems bent upon crossing the road. The drifts pile quite high before the road crews clean them off and conditions do get hazardous, especially if it's foggy.

Information

Lüderitzbucht Tours & Safaris (☎ 202719, fax 202863; e ludsaf@ldz.namib.com; Bismarck St; open 8am-1pm & 2pm-5pm Mon-Fri, 8am-noon Sat, 8.30am-10am Sun) provides reliable tourist information, organises visitor permits for Kolmanskop and sells curios, books, stamps and phone cards. The helpful **NWR**

office (☎ 202752; Schinz; open 7.30am-1pm & 2pm-4pm Mon-Fri) can help with national park information.

Several banks on Bismarck Street change cash and travellers cheques. **Extreme Communications I-café** (☎ 204256; Waterfront Complex; open 8am-5pm Mon-Fri, 9am-1pm Sat) charges US$3.50 per hour for email and Internet access.

Things to See

Just about every view in Lüderitz reveals its German Imperial and Art Nouveau architectural heritage. Prominent buildings include the **colonial train station** (cnr Bahnhof & Bismarck St), and the **Goerke Haus** (Diamantberg St; admission US$1.30; open 2pm-4pm Mon-Fri, 4pm-5pm Sat-Sun).

NAMIBIA

The prominent 1912 Evangelical Lutheran church, **Felsenkirche** *(open 5.30pm-7pm Mon-Sat summer, 4.30pm-6pm Mon-Sat winter)*, dominates Lüderitz from high on Diamond Hill. It was designed by Albert Bause, who implemented the Victorian influences he'd seen in the Cape, and the stained-glass panel over the altar was donated by Kaiser Wilhelm II himself. Go to see the late-afternoon sun shining through the extraordinary stained-glass work.

The **Lüderitz Museum** *(☎ 202582; Diaz St; admission US$1.30; open 3.30pm-5pm Mon-Fri)* details Lüderitz's diamond mining heritage and other aspects of its natural and cultural history.

AROUND LÜDERITZ
Kolmanskop Ghost Town
A popular trip from Lüderitz is the ghost town of Kolmanskop, 14km away, which was once a substantial diamond-mining town. It was named after an early Afrikaner trekker, Jani Kolman, whose ox-wagon became bogged in the sand here. It once boasted a casino, skittle alley and theatre with fine acoustics, but the slump in dia-

mond sales after WWI and the discovery of richer deposits at Oranjemund ended its heyday. By 1956 it was deserted. Several buildings have been restored, but many have already been invaded by the dunes.

Kolmanskop tours *(US$4/2 adult/child; open 9.30am & 10.45am Mon-Sat, 10am Sun)* last 45 minutes; pick up a permit from the Lüderitzbucht Tours & Safaris tourist office at least 30 minutes prior to each tour. Participants must provide their own transport from town. After the tour, you can eat a light lunch in the Ball Hall restaurant.

The Lüderitz Peninsula
The Lüderitz Peninsula, much of which lies outside the Sperrgebiet prohibited area, makes an interesting half-day excursion from town. The picturesque and relatively calm bay, **Sturmvogelbucht**, has a lovely beach and is viable for swimming, but the water temperature would only be amenable to a seal or a penguin. A Norwegian whaling station was sited there in 1914, but is now a rusty ruin.

At **Diaz Point**, 22km south of Lüderitz, is a lovely, classic lighthouse and a replica of

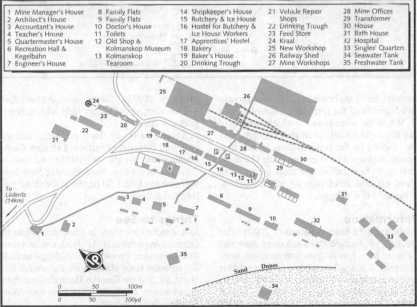

KOLMANSKOP GHOST TOWN

1 Mine Manager's House	8 Family Flats	14 Shopkeeper's House	21 Vehicle Repair	28 Mine Offices
2 Architect's House	9 Family Flats	15 Butchery & Ice House	Shops	29 Transformer
3 Accountant's House	10 Doctor's House	16 Hostel for Butchery &	22 Drinking Trough	30 House
4 Teacher's House	11 Toilets	Ice House Workers	23 Feed Store	31 Bath House
5 Quartermaster's House	12 Old Shop &	17 Apprentices' Hostel	24 Kraal	32 Hospital
6 Recreation Hall &	Kolmanskop Museum	18 Bakery	25 New Workshop	33 Singles' Quarters
Kegelbahn	13 Kolmanskop	19 Baker's House	26 Railway Shed	34 Seawater Tank
7 Engineer's House	Tearoom	20 Drinking Trough	27 Mine Workshops	35 Freshwater Tank

Diamond Dementia in the Desert

Although diamonds were discovered along the Orange River in South Africa as early as 1866, and had also turned up on guano workings on the offshore islands, it apparently didn't occur to anyone that the desert sands might also harbour a bit of crystal carbon.

In May 1908, however, railway worker Zacharias Lewala found a shiny stone along the railway line near Grasplatz and took it to his employer August Stauch, who knew exactly what it was. Stauch took immediate interest and to his elation, the state geologist Dr Range confirmed that it was indeed a diamond. Stauch applied for a prospecting licence from the Deutsche Koloniale Gesellschaft and set up his own mining concern, the Deutsche Diamanten Gesellschaft, to begin exploiting the presumed windfall.

This sparked off a frenzy, and hordes of prospectors descended upon Lüderitz with dreams of fabulous wealth buried in the sands. As a result, Lüderitz was soon rolling in dough, and service facilities sprang up to accommodate the growing population. In September 1908, after the diamond mania had escalated out of control, the German government intervened and proclaimed the Sperrgebiet. This 'closed area' extended from 26°S latitude southward to the Orange River mouth, and stretched inland for 100km. Independent prospecting was henceforth *verboten* and those who'd already staked their claims were forced to form mining companies.

In February 1909, a Diamond Board was created to broker diamond sales and thereby control prices. However, after WWI, the world diamond market was so depressed that in 1920, Ernst Oppenheimer of the Anglo-American Corporation was able to purchase Stauch's company, along with eight other producing companies, and combined them to form the Consolidated Diamond Mines (CDM). At this time, Anglo-American's CDM (and other diamond interests in Southwest Africa) were amalgamated into a new CDM, under control of De Beers South Africa, which set up its headquarters at Kolmanskop. In 1928, however, rich diamond fields were discovered around the mouth of the Orange River and, in 1944, CDM relocated to the purpose-built company town of Oranjemund. Kolmanskop was abandoned to the encroaching dunes.

In 1994, the British-Canadian company Namibian Minerals Corporation (Namco) was awarded offshore diamond-mining concessions at Lüderitz and Hottentots Bay by the Namibian government. These areas were estimated to hold a total of 27 million carats at a value of US$4 billion; the diamonds are recovered by vacuuming the diamondiferous sands beneath the sea bed. They're currently doing well, but it remains to be seen whether they'll affect De Beers' stranglehold on the market.

a cross erected in July 1488 by Portuguese navigator Bartolomeu Dias on his return voyage from the Cape of Good Hope. The point is frequented by sea lions, and from the nearby car park, you can observe the jackass penguin colony on **Halifax Island**. You can also observe cormorants, wading birds and even the occasional school of dolphins.

Grosse Bucht (Big Bay) at the southern end of the peninsula, is another wild and scenic beach. This normally cold, windy spot is favoured by flocks of flamingoes that feed in the tidal pools. It's also the site of a small but picturesque shipwreck on the beach. Just a few kilometres north lies the small seaside rock arch known as **Klein Bogenfels**.

Organised Tours

Weather permitting, **Atlantic Adventure Tours** (☎/fax 204030 or 202256; e sedina@ iafrica.com.na) sails daily with the schooner *Sedina* past the Cape fur-seal sanctuary at Diaz Point and the penguin colony on Halifax Island. The two- to three-hour trips cost US$22; book at the tourist office. Be sure to take warm gear.

Ghost Town Tours (☎ 204033; e kol mans@iafrica.com.na; Goerke Haus), which operates Kolmanskop Tours, also does day trips to Elizabeth Bay (US$27), deep in the Sperrgebiet, and a full day taking in Kolmanskop, Elizabeth Bay and the Lüderitz Peninsula (US$52). These trips run with a minimum of four people and permits must be issued at least a week in advance. Bring your passport.

Coastways (☎ 202002, fax 202003; e lewis cwt@iway.na; Waterfront, PO Box 77) runs day tours (US$78) to the 55m Bogenfels sea arch, Maerchental Valley and the ghost town of

AROUND LÜDERITZ

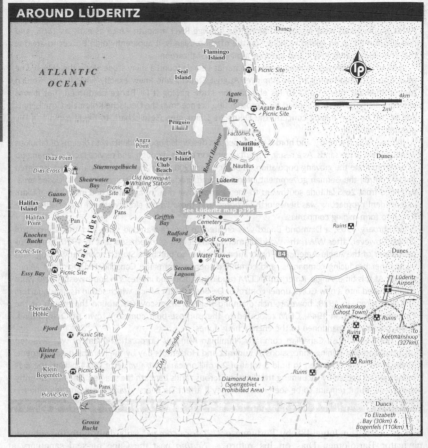

Pomona, also in the Sperrgebiet. This tour also requires at least four participants and must be booked a week in advance. The same company also operates the popular 4WD trail (US$42 per person per day) up the dune-studded coast to Spencer Bay, where participants drive their own vehicles to several untouched shipwrecks along an otherwise inaccessible coastline. It's normally fully booked up to a year in advance, so plan early.

Places to Stay

Shark Island (camping US$12 for four people, 5-bed bungalows US$67), operated by NWR, is beautifully situated but aggravatingly windy. It's connected to the town by a causeway, but is no longer an island, thanks

to the recent harbour reclamation project that attached it to the mainland.

Lüderitz Backpackers (☎ 202000, fax 202633; e luderitzbackpackers@hotmail.com; 7 Schinz St, dorm beds US$6.50-8, doubles US$17) includes all the usual backpacker amenities, including a kitchen, braai and good tourist information.

Haus Sandrose (☎ 202630, fax 202365; e sandrose@ldz.namib.com; 15 Bismarck St, PO Box 109; doubles US$29) has three very different rooms, arranged around a sheltered garden. Two of the units have self-catering facilities.

Kratzplatz (☎/fax 202458; e kratzmr@iway .na; 5 Nachtigal St; dorm beds US$5, singles/ doubles US$19/28 with breakfast) is a homely and informal B&B right in the town centre.

Hansa Haus Guesthouse (☎/fax 203581, 0811 280061; e mcloud@africaonline.com .na; 5 Mabel St, PO Box 837; singles/doubles US$16/26, family rooms from US$42) is a monumental hilltop home with a wonderful sea view and comfortable accommodation. Guest have use of the kitchen.

Nest Hotel (☎ 204000, fax 204001; e nest hotel@natron.net; w www.natron.net/tour /nest-hotel/index/; 820 Diaz St, PO Box 690; singles/doubles US$57/83), a bright place on the rocky coast south of the centre, features seaview rooms, a sheltered pool and a sauna.

Places to Eat

Diaz Coffee Shop (☎ 203147, cnr Bismarck St & Bay Rd; open 8am-5.30pm Mon-Fri, 8am-3pm Sat, 9am-3pm Sun; snacks from US$1) serves excellent toasted sandwiches, light meals, coffee and cakes.

Fairies' Coffee Nook (☎ 0812 456158; Waterfront Complex; open 8am-5.30pm Mon-Fri, 8am-1pm & 3.30pm-6pm Sat; breakfast US$3.20, sandwiches US$0.50-1), with a good sea view, serves up light meals, coffee and sweet snacks.

Badger's Bistro (☎ 202855; Diaz St; lunch US$2.50-5, mains US$3-7, lobster US$15) is a good spot for lunch or dinner, but the attached bar can be noisy. Crayfish is available only in season.

Ritzi's (☎ 0811 243353; Diaz St; mains US$6-10) is always fully booked, so reservations are essential. The specialities include local oysters, kingclip and crayfish, as well as excellent venison, beef and vegetarian options. Entry is through Badger's Bistro.

Legends (☎ 203110; Bay Rd; open noon-midnight daily; mains US$5-10) specialises in seafood – especially crayfish – but you can also order pizza, beef and other mains. It also has a pub with billiards and a big-screen TV. Takeaways are available.

Rumours Grill & Pizzeria (☎ 202655; Kapp's Hotel, Bismarck St; open lunch & dinner daily; mains US$5-9, crayfish from US$15) is a popular steak house that's known for its beef, pizzas and seafood. You can choose between the sports bar and the beer garden.

For self-catering, see the **Spar** and **OK** supermarkets.

Getting There & Away

Air Namibia flies five times weekly between Windhoek and Cape Town, stopping en route in Walvis Bay, Lüderitz and Oranjemund.

Star Line (☎ 312875) buses to Keetmanshoop (US$9, 4¾ hours) leave from the historic train station at 12.30pm on Monday, Wednesday and Friday.

FISH RIVER CANYON NATIONAL PARK

Nowhere else in Africa is there anything like Fish River Canyon. The Fish River, which joins the Orange River at the mouth of the canyon, has been gouging out this gorge for thousands of years and the results are both dramatic and enormous. The canyon measures 160km in length, and reaches up to 27km wide and 550m deep, but these figures don't convey the sort of response you're likely to have when you first gaze into its depths.

Inside Fish River Canyon National Park (admission US$2.50 per person plus US$2.50 per vehicle), the two main camps are Hobas, at the northern end, and Ai-Ais Hot Springs Resort, in the south. Pre-book all accommodation at NWR in Windhoek.

Hobas
☎ 063

The **Hobas Information Centre** (open 7.30am-noon & 2pm-5pm daily), at the northern end of the park, is also the check-in point for the five-day Fish River Canyon Trail. This popular route begins at **Hikers' Viewpoint**, 10km down a gravel road, which affords a fantastic view over the northern part of the canyon. The view from Main Viewpoint, a few kilometres to the south, features in nearly every tourist brochure ever published on Fish River Canyon. Both of these dramatic vantage points encompass the sharp river bend known as **Hell's Corner**.

The well-shaded **camping ground** (camping US$15 for four people) offers a kiosk, swimming pool and clean facilities, but there's no restaurant or petrol station.

Fish River Trail

The magical five-day, 85-km Fish River Trail hike (US$11 per person) between Hikers' Viewpoint and Ai-Ais is Namibia's most popular walk – with good reason. Due to flash flooding and heat in the summer months, it's open only from 1 May to 30

Fish River Canyon

The early San had a legend that the wildly twisting Fish River Canyon was gouged out by a frantically scrambling snake Koutein Kooru as he was pursued into the desert by hunters.

The geological story is only a bit different. Fish River Canyon is actually two canyons, one inside the other, which were formed in entirely different ways. It's thought that the original sedimentary layers of shale, sandstone and loose igneous material around Fish River Canyon were laid down nearly two billion years ago and were later metamorphosed by heat and pressure into more solid materials, such as gneiss. Just under a billion years ago, cracks in the formation admitted intrusions of igneous material, which cooled to form the dolerite dykes (which are now exposed in the inner canyon).

The surface was then eroded into a basin and covered by a shallow sea, which eventually filled with sediment – sandstone, conglomerate, quartzite, limestone and shale – washed down from the surrounding exposed lands. Around 500 million years ago, a period of tectonic activity along crustal faults caused these layers to rift and to tilt at a 45° angle. These forces opened a wide gap in the earth's crust and formed a large canyon. This was what we now regard as the outer canyon, the bottom of which was the first level of terraces that are visible approximately 170m below the eastern rim and 380m below the western rim. This newly created valley naturally became a watercourse (the Fish River, oddly enough) which began eroding a meandering path along the valley floor and eventually gouged out what is now the 270m-deep inner canyon.

September. Groups of three to 40 people may begin the hike every day of the season, but it's very popular so you'll have to book well in advance; officials may also require a doctors' certificate of fitness, issued less than 40-day before your hike. Hikers must arrange their own transport and accommodation in Hobas and Ai-Ais

Ai-Ais Hot Springs Resort

Ai-Ais Hots Springs Resort (camping US$15 for four people, 4-bed bungalows US$27, 2/4-bed flat US$42/36, mineral baths US$2.50; open to day visitors sunrise-11pm daily), whose name means 'scalding hot' in Nama, is known for its thermal baths that originate beneath the riverbed. They're rich in chloride, fluoride and sulphur, and are reputedly salubrious for sufferers of rheumatism or nervous disorders. The hot water is piped to a series of baths, Jacuzzis and an outdoor swimming pool.

Ai-Ais also has a shop, **restaurant** (open 7am-8.30am, noon-1.30pm & 6pm-8.30pm daily), petrol station, tennis courts, post office, and a grocers.

Getting There & Away

There's no public transport to either Hobas or Ai-Ais, but from mid-March to 31 October, hitchers should eventually be successful. Alternatively, take the train from Keetmanshoop to the Hoolog rail halt, which is within relatively easy hitching distance (43km)

from Hobas. However, don't even attempt this without camping gear and several days' supply of food and water.

AROUND FISH RIVER CANYON
Canyon Adventures

The friendly Canyon Adventures Guestfarm (formerly called Fish River Lodge) occupies a ranch cradled in the confluence of the Löwen and Fish River Canyons amid some of the most amazing geology imaginable. A highlight is the 4WD trip into the canyon (US$9) to swim in the river pools, do a 'garnet crawl', and see the bizarre petroglyphs in the rippled black dolerite.

From April to October, you can also do the five-day, 85km Löwenfish hiking trail (US$42), which takes in the Löwen Canyon and several days along Fish River Canyon, interrupted by ascents to the plateau and descents down scenic kloofs. Camps (no facilities) are sited at water sources along the way and on the last night you can stay at **Koelkrans Camp** (US$8 per person), with cooking facilities and hot showers. On the last day, hikers climb out of the canyon and follow a scenic route back to the farmhouse. Stages of this trip may also be done as one- to four-day hikes.

If you're driving, head west from Keetmanshoop and turn south on the D545; after 33km, bear left at the junction. After 32km more, you'll see the 'Fish River Lodge' sign west of the road. From here, it's 22km west

Fishermen mending their nets, Ilha de Moçambique, Mozambique

A boat moored near Maputo, Mozambique

Sossusvlei sand dunes, Namibia

Burchell's zebra, Etosha National Park, Namibia

Desert vegetation, Fish River Canyon National Park, Namibia

to the farmhouse on a rough track that's passable with 2WD. Transfers from Keetmanshoop cost US$42 per group return.

Fish River Lodge (*☎ 693007 or 266018, fax 693006; e frlodge@iafrica.com.na; w www .fishrivercanyon.ws; PO Box 1840, Keetmanshoop; bush camping US$5.50 per person, dorm beds US$8, singles/doubles from US$32 per person with breakfast*) offers very amenable accommodation in a magical wild setting. Dinner is available for US$8. Pre-bookings are essential.

Gondwana Cañon Park

Founded in 1996, the 100,000 hectare Gondwana Cañon Park was created by amalgamating several former sheep farms and removing fences to restore the wilderness country immediately east of Fish River Canyon National Park. Waterholes have been established and wildlife is now returning to this wonderful, remote corner of Namibia. Book accommodation (see the descriptions, following) through the **Cañon Travel Centre** (*☎ 061-230066, fax 251863, e nature.i@mweb.com.na; PO Box 80205, Windhoek*).

Cañon Lodge (*w www.natron.net/canyon lodge; singles/doubles US$65/100 with breakfast, mountain camp US$15 per person*), perfectly integrated into its boulder-strewn backdrop, is one of Namibia's most stunning accommodation options. The restaurant, housed in a restored 1908 farmhouse, is decorated with historic farming implements and rambling gardens. For an even quieter experience, opt for their rustic self-catering camp at the foot of the nearby hills. Activities include scenic flights (from US$58), horse-riding (US$15/hour) and sundowners (US$20); lunch/dinner cost US$7/13.

Cañon Roadhouse (*w www.natron.net/ canyon; camping US$6.50/site plus US$2.50 per person, singles/doubles US$50/84*) attempts to re-create a roadhouse out on the wildest stretches of Route 66 – at least as such a thing would exist in the collective imagination. Amenities include a swimming pool, petrol station and an acclaimed à la carte restaurant with an imaginative menu.

NOORDOEWER
☎ 063

The Orange River has its headwaters in the Drakensberg Mountains of Natal, South Africa, and forms much of the boundary between Namibia and South Africa. It was named not for its muddy colour, but for Prince William V of Orange, who was the Dutch monarch in the late 1770s. The road from Noordoewer to Rosh Pinah makes a very nice desert adventure.

Noordoewer, the main border crossing between Namibia and South Africa, lies astride the Orange River and is becoming a centre for viticulture, as well as canoeing and rafting adventures.

To change money, try the BP petrol station.

River Trips

Several companies, backed up by riverside camps, offer easy-going canoe trips on the Orange River. Trips are normally done in stages and last from one to six days. Possible stages include Noordoewer to Aussenkehr, the Fish River mouth, Nama Canyon (which has several serious rapids) and/or Selingsdrif. The following companies offer options:

Amanzi Trails (*☎ South Africa 21-559 1573, e colleen@amanzitrails.co.za, w www .amanzitrails .co.za*)

Felix Unite (*☎ 297161, 27-(0)82 495 8519, fax 297250, e carlosp@iafrica.com.na or bookings@felix.co.za, w www.felixunite .com*) PO Box 3, Noordoewer

Rivers Inc (*☎ South Africa 21-551 6659, 082 343 7641, e info@riversinc.co.za, w www.riversinc.co.za*)

Places to Stay & Eat

Camel Lodge (*☎ 297171, fax 297143; e nih@ mweb.com.na; B1, PO Box 1; camping US$3 per person, singles/doubles from US$15/22*) has been spruced up and now offers rooms with TV and air con. The swimming pool and *braai* facilities are available for an extra charge.

Orange River Lodge (*☎ 297012, fax 297230; e orlodge@iway.na; camping US$3.50 per person, singles/doubles US$20/28*) is an agreeable chalet complex beside the BP petrol station. Meals are available.

Abiqua Camp (*☎ 297255, fax 297259; e abiqua@iway.na; km13 Orange River road; camping US$4 per person*), on the riverbank, is the launch site for both the Amanzi Trails and Rivers Inc river trip operators. If no one is around when you arrive, check in at the white house 500m back along the access road.

South Africa

South Africa, the southern gateway to the region and the whole vast continent, is an exhilarating, spectacular and complex country. Geographically, its extremes include the arid semidesert of the Karoo, the snowcapped peaks of the Drakensberg Range, the lush subtropical coast of KwaZulu-Natal and the fertile temperate valleys of Western Cape.

World-class attractions abound. There's the Kruger National Park, with possibly the finest wildlife viewing in Africa, and Cape Town, a city of magnificent beauty nestling beneath imposing Table Mountain.

The influx of foreign visitors to the country in recent years has set off an explosion of tours and activities: dive with great white sharks, sip a cocktail while watching lions play, wander around a Zulu village or explore the Cape's elegant old wine estates.

The 'rainbow nation' is an economic powerhouse, a fact reflected in the outstanding and well-organised network of national parks and reserves. The road system is excellent and getting around is relatively easy: for budget travellers, hostels pepper the country, and a bus service links most of them.

South Africa's people are diverse – they speak 11 different languages – and with the transition to majority rule, that diversity is now respected. In the north of the country you can meet the Venda people, fabled ironworkers of mysterious origin and in the south the Cape Muslims, with roots in South Asia.

The 'new' South Africa is a young country still coming to grips with democracy and changing rapidly, both for good and bad – falling physical and psychological barriers built around skin colour on one hand, and the well-publicised crime problem on the other. It is an exciting time to come to South Africa and observe these changes at first hand.

Facts about South Africa

HISTORY

South Africa's history extends back to around 40,000 BC when the San people first settled Southern Africa. By the 3rd century

South Africa at a Glance

Area: 1,233,404 sq km

Population: 43.79 million

Capitals: Pretoria (administrative capital), Bloemfontein (seat of high court) and Cape Town (seat of parliament)

Head of State: President Thabo Mbeki

Official Languages: English, Afrikaans, Ndebele, South Sotho, North Sotho, Swati, Tsonga, Tswana, Venda, Xhosa and Zulu

Currency: rand (R)

Exchange Rate: US$1= R7.97

Highlights

- Cape Town – wandering the city; climb Table Mountain and sample the fruits of the Winelands

- Kruger National Park – experiencing the most convenient wildlife viewing in Africa

- Drakensberg Range – hiking through this rugged and spectacular escarpment

- The East Coast – watching whales; surfing world-class waves and discovering the Greater St Lucia Wetlands

- Zululand – experiencing traditional and modern Zulu culture; visiting important battlefields and outstanding national parks

- Transkei – revelling in the solitude of the largely undeveloped Eastern Cape, with its superb warm-water surf beaches and excellent hiking trails

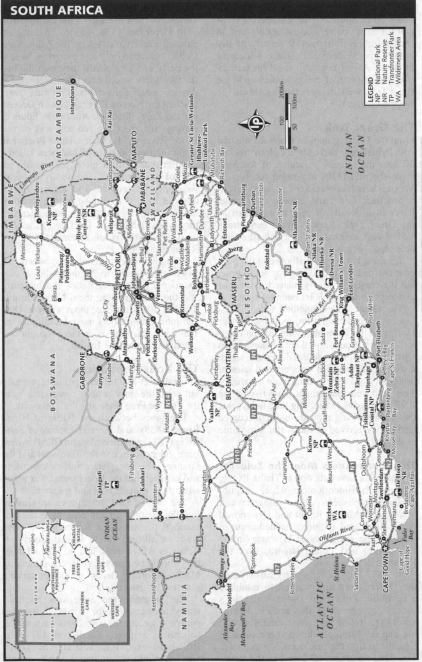

SOUTH AFRICA

SOUTH AFRICA

LEGEND
NP National Park
NR Nature Reserve
TP Transfrontier Park
WA Wilderness Area

SOUTH AFRICA

AD, Bantu-speaking peoples were well established in South Africa. Competing colonial European powers began settling here in small numbers from the 17th century, mostly in the Cape. Widespread colonial settlement of South Africa began in the 19th century (for a description of events leading up to the Great Trek, see History in the Facts about the Region chapter).

The Great Trek
From the 1820s, groups of Boers dissatisfied with British rule in the Cape Colony trekked off into the interior in search of freedom. From the mid-1830s increasing numbers of Voortrekkers (Fore-trekkers, pioneers) abandoned their farms and crossed the Orange River in a decade of migration known as the Great Trek. Reports from early treks told of vast, uninhabited – or at least poorly defended – grazing lands.

Tensions between the Boers and the government had been building for some time, but the reason given by many trekkers for leaving was the 1833 act banning slavery.

The Great Trek coincided with the *difaqane* (forced migration, explained under History in the Facts about the Region chapter) and the Boers mistakenly believed that what they found – deserted pasture lands, disorganised bands of refugees and tales of brutality – was the normal state of affairs. This mistaken assessment gave rise to the Afrikaner myths (still dying hard today) that the Voortrekkers moved into unoccupied territory or arrived at much the same time as the blacks.

The Voortrekkers Meet the Zulu
The Great Trek's first halt was at Thaba 'Nchu, near modern Bloemfontein, where a republic was established. After a disagreement, trek leaders Maritz, Retief and Uys moved on to Natal, and Potgieter headed north to establish the Republics of Winburg (in the Free State) and Potchefstroom, later the Republic of Transvaal.

By 1837 Piet Retief's party had crossed the Drakensberg and wanted to establish a republic. Zulu king Dingaan (Shaka's successor) agreed to this and, in February 1838, Retief and some others visited his capital Mgungundlovu (near modern Ulundi) to sign the title deed. It was a trap. The deed assigning all Natal to the Boers

was signed but immediately afterwards Dingaan's men massacred the entire party.

In December 1838 Andries Pretorius organised a revenge attack on the Zulus. Sarel Celliers climbed onto a gun carriage to lead the party in a vow that if they won the battle, the Boers would ever after celebrate the day as one of deliverance. Pretorius' party reached the Ncome River and on 16 December the Zulus attacked. After three hours of carnage the river ran red and was named Blood River by the Boers. Three Boers had slight injuries; 3000 Zulus had been killed.

After such a 'miraculous' victory (the result of good tactics and vastly superior weaponry) it seemed Boer expansion really did have that long-suspected stamp of divine approval, and the 16 December victory was celebrated as the Day of the Vow until 1994, when it was renamed the Day of Reconciliation.

Perhaps more miraculously, when Boers pushed on to Mgungundlovu they found the remains of Retief and his party and the deed granting them Natal. Despite this, the British annexed the republic in 1843 and most of the Boers moved north into the Transvaal, carrying with them yet another grievance against the British.

The Boer Republics
Several short-lived Boer republics sprang up but soon the only serious contenders were the Orange Free State and the Transvaal.

The years between the Battle of Blood River (1838), and the conventions of Sand River (1852) and Bloemfontein (1854), which gave independence to the Transvaal and the Orange Free State, were full of confusion and conflict, but the Boers were clear about what they wanted: land and freedom.

The aims of the black tribes were similar, but the British government, which commanded the strongest forces in the area, wasn't at all sure what it wanted. British officials in Africa often had no idea whether they should be restraining Boers, protecting blacks, enforcing British treaties or carving out new British colonies.

The Orange Free State was intermittently at war with the powerful Basotho people – sometimes with British assistance, sometimes without. Finally, in 1871, the British annexed Basotholand. The Transvaal Republic's problems were mostly

internal, with several leaders and breakaway republics threatening civil war until Paul Kruger (president of the Zuid-Afrikaansche Republiek; **ZAR – South African Republic**, 1883–1900) settled the issue with a short, sharp campaign in 1864.

The financial position of the republics was always precarious and their economies depended entirely on cattle. Most trade was by barter. Just when it seemed that the republics, with their thinly spread population of fiercely independent Boers, were beginning to settle into stable states, diamonds were discovered near Kimberley in 1869. Britain stepped in quickly and annexed the area.

The Boers were disturbed by the foreigners, both black and white, who poured in following the discovery and were angry that their impoverished republics were missing out on the money the mines brought in.

Meanwhile, Britain became nervous about the existence of independent republics in Southern Africa, especially as gold had been found in the Transvaal. The solution, as usual, was annexation and in 1877 the Transvaal lost its independence.

Anglo-Boer Wars

After the annexation, the Transvaal drifted into rebellion and the First Anglo-Boer War, known by Afrikaners as the War of Independence, broke out. It was over almost as soon as it began, with a crushing Boer victory at the Battle of Majuba in early 1881, and the republic regained its independence as the ZAR.

With the discovery of a huge reef of gold in the Witwatersrand (the area around Johannesburg) in 1886 and the ensuing explosive growth of Johannesburg itself, the ZAR was suddenly host to thousands of *uitlanders* (foreigners), black and white.

With little experience of towns, none of cities, and a deep suspicion of foreign ways, Kruger's ZAR government did its best to isolate the republic from the gold rush. The foreigners paid taxes but were not allowed to vote.

In 1899 the British demanded that voting rights be given to the 60,000 foreign whites on the Witwatersrand. Kruger refused, demanding that British troops massing on the ZAR borders be withdrawn by 11 October – if they weren't, he asserted, he would consider the republic to be at war.

The British, confident that their vastly superior numbers of experienced troops would win swiftly, took him on. Shocked to find that the Boers were no pushover, the British fell into disarray until reinforcements arrived. Lords Roberts and Kitchener led an army of 450,000 men against the 80,000 Boers from the ZAR, the Free State and the Cape. The Boers gave way rapidly and by 5 June 1900 Pretoria, the last of the major towns, had surrendered.

It seemed that the war was over but instead it entered a second, bitter phase. Commando raiders denied the British enemy control of the countryside. There was no possibility that the British could be defeated, but maintaining an occupying army would be an expensive proposition for them.

Without an enemy army to face, just commandos who could instantly become innocuous farmers, the British decided to exact reprisals. If a railway line was blown up, the nearest farmhouse was destroyed; if a shot was fired from a farm, the house was burnt down, the crops destroyed and the animals killed. The women and children from the farms were collected and taken to concentration camps – a British invention. By the end of the war 26,000 people, mainly children, had died of disease and neglect in the camps.

On 31 May 1902 the Peace of Vereeniging was signed and the Boer republics became British colonies.

British Rule

The British response after their victory was a mixture of appeasement and insensitive imperialism. It was essential for the Boers and British to work together. The non-whites were scarcely considered, other than as potential labour, despite the fact that they constituted about 80% of the combined population of the provinces.

Political awareness was growing, however. Mohandas (later Mahatma) Gandhi was working with the Indian populations of the Natal and Transvaal, and men like John Jabavu, Walter Rubusana and Abdullah Abdurahman laid the foundations for new non-tribal, black political groups.

Hard-up Boers flooded into the cities to find a world dominated by the English and their language. Worst of all, they were forced to compete for jobs with blacks. Partly as a

backlash to this, Afrikaans came to be seen as the *volkstaal* (people's language) and as a symbol of Afrikaner nationhood.

The former republics were given representative government in 1906-7, and moves towards union began almost immediately.

Union of South Africa

The Union of South Africa was established on 31 May 1910. The British High Commission Territories of Basotholand (now Lesotho), Bechuanaland (now Botswana), Swaziland and Rhodesia (now Zimbabwe) were excluded from the Union.

English and Dutch became the official languages – Afrikaans was not recognised as the official language until 1925.

The first election was held in September 1910. The South African National Party (soon known as the South African Party, or SAP), a diverse coalition of Boer groups under General Louis Botha and the brilliant General Jan Smuts, won the election and Botha became the union's first prime minister.

General Barry Hertzog raised some of the most divisive issues, championing Afrikaner interests, advocating separate development for the two white groups and independence from Britain. He and his supporters formed the National Party (NP).

Soon after the union was established a barrage of repressive legislation was passed. It became illegal for black workers to strike; skilled jobs were reserved for whites; blacks were barred from military service; and pass laws, restricting black freedom of movement, were tightened.

In 1912, Pixley ka Isaka Seme formed a national democratic organisation to represent blacks. It was initially called the South African Native Congress, but from 1923 it was known as the African National Congress (ANC).

In 1913 the Natives Land Act set aside 7.5% of South Africa's land for black occupancy. No black (and blacks made up over 70% of the population) was allowed to buy, rent or become a sharecropper outside this area. Thousands of squatters were evicted from farms and forced into increasingly overcrowded reserves, or into the cities.

In 1914 South Africa, as a part of the British Empire, found itself automatically at war with Germany and saddled with the responsibility of dealing with German South West Africa (now Namibia). South Africa's involvement on the British side prompted the last major violent Afrikaner rebellion – more than 300 men were killed. After the war, South West Africa became a part of South Africa under 'mandate' from the League of Nations.

Fusion

In 1924 the NP under Hertzog came to power, with an agenda that included promoting Afrikaner interests, independence and racial segregation. In the 1929 election the *swaartgevaar* (black threat) was made the dominant issue for the first time.

In reality, the NP and the SAP were not so far apart politically and, in 1933, the two formed a coalition (or fusion government), with Hertzog as the prime minister and Smuts as his deputy.

Fusion was rejected by Dr DF Malan and his followers. They formed the Purified National Party, which quickly became the dominant force in Afrikaner political life. The Afrikaner Broederbond, a secret ultra-nationalistic Afrikaner brotherhood, became the extraordinarily influential force behind the party. From 1948 to 1994 every prime minister and president was a member of the Broederbond.

At the far right, the Ossewa-Brandwag (Sentinels of the Ox-wagon, or OB) became a popular militaristic organisation with strong German sympathies and an obvious affinity with Hitler's doctrine of a master race.

Apartheid

The NP won the 1948 election on a platform of establishing apartheid (literally, the state of being apart). With the help of creative electoral boundaries it held power right up to the first democratic election in 1994.

Mixed marriages were prohibited and interracial sex was made illegal. Every individual was classified by race. The Group Areas Act enforcing the physical separation of residential areas was promulgated. The Separate Amenities Act created separate public facilities – separate beaches, separate buses, separate toilets, separate schools and separate park benches. The pass laws were further strengthened and blacks were compelled to carry identity documents at all times and were prohibited from remaining in towns, or even visiting them, without specific

permission. Thanks to the Dutch Reformed churches, apartheid was even given religious justification.

Black Action

In 1949 the ANC for the first time advocated open resistance in the form of strikes, acts of public disobedience and protest marches. These continued intermittently throughout the 1950s, with occasional violent clashes.

In June 1955, at a congress held at Kliptown near Johannesburg, a number of organisations, including the Indian Congress and the ANC, adopted a Freedom Charter setting out a vision of a nonracial democratic state.

On 21 March 1960 the Pan African Congress (PAC) called for nationwide protests against the hated pass laws. When demonstrators surrounded a police station in Sharpeville police opened fire, killing 69 people and wounding 160. To people in South Africa and the rest of the world, the struggle had now crossed a crucial line – there could no longer be any doubts about the nature of the white regime.

Soon after, the PAC and ANC were banned and the security forces were given the right to detain people indefinitely without trial. Prime Minister Verwoerd announced a referendum on whether the country should become a republic. A slim majority of white voters gave their approval to the change and in May 1961 the Republic of South Africa came into existence.

Nelson Mandela became the leader of the underground ANC and Oliver Tambo went abroad to establish the organisation in exile. As more black activists were arrested, the ANC and PAC began a campaign of sabotage through the armed wings of their organisations, respectively Umkonto We Sizwe (Spear of the Nation; usually known as MK) and Poqo (Pure). In July 1963 Nelson Mandela, along with a number of other ANC and communist leaders, was arrested, charged with fomenting violent revolution and sentenced to life imprisonment.

The Homelands

Verwoerd was assassinated in parliament in 1966 (there was apparently no political motive) and was succeeded by BJ Vorster, who was followed in 1978 by PW Botha. Both men continued to pursue the insane dream of separate black Homelands and a white South Africa.

The plan was to restrict blacks to Homelands that were, according to the propaganda, to become self-sufficient, self-governing states on the traditional lands of particular tribal groups. In reality, they had little infrastructure and no industry and were therefore incapable of producing sufficient food for the burgeoning black population. Under the plan, 13% of the country's total land area was to be the home to 75% of the population.

Intense and widespread suffering was the result as blacks could not even move beyond their Homeland without a pass and explicit permission.

Power proved irresistible to the leaders of Transkei, Bophuthatswana, Venda and Ciskei. Between 1976 and 1981 the collaborators accepted a nominal independence, and they then proceeded to crush all resistance to their rule and to that of the South African government.

International Conflict

In 1980 Robert Mugabe was elected prime minister of an independent Zimbabwe, and South Africa found itself the last white-controlled state in Africa. Increasing numbers of Western countries imposed sanctions and the ANC and PAC received direct support from the governments of black Africa (with the exception of Malawi and Swaziland). South Africa's white governing elite increasingly saw the country as a bastion besieged by communism, atheism and black anarchy.

Soweto Uprising

On 16 June 1976 the Soweto Students' Representative Council protests against the use of Afrikaans (considered the language of the oppressor) in black schools. Police opened fire on a student march, starting a round of nationwide demonstrations, strikes, mass arrests and riots that, over the next 12 months, took more than 1000 lives.

Steve Biko, the charismatic leader of the Black Consciousness movement, which stressed the need for psychological liberation and black pride, was killed in September 1977. Unidentified security police beat him until he lapsed into a coma – he went without medical treatment for three days and finally died in Pretoria. At the subsequent inquest,

SOUTH AFRICA

the magistrate found that no one was to blame.

South Africa was never the same again – a generation of young blacks committed themselves to a revolutionary struggle against apartheid and the black communities were politicised.

After changes to the constitution in 1983, the powers of the state president were increased and coloureds (mixed race) and Indians were given a token role in government. Blacks were given no role at all.

Violent protest built up steadily over the next two years until, in 1985, the government declared a state of emergency that was to stay in force for the next five years. The media was strictly censored and, by 1988, 30,000 people had been detained without trial. Thousands were tortured.

Botha repealed the pass laws, but this failed to mollify black protesters and created a white backlash. His reforms also failed to impress the rest of the world, and economic sanctions began to bite. Foreign banks refused to roll over government loans and the rand's value collapsed. In late 1989 Botha was replaced by FW De Klerk.

Reform

At his opening address to the parliament on 2 February 1990 De Klerk announced that he would repeal discriminatory laws and that the ANC, PAC and Communist Party were legalised. Media restrictions were lifted, and De Klerk undertook to release political prisoners. On 11 February he released Nelson Mandela, after 27 years in jail. During 1990 and 1991 virtually all the old apartheid regulations were repealed.

On 21 December 1991 the Convention for a Democratic South Africa (Codesa) began negotiations on the formation of a multiracial transitional government and a new constitution extending political rights to all groups.

The Codesa negotiations did not proceed smoothly but both the NP and the ANC were determined that free elections would take place at some time. However, thrashing out the details was complex and the ANC suspected the government of dragging out the process.

The talks, by now a negotiation between the NP and the ANC, excluded the smaller parties, including the predominantly Zulu Inkatha Freedom Party, which demanded a

federal structure for the new constitution. Right-wing whites, who wanted a *Volkstaat* (literally People's State; a Boer Homeland), joined them in an unlikely alliance.

Now, with white support drifting to the right-wing parties, the National Party needed to hurry negotiations. A compromise was reached and both sides accepted a five-year, post-election interim government of national unity.

Free Elections

Across the country at midnight on 26–27 April 1994, *Die Stem* (the old national anthem) was sung and the old flag was lowered. Then the new rainbow flag was raised and the new anthem, *Nkosi Sikelele Afrika* (God Bless Africa), was sung.

The ANC won 62.7% of the vote, less than the 66.7% which would have enabled it to overrule the interim constitution. As well as deciding the national government, the election decided the provincial governments, and the ANC won in all but two of the provinces. The National Party won 20.4% of the vote, enough to guarantee it representation in cabinet.

Today

In 1999, after five years of learning about democracy, the country voted in another election. Economics and political competence were major issues of debate. Fears that Nelson Mandela's retirement would hit the ANC's majority proved unfounded.

The New National Party (NNP) lost two-thirds of its seats and lost official opposition status to the Democratic Party (DP); the United Democratic Movement (UDM) also fared poorly. The ANC retained all of its provincial governments.

Thabo Mbeki, who took over leadership of the ANC from Nelson Mandela, became the new president in 1999. Mbeki, held in far less affection by the ANC grassroots than their beloved 'Madiba' (Mandela), has proved himself a shrewd politician, maintaining his political pre-eminence by isolating or co-opting opposition parties (the most incredible example being a power 'sharing' deal with the New National Party – the rebranded architects of apartheid).

New 'floor crossing' legislation forced through by the government in 2002 enabled MPs to switch parties on personal whim and

without recourse to their electorate. These laws helped Mbeki win total control of South African politics for the ANC in 2003 when it held for the first time a two-thirds majority in Parliament.

ANC dominance has raised fears of the advent of a de facto one-party state and an increase in self-interested and corrupt political cronyism. Its dominance does give the ANC the option to rewrite the constitution if it chooses.

It has not been all plain sailing for Mbeki, however. In the early days of his presidency his effective denial of the AIDS crisis invited global criticism. The purchase in 2002 of a US$68m presidential jet was seen as indulgent at a time when many citizens struggled to fill their stomachs.

White South African land owners and foreign investors were spooked in 2001 and beyond as Mbeki conspicuously failed to condemn the chaotic, violent and forced reclamation of white-owned farms in neighbouring Zimbabwe. This tacit support for Zimbabwean president Robert Mugabe created fears for the future of white-owned land in South Africa and led to an alarming devaluation of the rand.

Such concerns (currency scares aside) are long-term ones however, and for the majority of white South Africans rampant crime remains the number one concern; blacks also suffer from crime, but then they have done so for a very long time. For black South Africans economic inequality remains the big problem, and although the apartheid system is dead, economic apartheid is dying far too slowly for most.

GEOGRAPHY

South Africa is a big country, covering nearly 2000km from the Limpopo River in the north to Cape Agulhas in the south, and nearly 1500km from Port Nolloth in the west to Durban in the east. It's mostly dry and sunny, lying just south of the Tropic of Capricorn. The major influence on the climate is not the country's latitude, but its topography and the surrounding oceans.

The country can be divided into three major parts: the vast interior plateau (the highveld); the great escarpment at its edge (the Kalahari Basin); and a narrow coastal plain (the lowveld). Although Johannesburg is not far south of the tropics, its altitude

(around 1700m above sea level) and its distance from the sea moderates its climate. It is 1500km further north than Cape Town, but its average temperatures are only 1°C higher.

South Africa is divided into nine provinces: Gauteng, Limpopo, Mpumalanga, Free State, KwaZulu-Natal, Northwest, Northern Cape, Eastern Cape and Western Cape.

The Homelands no longer exist as political entities, but in this guide we sometimes refer to the old Homelands by name.

CLIMATE

The Western Cape has dry sunny summers with maximum temperatures around 26°C. It is often windy, however, and the southeasterly 'Cape Doctor' can reach gale force. Winters can get cold, with average minimum temperatures of around 7°C and the maximum around 17°C. There is occasional snow on the higher peaks.

The eastern plateau area (including Johannesburg) has a dry, sunny climate in winter with maximum temperatures around 20°C and crisp nights with temperatures dropping to around 5°C. Between October and April there are late afternoon showers often accompanied by spectacular thunder and lightning, but it rarely gets unpleasantly hot. Heavy hailstorms cause quite a lot of damage each year. It can, however, get very hot in the Karoo (the semidesert heart of all three Cape provinces) and the far north (the Kalahari).

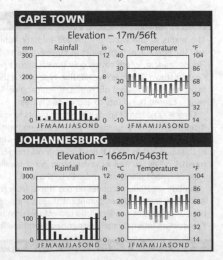

SOUTH AFRICA

SOUTH AFRICA

The coast north from the Cape becomes progressively drier and hotter. Along the south coast the weather is temperate, but further north the east coast gets increasingly tropical. KwaZulu-Natal and the Transkei region can be hot and very humid in summer, although the highlands are still pleasant; it's also a summer rainfall area. Mpumalanga and Limpopo Province lowvelds get very hot in summer, when there are spectacular storms. In winter the days are sunny and warm.

ECOLOGY & ENVIRONMENT

South Africa is ranked as the third most biologically diverse country in the world. A major environmental challenge for the government is to manage increasing population growth and urbanisation while protecting this diverse environment. The HIV crisis looks set to take a massive toll on South Africa's population figures. Currently growing at 2% per year, the population is predicted to begin falling by 2010 as life expectancy falls. With half of South Africa's people living in towns and cities, 30,000 hectares of farmland are being lost to the spread of urban centres annually.

This is putting more pressure on agricultural land, and overuse of woody vegetation for fuel, livestock grazing and soil cultivation have caused vegetation and soil degradation, particularly in former Homeland areas. Adding to the problem are both water and wind erosion, which are responsible for the loss of 500 million tonnes of topsoil each year.

The currently rising population also contributes to an increase in the demand for water. To try to meet demand, all major rivers in South Africa have been dammed or modified – a practice that disrupts local ecosystems.

Conservation of native fauna is an active concern and although we can only dimly imagine the extent of the loss since the arrival of Europeans, a significant amount remains. However, many species are threatened and extinction rates are high. An estimated 37% of the country's mammals and 36% of its freshwater fish species are threatened with extinction. Protected areas assist conservation, but only 6% of natural land habitat and 17% of the coastline in South Africa is under formal protection. Provincial funding of many national parks and reserves has been recently cut, making it harder for parks to protect their inhabitants.

FLORA & FAUNA

The world's flora is divided into just six floral kingdoms and South Africa is the only country with one of these kingdoms within its borders. This is the Cape Floral Kingdom in Western Cape with its characteristic fynbos (fine bush), primarily proteas, heaths and ericas – see the 'Fynbos' boxed text for more.

Fynbos

The plants of the world are divided into six floral 'kingdoms', including the Australian Kingdom and the Boreal Kingdom (most of Europe, Asia and North America). By far the smallest is the Cape Floral Kingdom, which covers only the southern tip of South Africa, from the Cape Peninsula east to Grahamstown. The major vegetation type here is the unique 'fynbos' (Afrikaans for fine bush), which takes on a sort of 'Lord of the Rings' appearance. Local conditions (including poor soil and frequent winds) caused the plants to evolve fine leaves.

Over 8000 different species of fynbos plants have been recorded in the Cape Floral Kingdom, making it the most densely speciated plant community in the world. The Cape Peninsula alone (including Table Mountain) contains over 2250 plant species in just 470 sq km – more species than in the whole of Britain, which is 5000 times bigger. Most species belong to the protea, erica (heather) and restios (reed) families, as well as seven other plant families found nowhere else in the world. More than 70% of fynbos plants are endemic to the area.

Fynbos vegetation is under serious threat from the spread of alien plants such as hakea, pine and Australian wattle. Other significant threats include fire, commercial forestry and the development of housing estates and farms. To protect this unique flora, there are calls to proclaim the Cape Floral Kingdom an internationally recognised Biosphere Reserve.

In the drier areas there are succulents, dominated by euphorbias and aloes, and annuals, which flower brilliantly after spring rainfall (see Namaqualand in the Northern Cape Province section later in this chapter).

In contrast to this wealth, South Africa is very poor in natural forests. Although forests were more widespread in the past, they were never particularly extensive. Today, only a few protected remnants remain (see Flora & Fauna in the Facts about the Region chapter).

You probably have a better chance of seeing the Big Five – buffaloes, lions, leopards, elephants and black rhinos – in South Africa than in any other African country. It is also home to the last substantial populations of black and white rhinos (with horns intact). For descriptions of fauna, see the colour Wildlife Guide.

There is also a spectacular variety of birds in South Africa. They range from the largest in the world (ostriches) and the largest flying bird (the kori bustard), to spectacularly coloured sunbirds, flamingos and the extraordinarily sociable weaver birds whose huge colonies live in 'cities' of woven grass.

National Parks & Reserves

National parks and reserves are among South Africa's premier attractions with spectacular scenery, abundant fauna and flora and reasonable prices. Most travellers, especially those with private transport, will find the parks more of a highlight than many of the towns and cities.

In addition to the countrywide South African National Parks Board, the provinces also have conservation bodies. However, unless otherwise indicated, the following parks fall under the control of the National Parks Board (only a small selection of the nation's parks is listed here).

In Kruger National Park (with exceptions) and Kgalagadi Transfrontier Park (formerly Kalahari-Gemsbok National Park), visitors are confined to vehicles so without a car you'll have to take a tour. Renting a car is the best way to get to and around the parks (4WD is not necessary).

If you want to walk in any of the other parks or reserves, you'll usually need permits from the appropriate authorities in advance, and you're nearly always restricted to staying overnight in official camp sites or huts.

The national parks all have rest camps offering a range of good-value accommodation, from cottages to camp sites. Most have restaurants, shops and petrol pumps. There's no need to book camp sites (except at busy holiday times), but it's advisable to book cottages ahead.

Entrances to parks and reserves normally close around sunset. Listed here are some of the main booking addresses; for others see the individual park entries later in this chapter.

Cape Nature Conservation (☎ 021-426 0723, W www.capenature.co.za) Private Bag X9086, Cape Town 8000. This organisation controls a surprisingly diverse range of reserves and wilderness areas in Western Cape.

Eastern Cape Tourism Board (☎ 043-701 9600, W www.ectourism.co.za) Corner Longfellow & Aquarium Rds, East London 5211. Covers park and reserves in the former Ciskei and Transkei regions.

Free State Dept of Environmental Affairs (☎ 051-403 3435) PO Box 264, Bloemfontein 9300

KwaZulu Wildlife (KZN Wildlife) (☎ 033-845 1000, W www.kznwildlife.com) PO Box 662, Pietermaritzburg, runs all parks in KwaZulu-Natal

South African National Parks Board (☎ 012-428 9111, fax 343 0905, W www.parks-sa.co.za) PO Box 787, Pretoria 0001

Private wildilfe reserves also abound and while entry to these generally costs more than their public equivalents, you can often get closer to the animals. Before deciding which private reserve to visit, it's worth asking a specialist travel agent about any special deals going. **Pathfinders Travel** (☎ 011-453 1113/4, fax 453 1483; Shop 16, Linksfield Terrace, Linksfield Rd, Benderwood, Johannesburg) is very helpful.

South Africa's national parks and private reserves include:

Western Cape

Bontebok National Park Proclaimed to protect the last herds of bontcbok, a beautiful antelope unique to the Cape, this park is small but pleasant. It is just south of Swellendam.

Cape of Good Hope Nature Reserve This reserve protects a dramatic coastline and the unique Cape Floral Kingdom, with some of the best examples of fynbos.

Cederberg Wilderness Area Administered by Cape Nature Conservation, Cederberg comprises 71,000 hectares of rugged valleys and peaks (up to 2000m), characterised by extraordinary sandstone formations. The vegetation is predominantly mountain fynbos, and includes the rare

Clanwilliam cedar. Mammals include baboons, rheboks, klipspringers and predators such as the honey badger and caracal.

De Hoop Nature Reserve De Hoop includes a scenic coastline, a freshwater lake and the Potberg Range. It's one of the best places to see both mountain and lowland fynbos. Fauna includes Cape mountain zebras, bonteboks and a wealth of birdlife. The reserve covers 41,000 hectares to the east of Bredasdorp and is administered by Cape Nature Conservation.

Karoo National Park This park, near Beaufort West encloses 32,000 hectares of classic Karoo landscape and a representative selection of its flora and fauna. There's a three-day hiking trail and excellent accommodation.

Northern Cape Province

Augrabies Falls National Park This park, 120km west of Upington, features the dramatic Augrabies Falls, where the Orange River drops into a solid granite ravine.

Goegap Nature Reserve 10km from Springbok, Goegap is famous for its extraordinary display of spring flowers and its nursery of more than 200 amazing Karoo and Namaqualand succulents. In addition to the flora, there are springboks, zebras and birds.

Kgalagadi Transfrontier Park Formerly Kalahari-Gemsbok National Park, this is not as famous as many other African parks, but it supports large populations of birds, reptiles, small mammals, springboks, gemsboks, blue wildebeests, red hartebeests and elands. These in turn support a large population of predators – lions, leopards, cheetahs, hyenas, jackals and foxes.

Richtersveld National Park Protecting 162,000 hectares of high-altitude, mountainous desert bordering Orange River in the province's north-western corner, Richtersveld offers spectacular countryside and flora. The park is very rugged and it will be a while before it is easily accessible.

Eastern Cape

Addo Elephant National Park Addo, north of Port Elizabeth, protects the last remnant of the great elephant herds that once roamed the province. It is small, but the unusual bush (spekboom, sneezewood and guarri) supports a high density of elephants. You would be unlucky not to see one of the 300 or so elephants living in the park.

Karoo Nature Reserve Just outside Graaff-Reinet, this reserve has extraordinary flora, with the weird Karoo succulents well represented. There's also wildlife, interesting birdlife and spectacular rock formations. There are a number of day walks and a two-day hike. The reserve is administered by Cape Nature Conservation.

Mountain Zebra National Park Only 6500 hectares in extent, this park was proclaimed to ensure the survival of the Cape mountain zebras. It covers the rugged northern slopes of the Bankberg Range and there are magnificent views across the mountains and the Karoo plains.

Transkei Area The Transkei coastline is largely untouched, but there are several conservation areas set aside. **Mkambati Nature Reserve** is a coastal reserve with some great scenery, including the Misikaba River Gorge. Other reserves include **Dwesa**, between Coffee Bay and Kei Mouth; **Hluleka**, on the Coffee Bay Trail; and **Silaka**, just south of Port St Johns.

Tsitsikamma Coastal National Park This coastal park encompasses a narrow band of spectacular coast between Plettenberg Bay and Jeffrey's Bay. It is traversed by one of the most famous walks in the country, the Otter Trail, which is an easy five day, 41km trail along the coast.

KwaZulu-Natal

Drakensberg Reserves Along with Golden Gate Highlands National Park in Free State, there are two main reserves in the dramatic Kwa-Zulu-Natal Drakensberg: **Giant's Castle Game Reserve** and **Royal Natal National Park**. Both have spectacular scenery, walking trails and good accommodation. In addition there are the Mkhomazi Wilderness Area, Mzimkulu Wilderness Area and Mzimkulwana Nature Reserve, all of which have excellent hiking.

Greater St Lucia Wetlands This complex of KZN Wildlife reserves centres on Lake St Lucia on the north coast. There are crocodiles and hippos, as well as good fishing and hiking trails. Other big game is being steadily introduced.

Hluhluwe-Umfolozi Park These large, adjoining game reserves have rhinos, lions and elephants. Umfolozi offers guided hiking.

Itala Game Reserve With facilities rivalling much more expensive private reserves, this is the KZN Wildlife's flagship reserve and is worth visiting.

Ndumo Game Reserve On the Mozambique border about 100km north of Mkuze, this remote reserve has black and white rhinos, hippos, crocodiles, antelopes and a wide range of birdlife.

Ntendeka Wilderness In the Zulu heartland, this is a beautiful area of grassland and indigenous forest, with some dramatic cliffs and hiking trails.

Mpumalanga

Blyde River Canyon Nature Reserve A spectacular 60km canyon follows the Blyde River down from the Drakensberg escarpment to the lowveld, and has a huge range of flora and fauna. Book the popular hiking trail through **Blyde River Canyon Nature Reserve** (☎ 013-758 1035, PO Box 1990, Nelspruit 1200).

Free State

Golden Gate Highlands National Park One of the spectacular Drakensberg reserves, this national park is close to the northern border of Lesotho.

QwaQwa Conservation Area This reserve is in the foothills of both the Maluti Mountains and the Drakensberg.

Limpopo

Kruger National Park Kruger is one of the best parks in Africa, if not the world. With all of the Big Five animals, inexpensive accommodation and walking trails (book early), it's not to be missed.

Lapalala Wilderness This private reserve north in the Waterberg Mountains has white rhinos, zebras, blue wildebeests and several antelope species, plus crocodiles. The rivers are bilharzia-free.

Lesheba Wilderness In the Soutpansberg Range, this private reserve has dramatic and varied country and there are plenty of animals, including rhinos.

Nwanedi National Park In the undeveloped Venda region, this park is on the northern side of the Soutpansberg Range and the country is in the lowveld rather than rainforest.

GOVERNMENT & POLITICS

South Africa's constitution became law in 1996. South Africa rejoined the (British) Commonwealth after withdrawing in 1961 when the country became a republic.

There are two houses of parliament: a National Assembly (400 members) and a Senate (90 members). Members of the National Assembly are elected directly (using the proportional representation method – there are no constituencies) but Senate members are appointed by the provincial legislatures. Each province, regardless of its size, appoints 10 senators.

The head of state is the president, currently Thabo Mbeki. The president is elected by the National Assembly (and thus will always be the leader of the majority party), rather than directly by the people.

There are also provincial legislatures, with memberships varying with population: Northern Cape is the smallest with 30 members, and the largest is Gauteng with 86. Each province has a premier. Provincial governments have strictly limited powers and are bound by the national constitution.

In addition to the Western-style democratic system there is a system of traditional leaders: a Council of Traditional Leaders, to which all legislation pertaining to indigenous law, traditions or customs must be referred.

Although the council cannot veto or amend legislation, it can delay its passage. In each province where there have been recognised traditional authorities (every province except Gauteng, Western Cape and Northern Cape), a House of Traditional Leaders will be established with similar powers to the council.

ECONOMY

South Africa's economy is a mixture of First and Third World with a marked disparity in incomes, standards of living, lifestyles, education and work opportunities. On one hand there is a modern industrialised and urban economy; on the other there is a subsistence agricultural economy that has changed little over a century or more.

Wealth is concentrated in the Pretoria, Witwatersrand, Vereeniging (PWV) area centred on Jo'burg (now the province of Gauteng). This area accounts for an estimated 65% of the country's gross domestic product (GDP) and 25% of the continent's gross product.

Until the discovery of diamonds at Kimberley (1869) and the gold reef on the Witwatersrand (1886), the economy was exclusively agricultural. Since then, mineral wealth has been the key to development. Mining accounts for more than 70% of exports and 13% of GDP.

Both inflation and massive unemployment remain problems, the former exacerbated by the sharp dip in the rand at the end of 2001. Economic growth in the new millenium has been stronger than the global average but is unequally shared.

Nonwhites have too seldom shared in the fruits of their labour and ensuring they do so in the future is a daunting task. The economy is still geared to a limitless pool of nonwhite labour (earning Third World rates).

The government is trying to hand some equity in the large corporations (such as the mining conglomcrates) to historically disadvantaged groups to redress some of this unfair distribution, but it's a slow, complicated process.

The spread of AIDS is likely to have a significant effect on the economy in years to come (see the boxed text 'One in Five Million').

POPULATION & PEOPLE

Of the population of 43.7 million, some 32 million are of Bantu origin, five million

SOUTH AFRICA

One in Five Million

South African Zackie Achmat is one in a million. Actually he's one among 4.7 million South Africans with HIV/AIDS.

What makes the extraordinarily brave Mr Achmat special, however, is that he has refused take AIDS drugs (which he could easily afford and which could probably save his life) in protest at the South African government's refusal to properly acknowledge the effects of the virus on its people or to supply the drugs to fight it.

Without the drugs, a significant segment of the working-age population will succumb to illness as the AIDS crisis in Southern Africa moves from what the UN calls 'the era of infection' to 'the era of sickness'.

The statistics are chilling: As much as 20% of the adult population could be infected. AIDS killed 360,000 people in 2001 and has already created 660,000 orphans.

But the statistics only hint at the likely human and economic impact of the pandemic. Instead of the usual population pyramid you see on census graphs, South Africa's looks set to become hourglass shaped – representing a population of predominantly elderly and young people as the economically active generation dwindles.

What this will mean for the future prosperity and stability of the country is anyone's guess. Sick leave among teachers and government workers is already increasing and in rural areas, illness from HIV is compounding the effects of poor harvests and drought.

Tales of unimaginable suffering – children missing school to care for dying parents, perhaps burying them in their gardens for the lack of mortuary fees – are heartbreakingly common.

The good news is that the government seems to be waking up to the problem, educational programmes are cutting infection rates, big corporations have pledged to supply workers with drugs and at last pregnant women seem set to get the drugs they need to prevent infection passing onto their children.

The long-term prognosis should be good. Treatment, and along with it the life expectancy of those who receive it, is constantly improving. And key workers should be the first to benefit. The question is, how many others will?

if you're a subsistence farmer in the Transkei, for example, will the government extend treatment to you and your family? Who, apart from Mr Achmat, is standing up for you?

white, three million 'coloured' (ie, mixed race) and one million of Indian descent. Some 60% of the whites are Afrikaner and most of the rest are of British descent.

Most of the 'coloured' population lives in Northern and Western Cape Provinces. Cape Muslims are South Africans of long standing. Although many were brought to the early Cape Colony as slaves, others were political prisoners from the Dutch East Indies. Most South Africans of Indian descent live in KwaZulu-Natal.

Limpopo, Mpumalanga and the Free State are the Afrikaner heartlands. People of British descent are concentrated in Kwa-Zulu-Natal and Western and Eastern Cape Provinces.

Although the Homelands no longer have any political meaning and were never realistic indicators of the area's cultural diversity, it's useful to have some idea of where the Homelands were and who lived (and still

live) in them. Zulus are the largest group (seven million), followed by the Xhosa (six million) and the various Northern Sotho peoples, most of whom are Tswana. The smallest group are the Venda (500,000).

The Homelands and their peoples were:

Homelands	People
Bophuthatswana	Tswana
Ciskei	Xhosa
Gazankulu	Tsonga
KwaNdebele	Ndebele
KwaNgwane	Swazi
KwaZulu	Zulu
Lebowa	Lobedu
QwaQwa	South Sotho
Transkei	Xhosa
Venda	Venda

Superficially, urbanised European culture doesn't seem to differ much from that found in other Western countries. However, the unique experience of the white people

The Zulu & the Xhosa

The Xhosa and the Zulu are two of the most important ethnic groups in South Africa. Both have played central roles in shaping the country's history and both are important constituents in the ethnic, linguistic and political make-up of modern day South Africa.

Zulu

The name Zulu (Heaven) comes from an early chief. His descendants were *abakwaZulu* (people of Zulu). Under a chief called Shaka, the Zulu became a large and dominant tribe, and since that time the *inoksa* (king) has been the leader of all the people. Before Shaka there was a looser organisation of local chiefs and almost self-sufficient family groups.

The Zulu *kraal* (village) is usually circular, often with a defensive wall of dead saplings and branches. The huts are hemispherical and made of tightly woven grasses. Inside the hut the right-hand side is for the men and the left-hand side is for the women, with ancestral spirits allocated a space at the rear.

In common with other peoples, the important stages of life – birth, puberty, marriage and death – are marked by ceremonies. The clothes people wear reflect their status and age. For example, girls may not wear long skirts until they become engaged. Animal skins are worn to reflect status, with a leopard-skin cloak signifying a chief.

Dancing and singing are important and if you see a large Zulu gathering, such as an Inkatha Freedom Party (IFP) demonstration you'll feel something of the stirring power of massed Zulu singing.

The Zulu traditionally believe that the creator of the world is Unkulunkulu (Old, Old Man), but his daughter uNomkubulwana is more important in day-to-day life as she controls the rain. Still more important are ancestors, who can make most things go well or badly depending on how assiduously a person has carried out the required sacrifices and observances.

Today Zulus maintain a strong sense of identity both culturally and politically. Zulus are proud of their mighty heritage and gather in huge numbers for several festivals including the annual Reed Dance and King Shaka Day festival.

The George hotel in Eshowe is the place to find out about attending these and other Zulu ceremonies or about visits to Zulu villages. For a slightly more contrived (but still well executed) portrayal of Zulu song and ceremony, Shakaland runs daily shows (see Zululand later in this chapter for more details).

Xhosa

The Xhosa, many of whom maintain a traditional lifestyle, are known as red people because of the red-dyed clothing worn by most adults. Different subgroups wear different colours and arrangements of beads. The Tembu and Bomvana favour red and orange ochres in the dyeing of their clothing, and the Pondo and Mpondomise use a very light-blue ochre (although chemical dyes are now much in use).

The Xhosa deity is known variously as uDali, Tixo and Qwamata, which also figured in the San religion and it is probable that the invading Xhosa adopted it from them. There's a pantheon of numerous minor spirits and a rich folklore persists in rural areas. A belief in witches (male or female) is strong and witch-burning still occurs. The Xhosa believe most witchcraft is evil, and their main fear is that people will be possessed by depraved spirits. The main source of evil is the *tokoloshe* which lives in water but is also kept by witches.

The *igqirha* (spiritual healer) holds an important place in traditional society because he or she can deal with the forces of nature and the trouble caused by witches. The *ix-hwele* (herbalist) performs some magic but is much more concerned with health issues. The *mbongi* are the holders and performers of a group's oral history and are something like a cross between a bard and a court jester.

While there is a hierarchy, the structure of Xhosa society is much looser than that of the Zulus.

Puberty rituals figure heavily for both men and women, and marriage customs and rituals also play a significant role.

Beadwork and jewellery are important. The *danga* is a long turquoise necklace that identifies the wearer to his/her ancestors. The *ngxowa yebokwe* is a goatskin bag carried over the left shoulder on important occasions.

An indication of the influence Xhosa have on modern day South Africa is the profusion of high-ranking ANC posts held by people of Xhosa descent, including former president Nelson Mandela.

of Africa has given them a self-awareness that has raised culture to an issue of central importance. Those of Afrikaner and British descent form distinct subgroups.

Despite the strength of traditional black culture in the countryside, the mingling of peoples in South Africa's urban areas means that old cultures are fading and others are emerging.

ARTS

Although South Africa is home to a great diversity of cultures, most were suppressed during the apartheid years. To an extent, the Homelands kept alive some of the traditional cultures, but in a static form. The day-to-day realities of traditional and contemporary cultures were ignored, trivialised or destroyed.

Many artists, black and white, were involved in the anti-apartheid campaign and some were banned. In a society where you could be jailed for owning a politically incorrect painting, serious art was forced underground and blandness ruled in the galleries and theatres. *Resistance Art in South Africa* by Sue Williamson gives an overview of South African art during these times.

It will take time for the damage to be undone, but there is hope. Many galleries are holding retrospective exhibitions of contemporary and traditional black artists, and musicians from around Africa perform in major festivals.

Jazz was about the only medium in which blacks and whites could interact on equal terms, and it remains tremendously important. Theatre was also important for blacks, both as an art form and as a way of getting political messages across to illiterate comrades.

Literature

Nadine Gordimer was awarded the Nobel Prize for Literature in 1991. Her first novel, *The Lying Days*, was published in 1953, and *The Conservationist* was the joint winner of the 1974 Booker Prize. Her more recent work explores the interracial dynamics of the country – look for *July's People* and *A Sport of Nature*.

JM Coetzee is another contemporary writer who has received international acclaim; he's a double Booker Prize winner for *The Life & Times of Michael K* (1983) and the bleakly brilliant *Disgrace* (1999).

Alan Paton was responsible for one of the most famous South African novels, *Cry the Beloved Country*, an epic that follows a black man's sufferings in a white, urban society.

Indaba My Children is an interesting book of folk tales, history, legends, customs and beliefs, collected and told by Vusamazulu Credo Mutwa. Published literature by non-white authors is in short supply although the situation is changing.

LANGUAGE

South Africa's official languages were once English and Afrikaans but nine others have been added. These are: Ndebele, South Sotho, North Sotho, Swati, Tsonga, Tswana, Venda, Xhosa and Zulu. The most widely spoken are English, Afrikaans, South Sotho, Xhosa and Zulu. (For more information on the official languages of South Africa and for some useful words and phrases, see the Language chapter at the back of this book.)

Facts for the Visitor

SUGGESTED ITINERARIES

The longer your trip in South Africa the better; it's a huge and diverse place with a vast amount of amazing places to see. If time is limited you will have some tough decisions deciding what to leave out. The following presumes you are starting from around either Cape Town or Jo'burg and is far from exhaustive.

In particular, don't forget the Transkei and the Wild Coast in Eastern Cape, which is well worth a detour. Don't forget also that from 2003, some international flights should be landing in Nelspruit, close to the Kruger National Park (and also handy for entry to Mozambique), so you may be able to plan an itinerary starting in the North of the country that avoids Jo'burg.

Two Weeks

A week probably isn't quite enough to explore beautiful and relaxed Cape Town with its vibrant nightlife, stunning Table Mountain and mouth-watering cuisine. Extraordinary beauty awaits you less than an hour's drive from the city centre. The Cape of Good Hope Nature Reserve has a rugged elemental charm (and fascinating flora). The more cultivated beauty of the wine country around the nearby

towns of Stellenbosch and Franschhoek, is a food and wine lover's paradise.

If you enter the country via Jo'burg, you could spend a few days in the city where the change – good and bad – in South Africa is happening first. Don't miss the excellent Apartheid Museum. Nearby Pretoria is more relaxed and worth a look, especially if you're there while the jacarandas are flowering in spring. Kruger National Park, South Africa's premier attraction with perhaps the best wildlife viewing in Africa, is a four-hour drive from Jo'burg. Book your accommodation well in advance, especially in the high season. A few days inside the park and a few days meandering along the scenic Blyde River Canyon in the Klein Drakensberg will have you planning your return trip.

One Month

Starting with two weeks around Cape Town, if you had a month you could extend your trip further to include some whale watching at Hermanus (make sure it's the right season – June to November) and then potter along the Garden Route's magnificent scenery, enjoy numerous outdoor activities from hiking to shark-cage diving and sample its bustling towns such as Knysna and Plettenberg Bay.

Alternatively, after spending time around Kruger, you could head down to KwaZulu-Natal where you'll find magnificent national parks, glimpses of Zulu culture and the subtropical city of Durban, where you can relax in the sun and surf or party in its lively bars and clubs. If you have time to spare, the spectacular Drakensberg Escarpment is a magnet for hikers.

The Big Trip

South Africa's large international airports and excellent air and road links into the entire region make it a logical entry point into Southern Africa.

Starting in the far South (Cape Town) is as practical as starting further north in Johannesburg and really just depends on how much of South Africa you want to see before heading into the rest of the region.

Top Tips

This is a huge country, with massive distances to cover and so much to see, so think very carefully about how you'll get around.

A car may be best, and hiring them can be dirt cheap especially if you book ahead or if there's a group of you.

If time is tight and you want to take in the main attractions north and south, internal flights, although not amazingly cheap will save you valuable time and energy.

The Baz Bus is a good, sociable alternative to car hire. Pricier than the coach lines but offering a door to door hostel service to a mainly young backpacker crowd, it can help you minimise travelling, waiting and general faffing time, although you'll still need to plan your itinerary around its timetable.

As far as the weather goes, don't assume you'll be basking in sunshine all the time. Outside the summer, Jo'burg nights can be freezing and Cape Town can endure cold, wet spells throughout much of the year.

PLANNING
When to Go

In many places, especially the lowveld, summer (December to February) can be uncomfortably hot. The warm waters of the east coast make swimming a year-round proposition. Spring (September to December) is the best time for wildflowers in the Northern and Western Cape Provinces and they are at their peak in Namaqualand (Northern Cape) from mid-August to mid-September. Winter (June to August) is mild except in the highest country, which experiences frosts and occasional snowfalls. Summer brings warmer weather but also rain and mist to the mountains.

Many people take their annual holidays from mid-December to late January, with several overlapping waves of holiday-makers streaming out of the cities. Then, as well as during the other school holidays, resorts and national parks are heavily booked and prices on the coast can more than double. The KwaZulu-Natal coast, especially south of Durban, is packed. The absolute peak time is from Christmas to mid-January but as the Cape in particular becomes increasingly popular with overseas visitors the season is starting as early as November.

Maps

Good maps are widely available. For a sturdy and helpful map of Cape Town, see Lonely Planet's *Cape Town City Map*.

South African Tourism (formerly Satour) hands out a reasonable countrywide map.

SOUTH AFRICA

The **Map Office** (☎ *011-339 4941; 40 De Korte St, Jo'burg*) sells government topographic maps for around US$6.90 a sheet.

The Michelin maps are excellent and the Map Studio series is recommended. The **Map Studio** has offices in Cape Town (☎ *021-510 4311)*, Jo'burg (☎ *011 807 2292)* and Durban (☎ *031-263 1203)* and also sells government topographic maps.

TOURIST OFFICES

South African Tourism handles international promotion, while the provincial authorities have their own tourist boards (of hugely varying standards) for local information.

Local Tourist Offices

Just about every town in the country has a tourist office, although some of the provincial organisations are very new at the job and have little practical information.

Tourist Offices Abroad

South African Tourism (W *www.southafrica .net)* produces some glossy guides, which can be fairly useful. They are free outside the country but expensive within South Africa.

South African Tourism offices abroad include:

Australia (☎ 02-9231 4444, fax 9231 2444, W www.southafrica.com.au) Level 6, 5 Elizabeth St, Sydney, NSW 2000
France (☎ 01 45 61 01 97, fax 01 45 61 01 96, e paris@southafricantourism.com) 61 Rue La Boëtie, 75008 Paris
Germany (☎ 69-929 1290, fax 28 0950, e info@ southafricantourism.de) An der Hauptwache 11D-60313 Frankfurt/Main 1, Postfach 101940, 60019 Frankfurt
UK (☎ 020-8971 9352, fax 8944 6705, e info@ south-african-tourism.org) 5 Alt Grove, London SW19 4DZ
USA (☎ 212-730 2929, fax 764 1980) 500 Fifth Ave, 20th floor, New York, NY 10110

VISAS & DOCUMENTS
Visas

Entry permits, entitling a 90-day stay, are issued free on arrival to nationals of many Commonwealth countries and the vast majority of West European countries, including Ireland, France, Germany, and also the USA.

Other nationalities may need a visa. Visas are usually free and multi-entry, but are not issued at the border, so you must get one in advance – South Africa has consular representation in most countries, but outside Southern Africa allow at least a couple of weeks for the process.

On arrival you might have to satisfy an immigration officer that you have sufficient funds for your stay. If you arrive by air, you should in theory have an onward ticket. An air ticket is best but overland travel seems to be acceptable. If you come by land, things are more relaxed.

Visa Extensions Apply for a visa extension or a re-entry visa at the **Department of Home Affairs** (☎ *012-324 1860; Sentrakor Bldg, Pretorius St, Pretoria • ☎ 021-462 4970; 56 Barrack St, Cape Town, also Jo'burg or Durban)*. Extensions applied for this way cost about US$57.

Visas for Onward Travel

If you need visas for neighbouring countries, the embassies and high commissions are generally open for applications from 7.30am to 12.30pm and 1.45pm to 4.30pm weekdays. However, visas are easily available at the Botswana–Zambia, South Africa–Mozambique and Botswana–Zimbabwe border crossings.

Botswana Visas cost US$5, and take between four and 14 days to process. Two passport photos needed.
Lesotho Visas cost US$2.30 and take 24 hours to issue. You'll need one photo.
Mozambique Visas cost from US$9. They take 24 hours to issue (or immediately at the border, although it's more expensive). You'll need two photos. Visas may be arranged at Nelspruit and Mbabane in Swaziland.
Namibia Visas cost US$16 and take two to three days. No photos are required.
Swaziland Same-day visas cost US$4.60. No photos required.
Zimbabwe Single entry visas cost US$61 and take a minimum of seven days to issue. One passport photo required.

Driving Licence & Permits

You can use your own driving licence if it has your photo, otherwise you'll need an International Driving Permit, obtainable from a motoring organisation in your country.

Student Card

A student card can be useful for discounts on some bus services and attractions, such

as museums and cinemas. Try to get an international student card (inquire at your educational institution) before you leave home.

Other Documents

If you have travelled through the yellow fever zone in Africa or South America (including Brazil), you must have a vaccination certificate to show you've been immunised against yellow fever.

EMBASSIES & CONSULATES
South African Embassies & High Commissions

South Africa has embassies and high commissions in the following African countries: Botswana, Kenya, Lesotho, Malawi, Mozambique, Namibia, Swaziland, Zambia and Zimbabwe. (Embassies for countries in this book are listed in the relevant country chapters.)

Elsewhere in the world, places with a South African embassy or high commission include:

Australia (☎ 02-6273 2424, fax 6273 3543, e info@rsa.emb.gov.au) Rhodes Place, Yarralumla, Canberra, ACT 2600
Belgium (☎ 02-285 4400, fax 02-285 4402, e embassy.southafrica@belgium.online.be) 26 Rue de la Loi, Box 7/8 Brussels 1000
Canada (☎ 613-744 0330, fax 741 1639, e rs africa@sympatico.co.za) 15 Sussex Dr, Ottawa, K1M 1M8
France (☎ 01 53 59 23 23, fax 01 53 59 23 33) 59 Quai d'Orsay, 75343 Paris
Germany (☎ 030-22 0730, fax 220 7310, e botschaft@suedafrika.org) Friedrichstrasse 60, Berlin 10117
Ireland (☎ 1-661 5553, e information@saedub lin.com) 2nd floor, Alexandra House, Earlsfort Centre, Dublin 2
Netherlands (☎ 70-392 4501, fax 346 0669, e info@zuidafrika.nl) Wassenaarseweg 40, The Hague
Sweden (☎ 08-243 950, fax 660 7136, e saemb .swe@telia.com) Linnégatan 76, 115 23 Stockholm
UK (☎ 020-7451 7299, fax 7451 7284, e general@southafricahouse.com) South Africa House, Trafalgar Square, London WC2N 5DP
USA (☎ 202-232 4400, fax 265 1607, e safrica@southafrica.net) 3051 Massachusetts Ave NW, Washington DC 20008 (also consulates in Chicago, Los Angeles and New York)

Embassies & Consulates in South Africa

Most countries have their main embassy or high commission in Pretoria, with an office or consulate in Cape Town that becomes the official embassy during Cape Town's parliamentary sessions. However, many countries also maintain consulates (which can arrange visas and passports) in Jo'burg.

Many consulates are only open in the morning. For a full list, see the Yellow Pages.

Australia (☎ 012-342 3781) 292 Orient St, Arcadia, Pretoria. Open from 8.45am to 12.30pm weekdays.
Belgium (☎ 011-447 5495) 158 Jan Smuts Bldg, 9 Walters Ave, Rosebank, Johannesburg (also represented in Pretoria and Cape Town). Open from 9am to noon weekdays.
Botswana (☎ 021-421 1045) 4th floor, Southern Life Centre, 8 Reibeeck St, City Bowl Open from 8am to 1pm weekdays.
Canada (☎ 012-422 3000) 1103 Arcadia St, Hatfield, Pretoria. Open from 8am to noon weekdays.
France (☎ 011-778 5600, e fconsjhb@cis.co.za) 3rd floor, Standard Bank Bldg, 191 Jan Smuts Ave (corner of Seventh Ave), Rosebank, Johannesburg (also represented in Pretoria and Cape Town). Open from 8.30am to 1pm weekdays
Germany (☎ 012-427 8999) 180 Blackwood St, Arcadia, Pretoria (also has a consulate in Cape Town). Open from 7.30 to 11am weekdays, except Wednesday (9am to 11.30am)
Ireland (☎ 012-342 5062) 1234 Church St, Colbyn, Pretoria. Open from 8.30am to 1pm weekdays
Lesotho (☎ 012-460 7648, fax 460 7649) 391 Anderson St, Menlo Park, Pretoria. Open from 9am to 4.30pm weekdays
Mozambique (☎ 012-401 0300) 529 Edmund St, Arcadia, Pretoria (Mozambique also has consulates in Jo'burg, Cape Town, Nelspruit and Durban). Open from 8.30am to 12.30pm weekdays
Namibia (☎ 012-481 9100) 197 Blackwood St, Arcadia, Pretoria. Open from 8.30am to 12.30pm weekdays
Netherlands (☎ 012-344 3910) 825 Arcadia St, Arcadia, Pretoria (also a consulate in Cape Town and an honorary consul in Durban). Open from 9am to noon weekdays
Swaziland (☎ 012-344 1910) 715 Government Ave, Arcadia, Pretoria (also a consulate in Jo'burg). Open from 9am to 12.30pm and 2.30pm to 4pm weekdays
UK (☎ 012-483 1200) 255 Hill St, Arcadia, Pretoria (also has consulates in Jo'burg and Cape Town). Open 8.45am to noon weekdays

USA (☎ 012-342 1048) 877 Pretorius St, Arcadia, Pretoria (also has consulates in Jo'burg and Cape Town). Open 8am to noon weekdays

Zambian (☎ 012-326 1847, fax 012-326 2140) 1159 Ziervogel St, off Hamilton St, Arcadia, Pretoria. Open 9am-12.30pm weekdays

Zimbabwe (☎ 011-838 5620) 17th floor, 20 Anderson St, Marshalltown, Johannesburg (also has a high commission in Pretoria ☎ 012-342 5126). Open 8.30am to noon weekdays, except Wednesday

CUSTOMS

South Africa, Botswana, Namibia, Swaziland and Lesotho are all part of the South African Customs Union, which means the internal borders are effectively open from a customs point of view. When you enter the union, however, you're restricted in the normal way to personal effects: 1L of spirits, 2L of wine and 400 cigarettes. Motor vehicles must be covered by a carnet. For information contact the **Department of Customs & Excise** (☎ 012-284308) in Pretoria.

MONEY

The unit of currency is the rand (R), which is divided into 100 cents. There is no black market.

The coins are: 1, 2, 5, 10, 20 and 50 cents; 1, 2 and 5 rand. The notes are: R10, R20, R50, R100 and R200. The rarely seen R200 note looks a lot like the R20 note, so take care. There have been forgeries of the R200 note and some businesses are reluctant to accept them.

Exchange Rates

At the time of going to print, the currency exchange rates were as follows:

country	unit		rand
Australia	A$1	=	R5.28
Botswana	P1	=	R1.54
Canada	C$1	=	R5.90
euro zone	€1	=	R9.35
Japan	¥100	=	R6.77
Malawi	Mk1	=	R0.09
Mozambique	Mtc100	=	R0.03
Namibia	N$1	=	R1.02
New Zealand	NZ$1	=	R4.60
UK	UK£1	=	R13.30
USA	US$1	=	R7.97
Zambia	ZK100	=	R0.16
Zimbabwe	ZW$100	=	R0.98

ATM Scams

Beware of ATM scams when you draw cash. Refuse any help or distraction from 'kindly' strangers while at an ATM and if you can, draw cash during office hours. Go for ATMs in shopping malls, preferably ones watched over by security guards. If possible draw cash with a friend so that if the machine swallows your card, one of you can report it inside while the other stays with the machine to watch for the card.

Exchanging Money

The Thomas Cook agent is Rennies Travel, a large chain of travel agencies, and there are American Express offices in the big cities. Neither charges commission on its own travellers cheques. Nedbank is associated with American Express. First National Bank and Nedbank are associated with Visa. Most other banks change travellers cheques in major currencies, with various commission charges.

Keep at least some of the receipts you get when changing money as you'll need to show them to reconvert your rands when you leave.

Credit cards, especially Visa and MasterCard, are widely accepted and cards with the Cirrus logo occasionally so. Most ATMs give cash advances.

Costs

With a depressed rand, South Africa is cheaper than ever to travel in. Inflation has been more than outstripped by the devaluation of the rand so it's great value by European, US and Australian standards.

Shoestring travellers will find self-catering while camping or staying in hostels, or bungalows is the cheapest option, often working out to US$4.60 to US$7 per person. Sit-down meals in restaurants work out to between US$5 to US$7 per person, less in pubs.

Mid-range travellers will find accommodation in self-catering cottages, B&Bs and hotels costs around US$25 to US$46 – the standard is usually high. Distances are large, so transport can be infrequent and expensive; hiring or buying a car can be worthwhile both for convenience and economy as fuel is cheap (see the Getting Around section later in this chapter, and the Getting Around the Region chapter).

Tipping

Tipping is pretty well mandatory because of the very low wages. Around 10% to 15% is usual.

Taxes & Refunds

Value Added Tax (VAT) is levied at 14%, but departing foreign visitors can reclaim VAT on goods being taken out of the country (so you can't claim back the VAT on food or car rental, for example).

To make a claim you need the tax invoices (usually the receipt, but make sure the shop is VAT registered and get a full receipt). The total value of your purchases must exceed R250 (US$28.50).

When you depart you'll have to fill out a couple of forms and show the goods to a customs inspector. There's an efficient system in place in the Cape Town Tourism offices and those of other major cities enabling you to process the paperwork beforehand.

At airports make sure you have the goods checked by an inspector before you check in your luggage. You pick up your refund cheque after you've gone through immigration.

POST & COMMUNICATIONS

Post

South Africa has reasonably good post and telecommunications facilities. Most post offices open from 8.30am to 4.30pm Monday to Friday and 8am to noon on Saturday. Aerograms and internal letters cost about US$0.25, postcards US$0.35 and airmail letters US$0.40 to send. Internal delivery can be very slow and international delivery isn't exactly lightning fast.

Telephone

Local telephone calls are fairly cheap. Phonecards are widely available (see under ekno Communication Card later in this section).

Long-distance and international telephone calls are very expensive. There are private phone centres where you can pay cash for your call without feeding coins into the slot of a public phone, but at double the rate. Calls from some hotels can also be charged at exorbitant rates.

All South African telephone books give full details of service numbers and codes.

The following are useful directory service numbers within South Africa:

Directory service	(☎)
Inquiries (local)	1023
Inquiries (national and international)	1025
Reverse-charge calls (national)	0020
Reverse-charge calls (international)	0900

When dialling overseas from South Africa, add ☎ 09 before the country code (see the list of codes under Post & Communications in the Regional Facts for the Visitor chapter). When making calls to South Africa from outside the country, dial the international access code, then ☎ 27, then the area code in South Africa (dropping the zero), and then the telephone number.

International calls are cheaper after 8pm on weekdays and between 8pm Friday and 8am Monday.

To avoid high charges when calling home, dial your 'Country Direct' number, which puts you through to an operator in your country. You can then either place a call on your 'phone home' account, if you have one, or place a reverse-charge call. To find out your Country Direct number, call a major telecommunications company in your country.

Lonely Planet's ekno card provides cheap international calls for travellers. You can join online at w www.ekno.lonelyplanet.com. The access numbers from South Africa are ☎ 0800-997285 or ☎ 0800-992921.

Mobile Phones The mobile (cell) phone network covers most of the country and mobile phone ownership is widespread. Mobile phone hire (try Jo'burg international airport or certain Vodacom shops) is cheap, but call charges are high. Some car rental firms throw in a mobile phone loan with rentals. A cheap alternative is to use your own phone (check ahead that it's compatible) and insert a local pay-as-you-go SIM card from one of the three mobile networks: Vodacam, MTN and Cell C. SIM cards are cheap, starting at about US$4.60.

Plenty of places sell top-up cards in denominations of about US$3.50 and up. Calls typically cost from US$0.35 per minute.

There are three different mobile networks in South Africa with varied prefixes; ☎ 072, ☎ 073, ☎ 082, ☎ 083, and ☎ 084.

Fax

You can fax most organisations and businesses. Phone books list fax numbers. You can send faxes from private phone centres.

Email & Internet Access

Internet access costs from US$2.30 to US$4.60 per hour and can be found almost anywhere in South Africa; many hostels offer email facilities.

DIGITAL RESOURCES

There's no better place to start your Web explorations than the Lonely Planet website (W www.lonelyplanet.com) where you'll find postcards from other travellers and the useful Thorn Tree notice board where you can post questions and read answers from other travellers.

The following websites are also worth a surf. (For regional listings, see also Internet Resources in the Regional Facts for the Visitor chapter).

Baz Bus (W www.bazbus.com) Transport specifically geared towards budget travellers (see also Bus in the Getting Around section later in this chapter)

Intercape Mainliner (W www.intercape.co.za) Coaches operating throughout Southern Africa (see also Bus in the Getting Around section later in this chapter)

South African National Parks (W www.parks-sa .co.za) Information and bookings for national parks around the country

South African Tourism (W www.southafrica.net) The government-run tourism organisation's international website

Womensnet (W www.womensnet.org.za) A government-sponsored women's Internet resource

BOOKS

This section covers books specific to South Africa. (For information on books about the Southern Africa region, see Books in the Regional Facts for the Visitor chapter.)

Lonely Planet

Lonely Planet also publishes *South Africa, Lesotho & Swaziland* with more detail on these three countries; *Cape Town*, an exhaustive guide to the city and Cape areas; and the classic *Africa on a Shoestring* for budget travellers.

Guidebooks

The Automobile Association (AA) publishes some handy paperback guides to caravan parks, guesthouses and hotels, available in most bookshops.

History & Politics

Long Road to Freedom, by Nelson Mandela, this extraordinary autobiography is almost compulsory reading for any visitor interested in South Africa's recent history.

The Mind of South Africa, by Allister Sparks, is a good introduction to white South African history.

My Traitor's Heart, by Rian Malan, is a brutally honest portrait of the Afrikaner mindset, the history that shaped it and a dissection of the tortured complexity of South African race relations. It is grisly, but compelling.

A History of South Africa, by Frank Welsh, is a worthy, compendious account of the country's colonial history.

General

Exploring Southern Africa on Foot: Guide to Hiking Trails, by Willie & Sandra Olivier, although it is out of print this book is outstanding if you can find it.

John Platter's South African Wine Guide, updated annually and incredibly detailed, covers all available wines.

The Safari Companion, by Richard Estes, is a highly recommended guide to the behaviour of the major African wildlife species.

Complete Guide to Walks and Trails in Southern Africa, by Jaynee Levy, is a thorough tome. Also look out for *Western Cape Walks,* by David Bristow.

NEWSPAPERS & MAGAZINES

Major English-language newspapers are published in the cities and sold across the country, although in Afrikaans-speaking areas and the ex-Homelands they may not be available in every little town.

The *Sowetan* is the biggest-selling paper in the country and is worth reading as a contrast to the white perspective of many other papers.

The best newspaper or magazine for investigative journalism, sensible overviews and high-quality columnists, not to mention a week's worth of Doonesbury and a good entertainment section, is the *Weekly Mail &*

Guardian (W www.mg.co.za). It also includes a shortened version of the international edition of the British *Guardian*, which includes features from *Le Monde* and the *Washington Post*.

RADIO & TV

The monolithic and conservative South African Broadcasting Corporation (SABC), formerly a government mouthpiece, serves up rather bland fare. The mainstream SABC radio stations (AM and FM) play dreary music and offer drearier chat, but the stations geared to a black audience are well worth channel surfing for some more interesting music.

SABC's SAFM (104-107FM) offers the most reliable reception nationwide and some reasonable drive-time news and current affairs. Richard Nwamba's weekly Saturday afternoon *African Connection* show plays a great mix of pan-African music. For the light entertainment equivalent to a frontal lobotomy, try the station's inane chatter and cheesy 80s rock.

If you're in the Cape, the much-loved Tim Modise hosts a talk show on Cape Talk 567 (MW), great for tuning into the public and political preoccupations of the day.

TV is even worse than radio, with daytime US soap operas playing in prime time, and local programs broadcast in many languages but without subtitles. Some exceptions include gritty urban soaps such as *Isidingo* and *Yizo Yizo*.

Pay-TV channel M-Net, offers a greater choice of movies and channels from around the world.

PHOTOGRAPHY & VIDEO

Films, cameras and accessories are readily available in larger towns. Processing standards are generally high. Print film (24 exposures) costs about US$6.90 plus US$5.60 for processing.

HEALTH

The extent of the HIV/AIDS crisis in South Africa (and the region) almost defies belief. Almost one in nine of its citizens are infected with HIV/AIDS. The virus is transferred through exposure to infected blood, blood products and body fluids. The most effective measure against HIV infection through sexual activity (short of abstinence) is to practice safe sex using condoms.

Malaria and bilharzia do occur in some areas and there's a possibility of hikers drinking contaminated water but otherwise visitors will experience few health problems. Good medical care is never too far away except in the remote areas, where air evacuation of emergency cases is routine. Make sure you have enough insurance (for more details, see Travel Insurance in the Regional Facts for the Visitor chapter).

Problem Areas

Malaria is mainly confined to the eastern part of the country (Limpopo, Mpumalanga, northern KwaZulu-Natal), especially on the lowveld, and around St Lucia and Swaziland. Parts of the Northwest Province may also be malarial. Bilharzia is also found mainly in the east but outbreaks do occur in other places, so you should always check with knowledgeable local people before drinking water or swimming in it.

While hiking in the ex-Homelands or wherever you find yourself drinking from streams (even if there is no bilharzia), make sure that there isn't an upstream village. Typhoid is rare but it does occur. Industrial pollution is common in more settled areas.

WOMEN TRAVELLERS

Many South African men, whatever their colour, have sexism in common. Modern ideas such as equality of the sexes haven't filtered through to many people, especially those away from the cities. There's a very high level of sexual assault and other violence against women in South Africa; as usual most victims (an estimated 60%) know their attackers. For most female visitors, paternalistic attitudes are the main problem rather than physical assault. There have been incidents of female travellers being raped, but these cases are rare and isolated, causing outrage in the local communities and indeed nationally.

A large part of the problem in South Africa is the leniency of the judicial system which repeatedly lets perpetrators of sex offences off with short prison sentences.

For more information, see Dangers & Annoyances later in this section, and Women Travellers in the Regional Facts for the Visitor chapter.

GAY & LESBIAN TRAVELLERS

South Africa's new constitution guarantees freedom of sexual choice and there are small but active and growing gay and lesbian communities and scenes in Cape Town (see Entertainment under Cape Town in the Western Cape section), Jo'burg and Durban. However, the new constitution is a radical legislative move and it will be a while before the more conservative sections of society begin to accept it.

Check out the **GaySA website** (W *www.gay southafrica.co.za*), which has entertainment and travel listings, but be warned that it also contains links to explicit erotic images.

The **Gay & Lesbian Organisation of Pretoria** (☎ *012-344 6501; 133 Verdoorn St, Sunnyside*) has been recommended. It has loads of information such as listings of guesthouses and tour companies.

In Cape Town, the Mother City Queer Project (W *www.mcqp.co.za*) runs the hugely popular December party and festival.

DISABLED TRAVELLERS

People with limited mobility will find the going tough in South Africa. It will certainly be easier to travel with an able-bodied companion. The good news is that there are a growing number of places with ramps, wheelchair access and wheelchair friendly bathrooms. South African Tourism publishes a guide with disability-friendly accommodation.

For information on travelling in South Africa with a disability, try the website W www.access-able.com. The **National Parks Board** website (W *www.parks-sa.co.za*) has useful mobility information for all its parks. See also Disabled Travellers in the Regional Facts for the Visitor chapter.

Titch Tours (☎ *021-686 5501, fax 686 5506;* e *titcheve@iafrica.com;* W *www.titch tours.co.za; 26 Station Rd, Rondebosch, Cape Town*), specialises in tours for visually impaired and physically disabled travellers. It has specialised equipment including a coach with wheelchair lift and hires cars fitted with hand controls for disabled people.

DANGERS & ANNOYANCES

Some specific things to watch out for are listed here. Also keep in mind the natural dangers, from freezing storms in the Drakensberg to crippling heat on the lowveld. For general advice see Dangers & Annoyances in the Regional Facts for the Visitor chapter.

Animals

Crocodiles occur in lowveld rivers and streams. Hippos can also be very dangerous. If you meet one (most likely on and near the KwaZulu-Natal north coast), do not approach it and be prepared to run away or climb a tree very fast. You are very unlikely to encounter lions, rhinos and elephants when you are walking, but do not leave your vehicle while in a wildlife reserve (for more information see the boxed text 'Close Encounters' in the Regional Facts for the Visitor chapter).

Crime

Crime is the national obsession, although the perception that crime rates rose from low levels following the ANC's first election victory is wrong. Violence has long been a problem, the only post-1994 difference being that the white community is now suffering from the crime that has long plagued non-whites.

Take care at all times. Daylight muggings are common in parts of Jo'burg, and that city's Metro train system has had a problem with violent crime. Generally, avoid the CBD areas of the bigger cities at night; if you need to go through the CBD at night take a taxi – don't walk.

It would be unwise for outsiders to venture into a township except with a trusted guide or as part of a tour.

Cape Town is reasonably safe and there are few places around the city that are off-limits during the day. As in all the big cities, the situation changes at night; ask about safety when you're there.

Most ATMs have security guards. If there's no guard around when you're withdrawing cash, watch your back or get someone else to watch it for you.

As a general rule avoid driving at night, keep your windows up and doors locked when driving, and consider hiring a mobile phone. Leave your car in secure parking at night and don't leave anything valuable in the car.

Car-jacking is a hazard but is more likely if you're driving something flash rather than a standard rental car.

Incidents such as taxi wars (between rival minibus taxi companies) have led to deaths. Once again, it's a matter of knowing the

current situation and avoiding being in the wrong place at the wrong time. There are very, very few wrong places and times.

Incidents of violent crime are far worse in Jo'burg than other cities and extra precautions are necessary (for more information, see Dangers & Annoyances in the Jo'burg and Pretoria sections later in this chapter).

EMERGENCIES
The countrywide contact numbers for emergency services are: ambulance (☎ 10177) and police (☎ 10111).

LEGAL MATTERS
Marijuana was an important commodity in the Xhosa's trade with the San. Today *dagga* or *zol* is illegal but widely available. There are heavy penalties for use and possession although many smoke it. The legal system doesn't distinguish between soft and hard drugs.

BUSINESS HOURS
Banking hours vary, but are usually from 9am to 3.30pm weekdays; many branches are also open 8.30am to 11am Saturday. Post offices usually open from 8am to 4.30pm weekdays and 8am to noon Saturday. Banks and post offices close for lunch in smaller towns.

Most shops are open from 8.30am to 5pm weekdays, and on Saturday morning. Bars usually close around 11pm, except in the major cities (where the closing times vary).

PUBLIC HOLIDAYS & SPECIAL EVENTS
South Africa's public holidays include:

New Year's Day 1 January
Human Rights Day 21 March
Easter March/April – Good Friday, Saturday & Easter Monday
Family Day 17 April
Constitution Day 27 April
Workers' Day 1 May
Youth Day 16 June
Women's Day 9 August
Heritage Day 24 September
Day of Reconciliation 16 December
Christmas Day 25 December
Day of Goodwill 26 December

South African (and Namibian) school holidays normally occur from mid-December to mid-January; around Easter; from late

July to early August; and for two weeks in mid-October.

ACTIVITIES
There are many 'adventure' or 'eco' outfits offering a range of activities, such as hiking, canoeing and rafting, and some have trips into other African countries. There are plenty of options, so shop around. Two of the larger 'alternative' South African companies are **African Routes** (☎ 031-569 3911, fax 569 3908; ⓦ www.africanroutes.co.za) based in KwaZulu-Natal and **Drifters** (☎ 011-888 1160, fax 888 1020) based in Gauteng.

In addition to longer trips, a lot of smaller outfits offer day trips and these can be excellent. Hostels often take bookings for adventure activities and travel, but remember that a particular hostel might have an agreement with a particular company.

Air Sports
Flying, hang-gliding, paragliding, ballooning and parachuting are all popular activities and can be amazingly cheap compared to other countries. Cape Town's Table Mountain is a spectacular spot to paraglide or hang-glide.

Bird-watching
With hundreds of endemic species, South Africa is a paradise for bird-watchers. The regional variation is huge so keen bird-watchers should aim to cover a range of habitats – Kruger National Park is particularly renowned. Even those with a passing interest will find that binoculars and a field guide are worthwhile investments.

Canoeing & Rafting
Being a dry country with few major rivers, the canoeing and rafting possibilities are limited. The Orange River is the giant among South African rivers, running west across the country for 2340km. Other major rivers include the Tugela (KwaZulu-Natal), the Komati (Mpumalanga) and the Olifants, Berg and Breede (Western Cape).

Rafting and canoeing trips on the Orange River (through a beautiful desert wilderness and undemanding rapids) in the far northwest, where it forms the border with Namibia, have become very popular.

The Tugela offers more challenging rafting, rainfall permitting. It is at its best from late December to mid-March.

SOUTH AFRICA

One of the biggest operators is **Felix Unite** (☎ 021-670 1300 Cape Town).

Diving
The KwaZulu-Natal north coast, particularly around Sodwana Bay, offers excellent warmwater diving and some good reefs. Most resort towns along Western Cape's Garden Route have diving schools.

Shark Diving Seeing sharks up close from the safety of a cage has proven hugely popular, particularly in Western Cape. There are, however, some ecological downsides to shark diving and you might want to think twice before doing it. The most obvious problem is that they are fed bait to attract them and so associate humans with food. Not a pleasant scenario.

Hiking
South Africa has an excellent system of hiking trails, usually with accommodation available. They are popular and most must be booked well in advance (for more details see Hiking under Activities in the Regional Facts for the Visitor chapter). Jaynee Levy's *Complete Guide to Walks & Trails in Southern Africa* has more detail.

There are many hiking clubs – contact the **Hiking Federation of South Africa** (☎ 012-327 0083; ◉ hanssteyn@yebo.co.za) – and several adventure travel outfits offer organised hikes.

Most trails are administered by the National Parks Board or the various Forest Regions, although the KwaZulu-Natal Nature Conservation (KZN Wildlife) controls most trails in KwaZulu-Natal. Some of the best-known trails and their booking details are:

Western Cape
Otter Trail Five days along the Garden Route coast; contact the National Parks Board (☎ 012 428 9111)
Outeniqua Up to eight days in indigenous forest near Knysna; contact the Forestry Department (☎ 044-382 5446)

Eastern Cape
Amatola Up to six days in the former Ciskei Homelands; contact Ken Agency (☎ 043-642 2571)
Wild Coast Three five-day sections along the Transkei coast; contact Wild Coast Trails (☎ 039-305 6455, ◉ communitytourism@euwildcoast.za.org, ⒲ www.wild-coast.co.za)

KwaZulu-Natal
Giant's Cup Up to five days in the southern Drakensberg; contact KZN Wildlife (☎ 033-845 1000). There are also wilderness trails and guided walks in Umfolozi, Mkuzi and Greater St Lucia National Parks; contact KZN Wildlife.

Mpumalanga
Blyde River Canyon Trail Up to five days in this spectacular area; contact Blyde River Canyon Nature Reserve (☎ 013-758 1035, PO Box 1990, Nelspruit 1200)
Kruger National Park There are 'wilderness trails and guided walks'; contact the National Parks Board (☎ 012-428 9111)

Free State
Rhebok
Two days in Golden Gate Highlands National Park; contact the National Parks Board (☎ 021-422 2810, 012-343 1991)

Limpopo
Mabudashango Four days in former Venda Homelands; contact the Department of Tourism (☎ 015-962 4724, Private Bag X50008, Thohoyandou, Limpopo)
Soutpansberg Up to two days in the Soutpansberg Range; contact Komatiland (☎ 012-481 3615 or 013-764 1058)

Mountain Biking
South Africans have discovered mountain biking and taken to it in a very big way. Some nature reserves and national parks are putting in mountain-bike trails, and some outfits offer trips.

Rock Climbing
There are some challenging climbs, especially in the KwaZulu-Natal Drakensberg. Contact the **Mountain Club of South Africa** (☎ 021-465 3412; ⒲ www.mssa.org.za) for addresses of regional clubs.

Surfing
South Africa has some of the best and least-crowded surfing in the world. Jeffrey's Bay is famous but there are myriad alternatives, particularly along the east and south coasts. April to July offers the best surfing conditions.

Boards and surfing gear can be bought in most big coastal cities. New boards cost about US$185 and good quality second-hand boards around US$100. If you plan to surf Jeffrey's Bay you'll need a decent-sized board – it's a big, very fast wave. **Wavescape** is worth a look online (⒲ www.wavescape.co.za).

WORK

The best time to look for work is from October to November, before the high season starts and before university students begin holidays. Employers face extremely tough penalties for taking on any foreigners illegally. So far this doesn't seem to have stopped travellers getting jobs in restaurants/bars in tourist areas, but it might change. Don't expect decent pay although tips can be good.

ACCOMMODATION

Both hostels and self-catering cottages (usually on farms) have become boom budget-accommodation industries. Accommodation is plentiful and generally of a high standard.

Many places have seasonal rates. The high season is usually during the summer school holidays, especially around Christmas and the New Year, and Easter. Prices can double or triple and some places require a minimum stay of a week.

Camping

Most towns have an inexpensive municipal caravan park charging around US$5 for a camp site, and often a resort from US$9 per site (more in high season). Many backpackers hostels have space for a few tents and usually charge around US$2.90 per site. In some rural backwaters of the ex-Homelands (where there are few official camp sites) you can still free-camp. *Always* ask permission from the nearest village or home before setting up your tent. This is not just good manners; you are at serious risk of robbery or worse if you ignore local sensibilities.

Self-Catering Cottages

The cheapest self-catering accommodation is usually in cottages, also known as chalets, cabins and rondavels (circular, often thatched, huts) which can be great value. You might find something for about US$23 a double.

Hostels

There's a huge number of usually excellent backpackers hostels all over the country. A dorm bed costs US$6.90 to US$9.20 a night and private rooms about US$18.50/22 a single/double.

B&Bs & Guesthouses

There is an enormous number of B&Bs and guesthouses and on the whole standards are extremely high.

Hotels

There are plenty of decent hotels, usually owned by one of the big South African chains, in the larger towns. Hotels in the small towns these days can be somewhat down-at-heel and old-fashioned.

FOOD

Although South Africa produces some of the best meat, fresh produce and seafood in the world, eating out can be hit or miss. Large steaks (admittedly, usually excellent), overboiled vegetables, heavy sauces and fried chips are all too often the restaurant staples. Things are changing rapidly for the better, however. The Winelands and Cape Town remain the best places to eat well.

Boerewors (farmers' sausage) is the traditional sausage and it's sold everywhere.

The staple for most blacks is rice or *mielie* (maize) meal, served in a variety of forms and often referred to as *pap*. Although it isn't especially appetising, it's cheap. Servings of rice and stew cost about US$1 around minibus taxi parks.

DRINKS

Pubs

There's a growing number of bars and pubs in South Africa, although choice is limited in the smaller towns. Durban, Pretoria, Bloemfontein and Cape Town have a decent range of drinking places.

There's not much to distinguish the available lagers, which include Castle, Amstel, Windhoek and Carlsberg. In the Cape, look out for Mitchell's Beers, which come from a couple of small breweries around the area. A beer costs between US$1 and US$1.75.

Wine

Wine was first made in South Africa in 1659. It is now an enormous industry, employing around 30,000 people in Western Cape. The wine is of a high standard, and it is very reasonably priced. If you buy direct from a vineyard you can get bottles for as little as US$1.85, and from US$3.45 and up in a restaurant or bottle store. Most restaurants have long wine lists.

South Africa offers excellent dry whites made from sauvignon blanc, riesling, colombard and chenin blanc. The most popular reds are cabernet sauvignon, pinotage (an interesting local cross of pinot and cinsaut, which was known as Hermitage), shiraz, cinsaut and pinot noir.

SPECTATOR SPORTS

Cricket fans tend to be English-speakers, but after South Africa's return to international sport in the 1992 World Cup, cricket occupied centre stage. The euphoria following South Africa's surprising success in the competition probably helped the Yes vote in the referendum on constitutional reform.

Rugby (Union, not League) was traditionally the Afrikaners' sport until the 1995 World Cup, which was hosted and won by South Africa. The entire white and coloured population went rugby mad – the black population's response was more muted. This may change as more black players compete professionally.

Soccer is the most popular sport among black South Africans. South Africa's national team *Bafana Bafana* (The Boys, The Boys) won the prestigious Africa Cup in 1996 (helped, it has been said, by Nigeria's boycott of the event), thereby giving South Africa three important victories in their three major sports since the country's readmittance to world sport.

There are traditional Afrikaner games, the most popular of which is *jukskei* – something like horseshoe-tossing but using items associated with trek wagons. Kroonstad (in Free State) is the centre for national competition.

SHOPPING

Indigenous crafts are on sale everywhere, from expensive galleries to street corners. There are some quality items among the junk. See what's available in a good shop in a big city, then look for a better price as you travel around the rural areas.

As well as traditional crafts there are 'township crafts', the product of extreme poverty and vivid imaginations. Items, often exquisitely crafted, such as karoo windmills or flowers made from soft-drink cans and toys made from wire, all make great gifts.

Getting There & Away

This section covers access into South Africa only from neighbouring countries. Information about reaching Southern Africa from elsewhere on the African continent and from other continents is outlined in the regional Getting There & Away chapter.

AIR

South Africa is the major air link in Southern Africa. (For more information, including discount travel agents around the world, see Air in the regional Getting There & Away chapter.)

Airports & Airlines

The main international airport remains Johannesburg International Airport (JNB), between Jo'burg and Pretoria, but an increasing number of international flights use Cape Town and Durban. There's also a small international airport at Nelspruit, close to the Kruger National Park.

South Africa is serviced by about 25 international carriers. The national carrier, South African Airways (SAA), has a good safety record and generally high standards.

Departure Tax

Airport departure and security taxes have risen sharply in recent years ranging from about US$8.80 for domestic and more than US$23 for international flights, although they are usually included in the ticket price.

Southern Africa

There are several flights to other countries within Southern Africa. Air Botswana has flights between Jo'burg and Gaborone.

SAA flies frequently (US$117 one way) between Moshoeshoe International Airport, 18km from Maseru in Lesotho, and Jo'burg. There are some deals on return flights.

SAA flies between Jo'burg and Swaziland and between Jo'burg and Maputo in Mozambique for about US$140. It also flies from Jo'burg to Harare for US$270.

Comair flies between Windhoek (Namibia) and Jo'burg or Cape Town for about US$103.

LAND
South Africa shares borders with Botswana, Lesotho, Mozambique, Namibia, Swaziland and Zimbabwe. Jo'burg is a major hub for road and rail transport. Fares given are one way.

Botswana
Border Crossings The main border crossings are Ramatlabama/Mmabatho, north of Mafikeng, open from 6am to 8pm; Skilpadshek, northwest of Zeerust, open from 6am to 10pm; and Tlokweng Gate/ Kopfontein, north of Zeerust, open from 6am to 10pm.

Bus From Jo'burg/Pretoria, **Intercape Mainliner** (☎ 012-654 4182) runs to Gaborone daily (US$18.50, seven hours). Minibus taxis run from Mafikeng (Northwest Province) to Gaborone (US$4); see also the Getting There & Away section in the Botswana chapter.

Lesotho
There are no direct buses between South African cities and Maseru. Take a bus to Bloemfontein or Ladybrand and catch a minibus taxi from there. Bloemfontein to Maseru is about US$3.

For information on land routes and border crossings as well as regional sections for details on hiking and horse trails through the Drakensberg into South Africa, see the Getting There & Away section in the Lesotho chapter.

Malawi
Translux runs from Jo'burg to Blantyre three times a week for US$57.

Mozambique
Bus From Jo'burg/Pretoria **Translux** (☎ 011-774 3333) runs daily to Maputo (US$24, seven hours). Also making daily runs for the same fare are **Intercape** and **Panthera Azul** (☎ 011-337 7409).

Train The *Komati* runs between Jo'burg and Komatipoort, on the Mozambique border (US$20/14/9 in 1st/2nd/3rd class). From here you need to change trains for Maputo (about US$3.45, 150km). The *Trans Lubombo* runs between Durban and Maputo, but check for current schedules as there have been recent disruptions to this train service (for more travel information, see the Getting There & Away section in the Mozambique chapter).

Namibia
Border Crossings The main crossing west of Upington is at Nakop (Ariamsvlei), open 24 hours. The main crossing on the west coast is between Vioolsdrif and Noordoewer (open 7am to 7pm). You can't cross the border between Namibia and South Africa in the Kgalagadi Transfrontier Park. The nearest alternative is to cross between Rietfontein and Klein-Menasse (open 8am to 4.30pm).

Bus From Cape Town, **Intercape Mainliner** (☎ 021-386 4400) runs to Windhoek four times a week (US$50, 20 hours). You can travel between Windhoek and Jo'burg (US$62), changing at Upington with Intercape. For more information, see Getting There & Away in the Namibia chapter.

Swaziland
The **Baz Bus** (☎ 021-439 2323, fax 439 2343; e info@bazbus.com) runs from Jo'burg/ Pretoria to Durban via Mbabane and Manzini, four times a week (US$26).

For details on land routes and border crossings, see the Getting There & Away section in the Swaziland chapter

Zambia
Translux runs to Lusaka from Pretoria (US$46) three times a week.

Zimbabwe
Border Crossings The only border crossing between Zimbabwe and South Africa is at Beitbridge on the Limpopo River, which is open between 5.30am and 8.30pm. Lengthy waits are not uncommon, particularly going from South Africa to Zimbabwe. Car drivers pay a toll at the border crossing to use the Limpopo Bridge when entering or leaving South Africa.

Bus There are four services a week from Jo'burg/Pretoria to Harare (US$40) with **Translux** (☎ 021-449 3333). Greyhound and Intercape Mainliner do the same run, but **Greyhound** (☎ 012-323 1154) also has a useful service six times a week from Pretoria to Bulawayo (US$25).

For more travel information, see under Getting There & Away in the Zimbabwe chapter. Given Zimbabwe's changing situation, **Zim Travel** (☎ 012-543 1236; e zim travel@africa.com) is worth trying for the latest information.

SEA

South Africa's **Safmarine** (☎ 021-408 6911, fax 408 6660; W www.safmarine.com) is actively seeking passengers for its container ships, which sail to many of the world's major ports. Fares are expensive (from US$2340/3600 a single/double between Cape Town and the UK), but they are negotiable. Also fares *from* South Africa seem to be lower than fares *to* South Africa.

You can also take a ship between Cape Town and Durban or between Durban and Port Elizabeth. Detailed information can be found on the Safmarine website.

ORGANISED TOURS

For tour and safari companies based outside Southern Africa that run trips around the region, see Organised Tours in the regional Getting There & Away chapter.

The most-common type of tour in South Africa and beyond is by big overland truck. Some get good reviews, others don't. Many travellers find them an excellent, cost-effective and sociable way to see the region. Some find being cooped up with up to 20 travellers for days or weeks can be too much like hard work.

A good way to get a feel for the different operators and other travellers' overland tour experiences is to read their opinions on Lonely Planet's Thorn Tree site. The following are just a small sample of the operators out there:

African Routes (☎ 031 569 3911, W www .africanroutes.co.za, PO Box 1835, Durban, 4000) A well-established operator running budget tours aimed at the 18 to 35 age bracket

All In Exclusive (☎ 011-465 7767, W www.allin exclusive.com) Small-scale, all-in tours of up to 15 days in eight-seater buses aimed at more senior travellers

Bundu Bus (☎ 011-675 0767, W www.bundu safaris.co.za, PO Box 697, Wilgeheuwel, 1735 Gauteng) Runs a range of tours of up to eight days in South Africa and into neighbouring countries

Drifters (☎ 011-888 1160, W www.drifters.co.za, PO Box 48434, Roosevelt) Another overland truck operator offering an incredible range of tours of up to a month

Nomad (☎ 021-426 5445, W www.nomadtours .co.za, 204 Long St, Cape Town) An established operator aiming at the budget market

Rovos Rail (☎ 012-315 8242, W www.rovos.co .za, Pretoria 0001, Gauteng) Restored steam trains pull luxurious carriages on opulent tours between Pretoria and Cape Town lasting up to a week

Getting Around

South Africa is geared towards travel by private car, with some very good highways but limited and expensive mainstream public transport. Hiring or buying a car is the best way to cover a lot of ground if time is short. If you don't have much money but time to spare there's the extensive network of (moderately uncomfortable) minibus taxis, and 3rd-class train seats.

AIR

South African Airways (SAA; W www.flysaa .com) is a domestic and international carrier flying daily to many destinations. Fares aren't cheap, but checking with a travel agent before you leave home can secure some good special deals on advance purchase tickets. Once you're in South Africa there are a few discount options – a 15% discount if you book and pay 14 days in advance and 50% off for 21 day advance purchases.

Domestic destinations covered include Jo'burg, Cape Town, Durban, Port Elizabeth, East London, Bloemfontein, Upington, Kimberley, Nelspruit, Springbok and Alexander Bay.

SAA flights can be booked centrally (☎ 0861-359 722, or international ☎ 27-11-978 5313).

British Airways Comair (☎ 011-921 0222; Jo'burg • ☎ 021-936 9000; Cape Town) flies to Cape Town, Durban, Jo'burg and Port Elizabeth. Routes include: Jo'burg to Cape Town (US$205); and Durban to Jo'burg (US$121).

Airport departure taxes total about US$8.70 for domestic flights and seem to rise fairly often. They are usually included in the ticket price.

BUS

Translux, part of the semi-privatised government transport service, runs long-distance buses between most major towns. The other main national operator is Greyhound. With the exception of City to City (a poor relation of Translux) and local services competing with minibus taxis, bus travel isn't cheap.

In the western half of the country Intercape Mainliner has useful services at fares a little lower than Translux.

Translux

Translux runs express services on the main routes. Tickets must be booked 24 hours in advance. You can get on without a booking if there's a spare seat, but you won't know that until the bus arrives. You usually can't book a seat to a nearby town, but prices for short sectors are exorbitant anyway – you're better off catching a local bus or a minibus taxi.

Computicket takes bookings, as do many travel agents. There are also reservations offices around the country including:

Cape Town	☎ 021-449 3333
Durban	☎ 031-308 8111
Jo'burg & credit card bookings	☎ 011-774 3333
Port Elizabeth	☎ 041-392 1333

There's a slight discount on fares during less busy times of the year.

Translux services include:

Jo'burg–Cape Town via Bloemfontein Daily, 19 hours (overnight). Stops (with fares from Jo'burg/Cape Town) include: Bloemfontein (US$21/41); Beaufort West (US$27.50/23); Worcester (US$41/12.60); and Cape Town (US$46).

Jo'burg–Cape Town via Kimberley Five a week, 18½ hours (overnight). Stops (with fares from Jo'burg/Cape Town) include Kimberley (US$18/33).

Jo'burg–Durban Several daily, eight or nine hours (daylight and overnight). Stops (with fares from Jo'burg/Durban) include: Harrismith (US$16/16); Pietermaritzburg (US$20/5.75); and Durban (US$21.50).

Jo'burg–East London Daily, 14 hours (overnight). Stops (with fares from Jo'burg/East London) include: Bloemfontein (US$21/22); Queenstown (US$25/10); King William's Town (US$33/10); and East London (US$33).

Jo'burg–Knysna Daily, 17½ hours (overnight) via Kimberley or Bloemfontein. Stops (with fares from Jo'burg/Knysna) include: Bloemfontein (US$20.50/28); Kimberley (US$18/32); Oudtshoorn (US$34/

8.60); Mossel Bay (US$42/8.60); George (US$42/10); and Knysna (US$42).

Jo'burg–Port Elizabeth Daily, 15 hours (overnight) via Graaff-Reinet. Stops (with fares from Jo'burg/Port Elizabeth) include: Bloemfontein (US$21); Graaff-Reinet (US$28.50/20); and Port Elizabeth (US$37.50).

Jo'burg–Umtata Four a week, 13½ hours (overnight). Stops (with fares from Jo'burg/Umtata) include: Pietermaritzburg (US$20/18); Kokstad (US$21.50/9.80); and Umtata (US$24).

Cape Town–Durban Daily, 20 hours. Stops (with fares from Cape Town/Durban) include: Paarl (US$10.40/53); Bloemfontein (US$40/25); Bethlehem (US$41/18.50); Pietermaritzburg (US$52.60/5.75); and Durban (US$52.50).

Cape Town–East London Daily, 15 hours (overnight). Stops (with fares from Cape Town/East London) include: Graaff-Reinet (US$25.60/21.50); Queenstown (US$32/9.80); King William's Town (US$24/9.80); and East London (US$35).

Cape Town–Port Elizabeth via Coastal Route Daily, 10½ hours (daylight). Stops (with fares from Cape Town/Port Elizabeth) include: Swellendam (US$10.40/25); Mossel Bay (US$12.60/11.90); George (US$15/10.40); Knysna (US$17.50/9.20); Plettenberg Bay (US$18.50/9.20); Storms River (US$19/7); and Port Elizabeth (US$24.50).

Cape Town–Port Elizabeth via Mountain Route Daily, 12 hours (overnight). Stops (with fares from Cape Town/Port Elizabeth) include: Robertson (US$12.60/24); George (US$15/$10.40); Knysna (US$17.50/9.20); Plettenberg Bay (US$18.50/9.20); and Port Elizabeth (US$25).

Durban–Port Elizabeth Daily, 14 hours (daylight). Stops (with fares from Durban/Port Elizabeth) include: Port Shepstone (US$8/25); Kokstad (US$10.50/25); Umtata (US$17/20); East London (US$20/15); Grahamstown (US$29/10); and Port Elizabeth (US$31).

Greyhound

Greyhound (**W** *www.greyhound.co.za*) offers services on much the same routes as Translux at much the same prices, although special deals are sometimes available. One of Greyhound's Jo'burg-Durban services runs through parts of Zululand to Richards Bay, then down the coast to Durban, which is handy.

Book through a travel agent or the following Greyhound offices:

Bloemfontein	☎ 051-447 1558
Cape Town	☎ 021-505 6363
Durban	☎ 031-309 7830
Jo'burg & credit card bookings	☎ 011-249 8900
Nelspruit	☎ 013-753 2100
Port Elizabeth	☎ 041-585 8648

SOUTH AFRICA

Intercape Mainliner

Intercape Mainliner *(Intercape;* ☎ *0861-287287)* is a major line in the western half of the country and generally charges less than Translux. Routes include: Port Elizabeth–East London (US$13); Cape Town–Port Elizabeth (US$25); Cape Town–Upington (US$25); Jo'burg–Upington (US$29); Upington Windhoek (Namibia) (US$34); and Cape Town–Windhoek (US$51).

City to City (Transtate)

City to City stops and offices are few and can be difficult to find. Buses often stop at train stations (ask about the 'railways bus'). It's worth using City to City because they are generally far cheaper than the major bus companies, but it's difficult to find current and reliable information about them. City to City's Jo'burg **information desk** *(☎ 011-337 6650)* can be of use.

Baz Bus

The **Baz Bus** *(☎ 021-439 2323, fax 439 2343;* **w** *www.bazbus.com)* is an excellent alternative to the major bus lines. Most hostels take bookings, or you can phone. While it's aimed at backpackers, its routes, organisation and service levels make it very useful for travellers on any budget.

The Baz Bus offers hop-on, hop-off fares and door-to-door service between Cape Town and Jo'burg via the Northern Drakensberg, Durban and the Garden Route. It also does a very useful loop from Durban up through Zululand and Swaziland and back to Jo'burg, passing close by Kruger National Park. No other mainstream transport options cover this route. Hop on, hop off fares from Cape Town include: Durban via Garden Route US$160; Jo'burg via northern Drakensberg US$190; Jo'burg via Swaziland US$230.

MINIBUS

If there's no bus, and you don't have a car, the only way to get between many places is to take a minibus taxi or hitch (see Hitching later in this section).

Minibus taxis tend to run on relatively short routes, generally only to neighbouring towns, although you'll nearly always find a few running to a distant big city. As well as the usual 'leave when full' taxis, there's a small but increasing number of door-to-door services, which you can book. These tend to run on the longer routes and, while they cost a little more, they're convenient.

Away from the big cities, robbery on taxis is not much of a problem. 'Taxi wars' between rival companies – involving often lethal shoot-outs – do occasionally happen, but given the number of taxis the incidence of attacks is very low. Cape Town's taxi war flares regularly and a few other areas have had trouble, including East London. Read the newspapers and ask around about the situation to be on the safe side.

A bigger problem is driver fatigue, so you'll be safer using a bus or train for long-distance trips (eg, Jo'burg to Cape Town).

TRAIN

Trains are a good way to get between major cities and 3rd class travel is very cheap.

The Blue Train

Some people come to South Africa just to ride on the famous *Blue Train* (☎ *012-334 8459;* **w** *www.bluetrain.co.za).* The original train ran between Pretoria/Jo'burg and Cape Town, offering 25 hours of luxury. More routes have since been added.

If you can't afford to take an entire trip (a de-luxe double from Pretoria to Cape Town starts at about US$1110), consider taking just a section. Low-season fares apply between the beginning of May and the end of August. Some travel agents in South Africa and in other countries take bookings.

Named Trains

Passenger services are all on 'name trains'. On overnight trips the fare includes a sleeping berth (more expensive private compartments can also be hired). Meals are à la carte.

First and 2nd class must be booked at least 24 hours in advance; you can't book 3rd class. Most stations and some travel agents accept bookings.

Routes & Fares Return fares are simply double the one-way fares (given here in 1st/2nd/3rd class). Note that these are most of the lines, however there are other lines with routes that double-up on some of the stops listed. Call **Spoornet** *(☎ 0860-008888)* for more information.

Algoa *Jo'burg–Port Elizabeth* Daily, 19 hours. Departs from Jo'burg and Port Elizabeth at 2.30pm.

Dusk, Cape Town, South Africa

Ground hornbill, Kruger National Park, South Africa

Kirstenbosch Botanic Gardens, Table Mountain, Cape Town, South Africa

Sunset, Lake Itezhi-Tezhi, Kafue National Park, Zambia

Hippopotamus, Lower Zambezi NP, Zambia

Great Zimbabwe ruins, Zimbabwe

Victoria Falls, Zimbabwe

Stops include: Kroonstad (US$10/6.35/3.45 from Jo'burg, US$33/22.50/14 from Port Elizabeth); Bloemfontein (US$16/11/6.35, US$25.50/18/11); Cradock (US$31/21/12.60, US$11.50/8/4.60); and Port Elizabeth (US$41/27/17).

Amatola Jo'burg–East London Daily, 20 hours. Departs from Jo'burg 12.45pm, departs from East London at noon. Stops include: Kroonstad (US$9.20/6.35/3.45 from Jo'burg, US$30/20/13 from East London); Bloemfontein (US$17/11/6.35, US$23/17/10); Queenstown (US$30/20/13, US$9.20/6.35/4); and East London (US$36.50/25/15.50).

Bosvelder Jo'burg–Messina Daily, 15 hours. Departs from Jo'burg at 6.50pm, departs from Messina at 2.45pm. Stops include: Pretoria (US$4/3.45/1.75 from Jo'burg, US$21/15/9 from Messina); Pietersburg/Polokwane (US$14/10/5.75, US$11.50/8/4.60); Louis Trichardt (US$19/13/7.50, US$6.35/4.60/2.30); and Messina (US$23/16.50/10).

Diamond Express Jo'burg-Bloemfontein via Kimberley Daily, 15 hours. Departs from Jo'burg at 7.35pm. The fare between Jo'burg and Kimberley is US$19/12.50/8.

Komati Jo'burg–Komatipoort Daily, 12 hours. Departs from Jo'burg at 5.45pm, departs from Komatipoort at 6.07pm. This service theoretically connects with a train to Maputo in Mozambique. There is also a shuttle bus that runs from Komatipoort to Maputo daily. Stops include: Pretoria (US$3.45/2.90/1.75 from Jo'burg, US$17.50/12.60/7.50 from Komatipoort); Middelburg (US$9.20/6.90/3.45, US$12.60/10/5.20); Nelspruit (US$17/11.50/6.35, US$8/6.35/2.30); and Komatipoort, (US$24/16.50/10).

Trans Karoo Jo'burg–Cape Town Daily, 27 hours. Departs from Cape Town at 9.20am, departs from Jo'burg at 12.30pm. Stops include: Kimberley (US$19/12.60/8 from Jo'burg, US$37/25/15.50 from Cape Town); Beaufort West (US$37.50/24/15, US$21/14/8.60); and Cape Town (US$55/36.50/23).

Trans Natal Jo'burg–Durban Daily, 13½ hours. Departs from both Jo'burg and Durban at 6.30pm. Stops include Newcastle (US$12.60/8.60/5.20 from Jo'burg, US$16/11/7 from Durban); Ladysmith (US$17.50/11.50/7, US$12/8/4.60); Pietermaritzburg (US$23.50/18/10, US$5.75/4.60/2.30); and Durban (US$28/18.50/11.50)

Trans Oranje Cape Town–Durban Weekly, 30½ hours. Departs from Cape Town on Monday at 6.50pm, departs from Durban on Thursday at 5.30pm. Stops include: Wellington (US$4/3.45/1.75 from Cape Town, US$68/46/29 from Durban); Beaufort West (US$20.50/14/9, US$50/37.50/22); Kimberley (US$28/19/11.50, US$26/18.50/11.50); Bloemfontein (US$43/ 29.50/18, US$30/20/13; Kroonstad (US$50/34/21, US$23/$17/10);

Ladysmith (US$67/41/25.50, US$12/8/4.60); Pietermaritzburg (US$67/46/29); and Durban (US$70/27/33).

Metro Trains

There are Metro services in and around several cities. Make sure you get local advice before using a Metro train – violent robbery is always a possibility, particularly between Pretoria and Jo'burg.

CAR & MOTORCYCLE

Most major roads are excellent and carry relatively little traffic, and off the big roads there are some interesting back roads to explore.

The country is crossed by national routes (eg, the N1), and some sections of these are freeways. A toll of between US$0.70 and US$2.50 is payable on some of these.

Petrol stations are often open 24 hours and fuel costs about US$0.45 a litre. Unleaded petrol is widely available.

Road Rules

South Africans drive on the left-hand side of the road. The main local road rule is the 'four-way stop', which can occur even on major roads. When you arrive at a four-way stop, you must stop. If there are other vehicles at the intersection, those that arrived before you cross first.

Hazards

South Africa has a horrific road fatality rate, caused mostly by dangerous driving. Hundreds of people die whenever there's a long weekend and the annual death toll is pushing 10,000. A further 150,000 people are injured on the roads annually. With a population of about 41 million – the vast majority of whom don't own cars – that's appalling.

Animals & Pedestrians In rural areas, particularly in the Eastern Cape, slow down and watch out for people and animals on the roads.

Crime Carjacking is a problem in Jo'burg and to a lesser extent in the other big cities (people have been killed for their cars). Stay alert, keep doors locked and windows wound up.

Other Drivers On highways, fast cars coming up behind you will expect you to

Car Guards

Parked cars are easy targets in crime-plagued South Africa and you'll see car guards in towns and cities across the country. Although probably incapable of stopping a gang of determined car thieves, the guards are good visible deterrents.

When you step out of your car you're likely to be hailed by a guard, often volunteers organised by local councils.

You may come back to your vehicle without sighting the guard (and we certainly caught them napping on more than one occasion), but you can be sure they will pop up before you have the chance to zoom off.

A couple of rand is a reasonable tip if you've parked for more than a few minutes.

move left into the emergency lane to let them pass. The problem is that there might be pedestrians or a slow-moving vehicle already in the emergency lane. Don't move over unless it's safe. It is becoming common for an overtaking car to rely on *oncoming* traffic to move into the emergency lane! This is sheer lunacy and you must remain constantly alert. Drivers on little-used rural roads often speed and they often assume that there is no other traffic. Be careful of oncoming cars at blind corners on country roads. Drink-driving is another major hazard. Avoid driving at night if you can.

Roads In the ex-Homelands beware of dangerous potholes, wash outs, unsignposted hairpin bends and the like.

You don't have to get very far off the beaten track anywhere in the country to find yourself on dirt roads. Most are regularly graded and reasonably smooth and it's often possible to travel at high speed – don't!

If you're travelling along a dirt road at 100km/h and you come to a corner, you won't go around that corner, you'll sail off into the veld. If you put on the brakes to slow down you'll probably spin or roll. If you swerve sharply to avoid a pothole you'll go into an exciting four-wheel drift, then find out what happens when your car meets a telegraph pole. Worst of all you could lose control as you move to the side of the road to avoid an approaching car, and have a head-on collision. As a rule, treat dirt like ice.

Rental

The major international companies, including **Avis** (☎ 0861-021111, 011-923 3674) and **Budget** (☎ 0800-016622 toll free) have offices or agents across the country. Their rates are high, but if you book through your local agent at home before you arrive they will be significantly lower – though still higher than the cheaper companies in South Africa.

Local companies come and go, but currently the larger ones include **Imperial** (☎ 0861-131000 toll free or ☎ Johannesburg 011-453 0005) and **Tempest** (☎ 011-396 1080), which has agents in the main cities and a few other places.

A step down from these are smaller and cheaper outfits that regularly burst onto the scene, and in a lot of cases fade just as rapidly. They normally offer very competitive rates. Tourist information offices are the best places to begin your inquiries.

For budget travellers, hostels can often organise a rental car deal through a broker with one of the major companies (such as Budget or Europcar) at far better rates than if you approached the company directly. For a small car (such as a 1.6L Toyota Corolla) you can expect to pay around US$27 to $US32 a day with insurance and other costs included – a bargain if there is a group of you.

It's also worth checking out the website ⓦ www.travelocity.com which often has good deals from the major rental agencies – cars in Jo'burg and Cape Town were going for as little as US$13 per day at the time of research, with air-conditioning and unlimited kilometres, a real bargain!

Camper Vans One way around South Africa's high accommodation and transport costs is to hire a camper van. Note that one-way rentals might not be possible with these vehicles.

One company with a range of deals is **African Leisure Travel** (☎ 011-792 1884; ⓦ www.africanleisuretravel.co.za; 2 Sambreelboom Ave, Randparkridge, Jo'burg, Gauteng). It has been in business for quite a while and its rates are good. As well as Toyota Landcruiser campers they have cheaper 'bakkie' campers, which sleep two in the back of a canopied pick-up. These include all the necessary camping gear.

Motorcycle Renting a bike isn't cheap but the idea of riding around South Africa is attractive. For more information, see Car & Motorcycle under Cape Town & the Peninsula section.

Purchase

An increasing number of travellers buy a car to tour South Africa, or the entire region, then sell it again after their trip. Cape Town and Jo'burg are the two main places for this (for more information, see the regional Getting Around chapter).

BICYCLE

South Africa is a good country to cycle around, with a wide variety of terrain and climate, plenty of camping places and many good roads, most of which don't carry a lot of traffic.

However, parts of South Africa are very hilly and even on main roads gradients are steep.

Away from cities you might have trouble finding specialised parts, although there are basic bicycle shops in many towns. Theft is a problem – bring a good lock and chain.

There is a boom in mountain biking (usually with support vehicles, *braais* (barbecues) and beer – see Activities in the Regional Facts for the Visitor chapter), so mountain bikes are sold everywhere. Touring bikes are harder to come by except in the major cities.

HITCHING

Hitching means taking a small but potentially serious risk, particularly in South Africa, and it's not a form of travel we can recommend. If you must hitch, do it in pairs and let someone know where you're going.

Hitching is, however, sometimes the only way to get to smaller towns, and even if you're travelling between larger towns the choice is sometimes to wait a day or two for a bus or hitch. Make it obvious that you're a clean-cut foreign visitor. It helps to carry a sign stating your destination.

Hitching is riskier in and around major cities. You are advised to catch public transport well beyond the city limits before you start to hitch.

LOCAL TRANSPORT

Getting around South Africa's often sprawling towns isn't easy. It's a major pain if you're hitching, especially if the town is bypassed by the freeway. The big cities and some of the larger towns have bus systems. Services often stop running early in the evening.

In Durban and some other places you'll find that mainstay of Asian transport, the *tuk-tuk* (motorised three-wheel vehicle), which run mainly in downtown or tourist areas.

Cape Town

CAPE TOWN & THE PENINSULA
☎ 021 • pop 3,140,600

Geographically isolated Cape Town, or Kaapstad, is one of the world's most beautiful cities. About 40km from the Cape of Good Hope, near the southern tip of Africa, it's dominated by a 1000m-high mountain with virtually sheer cliffs, surrounded by mountain walks, vineyards and beaches.

Cape Town is the most open-minded and relaxed city in South Africa and has nothing like the sense of tension that pervades Johannesburg. It is the capital of Western Cape and the parliamentary capital of the republic.

History

The first European to round the Cape (in 1487) was Portuguese sailor Bartholomeu Dias. He named it Cabo da Boa Esperanca (Cape of Good Hope). At this time the Cape was occupied by the Khoikhoi, relatives of the San people, who were semi-nomadic sheep and cattle pastoralists.

By the late 16th century the English and Dutch were starting to challenge the Portuguese, and the Dutch East India Company (VOC) established a base where ships could stock up on supplies. Jan van Riebeeck was chosen to lead an expedition and barter with the Khoikhoi for meat. He reached Table Bay on 6 April 1652, built a mud-walled fort and planted gardens that have now become the Botanical (Company's) Gardens. The colony was short of labour, so van Riebeeck imported slaves from East Asia.

Cape Town thrived, and was known as the Tavern of the Seas, a riotous port used by every navigator, privateer and merchant travelling between Europe and the East.

The population of whites did not reach a thousand until 1745, but small numbers of free (meaning non-VOC) burghers had begun to drift inland, driving the Khoisan

CAPE TOWN & THE PENINSULA

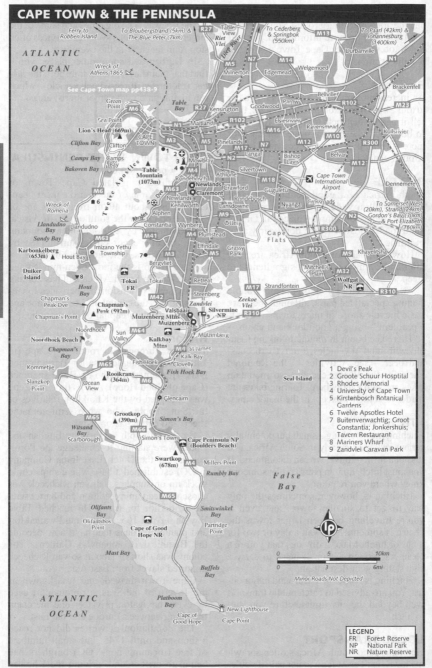

1 Devil's Peak
2 Groote Schuur Hospital
3 Rhodes Memorial
4 University of Cape Town
5 Kirstenbosch Botanical Gardens
6 Twelve Apostles Hotel
7 Buitenverwachting; Groot Constantia; Jonkershuis; Tavern Restaurant
8 Mariners Wharf
9 Zandvlei Caravan Park

LEGEND
FR Forest Reserve
NP National Park
NR Nature Reserve

(San and Khoikhoi peoples) from their lands.

By the end of the 18th century, Dutch power was fading and the British took the Cape in 1806. The slave trade was abolished in 1808 and the remaining Khoisan were given the explicit protection of the law in 1828, a move that contributed to Afrikaner dissatisfaction and the Great Trek (1834–40).

With the discovery of diamonds and gold in the centre of South Africa in the late 1800s and the ensuing growth of Johannesburg, Cape Town was no longer the single dominant metropolis in the country; as a major port it was, however, a beneficiary of this mineral wealth.

Cape Town avoided any direct role in the 1899–1902 Anglo-Boer War, although it did play a key role in landing British troops and their supplies. With the moves towards the union of the separate South African provinces after the war, Cape Town was made the seat of the legislature.

Many of the bitter battles fought over apartheid were played out in Cape Town, where following the National Party's 1948 victory, the right of coloureds to vote in the Cape was removed and the apparatus of apartheid was erected.

The newly elected National Party declared the western half of the Cape Province a 'coloured preference area', which meant no black could be employed unless it could be proved there was no suitable coloured person for the job. No new black housing was built. As a result, illegal black squatter camps mushroomed on the sandy plains to the east of Cape Town. Government bulldozers would flatten the shanties, and their occupants were dragged away and dumped in their Homelands. Within weeks, the shanties would rise again.

In mid-1963, following three years of unrest and demonstrations over the hated pass laws, which required blacks and coloureds to carry passbooks authorising them to be in a particular area, Nelson Mandela and other ANC leaders were arrested and imprisoned on Robben Island in Table Bay.

District Six, just to the east of the city centre, was the suburb that, more than any other, gave Cape Town its cosmopolitan atmosphere and life. It was primarily a coloured ghetto, but people of every race lived there. It was a poor, overcrowded, but vibrant community. The streets were alive and jazz was its lifeblood.

This state of affairs did not appeal to the government so, in 1966, District Six was classified as a white area. Fifty thousand people, some of whose families had been there for five generations, were evicted and dumped in bleak townships such as Athlone, Mitchell's Plain and Atlantis.

The government tried for decades to eradicate the squatter towns, such as Crossroads, which were focal points for black resistance to apartheid. In its last attempt between May and June 1986, an estimated 70,000 people were driven from their homes and hundreds were killed.

Happier days followed the fall of the apartheid regime. It was in Cape Town's parliament that Nelson Mandela was proclaimed the country's first democratically elected president.

Cape Town still lives with many of apartheid's legacies. Much of District Six, for example, is still empty wasteland although redevelopment is being undertaken, some by former inhabitants. A worse legacy is the continued suspicion and mistrust between the black and coloured communities, although progress is being made towards better understanding and integration.

Orientation

The city centre lies to the north of Table Mountain and east of Signal Hill, and the inner city suburbs of Tamboerskloof, Gardens and Oranjezicht are within walking distance of it. This area is referred to as the City Bowl. On the western side of Signal Hill, Sea Point is another inner suburb, densely populated with high-rise apartments, hotels, restaurants and bars.

Some suburbs and surrounding towns cling to the coast, such as exclusive Clifton and Camps Bays and, further south, Llandudno Bay, Hout Bay and Kommetjie. The False Bay towns from Muizenberg to Simon's Town can be reached by rail from the centre.

Most of the population lives in sprawling suburbs on the eastern side of Table Mountain; whites close to the mountain and blacks and coloureds on the bleak plain known as the Cape Flats (which includes Guguletu, Nyanga, Philippi, Mitchell's Plain and Khayelitsha).

SOUTH AFRICA

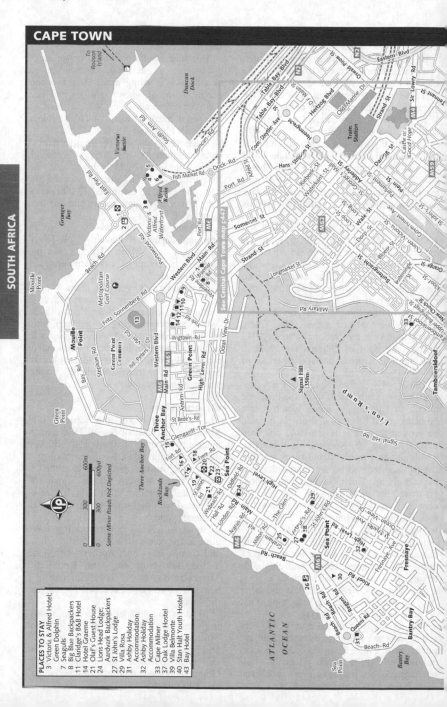

CAPE TOWN

See: Central Cape Town map (–447)

PLACES TO STAY
3 Victoria & Alfred Hotel;
   Green Dolphin
7 Seagulls
8 Big Blue Backpackers
11 Claridge's B&B Hotel
14 Hotel Graeme
21 Olaf's Guest House
24 Lions Head Lodge;
   Aardvark Backpackers
27 St John's Lodge
29 Villa Rosa
31 Ashby Holiday
   Accommodation
32 Ashby Holiday
   Accommodation
33 Cape Milner
37 Oak Lodge Hostel
39 Villa Belmonte
40 Stan Halt Youth Hostel
43 Bay Hotel

SOUTH AFRICA

CAPE TOWN

PLACES TO EAT
10 News Cafe
12 Giovanni's Deli World
16 L'Orient
17 Wow
18 Cafe Erte
19 Venezia
22 Maz Japanese Sushi Bar
30 New York Bagels
34 Saigon
36 Cafe Paradiso
41 La Med
42 Cafe Caprice
44 Blues; The Promenade

OTHER
1   Victoria Wharf Shopping
    Centre
2   BMW Pavilion-Imax
    Cinema
4   Bertie's Landing
5   Nelson Mandela Gateway
    & Embarkation Point for
    Robben Island Tours
6   Clock Tower
9   Dale Court
13 Green Point Stadium
15 Glengariff Pharmacy
20 Adelphi Shopping Centre;
    Rennies Foreign Exchange
23 Public Phones
25 Rennie's Travel (Thomas
    Cook)
26 Sea Point Pavilion Pool
28 Woolworths
35 Melissa's Food Shop
38 Wayne Motors
45 Dizzy Jazz Café; The
    Codfather

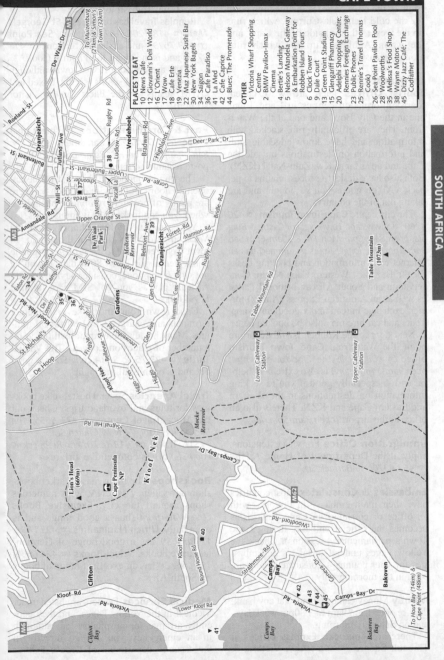

SOUTH AFRICA

The Cape of Good Hope (70km by road south of the city centre) is the meeting point for the cold Benguela Current, which runs up the west (Atlantic) side of the Cape, and the warm Agulhas Current, which runs along the east coast.

Information

Tourist Offices There are two excellent tourist information centres in Cape Town, one in the City Bowl and one at the Waterfront. They are efficiently run, stacked with information and have knowledgeable staff and information on destinations outside the Cape and up as far as KwaZulu-Natal (KZN). Both also have desks to process claims to get back VAT on goods you've bought and are taking out of the country.

The city centre **Cape Town Tourism** (☎ 426 4260; w www.cape-town.org; cnr Castle & Burg Sts; open 8am-6pm Mon-Fri, 8.30am-6pm Sat, 9am-1pm Sun, longer hours in summer) has an Internet café, information and booking desks for the Baz Bus, Western Cape Nature Conservation and South African National Parks, as well as an American Express (AmEx) foreign exchange bureau and a good craft shop. Tours and car hire may also be booked here.

Next door to the Robben Island departure point, the Waterfront **Cape Town Tourism** office (☎ 408 4500; The Clocktower Centre; open 9am-11pm daily) is also extremely helpful and is especially good if you're seeking information on destinations in the Western and Eastern Cape and KZN. There's also an office at the airport (open 7am-5pm daily).

Immigration Office For visa extensions, apply at the **Department of Home Affairs** (☎ 462 4970; 56 Barrack St).

Embassies & Consulates Most countries have their main embassy in Pretoria, with an office or consulate in Cape Town (this becomes the official embassy during Cape Town's parliamentary sessions). Check the Yellow Pages under Consulates & Embassies for your country's consulate. Many are open in the morning only.

Money Money can be changed at any bank; they're open from 9am to 3.30pm weekdays, and on Saturday morning.

There are **American Express offices** at Thibault Square (☎ 408 9700), Victoria &

Alfred Waterfront (☎ 419 3917) and at the Cape Town Tourism office.

Rennies Travel has branches at **St George's Mall** (☎ 418 1206; 182 Main Rd), **Sea Point** (☎ 439 7529); and at the **Waterfront** (☎ 418 3744) and is the agent for Thomas Cook.

ATMs are dotted all over town, although do beware of ATM scams (see the boxed text 'ATM Scams' in the Facts for the Visitor section).

Post & Communications The **main post office** (cnr Darling & Parliament Sts; open 8am-4.30pm Mon-Fri, 8am-noon Sat) has a poste restante counter.

The public phones in the post office are open 24 hours, but they're often busy. There are plenty of privately run phone businesses where you can make calls without coins.

You can rent mobile phones from the Vodacom and MTN desks at the airport. In town **Cellurent** (☎ 418 5656) offers mobile phone rental for US$1.80 a day. If you've got your own phone, consider buying a South African 'pay as you go' SIM card (around US$4.60).

Cape Town Tourism has several Internet terminals and charges US$1.80 for 30 minutes. Many hostels have email facilities as do a number of places on Long St. **The Virtual Turtle** (☎ 423 7508; 303A Long St) is a good bet and is open until midnight.

Travel Agencies Several hostels take bookings for tours and overland trips. Check out the **Africa Travel Centre** (☎ 423 5555; The Backpack Hostel, 74 New Church St).

STA Travel (☎ 418 6570; cnr Riebeeck & Loop Sts) offers competitive airfares.

Bookshops The main mass-market bookshop/newsagency is **CNA**, with numerous shops around the city. **Exclusive Books** (The Waterfront) has a good range and is open daily. **Ulrich Naumann's** (☎ 423 7832; 17 Burg St) has a good range of German-language books. **Select Books** (☎ 424 6955; 186 Long St) has an excellent range of books on South Africa.

Medical Services Doctors are listed under Medical in the Yellow Pages, and they generally arrange for hospitalisation, although in an emergency you can go directly to the casualty department of **Groote Schuur**

Hospital *(☎ 404 9111; cnr De Waal – M3 & Eastern Boulevard – N2)* to the east of the city. Phone the **police** *(☎ 10111)* to get directions to the nearest hospital.

There's a **Medi Travel Clinic** *(☎ 419 1888; Clock Tower Centre; open 9am-9pm daily)* next door to the tourist office on the Waterfront.

For medications, try the **Glengariff Pharmacy** *(Cnr Main Rd & Glengariff, Sea Point; open to 11pm daily)*.

Emergency The phone numbers for emergency services are:

ambulance	☎ 10177
fire brigade	☎ 535 1100
police	☎ 10111
Automobile Association (AA)	☎ 0800-10101
Lifeline	☎ 461 1111
Rape Crisis	☎ 447 9762

Dangers & Annoyances Cape Town is one of the most relaxed cities in Africa but common sense is still required. There has been a substantial increase in street crime in recent years. Take care in Sea Point late at night. Walking to or from the Victoria & Alfred Waterfront has been dangerous in recent years, however the completion of the new Convention Centre theoretically means security should be much tighter. Seek local advice before doing this or walking around the city centre at night.

The townships on the Cape Flats have an appalling crime rate and without a trustworthy guide, they are off limits.

Watch out for ATM scams in Cape Town. Some ATMs accept your card but don't give it back. While you're away getting help, your card and cash mysteriously disappear! Try to use ATMs attached to a bank and do so during business hours. Outside business hours, a queue in front of an ATM is a good sign. Don't allow a 'helpful' bystander to tell you how to operate the machine.

Swimming at all of the Cape beaches is potentially hazardous, especially for those inexperienced in surf. Check for signs warning of rips and rocks, and swim in patrolled areas.

The mountains in the middle of the city are no less dangerous just because they are in the city. Weather conditions can change rapidly, so warm clothing and a good map and compass are necessary. Also watch out for ticks here.

Museums

Bo-Kaap Museum The small but interesting Bo-Kaap Museum *(71 Wale St; US$0.60; open 9.30am-4.30pm Mon-Sat)* gives an insight into the lifestyle of a prosperous, 19th-century Muslim family. The house itself was built in 1763.

District Six Museum During the apartheid era the lively mixed-race suburb of District Six was bulldozed and the government changed the street grid and the names of the few remaining roads. Today, the simple District Six Museum *(☎ 461 8745; cnr Buitenkant & Albertus Sts; donation requested; open 9am-4pm Mon-Sat)* is as much *for* the former residents of this vanished area as it is about them. The floor is covered with a large-scale map of District Six. Walking tours of District Six's streets may be booked ahead for US$2.40, although tours take a minimum of five people.

Slave Lodge & Cultural History Museum This interesting museum *(☎ 461 8280; admission US$0.80; open 9.30am-4.30pm Mon-Sat)* at the mountain end of Adderley St is the former slave lodge of the VOC, but it has gone through several incarnations since then, including stints as the Supreme Court and the Legislative Assembly. There are displays on Cape history including information about slavery and pre-colonial African cultures, such as the Khoisan herders.

South African Museum This museum *(☎ 424 3330; US$0.90, free Wed; open daily)*, at the mountain end of the Botanic (Company's) Gardens, is the oldest and arguably the most interesting museum in South Africa.

There's a profusion of amazing objects including good displays on early man, some excellent San Rock art and fossilised human footprints thought to be more than 100,000 years old. There's also a planetarium here – a visit may help northerners understand the southern hemisphere night sky.

Townhouse Museum This museum *(Greenmarket Square; admission free; open 10am-5pm daily)* is an old Cape Dutch building housing dour Dutch and Flemish art from the 16th and 17th centuries. The museum is worth visiting for the views from the balcony overlooking the bustling square.

National Gallery

This small but exquisite gallery (☎ 465 1628; admission free; open 10am-5pm Tues-Sun) in the Botanical Gardens has some interesting temporary exhibitions which begin to redress the imbalance from the apartheid days. There is also a shop and a café.

Houses of Parliament

On Government Ave (Wale St end) are the Houses of Parliament (☎ 403 2537; admission free), which were opened in 1885. During the parliamentary session (usually January to June) gallery tickets are available; overseas tourists may have to present their passports.

During the recess (usually July to January) there are **guided tours** at 11am and 2pm weekdays. Go to the Old Parliament building entrance on Parliament St.

Castle of Good Hope

The Castle of Good Hope (☎ 469 1084; admission US$1.80) was constructed between 1666 and 1679 and is one of the oldest European structures in Southern Africa.

It is still a military base but visitors are welcome. There are a couple of museums with collections of furniture, paintings and interesting temporary exhibitions. Guided tours leave at 11am, noon and 2pm; entry is from Grand Parade. There's also a decent café, **De Goewerneur**.

Noon Gun & Signal Hill

Signal Hill separates Sea Point from the City Bowl. There are magnificent views from the 350m-high summit, especially at night. At noon (daily except Sunday) a cannon is fired, and can be heard throughout the city. Head up Kloof Nek Rd from the city and take the turn-off to the right at the top of the hill.

Table Mountain & Cableway

A waypoint beloved of seafarers, a giant barometer, the city's icon and a nature reserve floating 1000m above the city's heart – Table Mountain is all these things.

This imposing lump of rock is as good close up as it is from afar. You can salute its lovely outline with a sundowner from one of the many viewpoints around town or enjoy the inspirational views from its flat summit, where there are some good walks. Several tour operators in the city offer a number of high-adrenaline descents of the mountain, including *kloofing*, abseiling and paragliding. See the boxed text 'Climbing & Exploring Table Mountain' following for details about exploring the jewel in the Cape's crown.

The revolving cable cars (☎ 424 8181; W www.tablemountain.net; one way/return US$5.80/10.90; operating 8am to 9pm, later in peak season) enable you to take in the lovely panorama on the way up and down, but don't operate when it's dangerously windy, and there's not much point going up if the mountain has its tablecloth of cloud.

There's a small **restaurant** and shop at the top. To get to the lower cableway station, catch the Kloof Nek bus from outside OK Bazaars in Adderley St to the Kloof Nek terminus and connect with the cableway bus.

Robben Island

A tour of Robben Island, where former president Nelson Mandela was held prisoner for 27 years, is an unforgettable experience.

Tours (☎ 419 1300/413 4200; W www.robben-island.org.za; Nelson Mandela Gateway; Clock Tower Precinct; adult/child US$17.50/8.60), which leave from the Waterfront, are only possible on rather pricey official tours but they are well worthwhile.

What makes them special are the guides – ex-political prisoners, many of them held here during Mandela's imprisonment. Our guide, when asked how many years he had been in prison, answered 5,590 days (about 15 years). The guides are happy to answer any questions you ask them about their personal experiences. Their answers are direct, personal and often shocking.

Amazingly, the guides seem to be without bitterness and keep the memory of the prison's history and its criminal past alive out of a wish for reconciliation, not revenge. After the prison tour, a bus ride around the island reveals an interesting history, including the remnants of a leper colony, some WWII bunkers and two 19th-century churches. The view of Cape Town and Table Mountain from the island is stunning.

Tours to the island are hugely popular so booking ahead is essential.

Climbing & Exploring Table Mountain

Table Mountain commands surely some of the most spectacular views in the world. Look north and you're gazing over the angry Atlantic to tiny Robben Island, south and you're looking at the majestic cliffs of the Twelve Apostles and the rugged coast below.

Inland you'll see the city spread away from the mountain's mighty roots, in the middle distance the shanty towns of the Cape Flats and beyond them the looming silhouettes of the Hottentots-Holland mountains.

The 3km-long slab of the summit is also worth exploring. Consider the fairly flat hike to Maclear's Beacon, at 1086m the highest point of the mountain.

You're sure to encounter the fluffy, cute, rodent-like dassies (also known as rock hyraxes). They are not rodents in fact, but distant relatives of the elephant.

The mountain is also home to 110 invertebrates, including the Table Mountain ghost frog found here and nowhere else. There's plenty of birdlife up here too, including black eagles, rock kestrels and red-winged starlings.

Climbing Table Mountain is a good way to discover its secrets and you'll appreciate the thrill of those views all the more. It's a hard three-hour slog and only for the reasonably fit, but hugely rewarding. There are hundreds of routes up, but two or three firm favourites.

One of the most direct routes is up the Platteklip Gorge, starting about 1.5km east of the lower cableway station along Tafelberg Rd. It's straightforward enough although there are a couple of hair-raisingly steep sections towards the top.

If you want to ascend and descend via different routes and fit in a bit of botany at the same time, consider the (roughly five-hour) route from Kirstenbosch Botanic Gardens – up Skeleton Gorge (steep and tricky in places and a tough descent) and down Nursery Ravine.

It's best to get either a local guide (ask at Cape Town Tourism) or buy one of the local walking guides that detail various routes. The *Approved Paths on Table Mountain*, published by the Mountain Club of South Africa, is the ideal paper companion.

Don't assume it's an entirely safe place just because it's so close to the city – people have died up here. Take note of the weather forecast, go well equipped with warm clothes, don't walk alone, tell someone where you're going, take waterproofs and food and bear in mind that conditions, and visibility, on the mountain can quickly deteriorate.

You can get a one-way ticket back down on the cableway.

By car, take Kloof Nek Rd and turn off to the left (signposted).

Victoria & Alfred Waterfront

The Victoria & Alfred Waterfront (V&A Waterfront) is crammed with bland malls but it's still well worth visiting. Packed with restaurants, bars and at least a few interesting shops, it buzzes day and night.

One of the Waterfront's main charms is that the eating, drinking and shopping is done around a properly functioning (if small-scale) dock. Escape the mall muzak and wander the dry dock where fishing boats are scrubbed clean of barnacles, or just stand and watch yachts and liners coming and going. You may even spot the odd sunbathing seal.

Whatever else you do you don't miss a **cruise** into Table Bay. Try the **Waterfront Adventures** (☎ 418 5806) or **Waterfront Boat**

Company (☎ 418 0134; Port Captain's building, Pier Head), across from Bertie's Landing, for a variety of cruises. Half-hour cruises start at around US$3.50.

The **aquarium** (☎ 418 3823; admission US$5.20; open 9.30am-6pm daily) is well worth a visit. The kelp forest tank is wonderful. There's also a good shark tank.

Even if you're not heading out to Robben Island (see the boxed text 'Robben Island' earlier), pay a quick visit to the smart new **Nelson Mandela Gateway** (Clock Tower Precinct; open daily 8am-6pm; admission free), from which cruises to the island leave. There's some good audiovisual material on the events surrounding Mandela's imprisonment. It's no substitute for heading to Robben Island itself though.

Shuttle buses to the Waterfront run roughly every 15 minutes from Adderley St up Strand

St, with a stop near the Holiday Inn, to the centre of the waterfront and cost US$0.40. They also leave from near the Pavilion Pool in Sea Point. Parking here is straightforward. There's plenty of free open and paid covered parking.

At the time of writing it was still unsafe to walk between the city centre and the Waterfront, but security should improve vastly with the completion of the new convention centre nearby. Take advice locally.

Kirstenbosch Botanical Gardens

The Gardens (☎ 799 8800; w www.nbi.ac.za; Rhodes Dr, Constantia; admission US$1.80; open from 8am year-round, closing 7pm Sept-Mar, 6pm Apr-Aug) are among the most beautiful in the world. In 1895, Cecil Rhodes purchased the eastern slopes of Table Mountain and bequeathed the property to the nation on his death in 1902.

Kirstenbosch is devoted almost exclusively to indigenous plants and has about 9000 of Southern Africa's 22,000 plant species. Don't miss the desert plants in the conservatory. The information office (open daily) has maps and gives advice on various walks.

The gardens are a great place for a picnic and there are good-value Sunday afternoon concerts in the summer.

Rikki's taxis run out to the gardens for US$6.40 from the city centre.

Rhodes Memorial

Originally part of Kirstenbosch when it was owned by diamond magnate and empire-builder Cecil Rhodes, this area now houses the huge Rhodes Memorial, a classic example of the extremes of stuffy bombast that went into British Empire architecture and statuary, but impressive nonetheless.

The attached café is a lovely shaded spot for a coffee or a meal. The paths above the monument offer good city and bay views. It's also possible to walk to Kirstenbosch from here but the paths are not clearly marked and you'll need a good map.

Groot Constantia

Groot Constantia (☎ 794 5128) is the oldest vineyard in the Cape, and one of the grandest. It was built by Governor Simon van der Stel in 1692. In the 18th century, Constantia wines were exported around the world and were highly acclaimed. Fine wines are still produced here.

It's well worth visiting as much for the lovely old Cape architecture as for the wine or food. There are tours with tastings (10am-5pm daily).

Other nearby vineyards used to form part of the estate and are also worth a visit, including **Buitenverwachtig** (☎ 794 5190) which also offers tastings and has a top-notch restaurant. A visit to Groot Constantia could easily be combined with a visit to Kirstenbosch Botanical Gardens. Unfortunately there is no direct public transport to either.

Atlantic Coast

The Atlantic coast here has some of the most spectacular scenery in the world. The beaches include the trendiest on the Cape, with the emphasis on sunbathing rather than swimming – the water comes straight from the Antarctic.

For the areas south or west of the City Bowl, buses and minibus taxis run along Victoria Rd from the city to Hout Bay. Minibus taxis run along Main Rd to the end of Regent St in Sea Point but no further.

Bloubergstrand & Table View Bloubergstrand, 25km to the north of the city on Table Bay, is the site of the 1806 battle between British and Dutch forces that resulted in the second British occupation of the Cape. This is also the spot with the most dramatic (and photographed) view of Table Mountain.

Unfortunately, you'll need a car to get here. Take the R27 north from the N1.

Sea Point This is a bustling residential suburb and Main Rd is lined with restaurants and shops (and often choked with traffic). The coast is rocky and swimming is dangerous but there are four tidal swimming pools. Visit the **Sea Point Pavilion Pool** (admission US$0.80; open 8.30am-dusk), at the end of Clarens St.

Clifton There are four linked beaches at Clifton, accessible by steps from Victoria Rd. They're the trendiest, busiest beaches on the Cape. Fourth Beach, at the Camps Bay end, is the most accessible and is popular with families. First Beach is the place to be seen.

Camps Bay This bay is often windy and is not as trendy as Clifton, but it is more spectacular. The impressive Twelve Apostles of Table Mountain tumble into the sea above the broad stretch of white sand. There are no lifesavers, but strong surf, so take care. **La Med** *(☎ 438 5600)* next to the green where the paragliders float in to land from Lion's Head, is a great spot for sundowners, although there are better places to eat. For sundowners with sea views the (pricey) bar at **The Twelve Apostles Hotel** *(☎ 437 9001; Victoria Rd)* is hard to beat. You may even see whales.

Hout Bay As well as retaining something of a village atmosphere, Hout Bay is in a stunning setting. The southern arm of the bay is an important fishing port.

The **Mariners Wharf complex** is the best place to eat, drink and buy fresh seafood. The fish and chip places round the corner offer a good opportunity to enjoy the bustle of port life while you eat.

Chapman's Peak Drive south around the Bay, cut into the side of sheer mountain walls, used to be one of the world's great scenic drives until rock falls forced its seemingly indefinite closure.

Kommetjie This is just a smallish cray-fishing village but it's the focal point for surfing on the Cape, offering an assortment of reefs that hold a very big swell. Unfortunately, since rock falls forced the closure of Chapman's Peak Drive, it's a long way round from the city via False Bay and there's no public transport here.

False Bay

False Bay lies to the southeast of the city. Although the beaches on the eastern side of the peninsula are not quite as scenically spectacular as those on the Atlantic side, the water is much warmer.

During October and November, False Bay is a favoured haunt for whales and their calves; southern right, humpback and bryde (**bree**-dah) whales are the most commonly sighted.

On weekdays trains run between Cape Town and Fish Hoek via Muizenberg every half hour to 9pm; every hour one train continues through to Simon's Town. On weekends nearly all trains run through to Simon's Town, more or less hourly. Cape Town to

Muizenberg is US$0.90/0.50 in 1st/3rd class, Simon's Town is US$1.10/0.60.

Simon's Town (Simonstad) Named after Simon van der Stel, an early governor, this town was the VOC's winter anchorage. The British turned the harbour into a naval base in 1814 and it has remained one ever since.

There's an **information bureau** *(☎ 786 2436; 111 St George's St)*. Next door is the **Navy Museum** *(open 10am-4pm daily; admission free)*. **Seaforth Beach** is the nearest to Simon's Town and a good family swimming spot. A bit further on is the **Boulders**, an area with attractive coves among large boulders.

Don't miss the 3000-strong penguin colony 3km from the town centre around Boulder's Beach, part of the **Cape Peninsula National Park** *(☎ 786 2329; open 8am-6pm daily; admission US$1.20)*. There's a large boardwalk to the main colony but further round you can even share the beach with these endearing, but endangered, birds.

Cape of Good Hope Nature Reserve

This reserve *(☎ 780 9204; admission US$2.90; open 6am-6pm daily in summer, 7am-5pm in winter)* on the spectacular peninsula is another 'must see' while you're in the Cape. Make time to do more than head to the peninsula, have a coffee and leave. There are countless great walks and beaches offering a chance to see the Cape's unique flora (fynbos) up close as well as antelopes and abundant birdlife. Beware of the belligerent baboons.

Maps are available at the gate, and there are picnic places, a kiosk and restaurant. The tip of the peninsula is a dramatic place to be on a clear day. For the less mobile or the downright lazy, there's a funicular railway which heads to just below the lighthouse at the top.

The only public transport to the peninsula Cape is with Rikki's (see Getting Around later in this section).

Numerous tours include Cape Point on their itineraries. **Day Trippers** *(☎ 511 4766)* and the **Baz Bus** *(☎ 439 2323; US$31)* take along mountain bikes.

Botany lovers looking for an in-depth guided tour of the peninsula's flora should contact botanist, life-long Cape resident and mountaineer Elizabeth Ashton. She can be contacted through the Kirstenbosch Botanical Society *(☎ 671 5468)*.

Cape Flats

For the majority of Cape Town's inhabitants, home is in one of the grim townships on the Cape Flats: Guguletu, Nyanga, Philippi, Mitchell's Plain, Crossroads or Khayelitsha. Visiting without a companion who has local knowledge would be foolish. If a black friend is happy to escort you, you should have no problems, and tours have operated safely for years (see Organised Tours later in this chapter).

Diving

Cape Town has a wide variety of diving possibilities as the Agulhas and Benguela Currents create a unique cross-section of marine conditions. There are several dive operators, such as **Table Bay Diving** (☎ 419 1780/8822; Quay 5, V&A Waterfront). A certificate course costs about US$195.

Surfing

The Cape Peninsula has fantastic surfing possibilities: from gentle shorebreaks ideal for beginners to monsters for experts only.

In general, the best surf is along the Atlantic side, and there is a string of breaks from Bloubergstrand through to the Cape of Good Hope. Most of these breaks work best in southeasterly conditions.

The **Surf Zone** (☎ 423 7853; 45 cnr Castle & Berg Sts) in the city centre has a good stock of wetsuits and second-hand boards; it also hires boards and wetsuits.

Hiking & Walking

There are some fantastic hikes around the peninsula. Look out for Shirley Brossy's *Walking Guide for Table Mountain* and Mike Lundy's *Best Walks in the Cape Peninsula* (US$5.20). Cape Town Tourism also has information about various guided walks.

Walking up (or down) Table Mountain is definitely possible. See the boxed text 'Climbing and Exploring Table Mountain' earlier in this chapter.

Serious technical climbers should get in touch with the **Mountain Club of South Africa** (☎ 465 3412).

Other Activities

Several **canoeing** operators run short and long trips from Cape Town. **Felix Unite** (☎ 670 1300) is the major operator and has a good reputation.

Abseiling off Table Mountain (or Chapman's Peak, depending on the weather) with **Abseil Africa** (☎ 424 4760) costs US$29 (plus the cableway fare, if applicable). There are also day tours to **'Kamikazi Kanyon'** (US$46), which include hiking, *kloofing* and abseiling through a waterfall.

A number of operators also offer tandem paragliding trips off Lion's Head, which cost around US$51. Try **Hi-xposure** (☎ 439 5796)

Hostels are usually a good source of information on most activities and budget tour companies. **Day Trippers** (☎ 511 4766) gets excellent feedback.

Organised Tours

For a quick orientation on a fine day, you can't beat **The Cape Town Explorer** (book through Cape Town Tourism ☎ 426 4260), which runs an open-top double-decker bus. The two-hour city tour (US$9) between Dock Rd at the Waterfront and the train station departs six times a day.

Civair Helicopters (☎ 419 5182) offers spectacular flights around the city and peninsula. A 20-minute Cape Peninsula flight costs US$210 for one or two people or US$275 for three of four people.

One City Tours (☎ 387 5351) runs highly recommended township tours of the Cape Flats

Tana-Baru Tours (☎ 424 0719/073 237800) offers a two-hour walk or drive through Bo-Kaap (the Malay quarter). Tours cost US$11.50

For information on boat cruises, see Victoria & Alfred Waterfront earlier in this section.

Places to Stay

There are so many options in Cape Town that most people will easily find something that suits their pocket; keep in mind that the Cape starts filling up in November and in the high season – December to Easter – prices can double and many places are fully booked.

Places to Stay – Budget

Camping There are no central caravan or camping parks.

Zandvlei Caravan Park (☎ 788 5215; The Row; 2-person camp sites US$11.50), in Muizenberg, is about 2km from Muizenberg train station and about 1km from the beach.

CENTRAL CAPE TOWN

PLACES TO STAY
22 Metropole Hotel
30 Tudor Hotel
31 Greenmarket Square Hotel
35 Holiday Inn
57 Long St Backpackers
60 St Paul's Guesthouse
64 Travellers Inn
65 Cat & Moose
66 The Backpack & Africa Travel Centre
67 Zebra Crossing
84 Mount Nelson Hotel
85 Ashanti Lodge

PLACES TO EAT
2 Chilli 'n Lime
23 Savoy Cabbage
27 Cafe Mozart
28 Sunflower Health Deli
33 Surf Zone
54 Five Flies
55 Mr Pickwicks Deli
63 Long St Cafe
68 Rozenhof
69 Cafe Bar Deli

70 Naked on Kloof
77 Perseverance Tavern

ENTERTAINMENT
1 The Bronx
3 Cafe Manhattan
7 The Drunken Springbok
10 The Rockin' Shamrock
14 Artscape
32 Purple Turtle; Virtual Turtle
53 169 on Long
56 Mama Africa
58 The Lounge
59 Jo'burg
61 Marvel
62 Carnival Court
72 Little Theatre
79 The Stag's Head
83 Labia Cinema

MUSEUMS
21 Koopmans de Wet House
25 Bo-Kaap Museum
38 Townhouse Museum; Ivy Garden Restaurant

50 Slave Lodge & Cultural History Museum
73 South African Museum
76 District Six Museum
78 Rust-en-Vreugd
80 National Gallery
81 Jewish Museum
82 Bertram House

OTHER
4 Budget
5 Avis
6 STA Travel
8 Hertz
9 Imperial Car Rental
11 Rennies Foreign Exchange
12 BP Centre
13 Broadway Centre
15 Civic Centre
16 Jan & Maria van Riebeeck Statues
17 American Express; Trustbank Centre
18 British Airways Travel Clinic
19 ABSA Centre
20 Southern Life Centre

24 Tempest Car Rental
26 The African Music Store
29 African Image
34 Cape Town Tourism; Western Cape Tourism; Baz Bus Booking Office; Internet Cafe; Amex; National Parks Office
36 Ulrich Naumann's
37 Greenmarket Square; Cycles
39 Rennies Travel
40 BOB (First National Bank)
41 Woolworths
42 Golden Acre Centre
43 Main Bus Station
44 Castle of Good Hope
45 Grand Parade
46 Town Hall
47 Bus Information Kiosk
48 Lite Kem Pharmacy
49 Groote Kerk
51 Houses of Parliament
52 St George's Cathedral
71 Spar Supermarket
74 Botanical (Company's) Gardens; Public Gardens Tea Rooms
75 Department of Home Affairs

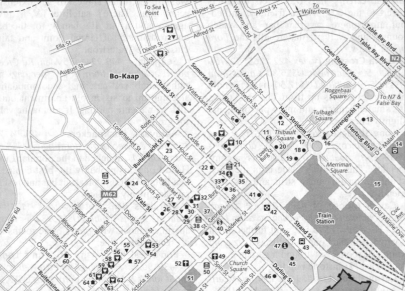

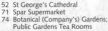

SOUTH AFRICA

Hostels & Budget Guesthouses There is an excellent and growing range of cheap hostels aimed at backpackers. Listed below are a few favourites. You'll find brochures about the rest at Cape Town Tourism.

City Bowl One of the best hostels in town, **The Backpack** (☎ 423 4530; e backpack@gem.co.za; w www.backpackers.co.za; 74 New Church St; dorm beds US$9.20-11.50, doubles US$32) has spacious doubles, although the dorm bunks are wobbly so go for the deluxe ones. Its website also includes information on tours and activities available from the Africa Travel Centre (based at the hostel).

Oak Lodge (☎ 465 6182, fax 465 6308; 21 Breda St, Gardens; dorm beds US$8, doubles and self-catering flats U$32) lets travellers revert to the 60s, with a friendly, chilled-out atmosphere, a great bar and video lounge, and wall art that recalls the *Lord of the Rings*.

Zebra Crossing (☎/fax 422 1265; 82 New Church St; dorm beds US$5.80 singles from US$11.50, doubles US$17.50) is a friendly place a few doors up from The Backpack. It's smaller, quieter and more personal, and slightly cheaper.

Long St Backpackers (☎ 423 0615; e longstbp@mweb.co.za; 209 Long St; dorm beds US$6.90-8, doubles US$18.50) is recommended. This bustling place is in the thick of things on this busy strip and it's very friendly.

Cat & Moose (☎ 423 7638; e catandmoose@hotmail.com; 305 Long St; dorm beds US$7.50, doubles $18.50), a bit further down Long St, near the Long St Baths, is a dizzying warren of rooms, set around a garden courtyard in a 1791 historic building.

Carnival Court (☎ 423 9003; e info@carnivalcourt.co.za; 255 Long St; dorm beds US$8; twins/doubles US$18.50/21) is a smart place in a handsome old building, funkily stripped back to wooden floors and bare brick with two large balconies from which to watch Long St's human wildlife.

Ashanti Lodge (☎ 423 8721; e ashanti@iafrica.com; 11 Hof St, Gardens; dorm beds US$10, singles US$19.50, doubles US$28) is a great place in a huge rambling mansion. There's a bar and café upstairs, a travel centre for backpackers, and a terrific view of Table Mountain.

Travellers Inn (☎ 424 9272; e travellersinn@intekom.co.za; 208 Long St; B&B singles/doubles US$17.50/23) is another central, basic but good-value guesthouse.

St Paul's Guesthouse (☎ 423 4420; 182 Bree St; singles/doubles/triples US$14/23/34.50) is very comfortable, spotless, cheap and close to Long St. It belongs to the local parish and the rooms are named after its former priests.

Waterfront, Green Point & Sea Point Areas In an imposing 1905 mansion **Big Blue Backpackers** (☎ 439 0807; 7 Vesperdene Rd, Green Point; dorm beds US$8, doubles with shared/private bathroom US$17.50/23), complete with chandeliers and grand staircases leading to 22 rooms, was in the final stages of an extensive renovation. There's satellite TV, a travel agency and a bar. It's handy for the bars and restaurants of Green Point and fairly close to the Waterfront.

Seagulls (☎ 439 9941; 35 Main Rd Greenpoint; apartments from US$23 per day) has rather drab self-catering accommodation sleeping up to six in old apartment buildings with secure parking. It's fantastic value for groups.

Aardvark Backpackers (☎ 434 4172; e aardbp@mweb.co.za; dorm beds US$8.60, rooms US$31), attached to the popular Lions Head Lodge, is probably the best choice in Sea Point. There's a pleasant bar and restaurant and plenty of life.

Claridges B&B Hotel (☎ 434 1171; 47 Main Rd; singles/doubles US$19/32) is a large apartment block with pretty basic rooms but it's reasonable value.

For a real bargain try **St John's Lodge** (☎ 439 9028; e stjohnslodge@mweb.co.za; cnr St John's & Main Rds; dorm beds US$7.50, singles/doubles US$15/18.50).

Camps Bay The **Stan Halt Youth Hostel** (☎ 438 9037; Roundhouse Rd, The Glen, Camps Bay; dorm beds US$5) is a national monument in a beautiful position with a great view. It only has dorms, and meals are available. This place is very easy-going and would be a good place to spend a few days recuperating from an overdose of nightlife. Take the Kloof Nek bus from outside OK Bazaars (US$0.40) to the top of Kloof Nek, then take the road to the right.

Places to Stay – Mid-Range

The **Bed 'n Breakfast Organisation** (☎ 683 3505) has members around the Cape Peninsula. Prices start at US$22/26 per person in the low/high seasons. You can pay a lot more than this. Alternatively, try the **Guesthouse Association** (☎ 762 0880; fax 797 3115) or the accommodation booking service at Cape Town Tourism.

Most of the good-value hotels are in and around the city centre.

City Bowl The small and recently renovated **Tudor Hotel** (☎ 424 1335; Greenmarket Square; singles/doubles from US$37/48.50) has a great position in the middle of town.

The **Metropole Hotel** (☎ 423 6363; 38 Long St; rooms from US$20) is a charming old-style hotel that has recently been revamped and has clean rooms (with TV, phone and bathroom). There are also executive rooms for about US$7 extra, but the standard rooms are better value. There's secure parking at night for an extra US$0.70 – well worth it.

Waterfront & Green Point Areas Close to the Waterfront, **Hotel Graeme** (☎ 434 9282; e hotelg@mweb.co.za; 107 Main Rd; B&B singles/doubles US$46/52) is bright and modern with a homely feel.

Dale Court (☎ 439 8774; e dalecrt@iafrica .com; 1 Exhibition Terrace Rd, Green Point; B&B singles/doubles US$40/43) is another appealing, comfortable mid-priced guesthouse boasting good breakfasts.

Sea Point With some lovely apartments, **Ashby Holiday Accommodation** (☎ 434 1879; e sylk@mweb.co.za 242 High Level Rd, Fresnaye; low/high season US$34/55) is close enough to the seafront to get a nostril full of sea spray if you leave the window open.

Villa Rosa (☎ 434 2768; e villaros@meb.co .za; 277 High Level Rd; singles/doubles from US$28/40, peak season from US$38/55) has very smart, well-equipped rooms in a lovely old house.

Lions Head Lodge (☎ 434 4163; e lion head@mweb.co.za; 319 Main Rd; rooms from US$29) is efficiently run and excellent value, with discounts for longer stays. There is also a pub and restaurant.

Hout Bay On Hout Bay, **Chapman's Peak Hotel** (☎ 790 1036; Main Rd, Hout Bay; rooms from US$57) isn't flash but it's a relaxed place.

Places to Stay – Top End

City Bowl The fantastically located **Greenmarket Square Hotel** (☎ 423 2050; Greenmarket Square; singles/doubles US$56/62) has been stylishly renovated and offers pretty good value. There's a pub and a restaurant attached and you can sit out with a drink overlooking the square's daytime hubbub.

The **Cape Milner** (☎ 426 1101; e cape milner@threecities.co.za; 2A Milner Rd, Tamboerskloof; high season singles/doubles from US$92/120) is not as well located for the city but nestles below the mountain and is a swish, modern place with a decent restaurant and bar. It's reasonably cheap for what you get.

Mount Nelson Hotel (☎ 483 1000; w www .mountnelsonhotel.orient-express.com; 76 Orange St; rooms mid-season from US$530) dates from 1899. Set in seven acres of parkland this hotel allows you to step back in time to the grand days of the British Empire. To pay for the privilege, however, you may have to auction one of your kidneys. The lavish afternoon tea buffet (US$9) is tempting even if you're not staying.

Holiday Inn (☎ 488 5100; Strand St; rooms US$110), in complete contrast, is a large, modern five-star hotel in the middle of the city. There are weekend specials.

As well as the hotels, there are some outstanding top-end guesthouses such as **Villa Belmonte** (☎ 462 1576; fax 462 1579; 33 Belmont Ave, Oranjezicht; singles/doubles from US$155/210), which is an ornate Italianate villa.

Waterfront Area The elegant **Victoria & Alfred Hotel** (☎ 419 6677, e res@vahot el.co.za; singles/doubles from US$140/200) is in the heart of the Waterfront and has lovely, large rooms, some with great mountain views.

Sea Point & Camps Bay The five-star **Bay Hotel** (☎ 438 4444; singles/doubles in the low season from US$122/148) has a smart contemporary look and is just across the road from lovely (but busy) Camps Bay beach. You'll pay more for a sea view.

Olaf's Guest House (☎ 439 8943; e olafs@icon.co.za; 24 Wisbeach Rd, Sea Point; doubles from US$87) is a stylish

and serene hideaway. The owner speaks German.

Places to Eat

Cape Town could easily claim to be the gastronomic capital of Southern Africa.

The biggest concentration of restaurants is at the Victoria & Alfred Waterfront, but the city centre is also worth sniffing out. Most of the inner neighbourhoods in the City Bowl also have an increasing number of good places to eat.

City Centre Near the corner of Long St, **Cafe Mozart** *(Church St; open 7am-3pm Mon-Fri, & Sat morning)* is a buzzing place. It's popular with locals at lunchtime and has live music.

Sunflower Health Deli *(111 Long St)* serves fresh juice combinations, tasty muffins and wholesome vegie snacks.

Mr Pickwick's Deli *(158 Long St)* is a licensed, deli-style café that stays open very late, patronised by a youngish alternative crowd.

Long Street Cafe *(259 Long St; mains around US$4)* is an appealing, spacious hangout as good for drinking as eating. You can kick off a night here or finish one as it stays busy till late.

Ivy Garden Restaurant *(Old Town House, Greenmarket Square; open 10am-4pm Mon-Sat)* is a good, reasonably priced lunchtime option in a pleasant courtyard, a bread roll's throw from the bustle of the square.

Five Flies *(☎ 424 442; 14-16 Keerom St; 2-/3-courses US$9/12)* is swanky and relaxed but pricey, although the food is irreproachable.

The Savoy Cabbage *(☎ 424 2626; 101 Hout St; mains from US$7)*, in pleasing barebrick and girder surroundings, serves the freshest food from an unpretentious, constantly changing menu. Good vegie options (try the *bobotie*), great service and decent wine make this one of Cape Town's finest restaurants.

Gardens & Tamboerskloof There is a batch of interesting places south of the city centre.

Public Gardens Tea Room *(Botanical (Company's) Gardens; open 7.30am-5pm daily)* is a restful, shaded spot for light refreshment.

Perseverance Tavern *(☎ 461 2440; 83 Buitenkant St)* is a Cape Town pub gem, built

in 1808, serving good, solid pub-style main courses for around US$4.

Naked on Kloof *(51 Kloof St; open 9am-11pm)* serves healthy wraps and fresh juices till late in sleekly modern surroundings.

Cafe Bar Deli *(Kloof St; open breakfast, late Mon-Sat)* is a big, funky place in a period building near the corner of Rheede St. The food is fresh, healthy and good value.

Rozenhof *(☎ 424 1968; 18 Kloof St; mains around US$6)* is one of the best restaurants in town, with small but interesting seasonal menus.

Other decent places further along Kloof St include the elegant Vietnamese restaurant **Saigon** *(Cnr Kloof & Camp Sts)* and two cafés: **Cafe Paradiso** *(110 Kloof St)* with a good sitting out area; and **Melissa's Food Shop** *(94 Kloof St)*, a lovely upmarket café/deli.

Waterfront Area The quality of the food here is generally good, especially the seafood, and it's a great place to eat outside on a warm evening.

Ferryman's Tavern, adjoining Mitchell's Waterfront Brewery, is a cheap and cheerful option serving freshly brewed beers and good-value pub meals.

Harrie's Pancakes *(Clocktower Centre; mains around US$4)* serves delicious savoury and sweet pancakes.

At **Cape Town Fish Market** *(☎ 418 5977; starters from US$1.00, mains US$4.60-7)* you can sharpen your appetite by gaping at the fish in the impressive fish counters before sampling it at the restaurant or the sushi bar. It's near the cinemas in Victoria Wharf.

Balducci's *(☎ 421 6002; Waterfront entrance to Victoria Wharf; mains US$5.80; sushi US$2-4.50)* offers good seafood and runs the excellent **sushi bar** adjacent.

Den Anker *(☎ 419 0249; Pierhead; mains US$5-7.50; open 11am-11pm)*, with great seafood, Belgian beer and a prime quayside setting, is a top choice.

Green Point The buzzy **News Cafe** *(83 Main Rd)* is good for bistro-style food or snacks.

Giovanni's Deli World *(103 Main Rd)* is a superb-deli-cum-café serving good coffee and ace sandwiches.

Sea Point Most eating places are within a stroll of each other along Main Road.

Café Erté (*Main Rd; open 11am-5am*) is a relaxed, gay-friendly bar and café, serving inexpensive, fresh food.

There are some good **coffee shops** at the Adelphi shopping centre, and the tiny but decent **Maz Japanese Sushi Bar**.

L'Orient (☎ 439 6572; 50 Main Rd; mains from US$6; open dinner Mon-Sat) is a good restaurant serving Malay and Indonesian fare.

Wow (66 Main Rd, sandwiches US$2-3) offers cheap, fast food for the health conscious, including juices, 'high protein' and 'workout' smoothies, salads and sandwiches.

Venezia (☎ 439 2758; 92 Main Rd; mains US$4.50-7; open dinner Wed-Mon, lunch Sun) is an excellent formal Italian restaurant.

New York Bagels (☎ 439 7523; 51 Regent Rd) is a great spot for breakfast lunch or dinner. You're allocated a charge card on arrival and make your choices from the large central food court.

Camps Bay Set back from the beachfront, **The Codfather** (☎ 438 0782; 37 The Drive) upstairs from the Dizzy Jazz Cafe is highly rated. Pick your own cut or size of fish at the counter or install yourself at the sushi carousel.

Cafe Caprice (☎ 438 8315; 37 Victoria Rd) is cool and sleek and right by the beach – this is where the beautiful people flock.

Entertainment

You can't do without the entertainment guide in the *Weekly Mail & Guardian* or in the entertainment section of the *Cape Argus*. For bookings, contact **Computicket** (☎ 918 8910; ⓦ www.computicket.com). It has outlets in the Golden Acre Centre on Strand St and the Waterfront.

Pubs & Bars Several pubs and bars are listed under Places to Eat.

Cantina Tequila (*Waterfront*) is very popular. **Quay 4 Bar** nearby is nearly always crowded. **The Lounge** (194 Long St), a small and relaxed place, tends to have an alternative gathering.

The Rockin' Shamrock (*Loop St*) and **The Drunken Springbok**, opposite each other, both occupy the tackier end of the nightlife spectrum.

Stag's Head Hotel (71 Hope St, Gardens) is a very popular grungy pub. It's one of the few English/Australian-style hotels in South Africa.

Clubs Wednesday, Friday and Saturday are the big club nights. The blocks around Bree, Loop and Long Sts and Waterkant are incredibly lively all night long on summer weekends. There's a good buzz, although the music can be rather house and techno heavy. Cover charges are about US$2.50.

Happening bars-cum-clubs of the moment at the time of research include **Jo'burg**, a small, dancy, chic place and **Marvel**, a laid-back joint with a chilled out crowd and beats to match. Both regularly host DJs and are close to each other on Long St.

Chilli 'n Lime (23 Somerset St) is a lively, mainly straight bar and club in the heart of the gay district.

169 on Long plays lots of R&B and is one of the few places on Long St where whites are in the minority.

Gay & Lesbian Venues There's an increasingly vibrant gay scene in Cape Town, with the occasional large-scale knees-up roughly every month or so. Your first stop should be Cape Town Tourism, where you can pick up a copy of the *Pink Map* and *Detail*, the free monthly gay lifestyle newspaper.

The Bronx (*cnr Somerset Rd & Napier St*) is a small bar and cabaret venue between the city and Green Point.

Cafe Manhattan (*cnr Waterkant & Dixon*) is an excellent gay-friendly bar and restaurant not far away.

Live Music Several music venues are listed under Places to Eat.

Mannenberg's (☎ 421 5639; The Clocktower Centre) is a buzzing live jazz venue attracting some of the best national and international performers and a refreshingly mixed black, white and coloured audience. Cover charges vary from US$3.50 up to US$12 depending on who's playing. You can sit and eat or just drink at the bar.

The Green Dolphin (☎ 421 7480; starters around US$5, mains around US$7), beneath Victoria & Alfred Hotel, is a good jazz venue and a popular restaurant, pitched at the tourist market. If it's busy you have to eat to see the band, although you can sit and listen at the bar.

SOUTH AFRICA

The **Dizzy Jazz Cafe** (☎ 438 2686; 41 The Drive) specialises in seafood platters eaten to the beat of live music, usually from around 9pm. If you're lucky there will actually be jazz, but this place is no stranger to middling cover bands so pick your night.

Mama Africa (cnr Long & Pepper Sts) is a lively restaurant/bar. There's live African music on the weekends. The music is better than the food.

City Hall (☎ 462 1250) is worth checking out for classical music. The Cape Town Symphony performs regular concerts here.

Artscape Complex also has classical music (see Cinema & Theatre).

Cinema & Theatre The best cinema for 'mainstream alternative' films is **Labia Cinema** (☎ 424 5927; 68 Orange St, Gardens).

At the Waterfront there are **Nu-Metro cinemas** for commercial fare and a giant-screen **IMAX cinema**.

Baxter Studio (☎ 685 7880; Woolsack Rd, Rosebank), and the **Little Theatre** (☎ 480 7100; Orange St, Gardens) are venues for non-mainstream theatre productions.

The various theatres in the **Artscape Complex** (☎ 421 7695; ⓦ www.artscape.co.za) on the foreshore host ballet, opera and mainstream theatre.

Shopping

The city centre and the Waterfront have it all, but if you hunger for a suburban mall, try stylish **Cavendish Mall**, off Protea Rd in Claremont. For African music head to **The African Music Store** (134A Long St).

Crafts Craft shops abound in town, but don't forget that few items come from this area, so you may be better off looking in the part of the country from which they originate. There are, however, some township-produced items, such as recycled tin boxes and toys, which make great gifts.

The **Siyakatala stall** in the craft market at the Waterfront sells good quality items made by self-help township groups. **African Image** (cnr Church & Burg Sts) has an interesting range of new and old craftworks and artefacts. Look out for the quirky, enchanting beadwork figures and toys, handmade by skilled craftswomen in the Cape's townships, at **Monkeybiz** in Cape Tourism's city centre office.

Markets There are also markets in **Greenmarket Square** (open daily) and at **Green Point** (open Sun), between the Waterfront and Sea Point.

Antiques & Collectables There are several good second-hand and antiquarian bookshops at the southern end of Long St and between Long and Burg Sts.

Wine The Cape produces many wines to extremely high standards, which are very cheap by international standards. Several companies will freight wine home for you, including **Vaughan Johnson's Wine Shop** (☎ 419 2121; Waterfront) and **Cellar in the City** at Cape Town Tourism's city centre office.

Getting There & Away

Air Cape Town has an increasingly busy international airport. Domestically, SAA flies between Cape Town and major centres (see the main Getting Around section earlier in this chapter).

There are many international airlines with offices in Cape Town. Following is a short list; for others, see the Yellow Pages:

Air Namibia (☎ 936 2755) Cape Town Airport
British Airways (☎ 936 9000) Cape Town Airport
KLM-Royal Dutch Airlines (☎ 670 2500) Slade House, Boundary Terraces, 1 Mariendahl Lane, Newlands
Lufthansa (☎ 934 8794) Cape Town Airport
Malaysian Airlines (☎ 934 8534) Cape Town Airport
SAA (☎ 936 1111, 24 hours) Cape Town Airport

Bus All long-distance buses leave from the main train station. Don't forget the **Baz Bus** (☎ 439 2323), which picks up from hostels; there's a booking desk at the city centre Cape Town Tourism office. The main bus lines are:

Greyhound (☎ 505 6363) Runs fewer routes from Cape Town than Translux, and prices are a bit higher.
Intercape (☎ 386 2488) Competitive operator with some extremely useful services, including along the west and south coasts.
Translux (☎ 449 3333) The Translux office is on the Adderley St side of the station block.

Johannesburg Translux, Greyhound and Intercape run to Jo'burg at least once a

day (US$46-52, 19 hours), via either Bloemfontein (12½ hours) or Kimberley (12½ hours).

Garden Route Translux runs at least once daily to Port Elizabeth (US$25, 12 hours) via Swellendam (US$10.50, 3¾ hours), Mossel Bay (US$12.50, six hours), George (US$15, seven hours), Knysna (US$17.50, eight hours), Plettenberg Bay (US$18.50, 8½ hours) and Storms River (US$19, nine hours).

Intercape runs the Garden Route twice daily. If you plan to visit several Garden Route towns, check out the options on the Baz Bus.

Mountain Route Like the Garden Route, the mountain route takes you east from Cape Town, but inland for the first half of the trip. Translux runs to Port Elizabeth (US$25, 11¾ hours) three times a week via Robertson (US$12.50, three hours).

Eastern Cape & Durban Translux services to Port Elizabeth connect with a daily bus to Durban via East London and Umtata. The total trip takes about 20 hours – consider finding a discount air ticket.

A slightly faster Translux service runs to Durban (US$52, 21½ hours) via Bloemfontein (US$40, 12½ hours).

West Coast & Namibia Intercape runs to Upington (US$25, 11½hours) via Citrusdal (US$14.50, 3¾ hours) and Clanwilliam (US$15.50, 4¼ hours). From Upington you can get an Intercape bus to Windhoek (Namibia) for US$30. Intercape also has a direct service between Cape Town and Windhoek (US$51, 20 hours), via Springbok (US$28, eight hours).

Minibus Taxi Most long-distance minibus taxis start picking up passengers in a distant township and make a trip into the train station's taxi ranks only if they need more people, so your choices can be limited. Not all townships are off-limits but the situation is volatile. *Do not* go into a township without accurate local knowledge, and preferably go with a black friend.

A minibus to Jo'burg costs about US$19.50, but it's a long, uncomfortable trip and potential driver fatigue makes it dicey.

Train The local area Metro service is the best way to get to the Winelands area (see the following Getting Around section).

Several long-distance trains run to/from Cape Town (☎ 0860-008888 for information and bookings). The *Blue Train* and *Trans Karoo* run to Pretoria via Kimberley; and the *Trans Oranje* goes to Durban via Kimberley and Bloemfontein (for fares and other details, see the main Getting Around section earlier in this chapter).

If you can't afford the time or money to take the expensive *Blue Train* all the way to Jo'burg, consider taking a sector.

Car & Motorcycle Major international companies such as **Avis** *(☎ 0861-021111 toll free; 123 Strand St)*, and **Budget** *(☎ 0800 016622 toll free; 120 Strand St)* are represented.

The larger local companies, such as **Imperial** *(☎ 0800 131000 toll free; cnr Loop & Strand Sts)*, and **Tempest** *(☎ 0860-031666 toll free; cnr Buitengragt & Wale St)* offer comparable service to the major companies at slightly lower rates.

The smaller, cheaper local companies come and go. You'll find plenty of brochures at Cape Town Tourism and at hostels – read the small print.

Hitching Although we do not recommend hitching, if you are planning on using your thumb, either start in the city centre or catch public transport to one of the outlying towns – the idea is to miss the surrounding suburbs and townships.

In the city centre, make a sign and start at the foreshore near the train station where the N1 (to Jo'burg), the N7 (to Windhoek) and the N2 (to the Garden Route) converge.

Getting Around

To/From the Airport The **Backpacker Bus** *(☎ 082 809 9185)* picks up at City Bowl hostels and runs to the airport. It costs US$15 for one person, but less for a group booking. **Homeland Shuttle and Tours** *(☎ 426 0294)* runs a daily, 24-hour airport service. Daytime prices start at US$10.50 but fall the more people jump aboard, down to as little as US$4 for five or more people. You can pay up to US$18.50 for a taxi.

Bus The main local bus interchange is on Grand Parade, where there's an **information office** (☎ 461 4365).

A bus (off-peak) to Sea Point costs US$0.30, to Camps Bay US$0.40, and to Hout Bay about US$0.70. Travelling short distances, most people wait at the bus stop and take either a bus or a minibus taxi – whichever arrives first.

Minibus You will find the minibus taxis cover most of the city. They are a cheap and efficient way of getting around and cost about the same as the municipal buses. The main rank is on the upper deck of the train station, accessible from a walkway in the Golden Acre Centre, or from stairways on Strand St. In the suburbs, you just hail them from the side of the road – point your index finger into the air.

Rikki's For Rikki's you can telephone (☎ 423 4888) or just hail one on the street – you can pay a shared rate of a few rand, or more if you phone for the whole van. Rikki's runs its tiny, open vans in the City Bowl and nearby areas. They run between 7am and 7pm daily except Sunday and go as far afield as Sea Point and Camps Bay. Sample fares from the city centre include: Camps Bay US$2.90; Tamboerskloof US$1; and the cableway station US$1.70. Rikki's also operates out of **Simon's Town** (☎ 786 2136). Simonstown to Boulders Beach costs US$0.60.

Train The information office for **Metro (local) trains** (☎ 449 4045) is in the main train station near the old locomotive opposite Platform 23. Note that services had been cut back at the time of research.

Local trains have 1st- and 3rd-class carriages. It's reasonably safe to travel in 3rd class (check the current situation), but don't do it during peak hours (crowds offer scope for pickpockets), on weekends (lack of crowds offer scope for muggers) or when carrying a lot of gear.

Probably the most important line for travellers is the Simon's Town (Simonstad) line that runs through Observatory (US$1/0.60 in 1st/3rd class) and then around the back of the mountain through upper-income white suburbs such as Rosebank, down to Muizenberg (US$0.90/0.60) and along the False Bay coast to Simon's Town (US$1/0.60).

Local trains run some way out of Cape Town to Strand (on the eastern side of False Bay) and into the Winelands to Stellenbosch (US$1.20/0.60) and Paarl (US$1.35/0.70).

Taxi There is a taxi rank at the Adderley St end of Grand Parade, or try **Unicab Taxis** (☎ 447 4402). There are often taxis near Greenmarket Square and outside the Holiday Inn on Strand St. Taxis, a good idea at night, cost about US$1.20 per kilometre.

Bicycle Many hostels hire bicycles, some of them in reasonable condition. Try also **Day Trippers** (☎ 511 4766).

Western Cape

WINELANDS

The wine-producing region around Stellenbosch is only one of the important wine-growing places in South Africa, but it is the oldest and most beautiful.

Although Jan van Riebeeck had planted vines and made wine, it was not until the arrival of Simon van der Stel in 1679 that wine-making seriously began. From 1688 to 1690, 200 French Huguenots arrived in the country. Granted land in the area, particularly around Franschhoek (French Corner), they gave the infant industry fresh impetus.

It is easy to see Stellenbosch and Paarl on day trips from Cape Town. Both are accessible by train, but Stellenbosch is the easiest to get around if you don't have a car. If you want to explore the wine routes, you'll need a car or bicycle.

Stellenbosch
☎ 021 • pop 67,500

Stellenbosch was established as a frontier town on the banks of the Eerste River by Governor van der Stel in 1679. It's the second-oldest town (after Cape Town) in South Africa, and one of the best preserved. Standing proudly in the middle of rugged mountain country, the oak-shaded town is full of architectural and historical gems.

The presence of the University of Stellenbosch, with over 12,000 students, means there is a thriving nightlife here.

WESTERN CAPE

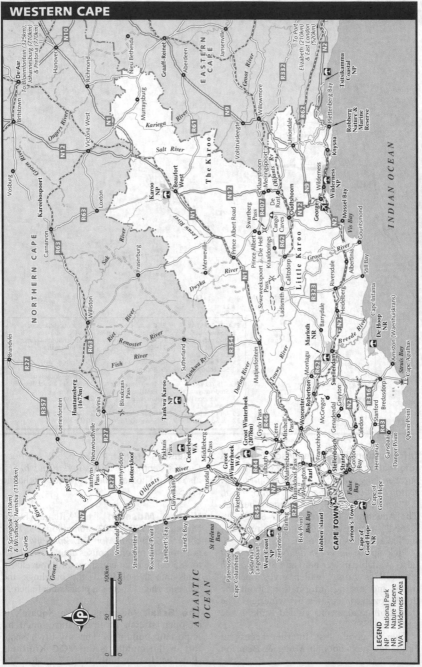

SOUTH AFRICA

LEGEND
NP National Park
NR Nature Reserve
WA Wilderness Area

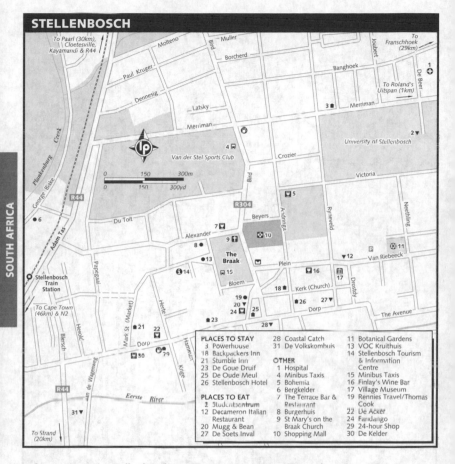

STELLENBOSCH

PLACES TO STAY
3 Powerhouse
18 Backpackers Inn
21 Stumble Inn
23 De Goue Druif
25 De Oude Meul
26 Stellenbosch Hotel

PLACES TO EAT
2 Studentsentrum
12 Decameron Italian Restaurant
20 Mugg & Bean
27 De Soets Inval

28 Coastal Catch
31 De Volkskombuis

OTHER
1 Hospital
4 Minibus Taxis
5 Bohemia
6 Bergkelder
7 The Terrace Bar & Restaurant
8 Burgerhuis
9 St Mary's on the Braak Church
10 Shopping Mall

11 Botanical Gardens
13 VOC Kruithuis
14 Stellenbosch Tourism & Information Centre
15 Minibus Taxis
16 Finlay's Wine Bar
17 Village Museum
19 Rennies Travel/Thomas Cook
22 De Akker
24 Fandango
29 24-hour Shop
30 De Kelder

Information The **Stellenbosch Tourism & Information Bureau** (☎ 883 8017; 36 Market St; open high season 8am-6pm Mon-Fri, low season 9am-5pm, and all year 9am-5pm Sat, 9.30am-4.30pm Sun) is extremely helpful. The **Adventure Centre** (☎ 882 8112), attached, specialises in booking adrenaline-fuelled activities in the area.

Pick up *Discover Stellenbosch on Foot* (also available in German) and *Stellenbosch & its Wine Route*, which gives opening times and tasting information about the three dozen or so nearby wineries. The tourist office also runs guided walks twice daily for US$5.75.

There's good, fast Internet access at **Fandango** next door to Mugg & Bean on Muel St.

Rennies Travel (☎ 886 5259; 1st floor, De Wet Centre, cnr Bird & Kerk (Church) Sts) also has a Thomas Cook currency exchange office.

Village Museum The Village (Dorp) Museum (☎ 887 2902; admission US$1.15; open 9.30am-5pm Mon-Sat, 2pm-5pm Sun) is a group of restored houses dating from 1709 to 1850. The main entrance, on Ryneveld St, leads into the oldest of the buildings, the Schreuderhuis. There's a pleasant café here.

The Braak Meaning 'Town Square', is an open stretch of grass surrounded by important buildings. The toy-town scale fort in the middle is the **VOC Kruithuis** (Powder House), built in 1777 to store the

town's weapons and gunpowder. Many old weapons are on display here. On the north-western corner the 1797 **Burgerhuis** is a fine example of the Cape Dutch style.

Bergkelder If you don't have the time or transport to tour the wine region, the Berg-kelder (☎ 888 3016; tours 10am, 10.30am (in German) and 3pm), a short walk from the train station; is a reasonable alternative, al-though far better wine awaits your tastebuds in the surrounding valleys. For US$1.30 you get a slide show, a cellar tour and pour-your-own tastings of up to six wines.

Activities There are 90 **walks** in the Stellen-bosch region – the tourist office has details.

Amoi Horse Trails (☎ 082 681 4285) offers tailor-made **horse rides**. There are two-hour morning and sunset rides and a four-hour ride with wine tasting and lunch. They'll match you with a horse to suit your skill level.

Organised Tours For wine tours **Easy Rider Wine Tours** (☎ 886 4651) is an estab-lished operator running daily, full-day tours to five wineries for US$25.

Places to Stay The **Backpackers Inn** (☎ 887 2020; e bacpac1@global.co.za; An-dringa St; dorm beds US$7.50) is central but was scruffy and long overdue for an overhaul when we visited.

Stumble Inn (☎ 887 4049; e stumble@ iafrica.com, 14 Mark St; camping US$4.50 per person, dorm beds US$6.40, doubles US$18.50) is a good hostel offering lots of in-formation and activities including discounted wine tours. This place also rents upmarket flats (US$29) nearby.

De Oude Meul (☎ 887 7085, 10a Mill St, singles/doubles US$36.50/50) above an antique shop is a comfortable, small-scale place popular with readers.

De Goue Druif (☎ 883 3555; 110 Dorp St; singles/doubles US$40/63) is a delight-fully rambling old house built in 1811 with comfortable suites.

Powerhouse (☎ 887 9809, 34 Merriman St; e phlodge@mweb.co.za; singles/doubles US$43/52), in a converted power station near the main campus, has smart, modern rooms plus a couple of 'yuppie backpacker' doubles nearby for US$17.50 per person.

Roland's Uitspan (☎ 883 2897; e info@ rolands.co.za; 1 Cluver Rd; singles/doubles US$24/40) is a friendly guesthouse, about 1.5km from the town centre, which has been recommended by readers. There's a lovely valley view from its deck.

Stellenbosch Hotel (☎ 887 3644; cnr Dorp & Andringa Sts; singles/doubles from US$50/69) is an idiosyncratic old pile with sections dating from 1743. The rather dour fixtures, including TVs that can't be much younger than the hotel, need updating.

Places to Eat Keep in mind that several of the nearby vineyards have good restaurants or cafés. For real budget snacks and meals the university's **Studentesentrum** (student centre) has several options.

Mugg & Bean (☎ 883 2972, Muel St) serves reasonably good coffee, and fairly standard snacks and meals.

Coastal Catch (☎ 887 9550, 137 Dorp St) is a decent fish and chip takeaway, with some plastic seating.

Decameron Italian Restaurant (☎ 883 3331, Plein St; mains US$4.50-7) has good, genuine Italian food. Prices are high, but it's worth it.

De Soete Inval (☎ 886 4842; 5 Ryneveld St; Mains US$4-5) serves a range of outstanding pancakes and some Indonesian fare, includ-ing rystafel with six dishes for US$6.40.

De Volkskombuis (☎ 887 2121; Aan de Wagenweg), to the south of town, is one of the best places in the Cape to sample trad-itional cuisine. Try the Cape country sampler (four traditional specialities) for US$5.80. Bookings are advisable.

Entertainment It's relatively safe to walk around at night, so you can check a few of the options before you settle.

The Terrace Bar & Restaurant (Alexander St; pub food from US$2.30) is worth a look.

Bohemia (☎ 882 8375, Cnr Andringa & Vic-toria Sts) is a cosy place with Turkish-style pipes and occasional live music.

De Kelder (63 Dorp St) has a nice atmos-phere and is apparently popular with German backpackers.

De Acker (cnr Dorp & Herte Sts; pub meals from US$3) is a classic student drinking hole with cheap grub.

Finlay's Wine Bar (Plein St) is a boisterous, cheerful place.

Cape Dutch Architecture

Drive around South Africa for just a short time and you'll realise how pervasive the Cape Dutch style of architecture is, even in newly built houses.

The style began to evolve in the late 17th century, partly thanks to Britain's wars with France, which forced it to turn to the Cape for wine. The burghers of the Cape prospered from the resulting boom and during the 18th and 19th centuries built the magnificent estates that stand today.

These houses share common features which include a *stoep* (essentially a large veranda) with seats at each end; a large central hall running the length of the house; and the main rooms symmetrically arranged on either side of the hall. They are invariably painted white and are crowned with a steep, reed-thatched roof.

Perhaps the most distinctive and appealing features are the gables above the front entrance and often also at each end. The front gable, extending above the roof line and almost always containing a dormer window, shows the influence of 18th-century Dutch styles.

Inside, the rooms are large and simply decorated. The main hall is often divided by a louvred wooden screen, thought to have derived from similar screens the Dutch would have seen in the East Indies.

The loveliest of all the manors (and certainly in the most stunning setting) is **Boschendal**, between Franschhoek and Stellenbosch, although **Groot Constantia** in Cape Town rivals its grace and splendour. Good examples and variations also include **Koopmans de Wet House** in central Cape Town, **Reinet House** in Graaf Reinet and **Burgerhuis** in Stellenbosch.

There are several good books on the subject including Phillida Brooke Simons' *Cape Dutch Houses and Other Old Favourites*.

Getting There & Away Buses to Cape Town are expensive (about US$2.30 with Translux, one hour) and you can't book this short sector. Translux stops here on the Mountain Route run between Cape Town and Port Elizabeth (see Getting There & Away in the Cape Town section).

Metro trains run the 46km between Cape Town and Stellenbosch; 1st/3rd class is US$1.20/0.60 (no 2nd class) and the trip takes about one hour. For inquiries phone **Stellenbosch train station** (☎ 808 1111). To be safe, travel in the middle of the day and not at weekends.

A minibus taxi to Paarl is about US$1.20, but you'll probably have to change minibus en route.

Getting Around Green Tri (☎ 082 899 1067) uses nothing but pedal power for its fun, eco-friendly tours of town (US$7, 30 minutes).

Boschendal

Boschendal vineyard lies between Franschhoek and Stellenbosch on the Pniel Rd (US$35), beneath some dramatic peaks. The **Cape Dutch homestead** (☎ 021-870 4210; open 9.30am-5pm daily), winery buildings and vineyard are almost too beautiful to be real. Sales and tastings (US$1.20) are available daily from 8.30am to 4.30pm.

Franschhoek
☎ 021

Cradled beneath stern mountains that mellow into wooded hills and vineyards, the gracious village of Franschhoek is a small piece of heaven. Unfortunately heaven doesn't come cheap, but hang the expense. The outstanding food, wine and guesthouses make this lovely old Cape settlement ideal for an epicurean spending spree.

The rather grudging **information centre** (☎ 876 3603; open daily in season) is in a small building on the main street. Pick up a map of the area's scenic walks.

There is an interesting **museum** (admission US$0.60) commemorating the French Huguenots who settled in the area, and several good wineries and restaurants.

Places to Stay Try the information centre for B&Bs and other accommodation in and around town. Farther flung farm B&Bs offer the best value, but you'll need wheels. Book as far ahead as possible to be sure of a more central bed in or near high season.

Franschhoek Group Accommodation
(☎ 876 2537/082 335 0123; e info@fgaccom modation.co.za; beds US$8; 15 Akademie St) is the only real budget option. It's a tad cheerless and barracks-like but also squeaky clean, central and great value.

The Cottage (☎ 876 2392; e scholtz@ scholtz.wcape.school.za; B&B singles/doubles US$18.50/38) is just a single, charming, great-value cottage. Book ahead.

La Fontaine Guesthouse (☎ 876 2112; e lafontaine@wam.co.za; 21 Dirkie Uys St; B&B singles/doubles US$49/74) has homely, comfortable rooms in a lovely, large old house and charming hosts – certainly one of the picks in town.

Klein Oliphant's Hoek (☎ 876 2566; e info@kleinoliphantshoek.com; 14 Akademie St; B&B high/low season from US$36/44), in a 19th-century mission building, lovingly decorated in a contemporary style, is great value and serves good food.

Rusthof Guest House (☎ 876 3762; e rusthof@kingsley.co.za; B&B from US$125) is plush and pricey but it does have very well-equipped rooms. The house is beautiful and the service is very warm and welcoming.

Places to Eat Don't ignore the restaurants at the many nearby wineries. **La Haute Cabriére Cellar Restaurant** (☎ 021-876 2630) is the acknowledged gourmet's paradise with a menu built around its wines. The handsomely positioned **La Petite Ferme** (☎ 876 3016) nearby on the Franschoek Pass is also popular. You'll have to book ahead for these two.

In town, **Delicious** (Huguenot Rd) is a great café.

Le Bon Vivant (☎ 072 117 3491, La Rochelle St; mains US$4.50-6.50) is new and highly recommended, offering simple but outstanding food and good wine, both far cheaper than some nearby competitors.

Topsi & Company (☎ 876 2952; 7 Reservoir St; Mains US$5.80-7) is a quirky place with an imaginative menu, where the waiters are also the chefs and cats lounge at random.

Getting There & Away It's possible, if you're fit, to cycle between Stellenbosch and Franschhoek, otherwise taxis are the best way of getting between towns.

Paarl
☎ 021 • pop 158,800
Paarl is a large commercial centre on the banks of the Berg River, surrounded by mountains and vineyards. There are actually vineyards and wineries within the town limits, including the huge Kooperatieve Wijnbouwers Vereniging (better known as the KWV), a cooperative that regulates and dominates the South African wine industry.

It's hard to tour Paarl's sprawling streets on foot and it's less touristy and far less lively than Stellenbosch or Franschhoek.

Information On the corner of Auret St, Paarl Tourism (☎ 872 3829; w www.paarl online.com; 216 Main St; open 9am-5pm Mon-Fri, 9am-1pm Sat, 10am-1pm Sun) is well stocked with brochures and can help find accommodation.

Paarl Museum The old parsonage (☎ 863 2537; 303 Main St; admission US$0.60; open 9am-5pm Mon-Fri, 10am-1pm Sat & Sun), dating from 1714, is worth a visit. It houses a good collection of Cape Dutch antiques and relics of Huguenot and early Afrikaner culture.

Paarl Mountain Nature Reserve This popular reserve is dominated by three giant granite domes looming over the town, which apparently glisten like pearls in the sun after a fall of rain – hence 'Paarl'.

A map showing walking trails is available from Paarl Tourism.

Places to Stay On the N45 towards Franschoek, **Berg River Resort** (☎ 863 1650; 2-person camp sites without electricity high/low season US$10.50/12.50) is 5km from Paarl.

Jacky's Place (☎ 872 8167; 6 Nantes St; singles/doubles US$26/31) is a small guesthouse with a homely feel and vine-covered verandas overlooking a well-tended garden.

Laborie Vineyard Guesthouse (☎ 807 3271; w www.kwv-international.com; singles/ doubles US$29/58) is in a handsome setting in this showcase vineyard.

Pontac Manor (☎ 872 0445; e pontac@ iafrica.com; 16 Zion St; low season singles/ doubles US$65/89) is a beautiful manor house dating back to 1723 with spacious, well appointed rooms.

SOUTH AFRICA

Places to Eat Several of the vineyards around Paarl have restaurants and they are probably the best places to eat if you're sightseeing.

De Malle Madonna (☎ 863 3925; 127 Main Rd; closed Mon) is a smart, welcoming place serving good coffee, tasty sandwiches and imaginative mains for around US$4.50.

Getting There & Away Several bus services come through Paarl but the bus segment between Paarl and Cape Town is much more expensive and inconvenient than the train, so take a train to Paarl and then link up with the buses.

Paarl is on Translux's Mountain Route between Cape Town and Port Elizabeth: Paarl to Port Elizabeth (US$24.50, 1¼ hours). Translux and Greyhound buses running between Cape Town and Jo'burg/Pretoria also stop in Paarl.

On weekdays there are Metro trains between Cape Town and Paarl (1st/3rd-class US$0.80/1.30; 1¼ hours) roughly every hour but they are sparser on weekends.

You can travel by train from Paarl to Stellenbosch, but you have to take a Cape Town–bound train and then change at Muldersvlei.

Bainskloof Pass

Bainskloof, north of Wellington (which adjoins Paarl), is one of the great mountain passes. The road and pass was developed by Andrew Bain between 1848 and 1852.

WEST COAST & SWARTLAND

The area immediately to the north of Cape Town straddling the N7 highway can be further divided into two areas – the West Coast and Swartland.

The coast, because of its relative barrenness and cold water, has only relatively recently been discovered by Capetonian holiday-makers, but new development is already changing the feel of this once sleepy area.

Most public transport through this area travels from Cape Town north along the N7, either going all the way to Springbok and Windhoek (Namibia), or leaving the N7 at Vanrhynsdorp and heading through Calvinia to Upington. Intercape Mainliner services both these routes. Getting to the coast by public transport can be difficult, however.

West Coast National Park

The West Coast National Park is one of the few large reserves along South Africa's coastline. It runs north from Yzerfontein to just short of Langebaan, surrounding the clear, blue waters of the Langebaan lagoon.

The park protects wetlands of international significance, as well as important seabird breeding colonies, and is famous for its wildflower display, usually between August and October.

Saldhana and Laanebaan are both burgeoning resorts with plenty of accommodation options and excellent conditions for watersports (constant wind and sheltered waters) including windsurfing and kitesurfing. It's worth starting your visit at Langebaan to pick up a map and local information from the **tourist information centre** (☎ 022-772 1515; Hoof St; open 9am-5pm Mon-Fri, 9am-noon Sat & Sun).

There's no accommodation in the park but Langebaan has several municipal **caravan parks**. They have chalets but don't allow tents.

Windstone Backpackers (☎ 022-766 1645; Route 45 near Langeenheid train station; dorm beds US$7.50, doubles US$22) has good facilities including an indoor pool but it's a fair trek from town.

Die Strandloper (☎ 022-772 2490) is an atmospheric open-air restaurant on the beach, specialising in seafood. It gets good reviews and you must book ahead.

No public transport runs to Langebaan. Saldhana is the nearest town with public transport to/from Cape Town.

Olifants River Valley

There are some acclaimed wineries on the intensively cultivated valley floor of the Olifants River. The eastern side is largely bounded by the spectacular Cederberg Range and the whole area is famous for spring wildflowers.

Cederberg Wilderness Area The Cederberg is a rugged area of valleys and peaks extending roughly north–south for 100km between Citrusdal and Vanrhynsdorp. Part of it is protected by the 71,000-hectare Cederberg Wilderness Area.

The Cederberg offers excellent hiking through an area famous for its weathered sandstone formations. This is a genuine

wilderness area – you are *encouraged* to leave the trails and little information is available on suggested routes. It's up to you to survive on your own.

There is a buffer zone of conserved land between the wilderness area and the farmland, where activities such as mountain biking are allowed. Pick up a copy of the mountain biking trail map (US$4) from the Citrusdal information centre (see Information following).

Information The main office is at Citrusdal. There's also an office at the Algeria Camping Ground. Entry to the Wilderness Area costs US$1.90. The Algeria entrance closes at 9pm.

Hiking permits (US$2.30 per day) must be booked through the **Chief Nature Conservator** (☎ 027-482 2812; Ⓦ *www.cape nature.org; Private Bag X6, Clanwilliam 8135*), Cederberg.

Ferdinands Tours (☎ 021-421 1662) in Cape Town runs two-day trips to the wilderness area.

Places to Stay You'll need to book the following camping grounds through the Chief Nature Conservator, Cederberg. There are basic huts for hikers in the wilderness area.

Algeria Camping Ground (camp sites US$9.20; 4-person chalets US$37) is in a beautiful spot alongside the Rondegat River. Rates are higher in peak periods.

Kliphuis State Forest has another good camping ground, near Pakhuis Pass on the R364, about 15km northeast of Clanwilliam.

Getting There & Away The Cederberg Range is about 200km from Cape Town. It is accessible from Citrusdal and Clanwilliam but the easiest route is from the signposted turn-off from the N7 north of Citrusdal.

Public transport into Algeria is nonexistent. It takes about two days to walk from Citrusdal to Algeria, entering the wilderness area at Boskloof. The Chief Nature Conservator's office in Citrusdal has information on this route.

Citrusdal
☎ 022

This small town makes a good base for exploring the Cederberg Range. There's a **Tourist Bureau** (☎ 921 3210; 39 Voortrekker St; open 8am-5pm Mon-Fri, 8am-1pm Sat), and the helpful **Sandveldhuisie Country Shop & Tea Room** (☎ 921 3210; Kerk St) also has information. Not far away is the office of the Chief Nature Conservator for the Cederberg Wilderness Area.

Intercape stops at a petrol station on the highway just outside town; Translux comes into town and stops at the Cederberg Hotel. Minibus taxis to Cape Town and Clanwilliam stop at the Caltex petrol station.

Much of the accommodation is out of town and there are plenty of farmstays in the area, either B&Bs or self-contained cottages. Contact the information centre for recommendations.

Clanwilliam
☎ 027

A popular little weekend resort, the attraction here is the town itself (which has some nice examples of Cape Dutch architecture) and the proximity to the Cederberg Range. Accommodation can be expensive and scarce in the spring wildflower season.

Clanwilliam Dam Municipal Caravan Park & Chalets (☎ 482 2133; camp sites US$5.50, doubles US$23) is well equipped and maintained.

Strassberger's Hotel Clanwilliam (☎ 482 1101; ⓔ strassberger@lando.co.za; Main St; singles/doubles US$24/42, in flower season US$32/57) is comfortable and good value; rates include breakfast.

All the buses that pass through Citrusdal also come through Clanwilliam. It's about 45 minutes between the two towns. Minibus taxis running between Springbok and Cape Town also pass through Clanwilliam.

BREEDE RIVER VALLEY
This attractive, bountiful area lies to the northeast of the Winelands on the western fringes of the Little Karoo. Though dominated by the Breede River Valley, this is mountainous country and includes some smaller valleys. The valley floors are intensively cultivated with orchards, vineyards and wheat.

The headwaters of the Breede (sometimes called the Breë), in the beautiful mountain-locked Ceres basin, escape via Mitchell's Pass, flowing southeast for over 300km before meeting the Indian Ocean at Whitesands.

Look out for the *Cape Fruit Routes* map in information centres. It covers places in

the Breede River Valley and also around the Winelands and east to the Montagu area.

Tulbagh

☎ 023

Tulbagh is one of the most complete examples of an 18th- and 19th-century village in South Africa, although many of the buildings were substantially rebuilt after earthquakes in 1969 and 1970.

Although most of Tulbagh's surviving buildings date from the first half of the 19th century, the Tulbagh Valley was first settled in 1699. The village began to take shape after the construction of a church in 1743.

The town's main street, Van der Stel St, is parallel to Church St, in which every building has been declared a national monument. There's an **information office** (☎ 230 1348; 4 Church St).

Oude Kerk Volksmuseum The Old Church Folk Museum (admission US$0.60; open 9am-5pm Mon-Fri, 10am-4pm Sat, 11am-4pm Sun) is made up of four buildings. Start at No 4; then visit the beautiful Oude Kerk itself (1743); follow this with No 14, which houses Victorian furniture and costumes; and then No 22, which is a reconstructed town dwelling from the 18th century.

Places to Stay & Eat Ask at the information centre about B&Bs and guesthouses (doubles average US$40) and farmstays (from US$11.50 per person self-catering).

Kliprivier Park Resort (☎ 230506; camp sites from US$8, double chalets from US$23), on the edge of town, is quite a pleasant spot with reasonable modern chalets.

De Oude Herberge (☎ 230 0260; 6 Church St; singles/doubles US$25/42) is a guesthouse surrounded by old buildings and built in traditional Cape style. There's no smoking and no children under 12 are permitted.

Paddagang Restaurant (☎ 230 0242; breakfast US$3.50; open breakfast, lunch & dinner) is in a beautiful old homestead with a vine-shaded courtyard. It serves snacks, light meals and a fine breakfast.

Getting There & Away Most minibus taxis leave from the 'location' (black residential area), on the hill just outside town, but you might find one at Tulbagh Toyota (the Shell service station) on the main street.

Robertson

☎ 023

Robertson is an attractive, prosperous, if somewhat dull little town. It's the centre for one of the largest wine-growing regions in the country and is also famous for horse studs. If you're staying overnight in the area, consider nearby McGregor or Montagu instead.

Ask at the **tourist bureau** (☎ 626 4437; cnr Piet Reteif & Swellendam Sts; open 9am-5pm Mon-Fri, Sat morning) about 'over-night' hiking trails (ie, more than one day) which take you into the mountains above Robertson, offering great views.

Places to Stay The tourist bureau can tell you about accommodation, including self-catering farm cottages which start at about US$10.50 per person.

Roberston Backpackers (☎ 626 1280; e roberstonbackpackers@yahoo.com; 4 Dordrecht Ave; camping US$3.50, dorm beds US$5.20, rooms US$12.60) is new, comfortable and friendly. The owners offer guided walks in the surrounding mountains and pick-ups from the bus stop.

Grand Hotel (☎ 626 3272; 68 Barry St; singles/doubles US$25/40), on the corner of White St, has a couple of cheerful bars downstairs and good food.

Getting There & Away Translux stops at the train station (for more details see Getting There & Away in the Cape Town section) on the run between Cape Town (US$12.50, three hours) and Port Elizabeth (US$24, 8¾ hours).

Minibus taxis running between Cape Town (US$4.60) and Oudtshoorn (US$12.50) stop at the Shell petrol station on the corner of Voortrekker and Barry Sts. These minibuses also run through Montagu (US$2.90).

McGregor

☎ 023

McGregor feels as if it has been forgotten. It's one of the best-preserved mid-19th century villages in the country, with thatched cottages surrounded by orchards, vegetable gardens and vineyards. There are about 30 wineries within half an hour's drive.

Vrolijkheid Nature Reserve, on the road between Robertson and McGregor, has about 150 species of birds. It has bird hides and an 18km circular walking trail.

The **Boesmanskloof Hiking Trail** begins at Die Galg, about 15km south of McGregor, and winds 14km through the Riviersonderend mountains to the small town of Greyton. For permits, contact **Vrolijkheid Nature Reserve** (☎ 023-625 1621).

Places to Stay Guesthouses are the major industry in this village and more are opening all the time. There are also self-catering cottages on nearby farms (the information centre in Robertson has a complete list).

Old Mill Lodge (☎ 625 1841; per person with half-board US$24) is a beautiful old building surrounded by a clutch of modern cottages. There's also a decent restaurant here

McGregor Country Cottages (☎ 625 1816; e countrycottages@lando.co.za; 4-person cottages US$50) is a lovely cluster of wheelchair-friendly cottages in an apricot orchard. The cottages are fully equipped and are great value.

THE OVERBERG

The Overberg (literally, Over the Mountains), is the area west of the Franschhoek Range and south of the Wemmershoek and Riviersonderend Ranges, which form a natural barrier with the Breede River Valley.

This area's wealth of coastal and mountain fynbos is unmatched; most species flower somewhere in the area between autumn and spring.

Coming from Cape Town by car, head to Gordon's Bay, from where the R44 skirts a magnificent stretch of coast facing out onto False Bay. It's a spectacular drive.

Hermanus

☎ 028 • pop 22,600

Hermanus is a popular seaside resort 122km from Cape Town. It was originally a fishing village, and still retains vestiges of its heritage, including an interesting **museum** at the old harbour. It's best known as a place for **whale-watching** close to the shore.

The **Hermanus Tourism Bureau** (☎ 312 2629; w www.hermanus.co.za; Old Station Bldg, Mitchell St; open 9am-5pm Mon-Sat) is helpful and laden with brochures.

The **Internet & Information Cafe** (☎ 313 0249; Waterkant Bldg, Main Rd) charges around US$1.20 for 15 minutes.

Whales Between June and November, southern right whales (Eubalaena australis) come to Walker Bay to calve. There can be up to 70 whales in the bay at once and the numbers visiting seem to grow every year. Humpback whales (Megaptera novaeangliae) are also sometimes seen.

Whales often come very close to shore and there are some excellent vantage points from the cliff paths that run from one end of Hermanus to the other. The best places are Castle Rock, Kraal Rock and Sievers Point.

Sharks Several operators run trips to Dyer Island, near Gansbaai, where Great White sharks patrol the waters. You'll get within metres of the sharks and it costs about US$80 for the day – ask at the tourism bureau for more information.

Places to Stay There's a huge amount of accommodation in Hermanus, yet it can still get fully booked during the busy times, so booking ahead is probably advisable. As well as the tourism bureau, two organisations can help with accommodation: **Whale Route Accommodation** (☎ 314 1567) and the **Hermanus Accommodation Centre** (☎ 313 0004).

Zoete Inval Travellers Lodge (☎/fax 312 1242; e zoetein@hermanus.co.za; 23 Main Rd; dorm beds US$7, singles/doubles US$19.50/ 26) is friendly, peaceful and comfortable.

Hermanus Backpackers (☎ 312 4293; e moobag@mweb.co.za; 26 Flower St, Westcliff; dorm beds US$8, singles/doubles US$11/ 20), in a huge, manic house, is a bustling place with a big kitchen and a great lounge area.

Moby's Traveller's Lodge (☎ 313 2361; e moby@hermanus.co.za; 8 Main Rd; dorm beds US$7; singles/doubles US$38/20) is central, big and can turn into a noisy party zone if the attached bar gets busy.

Windsor Hotel (☎ 312 3727, fax 312 2181; 49 Marine Dr; B&B singles/doubles low season US$40/50, high season US$44/86), is a large old place which seems to make its living from coach tours. Breakfast is included in the rates; sea-facing rooms cost more.

The Potting Shed (☎ 312 1712; e pot shed@hermanus.co.za; 28 Albertyn St; B&B singles/doubles US$29/46) is a comfortable mid-range guesthouse.

Auberge Bergundy (☎ 313 1202; e auberge@hermanus.co.za; 16 Harbour Rd; B&B

doubles from US$92) is a very stylish place built like a Mediterranean villa. There's an excellent restaurant attached.

The Marine Hermanus *(☎ 313 1000; Marine Dr; singles/doubles from US$120/200)* is a grand, old-style hotel that has been renovated. It's very comfortable and in a great spot.

Places to Eat A stroll along Main St and around Village Square will quickly turn up a place suitable for your palate.

St Tropez *(☎ 312 3221; 28 Main Rd; lunches under US$2.30, dinners around US$3.50)* has good-value lunches.

Burgundy Restaurant *(☎ 312 2800; 16 Harbour Rd; mains US$6.35-7.50)* is one of the most acclaimed restaurants in the province. Book ahead.

Bientang's Cave *(☎ 312 3554; Marine Dr; Mains US$4.50; open daily 11am-5pm)* is atmospheric and right over the sea. It really is a cave and you may sea whales up close as you dine.

There are a couple of interesting possibilities on High Street, which runs parallel to Main Rd.

Rossi's Pizzeria & Italian Restaurant *(☎ 312 2848; 10 High St; mains from US$4)* has a pleasant and relaxed atmosphere. It has a range of pasta dishes, pizzas and steak or line fish.

Getting There & Away One company, **Bernardus Niehaus** *(☎ 083 658 7848)*, runs a 24-hour private shuttle service between Hermanus and Cape Town (US$16, two hours).

Minibus taxis are rare. Ask at the tourist office.

Cape Agulhas

Cape Agulhas is the southernmost point of the African continent. On a stormy day it really looks like the next stop is the South Pole, but otherwise it isn't especially impressive.

There isn't much in the hamlet of Cape Agulhas, but **Struisbaai**, about 6km east, is a little larger and has a **caravan park**. There's also the luxurious **Arniston Hotel** *(☎ 028-445 9000; rooms per person with breakfast from US$50)* in **Waenhuiskrans** (also called Arniston).

De Hoop Nature Reserve

De Hoop (**huu**-op) is worth visiting. It includes a scenic coastline with lonely stretches of beach, rocky cliffs, a freshwater lake and the Potberg Range.

This is one of the best places to see both mountain and lowland fynbos and a diverse range of coastal ecosystems. Fauna includes the Cape mountain zebra, bontebok and a wealth of birdlife. The coast is an important breeding area for the southern right whale.

There is hiking and good snorkelling along the coast, and since it is to the east of Cape Agulhas, the water is reasonably warm.

Four-person **cottages** *(from US$30)* and **camp sites** *(US$10)* must be booked in advance *(☎ 028-542 1126)*.

Swellendam

☎ 028

As well as being a very pretty town with a real sense of history (it dates from 1746 and is the third-oldest European town in South Africa), Swellendam offers those with transport a good base for exploring quite a range of country. The Breede River Valley and the coast are within easy reach, as is the Little Karoo.

Swellendam is dotted with old oaks and on its southern side is surrounded by beautiful rolling wheat country, but it backs up against a spectacular ridge of the Langeberg Range.

Information The **tourism bureau** *(☎ 514 2770; Voortrek St; open 8am-5pm Mon-Fri, 9am-1pm Sat)* is in the old mission, or Oefeninghuis.

For permits to walk in **Marloth Nature Reserve** in the Langeberg Range contact the **Nature Conservation Department** *(☎ 514 1410)*. There are one-day, two-day and week-long hikes.

Drostdy Museum The centrepiece of this museum *(☎ 514 1138; admission US$1.20; complex open 9am-4.45pm Mon-Fri, 10am-3.45pm Sat & Sun)* is the beautiful *drostdy* (the former official government residence), which dates from 1746. There is also the Old Gaol; part of the original administrative buildings; the Gaoler's Cottage; a water mill; and Mayville, a residence dating from 1853. Some distance away, **Morgenzon** *(16 Van Oudtshoorn Rd)*, is an annexe of the museum. It was built in 1751 as a house for the secretary of the *landdrost* (an official representative of the colony's governor).

Places to Stay A 10-minute walk from
town, **Swellendam Caravan Park** (☎ 514
2705; 2-person camp sites around US$8.50)
is in a lovely spot near the Morgenzon
museum.

Swellendam Backpackers (☎ 514 2648;
5 Lichtenstein St; camp sites US$3.45, dorm
beds US$5.20, doubles US$15), serene and
comfortable, is a good place to unwind,
with a large grassed area out the back. It
also arranges local horseback and mountain
bike trails.

Roosje Van de Kaap (☎ 514 3001; 5
Drostdy St; B&B singles/doubles US$27/42)
is a friendly little guesthouse which has
four guest rooms overlooking a small pool.
A decent restaurant is attached.

Moolmanshof (☎ 514 3258; e moolmans
hoof@sdm.dorea.co.za; 217 Voortrek St; B&B
singles/doubles from US$23/34) is a beautiful
old home dating from 1798. The garden is
superb, the house is furnished with period
furniture and the rates are competitive.

Braeside (☎ 514 3325; e ctaylor@sdm.dorea
.co.za; 13 van Oudtshoornweg; B&B singles/
doubles US$34/46) is well appointed, has
breathtaking views and a great deck for
breakfasting or sipping sundowners.

Adin & Sharon's Hideaway (☎ 514 3316;
e adinbb@dorea.co.za; 10 Hermanus Steyn
St; B&B singles/doubles US$52/82) is an AA
accommodation award-winner priding itself
on attentive service with lots of snacks and
drinks thrown in.

Places to Eat Adjoining the Drostdy Museum, **Zanddrift Restaurant** is in a building
that dates from 1757. Breakfast is a must:
US$4 gets you a huge platter of omelette,
ham, cheese, paté, fruit and so on. The set-
menu dinners are also well rated locally.

The Connection (☎ 514 1988; Swellen-
grebel St; mains US$5), the sister restaurant to
Zanddrift, is also worth trying for similarly
good home-made fare.

Getting There & Away Intercape runs to
Cape Town (US$10.50, 3¼ hours); Mossel
Bay (US$10.40, 2¼ hours); Knysna (US$14,
4¼ hours); and Port Elizabeth (US$20, eight
hours).

Minibus taxis stop behind the Spar supermarket on Voortrek St. There's a daily service
to Cape Town (US$10.50) and Mossel Bay
(US$8).

Bontebok National Park

Bontebok National Park (☎ 314 2646; admission US$1.20), 6km south of Swellendam, is a
small chunk of land protecting the bontebok,
an unusually marked antelope. As a nice
place to relax, it's hard to beat.

There are six-berth **'chalavans'** (US$17,
plus US$2.30 per person) – book through the
National Parks Board or directly at Bontebok – and pleasant **camp sites** (2 people
US$7.50).

THE LITTLE KAROO

The Little (or Klein) Karoo is bordered in
the south by the Outeniqua and Langeberg
Ranges, and in the north by the Swartberg
Range. It runs east from Montagu for about
300km to Uniondale, and is more fertile and
better watered than the harsher Karoo to the
north. The Little Karoo is renowned for ostriches and wildflowers and for the spectacular passes that cut through the mountains.

Most people travelling between Cape
Town and the Garden Route use the N2, but
there's an interesting alternative: the Mountain Route running via Robertson, Montagu,
Oudtshoorn and George.

Montagu
☎ 023

Montagu, founded in 1851, lies just outside
the Breede Valley – once you pop through
the Kogmanskloof Pass near Robertson you
are in a very different world. It's a good place
to go if you want to escape the 20th century
and get a brief taste of the Little Karoo.

The helpful **information office** (☎ 614
2471) has information on accommodation
(including a range of B&Bs and self-catering cottages), walks, hikes and organised
tours of Zolani township (US$4.60). The
town prides itself on its three-hour **tractor
trips** (614 2471; US$4.60) which are a good,
if slightly surreal, way of seeing the valley.

Montagu Museum & Joubert House
The Montagu Museum (Long St) is in the
old mission church, and includes interesting
displays and some good examples of antique
furniture. Joubert House, also on Long St, is
the oldest house in Montagu (built in 1853)
and has been restored to its Victorian finery.

Montagu Hot Mineral Springs The
springs are about 3km from town; they are

hot (45°C) and renowned for their healing properties.

Places to Stay On the edge of town, **De Bos** (☎ 614 2532; camp sites US$2.90, backpackers barn US$4.60, single/double ensuite rooms US$14/17.50, single/double bungalows US$19/21) is an excellent, cheap guest farm in a stunning setting beneath the nearby mountains.

Mimosa Lodge (☎ 614 2351; e mimosa@lando.co.za; Church St; singles/doubles half-board from US$46/60) is an appealing guesthouse in a beautifully restored old building serving excellent dinners and breakfasts.

The information office has details on several B&Bs from about US$16.50 per person. There are also cheap self-catering farmhouses and cottages.

Places to Eat Out at Avalon Springs Hotel, **Romano's Pizzeria** is said by locals to have the best pizzas.

Mimosa Lodge is good for an upmarket dinner. **Montagu Country Inn** has a restaurant.

Getting There & Away Minibus taxis running between Oudtshoorn (about US$4.60) and Cape Town (US$7.50) stop near the police station.

Oudtshoorn
☎ 044 • pop 60,600

The tourist capital of the Little Karoo, Oudtshoorn is a large, sedate place with some nice old buildings built on the profits from the 19th century boom in ostrich feathers. The boom collapsed but Oudtshoorn is still ostrich crazy. It is also well situated as a base for exploring the very different environments of the Little Karoo, the Garden Route and The Karoo.

Oudtshoorn Tourism Bureau (☎ 279 2532; Baron van Rheede St; open 8am-5pm Mon-Fri, 9am-1pm Sat) is near Queen's Hotel.

Cango Wildlife Ranch & Cheetahland (☎ 272 5593; admission US$4.50; open 8am-5pm daily) has a good collection of wildlife and big cats (in rather small enclosures) including cheetahs, which you can pat for an extra US$3.50 (funds go to the Cheetah Conservation Foundation). The ranch is 3km from town on the road out to Prince Albert.

Ostrich Farms A number of ostrich show farms offer guided tours of about two hours: try **Safari Ostrich Farm** (☎ 272 7311), 6km from town on the Mossel Bay road; and **Highgate Ostrich Farm** (☎ 272 7115), 10km from town, signposted from the Mossel Bay road. Entry for both is US$4.

Cango Caves These impressive caves (☎ 272 7410) are 30km from town. There's a **restaurant** and curio complex. Tours cost from US$5.80.

Calitzdorp For a peaceful country break, head 19km up the valley from the country village of Calitzdorp to **The Retreat at Groenfontein** (☎ 044-213 3880; e groenfon@iafrica.com; singles/doubles US$40 for half-board), a delightfully restored Victorian farmhouse with well-trimmed gardens. The delightful hosts here make this an ideal bolt hole or base for hiking in the Swartberg Mountains.

Activities A good way to see the striking Swartberg pass is a day trip by minibus to the top followed by an exhilarating ride down by mountain bike. Most of the hostels offer this tour for around US$14.

Places to Stay In a large and relaxed house, **Backpackers' Oasis** (☎/fax 279 1163; e backpackersoasis@yahoo.com; 3 Church St; camp sites US$4 per person, dorm beds US$5.80, doubles US$16.50) has a good-sized yard and a decent pool. The staff can arrange local budget tours.

Backpackers' Paradise (☎ 272 3436; e paradise@isat.co.za; 148 Baron van Rheede St; dorm beds US$6.40, doubles from US$15) is an impressive hostel, although some of the doubles are a tad small and stuffy. This place also runs daily pick-ups from George.

Aan de Brug (☎ 272 2665; e stemmet@mweb.co.za; 76 Church St; B&B singles/doubles US$23/37) is a small, welcoming family-run place close to the town centre.

Shades of Africa (☎ 272 6430; e shades@pixie.co.za; 238 Jan van Riebeeck Rd; B&B singles/doubles US$43/72) is a little way from the centre but it's a beautiful, modern, artistically done place with lovely individual rooms and a pool.

Queen's Hotel (☎ 272 2101; e queens@xsinet.co.za; Baron van Rheede St; B&B singles/

doubles from US$60/82) is an attractive, stylish old-style country hotel.

Places to Eat Between the tourism bureau and Queen's Hotel, **Cafe Brule** does open sandwiches and tasty baguettes from US$1.80 to US$2.40.

Most places serve ostrich in one form or another.

Jemima's (☎ 272 0808; 94 Baron van Rheede St; mains US$5.80; open 10am-3pm & 6.30pm-10pm Tue-Sat, noon-2pm Sun) is clearly passionate about simple yet imaginative food. It must be one of the best places in South Africa and the prices aren't bad considering. Highly recommended and popular so book ahead.

Rock Art Cafe (☎ 279 1927; 62 Baron van Rheede St; mains US$2.30-6) is the choice for a few beers and some straightforward bar food. It opens till 2am nightly but closes during the day on Sunday.

Getting There & Away Translux fares from Oudtshoorn include: Knysna (US$8.60; stand-by available only, two hours); Bloemfontein (US$28, nine hours); Jo'burg (US$34, 15 hours).

There's no direct bus from Cape Town. Change at either Mossel Bay (with Translux) or George (Intercape and the Baz Bus).

Minibus taxis aren't easy to find – try Union St near the Spar supermarket, or contact the tourism bureau.

THE KAROO

For further information on The Karoo see The Karoo in the Eastern Cape section later in this chapter.

GARDEN ROUTE

The heavily promoted Garden Route encompasses a beautiful bit of coastline from Still Bay in the west to just beyond Plettenberg Bay in the east.

The narrow coastal plain is often forested, and is mostly bordered by lagoons which run behind a barrier of sand dunes and superb beaches. Inland, its boundary is the Outeniqua and Tsitsikamma Ranges.

Although the Garden Route is beautiful, and there's a wealth of places to see and things to do, it is also heavily (and tackily) developed in places. Most accommodation prices jump by at least 30% in mid-season

(late January to May) and more than double over the high season (December, January and Easter).

For information on the Tsitsikamma area, which is sometimes considered part of the Garden Route, see the Eastern Cape section later in this chapter.

Getting There & Away

Translux (☎ 021-449 3333) and **Intercape** (☎ 0861-287287) run at least daily from Cape Town to Port Elizabeth via the main Garden Route towns. Translux also runs a service from Jo'burg to Knysna via some Garden Route towns. (For fares and main destinations, see the main Getting Around section in this chapter.) If you plan to travel around the area, don't forget the Baz Bus, which drops and picks up at hostels along the Garden Route.

The weekly *Southern Cross* train between Cape Town and Port Elizabeth stops in some Garden Route towns (see the main Getting Around section earlier in this chapter).

Mossel Bay
☎ 044 • pop 49,400

Mossel Bay (or Mosselbaai) is a smallish town on a beautiful bay with the feel of a Mediterranean village. It has a low-key charm if you ignore the ugly industrial development on its outskirts. Perhaps the best thing about Mossel Bay is that many holidaymakers on the Garden Route skip it, so it's less clumsily developed (in the town centre at least) and you stand a better chance of finding decent, cheaper accommodation, especially midweek.

The first European to visit the bay was the Portuguese explorer Bartholomeu Dias in 1488. From then on, many ships stopped to take on fresh water and to barter for provisions with the Gouriqua Khoikhoi who lived in the area.

The **tourism bureau** (☎ 691 2202; Market St; open 9am-5pm Mon-Fri, 9am-1pm Sat) is efficient and informative.

Mossel Bay is off the highway and buses don't come into town – they'll drop you at the Voorbaai Shell petrol station, 7km from town. The hostels can usually collect you if you give notice.

Internet access is available from **Postnet** (*Bland St*).

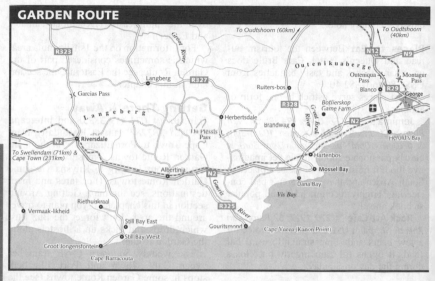

GARDEN ROUTE

Bartholomeu Dias Museum Complex

The highlight of this **Complex** (☎ 691 1067; open 8.15am-5pm Mon-Fri; 9am-4pm Sat & Sun) is the replica of the unbelievably tiny vessel that Dias used on his 1488 voyage of discovery. The replica was built in Portugal and sailed to Mossel Bay in 1988 to commemorate the 500th anniversary of Dias' trip.

Boat Trips The *Romonza* (☎ 690 3101) runs boat trips to Seal Island (US$4.50) departing from the harbour behind the train station. In late winter and spring it's not unusual to see whales on the trip. Several operators offer **shark cage diving** (US$69-80), enabling you to get right up close to the great whites which loiter just off shore. Try **Electrodive** (☎ 698 1976). There are also some great surf spots. Try **Billeon** (☎ 082 971 1405) for surf trips.

Places to Stay There are three municipal caravan parks, **Bakke** and **Santos** on the pretty Madiba beach and **Punt** near the surf. You can contact these places on ☎ 691 2915. They have chalets from US$30 and camp sites from US$8 per site.

Barnacles Ecno-Lodge (☎ 690 4584; e barnacles@mweb.co.za; 112 High St; dorm beds US$8, singles/doubles US$15/18.50), with its entrance off Hill St, is a big house with superb views over the bay. It's very

clean and you won't see better doubles in a backpackers.

Santos Express (☎/fax 691 1995; Santos Beach; dorm Beds US$7, singles/doubles US$10.50/17.50) is a line of old railway carriages right on the beach. The bar and restaurant are a stumble away. The berths are tiny and you'll need your own bedding for the dorms.

Mossel Bay Backpackers (☎ 691 3182; e marquette@pixie.co.za; 1 Marsh St; dorm beds US$7, doubles US$21, for bedding US$2.30) is part of the more comfortable **Huis Te Marquette B&B** (singles/doubles from US$31/52). You can also rent mountain bikes and boogie boards here.

Old Post Office Tree Manor (☎ 691 3738; singles/doubles US$38/75), not far from the museum, is a very comfortable hotel. A good breakfast is thrown in and there's a restaurant and a bar with lovely sea views.

There are many other guesthouses and B&Bs; the tourist bureau has a list.

Places to Eat In the Old Post Office Tree Manor the **Gannet Restaurant** (mains US$6.50) specialises in seafood and has a bright and informal atmosphere.

Jazzbury's (☎ 691 1923; 11 Marsh St; mains US$5) is an elegant place with a good African menu.

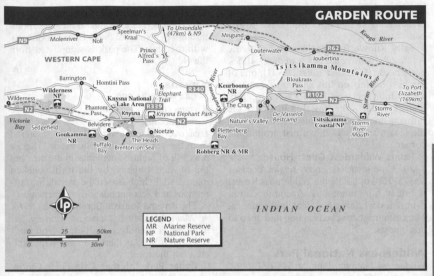

GARDEN ROUTE

LEGEND
MR   Marine Reserve
NP   National Park
NR   Nature Reserve

INDIAN OCEAN

The Bay Tavern *(Marsh St)* serves pub grub.

George
☎ 044 • pop 106,500

George, founded in 1811, lies on a coastal plateau at the foot of the Outeniqua Range. It's not especially interesting and unless you have a car, it's not convenient from the coastal area.

The **tourist office** *(☎ 801 9295; 124 York St; open 8am-5.30pm Mon-Fri, 9am-1pm Sat)* has lots of information and some handy maps.

Steam Train Museum and Outeniqua Choo-Tjoe One of the reasons to visit George is the famous *Outeniqua Choo-Tjoe*, a steam train running along a spectacular line to Knysna (US$5.20/7, one way 2½ hours; return trip 7½ hours). For more details, contact the **Steam Train Museum** *(☎ 801 8295; just off Courtenay St; open 7.30am-6pm Mon-Sat)*.

Places to Stay & Eat About a 20-minute walk from the town centre, **George Tourist Resort** *(☎ 874 5205; York St; camp sites from US$7.50, double rondavels from US$31, chalets from US$56)* is a large, well-run caravan park.

George Backpackers Hostel *(☎ 874 7807; 29 York St; camping US$5; dorm beds US$5.80,*

doubles US$15) has been recently renovated but is quite a long walk south of the centre of town.

Protea Landmark Lodge *(☎ 874 4488; 123 York St; singles/doubles US$46/55)* is comfortable but nothing special.

Keg & Lourie *(☎ 873 3482; 127 York St)* does tasty pub lunches.

The Kingfisher *(Courtenay St)* is the place for seafood and pasta at reasonable prices.

Wilderness
☎ 044

Wilderness is no longer an apt description for this popular holiday village. Still, it is on a beautiful stretch of coast with a lush mountain hinterland.

Wilderness Tourism Bureau *(☎ 877 0045 open 8am-5pm Mon-Fri, 8am-1pm & 3pm-5pm Sat in high season)* books B&B accommodation.

Eden Adventures *(☎ 877 0187)* offers canoe and mountain bike hire and arranges tours in the locality, including abseiling and kloofing (mucking about in ravines).

Places to Stay The excellent **Wild Welcome Backpackers** *(☎/fax 877 1307; e wildwelcome@hotmail.com; 479 10th Avenue; dorm beds from US$7.50, doubles from US$18.50)* has bike hire and organises loads of activities. It's in a terrific spot on a wooded

hillside overlooking the crashing waves on a breathtaking stretch of coast. There's also a bar.

Fairy Knowe Backpackers (☎ 877 1285; e fairybp@mweb.co.za; camping US$5, dorm beds US$7.50, doubles US$21), one of the best hostels on this stretch of coast, is set on four hectares. Follow signs to Fairy Knowe Hotel – the hostel is just over the railway line. The Baz Bus stops here and the steam train sets down just around the corner.

Palms Wilderness Guest House (☎ 877 1420; e palms@pixie.co.za; singles/doubles US$75/100) opposite the Wilderness Resort is pricey but sumptuous. Accommodation is in fancy whitewashed, thatched cottages. The restaurant attached is good and open to non-guests.

Wilderness National Park

Wilderness National Park (☎ 044-877 1197; admission US$2.30 per vehicle) encompasses the area from Wilderness in the west to Sedgefield in the east. There are several nature trails taking in the lakes, the beach and the indigenous forest.

Camp sites (from US$8.50) and two-bed **huts** (US$32) are available in the park; book through the National Parks Board or directly with the park. The park is signposted from the N2.

Knysna

☎ 044 • pop 34,900

Knysna (the 'k' is silent) is a bustling place with a holiday atmosphere. It's a beautiful area overlooking a large lagoon sheltered from the sea by the dramatic heads. There's a wealth of fantastic activities in the area but the town is blighted by the traffic-choked main road. In high season the crowds are horrendous and accommodation is expensive.

The **Knysna Tourism Bureau** (☎ 382 5510; 40 Main Rd; open 8.30am-5pm Mon-Fri, Sat morning) is friendly and efficient. You can't miss the office, as there's an elephant skeleton out the front.

Cyber Perk Internet Cafe (Spar Centre, Main Rd) has Internet access (US$2.30 per hour).

Activities There are excellent tours to the nearby Wiklokasia township run by Eco

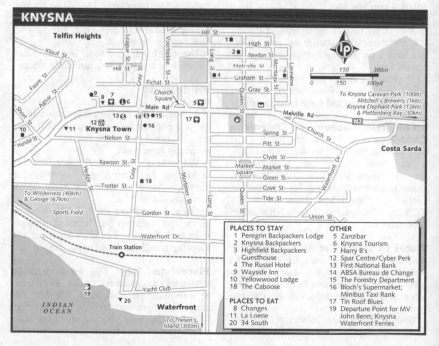

KNYSNA

To Knysna Caravan Park (100m),
Mitchell's Brewery (1km),
Knysna Elephant Park (12km)
& Plettenberg Bay (30km)

To Wilderness (40km)
& George (67km)

To Thesen's
Island (300m)

PLACES TO STAY
1 Peregrin Backpackers Lodge
2 Knysna Backpackers
3 Highfield Backpackers Guesthouse
4 The Russel Hotel
9 Wayside Inn
10 Yellowwood Lodge
18 The Caboose

PLACES TO EAT
8 Changes
11 La Loerie
20 34 South

OTHER
5 Zanzibar
6 Knysna Tourism
7 Harry B's
12 Spar Centre/Cyber Perk
13 First National Bank
14 ABSA Bureau de Change
15 The Forestry Department
16 Bloch's Supermarket; Minibus Taxi Rank
17 Tin Roof Blues
19 Departure Point for MV John Benn; Knysna Waterfront Ferries

Afrika (☎ 082 925 0716). The two-hour trip (US$19) includes a visit to local schools, a visit to a *sangoma* (witch doctor) and a beer in a shebeen.

The MV *John Benn* (☎ 382 1697) offers **cruises** on the lagoon for US$5.20. Bookings are essential.

Diving in the lagoon is interesting and there's a wreck to explore. Beneath Tapas Jetty you might meet the unique Knysna seahorses. **The Heads Adventure Centre** (☎ 384 0831; East Head) charges about US$200 for an open-water certificate course. It also rents gear and runs other activities including rock climbing and abseiling.

The **Forestry Department** (☎ 382 5466; Main Rd), in an office upstairs opposite Memorial Square, is where you book for walking trails and collect maps and information. The **Outeniqua Trail** is popular and takes a week to walk, although you can also do two- or three-day sections. Judith Hopley's *On Foot in the Garden Route* is a useful guide.

There are plenty more activities on offer in and around Knysna including a tour of Tsitsikama's forest canopy with **Treetop Tours** (☎ 042-281 1836), quad biking, canoeing, abseiling The Heads (visit Knysna Tourism for details) and for aspirant Rambos, the chance to test an arsenal of small arms at a couple of the local firing ranges.

Alternatively, enjoy a more sedate day out at the popular **Knysna Elephant Park** (☎ 044-532 7732; admission US$7) where you can hug and touch an elephant.

Places to Stay – Budget Simple, cheap and friendly **Knysna Caravan Park** (☎ 382 2011; camp sites US$4 per person), off Main Rd, is the closest to town and has camp sites only.

Highfield Backpackers Guesthouse (☎ 382 5799; e highfield@hotmail.com; 2 Graham St; dorm beds US$7, doubles US$18.50) is more like a decent guesthouse. It's clean and has a pool, bar and *braai* area.

Peregrin Backpackers Lodge (☎ 382 3747; 37 Queen St; camp sites US$4.50, dorm beds US$7.50, doubles US$18.50) is a clean hostel on a large property with a great view over the bay and something of a party reputation. Rates include breakfast.

Knysna Backpackers (☎ 382 2554; e kny back@netactive.co.za; 12 Newton St; dorm beds US$7; doubles US$19) is a large, smart, well-kept Victorian house on the hill a few blocks up from Main Rd; its prices also include breakfast.

Places to Stay – Mid-Range & Top End Taking its train theme to the extreme, **The Caboose** (☎ 382 5850; e knysna@caboose.co .za; cnr Gray & Trotter Sts; singles/doubles/ triples US$15/20/23) offers cheap, tiny but cosy compartments built exactly like train sleeper cabins.

Wayside Inn (☎/fax 382 6011; singles/ doubles US$31/48) is intimate, well-run and good value. It's just off Main Rd near the cinema.

The Russel Hotel (☎ 382 1052; e russel hotel@mweb.co.za; cnr Long & Graham Sts; singles/doubles low season US$29/46, high season US$57/80) is brand new and comfortable, and especially worth considering in the low season.

Yellowwood Lodge (☎ 382 5906; 18 Handel St; singles/doubles from US$52/57) is a beautiful old house with very comfortable double rooms and breakfast included.

Places to Eat & Drink There are plenty of snack and coffee places in town. All the familiar fast food chains are on Main Rd.

Knysna Oyster Company (Thesen's Island) is the place to go for cheap, fresh oysters.

Changes (☎ 382 0456; Pledge Square; mains US$3.50-4.50) is a popular gay-friendly restaurant serving consistently good food.

La Loerie (☎ 382 1616; 57 Main Rd; mains US$5) is a small but excellent French restaurant.

Paquita's (☎ 384 0408) is a bar and restaurant in a beautiful setting at The Heads, serving pasta from US$2.50 and steaks from US$5; it also does great soups, coffee and inexpensive snacks.

34° South (☎ 382 7268; mains US$4) at the Waterfront is a smart place for breakfast, dinner or lunch. There's fresh seafood and fabulous deli stuff for picnics.

If you're trying to kill a powerful beer thirst, the smart **Zanzibar**, the grungier **Tin Roof Blues** (with pool tables), and the dressy **Harry B's** are all good options on Main Rd.

Getting There & Away Intercape and Greyhound stop at the Engen/Toyota garage, Translux stops at the train station. Short hops

SOUTH AFRICA

along the Garden Route are most economic via minibus taxi.

The historic *Outeniqua Choo-Tjoe* steam train runs between Knysna and George every day except Sunday and public holidays (for details see the earlier George section).

Most minibus taxis stop in the car park behind Bloch's supermarket off Main Rd. Fares include: Plettenberg Bay (US$1.80); and Cape Town (US$11.80), which departs around 7.30am.

Plettenberg Bay
☎ 044

Plettenberg Bay (or just 'Plett') is a beautiful resort and a trendy destination, so things tend to be upmarket. In some ways it's a better (and certainly less traffic-choked) place to spend time in than Knysna – especially if you want to be on the beach (although take care of rip currents when swimming). The bay is also rich in marine life including dolphins, seals and whales.

The **tourism association** *(☎ 533 4065; shop 35, Melville's Corner, cnr Kloof & Main Sts; open 8.30am-5pm Mon-Fri, 9am-1pm Sat)* has useful information.

Activities For information on the surrounding nature reserves and **walks** contact **Cape Nature Conservation** *(☎ 533 2125; w www.capenature.co.za)*. A great way to see the reserve is on the two-day **canoeing trail** *(US$41 per person, with a 4-person minimum)* on the Keurbooms River, with secluded log cabin accommodation.

Mountain-bike trails are being developed in the area; the tourism association has details. **Equitrailing** *(☎ 533 0599)* offers **horse riding**. Adrenaline addicts may skydive above the bay *(Mike ☎ 082 905 7440)*.

Motor Glider Flights *(☎ 535 9112; US$32 for a 40-minute flight)* from Stanley Island about 12km east of Plett offers a sensational way to see that beautiful sweep of bay and you stand an excellent chance of seeing dolphins, seals and, in season, whales.

Ocean Safaris *(☎ 533 4963)* runs whale watching trips in the bay.

Contact the **Heads Adventure Centre** *(☎ 533 1158)* for diving.

Monkeyland *(☎ 044 574 8906; open 8am-6pm)*, 16 km east of Plett along the N2, is a good place for a diverting half-day strolling among playful primates.

If you have your own vehicle, the road running east of Plett is brilliant. Don't take the toll road, but turn off to Nature's Valley and the **Bloukrans Pass**. It's a beautiful drive.

Places to Stay There are backpackers hostels mushrooming all over the area.

Albergo *(☎ 313 4434; e albergo@mweb.co.za; 8 Church St; dorm beds US$7.50, doubles with bathroom US$18)*, near the town centre, is a well-run, friendly place.

Northando Backpackers *(☎/fax 533 0220; e mwdeois@mweb.co.za; 3 Wilder St; dorm beds US$7; doubles with shared/private bathroom US$18.50/21)* is spotless and spacious with a B&B feel.

Weldon Kaya *(☎ 533 2437; singles/doubles in rondavels from US$37/57)*, off the N2 at the corner of Piesang Valley Rd, is a bit out of town but is well worth the trip. The rondavels are quirky and beautiful and the beds huge and comfortable. The attached bar/restaurant is excellent.

Bayview Hotel *(☎ 533 1961; cnr Main & Gibb Sts; singles/doubles US$23/46)*, right in town, is modern, small and pleasant.

Beacon Island Resort *(☎ 533 1120; singles/doubles US$99/170)* is an expensive, carbuncular multistorey hotel on Beacon Island (linked to the rest of Plett by a causeway). Its position, right above the pounding waves, is spectacular.

Places to Eat By the beach near Lookout Rocks is **The Lookout** *(mains around US$5)*. If you're lucky, you may see dolphins playing in the surf here.

Weldon Kaya *(☎ 533 2437; mains around US$5)* is a pain to reach without wheels but it's worth the effort for its tasty, contemporary food.

Getting There & Away Buses and long-distance minibus taxis stop at or near the Shell Ultra City on the N2. The Baz Bus comes into town. Minibus taxis to Knysna (about US$1.75) leave from the corner of Kloof and High Sts. Other long-distance taxis stop at the Shell Ultra City.

Robberg Nature & Marine Reserve

Robberg protects a peninsula with a rugged coastline of cliffs and rocks. The peninsula acts as a sort of marine pit-stop for larger

mammals and fish, which linger here before moving on.

This reserve (☎ 044-533 2125) is 9km southeast of Plettenberg Bay. From Piesang Valley follow the airport road until you see the signs.

Northern Cape Province

Northern Cape is by far the largest but one of the least populated of South Africa's provinces. The mighty Orange River is a lifeline that runs through this area which becomes desert-like on the fringes of the Kalahari and in the Karoo. The Orange and its tributary, the Vaal, combine to create the longest and largest river in South Africa.

Intensely cultivated, irrigated farms line the river. To the north of the river, bordering Botswana, are sparsely wooded savanna and grasslands – cattle-ranching country. To the south, there's the Karoo with woody shrubs and succulents – sheep-farming country.

The Orange flows west to form the border between South Africa and Namibia, and this area is spectacularly harsh country. Namaqualand, world-famous for its spring flowers, lies south of here. To the north lies Augrabies Falls, and the Kgalagadi Transfrontier Park. If you can find the considerable amount of time and effort needed to get in and out of Kgalagadi your time in one of

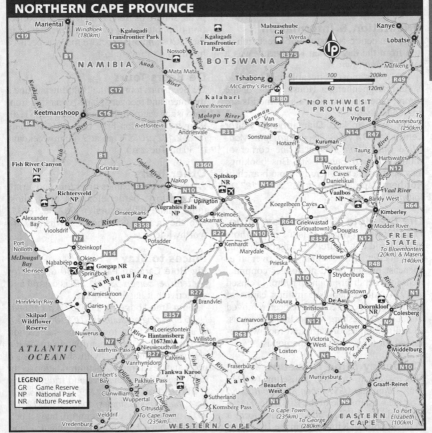

NORTHERN CAPE PROVINCE

LEGEND
GR Game Reserve
NP National Park
NR Nature Reserve

South Africa's greatest, but little known, national parks will be well rewarded.

KIMBERLEY
☎ 053 • pop 192,800

Kimberley, the capital of Northern Cape, owes its existence to the human fascination (and greed) for things that glitter. This was where the De Beers company began and Cecil Rhodes and Ernest Oppenheimer made their fortunes.

Diamonds were discovered in 1869, and by 1872 there were 50,000 miners in the vicinity. In 1871 diamonds were discovered at a small hill, which came to be known as **Colesberg Kopje** and later as Kimberley, and the excavation of the Big Hole commenced.

After a long trip across the Karoo, the relatively bright lights of this wealthy and friendly town are a welcome sight.

Orientation & Information
The town centre is a tangle of streets inherited from the days when Kimberley was a rowdy shantytown.

The city's most noticeable tall building is Harry Oppenheimer House, south of the centre, where South Africa's diamonds are graded and valued.

The well-stocked **Diamantveld Visitor Centre** (☎ 832 7298; open 8am-5pm Mon-Fri, & Sat morning) is near the corner of Bultfontein and Eureka Sts. Bus bookings may be made here. There is also a branch of **Northern Cape Tourism** (☎ 832 2657; 187 Du Toitspan Rd).

The Big Hole & Kimberley Mine
The 180m-deep Big Hole is the largest hole in the world dug entirely by manual labour.

Kimberley Mine, which took over after opencast mining could no longer continue, went to a depth of around 1100m. It closed in 1914. Altogether, 14.5 million carats of diamonds are believed to have been removed from under Colesberg Kopje. In other words, 28 million tonnes of earth and rock was removed for three tonnes of diamonds.

Kimberley Mine Museum
This excellent open-air museum (☎ 833 1557; admission US$2; open 8am-6pm daily) is on the western side of the Big Hole. Forty-eight original or facsimile buildings form a reconstruction of Kimberley in the 1880s and

De Beers Hall has a collection of diamonds. There's also a platform from where you can gape at the size of that hole – 150m down to the waterline and 800m deep in total.

The William Humphreys Gallery
It may seem unlikely but Kimberley can lay claim to one of the most interesting and absorbing galleries in the country. **The William Humphreys Gallery** (☎ 831 1724; admission US$0.60; open 10am-5pm Mon-Sat, 2pm-5pm Sun) has a varied and striking collection of contemporary works, mostly by black artists, among some older and rather staid Dutch, Flemish and English art.

Duggan-Cronin Gallery
The Duggan-Cronin Gallery (☎ 842 0099; Egerton Rd; admission US$0.60; open 9am-5pm Mon-Fri, 9am-1pm Sat, 2pm-5pm Sun), in the suburb of Belgravia, features a collection of photographs of black tribes taken in the 1920s and 30s – before many aspects of traditional life were lost.

De Beers Tours
De Beers runs tours of the Bultfontein Mine's treatment and recovery plants, departing from the visitor centre at the mine gate (US$1.20; 9am & 11am Mon-Fri). Underground tours (☎ 842 1321, US$7) are at 7.45am weekdays (9.30am Tuesday).

Other Tours
A wealth of companies offer tours covering local history, battlefields and even ghost tours. **Fikile Bili's tours** (☎ 082 862 8711) into the nearby Galeshewe townships are worthwhile.

Places to Stay
Big Hole Caravan Park (☎ 830 6322; sites per tent/per person US$3/1.20) is central and attractive but has little shade.

Gum Tree Lodge (☎ 832 8577; dorm beds US$5.80, singles/doubles US$10.50/18.50) is about 5km from town at the intersection of Hull St and the Bloemfontein road. It's a large, pleasant place with shady lawns, a pool and restaurant. Accommodation is in fairly basic flats with stove and fridge.

Stay-A-Day (☎ 832 7239; 72 Lawson St; dorm beds US$5, singles/doubles US$12.50/21) is an excellent, clean, central, budget bet. Doubles have bathroom, TV and tea- and

Cecil Rhodes

Cecil John Rhodes (1853–1902), the sickly son of an English vicar, was sent to South Africa in 1870 to improve his health. By 1887 he had founded the De Beers Consolidated Mines Company and could afford to buy Barney Barnato's Kimberley Mine for UK£5,000,000. By 1891, De Beers owned 90% of the world's diamonds and Rhodes also had a stake in the fabulous reef of gold discovered on the Witwatersrand (near Johannesburg).

Rhodes was not satisfied with merely acquiring personal wealth and power. He personified the idea of empire and dreamed of 'painting the map red' by building a railway from the Cape to Cairo (running through British territory all the way) and even of bringing the USA back under British rule. The times were right for such dreams and in 1890 he was elected prime minister of the Cape Colony.

Rhodes was successful in establishing British control in Bechuanaland (later Botswana) and the area that was to become Rhodesia (later Zimbabwe), but the gold mines there proved to be less productive than those on the Witwatersrand.

The Transvaal Republic in general, and Paul Kruger in particular, had been causing Rhodes difficulty for some time. It irked Rhodes that Kruger's republic of pastoralists should be sitting on the richest reef of gold in the world, and the republic was also directly in the path of British expansion.

The miners on the Witwatersrand were mainly non-Boers, who were denied any say in the politics of the republic. This caused increasing resentment, and in late 1895 Captain Leander Jameson led an expedition into the Witwatersrand with the intention of sparking an uprising among the foreigners.

The Jameson raid was a fiasco. All the participants were either killed or captured and Jameson was jailed. The British government was extremely embarrassed when it became apparent that Rhodes had prior knowledge of the raid and probably encouraged it. He was forced to resign as prime minister and the British government took control of Rhodesia and Bechuanaland, his personal fiefdoms. Rhodes' empire-building days were over.

After his death in 1902, Rhodes' reputation was largely rehabilitated by his will, which devoted most of his fortune to the Rhodes Scholarship. This still sends winning students from the Commonwealth and other countries to study at Oxford University.

coffee-making facilities. Accommodation proceeds go towards a local orphanage.

Diamond Protea Lodge (*☎ 831 1281; singles/doubles midweek US$28/40, weekends US$46/48*) has comfortable, well equipped rooms but few hotel facilities.

Places to Eat

The **Lemon Tree** (*Angel St*), close to the visitors centre, is a pleasant, cheap café.

Keg & Falcon (*meals around US$3*) conveniently located next to the Northern Cape Tourism office has tasty, affordable meals.

Halfway House (*Du Toitspan Rd*) near the corner of Egerton Rd is an atmospheric watering hole in a historic building.

15 on Dalham (*☎ 832 0608; 15 Dalham Rd; mains around US$6*) is an expensive restaurant serving inventive, tasty, home-made cuisine which it calls 'Boer Baroque'.

Getting There & Away

Air SA Express flies here regularly from Jo'burg. A seven-day advance ticket costs US$120. SA Airlink offers direct Cape Town services (seven-day advance ticket US$130).

Bus Many services run to/from Jo'burg, about six hours from Kimberley. The cheapest is Greyhound's daily service for US$13. The trip from Kimberley to Cape Town with Translux costs US$33 and takes 10 hours. Translux also runs to Knysna (US$32; 11 hours) via Oudtshoorn (US$23), Mossel Bay (US$32) and George (US$32).

Translux buses stop at the central Shell/ Civic Motors garage. Greyhound buses stop at the Shell Ultra City on the N12 – you'll have to get a bus, taxi or hitch there. Tickets may be booked at Tickets for Africa (*☎ 832 6040*) in the Diamentvelt Visitors Centre.

Minibus The minibus taxi area is around the **Indian shopping centre** (*Duncan St*). Destinations include: Bloemfontein (US$5.75); Jo'burg (US$10); Upington (US$9); and Cape Town (US$15). The long-distance taxis are near Crossley St.

Train For information on trains, contact **Spoornet** (☎ 086 000 8888; W www.spoor net.co.za).

The *Trans Karoo* runs daily to Cape Town (17¼ hours) and Jo'burg/Pretoria (8¾ hours).

The *Trans Oranje* between Cape Town and Durban also stops here.

Getting Around

A minibus taxi around town costs about US$0.20. For a taxi from the pub, there is **AA Taxi** (☎ 083 283 0558) and **Rikki's Taxi** (☎ 083 342 2533).

An antique tram runs between the mine museum (departing on the hour) and the town hall (departing at quarter past). The return fare is US$1.70.

AROUND KIMBERLEY
Wildebeeste Kuil

This small, rocky hillock, about 10km northwest of Kimberley on the R31 towards Barkly West, is rich in mythical, cultural and archaeological interest. The San people who hunted here, and made the profusion of rock carvings, are thought to have seen it as a kind of gateway to the spirit world.

The attached **visitor centre** (☎ 053-833 7069; admission with audio US$3; open Mon-Fri 10am-5pm, Sat & Sun 11am-4pm) offers an excellent audio tour around the sun-baked rocks. A Barkly West–bound minibus taxi is probably the best transport bet without a car, although getting back into Kimberley will be tiresome.

UPINGTON

☎ 054 • pop 62,300

Nestling on the banks of the Orange River, Upington is the principal town in the far north. It's an orderly, prosperous place, full of supermarkets and chain stores.

The surrounding area is intensively cultivated thanks to the limitless sunlight and irrigation water.

The helpful **tourist office** (☎ 332 6064) is in the rather meagre Kalahari Orange Museum. There's not much to see in the museum (a former mission church) apart from a few artefacts from Upington's early town life.

Places to Stay

A fair walk from town on the southern bank of the Orange River, **Eiland Holiday Resort** (☎ 334 0286; camp sites US$4.60, single/double rondavels US$12.50/18) has pleasant tent sites and a range of hut, chalet and rondavel choices. To get here, cross the bridge signposted for Prieska at the northern end of town.

Kalahari Junction Backpackers (☎ 332 7874; 3 Oranje St; camping US$4, dorm beds US$7.50, doubles US$19) is a smallish place which also runs day tours and two- to five-day tours into Kgalagadi Transfrontier Park.

Yebo Guesthouse & Backpackers (☎ 331 2496; 21 Morant St; dorm beds US$5.75, singles/doubles from US$10/19) is in a pleasant spot just north of the sports stadium with a swimming pool, kitchen and tidy rooms.

There are plenty of guesthouses charging from US$14 per person, alternatively the two Protea hotels stand opposite each other on the corner of Lutz and Schroder Sts. Both have weekend specials.

Oasis Protea Lodge (☎ 331 1125; singles/doubles US$41/51) is a comfortable if characterless place. **Upington Protea Hotel** (☎ 332 4414; singles/doubles US$40/48) is older.

Getting There & Away

Air SAA flies to/from Jo'burg and Cape Town. There is no public transport between the airport and Upington, although the hotels often lay on taxis for guests.

Bus Contact the **Intercape bus office** (☎ 332 6091; Lutz St). The Jo'burg service (US$29, nine hours) connects with one to Windhoek (US$34, 10 hours). Intercape also runs to/from Cape Town (US$25, 10½ hours).

Minibus Taxi You'll find minibus taxis, including many of the long-distance services, near Checkers supermarket on the corner of Mark and Basson Sts. Upington taxis can take a long time to fill but there is generally at least one per day to major destinations including Kimberley (US$11), Cape Town (US$18.50), Jo'burg (US$17.50) and Windhoek (US$22). **VIP Taxis** (☎ 027-851 8780) operates weekdays to Port Nolloth via Springbok (US$7.50).

Car If you want to see the Kgalagadi Transfrontier Park and are short of time, it makes sense to fly to Upington and hire a car. There's an **Avis agent** (☎ 332 4746) at the airport. **Tempest** (☎ 337 8560) is a

competitive rental firm. The Oasis Protea Lodge rents 4WD vehicles.

KGALAGADI TRANSFRONTIER PARK

In 1999, South Africa's Kalahari-Gemsbok National Park and Botswana's Mabuasehube-Gemsbok National Park merged and are now collectively known as the highly worthwhile Kgalagadi Transfrontier Park, one of Africa's largest protected areas. The relatively accessible South African section of the park lies in the triangular segment of the country between Namibia and Botswana, covering 959,103 hectares. The protected area continues over another 1,807,000 hectares on the Botswana side of the border (there are no fences). It's possible to venture into the Botswana side of the park (only accessible with groups of two 4WD vehicles or more and prior booking is compulsory), but you'll need a passport to enter from one country and leave from the other. For information and bookings on the Botswana side, contact the **Botswana Department of Wildlife & National Parks** (☎ 267-318 0774; e dwnp@gov.bw).

Although the countryside is semi-desert it supports large populations of birds, reptiles, small mammals and antelopes. These in turn support a large population of predators.

The Nossob and Auob Rivers (usually dry) run through the park and meet at Twee Rivieren. Much of the wildlife is concentrated around water holes in the river beds, making wildlife viewing remarkably rewarding.

Information

The best time to visit is in June and July when the weather is coolest (below freezing at night) and the animals have drawn in to the water holes.

The wet season is from September to October when many of the animals scatter across the plain to take advantage of the fresh pastures. November is quiet, and daily temperatures start to rise. Despite the fact that temperatures frequently reach 45°C in December and January, the chalets in the park are often fully booked.

The daily conservation fee is US$2.90/1.50 for adults/children plus US$0.60 per vehicle. All the rest camps have shops selling basic groceries, soft drinks and alcohol (no fresh vegetables). Petrol and diesel are available at each camp.

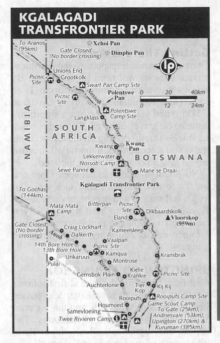

The entrance gates open from around 6.30am to 6.30pm depending on the time of year.

Fauna

About 215 species of bird have been spotted in the park, including the secretary bird, the kori bustard and the sociable weaver. There are also 19 predator species, including dark-maned Kalahari lions, cheetahs, leopards, wild dogs, hyenas, jackals, bat-eared foxes and suricates. The most numerous species is the springbok.

Places to Stay

There are rest camps at **Twee Rivieren**, **Mata Mata** and **Nossob**; all have a range of fully equipped **cottages** (3 people from US$38) and there are **huts** (2 people from US$34) with shared facilities at Mata Mata and Nossob. All the rest camps have **camp sites** (up to 6 people US$8.50). All accommodation, including tent sites, must be booked through the **National Parks Board** (☎ 012-428 9111; w www.parks-sa.co.za) in Pretoria.

A number of guesthouses, mostly farms, offer accommodation en route between

Upington and Kgalagadi Transfrontier Park. The tourist office in Upington has details.

Getting There & Away
There is no public transport, so those without private vehicles will need to join a tour. By car, it's a five- or six-hour drive from Twee Rivieren to Kuruman (385km) or Upington (358km) and you have to cover a significant distance on gravel, although the road is being sealed. Be careful driving on the dirt sections and if you stop, don't pull too far off the road or you might become stuck in the sand.

No petrol is available between Upington and Twee Rivieren, so make sure you start with a full tank. It's important to carry water, as you might have to wait a while if you break down – you can rapidly become dangerously dehydrated when the temperature is over 40°C.

UPINGTON TO SPRINGBOK
West from Upington the road at first follows the course of the Orange River and passes through oases of vineyards and the pleasant little towns of **Keimos** and **Kakamas**. The turn-off to Augrabies Falls National Park, 40km north of the road, is at Kakamas.

From Kakamas to **Pofadder** things are considerably duller, but then you enter a wide, bleak valley and, as you approach Springbok, dramatic piles of boulders litter the landscape – you have entered Namaqualand.

Augrabies Falls National Park
This national park (☎ 054-452 9200; admission adult/child US$1.80/0.90; gates open 6.30am-10pm) is more than just an impressive waterfall.

Certainly the falls can be spectacular but the most interesting facet of the park is the fascinating desert and riverine environments on either side of the river.

The three-day **Klipspringer Hiking Trail** (US$11.50 per person; closed mid Oct-Mar) runs along the southern bank of the river. Hikers must supply their own sleeping bags and food. Booking ahead is advisable.

Maps and information are available from the main park complex. There's no public transport available, although the Kalahari Adventure Centre picks up clients from Upington for US$18.50 per person (with a minimum of four people).

There's a **camping ground** (2-person sites US$10) and self-contained **chalets** (2 people US$34). Book through the **National Parks Board** (☎ 012-428 9111; W www.parks -sa.co.za) in Pretoria.

NAMAQUALAND
☎ 027
Namaqualand is a rugged plateau in the northwest of the province that overlooks a narrow, sandy coastal plain and the bleak beaches of the west coast. In the east it runs into the dry central plains that are known as Bushmanland.

The area is sparsely populated, mainly by Afrikaans-speaking sheep farmers, and in the northwest by the Namaqua, a Khoikhoi tribe famous for its metal-working skills.

The cold Benguela Current runs up the west coast and creates a desert-like environment. You'll see the characteristic kokerboom, an aloe that can grow to a height of 4m. In the north you'll see 'halfmens' or elephant trunk *(Pachydodium namaquanum),* weird tree-like succulents topped by a small 'face' of foliage. They always look to the north, and there's a legend that they are the transformed bodies of Khoikhoi who were driven south during a war. Those who turned around to look towards their lost lands were turned into trees.

Namaqualand can get cold in winter (average minimums around 5°C) and hot in summer (average maximums around 30°C).

Alluvial Diamonds
In 1925 a young soldier found a glittering stone near Port Nolloth. Prospectors converged on the area and it soon became clear (notably to Ernest Oppenheimer of De Beers) that an enormously rich source of diamonds had been discovered. Eventually De Beers acquired all the major mines.

The diamonds are harvested from gravel beds on the sea floor and from beneath the sandveld, a narrow, sandy plain between mountains and sea.

Despite strict security and laws, it's believed that substantial quantities of diamonds still find their way to illegal traders. You may meet locals who offer to sell you cheap diamonds – this is highly illegal, and you're likely to end up with a *slenter* (fake diamond). The bleak landscape and the presence of diamond miners and divers contribute

to a frontier atmosphere. If you want to check it out, the best place to go is **Port Nolloth**; stay at the friendly **Bedrock** (☎ 851 8865; e bedrock@icon.co.za), which has guesthouse accommodation.

Wildflowers

Although the wildflowers of the Western Cape are spectacular, they are overshadowed by the brilliance of the world-renowned Namaqualand displays.

Generally the Namaqualand flowers bloom a couple of weeks earlier than those further south. The flowers are at their peak between mid-August and mid-September, although the optimum time to visit varies from year to year.

The Namaqualand flora, which is part of the Palaeotropical kingdom, begins north of Vanrhynsdorp in Western Cape. There can be flowers on the plains between Nuwerus and Garies, but the major spectacle begins around Garies and extends to Steinkopf in the north. Springbok is considered the flower capital.

Another zone can be found in the Kamiesberg Range, east of Kamieskroon. The plain to the east of Springbok and north to Vioolsdrif produces more brilliant annuals.

The flower season brings hordes of people to the area and accommodation becomes scarce and expensive.

Getting There & Away

Aside from buses on the N7 and R27 (between Vanrhynsdorp and Upington) public transport is sparse. The major operators offer tours of Namaqualand from Jo'burg and Cape Town, but touring in your own car is the best way.

Kamieskroon

Kamieskroon is perched high in the mountains and is surrounded by boulder-strewn hills. There are some beautiful drives and walks in the area. For information contact the **Kamieskroon & Sandveld Tourism Forum** (☎ 672 1627).

About 18km northwest of Kamieskroon is the **Skilpad Wildflower Reserve** (☎ 672 1614; admission US$1.80). It often outdoes other nearby areas during the flower season.

The **Kamieskroon Hotel & Caravan Park** (☎ 672 1614; camp sites US$4.50, singles/doubles US$18/25) is a civilised hideaway. Rates are higher in flower season.

Springbok

Springbok, in a valley among harsh, rocky hills, considers itself the capital of Namaqualand. It explodes with colour in the flower season. On its outskirts, the first European-run **copper mine** was established in 1852. In modern times, this rough-and-tumble frontier town has been transformed into a busy service centre for the area's copper and diamond mines.

Orientation & Information The town is quite spread out, but most places are within walking distance of the small *kopje* (isolated hill) in the elbow of the main street's right-angled bend.

There's an **information centre** (☎ 718 2985; open 7.30am-4.15pm) on Voortrekker St opposite the Shell garage. **Springbok Lodge** (☎ 712 1321, Voortrekker St) is also a good place to collect information on the area (including where the best flowers are). You can get online at **Blue Chip** on Voortekker St near Springbok Lodge.

Springbok Museum In the 1920s Springbok had a large Jewish population. Most have moved away, however, and their synagogue has been converted into an interesting local museum open weekday mornings.

Places to Stay During the flower season accommodation in Springbok can fill up and prices rise. The information centre can tell you about overflow accommodation in private homes.

Springbok Caravan Park (☎ 718 1584; Goegap Rd; camp sites US$4 per person) is 2km from town on the road to the nature reserve. Occasional buses run past, otherwise it's a long walk.

Richtersveld Challenge (☎ 718 1905; e richtersveld.challen@kingsley.co.za; Voortrekker St; dorm beds US$7, doubles US$29), opposite the information centre, has one large dorm aimed at tour bus groups and some beautiful and good value B&B accommodation. Self-catering is an option.

Annie's Cottage (☎ 712 1451; 4 King St; B&B singles/doubles from US$25/34) is a quiet, upmarket place recommended by readers.

Springbok Lodge (☎ 712 1321; rooms from US$11.50 per person) has rooms and cottages behind the café and all over town. The cottages have been steadily upgraded

over the years and are simple but pleasant. Self-catering units are more expensive.

Places to Eat Eating options are pretty grim in town, but there is a **KFC** in the town centre.

Springbok Restaurant at the Springbok Lodge is informal and fun, if somewhat greasy. The menu is large and includes grills from US$3.50, breakfast, snacks and salads.

Getting There & Away There are weekday flights from Springbok to Cape Town (US$190) with **National Airlines** (*☎ 712 2061 in Springbok, • ☎ 021-934 0350 in Cape Town*).

Intercape's Windhoek (Namibia) to Cape Town service runs through Springbok, Springbok to Cape Town (US$28, six hours) and Springbok to Windhoek (US$37, 11½ hours).

Van Wyk's Busdiens (*☎ 713 8559*) runs a daily door-to-door taxi to Cape Town for US$19. Ordinary minibus taxis to Cape Town (also US$19.50) stop at the Caltex garage on Voortrekker St, or at the taxi rank behind First National Bank near the kopje.

Ask at the Springbok Lodge or the tourism information centre about car hire from local garages.

Goegap Nature Reserve

This reserve (*admission per vehicle US$1.20; open 8am-4pm Mon-Fri, also weekends during flower season*), 8km from Springbok, is famous for its spring flowers and its nursery of amazing Karoo and Namaqualand succulents. You may also see springboks, mountain zebras and varied birdlife.

Vioolsdrif

Vioolsdrif, on the N7 677km north of Cape Town, is the border crossing for traffic going to/from Namibia (the border is open 24 hours), and is the gateway to Richtersveld National Park.

The **scenic drive** from Steinkopf is spectacular and at Vioolsdrif there are great views of the Orange River carving its way through the desolate mountains with the narrow strip of farmland along its banks.

For more border crossing information, see under Land in the main Getting There & Away section earlier in this chapter.

Peace of Paradise (*☎ 761 8968; camp sites US$5.75 per person*) occupies a lovely setting 23km downstream along the river road from the border crossing. Canoes are available for guests.

Richtersveld National Park

This big national park (*☎ 831 1506; PO Box 406, Alexander Bay 8290*) is located in the northern loop of the Orange River to the northwest of Vioolsdrif and the N7. The park is the property of the local Namaqua people who continue to lead a semi-traditional, semi-nomadic pastoral existence.

The area is a mountainous desert and the hiking possibilities, though demanding, are excellent. Despite its apparent barrenness, the territory has a rich and prolific variety of succulent plants.

Most of the park is virtually inaccessible without a properly equipped expedition and local guides.

Eastern Cape

Eastern Cape is a diverse and largely undeveloped province. It includes the former Homelands of Ciskei and Transkei, so most of its population is Xhosa-speaking.

The long coastline extends from Tsitsikamma Coastal National Park, through Port Elizabeth and the Sunshine Coast to the Shipwreck Coast of the former Ciskei region. It then continues past East London and into the spectacular subtropical Wild Coast of the former Transkei.

Inland, the rolling green hills around Grahamstown are known as Settler Country, after the British migrants who settled the area in the early 19th century. The semidesert Karoo is further north on the plateau.

Although many of the roads within the former Ciskei and Transkei regions are of a reasonable standard, there is a real likelihood of children and livestock straying onto them.

NATURE'S VALLEY TO PORT ELIZABETH

Tsitsikamma Coastal National Park has beautiful forests, while the coast between Cape St Francis and East London is best known for its surf. The coast between the Great Fish River (east of Port Alfred) almost to East

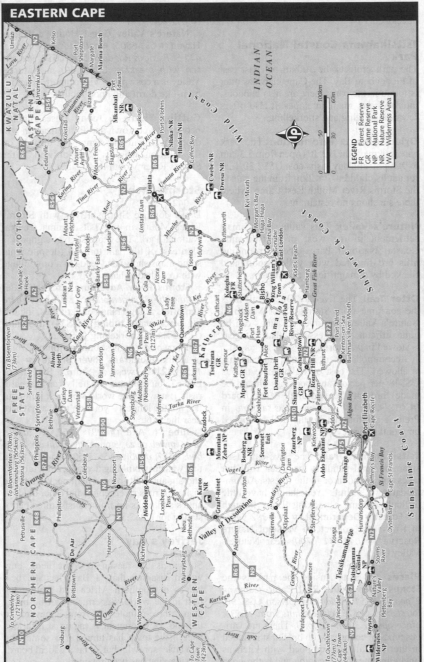

London was once part of Ciskei and is less developed.

Tsitsikamma Coastal National Park

The park protects the 100km of coast east of Plettenberg Bay. The Cape clawless otter is found in the park; there are also baboons, monkeys and small antelopes. It also offers rewarding **diving** and **snorkelling**.

Orientation & Information The park gate is 6km off the N2. It's open from 5.30am to 9.30pm, and day visits cost US$2.30/1.20 for adults/children. It's 2km from the gate to the Storms River Mouth Rest Camp, where there's a shop and restaurant.

Nature's Valley This valley has a small settlement in the west of Tsitsikamma Coastal National Park. The surrounding hills are forested with yellowwood, and flanked by a magnificent 5km beach.

Otter Trail The five-day Otter Trail hugs the coastline from Storms River Mouth to Nature's Valley. The river crossings can be quite difficult, so it is essential that your gear is stowed in waterproof bags.

Accommodation is in **huts**; no camping is allowed. The cost of walking the trail is US$48 per person and bookings should be made through the **National Parks Board** (☎ 012-428 9111; ⒲ www.parks-sa.co.za) in Pretoria. Unfortunately, the trail is booked up months ahead.

Tsitsikamma Trail The five-day Tsitsikamma Trail parallels the Otter Trail but takes you inland through the forests. Accommodation is in **huts**. You should have little difficulty getting a booking. Book through the **Forestry Department** (☎ 044-382 5466) in Knysna or contact **De Vasselot Nature Reserve** (☎ 044-531 6700) near Nature's Valley.

Places to Stay Inside the park is the **Storms River Mouth Rest Camp** (camping 2 people US$15, additional person US$2.90, forest huts US$23, chalets/huts from US$34; office open 7.30am-4.30pm). There are various types of cottages, with breakfast included in the rate; all are equipped with kitchens (including utensils), bedding and bathrooms.

Book through the **National Parks Board** (☎ 012-428 9111)

Nature's Valley Guest House & Hikers Haven (☎ 531 6805; Ⓔ patbond@mweb.co.za; 411 St Patrick's Rd; dorm beds US$7, per person with breakfast US$17.50) in Nature's Valley is a cosy place with a smart, spacious barn-like dorm and good facilities.

Getting There & Away Buses running between Cape Town and Port Elizabeth will drop you off at the signposted turn-off on the N2, from where it's an 8km walk to the Storms River Mouth Rest Camp.

Storms River
☎ 042

Don't confuse Storms River with Storms River Mouth in the Tsitsikamma Coastal National Park. The Storms River signpost is 4km east of the park turn-off (despite what some maps show) and leads to a tiny village with tree-shaded lanes.

Storms River Adventures (☎ 281 1836; Ⓔ adventure@gardenroute.co.za) is based here and offers a huge range of activities, including **black-water tubing** (US$34), **abseiling** (US$14) and **snorkelling** (US$52).

The world's highest **bungee jump** (216m) is at the **Bloukrans River Bridge** (☎ 281 1458), 21km west of Storms River. For US$57 you can have one hell of an adrenalin rush. It may be the world's highest jump but it is not the longest – you don't fall anywhere near the 216m.

Tube 'n Axe (☎ 281 1757; Ⓔ tube-n -axe@mweb.co.za; Storms River Village; dorm beds US$7, doubles US$17.50) is a new place that was busy building decking, a hot tub, bar and a giant multi-person hammock when we visited. It runs river tubing and other outdoor antics and picks up from Tsitsikamma petrol station for US$2.30.

Jeffrey's Bay
☎ 042

Surfing is the reason to come here! Few would disagree that 'J Bay' has the best waves in Southern Africa and among the best in the world. Supertubes can be better than a three-minute ride from Boneyards to the end. Development is raging at a furious pace – the town has turned into something of a tacky sprawl – but so far the local board-waxing vibe has been retained.

History of the Xhosa

Most of Eastern Cape is populated by groups of Nguni peoples (Zulu, Xhosa and Ndebele) who occupied the coastal savanna of South Africa, but those living west of the Great Fish River are relatively recent arrivals. It's not clear how the differences between the coastal Nguni and the Sotho of the highveld came about. Iron Age Bantus probably reached the Great Kei River by AD 1000.

The Xhosa first came into contact with Boers in the 1760s. Both groups were heavily dependent on cattle, and both coveted the grazing land in the area known as Zuurveld (the coastal strip from Algoa Bay to the Great Kei River).

In 1771, Governor van Plettenberg convinced some chiefs to consider the Great Fish River as the boundary between the Dutch East India Company's territory and the Xhosa's. Conflict was inevitable, and the first of nine major frontier wars broke out in 1779 – skirmishes and brigandage (by blacks and whites) were virtually continuous for the next century.

By the beginning of the 19th century, the Xhosa were under pressure in the west from white expansion, and in the east and north from peoples fleeing from the *difaqane* (forced migration). After the Sixth Frontier War (1834–35) the British declared the land between the Great Kei and Keiskamma Rivers the Province of Queen Adelaide, and allowed a limited degree of independence. In 1846, however, white colonialists invaded, beginning the Seventh Frontier War. In its aftermath, British Kaffraria was established, with King William's Town as its capital.

In 1840 the great leader Sandile had become the paramount chief of the Rharhabe (or Ciskei) Xhosa. He was to mobilise the Xhosa in their last increasingly desperate attempts to retain their land and resist white influence. He was a key figure in the Seventh, Eighth (1850–53) and Ninth Frontier Wars.

He was also involved in the 'Great Cattle Killing', the Xhosa suicide of 1857. A young girl, Nongqawuse, had visions suggesting the Xhosa could reconcile themselves with a spirit world that allowed the theft of their lands and destruction of their culture through the sacrifice of cattle and crops. In return the whites would be swept into the sea. The Xhosa followed Nongqawuse's visions and it's thought that from a Xhosa population of 90,000 in British Kaffraria, 30,000 died of starvation and 30,000 were forced to emigrate as destitute refugees.

In 1866, British Kaffraria became part of the Cape Colony. The Xhosa had been devastated by years of struggle, but in 1877–78 they once again fought for their independence in the Ninth Frontier War.

Information The small **publicity association** (☎ 293 2588) in the municipal buildings is open on weekdays and Saturday morning. The **Network Internet Cafe** is opposite the publicity association (US$2.30 per half hour).

Places to Stay The friendly and well-run **Jeffrey's Bay Backpackers** (☎ 293 1379; e backpack@netactive.co.za; 12 Jeffreys St; dorm beds US$5.75, singlcs/twins US$8/14) has four-bed dorms and private rooms. It also organises surfing lessons for around US$8.50 per hour.

Island Vibe Backpackers (☎ 293 1625; e ivibe@lantic.net; camping US$4.50, dorm beds US$7, doubles US$19) is a bit out of town (follow the signs), but is friendly and has panoramic bay views. The beach is just a hop and skip away.

Cristal Cove (☎ 293 2101; e cristal@lantic .net; 49 Flame Crescent; dorm beds US$7,

doubles US$14/16) may be the pick of the places in J Bay. It has self-catering, is backpacker friendly and excellent value. The friendly owners know lots about the surf (it's right by Supertubes).

Seashells Luxury Apartments (☎ 293 1104; e olive@corpdial.co.za; 125 Da Gama Rd; apartments US$34-63) has huge, plush apartments close to the beach.

Places to Eat Good places for coffee are the **cafés** in the Seafront Mall, and the **Coffee Mill** at the museum opposite the mall.

Sunflower Cafe (☎ 293 1682; 20 Da Gama Rd; breakfast/lunch US$1.80/2.50) doles out generous portions of hearty food, with vegie options.

The Breakers (☎ 293 1975; 23 Diaz Rd), overlooking the water, is a gem among the grease merchants so consider a minor splurge here. The menu offers mainly seafood, from US$6, as well as good pizza.

Getting There & Away The Baz Bus stops at the hostels. **Sunshine Express** (☎ 293 2221) runs to Port Elizabeth for US$8, door-to-door.

Minibus taxis depart from Bloch's supermarket; the fare to Humansdorp is US$1.20.

PORT ELIZABETH
☎ 041 • pop 1,065,900

Port Elizabeth's city centre is on steep hills overlooking Algoa Bay. It has pleasant beaches, a revamped seafront area, parks and some interesting historical architecture, which is unfortunately crumbling through neglect. Port Elizabeth (commonly known as 'PE') bills itself as the 'Friendly City' and lives up to the moniker.

It does have a less sunny side, however. Steve Biko, the Black Consciousness Movement leader was held and tortured here for 26 days. There are also some enormous townships around PE and Uitenhage, home to all the problems and violence associated with poverty and bad housing. This is far from the complete picture though, as the excellent township tours in PE will show.

Orientation & Information

The train station (for trains and buses) is just north of the Campanile, the bell tower, which you can climb for a donation. Walk up the steep hill to Donkin Reserve to orient yourself. The beaches are to the south.

Tourism Port Elizabeth (☎ 585 8884; ₩ www.ibhayi.com; Donkin Reserve; open daily) is in the lighthouse building in Donkin Reserve and has plenty of brochures and information.

For currency exchange try **AmEx** (☎ 365 1225; The Boardwalk). For travel bookings, contact **Rennies** (☎ 363 1185; The Bridge Shopping Centre).

Dangers & Annoyances

The city centre can be dangerous at night, although tougher policing has improved things recently. The thriving seafront area is safe.

Things to See & Do

Although **Settlers' Park** is virtually in the centre of the city, it includes 54 hectares of cultivated and natural gardens in the valley of the Baakens River. The main emphasis

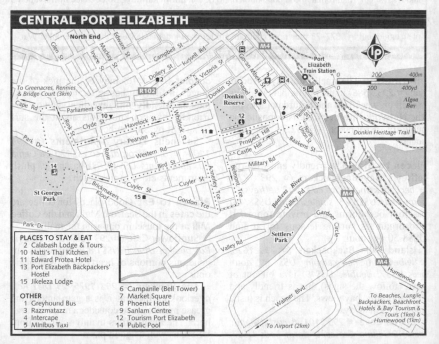

CENTRAL PORT ELIZABETH

PLACES TO STAY & EAT
2 Calabash Lodge & Tours
10 Natti's Thai Kitchen
11 Edward Protea Hotel
13 Port Elizabeth Backpackers' Hostel
15 Jikeleza Lodge

OTHER
1 Greyhound Bus
3 Razzmatazz
4 Intercape
5 Minibus Taxi
6 Campanile (Bell Tower)
7 Market Square
8 Phoenix Hotel
9 Sanlam Centre
12 Tourism Port Elizabeth
14 Public Pool

is on native plants and flowers, so it's also a good place for birdlife. The main entrance is on How St (off Park Dr, which circles St George's Park and its sporting fields).

Bayworld (☎ 584 0650; Beach Rd; admission museum/oceanarium US$1.20/1.80; complex open 9am-1pm & 2pm-5pm daily) has some interesting anthropological exhibitions; a tropical house and snake park; and an oceanarium, complete with performing dolphins.

Travellers have recommended the day and night **township tours** offered by **Molo Tours** (☎ 581 7085 or 082 970 4037; US$14). It's founder Mzolisi is well connected and gets you up close and friendly with the locals.

The **beaches** are to the south of the city centre. Take Humewood Rd; this becomes Beach Rd, then Marine Dr. Kings Beach stretches from the harbour breakwater to Humewood Beach; both of these are sheltered. Surfers and *Hobie Cat* (catamaran) sailors should make for Summerstrand, about 5km from the centre.

There are good **diving sites** around PE, including some wrecks and the St Croix Islands, a marine reserve. Several outfits, including **Ocean Divers** (☎ 583 1790; **w** www.odipe.co.za; The Boardwalk, Summerstrand) and **Pro Dive** (☎ 583 5316) offer diving trips. PADI courses start at US$170.

PE is also a good place to organise tours to **Addo Elephant Park** (see Port Elizabeth to Kei River later in this chapter). A number of outfits can arrange these, including **Bay Tourism & Tours** (☎ 584 0622), which charges about US$46, and **Tanaqua** (☎ 270 9924).

Places to Stay
There is a good range of accommodation in PE. The following covers just a few of the better places.

Tourism Port Elizabeth makes B&B bookings and you will find most places charge between US$14.50 and US$20 per person.

West of Summerstrand, about 7km from the city centre, **Pine Lodge** (☎ 583 4004; 2-person camp sites $US10) also has a range of self-catering options and motel rooms.

Within walking distance of the city centre **Port Elizabeth Backpackers Hostel** (☎ 586 0697; **e** pebakpak@global.co.za; 7 Prospect Hill; dorm beds US$7, doubles US$18.50) is a sociable place and offers free trips to the beaches.

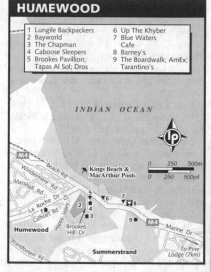

HUMEWOOD

1 Lungile Backpackers
2 Bayworld
3 The Chapman
4 Caboose Sleepers
5 Brookes Pavillion; Tapas Al Sol; Dros
6 Up The Khyber
7 Blue Waters Cafe
8 Barney's
9 The Boardwalk; AmEx; Tarantino's

Jikeleza Lodge (☎ 586 3721; 44 Cuyler St; camping US$5, dorm beds US$7, doubles US$18.50) is an excellent hostel. It's small and clean and the owners are a veritable gold mine of information on PE – ask about local township tours and tours to Addo and Kruger National Parks.

Lungile Backpackers (☎ 582 2042; **e** lungile@netactive.co.za; 12 La Roche Dr, Humewood; camping US$4, dorm beds from US$5.80, doubles US$17.50) is comfortable and offers value for money. It's on the beachfront and surfboards are available.

Calabash Lodge (☎ 585 6162; **e** calabash@iafrica.com; 8 Dollery St, Central; singles/twins without bathroom US$18.50/23, singles/doubles with bathroom US$20/29) is probably the best value in town. Calabash also runs some good township tours.

The compartments at **Caboose Sleepers** (☎ 584 0638; Brookes Hill Dr; singles/doubles/triples US$15/21/23) are modelled on train sleeper berths and although tiny are cheap.

Edward Protea Hotel (☎ 586 2056; **e** edward@pehotels.co.za; Belmont Terrace; singles/doubles from US$46/56), in the heart of the city, is a gracious Edwardian hotel with comfortable rooms. Breakfast is US$7.

The Chapman (☎ 584 0678; **e** chapmail@iafrica.com; 1 Lady Bea Crescent; singles/

doubles from US$42/55), is a splendid place overlooking the ocean. There are often weekend deals.

Places to Eat

There are plenty of places on the seafront in Humewood and in the tacky new Boardwalk complex.

Natti's Thai Kitchen (☎ 585 4301; 21 Clyde St; meals around US$5) is, according to locals, one of the best places to eat in PE.

Blue Waters Cafe (☎ 583 4110; Marine Dr, Summerstrand; mains US$3.50-6) is a bright, lively place overlooking the ocean.

Barney's (☎ 503 4500; The Boardwalk), next door to Blue Waters, is a decent British-style boozer serving pub grub.

Up the Kyber (☎ 582 220; MacArthur Baths Complex; mains US$4) is a bright modern curry house right on the seafront in the newly revamped pool area. It's cheap too, although the curries aren't spectacular.

Entertainment

The cluster of bars and restaurants on the beachfront or the Boardwalk is probably your best bet these days.

Tapas Al Sol and **Dros** are just two options inside Brookes Pavilion.

Barney's is a good, cosy pub, and when we visited the club of the moment was **Tarantino's**. Both are inside the rather bland Boardwalk.

Phoenix Hotel (Chapel St) is a grungy little pub which can get rough; it has live music some nights.

Razzmatazz (Morgan St) is a black club that has live jazz. Be careful in this area at night.

Getting There & Away

BA Comair (☎ 0800-011747 toll free) flies between Jo'burg and Port Elizabeth. **SA Airlink** (☎ 507 1111) flies daily from Port Elizabeth to Jo'burg (US$154), Bloemfontein (US$173), East London (US$98) and Cape Town (US$120).

Buses stop at the train station or the Greenacres shopping centre; the latter is a better place to disembark at night. PE has regular connections to the major South African cities. Contact the **Translux office** (☎ 392 1333; Ring Road, Greenacres), the **Intercape office** (☎ 0861-287 287; Fleming St), behind the old post office or the **Greyhound office** (☎ 363-4555; 6 Nile Rd), near the Greenacres Shopping Centre.

Most minibus taxis leave from the townships surrounding PE and can be difficult to find, although a few depart from the area under under the flyovers around the station. **Norwich** (☎ 585 7253) runs to Cape Town (US$23; 9 hours). **J Bay Sunshine Express** (☎ 581 3790; US$3.50) runs to Jeffrey's Bay and other stops along the coast.

The *Algoa* train runs daily to Jo'burg via Bloemfontein and the *Southern Cross* runs to Cape Town via some Garden Route towns. Contact **Spoornet** (☎ 507 2459)

All the big car-rental operators have offices in PE or at the airport: **Avis** (☎ 581 1306), **Budget** (☎ 581 4242) and **Imperial** (☎ 581 5826). Alternatively, try **Economic Car Hire** (☎ 581 5826; 104 Heugh Rd, Walmer).

Getting Around

There's no public transport to the airport; a taxi costs US$2.30 to US$3.50.

For local bus information, try **Algoa Bus Company** (☎ 404 1200). The bus marked 'UPE' runs to the beachfront from the city. The 'Greenacres' bus runs to the shopping centre of the same name.

For taxis, contact **Supercab** (☎ 457 5590) or **Hurter's Radio Cabs** (☎ 585 5500).

PORT ELIZABETH TO KEI RIVER
Addo Elephant National Park
☎ 042

If elephants are your thing, Addo beats the Kruger hands down. The park is home to 350 of them (the remnants of the huge herds that once roamed Eastern Cape) and you'd be unlucky not to see some. In fact, you may get closer than you thought here; it's not uncommon for these mighty beasts to amble so close they brush your car wing mirror.

There are exciting plans to extend the size of the 125,000-hectare park to almost 500,000 hectares (to be called the Greater Addo) – enough space to support a population of well over 2000 elephants as well as the existing populations of other animals including rhinos, buffaloes and leopards.

Addo is 72km north of Port Elizabeth near the Zuurberg Range in the Sundays River Valley.

Those without transport can take a tour from Port Elizabeth – contact Tourism Port Elizabeth for suggested operators. If you're driving yourself around the park it's possible to pay for a guide to join you in your vehicle for US$5.80 which is well worth the investment.

Information The entrance gate is open daily from 7am to 7pm. The park's roads are dirt and can become impassable after heavy rain, so call ahead (☎ 223 0556) if the weather is wet. Day visitors are charged US$2.30/1.20 per adult/child. There's a well-stocked **shop** *(open 8am-7pm daily)*.

Places to Stay & Eat There's a **camping area** *(2-person sites US$10)* and other accommodation, including **chalets** *(2 people US$32)* and **rondavels** *(2 people US$46)*. Book through the **National Parks Board** *(012-428 9111; [w] www.parks-sa.co.za)*. There's a communal kitchen and a **restaurant**.

Port Alfred
☎ 046

Port Alfred is a pleasant holiday village that's rapidly developing into a bustling resort. It makes a good base for exploring the lovely, remote beaches north of here. For surfers there are good right- and left-hand breaks at the river mouth, and for golfers there's a famous course, one of the four 'Royals' in South Africa. Other activities include two health spas and day trips as far as Grahamstown on the town's own diminutive train, the *Kowie Chu Chu*.

The **tourist information centre** *(☎ 624 1235; open 8.30am-5pm Mon-Fri)*, on the western riverbank between the two bridges, is well stocked with brochures detailing accommodation, walks and canoe trails.

Activities At the Halyards Hotel, **Kowie Dive** *(☎ 083 512 3437)* has **dive courses** for US$160, a resort course for US$46 and an introductory pool dive for US$9. Next door to the dive shop, the same company runs **Maximum Exposure** *(☎ 624 4432)*, a booking agency for all the adventure activities available in the area

The two-day **Kowie Canoe Trail** *(☎ 624 2230; US$7.50 per person)* is a fairly easy paddle upriver from Port Alfred. Phone well in advance for bookings and canoe hire.

Three Sisters Horse Trails *(☎ 675 1269)* offers beach and bush horse treks.

Places to Stay Near the bridge over the Kowie River, **Willows Caravan Park** *(☎ 624 5201; 2-person camp sites US$7.50)* has powered camp sites.

Station Backpackers *(☎ 624 5869; [e] backpack@thestation.co.za; dorm beds US$5.75; doubles from US$14)* is a smart new place with a bar, restaurant and pool table occupying the old railway station building on the eastern riverbank.

Amanzi Lodge *(☎ 072 123 1364, US$8 per person)* is a good budget option offering basic, functional rooms, sleeping up to four and equipped with kettle and microwave. It's near Halyards Hotel in the same unit as Kowie Dive.

Halyards Hotel *(☎ 624 2410; [e] reservations@halyardshotel.com; Albany Rd; singles/doubles from US$34/56)*, at Royal Alfred Marina overlooking the harbour, is an elegant wooden-boarded place with restaurant and pool.

Places to Eat For good lunch specials try **CJ's Bistro** *(Campbell St)*. **Buck & Hunter** has sizzling seafood dishes from US$4.50. **Butlers Pub & Restaurant** *(mains US$3.50-9, pub dishes served 11am-11pm)*, on the riverbank, is a pleasant place for a beer, a snack or a good meal.

Getting There & Away The Baz Bus stops on its run between Port Elizabeth and Durban.

Minibus taxis run from Biscay Rd, outside the Heritage Mall. Daily services run to destinations including Port Elizabeth (US$4.50), Grahamstown (US$2.50) and East London (US$4.50).

The Shipwreck Coast
This unspoiled stretch of coast, the graveyard for numerous ships, was once part of the Ciskei Homeland.

Mpekweni Sun *(☎ 040-676 1026; singles/doubles US$67)* is 11.5km east of the Great Fish River, beside the sea; there's a restaurant, several bars and a pool.

Shipwreck Hiking Trail This hiking trail from the Great Fish River to the Ncera River is 64km long, but it is possible to do

SOUTH AFRICA

any section. This is one of the few walking areas in South Africa where hikers can set their own pace, camp more or less where they choose and light fires. The trail is free and bookings are not required.

Hamburg The small village of Hamburg is at the wide river flats at the mouth of the Keiskamma River, near empty beaches that stretch into the horizon. The flats are home to many birds, especially migrating waders in summer. They also offer good fishing.

Oyster Lodge & Backpackers (☎/fax 040-678 1020; e oyster@magicmail.co.za; 279 Main Rd; camping US$4, dorm beds US$7, doubles US$18.50) is spacious, clean and welcoming with a big garden, a deck and *braai* area.

There's a daily minibus taxi between Hamburg and East London, about 100km east. The Baz Bus stops within about 10km of the lodge on the R72. The lodge can do a pick-up if you book ahead.

East London
☎ 043 • pop 559,100

This bustling port with 175,000 residents (or 750,000 if you count the residents of the sprawling Mdantsane township 15km from town) has a good surf beach and a striking bay which curves around to huge sand hills. After a few years of recession the town seems to be coming back as a family resort. While it's not the Eastern Cape's best seaside resort, you could certainly do worse. The main downtown street is Oxford St, with the city centre extending from about Argyle St south to Fleet St.

Information There's loads of information on the area at Tourism East London (☎ 701 9600; cnr Longfellow & Aquarium Rds; open 8am-4pm Mon-Fri) near the seafront. You can book accommodation for the Wild Coast at the Wild Coast Holiday Reservations office (☎ 743 6181) here.

Things to See & Do The small aquarium (adult/child US$1/0.50) on the beachfront is worth a look.

The East London Museum (cnr Oxford & Lukin Sts; admission US$0.60; open Mon-Fri, & Sat pm), about 2km north of the centre, has the world's only dodo egg, plus a coelacanth and displays on Xhosa culture.

There are sunset **river cruises** (☎ 735 2232; US$6) aboard the *Miscky* departing from the harbour.

You will find the best **surfing** is near Bats Cave, towards the southern end of Nahoon Beach.

Places to Stay With a reputation as a good place to party, Sugarshack Backpackers (☎ 722 8240; Eastern Esplanade; dorm beds US$6.50, doubles US$15) is basic but also offers free use of surfboards. It has a terrific spot right on the beach near the Holiday Inn Garden Court.

East London Backpackers (☎ 722 2748; e kaybeach@iafrica.com; 11 Quanza St; dorm beds US$6.50, doubles without/with bathroom US$15/18.50) is close to the seafront, neat and well kept. It boasts spacious rooms and dorms, a *braai* area and plunge pool.

Esplanade Hotel (☎ 722 2518, fax 722 5379; e esphotel@iafrica.com; Clifford St; B&B singles/doubles from US$19/33), near the beachfront, is a good mid-range hotel with B&B.

Osner Resorts (☎ 743 3433, e osacomm@iafrica.com) runs a virtual monopoly of the beachfront accommodation in town, most of it at fairly competitive rates and all booked through the same telephone and email addresses. The **Express Lodge** (cnr Fleet & Fitzpatrick Sts; singles/doubles/triples US$15/20/24, 4-person room US$28) is the best budget option. The **Kennaway Hotel** (Esplanade, singles/doubles US$30/35) and **Hotel Osner** (Court Crescent, singles/doubles US$24/31) are both comfortable seafront places.

The Regent (☎ 709 5000; e regent@mweb.co.za; 22 Esplanade; singles/doubles US$25/50, weekend specials US$21/33) is plush.

Places to Eat As authentically Gaelic as Mickey Mouse, O'Hagan's (Esplanade; mains US$3.50-5) is a popular Irish-themed, seafront eatery with some reasonable seafood options.

Ernst's Chalet Suisse (☎ 722 1840; Orient Beach shopping centre; dinner around US$6) is one of the best posh places in town, with some sumptuous seafood dishes.

The Deck next door offers a decent pub menu and a relaxed drinking ambience.

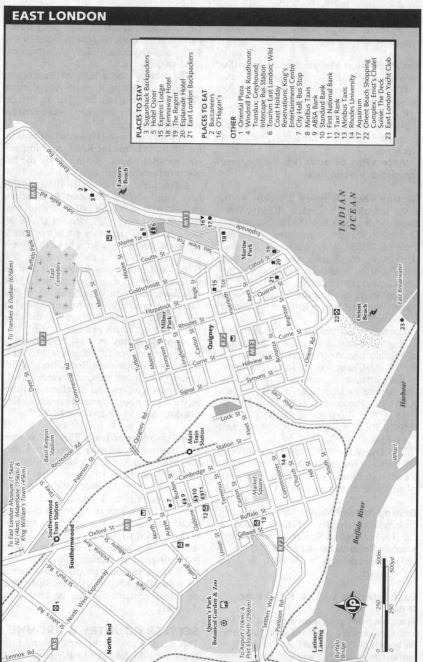

EAST LONDON

PLACES TO STAY
3   Sugarshack Backpackers
5   Hotel Osner
15 Express Lodge
18 Kennaway Hotel
19 The Regent
20 Esplanade Hotel
21 East London Backpackers

PLACES TO EAT
2   Buccaneers
16 O'Hagan's

OTHER
1   Oriental Plaza
4   Windmill Park Roadhouse;
    Translux; Greyhound;
    Intercape Bus Station
6   Tourism East London; Wild
    Coast Holiday
    Reservations; King's
    Entertainment Centre
7   City Hall; Bus Stop
8   Minibus Taxis
9   ABSA Bank
10 Standard Bank
11 First National Bank
12 Taxi Rank
13 Minibus Taxis
14 Rhodes University
17 Aquarium
22 Orient Beach Shopping
    Complex; Ernst's Chalet
    Suisse; The Deck
23 East London Yacht Club

SOUTH AFRICA

INDIAN OCEAN

Buccaneers, right next to Sugarshack Backpackers serves hearty, cheap steak-and-chips-style fare.

Entertainment Many restaurants have live entertainment on Friday or Saturday nights.

O'Hagan's is perfect for a beer on the balcony on a sunny afternoon.

Buccaneers is the place to test drive those new dancing trousers. It has a happy hour on Wednesday night and bands on weekends.

Vincent Park Cinemas is in the shopping complex at Vincent Park.

Getting There & Away Translux (☎ 700 1999) has buses to: Umtata (US$10, three hours); Port Elizabeth (US$12, four hours); Durban (US$18.50, nine hours); Jo'burg/Pretoria (US$33, 11½ hours); Graaf-Reinet (US$18.50, 6½ hours) and Cape Town (US$26, 15½ hours). Greyhound charges US$12 to Port Elizabeth and US$18 to Durban. Intercape, Translux and Greyhound depart from the Windmill Park Roadhouse on Moore St.

Long-distance minibus taxis to the north of East London leave around the corner of Buffalo and Argyle Sts. Minibus taxis for the old Ciskei and the local area depart by the corner of Caxton and Gillwell Sts. Destinations include King William's Town (US$1.30), Butterworth (US$3.50), Umtata (US$7), Port Elizabeth (US$8.50), Jo'burg (US$18.50), Queenstown (US$4.50) and Cape Town (US$23).

The *Amatola* (☎ 744 2719) train to Jo'burg (20 hours) begins its journey in East London. It runs via Bloemfontein (13 hours), from where there are connections to Cape Town.

Getting Around Most city buses, including the beach-bound route via Fleet St, stop at the City Hall on Oxford St. For information call **Amatola Regional Services** (☎ 722 1251).

There's a **taxi rank** (☎ 722 7901; cnr Union & Oxford Sts).

East London to the Kei River
☎ 043
There are many resorts on the coast north of East London and a couple of good backpackers hostels in **Cintsa**. The East Coast Resorts turn-off from the N2 will get you to most of them.

The first beaches to the north are centred on **Gonubie Mouth**, which has **caravan parks** and the **Gonubie Mouth Hotel** (☎ 740 4010; singles/doubles US$20/32), which has good-value rooms.

The next concentration of beaches is around **Haga-Haga**, a small village about 70km from East London. The tip of the very scenic Cape Henderson Nature Reserve adjoins Haga-Haga.

Northeast of Haga-Haga, reached by turning off the N2 onto the R349, are Morgan's Bay and Kei Mouth. Kei Mouth is the last resort before the Wild Coast.

Independent travellers will probably have heard about **Buccaneers Backpackers** (☎ 734 3012; camp sites US$4.50, dorm beds US$7, safari tents US$15, doubles US$18.50) in Cintsa long before they get to this part of the world. Many consider it to be the best in South Africa. You can use the canoes, surfboards and paddle-skis for free. It also organises many activities and trips in the area. Buccaneers has a daily shuttle service to East London. If you're driving from East London, take exit 26 from the N2; coming the other way take the Cintsa/Cefani exit.

Moonshine Bay (☎ 734 3590; camping US$4, dorm beds US$7, doubles US$15) lacks the party atmosphere of Buccaneers but it's a great place recommended by readers, with comfortable rooms and excellent facilities including a pool and tennis courts. East London airport pick-ups cost US$3.50.

The Strandloper Trails This trail starts in Kei Mouth and continues through to Gonubie, 65km south. The five-day trail (☎ 841 1046; w www.strandlopertrails.co.za; US$34 per person per trail; guides optional) has accommodation in trail huts along the route. The trail also offers an overnight canoeing section on the Kei River and a link through to Inkwenkwezi Game Reserve. Strandloper (or 'beach walker') is the name given to the original inhabitants of the east coast of Africa, a nomadic people who survived by harvesting shellfish. Strandloper middens shell remains can still be seen along the coast.

SETTLER COUNTRY & AROUND
This section covers the area around Grahamstown, the heart of Settler Country, as well as most of the old Ciskei Homeland.

Grahamstown

☎ 046 • pop 70,300

Grahamstown is the capital of Settler Country and the Borders and it still feels like a strange English transplant. The large student population breathes life into this otherwise conservative, Victorian-era town. The nearby township is a good place to get a closer look at township life and even to stay overnight with a local Xhosa family (see Places to Stay).

Information The efficient **Tourism Grahamstown** (☎ 622 3241; Church Square; open 8.30am-5pm Mon-Fri, 8.30am-12pm Sat) is next door to the town's booking office (☎ 622 5777).

GBS Travel (☎ 622 2235; 84 High St) handles bookings for local travel.

Albany Museum The museum has four components and entry to all of them costs US$0.60/0.50 for adults/children. The most interesting is the wonderfully eccentric **Observatory Museum** on Bathurst St. The **National History Museum**, on Somerset St, has some interesting Xhosa artefacts. The 1820 **Settlers Memorial Museum**, also on Somerset St, is devoted to the English settlers. Fort Selwyn, built in 1836 as a semaphore station, has been fully restored.

Fort Selwyn (☎ 622 2312) is open by appointment; the other places are open from 9.30am to 1pm and 2pm to 5pm Tue-Sat.

Grahamstown Festival The town hosts the very successful National Festival of Arts and an associated Fringe Festival. The festival runs for 10 days, beginning at the end of June; accommodation at this time can be booked out a year in advance. For more information, contact the **1820 Foundation** (☎ 622 7115/622 4341).

Grahamstown East Township Tours of the nearby township, including lunch with a local family, may be arranged through the **Umthathi Self-help Project** (☎ 622 4450) near the train station. Overnight B&B stays are also possible. Contact Mrs Habana (☎ 637 0776).

Places to Stay In tranquil grounds on a beautiful spot, **Grahamstown Caravan Park** (☎ 603 6072; camp sites US$3.50) is a bit of a trek from town.

Old Gaol Backpackers (☎ 636 1001; Somerset St; dorm beds US$5.80, doubles US$14) has rooms in the small, gloomy cells of this former jail opposite the university. It's central but pretty run down.

Graham Protea Hotel (☎ 622 2324; 123 High St; singles/doubles US$47/42) is comfortable enough and is in the centre of town, although street noise can be a minor problem in the rooms at the front.

Cock House (☎ 636 1287; 10 Market St; B&B singles/doubles US$41/68) is a cosy guesthouse in a National Monument building dating back to 1826. The thoughtful hosts can arrange activities around town, the rooms are exquisite and rates include a sumptuous breakfast.

Tourism Grahamstown offers information on other local B&Bs, including **township homestays**. Grahamstown is a convenient place to try one since accommodation is in secure houses with local families and costs about US$9.

Places to Eat Grahamstown has loads of cafés and there are some good-value options on campus including **The Monkey Puzzle**, **The House of Joy**, and the **Old Provost**.

La Galleria (☎ 622 3455; New St) is a well-regarded Italian place.

Dulcé (112 High St) serves good coffee, cakes and muffins.

Rat & Parrot (New St), a British-style boozer, serves standard pub meals. It's a good place for a beer and attracts a student crowd most nights.

Cock House Restaurant (meals US$3-6) is superb, with an ever-changing European-style menu.

Calabash (☎ 622 2324), attached to the Grahamstown Protea, serves hearty Xhosa hotpots for US$5.

Getting There & Away Translux stops on the corner of Bathurst and High Sts on the run from Port Elizabeth (US$8, standby only) to Durban (US$23, 11 hours), via King William's Town (US$4), East London (US$4.60) and Umtata (US$18.50). Greyhound stops here on the same run.

The minibus-taxi rank is in Market Square off Beaufort Street. Fares include: King William's Town (US$4); East London

(US$3.50, 2¾ hours); and Port Elizabeth (US$4.50, 6½ hours). Minibus taxis leave for the township from around town, including the area around the Grahamstown Protea Hotel on the High Street.

King William's Town
☎ 043

Established by the London Missionary Society in 1826, King William's Town (KWT) became an important military base in the interminable struggle with the Xhosa. After the Seventh Frontier War (1846–47), British Kaffraria was established with King William's Town as its capital. KWT remains the area's commercial and shopping capital.

The **library** (☎ 642 3450) has some tourist information.

East London is better for accommodation.

Bisho
☎ 040 • pop 150,800

Bisho, once the capital of Ciskei and now the administrative capital of Eastern Cape, was originally the black 'location' for nearby King William's Town. The centre of Bisho was built to house Ciskei's bureaucrats and politicians, so there is a compact bunch of suitably grandiose and ugly public buildings.

Amatola & Katberg Mountains

The area north and west of King William's Town is partly degraded grazing land and partly rugged mountains with remnant indigenous forest. It has some good walks, all of which must be booked with the Department of Forestry (☎ 043-642 2571) in King William's Town.

The six-day **Amatola Trail** (US$17.50 per person) begins at Maden Dam, 23km north of King William's Town, and ends at the Tyumie River near Hogsback. It is pretty tough.

The two-day **Evelyn Valley Loop Trail** starts and ends at Maden Dam. The scenery includes magnificent forests and numerous streams. It's a fairly easy hike.

The two-day **Zingcuka Loop Trail** begins and ends at the Tyumie River near Hogsback. It's fairly easy but there are some steep sections on the second day.

Ask about the **Wolf River Experience**, along the river and ending up at a Xhosa homestead.

Hogsback This is a small resort area high in the beautiful Amatola Mountains about 100km northwest of Bisho. There are some great forest walks and drives in the area taking in numerous waterfalls. You can buy booklets detailing walks from the Hogsback store.

Away with the Fairies (☎ 045-962 1031; e hogsback1@iafrica.com; camping US$4, dorm beds US$7, doubles US$14) is a majestic little getaway with a superb view of Hogsback Ridge. There are mountain bikes for hire and Sugarshack in East London can get you here.

The **Hogsback Inn** (☎ 045-962 1006; e hogsbackinn@xsinet.co.za Main Rd; low season half-board singles/doubles US$23/32) has pleasant cottages, a swimming pool and a huge, beautiful garden.

There's no public transport to Hogsback but Sugarshack Backpackers in East London shuttle out here for US$4.50.

Katberg About 110km northwest of Bisho, Katberg is a small town at the foot of a wooded range. The surrounding countryside is still very much as it was when this area was part of Ciskei – overworked, underfunded and almost medieval.

It's an interesting drive from Hogsback, 27km to the east. The road over the Katberg Pass is unsealed, so make sure you check locally before tackling it after a lot of rain, and definitely think twice if it has been snowing (which happens a couple of times each winter).

The luxurious **Katberg Hotel** (☎ 040-864 1010; singles/doubles from US$37/43) is 8km uphill from the village. Rates are higher during weekends.

Tsolwana Game Reserve

Tsolwana (☎ 040-842 2026; adult/child US$0.70/0.40 plus US$2.30 per vehicle) is 57km southwest of Queenstown, near Fort Beaufort. It protects a rugged Karoo landscape south of the spectacular Tafelberg (1965m), adjoining the Swart Kei River. The reserve has rolling plains interspersed with valleys, cliffs, waterfalls, caves and gullies.

There is a similarly diverse range of animals, including herds of antelopes, rhinos, giraffes and mountain zebras. The largest four-legged predator is the Cape lynx.

The park is managed in conjunction with the local Tsolwana people, who benefit

directly from the jobs and revenue produced. There are **lodges** and **huts** here from US$50 for a minimum of four people.

The Eastern Cape Tourism Board (☎ 040-635 2115) in Bisho administers the reserve.

THE KAROO

Although part of the vast Karoo region mostly lies in Western Cape, this semi-desert plateau also sprawls into Eastern and Northern Cape Provinces. Therefore the towns of Prince Albert, Beaufort West, and Matjiesfontein, plus the Karoo National Park, are found on the Western Cape map under Western Cape earlier in this chapter.

Graaff-Reinet
☎ 049 • pop 38,700

Graaff-Reinet is the quintessential Karoo town – it is often referred to, justifiably, as the gem of the Karoo. If you visit only one inland town in Eastern Cape, make it this pretty, green place nestling among ruggedly handsome hills.

The fourth-oldest European town in South Africa, its outstanding architectural heritage has been restored through the recognition of 220 National Monument buildings – more than any other town in South Africa.

If you have wheels consider driving up the hills above town (head northwest to the nature reserve) for outstanding views down onto Graaf-Reinet, the Valley of Desolation and across the yawning expanses beyond.

History In 1786 a *landdrost* was despatched to establish order in the lawless Cape interior. In 1795 the citizens of Graaff-Reinet drove out the *landdrost* and established a short-lived independent republic.

Between 1824 and 1840, the Boers' continuing dissatisfaction with Cape Town's control led to the Great Trek, and Graaff-Reinet became an important stepping stone for Voortrekkers heading north.

Orientation & Information The town lies within a bend of the Sundays River, overshadowed by the rocky Sneeuberg. The centre of town is easy to get around on foot.

The **publicity association** (☎ 892 4248; cnr Church & Somerset Sts; open 8am-12.30pm & 2pm-5pm Mon-Fri, 9am-noon Sat & Sun) is worth a visit, but the staff are disinterested

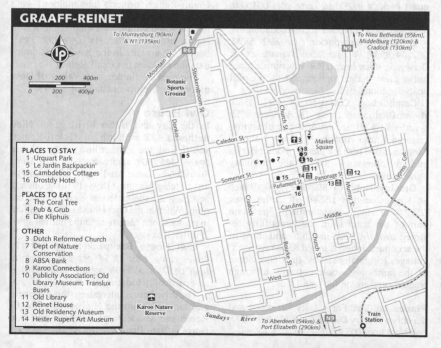

GRAAFF-REINET

To Murraysburg (90km) & N1 (135km)

To Nieu Bethesda (55km), Middelburg (120km) & Cradock (130km)

R63

N9

Mountain Dr

Stockenstroom St

Donkin

Botanic Sports Ground

0   200   400m
0   200   400yd

Caledon St

Church St

Market Square

Somerset St

Parliament St

Parsonage St

Cradock

Caruline

Bourke St

Church St

Murray St

Cypress Gve

Middle

West

Sundays River

Karoo Nature Reserve

To Aberdeen (54km) & Port Elizabeth (290km)

Train Station

N9

PLACES TO STAY
1   Urquart Park
5   Le Jardin Backpackin'
15 Cambdeboo Cottages
16 Drostdy Hotel

PLACES TO EAT
2   The Coral Tree
4   Pub & Grub
6   Die Kliphuis

OTHER
3   Dutch Reformed Church
7   Dept of Nature Conservation
8   ABSA Bank
9   Karoo Connections
10 Publicity Association; Old Library Museum; Translux Buses
11 Old Library
12 Reinet House
13 Old Residency Museum
14 Hester Rupert Art Museum

and seem to have pre-recorded answers to most inquiries.

Karoo Connections (☎ 892 3978; Church St.) operates tours into the Valley of Desolation, Nieu Bethesda and the Karoo Nature Reserve.

Museums All museums are open from 9am to 12.30pm and 2pm to 5pm weekdays, and in the morning on weekends. Entry to each is US$0.40.

The **Old Library** (cnr Church & Somerset Sts) houses paintings, Karoo fossils and a collection of photos and clothing from the 19th century.

The **Hester Rupert Art Museum** exhibits contemporary South African art.

Reinet House (Murray St) is a beautiful example of Cape Dutch architecture. It is furnished with 18th- and 19th-century furniture.

The **Old Residency** in Parsonage St is another well-preserved 19th-century house, displaying a large collection of historical firearms.

Places to Stay To the north of town, **Urquart Park** (☎ 892 2136; camp sites US$5.80, 2-person rondavels without bedding from US$9) has camp sites and other accommodation.

Le Jardin Backpackin' (☎ 892 5890, 082 64 4938; e backpackers@ananzi.co.za; Donkin St; dorm beds US$8) is a simple place but a great budget option and the helpful hosts are founts of local knowledge.

Cambdeboo Cottages (☎ 892 3180; e info@karoopark.co.za; 16 Parliament St; doubles US$21) are modest but charming restored Karoo cottages – all are National Monuments. There are plenty of other B&Bs and guesthouses – ask at the publicity association.

Drostdy Hotel (☎ 892 2161; 30 Church St; singles/doubles US$40/61; suites from US$71) is simply outstanding. The main part of the hotel is in the beautifully restored *drostdy*, built in 1806, and most of the accommodation is in old Karoo workers' cottages (originally slaves' quarters). Some of the suites are whole cottages, although some rooms are on the small side.

Places to Eat For a tasty breakfast and decent coffee, try **Die Kliphuis** (46 Bourke St; breakfast from US$1.80).

Pub & Grub (cnr Muller St), opposite the Dutch Reformed Church, has pub fare; a filling serve of steak and chips costs US$4.

The Coral Tree (☎ 892 5947; 3 Church St; mains US$4), serving an impressive range of home baked meals and snacks in smart surroundings, may well be the pick of places in town.

Drostdy Hotel (set-menu dinners US$9) is open to non-guests and offers dining in an 18th-century room illuminated by candelabra. There are set menus, and you can also order a la carte.

Getting There & Away The publicity association is the Translux agent. Translux stops here on the run between Cape Town (US$25.60, eight hours) and East London (US$21.50, seven hours).

Minibus taxis leave from Market Square. Major destinations include Port Elizabeth (US$18.50), Cape Town (US$8.50) and Jo'burg. For more information try calling **J Kane** (☎ 892 4390).

Karoo Nature Reserve

This reserve, which virtually surrounds Graaff-Reinet, protects mountainous veld and its flora is a highlight. Ask about its hiking trails and wildlife viewing at the Karoo Nature Reserve office (☎ 049-892 3453; Bourke St), upstairs in the provincial administration building in Graaff-Reinet.

The road overlooking the **Valley of Desolation** has simply outstanding views.

Owl House

In the tiny and isolated village of **Nieu Bethesda**, 55km north of Graaff-Reinet, you'll find the extraordinary Owl House (☎ 049-841 1603; admission US$1; open 9am-6pm daily) – home, studio and life's work of artist Helen Martins (1898–1976). Concrete and glass are the materials used in her creations. Whether the Owl House is a monument to madness or a testament to the human spirit is difficult to say.

Owl House Backpackers (☎ 049-841 1642; camp sites US$4 per person, dorm beds US$7, doubles in cottage US$17.50) is an ecofriendly lodging.

The drive here is interesting (there are several turn-offs from the N9 between Graaff-Reinet and Middelburg), but you can't buy petrol in Nieu Bethesda.

Mountain Zebra National Park

Mountain Zebra National Park, 26km from the small town of Cradock, is on the northern slopes of the 2000m Bankberg Range and has magnificent views over the Karoo. It's a small park protecting one of the rarest animals in the world – the mountain zebra *(Equus zebra)*.

In addition to the zebra, there are many antelope species. The largest predator is the caracal (or lynx).

There's a relatively limited network of roads around the park and visitors have to drive themselves. The Mountain Zebra Hiking Trail is closed.

Information The entrance gate is open from 1 October to 30 April between 7am and 7pm, and from 1 May to 30 September between 7.30am and 6pm. Day visits cost US$1.80/1 for adults/children. The main camp has a shop and restaurant.

Places to Stay The most interesting place to stay in the national park area is **Doornhoek** *(up to 4 people US$69)*, a restored historic farmhouse that was built in 1836. It is hidden in a secluded valley.

There are also **camp sites** *(2-person sites US$7.50)* and **cottages** *(2 people from US$34)*. Book online (**W** www.parks-sa.co.za) or through the **National Parks Board** in Pretoria (**☎** *012-428 9111)*.

Prince Albert

☎ 023

Prince Albert is a beautiful little town, dozing on the edge of the Karoo at the foot of the astounding **Swartberg Pass**, which presents one of the country's most memorable motoring challenges. You can easily visit on a day trip from Oudtshoorn or the coast. Alternatively, stay in Prince Albert and make a day trip to Oudtshoorn (see Oudtshoorn in the Western Cape section earlier in this chapter).

The town was founded in 1762 and there are some interesting examples of Cape Dutch, Victorian and Karoo styles of architecture. The small **tourism bureau** (**☎** *541 1366)* gives out a leaflet with accommodation and eating options. Don't miss visiting the rustic **Prince Albert Mill**, on the roadside en route to the Swartberg Pass.

Places to Stay & Eat On the southern (Swartberg Pass) edge of town, **Dennehof Karoo Guesthouse** (**☎** *541 1227; rooms per person from US$14.50)* is in the town's oldest house (1835).

Swartberg Hotel (**☎** *541 1332; 77 Church St; B&B singles/doubles from US$32/46)* has an old world charm.

Sampie se Plaasstal on the main street is a farm produce stall that is much, much better than most. It sells nuts, game meat, biltong, dried fruit (including *meëbos*, parchment-like pastry sheets) and some delicious homemade pastries.

Getting There & Away The nearest Intercape, Translux and Greyhound stop (on the run between Cape Town and Jo'burg/ Pretoria) is at Laingsburg, about 120km away, but you can arrange to be dropped at Prince Albert Road, the rail halt. Some places to stay in Prince Albert will collect you from here.

The nearest train station is Prince Albert Road, 45km northwest of Prince Albert. The daily *Trans Karoo* between Cape Town and Jo'burg via Kimberley stops there.

Beaufort West

☎ 023 • pop 32,400

Beaufort West is the archetypal stopover town. Most people will be happy to snatch a cold drink, petrol and perhaps some sleep – there's little to recommend staying longer. The **tourist bureau** (**☎** *415 1488; Church St)* is helpful.

There are many places offering 'overnight rooms'. **Donkin House** (**☎** *414 4287; 14 Donkin St; singles/doubles US$16/21)* offers a reasonable deal. It's fairly basic but friendly. **Hotel Formula 1** (**☎** *415 2421; 144 Donkin St; rooms sleeping up to 3 people US$23)* is bland, clean and cheap. **Ye Olde Thatch** (**☎** *2209; 155 Donkin St; doubles from US$23)* has secure parking and four guest suites. The **restaurant** here specialises in Karoo dishes. Other options in town are of the greasy, fast-food variety.

Beaufort West is a junction for many bus services. Most buses stop on Donkin St outside Oasis Hotel, which is the Translux agent.

Most minibus taxis stop at the BP station at the southern end of Donkin St, not far from the caravan park. Destinations include:

Oudtshoorn (US$5); King William's Town (US$9); and Cape Town (US$10.50).

The daily *Trans Karoo* train, which runs to Cape Town (8½ hours) and Jo'burg (16¼ Hours) via Kimberley (8 hours), stops here.

Karoo National Park

The Karoo National Park *(adult/child US$1.80/1; gates open 5am-10pm)*, north of Beaufort West, protects 33,000 hectares of impressive Karoo landscapes. The park has 61 species of mammal, the most common of which are dassies and bat-cared foxes. A rhino or two have been reintroduced and the park is also trying to breed the 'formerly extinct' quagga (a zebra sub-species).

There are two short nature trails and an 11km day walk. There are also 4WD guided trails, for one day or longer. There's a shop and a **restaurant**.

There are some excellent **camp sites** (US$10) and a range of **chalets** and **cottages** (from US$37). Book accommodation through the **National Parks Board** *(☎ 021-422 2810 in Cape Town; W www.parks-sa.co.za)* or directly with the park *(☎ 415 2838)*.

Matjiesfontein
☎ 023

Fascinating Matjiesfontein (sounds like 'Mahkeysfontein'), west of Prince Alfred, is a small railway siding that has remained virtually unchanged for 100 years; its impressive buildings seem incongruous in the bleak Karoo landscape.

As well as the attractive **old buildings** there's a **museum** in the train station.

The grand **Lord Milner Hotel** *(☎ 551 3011; singles/doubles from US$32/50)* is a period piece (no children under 12).

The daily *Trans Karoo* train between Cape Town (5½ hours) and Jo'burg (20 hours) stops here.

NORTHEASTERN HIGHLANDS

This bleak but atmospheric area is surrounded on three sides by the former Transkei and it also has a short border (but no crossing point) with Lesotho. It's high country, in the southern tail of the Drakensberg.

Rhodes & Tiffindell

Sleepy Rhodes, between Maclear and Barkly East on the R396, is a relaxing place that doesn't seem to have changed much during the last 100 years. The **Rhodes Hotel** *(☎ 045 974-9305; half-board doubles per person off season US$28)* is a good stop for a basic meal or a drink and makes a convenient base for keen trout anglers.

Nearby Tiffindell (2800m), an area of breathtaking mountain scenery, may still be South Africa's only ski resort complete with snow-making facilities which guarantees a season of a hundred or so days.

Tiffindell's **mountain hut** *(☎ 011-797 9090; summer per person with full board from US$34, 3-day winter all in winter ski packages per person US$150)* has accommodation. Summer activities include **mountain biking, horse riding, grass-skiing** and **rock climbing**. Winter rates include lift pass, equipment hire and emergency medical facilities. **Ben Macdhui** (3001m) nearby has ski lifts.

Aliwal North
☎ 051 • pop 25,500

Aliwal North is a largish town popular for its mineral baths and hot springs. For information on the local area, drop by the **Northeast Cape Tourism Association** *(☎ 41362)*.

The **spa complex** *(☎ 633 2951)* has camp sites for US$7 and double chalets from US$24. There are several other places to stay nearby.

Riverside Lodge *(☎ 633 3282; B&B singles/doubles US$29/41)*, close to the river and the bridge, is large and spacious with heavy wooden furniture. There's also a pub and grill with a good sundowner deck.

If you crave African-style food, **Ezibeleni**, on the corner of Grey and Murray Sts, has *samp* (maize porridge) and fish balls for about US$1.80.

A daily City to City bus stops here on the Jo'burg to Queenstown run. Translux, Greyhound and Intercape stop at Nobby's Restaurant (on the N6 near the junction with the R58). The minibus taxi and local bus stop is on Grey St, near the corner of Somerset St.

TRANSKEI

With natural boundaries (the Kei River and the Drakensberg), Transkei (or the former Transkei as it's now awkwardly known) was at least a logical subdivision of the country, unlike most of the other Homelands –

although it's officially incorrect to refer to it as a specific region these days. The former Transkei, at the forefront of the country's historical struggle for democracy, is home to many of South Africa's most notable political luminaries including Nelson Mandela, Thabo Mbeki and the late Oliver Tambo.

Transkei's major attraction is its coastline, where you'll find superb warm-water surf beaches and lush subtropical vegetation.

Nelson Mandela was born in Transkei, in the village of Mvezo on the Mbashe River. He spent most of his childhood in **Qunu**, 31km south of Umtata. There is a museum and cultural centre built on the site of Mandela's former school in Qunu, which details his life and struggle against apartheid.

Summers on the coast are hot and humid. Inland, summers can be hot, but many areas have winter frosts. Most rain falls in March and spring also sees heavy rains. Unsealed roads can be impassable after rain, especially near the coast.

History

The Xhosa peoples living east of the Kei River (that is, living trans-Kei from the Cape Colony) came under the domination of the Cape Colony government from about 1873, but it was not until 1894, with the defeat of Pondoland, that the whole of modern Transkei came under European rule.

In 1976, Transkei became an 'independent Homeland' (or in plainer English, another of apartheid's dumping grounds for those it dispossessed). If its independence had been internationally recognised it would have been classified as one of the world's poorest countries and one of Southern Africa's most densely populated regions.

Umtata
☎ 047 • pop 86,400

Umtata, the main town in Transkei, was founded in 1871 when Europeans settled on the Umtata River at the request of the Thembu tribe to act as a buffer against Pondo raiders. Today, Umtata is more like an oversized village, with the same violent crime problems that plague most South African cities. It isn't pretty but it's refreshingly free of racism and has a raw, African edge which is missing from most cities in South Africa.

Information The **Eastern Cape Tourism Board** (☎ 531 5290/2; e ectbwc@icon.co.za; 64 Owen St; open 8am-4.30 Mon-Fri) is helpful. Book Wild Coast hiking trails with the **Department of Nature Conservation** (☎ 531 1191; open 9am-5pm Mon-Fri). It's worth picking up A Guide to the Coast & Nature Reserves of Transkei (US$1.20).

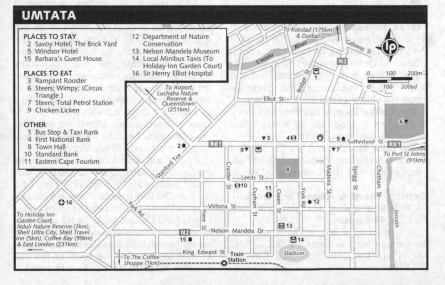

UMTATA

PLACES TO STAY
2 Savoy Hotel; The Brick Yard
5 Windsor Hotel
15 Barbara's Guest House

PLACES TO EAT
3 Rampant Rooster
6 Steers; Wimpy; (Circus Triangle)
7 Steers; Total Petrol Station
9 Chicken Licken

OTHER
1 Bus Stop & Taxi Rank
4 First National Bank
8 Town Hall
10 Standard Bank
11 Eastern Cape Tourism

12 Department of Nature Conservation
13 Nelson Mandela Museum
14 Local Minibus Taxis (To Holiday Inn Garden Court)
16 Sir Henry Elliot Hospital

Wild Coast Central Reservations (☎ 532 5344; 3 Beaufort St) books the various coastal hotels and resorts.

There is a Standard Bank and a First National Bank. It may be an idea to draw cash here before heading to the Wild Coast.

Things to See The new **Nelson Mandela Museum** (☎ 532 5110; open 9am-4pm Mon-Fri, 9am-noon Sat; admission free) is the highlight in town. It's a loving dedication to the great statesman, although its obsession with the small details of his life verges on the hagiographic. (The excellent Apartheid Museum in Jo'burg is better at highlighting Mandela's greatness by putting his life and actions in a clearer context.)

Places to Stay For a peaceful escape from Umtata's bustle, try **Barbara's Guesthouse** (☎ 531 1751; 55 Nelson Mandela Dr; singles/doubles US$33/46).

Savoy Hotel (☎ 531 0791; singles/doubles from US$21/24), out on the Queenstown bypass, is a big airy place, and is good mid-range value. More luxurious rooms are in the courtyard at the rear.

Windsor Hotel (☎ 531 0721; 36 Sutherland St; singles/doubles US$29/40) right in town is secure but nothing special.

Holiday Inn Garden Court (☎ 537 0181; rooms from US$50) is out of town on the East London side of the N2.

Places to Eat Fast-food joints are well represented. Noisy **Wimpys** can be found in the Munitata Building, on the corner of Sutherland and Owen Sts; at the Circus Triangle shopping mall on the Port St Johns road; and by the Holiday Inn Garden Court. There are numerous **chicken** eateries around town.

The Coffee Shoppe (Southerwood Shopping Centre, Errol Springs Rd) serves a fine cappuccino and light snacks.

The Brick Yard (☎ 531 0188; Cnr Stanford Terrace & Sutherland Sts; pizzas US$3-5) adjoining the Savoy Hotel serves good pizza.

Getting There & Away There are daily **SA Airlink** (☎ 536 0024) flights to Jo'burg for US$144 one way.

A City to City bus service runs daily between Jo'burg to Umtata (US$23, 12¼ hours) via KwaZulu-Natal and Kokstad (US$12).

Translux, Greyhound and the Baz Bus stop at the Shell Ultra City outside town. Translux runs to Durban (US$16, 5¾ hours), Port Elizabeth (US$19, 6½ hours), East London (US$10.50, 3¾ hours), Jo'burg/Pretoria (US$25, 11½ hours) and Cape Town (US$10.50, 20½ hours).

The Baz Bus passes through Umtata on its Port Elizabeth–Durban run – Monday, Tuesday, Wednesday, Friday and Saturday. It runs in the other direction Monday, Tuesday, Thursday, Friday and Sunday.

Local buses, and also minibus taxis to Transkei destinations, stop at the taxi park near Bridge St. Some sample fares: Port St Johns (US$2.30), Coffee Bay (US$2.30), Butterworth (US$2.90) and East London (US$7).

The Wild Coast

Notoriously dangerous for ships, the coastline played a key role in the decline of the Portuguese seafaring empire. Shipwrecked sailors were the first Europeans to visit this part of the world, and few were rescued or completed the harrowing journey to Cape Town or Lourenço Marques (now Maputo, Mozambique). A survivor's account of the trek from the São Bento, stranded at Msikaba (Mkambati) in 1564, to Maputo is among the earliest recorded shipwrecks and descriptions of the area.

An active policy of underdevelopment of the region during the apartheid era has largely preserved the sense of wilderness of the area and about 40,000 hectares of indigenous forest survives along the coast. While there is plenty of birdlife (and butterflies galore), animal sightings are increasingly restricted to the coastal nature reserves. An abundance of estuaries, deeply incised ravines and rolling grasslands interspersed with traditional villages and subsistence lifestyles makes this one of the most beautiful and interesting sections of coastline in South Africa.

Resorts and coastal towns are reached by gravel roads leading off the N2 and R61, with sealed roads to Port St Johns (PST) and Coffee Bay. The R61 links the towns of Mbizana, Flagstaff, Lusikisiki and Port St Johns to Port Edward and Umtata, while the N2 covers the inland region from Kokstad (and Port Shepstone) through Umtata to Kei Mouth and East London. A link road just south of Kokstad joins the N2 to the R61. To be safe, travel in

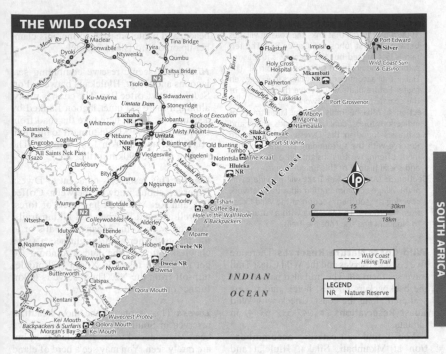

THE WILD COAST

SOUTH AFRICA

daylight hours. Motorists should be cautious of wandering animals.

Wild Coast Hiking Trail A walk or horse ride along this trail is an unforgettable experience – you may see bottlenose dolphins frolicking near the shore, or meet locals who welcome you into their villages. You'll certainly experience hauntingly quiet, starry nights.

There's never been a better time to explore sections of the Wild Coast Hiking Trail. A total revamp as part of a community tourism initiative aimed at promoting responsible tourism in the region is almost complete and will create a wealth of new options and tours for visitors.

The trail network has five distinct sections incorporating guided and catered horse, hiking and canoe trails. To walk the whole Wild Coast would take about three weeks; most people do only one section. The sections are in various stages of improvement but, generally speaking, improvements are being completed from north to south.

One word of warning: in the last couple of years there have been a couple of serious attacks on hikers on the trails south of Port St Johns. Be aware, but don't let this put you off hitting the trails, as attacks are a real rarity. Local advice and sensible precautions should be all you need to stay safe. If you're hiking, using local guides is a good idea; it's safer and you'll learn more. As a guest, respect local traditions and cultures.

For bookings and current information on the trails and travel in the region contact Wild Coast Trails (☎ 039-305 6455; e communitytourism@euwildcoast.za.org; w www.wild-coast.co.za).

Section 1: Amadiba Adventures is the most mature and successful part of the trail network. Amadiba covers the northern 25km of the Wild Coast, from Mzimba to Mtentu, immersing you in the landscape, culture and history of this pristine stretch of coastline.

Section 2: Pondoland Trails offers the choice of overnighting in coastal trail camps or traditional village accommodation. Multi-day horse and hiking trails are offered along this 85km stretch of the southern Pondoland coast with three major entry/exit points (Msikaba, Mbotyi and PSJ) along the way. The trail provides access to some of the most spectacular natural features and remote villages of the Wild Coast.

Section 3: PSJ – Coffee Bay Village Trails is a 100km hiking trail that links the coastal villages between Port St Johns and Coffee Bay. The terrain is less rugged but the scenery is just as inspiring as the northern sections of the trail. The Elalini Trail accommodates walkers in villages en route. Future plans will involve the upgrade of the coastal trail camp network.

Section 4: Mbashe Trails link the large tracts of indigenous forest, coastal grasslands, rivers and estuaries found in the Dwesa–Cwebe Nature Reserve with the surrounding cultural environment offering visitors insights into the natural and social history of this unique area.

Section 5: Mazeppa–Kei Trails will provide overnight village accommodation on a trail network covering the southern section of the Wild Coast from Kei Mouth to Mazeppa with a future link to Nqabara and the Mbashe Trails.

Wild Coast Nature Reserves There are five coastal reserves and the Wild Coast Trail traverses them all. The trail also passes near the backpackers hostels, hotels and resorts scattered along the coast. Check with **Wild Coast Reservations** (☎ 047-532 5344) in Umtata.

You'll find self-catering **accommodation** at Mkambati, Silaka, Hluleka and Dwesa Reserves, and there are **camp sites** at Cwebe and Dwesa. Sites cost about US$2.30 and **chalets** around US$5.80 per person, although during peak holiday times you might have to book a whole chalet for about US$14. Camp sites and accommodation must be booked at the **Eastern Cape Tourism Board** (☎ 043-701 9600). There is also an office in Umtata (☎ 047-531 5290) and information centres at Mzimba, Umtata and Kei Mouth, which can provide current information on roads and access to the reserves.

Mkambati You can canoe up the Msikaba River, and there are walking trails too. Entry to the reserve is US$0.60. A shop sells basic food. Turn off the R61 to Holy Cross Hospital just north of Flagstaff (also known as Siphaqeni). A link road from the N2 south of Kokstad will take you the 65km to Flagstaff. Local buses run from Durban to Mkambati and from Lusikisiki to Msikaba on the southern edge of the reserve.

Silaka Just south of Port St Johns, Silaka runs from Second Beach to Sugarloaf Rock.

There are often Cape clawless otters on the beach, and white-breasted cormorants clamber up onto Bird Island. Magic!

Hluleka A scenic reserve combining sea, lagoons and forest, Hluleka is between Port St Johns and Coffee Bay. The coast is rocky, although there's a quiet lagoon flanked by a saltmarsh. To get here take the road from Umtata towards PSJ, but turn off to the right at Libode, about 30km from Umtata. The reserve is about 90km further on.

Cwebe This reserve is adjacent to Dwesa Reserve, about midway between Coffee Bay and Kei Mouth. It has tracts of forest as well as good beaches and hiking trails. You can walk to the Mbanyana Falls or to the lagoon, where you might see a Cape clawless otter in the late afternoon. To get to Cwebe take the Xhora (Elliotdale) turn-off from the N2. The reserve is 65km further on.

Dwesa This is one of the most beautiful reserves in South Africa. Crocodiles have been reintroduced to the Kobole River, but are rarely seen. You may see a herd of eland come down to the beach near the Kobole estuary in late afternoon. The thick forests also contain dassies, samango monkeys and blue duikers. For Dwesa, turn off the N2 at Idutywa (40km northeast of Butterworth) on the road to Gatyana (Willowvale). Continue until you come to a fork with another sign to Gatyana – take the other, unmarked direction. After heavy rain this is no place for 2WD vehicles.

Coffee Bay
☎ 047

Coffee Bay is just a tiny hamlet but it's relaxed and is becoming popular with travellers. There is a theory that a ship wrecked here in 1863 deposited its cargo of coffee beans on the beach; hence the name. Coffee Bay's Xhosa name, *Tshontini*, refers to a dense wood nearby.

Three rivers flow into the sea near Coffee Bay: the Henga (Place of the Whale); the Mapuzi (Place of Pumpkins); and the Bomvu (Red).

Places to Stay & Eat Near the beach, **Bomvu Backpackers** (☎ 575 2073; camp sites

US$4, dorm beds from US$6, doubles US$15-18.50) is a chilled-out place that occasionally comes alive for full moon parties.

The Coffee Shack *(☎ 575 2048; camp sites US$3.50, dorm beds US$6.50; doubles US$16)* is well run and offers good value, even if it doesn't look too flash from the outside. There are surfboards, a windsurfer and horse riding can be arranged. Your host is an ex-surfing champ.

Ocean View Hotel *(☎ 575 2005; low/high season per person with half-board US$32/37)* has bungalow-style accommodation and a restaurant. It's just metres from the beach and some readers have raved about this place.

Hole in the Wall Backpackers *(☎ 575 0055, 083 317 8786; e holeitwb@iafrica.com); camping US$4, dorm beds from US$6, doubles US$15)*, inside the beachfront miniresort of the same name, is popular with readers. Guests may use the resort's facilities including swimming pool and volleyball court. Horse riding costs US$5.80 per hour. This place shares pick-up duties from Umtata with the Coffee Bay Backpacker outfits which lie about 8km north on a rutted dirt track.

Getting There & Away The backpackers hostels can collect you (US$4.50 each way) from the Shell Ultra City in Umtata. A minibus taxi from Umtata to Coffee Bay costs US$2.30 and takes about an hour.

To get to Coffee Bay by vehicle, take the sealed road that leaves the N2 at Viedgesville, south of Umtata. The turn off onto the decent dirt road to Hole in the Wall is well signposted.

KwaZulu-Natal

Despite being a relatively small province, KwaZulu-Natal manages to cram in most of the things visitors come to South Africa to see.

There's the spectacular Drakensberg Range in the southwest, a long coast of subtropical surf beaches, remote lowveld savanna in the far north, and historic Anglo-Boer War and Anglo-Zulu War battlefields. In the middle of it all is the Zulu heartland. The KwaZulu-Natal Nature Conservation (KZN Wildlife) organisation has many ex-

cellent parks, while Durban is a city with a holiday atmosphere and, in parts, an Indian flavour. If you're planning to spend much time in KZN's many nature reserves and wildlife parks, the KZN Wildlife office in Pietermaritzburg, or its kiosk in Durban, are worth stopping in at for bookings and information.

History

Just before the 1994 elections, Natal Province was renamed KwaZulu-Natal, in a belated recognition of the fact that the Zulu heartland of KwaZulu comprises a large part of the province.

Natal was named by Vasco da Gama, who sighted the coast on Christmas Day 1497. It was not until 1843 that Natal was proclaimed a British colony, and in 1845 it was made part of the Cape Colony.

In 1856 Natal was again made a separate colony. With the introduction of Indian labour in the 1860s and the development of commercial agriculture, and with railways linking Durban's port with the booming Witwatersrand in 1895, the colony began to thrive.

The recorded history of the province until the Union of South Africa is full of conflict: the *difaqane*, the Boer-Zulu and the Anglo-Zulu Wars; and the two wars between the British and the Boers.

DURBAN
☎ 031 • pop 2,396,100

Durban is a big subtropical city on a long surf beach. It is a major port, but is better known as a mecca for holiday-makers. The weather (and the water, thanks to the Agulhas Current) stays warm year-round. Over summer the weather is hot and very humid, with spectacular thunderstorms.

Durban is home to the largest concentration of Indian-descended people in the country – about 800,000.

History
Natal Bay, around which Durban is located, provided refuge for seafarers at least as early as 1685, and it's thought that Vasco da Gama anchored here in 1497.

In 1837 the Voortrekkers crossed the Drakensberg and founded Pietermaritzburg, 80km northwest of Durban. The next year, after Durban was evacuated during a Zulu

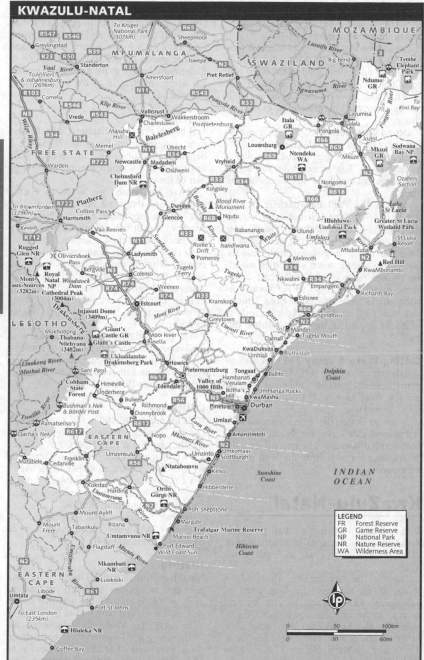

KWAZULU-NATAL

LEGEND
FR Forest Reserve
GR Game Reserve
NP National Park
NR Nature Reserve
WA Wilderness Area

raid, the Boers claimed control. It was reoccupied by a British force later that year, but the Boers stuck by their claim. The British sent troops to Durban but they were defeated at the Battle of Congella in 1842.

The Boers retained control for a month until a British frigate arrived (fetched by teenager Dick King who rode the 1000km of wild country between Durban and Grahamstown in 10 days) and dislodged them. The next year Natal was annexed by the British and Durban began its growth as an important colonial port city, although there were still elephant roaming the Berea Ridge into the 1850s.

In 1860 the first indentured Indian labourers arrived to work the canefields. Despite the iniquitous system – slave labour by another name – many more Indians arrived, including, in 1893, Mohandas Gandhi (see British Rule under History in the Facts about South Africa section earlier in this chapter).

Orientation

Marine Parade, fronting long surf beaches, is Durban's focal point. Most places to stay and eat are on the parade or in the streets behind it, and much of the entertainment is here as well.

West St starts as a mall, but further west it becomes one of downtown Durban's main streets. The city hall and the centre of the downtown area are about 1.5km west of the beach, straddling West and Smith Sts.

North of Durban and inland from Umhlanga Rocks is Phoenix, an Indian residential area named after Gandhi's commune.

A fair proportion of Durban's population, mainly black, lives in townships surrounding the city. These include Richmond Farm, KwaMashu, Lindelani, Ntuzuma and the Greater Inanda area.

Information

Tourist Offices The main information centre (☎ 304 4934; cnr Pine & Gardiner Sts, open 8am-5pm Mon-Fri, 9am-2pm Sat & Sun) is in the old train station in a complex known as **Tourist Junction**.

Pick up a copy of *What's on in Durban* and a free Durban map. There are various other useful agencies in the Tourist Junction complex, including an accommodation booking agency (**W** *www.bookabedahead.co.za*), a

Baz Bus office and a reservations office for both KZN Wildlife and the National Parks Board. A foreign exchange outlet at Tourist Junction was also being planned at the time of research.

Money There's a foreign exchange counter at **First National Bank** (cnr West & Gillespie Sts; open 11am-6pm Mon-Sat, 10am-3pm Sun).

Rennies Travel (☎ 305 5772), the Thomas Cook agent, has several branches including one at 333 Smith St, between Gardiner and Field Sts. **AmEx** (☎ 301 5541, 10th Fl, Nedbank Building, Durban Club Place) is nearby just off Smith Street.

Post & Communications Poste restante is at the **main post office** (West St); mail is normally held for a month. There's Internet access at Tourist Junction.

Emergency The emergency phone number in Durban is: ☎ 10111 from a landline or ☎ 112 from a mobile phone. Or call **ambulance** (☎ 10177), and **police** (☎ 306 4422). The private Entabeli Hospital number is (☎ 204 1300).

Dangers & Annoyances Many areas can be unsafe at night, especially in the Indian area (see Indian Area later in this section). At night, most people head to the restaurants in the northern suburbs such as Morningside or the big hotels and clubs along the beachfront.

The crowded beachfront Promenade has been a happy hunting ground for pickpockets, and violent robberies have occurred here at night, although the area has been much improved in recent years. Although you should be fine along the main beachfront area these days, it's probably still a good idea to get the local word when you're there.

Beachfront

Durban's prime attraction is its long string of surf beaches. Lifesavers patrol the beaches between 8am and 5pm – always swim in the patrolled area between the flags. Durban's 'Golden Mile' is actually 6km long; shark nets protect the warm-water beaches all the way from Blue Lagoon Beach (at the mouth of the Umgeni River) south to Addington Beach on The Point.

SOUTH AFRICA

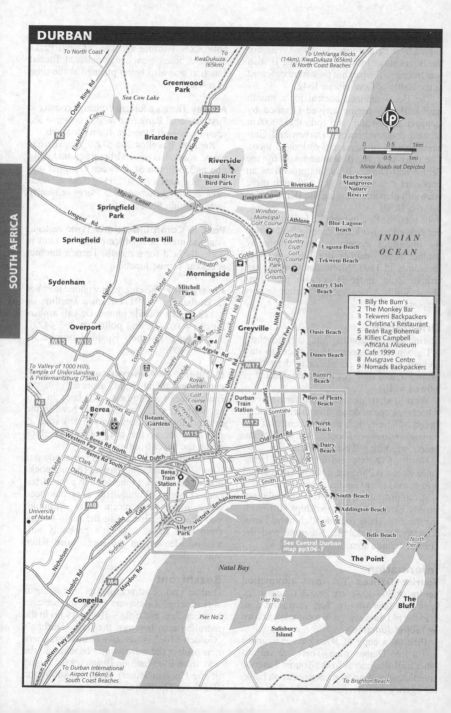

DURBAN

To North Coast

Greenwood Park

Sea Cow Lake

To KwaDukuza (65km)

To Umhlanga Rocks (14km), KwaDukuza (65km) & North Coast Beaches

Briardene

Riverside

Umgeni River Bird Park

Beachwood Mangroves Nature Reserve

Springfield Park

Springfield

Puntans Hill

Windsor Municipal Golf Course

Durban Country Club Golf Course

INDIAN OCEAN

Blue Lagoon Beach

Laguna Beach

Tekweni Beach

Sydenham

Morningside

Mitchell Park

Greyville

Country Club Beach

Overport

Oasis Beach

To Valley of 1000 Hills, Temple of Understanding & Pietermaritzburg (75km)

Dunes Beach

Battery Beach

Royal Durban Golf Course

Berea

Greyville Racecourse

Botanic Gardens

Durban Train Station

Bay of Plenty Beach

North Beach

Dairy Beach

Berea Train Station

University of Natal

Albert Park

South Beach

Addington Beach

Bells Beach

See Central Durban map pp506-7

The Point

North Pier

Natal Bay

Congella

Pier No 1

Pier No 2

Salisbury Island

The Bluff

To Durban International Airport (16km) & South Coast Beaches

To Brighton Beach

1 Billy the Bum's
2 The Monkey Bar
3 Tekweni Backpackers
4 Christina's Restaurant
5 Bean Bag Bohemia
6 Killies Campbell Africana Museum
7 Cafe 1999
8 Musgrave Centre
9 Nomads Backpackers

0   0.5   1km
0   0.5   1mi
Minor Roads not Depicted

The revamped **Promenade** fronts the surf. It's a good place to watch the crowds and there are a number of things to do. **Seaworld** *(☎ 337 3536; adult/child US$5.75/3; open 9am-9pm daily)*, near West Street, offers frequent shows in which fish, including sharks, penguins and seals are hand-fed daily by divers.

There are about a dozen **rickshaws** in Durban, which are usually found on the beachfront near Seaworld. A five-minute ride costs around US$1.20 plus US$0.60 for the mandatory photo.

City Centre

The impressive **city hall** (1910), a facsimile of Belfast's own in Northern Ireland, is worth a look inside and out. In the city hall building is the **Natural Science Museum** *(enter from Smith St; admission free; open 8.30am-4pm Mon-Sat, 11am-4pm Sun)*. Upstairs is the **Art Gallery**, which houses a good collection of contemporary works; especially good are the arts and crafts of Zululand. The **Local History Museum** *(admission free)* is in the courthouse (1863) behind the city hall (enter from Aliwal St). It has interesting displays on colonial life and a useful bookshop.

On the eastern side of the main post office is **Church Square**, with its old vicarage and the 1909 **St Paul's Church** at the rear on Pine St.

The **Workshop** *(Commercial Rd)*, a shopping centre, and the **Tourist Junction complex** nearby are in interesting former train station buildings. The excellent **KwaMuhle Museum** *(Ordnance Rd)*, in the former Bantu Administration building, has a permanent display with good oral history tapes on the 'Durban System' by which whites historically subjugated blacks.

Indian Area

The **Victoria Indian Street Market**, at the western end of Victoria St on the corner of Prince Edward St, has replaced the old Indian Market, which burned down. It is the main tourist attraction of the area but a walk through the nearby bustling streets is equally interesting – watch out for pickpockets.

Grey St, between Victoria and West Sts, is the main shopping area. Prices are low and you can bargain. Most Muslim shops close between noon and 2pm on Friday.

The big **Juma Mosque** *(☎ 306 0026; cnr Queen & Grey Sts)* is open to visitors on weekdays and Saturday morning; call for a guided tour. The **Alayam Hindu Temple** *(Somtseu Rd; open 7am-6pm daily)* is the oldest and biggest in South Africa. It's away from the main Indian area, north of the centre on Somtseu Rd, which runs between Snell Parade and NMR Ave.

Berea

The **Killies Campbell Africana Museum** *(☎ 207 3711; 220 Marriot Rd; admission US$1.80)*, near the corner of Musgrave Rd, in Berea, is an old home preserving an important collection of Zulu craft, art, furniture and paintings.

Activities

There's a multitude of good beaches with any number of **surfing** breaks. The online magazine *Zigzag* (W *www.zigzag.co.za)* is worth consulting.

Durban is a great place to learn how to sail. Readers have recommended the **Ocean Sailing Academy** *(☎ 301 5726; e academy@ oceansailing.co.za; 38 Fenton Rd)*. It offers a five-day course for aspiring yacht hands/skippers for US$274/345.

Organised Tours

Durban Africa *(☎ 304 4934)* conducts several walking tours of the city; the US$4.50 cost is well worthwhile. Tours leave from the Tourist Junction at 9.45am on weekdays; you must book in advance.

The **Durban Ricksha Bus** *(☎ 083 289 0509)* does tours of the city in an open-top, double-decker bus. It departs from behind Tourist Junction in the city centre at 1.30pm on Tuesday, Thursday & Sunday then heads to the seafront where it picks up more passengers at 2pm near the U Tours Coach Company stand. It costs US$4.60/2.30 for adults/children and gives visitors an excellent overview of the city.

Hostels are good places to organise budget tours and activities. The largest range is offered by Tekweni Eco-Tours, part of Tekweni Backpackers (see Places to Stay – Budget following).

The *Outdoor Adventure Guide* available free from Tourist Junction is a useful summary of more adrenaline fuelled options including paragliding, quadbiking, abseiling and horse riding.

Places to Stay – Budget

There's plenty of excellent budget accommodation in Durban but no central caravan parks, so if you're camping, you're better off staying at one of the many coastal resorts north or south of Durban.

Banana Backpackers (☎ 368 4062; 1st floor, 61 Pine St; dorm beds US$7, singles US$9, twins US$16, small doubles US$20), on the corner of Prince Alfred, is 1km from the beach. It's a big place but friendly and clean, and it gets good feedback from readers.

Tekweni Backpackers (☎ 303 1433; 167 Ninth Ave; dorm beds US$8, doubles US$20) is a popular and recently revamped place a manageable distance north of the centre in trendy Morningside. Tekweni Eco-Tours is also here and there's a small pool, Internet access and a bar. This place also offers some useful door-to-door bus services to town, the airport and towns in KZN, including Umhlanga and other coastal resorts.

Nomads Backpackers (☎ 202 9709; 70 Essenwood Rd, Berea; dorm beds US$7, doubles from US$18.50), run by friendly folk, is another good option. The doubles are large and clean and your hosts can offer some good advice on local partying and dining spots.

Places to Stay – Mid-Range

More information on mid-range to top-end places is available at Tourist Junction or through its bookings website **w** www.bookabedahead.co.za. There's an accommodation booking desk in the complex, and the staff should be able to find you a B&B from about US$19/25 a single/double.

The streets near the beach, especially Gillespie St, are the places to look for cheaper hotels and apartments.

Impala Holiday Flats (☎ 332 3232; 40 Gillespie St; flats from US$21) is good value in the low season, with tidy three- or four-bed flats. Take care though – it is in a slightly edgy area just away from the main beachfront.

Parade Hotel (☎ 337 4565; **e** paradehotel@eca.co.za; 191 Marine Parade; singles/doubles low season US$24/38) is typical of the comfortable beachfront hotels.

Tudor House Hotel (☎ 337 7328; West St; doubles US$23), east of Aliwal St, is away from the beach but great value. It has rather old fashioned double rooms with air-con, phone and TV, and breakfast is included.

CENTRAL DURBAN

CENTRAL DURBAN

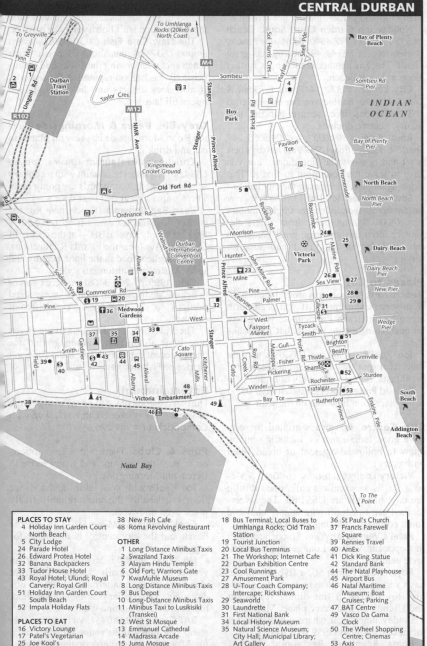

PLACES TO STAY
4 Holiday Inn Garden Court
   North Beach
5 City Lodge
24 Parade Hotel
26 Edward Protea Hotel
32 Banana Backpackers
33 Tudor House Hotel
43 Royal Hotel; Ulundi; Royal
   Carvery; Royal Grill
51 Holiday Inn Garden Court
   South Beach
52 Impala Holiday Flats

PLACES TO EAT
16 Victory Lounge
17 Patel's Vegetarian
25 Joe Kool's

38 New Fish Cafe
48 Roma Revolving Restaurant

OTHER
1 Long Distance Minibus Taxis
2 Swaziland Taxis
3 Alayam Hindu Temple
6 Old Fort; Warriors Gate
7 KwaMuhle Museum
8 Long Distance Minibus Taxis
9 Bus Depot
10 Long-Distance Minibus Taxis
11 Minibus Taxi to Lusikisiki
   (Transkei)
12 West St Mosque
13 Emmanuel Cathedral
14 Madrassa Arcade
15 Juma Mosque

18 Bus Terminal; Local Buses to
   Umhlanga Rocks; Old Train
   Station
19 Tourist Junction
20 Local Bus Terminus
21 The Workshop; Internet Cafe
22 Durban Exhibition Centre
23 Cool Runnings
27 Amusement Park
28 U-Tour Coach Company;
   Intercape; Rickshaws
29 Seaworld
30 Laundrette
31 First National Bank
34 Local History Museum
35 Natural Science Museum;
   City Hall; Municipal Library;
   Art Gallery

36 St Paul's Church
37 Francis Farewell
   Square
39 Rennies Travel
40 AmEx
41 Dick King Statue
42 Standard Bank
44 The Natal Playhouse
45 Airport Bus
46 Natal Maritime
   Museum; Boat
   Cruises; Parking
47 BAT Centre
49 Vasco Da Gama
   Clock
50 The Wheel Shopping
   Centre; Cinemas
53 Axis

Places to Stay – Top End

Many top-end places line the beachfront.

Holiday Inn Garden Court South Beach *(☎ 337 2231, fax 337 4640; 73 Marine Parade; singles/doubles US$43/49)* nearby has great views. There is another branch a bit further along at North Beach.

City Lodge *(☎ 332 1447; cnr Brickhill & Old Fort Rds; doubles midweek/weekends US$61/53)* has free, secure parking and luxury, generic doubles.

Royal Hotel *(☎ 304 0331, fax 304 5055; 267 Smith St; doubles from US$60)* is Durban's best hotel and boasts some fine dining, but you have to leave the beachfront to find it. This extravagant place is opposite the city hall.

Edward Protea Hotel *(☎ 337 3681, e reservations@proteaedward.co.za; singles/doubles from US$80/98)*, on the seafront, offers elegant, modern surroundings, great breakfasts (not included in the rates) and superior service.

Places to Eat

Beachfront Many hotels around the beachfront serve cheap meals. If you head north along North Beach Promenade, you get to an enclave of eating places that overlooks the sea.

Joe Kool's *(breakfasts US$2)* is a night (and day) spot that serves great 'recovery' breakfasts. It gets very lively at night.

Edward Protea Hotel *(breakfast from US$7)* is the place for a blow-out on the seafront.

City Centre Takeaways around the city have good Indian snacks, including bunny chow (a hollowed-out loaf of bread filled with curry).

Victory Lounge *(upstairs, cnr Grey & Victoria Sts)* is an excellent café, open during the day; biryanis are US$1.80. The sweet-toothed can finish off with sugary chai and some coronary-inducing ghee sweetmeats.

Patel's Vegetarian *(Grey St; open to 3pm)* just opposite Victory Lounge is a Gujarati-style eatery.

Royal Hotel *(Smith St)*, a five-star place, has a variety of excellent restaurants including Royal Grill, a fine-dining restaurant and Ulundi, a good curry place. Most have a Sunday lunch deal where a buffet or set menu costs around US$9 plus drinks.

Roma Revolving Restaurant *(☎ 332 3337; 32nd floor, John Ross House, Victoria Embankment; 3 courses with coffee & wine around US$12.50)* has an amazing view and the Italian food isn't horrifyingly expensive.

The New Cafe Fish *(☎ 305 5062; mains around US$7)* by the Yacht Club is a great lunch spot overlooking the docks and unsurprisingly has a good reputation for seafood. It also does dinners and has a bar which opens till late.

Greyville, Berea & Morningside Florida Rd in Morningside has several places to eat and drink.

Christina's Restaurant *(mains around US$4.50)* is a smart restaurant with a cookery school attached, so standards are pretty high. There's also a great deli next door.

Bean Bag Bohemia *(Windermere Rd; baguettes from US$3; mains around US$4.50)* – the sign simply says 'BBB' – at the corner of Campbell Ave (near the Florida Rd junction), serves excellent food in the light, healthy and spicy Australian/Californian style.

Cafe 1999 *(☎ 202 3406)* in Berea serves delicious Mediterranean food in starter-sized portions so you can try several different dishes.

The Musgrave Centre, close to the Berea hostels, is also a rich hunting ground for cheap, decent eats. Try **Little India** for good curries or **Fishmongers** for sushi.

Entertainment

Durban is a good place to party, with a range of venues. Many events can be booked with **Computicket** *(☎ 304 2753)*.

Pubs & Clubs There are a few options on or near the seafront and many more in Berea and Morningside.

Joe Kool's with pool tables and a dance floor is probably the most reliably lively place even mid-week.

Cool Runnings *(Milne St)*, between the beach and the city centre, is the place for reggae.

No 330 *(Point Rd)* is *the* place for Durban groovers. It's basically a dance club but masquerades as an 'alternative' club on Friday night. The regular beat includes techno, hip-hop, acid house and garage.

BAT Centre *(☎ 332 0451; Victoria Embankment)* is a funky little venue recommended for African music and jazz on the weekends. Call ahead to find out what's on.

The Florida Rd precinct of Morningside also attracts a late-night crowd, with several pubs and places to eat, including the big, buzzing **Monkey Bar**.

Billy the Bum's, right at the top of Windermere Rd attracts a smart, professional crowd which likes to party.

Gay & Lesbian Venues There's a small gay scene in Durban. **Axis** *(cnr Gillespie & Rutherford Sts)* is a popular gay nightclub.

The Bar *(open nightly)* is Durban's oldest gay club. There's a small cover charge.

No 330 (see Pubs & Clubs earlier), although mainly straight, is gay friendly.

Classical Music, Theatre & Dance A variety of musicians and exceptional gospel choirs play and sing on the city hall steps on Wednesday at 1pm.

The University of Natal's Music Department has free lunchtime concerts on Monday in **Howard College** (concerts also in the evenings).

Natal Playhouse *(Smith St)*, opposite the city hall, has dance, drama and music most nights.

KwaZulu-Natal Philharmonic Orchestra (☎ 369 9438) performs weekly in the city hall in spring.

Cinemas There are cinemas in the **Wheel Shopping Centre** *(Gillespie St)*, **The Workshop** *(Commercial Rd)*, and the **Musgrave Centre**.

Getting There & Away
Air Durban international airport is off the N2, about 15km south of the city. **SAA** (☎ 250 1111) is based at the airport.

Bus Most long-distance buses leave from the rear of the Durban train station. **Translux** (☎ 308 8111), **Greyhound** (☎ 309 7830) and **Intercape** (☎ 307 2115) all have offices here. A small operation, **Panthera Azul** (☎ 309 7798), runs to Maputo (US$24) Wednesday, Friday and Sunday departing at 7am. You can also book Translux and Greyhound at the bus office on the beachfront.

The **Baz Bus** (☎ 304 9099 or book through hostels) service between Cape Town and Jo'burg runs via Durban and the Garden Route. There's an office at Tourist Junction.

Amanzimtoti Singh's Tours (☎ 039-979 5447) runs several services to Amanzimtoti from the Dick King Statue (Victoria Embankment).

Bloemfontein Greyhound runs to Bloemfontein (US$18.50, 9½ hours) via Bethlehem (US$17.50) and Welkom (US$18.50).

Cape Town Translux has a daily service to Cape Town (US$40 21¾ hours) via Bloemfontein (US$25, 9½ hours).

Jo'burg Translux (US$21.50, eight hours) and Greyhound (US$19.50, eight hours) run at least daily. Eldo Coaches (☎ 307 3363), also at the station, seems to offer the cheapest daily service to Jo'burg for US$15.

Margate The Margate Mini Coach (☎ 039-312 1406) runs between Margate and Durban daily (US$7, 2½ hours). Its Flutterbus service runs down to the Wild Coast Sun Casino (just over the border in Eastern Cape).

Pietermaritzburg Translux runs several times daily to Pietermaritzburg.

Port Elizabeth Greyhound runs a daily service (US$23, 14¾ hours) via Umtata (US$17.50, 6½ hours) and East London (US$18, 10 hours).

Richards Bay Stallion Coaches (☎ 403 7725) runs to Richards Bay daily at 4.30pm and Friday and Sunday at 3pm (US$8, three hours). The bus departs outside St Paul's church on Pine St.

Minibus Taxi Some long-distance minibus taxis leave from ranks in the streets opposite the Umgeni Rd entrance to the Durban train station. Routes include the Swaziland border (US$11.50) and Jo'burg (US$14).

Other minibus taxis, running mainly to the south coast and the Transkei region in Eastern Cape, leave from around the Berea train station. Minibus taxis to other South African destinations leave from the taxi ranks just south of the train station between Alice St and Prince Edward and Umgeni Rd and Prince Edward.

Train Contact **Durban train station** (☎ 0860-00888; Umgeni Rd) for information.

The *Trans Natal* (Durban to Jo'burg via Newcastle and Ladysmith) runs daily except Tuesday and Saturday, and the weekly *Trans Oranje* (Durban to Cape Town via Bloemfontein and Kimberley) also runs from here. There are also commuter trains running down the coast as far as Kelso near Pennington and north to Stanger.

Car Durban has offices for **Avis** (☎ *0800-02 1111*) and **Budget** (☎ *0860-016622*), as well as lower-priced companies such as **Tempest** (☎ *368 5231*).

If you're driving into Durban, cheap, secure parking is available from US$0.60 a day at Maritime Parking by the Natal Maritime Museum.

Getting Around

To/From the Airport A bus (☎ *465 5573; US$2.90*) runs to the airport from near the corner of Aliwal and Smith Sts. Some hostels can get discounts and pick-ups for backpackers on the return trip. By taxi, the same trip costs around US$15. Many hostels also offer airport pick-ups.

Bus The main bus terminus and information centre (*Commercial Rd*) is across from The Workshop. **Mynah** (*307 3503*) covers Berea, the Botanical Gardens and the central and beachfront areas, roughly every 20 minutes on weekdays from 6am to late afternoon. All trips cost around US$0.50. There are also less-frequent full-size buses running more routes and travelling further from the city centre than Mynah. At off-peak times the most you will pay is US$0.50. Tourist Junction has a full and up-to-date list of operators.

Taxi A taxi between the beach and the train station costs around US$2.90. **Bunny Cabs** (☎ *332 2914*) runs 24 hours – the drivers we met were friendly. Other taxi companies are **Eagles** (☎ *337 8333*) and **Aussies** (☎ *309 7888*).

Rickshaw Asian-style three-wheelers congregate on the beachfront near Palmer St. Over short distances their fares are lower than taxis.

AROUND DURBAN

The **Valley of 1000 Hills** (also known as the Umgeni Valley) runs from the ocean at Durban to Nagle Dam, east of Pietermaritzburg. The rolling hills and traditional Zulu villages are the main reason visitors drive through here, usually on the R103, which begins in Hillcrest off the M13.

SOUTH OF DURBAN

There are some good beaches on the south coast between Durban and Transkei. There are also shoulder-to-shoulder resorts for much of the 150km, and in summer there isn't much room to move.

Commuter trains run from Durban down the coast as far as Kelso, on the northern edge of Pennington. (For details of the Margate Mini Coach, see Getting There & Away in the Durban section.)

Sunshine Coast

The Sunshine Coast stretches about 60km from Amanzimtoti to Mtwalume. All of the beaches are easily accessible from the N2, but the area suffers from its proximity to Durban.

The main town is **Amanzimtoti** (Sweet Waters), a jungle of apartment blocks. It merges into Kingsburgh to the south. **Winklespruit**, **Illovo** and **Karridene** beaches are nearby. The friendly **visitors centre** (☎/fax *031-903 7498; Beach Rd*) is in Amanzimtoti, not far from the Inyoni Rocks.

Further south are Umkomaas, Scottburgh, Park Rynie, Kelso and Pennington.

Inland from Park Rynie, off the R612 past Umzinto, the **Vernon Crookes Nature Reserve** (☎ *033-845 1000; admission US$1.20*) has a few animal species and some indigenous forest. If you walk through the reserve beware of ticks. There are two-bed **huts** (☎ *039-974 2222; US$20*).

Places to Stay At Illovo, the **Illovo Beach Caravan Park** (☎ *031-916 3472; camp sites high/low season US$32/16*) has a restaurant and swimming pool.

Villa Spa (☎ *031-916 4939*), a shady place with decent chalets, is also on Illovo Beach.

Blue Marlin (☎ *039-978 3361, fax 976 0971; 180 Scott St, Scottburgh; singles/doubles US$26/41*) is a cheerful place further south in Scottburgh.

There are plenty of B&Bs and in the low season you may get away with US$10.50 per person – ask at the various information centres.

Hibiscus Coast

This section of the south coast includes the seaside towns of Hibberdene, Port Shepstone, Shelly Beach, St Michaels-on-Sea, Uvongo, Margate, Ramsgate and Marina Beach. Port Shepstone is an unattractive industrial centre and Margate is a large resort town. For information on the towns in this area try **Tourism Margate** (☎ 039-312 2322; Main Beach, Margate).

The **Oribi Gorge Nature Reserve** (admission US$1.20) is inland from Port Shepstone, off the N2. The spectacular Oribi Gorge on the Umzimkulu River is one of the highlights of the coast. As well as the scenery, there are many animals and birds to witness. KZN Wildlife has huts and cottages available here. The **Oribi Gorge Hotel** (☎ 039-687 0253; B&B singles/doubles US$29/43) is near a viewing site overlooking the gorge.

The **Trafalgar Marine Reserve** off the coast near Margate protects ancient fossil beds, but for most visitors it is the surfing and especially sailboarding here that are the attractions.

Places to Stay There are plenty of hotels, resorts and self-catering apartments in Margate. It's a good idea to book something through an agency such as **Beach Holidays** (☎ 039-315 0265, 312 2543, fax 73753; W www.infocentre.co.za) or the **Information Centre for Holiday Accommodation** (☎ 039-315 0265).

Margate Caravan Park (☎ 039-312 0852), opposite the police station and sandwiched between the R620 and Valley Rd, is another option.

Sunlawns (☎ 039-312 1078; Uplands Rd; per person with half-board US$18.50) is a cheap hotel.

Villa Siesta (☎ 039-681 3343; camp sites high/low season US$18.50/5.80, 4-bed chalets high/low season from US$34/14) is in Anerley.

Mantis & Moon Backpackers (☎ 039-684 6256; e travels@saol.com; 7/178 Station Rd; dorm beds US$7, doubles US$18.50) is a great spot offering small dorms and garden shed–style cabins set amid shaded tropical grounds with a bar and Jacuzzi. It's close to large empty beaches and you can borrow surf boards for free. The Baz Bus stops here.

Port Edward

Port Edward adjoins the Transkei region of Eastern Cape. Just south of town is the interesting **Mzamba Village market** where a range of Xhosa crafts are sold.

Old Pont (☎ 039-311 2211; 2-person camp sites from US$10.50) is a good family resort.

Vuna Valley Backpackers (☎ 083 992699, camp sites US$5.80, dorm beds US$8, doubles US$18.50) not far from Port Edward is a large, mellow place. To get there from the highway at Port Edward, turn right onto Old Pont Rd and follow the signs.

NORTH OF DURBAN

The stretch of coast from Umhlanga Rocks north to Tugela Mouth is less developed than the south coast, and the beaches are better. With lots of time-shares and retirement villages, things aren't very lively.

Umhlanga Rocks

☎ 031

This big resort town (the name means Place of Reeds and you pronounce the 'h' like a 'sh') is about 15km north of Durban.

There's an **information kiosk** (☎ 561 4257; e info@umhlanga-rocks.com; open 8am-4.30pm Mon-Fri) on the mall, near the intersection of Lagoon Dr and Lighthouse St.

The **Natal Sharks Board** (☎ 566 0400; W www.shark.co.za; adult/child US$1.80/1.20) is a research institute dedicated to studying sharks and their danger to humans. Call for the latest opening times. The board is about 2km out of town, up the steep Umhlanga Rocks Drive (the M12 leading to the N3).

Places to Stay & Eat Umhlanga's many holiday apartments fill up in the high season, when you'd be lucky to rent one for less than a week, but otherwise it's possible to rent one for as few as two days. A two-bedroom apartment costs from US$40 per night in the low season (US$70 in the high season), and three-bedroom apartments cost from US$57 in the low season (US$90 in the high season). Contact **Umhlanga Accommodation** (☎ 561 2012; fax 561 3957).

Most hotels charge about US$51/69 a single/double. Along Lagoon Dr are **Umhlanga Rocks** (☎/fax 561 1321) and **Umhlanga Sands** (☎ 561 2323, fax 561 4408).

SOUTH AFRICA

Oyster Box Hotel (☎ *561 2233,* e *oyster box@iafrica.com, 2 Lighthouse Rd, singles/ doubles from US$62/92)* is lovely and right on the shore. Its restaurant has a good reputation, although the snack food served from its veranda is disappointing.

Swallows *(Protea Mall)* is a good place for a coffee, brunch or lunch.

Dolphin Coast
☎ 032

The Dolphin Coast starts at Umdloti Beach and stretches north to the Tugela River. It includes Tongaat, Ballito, Shaka's Rock, Umhlali (Salt Rock), Blythdale, Stanger, Zwinkwazi and Tugela Mouth. The coast gets its name from the pods of bottlenose dolphins that frolic offshore.

The **Dolphin Coast Publicity Association** (☎ *946 1997)* is near the BP service station, just where you leave the N2 to enter Ballito.

Places to Stay Well-located right on the beach, **Beach Bums Backpackers** (☎ *943 1401;* e *bsbeach@iafrica.com; 65 Casuarina Dr, Casuarina Beach, Tongaat: dorm beds US$7, doubles US$17.50)* boasts its very own shipwreck and great views from its upstairs lounge. The location is a bit isolated but it's a good place to relax.

Tugela Mouth The Tugela River, once an important natural boundary for local tribes, enters the sea here to end its journey from Mont-aux-Sources in the Drakensberg. There are several major battlefields near the mouth.

The **Ultimatum Tree,** where the British presented their demands to Cetshwayo's representatives, is nearby.

At this site in 1878, the British demanded that by mid-January 1879 the Zulu pay taxes and return all the cattle they had stolen. The cattle were not returned, precipitating the Anglo-Zulu War, which raged until August 1879 when Cetshwayo was captured (for more on Cetshwayo, see the boxed text 'The Zulu after Blood River'). Across the river there is a collection of war graves on the site of Fort Pearson.

ZULULAND
Zululand covers much of central KwaZulu-Natal. The area east of the N2 and north of the Mtubatuba–St Lucia road is known

as Maputaland and is covered later in this chapter.

This area is dominated by one tribal group, the Zulu. The name Zulu (Heaven) comes from an early chief. His descendants were known as *abakwaZulu,* or people of Heaven.

Richards Bay
☎ 035 • pop 82,200

This town feels as though it was meticulously planned for a boom that hasn't happened yet. It's spread out, with tourist-oriented facilities far from what passes for the centre. Unless you have business here there's not much reason to visit. The **publicity association** (☎ *788 0039; Anglers Rd)* has information on things to do in the area.

Imvubu Log Cabins (☎ *753 4122; Krewelk Rd; dorm beds US$11.50, 2-person chalets from US$40)* is a leafy resort with spacious, spotlessly clean log cabins.

Empangeni
☎ 035

Empangeni (m'pan-**gay**-nee) started out as a sugar town, but the huge eucalypt plantations nearby are rivalling the cane in importance to the town's economy. It's a jumping-off point for the coast and the inland areas of Zululand.

Harbour Lights (☎ *196 6239; camp sites US$7; backpacking accommodation US$8)* is a basic and rather unappealing caravan park off the N2 between Empangeni and Richards Bay.

Protea Hotel (☎ *772 3322,* e *proteaemp@ microweb.co.za, 64 Turnbull St, singles/doubles US$68/81)* is smart and comfortable and has a good restaurant attached.

Enseleni Nature Reserve
The small Enseleni Nature Reserve (open 8am-5pm daily) is 13km northeast of Empangeni on the N2 and has wildlife including crocodiles, hippos and zebras. It's possible to walk here but there's no accommodation.

Eshowe
☎ 035

This pleasant town is inland in the misty Zululand hills. The name Eshowe is said to be the sound the wind makes when passing through trees. Eshowe was Cetshwayo's stronghold before he moved to Ondini, and like Ondini, Eshowe was destroyed during

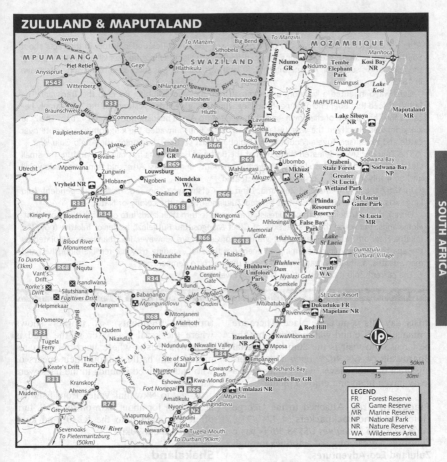

ZULULAND & MAPUTALAND

the Anglo-Zulu War. The British built Fort Nongqai in 1883, establishing Eshowe as the administrative centre of their newly captured territory.

The helpful **Eshowe Publicity Association** (☎ 41141) provides information. Alternatively **Zululand Eco-Adventures** (☎ 474 4919; **w** www.eshowe.com) at the George Hotel offers a huge range of local activities and tours, from adrenaline-fuelled activities like rocksliding to local tours into nearby Zulu communities.

The owner has extensive links with many of the local Zulu communities so this is a great place to head out on one of the semi-structured tours where you can chat with locals in a nearby village. At weekends there's a good chance of being guest of honour at a wedding or coming of age ceremony.

Things to See & Do In the mud-and-brick *Fort Nongqayi* you'll find the **Zululand Historical Museum** (*admission US$1.20; open 9am-5pm daily*). The Vukani Collection, a display of well-crafted woven pots is next door. From the museum you can walk to **Mpushini Falls**, which are supposed to be now free from bilharzia but you swim at your own risk.

On a lonely hill nearby (ask at the George Hotel) a cross made of railway sleepers marks the spot of the area's first Zulu convert to Christianity who was subsequently killed by his own tribe for doing so.

The **Dlinza Forest Reserve** is a 200-hectare stand of dense rainforest – on a

The Zulu After Blood River

After the disaster of Blood River (for more details, see The Great Trek under History in the Facts about South Africa section), the Zulu king Dingaan fled to Swaziland, where he was killed in 1840. During the reign of his successor, Mpane, much Zulu land was lost. He was succeeded by his son Cetshwayo in 1873.

Cetshwayo inherited a kingdom under threat from the land-grabbing Boers in the Transvaal. The British agreed that Boer encroachment was illegal but they gave little assistance to the Zulu, largely because they had a plan of their own – a British wedge into Africa heading north from Durban. The Zulu kingdom was directly in the way. In January 1879 the British invaded the kingdom in a dispute over cattle and taxes (see Tugela Mouth in the Dolphin Coast section), beginning the Anglo-Zulu War.

The Zulu decisively defeated the British at the Battle of Isandlwana but failed to capture the small station at Rorke's Drift, despite overwhelming superiority in numbers. After that things went downhill and on 4 July at Ulundi, Cetshwayo was defeated.

In 1887 the British annexed Zululand. Dinizulu, Cetshwayo's son and the last independent Zulu king, was exiled. In 1897 the British handed Zululand over to the colony of Natal.

During the apartheid era, the Zulu resisted attempts to turn their lands into one of the 'independent' Homelands, thanks to the political skills of Chief Mangosuthu Buthelezi, leader of Inkatha (now the Inkatha Freedom Party, IFP) and great-grandson of Cetshwayo. However, Inkatha was manipulated by the apartheid regime into becoming an enemy of the ANC, leading to some terrible bloodshed and many deaths, a situation that almost derailed the march to democracy.

The current Zulu monarch is King Goodwill Zwelithini.

misty day this is an eerie place. There are animals, birdlife and walking trails but the best reason to visit is the 20m-high **Aerial Boardwalk** (☎ 474 4029; open daily) offering great tree-top views, with guides, and a leafy haven to sit and enjoy a picnic.

Places to Stay Attached to the George Hotel, **Zululand Backpackers** (☎ 474 4919; dorm beds US$8, doubles US$18.50) is basic but offers a great range of activities through **Zululand Eco-Adventures**.

George Hotel (☎ 74919; e info@eshawe .com; B&B singles/doubles US$25/40) is a slightly ramshackle place. There's a restaurant and a good bar with its own microbrewed beers.

Getting There & Away Minibus taxis depart from the car park at the Kwik Spar on the main street. A fare to Empangeni is US$2.30. If you want to go deeper into Zululand, take a taxi to Melmoth (about US$2.30).

Nkwalini Valley

The Zulu nation was pretty much born here. KwaBulawayo, Shaka's military headquarters, once loomed over this beautiful valley but today it is regimented into citrus orchards and canefields rather than *impis*

(military regiments). A marker shows where the kraal was. Across the road is **Coward's Bush**, where warriors who returned from battle without their spears or who had received wounds in the back were executed.

To get to Nkwalini Valley from Eshowe, head north for about 6km on the R68, turn off to the right onto the R230, and keep going for about 20km.

Shakaland

Created as a set for the telemovie *Shaka Zulu* and managed by the Protea chain, this isn't exactly a genuine Zulu village. While it is obviously a stage-managed affair put on for the benefit of tour groups, the singing and choreography are genuinely impressive. The experience can also include **accommodation** (singles/doubles with half-board US$100/170).

Shakaland (☎ 035-460 0912 for bookings; shows 11am and 12.30pm; US$17.50 including lunch) is at Norman Hurst Farm, Nkwalini, a few kilometres off the R68 and 14km north of Eshowe.

KwaBhekithunga Zulu Kraal This craft centre (☎ 035-460 0644) on the road into Nkwalini is worth visiting for its crafts

such as beadwork and spears. There's accommodation in beehive huts from US$10 per person. The proceeds support a local health clinic. It's on the R34, down a dirt road turning 6km east of the intersection with the R66.

Ulundi

Ulundi, the former capital of the KwaZulu Homeland, is a rapidly growing town. The area has been the stronghold of many Zulu kings, and several are buried in the nearby Valley of the Kings. The town itself offers little to see, but there are important historical sites in the area. For information go to the **KwaZulu Monuments Council** (☎ 0358-702 050) in Ondini.

Close to Ulundi are **Fort Nolela**, near the drift on the White Umfolozi River where the British camped before attacking Ondini in 1879; and **KwaGqokli**, where Shaka celebrated victory over the Ndwandwe in 1818. Another place of great significance to the Zulu is eMakhosini, **Valley of the Kings**. The great *makhosi* (chiefs) Nkhosinkulu, Senzangakhona (father of Shaka, Dingaan and Mpande) and Dinizulu are buried here. The museum near Dingaan's kraal is also the place where Piet Retief and his party were tricked and slaughtered in 1838.

Ulundi Holiday Inn Garden Court (☎ 0358-701 012; singles/doubles from US$56/65) has weekend specials.

The minibus taxi rank is opposite the Holiday Inn. Routes include: Ondini (US$0.40); Vryheid (US$1.75); Eshowe (US$2.30); Durban (US$7); and Jo'burg (US$7.50).

Ondini

Ondini (High Place) was established as Cetshwayo's capital in 1873, but it was razed by British troops after the Battle of Ulundi (4 July 1879). It took the British nearly six months to defeat the Zulu *impis* but the Battle of Ulundi went the way of most of the campaign, with the number of Zulu deaths 10 to 15 times higher than the number of British deaths.

The **KwaZulu Cultural-Historical Museum** (admission US$1.20), has good exhibits on the battles, Zulu history and culture.

To get to Ondini, take the airport turnoff from the highway just south of Ulundi and keep going for about 5km on a dirt road. This road continues on to Hluhluwe-

Umfolozi Park. Minibus taxis occasionally pass Ondini.

Itala Game Reserve

This reserve (admission US$3.50/3.50 per person/vehicle) in northern Zululand has all the trappings of a private wildlife reserve but at much lower prices. It's a beautiful reserve and well worth visiting if you've not already had your fill of wildlife parks.

Animals include black and white rhinos, elephants, nyalas, hyenas, buffaloes, baboons, leopards, cheetahs and crocodiles. The diverse habitats support over 320 species of bird.

Ntshondwe (☎ 034-907 5105; camp sites US$2.70 per person, units with shared kitchen from US$22, chalets from US$21) is the main centre, with superb views of the reserve below. There are a few basic camp sites.

Itala is entered from Louwsburg, about 65km east of Vryheid on the R69, and about the same distance southwest of Pongola via the R66 and the R69.

MAPUTALAND
☎ 035

Maputaland is one of the wildest and most fascinating areas of South Africa. It takes its name from the Maputo River, which splits, on the border of Mozambique and South Africa, into the Usutu and Pongola Rivers. Maputaland is sparsely settled and much of it is protected in parks and reserves. It contains coral reefs, many wildlife reserves, the country's last free-ranging wild elephants in Tembe Elephant Park, and three huge lakes, including the Greater St Lucia Wetlands.

KwaMbonambi

KwaMbonambi is a tiny but lush and beautiful town off the N2 about 30km north of Empangeni and the same distance south of Mtubatuba. There would be no reason to stop here, except that it has two excellent hostels, making it an ideal base for travellers exploring St Lucia, Hluhluwe-Umfolozi and other attractions in northern Zululand and Maputaland.

Cuckoo's Nest (☎ 580 1001/2; 28 Albezia St; dorm beds US$6.50, doubles US$16.50) is a cheerful, carefree hostel with few rules, lots of activities and money off your bill if you can do the log walk across the pool. It

offers trips to Sodwana Bay and Hluhluwe-Umfolozi Parks.

Mtubatuba

This trading town gets busy on weekends. The main reason to visit Mtubatuba is because local buses and minibus taxis run through here on the way south to Durban and west into Zululand. Coming from those destinations, Mtubatuba is the stop for St Lucia, which is about 25km east; the trip costs US$0.70 by minibus taxi.

The **Paradiso Hotel** (☎ 550 0153; e *para diso@mtuba.co.za; B&B singles/doubles US$12.50/20)* is friendly with basic rooms.

Wendy's Country Lodge (☎ 550 0407; e *wendyb@iatrica.co.za; singles/doubles from US$34/52)* offers large, well-furnished rooms in a secure part of town close to the Illovo Sugar Mill.

Dumazulu Cultural Village

Probably the best of the 'Zulu experience' villages, Dumazulu (☎ 562 2260 for bookings; per person with half-board around US$80) is east of the N2, north of Mtubatuba. Four shows are held daily for about US$8. Lunch and dinner are available and there's a **lodge** (per person with half-board around US$80).

Isinkwe Backpackers Lodge (☎ 562 2258; e *isinkwe@saol.com; 104 Bush Rd; camping US$4, dorm beds US$6.50, doubles US$16.50)* is arguably one of the best backpackers hostels in South Africa. It's next to Dumazulu Cultural Village, off the N2 south of Hluhluwe (take the Bushlands exit). It's on a large, beautiful patch of virgin bush and has small but comfortable cabins, 'rustic' huts, tents and a dorm, all in a pleasant garden. There's a good kitchen and bar.

Hluhluwe-Umfolozi Park

The two reserves of Hluhluwe (shlu-shlu-ee) and Umfolozi were first proclaimed in 1897, and today they are among the best in South Africa. They don't adjoin, but a 'corridor' between them allows animals to move from one park to the other. Both reserves have lions, elephants, many rhinos (black and white), giraffes and a host of other animals and birds.

Several tours include Hluhluwe-Umfolozi Park. One inexpensive option is the three-day trip with Tekweni Eco-Tours (contact Tekweni Backpackers in Durban), which also takes in the Greater St Lucia Wetlands.

Entry to each reserve costs US$3.50 per person plus US$4 per vehicle.

Wilderness Trails In Hluhluwe there are driving trails but no walking trails except for a short one around the camp.

One of the main attractions in Umfolozi is the trail system in a 24,000-hectare wilderness area. Accompanied by an armed ranger and donkeys to carry supplies, hikers spend four days walking in the reserve. You need a party of eight people (no children under 12). Bookings are accepted up to six months in advance and it's advisable to book early, with alternative dates if possible. It costs US$225 per person, including all meals and equipment. A two-night weekend trip costs US$110 per person. Bookings are through KZN Wildlife (see Places to Stay & Eat).

Places to Stay & Eat The best place to stay is **Hilltop Camp** (huts per person from US$44, self-catering chalets per person US$22), in Hluhluwe, with stupendous views.

Mpunyane Restaurant serves game dishes at reasonable prices. There are bush lodges at **Muntulu** (US$49 per person), perched high above the Hluhluwe River, and at **Munya-waneni** (US$49 per person), which is secluded and self-contained. These sleep eight and cost a minimum of US$290.

In Umfolozi, there are 5-bed **huts** (from US$22 per person, minimum US$64) at **Mpila** and **Masinda**. There are also 2-bed **safari camps** (US$23 per person, minimum US$34).

Book all accommodation through the **KZN Wildlife** in Pietermaritzburg (☎ 033-845 1000; e *bookings@kznwildlife.com; w www.kznwildlife.com)*.

Getting There & Away The main entrance to Hluhluwe, at Memorial Gate, is about 15km west of the N2, about 50km northwest of Mtubatuba. Alternatively, just after Mtubatuba, turn left off the N2 onto the R618 to Nongoma and take the right-hand turn to the reserve after 17km. The Cengeni Gate is on the southeastern side of the park. Petrol is available at Mpila Camp in the park.

Greater St Lucia Wetlands

One of the world's great ecotourism destinations stretches for 80km from Sodwana Bay, in the north of Maputaland, to Mapelane

Nature Reserve at the southern end of Lake St Lucia. It's an under-hyped and largely unspoiled bit of South Africa and is well worth devoting at least a couple of days to exploring.

The area is gradually being consolidated as the Greater St Lucia Wetlands, and satisfies the criteria for listing as a UNESCO world heritage area. Rhinos, elephants, leopards and buffaloes have been introduced since 2001. Lions and wild dogs are also due to be introduced.

The park protects five interconnected ecosystems: marine (coral reefs, beaches); shore (barrier between lake and sea); Mkuze reed and sedge swamps; the lake (the largest estuary in Africa); and western shores (fossil corals, sand forest, bushveld and grasslands).

The main walks are the four-night guided St Lucia Wilderness Trail and the three-day Mziki Trail, both in the Cape Vidal area (see Tewati Wilderness Area later in this section), and the *Dugandlovu Hiking Trail* in False Bay Park (see False Bay Park later in this section). There are also day walks, detailed in KZN Wildlife literature available at the St Lucia Resort office.

All the parks and reserves in the area are administered by the KZN Wildlife. There is also private accommodation at St Lucia Resort, which is a sizeable holiday village.

Dangers & Annoyances You should be aware of crocodiles and hippos in this area – both are potentially dangerous. Be careful at night, as hippos roam. In more remote areas hippos may be encountered on shore during the day – treat them with respect and retreat quietly. Sharks sometimes venture up the St Lucia estuary.

Organised Tours Just about any tour in the area can be organised through St Lucia Tours & Charters (☎ 590 1259), next to the Dolphin supermarket. They include night drives (US$11), turtle- and whale-watching trips in season, as well as cultural tours to local townships and Zulu villages. Bibs Hostel (see Places to Stay & Eat later in this section) has loads of organised activities such as snorkelling at Cape Vidal (US$22) and hippo tours on the estuary (US$9).

One of the highlights is the trip on the *Santa Lucia*. It leaves from the wharf on the west side of the bridge on the Mtubatuba road at 8.30am, 10.30am and 2.30pm daily (US$7). Longer trips with more informative commentary operate on smaller boats, which leave from a jetty on the town side of the estuary.

St Lucia Resort This resort is the main centre for the area, with KZN Wildlife offices, shops, boat hire and other services, as well as a lot of private accommodation.

There are three ATMs in town: ABSA near the Wimpy, at the First National Bank next to the Dolphin supermarket, and at the Standard Bank.

About 2km north of St Lucia Resort on the road to Cape Vidal, the Crocodile Centre (admission US$1.80) has some good information on the area's ecosystems.

Places to Stay & Eat There are three KZN Wildlife **camping** areas (bookings ☎ 590 1340; e bookings@kznwildlife.com; w www.kznwildlife.com): **Sugarloaf** (camping per person US$7), **Eden Park** (camping per person US$5.80), and **Iphiva** (camping per person US$5.50).

Bibs Hostel (☎ 590 1056; e kgb@mega.co.za; dorm beds US$7, doubles US$18.50) is a huge barn converted into roofless backpacker cubicles and some rather musty guesthouse accommodation. It can be noisy but it has online terminals and organises heaps of activities. There are regular *braais*.

African Tale Backpackers (☎ 550 4300; 082 752 7791; e bookings@africantale.co.za dorm; US$5.80, singles/doubles US$8/16.50), on the road between Mtubatuba and St Lucia Resort, is a great, colourful place to hang out for a day or two. Accommodation options include genuine *umuzi* ('beehive' huts). It has a bar, Internet access, offers pick-ups from Richards Bay and into St Lucia and is a Baz Bus stop.

St Lucia Wilds (☎ 590 1033; 6-person apartments per person from US$7.50) is one of the real bargains in town, although don't expect any luxury; ask in town for directions.

St Lucia Namib Safari Lodge (☎ 590 1133, w www.namibsafari.co.za, self-catering per person from US$13.50) is new, clean and very pleasant indeed.

Kingfisher Lodge (☎ 590 1015, e stlucia kingfisherlodge@mweb.co.za; singles/doubles from US$32/50), next door, is an upmarket B&B in a lovely estuary setting. We've had

excellent feedback about this place from readers.

Santa Lucia (☎ 590 1151, ℮ rika@santalucia .co.za, singles/doubles from US$25/41.50) is a small, central guesthouse with friendly and helpful hosts.

St Pizza has a shaded outdoor area. For seafood try the upmarket **Lake View**.

Mapelane Nature Reserve This popular fishing spot (admission US$2.30), south across the estuary from St Lucia, will probably become the visitors centre for Mhlatuze State Forest when the area is developed for recreational use.

There are **camp sites** (US$6) and **log cabins** (US$21).

Although it's across the estuary from St Lucia, travel between the two centres is circuitous unless you have a boat. Mapelane is reached by 40km of sandy and sometimes tricky road from KwaMbonambi, off the N2 south of Mtubatuba. Follow the 'Kwa Mbonambi Lighthouse' sign.

Tewati Wilderness Area (Cape Vidal) The Tewati Wilderness Area (admission per person/vehicle US$2.30/2.90) takes in the land between the lake and the ocean north from Cape Vidal. The Eastern Shores State Forest runs south from Cape Vidal to St Lucia, and is administered as part of the Cape Vidal State Forest.

The Cape Vidal KZN Wildlife office is the starting place for the four-night **St Lucia Wilderness Trail**, a guided walk costing US$178 per person (minimum four people). Walks are available only from April to September.

There is a range of accommodation at the **Bhangazi** complex (☎ 590 1404; camp sites US$2.30/2.90, log cabins per person from US$21, minimum US$63, dorm cabins per person US$9, minimum US$36, 8-bed log cabin per person US$21, minimum US$84). From St Lucia Resort head north past the crocodile centre and through the entrance gates. Cape Vidal is about 30km further on.

False Bay Park This park (admission US$2.30) runs along the western shore of Lake St Lucia. As well as the lake's hippos and crocodiles, the park has several antelope species and other animals.

There are **camp sites** (camping per person US$4.50, minimum US$9.50) and rustic four-

bed **huts** (per person US$11, minimum US$22) on the Dugandlovu Trail, about 9km from the entrance gate; you can drive there. Book both of these direct (☎ 035-562 0425).

The main road into the park runs east from Hluhluwe village (not Hluhuwe-Umfolozi Park) off the N2. Hluhluwe village is also the nearest place to buy fuel and supplies.

Outside the park, **Sand Forest Lodge** (☎ 562 0509; ℮ sandforest@futurenet.co.za; camping US$4.50, bungalows US$11.50 per person, cottages from US$44) has its own grounds with walking trails, a pool, bar and tasteful cottage accommodation, as well as more rustic camping and cabins. Readers have highly recommended this place. It's just outside False Bay Park and makes a great alternative to KZN Wildlife accommodation.

St Lucia Park & Game Reserve This takes in the lake, the islands and Mapelane Nature Reserve. Lake St Lucia is a huge and meandering estuary with a narrow sea entrance. It is mainly shallow and the warm water is crowded with fish, which in turn attract huge numbers of water birds. However, the area is best known as a crocodile and hippo reserve.

St Lucia & Maputaland Marine Reserves These reserves combined cover the coastal strip and three nautical miles out to sea, running from Cape Vidal right up to Mozambique. The reserves include the world's most southerly coral reefs, especially around Sodwana Bay, and nesting sites of leatherback and loggerhead turtles.

Sodwana Bay

Sodwana Bay's appeal is in its isolation, the accessibility of Africa's most southerly coral reef, its walking trails, fishing and its magic coastal scenery. For divers, it offers warm water and some of the best marine life and visibility in South Africa.

The small **Sodwana Bay National Park** (day entry US$2.30) is on the coast east of Mkuze Game Reserve. There are some animals and the dunes and swamps are worth visiting, as are the offshore coral reefs. Over Christmas there are **turtle-viewing** tours.

For a more peaceful look at a similar ecosystem, head south to the adjoining Sodwana

Snorkelling & Diving

The coastline near Sodwana Bay is a diver's paradise. Predominantly soft coral over hard, the reef has one of the world's highest recorded numbers of tropical fish species. All of these wonders can be seen using scuba or snorkelling equipment, and excellent visibility and warm winter waters allow for year-round diving.

Popular snorkelling spots include: Cape Vidal; Two-Mile Reef off Sodwana Bay; Mabibi; and the Kosi Mouth with its famous 'aquarium', so named because of the diversity of fish. Scuba divers should head for Tenedos Shoal, between the Mlalazi River and Port Durnford, and Five-, Seven- and Nine-Mile Reefs. Courses are held at Two-Mile Reef.

Sodwana Bay Lodge specialises in NAUI diving packages (see under Sodwana Bay following).

State Forest, also known as **Ozabeni** *(entry US$2.30; camp sites US$3.50)*, which runs all the way down to Lake St Lucia. North of the lake is a prohibited area. Birdwatchers will go wild, as over 330 species have been recorded here.

At Sodwana Bay National Park, there is KZN Wildlife **accommodation** *(☎ 571 0051/2; camp sites from US$4.50, cabins per person from US$21, minimum US$61)*. There is a shop and fuel in this resort.

Sodwana Bay Lodge *(☎ 571 0095; singles/doubles with half-board from US$61/ 108)*, a private resort a few kilometres from the park on the road in, specialises in diving packages. A day's diving costs US$38 with equipment, PADI open water courses cost US$228 (see the boxed text 'Snorkelling & Diving').

Coral Divers *(☎ 571 0290; e coraldivers@ mweb.co.za; tents from US$8.50, cabins from US$16.50)* is an ideal destination for divers. PADI open water courses cost US$165. It offers pick-ups from Hluhluwe for US$11.50. Note that there's an additional nightly US$4 park fee and if you're driving, a daily US$2.30 parking fee on top of these rates.

The **MaaknJol Bar**, next door to Sodwana Bay Lodge, is the place to party in the area. It's a lively nightspot with pool tables and a disco where you're likely to find yourself knee deep in diving instructors.

Tongaland

The area north of Hluhluwe-Umfolozi Park up to the Mozambique border was once known as Tongaland, as it was settled by Mozambique's Tonga people. It's a distinct ecological zone: flat and hot with sandy soil and sluggish rivers harbouring crocodile and hippo. Forests of huge figs spread inland, especially along the Pongola River. Nearer the coast, palms grow among salt pans and thornveld.

Mkuze A small town on the N2 and the Mkuze River, Mkuze is west of a pass over the Lebombo Mountains. The road through the pass is one route to Sodwana Bay. **Ghost Mountain**, southeast of the town, was an important burial place for the Ndwandwe tribe and has a reputation for eerie occurrences.

The **Ghost Mountain Inn** *(☎ 573 1025; singles/doubles US$38/60, weekend specials per room US$34)* is an upmarket place.

Mkuzi Game Reserve This KZN Wildlife reserve *(admission per person/vehicle US$3.50/4; open sunrise-sunset daily)* lacks lions and elephants but just about every other sought-after animal is represented, as well as over 400 bird species. The hides at the pans and watering holes offer some of the best wildlife viewing in the country.

It's possible to arrange guided walks (US$6) and night drives (US$9).

There are self-contained **chalets** and a **safari camp** *(per person from US$24, minimum US$48)*. There are also **camp sites** *per person US$5.75)*.

Ndumo Game Reserve On the Mozambique border, about 100km north of Mkuze, Ndumo *(☎ 591 0032; admission per person/vehicle US$3.50/4)* has black and white rhinos, hippos, crocodiles, and antelope species, but it is the birdlife that attracts visitors. Guided walks and vehicle tours are available. There are self-catering **cottages** *(per person US$18.50)* and camping *(per person US$4.50)*.

Tembe Elephant Park South Africa's last free-ranging elephants are protected in the sandveld forests of this park *(admission per person/vehicle US$3.50/4)* on the Mozambique border. There are about 100 elephants as well as white rhinos and leopards.

SOUTH AFRICA

Getting to the park requires a 4WD. There is private **accommodation** (☎ 031-202 9090) in the park.

Coastal Forest Reserve

This reserve stretches from Mozambique in the north to Sodwana Bay in the south, and includes Lake Sibaya, Kosi Bay, Bhanga Nek, Black Rock, Rocktail Bay, Manzengwenya, Mabibi and Nine-Mile Beach. The reserve is administered by KZN Wildlife.

Lake Sibaya Nature Reserve The largest freshwater lake in South Africa is home to hippos, crocodiles and a large range of birds. The lake is popular for fishing – you can hire boats (complete with skipper) for fishing trips.

There is accommodation in cabins at **Baya Camp** (☎ 035-592 0142; US$14 per person) on the south side of the lake. The main route here is via the village of Mbazwana, south of the lake, either from Mkuze or from Mhlosinga, off the N2 north of Hluhluwe village.

Kosi Bay Nature Reserve On the coast near the Mozambique border, this remote reserve encompasses fig and raffia palm forests, mangrove swamps and freshwater lakes. There are pristine beaches and a coral reef with great snorkelling.

There are antelope species in the drier country and hippos, Zambezi sharks and some crocodiles in the lake system. A research station here studies leatherback turtles.

You can arrange a four-night guided walk around the Kosi estuarine system (US$33), stopping each night in remote camps that focus on different aspects of the reserve.

You can camp (per person US$7), hire 2-bed lodges (per person US$24).

To get here, take the Jozini turn-off from the N2 and head towards Ndumo Game Reserve, but turn hard right (east) just before Ndumo village – you might need a 4WD.

UKHAHLAMBA-DRAKENSBERG PARK

The awesome Drakensberg Range is a mountainous basalt escarpment forming the border between KwaZulu-Natal and Lesotho, and continuing a little way into Free State.

Drakensberg means Dragon Mountains; the Zulu named it *Quathlamba* (Battlement of Spears). The Zulu word is a more accurate description of the sheer and jagged escarpment, but the Afrikaans name captures something of its otherworldly atmosphere. People have lived here for thousands of years – there are many San rock-art sites to testify to this fact, yet some of the peaks and rocks were first climbed by Europeans less than 50 years ago.

Orientation The Drakensberg is usually divided into three sections, although the distinctions aren't strict. The northern Drakensberg runs from the Golden Gate Highlands National Park in the Free State (covered in that section) to the Royal Natal National Park. Harrismith (Free State) and Bergville are sizeable towns in this area.

The central Drakensberg's main feature is Giant's Castle Game Reserve, the largest national park in the area. Northwest of Giant's Castle are Cathedral Peak and wilderness areas. Bergville, Estcourt and Winterton are all adjacent to the central Drakensberg.

The southern Drakensberg runs down to the Transkei region of Eastern Cape. This area is less developed than the others but is no less spectacular. There's a huge wilderness area and the Sani Pass route into southern Lesotho. In the hills are some pleasant little towns, notably Underberg and Himeville.

Information As well as the various KZN Wildlife offices in the reserves, the **Drakensberg Tourism Association** (☎/fax 036-448 1557), which covers the northern and central Drakensberg, is based in Bergville. **Major Adventures & Tourist Association** (☎ 033-701 1628) in Underberg is another good source of information.

When to Go If you want to avoid most of the sharp frosts and, on the heights, snowfalls, you should visit in summer, although this is when most of the rain falls and views can be obscured by low cloud. However, what you lose in vistas you'll gain in atmosphere, as the stark and eerie peaks are at their best looming out of the mist.

Much of the rain falls in sudden thunderstorms so you should always carry wet-weather gear. Cold snaps are possible even in the middle of summer.

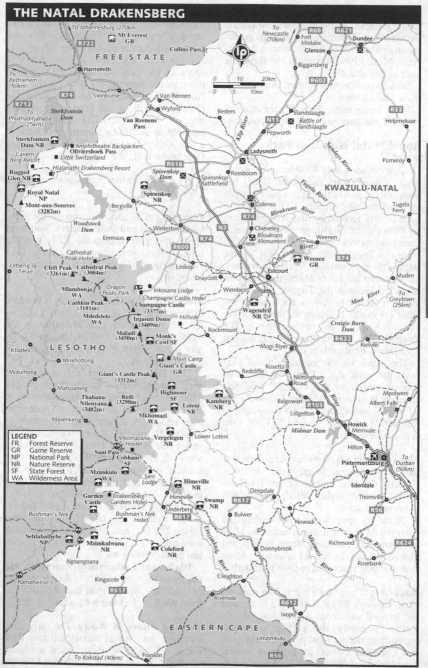

THE NATAL DRAKENSBERG

SOUTH AFRICA

LEGEND

FR	Forest Reserve
GR	Game Reserve
NP	National Park
NR	Nature Reserve
SF	State Forest
WA	Wilderness Area

Getting There & Away There is little public transport in the northern and central Drakensberg. The main jumping-off points are on or near the N3. See the entries for Estcourt, Mooi River, Winterton and Bergville later in this chapter.

Sani Pass is the best-known Drakensberg route into Lesotho.

Many roads in the Drakensberg area are unsealed and after rain some are impassable.

Royal Natal National Park
☎ 036

Despite covering only 8000 hectares, Royal Natal National Park (*admission US$1*) has some of the Drakensberg's most dramatic and accessible scenery. The southern boundary is formed by the Amphitheatre, an 8km stretch of cliff that is spectacular from below and even more so from the top. Here the Tugela Falls drop 850m in five stages (the top one often freezes in winter). Looming up behind is **Mont-aux-Sources**, so called because the Tugela, Elands and Western Khubedu Rivers rise here – the latter eventually becomes the Orange River and flows all the way to the Atlantic. The **Rugged Glen Nature Reserve** adjoins the park on the northeastern side.

The park's visitors centre is about 1km from the main gate. There's a bookstore here where you can pick up KZN Wildlife's excellent booklet *Royal Natal National Park* (US$1.25) and a good 1:20,000 topographical map *Mont-aux-Sources* (US$1.20). Fuel is available.

Flora & Fauna Broadly speaking, much of the park is covered in grassland. At lower altitudes there are valleys of small yellowwood forests. At higher altitudes grass yields to heath and scrub.

Of the six species of antelope, the most common is the mountain reedbuck. Most other animals, including otters, jackals and mongooses, are shy and not often seen. More than 200 bird species have been recorded.

Rock Art There are several San rock-art sites, although Royal Natal's are fewer and not as well preserved as those at Giant's Castle. The notable sites are Sigubudu Shelter, north of the road just past the main gate; and Cannibal Caves, on Surprise Ridge, outside the park's northern boundary.

Hiking Trails Except for the walk to Mont-aux-Sources, all of the 30-odd walks are day walks. Only 50 day visitors and 50 overnighters are allowed on *Mont-aux-Sources* each day. There are two ways to approach the summit. The easiest way is to drive to the Sentinel car park on the road from Phuthaditjhaba in the Free State (see QwaQwa Area in the Free State section later in this chapter). By doing this it's possible to get to the summit and back in a day. Otherwise, you walk up to Basotho Gate then take the road to the Sentinel car park.

There's a basic hut on the escarpment near Tugela Falls.

Climbing The park is a mecca for technical climbers and mountaineers. You must apply for a permit from the KZN Wildlife office before you attempt a climb. Take your passport if you plan to venture into Lesotho.

Places to Stay The main camp is **Tendele** (*2-bed chalets US$28*), with a variety of chalets. There are camp sites at **Mahai** (*☎ 438 6310; per person US$6.50*) and **Rugged Glen** (*per person US$5.75*) on the northeastern edge of the park.

The following places are outside the park: **Amphitheatre Backpackers** (*☎ 438 6106; e amphibackpackers@worldonline.co .za; camping US$4, dorm beds US$7, doubles from US$17*) is a great spot often recommended by readers. Commanding striking valley views in the Pocolane Nature Reserve off the Oliviershoek Pass, it's a very friendly, well-run place with a good bar and food. The owners run some excellent tours including a day trip into Lesotho.

Little Switzerland (*☎/fax 438 6220; 4-person chalets from US$49, full-board per person US$54*), just off the R74, near Oliviershoek Pass, is a large place with chalets and hotel-style rooms.

Hlalanathi Drakensberg Resort (*☎ 438 6308; camp sites US$3.50, double chalets from US$34*), off the road into Royal Natal from the R74, has camp sites and chalets.

Getting There & Away The only road that runs into Royal Natal National Park leaves off the R74, about 30km northeast of Bergville and about 5km from Olivier-

shoek Pass. (For information on the route to Mont-aux-Sources, see Hiking Trails earlier in this section).

Bergville
☎ 036

This small town is a handy jumping-off point for both the northern Drakensberg and the Midlands – if you have a car.

On the third Friday of each month there are cattle sales and this sleepy town takes on an altogether different atmosphere.

Drakensberg Inn (☎ 448 2946; e brizer@ futurenet.co.za; B&B singles/doubles US$23/ 42) in town has reasonable rooms, a restaurant, a bar and breakfast is included. Pick-ups from Ladysmith cost US$29.

The **Sanford Park Lodge** (☎ 448 1001, fax 448 1047; half-board singles/doubles around US$45/80), a few kilometres out of Bergville off the R616 to Ladysmith, has good rooms in thatched rondavels or in a big old farmhouse, and meals are included.

None of the long-distance buses run very close to Bergville. You'll have to get to Ladysmith and take a minibus taxi from there. Translux's Jo'burg/Pretoria–Umtata and Jo'burg/Pretoria–Durban services stop at Montrose. The daily Greyhound bus stops at Estcourt, Swinburne (Free State) and Ladysmith.

Minibus taxis run into the Royal Natal National Park area for about US$1.30 but few run all the way to the park entrance. The taxi rank is behind the supermarket.

Central Berg
☎ 036

In many ways the Central Berg is the most attractive part of the Drakensberg range. It also has some of the most challenging **climbs**: Cathkin Peak (3181m), Monk's Cowl (3234m) and Champagne Castle (3377m). The central area also includes the grand Giant's Castle Peak (3312m). Midway between Cathedral and Cathkin Peaks is Ndedema Gorge, where there is some fine **San rock art** to view.

The area between Cathedral Peak and Giant's Castle Game Reserve, in the Central Berg, comprises two wilderness areas: Mlambonja and Mdedelelo. Grey rheboks, klipspringers and mountain reedbucks can be found here.

Winterton This pretty little town is the gateway to the Central Berg and is not too far from the northern end.

There is a great little **museum** (Kerk St; open Wed & Fri afternoon, Sat morning) which concentrates on the geology, flora and fauna of the Drakensberg.

The **Bridge Hotel** (☎ 488 1554; e yarber@ mweb.co.za; dorm beds US$8, singles/doubles US$14/19) is a friendly local pub with some good, if basic, accommodation at the back.

Minibus taxis run to Bergville (US$2.30), Cathedral Peak State Forest (US$2.30) Estcourt (US$1) and Durban (US$11).

Cathedral Peak State Forest Cathedral Peak (3004m; admission US$1.80) lies between Royal Natal National Park and Giant's Castle Game Reserve, west of Winterton. It's part of a small chain of peaks that jut out east of the main escarpment. Cathedral Peak is a long-day's climb; no special equipment is required, although you need to be fit.

A trail begins near the hotel and the forest office is also nearby. Hikes of more than one day cost US$3.50 per person per night.

The KZN Wildlife has **camp sites** (☎ 488 1880; per person US$3.50). The **Cathedral Peak Hotel** (☎/fax 488 1888; doubles with half-board from US$102), some 42km from Winterton, is close to the escarpment. The hotel will collect you from Estcourt.

Monk's Cowl State Forest (Champagne Castle) The **office** (☎ 468 1103; admission US$1.80; camp sites per person US$4.50, overnight hiking per person US$3.50) is 3km beyond the Champagne Castle Hotel.

The **Inkosana Lodge** (☎ 468 1202; dorm beds US$8.50, doubles US$23, suites US$30) has very good information about hiking and is a useful base for treks. All rates include breakfast and pick-up from Winterton.

Dragon Peaks Park (☎ 468 1031, fax 468 1104; camping per person US$6.50) is a Club Caravelle resort with the usual maze of prices and minimum stays that depend on seasons and school holidays.

The **Champagne Castle Hotel** (☎/fax 468 1063; e champagnecastle@futurenet.co .za; per person with full board from US$47) is one of the best-known resorts and it's well located, right in the mountains at the end of the R600 to Champagne Castle. There are cottages, rondavels and units.

Giant's Castle Game Reserve

This reserve (admission US$2.30) was established in 1903. It's in high country: the lowest point is 1300m and the highest tooth of the Drakensberg in the reserve is the 3409m Injasuti Dome. With huge forest reserves to the north and south and Lesotho's barren plateau over the escarpment to the west, it's a rugged and remote place, despite the number of visitors it attracts.

Limited supplies (including fuel) are available at Main Camp and there's a basic shop near the White Mountain Lodge, but otherwise the nearest shops are in Estcourt, 50km away. There are three main areas, as well as trail huts and caves for hikers. Note that nowhere in the park are you allowed to cut or collect firewood, so bring a stove. Litter must be carried out, not burned or buried.

Flora & Fauna The reserve is mainly grassland, wooded gorges, high cliffs with small forests in the valleys, and some protea savanna. In spring there are many wildflowers.

The reserve is home to 12 species of antelope and altogether there are about 60 mammal species. The rare lammergeyer, or bearded vulture (Gypaetus barbatus), which is found only in the Drakensberg, nests in the reserve. **Lammergeyer Hide** is the best place to see the vultures. The fee for using the hide is US$13 per person (minimum US$34), and you must book.

Rock Art The reserve is rich in San rock art, with at least 50 sites. It is thought that San people still lived here at the turn of the 19th and 20th centuries.

The two main sites are Main Cave and Battle Cave (admission US$1.80). Main Cave (open 9am-3pm weekends & holidays) is 2km south of Main Camp.

On weekdays you have to go with a tour (US$4), which departs from the camp office at 9am and 3pm. Battle Cave is near Injasuti and must be visited on a tour, which leaves the camp daily at 9am. It's an 8km walk each way.

Hiking Trails There are many hiking trails, most of them loops from either Main Camp or Injasuti or one-way walks to the mountain huts. There are also walks between huts, so you can string together several two-day hikes, but you need to prebook the huts through the KZN Wildlife. The reserve's booklet Giant's Castle Game Reserve gives details and has a basic map of the trails.

Before setting out on a long walk you must fill in the rescue register; if you plan to go higher than 2300m you must report to the warden.

Places to Stay There's a range of accommodation at **Main Camp** (double bungalows from US$30), but you can't camp here.

Hillside (☎ 0363-24435; admission US$0.90, camp sites per person US$2.50), in the reserve's northeastern corner, is a long way from Main Camp, let alone the escarpment.

Injasuti Hutted Camp (☎ 036-431 7848; admission US$1.80, camp sites per person US$5, 2-bed safari camp per person US$9) is in a pleasant and secluded spot on the northern side of the reserve.

Getting There & Away The best way into Main Camp is via the dirt road from Mooi River, although the last section can be impassable when wet. It's also possible to get here by following the route for Hillside, taking the Hillside turn-off. However, until the road is sealed don't attempt it in wet weather.

To get to Hillside, take the Giant's Castle road from Estcourt, signposted at the Anglican church. Turn left at the White Mountain Lodge junction and after 4km turn right onto the Hillside road. Take the right turn at the two minor intersections that follow. Minibuses run between Estcourt and Mahlutshini – ask to be let off at the signposted Hillside Camp junction. From the junction it's about a 5km walk to the camp site.

Infrequent minibuses run between Estcourt and the villages near the main entrance (KwaDlamini, Mahlutshini, KwaMankonjane), but these are still several kilometres from Main Camp.

Injasuti is accessible from the township of Loskop, northwest of Estcourt; the road is signposted.

Southern Drakensberg Wilderness Areas

☎ 033

Four state forests – Highmoor, Mkhomazi, Cobham and Garden Castle – run from Giant's Castle south beyond Bushman's

Nek, to meet Lesotho's Sehlabathebe National Park. The big Mkhomazi Wilderness Area and the Mzimkulu Wilderness Area are in these state forests.

The wilderness areas are close to the escarpment, with the Kamberg, Loteni, Vergelegen and Mzimkulwana Nature Reserves to the east of them, except for a spur of Mzimkulwana that follows the Umkomazana River (and the road) down from Sani Pass, separating the two wilderness areas.

The wilderness areas are administered by KZN Wildlife. Entry to each is US$1.80 and hiking costs US$3.50 per night.

Kamberg Nature Reserve Southeast of Giant's Castle and a little away from the main escarpment area, this small KZN Wildlife reserve *(2232 hectares; admission US$1.80)* has a number of antelope species. The country in the Drakensberg foothills is pretty, but it's trout fishing that attracts most visitors.

Hiking costs US$3.50 per night. The cheapest accommodation is in **rest huts** *(per person US$20)*.

Take either road (west off the N3) from Rosetta or Nottingham Road.

Highmoor Part of the Mkhomazi Wilderness Area is in **Highmoor** *(admission US$1.80)*. The **forest office** *(☎ 033-263 6444)* is off the road between Rosetta and Kamberg; turn off to the south just past the sign to Kamberg, 31km from Rosetta. Camp sites with limited facilities cost US$4.50.

Loteni Nature Reserve This reserve *(admission US$1.80)* has a **Settlers Museum** and good day walks. There are **camp sites** *(☎ 702 0540; sites US$4.50)* and a variety of other **accommodation** *(from US$10)*. Overnight hiking costs US$3.50 per night.

The access road runs from the hamlet of Lower Loteni, about 30km northeast of Himeville or 65km southwest of Nottingham Road. The roads aren't great and heavy rain can close them.

Mkhomazi This is the southern part of Mkhomazi Wilderness Area. The 1200-hectare **Vergelegen Nature Reserve** *(admission US$1.80)* is along this road. There are no established camp sites. The turn-off to the state forest is 44km from Nottingham Road,

off the Lower Loteni/Sani Pass road, at the Mzinga River. From here it's another 2km.

Cobham The **Mzimkulu Wilderness Area** and the **Mzimkulwana Nature Reserve** are both in Cobham. The **forest office** *(☎ 702 0831; admission US$1.80)* is about 15km from Himeville on the D7 and it's a good place to get information on the many hiking trails in the area. There are basic **camp sites** *(with overnight hiking US$3.50)*.

Garden Castle State Forest The reserve's **headquarters** *(☎ 701 1823)* are 3km further on from the Drakensberg Gardens Resort Hotel, 30km west of Underberg. No camping is allowed at the headquarters, but there is a hut nearby on the Giant's Cup Hiking Trail (see later in this section), which you can use if it's not fully booked by hikers. Otherwise, there's a camp site at the **Drakensberg Gardens Resort Hotel**, or if you walk at least 3km into the reserve, pitching a tent counts as **wilderness camping** *(US$3.50)*.

Sani Pass This steep route into Lesotho, the highest pass in South Africa and the only road between KwaZulu-Natal and Lesotho, is one of the most scenic parts of the Drakensberg. At the top of the pass, just beyond the Lesotho border crossing, is Sani Top chalet (for details see the Sani Pass section of the Lesotho chapter). Various operators run 4WD trips up to the chalet – contact the information centres in the nearby towns of Underberg and Himeville.

Khotso Horse Trails *(☎ 701 1502)* has rides and treks in the area and has been highly recommended by readers.

There are two budget places at the bottom of the pass. **Sani Lodge** *(☎ 702 1401; camp sites US$3, dorm beds US$4.50, doubles US$11.50)*, 19km from Underberg, is small and quiet. This place is run by Russel Suchet, a good source of information on the many hiking (one-day or longer) possibilities that exist in this area.

Mkomazana *(☎ 702 0340/313; camping US$4, dorm beds US$4.50, rooms from US$11.50)*, another 5km along the road, is much larger. It's an old farm and in a beautiful spot – the only privately owned property in KwaZulu-Natal in a national park – and there's good walking in the area.

SOUTH AFRICA

Giant's Cup Hiking Trail The five-day, 60km Giant's Cup Trail runs from Sani Pass to Bushman's Nek and is one of the great walks of South Africa. It's designed so that any reasonably fit person can walk it, so it's very popular. Early booking (up to nine months ahead, through the KZN Wildlife) is advisable. The usual precautions for the Drakensberg apply – expect extremely severe cold snaps at any time of the year.

Camping is not permitted; there's accommodation in shared **huts** *(per person US$7)*. No firewood is available so you'll need a stove and fuel. Sani Lodge (see its listing under Sani Pass earlier in this section) is near the trailhead; arrange for the lodge to pick you up from Himeville or Underberg.

Bushman's Nek This is one of the border crossings into Lesotho. There are hiking trails up into the escarpment from here, including to Lesotho's Sehlabathebe National Park. You can walk in or hire a horse and trot across the border.

The **Bushman's Nek Hotel** *(☎ 701 1460; half-board rooms high season US$21 per person, chalets from US$22.50)*, east of the border, has rooms and four-person self-catering chalets.

Underberg
☎ 033

This quiet little town in the foothills of the southern Drakensberg is the centre of a farming community. The Underberg hiking club is a good source of information on the excellent hiking in the area. **Major Adventures & Tourist Information** *(☎ 701 1628)* on the main street next to the Underberg Inn is also worth a visit. Ask here about Sani Pass Day Tours (US$28). This office also books **Khotso Horse Trails** *(☎ 033-701 1502/082 412 5540; US$6.40 an hour, US$34 full-day, US$80 two days)*.

The **Underberg Inn** *(☎ 701 1412; singles/doubles with breakfast US$20/32)* is archaic but pleasant. **Mike's Restaurant** on the northern edge of town is recommended by locals.

Sani Pass Carriers *(☎ 701 1017)* runs a shuttle bus daily between Underberg, Kokstad (US$8.50) and Pietermaritzberg (US$11.50).

Minibus taxis run between Underberg and Himeville (US$0.40) and Pietermaritzberg (US$2.30), and occasionally to the Sani Pass Hotel.

The main routes to Underberg and nearby Himeville are from Pietermaritzburg on the R617 and from Kokstad on the R626, but it's possible to drive here from the northeast via Nottingham Road on an unsealed road.

Himeville
☎ 033

Not far from Underberg, this smaller but nicer town is above 1500m so winters are coolish.

There's a KZN Wildlife **camping ground** *(sites per person US$5)* in Himeville Nature Reserve *(admission US$1.20)* not far from town. The **Himeville Arms** *(☎/fax 702 1305; e himevillearms@futurenet.co.za; singles/doubles from US$28/49)* has good rooms, and breakfast is included.

Minibus taxis to Underberg (US$0.40) and twice-daily KZT buses to Pietermaritzburg are about the only regular transport from Himeville.

THE MIDLANDS

The Midlands run northwest from Durban to Estcourt and skirt Zululand to the northeast. This is mainly farming country with not a lot to interest visitors. The main town is Pietermaritzburg – KwaZulu-Natal's capital.

West of Pietermaritzburg there is pretty, hilly country, with horse studs and plenty of European trees. The various art galleries and potteries in this area are linked in a tourist route called the *Midlands Meander*. Pick up a brochure from one of the larger tourist offices.

Pietermaritzburg
☎ 033

After the defeat of the Zulu at the Battle of Blood River, the Voortrekkers began to establish their republic of Natal. Pietermaritzburg (PMB) was named in honour of leader Pieter Mauritz Retief, and was founded in 1838 as the capital. Here in 1841 the Boers built their Church of the Vow to honour the Blood River promise (see History in the Facts about South Africa section earlier in this chapter). The British annexed Natal in

PIETERMARITZBURG

PLACES TO STAY
20 Imperial Protea Hotel
21 Ngena Backpackers Lodge
22 City Royal Hotel

PLACES TO EAT
8 Ristorante Da Vinci
17 Upper Crust Patisserie

OTHER
1 Islamia Mosque
2 Hindu Temple
3 Hindu Temple
4 Voortrekker Museum
5 Modern Memorial Church
6 Elephant Pub & Grill
7 Crowded House
9 Old Colonial Buildings
10 Standard Bank
11 First National Bank
12 Statue of Gandhi
13 City Hall
14 Long-Distance Buses; City Buses
15 Publicity Association
16 Tatham Art Gallery (Old Supreme Court) & Cafe
18 Natal Provincial Administration Collection
19 Natal Museum
23 McDonald's Plaza; Greyhound Bus Stop; HDI Computers
24 Bus Station; KZT Buses
25 Minibus Taxis to Underberg
26 Minibus Taxis to Ladysmith
27 Minibus Taxis to Johannesburg
28 Macrorie House Museum

SOUTH AFRICA

1843 and retained Pietermaritzburg as the capital.

PMB rightly bills itself as 'the heritage city', as it has numerous historic buildings and a British colonial air.

Orientation The central grid of PMB contains most places of interest and is easy to get around. The northern end of the city, beyond Retief St, is a largely Indian commercial district. North of here is the Indian residential area of Northdale. To the southwest of the city is Edendale, the black dormitory suburb.

Just to confuse attempts at orientation, there were unspecified plans to change a number of major street names in PMB at the time of research, so beware!

Information The helpful **publicity association** (☎ 345 1348; e info@pmbtourism.co.za; 177 Commercial Rd; open 8am-5pm Mon-Fri, 8am-3pm Sat) is on the corner of Longmarket St.

HDI Computers (☎ 345 1133; Shop 4, McDonald's Plaza, 251 Commercial Rd; open 8am-5pm Mon-Fri, 8am-12.30pm Sat), tucked behind McDonald's, has Internet access.

KwaZulu-Natal Nature Conservation (KZN Wildlife) Office This is the office (☎ 845 1000; Queen Elizabeth Park; open 8am-4pm Mon-Fri) where you book most of the accommodation and walks for KwaZulu-Natal parks; it's a long way northwest of the town centre. You can make phone bookings with a credit card but it's better to visit to

collect the literature and chat to some of the knowledgeable and friendly staff.

To get to the office, head out to the Old Howick Rd (Commercial Rd) and after some kilometres you'll come to a roundabout – don't go straight ahead (to the Hilton), but take the road veering to the right. This road has a very small sign directing you to 'QE Park', which is 2km further on. Some minibus taxis running to the Hilton pass this roundabout.

Things to See & Do Two of the town's best features are its avenues of huge old jacaranda trees, and the maze of narrow pedestrian lanes running between Church and Longmarket Sts off the mall. There are a number of colonial-era buildings. The massive red brick city hall *(cnr Church St & Commercial Rd)*, is a good example, as is the old supreme court across the road.

The **Macrorie House Museum** *(cnr Loop & Pine Sts; open 9am-1pm Tues-Fri, 11am-4pm Mon)* displays items related to early British settlement. The **Natal Museum** *(☎ 345 1404; Loop St; open 9am-4pm Mon-Fri, 2pm-5pm Sat; admission US$0.50)* has a range of displays, including African ethnography. It's southwest of Commercial Rd.

The **Tatham Art Gallery** *(open 10am-6pm Tues-Sun)* is housed in the old supreme court. It has a collection of French and English 19th- and early 20th-century works. There's also a great café/restaurant (see Places to Eat).

The **Voortrekker Museum** *(☎ 394 6834; cnr Longmarket & Boshoff Sts; admission US$0.40; open 9am-4pm Mon-Fri, 9am-1pm Sat)* in the Church of the vow, built in 1841 in thanks at the Boer victory at Blood River. Afrikaner icons on display include Retief's prayer book.

The **Natal Provincial Administration Collection** *(☎ 453201; 330 Longmarket St)* has some of the finest examples of indigenous art, including beadwork, pottery and weaving. It is open by appointment only.

Places to Stay Hardly central, the **Msundzi Caravan Park** *(☎ 386 5342; 50 Cleland Rd; camp sites US$4)* is 5km from the train station. Head southeast on Commercial Rd, which becomes Durban Rd after the creek. Go left into Blackburn Road across the freeway then take the first right.

Ngena Backpackers Lodge *(☎ 345 6237; e ngena@sai.co.za; 293 Burger St; dorm beds US$9, doubles without/with bathroom US$25/30)* is pricey but well located. It's spotless and stylishly decorated, more like a guesthouse.

City Royal Hotel *(☎ 394 7072, fax 394 7080; 301 Burger St; singles/doubles US$29/37)* has modern, attractively furnished rooms, a restaurant, bar and secure parking. It's also quiet and the staff are friendly.

Imperial Protea Hotel *(☎ 342 6551; imperial@iafrica.com; 224 Loop St; singles/doubles US$63/69, specials from US$44)* is a pleasant enough place with secure parking, but it's expensive given that the fittings are worn and standards seem to be sliding. It needs a refit but will do if the City Royal Hotel is full.

The publicity association provides a full list of the many B&Bs in the area.

Places to Eat Near the long-distance bus stop, **Upper Crust Patisserie** *(Longmarket St)* is a reasonably good bakery.

Tatham Art Gallery Cafe *(1st fl, Tatham Art Gallery; open 10am-6pm Tues-Sun)* serves coffee, snacks and great home-made lunches including some good vegie dishes.

Ristorante da Vinci *(117 Commercial Rd)* is a cheap, decent Italian lunch and dinner place.

Entertainment With a small but very popular bar, **Ristorante da Vinci** (see under Places to Eat earlier) is open until very late.

Elephant Pub & Grill *(80 Commercial Rd)* is another popular watering hole.

Crowded House *(99 Commercial Rd; open 8pm-4am)* has a large, although not exclusive, student following.

Getting There & Away Transport options to/from PMB include the following:

Bus Greyhound, Intercape and Translux buses stop on Durban Rd. Translux goes to Bloemfontein (US$25, 8½ hours) via Bethlehem (US$18.50, 6¼ hours), and Jo'burg/Pretoria (US$20, 8¾ hours) via Harrismith (US$16.50, three hours). Greyhound has several daily services between Durban and Jo'burg/Pretoria via PMB, Ladysmith and Newcastle. The Durban–Kimberley run also stops in PMB. Intercape runs to

Cape Town (US$42, 20½ hours) Monday, Wednesday, Friday and Saturday. Book Translux and Greyhound at the publicity association (see Information earlier in this section).

Minibus Taxi Most minibus taxi ranks are near the train station. Fares include: Durban (US$2.30); Estcourt (US$2.30); Ladysmith (US$4.50); Newcastle (US$5.75); and Jo'burg (US$10.50). Other taxis depart from Market Square (behind the publicity association), and you might find taxis running to Umtata (Eastern Cape) and Maseru (Lesotho) here.

Train The weekly *Trans Oranje* (Durban–Cape Town) and the daily *Trans Natal* (Durban–Jo'burg/Pretoria) stop here (for more information, see the main Getting Around section earlier in this chapter).

Car If you're driving and heading north, the R103, running through pretty country between Howick and Mooi River is a picturesque alternative to the N3.

Avis (☎ *0861-102 1111*), **Budget** (☎ *0861-016622*) and **Imperial** (☎ *0800-131000*) have agents in Pietermaritzburg.

Getting Around The main rank for city-area buses is in the area behind the publicity association office on the corner of Longmarket St and Commercial Rd.

For a taxi call **Junior** (☎ *394 5454*) or **Unique** (☎ *391 1238*).

Mooi River
☎ 033

Mooi River is a nondescript town, but the surrounding countryside, especially to the west, is worth exploring. It's horse-stud country on rolling land dotted with old European trees.

Riverbank (☎ *263 2144*) is a caravan park in town. The **Argyle Hotel** (☎ *263 1106; singles/doubles US$17.50/30*) is inexpensive and was building backpacker accommodation at the time of research.

However, it's the country guesthouses in the area that visitors come for. One of the better-known places is **Granny Mouse Country House** (☎ *234 4071; rooms from US$39 per person*), near the village of Balgowan, south of Mooi River.

Greyhound buses between Durban and Jo'burg/Pretoria stop at the big truck stop on the Rosetta road near the N3, 1km from the centre.

The *Trans Oranje* and *Trans Natal* trains stop here. Book tickets at the goods office, across the tracks from the old station.

Estcourt
☎ 036

Estcourt is close to the central Drakensberg resorts and Giant's Castle Game Reserve, and it's on the Durban–Jo'burg/Pretoria bus route. It also has good train and minibus taxi connections.

About 30km northeast of Estcourt is the **Weenen Game Reserve** (☎ *354 7013; admission US$1.20/15 per person/vehicle*), which has black and white rhinos, buffaloes, giraffes and several antelope species. There are two good walking trails.

The municipal **caravan park** (☎ *352 3000; Lorne St*) is inexpensive and close to the town centre. **Val-U-Lodge** (☎ *352 6760; 86 Harding St; rooms from US$15*) has bland but very cheap rooms.

Greyhound buses leave from the information centre on the main street, as do Translux buses on the Durban-Jo'burg/Pretoria route.

Both the *Trans Oranje* and the daily *Trans Natal* trains stop here.

The main minibus taxi rank is at the bottom of Phillips St, downhill from the post office. Taxis beside the post office are for the local area only. Destinations include: Winterton (US$1); Ladysmith (US$1.80); Pietermaritzburg (US$2.30); Durban (US$3.50); and Jo'burg (US$6.40).

THUKELA

History buffs will be happy in Thukela, in the northwest of KwaZulu-Natal. The area is often described as the Battlefields Route as some of the more important conflicts in South Africa's recent history took place in the area. They include the Siege of Ladysmith, the Battle of Spioenkop, the defeat of the British by the Zulu at Isandlwana, the heroic Defence of Rorke's Drift and the battles of Majuba Hill and Blood River.

Colenso
☎ 036

There are several Anglo-Boer War battlefields near Colenso, a small and soporific

town about 20km south of Ladysmith. Colenso was the British base during the Relief of Ladysmith, and there is a **museum** relating to the Battle of Colenso (15 December 1899). The museum is in the toll house adjacent to the bridge. You can pick up the keys from the owners of the **Battlefields Lodge** *(☎ 422 2242/082 422 8634; 75 Sir George St; per person with breakfast US$12.50)*, which also runs tours and has good, secluded rooms and a swimming pool.

Spioenkop Nature Reserve
This 6000-hectare KZN Wildlife reserve *(admission US$1.20)* is handily positioned between most of the area's battlefield sites and is not too far from the Drakensberg for day trips. Animals in the two small wildlife reserves include white rhinos, giraffes and zebras. There's a swimming pool, and horse riding and tours of the Spioenkop battlefield are available.

There's a range of overnight options at **iPika** *(camp sites per person US$5, 4-bed bush camp per person US$15, 6-bed chalets per person US$11)*. Book these on ☎ 036-488 1578.

Ladysmith
☎ 036
Ladysmith (not to be confused with Ladismith in the Western Cape) was named after the wife of Cape governor Sir Harry Smith. The town achieved fame during the 1899–1902 Anglo-Boer War, when it was besieged by Boer forces for 118 days.

The **information office** *(☎ 637 2992; Murchison St; open Mon-Fri)* is in the town hall. Ask here about guided tours of the battlefields.

Things to See & Do The good **Siege Museum** *(open 9am-4pm Mon-Fri, 9am-1pm Sat)* is next to the town hall in the Market House (built in 1884), which was used to store rations during the siege. There's also a small information office here with the same opening times.

Outside the town hall are two guns, **Castor** and **Pollux**, used by the British in the defence of Ladysmith. Nearby is a replica of **Long Tom**, a Boer gun capable of heaving a shell 10km.

Across the river on the west side of town (there's a footbridge) is a **Sufi Mosque**, built by the Muslim community, which has been in Ladysmith almost since the town's inception.

South of town, near the junction of the N11 and R103, is an area generally known as **Platrand** (or Wagon Hill). There is a monument to the Boers who died trying to wrest Wagon Hill from the British on 6 January 1900.

Places to Stay You'll find the **Municipal Caravan Park** *(☎ 637 6050)* is on the northern side of town; follow Poort Rd over the hill, where it becomes the Harrismith road.

Near the town hall, on Murchison St, there are two venerable old hotels: the **Crown** *(☎ 637 2266; B&B singles/doubles US$32/25)* and the **Royal** *(☎/fax 637 2176; e royalhotel@ intekom.co.za; singles/doubles US$30/50)*.

The information office has details of farmstays and B&Bs. Prices start at around US$25 a double.

Getting There & Away Translux buses leave from the train station and run to Durban (US$9, 3½ hours) and Bloemfontein (US$16.50, 6¾ hours). Greyhound has daily services to Jo'burg/Pretoria and Durban. Book at the Shell service station on the corner of Murchison and King Sts, or at Destinations Travel (☎ 631 0831).

Both the *Trans Oranje* and the daily *Trans Natal* trains stop here.

The main minibus taxi rank is south of the centre near the corner of Queen and Lyell Sts. Taxis for Harrismith and Jo'burg are nearby on Alexandra St. Destinations include: Harrismith (US$2.20); Durban (US$6.40); and Jo'burg (US$8).

Majuba Hill
The first Anglo-Boer War ended abruptly 40km north of Newcastle, with the British defeat at **Majuba Hill** in 1881. The site has been restored and a map is available; there is a small entry fee.

Peace negotiations took place at **O'Neill's Cottage** in the foothills near Majuba. The cottage, used as a hospital during the battle, has been restored and has a **photographic display** *(open daily)*.

Isandlwana, Rorke's Drift & Fugitive's Drift
☎ 034
Don't miss **Isandlwana**, a haunting place of slaughter at the base of a sphinx-like

rock, where individual whitewashed stone cairns pepper the valley. On 22 January 1879 King Cetshwayo's Zulu army caught the British army napping and destroyed it in the first major engagement of the Anglo-Zulu war.

The randomly spaced positions of the cairns gives an idea of the panic and the ragged butchery that must have occurred. The **Isandlwana museum** *(St Vincent's)*, with artefacts taken from the battlefield, is just outside the site.

A small but extraordinary victory was wrested from the jaws of this bloody defeat at **Rorke's Drift**, 42km from Dundee, where 100 British soldiers held off 4000 Zulu, winning 11 Victoria Crosses for their efforts. There is a good museum, a trail around the battlefield, several memorials and the ELC Zulu craft centre. The rugs and tapestries woven here are world-renowned and not cheap.

About 10km south of Rorke's Drift is **Fugitive's Drift**. Two British officers were killed here attempting to prevent the Queen's Colours from falling into Zulu hands.

A number of companies offer tours of the battlefields (see Places to Stay) and it really is worth going on one if you have the time, especially to hear the detail of the incredible defence of Rourke's Drift.

Places to Stay About 20km east of Isandl-wana, the **Babanango Valley Lodge** *(☎ 350 062, fax 350160; singles/doubles US$124/195)* is outside Babanango town in a lovely setting. You need a car to get there: turn north off the R68 about 4km west of Babanango and continue on for about 12km (stay left at the fork).

Rattray's Historical Lodges *(☎ 034-642 1843; e fugdrift@trustnet.co.za)* operates three lodges in the area and runs some good tours to the battlefields.

Getting There & Away The battlefields are southeast of Dundee. Isandlwana is about 70km from Dundee, off the R68; Rorke's Drift is about 40km from Dundee, also accessible from the R68 or the R33 (the R33 turn-off is 13km south of Dundee). The road to Isandlwana is sealed but the roads to Rorke's Drift and Fugitive's Drift can be dusty and rough.

Blood River Monument

For information on the Battle of Blood River, see History in the Facts about South Africa section earlier in this chapter. The Blood River battlefield is marked by a full-scale re-creation of the 64-wagon *laager* (wagon circle) in bronze.

The cairn of stones was built by the Boers after the battle to mark the centre of their *laager*. The monument is 20km southeast of the R33.

Mpumalanga

Mpumalanga takes in both highveld and lowveld, with the dramatic Klein Drakensberg escarpment in between.

Down on the lowveld the world-famous Kruger National Park is bordered by a host of luxurious private game reserves to the west and Mozambique to the east.

Mpumalanga was once part of the Transvaal (it was called Eastern Transvaal for the first couple of years of the new South Africa). For more information on history, see the Gauteng and Limpopo sections.

EASTERN LOWVELD
☎ 013

To the north the lowveld is hot – extremely so in summer, when there are storms and high humidity. Further south the temperatures are more moderate and the scrubby terrain gives way to lush subtropical vegetation around Nelspruit and the Crocodile River. South of here, around Barberton, the dry country resumes with a vengeance – gold prospectors last century dubbed it the Valley of Death.

Much of the eastern lowveld is taken up by Kruger National Park and the private game reserves that border it.

Kruger National Park

This park is one of the biggest, oldest and quite simply one of the best wildlife parks in the world. A visit here is likely to be the highlight of your trip to South Africa.

The park boasts the greatest variety of animals of any park in Southern Africa (and perhaps the whole of Africa), with lions, leopards, elephants, buffaloes and rhinos (the Big Five) as well as cheetahs, giraffes, hippos and many varieties of antelope and smaller animals.

Altogether, these include 147 mammals, more than 500 birds, 114 reptiles and 49 species of fish.

Originally known as Sabie Game Reserve it was established in 1898 by the president of the South African Republic (ZAR), Paul Kruger. Since renamed and much expanded, it's now nearly two million hectares in extent (about the size of Wales) and forms part of a newer and even larger entity, the Great Limpopo Transfrontier Park (see the boxed text 'Africa's New Superpark').

Unlike some Southern Africa parks, Kruger does not offer a true wilderness experience (although the guided walking trails here come close) as the infrastructure is too highly developed and organised. However, this means you can explore at leisure,

without having to depend on organised tours or guides, although many of these are often well worthwhile.

Orientation Kruger stretches almost 350km along the Mozambique border and has an average width of 60km. There are eight entrance gates: Malelane and Crocodile Bridge on the southern edge, accessible from the N4 (the quickest direct route from Jo'burg); the Numbi and Paul Kruger Gates, accessible from White River and Hazyview (turn off the N4 just before Nelspruit); Orpen, which is convenient if you have been exploring Blyde River; Phalaborwa, accessible from Pietersburg/ Polokwane and Tzaneen; Punda Maria, accessible from Louis Trichardt; and Pafuri,

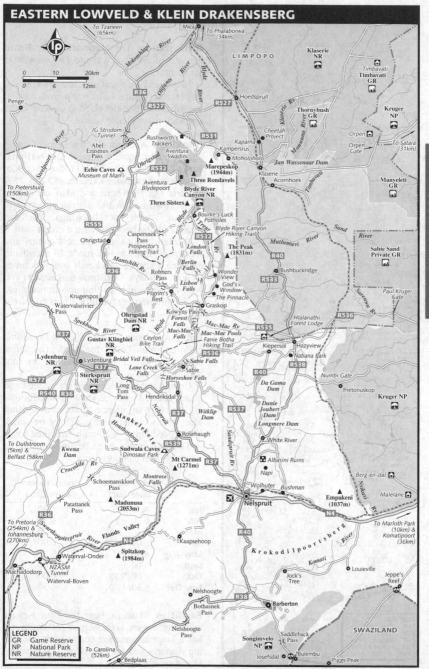

EASTERN LOWVELD & KLEIN DRAKENSBERG

SOUTH AFRICA

LEGEND
GR Game Reserve
NP National Park
NR Nature Reserve

KRUGER NATIONAL PARK

accessible from the Venda region of Limpopo Province.

Information The **National Parks Board** has an informative website (W *www.parks-sa.co.za*).

Maps and publications are sold at the larger rest camps. The map and animal identification booklet (US$4) on sale at the entrance gates is also useful.

Bookings Accommodation (except camp sites) can be booked through the **National Parks Board** (☎ *012-428 9111, fax 343 0905;* e *reservations@parks-sa.co.za; PO Box 787, Pretoria 0001*). There are also offices in Cape Town and at the Tourist Junction in Durban, which take bookings. You can make a phone booking with a credit card.

Written applications for rest camps and wilderness trails can be made 13 months in advance. Except at weekends and peak times (school holidays, Christmas and Easter) you won't have trouble getting accommodation. Night and morning wildlife drives cost from US$14.

Entry Admission is US$3.50/1.80 for adults/children, plus US$3 for a car (bicycles, motorcycles and open vehicles are not admitted).

Camps and entrance gates are opened and closed at fixed times, as shown in the following list. It is an offence to arrive at a camp after it has closed, and you may be fined. With speed limits of 50km/h on sealed roads and 40km/h on dirt, it can be time-consuming to travel from camp to camp.

	gates/camps open (am)	gates/camps close (pm)
Jan	4.30/5.00	6.30
Feb	5.30	6.30
Mar	5.30	6.00
Apr	6.00	6.00
May–Aug	6.30	5.30
Sept	6.00	6.00
Oct	6.00/5.30	6.00
Nov–Dec	5.30/4.30	6.30

Facilities Skukuza, near the Paul Kruger and Numbi gates, is the biggest rest camp and has a large information centre with interesting displays and the exceptional Stevenson-Hamilton library.

Africa's New Superpark

If you think the Kruger National Park is big and impressive, just look at the plans for Africa's new superpark. Known as the Great Limpopo Transfrontier Park, it will be formed by the merger of Kruger with adjacent conservation areas in Mozambique and Zimbabwe covering an initial 35,000 sq km, and ultimately a staggering 100,000 sq km.

The park is slowly coming into existence – the final agreements were signed in 2002 – but it's a huge and complex project aimed at improving the region's ecosystems, supporting greater populations of large mammals and hopefully re-establishing old migration patterns.

Some of the fencing dividing the Kruger Park and Mozambique has already come down and small numbers of animals have been moved from the Kruger Park into Mozambique, but it will take a few years before the park is running as intended.

When it's complete, visitors should be able to follow migrating elephants across international boundaries with minimal fuss and enjoy new attractions such as bird-rich tropical wetlands, lake cruises, and even richer wildlife viewing.

Before then, linking roads, bridges and wildlife corridors need to be established and local populations informed and involved. A number of problems, such as the cross-border spread of animal TB (caught for example by buffaloes in Mozambique from water infected by humans and passed up the food chain to lions in the Kruger) also need to be solved.

If the superpark scheme comes off as planned, however, it will be a major coup for conservation that will open exciting new areas of the region to visitors.

SOUTH AFRICA

There's an AA workshop for vehicle repairs, a doctor, a bank, a post office and photo-developing services. Letaba and Satara rest camps also have workshops, and there are staffed information centres at Letaba and Berg-en-dal. All camps have telephones and first-aid centres.

The larger camps have restaurants and shops stocking a range of essentials (including cold beer and wine) and maybe some fresh fruit and veg. If you are planning to self-cater, consider stocking up outside the park. The food in the restaurants does not have a great reputation for flavour or value.

Climate Summers are very hot with violent thunderstorms, and temperatures average 30°C. The park is in a summer rainfall area, with the rainfall generally decreasing as you go north. In winter, nights can be cold (sometimes falling below 0°C) and the days are pleasant.

Fauna Kruger takes in a variety of ecosystems. Most mammals are distributed throughout the park, but some show a preference for particular areas.

Impalas, buffaloes, Burchell's zebras, blue wildebeests, kudus, waterbucks, baboons, vervet monkeys, cheetahs, leopards and smaller predators are all widely distributed. Birdlife is prolific along the rivers, and north of the Luvuvhu River at the park's northern end.

The southwestern corner between the Olifants and Crocodile Rivers, where the rainfall is highest (700mm a year), is thickly wooded. It's favoured by white rhinos and buffaloes, but less so by antelopes and, therefore, by predators.

The grazing-rich eastern section south of the Olifants River, on the plains around Satara and south to the Crocodile River, attracts large populations of impalas, zebras, wildebeests, giraffes and black rhinos. Predators, particularly lions, prey on the impalas, zebras and blue wildebeests.

North of Olifants River the rainfall drops below 500mm and the veld's dominant tree is mopane, a favourite in the diet of elephants, which are common north of the Olifants.

Perhaps the most interesting area is in the far north around Punda Maria and Pafuri. This has a higher rainfall than the mopane country and supports a wider variety of plants (baobabs are particularly noticeable) and a higher density and greater variety of animals.

Wilderness Trails The seven guided trails offer a chance to walk through the park with knowledgeable armed guides. You'll see few big animals than in a car (you'll cover less ground and many animals will avoid your scent) but you'll learn, feel, hear, smell and

touch many things you wouldn't on a wild-life drive. Most trails last two days and three nights, departing on Sunday or Wednesday.

Accommodation is in huts and you don't need to provide food or equipment (although it is an idea to bring your own beer and wine).

Wilderness trails cost US$195 and must be booked well in advance. See Bookings earlier in this section for information.

Places to Stay Most visitors stay in **rest camps**. These have a wide range of facilities. Their restaurants are adequate. Most have shops, phones and fuel. The accommodation varies, but usually includes huts and self-contained cottages. Camping facilities are also available at most camps.

Bushveld camps are smaller, more remote camps without shops and restaurants, and **private camps** cater for groups which must take the entire camp. Bookings are essential for both types.

All huts and cottages are supplied with bedding and towels. Most have air-con or fans, and fridges. If you are staying in accommodation with a communal kitchen you have to supply your own cooking and eating utensils. Most tent sites are not equipped with power points.

Some of the better camps include Skukuza (for facilities and location); Lower Sabie (overlooking a dam on the Sabie River and a prime wildlife viewing spot); Olifants (for spectacular views down onto the Olifants River and some great wildlife viewing territory); and Punda Maria (an old-fashioned place in an attractive setting that's good for exploring the unique northern end of the park).

As a guide to prices: camping costs US$10 for two people, plus US$3 for each additional person. Most huts or safari tents with communal bathroom and kitchen cost between US$15 and US$23 for two people; bungalows with private bathroom and shared kitchen cost between US$41 and US$46 for two; self-contained chalets, rondavels and huts cost between US$23 and US$74; and the average price for a self-contained cottage sleeping six is US$114.

Less-mobile visitors will find some useful information on wheelchair friendly accommodation in the area on the National Parks Board website (**W** www.parks-sa.co.za).

Getting There & Away There are several options to/from Kruger National Park.

Air SA Airlink flies daily from Jo'burg to Skukuza for US$98, Nelspruit for US$125 and Phalaborwa for US$118; all fares are one way. There are also flights into the recently expanded Nelspruit international airport, with connecting buses into the park.

Bus & Minibus Taxi Nelspruit is the most convenient large town near Kruger, and it's well served by buses and minibus taxis to and from Jo'burg. However, from Nelspruit you still have a fair way to go to get into the park. Near Nelspruit and closer to Kruger (15km from Numbi Gate) is the small village of Hazyview, where there are a couple of backpackers hostels that pick up from Nelspruit.

A minibus taxi from Hazyview to Skukuza costs about US$1.80.

Train The *Komati* runs from Jo'burg to Komatipoort (via Nelspruit), about 12km from Crocodile Bridge Gate and takes 12 hours.

Car Skukuza is about 500km from Jo'burg and can be reached in five to six hours. Punda Maria is about 620km from Jo'burg and can be reached in about eight hours. Rental cars are available at Skukuza airport through **Avis** (**☎** 0860-102 1111) and also at Nelspruit and Phalaborwa (see the relevant sections later in this chapter).

Private Wildlife Reserves

The area just west of Kruger contains a large number of private reserves, usually sharing a border with Kruger and thus most of the animals. They are often extremely pricey – US$100 per person seems to be the starting price for many places. It is possible to find cheaper places, and these may be more enjoyable because accommodation is in bush camps.

Although the private reserves can be expensive, don't dismiss the idea out of hand. A couple of slightly pricier (but often all-inclusive) days spent in the right private reserve can be hugely rewarding. The rangers can be a wealth of knowledge and can train you in the art of wildlife watching before you head to the Kruger for your own self-guided trip.

There must be hundreds of operators running tours into the private parks so it's worth talking to a travel agent to help you find a good deal. The better-known reserves include those within the large Sabi Sand conservation area (such as Sabi Sabi), Idube, Londolozi and Mala Mala.

Inkwazi Bush Camp (☎ 015-793 1836; e niel@inkwazi.co.za; w www.inkwazi.co.za) is one of the best budget options. It offers accommodation, wildlife drives and walks with knowledgeable guides from US$57 per day/night (self-catered) or US$86 per day/night (all inclusive).

Transfrontiers (☎ 015-793 3816, 083 700 7987; w www.transfrontiers.com) runs good-value, nature-oriented walking safaris in some of the private reserves. An all-inclusive (except drinks), four-day, three-night trip costs US$265, including transfers to and from Jo'burg or Pretoria.

Nelspruit
pop 107,200
Nelspruit, in the Crocodile River Valley, is the largest town in Mpumalanga's steamy subtropical lowveld, and is the provincial capital. Its growth began only in the 1890s, when the ZAR decided to put a railway through to Delagoa Bay (Maputo) so it would have access to a non-British port. The recently upgraded airport, enabling the largest international jets to land and deliver Kruger-bound tourists direct, should spur further growth.

Information The **Nelspruit Publicity Association** (☎ 755 1988/9, 082 868 1444; Municipal Buildings; open 8am-4.30pm Mon-Fri 9am-5pm Sat, 10am-2pm Sun) is helpful.

If you're heading on to Mozambique, the efficient **Mozambique Consulate** (☎ 753 2089, 752 7396) can process visas in a day (if you apply at 9am) for US$9 – significantly cheaper than at the border.

Places to Stay The **Safubi River Holiday Resort** (☎ 741 3253; 45 Graniet St; 2-person camp sites US$9, chalets from US$34) is a tranquil place a long way from the town centre. To get there head west on the N4, go past Agaat St and turn left at the Caltex station.

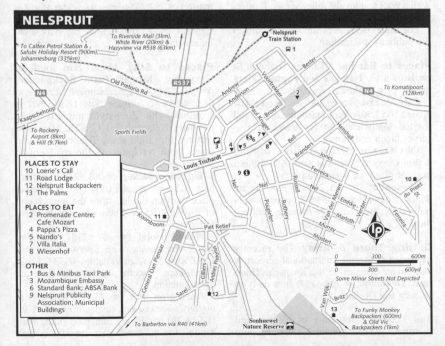

NELSPRUIT

PLACES TO STAY
10 Loerie's Call
11 Road Lodge
12 Nelspruit Backpackers
13 The Palms

PLACES TO EAT
2 Promenade Centre;
   Cafe Mozart
4 Pappa's Pizza
5 Nando's
7 Villa Italia
8 Wiesenhof

OTHER
1 Bus & Minibus Taxi Park
3 Mozambique Embassy
6 Standard Bank; ABSA Bank
9 Nelspruit Publicity
   Association; Municipal
   Buildings

Funky Monkey Backpackers (☎/fax 744 1310; 102 Van Wijk St; dorm beds US$6.40, doubles US$16.50) is a well-run hostel with a pool and bar. Ask the staff about the best nightspots in town.

Nelspruit Backpackers (☎ 741 2237; e nel back@hotmail.com; 9 Andries Pretorius St; camping US$4; dorm beds US$6.40, doubles US$16.50) is basic and laid-back. It offers free pick-ups, has a pool and bar and can arrange tours into the Kruger and Blyde River areas.

Old Vic Backpackers (☎ 744 0993; e old vic@mweb.co.za; 12 Impala St; dorm beds from US$8) is a good, basic place with a pool. It also runs tours.

Road Lodge (☎ 741 1805; w www.citylodge .co.za; cnr General Dan Pienaar & Koorsboom Sts; rooms US$23) has good-value rooms that sleep three. Breakfast is US$3.

The Palms Guest House (☎ 755 4374; 25 Van Wijk St; singles/doubles US$28/40) is a pleasant, friendly place with a pool and lush greenery.

Loeries Call (☎ 752 4844; e info@loeries call.co.za; 2 Du Preez St; singles/doubles US$39/51) is a beautifully furnished, upmarket place with a pool and lovely valley views. It offers pick-ups from town and airport.

For other B&B accommodation contact the publicity association.

Places to Eat Just off Louis Trichardt St on Brown St, **Nando's** and **Pappa's Pizza** are the pick of the fast food places.

Cafe Mozart (Promenade Centre; breakfast around US$3.50) offers a tasty breakfast, and toasted sandwiches go for US$2. It also serves lunch and dinner.

Villa Italia (☎ 752 5780; cnr Louis Trichardt & Paul Kruger Sts; mains around US$4.50) is a popular place for pasta and pizza.

Wiesenhof (☎ 755 2858; ABSA Square Building; mains from US$4.50) opposite Villa Italia offers a good range of cakes, coffees meals.

Getting There & Away The recently expanded Nelspruit international airport is 8km south of town on the Kaapsche Hoop road. **SA Airlink** (☎ 752 5257) flies daily to Jo'burg and Durban.

Bus Translux runs daily to Jo'burg and Pretoria (US$15, 5½ hours), and to Maputo

(US$14, 7 hours). Greyhound has a daily service to Jo'burg (US$16.50, 5½ hours). Translux and Greyhound depart from the Promenade Centre.

City to City runs direct from Nelspruit to Jo'burg daily for US$14.50.

Minibus Taxi The main minibus taxi park is near the train station. Destinations include: Barberton (US$1.20); Hazyview (US$1.70); Sabie (US$1.80); Komatipoort (US$5); Jo'burg (US$9) and Maputo (US$8).

Train The *Komati* runs once daily, except Saturday, between Jo'burg and Komatipoort via Nelspruit (10 hours).

Car For rentals, **Avis** (☎ 741 1087), **Budget** (☎ 741 3871) and **Imperial** (☎ 7041 2834) have offices at the airport.

Hazyview

Hazyview is a small village with large shopping centres. It is close to Kruger National Park's Numbi Gate (15km) and Paul Kruger Gate (43km).

For tourist information, **Panorama Information** (☎ 737 7414; open 9am-5pm Mon-Fri, 9am-12pm Sat), in the Simunye Shopping Centre close to the Pick 'n Pay, has some information.

Places to Stay About 2km south of Hazyview, **Kruger Park Backpackers** (☎ 737 7224; e krugback@mweb.co.za; dorm beds US$6.40, private huts US$16.50) is spacious with Zulu-style huts. It picks up from Nelspruit for US$15. If you're driving, turn right at the T-junction as you come from Nelspruit on the road out to Numbi gate.

Big 5 Backpackers (☎ 083 524 6615; dorm beds US$6.40, doubles US$17.50) is a genial place 3km up the hill from the intersection of R40 and R538. There are superb views to Kruger.

Numbi Hotel (☎ 737 7301; e hotel numbi@worldonline.co.za; 2-person camp sites US$7.50; B&B singles/doubles US$34/53) is a well-kept, peaceful place not far from the main junction.

Rissington Inn (☎ 737 7700; e riss ington@mweb.co.za; singles/doubles from US$39/75) is a lovely upmarket place with a pool and an excellent restaurant (worth

the trip even if you're not staying) 1km from town.

Getting There & Away Minibuses go to Nelspruit (US$1.80) and Sabie (US$1.80).

Komatipoort

This border town is at the foot of the Lebombo Mountains near the confluence of the Komati and Crocodile Rivers. It is only 10km south of Crocodile Bridge into Kruger.

Border Country Inn (☎ 790 7328; B&B singles/doubles US$28/44) is on the N4 close to the Mozambicam border crossing and Kruger. It has a lovely poolside terrace and bar, although the rooms are spartan.

It is fairly easy to cross the border here (open 6am–7pm daily). Visas for Mozambique are available at the border (US$21), in Jo'burg, Cape Town, Durban and in Nelspruit.

If you have a car you will need a breakdown warning triangle, seat belts and the relevant vehicle papers, especially for rental cars.

Barberton

Barberton, about 50km south of Nelspruit, is a quiet town in the harsh but interesting lowveld country of **De Kaap Valley**. It had South Africa's first stock exchange but today languishes in obscurity. The very helpful **information centre** (☎ 712 2121; W www.barberton.info; Market Square, Crown St; open 8am-1pm & 2pm-4.30pm Mon-Fri, 8.30am-noon Sat) has a brochure detailing the various restored houses.

The aerial cableway brings asbestos down from a mine in Swaziland, carrying coal in the other direction as counterweight.

Places to Stay There's a **caravan park** (☎ 712 3323; 3-person tent sites US$5, 2-person chalets with kitchens from US$18.50) with camp sites and chalets.

Fountain Baths Guest Lodge (☎ 712 2707; fax 712 3361; self-contained singles/doubles US$17.50/28), also called FB Holiday Cottages, is a good place to stay. It's at the southern end of Pilgrim St. Built in 1885, it used to be Barberton's public baths and swimming pool; it's popular so book ahead.

Hillside Lodge (☎ 712 4466; 62 Pilgrim St; per person with breakfast US$14) is a comfortable guesthouse with magnificent views and lovely gardens.

The Phoenix Hotel (☎ 712 4211; cnr Pilgrim & President Sts; singles/doubles US$16.50/29) is a clean, old-style country pub, exuding a certain faded elegance that dates from 1882. Breakfast is included.

Places to Eat Covering most tastes, **Gold Mine** (bar meals US$3) is next to the Checkers supermarket.

Bernstein's (mains around US$5.80; closed Sun), next door to the Phoenix Hotel, specialises in steaks.

Cocopan (Crown St) opposite the museum is a casual place with **John Henry's Pub** attached.

Victorian Tea Garden (light meals US$3) near the tourist office is a great place to relax.

Getting There & Away The scenic R40 from here to Swaziland (via the Bulembu border crossing) is unsealed and rough. Do not attempt the journey in a 2WD in the wet. The border closes at 4pm. It's further, but quicker, to enter Swaziland via Pigg's Peak from here if you're in a 2WD.

There is a minibus taxi rank by Emjindini, about 3km from town on the Nelspruit road, or you can find taxis in town. The fare to Nelspruit is US$0.80 and to Badplaas it costs US$1.20.

KLEIN DRAKENSBERG
☎ 013

The highveld ends suddenly at this escarpment which tumbles down to the eastern lowveld.

The Klein (Small) Drakensberg (as opposed to the main Drakensberg Range in KwaZulu-Natal) is not so much peaks as cliffs, and there are stunning views. As it is prime vacation territory there's a lot of accommodation, but it fills up at peak times. The population density is low, so there's little public transport.

Winters are cold, with occasional snowfalls. Summers are warm, but after the sweltering lowveld it's a relief to get up here.

Blyde River Canyon

The Blyde River Canyon Nature Reserve snakes north for almost 60km from Graskop, following the escarpment and meeting the Blyde River as it carves its way down to the lowveld. The Blyde's spectacular canyon,

SOUTH AFRICA

nearly 30km long, is one of South Africa's scenic highlights.

The following description, from north to south, begins near the Manoutsa Cliffs at the junction of the Tzaneen road (R36) and the R527 (sometimes marked on maps as a continuation of the R531).

Follow the R36 as it turns south and climbs up from the lowveld through the Strijdom Tunnel and scenic Abel Erasmus Pass.

If you return to the junction and proceed east along the R532 you come to the Aventura Blydepoort resort. There is a good view of the **Three Rondavels** from within the resort. The Rondavels are huge cylinders of rock with hut-like pointy 'roofs' rising out of the far walls of the canyon.

Bourke's Luck Potholes (admission US$1.20) are weird cylindrical holes carved into the rock by whirlpools in the river. They are interesting, although nothing mind-boggling. There is a good visitors centre with information on the geology, flora and fauna of the canyon.

The R532 follows the Treur River south to its source, and further on is a turn-off to the R534 loop road. This road leads to the spectacular viewpoints of **Wonder View** and **God's Window**. A few kilometres on you pass the **Pinnacle**, an impressive rock formation which juts out from the escarpment. The R534 rejoins the R532 about 3km north of Graskop.

Hiking Trails There are several great hiking trails in the area. The visitors centre at the Bourke's Luck Potholes is the best place to get maps and information. The Graskop information centre is also helpful. Fees on the overnight trails (the only way to get to the canyon floor) are US$3.50 per person per night. Book well in advance (☎ 759 5432).

Places to Stay As well as accommodation in the towns on top of the escarpment, there are several places to stay close to the canyon.

Aventura Blydepoort (☎ 769 8005; sites per tent/per person around US$3.50/4, 2-bed chalets from US$34, 4-bed chalets US$48) is a large resort with all the usual facilities.

Aventura Swadini (☎ 015-795 5141) is at the bottom of the escarpment, on the eastern side but still on the Blyde River, with the similar rates to Aventura Blydepoort.

Rushworth's Trackers (☎ 015-795 5033; basic camp sites US$2.30, cottages per person without/with half-board US$7.50/16.50) is also at the bottom of the escarpment, to the north of Swadini (and actually in Limpopo). It takes in the strikingly different ecosystems of the highveld and the lowveld. The reserve caters mainly to educational groups, but individuals are welcome.

To get to Trackers, take the R527 west from Hoedspruit and after about 20km turn south onto the small Driehoek road, just after you cross the Blyde River. After 6.5km you will see the Trackers signpost.

Graskop

On the edge of the Drakensberg escarpment, at the top of Kowyns Pass, Graskop is a pretty little town. Nearby there are spectacular views of the lowveld almost 1000m below. The town is well situated for visiting the area's highveld attractions and is less than 60km from Kruger National Park.

There is an **information centre** (☎ 767 1377/767 1833; Pilgrim St) inside the Spar supermarket.

Places to Stay There's camping at **Graskop Holiday Resort** (☎ 767 1126; 1-/2-person camp sites US$3/4, chalets from US$23). A walking trail that includes places described in Jock of the Bushveld starts here.

Summit Lodge (☎ 767 1058; e summit lodge@iafrica.com; 8 Market St; camping US$3.50, dorm beds US$5.75, rondavels US$16.50) has a pub, pool and restaurant attached. The dorm beds are in an old railway carriage.

Panorama Rest Camp (☎ 767 1091; e pan orus@lantic.net; 2-person camp sites US$5.80, 2-person chalets from US$24) is about 2km south of town on the road to Kowyns Pass. It's stunningly situated and the small swimming pool is right on the edge of the berg. The chalets have breathtaking views.

Graskop Hotel (☎ 767 1244; B&B singles/doubles US$17.50/29) is a spacious, stylishly designed place on the main street. There are also family rooms and a good coffee shop.

Places to Eat Well geared to tourist tastes, **Harry's Pancake Bar** (Louis Trichardt St; pancakes US$3) is a minor gastronomic delight. The savoury fillings are great.

Lonely Tree Pancake Cabin, a bit further along, is also highly recommended.

Leonardo's Trattoria (☎ 767 1078) across the road will satisfy those pizza and pasta cravings.

Getting There & Away There are no scheduled bus services to Graskop so the only option is a minibus taxi from the southern end of Main St. It costs US$1.30 to Sabie.

Sabie

Sabie is a small town, but it's the largest in this area. Tourists come for the cool climate, trout fishing and the extensive pine and eucalypt plantations. If you prefer your forests wild, these won't be much of an attraction.

You'll find information at **Panorama** (☎ 764 1125) next door to the Spar.

Things to See & Do The decent **Forestry Museum** (adult/student US$0.60/0.40; open daily) has displays on the local forests.

There are several waterfalls in the area. Off the R532 are the **Mac-Mac Falls** (named because of the number of Scottish names on the area's mining register) and **Forest Falls**, 10km from Graskop and reached by a walk through the forest.

There are several nature walks near Sabie and two excellent mountain-bike trails. **Sondelani Travel & Info** (☎ 764 3492; by the Woodsman, cnr Mac Mac Rd) can provide further information.

Places to Stay Out of town off Old Lydenburg Road, **Merry Pebbles** (☎ 764 2266; sites per tent low season US$10.50; double chalets US$29) has camping and self-contained chalets.

Sabie Backpackers (☎ 764 2118; fax 764 3130; Main Rd; dorm beds US$5.80, doubles US$14), newly opened is near the corner of Simmons St, is a clean little house with cooking facilities, a heated pool and bar.

Sabie Vallée Inn (☎ 764 2182; Tenth St; dorm beds US$5.80, cabins & rooms half-board US$23 per person) has backpacker dorms, self-catering log cabins and comfortable hotel rooms (rates for these are less if you stay two nights).

The area has a number of B&Bs. **Sabie Townhouse** (☎ 764 2292; Power St; singles/ doubles US$34/60) is the place in town for

a well-earned indulgence. Book ahead as it is popular.

Places to Eat Locals recommend the **Country Kitchen** (closed Mon & Sun dinner; mains US$4.50-10)

Woodsman (mains US$3.50-4.50) has a great Greek menu.

Loggerhead (full meals around US$5), near Sabie Falls, is a good steakhouse.

Getting There & Away Minibus taxis are your only bet. Sabie's minibus taxi park is behind the Spar supermarket on Main St. Most taxis run only in the local area. The fare to Hazyview is US$2.30; to Nelspruit it's US$3.50.

Mt Sheba Nature Reserve

If you're wondering how this area looked before most of the indigenous forest was destroyed, visit this reserve 15km off the R533 and about 10km west of Pilgrim's Rest. With its plentiful rain and mists, it's an evocative place. There are day walks in the area; pick up a brochure and map at the Mt Sheba Hotel, the Sondelani Travel & Info Centre in Sabie or from Pilgrim's Rest.

The luxurious **Mt Sheba Hotel** (☎ 768 1241; half-board singles/doubles US$92/133) in the nature reserve has great views.

Pilgrim's Rest

Gold was discovered here in 1873 and for 10 years the area buzzed with diggers working small-scale alluvial claims. When the big operators arrived in the 1880s, Pilgrim's Rest became a company town, and when the gold finally fizzled out in 1972 the town was sold to the government as a ready-made historical village.

The **information centre** (open 8.30am-12.45pm & 1.15pm-4.30pm daily) is on the main street. There are three **museums** and entry to all three costs US$1.20; buy tickets at the information centre. The **nature reserve** that surrounds the town is a good place for a walk.

The restored **District Six Miner's Cottages** (☎ 768 1211/768 1262; 4-bed cottage for 2 people US$20) are the cheapest accommodation option.

Royal Hotel (☎ 768 1100; B&B singles/ doubles US$55/91) is a Victorian-era place with ornate rooms.

Gauteng

Gauteng ('Place of Gold', in Sotho) takes in the area once known as the PWV – Pretoria, Witwatersrand and Vereeniging. The Witwatersrand (literally, Ridge of White Waters), is often shortened to 'the Rand', and it contains the world's richest gold reef.

Gauteng is the smallest South African province (about 19,000 sq km) but with around 10 million people it has the largest population. It has been claimed that Gauteng accounts for 25% of the gross domestic product of all Africa.

The area is rich in history, but for most visitors a quick visit to crime-plagued Johannesburg (Jo'burg) and more amenable Pretoria will be enough.

JOHANNESBURG
☎ 011 • pop 5,100,700

Johannesburg's sole reason for existence is the reef of gold that lies under the *highveld* (high open grassland), and its inhabitants are single-minded in their pursuit of the rand. Cultural assets (including good bars and restaurants) are pitifully thin on the ground.

This is the heart of the new South Africa, and this is where change – both good and bad – is happening first.

Unfortunately, it's the bad that gets most of the press and, to an extent, it's warranted – violent crime is rampant in the city centre and the inner suburbs of Hillbrow and Berea.

The statistics are simply horrifying. Businesses have fled to the suburbs (particularly

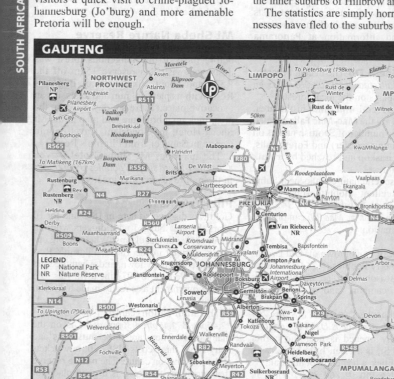

GAUTENG

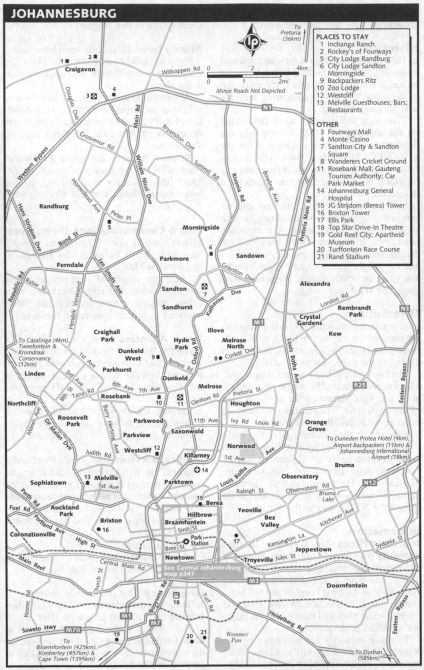

JOHANNESBURG

To Pretoria (36km)

0   2   4km
0   1   2mi
Minor Roads Not Depicted

PLACES TO STAY
1 Inchanga Ranch
2 Rockey's of Fourways
5 City Lodge Randburg
6 City Lodge Sandton Morningside
9 Backpackers Ritz
10 Zoo Lodge
12 Westcliff
13 Melville Guesthouses; Bars; Restaurants

OTHER
3 Fourways Mall
4 Monte Casino
7 Sandton City & Sandton Square
8 Wanderers Cricket Ground
11 Rosebank Mall; Gauteng Tourism Authority; Car Park Market
14 Johannesburg General Hospital
15 JG Strijdom (Berea) Tower
16 Brixton Tower
17 Ellis Park
18 Top Star Drive-In Theatre
19 Gold Reef City; Apartheid Museum
20 Turffontein Race Course
21 Rand Stadium

Craigavon
Witkoppen Rd
Douglas Dve
Main Rd
Bryanston Dve
Grosvenor Rd
William Nicol Dve
Summit Rd
Rivonia Rd
Bowling Ave
Pretoria Main Rd
N1

Western Bypass
Homestead Ave
Randburg
Peter Pl
Morningside
Sandown
Hans Strijdom Dve
Bond St
Jan Smuts Ave
Grayston Dve
Alexandra
Ferndale
Rabie St
Parkmore
Sandton
Katherine Dve
London Rd
N3
Republic Rd
Hendrik Verwoerd
Sandhurst
Crystal Gardens
Rembrandt Park
Kew
Craighall Park
1st Ave
Illovo
M1
Louis Botha Ave
Eastern Bypass
To Casalinga (4km), Tweefontein & Kromdraai Conservancy (12km)
Hyde Park
Melrose North
3rd Ave
Dunkeld West
Bompas Rd
Corlett Dve
Linden
8th St Tana Rd
6th Ave 7th Ave
Dunkeld
Parkhurst
Rosebank
Melrose
Pretoria St
R25
Northcliff
Glenhove Rd
Houghton
Roosevelt Park
Barry Hertzog Ave
Parkwood
11th Ave
Ivy Rd Louis Rd
Orange Grove
DF Malan Dve
Parkview
Saxonwold
To Duneden Protea Hotel (4km), Airport Backpackers (11km) & Johannesburg International Airport (18km)
Judith Rd
Westcliff
Killarney
1st Ave
Norwood
Louis Botha Ave
Bruma
Melville
1st Ave
Parktown
Louis Botha
Observatory
N12
Sophiatown
Raleigh St
Observatory Rd
Bruma Lake
Fuel Rd Portland Ave
Auckland Park
Brixton
Berea
Yeoville
Bez Valley
Kitchener Ave
Sydonia St
Coronationville
High St
Hillbrow
Braamfontein
Smit St
Kensington La
Jeppestown
Main Reef
Nasrec Rd
Bree St
Park Station
Troyeville Jules St
Central Main Rd
Newtown
Doornfontein
Church St
See Central Johannesburg map p547
M2
Booysens Ave
Soweto Hwy
M70
M1
M7
Turf Rd
Heidelberg Rd
Eastern Bypass
To Bloemfontein (425km), Kimberley (457km) & Cape Town (1395km)
Wemmer Pan
To Durban (585km)

north) and that's where you'll find most accommodation, bars and restaurants.

History

In 1886 George Harrison, a prospector, found traces of gold on the highveld, little realising he had stumbled on the only surface outcrop of the world's richest gold-bearing reef. He sold his claim for £10.

Thousands of diggers soon descended on the site and by 1889 Jo'burg was the largest town in Southern Africa. After the 1899–1902 Anglo-Boer War, which saw Jo'burg become a virtual ghost town, the city recovered quickly and huge new mines were developed.

Under black leadership, the vast squatter camps that sprung up around Jo'burg became well-organised cities, despite the atrocious conditions. In the late 1940s many of the camps were destroyed by the authorities and the people were moved to new suburbs known as the Southwestern Townships, now shortened to Soweto.

Orientation

Two communication towers on the ridges to the north of the city centre make good landmarks: the Hillbrow Tower; and the Brixton Tower, to the northwest of the city.

The city centre is laid out on a simple grid. Many people arrive in Jo'burg by bus or train at or near Park Station on the northern edge of the city centre. The northern suburbs are affluent, white middle-class ghettos.

Soweto (to the southwest) is the main township outside the city, but there are also large developments at Tokoza (south of Alberton), Kwa-Thema and Tsakane (south of Brakpan), Daveyton (east of Benoni), Tembisa (to the northeast) and Alexandra (inside the N3 freeway to the north).

Information

Tourist Offices The **Gauteng Tourism Authority** isn't terribly useful but does offer some brochures and information. It has two offices, the main one at Rosebank (☎ 340 9000; Shop 401, Upper Level, Rosebank Mall) and the kiosk in Sandton (☎ 784 9597; 1st Floor Medical Mews). There's also an information kiosk at the airport.

To make bookings for parks run by the National Parks Board, you'll need to contact the board's **Pretoria office** (☎ 012-428 9111) –

for more contact details, see the Pretoria section later in this chapter).

Money Banks are usually open from 9am to 3.30pm weekdays and 8.30am to 11am Saturday. There are foreign exchange counters at the airport.

American Express (AmEx) has 24-hour offices at the **airport** (☎ 390 1233); in **Sandton** (☎ 883 9009; 78A Sandton City Mall); and **Rosebank** (☎ 880 8382; Nedbank Gardens, 33 Bath Ave).

Rennies Travel is the agent for Thomas Cook with foreign exchange outlets (☎ 492 1990; 35 Rissik St • ☎ 390 1040; Jo'burg International Airport • ☎ 884 4035; Sandton City Mall).

Post & Communications The **main post office** (Jeppe St; open 8.30am-4pm Mon-Fri, 8am-noon Sat) is between Von Brandis St and Smal St Mall.

There are plenty of commercial phone services around the city. Check the rates before making a long-distance call. Most backpackers hostels have email facilities.

Travel Agencies There's a branch of STA Travel (☎ 716 3045; Student Union Bldg, University of Witwatersrand; open Mon-Fri 9am-4.30pm). You don't have to be a student to use its services but you'll need ID to get into the campus.

Rennies Travel (☎ 407 3343) has several offices around Jo'burg (see Money earlier in this section).

Medical Services Doctors are listed under 'Medical' in the Yellow Pages. If urgent medical attention is required go direct to the casualty department of **Johannesburg General Hospital** (☎ 488 4911) less than 1km north of Hillbrow. Otherwise ring the **Police Flying Squad** (☎ 10111) to get directions to the nearest hospital.

There is a **pharmacy** (☎ 883 7520; open to 10.30pm daily) in Sandton City Mall.

Emergency The emergency numbers in Jo'burg are: **ambulance** (☎ 403 4227); **fire brigade** (☎ 999); and **police** (☎ 10111).

The phones at the **Battered Women & Rape Crisis Centre** (☎ 642 4345) are staffed daily from 6am to 10pm. There's a **Lifeline service** (☎ 728 1347).

Soweto

The idea was simple. Move anyone who wasn't white as far away from the 'chosen race' as possible, but still close enough that they could be used as cheap labour.

Thus was born Soweto and the other townships circling Jo'burg which are still home for the majority of its inhabitants. Soweto is by far the biggest, sprawling over 150 sq km and housing 3.5 million souls. Given the lack of facilities like running water and electricity and the low-rise nature of the housing, it's an appalling overcrowding statistic.

Most white South Africans have never been inside a township and picture life here as one of unmitigated hostility, drugs, superstition, tribal warfare, depravity and violent crime.

In fact, some suburbs within the townships are much like suburbs anywhere, while others are as bad as any Third World slum.

In descending order of wealth, a tiny wealthy elite live in comfortable bungalows; the privileged live in monotonous rows of government-built houses; the lucky own a block of land, a prefabricated toilet and a tap; the fortunate live in shacks erected in backyards; the squatters build wherever they can; and at the bottom of the pile are the men who live in dorms in vast, dilapidated hostels.

The townships played a crucial role in the struggle against apartheid and a government that routinely used bullets, tear gas, bombs, imprisonment without trial, torture, and summary execution of men, women and children.

Soweto was in a virtual state of war from 1976, when the first protesting school students were killed in defiance of a proposal to use Afrikaans as the language of instruction. This terrible era of violence continued as an internal political war in the dying days of apartheid and many thousands died in the years leading up to the 1994 elections.

Since then Soweto's residents have been busy trying to meet basic aspirations – for work, decent housing, and a good future for their children.

Given the townships' recent history, the friendliness generally shown to white visitors is almost embarrassing. Caution is needed, however. The townships are still in a state of acute social trauma, and violent crime is commonplace. Visiting without a companion who has local knowledge is likely to be disastrous.

Organised tours, however, are safe and often unforgettable experiences. It may seem odd, even voyeuristic, treating these places as a tourist attraction, but to get any kind of appreciation for South African reality, you have to visit them. It's also another way of supporting local, black-owned businesses directly.

Most Soweto tours are designed to be educational, so they can be earnest and a little dry. You should plan to see the poignant Hector Pieterson monument, a squatter camp, Vilakazi St (Nelson Mandela's old house, Walter Sisulu's residence and Desmond Tutu's house), Regina Mundi Square, Soweto 'architecture' (including shacks, brick palaces, and – if you can – the inside of a shack) and the Freedom Charter on the side of a shipping container in Kliptown.

A night in a B&B-style homestay with a local family is a good way to get to know something of Soweto and its people. Your stay may well include a trip to a local shebeen. **Lolo's B&B** (☎ 985 9183; US$45) is a plush place in a 'larney' (posh) part of Soweto. Alternatively book Soweto B&Bs through the tour companies.

Max Maximum Tours (☎ 938 8703, 082 770 0247; day tours US$29; tours and overnight B&B US$39), run by longtime Soweto resident Max, is highly recommended. Also recommended is **Neng Kapa Neng** (☎ 936 9738, 082 649 6368).

Dangers & Annoyances Pay careful attention to your personal security in Jo'burg. The amount of violent crime is pretty scary; to avoid getting paranoid don't read the statistics in the local newspapers! Daylight muggings in the city centre and other inner suburbs, notably Hillbrow, are not uncommon and you must be constantly on your guard. You'd be crazy to walk around central Jo'burg at night – if you arrive after dark and don't have a car, catch a taxi to your final destination.

It's probably best to avoid Yeoville and Hillbrow altogether and stay out of the city centre at night, although the revamped area around the Market Theatre and Museum Africa seems safer these days.

Security measures ensure the city centre is pretty safe by day – as a rough rule of thumb, west of Rissik St and south of Jeppe St should be OK. Take great care outside Park Station.

Follow the usual rules: never advertise your wealth or tourist status; look like you know where you're going; don't carry anything (even in a money belt) that can't easily be replaced; and use your hotel or hostel safe.

If you have a car, lock doors, close windows and when you're at traffic lights leave a car's length between you and the vehicle in front so you can drive away if necessary. Avoid driving at night and fork out the extra cash for secure parking.

If you do get held up, don't be a hero. Don't scare them into shooting you first.

If you want (or have) to spend some time in Jo'burg, talk to hostel/hotel managers and, of course, other travellers about places that are off-limits. As a general rule avoid the city centre for at least the first couple of days you are here.

Anyone can get unlucky, but if you use a bit of common sense you'll significantly reduce your chances of becoming a statistic in the newspapers.

Apartheid Museum

Incongruously located next to the cheap fun-park thrills of Gold Reef City, the unmissable new Apartheid Museum (☎ 309 4700; Northern Parkway & Gold Reef Rd; adult/child US$3/1.50; open 10am-5pm Tues-Sun) is impressive and chilling from the very moment you are directed through one of two entry turnstiles (one designated for 'whites', the other for 'blacks').

Inside, the apartheid story is told with sensory verve through large, visually stunning displays and excellent audiovisual exhibits, including an electrifying BBC interview with Mandela made when he was on the run from the authorities.

Some graphic images and the sight of multiple nooses in memory of those hanged during the struggle hardly make for a fun day out, but it's an essential place to visit to get a feeling for what apartheid-era South Africa was like. In its own dark way it also underscores the miracle of post-apartheid reconciliation.

Museum Africa

The museum (☎ 833 5624; 121 Bree St; adult/child US$0.80/0.30; open 9am-5pm Tues-Sun), next to the Market Theatre, has some interesting but unimaginatively presented exhibitions on Johannesburg's recent history, a large collection of rock art, and various other exhibits.

Johannesburg Art Gallery

This gallery (☎ 725 3180; admission free; open 10am-5pm Tues-Sun), at the southern end of Joubert Park, is housed in a lovely little building and has exhibitions featuring contemporary work and retrospectives of black artists. It's an edgy walk here so you might consider getting a taxi to drop you at the front gate.

Market Theatre

The Market Theatre complex (☎ 832 1641; Bree St), to the west of the city centre, has live theatre venues, an art gallery, a coffee shop, some interesting shops, and Kippie's Bar (an excellent jazz venue).

There's usually some interesting theatre here – check out the Weekly Mail & Guardian entertainment section for more information.

Places to Stay

Some of the places to stay in central Jo'burg are excellent value but that's because crime has scared away customers; unless you need to stay in the city centre, you're better off in the 'burbs.

Places to Stay – Budget

Many hostels will pick you up from the airport or Park Station. If you make an arrangement to be picked up, make sure you stick to it so the hostel people don't make a wasted journey. The Baz Bus (see Getting There & Away later in this section) drops off at most hostels. The list below is a small selection; there are plenty more to choose from.

Zoo Lodge (☎ 788 5182; fax 788 5182; e zoolodge@iafrica.com; 233a Jan Smuts Ave, Parktown North; dorm beds US$9, singles/doubles US$17.50/23) was undergoing major renovations at the time of writing,

SOUTH AFRICA

CENTRAL JOHANNESBURG

PLACES TO STAY & EAT	5 Taxis to Upington,	10 St Mary's Anglican	16 Anglo Gold Building
3 Parktonian All Suite Hotel	Kimberley & Cape Town;	Cathedral	18 Kwa Indaba
12 Chinese Restaurants	Bulawayo (Zimbabwe);	11 Car Licensing	19 Kohinoor Music Store
17 Kapitan's	Maputo (Mozambique) &	Department	20 Johannesburg Library;
21 Guildhall Bar & Restaurant	Durban	12 Department of	Library Square
	6 Johannesburg Art Gallery	Home Affairs	22 City Hall
OTHER	7 Minibus Taxis to Lesotho,	13 Market Theatre;	23 Supreme Court
1 Civic Theatre	Bloemfontein, Kroonstad &	Kippies's Bar;	24 Weleda Pharmacy
2 Braamfontein Centre:	Ficksburg	Gramadoela's; Yard	25 Rennies Travel
Swaziland Consulate	8 Taxis to Soweto & Pretoria	of Ale	26 Metro Bus Terminal;
4 City to City Bus Office	9 Shell House	14 Museum Africa	Gandhi Square

which should transform this hitherto scruffy backpackers. There's also a travel agency attached.

Rockey's of Fourways (☎ 465 4219, fax 467 2597; e info@backinafrica.com, 22 Campbell Rd, Craigavon, Fourways; dorm beds US$9, singles/doubles from US$15.50/23), aka Catch 22, has friendly management, a good atmosphere and it's clean. Unfortunately it's miles from the centre.

Inchanga Resort (☎ 708 2505; e ivi@pixi .co.za; Inchanga Ranch, Inchanga Rd, Fourways; dorm beds US$8.50, US$7.50 for YHA members, lodges from US$29) occupies a secluded spot on a ranch, with a bar, swimming pool and friendly staff, about 2km down the road from Rockey's. The cabins are lovely. The dorms, a trudge across the paddock, are less so.

Backpackers Ritz (☎ 325 7125; e ritz@ iafrica.com; 1A North Road, Dunkeld West; dorm beds US$8.50, singles/doubles US$15/ 19) is far from the city but it's very relaxing with spacious grounds, some pleasant double/twin rooms and a good bar. Avoid the huge dorms or spend the night playing 'count the snorers'.

Airport Backpackers (☎ 394 0485; e airportbackpack@hotmail.com; camping US$4.50, dorm beds US$8, singles/doubles US$17.50/23) is a comfortable place 2km from the airport.

Places to Stay – Mid-Range

B&Bs Melville has several good guesthouses close to 7th street's many bars and restaurants (book ahead).

They include: **The Melville House** (☎ 726 3505; w themelvillehouse.com; 59 Fourth Avenue; singles/doubles from US$34/57); and **Melville Manor Guest House** (☎ 726 8765; e mnh@icon.co.za; 80 Second Avenue; singles/doubles from US$26/41).

The **Portfolio organization** (☎ 880 3414, fax 788 4802; w portfoliocollection.com) also lists high-quality B&Bs in the northern suburbs.

Hotels The **Duneden Protea Hotel** (☎ 453 2002; 46 Van Riebeeck Ave, Edenvale; singles/ doubles US$32/64) is close to shops and the airport but not to the city.

The City Lodge group, which charges about US$50/61 for singles/doubles, offers good value. These smart, if slightly dull, places include: **City Lodge Sandton Morningside** (☎ 884 9500; cnr Rivonia & Hill Rds, Sandton), close to shops; **City Lodge Randburg** (☎ 706 7800; cnr Main Rd & Peter Place, Bryanston West, Randburg); and **City Lodge JIA** (☎ 392 1750; w www.citylodge.co.za; Sandvale Rd, Edenvale), out near the airport.

Also look out for the comfortable and cheaper **Town Lodges** (singles/doubles around US$36/55, specials per room from US$24), administered by the same group.

Places to Stay – Top End
The Parktonian All Suite Hotel (☎ 403 5740; e accom@parktonian.co.za; 120 De Koorte St, Braamfontein; singles/doubles US$68/81) is the best place in the centre; it offers weekend specials for stays of more than a night.

Westcliff (☎ 646 2400; w www.westcliff hotel.orient-express.com; 67 Jan Smuts Ave, Westcliff; rooms from US$285) is a luxurious place on a hill looking across the suburbs, with excellent, spacious rooms and a great bar/pool area. Make sure you have a sundowner here.

Places to Eat
Jo'burg is packed with places to eat but unfortunately for those without cars, most are in the northern suburbs.

City Centre There's a shortage of cafés and cheap eating places in the city. Just finding somewhere to sit down is a major problem.

Guildhall Bar & Restaurant (☎ 836 5600; cnr Harrison & Market Sts) is a great pub with

balcony tables good for people-watching. The food is limited – cheap stews and pap – but hearty, cheap and good.

Kapitan's (☎ 834 8048; upstairs, 11A Kort St; mains from US$3), in one of the few remaining Indian streets, is a cheerful, old-fashioned restaurant serving authentic Indian food.

Gramadoela's (☎ 838 6960; Market Theatre complex; mains from US$5) is probably the best restaurant in the city. The menu is superb, with Cape Dutch/Malay specialities.

Melville Just northwest of Braamfontein, Melville is the hip place to see and be seen. You'll find a good selection of restaurants on Seventh St.

Sam's (Seventh St; dishes around US$4) serves delicious starter-sized portions from its extensive menu. Highly recommended.

Nuno's (☎ 726 2247; Seventh St between 1st & 2nd Ave; open 7am-1am daily), serves cheap, hearty Portuguese fare till late.

Soi (☎ 726 5775; Corner of 7th St & 3rd Ave; mains US$6.40) is a poseurs paradise serving well-presented Thai and Vietnamese food in smart surroundings.

Entertainment
The best guide to entertainment is the *Weekly Mail & Guardian*; you can't do without a copy.

For entertainment bookings, contact **Computicket** (☎ 083 915 1234). Since it has everything on its system, staff can also give advice about what's on.

The best bet for a beer in the city centre is the cosy, old fashioned **Guildhall Bar & Restaurant** (cnr Harrison & Market Sts).

Melville is Johannesburg's brightest nightspot. It's heaving with good bars and restaurants. Just go for a wander along 7th and 4th Avenues. **Buzz 9** and **Ratz**, next door to each other on 7th Avenue, are buzzing most nights playing high energy music to a smart, young crowd.

Xai Xai is a scruffy but friendly bar with an interesting, alternative crowd. It's a great place to round off a big night out with a couple of cleansing beers and some bar food from Nuno's next door (see Places to Eat).

Yard of Ale (Market Theatre complex), a classic place in the city centre, has reopened and is worth checking out.

In the Market Theatre Complex, **Kippie's Bar** (☎ 833 3316; admission US$3.50) is one of the best places to see South African jazz talent.

Bassline (☎ 482 6915; 7th St Melville; admission US$2.30) is an intimate little place that heaves with people on the weekend. There's often decent local and international jazz.

A visit to the **Market Theatre complex** (☎ 832 1641; Bree St) is worthwhile. It's Johannesburg's most important venue for live theatre, some of the productions are outstanding.

Shopping

Shopaholics will enjoy **Rosebank Mall** in Rosebank or **Sandton City Mall** in Sandton, an enormous and plush shopping centre a half-hour drive north of the city centre.

One of the best places to buy ethnic/African music is **Kohinoor**; there are a number of branches, including one at 54 Market St.

If you want to remind yourself that you're still in Africa, visit one of the *muti* (traditional medicine) shops, which sell herbs and potions prescribed by a *sangoma* (witchdoctor). **Kwa Indaba** is at two locations: 14 Diagonal St, and also on the corner of Koch and Twist Sts, opposite the Art Gallery.

Crafts You can buy traditional carvings, beadwork, jewellery and fertility dolls in Johannesburg's shopping malls, although prices are high.

Street vendors set up on the footpaths around town selling some good stuff among the tat. Bargaining is expected.

The market in the northern suburb of Rosebank, held every Sunday in the upper-level car park of the Rosebank Mall, is excellent for traditional crafts.

Getting There & Away

Air South Africa's major international and domestic airport is **Johannesburg International Airport** (JIA; ☎ 9216262 for flight inquiries). For details on domestic fares and destinations, see the main Getting Around section earlier in this chapter.

Numerous international airlines have offices in Jo'burg and the following list is a small sample – check the Yellow Pages for other contact details.

Air France (☎ 970 1526) Johannesburg Airport
British Airways (☎ 921 6391)
KLM-Royal Dutch Airlines (☎ 961 6700)
Qantas Airways (☎ 978 6414)
SAA (☎ 978 1111 reservations, 978 3370 international terminal, 978 3119 domestic terminal)

Bus International bus services leave Jo'burg for Botswana, Zambia, Mozambique and Zimbabwe (for more details, see Getting There & Away earlier in this chapter).

The main long-distance bus lines (national and international) depart from and arrive at the Park Station transit centre. There are booking counters for **Translux** (☎ 774 3333), **Greyhound** (☎ 249 8900) and **Intercape** (☎ 333 2312). **City to City**, the inexpensive government bus service, leaves from behind the Formule 1 Hotel.

Don't forget the **Baz Bus** (☎ 021-439 2323); phone the Cape Town number, or book through hostels. One major advantage of the Baz Bus in Jo'burg is its door-to-door service, dropping at most hostels. This avoids the hassle (and danger) of finding your way to a hostel from the bus station.

North Several services run north up the N1 via Pretoria. For example, Translux has at least one bus each day to Beitbridge (and on to Harare) via Pietersburg/Polokwane (US$13/19, 4¾ hours), and Louis Trichardt (US$14.50, 6¾ hours).

City to City runs daily to Venda (Sibasa) for US$10, and also to Giyani/Malamulele via Pietersburg (US$7.50). These services also stop at the major towns along the N1.

Kruger National Park The nearest large town to Kruger is Nelspruit, and Greyhound runs there daily (US$15, five hours). Translux also stops at Nelspruit (US$15) on its run to Maputo (Mozambique). City to City runs a slow service to Nelspruit for US$9.

KwaZulu-Natal Greyhound has four daily buses to Durban (US$21, seven hours). Translux runs at least one daily bus down the N3 to Durban (US$20, 7½ hours).

South Coast Translux runs from Jo'burg/Pretoria to East London (US$33, 14 hours) daily and also has five services weekly to Port Elizabeth (US$37.50, 15 hours). Greyhound has overnight buses from Jo'burg to Port Elizabeth (US$35, 14½ hours).

Translux runs to Knysna (US$42, 17½ hours) via Kimberley or Bloemfontein then Oudtshoorn (US$34), Mossel Bay (US$42) and George (US$42).

City to City buses leave for Umtata daily at 5.15 pm. The trip takes 12¼ hours.

Cape Town Translux has at least one bus daily running from Jo'burg/Pretoria to Cape Town (US$46, 19 hours) via Bloemfontein (US$21, six hours). Also, five services (not Tuesday and Thursday) run via Kimberley (US$18).

Greyhound has buses daily to Cape Town (US$46, 19 hours) via Bloemfontein (US$22), and to Kimberley (US$20).

Intercape has four services a week to Upington (US$29, 9½ hours). From Upington there is a connection to Cape Town (US$25, nine hours).

West Translux and **City Link** (☎ 773 2762) run daily to Mafikeng for US$9. The journey takes 5½ hours.

Intercape runs to Upington and from there to Windhoek (Namibia). However, there is no direct connection between the two services.

Minibus Taxi The main long-distance minibus taxi ranks cluster just inside the perimeter of the Park Station complex, where security is pretty tight. Be very careful, however, about venturing to the few taxis beyond the 'cordon' (such as the Lesotho-bound taxis). It may not seem far, but walking about laden with rucksacks is asking for trouble. Take a taxi round to these minibuses or use the left luggage facilities while you sort out a fare and get one of the taxi guys to help you with your bags if necessary.

Some destinations and approximate fares from Jo'burg include: Bulawayo in Zimbabwe (US$23); Cape Town (US$34); Durban (US$14); Gaborone in Botswana (US$12.50); Kimberley (US$11); Manzini in Swaziland (US$10.50); Maseru in Lesotho (US$10.50); Nelspruit (US$10.50); Pietersburg/Polokwane (US$11).

As well as these minibus taxis, which leave when they are full, there are a few door-to-door services which you can book. Durban (about US$16.50 from Jo'burg) is well served. Ask about these at hostels.

Train Trains from Johannesburg's Park Station travel to Maputo (Mozambique; change at Komatipoort). For more details, see the Getting Around section at the start of this chapter.

There are sometimes 25% discounts available on train tickets, making them very competitive with the major bus services. Contact **Spoornet** (☎ 0860-008888) for information.

The Main Line ticket office is open from 7.30am to 5pm weekdays and until 1pm Saturday.

The station's left-luggage department is open from 6am to 7pm daily (9am to 6pm on Sunday). For more information on trains from Jo'burg, see the Getting Around section in this chapter.

Car The major companies have counters at the airport and offices around the city. Operators and their toll-free numbers include: **Avis** (☎ 0861-021111); **Budget** (☎ 0861-016622); **Imperial** (☎ 0800-131000).

There aren't many budget-priced rental companies; your best bet is to ask at a hostel, which can often negotiate special deals.

For details on purchasing a car, see the Getting Around the Region chapter.

Hitching Although absolutely *not* recommended, especially around Jo'burg, some will do it anyway. Heading north, a popular place to hitch is on the N1 near the Killarney Mall shopping centre, a couple of kilometres northwest of Yeoville. The N12 running east towards Kruger National Park begins just east of Eastgate Mall. Heading south on the N1 (to Cape Town, for example) you could try your luck on one of the freeway on-ramps.

Also check on hostel notice boards for details of free or shared-cost lifts.

Getting Around

To/From the Airport Between 5am and 10pm, buses run every half-hour between Johannesburg International Airport and Park Station transit centre. Journey time is about 25 minutes and the fare is about US$9. There's also the **Magic Bus** (☎ 608 1662; US$22.50) which costs more but drops off at the more expensive hotels. Hire taxis aren't cheap (around US$23).

Buses also run from the airport to Pretoria. See Getting There & Away in the Pretoria section for details.

Bus For inquiries about local bus services, call or visit the information counter (☎ 403 4300) on Gandhi Square. Most services stop by 7pm and most fares are about US$0.60. Routes Nos 5 (Parktown, Houghton, Rosebank and Illovo), 22 (Yeoville and Bruma) and 67 (Braamfontein, Auckland Park and Melville) are useful.

The buses that run out to Sandton are not part of the municipal fleet; they're operated by **Padco** (☎ 474 2634). The Padco buses leave the city centre from the corner of Kruis and Commissioner Sts.

Minibus Taxi Fares differ depending on the route, but US$0.80 will get you around the inner suburbs and the city centre. It's easy to get a minibus taxi into the city centre and, if you're waiting at a bus stop, a minibus will probably arrive before the bus does. Getting a minibus taxi back from the city is more difficult.

Train For inquiries about Metro trains, call ☎ 773 5878 or ☎ 0800-127070 or visit the information office in the Park Station concourse. There has been a serious problem with violent crime on the metropolitan system, mostly on lines connecting with black townships. In recent times the line between Pretoria and Jo'burg has been particularly bad. Be careful.

Taxi There are hire taxi ranks in the city centre and at the airport. Taxis have meters but once you get an idea of distances and prices, try agreeing on a price rather than using the meter. **Maxi Taxi** (☎ 648 1212) is a reputable company.

PRETORIA
☎ 012 • pop 1,541,300

Although the two cities are less than 60km apart, Pretoria's history bears no relation to Johannesburg's and they have very different atmospheres. Pretoria is South Africa's national administrative capital and is a more relaxed place that in recent times has been shedding its conservative image. The Sotho-speaking citizens call the city 'Tshwane'.

History
The Great Trek reached its logical conclusion in the early 1850s when the British granted independence to the Zuid-Afrikaan-sche Republiek (ZAR; South African Republic) north of the Vaal River, and to the, then Orange, Free State between the Orange and Vaal Rivers.

In 1853 two farms on the Apies River were bought as the site for the republic's capital. The ZAR was a shaky institution though. There were ongoing wars with the black tribes and violent disputes among the Boers themselves. Pretoria, which was named after Andries Pretorius, hero of the Battle of Blood River, was the scene of fighting during the 1863–69 Boer Civil War.

The discovery of gold on the Witwatersrand in the late 1880s revolutionised the situation. A small community of farmers suddenly controlled some of the richest real estate in the world.

Orientation
The main east–west road is Church (Kerk) St which, at 26km, is claimed to be one of the longest straight streets in the world. Fortunately most of the sights, decent hotels and restaurants in the city centre are not far apart. Church St runs through Church Square (although traffic is diverted), the historic centre of the city, and east to the suburb of Arcadia, home of most of the hotels and embassies, as well as the Union buildings.

Information
Tourist Offices The **Pretoria Tourism information bureau** (☎ 337 4430; w www .pretoria.co.za; Church Square; open 7.30am-4pm Mon-Fri) close to Cafe Riche is thinly stocked with brochures and pretty hopeless. If you're lucky you might find a copy of the useful *Pretoria Guide*.

The **National Parks Board head office** (☎ 428 9111; w www.parks-sa.co.za; PO Box 787, Pretoria 0001, 643 Leyds St, New Muckleneuk) is southeast of the city centre. Bookings may be made here and there's some information.

Immigration Office Applications for visa extensions are made to the **Department of Home Affairs** (☎ 324 1860; 1st fl, Sentrakor Bldg, Pretorius St), near Church Square.

Money For currency exchange, try **AmEx** (☎ 346 2599; Brooklyn Mall). **Rennies Travel** (☎ 320 2240; Sanlam Centre, cnr Andries & Pretorius Sts) has a few branches. If you're

SOUTH AFRICA

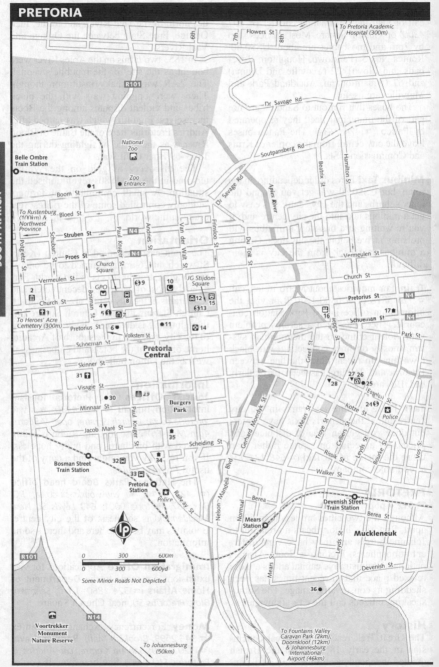

PRETORIA

To Pretoria Academic Hospital (300m)

Flowers St

6th
7th
8th

R101

Dr Savage Rd

Soutpansberg Rd

Beatrix St
Hamilton St

Belle Ombre Train Station

National Zoo

Zoo Entrance

Dr Savage Rd

Aapies River

1

Boom St

To Rustenburg (100km) & Northwest Province

Bloed St

Struben St

Proes St

Schubart St

Potgieter St

Paul Kruger St

Andries St

Van der Walt St

Frislsoo St

Du Toit St

N4

N4

Vermeulen St

Church St

Church Square

GPO

2

Church St

To Heroes' Acre Cemetery (300m)

3

Pretorius St

6

Schoeman St

Volkstem St

Bosman St

4

5

9

8

7

10

11

JG Stijdom Square

12

13

15

14

Pretoria Central

Vermeulen St

Church St

Pretorius St   N4

16

Schoeman St

17

Park St

Skinner St

31

Visagie St

30

Minnaar St

Jacob Maré St

Paul Kruger St

29

Burgers Park

35

Scheiding St

Greef St

Aapies St

27 26

28

25

Esselen St

24

Police

Mean St

Gerhard Moerdyk St

Troye St

Celliers St

Kotze St

Rissik St

Leyds St

Boukte St

Bosman Street Train Station

32

33

Pretoria Station

Police

34

Railway St

Nelson Mandela Blvd

Normaal

Berea

Walker St

Devenish Street Train Station

Berea St

Muckleneuk

0   300   600m
0   300   600yd
Some Minor Roads Not Depicted

Mears Station

Leyds St

Mears St

Vos St

Devenish St

R101

N14

Voortrekker Monument Nature Reserve

To Johannesburg (50km)

36

To Fountains Valley Caravan Park (2km), Doornkloof (12km) & Johannesburg International Airport (46km)

PRETORIA

PLACES TO STAY
17 Hotel 224
18 Sheraton Pretoria
20 La Maison
34 Manhattan Hotel
35 Kia Ora; Hole in the Wall
37 Mazuri Backpackers Lodge
38 That's It!
39 Pretoria Backpackers
40 Manor Protea Hotel
46 Hatfield Backpackers
47 North South Backpackers

PLACES TO EAT
4 Cafe Riche
27 Grapevine
28 Giovanni's; London Tavern
41 Bugatti's
48 Brasserie de Paris
50 The News Cafe
52 Greenfields

OTHER
1 Craft Stalls
2 Paul Kruger House; Pass Office
3 Dutch Reformed Church (Paul Kruger's Church)
5 Tourist Information Bureau
6 Department of Home Affairs
7 Taxi Rank
8 Bus Terminus
9 First National Bank
10 Mosque
11 Sanlam Centre; Rennies Travel
12 Taxi Rank
13 ABSA Bank
14 Tramshed Complex
15 State Theatre Complex
16 Sterland Cinemas
19 Swaziland Embassy
21 Australian Embassy
22 US Embassy
23 Pretoria Art Museum
24 ASBA Bank
25 Pharmacy
26 Web Weavers
29 Transvaal Museum of Anthropology & Geology
30 City Hall
31 Catholic Cathedral of the Sacred Heart
32 Long-distance Minibus Taxis
33 Greyhound, Translux & Intercape Terminal
36 National Parks Board Head Office
42 Hatfield Galleries; Odyssey Internet Cafe; Tings an' Times
43 First National Bank
44 STA Travel
45 Hatfield Plaza; Pick 'n' Pay
49 Hatfield Square; McGinty's; Drop Zone; Mozarellas
51 ABSA Bankteller
53 Cool Runnings
54 Brooklyn Mall; AmEx

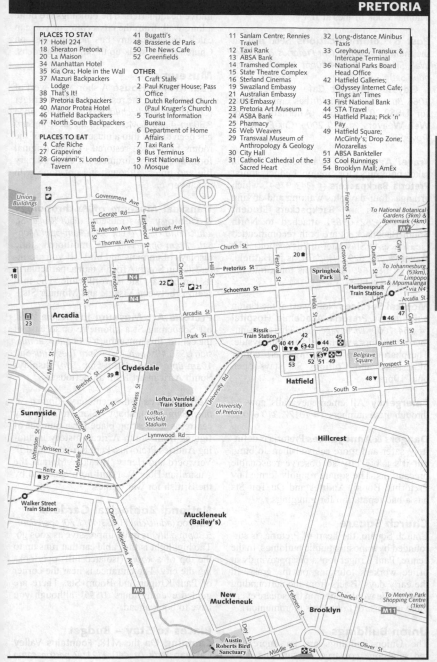

SOUTH AFRICA

flying in, there are also 24-hour AmEx and Thomas Cook offices at JIA.

Post & Communications Send mail at the **main post office** *(cnr Pretorius & Van der Walt Sts; open 8am-4.30pm Mon-Fri, 8am-noon Sat).*

Odyssey Internet Cafe *(☎ 362 2467; 1066 Burnett St, Hatfield)* has email access for US$2.20 per hour. Alternatively try **Web Weavers** *(☎ 440 2905, Cnr Esselen & Troye Sts).*

Travel Agencies The hostels in Pretoria take bookings for many budget tours; **Pretoria Backpackers** *(☎ 343 9754),* which arranges four-day-plus walking and driving Kruger tours and **Backpackers Student Travel** *(☎ 362 0989)* attached to North South Backpackers are both recommended (see Places to Stay later in this section). **STA Travel** *(☎ 342 5292; Hilda St)* is in Hatfield. **Jabu** *(☎ 082 649 6368)* runs tours into the nearby townships.

Medical Services Northwest of the Union buildings is **Pretoria Academic Hospital** *(☎ 354 1000; Dr Savage Rd).* There are numerous chemists in Hatfield and Sunnyside. The pharmacy on the northwestern corner of Esselen and Collings Sts stays open until 10pm.

Emergency All emergency calls now go through these numbers: *(☎ 10177, 310 6400).*

Dangers & Annoyances Pretoria is definitely safer and more relaxed than Jo'burg, but it's a big city so observe reasonable precautions. The square roughly formed by Pretorius, Boom, Andries and Du Toit Sts has a bad reputation for muggings.

Church Square
Church Square, the heart of Pretoria, is surrounded by imposing public buildings. In the centre, Paul Kruger looks disapprovingly at office workers lounging on the grass. In the early days, Boers from the surrounding countryside would gather in the square every three months for *achtmaals* (communion).

Union Buildings
The Union buildings are an impressive red sandstone construction surrounded by

gardens. They are the government's administrative headquarters. The buildings are quite a long walk from the city centre, or you can catch just about any bus heading east on Church St and walk up through the gardens.

Museums
Paul Kruger House A short walk west of Church Square, the residence of Paul Kruger *(Church St; adult/child US$1.30/0.60; open 8.30am-4.30pm Mon-Sat, 9am-4.30pm Sun)* has been turned into a museum. Some of the rooms have been restored to their original form, and others chronicle his extraordinary life and times, although it's not done with much verve.

Transvaal Museum of Anthropology & Geology This museum *(Paul Kruger St; adult/child US$1/0.60; open 9am-5pm Mon-Sat, 11am-5pm Sun)* has traditional static displays of animals and birds. If you are interested in South Africa's fauna, particularly its birdlife, a visit is worthwhile. The museum is between Visagie and Minnaar Sts.

Pretoria Art Museum In Arcadia Park, off Schoeman St a kilometre or so east of the centre, this museum *(☎ 344 1807; admission US$0.40; open 10am-5pm Tues, Thur-Sat, 10am-8pm Wed, 10am-5pm Sun)* displays South African art from all periods.

Heroes Acre This cemetery *(Church St; open 8am-6pm),* about 1.5km from the city centre, is the resting place for a number of figures from South African history including Andries Pretorius, Paul Kruger, Hendrik Verwoerd and Henry 'Breaker' Morant, the Australian Boer War anti-hero executed by the British for war crimes.

National Zoological Gardens
The zoo *(adult/child US$3.40/1.70; open 8am-5.30pm daily)* is quite impressive as zoos go. The highlight is the cable car that runs up to the top of a *kopje* (isolated hill) overlooking the city. The entrance is near the corner of Paul Kruger and Boom Sts. There are guided evening tours *(US$5),* although you have to book ahead.

Places to Stay – Budget
Camping On the M18, **Fountains Valley Caravan Park** *(☎ 440 2121; 2-person camp*

sites US$5.80) is a good facility with plenty of camp sites, a pool and tennis courts.

Hostels Competition between hostels is keen, so see what you can get in the way of (Jo'burg) airport pick-ups, free beers etc. Almost every hostel runs a travel and tour agency on the side.

Pretoria Backpackers *(☎ 343 9754, 083 302 1976; 425 Farenden St; camping US$5, dorm beds US$8.50, doubles US$18)* is a clean place with a lovely garden and conservatory area. The owners can also arrange budget tours.

Hatfield Backpackers *(☎ 362 5501, 0800-108102; 1226 Park St;* e *ata@mweb.co.za; camping US$6.40, dorm beds US$8, singles/ doubles US$16.50/19.50)* on the scruffy side perhaps but it's close to Hatfield's hotspots, offers airport pick-ups and has a large outdoor bar. Ask here about tours.

North South Backpackers *(☎ 362 0989;* e *northsouth@mweb.co.za; 355 Glyn St, Hatfield; camping US$4.50, dorm beds US$8, doubles US$21)* is an excellent, recommended hostel in a large comfortable suburban house. It's an easy walk to buzzing Burnett St, and the helpful owners can organise tours and bargain rental car deals. Lovers of peace and quiet can stay in comfortable budget doubles in a house nearby.

Kia Ora *(☎ 322 4803;* e *hostel@absamail .co.za; 257 Jacob Maré St; dorm beds US$7.50, singles/doubles US$16/18)* is central and built around the convivial Hole in the Wall, a pub with a great atmosphere inhabited by a good mixture of locals, white and black.

Mazuri Backpackers Lodge *(☎/fax 343 7782, 082 431 6077;* e *mazuri@ananzi.co.za; dorm beds US$6.40, doubles US$17.50)* is basic but friendly and cheap. The owner is the man to ask about trips into Venda.

Places to Stay – Mid-Range

That's It! *(☎ 344 3404;* w *thatsit.co.za; 5 Brecher St; B&B singles/doubles US$22/33)*, near the corner of Farenden St, is a very welcoming B&B in a leafy corner of Sunnyside. There's an immaculate back garden with a pool and a large outdoor eating area.

Hotel 224 *(☎ 440 5281;* e *hotel224@satic .co.za; doubles from US$29)* is a reasonably located high-rise hotel with some good views across town.

You can also contact the **Bed & Breakfast Association** *(☎ 430 3571)*; prices start at around US$22 for rooms.

Places to Stay – Top End

La Maison *(☎ 430 4341; 235 Hilda St, Hatfield; singles/doubles US$49/80)* is an enchanting historic house with three beautiful guest rooms. The owner is a cordon bleu chef.

Manhattan Hotel *(☎ 392 0000; Cnr Andries & Scheiding Sts; rooms US$48, suites US$50)* is a friendly, efficient and plush place close to the centre. It's also one of the few black-run places in town.

Manor Protea Hotel *(☎ 362 7077;* e *mp hotel@satis.co.za; cnr Burnett & Festival Sts, Hatfield; singles/doubles US$46/51)* provides standard corporate comfort that is smack in the middle of Hatfield's eating, drinking and partying heart.

Sheraton Pretoria *(☎ 429 9999; cnr Church & Wessels Sts; standard rooms US$75)* is a stunning, if snooty, place with a towering marble atrium.

Places to Eat

City Centre The best spot in the city for people watching is **Cafe Riche** *(☎ 328 3173; 2 Church St)*. It's an elegant marble-clad place with good, reasonably priced food and great coffee and croissants.

The **Tramshed complex** *(Van der Walt St)* is a good place to go for fast food such as burgers, pasta and curry.

Sunnyside Esselen St, to the southeast of the city, has numerous restaurants and takeaway joints, although the area is going downhill and many businesses and eateries have moved out.

Grapevine *(204 Esselen St)* is an excellent bakery. **Giovanni's**, upstairs across from the Sunnypark shopping centre, has good value Italian food. Downstairs, the **London Tavern** serves bar meals.

Hatfield Burnett St is blossoming into a swinging restaurant and café area.

Greenfields is very popular with the locals. **Bugatti's** is good for breakfast. **News Cafe** is good all day, and **Mozarella's** *(☎ 362 6464; mains US$4-4.50)*, serving pizza and pasta, is a great mid-priced option. A five-minute walk away (take care at night) is the swanky **Brasserie de Paris** *(☎ 362 2247;*

525 Duncan St; mains US$5.80-7) with high standards and prices.

Entertainment
Pubs & Bars The nightlife scene is progressively heading east, escaping the crime-ridden city centre and the increasingly seedy Esselen St.

There's a good buzz about Hatfield Square on Burnett St. It's packed with good eating and drinking places which overflow with diners and revellers most nights. **McGinty's** (open 11am-late daily) is an 'Irish' pub. **Cool Runnings** (Burnett St), with a studenty vibe, and **Tings 'an Times** (Hatfield Galleries, off Burnett St), with a friendly, mixed crowd, are two reggae joints close by. **Drop Zone** (Hatfield Square) a short stumble away, is Hatfield's pick-up place of choice and quickly gets packed.

Cinemas & Theatre There are several enormous cinema complexes.

Sterland (cnr Pretorius & Beatrix Sts) is the largest cinema complex. **State Theatre** (☎ 322 1665; cnr Prinsloo & Church Sts) hosts quite a range of high culture (opera, music, ballet and theatre). Check local newspapers for listings.

Getting There & Away
Bus Most inter-provincial and international bus services commence in Pretoria unless they are heading north. Most buses leave from the forecourt of Pretoria train station on Paul Kruger St.

Most **Translux** (☎ 315 2333) and **Greyhound** (☎ 323 1154) services running from Jo'burg to Durban, the south coast and Cape Town originate in Pretoria (for more information, see Getting There & Away under Johannesburg earlier in this chapter). Translux and City to City services running north up the N1 also stop here.

Intercape (☎ 654 4114) has services to Upington (US$29, 11½ hours), connecting with a service to Cape Town. From Upington you can also get an Intercape bus to Windhoek (Namibia), but there isn't a direct connection.

Fares for these operators are identical to those from Jo'burg. It's US$3.50 to travel between the two cities.

Translux fares from Pretoria include: Durban (US$20, 9½ hours); Kimberley (US$19, 7¼ hours); Nelspruit (US$15, 5½ hours); Beitbridge (US$23.50, seven hours); Bloemfontein (US$21, 7½ hours); Knysna (US$42, 18¾ hours); Port Elizabeth (US$35, 15½ hours); and Cape Town (US$46, 19 hours).

Train Pretoria has a train connection with Maputo (Mozambique; change at Komatipoort). For other train services, it may be necessary to get to Jo'burg first (for further details see the Getting Around section at the start of this chapter).

The **train station** (☎ 315 2757) is about a 20-minute walk from the city centre; all Main Line services can be booked here. Buses run along Paul Kruger St to Church Square, the main local bus terminus. Major services running through Pretoria include the *Trans Karoo* (to Kimberley and Cape Town daily) and the *Komati* (Jo'burg to Komatipoort Mon-Sun and the Bosvelder via Pietersburg to the Zimbabwe border daily). There are also services to Durban via Pietermaritzburg. The luxury *Blue Train* also runs to Cape Town on Monday, Wednesday and Friday.

There have recently been many violent robberies on the Metro system to Jo'burg, so we don't recommend it. A 1st-class train ticket to Jo'burg is US$1.80. The journey takes about 1¼ hours. On weekdays, trains run half-hourly from early in the morning, then hourly until 10pm. On weekends trains run about every 1½ hours. To find out the exact times, call ☎ 315 2007 in Pretoria or ☎ 011-773 5878 in Jo'burg.

Car The larger local and international companies are represented. **Swans** (☎ 0861-101 265); **Abba** (☎ 0861-101183) and **Budget** (☎ 0861-016622) all operate locally. **Buzz** (☎ 0860-072072) is pretty competitive with rates starting at US$18.50 per day with a daily 200km allowance.

Getting Around
To/From the Airport Many hostels offer airport pick-ups, some free, if you phone ahead. **Get You There** (☎ 346 3175) runs an hourly service from JIA day and night, dropping off at hotels and hostels for US$10.

Bus & Minibus Taxi The inquiry office (☎ 308 0839) and main terminus for local

buses is on the southeastern corner of Church Square. Some services, including the one to Sunnyside, run until about 10.30pm. The standard minibus fare around town is US$0.30. Long-distance minibus taxis leave from near the railway and bus stations just off Scheidling St.

Taxi There are ranks on the corner of Church and Van der Walt and at Vermeulen and Andries Sts, or call **Five Star** (☎ 320 7513/4). You'll pay about US$0.40 per kilometre.

AROUND PRETORIA
☎ 012
Doornkloof (Smuts' House)
General JC Smuts was a brilliant scholar, Boer general, politician and international statesman, and one of the architects of the Union of South Africa. His home, south of Pretoria, is now an excellent museum (☎ 667 1176; admission house/garden US$0.60/0.40; open 9.30am-4.30pm Mon-Sat, 9.30am-5pm Sun).

There's a small **cafeteria** with an outdoor tea garden, and a pleasant **caravan park** (☎ 667 1176; camp sites US$5.80).

There is no access by public transport. The house is signposted from both the N1 freeway (R28) and the R21.

Cheetah Research & Breeding Centre (De Wildt)
Just outside Pretoria, the Cheetah Research & Breeding Centre (☎ 504 1921) has excellent half-day tours for US$11.50. As well as cheetahs you'll probably see wild dogs, meerkats, honey badgers and lots of birds.

The only way to reach this centre is by car. It's about a 45-minute drive from Pretoria and is located just off the R513.

Pretoria National Botanical Gardens
The botanical gardens (open 6am-5.30pm daily; admission US$0.80) cover 77 hectares and are planted with indigenous flora from around the country. They are 11km east of the city centre.

To get there, catch the Meyerspark or Murrayfield bus from Church Square. By car, head east along Church St (R104) for about 9km, then turn right into Cussonia Rd; the gardens are on the left-hand side.

Voortrekker Monument & Museum
The imposing cube of the Voortrekker Monument (☎ 326 6670; admission US$2.30; open 9am-4.45pm) towers over the outskirts of Pretoria and is probably the one thing not to miss while you're in Pretoria. Built in 1938 to commemorate the Boers who trekked north into the heart of the African veld (open grassland) it's a striking, if cheerless, temple to Afrikaner nationalism and an encapsulation of the Afrikaner mindset.

Inside, beautifully rendered white marble bas reliefs depict Boer and Zulu butchering one another with languid, classical poise. They tell the story of the treks and the Battle of Blood River in which a few hundred farmers defeated an army of 12,000 Zulus. A staircase and lift lead to the roof and a panoramic view of Pretoria and the highveld.

The monument is 6km south of the city, just east of the N1 freeway. Getting here by public transport isn't easy. Catch the municipal Voortrekkerhoogte or Valhalla bus from Kruger St, near the corner of Church Square. Ask the driver to let you off at the entrance road to the monument, from where it is a 10-minute walk uphill.

Free State

The Free State consists largely of the plains of the Southern African plateau. In the east you'll find the weirdly eroded sandstone hills of the highlands.

The Free State's borders reflect the role it has played in South African history (for more details, see History earlier in this chapter). To the south is the Orange River, which the Voortrekkers crossed to escape the Cape colony during the Great Trek. The northern border is defined by the Vaal River, which was the next frontier of Boer expansion. To the east, across the Mohokare (Caledon) River, is Lesotho, where mountains and Moshoeshoe the Great's warriors halted Boer expansion. To the southeast, the Free State spills across the Caledon River as the mountains dwindle to grazing land, which was harder for Moshoeshoe to defend.

SOUTH AFRICA

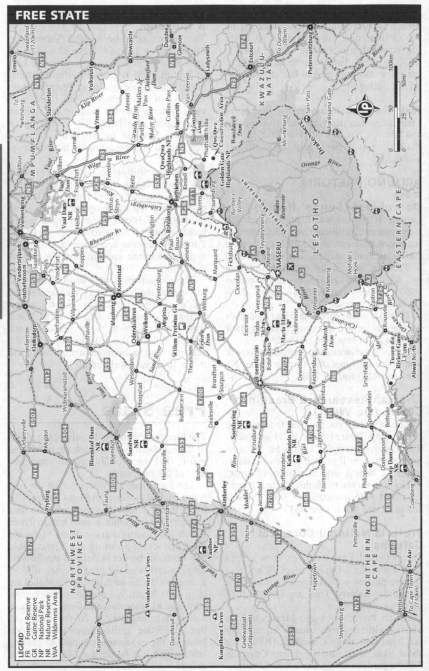

FREE STATE

SOUTH AFRICA

LEGEND
FR Forest Reserve
GR Game Reserve
NP National Park
NR Nature Reserve
WA Wilderness Area

Concentration Camps

During the 1899–1902 Anglo-Boer War the British invented the concentration camp in response to harassment by guerrilla bands that were helped by – and included – Afrikaner farmers. The British burned the farms of suspected combatants and sent Afrikaner women and children to concentration camps.

By the end of the war 200,000 Afrikaner women and children were prisoners. More than 26,000, mostly children, had died in the camps, accounting for about 70% of Afrikaner deaths in the war. There were also concentration camps for blacks and, of the 80,000 people interned, it is estimated that 14,000 died.

For Afrikaners, the image of a man returning from his defeated commando unit to find his farm destroyed and his children dead remains a powerfully emotive one. The loss of political independence and the destruction of family, home and farm left Afrikaners with little but the Bible, deep bitterness and a determination to survive against any odds.

SOUTH AFRICA

BLOEMFONTEIN
☎ 051 • pop 378,000
Bloemfontein (literally, Fountain of Flowers), known as 'Bloem', is the provincial capital and South Africa's judicial capital. As well as the legal community there is a university and a large military camp, so you can meet a wide range of people. Most of the blacks still live in the enclaves they were shunted into during the apartheid days. Botshabelo, on the Thaba 'Nchu road, is one of the largest 'locations' in the country.

History
In 1854 the Orange Free State was created, with Bloemfontein as the capital, and in 1863 Johannes Brand began his 25-year term as president. During Brand's presidency, Bloemfontein grew from being a struggling frontier town, in constant danger of being wiped out by Moshoeshoe the Great's warriors, to a wealthy provincial capital with railway links to the coast.

Orientation & Information
The central area is laid out on a grid and Hoffman Square is the centre of the downtown area. To the northeast is Naval Hill, from where there are good views of the town and surrounding plains.

Tourist information can be found at the friendly **Bloemfontein Tourist Centre** (☎ 405 8490; 60 Park Ave; **w** www.linx.co.za /bloemfontein), where there is also information on the rest of the Free State. There's an STA Travel branch and a Copy Centre here with cheap Internet and email access at US$1.80 per hour.

Museums
The most interesting display at the **National Museum** (cnr Charles & Aliwal Sts; admission US$0.60; open 7am-5pm Mon-Sat, 12.30pm-5.30pm Sun) is a re-creation of a 19th-century street.

The **National Women's Memorial & War Museum** (Monument Rd; admission US$0.70; open 9am-4.30pm Mon-Fri, 10am-4.30pm Sat, 2pm-4.30pm Sun), south of the centre, is devoted to the Anglo-Boer Wars and commemorates the Afrikaner women and children who died in British concentration camps (see the boxed text 'Concentration Camps').

President Brand St
If you head south down President Brand St from Voortrekker Rd, the **City Hall** (1934), with its reflecting pool, is on the right. On the next block, on the same side of the road, is **Fourth Raadsaal** (1929). Opposite is the **Appeal Court** (1893), which was the parliament house of the Orange Free State republic.

The **Old Government building** (1908) is on the corner of Elizabeth St and diagonally opposite, on the block between Maitland and St Andrew Sts, is the **Jubileum building and hall**.

Further down President Brand on the corner of Fontein St you'll find the **fire station** (1933) and the imposing **Supreme Court** (1906).

Just north of the corner of St Georges St, the **Old Presidency** is a grand Victorian-style building. Free State presidents once lived here in what must have seemed extraordinary opulence for the times. There's a **museum** (admission free; open afternoons Tues-Fri, Sun). On St Georges St just east of President Brand St is

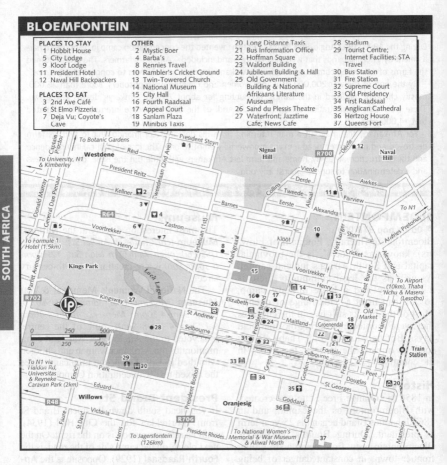

BLOEMFONTEIN

PLACES TO STAY	OTHER	20 Long Distance Taxis	28 Stadium
1 Hobbit House	2 Mystic Boer	21 Bus Information Office	29 Tourist Centre;
5 City Lodge	4 Barba's	22 Hoffman Square	Internet Facilities; STA
9 Kloof Lodge	8 Rennies Travel	23 Waldorf Building	Travel
11 President Hotel	10 Rambler's Cricket Ground	24 Jubileum Building & Hall	30 Bus Station
12 Naval Hill Backpackers	13 Twin-Towered Church	25 Old Government	31 Fire Station
	14 National Museum	Building & National	32 Supreme Court
PLACES TO EAT	15 City Hall	Afrikaans Literature	33 Old Presidency
3 2nd Ave Café	16 Fourth Raadsaal	Museum	34 First Raadsaal
6 St Elmo Pizzeria	17 Appeal Court	26 Sand du Plessis Theatre	35 Anglican Cathedral
7 Deja Vu; Coyote's	18 Sanlam Plaza	27 Waterfront; Jazztime	36 Hertzog House
Cave	19 Minibus Taxis	Cafe; News Cafe	37 Queens Fort

the **First Raadsaal**, the original parliament house, with its thatched roof and dung floors.

Places to Stay

Bloemfontein hosts important cricket and rugby games, and accommodation is scarce on match weekends.

Places to Stay – Budget

Two kilometres from the centre, **Reyneke Park** (☎ 523 3888; Petrusburg Rd; caravan sites US$8.50, chalets US$31) is well maintained and has four-person chalets.

Naval Hill Backpackers (☎ 430 7266; Delville St; e descover@iafrica.com; dorm beds US$7.50, singles/doubles US$10.50/16) is in an old water-pumping station. The industrial decor is stylish but noise carries,

there's not a lot of privacy and it's an oven on summer nights.

Places to Stay – Mid-Range & Top End

Formule 1 Hotel (☎ 831 2552; 200 Zastron St; 3-bed rooms US$22.50) has bland rooms with a double and a bunk, but it's good value.

Kloof Lodge (☎ 447 7603, fax 447 7746; e kloof@global.co.za; cnr Kellner & Kloof Sts; singles/doubles US$30/34) is a comfortable guesthouse with spacious rooms that come with bathroom, TV and phone; there's a cosy bar downstairs. It's popular so book ahead.

President Hotel (☎ 430 1111, fax 430 4141; 1 Union Ave, Naval Hill; singles/doubles US$42/48) is a fairly good value three-star place close to Naval Hill.

Hobbit House *(☎ 447 0663; 19 President Steyn St, Westdene; singles/doubles US$45/80)* is a self-styled 'boutique hotel' in a handsome 1920s house. Don't let the Tolkein-theme or the profusion of teddy bears put you off. The owners pride themselves on their faultless service and impeccable facilities and it's hard to beat.

City Lodge *(☎ 444 2974; cnr Voortrekker Rd & Parfitt Ave; singles/doubles US$45/52)* offers the usual, comfortable, corporate facsimile.

Places to Eat
There are a few places around the corners of Tweedelaan (2nd Ave) between Kellner and Zastron Sts, including a **St Elmo Pizzeria** *(pizzas US$3-5)*. **2nd Ave Cafe** *(cnr Tweedelaan & Kellner Sts; breakfast US$2.50-3.50)* offers cheap, hearty breakfast deals.

There are loads of places to eat at the Waterfront in King's Park. The lively **Jazztime Cafe** *(mains from US$4.50)* stands out, although the music can be too loud. Try the *zivas* (US$3), a Yemeni-style dough stuffed with a variety of fillings (such as Cajun chicken, feta and avocado) rolled and toasted. The cocktails here pack a punch.

Entertainment
Forget what other South Africans tell you about this being a dull town – Bloemfonteiners party down with a passion. Being a university town, Bloem has always had a fair range of places to drink but there's a particular buzz about the half-dozen or so places on Tweedelaan and Kellner Sts.

The Mystic Boer *(Zastron St)* is a brilliantly decorated place. Technicolor Boer commandos glare from the walls while Bloem's party people sit and chat on ammo boxes, or get down to music from the decks, which usually has an alternative flavour.

Barba's *(16 2nd Ave)* is packed at weekends with a young and cheerful crowd but there's always space to swig a beer or practice your dad-dancing. A great place to end up after a couple of sharpeners elsewhere.

News Cafe *(The Waterfront)* is one of several relaxed watering holes on the Waterfront.

Déjá Vu *(158 Voortrekker St)* is a good place to kick the evening off. And **Coyote's Cave**, with a good beer garden, is next door.

Getting There & Away
Bus Long-distance bus services arrive and leave from the tourist centre on Park Rd. **Translux** *(☎ 408 4888)* runs to Durban (US$25, nine hours), Jo'burg/Pretoria (US$21, 7½ hours), Port Elizabeth (US$24, 8½ hours), East London (US$22), Knysna (US$28, 12 hours) and Cape Town (US$38, 12½ hours).

Greyhound *(☎ 447 1558)* has similar services. **Intercape** *(☎ 447 1435)* runs to Jo'burg (US$22) and Cape Town (US$39).

Minibus Taxi Most minibus taxis leave from near the train station. Long-distance taxis leave about 100m south of the covered local minibus taxi stand. Destinations include Kimberley (US$5.80), Maseru in Lesotho (US$5.80) and Jo'burg (US$10.50). The Manguang Taxi Association *(☎ 051-448 5082)* has more details.

Train For train information call ☎ 086-000 8888.

The *Trans Oranje* (Durban–Cape Town), the *Amatola* (Jo'burg–East London) and the *Algoa* (Jo'burg–Port Elizabeth) all stop in Bloemfontein.

Getting Around
To/From the Airport The airport is 10km from the city centre. There's no public transport so you'll have to take a taxi (around US$11.50).

Buses & Taxis The public bus system services stop early in the evening. All buses run through Hoffman Square, and the **bus information office** *(☎ 448 4951; Central Park)* has timetables. To get to Naval Hill take bus No 2 to Union Ave and walk from there.

For taxis, try **President Taxis** *(☎ 522 3399)* or **Silver Leaf Taxis** *(☎ 430 2005)*.

NORTHERN FREE STATE & GOLDFIELDS
The Free State goldfields produce more than a third of the country's total gold output. The goldfields are centred on Welkom, Virginia and Odendaalsrus.

Kroonstad
☎ 0562
Kroonstad on the N1 is a typical large rural town, dating back to 1855. Sarel Celliers (of

the Blood River Vow) was one of the first settlers (for more details see History in the Facts about South Africa section).

The **Old Market building**, opposite the pretty **Magistrate's building** (cnr Mark & Murray Sts) is a national monument. Upstairs in the library there's the small **Sarel Celliers Museum**, and some tourist information.

Places to Stay & Eat Across the river from the town centre, **Kroon Park** (☎ 213 1942; sites per tent/person from US$6.40, chalets US$29) is more like a resort than a municipal caravan park.

Angelo's Trattoria (Reitz St) is good for Italian food, with pasta from US$2.50.

There's a **Spur** and a **KFC** on Buitekant St.

Getting There & Away Translux services between Jo'burg/Pretoria and East London, Knysna and Port Elizabeth stop at the Shell Ultra City on the highway, as does Greyhound's Jo'burg/Pretoria–Port Elizabeth service.

The *Amatola* (Jo'burg–East London) and *Algoa* (Jo'burg–Port Elizabeth) trains stop here. The minibus taxi park is opposite the train station.

SOUTHERN FREE STATE

The Southern Free State is dusty, harsh and dry, and the many windmills are reminiscent of parts of remote areas in Australia.

Tussen Die Riviere Game Farm

This reserve (☎ 051-763 1114; closed May-end Aug) has more animals than any other in the Free State, including white rhinos and hippos. For keen hikers, there are the Middelpunt (7km), the Klipstapel (12km) and the Orange River (16km) **hiking trails**; water must be carried on all of them.

There are **tent sites** and cheap **chalets** but no food is available. The entrance gate is on the road between Bethulie and Smithfield (R701), about 65km east of the N1.

Stokstert Hiking Trail

This overnight trail is in the Caledon River Conservancy Area, near Smithfield. This huge area includes the land of more than 60 farmers who have adopted conservation-based techniques. To book hikes write to: The Secretary, Caledon River Conservancy Area, PO Box 71, Smithfield 9966.

EASTERN HIGHLANDS

This is the most beautiful part of the Free State, stretching from Zastron in the south to Harrismith in the northeast. In addition to their tremendous scenery, the Eastern Highlands present important historical and archaeological interest.

Zastron
☎ 051

Zastron on the R726 is a quiet, dull little town. Its saving grace is its location at the foothills of the striking Aasvoëlberg and Maluti Mountains. There are some **San paintings** in the area; the best are in the Seekoei and Hoffman Caves. Contact the **tourist information office** (☎ 673 1018)

The **caravan park** (☎ 673 1397; tent sites US$5) is a few kilometres out of town. It's a nice walk down a wooded gorge.

The **Maluti Hotel** (☎/fax 673 2112; singles/ doubles US$17/27) isn't getting any younger but will do for a night. It has a fair to middling pub and restaurant.

There's no scheduled public transport to or from Zastron.

Ladybrand
☎ 051

Ladybrand on the R26 is the closest South African town to the main border crossing (16km from Ladybrand) into Lesotho. It's a pretty place and makes a good base for trips into Lesotho if you prefer the little luxuries that are so hard to find over the border.

The **tourist office** (☎ 924 5131; cnr Voortrekker & Church Sts; open 8am-5pm Mon-Fri) is helpful and has a wealth of information on the rock art in the area and local rock climbing routes.

There are some nice **sandstone buildings**, including the town hall and the Old Magistrate's Court. The **Catharina Brand Museum** has rock paintings and Stone Age tools. **Rose Cottage Cave** is the site of an ancient settlement thought to be 50,000 years old.

Places to Stay & Eat A peaceful resort 2km south of the town hall, **Leliehoek Holiday Resort** (☎ 924 0260; camp sites from US$6.40, chalets from US$14), is set in lovely grounds with a large swimming pool and rock climbing facilities.

Traveller's Inn (☎/fax 924 0191; 23A Kolbe St; singles/doubles/triples US$17.50/25/39) is

reasonably central and has spartan but clean rooms.

Cranberry Cottage *(☎ 924 2290; e cran cott@lesoff.co.za; singles/doubles from US$29/ 50, weekend specials US$22/38)* is the pick of the guesthouses in town with simple but beautifully decorated cottages in serene grounds.

Imperio Romano *(☎ 924 1184; 11 Church St; mains US$3.50-6)* is an excellent Italian restaurant with a pleasant, shaded courtyard.

Getting There & Away Minibus taxis gather near the church on Piet Retief St. Most run locally, including Ficksburg (US$2.30). For long-distance taxis head to Maseru Bridge (at the Lesotho border) for US$0.60.

Ficksburg
☎ 051

This town is in sandstone country and there are some fine buildings, including the town hall, the NG Kerk and the post office.

Ficksburg is the centre of the Free State's cherry industry and the **Cherry Trail** is a tourist route around the district. There are several orchards to visit, art and craft shops, some guest farms and hiking trails. **Ficksburg Tourism Office** *(☎ 933 2130)* has information.

Thom Park *(☎ 083 592 1267; Voortrekker Rd; camp sites US$4)* is the municipal caravan park.

Hoogland Hotel *(☎ 933 2214; Market Square; singles/doubles without bathroom US$14/23, with bathroom US$21/34)* near Voortrekker Rd is a decent, basic, good-value place.

Bella Rosa Guesthouse *(☎ 933 2623; 21 Bloem St; singles/doubles US$31/43)* is an outstanding guesthouse with a decent bar and restaurant and comfortable rooms with TVs and phones.

From Jo'burg, take a minibus taxi to Bethlehem and change there for Ficksburg.

Rustler's Valley
☎ 051

This remote valley in the heart of the conservative Free State is a haven for alternative lifestyle lovers. **Rustler's Valley** *(☎/fax 933 3939; W www.rustlers.co.za; camping US$3, dorm beds US$4.50, singles/doubles US$21/ 29)*, a resort in the valley of the same name, attracts a diverse crowd, including yuppies from Jo'burg and remnant hippies from all parts of the continent. It's a wonderful spot

with a decent café/restaurant and fantastical, fairytale gingerbread-style cottages.

You can walk up onto sandstone escarpments, climb imposing **Nyakalesoba** (Witch-doctor's Eye) and take horse rides into the labyrinthine dongas (steep-sided gullies).

There are also fairly regular parties and equinox festivals.

Getting There & Away If you've got wheels, the main turn-off is about 25km south of Fouriesburg on the R26 to Ficksburg. Head west on a dirt road that crosses the railway line. From the turn-off it is about 12km to Rustler's.

Alternatively, you can get to Ficksburg by taking a minibus taxi from Jo'burg to Bethlehem. At Bethlehem change buses for Ficksburg and call Rustler's to see if they can pick you up (they charge a small fee for this).

Fouriesburg
☎ 058

This is another town on the scenic R26, only 10km from the Calendonspoort border crossing into Lesotho and 50km from the Golden Gate Highlands National Park.

The **Brandwater Hiking Trail** is a five-day circular walk from the Meiringskloof Caravan Park, 3km from Fouriesburg, through varied sandstone country.

Camelroc Guest Farm *(☎ 223 0368; camping US$3.50, beds with breakfast US$15 per person, self-catering chalets US$35)* is a good base if you're heading into Lesotho as it's right by the Caledonspoort border crossing.

Golden Gate Highlands National Park

Golden Gate preserves the spectacular scenery of the foothills of the Maluti Mountains. There are also several animal species in the park, including grey rheboks, elands, oribis, Burchell's zebras, jackals and baboons.

Winters can be very cold here, with frost and snow; summers are mild but there's a good chance of rain and cold snaps are possible – if you're walking take warm clothing.

Rhebok Hiking Trail This circular, one-day trail (26km) is a great way to see the park. There are some steep sections so hikers need to be reasonably fit. The trail must be booked through the **National Parks Board** *(W www.parks-sa.co.za)*.

Places to Stay & Eat One option is **Glen Reenen** *(camp sites US$7.50, 3-bed bungalows from US$32)* which you can book through the **National Parks Board** (**w** *www.parks-sa.co.za*).

Getting There & Away The R711 is a sealed road into the park from Clarens, between Bethlehem and Fouriesburg. Alternatively, midway between Bethlehem and Harrismith on the R49 (N5), head south on the R712 and after a few kilometres turn west on a dirt road, or continue south on the R712 and head west about 7km before Phuthaditjhaba, QwaQwa.

QwaQwa
☎ 058

QwaQwa (master the 'click' pronunciation and you'll win friends) was once a small and extremely poor Homeland east of Golden Gate Highlands National Park.

Phuthaditjhaba, a burgeoning town with acres of new housing mushrooming on the outskirts, is a pretty ragged, unlovely place adjacent to the town of Witsieshoek and about 50km south of Harrismith. It has an **information centre** (☎ 713 5093, 713 5302) where you'll find details of hiking trails in the area. The **QwaQwa Conservation Area** covers 30,000 hectares in the foothills of both the Maluti Mountains and the Drakensberg. There are three excellent hiking trails: the Sentinel, the Fika Patso and the two-day Metsi Matsho.

Places to Stay In Phuthaditjhaba, **QwaQwa Hotel** *(☎ 713 0903; singles/ doubles with breakfast US$17/18)* is clean but uninspiring, set in the middle of an ugly shopping precinct.

Getting There & Away Minibus taxis to Harrismith cost US$1.30 and to Bethlehem the fare is US$4.

Bethlehem
☎ 058 • pop 37,700

Voortrekkers came to this area in the 1840s and Bethlehem was established in 1864. It's now a large, rather soulless town and the main centre of the eastern Free State.

The **tourist office** *(☎ 303 5732; Municipal Offices, East Miller St; open 7.30am-4.30pm Mon-Fri)* is close to the Pick 'n' Pay. There's a more central office but with sporadic opening hours and an uncertain future on the corner of Muller and High Sts.

As usual for this area, there are some impressive sandstone buildings, including the **Old Magistrate's Office** *(cnr Louw & Van der Merwe Sts)*, and the **NG Moederkerk** in the centre of town.

Places to Stay & Eat The tourist office has a full list of B&Bs.

Loch Athlone Holiday Resort *(☎ 303 4981; camping US$5.75, chalets per person from US$9)* is about 3km from the town centre.

Park Hotel *(☎ 303 5191; 23 Muller St; budget singles from US$13, standard doubles US$23)*, on the corner of High St, offers a range of accommodation and some good budget deals.

Fisant & Bokmakierie *(☎ 303 7144;* **e** *fisantBB@hotmail.com; 8 & 10 Thoi Oosthuyse St; singles/doubles US$28/36)* is an award-winning, comfortable and friendly guesthouse.

O'Hagen's *(Theron St)* serves better-than-average pub grub while **Nix Pub** *(Kerk St)* is a cosy place for a drink.

Getting There & Away Translux runs to Durban (US$18.50, five hours) and Cape Town (US$41, 16½ hours), as does Greyhound, with similar fares. Buses stop at Top Grill, on the corner of Church and Kerk Sts. Minibus taxis depart around the corner of Cambridge and Gholf Sts, north of the town centre on the way to the train station.

The weekly *Trans Oranje* (Cape Town–Durban) train stops here.

Northwest Province

The wide, hot plains of the Northwest Province were once covered entirely in scrub vegetation and thorn trees, but this is now an important agricultural territory. The dominant crop is mielies (maize) and the region also boasts the world's largest platinum mines, near Rustenburg.

San **rock art** sites attest to the original inhabitants of the area, but when the first white missionaries arrived in the 1830s the area was settled by Batswana. The Batswana were dispersed by Ndebele, who were themselves swept up in the wave of disruption

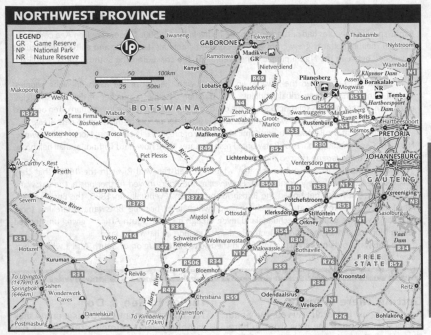

NORTHWEST PROVINCE

LEGEND
GR Game Reserve
NP National Park
NR Nature Reserve

unleashed during the *difaqane* (for more details see History in the Facts about the Region chapter).

As part of the apartheid regime's Homeland policy, the Batswana were relocated to Bophuthatswana (known as Bop); Northwest Province takes in most of the area once covered by Bop.

RUSTENBURG
☎ 014 • pop 120,900

Rustenburg is a large, dull, prosperous town at the western edge of the Magaliesberg Hills. Founded by Voortrekkers in 1841, it is the third-oldest town north of the Vaal River.

There's a good **tourist information centre** (☎ 597 0904; cnr Kloof St & Nelson Mandela Dr; open 8am-6pm Mon-Fri, 8am-noon Sat).

Things to See & Do

The **museum** (open 8.30am-4.30pm Mon-Fri, 9am-1pm Sat, 3pm-5pm Sun) is small but interesting, concentrating on the early Boer settlers. The original flag of the Zuid-Afrikaansche Republiek (ZAR; South African Republic) is on display.

Paul Kruger's farm, **Boukenhoutfontein**, just north of town, is worth visiting. A small section of the farm and several buildings have been preserved. These include a pioneer cottage built in 1841 and the main family homestead built in 1875, which is a fine example of Colesberg Cape Dutch style.

The **Rustenburg Nature Reserve**, at the western end of the Magaliesberg, is dominated by rocky ridges and wooded ravines.

Places to Stay & Eat

The plush **Hunter's Rest Hotel** (☎ 537 2140; B&B US$49) is an attractive resort 14km south of Rustenburg on the R30 with a large swimming pool, golf course and horse riding.

Ananda Country Lodge (☎ 597 1742; singles/doubles US$27/43) has camping facilities. It's 7km from town, close to a spectacular, looming *kloof* (ravine). Contact the owners for detailed directions.

As for eating out, **Karl's Bauernstube** (☎ 537 2128) has a good reputation. Otherwise you're stuck with standard fast-food places.

The Batswana

Bantu-speaking peoples had settlements on the highveld by AD 500. These were Iron Age communities and their inhabitants grew crops and kept domestic animals. Linguistic and cultural distinctions developed between the Nguni people, who lived along the coast, and the Sotho-Tswana, who lived on the highveld.

The Batswana (also called the Tswana), in common with the rest of the Bantu-speaking peoples, formed clans within a larger tribal grouping. Oral tradition describes a number of dynastic struggles, often with competing sons splitting clans on the death of the old chief. This segmentation often occurred peacefully, partly because there was sufficient land available for people to move on to new areas.

By the 19th century, Batswana tribes dominated much of present-day Limpopo, Northwest Province, Northern Cape and large parts of Botswana. Fresh pastures were now hard to find, and all hell broke loose during the *difaqane* (forced migration).

Such was the devastation when the first whites crossed the Vaal River in the 1830s that they believed the land was largely uninhabited. However, as the Boers moved further north, the Batswana fought back. They also petitioned the British for protection. Eventually, in 1885, the British established the British Protectorate of Bechuanaland, which later became Botswana. Mafeking (now Mafikeng) was the capital of Bechuanaland, even though it was in South Africa – giving unintended recognition to the fact that the protectorate did not include all Batswana land.

The Batswana outside Bechuanaland found themselves in the Union of South Africa when it was created after the Boer War.

Getting There & Away

Rustenburg is not well served by South Africa's buses. Intercape runs from Jo'burg/Pretoria to Rustenburg (en route to Windhoek) four times a week (US$11).

SUN CITY

☎ 014

Sun City *(admission US$5.80)* is an extraordinary temple to gambling, mildly risque shows, Disney-esque interpretations of Africa and Vegas-style kitsch. There are also excellent golf courses, swimming pools, sports facilities, restaurants and high-quality accommodation. Such extravagance has always sat incongruously in such a relatively poor country, but these days it's also a refreshingly mixed place that's enthusiastically enjoyed by South Africa's black as well as white affluent classes. It's also a substantial local employer.

Entry to Sun City includes 'chips' worth US$3.50. You don't have to use these for gambling; you could put them towards a meal or entry to the impressive beach and Valley of the Waves, for example.

Information

The **Welcome Centre** (☎ 557 1544) at the entrance to the Entertainment Centre dispenses information and a useful bird's eye map.

Things to See & Do

The **Entertainment Centre** is a pretty tacky gambling venue aimed primarily at daytrippers and slot-machine addicts. There is also a bank, bingo hall, a number of reasonably priced restaurants, cinemas, shops and the 7000-seat Superbowl. The **Sun City Hotel** has a more sophisticated casino area, ranks of slot machines, restaurants and nightclubs.

The spectacular centrepiece of Sun City is **The Lost City**, an extraordinary piece of kitsch. There's also the **Valley of the Waves** where there is (surprise!) a large-scale wave machine. This is probably the best reason for non-gamblers to come to Sun City.

There's golf at the superb **Gary Player Country Club** (☎ 557 1528) and **Lost City Golf Course** (☎ 557 3700).

Waterworld on the shores of a large artificial lake has facilities for parasailing, water-skiing and windsurfing. Alternatively, you can play bowls (indoor and outdoor), go horse riding, work out in a gym, or play tennis or squash.

Places to Stay & Eat

Sun City Cabanas *(standard rooms from US$130)* is a laid-back place that has the cheapest (that is, relatively speaking) accommodation.

Sun City Hotel (*standard rooms from US$194*) is a lively place. It's the oldest and least expensive of the five-star hotels.

These hotels, and the occasional special package deal, can be booked through **Sun City** (☎ *557 8100*) or **Sun International central reservations** (☎ *011-780 7800*) in Jo'burg.

All the hotels have a selection of **restaurants**. In the **Entertainment Centre**, expect to pay from US$5 to US$7.50 for a straightforward meal.

Getting There & Away

Pilanesberg airport is about 9km northwest of the entrance to Sun City. **SA Airlink** (☎ *011-978 1111*) in Jo'burg flies daily from Jo'burg.

Several tour operators make the trip from Pretoria and Jo'burg; ask at your hostel to find out what's on offer.

Sun City is surprisingly poorly signposted. From Jo'burg it's around a two-hour drive, depending on which route you take. The most straightforward route is via Rustenburg on the R565.

PILANESBERG NATIONAL PARK
☎ 014

The superb Pilanesberg National Park surrounds Sun City and makes an accessible wildlife-watching destination from Pretoria or Jo'burg. The 500-sq-km park protects country of attractive rocky outcrops, ridges and craters, mostly covered in sparse woodland inside an unusual complex of extinct volcanoes.

Pilanesberg is home to white and black rhinos, elephants, giraffes, hippos, buffaloes, a wide variety of bucks, zebras, leopards, jackals, hyenas and even a few cheetahs. Given its size, there's a good chance of seeing a wide range of wildlife, which tends to concentrate around the two main watering holes.

Orientation & Information

Signposting in this area is less than terrific but you can't really go wrong once you get to Sun City, because the Pilanesberg are the only significant hills in the area.

Information is available at the **Manyane Gate** (*office open 7.30am-1pm & 2pm-8pm daily*). If you are planning on staying overnight in the park, unless you are staying at Kwa Maritane, Tshukudu or Bakubung Lodge, you must enter the park through this gate.

While inside the park it's worthwhile stopping at **Pilanesberg Centre** for refreshments and a look at the map where other visitors have stuck coloured pins to denote recent wildlife sightings.

The entrance fee is US$1.80/1 for adults/children plus US$2.30 per vehicle. Gates into the park proper (ie, beyond the Manyane Complex) are closed from 6pm to 6am from April to August and from 7pm to 5.30am from September to March.

Gametrackers Wildlife Adventures (☎ *557 5830*) runs trips into the park for around US$18.50.

Places to Stay & Eat

Manyane Complex & Caravan Park (*camping US$14, safari tents US$32, 4-person chalets US$86*) near the Manyane Gate has expensive camp sites and chalets. There's also a very basic shop and a restaurant, although the food is pretty average.

You can book through **Golden Leopard Resorts** (☎ *555 6135*; e *goldres@iafrica .com*).

Kwa Maritane (☎ *557 1820*) and the **Bakubung Lodge** (☎ *557 1861*) are a couple of upmarket time-share resorts that also have hotel accommodation. Rates at both of these places start at around US$114/148 for singles/doubles.

MAFIKENG
☎ 018

Mafikeng and Mmabatho were twin towns about 3km apart until Mmabatho was officially merged into Mafikeng. Mafikeng is most famous for its role in the 1899–1902 Anglo-Boer War, when British forces under Colonel Baden-Powell were besieged by the Boers. Mmabatho was built as the capital of Bophuthatswana and became capital of Northwest Province after 1994. It was developed as Bop's showcase and has some suitably grandiose (and ugly) buildings.

Orientation & Information

It's easy to get around Mafikeng on foot. Most shops and banks are grouped around the central bus and car park. It's a hot and dusty 5km walk from the centre to the

Megacity shopping mall in Mmabatho; you're better off catching one of the numerous local buses.

The grand **Mafikeng Tourism Information Centre** *(☎ 381 3155; Lichtenburg Rd; open Mon-Fri)* is worth a visit.

First National Bank *(Robinson St)* has a branch in Mafikeng between Main and Shippard Sts.

Places to Stay

Cooke's Lake Camping Ground *(sites US$1.80 per person)* is dusty and unattractive but cheap.

St Joseph's Centre at **St Mary's Mission** *(☎ 383 2646; dorm beds US$5.80)* in Lomanyaneng, about 2km south of the train station, sometimes has beds.

If you have the money, it's definitely worth considering the opulent **Tusk Mmabatho Resort** *(☎ 389 1111; e mmabatho@tusk -resorts.co.za; singles/doubles US$59/85)*. There's a pool, tennis courts and a cinema here.

Places to Eat

Cafe Farma *(☎ 381 4906; Nelson Mandela Dr)* is good for breakfast and light meals.

Cafe 43 North *(☎ 381 6463; 43 Nelson Mandela Dr)* is the perfect place to relax and enjoy lunch.

Getting There & Away

People often come through Mafikeng on their way to/from Botswana. Ramatlabama, 26km to the north, is the busiest border crossing and lies on the main route to/from Lobatse and Gaborone.

City Link *(☎ 381 2680)* runs daily buses between Megacity shopping mall in Mmabatho and Jo'burg (US$9).

Minibus taxis leave from the forecourt of the Mafikeng train station. As usual, most leave early in the morning. You can take one to the border crossing at Ramatlabama (about US$0.60) or all the way to Gaborone (US$4.50). Taxis to Jo'burg cost about US$6.40.

Getting Around

Numerous city buses go between Mafikeng (from the corner of Main St and Station Rd) and Mmabatho (Megacity shopping mall) for a few rand. Buses also run out to Lotlamoreng.

AROUND MAFIKENG
Lotlamoreng Dam & Cultural Village

This village *(☎ 382 2095; admission free)*, 5km west of Mafikeng on the Vryburg Road, was formed to give an insight into traditional local cultures. These days, sadly, it seems to be on the wane. It's worth a visit, however, to see and buy the good stone carvings which a couple of local artists still make.

Limpopo

Limpopo, formerly Northern Province, is a combination of high-veld and lowveld but most of it is savanna and it's very hot in summer. This is the Afrikaner frontier, although the formerly conservative feel of this province is changing along with many of the road and town names.

A large part of Kruger National Park is in Limpopo, but the park is covered as a whole in the Mpumalanga section earlier in this chapter.

History

This area was not densely populated but it was, and still is, home to a considerable number of different peoples, including the Ndebele (north of Pretoria), the Venda (in the northeast), the Langa (in the Waterberg) and the Batswana of the Sotho group (in the southwest).

The Voortrekkers first crossed the Vaal River (which forms the northern border of Free State) in 1836 and bloody conflicts between blacks and whites followed. In 1852 the British granted independence to the trekkers north of the Vaal River, and in 1853 the name Zuid-Afrikaansche Republic (ZAR; South African Republic) was adopted.

THE N1 HIGHWAY

The wide, mostly straight (but heavily tolled) N1 highway from Jo'burg and Pretoria to the Zimbabwe border divides Limpopo. The province's main towns line this route, including the provincial capital Pietersburg/Polokwane.

Translux, Greyhound and City to City buses run along the N1, and the *Bosvelder* train stops at towns along the N1.

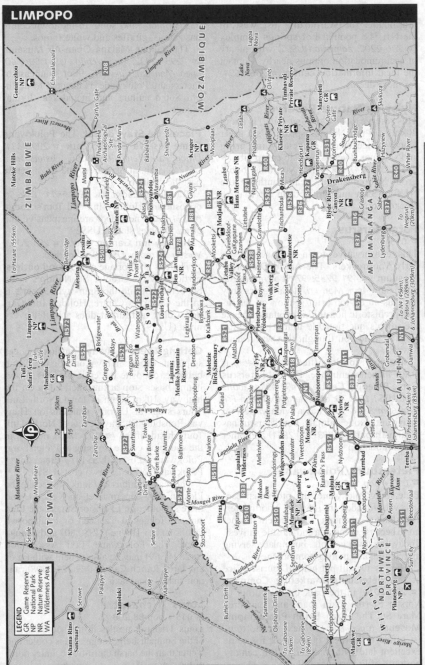

Warmbaths

Warmbaths (or Warmbad), just west of the N1, is a popular **hot springs** complex (☎ 736 2200; admission US$5) with plenty of accommodation options nearby. Contact the local **information centre** (☎ 736 3694) for more details.

Nylsvley Nature Reserve

This reserve (open 6am-6pm daily) is about 20km south of Naboomspruit. It's a great place to see birds, especially in spring and summer. There's a basic **camp site** (☎ 014-743 1074), for which you must book. From Naboomspruit, head south on the N1 for 13km and turn left on the road to Boekenhout.

Potgietersrus
☎ 015

This conservative town was settled by early Voortrekkers. The **Arend Dieperink Museum** (☎ 491 9735; 97 Voortrekker Rd; open 8am-4pm Mon-Fri) tells their story and has an all-too brief section on the area's prehistoric hominid inhabitants (hence the town's questionable tourist marketing slogan: 'And you thought this was a dead town!').

The small **tourist office** (☎ 491 8458) is at the museum entrance. The **Potgietersrus Game Breeding Centre** (☎ 491 4314; adult/child US$1.15/0.70; open 8am-4pm Mon-Fri, 8am-6pm Sat & Sun) has a wide variety of native and exotic animals. Potgietersrus has a **caravan park** (☎ 083 340 2861) and other accommodation.

Pietersburg/Polokwane
☎ 015 • pop 105,900

Pietersburg/Polokwane, the provincial capital, was founded in 1886 by Voortrekkers who had to abandon a settlement further north because of malaria and 'hostile natives'. Today, the town is a big, busy place serving agricultural and mining communities.

There's a small but helpful tourist office at the **Pietersburg Marketing Company** (☎ 290 2010) in the park on the corner of Vorster St (the main road) and Landdros Mare St. The **Hugh Exton Photographic Museum** (open Sun-Fri) next to the tourist office is worth a quick look for some excellent late 19th and early 20th century portraits of Pietersburg folk.

The **Polokwane Game Reserve** (☎ 290 2331; Union Park) south of the town centre has zebras, giraffes and white rhinos.

The **Bakone Malapa Open-Air Museum** (☎ 295 2432; adult/child US$1.50/0.40; open Mon am, Tues-Fri), 9km southeast of Pietersburg/Polokwane, is devoted to northern Sotho culture and includes a 'living' village.

Places to Stay & Eat The **Polokwane Game Reserve Caravan Park** (☎ 290 2331; Union Park; tent sites US$5, chalets from US$26) is about 3km from the town centre past the stadium.

Traveller's Lodge (☎ 291 5511; Bok St) opposite the Holiday Inn and **Tom's Lodge** (☎ 291 3798) next door are inexpensive and clean. Doubles start at US$29.

Holiday Inn Garden Court (☎ 291 2030; Vorster St; rooms US$48) is spotless.

There is no shortage of **fast food outlets**, particularly on Grobler St. **Nando's** is on Schoeman St and the Spur-style **Speer's** is in the Checkers Centre. **Holiday Inn Garden Court restaurant** does a buffet every night (US$9).

Getting There & Away Translux services stop at its offices in town outside the Azmo building, opposite the civic gardens. Greyhound buses stop at the Shell Ultra on the highway, 10km south of town. North Link Tours stops at Library Gardens on Hans van Rensburg St. Buy tickets at **North Link Tours head office** (☎ 291 1867) nearby in the shopping centre. Jo'burg to Pietersburg/Polokwane costs US$14; Pietersburg/Polokwane to Phalaborwa costs US$9.

The main minibus taxi rank is opposite the Pick 'n' Pay supermarket on Kerk St, and there's another on Excelsior St near the train station. To get to Tzaneen or Phalaborwa take a taxi to Boyne (US$0.80) and change there. The Polokwane Taxi Association (☎ 289 9369) may be able to help with times and fares. **Ranch Cab** (☎ 083 721 5598) runs non-shared local taxis.

Louis Trichardt
☎ 015 • pop 88,200

Louis Trichardt nestles in the southern side of the Soutpansberg Range, and is cooler and wetter than the harsh thorn-tree country north of the range.

The large and informative **tourist office** (☎ 516 0040) is on the corner of Songoswi Street (formerly Trichardt Street) and the N1.

The military folly known as **Fort Hendrina**, a kind of prefabricated iron pillbox, is just behind the municipal buildings on Erasmus St. The **Indigenous Tree Park** is close to the caravan park and, off the south end of Erasmus St, there's also a **bird sanctuary**.

Places to Stay There's a municipal **caravan park** (☎ 072 453 4633) near the town centre off Grobler St.

Carousel Lodge (☎ 516 4482; dorm beds US$8, singles/doubles US$14/21), down a side street off Rissik St, has cheap if rather dim and musty rooms, some with kitchen and bathroom.

Bergwater Hotel (☎ 516 0262; 5 Rissik St; singles/doubles US$30/42) includes breakfast in its rates. Weekend rates are slightly lower.

Clouds End Hotel (☎ 517 7021; singles/doubles US$26/46), an old fashioned place in pleasant grounds 3km north of town, offers 'booze and snooze' and a set-menu restaurant.

Inn on Louis Trichardt (☎ 517 7020; singles/doubles US$32/57) is a lovely spot about 11km north of town.

Places to Eat On Songoswi St, **Gateway Bakery** is dependable, and **Ricky's Supermarket** (Baobab St) has pizza for US$2.75 and home-made pies and cakes. There's a **Spur** (Krogh St) and a **KFC** (Songoswi St) but if you want to go upmarket try **Cafe d'Art** (Krogh St).

Getting There & Away Greyhound and Translux buses stop at the tourist office; the fare to Jo'burg is US$13. **Louis Trichardt Travel Agency** books bus tickets (☎ 516 5042)

The minibus taxi park is in the OK Bazaar supermarket car park off Burger St, a block northeast of Trichardt St. Fares from Louis Trichardt include: Thohoyandou (US$2.30); Pietersburg/Polokwane (US$3); Messina (US$5); and Jo'burg (US$11.50).

Around Louis Trichardt

Soutpansberg Hiking Trails There are two good hikes in the Soutpansberg – the two-day **Hangklip Trail** and the two-day **Entabeni Circular Route** (52km), about 40km

east of Louis Trichardt. Trail fees are from US$4.50 per person per day. To book either of these hikes, contact the **Sabie Forestry Office** (☎ 012-481 3615).

Lesheba Wilderness On the top of the western Soutpansberg Range, Lesheba Wilderness is home to white rhinos, leopards, baboons and zebras. This is dramatic, varied country, with grassland and forests, plains and the cliffs of the Sand River Gorge.

There are 4WD tours and 10 well-marked walking trails. Accommodation is in self-catering **cottages** (from US$29 per person) or in the sumptuous Venda Village **guesthouse** (per person US$98). You have to book (☎ 593 0076, fax 593 0076; w www.lesheba.co.za).

Ben Lavin Nature Reserve This reserve (☎ 015-516 4534; day visitor admission US$3.50; open 6am-6pm daily) has four marked hiking trails through varied terrain and habitat, all of which are rewarding. The Tabajwane Trail (8km) is good for wildlife viewing and the Fountain Trail follows the Doring River; there are hides at water holes. Mountain bike hire is also available

There are **tent sites** (per person US$4.50), or you can stay in **luxury tents** (per person US$18.50), **huts** (singles/doubles US$16/25) or **lodges** (singles/doubles US$26/40).

Messina
☎ 015

The closest town to the Zimbabwe border, Messina is hot and dusty, with a frontier feel. The theoretically 24-hour **border** is 12km away at Beitbridge and should be open from around 5am to 10pm at least. If you're planning a trip into Zim, it's worth checking the changeable visa situation ahead of time (try Visa Services in Jo'burg, ☎ 011-447 7055).

The helpful **Far North Tours and Safaris** (☎ 534 3500) runs Messina's tourist information office and also hires cars and 4WD vehicles. You can change money at the **First National Bank**, **ABSA** or **Standard Bank**. Internet access may be found at **Postnet** opposite ABSA or at the **Computer Shop** on the N1.

Places to Stay & Eat The **Baobab Caravan Park** (☎ 534 3504; sites US$4.50, plus per person US$1.75) is on the southern outskirts of town. You may also want to consider staying

in the **Messina Nature Reserve** (☎ 534 3235), 5km south of town, which protects some large and interesting baobabs.

Impala Lielie Motel (☎ 534 0127; single/double/triple rondavels US$17.50/20/22), next door, has a pool and restaurant.

Limpopo River Lodge (☎ 534 0204; singles/doubles US$13/21) has basic rooms with TV, air-con and bathroom.

All the usual fast food choices lie just off the main road. **Pot Belly** offers good value breakfasts and **Kremetart** serves good but expensive lunches and dinners.

Getting There & Away At the time of research Translux and Greyhound were only stopping at Beitbridge on the other side of the border. **Translux** runs from the border to Jo'burg (US$17.50, 8¼ hours) Bulawayo (US$23, 4½ hours) and Harare (US$26, 8½ hours).

Taxis between the border and Messina cost about US$1.20. There are a few taxis to Sibasa for US$3. There are many more minibus taxis at the border than in Messina. The **Beitbridge/Johannesburg Taxi Association** (☎ 01553 00086/082 868 6667) has further information on services south.

THE VENDA REGION

The Venda region, the Homeland of the Venda people under apartheid, is a fascinating place to visit for its cultural insights and scenery. The forest-covered Soutpansberg Range is strikingly lush compared with the hot, dry lowveld in the north of the area.

A good way to see the area is to take a tour. Several interesting tours run from Thohoyandou. Local expert Bethuel Mashwana runs tours (☎ 962 1500; half/full-day per person US$22.50/25). The highlight of the Southern Venda day tour is meeting Noria Mabasa, a woman who sculpts traditional Venda characters in clay and wood.

Thohoyandou/Sibasa
☎ 015 • pop 44,700
Created as the capital of the Venda Homeland, Thohoyandou has a small casino, some impressive public buildings, a shiny new shopping mall, but little else. Public transport arrives at and leaves from Sibasa a few kilometres north.

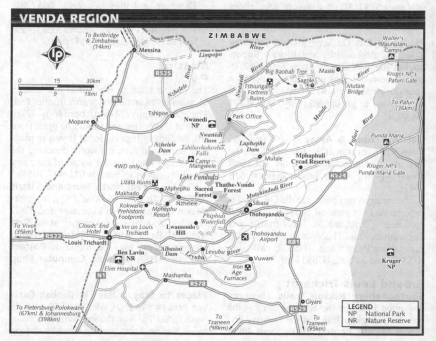

VENDA REGION

The Venda

Historians disagree about when the Venda people arrived and where they came from. They share aspects of Zimbabwean culture, and mining and metalworking have long been important elements in their economy and culture. The Lemba people, another group living in Venda, appear to have had contact with Islam.

It is certain that in the early 18th century a group of Senzi and Lemba, led by Chief Dimbanyika, crossed the Limpopo River and moved up the Nzhelele, a Limpopo tributary, and into the Soutpansberg, calling their new land Venda, believed to mean Pleasant Land.

At Lwandali they set up a chief's kraal and called it Dzata. When Dimbanyika died, some of his people moved south down the Nzhelele where they established another Dzata. Under the new chief, Thohoyandou, the Venda flourished until Thohoyandou disappeared mysteriously and this Dzata was abandoned as his offspring fought for succession.

Several invaders then tried to take over the Venda lands – first the Boers under Paul Kruger, then the Swazis, the Pedi and the Tsonga. The Venda, however, managed to avoid being overrun throughout the 19th century. Their relative isolation was partly due to the geography of the Soutpansberg, which made attack difficult, and partly to the tsetse fly, which made this area unattractive to graziers.

The Boer army conquered Venda in 1898. If the Venda had been able to hold out for another year, the defeat of the Boer republics in the 1899–1902 Anglo-Boer War may have given them time to negotiate a place in the Union of South Africa. Instead, Venda was absorbed into the Transvaal, and was granted 'independent Homeland' status in 1979. Today the area is part of Limpopo but retains its unique culture.

Places to Stay & Eat Neither Thohoyandou or Sibasa has much in the way of accommodation.

Thohoyandou Aventura (☎ 962 3095; camp sites US$5 plus per person US$2.30, double chalets US$23) is one option.

Bougainvillea Lodge (☎ 962 4064; singles/doubles from US$22.50/26) is a motel-style place about 1km from Thohoyandou, up the hill towards Sibasa. It's friendly, clean and comfortable.

Getting There & Away Translux runs daily between town and Jo'burg/Pretoria (US$21). City to City runs daily between Pretoria and Thohoyandou/Sibasa (US$9) departing at 8am. The Magweba company runs a daily bus, usually only during school term times, from Sibasa to Sagole (US$0.90).

In Thohoyandou minibus taxis congregate in the car park opposite the Venda Sun Hotel. The fare to Sibasa is US$0.30. The main taxi park is in Sibasa. Fares include: Mphephu Resort (US$0.50); Sagole Spa (US$1.20); Louis Trichardt (US$2.30); Messina (US$2.30); and Jo'burg (US$8.50).

Nwanedi National Park

The main attraction of this park is fishing and there's a walk to the scenic Tshihovhohovho Falls. You may spot white rhinos and blue wildebeests; there are also lions and cheetahs kept in enclosures.

There are **tent sites** (US$4.50) and four-person **chalets** (from US$15). Basic supplies are available and there's a **restaurant**.

You can get to the park from Thohoyandou via the Nwanedi Gate, but there's a good chance of getting lost. It's simpler to come via Tshipise, and enter from the west. Tshipise is the nearest place to buy fuel.

Sagole

This Venda town is near the hot springs spa of the same name. To the northwest are the ruins of the **Tshiungane stone fortifications** and nearby, in caves, are the remains of dwellings with clay grain bins built into the rocky walls. What is believed to be the biggest **baobab** in Africa is in the same area.

Sagole Spa (tent sites US$3, cottages US$26) has plunge pools fed by the nearby hot spring. Make bookings through **Acacia Park** (☎ 014-736 3649) in Thohoyandou.

Mphephu Area
☎ 015

Known for its hot springs, **Mphephu Resort** (☎ 973 0282; camping US$5.80 plus per person US$2.30, chalets from US$34) is 34km west of

Thohoyandou. There is a licensed **restaurant** in the resort.

Lake Fundudzi

This lake is sacred; its water is believed to come from the great sea that covered the earth before land was created. The python god, who holds an important place in the rites of Venda's matriarchal culture and once required human sacrifice, lives here. The lake is 35km northwest of Thohoyandou but you can't visit it without permission (which is unlikely to be granted).

Vuwani & Mashamba

South of Vuwani, you can see the remains of Iron Age furnaces where the Venda smelted high-grade iron for centuries. Many of their metalworking skills have been lost, but pottery making continues. Mashamba village also has several metal-casting foundries.

THE WATERBERG

The wild Waterberg, west of the N1, gets its name from the many swamps, springs and streams in the range. It stretches from Thabazimbi in the south to the Lapalala River in the northeast. The area's main town is **Vaalwater**.

From Vaalwater, there's a very scenic circular drive on a dirt road. Head northwest on the R517 for 10km, then turn south for 37km. At the prominent junction turn right for 20km to the **Palace of the Vultures**, a colony of Cape vultures (*Gyps coprotheres*). Return to the junction but continue straight ahead over Rankin's Pass. Here, take the Tweestroom road back to the R517 and turn left to Vaalwater or right to Nylstroom.

Northeast of Vaalwater is the pleasant little town of **Melkrivier** (Milk River) on the banks of the Lapalala.

There are several private reserves. **Lapalala Wilderness** (☎ *014-755 4395 for bookings*) is one of the best and has a wilderness area where you can hike. To get there from Nylstroom, take the R517 to Vaalwater and from there head to Melkrivier. **Touch Stone Game Ranch** (☎ *014-765 0230*), has all of the 'big five' and is southeast of Marken off the R518.

THE EAST

Eastern Limpopo is an attractive, culturally rich area, being the traditional home of the Tsonga, Shangaan and Lobedu people. It's also popular for a north–south traverse through Kruger National Park, or a visit to one of the many private reserves in the Hoedspruit area.

Letaba District

The Letaba Valley is east of Pietersburg/ Polokwane, between two chunks of the former Lebowa Homeland.

Tzaneen is the main town in the area and most places of interest are easily reached by car from there. The valley is subtropical and lush, with tea plantations and tropical fruits, the hills are thick with plantation forests.

The Magoebaskloof

The Magoebaskloof (ma-**ghoo**-bas-kloof) is the escarpment on the edge of the highveld, and the road drops through some magnificent country down to Tzaneen and the lowveld. There are waterfalls in the area, including **Debengeni Falls** in the De Hoek State Forest. You are able to swim in the pool at the bottom but be careful, as many people have drowned here. To get there, turn west off the R71 at Bruphy Sawmills.

The **Woodbush State Forest** is the largest indigenous forest in the Limpopo. It is home to leopard, among other animals.

There are several challenging **hiking trails**, through some beautiful country in this area. Two trails we recommend are the two-day Debengeni Falls Trail (21km) and the three-day Dokolewa Waterfall Trail (37km); both are rated moderately difficult. Book through **South African Forestry Company Ltd** (*Safcol;* ☎ *012-481 3615*) in Pretoria.

Places to Stay There are lovely valley views from the smart **Magoebaskloof Hotel** (☎ *276 4776;* Ⓦ *magoebaskloof.co.za; singles/ doubles from US$45/62*).

Tzaneen
☎ **015**

Tzaneen, the largest town in the Letaba region, makes a reasonable base. **Harvey Travel** (☎ *307 1294; Oasis Mall off Voortekker St*) doubles as the tourism information office.

Places to Stay & Eat On the George's Valley road (the R528), **Satvik Backpackers Village** (☎ *307 3920, 082 9711171;* Ⓔ *satvik@pixie.co.za; dorm beds US$8,*

doubles US$18.50) has farm accommodation in converted workers' cottages.

Fairview Caravan Park (☎ 307 2679; camp sites US$5.80, chalets from US$25) is a smart, shaded, well-kept place 1km from the town centre, after a turn-off from either the Phalaborwa road or Danie Joubert St.

Tzaneen Country Lodge (☎ 304 3290; singles/doubles US$49/67) 16km east of Tzaneen on the R71 is a good, if pricey, upmarket option. Its pub is also a good bet for a lunch stop.

Coach House (☎ 306 8000; set menu US$17.50) offers an excellent five-course set menu.

Getting There & Away The minibus taxi park is located behind the OK Centre, off the main street in the centre of town. To get to Pietersburg/Polokwane (US$2), take a taxi to Boyne and change there; to get to Louis Trichardt (US$2.30) take a taxi to Duivelskloof and change there. Taxis to Phalaborwa cost about US$2.30.

Wolkberg Wilderness Area

South of Tzaneen in the northern tail of the Drakensberg Range, this wilderness area (☎ 015-295 9713) has hiking trails and, in the valleys to the south and east, strands of indigenous forest. Book the hiking trails (a permit is essential) through **Safcol** (☎ 012-481 3615) in Sabie.

There is a **camp site** on the western side of the Serala Forest Station. You can't drive in the wilderness area, so plan your trip well. Fires aren't permitted – you'll need a gas or fuel stove.

The **Coach House** (☎ 015-306 8000; singles/doubles from US$80/152), about 15km south of Tzaneen, near the New Agatha Forest, is an upmarket refurbished old hotel with good views and a reputation for good food and wine.

Hans Merensky Nature Reserve

This nature reserve is bordered by the Letaba River but you risk contracting bilharzia if you swim in the river, not to mention the risk from larger denizens – crocodiles and hippos. You'd have to be lucky to see a lion or a leopard, but there is plenty of other wildlife.

There are several **hiking trails** of up to four days. To book the trails write to the reserve

at Private Bag X502, Letsitele 0885, or call ☎ 015-238633.

Modjadji Nature Reserve

This small nature reserve protects forests of the ancient Modjadji cycad. In the summer mists this place takes on an ethereal atmosphere.

Take the Ga-Kgabane turn-off from the R36 about 10km north of Duivelskloof; the turn-off to the reserve is a few kilometres further on.

Phalaborwa

☎ 015 • pop 111,100

Phalaborwa is a neat, well-planned copper mining town and also a major gateway to the Kruger Park. There is an interesting mix of cultures – Tsonga, Shangaan, Pedi, Sotho, Venda and Afrikaners. The majority of blacks live in the nearby townships of Namakgale, Lulekani, Majeje and Namakushan.

The Phalaborwa Gate into Kruger National Park is 3km from town. Phalaborwa is a good place to stay if the park's accommodation is booked out as you can join dawn and night drives and walks inside the park.

Tourist information was in a mess at the time of research, including outdated road signs, although a tourist office near the Kruger Park gate was set to open. If all else fails try the overworked **Kruger Parks office** (☎ 781 1037) in the main shopping mall or the **tourism hotline** (☎ 780 6392) during office hours on weekdays.

Places to Stay & Eat There's friendly, clean budget accommodation at **Elephant Walk** (☎ 781 2758, 082 495 0575; 30 Anna Scheepers St; tent sites US$3.50, dorm beds US$6.40, singles/doubles from US$16.50). It also offers self-catering cottages and the owner, Christa, organises various tours.

Daan & Zena's Guesthouse (☎ 781 6049; e daan-zena@lantic.net; 15 Birkenhead St; doubles from US$26) is a cheap, cheerful and helpful B&B.

Selati Lodge (☎ 789 2021; e selati@lantic .net; Rooibos St; singles/doubles US$32/44) is a tranquil place with cheaper weekend deals and a good lapa for sundowners.

Bed in the Bush (☎ 781 1139; singles/ doubles US$39/67) about 7km from town is a smart, contemporary lodge offering simple bush living. You sleep almost in the open and

SOUTH AFRICA

there's a good chance of mingling with wildlife. There's also some exquisite local pottery on sale here.

Sefapane Lodge (☎ 781 7041; e reserva tions@sefapane.co.za; Copper Road; singles/ doubles US$36/57) has some spacious, elegant rondavels with bathroom, aircon and fridge. There's also a decent restaurant (book for dinner).

Buffalo Express (mains US$3.50-5), just off the road to the Kruger gate, is a decent (if meat heavy) eating option.

Getting There & Away SAA flies direct to Jo'burg daily.

Translux runs daily between Phalaborwa and Pretoria/Jo'burg (US$20, seven hours). **City to City** also runs a less direct Jo'burg service (US$14). The National Parks office in the main shopping mall was selling bus tickets at the time of writing.

There aren't many minibus taxis in this area. Some run to Tzaneen (US$3) and south to Hoedspruit (US$2.30). There's a taxi park near the corner of Sealene Rd and Mellor Ave, about 300m southwest of the centre.

Avis (☎ 781 3169) has a car rental office in town.

Cheetah Breeding Project

The Hoedspruit Research and Breeding Centre (☎ 793 1633; US$3.50; open 8am-4pm Mon-Sat) is south of the small town of Hoedspruit on the R40. Admission includes a video and guided tour.

Private Reserves

A large number of private reserves, many of which share a border with Kruger, cluster to the west of the park. The best-known private reserves are just north of the Kruger Gate in Mpumalanga (see the Mpumalanga section earlier in this chapter).

The reserves around Hoedspruit and Kruger National Park's Orpen and Phalaborwa Gates are generally cheaper than those to the south. Better-known reserves include **Manyeleti** near Orpen Gate; **Klaserie** east of Hoedspruit, which contains similar fauna to Kruger; and **Timbavati**, which is known for its amazing population of white lions.

Swaziland

Tiny Swaziland, one of the few remaining African monarchies, is a friendly place. Free of the baggage of crime and racial animosity (past or present) endured by South Africa, you can feel those faint undercurrents of tension fade away almost as you cross the border.

The country's lovely national parks and some excellent handicrafts are other good reasons to visit. Swaziland makes a relaxing stopover on the trip between Mozambique and South Africa.

Facts about Swaziland

HISTORY

The area that is now Swaziland has been inhabited for a long time – in eastern Swaziland archaeologists have discovered human remains dating back 110,000 years – but the Swazi people arrived relatively recently.

During the great Bantu migrations into Southern Africa, one group, the Nguni, moved down the east coast. A clan settled in the area near what is now Maputo in Mozambique, and a dynasty was founded by the Dlamini family. (For detailed information on the Bantu migrations, see History in the Facts about the Region chapter.)

In the mid-18th century increasing pressure from other Nguni clans forced King Ngwane III to lead his people south to lands by the Pongola River, in what is now southern Swaziland. Today, Swazis consider Ngwane III to have been the first king of Swaziland.

Clan encroachment continued and the next king, Sobhuza I, also came under pressure from the Zulu. He withdrew to the Ezulwini Valley, which remains the centre of Swazi royalty and ritual today. Trouble with the Zulu continued though the next king, Mswazi (or Mswati), managed to unify the whole kingdom and by the time he died in 1868, a Swazi nation was secure. Mswazi's subjects called themselves people of Mswazi, or Swazis.

Highlights

- Mkhaya Game Reserve – seeing rare black rhinos in the wild
- Usutu River – shooting white-water rapids, including a 10m waterfall
- Ezulwini Valley – spending time in the centre of Swazi royalty and culture
- Malolotja Nature Reserve – hiking in a genuine, unspoiled wilderness
- Mlilwane Wildlife Sanctuary – wandering around this accessible and enchantingly pretty sanctuary and relax in its comfortable, bargain lodges

European Interference

During the same period the Zulu were coming under pressure from both the British and the Boers, creating frequent respites for the Swazis. However, the arrival of increasing numbers of Europeans from the mid-19th century brought new problems. Mswazi's successor, Mbandzeni, inherited a kingdom

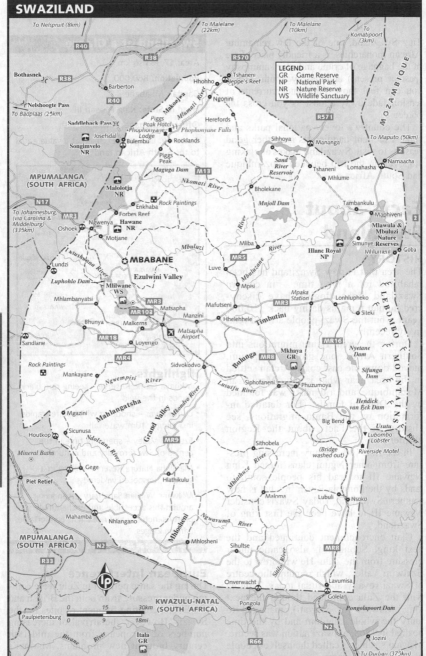

rife with European carpetbaggers – hunters, traders, missionaries and farmers, many of whom leased large expanses of land.

The Boers' South African Republic (ZAR) decided to extend its control to Maputo along with Swaziland which was in the way. Before this could happen, however, the British annexed the ZAR itself in 1877.

The Pretoria Convention of 1881 guaranteed Swaziland's 'independence', but also defined its borders, and Swaziland lost large chunks of territory. 'Independence' in fact meant that both the British and the Boers had responsibility for administering their various interests in Swaziland, and the result was chaos. The Boer administration collapsed with the 1899–1902 Anglo-Boer War and afterwards the British took control of Swaziland as a protectorate.

During this troubled time, King Sobhuza II was only a young child but Labotsibeni, his mother, acted ably as regent until her son took over in 1921. Throughout the regency and for most of Sobhuza's long reign, the Swazis sought to regain their land, a large portion of which was owned by foreign interests. Labotsibeni encouraged Swazis to buy the land back, and many sought work in the Witwatersrand mines (near Johannesburg) to raise money. By the time of independence in 1968, about two-thirds of the kingdom was again under Swazi control.

Independence

In 1960, King Sobhuza II proposed the creation of a legislative council composed of elected Europeans, and a national council formed in accordance with Swazi culture. One of the Swazi political parties formed at this time was the Mbokodvo (Grindstone) National Movement, which pledged to maintain traditional Swazi culture, but also to eschew racial discrimination. When the British finally agreed to elections in 1964, Mbokodvo won a majority and, at the next elections in 1967, won all the seats. Independence was achieved on 6 September 1968.

The country's constitution was largely the work of the British. In 1973, the king suspended it on the grounds that it did not accord with Swazi culture. Four years later, the parliament reconvened under a new constitution which vested all power in the king. Sobhuza II, then the world's longest-reigning monarch, died in 1982.

The young Mswati III ascended the throne in 1986 and continues to represent and maintain the traditional way of life, and to assert his pre-eminence, for better and often worse, as absolute monarch. (See the boxed text 'Absolute Power' later in this chapter).

Attempts by unions and (officially illegal) opposition groups to press for democratic change have met with legislation to curb their activities.

GEOGRAPHY

Swaziland, although tiny, has a wide range of ecological zones, from rainforest in the northwest to savanna scrub in the east.

The western edge of the country is highveld, consisting mainly of short, sharp mountains. There are large plantations of pine and eucalyptus. The mountains dwindle to middleveld into the heavily populated centre of the country. The eastern half is scrubby lowveld, lightly populated because of malaria, which is still a risk, but now home to sugar estates. To the east, the harsh Lebombo Mountains form the border with Mozambique.

CLIMATE

Most rain falls in summer, usually in torrential thunderstorms and mostly in the western mountains. Summers on the lowveld are very hot, with temperatures often over 40°C; in the high country the temperatures are lower and in winter it can get cool. Winter nights on the lowveld are sometimes very cold.

The rains usually begin around early December and last until April. May to August are the coolest months, with frosts in June and July.

MBABANE
Elevation – 1163m/3816ft

FLORA & FAUNA

Although small in size, Swaziland is rich in flora and accounts for 14% of the recorded plant life in Southern Africa. The remoteness of parts of the countryside

Absolute Power?

When you're an absolute monarch you don't have to court popularity. Just as well for Swaziland's King Mswati III.

He's done quite a bit to upset various people recently, most notably his decision in 2002 to purchase a royal jet aircraft, in the teeth of angry objections from foreign governments, agencies and even his own parliament.

His courtiers said the purchase would assist in the king's successful AIDS fundraising work – a hard argument to swallow when set against the plane's US$45 million price tag and at a time when many Swazis struggled to get enough to eat.

It was also counterproductive. The USA, among others, threatened to withdraw aid and to forbid the king entry to the US if the purchase went ahead.

The other source of recent discontent with the king came after the 2002 Reed festival, during which (in keeping with tradition) he chose a young woman, 18-year-old Zena Mahlangu, to become his 10th wife.

Zena's mother tried to take the king to court, accusing him of abducting and holding Zena against her will, something the king's aides strenuously denied. Refusing to let anyone speak to Ms Mahlangu, they blocked moves to try the king as unconstitutional.

The crisis rapidly went beyond being merely a question of whether Ms Mahlangu was being coerced or not, and soon descended into a constitutional and legal farce. The chief justice and two other leading judges were told by the attorney general to resign for refusing to throw the case out; the attorney general was in turn sacked, seemingly as a scapegoat for the outcry generated. Soon afterwards, lawyers and judges went on strike in protest at the king's refusal to subject himself to the rule of law.

Such clashes are perhaps inevitable. Reformers must reckon with the fact that the king is a highly revered figurehead; he is the *Ngwenyama* (The Lion), a descendent of the great kings (and the odd queen mother) who secured the independence of the Swazi nation. Looked on sympathetically, a Swazi king's power and the clan links that marrying so many wives bind him to, might be seen as the source of Swaziland's relative stability and the foundation of its continued independence.

This status is something Mswati has used to his advantage as he resists pressure for constitutional reform. It's his licence, it seems, to do pretty much whatever he pleases.

means there are probably species that have not yet been brought to the attention of botanists. Nature reserves, particularly those administered by the National Trust Commission, help to conserve indigenous plants.

Swaziland has about 121 species of mammals, representing a third of nonmarine mammal species in Southern Africa. These days the larger animals are restricted to the nature reserves and private wildlife reserves dotted around the country. Many species (such as elephants, warthogs, rhinos and lions) have been reintroduced. Mongooses and large-spotted genets are common throughout the country, while hyenas and jackals are found in the reserves. Leopards are present, but you'd be lucky to see one.

The most common of the 19 recorded species of bat is the little free-tailed bat, which can be found roosting in houses in the lowveld and middleveld.

National Parks & Reserves

The five main reserves reflect the country's geographical diversity. Easiest to get to is Mlilwane Wildlife Sanctuary in the Ezulwini Valley. Hlane Royal National Park and Mkhaya Game Reserve are also well worth visiting. These three reserves are privately run as part of the **Royal Swazi Big Game Parks organisation** (☎ 528 3944; e reservations@biggame.co.sz; w www.biggame.co.sz).

The booking office of the **National Trust Commission** (☎ 416 1179; w www.sntc.org.sz) is run from reception at the Mantenga Nature Reserve, near Lobamba. It runs Mantenga, Hawane, Malolotja and Mlawula Nature Reserves. Malolotja is a rugged highlands reserve with some very good hiking trails. Mlawula is in harsh lowveld country near the Mozambican border.

GOVERNMENT & POLITICS

Swaziland is governed by a parliament, but final authority is vested in the king, who can

dissolve parliament at any time. He appoints half of the 30 senators, and a third of the 60 members of the Assembly. The other members of the Assembly are elected in the constituencies, first by a show of hands and then by ballot. These members elect the other half of the Senate. The real power is vested in the king and the 16-person Council of Ministers.

Democracy activists have tried, and so far have failed utterly, to encourage the king to move to a more democratic system.

It's difficult to say whether the average Swazi wants radical political change given that opposition parties remain officially illegal and there are few organised vehicles for ordinary Swazis to make their will known or air their grievances.

ECONOMY

Swaziland is a poor country by world standards. The major export is sugar, and forest products are also important. Nearly 75% of the population works in agriculture, mostly at a subsistence level. The country is not self-sufficient in food, however, and in recent years drought has hit crop yields.

It's a problem that hits subsistence farmers hardest and is exacerbated by increasing instances of illness and death brought on by infection with HIV.

POPULATION & PEOPLE

Almost all people here are Swazi. The rest are Zulu, Tsonga-Shangaan and European. There are also a number of Mozambican refugees, of both African and Portuguese descent. About 5% of Swazis live and work in South Africa.

The dominant clan is the Dlamini and you'll meet people with that surname all over the country. There's a good chance you'll meet a prince in Swaziland. There are a lot of princes and they come from all walks of life.

The population, which was about 85,000 in 1904, today hovers around one million people, although the future for many of them looks bleak. The HIV/AIDS pandemic here is almost beyond comprehension – 33% of Swazi adults are thought to be infected – making a horrific reversal of its population statistics in the next couple of decades seem certain.

LANGUAGE

The official languages are Swati and English, and English is the official written language.

The Swazi

The ancestors of modern-day Swazis were part of the general, gradual migration of Bantu language speakers from Central Africa who broke from the main group and settled in Mozambique, finally moving in the mid-18th century into what became known as Swaziland. Today, Swazis still share a close cultural and linguistic heritage with other Southern African peoples including the Zulu and the Ndebele.

Swazis make up a little over half Swaziland's population, many of them subsistence farmers (although many more Swazis also live in Mozambique and South Africa) and there's a strong sense of Swazi identity. Social and cultural cohesion is maintained by a system of age-related royal regiments. Boys graduate from regiment to regiment as they grow older, an arrangement that minimises the potentially divisive differences between clans while emphasising loyalty to the king and nation.

Colourful ceremonies (and traditional dress, which is still commonly worn) also underline Swazis' unique identity. The most important ceremony, Incwala, is an annual festival of thanksgiving, prayer, atonement and a rite underlining the king's exalted status. Umhlanga is a reed dance, attended by unmarried girls, from whom the king chooses new brides (see the boxed text 'Swazi Ceremonies' later in this chapter).

For ordinary citizens, marriage arrangements are traditionally initiated by a request to the fathers of the couple by the mothers of the couple. Traditional marriage allows for the husband to take a number of wives, although many Swazis also follow Western marriage conventions, rejecting polygamy, but permitting divorce.

It's not hard to experience something of normal Swazi life. Myxo's Place (see Places to Stay & Eat under Manzini later in this chapter) offers tours to local villages where you can stay among rural Swazis living in the traditional way.

For some useful words and phrases in Swati see the Language chapter at the back of this book.

Facts for the Visitor

SUGGESTED ITINERARIES
One Week

With only a week at your disposal, a half-day in Mbabane is plenty. Spend a few days poking around the pretty Ezulwini Valley and Lobamba, and make a trip into the Mlilwane Wildlife Sanctuary; you'll probably see zebras, giraffes, many antelope species and a variety of birds. If you have time and you want to see rare black rhinos in the wild, continue east to Mkhaya Game Reserve.

Two Weeks

With two weeks you'd have plenty of time to do the above and take in some more wildlife at the extensive Hlane Royal National Park and Mlawula Nature Reserve. On your circular route back to Mbabane, you could drop in to Piggs Peak, an area known for its handicrafts, or hike in Malolotja Nature Reserve, an unspoiled wilderness area. Alternatively you could do this route clockwise, starting in Mbabane and heading north to Malolotja.

The Big Trip

While on an extended tour of the region, it's well worth diverting into Swaziland for its friendly people, relaxed atmosphere, unique culture and numerous, pretty and accessible wildlife parks and reserves. See The Big Trip in the regional Facts for the Visitor section earlier in this book.

PLANNING
Maps

The free maps in various brochures at Mbabane's tourist office are okay for getting around this tiny country. A good 1:250,000 scale map is available from the **Surveyor-General's office** at the **Ministry of Works** *(PO Box 58)* in Mbabane. If you're serious about hiking, there are also 1:50,000 scale maps.

Tourist Offices

Swaziland is not that well served by official tourism services either internally or exter-

nally. The Swazi National Trust and Royal Swazi Big Game Parks websites offer some very useful parks information; for accommodation information and bookings try the Ministry of Tourism website (see Digital Resources later in this section for details).

The most reliable and helpful **tourist office** *(☎ 442 4206)* in Swaziland is in the Ezulwini Valley.

VISAS & DOCUMENTS

Most people don't need a visa to visit Swaziland. Basically if you don't need a visa to enter South Africa, you won't need one for Swaziland. Anyone staying for more than 60 days must apply for a temporary residence permit from the **Chief Immigration Officer** *(☎ 404 2941; PO Box 372, Mbabane)*.

No vaccination certificates are required unless you have recently been in a yellow-fever area.

Hostel cards, student cards and seniors cards are of little use in Swaziland.

EMBASSIES & CONSULATES
Swazi Embassies

Swaziland has diplomatic representation in Kenya, Mozambique and South Africa (embassies for countries in this book are listed in the relevant country chapters). Elsewhere in the world, places with Swazi diplomatic representation include:

Canada *(☎ 613-567 1480)* 130 Albert St, Ottawa, Ontario KIP 5G4
Germany *(☎ 0211-350 866)* Worringer Strasse 59, Dusseldorf 40211
UK *(☎ 020-7630 6611)* 20 Buckingham Gate, London SW1E 6LB
USA *(☎ 202-362 6683)* Suite 3M, 3400 International Dr, Washington DC 20008

Embassies & Consulates in Swaziland

The Mozambican embassy in Mbabane, near the Mountain Inn, issues one-month visas for US$10.70 (considerably less than you would pay in Johannesburg). It can be done in a day and you'll need two photos. Other diplomatic representation in Swaziland includes:

Denmark *(☎ 404 3547, fax 404 3548; e citrus@ realnet.co.sz)* Ground floor, Sokhamlilo Bldg, Johnson St, Mbabane; open 8am to noon and 2pm to 5pm weekdays
Germany *(☎ 404 3174)* 3rd floor, Lilunga House, Giltillan St, Mbabane; open 9am to 12pm

weekdays; inquiries and visas handled in Maputo, Mozambique

Mozambique (☎ 404 3700) Princess Dr, Mbabane; open 9am to 1pm weekdays

South Africa (☎ 404 4651) The New Mall, PO Box 2507, Mbabane; open 8.30am to 12.30pm weekdays

The Netherlands (☎ 404 5178) Lot 234 Gilfillan St, Mbabane; open 8.30am to 12.30pm weekdays.

UK (☎ 404 2581/2/3) 2nd floor, Lilunga House, Gilfillan St, Mbabane; open 8am to 1pm weekdays

USA (☎ 404 6441) Central Bank Bldg, Warner St, Mbabane; open 8am to 12.30pm Wednesday and Friday

CUSTOMS

Customs regulations are similar to those for South Africa. (See Customs under Facts for the Visitor in the South Africa chapter earlier in this book.)

MONEY

Currency

The unit of currency is the lilangeni (the plural is emalangeni – E), which is fixed at a value equal to the South African rand. Rands are accepted everywhere and there's no need to change them, although a few places don't accept South African coins. Emalangeni are difficult to change for other currencies outside Swaziland. (For more details on exchange rates, see Money under Facts for the Visitor in the South Africa chapter.)

Exchanging Money

Several banks change travellers cheques. Banking hours are generally from 8.30am to 2.30pm weekdays, and until 11am Saturday. The bank at Matsapha airport, near Manzini, opens for flights.

Only a few ATMs accept international credit or debit cards. The most convenient are at Standard Bank in Swazi Mall, Mbabane and inside the Royal Swazi Hotel's casino. Most banks ask to see the receipt of purchase when cashing travellers cheques. First National bank charges a flat US$2.30 to cash travellers cheques.

Costs

Costs are similar to those in South Africa, although food is a little cheaper. The wildlife reserves here are particularly good value.

POST & COMMUNICATIONS

Post offices are open from 8am to 4pm weekdays, and until 11am Saturday.

There are no area codes within Swaziland. The international country code is ☎ 268; to call Swaziland from South Africa dial the prefix ☎ 09-268. International calls are most easily made using MTN phone cards.

Internet facilities are scarce outside Mbabane. A couple of places in Ezulwini Valley have Internet facilities.

DIGITAL RESOURCES

A couple of websites worth a surf include:

Ministry of Tourism (W www.mintour.gov.sz /szcomplete) Best used for details about Swaziland's hotels, restaurants and other facilities

Swaziland National Trust Commission (W www .sntc.org.sz) Helpful site with information about Malolotja and Mlawula Nature Reserves as well as Swaziland's cultural heritage

Swazi.com (W www.swazi.com) Slightly chaotic portal to many other Swazi sites

Swaziland Internet Dictionary (W www.directory .sz/internet/) Simple, easy-to-use search engine and directory for all things Swazi

For a more comprehensive listing of websites, see Digital Resources in the Regional Facts for the Visitor chapter.

BOOKS

Swaziland Jumbo Tourist Guide, by Hazel Hussey, has some useful information between a lot of glossy ads.

The Kingdom of Swaziland, by D Hugh Gillis, is a history (to independence) of the kingdom seeking to maintain its traditional way of life in the face of an overwhelming European influence.

All the King's Animals: The Return of Endangered Wildlife to Swaziland, by Cristina Kessler and Mswati III, contains some terrific photography. It's the story of the conservationist Ted Reilly and the successful reintroduction of endangered wildlife into the kingdom.

NEWSPAPERS & MAGAZINES

There are two English-language daily newspapers – the *Times of Swaziland* and the *Swazi Observer*. The *Times*, a virtual mouthpiece for royalty and a would-be lurid tabloid, is a fascinating read as much for what it doesn't say as what it does.

SWAZILAND

PHOTOGRAPHY & VIDEO

Film and photographic accessories are available in Mbabane and Manzini.

Don't take photos of soldiers, police, airports or government buildings.

HEALTH

Beware of both bilharzia and malaria. (For more information on how to avoid contracting these potentially deadly diseases, see Health in the Regional Facts for the Visitor chapter.) Malaria is a risk in low-lying areas of the country generally and you'll be at highest risk from November to April.

If you need medical assistance there is the **Mbabane Government Hospital** (☎ 404 2111), the **Raleigh Fitkin Hospital** (☎ 505 2211) in Manzini and the **Piggs Peak Government Hospital** (☎ 437 1111).

PUBLIC HOLIDAYS & SPECIAL EVENTS

Public holidays observed in Swaziland are:

New Year's Day – 1 January
Easter (March/April) – Good Friday, Holy Saturday and Easter Monday
King Mswati III's Birthday – 19 April
National Flag Day – 25 April
King Sobhuza II's Birthday – 22 July
Umhlanga Dance Day – August/September
Somhlolo Day (Independence) – 6 September
Christmas Day – 25 December
Boxing Day – 26 December
Incwala Day – Late December/early January

Sibhaca dancing developed fairly recently, but it is very popular. Local competitions are held frequently, and the Mbabane tourist office has details. The Sun hotels in the Ezulwini Valley sometimes have performances.

The most important cultural events in Swaziland are the Incwala ceremony, held sometime between late December and early January, and the Umhlanga (Reed) dance held in August or September (see the boxed text 'Swazi Ceremonies' later in this chapter). The venue for both is near Lobamba in the Ezulwini Valley. Ask at the tourist office in Mbabane for exact dates. Photography is not permitted at the Incwala, but it is at the Umhlanga dance.

ACTIVITIES

Although Swaziland is a small country, there are plenty of activities to keep you going for a few days. Swaziland offers some terrific white-water rafting (in the

---

Swazi Ceremonies

Incwala

The Incwala (sometimes Ncwala) is the most sacred Swazi ceremony. During this 'first fruits' ceremony the king gives his people permission to eat the first crops of the new year.

Preparation for the Incwala begins some weeks in advance. *Bemanti* (learned men) journey to the Lebombo Mountains to gather plants, other groups collect water from Swaziland's rivers and some travel to the Indian Ocean (where the Dlamini clan lived long before the Swazi nation came into being) to skim foam from the waves.

On the night of the full moon, young men all over the kingdom begin a long trek to the Royal Kraal at Lobamba. They arrive at dawn and build a *kraal* (a hut village) with branches gathered on their journey. Participants sing songs prohibited during the rest of the year, and the *bemanti* arrive with their plants, water and foam.

On the third day a bull is sacrificed. On the fourth day, the king breaks his retreat and dances before his people. He eats a pumpkin, the sign that Swazis can eat the new year's crops. Soon after, the rains are expected to fall.

Umhlanga

Not as sacred as the Incwala, the Umhlanga (Reed) dance serves a similar function in drawing the nation together and reminding the people of their relationship to the king. It is something like a week-long debutante ball for marriageable young Swazi women and a showcase of potential wives for the king.

On the sixth day they perform the reed dance and carry their reeds to the queen mother. They repeat the dance the next day. Princesses wear red feathers in their hair.

rainy season), horse riding and mountain biking.

For hikers, as well as walking trails in several parks, there are countless ancient walking tracks, so you can set out and explore the country on foot. Make sure you are well prepared and seek local advice on conditions.

ACCOMMODATION

There are few designated camp sites in Swaziland except in some of the national parks and reserves. Away from the population centres it's usually possible (and safe) to camp, but *always* ask permission from local people.

At the time of writing, there were no central hostels in Mbabane, but there are some good ones around Manzini. If you're stuck for a room in rural areas, you could try the local school, where you'll probably be welcomed.

Many of the country's hotels are geared towards South African tourists and are expensive.

Food

Although not exactly a gourmet's paradise, you won't eat badly in Swaziland. There's a good range of places to eat in Mbabane and the tourist areas of the Ezulwini Valley. Portuguese cuisine, including seafood is possible to find. In more remote areas, African staples such as stew and pap (also known as *mealie* meal) are common as is that South African favourite Bunny Chow (stew inside a hollowed-out loaf).

SHOPPING

Swaziland's handicrafts include jewellery, pottery, weapons and implements. Be aware that some readers have reported weapons being confiscated at customs, so think about how you're going to ship that Swazi ceremonial spear home before you buy it.

Woven grasswares such as *liqhaga* (grassware 'bottles') and mats are popular, as are wooden items, ranging from bowls to knobkerries.

Getting There & Away

This section covers travel between Swaziland and its neighbours, South Africa and Mozambique. (For information on reaching Swaziland from elsewhere on the African continent and from other continents, see the regional Getting There & Away chapter.)

AIR

A US$2.30 departure tax is levied at Matsapha airport.

Swazi Airlink (☎ 518 6192 • Swazi Plaza ☎ 404 3157) is a joint venture between SAA and the Swazi government operating out of Matsapha airport, north of Manzini. It's also an SAA agent. Schedules and tickets often refer to the airport as Manzini. It flies daily between Swaziland and Johannesburg (one-way, seven-day advance/three-day advance/full-fare tickets cost US$72/90/113).

Swazi Express Airways (☎ 518 6840; W www.swaziexpress.com) flies four times a week to Durban and twice a week to Maputo in Mozambique.

LAND

Swaziland's border crossings are all with South Africa, with the exception of the one between Namaacha and Lomahasha in the extreme northeast, which is the entry point to Mozambique (open from 7am to 8pm). Another crossing to Mozambique further south, Goba Fronteira, was due to open in 2003, but don't count on it.

The main border crossings with South Africa are: **Oshoek/Ngwenya** (open 7am-10pm); **Mahamba** (7am-10pm); **Golela/Lavumisa** (7am-10pm); **Josefsdal/Bulembu** (8am-4pm); **Pigg's Peak** (7am-8pm); and **Houtkop/Sicunusa** (8am-6pm).

Bus & Minibus Taxi

The **Baz Bus** (☎ South Africa 021-439 2323) runs from Jo'burg/Pretoria to Durban via Mbabane and Manzini four times a week, returning the next day.

Zulu Kayalami is a big bus transport group operating between Mbabane, Durban and Johannesburg charging similar rates to the minibus taxi operators. Most hostel managers will be able to help organise a seat.

Minibus taxis operate directly between either Mbabane or Manzini and a number of South African destinations (although many run only every other day or even once weekly) including Johannesburg (US$10.50; at least three times weekly, usually Sunday,

Monday and Tuesday) and Nelspruit (US$11.50; Sunday, Monday and Tuesday), Piet Retief (US$6; Sunday), Durban (US$11.50; Monday, Tuesday and Friday). There's also a daily service to Mozambique (US$4; 2½ hours).

Generally speaking, Manzini is best for Durban and Mozambique connections and Mbabane is best for destinations to Jo'burg and the north.

Car & Motorcycle
There's a US$0.60 road tax for vehicles entering Swaziland.

Getting Around

MINIBUS TAXI
There are a few infrequent (but cheap) domestic buses, most of which terminate at the main stop in the centre of Mbabane where most of them arrive and depart.

Generally you'll find minibus taxis the best public transport, although they often run shorter routes. Some sample fares include Manzini (US$0.50), Big Bend (US$1.20), and Pigg's Peak (US$0.90).

There are also nonshared taxis in some of the larger towns.

CAR & MOTORCYCLE
Most roads are quite good and the main ones are being improved rapidly (by Swazi standards). Drive slowly on the gravel roads (see Car & Motorcycle under Getting Around in the South Africa chapter for more advice). Driving down the Ezulwini Valley has improved substantially with the addition of the MR3 dual carriageway.

Away from the few population centres, the main dangers are people and animals on the road. Wearing seat belts is compulsory. You must pull over and stop for official motorcades. The speed limit is 80km/h on the open road and 60km/h in built-up areas.

Many petrol stations are open 24 hours and the price of petrol is similar to that of South Africa. There are Automobile Association (AA) agents in Manzini, Piggs Peak and Mbabane.

Rental
Swaziland is so small that hiring a car will allow you to cover much of the country in a

couple of days. Rates are similar to those in South Africa.

Avis (☎ 518 6226) and **Imperial** (☎ 518 4862) are at Matsapha airport, near Manzini. **Affordable Car Hire** (☎ 404 9136; Swazi Plaza, Mbabane) can offer competitive rates. You have to be 23 years old to hire cars from most hire companies.

HITCHING
Hitching is easier here than in South Africa because the skin colour of the driver and the hitchhiker aren't factors in the driver's decision to offer a lift. You might wait a long time for a car on back roads, and everywhere you'll have lots of competition from locals.

ORGANISED TOURS
Bundu Bus (☎ South Africa 011-675 0767; W www.bundusafaris.co.za; PO Box 697, Wilgeheuwel, 1735 Gauteng, South Africa) is a South African operator that runs a seven-day South African tour including a day and a half in Swaziland.

Swazi Trails (☎/fax 416 2180; W www .swazitrails.co.sz; Mantenga Craft Centre, Ezulwini Valley, Swaziland) specialises in one-day or half-day tours around the country, including white-water rafting, cultural tours and hiking.

Thompsons Indaba Safaris (☎ South Africa 013-737 7115; W www.thompsonssa .com; 781 Goshawk Ridge, Hazyview, 1242, South Africa) offers a two-night, three-day tour for R2615 (US$300).

Mbabane

pop 50,000
Mbabane (pronounced mba-**baa**-nay), the largest town in Swaziland, is pretty nondescript and there isn't that much to see or do here. The adjacent Ezulwini Valley has plenty of attractions and Mbabane is a relaxed place in a nice setting in the Dlangeni Hills.

The hills make Mbabane cooler than Manzini, one reason why the British moved their administrative centre here from Manzini in 1902.

Orientation
Despite recent development, Mbabane is a reasonably pleasant town. The main

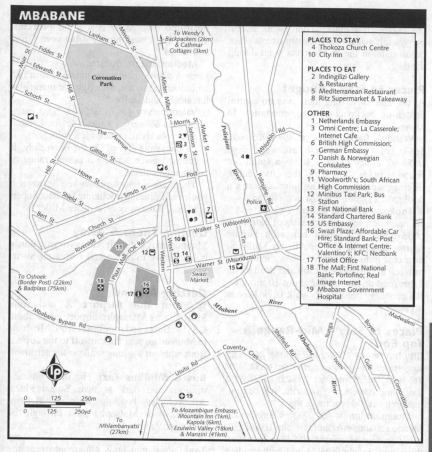

MBABANE

PLACES TO STAY
4 Thokoza Church Centre
10 City Inn

PLACES TO EAT
2 Indingilizi Gallery
  & Restaurant
5 Mediterranean Restaurant
8 Ritz Supermarket & Takeaway

OTHER
1 Netherlands Embassy
3 Omni Centre; La Casserole;
  Internet Cafe
6 British High Commission;
  German Embassy
7 Danish & Norwegian
  Consulates
9 Pharmacy
11 Woolworth's; South African
   High Commission
12 Minibus Taxi Park; Bus
   Station
13 First National Bank
14 Standard Chartered Bank
15 US Embassy
16 Swazi Plaza; Affordable Car
   Hire; Standard Bank; Post
   Office & Internet Centre;
   Valentino's; KFC; Nedbank
17 Tourist Office
18 The Mall; First National
   Bank; Portofino; Real
   Image Internet
19 Mbabane Government
   Hospital

street is Allister Miller St. Swazi Plaza, a large, modern shopping centre with most services and a good range of shops, is off Western Distributor Rd. The Mall, another shopping area, is across Plaza Mall St.

Information

The **tourist office** (☎ 404 2531; Swazi Plaza) has meagre brochure information available and seems to be sporadically staffed. Be sure to pick up a copy of the free monthly *What's On in Swaziland?* for current listings and other information. Alternatively try better-resourced **tourist office** in the Ezulwini Valley (☎ 442 4206).

Royal Swazi Big Game Parks (☎ 528 3944) has information on the main National Parks. The offices are in hard-to-reach Malkerns.

Money There is a **Standard Bank** with a 24-hour international ATM (Swazi Plaza), and a **First National Bank** (The Mall).

Post & Communications The best way to make international calls is with E15 to E50 (roughly US$1.20 to US$5.80) phone cards from Post Offices and shops. Internet access is available in a few places in town for around US$1.50 per half hour. The most convenient is **Real Image** (The Mall).

Emergency The contact numbers for emergency services are: fire (☎ 43333); **Mbabane Clinic Service** (☎ 404 2423); **Mbabane Government Hospital** (☎ 404 2111); and **police** (☎ 404 2221). The police emergency number is ☎ 999.

SWAZILAND

Dangers & Annoyances Mbabane is becoming unsafe at night, so don't walk around by yourself away from the main streets. Take precautions in the back streets even during the day.

Places to Stay – Budget

At the time of writing there was no central hostel or backpacker accommodation in town.

Wendy's Backpackers (☎ 404 3905, 602 3691; Lot 1120, Dalriach East; dorm beds US$6.90, doubles US$17.50) is a small but friendly place 2km from the city centre, offering weekend walking tours. There's a pool, and a light breakfast is included.

Thokoza Church Centre (☎ 404 6681; Polinjane Rd; rooms with/without bathroom US$5/3.90) is a good bet with simple rooms. To get here from Allister Miller St turn east onto Walker St, cross the bridge, turn left at the police station and head along a dirt road up the hill for about 10 minutes. It's probably not safe to walk back here at night.

Places to Stay – Mid-Range & Top End

City Inn (☎ 404 4278/2406; Allister Miller St; singles/doubles without bathroom US$13.80/16, with bathroom from US$23/28.50) is a long-time travellers' favourite. It's central, but pretty run-down these days.

Mountain Inn (☎ 404 2781; e info@mountaininn.sz; singles/doubles from US$62/77, poolside doubles around US$75), 4km from the centre, is comfortable and commands a great view over the Ezulwini Valley. Rates include breakfast.

Cathmar Cottages (☎ 404 3387; e cathmar@africaonline.co.sz; Pine Valley Rd; cottage accommodation from US$7) offers cosy, self-catering places and a pool 3km north of Mbabane. To get there, follow signs to Pine Valley, turn right into Fonteyn Rd, left into Mseni Drive and left into Lukhalo St.

Kapola (☎ 404 8266; singles/doubles US$26/48) is a guesthouse 6km from Mbabane, just off the main highway to Manzini. It has comfortable rooms and hillside views, but is only really a practical accommodation option if you're driving. You'll see the multicoloured flags on its garden wall close to the road.

Places to Eat & Entertainment

Portofino (The Mall) is a good breakfast option. Large servings cost between US$2 and US$3.

Mediterranean (Allister Miller St; open lunch & dinner; mains around US$4) is in fact an Indian restaurant, although the menu also has steaks and seafood.

Valentino's (☎ 404 7498; Swazi Plaza; mains from US$4.60) serves a mean seafood platter and is probably the place for a splurge.

La Casserole (Omni Centre; open daily) is a licensed place serving a decent range of continental cuisine.

There are a few supermarkets in town if you're self catering, including the Ritz Supermarket & Takeaway on Allister Miller St.

Getting There & Away

Minibus taxis to South Africa (mostly northbound) leave from the taxi park near Swazi Plaza.

Getting Around

To/From the Airport A taxi from Mbabane to Matsapha airport costs about US$14. Buses and minibuses from Mbabane to Manzini go past the turn-off to the airport, from where it's a long walk to the terminal.

Bus & Minibus Taxi The main bus and minibus taxi park is near Swazi Plaza. All vehicles heading towards Manzini (US$0.60) or Matsapha pass through the Ezulwini Valley.

Taxi Nonshared taxis congregate near the bus rank by Swazi Plaza. At night you can usually find one near the City Inn, or try calling ☎ 404 0965 or ☎ 404 0966. Nonshared taxis to the Ezulwini Valley cost at least US$5.80, more to the far end of the valley, and still more at night.

Around Mbabane

EZULWINI VALLEY

The royal valley begins just outside Mbabane and extends down past Lobamba village, 18km away. Most of the area's attractions are near Lobamba. It's a pretty valley, but it's becoming crowded with hotels and other development. The **tourist office** (☎ 442 4206) in the Ezulwini Valley is helpful.

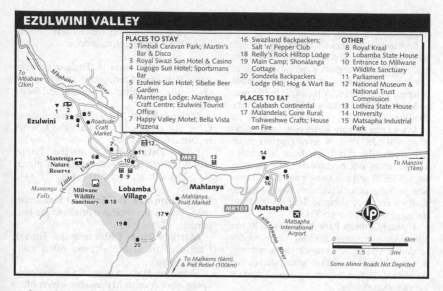

EZULWINI VALLEY

PLACES TO STAY
2 Timbali Caravan Park; Martin's Bar & Disco
3 Royal Swazi Sun Hotel & Casino
4 Lugogo Sun Hotel; Sportsmans Bar
5 Ezulwini Sun Hotel; Sibebe Beer Garden
6 Mantenga Lodge; Mantenga Craft Centre; Ezulwini Tourist Office
7 Happy Valley Motel; Bella Vista Pizzeria

16 Swaziland Backpackers; Salt 'n' Pepper Club
18 Reilly's Rock Hilltop Lodge
19 Main Camp; Shonalanga Cottage
20 Sondzela Backpackers Lodge (HI); Hog & Wart Bar

PLACES TO EAT
1 Calabash Continental
17 Malandelas; Gone Rural; Tishweshwe Crafts; House on Fire

OTHER
8 Royal Kraal
9 Lobamba State House
10 Entrance to Mlilwane Wildlife Sanctuary
11 Parliament
12 National Museum & National Trust Commission
13 Lothiza State House
14 University
15 Matsapha Industrial Park

Lobamba

This is the heart of Swaziland's royal valley. The British-built royal palace, the Embo State Palace, isn't open to visitors, and you are not allowed to take photos of it. Swazi kings now live in the Lozitha State House about 10km from Lobamba.

You can see the monarchy in action at the **Royal Kraal** in Lobamba during the Incwala ceremony and the Umhlanga dance (see the boxed text 'Swazi Ceremonies' earlier in this chapter for more details).

The **National Museum** (admission US$1.20; open daily) has some interesting displays on Swazi culture and a traditional beehive village. The **National Trust Commission office** (☎ 416 1179), where you can make bookings for Mlawula and Malolotja Nature Reserves, is here.

Next to the museum is the **parliament**, which is sometimes open to visitors. Across the road from the museum is a memorial to King Sobhuza II, the most revered of Swazi kings, plus a small **museum** devoted to him.

Mlilwane Wildlife Sanctuary

This lovely sanctuary (adult/child US$2.30/1.20), near Lobamba, is a private reserve created by Ted Reilly on his family farm in the 1950s. Reilly went on to open Mkhaya Game Reserve, and he also supervised the establishment of Hlane Royal National Park. The reserve is dominated by the precipitous Nyonyane (Little Bird) peak and there are several nice walks around it.

Zebras, giraffes, many antelope species, crocodiles, hippos and a variety of birds can be seen; in summer, the wildlife viewing also include the black eagle (Aquila verreauxii).

There are plenty of guided trips through the reserve: walks cost US$1.80 per hour, mountain biking costs US$5.20 per hour and horse riding costs US$8.70 per hour; there are also night drives. Watching the hippos from the restaurant is great entertainment, especially at feeding time (3pm).

The main entrance is 2km southeast of the Happy Valley Motel on the old Mbabane–Manzini road; it is signposted from the turn-off.

At the gate you can get a sanctuary map, and ask about night access via an alternative gate.

Places to Stay – Budget Mlilwane Wildlife Sanctuary has **camping** and **caravanning** (US$4 per person), but it has no electricity. There are also **beehive huts** (per person US$11.50) in the sanctuary's **Main Camp**, and more-luxurious **camp huts** (per person US$16) with bathroom and fridge. Book through the **Royal Swazi**

SWAZILAND

Big Game Parks office (☎ 528 3944; W www .biggame.co.sz).

Sondzela Backpackers (HI) Lodge (☎ 528 3117; dorm beds US$6, private singles/doubles US$11.50/17) is a great place just south of the camp. It's roomy, with a large veranda offering great views. A pick-up shuttle runs to Malandela's restaurant in Malkerns, where the Baz Bus stops.

Mantenga Nature Reserve (central reservations ☎ 528 3944; W www.biggame.co.sz) just down the dirt track from Mantenga Lodge, rents out beehive huts to campers for US$3.50 and has some great tented chalets looking onto Execution Rock (people really were once flung to their deaths from its jagged peak) for US$21.

Timbali Caravan Park (☎ 416 1156; e tim bali.co.sz; camp sites US$5.80, single/double rondavels US$32/52), outside the sanctuary, is a well-run place with a restaurant (closed on Monday) and a swimming pool. There's a supermarket nearby.

Places to Stay – Mid-Range With spacious accommodation **Shonalanga Cottage** (US$20.20 per person with breakfast) is in the sanctuary. There's a fully equipped kitchen. Book through **Big Game Parks** (☎ 528 3944).

Mantenga Lodge (☎ 416 2168, fax 416 2516; e mantenga@africaonline.co.sz; singles/ doubles US$38/51, single/double chalets US$46/59) is outside the sanctuary, off the main valley road on a wooded hillside near Mlilwane. The chalets offer lovely valley views. To get here, take the turn-off at Lobamba for Mlilwane Wildlife Sanctuary, and right at the T-intersection (look out for the Mantenga Craft Centre sign).

Places to Stay – Top End The Sun group's hotels offer the most opulent accommodation in the country. There's the **Royal Swazi Sun & Casino** (☎ 416 1001; e swazisun@sunsit.co.za; singles/doubles from US$120/130); the **Lugogo Sun** (☎ 416 1101) in the grounds of the Royal Swazi; and the **Ezulwini Sun** (☎ 416 1202; e swazi sun@sunint.co.sz; singles/doubles from US$83/ 90), across the road from the other two. At the Royal Swazi there's a golf course and a cinema.

Reilly's Rock (☎ 528 3944; e reserva tions@biggame.co.sz; singles/doubles with half-board from US$98/149), inside Mlilwane, offers fantastic hilltop views from colonial bungalows and attentive service.

Places to Eat Next to Timbali Caravan Park, **Calabash Continental** (☎ 416 1187; open daily) specialises in German and Swiss cuisine.

Malandelas (☎ 528 3115), next door to Gone Rural, is one of Swaziland's better restaurants with a cosy bar.

Bella Vista Pizzeria at the Happy Valley Motel has large vegetarian pizzas (US$3) and hearty seafood pizzas (US$4).

Entertainment The **Ezulwini Sun** sometimes has music, food and drinks in the beer garden.

Martin's Bar & Disco near the Timbali Caravan Park is a basic, but often busy, watering hole.

House on Fire is a fantastically decorated space next door to Malandelas which often has music, live or otherwise. Call Malandelas to find out what's on.

Getting There & Away During the day you could get on a Manzini-bound bus, but make sure the driver knows you want to get off in the valley. Even some nonexpress buses aren't keen on stopping. Nonshared taxis from Mbabane cost at least US$5.80. At night you'll have to negotiate.

MALKERNS

About 7km southeast of Lobamba there is a turn-off to the fertile Malkerns Valley, known for its art and craft outlets. At **Tishweshwe Crafts** (☎/fax 528 3336), 1km from the turn-off, lutindzi grass is woven into baskets and mats. **Gone Rural** (☎ 528 2001), next door, sells similar goods. Swazi Candles is based near Malkerns, and Baobab Batik is near Nyanza Stables on the Manzini road.

Places to Stay

Ecovision Swaziland (☎/fax 528 3561; e eco vision@zanet.co.za; old Ezulwini Rd; dorm beds US$7.50, doubles US$19.50), on the same road as Swazi Candles, is basic, but comfortable. It aims to let visitors sample Swazi culture. Local drumming groups and church choirs sometimes practice here. The owner also organises tours into Mozambique.

MANZINI

Manzini is now the country's industrial centre, but between 1890 and 1902 it was the administrative centre for the squabbling British and Boers. During the Anglo-Boer War a renegade Boer commando burnt it down.

Manzini's city centre isn't large, but it feels like a different country from easy-going rural Swaziland. There are reckless drivers, city slickers and a hint of menace. Be careful at night.

The market on Thursday and Friday mornings is highly recommended. Get there at dawn if possible, as people bring in their handicrafts to sell to retailers. The covered area above the clothes stalls is a good place to get cheap handicrafts and Swazi ornaments.

Apart from the market, there's not much to keep travellers here for long.

Places to Stay & Eat

Swaziland Backpackers (☎ 518 7225; e info@swazilandbackpackers.com; camp sites US$3.45, dorm beds US$5.80, doubles US$16) is a well-run, clean place, adjacent to the lively locals' watering hole the Salt 'n' Pepper Club. It has a bar and email facilities. The Baz Bus stops here.

Myxo's Place (☎ 505 8363; camping US$4.60, dorms US$6.90, doubles US$17.50), just off the Big Bend Road, is a chilled-out place run by Myxo, a Swazi. If you've time, Myxo runs two-day trips (around US$40 per person) to a local village where you can sleep and eat in the traditional Swazi way and spend some time among the villagers.

Mozambique Hotel (☎ 505 2489; Mahleko St; singles/doubles US$10.50/17.50) has average rooms, but there is a good bar and a popular Portuguese restaurant.

Takeaways abound in Bhunu Mall, including **Chicken Licken**, **King Pie** and **Steers**.

Getting There & Away

A nonshared taxi to Matsapha airport costs around US$7. The main bus and minibus taxi park is at the northern end of Louw St. Buses run up the Ezulwini Valley to Mbabane for US$0.30. Taxis to Mozambique leave from the car park next to KFC. Some sample fares include Jo'burg (US$10.50), Durban (US$11.50), Rustenburg (US$12.50), and Pretoria (US$10.50). Most long-distance taxis leave early in the morning.

MHLAMBANYATSI

Mhlambanyatsi (literally, Watering Place of the Buffalo) is 27km from Mbabane. The popular **Foresters Arms** (☎ 467 4177, fax 467 4051; per person with half-board around US$39) is likely to be full of locals on the weekend, when they drift here from Mbabane for home-made bread and Sunday lunch. You can go sailing, windsurfing or canoeing on the nearby **Lupholho Dam**, on the Mbabane road.

Northwestern Swaziland

NGWENYA

Ngwenya (Crocodile) is 5km east of the Oshoek border crossing on the road to Mbabane. At the **Ngwenya glass factory** (showroom open 7am-4pm daily), recycled glass is used to create African animals and birds as well as vases and tableware. **Endlotane Studios** (☎ 444 5447; open 8am-5pm daily) is 1km further up the road. Its tapestries are hung in galleries throughout the world.

MALOLOTJA NATURE RESERVE

This reserve in the hilly northwest, managed by the **reserve office** (☎ 442 4241; admission US$2.30; gates open 6am-6pm), has mainly antelope species. Over 280 species of bird have also been recorded here; a number of them rare. Several of the plant species here are only found in this part of Africa, such as the woolly Barberton and Kaapschehoop cycads. The Nkomati River cuts a gorge through the park and continues east in a series of falls and rapids until it meets the lowveld.

The reserve has one of the world's oldest known mines, dating from 41,000 BC. You can visit the mine by vehicle, but you must be accompanied by a ranger.

There's camping at the established **camp sites** (US$4.50) and on the **trails** (US$2.30). There are also fully equipped **cabins** (US$35) for two people. Book through the **National Trust Commission** (☎ 416 1178, 416 1151) in the National Museum, Lobamba. The park entrance is about 35km from Mbabane on the Piggs Peak road.

Hiking Trails

The reserve is a true wilderness area, rugged and in most parts unspoiled. There are hiking trails, from short day-walks to a week-long trail, extending from Ngwenya in the south to the Mgwayiza Range in the north.

For the extended trails, you must obtain a free permit and map. You can get a more detailed map for US$0.60 from the reserve office. You need to bring all your own food, and a camp stove as fires are not permitted outside the base camp.

PIGGS PEAK

This small town is the centre of Swaziland's logging industry and there are huge pine plantations in the area. The town was named after a prospector who found gold here in 1884.

West of Piggs Peak are **Bulembu** and the Havelock asbestos mine – carrying asbestos via a cableway to Barberton 20km away.

As well as its scenery, including the **Phophonyane Falls** about 8km north of town, this area is known for its handicrafts. At the Highlands Inn in Piggs Peak, **Tintsaba Crafts** displays a good range; there are several other craft centres in the district, including a couple of excellent shops just up from Piggs Peak Hotel (signposted from Phophonyane).

Places to Stay

Highlands Inn (☎ 137 1111; singles/doubles with breakfast from US$18.50/36), about 1km south of the town centre on the main road, is the only place to stay in town. The rooms are clean, but aren't great value. There's a pleasant garden area.

Phophonyane Lodge (☎ 437 1319; e lungile@phophonyane.co.sz; double safari tents/cottages from around US$43/58) is one of the best places to stay in Swaziland. It's in its own nature reserve of lush forest on the Phophonyane River. This isn't a malarial area, but there are plenty of mosquitoes in summer, so bring repellent. On weekends the minimum stay is two nights, and prices rise during holidays. There are cooking facilities or you can eat in the tiny restaurant. Day visitors pay US$1.20.

Getting There & Away

Roads in the northwest of the country are mainly dirt, but they're in reasonable condition. If you're driving, beware of buses between Piggs Peak and Tshaneni – they speed and hog the gravel road.

There's an express sprinter bus to Mbabane for US$1.20. The bus and minibus taxi rank is next to the market at the top end of the main street.

There are a few nonshared taxis in Piggs Peak. The fare to Mbabane is US$21.

Eastern Swaziland

The northeastern corner of Swaziland is a major sugar-producing area. It's hot and in the arid foothills of the Lebombo Mountains the scenery approaches what most people think of when they say 'Africa'.

This area has three notable parks and reserves: Hlane, Mlawula and Mkhaya. The towns of Tshaneni, Mhlume, Tambankulu and Simunye are the main population centres in the country's northeast. **Simunye** is a neat, lush town with excellent facilities.

The Sand River Reservoir, west of Tshaneni, has no facilities, but you can camp there. Don't swim in the water or drink it untreated as it's full of bilharzia.

SITEKI

This trading town isn't really on the way to anywhere any more, but it's a nice enough little place and a bit cooler than down on the plains. There are good views from the steep road on the way up here.

The town was originally named when Mbandzeni (great-grandfather of the present king) gave his frontier troops permission to marry – Siteki means Marrying Place.

The **Siteki Hotel** (☎ 343 4126; per person US$16) has accommodation, and the host is knowledgeable about the surrounding area.

HLANE ROYAL NATIONAL PARK

This park (adult/child US$2.30/1.20) – Hlane means Wilderness – in the northeast is near the former royal hunting grounds. There are white rhinos and many antelope species. Elephants and lions have been reintroduced. There are guided walking trails (US$1.80 per person per hour). The park entrance is about 4km from Simunye.

Places to Stay

There's **camping** (US$4 per person), but no electricity.

Ndlovu Rest Camp *(huts from US$17 per person)* has thatched huts with communal facilities and no electricity.

Bhubesi Rest Camp *(huts from US$17 per person)* has self-contained huts with electricity. Book for both through the Royal Swazi Big Game Parks office *(☎ 528 3944)*.

MLAWULA NATURE RESERVE

Mlawula *(US$2.30/1.20 per person/vehicle)* is a 16,000-hectare reserve in harsh, but beautiful, country taking in both plains and the Lebombo Mountains. Shy hyenas and antelopes hide in remote areas. Snakes include the deadly trio of black mambas, puff adders and spitting cobras. Aquatic dangers include both crocodiles and bilharzia. Watch out for ticks too.

The reserve's entrance is about 10km north of Simunye. There's camping *(adults from US$2.30)* and tented accommodation *(US$14/tent)*. Call for bookings *(☎ 383 8885; e mlawala@sntc.org.sz or e mlawula@africaonline.co.za)*, or see the National Trust Commission in Lobamba.

MKHAYA GAME RESERVE

This is a private reserve *(☎ 528 3943/4)* off the Manzini–Big Bend road, near the hamlet of Phuzumoya.

The reserve is on cattle farms that have been rehabilitated, although the area had always been popular with hunters. Mkhaya takes its name from the mkhaya tree (or knobthorn, *Acacia nigrescens*), which abounds on the reserve. Mkhayas grow only on fertile land, and are valued not only for their fruit, from which Swazis brew beer, but for the insects and birdlife they support.

Although small, Mkhaya has a wide range of animals, including white and black rhinos, roan and sable antelopes, and elephants. You have a good chance of meeting a black rhino in the wild here too.

There are also herds of the indigenous and rare Nguni cattle which make the reserve economically self-supporting. The Nguni is an old breed, and centuries of natural selection have made it heat tolerant, disease immune, self-sufficient and, importantly, tick resistant.

Wildlife Drives

The wildlife reserve organises a couple of good-value day tours. A one-day drive (mini-mum two people) in a 4WD, with lunch, costs US$20; a half-day costs US$14.

White-Water Rafting

One of Swaziland's highlights is white-water rafting on the Usutu River. This largely sluggish river turns to rapids through the narrow Bulungu Gorge near the reserve.

At one stage you'll have to portage a 10m waterfall. The second half of the day is a sedate trip through scenic country with glimpses of the 'flat dogs' (crocodiles) sunning on the riverbanks.

Swazi Trails *(☎/fax 416 2180; e tours@swazitrails.co.sz)* runs full-day trips in two-person 'crocodile rafts' for US$29 per person. Prices include lunch and all equipment.

Places to Stay

Stone Camp *(per person from US$60)* provides safari tents, and the price includes three meals, wildlife drives and walks. The camp is like a comfortable 19th-century hunting camp. The floors of the tents are on sand allowing you to see ant trails and the tracks of small nocturnal visitors.

Nkonjane *(Swallow's Nest; cottage per person US$60)* is a luxurious stone cottage. Rates increase on weekends. Book accommodation through the Royal Swazi Big Game Parks office *(☎ 528 3944)*.

Note that you can't visit without pre-booking, nor drive in alone; you'll be met at Phuzumoya at a specified pick-up time.

BIG BEND

Picturesque Big Bend is a neat sugar town on – not surprisingly – a big bend in the Lusutfu River and is a popular stopover with South Africans. It may pay to book accommodation ahead.

The New Bend Inn Hotel *(☎ 363 6725; B&B singles/doubles US$17.50/24.50)*, on a hill just south of town and with great views across the river, is good value. There's a restaurant and a pleasant outdoor bar overlooking Big Bend.

Next to the Lubombo Restaurant, Lismore Lodge *(☎ 363 6019; doubles US$20)* has small, comfortable good-value doubles.

One of Swaziland's best restaurants, Lubombo Lobster, a few kilometres south of Big Bend, has an excellent reputation for seafood. The seafood curry, crayfish and calamari are all recommended.

Victoria Falls

When David Livingstone first saw the Victoria Falls in 1855 he wrote in his journal 'on sights as beautiful as this, angels in their flight must have gazed'. He named the falls after the queen of England, but they were (and still are) known as *Mosi-oa-Tunya* in the Kololo language and *Chinotimba* by the Nambya. Both terms are loosely translated as 'The Smoke that Thunders'; in fact, on a clear day the spray can be seen from 50km away.

Victoria Falls is 1.7km wide (Niagara Falls is 1km) and 108m high (Niagara is 58m), with an annual average flow of one million litres per *second*. At the peak (March to May) the flow can be nine times higher, while in the dry season (September to December) the volume of water is often only 4% of the peak. Not surprisingly, the falls are regarded as one of the seven natural wonders of the world.

The Victoria Falls straddle the border between Zimbabwe and Zambia, and is easily accessible from both countries – as well from Namibia and Botswana. See the 'Zim or Zam?' boxed text below for some tips about visiting the falls.

Zim or Zam?

For many, the big question is: Do I visit the falls from Victoria Falls town (Zimbabwe) or Livingstone (Zambia)? The short answer is: Visit the falls from both sides and, if possible, stay in both towns.

The paths are longer and more hilly on the Zambian side of the falls but the surrounding forest is more pristine. From Zambia you can view the falls from upstream and downstream, and from above and from below. During the dry season, the views are far less spectacular on the Zambian side, but visitors can easily walk over to Livingstone Island in the middle of the falls. One disadvantage is that the falls are 11km from Livingstone town, but admission is cheaper on the Zambian side, which is conducive to more than one visit.

From the Zimbabwean side, the falls are a short walk from town (with comprehensive tourist facilities) and the paths are shorter and flatter. And by standing opposite the falls the overall view is far more complete.

What to Bring

Ironically, you'll need to bring drinking water during the hot season (September to December). Stalls at the car parks on both sides sell drinks, but there's nowhere to buy food or drinks once you're inside either national park surrounding the falls.

When the water volume is high (February to July), you'll need a decent umbrella and raincoat to protect yourself from the dense spray. Both can be hired from an enterprising place in Victoria Falls town (see that section for details) and at stalls in the car parks on both sides. And during this time, please don't wear anything that will cause a scandal if wet!

Also remember that tickets from both sides are for one visit only, so plan your trip accordingly.

Zambia

Zambia, which shares a border with Zimbabwe along the Zambezi River, is often undeservedly forgotten when talking about, and visiting, Victoria Falls. Try to visit the falls from both sides and take a trip to the historic town of Livingstone as well. For general information about Zambia, eg, visas and money, refer to the Facts for the Visitor section in the Zambia chapter.

LIVINGSTONE
☎ 03

Zambia's tourist capital is also a major hub for travellers in Southern Africa. Livingstone lies a short distance from the falls and is not too far from some high-quality national parks. It is more historical and 'African' than Victoria Falls town, over the border in Zimbabwe, and usually cheaper.

Information

The **Tourist Centre** (*☎ 321404; Mosi-oa-Tunya Rd; open 8am-1pm & 2pm-5pm Mon-Fri, 8am-12pm Sat*) is mildly useful, but has few brochures and maps to give away or even sell.

Barclays Bank (*cnr Mosi-oa-Tunya Rd & Akapelwa St*) and **Standard Chartered Bank** (*Mosi-oa-Tunya Rd*) accept major brands of travellers cheques (in US dollars only), but charge US$15 commission. Both offer cash

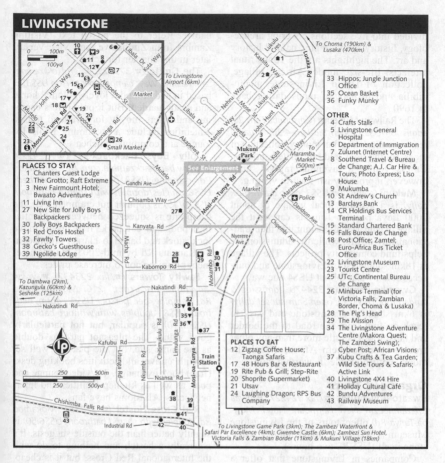

LIVINGSTONE

33 Hippos; Jungle Junction
   Office
35 Ocean Basket
36 Funky Munky

OTHER
4 Crafts Stalls
5 Livingstone General
   Hospital
6 Department of Immigration
7 Zulunet (Internet Centre)
8 Southend Travel & Bureau
   de Change; A.J. Car Hire &
   Tours; Photo Express; Liso
   House
9 Mukumba
10 St Andrew's Church
13 Barclays Bank
14 CR Holdings Bus Services
   Terminal
15 Standard Chartered Bank
16 Falls Bureau de Change
18 Post Office; Zamtel;
   Euro-Africa Bus Ticket
   Office
22 Livingstone Museum
23 Tourist Centre
25 UTc; Continental Bureau
   de Change
26 Minibus Terminal (for
   Victoria Falls, Zambian
   Border, Choma & Lusaka)
28 The Pig's Head
29 The Mission
34 The Livingstone Adventure
   Centre (Makora Quest;
   The Zambezi Swing);
   Cyber Post; African Visions
37 Kubu Crafts & Tea Garden;
   Wild Side Tours & Safaris;
   Active Link
40 Livingstone 4X4 Hire
41 Holiday Cultural Café
42 Bundu Adventures
43 Railway Museum

PLACES TO STAY
1 Chanters Guest Lodge
2 The Grotto; Raft Extreme
3 New Fairmount Hotel;
   Bwaato Adventures
11 Living Inn
27 New Site for Jolly Boys
   Backpackers
30 Jolly Boys Backpackers
31 Red Cross Hostel
32 Fawlty Towers
38 Gecko's Guesthouse
39 Ngolide Lodge

PLACES TO EAT
12 Zigzag Coffee House;
   Taonga Safaris
17 48 Hours Bar & Restaurant
19 Rite Pub & Grill; Step-Rite
20 Shoprite (Supermarket)
21 Utsav
24 Laughing Dragon; RPS Bus
   Company

advances (in kwacha only) with Visa and MasterCard over the counter and through their automated teller machines (ATMs). The **bureaux de change** dotted along Mosi-oa-Tunya are quicker and offer slightly better exchange rates. Do *not* change money on the street, though buying/selling kwacha with Zimbabwean dollars at the minibus terminal along Senanga Rd is accepted by the authorities and safe.

The **Post Office** (*Mosi-oa-Tunya Rd*) has a poste restante and fax service. **Zamtel**, next door, provides plenty of telephone booths; otherwise, try the two Internet centres (see following). To call Livingstone from Victoria Falls town in Zimbabwe, simply add ☎ 8 to the local number (ie, not the Zambian or Livingstone area codes).

The new **Zulunet** Internet centre (*Mosi-oa-Tunya Rd*) is impressive, while **Cyber Post** (*216 Mosi-oa-Tunya Rd*), near The Livingstone Adventure Centre, is also reliable and cheap, about US$1 per 30 minutes.

Photo Express (*Liso House, 106 Mosi-oa-Tunya Rd*) sells print and slide film, and develops 24/36 exposure print (only) film for US$4/5.50.

We hope you won't need to contact the **police** (☎ 320116; *Maramba Rd*) or the **Livingstone General Hospital** (☎ 321475; *Akapelwa St*).

Things to See
The large but tidy **Livingstone Museum** (*Mosi-oa-Tunya Rd; admission US$3; open 9am-4.30pm daily*) is the oldest museum in

Zambia. It contains a worthwhile collection, divided into five sections covering archaeology, history, ethnography, natural history and art. The highlights are the Tonga ritual artefacts, life-size model African village, collection of David Livingstone memorabilia and display of maps dating back to 1690.

The **Railway Museum** *(Chishimba Falls Rd; admission US$5; open 8.30am-4.30pm daily)* features a charming, but motley, collection of locos, rolling stock and rail-related antiques. Unless you're a ravenous railway buff, however, it probably isn't worth visiting.

Mukuni *(admission US$3; open dawn-dusk daily)* is a genuine local village of about 7000 Leya people. Tourists can visit the village to gain a small insight into their traditional way of life, while the admission fee helps fund community projects. The village is 18km southwest of Livingstone and only accessible by taxi (about US$4 one way).

Gwembe Castle *(☎ 324470; admission & guided tour US$3.50; open 8am-sunset daily)* is 6km south of Livingstone and easy to reach on foot from the road to the border and falls. It offers little more than any other croc farm in Southern Africa, though the mock Scottish 'castle' is worth a look.

Organised Tours

Bwaato Adventures *(☎/fax 324227; e bwaato@zamnet.zm; New Fairmount Hotel, Mosioa-Tunya Rd)* offers tours of the Livingstone Museum (US$15, one hour) and of Livingstone itself (US$20, two hours).

Companies in Livingstone that offer a plethora of adventure activities and tours in and around Livingstone and Victoria Falls are listed under Activities later in this chapter.

Special Events

The annual **Livingstone Festival** (three days in late August) features numerous concerts, including traditional dancing, and exhibitions around town.

Places to Stay

Currently, accommodation in Livingstone (only) does not attract the normal 17.5% Value Added Tax (VAT).

Places to Stay – Budget

Jolly Boys Backpackers and Fawlty Towers sometimes offer set-price deals to entice

visitors from Victoria Falls town in Zimbabwe. Refer to the boxed text 'Visiting Zambia from Zimbabwe (and Vice Versa)' later in this chapter for details.

The Grotto *(☎ 323929; e grotto@zamnet.zm; Kashitu Way; camping per person US$3)* is based in and around a lovely colonial home and shady garden. But it only offers camping and caters mostly for overland trucks. Amenities include a swimming pool, TV lounge and communal kitchen.

Jolly Boys Backpackers *(☎ 324229; w www.backpackzambia.com; 559 Mokambo Rd; camping US$3 per person, dorm beds US$6, singles/doubles with shared bathroom US$10/15)* is popular but cramped – eg, the camp site is squeezed between the (enticing) pool and car park. It plans to move lock, stock and barrel to a larger premises at 34 Kanyata Rd by mid-2003, but management promises not to increase prices.

Fawlty Towers *(☎/fax 323432; w www.adventure-africa.com; 216 Mosi-oa-Tunya Rd; camping per person US$5, dorm beds from US$8, doubles with/without bathroom US$30/20)* is popular, but not particularly good value. The pleasant gardens double as the camp site, but the place is well set up with a travel and activities booking desk, (free) book exchange, TV/video lounge and pool, as well as kitchen facilities and Internet access. All rooms have fans.

Red Cross Hostel *(☎ 323381; Mokambo Rd; doubles with shared bathroom US$6.50)* is slightly better than the outside suggests. It's not really a hostel, and nothing to do with the International Red Cross, but it is cheap, clean and friendly. Rooms have a mosquito net, but no fan.

Gecko's Guesthouse *(☎ 322267; e gecko@zamnet.zm; 84 Limulunga Rd; camping per person US$2.50, dorm beds US$6, singles/doubles with fan & shared bathroom US$13/20)* is clean and friendly, but looking a bit forlorn these days. It's aimed at couples and families, and anyone else who wants to avoid overland trucks. The camp site is small but it does offer single rates for the rooms. Facilities include a kitchen, pool and a convivial bar and restaurant.

Places to Stay – Mid-Range

Living Inn *(☎ 324203; 95 John Hunt Way; singles/doubles with bathroom & fan from US$14/17)* is on the corner with Akapelwa

St and easy to miss. The rooms, which overlook a tiny courtyard, are musty, but the hotel was (at long last) being renovated at the time of research.

Ngolide Lodge (☎ 321091; W www.zambia tourism.com/ngolide; 110 Mosi-oa-Tunya Rd; singles/doubles with bathroom & TV US$38/50) has a thatch roof, airy courtyard and motel-style rooms, which are a bit cramped. Staff are friendly and efficient, and the whole place is comfortable without being luxurious.

New Fairmount Hotel (☎ 320723; Mosi-oa-Tunya Rd; singles US$24, doubles US$29-33) is a colonial-style place stuck in a 1960's time warp. It's unappealing from the outside but the rooms are OK, though a touch pricey. All come with bathroom and breakfast. The single rooms face the noisy main road.

Chanters Guest Lodge (☎ 323412; Lukulu Cres; singles/doubles with bathroom & breakfast US$19/21) is similar to a number of homely lodges on the Zimbabwean side at Victoria Falls town. The rooms at Chanters are unremarkable, but contain a fan and TV. It is a little inconvenient, however.

The Zambezi Waterfront (☎ 330696; W www.safariparx.com/lodges/zwfmo.htm; camping per person US$5, single/double pre-set tents US$30/40, single/double chalets with breakfast from US$55/80) is along the majestic Zambezi River, only 4km from Livingstone. It offers a shady, grassy camp site, pre-erected tents on raised wooden platforms, charming chalets and an enticing pool. The only downside is that you'll have to charter taxis to and from Livingstone.

Places to Stay – Top End

Most upmarket hotels and lodges in the area are a fair way from Livingstone. Some are mentioned in The Zambezi Waterfront section in the Zambia chapter.

Zambezi Sun (☎ 321122; singles/doubles with breakfast US$160/170) boasts the best location on either side of the falls – in fact, it is actually *inside* the Mosi-oa-Tunya National Park. This huge complex, with restaurants, bars and a casino, is worth wandering around if you're not staying there. The hotel is about 300m before the entrance to the Zambian side of the falls.

Places to Eat

Funky Munky (☎ 320120; 216 Mosi-oa-Tunya Rd; snacks/mains from US$1.50/2.50) offers salads, baguettes and pizzas (US$2/3 for small/large 'uns) in a laid-back, comfortable setting. Definitely recommended.

Hippos (Limulunga Rd; mains about US$3) is a raucous bar-cum-restaurant at the back of Fawlty Towers. The two-course set-price meals (US$4) are good value, and many à la carte dishes have an appealing Spanish influence.

Ocean Basket (☎ 321274; 82 Mosi-oa-Tunya Rd; starters/mains about US$3/4) is a huge, new place that (not surprisingly) specialises in fish. Most fillets can be grilled in a 'Cajun style'.

Rite Pub & Grill (☎ 320398; Mosi-oa-Tunya Rd; snacks US$1, mains US$3.50) is a sparkling new place in a grubby part of town. It offers all sorts of tasty meals in a kitsch Wild West setting. Let's hope it becomes successful, because similar places in Livingstone have bitten the dust over recent years.

48 Hours Bar & Restaurant (Mosi-oa-Tunya Rd; snacks/mains US$2/4) has a cosy indoor bar (and outdoor tables) that sells the coldest beer in town. The restaurant at the back offers a limited choice of Western meals at reasonable prices in a quiet setting.

Zigzag Coffee House (Mosi-oa-Tunya Rd; breakfast about US$2, mains from US$3; open 8am-5pm daily) is an alluring hang-out with tables on the footpath and comfy sofas inside. It offers an eclectic range of dishes, from tacos to tandoori, and is ideal for a coffee or milk shake. The window is a mine of local information and there's a book exchange.

Laughing Dragon (☎ 097-846919; Mutelo St) is the only authentic Chinese eatery in town, while **Utsav** (☎ 322259; Mosi-oa-Tunya Rd) is *the* place for a curry. Both offer tempting 'backpackers specials' for about US$3.

The well-stocked **Shoprite** supermarket (Kapondo St) contains a decent **bakery**.

Entertainment

The Pig's Head (Kabompo Rd) is a British-style pub that attracts homesick Brits, as well as a number of other expats eager for a cold beer. The 'pub grub' is tasty.

The Mission (Mosi-oa-Tunya Rd) specialises in cocktails, which can be enjoyed in the outdoor, undercover bar while watching international sports on TV or by the swimming pool (guests: US$1).

Step-Rite (Kapondo St), just around the corner from the Rite Pub & Grill, is a sweaty

VICTORIA FALLS

Visiting Zambia from Zimbabwe (and Vice Versa)

From Victoria Falls town in Zimbabwe, it's a short walk (1km), or taxi ride, to the Zimbabwean border post. From there, walk (about 1.3km), or take a ride in a taxi or on a rickshaw (U$1) over the magnificent Victoria Falls Bridge to Zambia. Minibuses and shared taxis (US$1) leave regularly from the Zambian border into Livingstone. But don't walk to Livingstone (and think twice about cycling) because muggings along this road are common.

Alternatively, most travel agencies in Victoria Falls town and Livingstone offer transfers for about US$25 per person, but this is spectacularly poor value. Jolly Boys Backpackers and Fawlty Towers (both in Livingstone) sometimes offer excellent deals: for US$20 per person, you'll get a transfer from Victoria Falls, a free Zambian transit visa (valid for seven days and extendable, if you need one) and two night's accommodation in a dormitory. Contact Backpackers Bazaar in Victoria Falls for details and bookings (see Travel Agencies under Victoria Falls later in this chapter).

If you just want to admire the bridge, or take a day trip to Zambia or Zimbabwe, tell the immigration officials on both sides so you don't have to buy another visa on return (if you needed one anyway). If you would normally have to buy a visa for either country, ask for a day visa (US$10).

Money-changers hang around the Zambian border and at the minibus station in Livingstone (where the exchange rate is better). Both borders are open daily from 6am to 8pm.

and sleazy open-air disco. Other lively places to meet locals over a drink are **Mukumba** *(John Hunt Way)* and the **Holiday Cultural Café** *(Chishimba Falls Rd)*, which also offers traditional music and food every evening in a shady garden.

Shopping
African Visions *(216 Mosi-oa-Tunya Rd)*, near the Livingstone Adventure Centre, is a charming place selling quality fabrics and crafts from all over Africa.

Kubu Crafts *(Mosi-oa-Tunya Rd)* offers a vast selection of classy souvenirs. You can admire your purchases while sipping a tea or coffee in the shady (but noisy) **tea garden**.

The **craft stalls** in the southern corner of **Mukuni Park** *(Mosi-oa-Tunya Rd)* are a pleasant, hassle-free place to browse.

Getting There & Away
Air Flying to Lusaka several times a week for US$135 one way are **Nationwide** *(☎/fax 323360; **W** www.nationwideair.co.za; Zambezi Sun hotel)* and **Zambian Airways** *(☎ 322967; Livingstone Airport)*. Nationwide also plans to start flights to Arusha (near Mt Kilimanjaro) in Tanzania for about US$260. **South African Airways** flies every day to Johannesburg (Jo'burg) for US$106.

Tickets for all flights can be booked at **Southend Travel** *(☎ 320241; **e** southend@zamnet.zm; Liso House, 106 Mosi-oa-Tunya Rd)*.

Bus From Livingstone, buses and minibuses go to several cities in Zambia as well as into Botswana.

Domestic Several private companies offer comfortable buses to Lusaka (US$8, seven hours), via Choma (US$5, three hours), for almost identical prices. **CR Holdings Bus Services** has five buses a day from its terminal on the corner of Mosi-oa-Tunya Rd and Akapelwa St; **Euro-Africa** buses run once a day (at about 8.30am) from the ticket counter in front of the post office; and **RPS** operates buses (at 6.30am and 2pm) from its office near the Laughing Dragon restaurant (Mutelo St).

Minibuses to Lusaka leave from the minibus terminal along Senanga Rd, while a few also depart from outside the post office (Mosi-oa-Tunya Rd). Jolly Boys Backpackers (see Places to Stay earlier) runs a 'backpackers bus' (US$11) between Livingstone and Lusaka, but only with a minimum number of passengers. Contact them for details.

Most other public buses leave from **Maramba Market** in Maramba township, about 800m east of the post office. From there, one bus heads to Sesheke (US$7, six hours) every day at 10pm, and another goes to Mongu (US$10, 10 hours), via Senanga, late in the evening every Monday and Thursday.

Minibuses to Sesheke and the Botswana border at Kazungula (US$4, 1½ hours) also leave from a lay-by in Dambwa, along the

main road 3km west of Mosi-oa-Tunya Rd. Get there at around 7am.

International For information about travelling to Botswana, and crossing the Zambia–Botswana border at Kazungula, see the Getting There & Away section in the Zambia chapter. For details about crossing into Zimbabwe along the Victoria Falls Bridge, refer to the boxed text 'Visiting Zambia from Zimbabwe (and Vice Versa)' earlier.

Train The *Zambezi Express* leaves Livingstone for Lusaka (US$4/5/7/8 for economy/standard/1st class/sleeper, 15 hours), via Choma, on Tuesday, Thursday and Sunday at 7pm. Reservations are available at the **train station** (☎ 320001), signposted off Mosi-oa-Tunya Rd.

Getting Around

The renovated Livingstone Airport is 6km northwest of town. It is only accessible by taxi (about US$4 one way) or by shuttle buses (US$10) offered by UTc and Bwaato Adventures (see Activities later in this chapter).

Livingstone 4X4 Hire (☎ 320888; **w** www.4x4hireafrica.com; *Industrial Rd*) is the only place in town to hire a 4WD. It charges from US$53 per day, plus US$0.40 per kilometre, or US$96 per day with unlimited kilometres (if rented for at least four days). Rates include insurance, but not petrol. A driver-cum guide costs from an extra US$20 per day.

A.J. Car Hire & Tours (☎/fax 322090; **e** ajcarhire@zamnet.zm; *Liso House, 106 Mosi-oa-Tunya Rd*) charges US$59 per day, plus US$0.60 per kilometre, for a 2WD, plus US$10 per day for insurance. A driver will cost an extra US$10 per day.

Active Link (☎ 322753; *131 Mosi-oa-Tunya Rd*), which shares an office with Wild Side Tours & Safaris, can also arrange car and bicycle rental.

Bikes can ridden into Zimbabwe, but keep the receipt with you. And bear in mind that cyclists have been mugged while riding to and from the Zambian border and the falls.

MOSI-OA-TUNYA NATIONAL PARK

Zambia's smallest national park surrounds the Zambian side of Victoria Falls, about 11km from Livingstone. The park is divided into two smaller sections – one immediately surrounding the Victoria Falls, and a game park nearer Livingstone.

Victoria Falls World Heritage National Monument Site

This pretentiously named park (☎ 321396; *admission per person/vehicle US$10/3, open 6am-6pm daily*) is about 100m before the Zambian border post (if coming from Livingstone). The admission price is also payable in kwachas, South African rands and UK pounds. From the unpretentious entrance, an obvious path leads 200m to a car park. There you'll find the **Visitors Information Centre**, with modest displays about local fauna, geology and culture, and a mass of **craft stalls**.

Opposite the Information Centre is the **ticket booth** (☎ 321396), from where a network of paths leads through the thick vegetation to the various viewpoints. You can walk upstream along a path mercifully free of fences – and warning notices (so take care!) – to watch the Zambezi waters glide smoothly through rocks and little islands towards the lip of the falls.

For close-up views of the **Eastern Cataract**, nothing beats the hair-raising (and hair-wetting) walk across the **footbridge**, through swirling clouds of mist, to a sheer buttress called the **Knife Edge**. If the water is low, or the wind is favourable, you'll be treated to a magnificent view of the falls, as well as the yawning abyss below. Otherwise, your vision (and your clothes) will be drenched by spray. Then you can walk down a steep track to the banks of the great Zambezi to see the huge whirlpool called the **Boiling Pot**.

Like its counterpart on the Zimbabwean side, the park is open again in the evenings during (and just before and after) a full moon in order to see the amazing **lunar rainbow**. Tickets cost an extra US$10. Contact the ticket booth for more information.

Livingstone Game Park

Upriver from the falls, and only 3km southwest of Livingstone, is this tiny wildlife sanctuary (*admission per person/vehicle US$20/3; open 6am-6pm daily*). OK, it's not South Luangwa, but it is easy to reach and home to a surprising range of animals, including zebras, giraffes, buffaloes, elephants and antelopes. And it's the only place in Zambia that boasts white rhinos.

VICTORIA FALLS

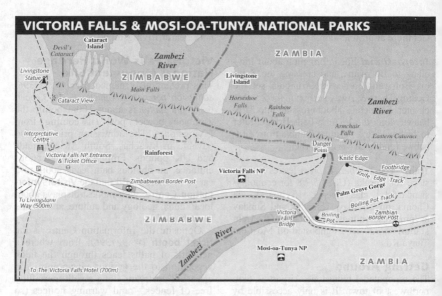

VICTORIA FALLS & MOSI-OA-TUNYA NATIONAL PARKS

Most visitors without their own car join a wildlife drive organised in Livingstone (see Activities later in this chapter). Otherwise, walk (or take a taxi) to the park entrance from Livingstone and hitch a ride into the park.

Getting There & Away

The Zambian side of the falls is 11km south of Livingstone and along the main road to the border with Zimbabwe. Plenty of minibuses and shared taxis ply the route from the minibus terminal along Senanga Rd in Livingstone. Don't walk (and think twice about cycling) because some people have been mugged.

ACTIVITIES

A plethora of companies in Victoria Falls town (Zimbabwe) and Livingstone (Zambia) offer a *staggering* array of tours and activities. In fact, some travellers have so much fun (and spend so much money) bungee jumping or rafting that they forget to visit the falls!

All activities listed in this section can be booked and started from either town for the same cost, but confirm any extra government charges and taxes. Included in all rates are transfers to and from your hotel and national park entrance fees (if required), but most prices do *not* include a visa (if required) for Zimbabwe, Zambia or Botswana. Full-day trips normally include one or two meals and

often unlimited drinks at the end of the trip. All prices are per person, and all payments are normally required in US dollars.

If money is tight, and you just can't decide what to do, try a whirlwind combination. Depending on the season and level of competition (which is fierce at times), you can get a 'combo' (including canoeing, game drive and booze cruise) for under US$100.

Travel Agencies

Any activity can be booked at any travel agency or tour/activity company in Livingstone or Victoria Falls, but it's often better (if possible) to book at the company office rather than any old travel agency. The original company can provide, for example, more reassuring information about the activities and offer special deals or discounts that may not be passed on by the travel agency.

Travel agencies have offices that you can visit and their addresses are listed here. While the original tour/activity companies are certainly happy to accept booking by telephone, fax or email, they do not have walk-in offices.

Agencies & Companies in Victoria Falls

Several of the travel agencies listed here also have offices in the Sprayview Hotel. The area code is ☎ 013.

VICTORIA FALLS

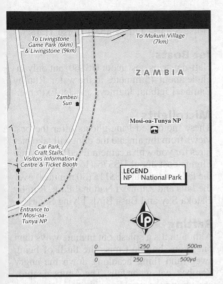

To Livingstone
Game Park (6km)
& Livingstone (9km)

To Mukuni Village
(7km)

ZAMBIA

Zambezi
Sun

Mosi-oa-Tunya NP

Car Park,
Craft Stalls,
Visitors Information
Centre & Ticket Booth

Entrance to
Mosi-oa-
Tunya NP

LEGEND
NP   National Park

0   250   500m
0   250   500yd

Bad Dog Rafting (☎ 42383) next to Kandahar/
Adrift, Parkway
Bundu Adventures (☎ 011 210946, W www
.bundu-adventures.com) Parkway
Bush Birds Flying Safaris (☎/fax 42210)
Dabula Safaris (☎ 44453) Inyathi Valley Motel &
Rest Camp, Parkway
Frontier Adventures (☎/fax 43587, e frontadv@
telcovic.co.zw) Parkway
Ivan Carter Safaris (☎/fax 45821, e cat@mweb
.co.zw)
Kalambeza Safaris (☎ 45938, e kalambez@
mweb.co.zw) Parkway
Kandahar/Adrift (☎ 43589, W www.adrift.co.uk)
Parkway
Safari Par Excellence (☎ 42054, W www.safari
parx.com) The Mall
Senanga Horse Safaris (☎ 45989)
Shearwater (☎ 45806, W www.shearwater
adventures.com) Parkway
Southern Cross Aviation (☎ 44618, e sca@zol
.co.zw)
Touch Adventure (☎ 40073, W www.touch
adventure.com)
United Air Charter (☎ 43383, W www.uaczam
.com)
UTc (☎ 43420, e pats@utcvfa.co.zw) Parkway
Zambezi Helicopter Company (☎ 43569)
Zambezi Horse Trails (☎ 011-209115, e horse
saf@telcovic.co.zw)

Agencies & Companies in Livingstone
The area code for the following is ☎ 03 or
☎ 8 if calling from neighbouring Victoria
Falls town.

African Extreme (☎ 324231)
Batoka Sky (☎ 323672)
Bundu Adventures (☎ 324407, W www.bundu
-adventures.com) Industrial Rd
Bushtracks Africa (☎ 323232, e victoriafalls@bush
tracks.com)
Bwaato Adventures (☎/fax 324227, e bwaato@
zamnet.zm) New Fairmount Hotel, Mosi-oa-
Tunya Rd
Del Air (☎/fax 323095, e delair@zamnet.zm)
Jet Extreme (☎ 321375, W www.jetextreme.com)
Makora Quest (☎ 324574, W www.bookorbuy
.com/makoraquest) The Livingstone Adventure
Centre, Mosi-oa-Tunya Rd
Raft Extreme (☎ 323929, W www.raftextreme
.com) The Grotto, Kashitu Way
Safari Par Excellence (☎ 326629, W www.safari
parx.com) The Zambezi Waterfront
Taonga Safaris (☎/fax 324081) Zigzag Coffee
House, Mosi-oa-Tunya Rd
The Zambezi Swing (☎ 323454) The Livingstone
Adventure Centre, Mosi-oa-Tunya Rd
Touch Adventure (☎ 321111, W www.touch
adventure.com)
UTc (☎/fax 324413, e utczam@zamnet.zm)
Mosi-oa-Tunya Rd
Wild Side Tours & Safaris (☎ 323726, W www
.wildsidesafaris.com) 131 Mosi-oa-Tunya Rd
Zambezi Jetboat Journeys (☎/fax 42233)

Abseiling
All-day fun on a rope, including abseiling,
rock climbing and cable swings, in a scenic
canyon off Batoka Gorge costs US$85/95 for
a half/full day. Run by The Zambezi Swing.

Bungee Jumping
Why not jump off Victoria Falls Bridge with
a rubber band tied around your ankles? The
second-highest (111m) jump in the world is
also one of the most spectacular. African
Extreme jumps cost about US$90.

Canoeing & Kayaking
Half/full-day trips along the Zambezi cost
from US$65/75, while tandem kayaking is
US$135 per day. Overnight jaunts cost about
US$140, and three-night trips cost from
US$425. Run by Bundu Adventures, Makora
Quest, Frontier Adventures, Kandahar/Adrift,
Raft Extreme and Safari Par Excellence.

Fixed Wings Flights
Flights in small fixed-wing aircraft run for 25
minutes (US$55) over the falls or 40 minutes
(US$75) over the falls and Zambezi National
Park. Run by United Air Charter, Del Air and
Southern Cross Aviation.

VICTORIA FALLS

Wildlife Drives

Zambezi and Hwange National Parks are accessible from Victoria Falls town, Mosi-oa-Tunya National Park is easy to reach from Livingstone, and trips to Chobe National Park (Botswana) are available from both towns.

Half/full-day trips to Zambezi and Mosi-oa-Tunya National Parks start at US$30/65, and three-hour sunset and evening drives (US$50) are also available. Trips include food and, usually, drinks. Day trips to Hwange cost US$130 to US$160, while overnight (US$230) and two-/three-night (US$400/450) trips can also be arranged.

Day trips to Chobe cost US$120 to US$150, but check to see if a Botswana visa (if required) is included. And note: if you take an overnight tour to Chobe (US$250), you'll be slugged for another visa (if required) back to Zimbabwe or Zambia.

Wildlife drives are run by Ivan Carter Safaris, UTc, Dabula Safaris, Bwaato Adventures, Senanga Horse Safaris, Bushtracks Africa and Wild Side Tours & Safaris. Trips to Chobe are also offered by **Travel Junction** (☎ 41480; e *junction@mweb.co.zw, Livingstone Way, Victoria Falls)*, and Jolly Boys Backpackers and Fawlty Towers (see Places to Stay under Livingstone earlier).

Helicopters

The aptly named 'Flight of the Angels' is a 12 to 15 minute joy ride (US$75) over the falls or 30 minutes (US$140) across the falls and Zambezi National Park. Run by the Zambezi Helicopter Company, United Air Charter and Del Air.

Hiking

Hiking with guides around the Zambezi National Park (from Victoria Falls), or Mosi-oa-Tunya National Park (from Livingstone), costs US$35 to US$45 for two hours and about US$55/100 for a half/full day. Wear neutral, natural colours. Run by Ivan Carter Safaris, Dabula Safaris and Bwaato Adventures.

Horse Riding

A great way to see some wildlife is on the back of a horse. Two-/three-hour rides cost about US$40/50, while one-day rides (US$85) can also be arranged. Wear long trousers and proper shoes. Riders often have

to be over 15 years old. Run by Senanga Horse Safaris and Zambezi Horse Trails.

Jet Boats

Half-day trips cost about US$60, but only include about 45 minutes in the water. Run by Zambezi Jetboat Journeys and Jet Extreme.

Microlights

These motorised hang-gliders offer the best views from the air, and the pilot will take pictures for you with a camera fixed to the wing. Flights cost about US$75 (15 minutes) over the falls and about US$115 (30 minutes) over the falls and Zambezi National Park. Run by Batoka Sky and Bush Birds Flying Safaris.

Rafting

Although it's a splash-out in more ways than one, you shouldn't miss the thrill of being swept and flung headlong down the angry Zambezi below the falls. The Zambezi rapids are among the world's wildest – but safest.

High-water runs through Rapids 11 to 18 (or 23), which are relatively mundane and can be done between 1 July and 15 August, though in high rainfall years they may begin as early as mid-May. Wilder low-water runs operate from roughly 15 August to late December, taking in the winding 22km from rapids four to 18 (or 23) if you put in on the Zimbabwean side, and from Rapids one to 18 (or 23) if you put in on the Zambian side.

The day is exhausting, but reserve some energy for the climb out of the gorge. The revelry often continues into the evening as video footage of your day's adventures is shown at an appropriate bar.

If it's hot, you can go rafting in shorts and T-shirt, but don't forget to protect yourself from sunburn. Some companies provide long-sleeved wetsuits when the weather is colder, and some may require you to wear shoes (which will get soaked).

Full-day trips cost about US$85, and overnight trips about US$145. Longer jaunts can be arranged and cost US$320/500 for three/five days. Run by Bad Dog Rafting, Bundu Adventures, Frontier Adventures, Raft Extreme, Safari Par Excellence and Touch Adventure.

River-Boarding

What about lying on a boogie board and careering down the rapids? 'Waterfall surfing',

as it's sometimes called, costs from US$85/115 for a half/full day. The best time of year for river-boarding is February to June. Run by Bundu Adventures, Frontier Adventures, Raft Extreme and Shearwater.

River Cruises
It's easy enough to spot wildlife from a boat, though some passengers seem more interested in the free drinks – which is why these are often called 'booze cruises'. The options are a breakfast cruise (US$30, three hours) including food; lunch cruise (US$30, two hours) including food and drinks; sunset cruise (US$20/30, two/three hours) including drinks; and dinner cruise (US$35, three hours) including food and drinks. Run by UTc, Dabula Safaris, Taonga Safaris, Wild Side Tours & Safaris, Kalambeza Safaris, Safari Par Excellence and Bwaato Adventures.

Steam Trains
Rail buffs with plenty of cash will love a train trip across the majestic Victoria Falls Bridge. These are run by **Victoria Falls Safari Express** (☎/fax 44682; w www.samara.co.zw/victoriaexp; Train Station, Victoria Falls) and cost from US$40 to US$110 (including food and drinks). But trains only run with at least 10 passengers.

Zimbabwe

For general information about Zimbabwe, eg, visas and money, refer to the Facts for the Visitor section in the Zimbabwe chapter.

VICTORIA FALLS
☎ 013 • pop 17,000
The town Victoria Falls is more recognised and offers better facilities than Livingstone (in Zambia) so many travellers visit the falls from the Zimbabwean side, though the Zambian side also has much to offer. The town was built for tourism and has developed into an archetypal tourist trap. Often known simply as Vic Falls, it has no history or ambience, but lies within easy walking distance of the falls.

Information
Tourist Offices The **Victoria Falls Publicity Association** (☎ 44202; Parkway; open 8am-1pm & 2pm-5pm Mon-Sat) gives away a few brochures and can book local accommodation (for no charge). The general **Information Office** at the airport has telephones and can also help with accommodation bookings (for no charge).

The **Zimbabwe Tourism Authority** (☎ 44376; e zta@vicfalls.ztazim.co.zw; 258 Adam Stander Dr; open 8am-4.30pm Mon-Fri) is responsible for the rest of the country.

Money The better **bureaux de change** are near Frontier Adventures along Parkway, and in and around the Trading Post Shopping Centre. The bureaux de change at the airport only offer the official rates, so use US dollars until you get into town.

Barclays Bank (off Livingstone Way), and the nearby **Standard Chartered Bank**, offer cash advances with Visa and MasterCard and have ATMs.

Post & Communications The **Post Office** (off Livingstone Way) is an efficient place to send home that spindly giraffe carving that you bought on impulse. Telephone calls can be made at **telephone offices** and travel agencies upstairs in Soper's Arcade.

Three cheap and reliable places to check on your cyber-mail from home are **eWorld Internet Centre** (The Mall), **The Econet Shop** (Galleria Shopping Centre, The Mall) and **Shearwater** (Parkway).

To dial Livingstone you don't need the country or city code – simply dial ☎ 8, then the local number.

Travel Agencies The best place for independent advice about activities and accommodation in Vic Falls and Livingstone is **Backpackers Bazaar** (☎/fax 45828; e backpack@telcovic.co.zw; off Parkway; open 8am-5pm Mon-Fri, 8am-4pm Sat-Sun) is It also has a book exchange.

A new rival, **Travel Junction** (☎ 41480; e junction@mweb.co.zw; Trading Post Shopping Centre, Livingstone Way) provides similar services, but concentrates more on tours, hotel bookings and tickets for long-distance buses around Southern Africa.

Raincoat Hire Available for rent at **Raincoat & Camping Equipment Hire Services** (☎ 43570; off Parkway) are sleeping bags, cooking equipment and tents, as well as umbrellas, binoculars and raincoats for US$1 each.

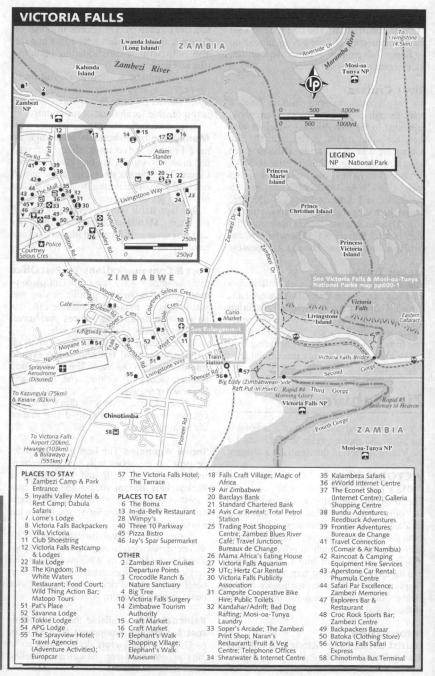

VICTORIA FALLS

PLACES TO STAY
1 Zambezi Camp & Park Entrance
5 Inyathi Valley Motel & Rest Camp; Dabula Safaris
7 Lorrie's Lodge
8 Victoria Falls Backpackers
9 Villa Victoria
11 Club Shoestring
12 Victoria Falls Restcamp & Lodges
22 Ilala Lodge
23 The Kingdom; The White Waters Restaurant; Food Court; Wild Thing Action Bar; Matopo Tours
51 Pat's Place
52 Savanna Lodge
53 Tokkie Lodge
54 APG Lodge
55 The Sprayview Hotel; Travel Agencies (Adventure Activities); Europcar

57 The Victoria Falls Hotel; The Terrace

PLACES TO EAT
6 The Boma
13 In-da-Belly Restaurant
28 Wimpy's
40 Three 10 Parkway
45 Pizza Bistro
46 Jay's Spar Supermarket

OTHER
2 Zambezi River Cruises Departure Points
3 Crocodile Ranch & Nature Sanctuary
4 Big Tree
10 Victoria Falls Surgery
14 Zimbabwe Tourism Authority
15 Craft Market
16 Craft Market
17 Elephant's Walk Shopping Village; Elephant's Walk Museum

18 Falls Craft Village; Magic of Africa
19 Air Zimbabwe
20 Barclays Bank
21 Standard Chartered Bank
24 Avis Car Rental; Total Petrol Station
25 Trading Post Shopping Centre; Zambezi Blues River Café; Travel Junction; Bureaux de Change
26 Mama Africa's Eating House
27 Victoria Falls Aquarium
29 UTc; Hertz Car Rental
30 Victoria Falls Publicity Association
31 Campsite Cooperative Bike Hire; Public Toilets
32 Kandahar/Adrift; Bad Dog Rafting; Mosi-oa-Tunya Laundry
33 Soper's Arcade; The Zambezi Print Shop; Naran's Restaurant; Fruit & Veg Centre; Telephone Offices
34 Shearwater & Internet Centre

35 Kalambeza Safaris
36 eWorld Internet Centre
37 The Econet Shop (Internet Centre); Galleria Shopping Centre
38 Bundu Adventures; Reedbuck Adventures
39 Frontier Adventures; Bureaux de Change
41 Travel Connection (Comair & Air Namibia)
42 Raincoat & Camping Equipment Hire Services
43 Aperstone Car Rental; Phumula Centre
44 Safari Par Excellence; Zambezi Memories
47 Explorers Bar & Restaurant
48 Croc Rock Sports Bar; Zambezi Centre
49 Backpackers Bazaar
50 Batoka (Clothing Store)
56 Victoria Falls Safari Express
58 Chinotimba Bus Terminal

VICTORIA FALLS

Laundry Near the Kandahar/Adrift office, **Mosi-oa-Tunya Laundry** *(Parkway)* will clean the collective grime from your clothes for about US$3 per (large) machine-load.

Photography For photo development, **Zambezi Memories** *(Safari Par Excellence, The Mall)* and **The Zambezi Print Shop** *(Soper's Arcade)* develop print (not slide) 24/36 exposure film from US$4/6.

Medical Services If you need medical attention, visit the **Victoria Falls Surgery** *(☎ 43356; West Dr; open 9am-4pm Mon-Fri, 9am-1pm Sat)*. For genuine emergencies, contact **Medical Air Rescue Service** *(MARS; ☎ 44764)* or the **police** *(☎ 44206; Livingstone Way)*.

Dangers & Annoyances Elephants like wandering through camping grounds at night, and the cute (but shifty) baboons seem to outnumber tourists these days. Don't walk or even cycle along Zambezi Dr to the Big Tree, because of the danger of being mugged. The touts and beggars along Livingstone Way, and at the entrance to Soper's Arcade, may seem aggressive but they are harmless.

Paradoxically, water shortages are common, so hotels often ask guests to keep water usage to a minimum in the dry season. There is little or no street lighting, so take a taxi, or walk in a group, after dark.

Victoria Falls National Park

The *raison d' etre* for the town of Victoria Falls is the national park *(☎ 42204; admission US$20; open 6.30am-6pm daily)* that surrounds the Zimbabwean side of the falls. Admission is payable only in US dollars.

Immediately past the entrance is the **Victoria Falls Interpretative Centre**, which desperately needs some renovation and imagination. Once you reach the rim, a network of surfaced tracks takes you to a series of viewpoints. One of the most dramatic is **Cataract View**, the westernmost point. It's poorly signposted and requires climbing down a steep stairway. Another track leads to the aptly-named **Danger Point**, where a sheer, unfenced 100m drop-off will rattle your nerves. From there, you can follow a side track for a view over the gracefully precarious **Victoria Falls Bridge** (also called the Zambezi Bridge).

While walking through the rainforests, note the profusion of unusual species growing in this unique little enclave – ebony, ferns, fig trees and a variety of lianas and flowering plants. Also, watch for bushbucks, which may be seen browsing right up to the lip of the gorge.

During a full moon (and the day before and after) 'Moonlight View' guided tours (US$30 extra, about 1½ hours) start at about 6.30pm. This gives you a once-in-a-lifetime chance of seeing a **lunar rainbow**. Take a torch for walking around, and catch a taxi home.

Things to See

Zambezi Dr heads north from near the entrance to the falls to the **Big Tree**, which is, well, a big tree. In fact, it's a baobab with a 20m circumference. Although there's little else to do, it features high on the itinerary of most tours. Don't walk or cycle there because of the danger of being mugged.

The impressive new **Victoria Falls Aquarium** *(Livingstone Way; admission US$5; open daily 9.30am-5.30pm)* is apparently the largest freshwater aquarium in Africa. It's worth a visit for the bright and imaginative displays about the aquatic life in the Zambezi River.

The new **Elephant's Walk Museum** *(Elephant's Walk Shopping Village, off Adam Stander Dr; admission free; open 8am-5pm daily)* houses a small but worthwhile private collection about the culture of several local ethnic groups.

The **Falls Craft Village** *(☎ 44309; Adam Stander Dr; admission US$8; open 8am-5pm daily)* is a touristy mock-up of a traditional Zimbabwean village. It offers the chance to watch craftspeople at work, consult with a *nganga* (fortune teller) and see some remarkable 'pole dancing' (but not the sort you might find in a Western strip joint!). The booklet (free with admission) is informative, so a guide is not necessary.

The **Crocodile Ranch & Nature Sanctuary** *(☎ 44604; Parkway; admission with guided tour US$5; open 8am-5pm daily)* offers lots of crocs, as well as lions and leopards. It shows informative videos, and houses a museum, aviary and insect collection. Try to get there for the lion feeding (4pm daily) or while the crocs chow down (11.15am and 3.45pm daily). It's 4km north of town. It may not be safe to walk, so charter a taxi (US$3 one way) or join an organised tour (US$15).

Places to Stay

Unlike the rest of Zimbabwe, most hotels and camp sites quote – and usually require payment – in US dollars. While the US dollar rates are reasonable, very few places even offer 'local rates'.

Places to Stay – Budget

Victoria Falls Backpackers (☎ 42209, w www .victoriafallsbackpackers.com; 357 Gibson Rd; camping per person US$4, dorm beds US$6-8, chalets & rooms per person US$10-15) is superbly set up for budget travellers. Among the shady gardens are a TV lounge, swimming pool, laundry and guests' kitchen. It's inconvenient but the owner rents bikes to guests (only) for US$3 per day (free to long-term guests). All rooms come with shared bathroom and breakfast. Singles may be asked to pay a supplement if it's busy, or pay for the double room/chalet. It's signposted along the streets as '357 Gibson Rd'.

Club Shoestring (☎ 40167; 12 West Dr; camping per person US$3, dorm beds US$7, doubles with bathroom US$20) is a laid-back place that caters almost exclusively to the overland truck crowd. Staff can be surly, the place is always noisy, the camp site isn't private and the doubles are poor value, but guests don't seem to care. The pool, bar and communal kitchen are bonuses.

Pat's Place (☎ 45893; 209 West Dr; dorms US$4, doubles with bathroom & fan US$12) is a small, friendly and secure option at the back of a family home. Guests can use the kitchen and swimming pool. Ask if you can pay the 'local rate', which may end up costing you considerably less (if you change at the unofficial rate).

Savanna Lodge (☎/fax 42115; e savanna@ telcovic.co.zw; 68 Courtney Selous Cres; dorm beds US$8, doubles with shared bathroom US$20 – all with breakfast) offers basic but comfortable rooms with a fan, as well as cramped dormitories. The tranquil garden and pool are surrounded by massive, eerie carvings. All rates include breakfast.

Victoria Falls Restcamp & Lodges (☎ 40509; off Parkway; camping per person US$5, dorm beds US$6, single/double chalets with shared bathroom US$14/16, single/double cottages with bathroom US$18/20) is the dreary, former government-run camping ground. It has, at long last, been renovated, complete with pool, volleyball court and pristine lawns, but the rooms are still sparsely furnished. One huge advantage is the excellent location.

Tokkie Lodge (☎/fax 43306; w www.safari south.co.zw; 224 Reynard Rd; camping per person US$3, singles with breakfast US$15, doubles with/without breakfast US$20/16) is the former Settler's Retreat, currently only signposted as '224 Reynard Rd'. Like many other homely lodges, it features a garden, TV lounge, pool, braai and guests' kitchen, but is closer to the town centre than most. All rooms come with fans and shared bathroom.

Places to Stay – Mid-Range

All places listed here have a swimming (or plunge) pool, and all rooms have fans.

Lorrie's Lodge (☎ 42139; 397 Reynard Rd, rooms with TV & with/without bathroom US$20/15) is a large, quiet and shady home with a TV lounge, communal kitchen and friendly staff. You can also book at Backpackers Bazaar in town, and ask there about a lift to the lodge.

Villa Victoria (☎ 44386; 165 Courtney Selous Cres; singles/doubles US$20/40) offers large, clean rooms, though some contain a private bathroom and others don't. Guests have access to a TV lounge, braai and kitchen facilities.

APG Lodge (☎ 43440, fax 42349; Nyathi Rd; doubles with bathroom & air-con about US$50) is one of a dozen or more places signposted along or just off Mopane St. This bright place offers lovingly-furnished rooms and a sparkling bathroom, as well as a communal kitchen and TV lounge. Ask about paying the 'local rate' (which could work out to be about one-tenth the US$ rate).

Inyathi Valley Motel & Rest Camp (☎ 42345; 951 Parkway; camping per person US$7, rooms with 3/4 beds & shared bathroom US$35/40, double cottages with kitchen & bathroom US$60) is a huge, quiet camping ground, complete with pet warthogs. It's not far from town, but don't walk back at night: you may bump into an elephant!

Places to Stay – Top End

All places listed here have a swimming pool and en suite facilities, and rates include breakfast.

The Sprayview Hotel (☎ 44344; e sprayvw@ africaonline.co.zw; Livingstone Way; singles/ doubles US$60/90) is an ugly, motel-style

place that is better than the outside suggests. The rooms are large and well-furnished, but the breakfast is perpetually unappetising.

Ilala Lodge (☎ 44737; **w** www.ilalalodge .com; 411 Livingstone Way; singles/doubles from US$200/286) is the closest place on this side to the falls. It features a sunny terrace bar, green lawns and surrounding bushland that creates a natural atmosphere.

The **Victoria Falls Hotel** (☎ 44751; **e** reservations@tvfh.zimsun.zo.zw; Mallet Dr; singles/doubles from US$347/386) is superb. It oozes history and elegance, and the setting, overlooking the gorge and bridge, is nothing short of spectacular. At least take a stroll along the stylish corridors and around the sumptuous lounge rooms.

The **Kingdom** (☎ 44275; **e** kingdom@kingdom.zimsun.co.zw; Livingstone Way; doubles US$228) would even look bizarre in Las Vegas. The rooms are nothing special, but it's worth visiting for its sheer vulgarity.

Places to Eat
Naran's Restaurant (Soper's Arcade; snacks/mains from US$0.50/US$1; open 8.30am-5pm Mon-Sat) is the best value in town. It offers sandwiches, as well as curries and samosas, though hungry adventure-junkies flock there for the hearty 'all-day breakfast'.

Wimpys (cnr Livingstone Way & Parkway; meals US$1.50-3) is more of a landmark than a recommended eatery, but tourists flock there for familiar Western food in a clean setting.

Pizza Bistro (☎ 44396; back of Soper's Arcade; meals US$1-2) features charming decor and good service. It offers pizzas, crepes, pasta and baked spuds, and does free deliveries until 9pm.

Three 10 Parkway (☎ 43468; 310 Parkway; breakfast US$1.50, snacks/mains about US$1.50/2.50; open 7.30am-3pm Wed-Mon) is an enticing place that serves small but tasty dishes at slightly higher-than-normal prices. The garden setting is a world away from the touts down the road.

Zambezi Blues River Café (Trading Post Shopping Centre, Livingstone Way; meals US$1-2.50) is convenient, breezy and open from 7am for breakfast (US$1.50). The menu is extensive, but it's a little pricey.

In-da-Belly Restaurant (☎ 332077; Victoria Falls Restcamp & Lodges, off Parkway; meals US$1.50-2) is excellent. The service is almost faultless, the meals (including breakfast) are

large and tasty, and the setting is quiet. You may end up going back there several times.

The Terrace (Victoria Falls Hotel, Mallet Dr; high teas US$3, meals from US$4) overlooks the hotel garden and mighty Victoria Falls Bridge. So, why not indulge yourself in a spot of afternoon tea with cucumber sandwiches, hey what? One reader suggested that the ladies may want to visit the restaurant's bathroom 'to pamper themselves with moisturiser and hot towels'.

The White Waters Restaurant (The Kingdom Hotel, Livingstone Way; buffet breakfast/dinner US$4/8) offers a remarkable spread in an extraordinary setting. The hotel complex is also home to a **food court** with several outlets selling Western food.

The Boma (☎ 43201; Victoria Falls Safari Lodge, Squire Cummings Rd; meals US$2-4, dinner buffet US$9) is consistently recommended by readers. Guests can enjoy the four-course African buffet, including warthog, ostrich and mopane worms (uggh!), or choose à la carte. A Ndebele choir performs in the background during the evening. Contact them about free transfers to and from your hotel (for the buffet only). Travel agencies and hotels offer a deal for US$20, including transport, food and drinks, but it's cheaper to get a taxi there and pay for your meal and drinks in Zimbabwe dollars.

For self-catering, visit the well-stocked **Jay's Spar Supermarket** (Courtney Selous Cres) or the **Fruit & Veg Centre** (Soper's Arcade).

Entertainment
Most rafters and bungee jumpers end up reliving their exploits at the **Wild Thing Action Bar** (Kingdom Hotel complex, Livingstone Way). Not surprisingly, the prices are as high as some of the customers.

A cheaper place for a drink is the **Croc Rock Sports Bar** (Zambezi Centre, off Courtney Selous Cres), which turns into a nightclub most evenings. Sports fans should settle on a stool in front of the TV at the **Explorers Bar & Restaurant** (back of Soper's Arcade).

More authentic is **Mama Africa's Eating House** (Lawley Rd; open 2.30pm-late daily). This vibrant place sells cocktails and meals (US$2 to US$3), which can be enjoyed in the outdoor bar or around a bonfire at night.

Magic of Africa (Falls Craft Village, Adam Stander Dr; US$20) offers a show between

6.30pm and 8pm every evening, with traditional dancing, but no food. However, you're better off at The Boma (see Places to Eat).

Shopping

Adam Stander Dr is a tourist trap full of souvenir stalls (and touts) selling mass-produced and over-priced goods, so the **craft markets** (Adam Stander Dr; & behind Elephant's Walk Shopping Village) are cheaper. Regional specialties to look out for include Tonga stool seats with roughly carved wooden bases.

Head to **Batoka** (Livingstone Way) for all your safari gear, boots and all, at surprisingly reasonable prices. Classy souvenirs are sold at the **Trading Post Shopping Centre** (Livingstone Way) and the snooty **Elephant's Walk Shopping Village** (off Adam Stander Dr).

Getting There & Away

Air For US$156 one way, **Air Zimbabwe** (☎ 44316; off Livingstone Way) flies between Vic Falls and Harare every day.

To Jo'burg, Air Zimbabwe (US$330) flies four times a week; **Comair** (part of British Airways) goes every day (US$298); and **South African Airways** (☎ 011-8086/8; airport) travels most days for about the same price as Comair. **Air Namibia** flies to Windhoek US$385/335 (one way/return) three days a week, but Air Botswana has suspended flights to Maun.

The agency for Comair and Air Namibia is **Travel Connection** (☎ 42053; e barn nvfa@pci.co.zw; Flame Lily Court, Fox Rd).

Bus & Minibus The grubby **Chinotimba Bus Terminal** in Chinotimba township caters for local 'African' buses.

Domestic To Bulawayo (US$3, seven hours), via Hwange town and Safari Crossroads, minibuses leave every two or three hours. There's no timetable; it's just fill and go. Six buses also travel every day between Vic Falls and Bulawayo at fixed times; the first (5am) continues to Harare.

Africa Link recently commenced a coach service to the Holiday Inn at Bulawayo (US$17, five hours) three times a week. Bookings are available at Backpackers Bazaar and **Matopo Tours** (☎ 42209; The Kingdom Hotel complex, Livingstone Way). The bus will stop at Hwange town and the Hwange Safari Lodge.

UTc (☎ 43420; e pats@utcvfa.co.zw; Parkway) runs daily shuttle buses to Hwange Safari Lodge (US$36 per person, minimum of two) at 1pm and 3.30pm.

To/From Botswana & Namibia Africa Link (see earlier) operates daily shuttle buses to the Zimbabwe–Botswana border (US$10 per person). **Travel Junction** (☎ 41480; e junction@mweb.co.zw; Livingstone Way) offers a better service to the border (US$10), because no minimum number of passengers are required and the minibus continues to Kasane (US$15). With more than two passengers it will carry on to Maun (US$35 per person), and twice a week it goes as far as Windhoek (US$50).

Otherwise, **InterCape** buses leave Vic Falls on Sunday and Wednesday for Windhoek (US$50, 20 hours), and return from the Namibian capital on Monday and Thursday. It travels via the Caprivi Strip. Book at Travel Junction or **Matopo Tours** (see earlier).

To/From South Africa Twice a week, **Africa Link** (see earlier) runs buses between Jo'burg (Crowne Plaza Hotel) and Bulawayo (Holiday Inn) for US$52. They are timed to connect with the train to/from Vic Falls – if not, basic accommodation in Bulawayo is included. Book at Backpackers Bazaar or Travel Junction in Victoria Falls (see Travel Agencies under Zimbabwe earlier) or any hostel or travel agency in Jo'burg catering to backpackers.

To/From Zimbabwe For information about crossing to Zambia along the Victoria Falls Bridge, refer to the boxed text 'Visiting Zambia from Zimbabwe (and Vice Versa)' earlier in this chapter.

Train Until the early 1990s, a romantic highlight of a trip to Zimbabwe was riding the steam train between Bulawayo and Victoria Falls. However, all current services are by diesel power, which means that cancellations are not uncommon.

The *Mosi-oa-Tunya* train leaves Vic Falls every day at 6.30pm for Bulawayo (US$4/3/1 for 1st/2nd/economy class, 12 hours). Bedding (if available) is cheap. Make reservations at the **ticket office** (☎ 44391; open 7am-12pm & 2pm-4pm Mon-Fri, 7am-10am Sat-Sun) inside the train station.

Hitching The roads between Vic Falls and Bulawayo, and Vic Falls and Kazungula, aren't busy, but you would count yourself very unlucky if you didn't find something. To both places, wait at the Kazungula turn-off about 800m past the Sprayview Hotel.

Getting Around

To/From the Airport The inadequately small **Victoria Falls Airport**, which caters to domestic and international flights, is 20km southeast of town along the Bulawayo road. (The Sprayview Aerodrome in town is used for pleasure flights.)

Most hotels and travel agencies offer transfers to the airport (and from the airport if booked in advance) for US$8 to US$13 per person. **Backpackers Bazaar** (☎/fax 45828; e backpack@telcovic.co.zw; off Parkway) can arrange a taxi for US$12 per vehicle, and **Travel Junction** (☎ 41480; e junction@mweb.co.zw; Livingstone Way) offers a minibus for US$10 per person (no minimum required). Chartering a taxi yourself will cost about US$20 – but bargain *hard*.

Taxi Taxis are distinguishable from private cars by the small word 'taxi' painted somewhere on the bonnet. A taxi around town costs about US$1; slightly more after dark. None of them use meters, so you'll have to bargain.

Car Rental Tourists pay the 'foreigners rates' in US dollars at **Avis** (☎ 44532; Total Petrol Station, 251 Livingstone Way; airport ☎ 43506) and **Europcar** (☎/fax 44598; e vicfalls@europcar.co.zw; Sprayview Hotel, Livingstone Way). **Hertz** (☎ 44772, fax 42097; UTc Centre, Parkway), however, allows foreigners to pay the 'local rates' in Zimbabwean dollars.

Otherwise, try **Aperstone** (☎ 40232; e aperstone@katamail.com; 2nd floor, Phumula Centre, The Mall). It charges from US$30 per day, plus US$0.30 per kilometre and US$11 per day for insurance. The rates are cheaper for longer rentals.

Refer to the Getting Around section in the Zimbabwe chapter for more information about the costs of, and conditions for, renting cars.

Bicycle Rental Try **Campsite Cooperative Bike Hire** (Parkway) which charges US$1 per hour (minimum of two) and US$5 per day. If you take a rented bike to Zambia, make sure you take a receipt to show the immigration officials. And note that muggings along the road to Livingstone are not uncommon.

ZAMBEZI NATIONAL PARK

This national park (admission US$10; open 6am-6.30pm daily) consists of 40km of Zambezi River frontage and a spread of wildlife-rich mopane forest and savanna. The park is best known for its herds of sable antelopes, but is also home to lions, giraffes and elephants. Most visitors to Victoria Falls don't realise that so much wildlife is so accessible.

Tour operators offering wildlife drives, horse riding and hiking from Victoria Falls use this park, though independent visitors may only **hike** on their own between the riverbank picnic areas Nos 1 to 25, near the park's eastern boundary. **Fishing** for yellow bream and tiger fish is fruitful, and no licences or permission are required.

All lodges (US$2 to US$3) and camp sites (ZW$125 per person) are run by National Parks & Wildlife Zimbabwe (NPWZ) and can be booked through the office in Harare, see the Zimbabwe chapter for details.

The six self-contained lodges at **Zambezi Camp** are located on the riverbank at the park entrance about 5km from Victoria Falls town. There is no restaurant, so bring your own food or eat out in Vic Falls.

There are also three so-called 'fishing camps': **Kandahar** (open all year), **Mpala-Jena** and **Sansimba** (both only open 1 May to 31 October). Each is serenely located along the river and set up (but not exclusively) for anglers.

Visitors may also camp overnight at the 'exclusive camps' (available to one group of 12 at a time): **Chundu I** and **Chundu II** (between Mpala-Jena and Sansimba), which occupy a lovely stretch of riverbank; **Chomuzi** (40km west of the park entrance); and **Siamunungu** (7km west of Chomuzi).

All visitors must have a rented/chartered/private vehicle, though hitchers could look for a lift from the park entrance, only 5km northwest of Vic Falls.

Zambia

For independent travellers, Zambia can be a challenge: distances between major towns and attractions are long and getting around by car or public transport takes time and patience. But for many, this challenge is part of Zambia's appeal; this is the 'real' Africa, so rare among the increasingly developed and Westernised parts of Southern Africa.

Zambia has several large and genuinely wild national parks where visitors with less time and more money can luxuriate at some of the finest safari lodges in Southern Africa. On top of this, Zambia shares (with Zimbabwe) the Zambezi River, along which are two of the region's major highlights: the Victoria Falls and Lake Kariba. (For further details on Victoria Falls and Livingstone see the Victoria Falls chapter.) And it may sound like a cliché, but Zambians *are* very friendly and welcoming.

So, if you like your travel to be easy, and your wilderness neatly bundled into a homogenised and Westernised version of 'Africa', then much of Zambia may not appeal. But if you enjoy a raw edge and a genuine Africa with few tourists, Zambia will be the place you're looking for.

Facts about Zambia

HISTORY

The precolonial history of the area that became Zambia, along with the rest of Southern Africa, is covered under History in the Facts about the Region chapter.

The Slave Trade & Early Europeans

The first Europeans to enter what is now Zambia were Portuguese explorers. In the 1790s several of them travelled from Angola as far as the headwaters of the Zambezi River. Around the same time another group of Portuguese pushed inland from Mozambique to the Mweru and Bangweulu Lakes.

The Portuguese generally followed routes established many centuries earlier by Swahili–Arab slave-traders who had penetrated the region from their city-states on the east coast of Africa. Often in collaboration with the chiefs of powerful tribes,

Zambia at a Glance

Area: 752,615 sq km
Population: 10.4 million
Capital: Lusaka
Head of State: President Levy Mwanawasa
Official Language: English
Currency: kwacha (k)
Exchange Rate: US$1=k4930

Highlights

- South Luangwa National Park – soaking up the wildlife and bush in one of the most majestic parks in Africa

- Lower Zambezi National Park – gazing in awe at elephants strolling along the bank and at fish eagles soaring overhead, while canoeing down the river

- Kafue National Park – exploring vast, classic wildlife country in Zambia's largest national park

- Northern Zambia – wandering around and wondering at the hills, lakes, wetlands and waterfalls, with rarely another tourist in sight

- Livingstone – visiting this historic town near the mighty Victoria Falls, or organising local adventure activities

- Lake Kariba – boating or fishing, or just relaxing at a resort along one of the world's largest artificial lakes

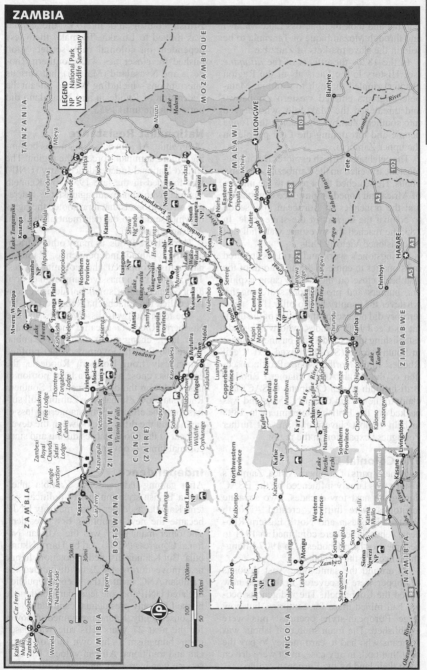

ZAMBIA

LEGEND
NP National Park
WS Wildlife Sanctuary

the slave-traders captured many people from Zambia and took them across Lake Malawi and through Mozambique or Tanzania to be sold in the slave markets of Zanzibar.

In the 1820s the effects of the *difaqane* (see History in the Facts about the Region chapter) rippled through to Zambia. Matabele migrants entered western Zimbabwe and threatened the Makololo, who moved into southern Zambia, displacing the Tonga people and threatening the Lozi people on the upper Zambezi.

The celebrated British explorer David Livingstone travelled up the Zambezi in the early 1850s. He searched for a route to the interior of Africa and hoped to introduce Christianity and the principles of European civilisation to combat the horrors of the slave trade. In 1855 he reached the awesome waterfall that he christened Victoria Falls.

Livingstone's work and writings inspired missionaries to come to the area north of the Zambezi; close on their heels came explorers, hunters and prospectors searching for whatever the country had to offer. The 'new' territory did not escape the notice of the ubiquitous Cecil John Rhodes, who was already establishing mines and a vast business empire in South Africa. (See the boxed text 'Cecil Rhodes' in the Northern Cape Province section of the South Africa chapter.) Rhodes' British South Africa Company (BSAC) laid claim to the area in the early 1890s and was backed by the British Government in 1895 to help combat slavery and prevent further Portuguese expansion in the region.

The Colonial Era

Like many parts of Southern Africa, Zambia's history was largely influenced by the BSAC during the next few decades. Two separate territories were initially created – North Western Rhodesia and North Eastern Rhodesia – but these were combined in 1911 to become Northern Rhodesia. In 1907 Livingstone became the capital.

At around the same time, vast deposits of copper were discovered in the area now called the Copperbelt. The indigenous people had mined there for centuries, but now large European-style opencast pits were established. The main source of labour was Africans who had to earn money to pay the new 'hut tax'; in any case, most were driven from their land by the European settlers.

In 1924 the colony was put under direct British control and in 1935 the capital was moved to Lusaka. To make them less dependent on colonial rule, settlers soon pushed for closer ties with Southern Rhodesia and Nyasaland (Malawi), but various interruptions – including WWII – meant the Federation of Rhodesia and Nyasaland did not eventuate until 1953.

Nationalist Resistance

Meanwhile, African nationalism was becoming a more dominant force in the region. The United National Independence Party (UNIP) was founded in the late 1950s by Kenneth Kaunda, who spoke out against the federation on the grounds that it promoted the rights of white settlers to the detriment of the local African population.

Through the 1960s, as many other African countries gained independence, Zambian nationalists opposed the colonial forces. This resulted in a massive campaign of civil disobedience and a small but decisive conflict called the Chachacha Rebellion.

The federation was dissolved in 1963 and Northern Rhodesia became independent a year later, changing its name to Zambia. While the British Government had profited enormously from Northern Rhodesia, the colonialists chose to spend a large portion of this wealth on the development of Southern Rhodesia (now Zimbabwe). Zambia still suffers from the effects of this staggering loss of capital and the difference between the development of the two countries during and since colonial times is obvious.

Independence

After gaining independence, Zambia inherited a British-style multiparty political system. Kaunda, as leader of the majority UNIP, became the new republic's first president. The other main party was the African National Congress (ANC), led by Harry Nkumbula. But Kaunda disliked opposition. In one neat move during 1972, he disbanded the Zambian ANC, created the 'second republic', declared UNIP the sole legal party and made himself the only presidential candidate.

Consequently, Kaunda remained in power for the next 27 years. His rule was based upon 'humanism' – his own mix of Marxism and traditional African values. The civil service was increased, and nearly all private

businesses (including the copper mines) were nationalised. But corruption and mismanagement, exacerbated by a fall in the world copper price, meant that by the end of the 1970s Zambia was one of the poorest countries in the world. The economy continued to flounder while Zambia's trade routes to the coast through neighbouring countries (eg, Zimbabwe and Mozambique) were closed in retaliation for Kaunda's support for several liberation movements in the region.

The 1980s

By the early 1980s two important events occurred that had the potential to significantly improve Zambia's economy: Rhodesia gained independence (and became Zimbabwe), which allowed Kaunda to take his country off a war footing; and the Tazara railway to Dar es Salaam (Tanzania) was completed, which gave Zambia unencumbered access to the coast. Yet the economy remained on the brink of collapse: foreign exchange reserves were almost exhausted, serious shortages of food, fuel and other basic commodities were common and unemployment (and crime) rates rose sharply.

In 1986 an attempt was made to diversify the economy and improve the country's balance of payments. Zambia received economic aid from the International Monetary Fund (IMF) but the IMF conditions were severe and included cutting basic food subsidies. Subsequent price rises led to country-wide riots in which many people lost their lives. Kaunda was forced to restore subsidies.

Turning Point

The winds of change blowing through Africa during the late 1980s, coupled with Zambia's disastrous domestic situation, meant something had to give. Following another round of violent street protests against increased food prices in 1990, which quickly transformed into a general demand for the return of multiparty politics, Kaunda was forced to accede to public opinion.

He announced a snap referendum in late 1990 but, as protests grew more vocal, he was forced to legalise opposition parties and announce full presidential and parliamentary elections for October 1991. Not surprisingly, UNIP (and Kaunda) were resoundingly defeated by the Movement for Multiparty Democracy (MMD), led by Frederick Chiluba, a

former trade union leader. Kaunda admirably stepped down without complaint, which may have saved Zambia from descending into anarchy.

President Chiluba moved quickly to encourage loans and investments from the IMF and World Bank. Exchange controls were liberalised to attract investors, particularly from South Africa, but tough austerity measures were also introduced. Once again, food prices soared. The civil service was rationalised, state industries privatised or simply closed, and thousands of people lost their jobs.

By the mid-1990s, the lack of visible change in Zambia allowed Kaunda to confidently re-enter the political arena. He attracted strong support and soon became the UNIP leader. Leading up to the 1996 elections, the MMD panicked and passed a law forbidding anyone with foreign parents to enter politics (Kaunda's parents were from Malawi). Despite intercessions from Western aid donors and world leaders like Nelson Mandela – not to mention accusations that Chiluba's parents were from Congo (Zaïre) – the law was not repealed. The UNIP withdrew all its candidates in protest and many voters also boycotted the election. Consequently, Chiluba and the MMD won easily, and the result was grudgingly accepted by most Zambians.

In October 1997 a bungled coup attempt allowed Chiluba to announce a state of emergency, and many opposition figures were arrested. Kaunda, who claimed the coup was a set-up, was placed under house arrest until March 1998. This endeared him further to UNIP supporters and MMD opponents.

Zambia Today

The political shenanigans continued unabated at the start of the new millennium: in mid-2001, Vice-President Christon Tembo was expelled from the parliament by Chiluba, so he formed an opposition party, the Forum for Democratic Development (FDD). Later, Paul Tembo, a former MMD national secretary, joined the FDD, but was assassinated the day before he was due to front a tribunal about alleged MMD corruption.

Chiluba was unable to run for a third presidential term in December 2001 (though he badly wanted to change the constitution so he could). He anointed his former vice-president, Levy Mwanawasa, as his successor,

ZAMBIA

but Mwanawasa only just beat a coalition of opposition parties known as the United Party for National Development (UPND). Again, allegations from international observers about the MMD rigging the results and buying votes fell on deaf ears. Meanwhile, Mwanawasa wants Chiluba to be charged with massive embezzlement while in office. At the time of writing, the Supreme Court in Lusaka was deciding about lifting Chiluba's immunity from prosecution (as a former president).

Zambia continues to be burdened with a massive international debt, high unemployment, rapidly growing population, tragic AIDS/HIV pandemic, and an ineffectual, corrupt government. And Zambia's woes will remain for as long as the political and economic crises continue in neighbouring Zimbabwe, Angola and Congo (Zaïre).

GEOGRAPHY

Landlocked Zambia is one of Africa's most eccentric legacies of colonialism. Shaped like a contorted figure of eight, its borders do not correspond to any tribal or linguistic area. And Zambia is huge: about the size of France, England and the Republic of Ireland combined.

Zambia sits on an undulating plateau, sloping to the south. To the north, the plateau drops steeply to Lake Tanganyika, one of the Rift Valley lakes that Zambia shares with Tanzania, Burundi and Congo (Zaïre).

Zambia's main river is the Zambezi, which rises in the west of the country. It forms the border between Zambia, Namibia, Botswana and Zimbabwe, and flows into the Victoria Falls and Lake Kariba. Other major rivers include the Kafue, which starts in the highlands between Zambia and Congo (Zaïre) and flows into the Zambezi southeast of Lusaka; and the Luangwa, which rises near the Tanzanian border and also flows into the Zambezi.

CLIMATE

Zambia's altitude creates a temperate climate. There are three distinct seasons: cool and dry from May to August (the most comfortable time to visit); hot and dry from September to early/mid-November (the best time to see wildlife); and warm and wet from early/mid-November to April (ideal for bird-watching, though some camps and lodges in the

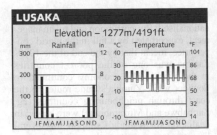

LUSAKA
Elevation – 1277m/4191ft

national parks close). Rainfall is higher in the north of the country.

ECOLOGY & ENVIRONMENT

Although the population is growing rapidly, it is still relatively sparse, so Zambia doesn't suffer many of the environmental problems encountered by its neighbouring countries. However, around the main urban areas, ie, Lusaka, Livingstone and the Copperbelt, denudation of local vegetation is apparent. And unsustainable deforestation (and associated soil erosion) in the countryside is a pressing environmental problem.

During the 1970s and 1980s, many Zambian parks were effectively abandoned and poaching became a major problem. Then, under pressure from international conservation organisations, the government slowly realised that tourism was a major source of foreign currency for the government (and local people) – and that this depended on healthy national parks. Despite successes in some parks, notably South Luangwa, Lower Zambezi and Mosi-oa-Tunya National Parks, poaching and poor management remain major problems. And the detrimental impact of tourism is obvious along the Zambezi River (particularly near Victoria Falls), where lodges continue to be built unabated and dozens of cruise boats shuttle along every day looking for the diminishing wildlife.

FLORA & FAUNA

The main vegetation zones are miombo woodland, which covers the plateau areas (about 65% of Zambia); mopane woodland in the hotter, lower parts of the country, such as the Zambezi and Luangwa Valleys; and acacia woodland and semi-evergreen forest in the south and west.

Because of Zambia's diverse landscape, plentiful water supplies, and position between eastern, southern and central Africa,

the diversity of animal species is huge. The rivers, of course, support huge populations of hippos and crocs, and the associated grasslands provide plenty of fodder for huge herds of zebras, impalas and pukus (antelopes common in Zambia, but not elsewhere). Other antelopes found in Zambia include waterbucks and lechwes; in fact, vast herds of rare black lechwes live near Lake Bangweulu and endemic Kafue lechwes settle in the area around the Kafue River. Kasanka National Park is one of the best places in Africa to see rare water-loving antelopes called sitatungas. Two more endemic species are Thornicroft giraffes and Cookson's wildebeests, both found in South Luangwa National Park.

These antelopes naturally attract predators, so most parks contain lions, leopards, hyenas (which you'll probably see) and cheetahs (which you probably won't). The other two big drawcards – buffaloes and elephants – are also found in huge herds in the main national parks.

Bird lovers can go crazy in Zambia, where about 750 species have been recorded. Twitchers used to the 'traditional' Southern African species listed in the *Roberts* and *Newman's* field guides will spend a lot of time identifying unusual species – especially in the north and west. Most notable are the endangered shoebill storks (found in the Bangweulu Wetlands); fish eagles (Zambia's national bird); and the endemic Chaplin's barbets.

National Parks & Reserves

Zambia boasts 19 national parks and reserves, but after decades of poaching, clearing and general bad management, many are just lines on the map that no longer protect (or even contain) much wildlife. However, four national parks do accommodate healthy stocks of wildlife, and are among the best in Southern Africa: ie, South Luangwa, Lower Zambezi, Kafue and Mosi-oa-Tunya.

In a scheme unique in Zambia (and unusual in Southern Africa), Kasanka National Park has been leased to a private operator since 1990. This park is now fully funded by donations and tourism, and functions very well. Another example of successful cooperation between an eco-friendly tour operator, an international conservation group (the World Wide Fund), and the Zambian park authorities, is the renovation of the previously neglected Lochinvar National Park.

Zambia also has 34 vaguely-defined game management areas (GMAs). These mainly act as 'buffer zones' around the major national parks, and are used mostly for commercial hunting. All GMAs and national parks/reserves (except Kasanka) are administered by the semi-autonomous Zambia Wildlife Authority (ZAWA) – see the Lusaka section later in this chapter for contact details.

Admission fees to the parks vary, so they're listed in the appropriate sections later in this chapter. Each ticket is valid for 24 hours from the time you enter the park, but if you're staying inside the park at official accommodation this admission fee is valid for seven days. Taking a vehicle inside the park costs between US$15 and US$30 per day, depending on the size and weight (of the vehicles, not the passengers). Landing a plane costs US$30 per aircraft, and using a private boat is US$20 a day. Unlike Zimbabwe, ZAWA is not responsible for any camp sites or lodges in or outside any of the parks mentioned in this chapter.

GOVERNMENT & POLITICS

Zambia is a multiparty parliamentary democracy that holds elections for president and members of parliament every five years. The country is ruled by the Movement for Multiparty Democracy (MMD) led by President Mwanawasa. Many of the 30 or more opposition parties, including the UNIP and FDD (see History earlier in this chapter), joined together to form the United Party for National Development (UPND), under Anderson Mazoka, but failed to dislodge the MMD.

ECONOMY

Zambia's economy is dominated by agriculture, with 50% of produce from subsistence farmers and the rest from large commercial farms. But the country still needs to import a lot of food and the economy is largely dependent on international aid.

Zambia is the world's fourth-largest supplier of copper and the leading producer of cobalt. In fact, these two minerals account for about 75% of the country's foreign exchange and employ about 5% of the population. Following the copper price slump of the 1970s,

the industry plunged into severe debt, effectively taking the country with it, but things will improve following the recent, overdue privatisation of the mines in the Copperbelt region. A notable growth industry is tourism, which now earns the country about US$100 million per year.

The economy has improved since 2000: GDP is now positive and the inflation rate has reduced to a manageable 30% per annum. But the monthly wages of those fortunate enough to have a job remain appallingly low: about US$25 for an unskilled labourer and US$60 for a skilled worker in the city.

POPULATION & PEOPLE

The population density is nearly 14 people per sq km, making Zambia one of the most thinly populated countries in Africa. However, about half the population is concentrated in urban areas (mostly Lusaka and the cities in the Copperbelt) – a high percentage for a developing country. This is noticeable as you travel through rural areas; you may go for hours without seeing more than a couple of small villages.

Intermarriage among the 73 officially recognised ethnic groups (tribes) is common, and Zambia is justifiably proud of its almost complete lack of tribal problems. The groups are (in order of size) the Bemba, originally from the Congo (Zaïre) and now settled in

The Lozi

A significant part of the Western Province, often called Barotseland, is home to the Lozi people who migrated there in the 17th century from the central Congo (Zaïre) area. They settled around the upper Zambezi River, and over the next century established a stable and well-organised system of rule and administration.

When Zambia became independent, the new government took control over Barotseland from the British. This fuelled an ongoing Lozi bitterness towards the central government in Lusaka, and self-rule for Barotseland remains high on the political agenda of the *litunga* (king) in Mongu, the regional capital.

Many of the 600,000 Lozi people are farmers, who expertly utilise the fertile land in the Zambezi flood plain, while others produce some of the finest baskets in Southern Africa.

northern Zambia and the Copperbelt; the Tonga, who are linked to other groups in Zimbabwe and live in southern Zimbabwe; the Nyanja, a collective term for about 1.5 million people living in eastern Zambia; the Ngoni, descendants of Zulus from South Africa now settled in the east around Chipata; and the Lozi (see the boxed text following).

ARTS
Music & Dance

All of Zambia's ethnic groups have their own musical traditions. The Lozi are famous for the large drums played during the remarkable Ku'omboka ceremony (described in the Western Zambia section later in this chapter), while the Bemba are also renowned drummers. Other traditional musical instruments used by most groups include large wooden xylophones, often with gourds underneath the blocks for resonance, and tiny thumb pianos, with just a few keys made from flattened metal.

The most notable traditional dance is the *makishi*, which features male dancers wearing masks of stylised human faces with grass skirts and anklets. It probably originated in the Congo (Zaïre) region and was brought to northwestern Zambia by the Luvale or Luchasi people, before being adopted by other ethnic groups. *Makishi* is now found in many parts of Zambia, mainly at boys' initiation ceremonies. But any local celebration seems to be a good excuse for the men to strut their stuff.

Contemporary musicians who have achieved some international fame include Larry Maluma and Ricki Ilonga, both exponents of a traditional style called *kalindula* (a rumba-inspired sound). Other popular musicians who play traditional styles include the Sakala Brothers from the Eastern Province and Mpunda Mutale from the Northern Province. Younger Zambians prefer reggae – both the hard Jamaican style and the softer version popular in Southern Africa. Many Zambians also admire Congo-style rhumba music (also called *kwasa kwasa*), which is invariably played long and loud at local bars and nightclubs.

For more information, see the special colour section 'Beats of Southern Africa'.

Arts & Crafts

Zambia boasts a thriving contemporary art scene. One of the country's most famous and

respected painters is the late Henry Tayali. His works – described by critics as 'crowded social realism' – have inspired many other Zambian painters and enjoyed a popular following among ordinary folk. If you want to know more about the local art scene, the studio and exhibition centre named after him in Lusaka is worth a visit.

Other internationally recognised artists include Agnes Yombwe, who works with purely natural materials and uses traditional ceramics and textile designs in her striking sculptures; Shadreck Simukanga, arguably the finest painter working in Zambia; and the country's best known artist, Stephen Kapata. Prominent sculptors include Eddie Mumba and the prolific Friday Tembo.

Zambian artistry includes skilfully woven baskets from Barotseland (Western Province), malachite jewellery from the north and woodcarvings from Mukuni village near Livingstone. Much of these crafts are sold in markets around the country, as well as in souvenir shops found in the more touristy areas.

Theatre
Lusaka's theatre scene is thriving, and many Zambian writers produce plays and other dramas, from slapstick comedy to hard political comment. There's nearly always something entertaining at the Lusaka Playhouse (see Entertainment in the Lusaka section later in this chapter).

LANGUAGE
Of the 70 languages and dialects spoken in Zambia, seven are recognised by the government as official 'special languages'. These include Bemba (mainly spoken in the north); Tonga (in the south); Nyanja (in the east), which is similar to Chichewa spoken in Malawi; and Lozi (in the west).

As a lingua franca, and the official, national language, English is widely spoken across Zambia. The Language chapter at the back of this book contains some useful words and phrases in Chichewa and Lozi.

Facts for the Visitor

SUGGESTED ITINERARIES
One consideration is your method of travel; independent travellers simply cannot reach the sort of remote places that are easily accessible by private vehicle or organised tour. Also, the bizarre shape of Zambia will no doubt frustrate your travel plans.

With only one or two weeks, it's best to concentrate on one of *the* attractions of Southern Africa – Victoria Falls – and visit one or two national parks, probably Lower Zambezi and Kafue. With extra time and money, head to South Luangwa National Park, Siavonga (the main town along the mighty Lake Kariba), the Copperbelt region and Kasanka National Park. If you're travelling to/from Tanzania or Malawi, or have even more time up your sleeve, explore the Northern Province, including the Bangweulu Wetlands and the dramatic southern tip of Lake Tanganyika.

The Big Trip
Most travellers come to Zambia as part of a lengthy jaunt around Southern Africa, eg, between Botswana and/or Namibia and/or Tanzania and/or Malawi. In this case, the best itinerary would be Livingstone, Lusaka, Kafue National Park, Siavonga, South Luangwa National Park, Bangweulu Wetlands and Lake Tanganyika. Easier, and even more spectacular, is the circular route through Zambia and Zimbabwe: eg, Livingstone, Lusaka, Lower Zambezi National Park and Siavonga; and, in Zimbabwe, Kariba, Harare, Eastern Highlands, Masvingo, Bulawayo, Hwange National Park and back to Victoria Falls.

Travel Tips
Zambia is deceptively large and transport is frustratingly slow. The Tazara railway from Tanzania will save considerable time across northern and eastern Tanzania. And don't ignore the Copperbelt region just because it's a little out of the way.

PLANNING
When to Go
From May to August, conditions are dry and comparatively cooler, and the landscape is green and lush. This is not a great time to see wildlife, however, because there are so many waterholes to choose from (though by August, wildlife viewing does improve). From September to early/mid-November, temperatures are uncomfortably hot and the landscape is dramatically arid, but this is the best time to watch wildlife. During the rainy season (November to April), many rural

ZAMBIA

roads are impassable and some lodges and camps in some national parks are closed. But this is the best time for bird-watching (particularly November and December).

Refer to the Victoria Falls chapter for details about the best time to visit this magnificent site.

Maps

Macmillan's *Traveller's Map* (1:2,200,000) is the best map of Zambia, and includes detailed – but fairly dated – maps of several cities, national parks and tourist areas. Also worthwhile is the *Zambia Map Pack* published by Directory Publishers, which includes maps of Zambia, Kitwe, Ndola, Livingstone and Lusaka. Both are available at bookshops in Lusaka. If you're trekking or driving into more remote regions, detailed survey maps at various scales (for US$1 to US$2 each) are available from the Map Sales office in Lusaka (see that section for details).

TOURIST OFFICES

The regional tourist offices in Lusaka and Livingstone are worth visiting for specific inquiries, but provide limited information about Zambia in general. Refer to the relevant sections for contact details.

The **Zambia National Tourist Board** (ZNTB) has two international offices: in the UK (☎ *020-7589 6343, fax 020-7225 3221;* e *zntb@aol.com; 2 Palace Gate, Kensington, London W8 5NG*); and in **South Africa** (☎ *012-326 1847;* e *zahpta@mweb.co.za; 589 Ziervogel St, Arcadia, Pretoria*). The official ZNTB web site – w www.zambiatourism.com – is outstanding, and provides links to dozens of lodges, hotels and tour agencies.

The **Tourism Council of Zambia** (e *tcz@zamnet.zm*) is an umbrella group of private companies throughout the country involved in the promotion of tourism.

VISAS & DOCUMENTS

All foreigners visiting Zambia need visas, but for most nationalities tourist visas are available at major borders, airports and sea ports. But it's important to note that you should have a Zambian visa *before* arrival if travelling by train or boat from Tanzania.

Citizens of the following countries can obtain tourist visas on arrival for free: Australia, Canada, Denmark, Finland, Ireland, Namibia, Norway, South Africa, Sweden

and Zimbabwe. For all other nationalities, tourist visas are issued on arrival, but cost about US$25 for a transit visa (valid for seven days), US$25/40 for a single/double-entry visa (valid for three months) and US$80 for a multiple-entry visa (valid for three months). Brits, however, are slugged US$65/65/80/80 for transit/single/double/multiple-entry visas. Note that multiple-entry visas are useful, eg, if you plan to travel to/from Zimbabwe several times. Payment can be made in US dollars, UK pounds, euros, South African rands, Botswana pula or Namibian dollars, regardless of which border you use.

Tourist and business visas can also be obtained from Zambian diplomatic missions abroad, and application forms can be downloaded from the website run by the Zambian High Commission in London at w www.zhcl.org.uk.

If you arrive in Zambia on an organised tour, tourist visas are normally issued free for all nationalities on arrival – in any case, your tour operator should be aware of the regulations and arrange everything. The 'Visiting Zambia from Zimbabwe (and Vice Versa)' boxed text in the Victoria Falls chapter explains how to obtain a free seven-day (extendable) transit visa when travelling from Zimbabwe. But if you come to Zambia from Zimbabwe on a free-visa transfer from Victoria Falls, make sure you keep all your paperwork, because you may be asked later why there is no indication on your passport that you have paid for a Zambian visa, and then forced to buy one. This has happened to unlucky readers travelling to Tanzania from Kapiri Mposhi by train.

Visa Extensions

Extensions for all types of tourist visas are possible at any Department of Immigration office in any main town in Zambia, though you're likely to be more successful in Lusaka (Memaco House, Cairo Rd) and Livingstone (Mosi-oa-Tunya Rd). Normally, a three-month extension can cost up to US$100 (depending on your nationality), but one reader was astounded to get a three-month, multi-entry visa extension for only US$2 – but didn't tell us which immigration office!

If the paperwork seems overwhelming, and the fees exorbitant, simply cross into Zimbabwe, Mozambique or Malawi (the easiest

options) and obtain a new visa when you return to Zambia.

Visas for Onward Travel

It's always best to visit any embassy or high commission in Lusaka between 9am and noon from Monday to Friday. You will probably need two passport-sized photos.

Your chances of obtaining a visa for Congo (Zaïre) or Angola are extremely remote in Lusaka, so get it before you arrive in Zambia.

Visas for Zimbabwe, Malawi, Namibia, Tanzania and Botswana are easy to obtain on arrival at the border of these countries for most visitors. So the high commissions in Lusaka for these countries will only issue visas to the few nationalities that need them before arrival. However, if you're travelling by train or boat to Tanzania, check with the Tanzanian high commission in Lusaka about whether you need a visa beforehand. If so, three-month visas cost from US$25 to US$50 (depending on your nationality). The visa is usually ready later the same day if you apply before noon.

For Mozambique transit visas (valid for seven days) cost US$11, single-entry visas (for one month) cost US$20, and multiple-entry visas (for three months) cost US$40. Visas are ready in two days, but for an extra fee you can get same-day service.

Other Documents

Hostel cards and senior cards are useless, though student or youth cards may be useful for buying tickets on major international airlines and the Tazara railway between Zambia and Tanzania.

A yellow fever certificate is not required before entering Zambia, but it *is* often requested by Zambian immigration officials if you have come from a country with yellow fever. And it is certainly required if you're travelling from Zambia to South Africa (and, possibly, Zimbabwe). For all sorts of reasons, it pays to get a jab before you come to Southern Africa and carry a certificate to prove it.

EMBASSIES & CONSULATES
Zambian Embassies & High Commissions

Zambia has high commissions in Botswana, Malawi, Mozambique, Namibia, South Africa and Zimbabwe – see the relevant

chapters in this book for contact details. Elsewhere in Africa, Zambian embassies and high commissions are located in Angola, Kenya and Tanzania, as well as:

Belgium (☎ 02-343 5649, fax 02-347 4333) 469 Ave Moliere, 1060 Brussels
Germany (☎/fax 0228-376811, fax 0228-379536) Mittelstrasse 39, Bad Ogdensburg, 5300 Bonn 2
UK (☎ 020-7589 6655, fax 020-7581 1353, W www.zhcl.org.uk) 2 Palace Gate, London W8 5NG
USA (☎ 202-265 9717, e zambia@tnm.com) 2419 Massachusetts NW, Washington DC 20008

Embassies & High Commissions in Zambia

The following countries have embassies or high commissions in Lusaka (area code ☎ 01). The British High Commission looks after the interests of Aussies and Kiwis because the nearest diplomatic missions for Australia and New Zealand are in Harare. The nearest French embassy is also in Harare. (See that section in the Zimbabwe chapter for contact details.)

Botswana (☎ 250019, fax 253895) 5201 Pandit Nehru Rd
Canada (☎ 250833) 5119 United Nations Ave
Congo (Zaïre) (☎ 235679, fax 252080) 1124 Parirenyetwa Rd
Germany (☎ 250644) 5209 United Nations Ave
Malawi (☎ 265764, fax 265765) 31 Bishops Rd, Kabulonga
Mozambique (☎ 239135, fax 220345) 9592 Kacha Rd, off Paseli Rd
Namibia (☎ 260407, fax 263895) 30B Mutende Rd, Woodlands
Netherlands (☎ 253819) 5208 United Nations Ave
South Africa (☎ 260999, fax 263001) 26D Cheetah Rd, Kabulonga
Tanzania (☎ 253222, fax 254861) 5200 United Nations Ave
UK (☎ 251133) 5210 Independence Ave
USA (☎ 250955) cnr Independence & United Nations Aves
Zimbabwe (☎ 254006, fax 253582) 11058 Haile Selassie Ave

CUSTOMS

There are no restrictions on the amount of foreign currency that tourists can bring in or take out of Zambia. Import or export of Zambian kwacha, however, is technically forbidden, but if you bring in/out a small amount (say, US$25 worth) it's unlikely to be a problem.

MONEY
Currency
Zambia's unit of currency is the kwacha (k), sometimes listed as 'ZK' (Zambian kwacha) or 'kw'. Bank notes come in denominations of k10,000, k5000, k1000, k500, k100 and k50, but k20 notes are extremely rare and virtually worthless. One hundred ngwee equals one kwacha, so, not surprisingly, ngwee coins have become souvenirs.

Inflation is high in Zambia, so quoting costs of transport, hotels etc in kwacha is not helpful, because prices will have undoubtedly changed by the time you arrive. Therefore, we have used US dollars (US$) throughout this chapter, except of course, for minor costs. Although the actual exchange rate will have altered by the time you reach Zambia, the cost of travel in US dollars (or any other hard currency) will not have altered that much.

Most tourist-oriented places in Zambia quote prices in US dollars, but you must by law pay in kwacha – except for international air fares, top-end hotels/lodges, visas and most organised tours. In reality however, US dollars are commonly (and gratefully) accepted by most hotels, budget camp sites, tour operators and national park rangers.

Exchange Rates
As a guide, the exchange rates in mid 2003 for larger notes (eg, US$50 and US$100) in major Western and regional currencies are listed here. The rates for smaller notes are about 10% less.

country	unit		kwacha
Australia	A$1	=	k3268
Botswana	P1	=	k952
Canada	C$1	=	k3650
euro zone	€1	=	k5797
Japan	¥100	=	k4187
Malawi	MK1	=	k55.15
Mozambique	Mtc100	=	k21.20
New Zealand	NZ$1	=	k2847
South Africa	R1	=	k622
Tanzania	Tsh100	=	k491
UK	UK£1	=	k8219
USA	US$1	=	k4930
Zimbabwe	ZW$100	=	k608

Exchanging Money
The best currencies to take to Zambia (in order of preference) are US dollars, UK pounds and South African rands. Euros have yet to take off and the currencies of most neighbouring countries are worthless in Zambia, except at the relevant borders. The exception is Botswana pula, which can also be exchanged in Lusaka.

In the cities and larger towns, you can change cash and travellers cheques (see following) at branches of Barclays Bank and Standard Chartered Bank. In smaller towns, try the Zambia National Commercial Bank.

Foreign exchange offices – almost always called a bureau de change – are easy to find in all cities and larger towns. Their rates for cash and travellers cheques (if accepted) are around 5% better than the banks' rates; service is also faster and there are no additional fees.

There is no black market. You might get a few kwacha more changing money on the street, but it's illegal and there is a chance that you'll be ripped off, robbed or set up for some sort of scam. However, moneychangers at the borders are more or less legitimate, but may take (slight) advantage of your ignorance about the current exchange rates. If you can't change cash at a bank or bureau de change, try a hotel or a shop that sells imported items.

Travellers Cheques It's worth avoiding travellers cheques for several reasons: they are not accepted at all bureaux de change, and they attract high charges and lower exchange rates (5% to 8% lower than for cash). Commission rates vary, so it's always worth shopping around. The standard commission charged by Barclays and Standard Chartered banks is about 1%, but often with a minimum of US$15. If you're likely to be charged a ridiculous commission – eg, US$15 (!) on a US$20 travellers cheque – try negotiating a lower commission. One reader did so and paid only US$2 commission at a bank for a US$20 travellers cheque.

You can pay for some items (such as tours, activities, hotels and lodges) directly with travellers cheques, but a few hotel and tour operators have a nasty habit of adding a surcharge (up to US$20) for this.

When you change travellers cheques at a bank, and at some bureaux de change, staff may check your original purchase receipt. Barclays, American Express, Thomas Cook and Visa are by far the most accepted brands.

Credit Cards You can obtain cash (kwacha only) over the counter at Barclays and Standard Chartered banks in the cities and larger towns with a Visa card (but less reliably with MasterCard). But it can take most of the day and you may be slugged a fee of about US$10. Larger branches of both banks have automated teller machines (ATMs) that accept Visa and MasterCard, but only kwacha can be withdrawn, and ATMs have a habit of malfunctioning.

Some shops, restaurants and better hotels/lodges accept major credit cards, though Visa seems to be the most readily recognised. A surcharge of 5% to 10% may be added to your bill if you pay with a credit card, so you're probably better off using your card to draw cash and paying with that.

Costs

If you're travelling on a tight budget you may find Zambia a tad more expensive than some other countries in Southern Africa. As an example, camping costs about US$5 per person (but double that in most national parks), while dormitory beds in hostels cost around US$6 per person. Reasonable singles/doubles in modest hotels cost about US$13/18. Local-style meals at cheap restaurants are available for about US$1, and Western meals in better restaurants start from US$2 to US$3.

Public transport can seem expensive too, but that's mainly because the distances between destinations in Zambia are great. Generally, the cost of bus travel per 100km is only slightly higher than elsewhere: less than US$2 on ordinary buses and lower classes of trains, and up to US$3 for 'luxury' or 'express' buses and first-class train travel.

So, if you're travelling on a very tight budget, you can get away with US$10/8 per person per day travelling as a single/double, but US$20/15 is more realistic. If you want to stay in decent hotels straddling the budget and mid-range, eat Western meals, travel first class on trains and use private buses, allow about US$40/30 per person per day travelling as a single/double. Add to this the costs of activities (eg, rafting trips cost up to US$100 per day), flights, car rental (about US$50 per day), national park admission fees (US$15 to US$20 per day), organised tours and souvenirs.

Taxes

The Value Added Tax (VAT) of 17.5% is added to almost everything. This tax is included in all prices listed in this chapter (and in the Zambian section of the Victoria Falls chapter) and in all prices quoted to you in the country. To encourage tourists from Victoria Falls town in Zimbabwe, there is no VAT on accommodation in Livingstone (only).

In more upmarket hotels and restaurants an arbitrary 10% 'service charge' is usually added to your bill.

POST & COMMUNICATIONS
Post

Postcards and normal letters (under 20g) cost k1800 to send to Europe and k2200 to the USA, Canada, Australia and New Zealand. Sending international letters from Lusaka is surprisingly quick (three or four days to Europe), but from elsewhere in the country it's less reliable and much slower. Parcels up to 1kg to Europe cost US$6 by airmail and US$7.50 to the USA, Canada, Australia and New Zealand. The cost is about half this for surface mail.

Poste restante service is available at the main post office in Lusaka (see Information in the Lusaka section for details) for a negligible fee.

Telephone & Fax

Almost all telecommunication services are provided by the government monopoly, Zamtel. Public phones operated by Zamtel use a token, which are available from post offices (k500) or local boys (k1000) hanging around phone booths. These tokens last three minutes but are only good for calls within Zambia. Phone booths operated by Tele2africa use phone cards (from US$5), available from post offices and grocery shops; these phone cards can be used for international calls. But it's often easier to find a 'phone shop' or 'fax bureau', from where all international calls cost about US$3 per minute.

Zamcell offers the largest mobile (cell) phone network. It's almost impossible to rent mobile phones in Zambia, and check with your mobile phone company at home about access in Zambia. Numbers starting with ☎ 095, ☎ 096 and ☎ 097 are mobile phone numbers.

International services are generally good, but reverse-charge (collect) calls are not

possible. The international access code for dialling outside of Zambia is ☎ 00, followed by the relevant country code. If you're calling Zambia from another country, the country code is ☎ 260, but drop the initial 0 for the area code.

Email & Internet Access

Zamnet is the country's largest Internet service provider. Internet centres are in Lusaka and Livingstone (see Internet Resources under Lusaka and Livingstone for details), and a few upmarket lodges allow guests (only) to use their Internet facilities for a small charge. Access at an Internet centre is cheap – about US$1 for 30 minutes – but irritatingly slow at times.

DIGITAL RESOURCES

Your first 'cyber-stop' should be the outstanding website run by the Zambia National Tourist Board: W www.zambiatourism.com. Other websites worth checking out include:

Zambia Online (W www.zambia.co.zm) has excellent links, and offers chat rooms with Zambians

Zambiz (W www.zambiz.co.zm) is ideal for all business, including booking lodges and tours

Zamnet (W www.zamnet.zm) provides links to all major national newspapers and several other useful sites

Other useful addresses are given throughout this chapter. For a more comprehensive listing, see also Digital Resources in the Regional Facts for the Visitor chapter.

BOOKS

The following titles are books specific to Zambia. Titles on the Southern Africa region are covered under Books in the Regional Facts for the Visitor chapter.

Lonely Planet

Zambia provides considerably more detail about the country, while *Africa on a Shoestring* includes general coverage of Zambia and everywhere else in the southern part of the continent.

General

The Africa House, by Christina Lamb, tells the story of Stewart Gore-Brown and his grand plans for a utopian fiefdom in a remote part of Zambia during the 1920s. His country mansion at Shiwa Ng'andu still stands (see Northern Zambia later in this chapter).

Although a personalised selection of observations on wildlife and humans, *Kakuli* by Norman Carr, also raises deeper issues and suggests some practical solutions to current conservation problems. The author spent a lifetime working with animals and people in the South Luangwa National Park (see South Luangwa National Park later in this chapter).

Spirit of the Zambezi, by Jeff & Fiona Sutchbury, is a personal and knowledgeable account of three decades living and working in, on and around the great river between Zambia and Zimbabwe. It's illustrated with beautiful photos.

Mark & Delia Owens (authors of the famous *Cry of the Kalahari*) based *Survivor's Song* in the North Luangwa National Park. They launch themselves single-mindedly into the hard fight against elephant poachers, putting their lives and relationship seriously on the line.

Zambia, by Richard Vaughan, is a highly recommended coffee-table book with superb photographs. It covers the magnificent landscape and wildlife, but also the less 'touristy' aspects such as city life and mining.

NEWSPAPERS & MAGAZINES

Zambia's national newspapers are all fairly boring and almost entirely full of advertisements. The *Daily Times* and the *Daily Mail* are dull, government-controlled rags; in contrast, the independent *Post* (W www.post.co.zm) continuously needles the government. Copies of the *Weekly Telegraph* and the *Guardian Weekly,* published in the UK but printed in South Africa, are available in Lusaka and Livingstone.

The *Lowdown* (W www.lowdown.co.zm; k2500) magazine is aimed at expats and well-off residents in Lusaka. For visitors, it does contain useful information, such as restaurant reviews and lists of upcoming events and attractions in the capital, as well as handy adverts for package deals at national parks around Zambia.

RADIO & TV

Both of the radio stations run by the Zambia National Broadcasting Corporation (ZNBC) offer Western and African music, as well as news and chat shows in English. The cities

and larger towns also have private commercial radio stations, while the BBC World Service can be heard in Lusaka (on 88.2FM) and Kitwe (89.1FM).

ZNBC also shows a few programmes on the solitary government-controlled television station every evening, but anyone who can afford a TV set will probably subscribe to satellite TV from South Africa. Rooms in most decent hotels contain TVs that pick up one or two international channels, such as the BBC and Supersports.

PHOTOGRAPHY & VIDEO

In Lusaka and Livingstone, a roll of 24/36 exposure print film costs about US$3.50/5, while a roll of 36 exposure slide film is about US$9 (without processing). Developing and printing 24/36 exposure print film costs about US$4/5.50, but developing slide film is almost impossible. Bring everything you need for video cameras.

Zambian officials do not like foreigners photographing public buildings, bridges, airports or anything else that could be considered strategic. If in doubt, ask; better still, save your camera for the national parks.

HEALTH

Most general aspects covered under Health in the Regional Facts for the Visitor chapter apply to Zambia. In Zambia malaria is a problem, and minor outbreaks of cholera and yellow fever are sometimes reported. Bilharzia is common in most rivers and lakes, so avoid swimming unless you're told by a knowledgeable local that it's OK.

Like every country in Southern Africa, the AIDS/HIV pandemic continues to have a massive economic and social impact. About 90,000 Zambians die each year (including some 13,000 teachers), while about 20% of the population are HIV positive. About 50% of all children under 16 have lost at least one parent to AIDS.

Medical facilities in Zambia are poor, and state-run hospitals suffer from severe shortages. The cities and larger towns have hospitals, private clinics and chemists (pharmacies).

DANGERS & ANNOYANCES

Generally, Zambia is very safe, though in the cities and tourist areas there is always a chance of being targeted by robbers or con-artists. As always, you can reduce the risk considerably by being sensible.

For as long as the seemingly endless civil strife continues in Congo (Zaïre), avoid any areas along the Zambian/Congo (Zaïre) border especially around Lake Mweru. Foreign embassies in Zambia warn of landmines (left over from the Rhodesian civil war) in the Sinazongwe area along the shores of Lake Kariba. Avoid trekking off the beaten track in this area.

The possession, use and trade of recreational drugs is illegal in Zambia and penalties are harsh: in 1999, two Kiwi travellers were given six months in jail with hard labour after being caught with a relatively small amount.

It's also worth noting that some travellers with an Asian background have reported annoying glares and racial slurs from Zambians.

BUSINESS HOURS

Government offices are open from 8am (or 9am) to 4pm (or 5pm) Monday to Friday, with an hour for lunch sometime between noon and 2pm. Shops keep the same hours, but also open on Saturday. Banks operate weekdays from 8.15am to 2.30pm, and from 8.15am to 11am on the first and last Saturday of each month. Post offices open from 8am (or 9am) to 4pm (or 4.30pm) weekdays.

PUBLIC HOLIDAYS & SPECIAL EVENTS

During the following public holidays, most businesses and government offices are closed:

New Year's Day 1 January
Youth Day March – second Monday
Easter March/April – Good Friday, Saturday & Easter Monday
Labour/Workers' Day 1 May
Africa (Freedom) Day 25 May
Heroes' Day July – first Monday
Unity Day July – first Tuesday
Farmers' Day August – first Monday
Independence Day 24 October
Christmas Day 25 December
Boxing Day 26 December

One remarkable festival to look out for is **Ukusefya pa Ng'wena**, practised by the Bemba people of northern Zambia. This programme of music, drama and dance, which is held near Kasama over four days in August, commemorates the victory of

the Bemba over the marauding Ngoni in the 1830s.

N'cwala is a Ngoni festival held near Chipata in eastern Zambia on 24 February. At this time, food, dance and music are all enjoyed by participants who celebrate the end of the rainy season and pray for a successful harvest.

Refer to the boxed text 'The Ku'omboka Ceremony' in the Northern Zambia section later in this chapter for details about this remarkable event.

Details about these and other festivals are on the official Zambian tourism website: **w** www.zambiatourism.com.

ACTIVITIES

More information about the various activities mentioned here is included under the relevant sections later this chapter and in the Victoria Falls chapter.

Companies in Livingstone (and Victoria Falls town in Zimbabwe) offer a bewildering array of activities, such as **white-water rafting** in the gorge below the falls or **river boarding** and **canoeing** on the quieter waters above the falls. Those with plenty of nerve and money can try **bungee jumping** or **abseiling**, or take a ride in a **microlight** or **helicopter**. The less adventurous may want to try some **hiking** and **horse riding**.

Canoeing is also a great way to explore the Zambezi River and can be arranged in Siavonga (or Kariba in Zimbabwe). **Fishing** along the Zambezi, at several lakes in northern Zambia, is also popular; the tigerfish are almost inedible, but provide a tough contest for anglers. Fishing and **boating** are also possible on Kariba, Bangweulu and Tanganyika Lakes. Kasanka, Lower Zambezi and South Luangwa National Parks also offer activities for visitors.

Many tour companies in Livingstone offer short **wildlife drives** in Mosi-oa-Tunya National Park near Victoria Falls, while companies in Lusaka and Livingstone can also arrange longer **wildlife safaris** to more remote national parks. In some parks (eg, Kasanka and South Luangwa), you can turn up and arrange wildlife drives or **walking safaris** on the spot.

ACCOMMODATION

Prices for all accommodation listed in this chapter, and in the Zambian section of the Victoria Falls chapter, are for the high (dry) season – ie, April/May to October/November – and are based on the 'international rates'.

It's worth noting that prices for rooms with private bathrooms are about 50% higher than rooms without, and that all accommodation in Lusaka is about 50% higher than anywhere else in Zambia. Most hotels in the mid- and top-end range include breakfast in their rates.

Budget

Most cities and larger towns have camp sites where you can pitch your tent, but most are way out in the suburbs. Camping is also possible at privately run camp sites at the national parks, though most are located just outside the park boundaries to avoid admission fees (until you actually want to visit the park). Unlike Zimbabwe, no camp sites are run by the national wildlife authority. There's little to stop you pitching your tent in the wild – except the chance of being interrupted by a hungry lion or rhino, of course.

The few youth hostels around Zambia are not part of any international organisation, so hostel cards are useless. But many hostels in Lusaka and the major tourist areas are well set up with swimming pools, bars, restaurants and travel agencies offering organised tours.

Some of the cheapest hotels in the cities are actually brothels. The better budget hotels charge by the room, so two, three or even four people travelling together can get some real (if crowded) bargains. Single travellers may find some prices steep, though negotiation is always possible.

Mid-Range to Top End

All national parks are dotted with expensive privately operated lodges and 'camps' (a confusing term often used to describe expensive lodges). They offer the same sort of luxury and exclusivity as other lodges and camps in southern and eastern Africa – all at US$200 or more per person per night (twin share). Foreigners usually pay the 'international rates' for lodges/camps, while tourists from Southern Africa get a 'regional rate' of 25% less, and Zambians pay about half the 'international rates'. These rates usually include all meals, drinks and activities, such as wildlife drives, but not transfers by road, air and/or boat. Lodges/camps should be booked in advance, either directly by phone,

fax or email, or through an agent in Lusaka or abroad. Some lodges/camps close in the wet season (November to April); if they're open, discounts of up to 50% are common.

FOOD

The national dish is unquestionably *nshima*, a bland but filling maize porridge-like substance. It's eaten with your fingers and always accompanied by a 'relish', such as beans or vegetables (in inexpensive eateries), or chicken or fish (in slightly better restaurants). Most other cheap meals are an unimaginative and unhealthy choice of fried eggs, fried sausages, fried chicken and burgers – all laden with chips (French fries).

In the cities and larger towns, many restaurants – especially in the hotels – offer Western meals like steak and schnitzel. Prices start from US$2, depending on the surroundings as much as the food itself, and whether you eat in or takeaway. More elaborate French and Italian cuisine is also available from better hotels, while several restaurants in Lusaka serve Chinese and Indian food. At most top-end establishments, main courses start from about US$5.

Most cheaper restaurants serve meals without meat, because locals can't afford anything but *nshima,* rice and vegetables anyway. In the cities and larger towns, it's not hard to find an Indian- or Chinese-owned restaurant offering one or two meatless dishes.

In better restaurants a 10% 'service charge' is often added (which technically means tipping is not required), as well as the normal 17.5% VAT (which some places cheekily round up to 20%). All prices in this chapter, and the Zambian section of the Victoria Falls chapter, include all charges and taxes.

Self-catering

Markets and stalls on the roadside sell fresh vegetables and fruit, while supermarkets in the cities and larger towns are well stocked.

DRINKS

Tea, coffee, soft drinks (sodas) and bottled mineral water are widely available and inexpensive. Beer is served pleasingly cold, but is nothing to get excited about: Mosi Lager is arguably tastier than the ubiquitous Castle (from South Africa) and the locally-brewed Rhino Lager. Traditional beer made from maize is sold commercially in cardboard cartons, but make sure you shake the carton before drinking.

SHOPPING

Visitors to Zambia continue to be delighted with the variety of reasonably priced souvenirs available in markets and speciality shops in Lusaka, Livingstone, Kitwe and Ndola. Charming mementoes include baskets made by the Lozi people in western Zambia and carvings by the Leya in and around Livingstone. Copper items are sold throughout Zambia, but paradoxically most of the stuff for sale in the Copperbelt region is made from metal processed in Congo (Zaïre). Ladies may wish to buy a *chitenje*, a multicoloured and multipurpose sheet of material used as a scarf and sarong.

Getting There & Away

Information about travelling to Southern Africa, including Zambia, from elsewhere in the continent, and from some Western countries, is included in the regional Getting There & Away chapter earlier in this book.

AIR

Zambia's main international airport is in Lusaka, though some international airlines fly to the new airport at Livingstone (for Victoria Falls) and Mfuwe (for the South Luangwa National Park). The major domestic and international carrier is Zambian Airways (**w** www.africa-insites.com/zambianairways).

Departure Tax

The departure tax for all international flights is US$20. This tax is *not* included in the price of your airline ticket and must be paid at the airport (in US dollars only).

Southern Africa

Zambia is well connected to the region. Zambian Airways flies daily between Lusaka and Harare (US$155/305 one way/return), while Air Zimbabwe (**w** www.airzim.co.zw) also flies to Lusaka (US$150/295) from Harare on the way to Nairobi each Thursday.

Air Malawi connects Lusaka with Lilongwe three times a week (US$150/200) and with Blantyre (US$185/299) twice a

ZAMBIA

week. Comair (a subsidiary of British Airways) and South African Airways both fly daily between Lusaka and Johannesburg for about US$200/295.

Refer to the Victoria Falls chapter for information about international flights to/from Livingstone.

LAND
Border Crossings
Zambia shares borders with eight countries, so there's a huge number of crossing points. All are open daily from 6am to 6pm, though the border closes at 8pm at Victoria Falls and at 7pm at Chirundu.

The following borders issue visas to foreigners on arrival.

Botswana These two countries share what is probably the world's shortest international boundary: 750m across the Zambezi River at Kazungula. The pontoon (car ferry) across the Zambezi is 65km west of Livingstone and 11km south of the main road between Livingstone and Sesheke.

Congo (Zaïre) The main border is between Chililabombwe (Zambia) and Kasumbalesa (Congo), but visas are not issued to tourists in Lusaka

Malawi Most foreigners use the border at Mchinji, 30km southeast of Chipata, because it's along the road between Lusaka and Lilongwe

Mozambique The main border is between Mlolo (Zambia) and Cassacatiza (Mozambique), but most travellers choose to reach Mozambique through Malawi

Namibia The only border is at Katima Mulilo (Zambia), on the northern bank of the Zambezi, while the Namibian border is near the Namibian town with the same name

Tanzania The main border by road, and the only crossing by train, is between Nakonde (Zambia) and Tunduma (Tanzania)

Zimbabwe There are three easy crossings: at Chirundu, along the road between Lusaka and Harare; between Siavonga (Zambia) and Kariba (Zimbabwe), about 50km upstream from Chirundu; and between Livingstone (Zambia) and Victoria Falls town (Zimbabwe).

Botswana
Several *very* crowded minibuses (US$4, 1½ hours) leave Livingstone every day for the terminal used by the pontoon ferry to Kazungula. The pontoon carries motorbikes/cars/4WDs for US$10/20/30, while foot passengers pay k2000. Payment is also possible in kwacha, Botswana pula or South African rands. From the Botswana border, minibuses regularly leave for Kasane.

A quicker and more comfortable (but more expensive) way to reach Botswana from Zambia is to cross from Livingstone to Victoria Falls (in Zimbabwe), from where shuttle buses head to Kasane – refer to the Victoria Falls chapter for details.

Buses to Gaborone, via Kasane and Francistown, leave several days a week from Lusaka (see that section for details).

Malawi
Direct buses between Lusaka and Lilongwe are infrequent and slow, so it makes sense to do this trip in stages. From the BP petrol station on the main street in Chipata, regular minibuses (US$2) run the 30km to the Zambian border. The two border crossings are 12km apart, connected by shared taxis and pick-ups (US$2), which continue to Mchinji, from where minibuses run to Lilongwe.

Mozambique
There is no public transport between Zambia and Mozambique and the only common border leads to a remote part of Mozambique. Most travellers, therefore, chose to visit Mozambique from Lilongwe in Malawi (see earlier).

Namibia
Every day, at least one bus and several minibuses leave Livingstone for Sesheke (US$7, six hours). The trip can take longer, because the road between the pontoon ferry terminal across to Kazungula and Sesheke is a shocker. The bus may terminate in Sesheke or continue another 5km to the pontoon (car ferry). The pontoon carries motorbikes/cars/4WDs for US$10/20/30, while foot passengers travel for free; payment is also possible in Botswana pula, Namibian dollars and South African rands. If the pontoon isn't operating, foot passengers pay about US$1.50 to cross by dugout canoe and vehicles are stuck at the border.

From the Namibian side, it's a 5km walk to Katima Mulilo, from where minibuses depart for other parts of Namibia.

Alternatively, cross from Livingstone to Victoria Falls (in Zimbabwe) and catch a shuttle bus to Windhoek – see the Victoria Falls chapter for details.

South Africa
There is no border between Zambia and South Africa, but several buses travel daily

between Jo'burg and Lusaka (see that section for details), via Harare and Masvingo in Zimbabwe. But make sure you have a Zimbabwean visa (if you need one before arrival) and a yellow fever certificate for entering South Africa (and, possibly, Zimbabwe).

Tanzania

Although travelling by bus is quicker, the train is more comfortable.

Bus Comfortable, but frighteningly speedy, buses leave Lusaka for Dar es Salaam once or twice a week, but services are less reliable these days. Alternatively, walk across the border from Nakonde, and take a minibus from Tunduma to Mbeya in Tanzania.

Train The Tazara railway company usually operates two international trains per week in each direction between Kapiri Mposhi (207km north of Lusaka) and Dar es Salaam. The 'express train' (42 to 45 hours) leaves Kapiri Mposhi at 5.30pm on Tuesday, while the 'interstate train' (50 to 52 hours) leaves Kapiri Mposhi at noon on Friday. The fares on both trains are about US$28/19/11 in 1st/2nd/3rd class (1st and 2nd class are sleeping compartments). A discount of 50% is possible with a student card.

Tickets are available on the spot at the New Kapiri Mposhi (Tazara) train station in Kapiri Mposhi and up to three days in advance from **Tazara House** (☎ 01-222280, *Independence Ave, Lusaka*). If there are no more seats left at the Lusaka office, don't despair because we've heard from travellers who easily bought tickets at Kapiri Mposhi, and upgraded from one class to another while on board.

It's prudent to get a Tanzanian visa in Lusaka (or elsewhere) before you board the train; at least, contact the Tanzanian High Commission in Lusaka about getting a Tanzanian visa on the train or at the border. You can change money on the train but take care because these guys are sharks. The buffet car on the train uses the currency of the country it's passing through at the time.

Zimbabwe

Plenty of buses travel every day between Lusaka and Harare, via Chirundu – see

---

The Lake Tanganyika Ferry

The massive *Liemba* ferry links the Zambian port of Mpulungu with Kigoma and other smaller places in Tanzania. The timetable is flexible, but the ferry normally departs Kigoma at 4pm on Wednesday. After about 40 hours it arrives in Mpulungu, from where it returns to Kigoma at 2pm on Friday. The ferry has ceased continuing to Bujumbura because of hostilities in the Burundian capital.

The fare between Mpulungu and Kigoma is US$55 for 1st class (in an upper-deck cabin with two beds), US$40 for 2nd class (a lower-deck cabin with six beds) and US$40 for economy class (a seat on the lower deck, if you're lucky). Fares must be paid for in US dollars, Zambian kwacha or Tanzanian shillings. Get your Tanzanian or Zambian visa before you leave; at least check the visa requirements for boat travel at the appropriate high commissions. Meals are available on the ferry.

---

the Lusaka section for details. If you're travelling from Siavonga, take a minibus or charter a car to the border, and walk (or take a shared taxi) across the impressive Kariba Dam to Kariba, from where buses leave daily to Harare. Most travellers cross at Livingstone – see the Victoria Falls chapter for details.

Getting Around

AIR

The main domestic airports are at Lusaka, Livingstone, Ndola, Kitwe, Mfuwe, Kasama and Kasaba Bay, though dozens of minor air strips cater for chartered planes.

Most domestic airlines have folded in the past few years, so the only scheduled internal flights are offered by **Zambian Airways** (W *www.africa-insites.com/zambianairways*) and occasionally, **Nationwide** (W *www .nationwideair.co.za*). The other major internal airline, **Travel International Air Charter** (*TIAC*, W *www.zambiz.co.zm/tiac*) temporarily suspended internal flights at the time of writing, but may be up and running by the time you to get to Zambia. Tickets for all airlines can be booked through any travel agent in Zambia.

The schedule for Zambian Airways is:

between	schedule	fare (US$) (one way)
Lusaka & Kitwe	daily	95
Lusaka & Ndola	daily	95
Lusaka & Mfuwe	Tues, Thur, Fri & Sun	145
Lusaka & Livingstone	Mon, Fri & Sun	135

Charter flight companies cater for guests staying at upmarket lodges/camps in national parks. Charter flights only leave with a minimum number of pre-booked passengers and fares are always high, but it's sometimes worth looking around for a last-minute stand-by flight. Check for special deals advertised in *The Lowdown* magazine in Lusaka, or contact one of these companies based at the airport in Lusaka (area code ☎ 01):

Airwave Avocet (☎ 770502, ⓔ avocet@zam net.zm)
Proflight Air Services (☎ 271035, ⓦ www.pro flight-zambia.com)

Departure Tax
The departure tax for domestic flights is k55,000. It is *not* currently included in the price of airline tickets bought in or outside of Zambia, and must be paid at the airport in kwacha.

BUS & MINIBUS
Distances are long, buses are often slow and many roads are badly potholed, so travelling around Zambia by bus and minibus can exhaust even the hardiest of travellers.

All main routes are served by ordinary public buses, which run on a fill-up-and-go basis or have fixed departures (these are called 'time buses'). 'Express buses' are faster – often terrifyingly so – and stop less, but cost about 15% more. In addition, several private companies run comfortable European-style express buses along the major routes, eg, between Lusaka and Livingstone, Lusaka and Chipata, and Lusaka and the Copperbelt region. These fares cost about 25% more than the ordinary bus fares and are well worth the extra kwacha. Tickets for these buses can often be bought the day before.

Many routes are also served by minibuses, which only leave when full – *really* full. Their fares can be more or less the same as ordinary buses. In remote areas the only public transport is often a truck or pick-up.

TRAIN
The Tazara trains between Kapiri Mposhi and Dar es Salaam in Tanzania (see the Getting There & Away section earlier in this chapter) can also be used for travel to/from northern Zambia. While the Lusaka–Kitwe service does stop at Kapiri Mposhi, the Lusaka–Kitwe and Tazara trains are not timed to connect with each other, and the domestic and international train terminals are 2km apart.

Zambia's only other railway services are the 'ordinary trains' between Lusaka and Kitwe, via Kapiri Mposhi and Ndola, and the 'express trains' between Lusaka and Livingstone. Refer to the relevant sections for schedules and costs.

These domestic trains are unreliable and slow, however, so buses are invariably better. Conditions on the trains vary, but generally range from slightly dilapidated to ready-for-scrap. Most compartments have no lights or locks, so take a torch and something to secure the door at night.

Tickets for all classes on domestic trains (but not the Tazara service) can be bought up to 30 days in advance. On the 'express train' between Lusaka and Livingstone, a 'sleeper' is a compartment for two people; 1st class is a sleeper for four; 2nd (or 'standard') class is a sleeper for six people; and 'economy' (or 3rd) class is a seat only. On the 'ordinary train' between Lusaka and Kitwe, 'standard' (2nd) class is also just a seat.

CAR & MOTORCYCLE
If you're driving into Zambia in a rented or privately-owned car or motorcycle, you will need a carnet; if you don't have one, a free Customs Importation Permit will be issued to you at major borders instead. Compulsory third-party insurance for Zambia is available at major borders (or the nearest largest towns) and costs about US$6 per month.

While it is certainly possible to get around Zambia by car or motorbike, many sealed roads are in bad condition and dirt roads can range from shocking to impassable – especially after the rains. If you haven't driven in Africa before, this is *no* place to start. Wearing a seat belt in the front seat is compulsory.

Petrol costs about US$0.80 per litre; diesel is slightly less. Distances between towns with filling stations are great and supplies are not always reliable, so fill up the tank whenever you can.

Rental

Cars can be rented from international and Zambian-owned companies in Lusaka, Livingstone, Kitwe and Ndola – for details refer to these sections later in this chapter. But renting in Zambia is expensive, so consider renting a car in Zimbabwe and taking it across to Zambia (see Car & Motorcycle in the Zimbabwe chapter for details).

For example, **Imperial Car Rental** (**w** www .zambiatourism.com/imperial) charges from US$41 per day for the smallest vehicle, plus US$0.35 per kilometre (less per day for longer rental periods). Add to this insurance (from US$12 per day) and petrol. Other companies, such as **Avis** (**e** avis@zamnet.zm), charge even more, but can arrange a driver for about US$50 extra per day, plus a daily and/or overnight allowance.

Most companies insist that drivers are at least 23 years old and have held a licence for at least five years; you can drive in Zambia using your driving licence from home as long as it's in English. Vehicles can be taken to Zimbabwe, Tanzania, Malawi and Mozambique if you give the car rental company enough notice.

HITCHING

Despite the general warning (see under Hitching in the Getting Around the Region chapter), hitching is a common way to get around Zambia. Some drivers, particularly expats, may offer you free lifts, but you should expect to pay for rides with local drivers (normally about the same as the bus fare, depending on the comfort of the vehicle). In such cases, agree on a price beforehand.

LOCAL TRANSPORT

The minibuses that ply the main roads in all cities and larger towns are a quick and easy to get around. For more comfort, however, taxis are also very good value. They have no meters, of course, so rates are negotiable.

ORGANISED TOURS

Tours and safaris around Zambia invariably focus on the national parks. Since many of these parks are hard to visit without a vehicle, joining a tour might be your only option anyway. Budget-priced operators run scheduled trips, or arrange things on the spot (with enough passengers), and can often be booked through a hostel or camp site. The upmarket companies prefer to take bookings in advance – directly, or through an agent in Zambia or your home country.

Companies running tours around Zambia as part of wider trips around Southern Africa are listed in the regional Getting There & Away chapter. Most Zambian tour operators are based in Lusaka and Siavonga (see those sections later), as well as Livingstone (see the Victoria Falls chapter). Several companies in Lilongwe (see the relevant section in the Malawi chapter) may also offer tours to South Luangwa National Park.

Lusaka

☎ 01 ● pop 1.2 million

The capital of Zambia is a big city, part modern and part traditional African, where dusty markets sit alongside high-rise blocks. Although Zambia is a fascinating country, Lusaka will never be a highlight for tourists. There are few notable buildings, monuments or other sights, but it does boast a lively ambience and genuine African feel. The markets are fascinating, there's a healthy arts scene and the nightlife throbs at weekends. If you have to be in Lusaka for a few days (eg, while waiting for yet another visa), you'll have no trouble passing the time pleasantly enough.

Orientation

The main street, Cairo Rd, is lined with shops, cafés, supermarkets, travel agencies, banks and bureaux de change. To the north is a major traffic circle and landmark, the North End Roundabout; to the south is the cunningly-named South End Roundabout. East of Cairo Rd are the wide jacaranda-lined streets of the smarter residential suburbs and the area officially called the Diplomatic Triangle (not surprisingly, home to many embassies and high commissions). West of Cairo Rd are the 'high density housing zones' (read 'townships').

Maps & Magazines The dusty **Map Sales** office (open 8.30am-3.30pm Mon-Fri) is

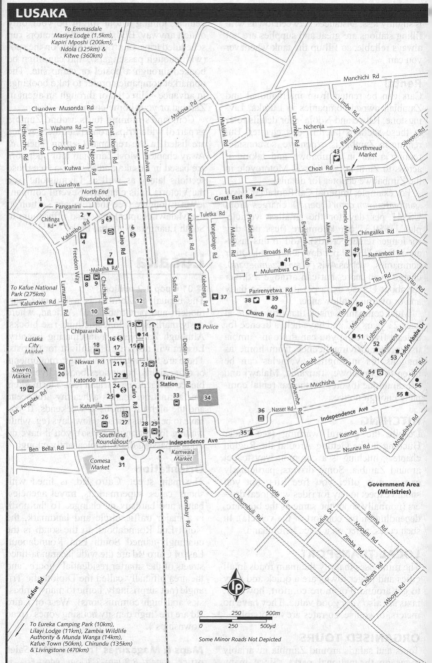

LUSAKA

To Emmasdale
Masiye Lodge (1.5km),
Kapiri Mposhi (200km),
Ndola (325km) &
Kitwe (360km)

Manchichi Rd

Chandwe Musonda Rd

Mukosa Pd

Makisni Rd

Limbe Rd

Luzambe Rd

Nchenja

Pasuli Rd

Sibwoni Rd

Washama Rd

Chishango Rd

Nchonchi Rd

Nwayi Rd

Musonda Ngosa Rd

Great North Rd

Wamululwa Rd

43

Northmead Market

Kutwa

Luanshya

Chozi Rd

North End Roundabout

1

Panganini

Great East Rd

42

Tuletka Rd

Omelo Mumba Rd

Chingalika Rd

2

Chifinga Rd

Kalambo Rd

3

5

6

Cairo Rd

Kabelenga Rd

Iongolongo Rd

Makishi Rd

Provident

Bwinjimfumu Rd

Mwiiwa Rd

Namambozi Rd

49

4

7

Broads Rd

41

Tito Rd

To Kafue National Park (275km)

Freedom Way

Malasha Rd

Chachacha Rd

Mulumbwa Cl

Kalundwe Rd

Lumumba Rd

8

9

Sadzu Rd

Kabelenga Rd

Parirenyetwa Rd

37

Tito Rd

50

Tito Rd

10

12

38

39

Mwenya Rd

Libwa Rd

Addis Ababa Dr

Lusaka City Market

Chiparamba

11

13

14

Church Rd

40

51

52

Hanswena Rd

53

Suez Rd

Soweto Market

18

16

17

15

Police

Deen Kinathi Rd

Chilubi

Nyakaseya Ituna Rd

54

56

19

20

Nkwazi Rd

21

22

23

Muchisha

55

Katondo Rd

24

25

Train Station

33

34

Dushambe Rd

36

Nasser Rd

Independence Ave

Katunjila

26

27

28

29

32

35

Kombe Rd

Moggadishu Rd

Ben Bella Rd

South End Roundabout

30

Independence Ave

Nsunzu Rd

Comesa Market

31

Kamwala Market

Government Area (Ministries)

Chilumbvuli Rd

Obote Rd

Indus St

Burma Rd

Mopani Rd

Kafue Rd

Bombay Rd

Zimba Rd

Chibwa Rd

Mboya Rd

To Eureka Camping Park (10km),
Lilayi Lodge (11km), Zambia Wildlife
Authority & Munda Wanga (14km),
Kafue Town (50km), Chirundu (135km)
& Livingstone (470km)

0   250   500m
0   250   500yd

Some Minor Roads Not Depicted

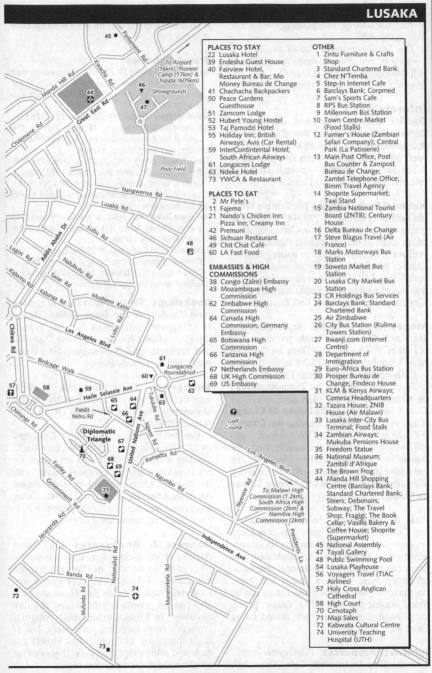

LUSAKA

ZAMBIA

PLACES TO STAY
22 Lusaka Hotel
39 Endesha Guest House
40 Fairview Hotel, Restaurant & Bar; Mo Money Bureau de Change
41 Chachacha Backpackers
50 Peace Gardens Guesthouse
51 Zamcom Lodge
52 Hubert Young Hostel
53 Taj Pamodzi Hotel
55 Holiday Inn; British Airways; Avis (Car Rental)
59 InterContinental Hotel; South African Airways
61 Longacres Lodge
63 Ndeke Hotel
73 YWCA & Restaurant

PLACES TO EAT
2 Mr Pete's
11 Fajema
21 Nando's Chicken Inn; Pizza Inn; Creamy Inn
42 Premuni
46 Sichuan Restaurant
49 Chit Chat Café
60 LA Fast Food

EMBASSIES & HIGH COMMISSIONS
38 Congo (Zaïre) Embassy
43 Mozambique High Commission
62 Zimbabwe High Commission
64 Canada High Commission; Germany Embassy
65 Botswana High Commission
66 Tanzania High Commission
67 Netherlands Embassy
68 UK High Commission
69 US Embassy

OTHER
1 Zintu Furniture & Crafts Shop
3 Standard Chartered Bank
4 Chez N'Temba
5 Step-In Internet Cafe
6 Barclays Bank; Corpmed
7 Sam's Sports Cafe
8 RPS Bus Station
9 Millennium Bus Station
10 Town Centre Market (Food Stalls)
12 Farmer's House (Zambian Safari Company); Central Park (La Patisserie)
13 Main Post Office, Post Bus Counter & Zampost Bureau de Change; Zamtel Telephone Office; Bimm Travel Agency
14 Shoprite Supermarket; Taxi Stand
15 Zambia National Tourist Board (ZNTB); Century House
16 Delta Bureau de Change
17 Steve Blagus Travel (Air France)
18 Marks Motorways Bus Station
19 Soweto Market Bus Station
20 Lusaka City Market Bus Station
23 CR Holdings Bus Services
24 Barclays Bank; Standard Chartered Bank
25 Air Zimbabwe
26 City Bus Station (Kulima Towers Station)
27 Bwanji.com (Internet Centre)
28 Department of Immigration
29 Euro-Africa Bus Station
30 Prosper Bureau de Change; Findeco House
31 KLM & Kenya Airways; Comesa Headquarters
32 Tazara House; ZNIB House (Air Malawi)
33 Lusaka Inter-City Bus Terminal; Food Stalls
34 Zambian Airways; Mukuba Pensions House
35 Freedom Statue
36 National Museum; Zambili d'Afrique
37 The Brown Frog
44 Manda Hill Shopping Centre (Barclays Bank; Standard Chartered Bank; Steers; Debonairs; Subway; The Travel Shop; Fragigi; The Book Cellar; Vasillis Bakery & Coffee House; Shoprite (Supermarket)
45 National Assembly
47 Tayali Gallery
48 Public Swimming Pool
54 Lusaka Playhouse
56 Voyagers Travel (TIAC Airlines)
57 Holy Cross Anglican Cathedral
58 High Court
70 Cenotaph
71 Map Sales
72 Kabwata Cultural Centre
74 University Teaching Hospital (UTH)

behind, and beneath, the government offices at the junction of Independence Ave and Nationalist Rd.

The Lowdown magazine is available at bookshops and grocery shops at the **Manda Hill Shopping Centre** (*Great East Rd*) and around the Diplomatic Triangle.

Information

Tourist Offices The head office of the **Zambia National Tourist Board** (☎ 229087; e *zntb@zamnet.zm; Century House, Cairo Rd; open 8am-1pm & 2pm-5pm Mon-Fri, 8am-12pm Sat*) has friendly enough staff but information is limited to Lusaka.

National Parks Offices The **Zambia Wildlife Authority** (*ZAWA;* ☎ 278244; e *zawares@coppernet.zm; Kafue Rd*) is in Chilanga, about 16km south of the city centre. Paradoxically, staff seem more interested in issuing hunting licences than helping foreigners visit national parks. The ZAWA office is accessible on the minibus to Chilanga or Kafue town from the City Bus Station or South End Roundabout.

Money Along Cairo Rd, the **Barclays** and **Standard Chartered Bank** have several branches (with ATMs). Both banks also have branches (with ATMs) at the Manda Hill Shopping Centre (Great East Rd).

To change cash, try the **Zampost Bureau de Change** (*inside the main post office, cnr Cairo & Church Rds*); **Delta Bureau de Change** (*Cairo Rd*); or **Prosper Bureau de Change** (*Findeco House, South End Roundabout, Cairo Rd*), which also offers reasonable rates for American Express travellers cheques. The only bureau de change open on Saturday afternoon and Sunday is **Mo Money Bureau de Change** (*Fairview Hotel, Church Rd*).

Post & Telephone The **main post office** (*cnr Cairo & Church Rds; open 8am-5pm Mon-Fri, 8am-12.30pm Sat*) contains Zambia's only reliable poste restante. International calls and faxes can be made at the **Zamtel** telephone office upstairs, while a dozen telephone booths (using tokens and phonecards) can be found outside the post office. Other 'phone shops' and 'fax bureaus' are dotted along Cairo Rd.

Internet Resources For 'cyber-mail', visit the **Step-In Internet Cafe** (*Cairo Rd*), which doubles as a telephone centre, or the incredibly popular and modern **Bwanji.com** (*Cairo Rd*).

Travel Agencies

Bimm Travel Agency (☎ 234372, W www.bimm.co.zm, Luangwa House, Cairo Rd), just south of the post office, is reliable and locally-run. It can also arrange car hire.

Steve Blagus Travel (☎ 227739, fax 225178, e sblagus@zamnet.zm, Nkwazi Rd) is the agency for American Express, Air France and a dozen upmarket lodges/camps.

The Travel Shop (☎ 253194, fax 250746, e travelshop@zamnet.zm, Manda Hill Shopping Centre, Great East Rd) is another agency for lodges/camps and safari companies, and it sells discounted airline tickets.

Voyagers Travel (☎ 253048, W www.zambiatourism.com/voyagers, Suezz Rd) arranges flights, hotel reservations and car hire.

Zambian Safari Company (☎ 228682, fax 222906, e reservations@zamsaf.co.zm, Farmers House, Cairo Rd) is also a booking agency for upmarket lodges/camps throughout Zambia.

Bookshops The best bookshop in Lusaka (and Zambia) is **The Book Cellar** (*Manda Hill Shopping Centre, Great East Rd*). It sells novels, coffee-table books about Zambia, and regional guidebooks, including those published by Lonely Planet.

Emergency Conditions and medical supplies are less than ideal at the major **University Teaching Hospital** (☎ 251200; *Nationalist Rd*).

Far better is the private clinic **Corpmed** (☎ 222612; *Cairo Rd*), behind Barclays Bank. Doctors available after hours are listed on the front door, and the company works with the countrywide emergency service **Medical Air Rescue Service** (*MARS;* ☎ 234290). Other emergency numbers are for the **police** (☎ 991; *Church Rd*) and **ambulance** (☎ 992).

Dangers & Annoyances Like most African cities, pickpockets take advantage of crowds, so be alert in the markets and bus stations and along the busy streets immediately west of Cairo Rd. There are usually enough people around during the day anywhere in Lusaka to dissuade potential criminals from targeting foreigners, but at night things are different. Most streets are dark and often empty, so even if you're on a tight budget, take a taxi at night.

Things to See & Do

The downstairs galleries in the **National Museum** (Nasser Rd; admission US$2; open 9am-4.30pm daily) are a perfect snapshot of Zambia, both past and present. The highlights are probably the impressive displays of contemporary Zambian paintings and sculpture. Upstairs are exhibits of cultural, ethnographical and archaeological interest; don't miss the display about witchcraft.

If you enjoyed the paintings and sculptures at the museum, head for the laid-back **Tayali Gallery** (Showgrounds, off Great East Rd; admission free; open 9am-5pm Mon-Fri, 10am-4pm Sat). This is where Zambian artists meet and work, and regularly display their artistic endeavours.

The **Town Centre Market** (Chachacha Rd; open daily 7am-7pm) is chaotic and, frankly, malodorous, but fascinating. Zambians get their bargains here, whether it's fruit and vegies, new and second-hand hardware, tapes or clothes. The market is relaxed and tourists don't get hassled.

The **Lusaka City Market** (Lumumba Rd; open 7am-5pm daily) is large and lively, but not as atmospheric (or smelly) as the Town Centre Market. The nearby **Soweto Market** (Los Angeles Rd; open 7am-7pm daily) is the largest market in Lusaka, but is more functional and lacks the traditional ambience of the other two. This is one place where you are most likely to be relieved of your valuables – so be careful.

The **Munda Wanga Wildlife Park & Sanctuary** (☎ 278456; e sanctuary@zamnet.zm; Kafue Rd, Chilanga; admission US$2; open 9am-4pm daily) has been recently taken over by new managers who thankfully care more about animal welfare than lining their pockets. The sanctuary features plenty of regional flora and fauna, though the American Black Bears look a little out of place. For visitors, the pool and bar are welcome additions. It's about 16km south of central Lusaka and accessible on any minibus heading towards Chilanga or Kafue town from the City Bus Station or South End Roundabout.

The spotlessly clean **Public Swimming Pool** (off Nangwenya Rd; admission US$1; open 9am-5pm Tues-Sun) is surrounded by a pleasant shaded area and is a great place to relax and unwind. **Horse riding** among wildlife can be arranged at **Lilayi Lodge** (see Places to Stay later) for about US$25 per person (two hours).

Places to Stay – Budget

Chachacha Backpackers (☎ 222257; w www.zambiatourism.com/chachacha; 161 Mulumbwa Close; camping per person US$3, dorm beds US$6, singles/doubles with shared bathroom US$12/14) is by far the most popular place for budget travellers. The garden, pool and bar are inviting, and other facilities include a restaurant (serving basic meals), a TV lounge, laundry service, a communal kitchen, baggage store and Internet access. Like most hostels in Southern Africa, however, it can be noisy, crowded and scruffy. On the other hand, it's a mine of information and a great spot to organise budget-priced tours. The singles/doubles should be reserved in advance, and if you do book ahead for any sort of accommodation ask about a free transfer from the bus or train stations.

YWCA (☎ 252800; Nationalist Rd; doubles with shared bathroom US$18) offers budget accommodation with a local feel for men and women. It's basic but very clean and friendly – and often full. The **restaurant** serves basic meals and is open to the public.

Emmasdale Masiye Lodge (☎ 096 767922; Great North Rd; singles/doubles with bathroom US$11/20, flats with bathroom & kitchen US$25) is 2.5km north of the North End Roundabout. The rooms are acceptable, while the flats (which sleep up to four) are a real bargain if you're in a group. Cheap food and grog are available, though the bar gets crowded some nights.

Peace Gardens Guesthouse (☎ 097 850101; 4 Tito Rd; doubles with bathroom US$15) is more of a popular bar-cum-restaurant than a guesthouse. The few tatty, musty rooms at the back of the gardens are nothing special, but they're good value for central Lusaka.

Hubert Young Hostel (☎ 250538; Church Rd; singles/doubles with shared bathroom US$4/5, suites with bathroom US$7-12) is fairly grubby and noisy at times, but safe and convenient. The rooms are certainly unpretentious, but the staff (when you can find any) are friendly. Breakfast costs an extra US$1, and guests can order local-style meals.

Eureka Camping Park (☎ 272351; w www.zambiatourism.com/eureka; camping per person US$5, chalets with shared showers

US$20-25, chalets with private bathroom US$30) is about 12km south of the city centre. The camp site is grassy and the security is good, while the swimming pool and bar (which sells snacks) are nice touches. Also, firewood is for sale. Minibuses from the City Bus Station or South End Roundabout go past the gate.

Pioneer Camp *(☎ 097 771936; W www .zambiatourism.com/pioneer; Palabana Rd, off Great East Rd; camping per person US$5, double chalets without/with bathroom US$20/30)* is signposted 5km south of Great East Rd and 17km east of the Manda Hill Shopping Centre. If you don't want to self-cater, there's a bar and **restaurant**. The friendly owners offer free transfers to/from the city on weekdays; otherwise, contact them beforehand for current advice about how to reach the camp by minibus.

Places to Stay – Mid-Range
All rooms in the hotels listed below contain a private bathroom, fan and TV, and all rates include breakfast.

Longacres Lodge *(☎ 254847; off Haile Selassie Ave; doubles US$33, suites US$53)* is a revamped government hostel with functional rooms. In mid-2002 it virtually doubled its prices overnight and is now exceedingly poor value. Hopefully, sense will prevail and the rates will drop soon.

Ndeke Hotel *(☎ 252779; off Los Angeles Blvd; singles/doubles US$30/50)* is also overpriced, but still popular with business groups and frustrated tourists who wish someone would build a reasonably priced mid-range hotel in the city centre. Many rooms are tiny, but the swimming pool is an attraction.

Zamcom Lodge *(☎ 253945; Church Rd; doubles US$35)* is new and not well known yet – even by taxi drivers. The rooms in this motel-style complex have no charm, but they also have no dirt or mosquitoes. Importantly, it offers the best value for a mid-range hotel in central Lusaka.

Endesha Guest House *(☎ 225780; Parirenyetwa Rd; doubles US$32-US$40)* is a cosy pension with only a handful of rooms (so book ahead). The 'standard' rooms have unattached, but private, bathrooms, while the more expensive rooms have a private bathroom inside. The bar is cosy and a great place to meet some interesting characters.

Fairview Hotel *(☎ 222604; e fairview@ zamnet.zm; Church Rd; singles/doubles US$62/ 67)* offers small, comfortable and well-furnished rooms within walking distance of the city centre. The attached **restaurant** is only just adequate, but the **terrace bar** is inviting.

Lusaka Hotel *(☎ 229049; e lushotel@zam net.zm; cnr Cairo & Katondo Rds; singles/ doubles US$47/52, doubles with air-con US$57)* is, remarkably, the *only* hotel in the city centre. It boasts a little (but not much) colonial charm and almost top-end facilities for a mid-range price. But the rooms are small and some are noisy.

Places to Stay – Top End
All rooms in the hotels listed here have a bathroom, air-conditioning and TV, and all rates include breakfast. The three hotels in the city also offer a business centre, swimming pool, travel desk and bookshop.

Holiday Inn *(☎ 251666; e holinn@zamnet .zm; cnr Church Rd & Independence Ave; singles/doubles US$120/150)* is convenient, popular and features several Western-style restaurants and bars. Discounted rates of about US$105/130 are possible with little prompting.

InterContinental Hotel *(☎ 250000; e lusaka@interconti.com; Haile Selassie Ave; singles/doubles from US$160/180)* offers the sort of amenities and rooms found in most of the hotels run by this chain throughout the world.

Taj Pamodzi Hotel *(☎ 254455; e pam odzi@zamnet.zm; Church Rd; singles/doubles US$80/90)* is a large multistorey complex with comfortable rooms offering views and all the mod cons. It looks a bit dated, but extensive renovations at the time of research should bring the hotel into the 21st century.

Lilayi Lodge *(☎ 279022; W www.lilayi .com; singles/doubles from US$80/90, about US$150/239 including meals and activities)* is one of Lusaka's finest options. The bungalows in this private wildlife reserve are very comfortable, and the gardens and pool are lovely. It offers horse riding (see Activities earlier in this chapter) and the chance to learn to play (horse) polo. The lodge is about 8km off Kafue Rd and about 13km south of the city centre, and only accessible by taxi or private/rented car.

Places to Eat

Several **food stalls** at the Town Centre Market (*Chachacha Rd*) serve cheap local food, but the scavenging dogs roaming the increasing piles of rubbish around the market may affect your appetite. Cleaner **food stalls** are dotted around the Lusaka Inter-City Bus Terminal (*Dedan Kimathi Rd*).

Fajema (*Cairo Rd; meals about US$2*), just back from the main road, is a far better place to try some tasty Zambian food while sitting inside a restaurant.

Junk-food junkies can flock to the corner of Cairo and Nkwazi Rds, where **Pizza Inn**, **Nando's**, **Chicken Inn** and **Creamy Inn** all share the same premises.

Alternatively, jump on the next minibus to the Manda Hill Shopping Centre (Great East Rd). At this huge, modern complex you'll find **Steers** (*US$3 for 'combo' burgers*), **Debonairs** (*US$2.50/3.50 for small/large pizzas*) and the incredibly popular **Subway**.

Fragigi (*☎ 255492; Manda Hill Shopping Centre, Great East Rd; sandwiches US$2.50, salads US$3*) is a pleasant and busy café where expats with time on their hands fritter away the afternoon. **Vasillis Bakery & Coffee House** (*Manda Hill Shopping Centre, Great East Rd; snacks about US$1.50*), nearby, serves tasty coffee and pastries, which can be enjoyed at the outside tables.

La Patisserie (*Central Park, cnr Cairo & Church Rds; snacks about US$1*), near Farmer's House, is a clean and modern bakery that sells sandwiches, rolls, pies and cakes. It's a welcome respite from the surrounding chaos along Cairo Rd.

LA Fast Food (*Longacres Roundabout, Haile Selassie Ave; meals US$2-3*) is an ideal place to grab a meal if you have to wait a while for your visa from any of the nearby embassies. Allow some time to plough through the confusing array of menus on the counter offering Chinese food, burgers, steaks and a hundred variations of 'chicken and chips'.

Premuni (*☎ 224609; 61 Great East Rd; meals US$3-6; open Wed-Mon*) is a large restaurant complex with a garden and outdoor tables. It offers 'multi-cuisine', in essence an eclectic range of dishes from Asia, Europe and Africa. The array of meatless options will delight frustrated and hungry vegetarians.

Sichuan Restaurant (*☎ 253842; Showgrounds, off Great East Rd; starters US$2-3, mains US$5-10*) is somewhat bizarrely situated in a warehouse at the Showgrounds. However, the prices are reasonable and the range of meals is tempting – where else in Zambia are you likely to be offered deep-fried crocodile meat and teppenyaki sizzling chicken?

Mr Pete's (*☎ 223428; Panganini Rd; meals US$5-9*) is a perennial favourite among hungry, meat-loving expats. It serves large dishes of beef, chicken and fish, though most guests seem to come for the specialty: barbequed spare ribs. It's in an unsavoury area chock-a-block with garages and spare parts shops, so take a taxi after dark.

Chit Chat Café (*☎ 234324; 5 Omelo Mumba Rd; meals about US$4; open 10am-6pm Mon-Thurs, 10am-10pm Fri & Sat*) is set up entirely for expats living in the surrounding leafy suburbs, so it charges accordingly. Still, it's a pleasant oasis within walking distance of a few places to stay.

Entertainment

Sam's Sports Cafe (*Malasha Rd*) is an ideal place to meet some entertaining locals while enjoying some cheap drinks. It's not particularly obvious from the street, so look for the bar behind the wooden panelling.

The Brown Frog (*Kabelenga Rd; open 11am-11pm daily*) is a British-style pub in an unremarkable warehouse. It's popular with South Africans and other expats, who come to play darts, pour coins into the video jukebox, and (most evenings) dance to live music. There's no cover charge for local bands, though you may have to pay about US$2 to see a big-name act.

Chez N'Temba (*Freedom Way; admission US$1-2*) is the best nightclub in the city centre, but offers mostly hardcore rhumba. It warms up at midnight and rocks until dawn, especially between Thursday and Sunday.

Zambili d'Afrique (*National Museum; Nasser Rd*) offers regular cultural evenings. The emphasis is on contemporary and traditional music and dance, and many readers have been delighted about how authentic and untouristy it is.

A healthy local performing arts scene means there's nearly always something on at the **Lusaka Playhouse** (*Church Rd; tickets about US$3*), but mostly on Friday and Saturday evenings. Programmes are advertised on posters around town and mentioned in *The Lowdown* magazine.

Shopping

The swish **Manda Hill Shopping Centre** (*Great East Rd*) is easy to reach by minibus from along Cairo Rd or from the Millennium Bus Station, or by taxi (US$2). As well as banks, bookshops, restaurants and fast-food outlets, the shopping centre boasts a huge **Shoprite** supermarket. Another Shoprite is along Cairo Rd.

Zintu Furniture & Crafts Shop (*Panganini Rd*) is the best place for quality souvenirs in the city centre. The choice is limited, but the carvings, fabrics and pottery on offer are well made and reasonably priced.

Kabwata Cultural Centre (*Burma Rd; open 9am-5pm daily*) is a scruffy collection of huts and stalls southeast of the city centre. Prices are cheap, however, because you can buy direct from the workers who live there. The specialties are carvings, baskets, masks, drums, jewellery and fabrics.

Zambili d'Afrique (*National Museum; Nasser Rd*) is a smart souvenir shop with a wide choice of imaginative items. Most are made for Western tastes and are not the sort of things you'll see in the markets. Lusaka's **markets** are covered in Things to See & Do earlier in this chapter.

Getting There & Away

Air For details about international and domestic flights to/from Lusaka, see Getting There & Away and Getting Around earlier in this chapter. The following major regional, domestic and international airlines have offices in Lusaka:

Air France (Steve Blagus Travel) – see Travel Agencies earlier
Air Malawi (☎ 228120) ZNIB House, Independence Ave
Air Zimbabwe (☎ 221750) Kariba House, 32 Chachacha Rd
British Airways (Com Air) (☎ 250579) Holiday Inn, Church Rd
KLM & Kenya Airways (☎ 255145) Comesa Headquarters, Ben Bella Rd
South African Airways (☎ 254350, ✉ saa@zam net.zm) InterContinental Hotel, Haile Selassie Ave
TIAC (Voyagers Travel) – see Travel Agencies earlier
Zambian Airways (☎ 225151, ✉ roanhq@zamnet .zm) Mukuba Pensions House, Dedan Kimathi Rd

Bus & Minibus To avoid some inevitable confusion and frustration, take a taxi to whichever station your bus/minibus leaves from. And if you arrive in Lusaka by bus/minibus in the middle of the night, do what the locals do and stay the rest of the night on the bus to avoid walking around any bus station after dark.

Domestic From in front of the massive and chaotic **Lusaka City Market Bus Station** (*Lumumba Rd*) buses and minibuses leave for nearby towns such as Chirundu (US$3) and Kapiri Mposhi (US$4.50), and destinations are more or less signposted. Public transport to other places, including Siavonga (US$3.50), leave from the **Soweto Market Bus Station** (*Los Angeles Rd*), where *nothing* is signposted, so you'll have to ask and ask again for the bus/minibus you want.

To add to the confusion, minibuses to places not far south of Lusaka, such as Kafue town (US$1), via Chilanga, leave from the **City Bus Station** (*off Chachacha Rd*), also called the Kulima Towers Station. And minibuses to the north (eg, the Manda Hill Shopping Centre) depart from the **Millennium Bus Station** (*Malasha Rd*).

All long-distance public buses (and a few private ones) use the **Lusaka Inter-City Bus Terminal** (*Dedan Kimathi Rd*), where there is a left luggage office and inquiries counter. From this terminal, buses and minibuses go several times a day to Ndola (US$5, four hours), Kitwe (US$5, five hours), Livingstone (US$8, seven hours) and Chipata (US$7/10 ordinary/express, eight hours), while buses operated by **JR Investments** go to Mongu (US$10, 12 hours) on Tuesday and Friday. It's certainly worth double-checking the schedules and booking your tickets one or two days before you leave.

The **RPS** bus company uses a chaotic lay-by along Freedom Way, and is worth avoiding because most buses leave at about 5am (or earlier). It offers buses to Kasama (US$10/13 ordinary/express, 14 hours) most days; to Mpulungu (US$16, 18 hours) three times a week; to Chipata (US$10) and Mongu (US$10) every day; and to Livingstone (US$7) at 7am and 1.30pm every day.

Euro-Africa has a station near South End Roundabout, on a back street between Cairo Rd and the railway line. Every day, it runs three buses and/or minibuses to Kitwe (US$6), via Ndola (US$5); one to Livingstone (US$8); and three or four to Kapiri Mposhi (US$4).

The bright yellow buses operated by **Marks Motorways** leave from a similarly coloured bus station along Nkwazi Rd. Every day, four buses head to Kitwe, via Ndola; one travels (at 8am) to Livingstone; and two leave (at 6am and 2pm) for Chipata. Fares are about the same as those charged by other private bus companies.

Buses operated by **CR Holdings Bus Services** depart from a spot just up from the train station. Every day, several comfortable buses leave for Kitwe, via Ndola, as well as Livingstone; and one goes to Mongu and Chipata. Fares are the same as those charged by other companies.

Another option worth considering is the **Post Bus**, which carries mail (and passengers) to Kasama (US$10) from outside the main post office (*cnr Cairo & Church Rds*) at 7am on Monday, Wednesday and Friday. Tickets are available in advance at the **post bus counter** (*open 7am-noon Mon-Fri, 7am-11am Sat & Sun*) inside the post office.

International All buses mentioned here (unless stated otherwise) leave from the **Lusaka Inter-City Bus Terminal** (*Dedan Kimathi Rd*).

To Botswana, **Smalls Transporters** provides buses to Gaborone (US$29, 22 hours), via Kasane (US$11) and Francistown (US$23) on Saturday and Tuesday, while **Bensten Express** also travels to Gabs on Monday and Thursday for about the same price.

For South Africa, **City to City** has buses every day to Johannesburg (US$27, 26 hours). **JR Investments** and **Vaal Africa** also travel to Jo'burg every day, but their buses are not as comfortable as those offered by City to City, though tickets are slightly cheaper. In addition, the reliable **Translux** buses travel to Jo'burg twice a week. All buses between Lusaka and Jo'burg travel via Harare, Masvingo and Pretoria.

To Zimbabwe, take any bus going to South Africa, or a **Trans Frontiers** bus directly to Harare (US$12, nine hours) on Monday, Wednesday and Saturday.

Buses to Dar es Salaam (US$35, 24 hours) run once or twice a week from the Comesa Market along Lumumba Rd, but services are less reliable these days (so take the train).

Train The *Zambezi Express* to Livingstone (US$4/5/7/8 economy/standard/1st class/sleeper, 15 hours), via Choma, leaves Lusaka at 6pm on Monday, Wednesday and Friday. Tickets are available from the **reservations office** inside the **train station** (*between Cairo & Dedan Kimathi Rds*) from 3pm to 5pm on the day of departure. Get there early and be prepared to hustle and bustle. Slow, ordinary trains to Kitwe (US$4/3/3 economy/standard/1st class, eight hours), via Kapiri Mposhi and Ndola, depart every day at about 10am.

Information about the Tazara train between Kapiri Mposhi and Dar es Salaam (Tanzania) is included in the Getting There & Away section earlier in this chapter.

Hitching Although we don't recommend hitching, many locals do it. There are several recognised places to wait for lifts: for eastern Zambia, including Chipata, wait just beyond the airport turn-off; for places to the south, go to the Chirundu–Livingstone junction 10km past Kafue town; and to the north, try at the junction north of Kapiri Mposhi.

Getting Around

To/From the Airport The international airport is about 16km northeast of the city centre. Taxis from the airport to central Lusaka cost about US$20, but *to* the airport drivers charge around US$12. There's no airport bus, but the upmarket hotels send courtesy minibuses to meet international flights, so you may be able to arrange a ride into town with the minibus driver (for a negotiable fee).

Bus & Minibus Local minibuses run along Lusaka's main roads, but there are no route numbers or destination signs, so the system is difficult to work out. See Bus & Minibus in the Getting There & Away section earlier for explanations about the confusing array of bus and minibus stations.

Otherwise, it is possible to flag down a minibus along a route. For instance, from the South End Roundabout, the 'Kabulonga' minibus goes along Independence Ave to Longacres Roundabout and then back towards the city along Los Angeles Blvd and Church Rd; the 'Chakunkula' or 'Chelston' minibus shuttles down Kafue Rd to Kafue town; and the 'Chilanga' minibus heads to Chilanga, via Kafue Rd. The standard fare is k1000 to k1500.

Car & Motorcycle Several international car rental companies, such as **Avis** (☎ 097 773978) and **Imperial** (☎ 271221), have counters at the airport, while **Avis** (☎ 251652) also has an office at the Holiday Inn (cnr Church Rd & Independence Ave).

Bimm Travel Agency (see Travel Agencies earlier) offers the cheapest rates. Vehicles cost from US$35 per day and US$0.35 per kilometre, plus US$10 per day for insurance, but the company inexplicably charges extra for keeping the car outside of Lusaka overnight.

Taxi Official taxis can be identified by the numbers painted on the doors, but hundreds of unofficial taxis also cruise the streets. Taxis can be hailed along the street or found at ranks near the main hotels and markets, and outside the Shoprite supermarket on Cairo Rd. Fares are negotiable, but, as a guide, US$2 to US$3 will get you from the train station to Manda Hill Shopping Centre.

The Copperbelt

The Copperbelt Province is the industrial heartland of Zambia and the main population centre outside of Lusaka. The world copper market slumped during the 1970s, so vast open-cast mines cut back production, thereby creating high unemployment in the area. But by 2001 most mines had become privatised and billions of dollars will be invested. The region is rarely visited by tourists, but it does provide an accessible view of rural Zambia for anyone not heading further east or north.

KAPIRI MPOSHI

This small but busy town, about 200km north of Lusaka, is at the southern end of the Tazara railway from Dar es Salaam (Tanzania) and at the fork in the roads to Lusaka, the Copperbelt and the Northern Province. If you get stuck at Kapiri Mposhi, there are some local **resthouses** along the main street, but the best option is the **Kapiri Motel** (singles/doubles with bathroom US$10/13).

If you're coming from Tanzania, there's a passport check before you can get out of the station, then a mad rush for buses (from outside the station) to Lusaka and elsewhere. Thieves and pickpockets thrive in the crowds and confusion, so take great care.

Buses and minibuses from Lusaka leave regularly (see Lusaka earlier in this chapter for details) than are a quicker and more convenient option than the local train from the capital. Note that the train station for the daily Lusaka–Kitwe service, which stops at Kapiri Mposhi, is about 2km from the **Tazara station** (☎ 05-271021). Refer to the Getting There & Away section earlier in this chapter for details about the trains from Kapiri Mposhi to Dar es Salaam.

NDOLA
☎ 02 • pop 500,000

About 325km north of Lusaka, Ndola is the capital of the Copperbelt region. So, it makes sense to visit the city's only real attraction: the **Copperbelt Museum** (Buteko Ave; admission US$3; open 9am-4.30pm daily) at the northeastern end of the main road (Buteko Ave). It showcases this local industry and, surprisingly, includes one of the best butterfly collections in Southern Africa.

Royal Hotel (☎ 621841; Vitanda St; singles US$15-20, doubles US$25-30), still sometimes referred to as the 'Travellers Lodge', is the best value in town. All rooms come with bathroom and breakfast. It's 1km north of the public bus station and 200m southwest of the train station.

New Savoy Hotel (☎ 611091; e savoy@zamnet.zm; Buteko Ave; singles/doubles with bathroom US$35/45) is a little bit classier and pricier than the Royal, and features an attractive terrace bar and pool. It's just north of the museum and 600m north of the public bus station.

Michelangelo's Café (Broadway), 1km west of the museum, is the best place in the region for Western delights, including drinkable coffee and edible pizzas.

Every day, **Zambian Airways** (☎ 621466) and/or **TIAC** (☎ 621096) offers flights between Lusaka and Ndola (US$75 to US$95 one way) though TIAC flights were temporarily suspended in early 2003. Zambian Airways also flies from Ndola to Kasama (US$125) and Kasaba Bay (US$165) on Tuesday and Friday. The airport is 3.5km south of the public bus station.

See Getting There & Away under Lusaka earlier in this chapter for information about buses and trains between Lusaka and Ndola. From the **public bus station** (off Chisokone Ave), three blocks south of Buteko Ave,

minibuses also run every few minutes to Kitwe. The **train station** (☎ 617641; off President Ave North) is 700m north of the museum. **Avis** (☎ 620741) and **Imperial** (☎ 620604) both have offices at the airport.

KITWE
☎ 02 • pop 700,000
About 60km northwest of Ndola is Zambia's second-largest city and the centre of the country's mining industry. Kitwe is pleasant, but the main reason to visit is the extensive **market** (Chisokone Ave; open 7am-7pm daily), one block west of the main street (Independence Ave).

The **YMCA** (☎ 211710; Independence Ave; doubles with breakfast & without/with bathroom US$15/25) is friendly but some rooms do face the noisy bar/restaurant. It's 1.5km north of the city centre.

Lothian House (☎ 222889; Chandamali Rd; singles/doubles with breakfast from US$15/20) is a former government hostel with musty but clean rooms. The more expensive rooms contain a private bathroom. It's 1km northeast of the city centre.

Sherbourne Guesthouse (☎ 222168; e sherbo@zamnet.zm; 20 Pamo Ave; singles/doubles with bathroom & breakfast from US$60/70) is 500m northeast of the city centre. The better rooms are in the main building, while the cheaper rooms are in the annex. It also has an excellent **restaurant**.

Arabian Nights (☎ 221097; 9th Ave; mains US$7-12) is worth the walk (800m) south of the southern end of Independence Ave. It serves European and Indian cuisine, and even a few Cajun dishes.

Zambian Airways (☎ 231316) flies to Lusaka daily (US$95 one way) from the airport, 3.5km east of the city centre. Refer to the Lusaka section earlier for details about buses and trains to Kitwe. The **public bus station** is 500m west of Independence Ave, and the **train station** (☎ 223078) is at the southern end of Independence Ave. **Avis** (☎ 224266) has an office at the airport, and **Imperial** (☎ 225056; 17 Enos Chomba Rd) is just east of Independence Ave.

CHIMFUNSHI WILDLIFE ORPHANAGE
On a farm 70km northwest of Chingola is this magnificent chimpanzee sanctuary (☎ 02-311255; w www.chimfunshi.org.za; admission US$5; open 8am-12pm daily). It is home to about 80 adult and young chimps confiscated from poachers and traders in nearby Congo (Zaïre) or brought from other parts of Africa, and apparently the largest of its kind in the world. This is not a natural wildlife experience, but it's still fascinating to observe the chimps as they feed, play and socialise.

The sanctuary is *not* interested in mass tourism, so only small numbers of visitors are allowed. And *please* do not come if you're sick in any way; the chimps can easily die of a simple disease like the 'flu. Visitors can stay at the **camp site** (US$10 per person) or **dormitory** (US$20) at the education centre, which has self-catering facilities. Bookings are essential through the **Friends of Chimfunshi** (☎/fax 0136-909368; e chimfunshiusa@aol.com; PO Box 3555, Kempton Park 1620, South Africa) or the local **office** (☎ 02-311293, fax 02-311100).

By car, take the crumbling dirt road – only really passable by 2WD with high clearance – towards Solwezi for about 50km from Chingola, then turn right at the signposted junction and follow it for 19km. Buses between Chingola and Solwezi can drop you off at the junction, from where you'll have to hike to the sanctuary.

Northern Zambia

Northern Zambia starts once you've passed the 'Pedicle' – the great tongue of Congo (Zaïre) territory that almost splits Zambia in two. The north is a beautiful and sparsely populated area of hills, valleys, lakes, rivers, wetlands and waterfalls, where you rarely meet another tourist. Distances between towns are long, and some sights are way off the beaten track, so it's easier to get around in a private/rented vehicle, though public transport is not hard to find.

SERENJE
Serenje is an unremarkable town, but you may find yourself changing buses or refuelling there. In the town centre, 3km north of the Great North Rd, there are some unappealing **resthouses** and a **bank**, but you're better off basing yourself at the junction along the main road, where there's a petrol station, shop and basic **restaurant**. At this junction, the **Siga-Siga Motel** (doubles with shared

ZAMBIA

bathroom US$8) offers basic but clean rooms and a friendly manager who can advise on local transport.

All buses between Lusaka and the Northern Province pass through Serenje. The Tazara train also stops at the Serenje train station, 3km north of the town centre.

KASANKA NATIONAL PARK

Zambia's only privately managed national park (W www.kasanka.com; admission US$10; open 6am-6pm daily) is highly recommended. During the months of November and December, this 450-sq-km park is home to five *million* migratory fruit bats, which blanket the sky for several minutes at dusk. It is also renowned for its vast numbers of swamp-loving sitatungas. (In fact, Kasanka is one of the best places in Africa to see these shy antelopes.)

Activities such as **boat rides**, **bush walks** and **canoeing** trips can be arranged at both camps (see Places to Stay). All profits from the park help fund projects that benefit the community and local environment.

Places to Stay

The only places to stay are **Wasa Camp** (☎/fax 01-253439; e kasanka@aol.com), which also acts as the park headquarters, and **Luwombwa Camp** (same contact details). Both offer simple self-catering rondavels with/without a bathroom for US$30/20 per person, or US$150 per person with full board, transfers (from the nearest airstrip) and several activities. Wasa is open all year, while Luwombwa is more likely to be closed in the wet season. Camping (US$10 per person) may be possible at the **Musande Campsite**, but check first.

Getting There & Away

From Lusaka, take a bus towards Mansa, or any bus heading north and change at Serenje for a minibus to Mansa. After turning off the Great North Rd, ask the driver to drop you off at the gate to Kasanka National Park near Mulembo village – not at Kasanka village. From the gate it's a pleasant 12km hike to Wasa Camp or radio for a lift from the gate (US$10 per vehicle).

With your own wheels, continue north along the Great North Rd from Serenje for 36km, turn left towards Mansa, and then drive 55km to the gate.

BANGWEULU WETLANDS

South and east of **Lake Bangweulu** is a vast seasonally flooded area known as the Bangweulu Wetlands (or Bangweulu Swamps). This fascinating and rarely visited part of Zambia supports vast herds of black lechwes (antelopes with long, curved antlers). About 400 species of birds have also been noted, including the strange and rare shoebill storks. The ideal time for bird-watching is April to June, though July and August are still pretty good. May to July is best for seeing the lechwes.

Shoebill Camp (☎/fax 01-253439; W www.kasanka.com; camping per person US$10, self-catering chalets with shared bathroom per person US$30, including meals, transfers from the nearest airstrip and several activities per person US$150; open Apr-Nov) is in the heart of the wetlands. It's not particularly great value, but you pay for the splendid position, with only birds, hippos, lechwes and the occasional passing fishermen for company. Booking are essential, especially if you want meals and need to be taken to the camp by boat.

The only way into the wetlands is by vehicle (2WD is normally OK) and chartered planes. From the Kasanka park gate (where you can get help with directions), dirt roads lead via Lake Waka-Waka and Muwele to the Chikuni ranger post, from where you can drive to Shoebill Camp if it's dry. In the wet, you'll have to travel the last 2km by boat.

SAMFYA

Perched on the western shore of Lake Bangweulu, about 10km east of the main road between Mansa and Serenje, is Samfya. This small trading centre and lake transport hub is small enough to get to know people and large enough to have resthouses, restaurants and bars. Just outside town is the majestic, sandy **Cabana Beach**.

Transport Hotel (singles/doubles with shared bathroom US$3/4, doubles with bathroom US$10), at the port, offers basic rooms. A bar and **restaurant** is next door.

Bangweulu Lodge (☎ 02-830124; camping per person US$5, singles/doubles with shared bathroom US$15/25) offers comfortable accommodation along Cabana Beach. Staff can arrange **boat trips** for any anglers who want to fight tigerfish. Look for the signs about 2km from town.

Samfya is regularly served by minibuses from Serenje. Buses from Lusaka may drop you into town or at the junction 10km away, from where local pick-ups shuttle passengers to and fro. Ask around about jumping on a **passenger boat** around the lake.

SHIWA NG'ANDU

The vast estate of Shiwa Ng'andu (admission US$1; open 9am-4pm daily) was established in the 1920s by Stewart Gore-Brown, a paternalistic British aristocrat. At its heart is the incongruous, abandoned mansion of **Shiwa House**, described in *The Africa House* by Christina Lamb (see Books in the Facts for the Visitor section earlier in this chapter).

Kapishya Hot Springs is about 20km west of Shiwa House, but still on the Shiwa Ng'andu estate. You can swim to your heart's content (the water never gets cold) at these marvellous springs. From the lodge (see following), **walking**, **fishing** and **canoeing** trips are also offered, as well as safaris to the North Luangwa National Park (see the Eastern Zambia section later in this chapter).

Kapishya Lodge (☎ 01-228682; e *reservat ions@zamsaf.co.zm; camping per person US$5, self-catering chalets per person US$35, with meals & activities per person US$100*) overlooks the river. Bring your own food for the staff to prepare, or the friendly management can provide meals with enough notice.

To reach Shiwa House, head along the highway by bus (or car) from Mpika for about 90km towards Chisoso. Look for the signpost to the west, from where a dirt road (13km) leads to the house. There is no public transport along this last section.

KASAMA
☎ 04

Kasama is the capital of the Northern Province and the cultural centre for the Bemba people. You might find yourself stuck there overnight if you're travelling between Lusaka and Mpulungu, or getting off the Tazara train before exploring the north.

If so, try the **Elizabeth Guesthouse** (*singles/doubles with shared bathroom US$6/ 12*) near the Tazara station. Close by, **Kapongolo Resthouse** (*doubles with bathroom & breakfast US$12*) offers small but clean rooms.

Thorn Tree Guesthouse (☎/fax 221615; e *kansato@zamnet.zm; 612 Zambia Rd;*

singles US$15-20, doubles US$25) offers very comfortable rooms (all with breakfast) in lush and colourful gardens. The **restaurant** is recommended. As you reach Kasama from Lusaka, turn left at the first crossroads, keep right at the forks and continue past the Heritage Centre for 1km.

Every Tuesday and Friday, **TIAC** airlines used to do a loop connecting Kasama with Ndola (US$125 one way), Lusaka (US$160) and Kasaba Bay (US$40), but flights were temporarily suspended in early 2003. Most days, buses and minibuses leave for Lusaka (US$10/13 ordinary/express, 14 hours), via Serenje. From Kasama, minibuses also run to Mpulungu, via Mbala. The Tazara train station is 5km south of the town centre.

MBALA

Mbala is perched on the edge of the Great Rift Valley. From this small town, the road north drops over 1000m in less than 40km down to Mpulungu and Lake Tanganyika.

The main reason to come is the **Moto Moto Museum** (*admission US$5; open 9am-4.45pm daily*), about 3km from the town centre. This huge and fascinating collection of artefacts centres on the Bemba people.

Grasshopper Inn (☎ 04-450589; *singles/ doubles with bathroom US$7/10*) is about 750m off the main street. The rooms are simple, but clean, and the bar and **restaurant** are appealing.

Old Soldier's Restaurant (*meals about US$1.50*), along the main street, offers good company and helpful information about local attractions.

All buses/minibuses travelling between Mpulungu and Kasama stop in Mbala.

KALAMBO FALLS

About 40km northwest of Mbala, and along the border between Zambia and Tanzania, is the 221m-high Kalambo Falls (*admission free; permanently open*). Twice as high (but nowhere near as expansive) as the Victoria Falls, Kalambo is the second-highest single drop waterfall in Africa (after Tugela Falls in South Africa). From spectacular viewpoints near the top of the falls, you can see the Kalambo River plummeting off a steep V-shaped cliff cut into the Rift Valley escarpment into a deep valley, which then winds down towards Lake Tanganyika.

There is nowhere to stay, so you'll have to daytrip from Mbala. If you don't have a vehicle, ask around the Old Soldier's Restaurant in Mbala (see earlier), where someone will take you for a negotiable US$20 to US$30 per person return.

Alternatively, the falls are accessible by boat from Mpulungu. A daily taxi boat serves villages along the lakeshore east of Mpulungu, but just getting to Nyamba village (the start of the walk) can take all day. So, it's better to hire a private boat from the Mpulungu harbour for about US$20 per day plus fuel (around US$15), though the lodges around Mpulungu (see that section following) charge about double this.

It takes about two hours on foot from Mpulungu to Nyamba, from where the two to three hour walk one way starts to the falls. A local guide (about k5000) is essential and can be arranged in Nyamba. This part of Zambia is always hot, so start early and be prepared.

MPULUNGU
☎ 04

Zambia's only international port is the terminal for the ferry across Lake Tanganyika to Tanzania (see the Getting There & Away section earlier in this chapter). Mpulungu is also a lively crossroads between Eastern, Central and Southern Africa. Although it's always very hot, don't be tempted to swim in the lake because there are a few crocs.

Places to Stay

Nkupi Lodge (☎ 455166; camping per person US$4, rondavels with shared bathroom per person US$10) is a long-time favourite, about 1.2km northeast of the town centre. A **bar/restaurant** is attached but the choice of meals is limited.

Harbour Inn (singles/doubles with bathroom US$6/12), between the port and bus station, offers comfortable and clean rooms. A popular bar is attached.

Tanganyika Lodge (☎ 455130; camping per person US$5, chalets with shared bathroom per person US$12-15) is in a superb spot about 6km west along the lake. A bar and **restaurant** are attached, and staff can help arrange fishing **boats** to Kalambo Falls. Look for the signpost along the main road about 5km before town. Otherwise, jump in any taxi boat going towards Kasakalbwe village from near the Mpulungu market.

Getting There & Away

Most buses/minibuses tie in with the Lake Tanganyika ferry – see the Getting There & Away section earlier in this chapter for details. To/from Lusaka, RPS buses (US$16, 18 hours) travel three times a week via Kasama and Mbala. Alternatively, take the Tazara train to Kasama, from where minibuses leave when bursting. Minibuses also depart from near the BP petrol station in Mpulungu for Mbala.

NSUMBU (SUMBU) NATIONAL PARK

This frequently overlooked park (admission US$10; open 6am-6pm daily) covers a beautiful area of hilly grassland and escarpment, bisected by several rivers and wetland zones, on the southern shore of Lake Tanganyika. Like other remote parks in Zambia, Nsumbu was virtually abandoned in the 1980s and wildlife was decimated by poaching. But recently conditions have improved, and herds of elephants and buffaloes are now seen regularly. Other animals include bushbucks, waterbucks and pukus, all of which are easy prey for the commonly-seen lions and elusive leopards.

Most visitors come for the seriously good **fishing**, especially to catch large and feisty Goliath tigerfish. Bring your own fishing gear, though you can charter a boat through the lodges listed here.

Kasaba Bay Lodge (☎ 01-263973, fax 01-265560; with all meals per person US$200; open all year) is at the northern tip and near the airstrip. It caters mainly for anglers, so if you don't like fishing you'll have nothing to talk about to anyone else staying there.

Nkamba Bay Lodge (☎ 01-288884, fax 01-287677; rooms with bathroom & breakfast per person US$65; open all year) is better value compared to the other lodges, but still nothing fantastic. The views are spectacular.

Ndole Bay Lodge (☎ 02-711150; e ndole bay@coppernet.zm; camping per person US$15, 4 bed chalets with full board per person US$125) is spectacularly located on the lakeshore just outside the northwestern boundary of the park. This is probably the best place to arrange activities, including boat hire for wildlife viewing or angling, bird walks (free for guests), wildlife drives and various water sports. Campers can also eat at the lodge.

Each lodge arranges transfers for guests from the airstrip, or across the lake from Mpulungu. **TIAC** airlines used to do a loop on Tuesday and Friday linking the Kasaba Bay airstrip, near Kasaba Bay Lodge, with Kasama (US$40 one way), Lusaka (US$200) and Ndola (US$165), but flights were temporarily suspended in early 2003. Hardy overlanders can drive, but come from the southwest, via Mporokoso, where the roads are not so treacherous. If travelling independently, charter a boat from Mpulungu.

NAKONDE

Nakonde, on the southern side of the border between Zambia and Tanzania, is full of hustlers and worth avoiding if you can. If you do get stuck, there are a few unappealing **resthouses**, such as the **Lwabazi Inn**, but these often fill on the nights before and after the Tazara train comes through.

Eastern Zambia

This section covers the area to the east of Lusaka, including the border towns of Chirundu and Chipata, and the Lower Zambezi and South Luangwa National Parks.

CHIRUNDU

This border town on the main road between Lusaka and Harare has a few shops and bars, as well as a **bank** and a clutch of money-changers (mostly at the border). The only reason to stay is if you're going to arrange a canoe trip along the Zambezi River – see the Middle Zambezi Canoe Safaris section in the Zimbabwe chapter for details – or planning to explore the Lower Zambezi National Park (following).

Nyambadwe Motel (doubles without/with bathroom US$12/15), right on the border in Chirundu, is noisy and unappealing, but certainly convenient. The dearer rooms with a bathroom are worth paying extra for.

Gwabi Lodge (☎ 01-515062; camping per person US$5, chalets with bathroom & breakfast US$20-30), 11km from Chirundu towards the Lower Zambezi National Park, has marvellous lush grounds, though the camping area is a bit dusty. Other attractions are the bar, **restaurant**, swimming pool and terrace with one of the best views in Africa. **Boat rides** are also available. Head north through the truck park just before the border, then along the dirt road. Unless you've got your own wheels, you'll have to hitch or walk.

Minibuses leave regularly for Chirundu from Lusaka (US$3, 3½ hours).

To reach Siavonga (on Lake Kariba) from Chirundu, catch a minibus towards Lusaka, get off at the obvious turn-off to Siavonga and wait for something else to come along.

LOWER ZAMBEZI NATIONAL PARK

Zambia's newest national park (admission US$20; open 6am-6pm daily) covers 4092 sq km along the northwestern bank of the Zambezi River opposite the Mana Pools National Park in Zimbabwe. Overlooked for many years, this is now one of Zambia's premier parks, with a beautiful flood plain alongside the river, dotted with acacias and other large trees, and flanked by a steep escarpment on the northern side, covered with thick miombo woodland.

The best wildlife viewing is on the flood plain and along the river itself, so **boat rides** are a major feature of all camps and lodges. Seeing groups of elephant swim across the river, or hundreds of colourful bee-eaters nesting in the steep sandy banks, could be the highlight of your trip. The best time to visit is March to December.

The main entrance is at **Chongwe Gate** along the southwestern boundary, though there are gates along the northern and eastern boundaries for hardy travellers.

Places to Stay

We can only mention a few of the numerous places to stay in and outside of the park. The rates listed here are per person in the high season (April to October) staying in twins/doubles; single supplements are usually 30% extra. (The rates for camping are also per person.) Also, add on transfers – eg, about US$90 per person return by road from Lusaka.

Community Campsite (camping US$5; open all year) is a basic place a few kilometres before Chongwe Gate. It's mainly set up for travellers with their own vehicles. Run by local people, the modest profits are put back into the community.

Lower Zambezi River Camp (☎ South Africa 031-5639774; ℮ info@kiambi.co.za; camping US$10, tented rooms with bathroom

ZAMBIA

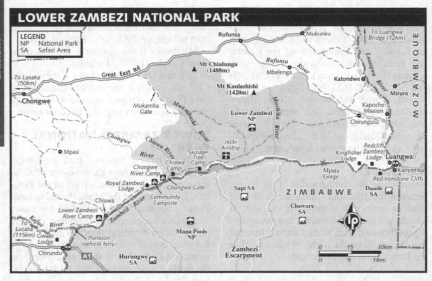

LOWER ZAMBEZI NATIONAL PARK

US$25; open March–mid-Jan) is the only budget place inside the park. It offers a swimming pool, communal kitchen and shady riverside camp site, and can arrange river cruises and canoe trips. Follow the signs from the Chirundu border for 23km.

Royal Zambezi Lodge (☎/fax 01-274901; W www.royalzambezi.com; camping US$35, chalets including meals & activities US$250; open all year) is a few kilometres southwest of Chongwe Gate. It offers luxurious walk-in tents, a **restaurant** overlooking the river and a splendid aerial bar built around the branches of a tree. Wildlife drives and boat rides are easy to arrange.

Chongwe River Camp (☎ 02-228682; W www.chongwe-river.com; camping US$12, chalets including meals & activities US$190; open all year) is on the confluence of the Zambezi and Chongwe Rivers, almost at Chongwe Gate. It offers a handful of tented thatched chalets with self-catering facilities and two camp sites.

Chiawa Camp (☎ 01-261588; W www .chiawa.com; including meals and activities US$400; open Apr-Oct) is a luxurious lodge inside the park at the junction of the Chiawa and Zambezi Rivers. The large, walk-in tents feature pine-clad private bathrooms, while the food is always top quality. The bar/lounge has an upstairs deck with majestic views over the river.

Sausage Tree Camp (☎ 01-272456; W www.sausagetreecamp.com; including meals & activities US$395; open May–mid-Nov) is further downstream from Chiawa Camp. The six tented chalets are cool and elegantly furnished in a Bedouin-style, each in its own private clearing, with minimal furniture and open-air bathrooms. Rates do sometimes drop as 'low' as US$175; check with travel agents in Lusaka and adverts in *The Lowdown* magazine.

Redcliff Zambezi Lodge (☎ 01-223641; W www.redcliff-lodge.com; including meals & activities US$175; self-drive packages with meals but no activities from US$90; open all year) offers six luxury chalets, as well as an inviting pool, for sports fishermen. Packaged deals are sometimes advertised in *The Lowdown*, eg, a 'two night getaway' for US$275 per person including transport by road and boat from Lusaka. If you have a private vehicle, contact them about a (free) boat transfer from near Luangwa.

Kingfisher Lodge (☎ 01-290146; e rshen ton@zamnet.zm; self-drive & self-catered US$50, with transport from Lusaka included US$120; open all year) is a small and secluded place, nestled under spectacular hills and cliffs. It caters for more budget-minded travellers and offers affordable hiking and fishing trips. Prices include boat transfers.

Getting There & Away

There's no public transport to Chongwe Gate, nor anything to the eastern and northern boundaries, and hitching is very difficult. Most people visit the park on an organised tour, and/or stay at a lodge that offers wildlife drives and boat rides as part of the deal.

For budget travellers, Chachacha Backpackers (see Places to Stay under Lusaka earlier in this chapter) operates popular five-day safaris from Lusaka. These are great value: US$380 per person includes transport from Lusaka, river cruises, canoe trips, bush walks, wildlife drives and fishing trips.

Getting Around

Drivers can reach the park independently and use the track from Chongwe Gate that runs alongside the Zambezi, but if you're going anywhere east of Jecki Airstrip you'll need a 4WD vehicle. There are several loops inside the park for wildlife-viewing, but these change from year to year, so pick up a guide at any of the gates.

One adventurous way to visit the park is by canoe along the Zambezi. Most of the lodges listed previously offer two/three-day canoe trips, with stops at seasonal camps along the river or makeshift camps on midstream islands. Otherwise, check the Middle Zambezi Canoe Safaris section in the Zimbabwe chapter for information about canoe trips along this part of the mighty Zambezi.

LUANGWA BRIDGE

The Great East Road crosses the Luangwa River on a large suspension bridge about halfway between Lusaka and Chipata. The nearby settlement of Luangwa Bridge serves as an ideal pace to break up the journey though there's little more than a few shops and souvenir stalls – but no petrol station. (Luangwa Bridge is about 80km north of Luangwa village, which is near the eastern end of the Lower Zambezi National Park, and far from the South and North Luangwa National Parks.)

Luangwa Bridge Camp (☎ 01-290146; **w** www.zambiatourism.com/changachanga; camping per person US$3, singles/doubles chalets with shared bathroom US$15/25) is on the western side of the river, about 3km south of the main road. This is an excellent place to base yourself for a couple of days of rest and relaxation. It features clean ablution blocks, cooking facilities and shady lawns, as well as a bar, restaurant and plunge pool. The chalets are built on a hill with river views, while the camp site is shady and clean. Short and long **hikes** and **canoe trips** can be arranged at the camp.

Get off any bus between Lusaka and Chipata at the place called 'Luangwa station', from where it's a 3km walk to the camp.

CHIPATA

☎ 062

Chipata is the primary town near the Zambian side of the border with Malawi, and a base from which to venture into the South Luangwa National Park. Many travellers rush through, but it's worth staying overnight, if only to recover from the arduous bus trip from Lusaka. Chipata is lively and friendly, and boasts a large **market** (500m north of the town centre), as well as several bars, cafés, petrol stations and banks.

Places to Stay & Eat

Camping Ground (☎ 254226; **e** wcsz@zam net.zm; Parerenyatwa Rd; camping per person US$3), run by the Wildlife Society of Zambia, is about 1.2km southeast of the bus station – turn off the main street at the BP petrol station along the main street (Umodzi Hwy) and continue east for two blocks.

Kapata Resthouse (☎ 21078; Umodzi Hwy; doubles with shared bathroom US$6) is about 150m north of the bus station and 1km north of the town centre. It's cheap, safe and fairly clean, and food is available.

Pine View (☎ 22143; off Umodzi Hwy; doubles without/with bathroom US$10/13) is probably the best option. The rooms are clean and face a large courtyard and pleasant garden. Walk (200m) east along the unnamed street opposite the Shoprite supermarket along the main street.

My Own Favourite Restaurant (meals about US$2), near the market, was recommended by one reader because it was clean and the food was tasty.

Getting There & Away

Several bus companies in Lusaka offer services to Chipata – refer to Getting There & Away under Lusaka earlier in this chapter for details. See South Luangwa National Park later in this chapter for details about travelling between Chipata and the park, and the

general Getting There & Away section earlier in this chapter for information about crossing the border to Malawi.

SOUTH LUANGWA NATIONAL PARK
☎ 062

For scenery, variety of animals, accessibility and choice of accommodation, South Luangwa (admission per person/vehicle US$25/15; open 6am-6pm daily) is the best park in Zambia and one of the most majestic in Africa. Vegetation ranges from dense woodland to open grassy plains, and mammals include lions, buffaloes, Cookson's wildebeest, kudus, bushbucks, waterbucks, impalas and pukus. This 9050-sq-km park also contains endemic Thornicroft's giraffes, many leopards, and one of the continent's largest numbers of elephants. The birdlife is also tremendous: about 400 species have been recorded. But the insectlife is also plentiful, so take precautions against malarial mosquitoes and tsetse flies.

The wide Luangwa River is the lifeblood of the park. It flows all year, but gets very shallow in the dry season (May to October). At this time, the vast sandbanks are exposed, but usually covered by groups of hippos and/or crocs basking in the sun. Steep exposed banks mean animals often have to drink at the park's numerous oxbow lagoons, formed as the river continually changes its course.

The focal point is Mfuwe, a village with shops, as well as a petrol station and market. About 1.8km further on is **Mfuwe Gate**, the main entrance to the park, where a bridge crosses Luangwa River and several cheaper lodges/camps and camp sites are set up. This part of the park can get comparatively busy with vehicles, but only because it's the best wildlife-viewing area. But in Zambia everything is relative: compared to rush-hour-rally-style safaris in Kenya, it's positively peaceful around Mfuwe. (Note that lots of wild animals in this area makes walking around at night very dangerous.)

Although South Luangwa is hard to visit on the cheap, there are more options for the budget-conscious here than most other parks in Zambia. But remember: one-night's budget accommodation, park fees, meals and a wildlife drive will give you little change from US$100. If this is out of your range, it's probably not worth coming.

Most of park is inaccessible between November and April (especially February and March), so many lodges close at this time.

Activities
Unlike other parks in Zambia, boat trips are not available in South Luangwa, but all lodges/camps run excellent day or night **wildlife drives** (all year) and **walking safaris** (June to November). These activities are included in the rates charged by the upmarket places, while the cheaper lodges/camps can

---

Norman Carr & South Luangwa

The history of South Luangwa National Park is inextricably linked with the story of Norman Carr, a leading wildlife figure whose influence and contribution to conservation has been felt throughout Africa.

One year after the North and South Luangwa Game Reserves were created in 1938 to protect and control wildlife populations, Carr became a ranger there. With the full backing of the area's traditional leader, Carr created Chief Nsefu's Private Game Reserve in 1950 and opened it to the public (until this time reserves had been for the animals only). All visitor fees were paid directly to the chief, thus benefiting the wildlife and the local community.

Carr was years ahead of his time in other fields too: he built Nsefu Camp, the first tourist camp in Zambia and developed walking safaris. In the following decades, other game reserves were created, more tourists came to Luangwa parks and more camps were built along the river.

In 1972 Nsefu and several game reserves were combined to form the South Luangwa National Park, but poaching of elephants and rhinos soon became an increasing problem. So, in 1980 Carr and several others formed the Save the Rhino Trust, which helped the government parks department to deter poachers.

In 1986 Carr opened yet another camp, Kapani Lodge, and continued operating safaris from this base. He retired from 'active service' in the early 1990s, but died in April 1997, aged 84.

ZAMBIA

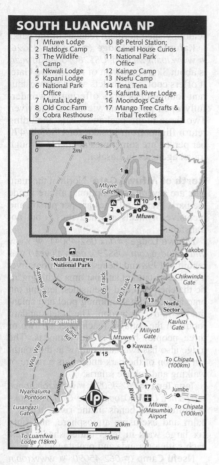

SOUTH LUANGWA NP

1	Mfuwe Lodge	10	BP Petrol Station;
2	Flatdogs Camp		Camel House Curios
3	The Wildlife	11	National Park
	Camp		Office
4	Nkwali Lodge	12	Kaingo Camp
5	Kapani Lodge	13	Nsefu Camp
6	National Park	14	Tena Tena
	Office	15	Kafunta River Lodge
7	Murala Lodge	16	Moondogs Café
8	Old Croc Farm	17	Mango Tree Crafts &
9	Cobra Resthouse		Tribal Textiles

Most lodges/camps in South Luangwa are along the banks of the river or at an oxbow lagoon. Several lodges/camps also have smaller 'bush camps' deep in the park, where they operate walks or drives away from the busier areas. Despite the rustic title, most 'bush camps' are very comfortable, with large tents, private bathrooms and excellent food. Joining a **walking safari** for a few days from one bush camp to the next is a popular and wonderful way to really experience the sights, sounds and smells of the bush.

Several budget places are just outside the park boundary, so you don't pay admission fees until you actually enter the park. Note that some lodges/camps open only in the high season (April to November), but those in and around Mfuwe are open all year. Places that open in the low (or 'green') season offers substantial discounts – often up to 40%. The rates listed here are per person in the high season for double/twin rooms; single supplements usually cost 30% more. The camping rates are also per person.

Moondogs Café, next to the Mfuwe (Masumba) airport, has a radio link with Flatdogs and the other lodges, so you can check availability and possible transfers.

Places to Stay – Budget & Mid-Range

All places mentioned here are outside the park and open all year.

Cobra Resthouse *(singles/doubles with shared bathroom US$3/6; Mfuwe)* is particularly useful if you arrive after dark or need to catch a crack-of-dawn minibus out. For this price, however, amenities are fairly basic.

Flatdogs Camp *(☎ 45068; W www.zambia tourism.com/flatdogs; camping US$5, chalets with bathroom US$25)* gets consistently good reviews for its excellent facilities, including a restaurant, bar, pool and shop. The self-catering chalets are surprisingly luxurious and everyone loves to watch wildlife along the river from the camp. Wildlife drives and walking safaris can be organised at affordable rates.

Old Croc Farm *(☎ 45074; e mfucroc@super -hub.com; camping US$3, chalets with shared bathroom US$12)* is based in the old site once occupied by Flatdogs. It's an appealing and reasonably shady spot along the river, with a pool and bar/restaurant serving unexpectedly good coffee and cakes. Wildlife drives and

organise things with little notice. A two-hour morning or evening wildlife drive normally costs US$25, while a **night drive** (US$30) offers the chance to spot an elusive leopard. These costs are based on three or four people in the car; you may be able to team up with others – but don't bank on it.

Places to Stay

We can only list a few of the numerous camp sites and lodges/camps in and around the park. When you're deciding where to stay, consider the size of the lodge/camp. It's not necessarily a question of quality, but more one of atmosphere. Some visitors like the intimate, exclusive feel of the smaller places, while others prefer the facilities and livelier atmosphere of the bigger lodges/camps.

walking safaris can be arranged, and transfers from Mfuwe are available.

The Wildlife Camp (☎/fax 45026; ⓦ www .wildlifecamp-zambia.com; camping US$5, tent hire US$10, self-catering chalets with bathroom US$22) is a spacious, quiet and secluded place, about 5km west of Mfuwe village. The self-catering chalets sleep up to three people, while the separate camp site has its own bar (with meals), pool and communal kitchen. The owners are admirably committed to local wildlife conservation. Check *The Lowdown* magazine in Lusaka for packages from US$80 per person per day including meals and activities.

Marula Lodge (☎ 45073; ⓔ marula@zam net.zm; chalets with bathroom & 2 bedrooms US$25) is about 400m east of Mfuwe Gate. It's a no-frills place offering good value and a quiet location. There's a swimming pool and restaurant, but no bar (so bring your own poison).

Places to Stay – Top End
South of Mfuwe Gate The following places are south or southwest of Mfuwe Gate and all (except the Luamfwa) are outside the park. All rates are per person and inclusive of meals and activities – but not transfers to/from the lodge/camp.

Luamfwa Lodge (☎ 01-261732; ⓦ www .luamfwa.com; US$130; open May-Dec) is in the far south of the park, about 65km southwest of Mfuwe village. It has a pool and bar/restaurant, and offers wildlife drives and walks. Special weekend packages are often advertised in *The Lowdown*.

Kapani Lodge (☎ 062-45015; ⓦ www .normancarrsafaris.com; cottages per person US$340; open all year) is about 4km southwest of Mfuwe Gate. The most famous of the top-end lodges is this classic Luangwa camp built by Norman Carr (see the boxed text 'Norman Carr & South Luangwa' earlier) with thatched cottages overlooking a lagoon frequented by weed-munching hippos. Kapani has three bush camps in the park and runs highly rated walking safaris.

Nkwali Lodge (☎ 062-45090; ⓦ www.robin popesafaris.net; US$300; open Apr-Dec) has six tastefully designed and spacious chalets with delightful, open-air bathrooms. The bar and restaurant overlook the river and the camp's private water hole. It's run by Robin Pope Safaris, which offers highly regarded walking safaris in the Nsefu sector and in the seldom visited northern reaches of the park.

Kafunta River Lodge (☎/fax 062-45026; ⓦ www.luangwa.com; US$280; open all year) is about 8km southwest of the Mfuwe Gate. It offers cool, airy chalets and a vast restaurant-lounge-deck area offering a wonderfully open panoramic view over the river. Two/three-night package deals including return flights from Lusaka for US$380/470 per person are sometimes available through travel agencies in Lusaka.

North of Mfuwe Gate North of the main gate are several other options; all are inside the park. Again, all rates are per person and inclusive of meals and activities – but not transfers.

Mfuwe Lodge (☎/fax 062-45041; ⓦ www .mfuwelodge.com; US$295; open all year) was rebuilt in 1998 and the results are impressive: a central restaurant and bar area, with gigantic thatched roof and open sides, leading out onto a deck with swimming pool and splendid views over a lagoon. The hotel-standard rooms in the cottages (each cater for two or three people) have private verandas. The lodge also has two bush camps in the southern section of the park and offers a range of walking and vehicle safaris.

Tena Tena (☎ 062-45090; ⓦ www.robinpope safaris.net; US$300; open June-Oct) overlooks beautiful wide bends in the river. It has a calm and exclusive atmosphere, and only six large walk-in tents under shady trees, each with a veranda and private view.

Nsefu Camp (☎ 062-45090; ⓦ www.robin popesafaris.net; US$395; open June-Oct) offers gorgeous river views. Nsefu was the first camp in Luangwa, and the six original bungalows (though completely renovated) retain their historic atmosphere. This area is the Nsefu sector, the only part of the park on the eastern bank of the river, so the Tena Tena and Nsefu lodges do boast some extra exclusivity.

Kaingo Camp (☎ 062-45064; ⓦ www.kain go.com; US$325; open mid-May–Oct), on the western bank of the Luangwa, is small, exclusive, relaxed and friendly, with five delightful cottages surrounded by bush overlooking the river. Skilled guides operate walks and wildlife drives, and there's also a bush camp that can be reached on a walking safari from the main camp.

Places to Eat

All the lodges/camps and camping grounds provide meals – from simple snacks to haute cuisine at the top-end lodges/camps. There are also a couple of basic **eateries** in Mfuwe village. The best is **Camel House Curios** *(meals US$2.50-4)*, at the BP petrol station, which offers Western-style food and excellent coffee.

If you're travelling by air, or have your own vehicle, take time to visit the incongruous but splendid **Moondogs Café**, next to the Mfuwe (Masumba) airport. All sorts of delicious items, including tacos, waffles and salads grace the menu.

Shopping

Most of the lodges/camps have souvenir shops selling the usual array of carvings. Other locally-made mementoes include ceramics and elephant-dung paper (mostly made in Malawi, however). Splendidly decorative fabrics are available from **Camel House Curios** at the BP petrol station in Mfuwe village, and all proceeds go directly to the makers.

The well-stocked **Mango Tree Crafts**, along the road between Mfuwe village and the airport, is home to **Tribal Textiles**, where most of the local fabrics on sale in the region are made. Short (free) walks around the factory are permitted.

Getting There & Away

Most people reach South Luangwa by air. Mfuwe (Masumba) airport is about 20km southeast of Mfuwe Gate and served by chartered flights from Lusaka and, occasionally from Lilongwe (Malawi). **Zambian Airways** *(☎ 062-45060)* also offers flights between Lusaka and Mfuwe on Tuesday, Thursday, Friday and Sunday for US$145 one way. Most lodges will meet clients who have made reservations.

Mfuwe Gate and the surrounding camps are (normally) easy to reach from Chipata in a 2WD vehicle. In the dry season the dirt road is usually poor and the drive takes about three hours. In the wet season, however, the drive can take all day (or be impassable), so seek advice before setting off. Hitching may be possible, but make sure your lift goes all the way to Mfuwe village or gate.

Minibuses leave when *really* full several times a day between Chipata and Mfuwe village. Fares are squarely priced for foreigners (about US$8). From Mfuwe village, it's easy to walk (about 1km) to Flatdogs and Old Croc Farm, or hitch to The Wildlife Camp – but, we repeat, do *not* walk at night. Otherwise, offer some extra kwacha to the minibus driver to take you to one of these three camp sites or to Mfuwe Gate.

Some travellers have hitched all the way from Chipata – but start at dawn. The junction by the Chipata Motel is the best place to wait for a lift; in Mfuwe, wait outside the BP petrol station.

If you're in a group, consider chartering your own minibus from Chipata for a negotiable US$60 to US$70 one way. Or just take the easy way out and fly. The airfare may seem steep (it is), but it beats the hell out of two days of torture on buses and minibuses from Lusaka which may cost you about US$50 anyway (with bus fares, food and accommodation). Some travellers who endured the torturous trip from Lusaka, bit the bullet, found the credit card, and bought a flight out of Mfuwe back to Lusaka.

NORTH LUANGWA NATIONAL PARK

This park *(admission US$15; open 6am-6pm daily)* is large, wild, remote and spectacular, but nowhere *near* as developed or set up for tourism as its southern counterpart. This may change sometime in the future, because facilities in the park (and at several local villages) are slowly being improved with help from the German development agency, Volunteers. Currently, all accommodation should be pre-booked, because no lodge/camp in the park is open to the general public.

Buffalo Camp *(☎ 01-228682; ⓔ reservations@zamsaf.co.zm; self-catering chalets per person US$50, with meals & activities per person US$200, each with bathroom; open all year)* is a quiet, secluded place run by knowledgeable and helpful staff. Book ahead for the 'self-catering rates', because these are normally only available when there's a paucity of big-spending guests on the all-inclusive package. Transfers for those without vehicles are possible (for little or no charge) through Kapishya Lodge (see under Shiwa N'gandu in the Northern Zambia section).

Mwaleshi Lodge *(ⓔ remote.africa@stratosmail.net; including meals and activities per*

person US$300; open June-Oct) is relaxed and luxurious.

Most guests on organised tours fly in and out on chartered planes. Despite the proximity of the two parks, road access between North and South Luangwa is not easy. It is possible to reach the main gate to North Luangwa from the highway, about 65km north of Mpika. But this is no doddle – the track is rough and rarely used, and plunges steeply down the Muchinga Escarpment into the Luangwa Valley. High clearance in a 4WD is essential.

Southern Zambia

This section covers the area between (but not including) Livingstone and Kafue National Park, as well as Lake Kariba. The Victoria Falls chapter provides detailed information about Livingstone and the magnificent falls.

THE ZAMBEZI RIVERFRONT
☎ 03

The Zambian shore of the Zambezi River upstream of Victoria Falls is fast becoming one of the country's major tourist areas. Numerous places to stay all overlook the river, and most are accessible from along the main road between Livingstone and Sesheke. It's usually necessary to book accommodation in advance, either directly or through an agent in Lusaka or overseas. All places listed here are shown on the inset map attached to the general Zambia map at the beginning of this chapter.

Places to Stay – Budget & Mid-Range

Jungle Junction *(☎ 324229; W www.jungle junction.net; camping per person US$6, huts per person for 1/2/3 days including all meals, activities & return transfers from Livingstone from US$75/100/125)* is about 50km from Livingstone and 8km from Kazungula. Located on a lush island in the middle of the Zambezi, there is probably nothing else like it anywhere in Southern Africa. Everyone who stays just loves the palm trees and the hammocks, as well as the all-round mellow atmosphere. Facilities were renovated in 2002 and prices have increased, however, so it's no longer such great value. Campers can bring their own tent (or rent one), but have to pay

US$20 for a return transfer from Livingstone. You can also book in person at the **office** inside Hippos restaurant/bar in Livingstone (see the Victoria Falls chapter for details).

Places to Stay – Top End

All rates listed here are per person, and transfers (if included) are from Livingstone.

Thorntree Lodge *(☎ 312213; W www.safari parx.com/lodges/ttlmo.htm; with meals, activities & transfers US$200)* is about 10km west of Livingstone and 2km off the main road. Comfortable chalets and large walk-in tents provide front-row views of elephants crossing the Zambezi, and the bar overlooks a watering hole where animals from the wildlife park often come to drink.

Tongabezi Lodge *(☎ 323235; W www.tonga bezi.com; including meals, activities & transfers from US$295)*, about 6km further west of Thorntree Lodge, is one of the most imaginative options along the riverfront. The large luxury tents are tastefully decorated and the secluded houses are completely open to views across the river.

Chundukwa Tree Lodge *(☎ 324006; W www.zambiatourism.com/chundukwa; including meals, activities & transfers US$150)*, about 20km west of Livingstone and 2km off the main road, is small and friendly. Most rooms are built in or around the mammoth trees. Canoeing, horse riding and trips to Kafue National Park can be easily arranged.

Kubu Cabins *(☎/fax 324091; e kubu@ zamnet.zm; with breakfast & dinner from US$120)* is a popular and long-standing place about 28km west of Livingstone and 5km off the main road. You can chose from delightful thatched rooms, or comfortable walk-in tents at the associated and grandly-named 'Livingstone Explorers' Club'. All sorts of activities, such as bird-watching, canoeing and walking safaris, are offered (for extra).

The Zambezi Royal Chundu Safari Lodge *(☎/fax 321772; W www.royalchundu.com; chalets including meals US$120, tree houses with breakfast & dinner US$85)* is next along from Kubu Cabins, but a tortuous 12km off the main road. This lodge offers charming riverfront chalets, though it lacks the relaxed atmosphere of some other places along the river. The tree houses on the river's edge have better views – but a longer walk to the bathroom!

Getting There & Away

Anyone without a private/rented vehicle, will probably have to charter a taxi from Livingstone if transfers are not included.

CHOMA
☎ 032

This busy market town, 188km northeast of Livingstone, is the capital of the Southern Province. Most visitors pass through at high speed on their way to Lusaka or Livingstone, but Choma is a pleasant stopover and staging post for trips to Lake Kariba and Kafue National Park.

For anyone interested in regional history, the excellent **Choma Museum & Craft Centre** (admission US$2; open 9am-4pm daily) is well worth a visit. Based in a former school dating from the 1920s (one of the oldest preserved colonial buildings in Zambia), the exhibits concentrate on the Tonga people, most of whom were forcibly relocated when the Kariba Dam was built. It also houses contemporary art exhibitions and a **craft shop**. The museum is about 1.5km north of the town centre and along the road towards Lusaka.

Choma Motel (☎ 20189; Livingstone Rd; singles/doubles with bathroom & breakfast US$15/18) along the southern edge of the town centre is a charmless motel set up for truck drivers, but it's clean and reasonably quiet.

Gwembe Safaris (☎ 20169; W www.zambia tourism.com/gwembe; camping per person US$5, single/double chalets with shared bathroom US$35/45) is signposted 1km south of town and is a further 2km off the main road. The camping ground is grassy and shady, and the shared bathrooms are spotless. Breakfast costs an extra US$3, and dinner is US$10.

All daily buses and trains between Livingstone and Lusaka stop at Choma.

LAKE KARIBA

The Zambian side of Lake Kariba is not *nearly* as developed or as popular as the southern and eastern shores in Zimbabwe. The Zambia side is more relaxed and authentic, but a bit rough around the edges.

Refer to the Lake Kariba section in the Zimbabwe chapter for information about the creation of this huge artificial lake.

Chikanka Island

This beautiful private island, about 10km from Sinazongwe, offers excellent self-catering **chalets** (singles/doubles with bathroom US$40/60), and **camping** (per person US$10) on a separate site. Meals are hard to arrange, so bring your own food and the staff in the kitchen will cook it for you. **Fishing boats** can be hired for trips around the lake. Boat transfers (US$10 per person; minimum of US$40) leave from near Sinazongwe. Reservations are essential and can be made through Gwembe Safaris (see Choma earlier).

Siavonga
☎ 01

Siavonga is the main town and resort along the Zambian side of Lake Kariba. Just a few kilometres from the massive Kariba Dam, Siavonga is a quiet and low-key village in contrast to Kariba town (in Zimbabwe) opposite.

The tiny **bank** at the end of the laneway east of the petrol station changes money, and so do the moneychangers at the turn-off to Siavonga along the road between Lusaka and the border. For reasons probably only known

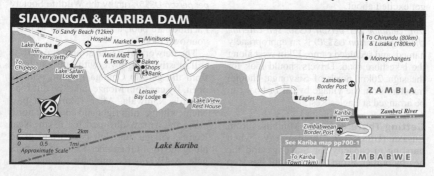

SIAVONGA & KARIBA DAM

To Sandy Beach (12km)
To Chirundu (80km) & Lusaka (180km)
Lake Kariba Inn
Hospital Market Minibuses
Ferry Jetty
To Chipepo
Lake Safari Lodge
Mini Mart & Tendi's
Bakery
Shops
Bank
● Moneychangers
Leisure Bay Lodge
Zambian Border Post
ZAMBIA
Lake View Rest House
■ Eagles Rest
Zambezi River
Kariba Dam
0   1   2km
0   0.5   1mi
Approximate Scale
Zimbabwean Border Post
See Kariba map pp700-1
Lake Kariba
To Kariba Town (1km)
ZIMBABWE

ZAMBIA

to Zambian and Zimbabwean immigration officials, moneychangers do not actually operate on either side of the border.

Tours *(free, but donations welcome)* of Kariba Dam are run by the dam authorities (as it were). These tours can be arranged through your hotel/lodge or directly with the relevant authority (☎ 511079). If you visit the dam, make sure you tell the Zambian immigration officers if you're not going on to Zimbabwe.

Eagles Rest (see following) offers three-hour **cruises** along the lake for US$120 per boat including food (maximum of eight), and speedboats for US$60 per hour. Eagles and Lake View Rest House also rent out **canoes** (US$6.50 per person per hour).

Places to Stay & Eat The **Eagles Rest** (☎ 511168; **W** www.eagles-rest.com; *camping per person US$6.50, chalets with bathroom & fan per person from US$30*) is highly recommended. The chalets are self-catering, though snacks and meals are available in the **bar/restaurant**, and the camp site is secluded and shady. There's a pool and plenty of space to relax. If you book in advance, you may be able to cadge a lift from Siavonga or even Lusaka.

Leisure Bay Lodge (☎/fax 511136; *singles/doubles with bathroom & breakfast US$20/28*) faces a beach along the lakeshore. The unremarkable rooms contain a TV, mosquito net and outdated air-conditioning. Guests can pre-order meals (US$4). Note that the small sandy beach is often commandeered by resident hippos!

Lake View Rest House *(doubles with bathroom US$7)* offers very basic but cheap rooms with a mossie net (but no fan) along a small rocky peninsula. The breezy bar is worth a try, though the meals are nothing to get excited about.

Sandy Beach (☎ 511353; **e** eagles@zamnet.zm; *camping per person US$6, self-catering chalets per person US$30*) is an appropriately named, and secluded camp, 12km west along the lakeshore road. Drivers should look for the sign 20km north of Siavonga, though transfers from the village by car or boat can be arranged at Eagles Rest.

Getting There & Away Minibuses from Lusaka (US$3, three hours) leave when bursting to capacity for Siavonga and the nearby border. From the makeshift bus stop

in Siavonga, you can easily walk to Leisure Bay Lodge or Lake View Rest House. There are no taxis in Siavonga, but your hotel may be able to arrange a private car to the border; otherwise, take the Lusaka minibus, which detours to the border.

For the adventurous, a local ferry runs once or twice a week between Siavonga and **Chipepo** (US$10 one way, 12 hours). There's no official accommodation in Chipepo, so ask about for a **room** in a private home. Check at the ferry jetty in Siavonga about the current timetable (if there is one).

LOCHINVAR NATIONAL PARK

This small (410-sq-km) park *(admission US$15; open 6am-6pm daily)*, northwest of Monze, consists of grassland, low wooded hills, and the seasonally flooded Chunga Lagoon – all part of a huge flood plain called the Kafue Flats. You may see buffaloes, wildebeest, zebras, kudus and some of the 30,000 Kafue lechwes residing in the park. Lochinvar is also a haven for birdlife, with more than 400 species recorded. An excellent selection of wetland birds (including wattled cranes) occur near the ranger post along the edge of Chunga Lagoon.

Lochinvar was virtually abandoned in the 1980s. Plans to rehabilitate the park and the lodge were announced in 1999, but almost immediately stalled through a lack of funds and a dearth of tourists. By late 2001 however, a tour operator, **Star of Africa** (**W** www.star-of-africa.com), had started to redevelop the park. It also built the superb **Lechwe Plains Tented Camp** *(with meals & activities per person US$305)*, under a clump of acacia trees along the shores of the Chunga Lagoon. Otherwise, you can stay at the **camp site** (☎ 062-254226; **e** wcsz@zamnet.zm; *camping per person US$5*), run by the Wildlife Society of Zambia, about 2km west of the park gate. Facilities are poor, and don't forget to bring your own food.

The network of tracks around the park is still mostly overgrown, with only the track from the gate to Chunga Lagoon reliably open. By car from Monze, take the dirt road towards Namwala. After 15km, just past Nteme village, turn right and continue north along the narrow dirt road for 13km. Near Kembe village, turn left (west) and grind along the road for another 13km to the park gate. A 4WD is recommended at any time

LOCHINVAR NATIONAL PARK

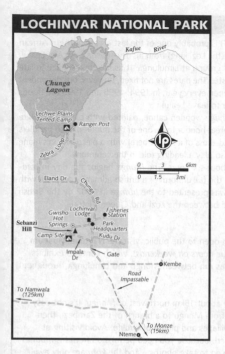

Kafue River

Chunga Lagoon

Lechwe Plains Tented Camp
Ranger Post

Zebra Loop

Eland Dr

Chunga Rd

0   3   6km
0   1.5   3mi

Gwisho Hot Springs
Lochinvar Lodge
Sebanzi Hill
Camp Site
Fisheries Station
Park Headquarters
Kudu Dr
Impala Dr   Gate
Kembe
Road Impassable
To Namwala (125km)
To Monze (15km)
Nteme

anywhere *inside* the park. For those without wheels, minibuses go to Namwala, but after the first junction at Nteme you'll have to walk or hitch. Star of Africa is likely to open an airstrip in the park soon for guests at the Lechwe Plains Tented Camp.

Western Zambia

This section covers most of the Western Province, including Barotseland, plus various other places along the Upper Zambezi. Most of this area is ideal for travellers with plenty of time, patience and endurance.

Make sure you read the general Getting There & Away section earlier in this chapter if you intend to cross the border into Namibia or Botswana.

SESHEKE

Sesheke is on the northeastern bank of the Zambezi River, 200km upstream from Livingstone and virtually opposite the Namibian town of Katima Mulilo.

Council Resthouse *(doubles without/with bathroom US$6/8)*, just off the main street and opposite the hospital, offers basic rooms. Meals are available and the bar sells cold beers to accompany wonderful views at sunset.

Brenda's Best & Baobab Bar *(camping per person US$5)* is a newish place almost next door to the resthouse. It offers a relaxing but basic camp site with a popular bar built around a massive baobab. **Canoes** can be hired for leisurely floats along the river.

At least one bus a day and several minibuses link Sesheke with Livingstone (US$7, six hours), but this trip is laborious and arduous. Occasional minibuses also link Sesheke with Katima Mulilo (see following).

KATIMA MULILO

This small village (not to be confused with Katima Mulilo in Namibia) is on the Zambian bank of the Zambezi and about 6km from Sesheke. The Namibian border is just south of the village.

Mulatiwa Guesthouse *(rooms US$5-20)* is a friendly place near the pontoon (car ferry). It offers all sorts of rooms – from those used by 'ladies of the night' to the 'VIP rooms' with a private bathroom. At the guesthouse, you can buy food and drink, change money and seek advice about onward transport.

Katima Mulilo is only linked to the outside world by minibus from Sesheke.

NGONYE FALLS

Ngonye Falls *(admission free; permanently open)*, also called Sioma Falls, is an impressive 1km-wide chain of waterfalls, rapids and rocky islands cutting across the Zambezi. It would be a major attraction if it wasn't so difficult to reach; imagine something almost as majestic as the Victoria Falls, but with almost no other person (local or foreign) in sight.

Maziba Bay Lodge *(☎/fax 015-7810205; camping per person US$10, chalets with bathroom including meals & activities per person from US$150)*, 8km south of the falls, offers large, luxurious chalets overlooking an idyllic sandy beach. Rates include a trip to the falls and all sorts of other activities.

The falls are less than 1km east of the main dirt road between Sesheke and Senanga. For drivers, access is not difficult from Sesheke, but far more problematic from Senanga (see following). Otherwise, hitch a ride and ask to be dropped by the turn-off (look for the 'Wildlife Department' sign).

ZAMBIA

The Ku'omboka Ceremony

The *ku'omboka* (literally, 'to move to dry ground') is probably one of the last great Southern African ceremonies. It celebrates the move of the *litunga* (the Lozi king) from his dry-season palace at Lealui, near Mongu, to his wet-season palace on higher ground at Limulunga. It usually takes place in late March or early April, and sometimes ties in with Easter. The dates are not fixed, however, but dependent on the rains. In fact, the *ku'omboka* does not happen every year: in 1994, 1995 and 1996 the floods were not extensive enough to require the *litunga* to leave Lealui.

Central to the ceremony is the *nalikwanda*, a huge wooden canoe, painted with black and white stripes, that carries the *litunga*. It is considered a great honour to be one of the hundred or so paddlers on the *nalikwanda*, and each paddler wears a head-dress of a scarlet beret with a piece of lion's mane and a knee-length skirt of animal skins. Drums also play a leading role in the ceremony.

The journey from Lealui to Limulunga takes about six hours. The *litunga* begins the day in traditional dress, but during the journey changes into the full uniform of a British admiral, complete with all regalia and ostrich-plumed hat. The uniform was presented to the *litunga* in 1902 by the British King Edward VII, in recognition of treaties signed between the Lozi and Queen Victoria.

Visiting the Palaces

Limulunga Because the **Litunga's Palace** is not open to the public, visit the **Nayuma Museum** *(admission US$1; open 8am-5pm Mon-Fri, erratic hours on weekends)*, which contains exhibits about the Lozi, *litunga* and *ku'omboka*. Minibuses run between Mongu and Limulunga throughout the day.

Lealui The *litunga's* **Main Palace** is on the plain about 15km northwest of Mongu. It's not easy to reach, but the journey by boat (along a canal from Mongu to a branch of the Zambezi, then upstream to Lealui) is spectacular, passing local villages and plenty of birdlife. Avoid visiting at weekends, when the *litunga's* *kotu* (court) is closed, because you need permission from his *indunas* (advisors) to get a close look at the palace and even to take photos – and the *kotu* are only available from Monday to Friday.

Public longboats between Mongu harbour and Lealui (US$2, one hour) leave once or twice a day. Alternatively, charter a longboat to Lealui for about US$80 return or a smaller slower boat for about US$30 return. Prices include fuel and are negotiable. Buses do the trip in the late months of the dry season (March to April).

SENANGA

If you're coming from Lusaka, Senanga has a real 'end of the line' feel. It is the best place to break up a journey between Mongu and Ngonye Falls or Sesheke.

The rooms at the **Council Resthouse** *(per person from US$8)* are basic, so a better option is **Senanga Safaris** *(☎ 07-230156; camping per person US$5, doubles with bathroom & breakfast US$20)*. It offers comfortable rondavels with splendid views over the Zambezi plains – spoilt only by the giant satellite TV dish in the garden. The bar sells cold beer and the **restaurant** serves expensive meals. Several cheaper **restaurants** are dotted along the main street nearby.

Minibuses and pick-ups run between Senanga and Mongu (US$4, two to three hours) several times a day. About 30km south of

Senanga (and accessible by minibus), a pontoon carries passengers (normally free) and vehicles (US$20/30 for 2/4WD) across the Zambezi to Kalongola. Often the ferry doesn't operate between February and June, so passengers take a small boat, but car drivers may have to charter a larger, different pontoon.

MONGU

☎ 07

The largest town in Barotseland, and the capital of Western Province, is on high ground overlooking the flat and seemingly endless Liuwa Plain. The town itself is spread out, but boasts a pleasant lively feel, so a walk along the main street is always interesting. From a harbour on the southwestern outskirts of town, an 8km canal runs westwards

to meet a tributary of the Zambezi. Around the harbour is a fascinating settlement of reed and thatch buildings, where local fishermen sell their catch and passenger boats take people to outlying villages.

Mongu really comes alive once a year, when thousands of people flock there for the annual **ku'omboka ceremony** (see the boxed text earlier). Not surprisingly, the prices for rooms (if you can find one) skyrocket at this time.

Places to Stay & Eat
Lumba Guesthouse (*☎ 221287; Kanyonyo Rd; singles/doubles from US$7/10*) is 300m northeast of (and over the Lusaka road from) the public bus station. Single travellers may want to pay extra for a double with a bathroom. Meals are available to the public.

Winters Resthouse (*Senanga Rd; doubles US$6-9*) is a decent budget place 1.3km north of the public bus station and past the market. Get a room at the far end of the yard to escape the noisy bar. The more expensive rooms contain a bathroom.

Lyamba Hotel (*☎ 21138; Lusaka Rd; doubles with breakfast US$15*) is a bit run-down, but good value, and guests can enjoy fine views from the garden. It's 1.2km west of the public bus station and past the post office.

Mongu Lodge (*☎ 221501; Mwanawina St; singles/doubles with shared bathroom US$7/12, doubles with bathroom & air-con US$15, all with breakfast*) is just south of the Lyamba. It's worth paying extra for the renovated rooms with a bathroom and air-con.

Getting There & Away
The **public bus station** is on the southeastern edge of town, behind the Catholic church. Several companies offer buses between Lusaka and Mongu (US$10, 12 hours) at least every day. Those run by **RPS** and **JR Investments** leave from stands along Senanga Rd in Mongu at about 4am. Book your ticket (at least) the day before and sleep on the bus before departure.

A bus travels between Livingstone and Mongu (US$10, 10 hours) twice a week via Sesheke, Kalongola and Senanga, but you're advised to break up this horror journey in Senanga. Better still, go to Lusaka from Livingstone and take the bus along the tarred road from Lusaka.

Minibuses and pick-ups leave on a fill-up-and-go basis from near the Caltex filling station in Mongu for Senanga (US$4, three hours), from where minibuses head to Sesheke.

KAFUE NATIONAL PARK
Kafue National Park (*admission per person/vehicle US$15/5; open 6am-6pm daily*) is about 200km west of Lusaka. Covering more than 22,500 sq km (nearly the size of Belgium), it's the largest park in Zambia and one of the biggest in the world. Vegetation includes riverine forest around Lake Itezhi-Tezhi and Kafue River and its main tributaries (the Lunga and Lufupa); areas of open mixed woodland; and the vast seasonally flooded grasslands of the Busanga Plains on the northern edge.

This is classic wildlife country and the foremost park for spotting The Big Five. Elephants and buffaloes are often seen in wooded areas, particularly around Chunga Camp. Carnivores include lions and hyenas, and the northern part of the park is noted for the number of leopards, cheetahs and wild dogs. Antelope species include impalas,

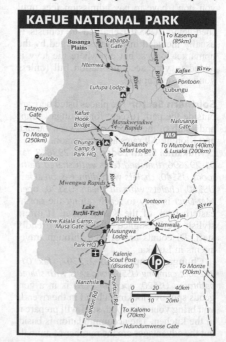

KAFUE NATIONAL PARK

roans, kudus, sables, red lechwes and sitatungas, and the rivers contain huge numbers of crocs and hippos. Birdlife is also prolific, with more than 400 species recorded.

The main road between Lusaka and Mongu runs though the park, dividing it into northern and southern sectors. (You don't pay park fees if you're in transit.) There are several gates, but three main ones: **Nalusanga Gate**, for the northern sector along the eastern boundary; **Musa Gate**, near the New Kalala Camp, for the southern sector; and **Tatayoyo Gate**, for either sector if you're coming from the west. Rangers are also stationed at the two park headquarters: at Chunga Camp and another 8km south of Musa Gate.

Some lodges/camps arrange **walking safaris**, but visitors are not allowed to walk in the park without an armed ranger. Most guests feel safer exploring the park in a 4WD, during a day or night wildlife drive, or by boat.

Places to Stay

We can only list a few of the numerous camp sites and lodges/camps offered in and around the park. Several lodges/camps are just outside the park boundaries, which means that you don't have to pay admission fees until you actually visit the park. The inexplicable 'bed levy' (US$10) charged to tourists is usually included in the rates charged by the upmarket lodges, but elsewhere the levy is added to your accommodation bill (unless you're just camping).

Southern Sector The places listed here are outside the park (except for Chunga Camp) and south of the main road between Lusaka and Mongu. All rates are per person.

Mukambi Safari Lodge (☎ 01-293848, fax 01-292696; thatched tents with shared bathroom US$40, chalets with dinner & breakfast US$80, chalets with all meals US$90; open Mar-Dec) is easy to reach, along the northeastern bank of the Kafue River. It offers stylish well-designed chalets and friendly staff. Discounts are offered through travel agents in Lusaka.

Chunga Camp (☎ 01-272307, fax 01-272308; camping US$5, rondavels with shared bathroom US$20; open all year) is in a gorgeous spot overlooking a bend in the river. If you bring your own food, staff will prepare it in the kitchen. The accommodation is basic, but the advantages are the number of animals

in and around the camp (so be careful at all times), and the proximity to the park headquarters for arranging walking safaris and wildlife drives.

New Kalala Camp (☎/fax 01-254461; camping US$10, chalets with shared bathroom US$30; open all year) is a low-key spot with unremarkable chalets near Lake Itezhi-Tezhi and Musa Gate. The pool, bar, restaurant and shady camp site are pluses. Boat trips can be easily arranged.

Musungwa Lodge (☎ 01-273493, e zam ker@zamnet.zm; camping US$10, singles/ doubles with bathroom & half-board US$75/ 130; open June-Oct) is a large place near New Kalala Camp. Originally built as a lakeside resort, it features comparatively lush gardens with a big swimming pool and tennis court. The comfortable rooms contain verandas overlooking the lake. The lodge can also offer wildlife drives and boat trips.

Northern Sector Several lodges/camps are also inside the northern section of the park, north of the main road from Lusaka. Again, all rates are per person.

Lufupa Lodge (☎ 01-227739; e sblagus@ zamnet.zm; camping US$12, chalets with bathroom & all meals US$95; open June-Oct) is at the confluence of the Lufupa and Kafue Rivers. It's a large place in a lovely position, with comfortable rondavels and an inviting swimming pool. The lodge offers boat rides, walking safaris and wildlife drives, and the guides are reportedly adept at spotting elusive leopards. Campers can hire a tent if arranged with plenty of notice for an extra US$10 per night, and eat in the restaurant.

Ntemwa (☎ 01-265814; including meals & activities US$275; open June-Oct) is yet another super-luxurious camp with enormous tents and excellent meals. Guests have raved about the quality of the activities, particularly the walks and drives.

Getting There & Away

Most guests of the top-end lodges/camps fly in on chartered planes. Transfers from the airstrip to the lodges/camps are often included in the rates.

For drivers, the main road into Kafue National Park is along the road between Lusaka and Mongu. About 35km west of Nalusanga Gate, a road leads southwest towards Lake

Itezhi-Tezhi. The road is shockingly pot-holed and only accessible by a 4WD with high clearance. Just past Itezhitezhi village is Musa Gate, from where the road crosses Lake Itezhi-Tezhi to the New Kalala Camp and Musungwa Lodge.

If you're staying at Mukambi Safari Lodge, continue west along the main road from Lusaka until about 10km before Kafue Hook Bridge and look for the signposted turn-off to the south. On the western side of the bridge, a main track leads into the northern sector of the park, and a dirt road leads southeast to Chunga Camp.

There's no public transport in the park, but you could get off the bus between Lusaka and Mongu and reach Mukambi Safari Lodge on foot, or get off at the Chunga junction and wait for a lift to Chunga Camp. Alternatively, take the slow, daily bus, or one of the more regular minibuses, from Lusaka to Itezhitezhi village (US$8, six hours). From the village bus stop wait around for a lift (because of the number of wild animals it may not be safe to hike).

The easiest way of reaching the park – and getting around it – is on an organised tour, but surprisingly few are offered by agencies in Lusaka or Livingstone. Chachacha Backpackers (see Places to Stay under Lusaka) promises to recommence tours if/when the roads to and around the park improve. Otherwise, contact Jolly Boys Backpackers (see Places to Stay under Livingstone in the Victoria Falls chapter) about what it might have on offer.

Zimbabwe

Tradition, culture and soul, combined, with an impressive (but crumbling) infrastructure, make Zimbabwe an appealing African destination, despite occasional political upheavals and the disastrous land reform policies. The Africa that most travellers envisage is all around: a landscape studded with *kopje* (rocky hills), face-to-face encounters with the Big Five in various national parks, and the 'Smoke that Thunders' at Victoria Falls. But few allow enough time to include the haunting shores of Lake Kariba and the Zambezi River, or the lush, mist-shrouded Eastern Highlands. And like explorers from yesteryear, many travellers fail to realise that the greatest sub-Saharan structure – Great Zimbabwe – is easy to visit.

Of course, the country has serious and well-publicised economic and political problems. While these have undoubtedly brought misery to thousands of Zimbabweans, it is *still* a great time to visit: the dramatic decline in tourism means that you may have a national park (and its wildlife) to yourself, and changing money at the unofficial (but accepted) exchange rate makes Zimbabwe one of *the* bargains on earth. Despite the hardships, and contrary to the situation portrayed by the hysterical Western media, Zimbabwe remains relatively safe (if you stay away from politics). Importantly, the people remain friendly and remarkably stoic.

Facts about Zimbabwe

HISTORY
The precolonial history of the area that became Zimbabwe, along with the rest of Southern Africa, is covered in the History section of the Facts about the Region chapter.

The Shona Kingdoms & the Portuguese
Historians believe that in the 11th century, the Great Zimbabwe society encountered Swahili traders who had been plying the Mozambique coast for over four centuries. They traded gold and ivory for glass, porcelain

Zimbabwe at a Glance

Area: 390,580 sq km
Population: 13 million
Capital: Harare
Head of State: Robert Mugabe
Official Language: English
Currency: Zimbabwe dollar (ZW$)
Exchange Rate: US$1 = ZW$57.44 (official); about ZW$600 (black market)

Highlights

- Bulawayo – strolling around the museums and art galleries in Zimbabwe's loveliest city

- Mana Pools National Park – paddling among the hippos along the Zambezi River, and walking unaccompanied among elephants and lions

- Great Zimbabwe – discovering Africa's largest stone ruins (after the pyramids) and the greatest archaeological site in Southern Africa

- Matobo National Park – roaming around a surreal landscape of caves, ancient rock art and balancing boulders

- Hwange National Park – observing the Big Five in Zimbabwe's largest, most accessible and most wildlife-packed park

- Victoria Falls – staying at this convenient, modern town while planning numerous adventure activities and tours

ZIMBABWE

LEGEND
GS   Game Sanctuary
NP   National Park
RP   Recreational Park

and cloth from Asia, and Great Zimbabwe became wealthy and powerful. However, by the 15th century, its influence was in decline because of overpopulation, overgrazing, political fragmentation and uprisings.

During Great Zimbabwe's twilight period, Shona dynasties fractured into autonomous states. In the 16th century Portuguese traders arrived in search of riches and golden cities in the vast empire of Mwene Mutapa (Monomatapa to the Europeans), where they hoped to find King Solomon's mines and the mysterious land of Ophir.

Alliances between Shona states led to the creation of the Rozwi state, which encompassed over half of present-day Zimbabwe. This state continued until 1834 when raiders known as the Ndebele (Those Who Carry Long Shields), under the command of Mzilikazi, invaded from the south and assassinated the Rozwi leader. Upon reaching the Matobo Hills, Mzilikazi established a Ndebele state. After Mzilikazi's death in 1870, his son Lobengula ascended the throne and relocated the Ndebele capital to Bulawayo.

Lobengula soon found himself face to face with the British South African Company (BSAC). In 1888 Cecil Rhodes, the company's founder, coerced him to sign the Rudd Concession, which granted foreigners mineral rights in exchange for 10,000 rifles, 100,000 rounds of ammunition, a gunboat and £100 each month.

But a series of misunderstandings followed. Lobengula sent a group of Ndebele raiders to Fort Victoria (near Masvingo)

to prevent Shona interference between the British and the Ndebele. The British mistook this as aggression and launched an attack on Matabeleland. Lobengula's *kraals* (hut villages) were destroyed and Bulawayo was burned. A peace offering of gold sent by Lobengula to the BSAC was commandeered by company employees. Ignorant of this gold token, the vengeful British sent the Shangani River Patrol to track down the missing king and finish him off. In the end, Lobengula died in exile of smallpox.

Without their king, the Ndebele continued to resist the BSAC and foreign rule. In the early 1890s they allied themselves with the Shona, and guerrilla warfare broke out against the BSAC in the Matobo Hills. When Rhodes suggested a negotiated settlement, the Ndebele, with their depleted numbers, couldn't refuse.

Meanwhile, finding little gold, the colonists appropriated farmlands on the Mashonaland plateau. By 1895 the new country was being called Rhodesia, after its heavy-handed founder, and a white legislature was set up. European immigration began in earnest: by 1904 there were some 12,000 settlers in the country, and seven years later the figure had doubled.

The First Chimurenga

The government of Rhodesia was set up 'for, by and of' the whites. The Ndebele had effectively been quashed, but trade between the Shona and Europeans continued until it became apparent that the colonists intended to control both African and Rhodesian interests. Spotting a weakness in the BSAC army, the Ndebele came back with a vengeance, gathering forces and single-mindedly attempting to drive the enemy from their land forever. This warlike spirit proved contagious; the Shona, traditional enemies of the Ndebele, joined in, and by 1896 the First Chimurenga, ('War for Liberation') had begun. Although the revolt gained some momentum, it was stalled in 1897 when its leaders were captured and subsequently hanged.

Beginnings of Nationalism

Conflicts between black and white came into sharp focus after the 1922 referendum in which the whites chose to become a self-governing colony rather than join the Union of South Africa. Although Rhodesia's constitution was in theory nonracial, suffrage was based on British citizenship and annual income, so few blacks qualified. In 1930 white supremacy was legislated in the form of the Land Apportionment Act, which disallowed black Africans from ownership of the best farmland, and a labour law that excluded them from skilled trades and professions. Poor wages and conditions eventually led to a rebellion, and by the time Southern Rhodesia, Northern Rhodesia and Nyasaland were federated in 1953, mining and industrial concerns favoured a more racially mixed middle class as a counterweight to the radical elements in the labour force.

Two African parties soon emerged – the Zimbabwe African People's Union (ZAPU) under the leadership of Joshua Nkomo, and the Zimbabwe African National Union (ZANU), a breakaway group under the leadership of Ndabaningi Sithole. Following the federation's break-up in 1963 – which paved the way for the independence of Northern Rhodesia (Zambia) and Nyasaland (Malawi) – the ZAPU and ZANU were banned and their leaders imprisoned.

Ian Smith & the Second Chimurenga

In 1964 Ian Smith took over the Rhodesian presidency and began pressing for independence. British prime minister Harold Wilson countered by outlining conditions to be met before Britain would agree: guarantee of racial equality, course towards majority rule, and majority desire for independence. Smith realised the whites would never agree, so in 1965 he made a Unilateral Declaration of Independence.

Britain reacted by declaring Smith's action illegal and imposed economic sanctions (which were also adopted by the UN in 1968). However, the sanctions were ignored by most Western countries and even by British companies. By this stage, both ZANU and ZAPU had opted for guerrilla warfare. Their raids struck deeper into the country with increasing ferocity, and whites, most of whom had been born in Africa and knew no other home, abandoned their properties.

On 11 December 1974 South Africa's John Vorster and Zambia's Kenneth Kaunda persuaded Smith to call a cease-fire and release high-ranking nationalists – including Robert Mugabe – and to begin peace negotiations.

The talks, however, broke down; ZANU split and Mugabe fled to Mozambique. The following year, ZANU chairman Herbert Chitepo was assassinated in Lusaka by Rhodesian intelligence.

The nationalist groups fragmented and re-formed. ZANU and ZAPU created an alliance known as the Patriotic Front (PF), but the expected spirit of cooperation was never realised. Similarly, ZIPRA and ZANLA (the military arms of ZAPU and ZANU respectively) combined to form the Zimbabwe People's Army.

Smith, facing a wholesale white emigration and a collapsing economy, was forced to try an 'internal settlement'. Sithole, and the leader of the ANC, Abel Muzorewa, joined a so-called 'transitional government' in which whites were guaranteed 28 out of the 100 parliamentary seats; veto over all legislation for 10 years; guarantee of their property and pension rights; and control of the armed forces, police, judiciary and civil service. And an amnesty was declared for PF guerrillas.

The effort was a dismal failure. Indeed, the only result was an escalation of the war, now known as the Second Chimurenga. To salvage the settlement, Smith entered into secret negotiations with Nkomo, offering to ditch both Sithole and Muzorewa, but Nkomo proved to be intransigent. Finally, Smith was forced to call a general, nonracial election and hand over leadership to Muzorewa, but on much the same conditions as the 'internal settlement'.

Independence

On 10 September 1979 delegations met at Lancaster House, London, to draw up a constitution favourable to both the PF of Nkomo and Mugabe, and the Zimbabwe–Rhodesian government of Muzorewa and Smith. Mugabe, who wanted ultimate power, initially refused to make any concessions, but after 14 weeks the Lancaster House Agreement was reached. It guaranteed whites (then 3% of the population) 20 of the 100 parliamentary seats.

In the carefully monitored election of 4 March 1980, Mugabe prevailed by a wide margin and Zimbabwe and its majority-rule government joined the ranks of Africa's independent nations.

Soon after, the economy soared, wages increased, and basic social programmes –

notably education and healthcare – were initiated. However, the initial euphoria, unity and optimism quickly faded: a resurgence of rivalry between ZANU (run mostly by Shona people) and ZAPU (mostly by Ndebele) escalated into armed conflict, and the ZAPU leader Nkomo was accused of plotting against the government. Guerrilla activity resumed in ZAPU areas of Matabeleland, and Mugabe deployed the North Korean-trained Fifth Brigade in early 1983 to quell the disturbances. The brigade launched an orgy of killing; innocent villagers were gunned down and prominent members of ZAPU were eliminated in order to root out dissidents. About 20,000 people are believed to have died.

Nkomo, meanwhile, fled to England until Mugabe (realising the strife threatened to erupt into civil war) publicly relented and guaranteed his safe return. Talks resulted in a ZAPU–ZANU confederation (called ZANU–PF) and amnesty for the dissidents, thereby masterfully sweeping the matter – but not the underlying discontent – under the rug.

Increasing Taxes & Tensions

Despite tragic experiments with one-party socialism in neighbouring countries, President Mugabe's Marxist dream remained alive. In 1988 the abolition of the law that guaranteed 20 parliamentary seats to whites, and the imposition of strict controls on currency, foreign exchange and trade, were steps in this direction.

In the 1990 elections, ZANU–PF was challenged by the newly formed Zimbabwe Unity Movement (ZUM), which promoted free enterprise and a multiparty democratic state. A gerrymander engineered by Mugabe, however, enabled ZANU–PF to post a landslide victory. Soon afterwards, Patrick Kombayi, a ZUM candidate, was wounded in an assassination attempt and those with ZUM ties immediately sought a low profile. In 1990, despite Mugabe's persistence, members of parliament voted against the implementation of Marxism in Zimbabwe.

In 1995, with his popularity waning and elections due, Mugabe revealed a US$160 million 'anti-poverty programme'. The election, however, was characterised by general apathy and voter turnout was poor, so Mugabe won. A year later, government officials had ripped off the War Victims' Compensation Fund. Veterans began demonstrating

Land Reform

When Rhodes and his private army advanced into Zimbabwe, and granted land to other white settlers, they no doubt thought they were securing investments for future generations. But the inequality remained intolerable: by the mid-1990s, whites owned about 70% of the arable land but made up less than 1% of the population. Yet 'white' farms form the backbone of the economy, and to simply redistribute this profitable land to subsistence farmers, who lack the skills to utilise it, would have serious implications.

When independence was declared, the Lancaster House Agreement guaranteed that private land-holdings could not be nationalised without fair compensation. This was reviewed in 1990, and in 1996, after written assurances that the takeover would be handled in a 'rational' way, the IMF promised to finance any shortfalls.

However, in November 1998, the government announced it would seize 1503 white-owned farms. Promising compensation, amid rumours of US$2 million being spent each day defending the regime in Congo (Zaïre), the government then stated it could only afford to compensate farmers for improvements (houses, barns and other structures) made during their ownership, but not for the full value of the farms. This led to breakdowns in negotiations with the IMF, and while some farmers freely gave up their land, for others the compensation (or lack of it) was unfair and lawsuits followed.

In early 2000, Mugabe, hoping to consolidate his power, held a referendum about land reform and redistribution, but the populace responded with a resounding 'no'. Although shaken, Mugabe remained confident that land reform would bring him popularity and votes, and published his own constitutional clause to allow for the seizure of farms. For many, this indicated approval to invade and 'reclaim' white properties.

Between February 2000 and October 2002, 600 white-owned farms were seized and more than 12 white farmers were killed. The rarely-mentioned statistic is that 150,000 black farm workers have also lost their jobs and/or homes. The so-called 'war veterans' (who ostensibly fought for Zimbabwean independence, although many farm-invaders were too young to have done so) were promised much of the land, but the opposition media believes that about one-third has been given to relatives, friends and political allies of Mugabe, including his wife, Grace.

and demanding their rightful compensation; their demands culminated in a confrontation with Mugabe at the 1997 Heroes' Day rally. Mugabe hastily promised money for the veterans, and an increase in income and fuel taxes was announced.

Already heavily burdened by excessive taxes, the normally passive Zimbabweans found the new tax levies unsustainable. They rebelled and boycotted work. Throughout the country, all colours united in a peaceful demonstration of disapproval, but in Harare, police attempted to halt the demonstration by firing tear gas into the crowds. The parliament soon rejected the proposed income-tax increase and mandated that the fuel price be dropped. The president and his ministers were incensed.

Meanwhile, the Zimbabwe dollar lost over 50% of its value. The increased cost of imports caused immediate price hikes for most goods, including basic foodstuffs. In Harare, protesters again took to the streets and rioting

ensued. The Zimbabwe Congress of Trade Unions (ZCTU) called on the government to address the problems or face a two-day work stoppage. The government simply threatened 'stern action' if the boycott went ahead. Undaunted, workers stayed home on 3 and 4 March 1998. Riot police came out in force and waited for a demonstration that never happened.

Zimbabwe Today

In 1999 thousands attended a ZCTU rally to launch the Movement for Democratic Change (MDC). Morgan Tsvangirai, the secretary general, stated he would lead a social democratic party fighting for workers' interests. Mugabe immediately realised that the MDC was a significant threat and tried to outlaw the party and discredit Tsvangirai.

Most Zimbabweans and all international monitors had desperately hoped for a change of government during the presidential elections in April 2002. But

ZANU–PF's consistent use of intimidation and violence against voters in the lead up to the elections resulted in a narrow victory for the ruling party. According to international aid agencies, one successful political tool used by ZANU–PF is to deliberately stall or halt the distribution of food aid to MDC voters and to areas that had previously voted for the MDC.

This election result, and the continuing expulsion of white farmers through the land reform programme, led to the Commonwealth debating the expulsion of Zimbabwe. Mugabe has also been publicly shunned by the Southern African Development Community (SADC). He has few political allies left.

GEOGRAPHY

Landlocked Zimbabwe is roughly three times the size of England and half as big as Texas. It lies within the tropics and consists of highveld and middleveld plateaus between 900m and 1700m above sea level. A low ridge running northeast to southwest across the country marks the divide between the Zambezi and Limpopo–Save River systems.

The northwest consists mostly of plateaus, characterised by bushveld dotted with *kopjes* and bald knob-like domes of smooth rock known as *dwalas*. The hot, dry lowveld of southern Zimbabwe is mainly the level savanna of the Save Basin, sloping almost imperceptibly towards the Limpopo.

The predominant mountainous region is the Eastern Highlands, which straddles the Zimbabwe–Mozambique border. Zimbabwe's highest peak, Nyangani, rises to 2592m near the northern end of the range.

CLIMATE

Zimbabwe stretches over a high plateau and enjoys a pleasantly temperate climate during the dry season. The cooler, drier months (May to October) are similar to the Mediterranean summer, with warm, sunny days and cool, clear nights. It never snows, though overnight frosts and freezing temperatures are not uncommon.

The lowveld and the Zambezi Valley experience hotter and more humid temperatures, but in winter there's still very little rainfall. Most of Zimbabwe's rain falls in brief afternoon deluges and electrical storms in the relatively humid and warmer months from November to April.

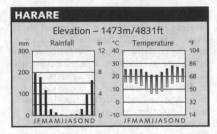

ECOLOGY & ENVIRONMENT

The usual ecological problems faced by countries in Southern African – eg, land degradation, urban sprawl, soil erosion, poaching, and slash-and-burning farming – have been exacerbated by the ill-devised land reform programme and Zimbabwe's ongoing political and economic crises.

The Elephant 'Problem'

Zimbabwe's 70,000 elephants are not endangered, but according to some the country faces ecological disaster because of their destructive habits. For instance, Zambezi Valley elephants have already proven a menace by destroying thousands of hectares of crops. But others claim that crops are often planted in areas that have always been frequented by elephants and that popular water holes are often drained by farmers.

Some have even suggested that elephant numbers could be reduced by culling (to half the current number) and trophy hunting. Currently, hunters pay about US$20,000 to shoot a bull elephant, providing badly needed revenue. On the other hand, conservation groups contend that the elephant population is sustainable.

In late 2002 Cites (the Convention on International Trade in Endangered Species) allowed Zimbabwe and several other Southern and Eastern African countries to sell ivory already collected and stockpiled through natural causes. Conservationists believe this will give poachers the green light to start illegally slaughtering more of these endangered beasts (see Ecology & Environment in the Facts about the Region chapter).

Conservation Efforts

In 1989 increasing disquiet over the government's 'shoot to kill' policy to combat poaching gave rise to Campfire (the Communal Areas Management Programme for

Indigenous Resources). This channelled revenue from hunting on communal lands, where wildlife had become a nuisance to subsistence farmers, back into the communities. Since its inception, Campfire participation has prospered and the amount of land in Zimbabwe dedicated to conservation has more than doubled. Poaching has also slowed and populations of endangered species including rhinos – are rising. About 90% of Campfire's revenue is derived from leases on sport hunting and tourism concessions to commercial safari operators, as well from foreign sources.

Control of wildlife on private ranches has been ceded to ranchers since 1975, but the Ministry of Environment and Tourism still hopes to place it under the care of the district councils and Campfire. However, alleged government mismanagement of elephant and rhino translocation projects, the policy of 'indigenisation' (granting new licences only to black Zimbabweans) of the safari industry, and the government's continued attempts to take over white-owned farms, have cast a veil of uncertainty over private conservation.

If you're interested in learning more about Zimbabwe's ecological problems, contact **Wildlife & Environment Zimbabwe (w** www .zimwild.org). This organisation educates Zimbabweans about the environment and assists projects involved in soil erosion and the protection of endangered species.

FLORA & FAUNA

The vegetation is uniform throughout Zimbabwe. Most of the central and western plateau is covered with bushveld (thorny acacia savanna) and miombo (dry open woodland), while the drier lowlands of the south and southeast are characterised by thorny scrub and baobabs. Among all this are towering cactus-like euphorbias resembling pipe organs, 30 diverse species of aloes, wildflowers (that bloom between September and November), jacarandas (whose flowers bury the streets of Harare, Bulawayo and Mutare in October), and a host of succulent tropical flowers and palms.

Most of the animals highlighted in the colour 'Wildlife Guide' section are represented in Zimbabwe. The largest lizards are the leguans (or water monitors), docile creatures that are often over 2m long. Other reptiles include geckos, chameleons and legless snake lizards. The rivers, dams and lakes are home to 117 species of fish; most visitors prefer bream on their plate, while anglers love the fight put up by the powerful tigerfish.

Twitchers will be delighted with the hundreds of bird species found all over the country, including buff-spotted fluff tails and stripe-cheeked bulbuls. Matobo National Park, for example, is home to one-third of the world's eagle species.

National Parks & Wildlife Reserves

Zimbabwe's national parks and reserves offer larger animal populations, and as much variety of species, as most countries in Southern and Eastern Africa. (And with the current paucity of tourists, you will have stretches of the parks and reserves to yourself.) Some 13% of Zimbabwe's surface area is protected, or semiprotected, in national parks or safari areas. This doesn't include privately protected areas such as game ranches and nature conservancies, as well as recreational parks – all of which would increase the percentage considerably.

Visiting Parks & Reserves Despite the hefty increases (for foreigners) in admission fees to most national parks (and reserves), a substantial part of the revenue ends up in the central treasury (to pay for imports) and very little returns to the parks. As a result, some parks face constant problems: eg, artificially pumped water holes often go dry, facilities are becoming increasingly shabby, and the reservations system has its difficulties.

Admission fees to all government-run parks are valid for 24 hours if you're just visiting for the day, but valid for up to seven days if you have pre-booked accommodation inside the park for that amount of time. If you stay longer than seven days, you must pay an extra fee at the gate on departure. Admission fees vary for each park (see the relevant sections for details). The only standard fee is for vehicles: those with more than six seats pay US$6 per vehicle per entry (ie, valid for the length of your stay in the park); other vehicles are free. For obvious safety reasons, motorbikes are not allowed in the parks.

Some activities, such as walking safaris, horse riding and wildlife drives, are offered by the national parks. But costs are high,

and payment is often required in US dollars. While foreigners can pay for national park accommodation in local currency, admission fees for visitors and their vehicles (if required) must be paid in US dollars.

Note that hitching is forbidden in all national parks, though park officials realise that not everyone has a vehicle and usually tolerate discreet or informal hitching that originates from *outside* the park. Cats and dogs are forbidden inside all parks.

The Accommodation section later in this chapter has information about booking lodges and camp sites run by National Parks & Wildlife Zimbabwe (NPWZ).

GOVERNMENT & POLITICS

The Republic of Zimbabwe is (in theory) a parliamentary democracy. The president, who is the official head of state and commander-in-chief of the armed forces, is (ostensibly) elected by national popular vote every six years. Since independence in 1980, the ruling party has been the Shona-dominated ZANU–PF and the president has been Robert Mugabe. The main opposition party is the multiracial MDC, led by Morgan Tsvangirai.

Of the 150 members of parliament, 120 are elected by the people every five years – one from each constituency throughout the country. Eight members are provincial governors and 10 are chiefs, who are elected by an electoral college of other chiefs (though only the president can authorise the title of 'chief'). The remaining 12 are directly appointed by the executive president.

Zimbabwe is divided into eight provinces, each with its own local government headed by a state-appointed governor.

ECONOMY

About 70% of Zimbabwe's population depends on agriculture, but it's mostly at the subsistence level and accounts for only 20% of the Gross National Product (GNP). The staple food crop is maize, while cotton, coffee, tea, tobacco, wine grapes and sugar cane are the main cash crops. Livestock, the main indicator of wealth in pre-colonial Zimbabwe, remains a major commodity.

Zimbabwe was once the world's second-largest producer of tobacco (after Brazil), and the evil weed contributed 31% (US$400 million) of Zimbabwe's annual foreign currency earnings. However, the land reform programme has brought about a 75% decline in tobacco production.

Ideally, tourism would total about 6% of the GNP, but tourism revenue declined from about US$400 million per year in the mid-1990s to US$81.4 million in 2001. About 30,000 jobs have been lost in the tourism industry since mid-1999.

In short, the economy is in shambles. The currency desperately needs to be devalued, but this would result in higher food prices, and subsequent civil unrest that would threaten Mugabe's power base. International agencies believe that an absolute minimum of ZW$35,000 per person per month is needed to buy basic supplies, yet the minimum monthly wage is ZW$15,000 (one kilogram of rice costs around US$600.) Not surprisingly, teachers (paid ZW$25,000 per month) went on strike in 2002, and were subsequently intimidated by ZANU–PF thugs.

During 2001 and 2002, the economy actually *shrank* by about 11%. Importing fuel costs about US$600 million a year, but foreign currency reserves are almost non-existent. In apparent desperation, Mugabe visited Libya in 2002, and the opposition media in Zimbabwe strongly believe that President Gaddafi gave Mugabe fuel supplies in return for vast amounts of Zimbabwean land and significant interests in government-run businesses.

One haunting memory of a visit to Zimbabwe will be the queues: people lining up for bread, paraffin oil (for cooking) and maize meal (the staple food) and – perhaps more poignantly – the longer queues outside passport offices and lottery agencies.

POPULATION & PEOPLE

About 65% of the population live in rural areas. Only a few years ago, the average life expectancy was nearly 60 years; today, with the onslaught of AIDS, it's about 40 years. With a growth rate of 2.5% per annum, about 40% of the population are under 18 years old.

Most Zimbabweans are of Bantu origin; 9.8 million belong to various Shona groups and about 2.3 million are Ndebele. The remainder are divided between the Tonga (or Batonga) people of the upper Kariba area, the Shangaan (or Hlengwe) of the Lowveld, and the Venda of the far south. Europeans (18,000), plus Asians (10,000), and mixed

Europeans and Africans (25,000) are scattered around the country.

ARTS

Visitors are often surprised by the degree of artistic talent Zimbabweans take for granted. Even the most humble pot or basket created in a remote village displays artistic sensitivity and attention to detail, and artists are highly esteemed in Zimbabwean society.

Information about Zimbabwean music is outlined in the special colour section 'Beats of Southern Africa' earlier in this book.

Literature

Although oral traditions perpetuated a large body of stories, legends, songs and poetry, the first written works by black authors didn't appear in print until the publication (in Shona) of *Feso*, by S Mutswairo, in 1956. The first Ndebele novel, published in 1957, was *Umthawakazi*, by PS Mahlangu.

Subsequent works dealt with pre-colonial traditions, myths and folk tales, and focused on the experiences of blacks under a white regime. The first serious treatise on this topic was Stanlake Samkange's *On Trial for My Country*, published in 1966.

Since independence, Zimbabwean literature has focused on the liberation effort and the struggles to build a new society. The 1992 Commonwealth Prize for Literature went to Zimbabwean writer Shimmer Chinodya for *Harvest of Thorns*, an epic novel of the Second Chimurenga. Another internationally renowned writer is Chenjerai Hove, who wrote the war-inspired *Bones*, the tragic *Shadows*, and the humorous *Shebeen Tales*.

Tsitsi Dangarembga's *Nervous Conditions* is also highly acclaimed. Set in eastern Zimbabwe, it relates the story of a young woman attending a mission school in Rhodesia during the 1960s.

Traditional Crafts

Even before Arab traders brought cloth from India, Zimbabweans were spinning and weaving garments from wild cotton that grew on the plateau. They were also making blankets, mats and clothing from strands of the soft and pliable tree bark known as *gudza*. Zimbabwean women have also developed nontraditional crafts, such as crochet and batik.

Pottery, another traditional female activity, has been an enduring art form. Intricately designed pots have always played a practical role in everyday life. They are used for storage, cooking, serving, carrying, preparing curdled milk and even brewing yeast beer.

Traditionally, hoes, axe handles, ladles, bowls and penis sheaths, were all carved from wood in simple and practical designs. Spear and dagger handles were decoratively rendered and shields were mounted on carved wooden frames. Even small canoes were typically hewn out of a single piece of wood.

Wooden stools, whose intricate decorations reach their highest level in the Tonga culture

The Shona & Ndebele

The Shona people, which dominate the ruling and political classes in Zimbabwe, originate from the Congo (Zaïre) region. As explained in the History section earlier in this chapter, they developed the Rozwi state, which built Great Zimbabwe. Now based in the northern and eastern parts of the country, the Shona are famous for their sculptures (see the 'Shona Sculpture' boxed text later in this chapter) and wood carvings. Shona groups playing traditional music with unique instruments, such as the *mbira* (thumb piano), are renowned throughout Southern Africa. Rural Shona, who live in remote settlements headed by chiefs, often still believe in ancestral spirits.

The Ndebele, including the Kalanga, occupy an area around central and western Zimbabwe, including Bulawayo and Victoria Falls. They are descended from the Zulus of South Africa. Music and singing are an integral part of the Ndebele culture, and their multipart harmony groups are renowned throughout Southern Africa and beyond. Similar to their Zulu cousins, Ndebele women are sometimes traditionally adorned with beads and rings, and their family homes are brightly painted.

Historically, the minority Ndebele has been discriminated against by the Shona, but relations are currently peaceful. Yet the rivalry between Shona-dominated Harare and Ndebele-dominated Bulawayo is more ethnic than economic.

Shona Sculpture

As a relatively recent addition to Zimbabwe's cultural arts, Shona sculpture has garnered significant international recognition, though they have no functional or ceremonial value, nor has the Shona any exclusive rights to the genre.

Shona sculptures weld African themes and ideas with European artistic training. They represent stylised animals, gods, spirits, ancestors and totems, as well as humans. A recurring theme is the metamorphosis of man into beast – the prescribed punishment for violation of social interdictions (such as eating one's totem animal).

The best place to buy sculptures, and to watch artisans at work, is the **Gallery of Shona Sculpture** at Chapungu Kraal in Harare (see Harare later in this chapter for details).

of western Lake Kariba, are also carved from a single piece of wood. Historically, only men were allowed to sit on them and male heads of households used them as 'thrones' from which to oversee family affairs.

LANGUAGE

The official language of Zimbabwe is English. It's used in government, legal and business proceedings, but is the first language for only about 2% of the population. Most Zimbabweans speak Shona (mainly in the north and east) or Ndebele (in the centre and west). Another dialect, Chilapalapa, is actually a pidgin version of Ndebele, English, Shona and Afrikaans, and isn't overly laden with niceties, so most people prefer you sticking to English.

For more information about the indigenous languages of Zimbabwe, and some useful words and phrases in Shona and Ndebele (Sindebele), see the Language chapter at the back of this book.

Facts for the Visitor

SUGGESTED ITINERARIES

With one or two weeks, it's best to base yourself in one or two places – eg, Harare, Masvingo (for Great Zimbabwe), Bulawayo (also for Matobo National Park) or Mutare (for the Eastern Highlands) – but make sure

you also visit Victoria Falls. With three or four weeks, spend longer at (and around) these places, and add in Gweru, Kariba and Hwange, Nyanga or Mana Pools National Parks. Alternatively, try a semicircular route: ie, Victoria Falls, Hwange National Park, Bulawayo, Gweru, Masvingo, Mutare, the Eastern Highlands, Harare, Kariba and Mana Pools National Park.

The Big Trip

Most travellers come to Zimbabwe as part of a lengthy jaunt around Southern Africa. If you're crossing Zimbabwe between Mozambique and Botswana (or Namibia), perhaps visit Mutare, the Eastern Highlands, Masvingo, Gweru, Bulawayo, Hwange National Park and Victoria Falls. Otherwise, try the circular route through Zimbabwe and Zambia: ie, Harare, the Eastern Highlands, Masvingo, Bulawayo, Hwange National Park and Victoria Falls; and then through Zambia, via Livingstone, Lusaka, the Lower Zambezi National Park and Siavonga, before returning to Zimbabwe at Kariba town.

Travel Tips

Allow plenty of time because petrol shortages have caused a reduction in the number of buses and minibuses. Obtain current and accurate information about exchange rates before you come, if possible.

PLANNING
When to Go

Generally, the dry winter months (May to October) are the most comfortable for travelling, but you'll miss the green landscapes that characterise the hotter and wetter summer season (November to April). In winter night-time temperatures can fall below freezing, while in summer daytime temperatures can climb to 35°C, but may be tempered by afternoon thunderstorms.

Winter is often the best time for wildlife viewing because animals tend to congregate around a diminishing number of water holes, and are therefore easier to glimpse. Tourist spots can be quite crowded during the South African and Namibian school holidays (see the South Africa and Namibia chapters).

Maps

The useful series of 'Tourist Maps' (which were once distributed for free by tourist

offices in Zimbabwe) cover the cities and most national parks. These maps are available for about US$1 each from the tourist offices and better bookshops, which also sell detailed maps of Zimbabwe. More detailed maps of the cities and national parks are available at the **Surveyor General** in Harare (see Harare later in this chapter for details).

TOURIST OFFICES
Local Tourist Offices
The government-run tourist organisation is the **Zimbabwe Tourism Authority** *(ZTA;* ☎ *04-758712, fax 758826;* **W** *www.zimba bwetourism.co.zw; 1 Union Ave, Harare).* This office, and the other ZTA offices in Bulawayo and Victoria Falls, deal with all of Zimbabwe; for specific inquiries about the place you're visiting, contact one of the regional tourist offices. These offices (often called 'publicity associations') are in Harare, Bulawayo, Kwe Kwe, Gweru, Kariba, Victoria Falls, Nyanga, Masvingo and Mutare (see the relevant sections for contact details). Some offices are considerably more helpful than others, but they all distribute brochures and try to answer queries.

Tourist Offices Abroad
Germany (☎ 069-920 7730, fax 920 7731) An der Hauptwache, 60313 Frankfurt am Main
South Africa (☎ 011-331 3137, fax 616 8692) 2nd floor, Finance House, Oppenheimer Rd, Bruma Park, Johannesburg
UK (☎ 020-7240 6169, fax 7240 5465, **e** zta .london@btclick.com) 429 The Strand, London WC2R 0SA
USA (☎ 212-486 3444, fax 486 3888) 128 East 56 St, New York 10022

VISAS & DOCUMENTS
Visas
Visas are required by citizens of all countries, but are available to most visitors on arrival at international airports and major borders. Citizens of the following countries can obtain free tourist visas on arrival: Botswana, Canada, Ireland, Namibia, Norway, Sweden, South Africa, UK and Zambia. Visitors from Australia, Israel, Japan, South Korea, New Zealand, Poland, Switzerland, the USA, and the EU can obtain tourist visas on arrival for a fee. Others must apply at a Zimbabwean embassy or high commission, or a British embassy in the absence of a Zimbabwean diplomatic mission (although this may

change in the near future, due to strained relations between Zimbabwe and the UK.)

Tourist visas on arrival, or from Zimbabwean diplomatic missions, cost US$30 for single-entry (valid for 90 days) and US$45 for double-entry (valid for six months). Multiple-entry tourist visas (valid for six months) cost US$55, but are only issued at Zimbabwean diplomatic missions. Visas on arrival can be paid (in cash) in US dollars, UK pounds, South African rands, Namibian dollars or Botswana pula.

Consider buying a double- or multiple-entry tourist visa if you're planning to go in and out of Zimbabwe a few times, eg, daytripping to Zambia from Victoria Falls or Kariba, or visiting Chobe National Park in Botswana from Vic Falls.

The boxed text 'Visiting Zambia from Zimbabwe (and Vice Versa)' in the Victoria Falls chapter has information about day visas if you're travelling between Victoria Falls (Zimbabwe) and Livingstone (Zambia).

Visa Extensions All tourist visas can be extended by one month (US$20 per month), but only three times. Extensions are possible at any office of the Department of Immigration Control, but you're more likely to be successful in Harare. The process is usually hassle-free, but if the paperwork becomes overwhelming and time-consuming, just leave the country, say to Zambia or Malawi, and get another Zimbabwean visa when you return.

Visas for Onward Travel Harare is one of the better places in Southern Africa to pick up visas for regional countries. Requirements constantly change, but nearly all require a fee (most in US dollars) and two passport-sized photos. The opening times of the main embassies and high commissions are listed in the Embassies & High Commissions in Zimbabwe section later.

Visas for Zambia, Namibia, Malawi, South Africa and Botswana are easy to obtain on arrival for most visitors. Consequently, the high commissions for these countries in Harare will only issue visas to the few nationalities that need them before arrival.

For Mozambique, transit visas (valid for seven days) cost US$11, single-entry visas (one month) cost US$20, and multiple-entry visas (three months) cost US$40. Visas are

ready in three days, but are available sooner for extra costs: about double the normal fee within 24 hours, and triple the fee to collect the visa on the same day.

Other Documents

Vaccination for yellow fever is not required for entry to Zimbabwe unless you have recently been to an infected area. According to some Zimbabwean authorities, however, Zambia is an 'infected area', though you probably won't be asked to show proof of yellow fever vaccination while crossing the border from Zambia to Zimbabwe. You probably *will* be asked to show a certificate if visiting South Africa from Zimbabwe or Zambia. For all sorts of reasons, get a jab before you come to Southern Africa and carry a certificate to prove it.

A few museums and tourist attractions accept senior or youth/student cards, but won't advertise the fact, so ask. A youth/student card may also be useful for buying tickets on major international airlines. A seniors' card will get you a 20% discount on domestic train travel.

EMBASSIES & CONSULATES
Zimbabwean Embassies & High Commissions

Zimbabwe has high commissions in Botswana, Malawi, Mozambique, Namibia, South Africa and Zambia (see the relevant chapters for details). Zimbabwean diplomatic missions are also in:

Australia (☎ 02-6286 2700, fax 02-6290 1680, e zimbabwe@dynamite.com.au) 11 Culgoa Circuit, O'Malley, Canberra, ACT 2606
Canada (☎ 613-237 4388, fax 613-563 8269, e zim.highcomm@sympatico.ca) 332 Somerset St West, Ottawa, Ontario K2P OJ9
France (☎ 01 56 88 16 00, fax 01 56 88 16 09) 12 Rue Lord Byron, Paris 75008
Germany (☎ 0228-356071, fax 0228-356309) Villichgasse 7, 5300 Bonn 2
UK (☎ 020-7836 7755, fax 020-7379 1167) 429 The Strand, London WC2R OSA
USA (☎ 202-332 7100, fax 202-438 9326) 1608 New Hampshire Ave NW, Washington, DC 20009

Embassies & High Commissions in Zimbabwe

The following embassies and high commissions are based in Harare (area code ☎ 04).

Australia (☎ 253661, W www.zimbabwe.embassy .gov.au) 29 Mazowe St
Botswana (☎ 729551) 22 Phillips Ave. Open 8am to 12.30pm, Monday, Wednesday and Friday.
Canada (☎ 252181) 45 Baines Ave
France (☎ 703216) First Bank Building, 74-76 Samora Machel Ave
Germany (☎ 308655) 14 Samora Machel Ave West
Malawi (☎ 752137) Malawi House, 42-44 Harare St. Open 8am to 1pm and 2pm to 5pm, Monday to Friday.
Mozambique (☎ 253871) 152 Herbert Chitepo Ave. Open 8am to 12pm, Monday to Friday.
Namibia (☎ 885841) 69 Borrowdale Rd. Open 8am to 1pm and 2pm to 5pm, Monday to Friday.
South Africa (☎ 753147, e sahcomm@internet .co.zw) 7 Elcombe Ave. Open 8am to 12pm and 1.15pm to 3pm, Monday to Friday.
UK (☎ 772990) 7th floor, Corner House, cnr Leopold Takawira St and Samora Machel Ave
USA (☎ 250594) Arax House, 172 Herbert Chitepo Ave
Zambia (☎ 773777, fax 773782) 6th floor, Zambia House, 48 Union Ave. Open 8am to 12.30pm and 2pm to 4.30pm, Monday to Friday.

CUSTOMS

Visitors may import a maximum of US$250 in nontrade items, excluding personal effects. Travellers over 18 years of age can also import up to five litres of alcohol, including two litres of spirits.

On arrival, you must complete a form issued by the Zimbabwe Revenue Authority. On this form, list the number and value of expensive items that you're bringing into the country, eg, still/video camera, laptop and jewellery, and the approximate amount of foreign currency you have. Theoretically, you must keep this form until you leave Zimbabwe, but there's a good chance you won't be asked to provide it when you leave.

MONEY
Currency

The unit of currency is the Zimbabwe dollar (ZW$1 = 100 cents). Notes come in denominations of ZW$5 (rare), ZW$10, ZW$20, ZW$50, ZW$100 and ZW$500. Coins to the value of 50 cents, ZW$1 and ZW$2 will occasionally be given to you in change.

Exchange Rates

The official bank rates listed here are what you'll be charged if you use a credit card

ZIMBABWE

ZIMBABWE

Costs & Currencies

For as long as the political crisis in Zimbabwe continues, the economic situation will remain a shambles. In short: *only* take cash (preferably in US dollars), and obtain accurate advice as soon you can from fellow travellers and Zimbabwean tourist workers about the current exchange rates.

During 2001 and 2002, the inflation rate peaked at 140% per annum, and during late 2002 the unofficial (black market) exchange rate with the US dollar almost doubled within two months. So, in an attempt to provide accurate prices in this chapter (and the Zimbabwe section of the Victoria Falls chapter) we have listed all costs in US dollars, with the exception of a few minor items that cost less than one US dollar. But the local currency should be used for all food, drinks, museum admission fees, public transport, and budget accommodation. On the other hand, US dollars are required to pay for some hotels, all upmarket lodges, most organised tours, all foreign visas, and admission fees to all national parks.

In calculating some prices, we used the unofficial exchange rate of US$1 = ZW$600, though these rates change daily and will have probably increased markedly by the time you visit. In any event, as long as the economic crisis continues (and it will indefinitely), and you can change money at the unofficial (but accepted) exchange rate, Zimbabwe will remain exceptionally good value.

and possibly travellers cheques. Always change cash at the unofficial (black market) rate, though not all currencies have a black market rate.

country	unit		official	unofficial
Australia	A$1	=	ZW$31.06	–
Botswana	P1	=	ZW$9.09	ZW$44
Canada	C$1	=	ZW$36.19	–
euro	€1	=	ZW$55.66	ZW$320
Japan	¥100	=	ZW$46.78	–
Malawi	MK1	=	ZW$9.10	–
Mozambique	Mtc100	=	ZW$2.40	–
Namibia	N$	=	ZW$6.24	ZW$39
New Zealand	NZ$1	=	ZW$27.24	–
South Africa	R1	=	ZW$5.44	ZW$33
UK	UK£1	=	ZW$89	ZW$1000
USA	US$1	=	ZW$57.44	ZW$600
Zambia	k100	=	ZW$13.33	–

Exchanging Money

If you're travelling independently and using credit cards or travellers cheques, Zimbabwe will be horrendously expensive, but if you use the unofficial black market rate, you'll find that it's one of *the* cheapest places on earth. Remember: many things that tourists pay for in Zimbabwean dollars are linked to the unofficial exchange rate.

If you don't have cash, change as much as you need for Zimbabwe in Zambia, Namibia, Botswana or South Africa in the relevant currencies, and then use the unofficial rates in Zimbabwe. (Exporting large quantities of local currency from these countries may be illegal, however. See the relevant chapters

for details.) Otherwise, ask someone to send you some US dollars through Western Union (which is affiliated with most major post offices in Zimbabwe), but confirm that the Western Union branch in Zimbabwe will give you US dollars in cash. Alternatively, pay for a mid-range/upmarket hotel or organised tour with travellers cheques and plead for change in US dollars cash. If all else fails, those on a budget may want to give Zimbabwe a miss.

Travellers Cheques All major brands of travellers cheques in US dollars or UK pounds can be exchanged for Zimbabwe dollars at all major banks and larger bureaux de change. However, you will probably be offered the official exchange rate; at best, the bank or bureau de change will offer a combination of 60% of the official rate and 40% of the unofficial rate. In any event, the exchange rate for travellers cheques will be *far* less than you would get for cash.

Zimbank charges 2% commission, while Barclays and Standard Chartered banks charge 1%. Barclays offers the best rates on Visa travellers cheques, but you must show proof of purchase – you know, the piece of paper they tell you to keep separate from your cheques.

ATMs Generally speaking, automatic teller machines (ATMs) at Barclays Bank accept Visa, and Standard Chartered Bank take MasterCard and any card with a Cirrus logo. But Zimbabwean banks will happily use the

official rate (or, possibly, offer the 60/40 rate mentioned earlier) – and you won't know until you get home and check your credit card account. Also, your daily withdrawal limit is only ZW$9000, which will not go far.

Credit Cards The bad news continues with credit cards. You *may* get the 60/40 rate mentioned earlier obtaining cash advances over the counter, but you will almost certainly be charged the official rate if you charge anything to a credit or debit card. So the memories of your travel around Zimbabwe will be severely tarnished if you're hit with a US$450 Visa bill for a US$25 cruise.

MasterCard and Visa are accepted by most establishments catering to tourists and business people. American Express is less common.

Black (Parallel) Market Official rates are accurately listed to the second decimal point on electronic noticeboards outside most banks and bureaux de changes. Simply ignore the official rates and take your cash into any of the numerous bureaux de change (banks will only offer the official or 60/40 rate mentioned earlier). Some bureaux de change may feign ignorance of the unofficial – and so-called 'parallel' – exchange rate, so simply ask again or find another bureau de change. Be confident: show your US dollar note(s) and say 'I have US$100 (or whatever). What rate can you offer?'. Rates are generally about 2% better for larger notes, eg, US$50 and US$100.

Don't change too much, because the rates normally go up rather than down, and the biggest note is ZW$500 so you'll need a bag to carry the equivalent of US$200 in Zimbabwe dollars. But make sure that you change enough in the cities and larger towns – namely Harare, Bulawayo, Mutare, Kariba and Victoria Falls – to last a few days in the countryside, because bureaux de change that accept the decent parallel rate are harder to find in smaller towns. If you can't locate anywhere to change cash, make discreet inquiries with the owner (not any staff member) at a larger hotel or travel agent.

Ask the bureau de change to give you a receipt at the *official* rate, so that you can pay for some hotels in Zimbabwe dollars rather than US dollars (see Accommodation later in this chapter). And, finally, always be careful

when walking out of a bureau de change, and never *ever* change money on the street. One reader spent three days over Christmas in the 'biggest hellhole of a prison cell' after being caught changing money on the street.

Costs

Many hotels and tour operators, and all national parks, employ a two-tier (or even three-tier) pricing system, in which foreigners pay at least three times more than Zimbabweans and 'regional visitors' (ie, citizens of all countries in Southern Africa) pay about twice as much as Zimbabweans. (See Accommodation later in this chapter.)

But if you travel independently, stay in budget and mid-range hotels, use public transport, and change money at the unofficial (parallel) exchange rate, you will probably leave Zimbabwe with plenty of change. (Or why not treat yourself and upgrade to a better class of accommodation and transport?) Because of the fluctuating unofficial exchange rate, it's pointless estimating how much you may spend per day, but extras to be wary of include internal air fares, souvenirs, activities or tours and national park admission fees.

At the unofficial rate of US$1=ZW$600, tasty Western meals in classy restaurants cost US$1 to US$2, while a plate of Zimbabwe-style food is about ZW$200. You'll be able to afford to wash your meal down with one (or three) bottles of tasty Zambezi lager (ZW$250 each). A public bus from Harare to Mutare (six hours) costs US$3, while more comfortable private buses cost twice as much. A first-class sleeper on the overnight train between Bulawayo and Victoria Falls only costs US$3 – so why not book a compartment to yourself?

Accommodation operated by the national parks is also ridiculously cheap: about ZW$125 per person for camp sites and US$2 to US$3 per chalet, cottage or lodge. Privately-run camp sites and hostels charge about US$4 per person for camping and about US$5 for a dormitory bed. Decent budget rooms cost about US$4/5 for singles/doubles, while top-end hotels charge US$50 to US$150 per person. Safari lodges can cost up to US$300 per person per day including meals, drinks and activities.

Prices for accommodation, meals and activities are higher in Victoria Falls, where operators of hotels, camp sites and travel

agencies regularly insist on payment in US dollars.

Tipping & Bargaining

Some restaurants automatically add a 10% 'service charge' to the bill; if so, no tip is required. Most prices at markets and street stalls are negotiable, and vendors will happily 'sell' you things in exchange for clothes (especially designer brands), caps, pens and electronic items.

Taxes

A 15% 'tourist tax' is usually added to the rates charged by upmarket hotels and lodges, tour operators and car rental agencies, but should be included in the rates quoted to you. (The tax is also included in all rates listed in this chapter and the Zimbabwe section of the separate Victoria Falls chapter.) A further 2% 'tourist levy' is charged on *all* accommodation and car rentals. Again, this should be included in the rates quoted to you (and is included in the rates listed here).

If you want to pay for an activity or tour in Zimbabwe dollars rather than US dollars, you may be slugged *another* 15% tax. This is a futile attempt by the government to offset the unofficial (parallel) exchange rate.

If all this sounds confusing (and it is!), the Goods & Services Tax (16 to 19%) was due to be replaced by a Value Added Tax (VAT) sometime in 2003. However, the government has far more serious economic and political problems to deal with, so this tax overhaul is unlikely to be implemented in the immediate future.

POST & COMMUNICATIONS
Post

Sending letters and postcards by surface mail to Europe and the UK costs ZW$50, and ZW$55 to the rest of the world. For airmail, it's only ZW$70 to Europe and the UK and ZW$90 for anywhere else.

Poste restante services are available in all cities and larger towns, but the post offices at Harare and Bulawayo are the most efficient.

Telephone

The local telephone system may be the butt of many jokes but it is improving – or so they say. Although there are lots of public telephones, glitches mean long queues and bad connections.

As a result, the mobile (cell) phone network is flourishing. If you have international roaming it's possible to purchase prepaid calls for your mobile at phone shops in the cities and larger towns. Another option is to hire a mobile phone from **EcoNet** (☎/fax 04-790797; e gsm@hircit.co.zw), which has stores in all classy shopping centres in Harare and Bulawayo. It offers a 'buy back' system for about US$50, excluding recharge cards (available from vendors on every street corner). Mobile phone numbers are prefixed with ☎ 011, ☎ 023 or ☎ 091.

Phonecards are sold at post offices for ZW$100 and ZW$200, but many telephone booths are empty, vandalised shells. Your best bet is to look for one of the plethora of 'phone shops' or 'communication centres'. Better still, visit an Internet centre because the queues are shorter. Reverse-charge calling is available but, if possible, wear the cost while in Zimbabwe: international calls from Zimbabwe cost less than US$1 per minute to anywhere in the world.

If calling from overseas, the country code for Zimbabwe is ☎ 263, but drop the initial 0 for the area codes. The international access code from within Zimbabwe is ☎ 00. Other useful numbers to remember are the **international operator** (☎ 966), the **national operator** (☎ 962) and **international inquiries** (☎ 965).

Fax

Public fax services are available at post offices in cities and larger towns. No fee is usually charged for receiving faxes, and the post office should (in theory) ring you when a fax arrives if you give them your contact details.

Email & Internet Access

Internet centres and cafés are springing up all over Zimbabwe, though connections can be frustratingly slow. Internet use is popular, so start your surfing before 10am or you may have to wait several hours. Costs are cheap: about US$1 for 30 minutes.

DIGITAL RESOURCES

For up-to-date information about Zimbabwe, try the following websites:

All Zimbabwe Includes useful information about recent political events, and offers numerous links. **W** www.allzimbabwe.com

Travel Zimbabwe The most comprehensive coverage of, and links to, the tourism industry, but practical information is dated. **W** www.travelzim.com

Zwnews.com No-holds-barred political reports about the Mugabe regime. **W** www.zwnews.com

Other useful addresses are given throughout this chapter. For a more comprehensive listing, see also Digital Resources in the Regional Facts for the Visitor chapter.

BOOKS

This section covers books specific to Zimbabwe. For details on books about the Southern Africa region, see Books in the Regional Facts for the Visitor chapter.

Lonely Planet

Songs to an African Sunset: A Story of Zimbabwe, by Sekai Nzenza Shand, is an excellent introduction to Shona traditions and culture. Shand tells of her childhood in Zimbabwe, and of her return to the country after spending many years living in the West. Packed with cultural information about rural life, it also gives an insight into the lives of middle-class urban Zimbabweans. *Songs* is one of many titles in Journeys, Lonely Planet's travel literature series.

Our separate *Zimbabwe* guide obviously provides far more in-depth coverage of the country than we can provide in this chapter.

Guidebooks & Coffee-Table Books

Great Zimbabwe Described & Explained, by Peter Garlake, attempts to sort out the history, purpose and architecture of the ancient ruins at Great Zimbabwe.

The Painted Caves – An Introduction to the Prehistoric Art of Zimbabwe, by Peter Garlake, is a detailed guide uncovering major prehistoric rock-art sites in Zimbabwe.

Beneath a Zimbabwe Sun is a classy souvenir book containing plenty of awesome photos. The hardback and paperback versions are available throughout Zimbabwe.

This is Zimbabwe, by Gerald Cubitt & Peter Joyce, is a glossy coffee-table style book, also available in Zimbabwe.

History & Politics

The Great Betrayal, by Ian Smith, is the autobiography of colonial Rhodesia's most controversial leader chronicling a tumultuous, emotion-charged period in Zimbabwean history.

Mugabe, by Colin Simpson & David Smith, is a biography of the Zimbabwean president tracing his controversial rise to power.

The Struggle for Zimbabwe: The Chimurenga War, by David Martin & Phyllis Johnson, is a popular history of the Second Chimurenga, the tragic war that led to the country's independence.

NEWSPAPERS & MAGAZINES

The two major daily newspapers – the *Chronicle* (from Bulawayo) and *The Herald* (Harare) – are shamelessly pro-Mugabe. One of the few sane and independent voices in Zimbabwe is *The Daily News* (**W** www.dailynews.co.zw). If you can't find a copy on the street corner it's probably because the editorial office or printing press has been vandalised or bombed, or the newspaper's distributors or vendors have been intimidated by ZANU–PF thugs.

Two journalists from *The Standard* (published each Sunday in Harare) were detained and tortured in 1999 following publication of a story about an alleged coup plot against the government. The *Standardplus* entertainment supplement is useful.

Kingston's bookshops, which can be found in all cities and major towns, often stock international magazines, mainly *Newsweek*, and newspapers such as *The Weekly Telegraph*, which is published in the UK but printed in South Africa. All are very cheap.

RADIO & TV

Radio and television broadcasts are overseen by the government-run Zimbabwe Broadcasting Corporation (ZBC).

The one remaining television station, ZTV, is hopelessly pro-Mugabe. It offers 75% local content, but runs on a shoestring budget, so it's virtually unwatchable. Budget hotels only offer ZTV, while mid-range places pick up at least one free-to-air station from South Africa. Top-end places offer the full array of satellite channels through DsTV. (Note: some hotels advertise rooms with DsTV, but fail to deliver because they can't pay the bills.)

ZIMBABWE

ZBC also runs four pro-government radio stations. Several other private stations also operate in the cities, eg, 105FM in Harare is enjoyed by jazz aficionados. International radio services, such as Voice of America and the BBC World Service, are easy to pick up on a short wave radio; otherwise, the BBC also broadcasts on 92.8FM in Harare.

PHOTOGRAPHY & VIDEO

Print and slide film and basic photographic accessories are easy to buy in all cities and larger towns. Prices, however, are not necessarily lower in Zimbabwe than your own country: eg, a roll of 24/36 exposure print film costs about US$3/5, while developing (within 24 hours) will cost about the same. Slide film can be bought and developed in Harare, Bulawayo, Mutare and Victoria Falls, but it's expensive. Bring all your own video equipment.

HEALTH

Bilharzia is a problem in most dams and lakes, including Lake Kariba; the exception is any high level fresh water in the Eastern Highlands. Malaria is increasingly prevalent in Victoria Falls, Hwange National Park and Lake Kariba. Outbreaks of cholera have been reported in remote areas during the wet season (November to April), but these are well reported in the local newspapers so it's easy to avoid infected areas.

Harare and Bulawayo have excellent general hospitals, but for potentially serious problems or complications, it's probably best to visit Johannesburg (Jo'burg) or return home. Doctors are listed in the front of telephone directories for all cities and larger towns in Zimbabwe. Pharmacies and chemists are found in all cities and major towns, but they won't dispense any medicines and drugs without a doctor's prescription.

An estimated 25% of Zimbabwean adults – and 40% of women – are HIV positive. And about 600,000 children have been orphaned and forced to leave school early to find work (in lieu of a working parent) or look after sick relatives.

In hospitals and private clinics, medical equipment is well sterilised and blood products are carefully screened, so there's little chance of infection from needles or transfusions. However, bush clinics operate on limited budgets and proper equipment

may not always be available, especially in emergency situations.

GAY & LESBIAN TRAVELLERS

Homosexual activities for men is illegal and officially punishable by up to five years in jail (though penalties are invariably not nearly as severe), yet lesbianism is not illegal.

For information about gay and lesbian clubs and meeting places in Zimbabwe, contact **Gays and Lesbians of Zimbabwe** *(☎ 04-741 736, fax 778 165;* e *galz@samara.co.zw; 35 Colenbrander Road, Milton Park, Harare).*

DANGERS & ANNOYANCES

Zimbabwe remains one of Africa's safest countries despite the political crisis that is often exaggerated by the Western media. Very occasionally, the remarkably passive Zimbabweans can vent their frustrations by marching or even rioting, but there's no call for paranoia. Just stay away from *anything* remotely political.

During the early 1990s drought forced many people to migrate to the cities, but most lacked marketable skills and few were successful. Some turned to crime, which has conversely created a growth industry: security firms. Because security guards seem to stand outside almost every shop, hotel and restaurant in the country, there is little or no crime. Crowded places that warrant special caution for petty theft, however, are bus terminals, markets, discos and parks. Most camp sites have guards, but occasionally things go missing.

Racism still exists, but the issue is not merely, umm, 'black and white': the long-standing animosity between the Shona and the minority Ndebele peoples has also caused untold grief in the past. And the government-led land reform programme, and the very occasional crimes committed against tourists, are mainly economic – ie, poor against rich, rather than black against white.

Most Zimbabweans are paid on the last Friday of each month, so almost immediately thousands flock to the nearest beer hall or *pungwe.* Unfortunately, this invariably brings parts of the country to a complete standstill the next day as staff are too drunk or hungover to work. Needless to say, lone women should be especially vigilant at this time.

Although you're not likely to be blatantly offered *mbanje* (marijuana) on the streets,

it, along with all other drugs, is illegal – if you're caught, the penalties will be severe. The numerous road blocks in eastern and central Zimbabwe are set up to halt the smuggling of drugs from Mozambique.

Finally, power blackouts are not uncommon, so bring a torch, and carry candles for an enforced 'romantic' evening in your hotel room.

EMERGENCIES

We hope you'll never need to contact any of the following countrywide, toll-free telephone numbers: **ambulance** (☎ 994), **fire brigade** (☎ 993) or **police** (☎ 995).

The **Medical Air Rescue Service** (MARS; ☎ 734531) is a private company providing air evacuation and ambulance services throughout Zimbabwe and other countries in Southern Africa. Contact details are listed in the Harare and Bulawayo sections of this chapter, and in the Zimbabwe section of the Victoria Falls chapter.

BUSINESS HOURS

Shops are generally open from 8am to 1pm and 2pm to 5pm weekdays (Monday to Friday), and from 8am to noon on Saturday, but some close earlier on Wednesday. Banks operate from 8.30am to 3pm weekdays, except Wednesday when they close sometime between 12pm and 1pm, and from about 8.30am to about 11am on Saturday. Post offices open from 8.30am to 4pm weekdays and 8.30am to 11.30am on Saturday.

PUBLIC HOLIDAYS & SPECIAL EVENTS

During the following public holidays, most government offices and businesses are closed:

New Year's Day 1 January
Easter March/April – Good Friday, Easter Sunday and Easter Monday
Independence Day 18 April
Workers' Day 1 May
Africa Day 25 May
Heroes' Day 11 August
Defence Forces' Day 12 August
National Unity Day 22 December
Christmas Day 25 December
Boxing Day 26 December

Several readers have been pleased that their visit to Zimbabwe had coincided with the festivals in Bulawayo, Harare

and Chimanimani – see those sections for details. The official tourism website – w www.zimbabwetourism.co.zw – lists other upcoming special events.

ACTIVITIES

Refer to the relevant sections in this chapter, and the Victoria Falls chapter, for details about the activities listed here.

Victoria Falls is the epicentre of activities in Zimbabwe, if not all of Southern Africa. The adventurous can get their adrenalin pumping with **white-water rafting, abseiling** and **bungee jumping**; the less excitable can enjoy **wildlife drives** and **horse riding**. Other activities include **canoeing** along the Zambezi River in and around Mana Pools National Park, **fishing** in Lake Kariba, **boating** in Lake Mutirikwe, **hiking** in Chimanimani National Park, and **walking safaris** in Hwange National Park.

A round of **golf** is inexpensive. Try the renowned Royal Harare Golf Club, or one of the most spectacular courses in the world at Leopard Rock (Bvumba Mountains), where it's hard to concentrate on putting while you're admiring the awesome views. And on every golf course in Zimbabwe, watch out for warthogs in the bunkers and crocs in the water hazards!

ACCOMMODATION

Despite the 'foreigners must pay in foreign currency' signs adorning many foyers, hotels will happily ignore this and allow foreigners to pay the 'local rates', ie, rates charged to Zimbabweans in local currency. Some hotels will ask you to sign in as a Zimbabwean (to fool the hotel inspectors), while other hotels may allow you to pay the 'local rates' in Zimbabwe dollars because any business is welcome.

A few other hotels may allow you to pay the 'local rate' in Zimbabwe dollars if you can prove that you've changed money at the official bank rate. So when you change money at a bureau de change – at the unofficial (parallel) rate – ask for a receipt showing that you 'changed' at the *official* rate. This is farcical, of course, because the hotel knows that you haven't been stupid enough to change money at the official rate; if you had, the cost of staying at their modest one-star hotel with no bathroom, TV or breakfast would cost you about US$100!

ZIMBABWE

The few budget and mid-range hotels that stubbornly charge foreigners in US dollars have little or no idea about the true value of the US$. Consequently, they may charge foreigners US$65 for a double room, while an identical place next door charges ZW$5000 (about US$9 at the unofficial rate). It pays to check out a few hotels and even telephone a few before you arrive. And always confirm the rates and agree to which currency you will use.

'Half-board' means breakfast and dinner, while 'full board' includes three meals. 'All inclusive' means that meals and activities, and sometimes drinks, are part of the rate, but transport to the hotel or lodge is rarely included.

Budget

Most cities and larger towns offer well-maintained camping grounds with clean ablutions, but some are located along noisy roads. Privately-run camping grounds are often *far* better than those run by local councils, because the latter often serve as picnic sites during the day so security and privacy can never be guaranteed. In some cases, hotels and hostels will allow you to camp, and use their facilities for a fee.

Camping in rural areas or on communal lands is generally discouraged and often prohibited. However, if you're caught without accommodation, ask property owners or village chiefs before setting up camp.

Before you think about bringing camping equipment, however, it's worth noting that hotels and hostels are *so* cheap in Zimbabwe that camping will rarely save you any more than a few US dollars a week.

Information about camping in the national parks is detailed later in this chapter.

Happily, a growing number of backpacker hostels are available. Most offer dormitory beds, double rooms and camp sites, as well as a wide range of amenities, such as a bar, swimming pool and restaurant, and useful services like Internet access, transfers to and from transport terminals, and budget tour bookings. Hostels are mostly found in popular tourist spots, such as Victoria Falls, Bulawayo and Harare.

Mid-Range

All cities and towns offer budget-priced hotels, but the cheapest places are likely to

be used by, umm, 'working ladies' and their clients. Most mid-range hotels are comfortable and clean, and usually offer rooms with a bathroom, TV and breakfast. Most allow foreigners to pay the 'local rate' in Zimbabwean dollars, but a few (which we have often excluded from this chapter) will charge 'foreigner rates' in US dollars.

Most better mid-range hotels, and all top-end places, are rated on a zero to five-star scale based on an elaborate points system, and almost all charge 'foreigner rates' in US dollars. Some hotels, however, may be persuaded to accept you as a 'Zimbabwean', so with a bit of gumption and luck you may be able to check into a four-star hotel with all the amenities that a budget traveller can only dream about for US$10 per person (at the unofficial rate).

Top End

Most national parks are dotted with exclusive, privately-operated lodges and 'camps' (a confusing term often used to describe expensive lodges). They offer the same sort of luxury and exclusivity as other lodges and camps in Southern and Eastern Africa. The daily rates of US$200 or more per person per night (twin share) are usually all inclusive, but single supplements of about 30% are usually charged. These places must be booked in advance, either directly or through an agent in Zimbabwe or abroad. Some close during the wet season (November to April).

National Park Accommodation

National Parks & Wildlife Zimbabwe (NPWZ), which operates all of Zimbabwe's national parks and reserves, offers an impressive range of accommodation, including 250 chalets, cottages and lodges, and dozens of camp sites.

The three types of accommodation are listed here. Each contains one or two bedrooms with two single beds in each. Linen and towels are provided, and all rooms are serviced daily by maids (who work from 7am to 12.30pm and 2pm to 5.30pm).

Chalets are the most basic (and cheapest) option, but usually contain a fridge, pots and pans (but no crockery or cutlery). Guests must use an ablutions block and have access to a communal kitchen.

Cottages contain a private bathroom and well-appointed kitchen (but no crockery or cutlery).

The only exception is at Hwange Main Camp (Hwange National Park), where the cottages don't have a private bathroom.

Lodges have a private bathroom and well-appointed kitchen (with crockery and cutlery)

National park camping grounds offer *braai* (barbecue) pits and ablutions blocks (hot showers are possible with *donkey boilers*), but larger camps cater more to caravans than tents. Most camping grounds consist of a patch of flat and hard dirt (rarely grass), so use a tent with hardy pegs. Most camping grounds are accessible by 2WD, except perhaps in the wet season (November to April) when the grounds may close anyway. It always pays to check the accessibility of the camping ground before booking (see later).

Some national parks also offer small 'exclusive camps'. This does not imply any extra luxuries at all, but means that you can't use the camping ground if it's even partially booked by someone else. Some of these exclusive camps are only accessible by 4WD.

Bookings Thankfully, all guests pay the same rates and foreigners can pay in Zimbabwe dollars – but admission fees to the national parks are payable in US dollars. Although the NPWZ may not advertise the fact, guests staying seven consecutive nights at any type of accommodation run by the NPWZ in any park may get one night free, ie, seven nights for the price of six.

If you're staying in the same national park (even at different camping grounds or lodges within that park) for more than three days, you *must* pre-book accommodation at the NPWZ offices in Harare or Bulawayo. If you want to stay in the same park for less than three days, it *may* be possible (if there are vacancies) to turn up at the local rangers office or park gate and get a lodge, chalet, cottage or camp site – but this can only be confirmed after 2pm. For late bookings, it's better to ring the NPWZ office in Harare, obtain a reference number, and pay for your accommodation at the rangers office. These days, vacancies are more likely, and same-day bookings are more accepted by the NPWZ, because of the dearth of tourists.

Reservations for national park accommodation are available through the NPWZ offices in Harare and Bulawayo (see those sections for contact details). The reservations system isn't exactly a well-oiled machine, so

book early and hang on to your receipt. Bookings are more reliable at the central office in Harare, because for all parks (except Matobo National Park) the office in Bulawayo checks with Harare anyway.

Reservations for all types of accommodation are available up to 12 months in advance by phone, fax, letter or email. If booking from outside of Zimbabwe, payments must be made to either booking office one month before your stay. If booking from within Zimbabwe, but outside of Harare or Bulawayo, payment must be made two weeks before your stay. The limit is one week if you book from Harare or Bulawayo.

The best idea is to plan ahead, and book and pay for your lodge, chalet, cottage or camp site while visiting Harare or Bulawayo; simply pay by cash in person at the office. Otherwise, payments can be made to either office: by bank draft or cheque made out to the 'National Parks Central Booking Office'; by direct debit into the 'Parks & Wildlife Conservation Fund' bank account (details from the booking offices); or by faxing a copy of your Visa or MasterCard with a covering letter authorising the NPWZ's bank to deduct the charges from your credit card. However, using a credit card in Zimbabwe is *not* recommended (see Money earlier in this chapter). Always make sure accommodation is available before sending any money, and keep your receipt to show when you enter the park. No refund is available if the reservation is cancelled within 14 days.

If the NPWZ staff tell you everything is full, don't despair: the reservation system accepts bookings without payment, and some travellers don't pay before the deadline and others don't turn up at the lodge, chalet, cottage or camp site. Keep trying. Extensions are only possible through the office in Harare, even if you're already inside the park.

In the good ol' days of boom tourism, the NPWZ had to use a draw or lottery system for bookings during the hectic school holidays in January, April and May, August and September, and December, but most parks have permanent vacancies.

FOOD

Zimbabwean cuisine is mostly the legacy of bland British fare – soggy sausages, greasy eggs and fatty chips (French fries) – as well as stodgy African dishes, such as the dietary

ZIMBABWE

staple *sadza*, the white maize meal porridge most locals are raised on. The second component is meat (or *nyama*), though *sadza ne nyama* is more likely to be *sadza* with meat gravy only.

Zimbabwe is one of the world's great beef producers and meat is available nearly everywhere. Popular fish include bream and the whitebait-like dried *kapenta*, both plentiful in Lake Kariba, and trout from rivers and dams in the Eastern Highlands.

In the cities and larger towns, especially around transport terminals, lots of small eating halls serve plain but filling fare – usually *sadza ne nyama*, chips, sausage rolls, meat pies, sandwiches and burgers. Junk-food junkies will not suffer withdrawal symptoms, because even the smallest town has at least one Chicken Inn, Baker's Inn, Creamy Inn or Pizza Inn (often all combined into one outlet). The spicy *peri peri* chicken meals sold at the ubiquitous Nando's are hard to resist.

The cities and bigger towns also offer a variety of trendy coffee houses and a range of restaurants serving Chinese, Indian and continental cuisine. Most mid- to upper-range restaurants offer decent vegetarian options. All tourist hotels harbour comparatively expensive restaurants serving European dishes. But why not dine out somewhere elegant when a classy three-course meal may set you back only US$3 (at the unofficial rate)?

DRINKS
Nonalcoholic Drinks

In all cities and larger towns, the water is treated and safe to drink, but not so in remote lodges and camp sites in the national parks and in smaller towns in the Eastern Highlands. Otherwise, plastic bottles of mineral water, boxed fruit juices and soft drinks (sodas) are widely available.

Although tea and coffee are grown in the Eastern Highlands, the best is exported. An increasing number of cafés and restaurants serve real local or imported coffee, while others sell a revolting blend made of 10% instant coffee and 90% chicory. Although it isn't the optimum-quality stuff, Nyanga tea is acceptable and available throughout the country.

Alcoholic Drinks

The tipple of the masses is *chibuku*, which, as its advertising asserts, is 'the beer of good

---

Pungwes

The exact origin of the word *pungwe* is unknown, but probably derived from the Shona word *ngwe*, meaning 'from darkness to light'. It was first used in the 1960s and referred to all-night discos. However, during the Second Chimurenga (1972–80), all-night celebrations of nationalistic unity between villagers and guerrillas, accompanied by morale-inspiring song and dance, came to be known as *pungwes*. Nowadays, any sort of event may be advertised as a *pungwe*, meaning it begins in the evening and carries on through the night.

---

cheer'. Served up in large plastic containers which, after the 1991 Gulf War, came to be known as *scuds*, it has the appearance of vomit, the consistency of thin gruel and a deceptively mellow build up to the knockout punch. It's sold mainly in roadside and township beer halls, and is distinctly a male social scene.

The beer you will more commonly see and drink is lager, which is always served cold. A popular brand is the South African-owned Castle, though the domestically-brewed Zambezi and Bohlinger lagers are superb.

Although the climate isn't suited to grape growing, Zimbabwe does sustain a limited wine industry, particularly east and southeast of Harare. The largest and most renowned winery is Mukuyu, near Marondera.

SHOPPING

One of the most frustrating things about visiting Zimbabwe is reconciling your baggage allowance with the amazing range of souvenirs you can purchase. From wire helicopters with rotating rudders to life-size carvings – you'll find it all. What's more, most of it is remarkably good value. Even when you've broken the bank you can still get more by trading anything and everything, from half a tube of toothpaste to a broken pen.

Zimbabweans set up stalls anywhere a tourist is likely to walk or drive past. The most popular items (especially at Victoria Falls) are wood carvings, including life-size (well, almost) giraffes. Most carvings are not made of mahogany or teak, however, but low-grade wood, which is then stained or polished. Other charming mementoes

include jewellery from precious and semi-precious stones, crocheted table cloths (best along Lake Kariba) and stone sculptures (from Harare and Bulawayo).

An increasing number of cooperatives and welfare societies have been established so that profits from goods sold at certain souvenir shops are directed back to the community or the disadvantaged. For example, **Jairos Jiri Crafts**, which has outlets in all cities and larger towns, sells batiks, carvings and wall hangings made by disabled and blind Zimbabweans.

Getting There & Away

Information about travelling to Southern Africa (including Zimbabwe) from elsewhere in the continent, and from some Western countries, is included in the regional Getting There & Away chapter earlier in this book.

AIR
Airports & Airlines

International airports are in Harare, Bulawayo and Victoria Falls.

With the exception of British Airways and South African Airways, most major international airlines deserted Harare after the political crisis worsened in early 2000. **Air Zimbabwe** (W www.airzim.co.zw) is still functioning and offers services throughout regional Africa and to major cities in Europe. Despite general shortages, fuel is found for all airlines, so cancellations are rare.

Departure Tax

From late 2002 the international departure tax of US$30 was included in the price of all tickets, whether bought in or outside of Zimbabwe.

Southern Africa

Zambian Airways (W www.africa-insites.com /zambianairways) flies daily between Harare and Lusaka (US$155/305 one way/return), while **Air Zimbabwe** (W www.airzim.co.zw) also links the two cities (US$150/295) on flights between Harare and Nairobi on Thursday, and between Harare and Jo'burg daily (US$195/265).

In addition, Air Zimbabwe flies between Bulawayo and Jo'burg twice a week, and between Harare and Lilongwe (Malawi) on Sunday. South African Airways offers flights several times a day between Harare and Jo'burg (US$190/290), and twice a week between Bulawayo and Jo'burg, while Mid Airlines flies most days between Harare and Jo'burg for about the same price. **Air Botswana** travels between Harare and Gaborone three times a week.

Refer to the Zimbabwe section of the Victoria Falls chapter for details about international flights to and from the town of Victoria Falls.

LAND

Because of a lack of demand and fuel, no trains currently run between Zimbabwe and any neighbouring country; nor are international train services likely to recommence in the immediate future.

Border Crossings

The following borders issue visas (if required) to foreigners on arrival. Each border is open daily and, unless stated otherwise, operates from 6am to 6pm.

Botswana The two most commonly used borders are at Kazungula, near Kasane, and between Plumtree and Ramokgwebana. There's also a minor crossing at Pandamatenga, west of Hwange town.

Mozambique The most direct crossings are at Nyamapanda, and at Machipanda, near Mutare.

Namibia There is no common border, so you have to travel through Kazungula in Botswana.

South Africa The only crossing is at Beitbridge (open 6am to 8.30pm), where car drivers pay a US$10 toll (in US$ or rand) either way. Zimbabwean officials are keen to catch locals trying to smuggle in South African goods without paying duty, but foreign travellers encounter few problems. The kilometre-long queues can now be avoided after the recent construction of a two-lane highway. This border operates 24 hours a day during the Christmas and Easter holidays.

Zambia The three main crossings are at Chirundu, along the main road between Harare and Lusaka; Kariba, about 50km upstream from Chirundu; and Victoria Falls (open 6am-8pm).

Botswana

There are no direct buses between Harare and Gaborone. The quickest way, therefore, across the border is to catch one of several daily buses or minibuses from Bulawayo – see

ZIMBABWE

Bulawayo for details. The Victoria Falls town section of the Victoria Falls chapter contains information about public transport between Victoria Falls and Botswana, via Kazungula and Kasane. There is no public transport across the border via Pandamatenga.

Mozambique

Using local transport or hitching across the border at Nyamapanda is not difficult, though it's quicker and not much more expensive to catch the direct bus between Harare and Lilongwe in Malawi (see the Harare section for details) and get off at Tete in Mozambique. Refer to the Mutare section for information about crossing the border at Machipanda.

Malawi

Refer to the Harare section for details about direct buses between Harare and Lilongwe, via Blantyre. But note that all buses between Zimbabwe and Malawi pass through Mozambique, for which you must have at least a transit visa.

Namibia

There's no direct public transport from Harare to anywhere in Namibia. So, drive or hitch to Kazungula (Botswana) from Victoria Falls, drive or hitch across the free transit route through Chobe National Park to the Namibian border at Ngoma Bridge. From there, it's a short drive or hitch to Katima Mulilo. Check the Victoria Falls chapter for information about private transport from Victoria Falls to Windhoek.

South Africa

Luxury buses (offering a TV, video, reclining seats, air-conditioning, a toilet and free soft drinks) to Jo'burg leave daily from Harare and Bulawayo – see those sections for details. Otherwise, it's easy enough to use buses or minibuses from Bulawayo or Masvingo (refer to those sections for information).

All buses between Lusaka and Jo'burg also pick up and drop off passengers at Harare and Masvingo, and all buses between Lusaka or Harare and Jo'burg stop at Pietersburg/Polokwane and Pretoria in South Africa.

Refer to the Victoria Falls chapter for information about direct transport between Jo'burg and Vic Falls.

Zambia

Plenty of buses travel every day between Harare and Lusaka, via Chirundu (see the Harare section for details).

From Kariba town to Siavonga (on the Zambian side of Lake Kariba), arrange a taxi to the border, take the same or another taxi (or walk) along the impressive Kariba Dam between the two countries, and then wait for a minibus to Siavonga.

Many travellers, however, cross at Victoria Falls (see the Victoria Falls chapter for details.)

Getting Around

The land-hungry colonists left convenient rail links between the four largest cities, as well as Victoria Falls, and a superb network of paved roads that used to be among the finest in Southern Africa. The main concerns about travelling in Zimbabwe are the result of a lack of foreign currency: poorly maintained roads and trains, and fuel shortages for public and private transport.

Try to avoid travelling by bus, minibus or train on the weekends after pay day (last Friday of the month), or at the beginning and end of school holidays, when it's pandemonium at every bus or train station in the country.

AIR

Lack of demand and fuel has severely curtailed domestic airline schedules. At the moment, only Air Zimbabwe flies between Harare and Bulawayo, and Harare and Victoria Falls. See the relevant sections for details about schedules and costs. Air Zim does not plan to restart flights to/from Hwange or Kariba. See the relevant sections for details about schedules and costs. Neither airline plans to restart domestic flights to/from Hwange or Kariba.

Similarly, charter flight companies catering to guests staying at upmarket lodges in the national parks are also suffering. Charter flights only leave with a minimum number of pre-booked passengers and costs are always high, but it's sometimes worth checking around for a last-minute standby. Ask travel agencies in Harare and Bulawayo, or contact one of these companies:

Eagle Air Services (☎ 031-3047, fax 011-410540) Chiredzi (in the southeast)

Falcon Air (☎ 04-780956, fax 04-780982) Charles Prince Airport, Harare

United Air Charters (☎ 04-302841, e reserva tions@hunting.co.zw) Charles Prince Airport, Harare

Domestic Departure Tax

The domestic departure tax of US$5 is included in the prices of tickets purchased inside and outside of Zimbabwe.

BUS & MINIBUS

Zimbabwe offers three types of public transport: luxury coaches, express public buses, and 'local' public buses/minibuses (commonly known as 'African' or 'chicken' buses). The less desirable fourth alternative is a pick-up or overland truck.

Luxury Coach

The only luxury coach company still operating is **Blue Arrow** (w *www.bluearrow.co.zw*), which offers buses most days between Harare and Bulawayo, and Harare and Mutare. Fares cost about twice as much as express or local 'African' buses, but are definitely worth the extra. Tickets can be bought in advance from Blue Arrow offices (where the buses also arrive and depart) in each city.

Express Buses

Express buses are comfortable (but not luxurious) and run by private Zimbabwean companies. They're relatively efficient and quick, and operate according to published timetables between most places of interest to visitors. These buses sometimes leave from private bus stations or offices, eg, at Roadport in Harare, but mostly from public bus terminals. Tickets can be bought one or two days in advance. Major companies include Tenda, Kukura Kurerwa (KK) and Power Coach Express.

Local ('African') Buses & Minibuses

Local buses and minibuses travel just about anywhere people are living. These buses and minibuses are always crowded and uncomfortable, but despite major hikes in fuel prices they remain cheap. You're more likely to meet Zimbabweans on local buses and minibuses than on express buses, and

the excitement of a foreigner on board will scarcely be containable for many people.

Local buses normally depart from the *musika* ('station' in Shona) or *renkini* ('station' in Ndebele) often near the market outside the city or town centre. Larger cities and towns also have an 'in-town' bus station, where you can be picked up or dropped off, but the problem will be finding a seat – or even standing space – once the bus has left the original bus station. Commuter 'omnibuses' (or minibuses) also cover intercity routes, but are far more cramped and uncomfortable.

Although you may hear vague murmurings about departure times or average numbers of local buses and minibuses per day, local buses follow no real timetables – so don't get flustered if no one seems to have specific information. Between major population centres, buses depart when full throughout the day, usually until mid- or late afternoon, but if you're unsure about departures or heading for a small town or village, turn up as early as possible. Sometimes the only bus of the day leaves at 5.30am!

Tickets for local buses and minibuses are always bought on board from a ticket collector. Keep the ticket because it'll be checked several times throughout the journey and possibly collected at the end of the trip.

TRAIN

Zimbabwe has a useful railway network that connects Harare, Bulawayo, Victoria Falls, Mutare and Chiredzi. Zimbabwean rolling stock includes 1920s passenger cars, complete with beautiful brass and wood-trimmed interiors, even in 2nd class. Newer trains have showers in 1st class and blaring video screens in 2nd class. All intercity trains run at night, and because of the relatively short distances covered, move very slowly in order to arrive at a convenient hour. However, despite the excruciating time they allow, trains regularly run late.

Sexes are separated at night, unless you say you're married or reserve a family or two-person compartment in advance (for an extra charge). First-class compartments (usually called 'sleepers') hold four berths, while second-class compartments hold six adults. It's worth noting that children under seven years are not counted as an 'adult', and most Zimbabwean women have at least one child.

ZIMBABWE

Fares are so cheap (if you have changed money at the unofficial rate) that it's certainly worth booking an entire compartment to yourself. Bedding (ZW$80) is available, but order it early from the steward on the train because demand always exceeds supply. As well as sleeping compartments, most services offer 'standard' (2nd class) and/or 'economy' (3rd class) seats, which are comfortable but crowded and difficult for sleeping.

The restaurant on the Bulawayo to Victoria Falls line is available to 1st- and 2nd-class passengers, and snack bars are available on all services (though it's best to bring your own food and water anyway). Always be wary of thieves who have been known to board and disembark trains in the dead of night and snatch things through windows at stations. And the enormous thud you may hear in the middle of the night on the service between Bulawayo and Victoria Falls is the train striking an elephant in Hwange National Park.

All tickets must be booked in advance; they're not available on the train unless you jump on at a remote location without a ticket office. Tickets for all classes can be reserved up to 30 days in advance, but must be paid for 24 hours before departure. Anyone over 60 with an international ID card, and willing to travel between Monday and Thursday, receives a discount of about 20%. A 20% peak-period surcharge applies to all travel on Friday and Sunday. (Fares listed in this chapter, and the Zimbabwe section of the Victoria Falls chapter, are for off-peak travel.)

Seat and compartment numbers may not be indicated on your ticket, so check the listings on the board at the platform about one hour before departure.

Refer to the Harare, Bulawayo and Mutare sections, and the Victoria Falls chapter, for information about the schedules and costs of domestic train services. Railway buffs with heaps of money may also be interested in the steam trains that travel across the border at Victoria Falls – see that chapter for details.

CAR & MOTORCYCLE

Driving a car is an ideal way of getting around because roads are generally good, public transport can be infrequent or nonexistent to and around national parks, and petrol (when available – see the boxed text 'The Fuel Crisis' following) is inexpensive.

Renting a car in Zimbabwe is also amazingly cheap if you have changed money at the unofficial rate and can find a rental agency that allows you to pay the 'local rate' in Zimbabwe dollars.

Drivers of foreign-registered vehicles (including rented cars) have to procure a temporary import permit at the border, which must also be presented to officials on departure. Third-party insurance is also compulsory for all vehicles entering Zimbabwe and is available at the major borders (about US$20 per month). You may also need to produce a police clearance from whichever country you bought the car to prove that the car is not stolen, but this is usually only required if the car was bought in Southern Africa.

Hire cars can be brought into Zimbabwe with permission from the rental company, but you need a sheet known as a 'Blue Book', detailing the vehicle's particulars, as well as proof of insurance in the vehicle's registered country. The hire company will provide the relevant paperwork.

Seat belts must be worn by drivers and front-seat passengers, but almost every Zimbabwean ignores this law. Speed traps operate throughout the country, seemingly for no other purpose than as a tidy piece of revenue raising. Fines are reasonably inexpensive, but always be on your guard for a scam. Motorists must use headlights between 5.30pm and 5.30am every day. In most national parks and reserves private cars are not allowed to drive after sunset and motorbikes are banned for safety reasons. Petrol – which is called 'blend' because it's mixed with sugar cane ethanol – costs about US$0.20 per litre; diesel a little more. Driving (in theory) is on the left-hand side of the road.

Rental

All foreigners can use their driving licence from their home country for up to 90 days in Zimbabwe as long as it's written in English. The minimum driving age required by rental companies varies, but is usually between 23 and 25 years. The maximum age is normally about 65 years.

International agencies, such as Avis and Budget, will charge you 'foreigners rates' and insist on payment in US dollars – from US$40 per day plus all the extras. However, some independently owned outlets of Europcar (especially in Harare) and Hertz

The Fuel Crisis

Thanks to Zimbabwe's declining economic situation, petrol and diesel shortages are a problem. If you're travelling away from major towns and cities, it's always wise to have several jerry cans with extra fuel. Fill up whenever possible, even if it means waiting two hours in a line around the block with 200 other frustrated drivers. Car rental companies may be able to get fuel when no-one else can – or they can at least loan you a jerry can or two for emergency supplies. Fuel shortages don't last long (maybe two or three days) and are often localised: eg, diesel may run out in Victoria Falls, but not in Bulawayo, where petrol may be non-existent. However, in any Zimbabwean town at any time, petrol may not be available at all.

(in Mutare and Victoria Falls) allow foreigners to pay the 'local rates' in Zimbabwe dollars. But you may need to show receipts from a bank or bureau de change to 'prove' that you changed money at the official rate (see Money in the Facts for the Visitor section earlier).

As an example, **Europcar** (W *www.europ car.co.zw*) charges from US$13 per day, plus US$0.20 per kilometre and insurance of US$4 per day, with a deposit of ZW$100,000. Weekend rates (two days) are great value: US$30 including 100 free kilometres and insurance. The rates charged by Hertz are sometimes negotiable. They start at US$14 per day, plus US$0.20 per kilometre (or perhaps with 100 free kilometres if you're lucky), plus insurance (US$4 per day), and a deposit of ZW$88,000.

The cheapest option in Harare and Bulawayo is undoubtedly **Transit Car & Truck Hire**. Reliable, 10- to 12-year-old vehicles cost about US$4 per day, plus US$0.05 per kilometre and insurance (US$1.50 per day). For rentals between three and six days it charges US$11 per day including 200 free kilometres and insurance. The deposit is ZW$100,000, but the company happily accepts a signed, but incomplete, credit card imprint instead.

Renting a 4WD is not cheap and agencies will not allow foreigners to pay 'local rates' in Zimbabwe dollars. One company that has been recommended by readers is **Cameron**

Harvey Safaris (π/fax Harare 04-860978, π Bulawayo 09-860978; e *camhar@africaon line.co.zw*). It offers 4WDs from US$70 per day (discounts for longer hire), including insurance and unlimited kilometres. It also rents associated camping equipment.

All rates quoted by rental companies (and listed in this chapter) do not include petrol, insurance or the 2% tourism levy. You will also be slugged extra if you use more than one driver, buy theft insurance, cross the border into another country, pick up the car at an airport (5%) or 'drop off' (eg, hiring a car in Harare but returning it to Bulawayo, or vice versa, costs US$50). Most agencies will allow their vehicles to travel to Zambia, Botswana and South Africa, but give the agency plenty of notice so they can sort out the paperwork and extra insurance.

Some rental companies insist on a deposit of ZW$420,000 in cash or with a credit card. This is problematic, because you may not pass the credit card check, which is done at the *official* rate (ie, about US$7500!) or you won't want to change and carry that much in cash. Most branches of Hertz and Europcar, however, are reasonable and can work out a compromise: eg, you provide a signed, but incomplete, credit card slip which you destroy when you return the car, or you can leave a smaller deposit in hard currency.

It's important to note that most collision damage waiver (CDW) insurance policies do not cover 2WD vehicles travelling on rough roads in national parks, especially in Mana Pools National Park.

Vehicles can be rented in Harare, Bulawayo, Mutare, Kariba and Victoria Falls. Refer to the relevant sections in this chapter and the Victoria Falls chapter for contact details of some rental agencies in these places.

HITCHING

Despite the general advice about hitching in the Getting Around the Region chapter earlier in this book, many locals hitch due to infrequent or nonexistent public transport, or because they simply cannot even afford the bus, minibus or train fare. Competition for lifts can be fierce, so always allow plenty of time to get around. You may end up jumping on a bus, minibus and truck anyway, for which you'll have to pay the normal fare.

To hitch a ride, don't use your thumb in the Western or South African style; instead, stick

your hand out at a 45° angle from your body. Many drivers charge passengers to help pay for fuel, but the rate should never exceed the equivalent bus, minibus or train fare. Always ask about charges before you climb in.

Although it's better to hitch in pairs, it is possible for women to hitch alone if there are women and/or children in the car, but it's not worth the risk of accepting a lift from a car full of men. Always try to ascertain the driver's degree of sobriety; drink-driving is a serious problem in Zimbabwe, especially on weekends and public holidays. Hitching isn't permitted within national parks and reserves for obvious safety reasons, but there's nothing stopping you hitching to a national park gate and then asking around for a lift into the park from there.

BOAT
Zimbabwe is a landlocked country, so the only boats offering any transport are the passenger ferries along Lake Kariba. Due to a habitual lack of demand and fuel, regular schedules for these ferries have been suspended indefinitely – refer to the Kariba section later in this chapter for details.

LOCAL TRANSPORT
Bus & Minibus
In all cities and larger towns, bus services connect the centre with suburban areas. Try to board at the terminal, otherwise the bus will be packed to overflowing when it drives past. Once people are hanging out the windows and doors, the driver won't bother to stop to pick up more. Local bus (and minibus) fares are about ZW$50.

More common are minibuses, usually called 'commuter omnibuses'. They generally leave when full (between 15 and 22 people) from bus terminals or makeshift stops along the city streets, but they can be flagged down along the roadside. Destinations are written on or near the front windscreen. The downside is that minibuses offer little or no room for luggage.

Taxi
To save your weary legs during the day, and to ensure your safety at night, take a taxi. They're very cheap: less than US$1 to anywhere within a city or town centre and about US$2 to the suburbs from a city or town centre. Most taxis in Bulawayo are

metered, and a few are in Harare, but elsewhere in Zimbabwe most taxis don't bother with meters. Therefore, you will have to negotiate a fare.

ORGANISED TOURS
Organised tours of national parks are ideal for anyone without a private vehicle, though renting a car may be cheaper. All sorts of other tours – including bushwalking, rail tours, canoe/raft trips, wildlife drives and bird-watching – are available from tour operators in Zimbabwe and from foreign specialist agencies. Almost all tours run by private companies in Zimbabwe charge 'foreigners prices' in US dollars, but a few tours, including some offered by the national parks, charge foreigners the 'local rates' in Zimbabwe dollars. You may not save much money booking a tour before you arrive, but it is imperative these days (because of a lack of tourists) to find out if the tour company is still operating and has the required minimum number of passengers to start the trip.

Several reliable Zimbabwean tour agencies are listed in the Harare, Bulawayo, Mutare and Kariba sections of this chapter, and in the Victoria Falls chapter.

Harare

☎ 04 • pop 2 million

Harare is the capital and heart of the nation in nearly every respect. Bequeathed a distinctly European flavour by its colonisers, it continues to be Zimbabwe's showpiece city and commercial centre. Harare is certainly more attractive than most other regional African cities (eg, Lusaka), and has enough attractions and restaurants to keep most weary and jaded travellers deliriously happy for several days. You won't even have to venture too far from Harare to observe some of Zimbabwe's magical wildlife and landscapes – see the Around Harare section later.

Orientation
The city centre is formed by the collision of two grids, and further confused by a complicated one-way traffic system. But the city is compact and easy to get around on foot. Most decent shops, restaurant, bars and banks are between Samora Machel Ave and Robert Mugabe Rd, while classier homes, shops and

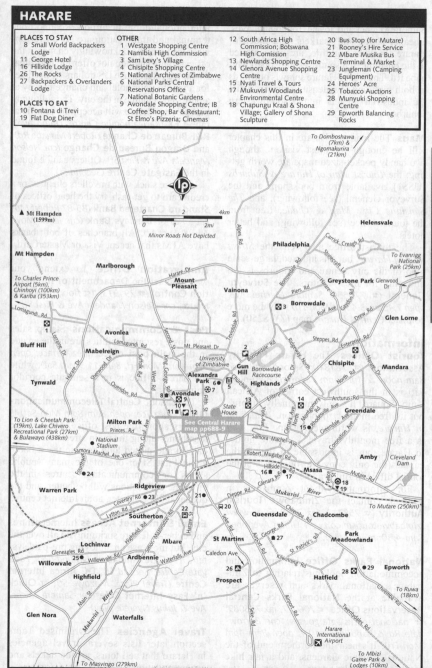

HARARE

PLACES TO STAY
8 Small World Backpackers Lodge
11 George Hotel
16 Hillside Lodge
26 The Rocks
27 Backpackers & Overlanders Lodge

PLACES TO EAT
10 Fontana di Trevi
19 Flat Dog Diner

OTHER
1 Westgate Shopping Centre
2 Namibia High Commission
3 Sam Levy's Village
4 Chisipite Shopping Centre
5 National Archives of Zimbabwe
6 National Parks Central Reservations Office
7 National Botanic Gardens
9 Avondale Shopping Centre; IB Coffee Shop, Bar & Restaurant; St Elmo's Pizzeria; Cinemas

12 South Africa High Commission; Botswana High Comission
13 Newlands Shopping Centre
14 Glenora Avenue Shopping Centre
15 Nyati Travel & Tours
17 Mukuvisi Woodlands Environmental Centre
18 Chapungu Kraal & Shona Village; Gallery of Shona Sculpture

20 Bus Stop (for Mutare)
21 Rooney's Hire Service
22 Mbare Musika Bus Terminal & Market
23 Jungleman (Camping Equipment)
24 Heroes' Acre
25 Tobacco Auctions
28 Munyuki Shopping Centre
29 Epworth Balancing Rocks

eateries are dotted around the area between Samora Machel and Josiah Tongogara Aves. Cheaper shops and markets, and much of Harare's seedier nightlife, are concentrated in the bustling area southwest of Robert Mugabe Rd. The rest of Harare sprawls outwards in both high and low-density suburbs, while the industrial area is in the southwestern suburbs.

Maps The maps of Harare in this chapter will be enough for most visitors, though two handy pocket-sized maps are worth getting: the *Tourist Map of Harare & Suburbs* (US$1), available from bookshops and the Surveyor General (see following); and *The Sunshine City: Map & Guide*, free from the tourist office (see following) and better hotels.

The tourist office also sells the *Street Map of Harare*, but this indexed, large-scale map of the city centre and suburbs is too unwieldy for most visitors. The **Surveyor General** (☎ 775550; *Samora Machel Ave; open 7.45am-3.45pm Mon-Fri*) sells the more compact *Central Harare* map (ZW$250).

Information

Tourist Offices The **Harare Publicity Association** (☎ 781810; *Second St; open 8am-noon & 1pm-4pm Mon-Fri, 8am-noon Sat*) is in the southwest corner of African Unity Square. It's only marginally helpful, but its free monthly publication, *What's on in Harare*, is worth picking up. *Time Out* is a free monthly 'travel & leisure guide' to Harare, but is impossible to find in the capital (the only copy we found was at the tourist office in Bulawayo!).

For information about Zimbabwe in general, contact the **Zimbabwe Tourism Authority** (☎ 758712, fax 758826; W www .zimbabwetourism.co.zw; *1 Union Ave; open 8am-4.30pm Mon-Fri*).

National Parks Office Information and accommodation bookings relating to Zimbabwe's national parks and reserves are available at the **National Parks Central Reservations Office** (☎ 706077, fax 726089; e national-parks@gta.gov.zw; *cnr Borrowdale Rd & Sandringham Dr; open 8am-4pm Mon-Fri*). It's near the northern end of the National Botanic Gardens, and a fair hike from town, so take a taxi.

Money The bureaux de change at the international/domestic airport, Roadport bus terminal and train station are set up for unwary visitors who unknowingly change at the official rate. They do not offer the unofficial exchange rate, so use US dollars (if need be) for a taxi to your hotel and change money at a bureau de change in the city. The following bureaux de change will accept the unofficial rate: **CFX** (*Karigamombe Centre, Union Ave*); **R&F Bureau de Change** (*Robert Mugabe Rd*); and **Dragon Bureau de Change** (*cnr Nelson Mandela Ave & First St*). Others can be found in the **Eastgate Centre** (*Second St*).

If you're stuck with travellers cheques, or a credit card to get cash, try the head offices of **Standard Chartered Bank** (*85-87 Robert Mugabe Rd*) or **Barclays Bank** (*cnr Jason Moyo Ave & First St*). All branches of both banks have ATMs that accept Visa or MasterCard.

Immigration Office To extend your visa, contact the **Department of Immigration Control** (☎ 791913; *1st floor, Linquenda House, cnr Nelson Mandela Ave & First St*).

Post & Communications Stamp sales and poste restante facilities are in the arcade in the **main post office** (*Inez Terrace; open 8am-4pm Mon-Fri, 8am-11.30am Sat*), while the parcel office is in a separate corridor downstairs.

The chaotic **Central Telecommunications Office** (*Inez Tce; open 8am-8pm Mon-Sat*) is upstairs above the post office. Most public telephones along the main streets were vandalised and gutted long ago, so use a booth along First St or one of the many 'public shops' or 'communication centres' in the city. The connections will be better, and the queues will be shorter, at an Internet centre.

Email & Internet Access Internet centres and cyber-cafés are springing up all over the city, but most use an annoying pre-paid system. Try **Cafe Zimbabwe** (*ground floor, Eastgate Centre, Second St*), **DC Africa Internet Centre** (*Travel Plaza, Mazowe St*), or **Quick 'n' Easy Internet Cafe** (*cnr Samora Michel Ave & Julius Nyerere Way*).

Travel Agencies The Organised Tours section later lists several travel agencies in Harare that sell tours, airline tickets and accommodation.

Bookshops As usual, the ubiquitous **Kingston's** bookshops *(cnr Second St & Jason Moyo Ave; • cnr Union Ave & Julius Nyerere Way, near the Zambian High Commission)* offer the best selection. For used books, check out **Treasure Trove** *(26C Second St)*, an Ali Baba's cave full of second-hand books, used clothing, and sports and camping gear.

The Book Café *(Fife Avenue Shopping Centre, Fife Ave)* offers an appealing selection of African literature and reference material, and is *the* place for literary buffs with a healthy appetite.

Photography Probably the best place in Zimbabwe for all your photographic needs, **Strachan's Photo Shop** *(66 Nelson Mandela Ave)* sells all sorts of films and accessories, and offers one-hour photo processing. You can admire or admonish your photographic skills at the Strachan's Tea Terrace upstairs.

Laundry Dry cleaners can be found in most shopping centres, but the only place to do it yourself is the **Fife Avenue Laundrette** *(Fife Avenue Shopping Centre, Fife Ave; open daily)*. Otherwise, there's a good chance your hotel will be able to scrub the dirt off your shirts and skirts.

Camping Equipment Limited camping equipment is sold (but cannot be rented) at **Fereday & Sons** *(Robert Mugabe Rd)*. **Jungleman** *(☎ 011-600889; e jungleman@ zimweb.co.zw; 41 Coventry Rd)* also sells camping gear. **Rooney's Hire Service** *(☎ 771557; 124 Seke Rd)* rents sleeping bags, tents and other camping equipment, but is more suited to the needs of upmarket mobile safari companies.

Emergency The **Parirenyatwa Hospital** *(☎ 701555; Leopold Takawira St)* is large and central, but most expats recommend the **Avenues Clinic** *(☎ 251180-99; cnr Mazowe St & Baines Ave)*. Night pharmacies are listed in *The Herald*. For emergencies, contact the **police** *(☎ 733033; cnr Inez Tce & Kenneth Kaunda Ave)* or the **Medical Air Rescue Service** *(MARS; ☎ 734531)*.

Dangers & Annoyances According to some expats, Harare now rivals Nairobi ('Nai-robbery') and Jo'burg for crime, but

Keep Out

Chancellor Ave is the site of the Executive President's residence and the State House. It's off limits and barricaded between 6pm and 6am. Don't wander in there between these hours; the guards are under orders to shoot first and ask questions later.

this is an exaggeration. Violent crimes in Harare (and throughout Zimbabwe) have been dramatically reduced because security guards are posted almost *everywhere*. There are still problems – especially in quieter areas around the northern city centre and the chaotic Mbare Musika Bus Terminal – but things have vastly improved. However, never walk around the city at night.

National Archives of Zimbabwe
Founded in 1935, this building *(Ruth Taylor Rd, off Borrowdale Rd; small admission fee charged; open 8.30am-4pm Mon-Fri, 8am-noon Sat)* is the repository for the history of Rhodesia and modern Zimbabwe. It features colonial artefacts and photos, accounts of early explorers and settlers, and a display about the Second Chimurenga. Prints of excellent oil paintings of Victoria Falls, among other places, are sold at the entrance.

Take any bus marked Borrowdale, Hatcliffe or Maryborough from the Market Square Bus Terminal. The main building, 3km from the city centre, is easy to spot from along Borrowdale Rd and the entry is well signposted.

Zimbabwe Museum of Human Sciences
This small museum *(Civic Centre, between Pennefather Ave & Raleigh St; admission US$1; open 9am-4pm daily)* is not as interesting as its counterpart in Bulawayo, though there are enough fossils and dioramas to keep most museum buffs happy for an hour or so. The highlights are the archaeological displays and the exhibits of traditional Shona crafts, arts and music. The museum is a 10-minute walk west of the city centre.

National Gallery of Zimbabwe
This collection *(cnr Julius Nyerere Way & Park Lane; admission ZW$50; open 9am-5pm daily)*

CENTRAL HARARE

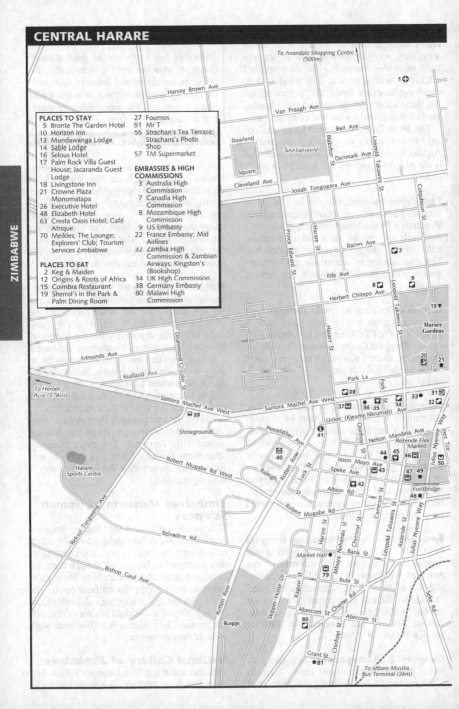

PLACES TO STAY
5 Bronte The Garden Hotel
10 Horizon Inn
13 Mundawanga Lodge
14 Sable Lodge
16 Selous Hotel
17 Palm Rock Villa Guest House; Jacaranda Guest Lodge
18 Livingstone Inn
21 Crowne Plaza Monomatapa
26 Executive Hotel
48 Elizabeth Hotel
63 Cresta Oasis Hotel; Café Atrique
70 Meikles; The Lounge; Explorers' Club; Tourism Services Zimbabwe

PLACES TO EAT
2 Keg & Maiden
12 Origins & Roots of Africa
15 Coimbra Restaurant
19 Sherrol's in the Park & Palm Dining Room

27 Fournos
51 Mr T
55 Strachan's Tea Terrace; Strachans's Photo Shop
57 TM Supermarket

EMBASSIES & HIGH COMMISSIONS
3 Australia High Commission
7 Canadia High Commission
8 Mozambique High Commission
9 US Embassy
22 France Embassy; Mid Airlines
32 Zambia High Commission & Zambian Airways; Kingston's (Bookshop)
34 UK High Commission
38 Germany Embassy
80 Malawi High Commission

To Avondale Shopping Centre (500m)

Harvey Brown Ave

Van Praagh Ave

Beit Ave

Rowland

Sportsground

Square

Cleveland Ave

Josiah Tongogara Ave

Baines Ave

Prince Edward St

Harare St

Fife Ave

Herbert Chitepo Ave

Leopold Takawira St

Harare Gardens

Edmonds Ave

Rudland Ave

To Heroes' Acre (3.5km)

Samora Machel Ave West

Samora Machel Ave West

Union (Kwame Nkrumah) Ave

Showgrounds

Pennefather Ave

Nelson Mandela Ave

Rezende Flea Market

Jason Moyo Ave

Speke Ave

Robert Mugabe Rd West

Raleigh Rotten Row St

Luck St

Albion Rd

Robert Mugabe Rd

Footbridge

Harare Sports Centre

Rekayi Tangwena Ave

Belvedere Rd

Bishop Gaul Ave

Market Hall

Bute St

Kaguvi St

Mbuya Nehanda St

Bank St

Leopold Takawira St

Rezende St

Julius Nyerere Way

Abercom St

Charter Rd

Abercom St

Chinhoyi St

Rotten Row

Skipper Hoste Dr

Kopje

Grant St

To Mbare Musika Bus Terminal (2km)

To Mbare Musika Bus Terminal (2km)

ZIMBABWE

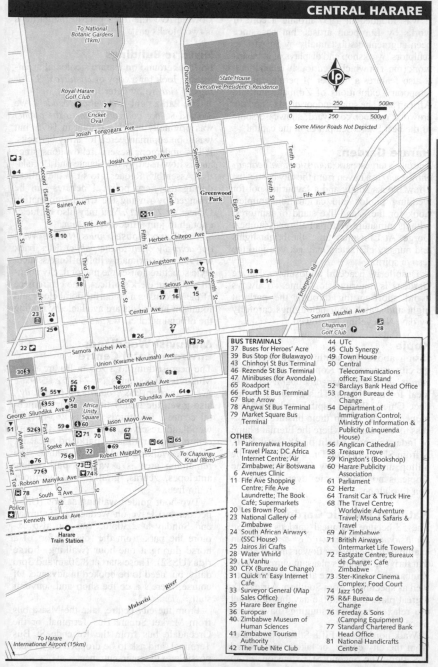

ZIMBABWE

CENTRAL HARARE

BUS TERMINALS
37 Buses for Heroes' Acre
39 Bus Stop (for Bulawayo)
43 Chinhoyi St Bus Terminal
46 Rezende St Bus Terminal
47 Minibuses (for Avondale)
65 Roadport
66 Fourth St Bus Terminal
67 Blue Arrow
78 Angwa St Bus Terminal
79 Market Square Bus
   Terminal

OTHER
1 Parirenyatwa Hospital
4 Travel Plaza; DC Africa
   Internet Centre; Air
   Zimbabwe; Air Botswana
6 Avenues Clinic
11 Fife Ave Shopping
   Centre; Fife Ave
   Laundrette; The Book
   Café; Supermarkets
20 Les Brown Pool
23 National Gallery of
   Zimbabwe
24 South African Airways
   (SSC House)
25 Jairos Jiri Crafts
27 Water Whirld
29 La Vanhu
30 CFX (Bureau de Change)
31 Quick 'n' Easy Internet
   Cafe
33 Surveyor General (Map
   Sales Office)
35 Harare Beer Engine
36 Europcar
40 Zimbabwe Museum of
   Human Sciences
41 Zimbabwe Tourism
   Authority
42 The Tube Nite Club

44 UTc
45 Club Synergy
49 Town House
50 Central
   Telecommunications
   office; Taxi Stand
52 Barclays Bank Head Office
53 Dragon Bureau de
   Change
54 Department of
   Immigration Control;
   Ministry of Information &
   Publicity (Linquenda
   House)
56 Anglican Cathedral
58 Treasure Trove
59 Kingston's (Bookshop)
60 Harare Publicity
   Association
61 Parliament
62 Hertz
64 Transit Car & Truck Hire
68 The Travel Centre;
   Worldwide Adventure
   Travel; Msuna Safaris &
   Travel
69 Air Zimbabwe
71 British Airways
   (Intermarket Life Towers)
72 Eastgate Centre; Bureaux
   de Change; Cafe
   Zimbabwe
73 Ster-Kinekor Cinema
   Complex; Food Court
74 Jazz 105
75 R&F Bureau de
   Change
76 Fereday & Sons
   (Camping Equipment)
77 Standard Chartered Bank
   Head Office
81 National Handicrafts
   Centre

is in the southeast corner of Harare Gardens. It was founded in 1957 around a core of works by European artists, but has since been augmented substantially by an African sculptors' workshop and displays of local artwork (most of which is curiously unlabelled). It also features a number of permanent and temporary exhibitions of Zimbabwean and African art. The small indoor display, and the crowded outdoor courtyard, showcase some of the best Shona sculptures in the capital.

Harare Gardens

The city's largest park (admission free; permanently open) is a haven from the city bustle just a few blocks south, and a favourite spot for wedding photos and canoodling couples. Look for the island-like stand of rainforest with its miniature Victoria Falls and Zambezi Gorge. At Christmas time, the bright lights and nursery characters may get you into the festive spirit.

Despite its peaceful atmosphere, Harare Gardens is notorious for crime, so always avoid short-cutting through the park at night and watch your belongings carefully by day. No cycling is allowed.

Kopje

Rising above the southwestern corner of the city centre is the Kopje (off Rotten Row; admission free; permanently open), which is ideal for city views. This granite hill was once Chief Mbare's capital, and at its foot pioneers first set up their businesses. Access to the summit, where the Eternal Flame of Independence was lit on 18 April 1980, is from Skipper Hoste Dr, which circles the hilltop, and Rotten Row. Unfortunately, the Kopje is no longer safe, even by day, so don't go alone.

National Botanic Gardens

The 58-hectare botanical gardens (Fifth St; admission free; open dawn-dusk daily) contain examples of the diverse flowers and greenery that thrive in Harare's pleasant climate. Most Zimbabwean species are also represented, as well as specimens from Southern Africa. It's a great place to spend the day, but don't get too relaxed because muggings have taken place here, too.

Walk north along Fifth St for 30 minutes from the city centre, or take a northbound bus along the Second St Extension. From the junction of Second St Extension and Downie Ave, the main gate to the gardens is two blocks east.

Historic Buildings

For background on Harare's colonial architecture, look for a copy of *Historical Buildings of Harare* by Peter Jackson.

The **Parliament** (cnr Nelson Mandela Ave & Third St; not normally open to the public) was originally built as a hotel in 1895, but was soon commandeered for army barracks. It has undergone several renovations since and is now used by the Senate and Legislative Assembly. Requests to sit in the gallery during the fiery political debates can be arranged by ringing the Chief Information Officer (☎ 700181). You may also be lucky enough to join a free weekly tour.

The **Town House** (Julius Nyerere Way; not normally open to the public) dates back to 1933. This primarily Italian Renaissance-style structure houses the mayoral, city council and town clerk's offices. The centrepiece of the gardens is a colourful floral clock and fountain. Free visits are available by ringing the official number (☎ 752577).

Mukuvisi Woodlands Environmental Centre

The nearest thing to a zoo in Harare is the Mukuvisi Woodlands (☎ 747152; Glenara Ave; admission US$1; open 8am-5pm daily), also given the trendy title of 'environmental centre'. Two-thirds of this 265-hectare woodland reserve, 7km east of the city centre, is natural msasa **parkland**, ideal for picnics, walking and bird-watching. The remaining area is a **wildlife park** where antelopes, zebras, giraffes and warthogs roam free.

Two-hour guided **walking safaris** (US$2 per person) leave on Wednesday, Saturday and Sunday at 2.30pm. You can also explore the park from the (dis)comfort of a horse during a one-hour (walking) **horse ride** (US$2). These start at 8.30am and 3pm daily, but need to be booked in advance. Of course, there's a coffee shop and souvenir stall.

From the city centre, take the Msasa bus from Market Square Bus Terminal, or the Greendale bus from the Rezende St Bus Terminal, and ask to be dropped off as near possible to the main entrance.

Chapungu Kraal & Shona Village

This endearing place *(Chapungu Sculpture Park; Felice St; admission ZW$200; open 8am-6pm Mon-Fri, 9am-5.30pm Sat & Sun)* is an attempt to create a cultural theme park for tourists. One highlight is the reconstructed Shona village, accessible during a half-hour guided tour (ZW$200 extra) that explains the motivation behind the granite, jasper and verdite works of Zimbabwe's most renowned artists. And don't forget to check the artisans at work at the **Gallery of Shona Sculpture**.

It's a good idea to time your visit around a performance of **African dance** *(admission included in the general ticket; 3pm Sat & Sun)*. Then perhaps enjoy a cuppa at the **tea garden** or detour to the Flat Dog Diner next door (see Places to Eat later).

The complex is 8km east of the city centre. Public transport is problematic, so take a taxi.

Heroes' Acre

On a hill overlooking Harare is the obelisk of Heroes' Acre *(☎ 774208; Fourth Ave; admission free; open dawn-dusk daily)*. This dominating monument serves as a memorial to the ZIPRA and ZANLA forces who died during the Second Chimurenga (see History at the start of this chapter). Permits used to be issued (free and without hassle) by the **Ministry of Information & Publicity** *(10th floor, Linquenda House, cnr Nelson Mandela Ave & First St)*, but are not required these days.

Guided tours are offered free of charge if arranged in advance (or on the spot if there aren't many visitors).

Heroes' Acre lies off the road to Bulawayo, 5km west of the city centre. Catch the Warren Park bus from the stop near the corner of Chinhoyi St and Samora Machel Ave West.

Tobacco Auctions

As explained under Economy in the Facts about Zimbabwe section earlier in this chapter, tobacco used to be one Zimbabwe's major foreign-exchange earners. Harare still serves as the major trading centre in Southern Africa for the evil weed and is home to the world's largest tobacco auction floor *(☎ 668921; Gleneagles Rd; open 8am-noon Mon-Fri, April-Oct)*. Tourists are welcome during auctions, and guided tours are often provided, but it's prudent to ring first to find out the times of the auctions and tours. The complex is 8km southwest of the city centre and accessible by the Highfield bus from the Fourth St Bus Terminal.

Activities

To cool off (but not necessarily to escape the crowds), visit the Olympic-sized **Les Brown Pool** *(Harare Gardens; admission ZW$200; open about 10am-6.30pm daily)*, behind the Crowne Plaza Monomatapa hotel. It's mainly used by local kids, so the site of a bikini clad foreign women is bound to cause a stir. Better is **Water Whirld** *(Samora Machel Ave; admission US$1; open 9am-6pm daily)*, 1.5km east of the city centre. It offers water slides and an artificial beach during the day, and a disco in the evening.

The most famous of the seven golf courses around Harare is the internationally acclaimed **Royal Harare Golf Club** *(☎ 702920; Fifth St; open 6am-6pm daily)*, a 15-minute walk north of the city centre. Guests are welcome for a small temporary membership fee.

For a sanitised 'taste of Africa', visit the **Mbizi Game Park & Lodges** *(see Places to Stay later; admission US$1; open 9.30am-5.30pm daily)*, about 22km southeast of Harare. It offers **walking safaris** and **wildlife drives** (with your own vehicle) through the wildlife park, as well as **fishing, canoeing** and **mountain biking** for less than US$1 per person per hour. It's not really accessible by public transport, so take a taxi.

Organised Tours

It's easy enough to get around Harare independently, but joining an organised tour of places near the capital (see the Around Harare section later) is worthwhile. However, the paucity of visitors these days means that tours do not run frequently. The costs of local tours depend on the number of passengers, and most charge in US dollars. These companies also sell tours and accommodation throughout Zimbabwe.

Jungleman Tours & Safaris *(☎/fax 333058)* offers interesting trips to local villages, the tobacco auctions and nearby wildlife parks

Msuna Safaris & Travel *(☎ 705716, fax 704792, e musuna@mweb.co.zw)* Ground floor, The Travel Centre, 93-5 Jason Moyo Ave, can book any tour and lodge around the country

Nyati Travel & Tours *(☎ 495804, fax 498553, w www.nyati.co.zw)* 29 Rhodesville Ave, offers

tailor-made tours, and specialises in canoeing trips and cultural tours

United Touring Company (UTc, ☎ 770623, fax 770643, **e** utczim@utc.co.zw) 4 Park St, is a reliable, but more upmarket, company that offers local village tours and cruises along Lake Chivero

Worldwide Adventure Travel (☎ 734724, fax 704794, **w** www.worldwideadventure.net) 5th floor, The Travel Centre, 93-5 Jason Moyo Ave, sells budget-priced safari trips and adventure activities all around Zimbabwe and Southern Africa

Special Events

The primary festival in the capital is the **Harare International Festival for the Arts** (one week in early May), which features international performers, as well as dance and music workshops. Other special events include the **Zimbabwe International Book Fair** (late July/early August), the **Zimbabwe Agricultural Society Show** (end of August) and the **Zimbabwe International Film Festival** (first two weeks in September). Check the local newspapers and posters around town for details.

Places to Stay – Budget

Hillside Lodge (☎ 747961; 71 Hillside Rd; camping per person US$3, dorm beds US$4.50, singles/doubles with shared bathroom US$8/10) is an old colonial home with a bar, swimming pool and communal kitchen, as well as Internet access and bike hire. Camping is in the large garden, and you can even sleep in a tree house. Ring to ask about a pick-up from the city. Otherwise, take the Msasa, Tafara or Mabvuku bus from the corner of Speke Ave and Julius Nyerere Way, get off at the Children's Home, and walk up Robert Mugabe Rd to Helm Rd which leads to Hillside Rd.

Sable Lodge (☎ 704959; **e** sable2000@mail.com; 95 Selous Ave; singles/doubles with shared bathroom US$6/7) is friendly, clean and convenient. Guests have access to cooking facilities, as well as a TV lounge and tempting pool, but it isn't great value.

Mundawanga Lodge (☎ 721678; 94 Selous Ave; singles/doubles with shared bathroom US$1.50/3) is opposite the Sable. The Mundawanga offers large, clean rooms with two beds and a table – and absolutely nothing else. There are so many rooms, that you'll be guaranteed somewhere to sleep if all else fails.

The Rocks (☎/fax 576371; 10 Caledon Ave; camping per person US$3, dorm beds US$5, doubles with/without bathroom US$15/12) is an overlanders' paradise set in 2.5 hectares of bushland. It revolves around an immense outdoor bar where there's always someone to drink with. The camp site is well set up, and tents are also available for hire. Take the Hatfield minibus from the Mobil petrol station on the corner of Robson Manyika Ave and Julius Nyerere Way, or the Zengeza or St Mary's bus from the Angwa St Bus Terminal.

Backpackers & Overlanders Lodge (☎/fax 575719; **e** conxshon@samara.co.zw; Kilwinning Rd; camping per person US$3, dorm beds US$5, doubles with/without bathroom US$13/11) is, as the name implies, a backpacker haven, but others have also enjoyed their stay. It also offers a bar-restaurant and pool, as well as snooker tables and volleyball courts, surrounded by a large garden. Although inconvenient, it does offer free transfers to and from the airport and city centre.

Palm Rock Villa Guest House (☎ 724550; 39 Selous Ave; dorms per person US$1, singles/doubles with shared bathroom US$2/3, suite with kitchen & bathroom US$3.50) is central, popular and ideal for budget travellers. Facilities in this converted old house include laundry service and a TV lounge and communal kitchen. The one suite is worth booking ahead. This part of Selous Ave is a bit unsavoury, however, so take a taxi at night.

Jacaranda Guest Lodge (☎ 700408; 41 Selous Ave; dorms per person US$2, singles/doubles with shared bathroom US$3/4) is next to the Palm Rock Villa. Although the Jacaranda isn't as good, it is a useful backup if the Palm Rock Villa is full. Only one room has a private bathroom.

Small World Backpackers Lodge (☎ 335176, fax 335341; 25 Ridge Rd; dorm beds per person US$6, doubles with/without bathroom US$20/15) is a charming, converted family home with clean and comfy rooms. Other amenities include a bar, swimming pool and snooker table, as well as shady gardens and Internet access. From opposite the King George Rd entrance to the Avondale Shopping Centre, walk west for 10 minutes along Ridge Rd; it's on the corner of Argyle Rd, but deliberately not signposted. Transfers (US$3 per person) are available from the airport and bus and train stations if arranged in advance.

Places to Stay – Mid-Range

All hotels listed in this section offer rooms with a TV and private bathroom. Currently, all foreigners can pay the 'local rate' in Zimbabwe dollars.

Executive Hotel *(☎ 701807; 126 Samora Machel Ave; doubles with breakfast US$6)* is an ugly, high-rise motel-style place with large rooms. It's noisy, but good value and convenient.

Selous Hotel *(☎ 727940; e selhotel@ samara.co.zw; cnr Selous Ave & Sixth St; singles/doubles with breakfast US$9/10)* is another decent option. It's not as good as the outside might suggest, and the place needs a spit and polish, but it's quiet. There's also plenty of rooms, so it's never full.

Horizon Inn *(☎ 724900; cnr Fife Ave & Second St; singles/doubles US$6/7, family room with 4 beds & kitchen US$9)* is a bright, modern, but ultimately charmless, place in a convenient location. Because it is remarkably good value, however, it's often full – so book ahead. Breakfast comes with all rooms.

George Hotel *(☎ 336677; e lezalo@yahoo .com; 20 King George Rd; doubles US$8)* offers large rooms in a very convenient location opposite the excellent Avondale Shopping Centre. But make sure you get a room away from the noisy pubs at the front of the hotel. An ordinary breakfast costs another US$1.

Livingstone Inn *(☎ 738593; cnr Third St & Livingston Ave; singles/doubles with breakfast US$6/7)* is a motel (painted light-green) along a leafy street. It's old fashioned and simple, but convenient and good value.

Places to Stay – Top End

All places listed here offer rooms with all the facilities expected, including breakfast.

Bronte The Garden Hotel *(☎ 796631, fax 721429; 132 Baines Ave; singles/doubles US$41/61 to US$73/94)* is a gorgeous pocket of colonial greenery. It's spotless and quiet, and features extensive gardens, as well as a pool and bar. Not surprisingly, it's popular – so book in advance. The cheaper rooms, however, in the annexe opposite are overpriced and not nearly as enticing.

Meikles *(☎ 707721; w www.meikles.com; cnr Jason Moyo Ave & Third St; singles/doubles US$210/240)* served as the foreign correspondents' watering hole during Zimbabwe's liberation war. This five-star place boasts a pool and numerous restaurants and bars, but the attitude may be too stuffy for some. The rates also include morning tea.

Mbizi *(☎ 700676; w www.mbizi.co.zw; including transfers, activities, breakfast & dinner per person US$120)* is 10km southeast of the airport and 22km from Harare. This wonderful place offers plenty of activities for guests and the public (see Activities earlier), as well as a unique pool surrounded by stunning gardens. It's really only accessible by taxi.

Cresta Oasis Hotel *(☎ 704217; e gm oasis@cresta.co.zw; 124 Nelson Mandela Ave; singles/doubles US$80/100)* is a three-star place offering high standards and a quiet location. There was plenty of renovation going on at the time of research, so the standards and facilities should improve even further.

Places to Eat

Harare boasts a surprising number of enticing and inexpensive restaurants and cafés. This is one of the best places in Southern Africa to splurge on Western delights at classy restaurants, or just load up with junk food.

Restaurants Origins & Roots of Africa *(☎ 721494; 73 Livingstone Ave; meals under US$1)* has a rather pretentious name, but is a modest place offering a range of traditional food. The flashy Mercedes cars parked outside indicate the restaurant's popularity among all Zimbabweans, and is not an indication of the prices.

Flat Dog Diner *(☎ 480883; Felice St; meals US$3-4)* offers good pub grub, with seafood a specialty. You can sit in the lush garden, on the veranda, or on the colourful indoor seating. Perhaps combine it with a visit to Chapungu Kraal next door (see the relevant section earlier). Specials are advertised in *The Daily News*.

Keg & Maiden *(☎ 700037; Harare Sports Club, off Fifth St; meals US$3-4)* has an unbeatable location overlooking the cricket oval. Although a little pricey, it does offer several vegetarian choices, and homesick Brits flock there for the bangers and mash. It features live music on Saturday night.

Café Afrique *(☎ 790861; Cresta Oasis Hotel, 124 Nelson Mandela Ave; salads US$1, grills US$3)* offers a diverse range of Zimbabwean and continental dishes. The buffet lunch (US$3) is popular with well-heeled city workers.

ZIMBABWE

Fontana di Trevi *(☎ 703038; 7 King George Rd; meals from US$3)* is an upmarket Italian restaurant, notable for its exotic buffet (US$4) of Ethiopian food on Sunday evening, and live music on Friday night.

Coimbra Restaurant *(☎ 700237; 61 Selous Ave; meals US$2-3)* is secluded, behind a bright yellow gate. It's popular with expats, though most times there will be more staff than diners. The best pick of the menu is the Portuguese-style chicken with lashings of spicy *peri peri* sauce.

Cafés The Book Café *(☎ 792551; Fife Avenue Shopping Centre, Fife Ave; meals about US$1; open 10am-10.30pm daily)* is a perfect place to relax over a drink or delicious home-cooked meal. Most evenings have a theme: eg, Wednesday is 'Africa night', with appropriate food and music, and Saturday afternoon features jazz and blues. Most daily specials cost under US$1.

Fournos *(☎ 708348; 144 Samora Machel Ave; snacks under US$1, meals from US$1.50)* is probably the best café in the city area. Try one or more of the fresh pastries, tasty samosas or scrumptious sandwiches. You can eat on an outdoor (but noisy) streetside table or in the welcome air-conditioning inside.

IB Coffee Shop, Bar & Restaurant *(Avondale Shopping Centre, King George Rd; meals US$1-2)* is arguably the best café in the suburbs. This Italian bakery (hence the initials) serves sandwiches and salads (US$1), as well as an excellent (but limited) range of Asian and continental dishes. It's open early for breakfast and a perfect place to relax after visiting a nearby cinema.

Strachan's Tea Terrace *(66 Nelson Mandela Ave; meals about US$1; open 8am-4.30pm Mon-Fri, 8am-11.30am Sat)* serves home-baked muffins, baguettes, quiches and cakes on a pleasant shaded terrace, where you can leaf through 12-year-old copies of *Newsweek*. It offers a few meals for lunch, as well as the recommended 'full breakfast' (US$1) with muesli, yoghurt and fresh juice.

Sherrol's in the Park *(☎ 705323; Harare Gardens; light meals about US$1; open 10am-5pm daily)* is a perfect place to drink coffee or enjoy a sandwich or burger while writing postcards or watching the locals stroll by. The attached **Palm Dining Room** *(meat dishes US$1.50, fish US$3; open lunch Mon-Sat,*

dinner Tues-Sat) is an intimate and classy place serving superb Italian food.

The Lounge *(Meikles Hotel, cnr Jason Moyo Ave & Third St; snacks US$2)* is the place to enjoy a spot of tea. While listening to the piano player tickle the ivories, why not indulge in a 'traditional tea' (US$1.50), including a three-tiered tray of sandwiches, cakes and scones?

Fast Food St Elmo's Pizzeria *(☎ 334980; Avondale Shopping Centre, King George Rd; small/large pizzas US$2/3, other dishes about US$2)* offers what are probably the tastiest pizzas anywhere between Jo'burg and Nairobi. The variety of toppings is imaginative, the servings are large and the waiters are attentive. Nonpizza lovers can also enjoy pastas and fresh salads.

The major shopping centres, including **Avondale Shopping Centre** *(King George Rd)* and **Sam Levy's Village** *(Borrowdale Rd)*, are all crammed with the usual fast-food outlets, eg, Debonairs (for pizzas) and Nando's (for chicken). Junk-food heaven is at the **food court** in the Ster-Kinekor Cinema complex *(Robert Mugabe Rd)*, where a visit to any of the nine fast-food outlets will guarantee to play havoc with your waistline.

Mr T *(cnr Angwa St & George Silundika Ave)* is about the only healthy fast-food place in the city centre.

Self-Catering Every shopping centre listed on both maps of Harare have large, well-stocked supermarkets. In the city centre, try **TM Supermarket** *(cnr Nelson Mandela Ave & Second St)* or visit the **Fife Ave Shopping Centre** *(Fife Ave)*, which is home to six supermarkets.

Entertainment

Harare is a great place to shake your booty to live African bands or to Western-style electronic music at a disco. For information about upcoming events, and to find out what's hot and what's not, check the listings in *The Daily News* and the weekly *Standardplus* supplement in *The Standard*.

Never walk to or from any of these (or any other) late-night spots after dark; always take a taxi.

Bars & Clubs Harare Beer Engine *(cnr Samora Machel Ave West & Park St)* brews

its own beer. After extensive research (!), we conclude that the Lighthouse Lager is the tastiest drop.

Explorers' Club *(Meikles Hotel, cnr Jason Moyo Ave & Third St)* is the place to go if you miss the golden days of the British colonial empire.

La Vanhu *(cnr Sixth St & Samora Machel Ave)* is very popular with the young hip crowd (though patrons must be over 23). It gets jam-packed on Wednesday, Friday and Saturday nights (when it's frequented by very discreet gays).

For something more 'African', step into **The Tube Nite Club** *(125 Mbuya Nehanda St)*, which gets thumping on Wednesday, Friday and Sunday night; or **Club Synergy** *(cnr Jason Moyo Ave & Park St)*, which also caters to the young and trendy set.

Places to catch local bands playing African music include **George Hotel** *(20 King George Rd)* and **Elizabeth Hotel** *(cnr Julius Nyerere Way & Robert Mugabe Rd)*, especially on Friday and Saturday night. Jazz fans should immediately head to **Jazz 105** *(cnr Second St & Robson Manyika Ave)*.

Cinemas Cinemas offering recent films, and cheap and comfortable seats (ZW$200), include the **Ster-Kinekor Cinema** complex *(Robert Mugabe Rd)*, opposite the Eastgate Centre, and the **Elite 100**, **Vistarama** and **7 Arts** cinemas, all at the **Avondale Shopping Centre** *(King George Rd)*.

Shopping
Harare is packed with shops and galleries selling gifts and souvenirs. While some places are convenient, they're not cheap, and similar or superior items can often be found at informal markets, such as the **Mbare Musika Market** *(open 6am-6pm daily)* in Mbare township, 5km south of the city centre. But be very careful with your belongings, because petty theft is rampant here.

Jairos Jiri Crafts *(cnr Julius Nyerere Way & Second St)*, opposite the national gallery, sells decent souvenirs at reasonable prices, and profits help fund welfare programmes for the disabled and blind. The **National Handicrafts Centre** *(Grant St; open 9.30am-5pm daily)* offers more imaginative mementoes, such as musical instruments and weavings. Shona sculptures can be bought at the **Gallery of Shona Sculpture** at

Chapungu Kraal (see the entry earlier in this section).

Everyday items at bargain prices can be bought at the **Rezende Flea Market** *(Julius Nyerere Way; open 8am-6pm daily)*.

Getting There & Away
Air For details about international flights to and from Harare, see the Getting There & Away section earlier in this chapter.

Air Zimbabwe offers two flights a day to Bulawayo for US$142 one way, which can drop to as little as US$53 on weekends, and one daily flight to Victoria Falls (US$156).

Because of a lack of business visitors and tourists, many international airlines have stopped flying to Harare and no longer operate offices in the city. But a few offices still remain:

Air Botswana (☎ 733837, ⓔ airbotsw@africa online.co.zw) Travel Plaza, 29 Mazowe St
Air Zimbabwe (☎ 251835) Travel Plaza, 29 Mazowe St; (☎ 253751) cnr Speke Ave and Third St
British Airways (☎ 747400) 5th floor, Intermarket Life Towers, Jason Moyo Ave
South African Airways (☎ 794511) 1st floor, SSC House, cnr Julius Nyerere Way and Second St
Zambian Airways (☎ 753510) Ground floor, Zambia House, 48 Union Ave, below the Zambian High Commission

Bus Buses for domestic and international travel depart from **Roadport** *(☎ 702828; Fifth St)* bus terminal.

Domestic Ramshackle local 'African' buses leave from the massive and chaotic **Mbare Musika Bus Terminal** in Mbare township, 5km south of the city centre. From there, buses to most places around Zimbabwe leave every two or three hours, while those to Bulawayo (US$4, six hours) and Mutare (US$3, five hours) depart every 30 to 60 minutes from dawn to dusk. Take care as robberies at this terminal are common, even during the day. Most locals feel safer flagging down buses to Bulawayo from outside the Showgrounds *(cnr Samora Machel Ave West & Rekayi Tangwena Ave)*; and to Mutare from near the so-called 'Coke Corner' *(cnr Seke & Dieppe Rds)*.

You are *far* better off paying a fraction more for a comfortable express bus from the small and crowded, but safe and convenient, **Roadport** *(☎ 702828; Fifth St)*. From there,

ZIMBABWE

Power Coach Express offers buses to Kariba (US$2, seven hours) every two hours; Tenda goes to Mutare (US$3) daily (except Saturday) at 8am, 10am and 11am; and Munenzwa Bus Service travels twice a day to Bulawayo (US$4) and three times to Mutare (US$3).

Blue Arrow (☎ 729514; e barrow@africa online.co.zw; Chester House, Speke Ave) offers the most comfortable buses to and from Harare. To Bulawayo (US$10, six hours), buses travel via Gweru (US$6, four hours) every day, and via Gweru and Kwe Kwe (US$5, three hours) three times a week. To Mutare (US$6, four hours), buses leave on Wednesday, Friday and Sunday. Tickets are available in advance from the Blue Arrow office, which also acts as the point of arrival and departure.

International All buses listed here leave from **Roadport** (☎ 702828; Fifth St). This terminal is hopelessly overcrowded, get there early and line up aggressively for tickets.

To Lusaka, Rwenzori (US$6) offers daily buses, Trans Frontiers (US$6.50) has services three times a week, and Dzimiri Buses (US$8) goes every day but Friday. Munorurama International travels daily (except Monday) to Lilongwe (US$9), via Blantyre (US$8), both in Malawi, and Tete in Mozambique.

To Jo'burg, Munorurama International (US$6), Greyhound (US$9) and Express Motorways (US$9) have daily buses, while Translux also goes to Jo'burg five days a week. The most comfortable option to Jo'burg is on the daily bus offered by City City (US$6), but these services are often booked out days in advance.

Train The **train station** (Kenneth Kaunda Ave) has a bureau de change (which does not offer the unofficial rates) and an information counter (open about 7am to 8pm daily).

Every day, the Umguza Express leaves at 8pm for Bulawayo (US$4/2/2 for sleeper/standard/economy class, nine hours), via Kwe Kwe (US$2/1/1, four hours) and Gweru (US$2/1/1, five hours). Also, the Pungwe Express departs daily at 9.30pm for Mutare (US$2/1/1, 8½ hours).

Reservations are available at the **ticket office** (☎ 786034; open 8am-1pm, 2pm-4pm & 7pm-9.30pm Mon-Fri, 8am-11.30am & 7pm-9.30pm Sat, 7pm-9.30pm Sun) inside the train station.

Getting Around

To/From the Airport All international and domestic airlines use the Harare International Airport, 15km southeast of the city centre. Charter flights and other light aircraft operate out of Charles Prince airport, 18km northwest of central Harare.

If there are enough passengers, **Tourism Services Zimbabwe** (☎ 707221; Meikles Hotel, cnr Jason Moyo Ave & Third St) may run shuttle buses from 6am to 6pm daily between the airport and city centre (about US$5 per person) – but check first. Otherwise, a taxi will cost about US$5 anyway.

Minibus Local minibuses can get very crowded at times, but they are an inexpensive way of getting around. Theoretically, you can flag them down, but your chances of squeezing on – or even inspiring a driver to stop for you – are inversely proportional to the number of stops you are from the terminal. On weekends, minibuses are supplemented by shared taxis, which charge the same fare (ZW$50). Almost every minibus going towards the city will drop you off in the city centre, but knowing which minibus to catch to the suburbs – and finding it's departure point in the city – is an art. The main terminals are:

Angwa St (cnr Angwa St and Robson Manyika Ave) is where buses leave for Hatfield and places to the southeast

Chinhoyi St (Speke Ave, between Cameron and Chinhoyi Sts) is a major terminal for places east of Harare, but nothing much is signposted, so ask and ask and…

Fourth St (Robert Mugabe Rd) has minibuses to Hatcliffe and Mbare, but it seems empty most of the time

Market Square (between Harare and Mbuya Nehanda Sts) is the largest and most organised terminal and offers (signposted) buses to Hatcliffe, Borrowdale, Highlands, Greystone Park and Epworth.

Rezende St (Rezende St) has minibuses to Mount Pleasant, via Second St

For Avondale, catch the minibus from the corner of Speke Ave and Leopold Takawira St.

Car & Motorcycle Major international car rental companies in Harare include **Europcar** (☎ 752559; e carhire@europcar.co.zw; 19 Samora Machel Ave West) and **Hertz** (☎ 706254; e admin@hertz.co.zw; Beverley

Court, Nelson Mandela Ave). By far the cheapest option is **Transit Car & Truck Hire** (☎ 706919; e transit@acacia.samara.co.zw; 80 George Silundika Ave). Refer to Car & Motorcycle in the Getting Around section earlier in this chapter for details about the costs of renting a car.

Taxi Always take a taxi at night, and even consider using one during the day to save your legs. It's easy enough to flag down a taxi along any street, or organise one at a taxi stand (eg, outside the main post office, Inez Tce). Otherwise, ring **Rixi Taxi** (☎ 753080) if you're in the city centre or **Avondale Taxis** (☎ 366616) if you're in the northern suburbs. These taxis use a meter without prompting, so their fares are paradoxically higher than set fares offered by unofficial, private cars-cum-taxis. A trip from the city centre to Mbare or Avondale will cost about ZW$500 in an unofficial taxi; double that in an official one.

AROUND HARARE

Most places listed in this section can be visited on day trips by public bus or minibus from the capital, though joining an organised tour (see Organised Tours in the Harare section earlier) or hiring a car is worthwhile.

Epworth Balancing Rocks

Although better examples of balancing rocks can be found all over Zimbabwe, those at Epworth (off Chiremba Rd; admission with guided tour US$1; open 6am-6pm daily), 13km southeast of Harare, are probably the most famous. The main attraction is the group known as the 'Bank Notes', which were catapulted to rock stardom by being featured on Zimbabwe's bank notes.

Take the Epworth bus from the Fourth St or Angwa St bus terminals and get off at either the Munyuki Shopping Centre or Epworth Primary School turn-off (from where it's 500m to the park entrance).

Ewanrigg National Park

This small national park (admission US$5; open 6am-6pm daily), 40km northeast of Harare, consists of 240 hectares of elaborate gardens and woodland. The gardens are characterised by an array of prehistoric-looking aloes, cacti and palm-like cycads, and during winter the slopes glow with the brilliant red

and yellow blooms of the succulents and the variegated hues of tropical flowers. The best time for blooms is June to October. But don't go on Saturday or Sunday, because the crowds will easily spoil the tranquillity.

Take the Shamva bus from the Mbare Musika Bus Terminal as early in the morning as possible and get off at the Ewanrigg turn-off, which is a 3km walk to the gardens.

Lion & Cheetah Park

This park (admission per adult/vehicle US$13/3; open 8am-5pm daily) sits on a private estate, 24km west of Harare and just off the road to Bulawayo. It's the only place close to Harare where visitors can 'ooh' and 'aah' at the variety of big cats (many of which are offspring from orphans that have lived in the park since 1968). You can also see baboons, crocodiles, giraffes and elephants, and even Tommy, a 250-year-old tortoise. Visitors must have a rented, chartered or private vehicle; walking and hitching are not permitted.

Lake Chivero Recreational Park

This 5500-hectare park is 32km southwest of Harare. It focuses on the 57-sq-km **Lake Chivero** (formerly Lake McIlwaine), where day-trippers from Harare love to spend their weekends fishing, boating and partying. But avoid swimming: if the crocs don't get you, the nasty bilharzia bugs might.

Along the northern shore, **Kuimba Shiri Bird Sanctuary** (admission US$1; open 10am-5pm Mon-Wed & Fri, 9am-5pm Sat & Sun) boasts over 450 types of birds, apparently the largest variety of indigenous species in Africa. **The Admiral's Cabin** (see later) offers all sorts of activities, such as **horse riding** and **boat/canoe hire**. The UTc travel agency (see Organised Tours in the Harare section earlier) offers two-hour **boat cruises** on the lake for about US$25 per person.

The quieter southern shore is dominated by the 1600-hectare **Chivero Game Park** (admission US$10; open dawn-dusk daily), where antelopes, zebras, giraffes and several well-protected white rhinos roam free. (One awestruck reader spent an hour watching two rhinos graze just three metres from the veranda of her chalet.)

Bushman's Point, at the end of the southern shore drive, has a designated **walking** area within the park, and several impressive **rock paintings**.

ZIMBABWE

Places to Stay & Eat National Parks Accommodation *(camping per person ZW$125, lodges with 2/4/5 beds US$2/3/4, chalets with 1/4/5 beds US$1/2/3)* is along the northern shore. Guests can use the swimming pool and *braai* pits.

The Admiral's Cabin *(☎ 062-2309;* e *bird park@mango.zw; camping per person US$3, chalets with breakfast per person US$12)* offers comfortable accommodation inside the bird sanctuary. A bar and **restaurant** are attached.

Getting There & Away One bus leaves daily at about 8am from the Mbare Musika Bus Terminal in Harare for the northern shore. Otherwise, buses from Mbare run every 30 minutes along the Bulawayo road, from where you can get within walking distance of the lake and accommodation. UTc in Harare (see Organised Tours in the Harare section) *may* offer a shuttle bus between its office and the Admiral's Cabin if enough passengers make it worthwhile.

To the northern shore, take the Bulawayo road, turn south at the Shell Turnpike petrol station, 5km northeast of the Manyame Bridge. From there it's 3km to the accommodation options listed earlier. To the southern bank, use the turn-off at Manyame Bridge. The southern shore isn't connected by road to the northern shore.

For Bushman's Point you must pass through the game park, where walking and hitching are prohibited. Therefore, access is only available by private, chartered or rented vehicle, though the rangers *may* arrange a lift for you.

Domboshawa & Ngomakurira

Domboshawa ('Red Rock' in the Shona language), 23km northeast of Harare, is renowned for its rock paintings. From the small **museum** at the car park, a well-marked 15-minute walk takes you to the **Domboshawa Caves** *(admission US$2; open 6am-6pm daily)*, where the paintings are concentrated.

Ngomakurira *(admission US$2; open 6am-6pm daily)*, 10km north of the turn-off to Domboshawa, offers even more spectacular rock paintings (especially photogenic in the afternoon).

For the Domboshawa Caves, take the Domboshawa bus from in front of Kingston's bookshop along Second St and walk 5km to the hill from Domboshowa village. Alternatively, take the Bindura-via-Chinamora bus from Mbare Musika Bus Terminal, get off at the turn-off 4km north of Domboshawa village and walk 1km east to the base of the rock. For Ngomakurira, stay on the Bindura-via-Chinamora bus, get off at Sasa Rd and walk 2km to the base of the mountain.

Northern Zimbabwe

The major attractions in this part of the country are the eastern section of Lake Kariba and the Mana Pools National Park, though the Chinhoyi Caves and Matusadona National Park are also worth the effort.

KARIBA
☎ 061 • pop 15,000

The name of the primary town along the Zimbabwean side of Lake Kariba (and the lake itself) is derived from *kariwa*, the Shona word for 'trap'. The name is rather appropriate because the town of Kariba is a bit of a tourist trap, as well as a playground for rich, water-loving Zimbabweans from Harare. It's also one of the hottest places in Southern Africa, and temperatures often reach over 40°C in summer (November to April). But

---

That Dam(n) Wall

On 17 May 1960, under the watchful eye of the British Queen Mother, the switch was flipped on the first generator on Lake Kariba. Until Egypt's Aswan High Dam was completed in 1971, Kariba was Africa's largest hydroelectric project. The dam at full capacity now covers 5200 sq km and holds 186 billion cubic metres of water. The wall is 128m high and 617m long.

If you want to visit the Kariba Dam wall *(admission free; open 6am-6pm daily)* independently, tell the Zambian or Zimbabwean immigration officials your intentions so that you don't have to pay any extra visa fees. (The Zimbabweans may ask you to leave your passport with them.) Then stroll along the hulking concrete mass, which eerily vibrates to the rhythm of the generators. Otherwise, arrange a tour in Kariba (see under Organised Tours later) or Siavonga (see the Zambia chapter for details).

The Curse of Kariba

For a long time the Tonga people around Kariba, who probably migrated from Lake Malawi during the 15th or 16th centuries, lived in a naturally protected enclave below the Zambezi Escarpment. Superimposed international boundaries inflicted the first blow to their culture, but it was the damming of the Zambezi River to form Lake Kariba that drove the deepest wound.

As construction began in 1955, the Tonga called upon Nyaminyami, the fish-headed and serpent-tailed Zambezi River god, to intervene. But did the god deliver? On Christmas Eve 1955 the river rose dramatically, sweeping away a pontoon bridge and swamping the foundations. Soon after, scorching temperatures stifled work and slowed progress to a crawl. In July 1957 a torrential storm sent floodwaters roaring through the work site, once more damaging the foundations. The following March there was yet another climatic anomaly – a once-in-a-millennium flood again destroyed the foundations and suspension bridge. (In all, 86 project workers died during construction, including those buried alive and still entombed within the dam wall.)

In 1958 Nyaminyami apparently relented: the project was completed, the waters began to rise over the valleys and 50,000 displaced and disgruntled Tonga were resettled on higher ground.

ZIMBABWE

Kariba is *the* place in Zimbabwe to organise water activities around the lake and along the Zambezi River.

Kariba's three-dimensional sprawl can easily leave visitors disoriented and frustrated. There is no town centre, and everything lies along a 15km stretch of lakeshore between the airport and the Zambian border. Mahombekombe is the (poor) township, while the cooler, more prestigious (and wealthy) Kariba Heights disappears into the clouds 600m above the shore.

Information

The **Kariba Publicity Association** (☎ 2328; W www.karibapa.co.zw; open 8am-5pm daily) is in the Kariba Dam Observation Point building, a steep 15-minute walk uphill from Lake Drive. The staff are friendly, but can't help with much. The noticeboard inside the tourist office also offers some limited information about local tours and attractions. However, the observation point *is* still worth visiting for the views, as well as the displays about the dam construction and Operation Noah (see the boxed text 'Operation Noah Monument' later in this section).

The only bank in town is **Barclays Bank** (*Kariba Heights*), though Barclays also has an **ATM** at the Total petrol station at the turn-off along Lake Drive. If you have cash, try **R&F Bureau de Change** (*Nhoro Cres, Mahombekombe*), beside the Spar Supermarket, or **Dragon Bureau de Change** (*The Heights Shopping Centre, Kariba Heights*). There are two **post offices** (*Kariba Heights & Mahombekombe*), but no Internet centres anywhere.

The **National Parks & Wildlife Zimbabwe** office (☎ 2257; open 7am-5.30pm daily) can provide some useful brochures and helpful information about local national parks. It's worth visiting if you're heading to one.

Things to See & Do

The quaint **Church of Santa Barbara** (*Kariba Heights; admission free; open 8am-6pm daily*) is dedicated to the patron saint of Italian military engineers, as well as to the Virgin Mary and St Joseph (the patron saint of carpenters). Workers from the Italian company that helped create Kariba Dam built the church in memory of 21 colleagues who died during construction.

If you've seen one croc farm, you have seen most of what is on offer at the **Lake Crocodile Park** (☎/fax 2822; 135 Lagoon Dr; admission ZW$300; open 8am-5pm daily). It's 12km east of Kariba Heights and hopelessly inconvenient without private transport. Phone ahead for feeding times.

Activities

All sorts of activities can be organised at Kariba, and most are amazingly affordable because some operators charge everyone the 'local rate' and accept payment in Zimbabwe dollars.

Refer to the Middle Zambezi Canoe Safari section later in this chapter for a list of companies offering canoe trips along the Zambezi River and around Lake Kariba.

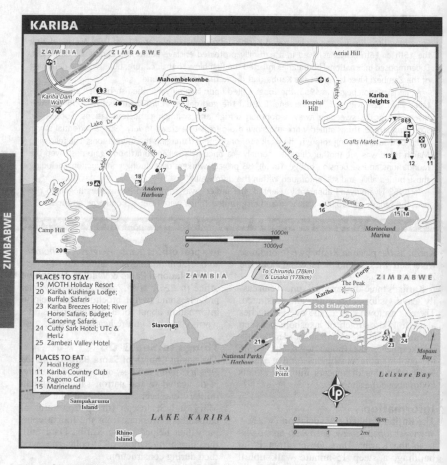

KARIBA

PLACES TO STAY
19 MOTH Holiday Resort
20 Kariba Kushinga Lodge;
     Buffalo Safaris
23 Kariba Breezes Hotel; River
     Horse Safaris; Budget;
     Canoeing Safaris
24 Cutty Sark Hotel; UTc &
     Hertz
25 Zambezi Valley Hotel

PLACES TO EAT
7 Hoal Hogg
11 Kariba Country Club
12 Pagomo Grill
15 Marineland

Houseboats & Speedboats A houseboat
is an ideal way to fully explore the lake and
to fish for bream or inedible, bony and feisty
tigerfish. The rates for houseboats (which
should be booked in advance) normally
include crew, but not fuel and national park
admission fees.

Al Cove (☎ 3338; e rstubbs@ecoweb.co.zw;
The Heights Shopping Centre, Kariba Heights)
charges US$7 per person per day for a
boat carrying 10 people. Other operators
can be found in Andora Harbour, such
as **Kariba Houseboats** (☎ 2766; e house
boats@zol.co.zw).

Kariba Marina (☎ 2475; e karibamarina@
zol.co.zw; *Chawara Marina)* offers speedboats
from US$15/20 (half/full-day). **Kingdom
Calls** (☎/fax 2845; e ctrhouseboats@zol.co.zw;

Marineland Marina) is another operator that
rents speedboats.

Wildlife Drives Several companies offer
wildlife drives around Matusadona National
Park. The best time for wildlife viewing is
between July and November.

Kasambabezi Wilderness Touch (☎/fax
2224; *Caribbea Bay Hotel)* arranges wildlife
drives for US$75 per person.

River Horse Safaris (☎ 2447; w www
.riverhorse.co.zw; *Kariba Breezes Hotel)* specialises in a full-day, four-in-one 'combo'
including a wildlife drive, walking safari,
canoe trip and lake cruise (about US$100
per person).

Buffalo Safaris (☎ 3041; e buffalo@harare
.iafrica.com; *Kariba Kushinga Lodge)* provides

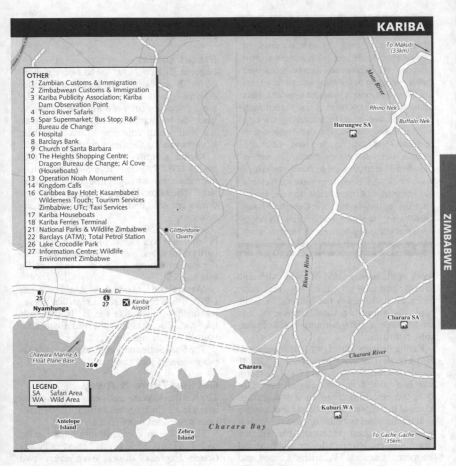

KARIBA

OTHER
1 Zambian Customs & Immigration
2 Zimbabwean Customs & Immigration
3 Kariba Publicity Association; Kariba Dam Observation Point
4 Tsoro River Safaris
5 Spar Supermarket; Bus Stop; R&F Bureau de Change
6 Hospital
8 Barclays Bank
9 Church of Santa Barbara
10 The Heights Shopping Centre; Dragon Bureau de Change; Al Cove (Houseboats)
13 Operation Noah Monument
14 Kingdom Calls
16 Caribbea Bay Hotel; Kasambabezi Wilderness Touch; Tourism Services Zimbabwe; UTc; Taxi Services
17 Kariba Houseboats
18 Kariba Ferries Terminal
21 National Parks & Wildlife Zimbabwe
22 Barclays (ATM); Total Petrol Station
26 Lake Crocodile Park
27 Information Centre; Wildlife Environment Zimbabwe

LEGEND
SA Safari Area
WA Wild Area

experienced guides and has better than average access to Matusadona. **United Touring Company** (UTc) offers similar tours as the others, and has convenient offices at the **Caribbea Bay Hotel** (☎ 2453) and **Cutty Sark Hotel** (☎ 2332).

Organised Tours

Tourism Services Zimbabwe (☎ 2452, ext 1542; Caribbea Bay Hotel) offers tours of the Lake Crocodile Park (US$2 per person) and Kariba Dam wall (US$3).

Ask your hotel to book you on a two-hour **lunch cruise** (US$6) or **sunset cruise** (US$4); these are run by several local companies. **UTc** (see earlier) also offers full-day **cruises** (US$6) around the islands in Lake Kariba.

Places to Stay

MOTH Holiday Resort (☎ 2809; Sable Dr; camping per person ZW$150, pre-erected tents & dormitory beds per person ZW$300, doubles with fan & shared bathroom US$1, self-contained chalets with fan & bathroom US$4) is the only place within walking distance of the shops and bus stop in Mahombekombe. The camp sites are quiet and shady, and the simple but pleasant chalets accommodate four to six people. It also sells braai packs and firewood, hires tents, and offers a laundry service and book exchange.

Kariba Kushinga Lodge (☎ 2645; e kushinga@zol.co.zw; camping per person US$2, A-frame chalets with shared bathroom per person US$5, self-catering rondavels with bathroom & fan from US$20) is near the

Operation Noah Monument

Construction of the lake caused problems not only for the Tonga people but also for animals trapped on intermediate islands threatened with inundation by the rising waters. So, a team of 57 wildlife experts mounted a rescue project dubbed Operation Noah. They worked from March to December 1959 tracking, trapping and relocating over 5000 creatures representing at least 35 species, including lions, rhinos and reptiles (such as black mambas!). The project resulted in artificially dense concentrations of wildlife along the southern shore, particularly at Matusadona National Park. To commemorate this marvellous feat, the **Operation Noah Monument** (admission free; permanently open) was erected just up from Kariba Heights.

shore at the western end of town. Although friendly and well set up, it's not great value and a bit remote. On the plus side are the pool, restaurant-bar with lake views, and shady gardens. The A-frames are comfortable, but rustic.

Kariba Breezes Hotel (☎ 2771; e breezes@ mweb.co.zw; camping per person US$0.50, backpacker lodges per person US$1-2, rooms with bathroom & breakfast per person US$6-7) is the best mid-range choice. Although much of the 1950s colonial-style architecture is ugly, the hotel is being upgraded. Amenities include a great **restaurant**, bar and two swimming pools (open to the public), and the rooms contain a TV, fan and air-con, and most have lake views.

Cutty Sark Hotel (☎ 2321; e cutty@africaon line.co.zw; budget singles/doubles with shared bathroom US$7/8, deluxe singles/doubles with bathroom from US$10/14) affords a terrific position with views of the lake and distant hills. Most budget rooms have a fan, balcony, TV and air-con, while the deluxe rooms also contain a pretty bathroom. All rooms come with breakfast.

Zambezi Valley Hotel (☎/fax 2926; singles/doubles with fan US$5/7, with air-con US$6/8) is in Nyamhunga township, about 4km east of Kariba Heights. It provides an African-style atmosphere, but is nowhere near the lake. Rooms, which feature a TV and air-con, are set around a pleasant courtyard and all come with breakfast. One

advantage is its accessibility by local bus and minibus.

Places to Eat

Pagoma Grill (☎ 2894; Kariba Heights; meals US$1.50) serves up light snacks and grilled dinners in a tasteful setting, but ironically most dishes on offer are *not* fish. If you've made the trek up to Kariba Heights anyway, it's well worth enjoying a nice cold beer while savouring the views from the terrace.

Kariba Country Club (Kariba Heights; meals US$2-3; open Tues-Sun) welcomes nonmembers for a negligible 'daily membership'. The home-cooked meals are tasty, the drinks are cold and the views are typically awesome.

Hoal Hogg (Kariba Heights; meals US$1-2), behind Barclays Bank, offers hot and cold (soft) drinks, and simple meals, in a charming garden setting. A few souvenirs are for sale inside.

Marineland (Marineland Marina; meals US$2-3) has a classy restaurant that serves reasonably-priced fish meals. It also sells take-away burgers and the old British favourite of fish and chips.

The **Spar Supermarket** (Nhoro Cres, Mahombekombe) is well stocked.

Getting There & Away

The Kariba Airport stands empty and forlorn because all flights to and from Kariba have been suspended indefinitely.

The only bus company that links Kariba with Harare (US$2, seven hours) is Power Coach Express. Buses leave every two hours between 6am and 2pm from outside the Spar Supermarket (Nhoro Cres, Mahombekombe).

A lack of fuel and demand has halted all scheduled passenger ferry services across the lake between Kariba and Mlibizi. **Kariba Ferries** (☎ 04-65476; Andora Harbour) still occasionally operates car and passenger ferries between Kariba and Mlibizi, but you'll have to contact the company directly or ask around Kariba town for information about departure times and costs.

The distance between the Zimbabwean and Zambian immigration offices is deceptively long (3km) and steep at times. However, if you take a shared or chartered taxi, you won't be able to see or appreciate the dam.

Getting Around

Huge buses and crowded minibuses link Nyamhunga with Mahombekombe and Kariba Heights every 30 to 60 minutes during daylight hours. However, the buses and minibuses don't go anywhere near the accommodation listed earlier (except the MOTH Holiday Resort and Zambezi Valley Hotel). **Mountain bikes** can be hired for US$2 per day at the MOTH Holiday Resort, but the roads around town are steep.

Without a vehicle Kariba may seem intimidating, but most locals are in the same boat. Hitching has become the normal method of getting around, but competition for lifts is fierce. Otherwise, order a taxi through **Taxi Services** (☎ 2454), which operates from the Caribbea Bay Hotel. Cars can be rented through **Budget** (☎ 2433; Kariba Breezes Hotel) or **Hertz** (☎ 2321; Cutty Sark Hotel).

MATUSADONA NATIONAL PARK

Those photos in brochures and postcards of 'drowned trees' before a wild mountain backdrop were taken at Matusadona National Park (admission US$10; open 6am-6pm daily). These trees are dead, victims of the rising waters of Lake Kariba during the late 1950s.

Matusadona (1410 sq km) lies along the southern shore of Lake Kariba and is sandwiched between the Sanyati and Ume Rivers. Much of the wildlife displaced by Operation Noah while building the lake eventually settled at Matusadona. The park is now renowned for its (endangered) black rhinos, impalas, hippos, (reintroduced) cheetahs and elephants (which often make their way through the streets of Kariba town at night). Matusadona is also home to one of the largest collections of wild lions in Africa and massive herds of buffaloes.

The bad news is that the park is almost impossible to reach independently and difficult to get around without a 4WD.

Places to Stay

Staying at any normal camp site run by National Parks & Wildlife Zimbabwe (NPWZ) costs ZW$125 per person, while the rate at the so-called 'exclusive camps' (maximum of 12 people) is ZW$375 per person. Chalets (maximum 12 people) cost US$9 per chalet.

Most people stay at **Tashinga Camp** at the park headquarters, which has an air strip and rents camping equipment. Another decent camp site is **Changachirere**, on the shore near Spurwing Island.

The 'exclusive camps' include **Ume** and **Mbalabala** (both on the estuary of the Ume River) and **Muuyu** (at Elephant Point, not far from Tashinga). Each of these three camps also have two six-bed self-catering chalets.

Sanyati River Camp (Sanyati Bridge Camp; ☎ 04-747422; camping per person US$4, double rondavels US$15) is along the Siabuwa Road at Sanyati Bridge. As part of the Communal Area Management Programme for Indigenous Resources (Campfire), it's an excellent place to experience traditional Zimbabwean life. Shona-style meals are available on request.

Sengwa Camp (Sanyati West Camp; ☎/fax 06-2281; W www.sengwa.com; including meals & activities per person US$110, return transfer from Kariba town US$50) is accessible by boat (one hour) or road (10 hours) from Kariba. The comfortable tents feature minimal furnishings, but the advantages are the exclusivity and tranquillity.

Lake Wilderness Safari Lodge (☎ 061-3041; e buffalo@harare.iafrica.com; budget accommodation per person US$65, suites including meals & activities per person from US$130) is a spectacular place occupying a houseboat. It offers a vast range of activities, and transfers from Kariba town.

Getting There & Away

Access to Matusadona is virtually impossible by public transport or hitching (but let us know if you were successful!). For most of the year, a 4WD is needed for the final stretch of dirt road into Tashinga, and for getting around the park. The main Chifudze River Gate to the park is 10km along the turn-off from the road to Siabuwa.

Refer to the Kariba section earlier for a list of tour operators offering wildlife drives around Matusadona. Otherwise, one truly exhilarating way to visit the park is by canoe (see the Middle Zambezi Canoe Safaris section later).

MANA POOLS NATIONAL PARK

This magnificent 2200-sq-km national park (admission US$15; open 6am-6pm daily) is a Unesco World Heritage Site, and its magic stems from its remoteness and pervading sense of the wild and natural. The word

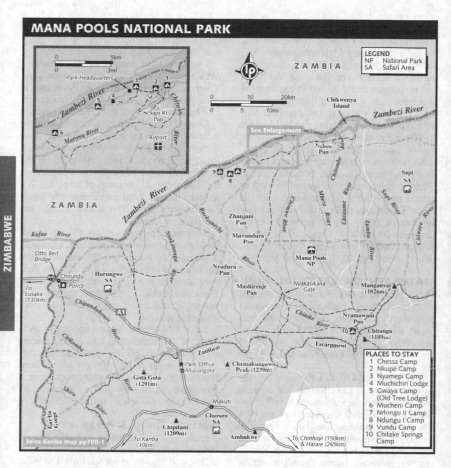

MANA POOLS NATIONAL PARK

LEGEND
NP National Park
SA Safari Area

ZAMBIA

Park Headquarters
Zambezi River
Sapi #1 Pan
Murowa River
Airport

Chikwenya Island
Zambezi River
See Enlargement
Nzhou Pan

Sapi SA

ZAMBIA

Zambezi River
Kafue River
Nyakasanga River
Ruckomechi
Zhanjani Pan
Mavundura Pan
Chitenje River
Mkera River
Chinume River
Zambu River
Chiwore River

Otto Beit Bridge
Chirundu Police
To Lusaka (130km)
Hurungwe SA
Chipandahauri River
A1
Nyadura Pan
Mana Pools NP
Mashirenje Pan
Nyakasikana Gate
Chitake River
Manganyai (1026m)
Nyamawanii Pan
Chitanga (1109m)

Chisombe River
Zambezi River
Escarpment

Park Office Marongora
Chemakunguwo Peak (1239m)

Gota Gota (1291m)
Makuti
Shiru River
Charara SA
Kariba Gorge
Chipitani (1209m)
Ambakwe

To Kariba (30km)
To Chinhoyi (150km) & Harare (265km)

Joins Kariba map pp700-1

PLACES TO STAY
1 Chessa Camp
2 Nkupe Camp
3 Nyamepi Camp
4 Muchichiri Lodge
5 Gwaya Camp (Old Tree Lodge)
6 Mucheni Camp
7 Ndungu II Camp
8 Ndungu I Camp
9 Vundu Camp
10 Chitake Springs Camp

'mana' means four in the Shona language, and refers to the four pools around the park headquarters that are popular with crocs and hippos. This is one park in Zimbabwe where you're almost guaranteed to see plenty of hippos, crocs, zebras, antelopes and elephants.

For many visitors, the attraction is the **fishing** and exploring on foot and by canoe. Mana Pools is the only park in Zimbabwe where visitors can go on **walking safaris** alone (ie, without an armed guard). Walking is allowed between 6am and 6pm daily, but take the normal precautions because the animals are still wild and potentially dangerous. Twitchers will be happy spotting some of the park's 350 species of birds.

Visitors may catch up to six fish per person per day from the Zambezi River

without a licence. Three-person canoes can be hired from the Nyamepi Camp (US$7 per day), though you will need a vehicle to transport the canoes to the river. See the Middle Zambezi Canoe Safaris section later for details about trips along the Zambezi and through Mana Pools National Park.

Information

As well as pre-booked accommodation, you will also need to obtain a special 'permit' – in effect, the normal admission fee (US$15) – from the **Mana Pools National Park Office** (☎ 063-512) in Marongora. You must pick up the permit before 3.30pm on the afternoon of your first night staying in the park, and then reach the **park headquarters** (☎ 063-533; open 6am-6pm daily), near Nyamepi Camp,

before 6pm. En route the permit will be scrutinised four times, so don't even consider trying to sneak past without one; you'll also have to produce it three more times to get out of the park. Note that to get a permit you must convince the officer that you have access to a *private* vehicle, because most car-rental agencies won't insure (or even allow) their 2WDs along any of the roads inside the park.

If you don't have a private or rented vehicle and you haven't been able to pre-book accommodation, hitch or take any bus from Chirundu to Marongora and hope there's a lift available from the park office. If there are vacancies at the lodges or camp sites inside the park, and you have secured a guaranteed lift around the park, the rangers may be able to sort out accommodation and a permit for you. (Hitchhikers cannot be added to a driver's permit, so buy a permit valid beyond your intended stay, thus allowing time to find another lift out of the park.)

Places to Stay

Camping is only available between 1 May and 31 October. Lodges remain open all year, but access roads may be impassable, so check before setting out in the wet season (November to April). The camps are run by NPWZ, which charges about US$1 per person for camping and US$4/6 per lodge with four/eight beds.

Nyamepi Camp, near the park headquarters, is the most popular and largest (with 30 camp sites), and has showers, toilets and sinks. Firewood is sold at the park headquarters, but campers are asked to bring their own stoves and fuel instead. **Vundu Camp**, 13km upstream of Nyamepi, has lodges with a cooking and lounge area, and an ablutions block with hot water and showers.

There are also several smaller camp sites: **Mucheni Camp** (8km upstream of Nyamepi), **Chessa Camp** (3km east of Nyamepi), **Nkupe Camp** (between Nyamepi and Chessa), **Gwaya Camp** (1km upstream from Muchichiri Lodge), and **Ndungu I Camp** and **Ndungu II Camp** (near Vundu). The two **Chitake Springs Camps**, 50km inland near the Zambezi Escarpment, are very remote and only accessible by 4WD.

There are no shops, restaurants or petrol supplies inside the park. Water should be treated before drinking and fruit is banned.

Getting There & Away

All visitors must stop at Marongora, 16km northwest of Makuti, to pick up a permit (see earlier). From the park office, it's about 6km to the turn-off northeast along the very rough road (30km) to the main Nyakasikana Gate. From there, the track heads north another 42km to the park headquarters.

Vehicles are usually only allowed into the park during the dry season (1 May to 31 October), though lodges open all year because they're accessible by boat and canoe. Because the track between the Harare–Chirundu road and the main gate is particularly bad, 4WDs are required.

MIDDLE ZAMBEZI CANOE SAFARIS

For many locals, the Zambezi River *is* the highway system around this stretch of northern Zimbabwe. To take advantage of this awesome wilderness route, several companies run canoe trips between Kariba and Kanyemba (on the river junction with Zimbabwe, Zambia and Mozambique).

The trip is normally done in stages: ie, Kariba to Chirundu (three days), Chirundu to Mana Pools National Park (three to four) and Mana Pools to Kanyemba (four to five). Any combination is possible, but if you can do only one stage, the Chirundu to Mana Pools segment offers the best scenery and diversity of wildlife, and the departure point is accessible by public transport. July to October are peak months for wildlife viewing. Some readers have even complained about too *much* wildlife at times, because thirsty hippos and frisky elephants can be dangerous obstacles.

Most canoe safaris include transport to and from Kariba or Harare and visas (if required). You can always save some money by making your own way to Kariba, Chirundu or Siavonga (in Zambia) if you've booked your trip elsewhere, or simply book and start the canoe trip in Kariba town. There are places to stay and eat at the Chirundu villages on the Zimbabwean and Zambian sides.

Most canoe safaris run from April/May to October/November, but some operate year-round. Since Zimbabwe limits the number of operators allowed on each of the three segments (and restricts their days of operation), some companies run from the less regulated Zambian side of the river.

ZIMBABWE

Please encourage your operator to observe good environmental practice if this is the case.

Finally, two points to remember. Firstly, the currents along this part of the Zambezi are deceptively strong. Secondly, all canoeists *must* stay within the territorial waters, and remain close to the bank, of the country they started in. Operators from Zambia are not permitted to cross the invisible border along the Zambezi into Zimbabwe (or vice versa), despite what they may claim.

Canoe Safari Operators

All the rates listed here are per person (but negotiable), and include transport from the booking office, guides, canoes, food and tented accommodation. Rates usually do not include admission fees (if required) to Mana Pools National Park. The high season is about July to October.

Buffalo Safaris (☎ 061-3041, e buffalo@harare .iafrica.com) Kariba Kushinga Lodge, Kariba – from Kariba to Chirundu, it charges US$250/ 315 low/high season; US$470/620 from Kariba to Mana Pools; and US$650/977 from Kariba to Kanyemba. Costs are lower if you start in Chirundu.

Canoeing Safaris (☎ 061-2265, W www.cansaf .com) Kariba Breezes Hotel, Kariba – trips for three/four/six days cost US$275/435/500. The more luxurious 'Denda Trail' over four days (US$500) along the shores of Mana Pools only operates between April and November.

Kasambabezi Wilderness Touch (☎/fax 061-2224) Caribbea Bay Hotel – offers all sorts of options: Kariba to Chirundu (US$285), Chirundu to Mana Pools (US$350), Mana Pools to Kanyemba (US$450) and Kariba to Kanyemba (US$500). A more sedate one-day paddle near Kariba costs US$75.

River Horse Safaris (☎ 061-2447, W www.river horse.co.zw) Kariba Breezes Hotel, Kariba – offers one-day canoe trips down the gorge for US$75 and two-/three-/four-day excursions for US$120/300/395.

Safari Par Excellence (☎ 013-42054, W www.safari parx.com) The Mall, Victoria Falls – runs several trips with overnight stops in riverside lodges for about US$200 per day. The popular four-day 'Island Trail' is more affordable at US$450.

Tsoro River Safaris (☎/fax 061-2926, e tsoro@ zol.co.zw) Kariba – operates small canoeing trips with new equipment and experienced guides for about US$100 per day. The office is along the road up to the Kariba Dam Observation Point.

CHINHOYI CAVES NATIONAL PARK

This small but worthwhile 'roadside' national park *(admission US$5; open 6am-6pm daily)* is 115km northwest of Harare. It's riddled with limestone and dolomite caves and sinkholes, which have been used for storage and refuge by traditional people for nearly 1500 years. The focus is **Sleeping Pool** or Chirorodzira (Pool of the Fallen), so named because locals were cast into the formidable hole by the invading Ngoni tribes in the early 19th century. The pool maintains a constant temperature of 22°C.

From **Dark Cave** (the rear entrance to Chirorodzira), the views through the sombre shadows to the sunlit waters far below reveal a magical effect. The clear water admits light so perfectly that the water line disappears and the pool takes on the appearance of a smoky blue underworld.

Caves Motel (☎ 067-22340, fax 22113; singles/doubles with breakfast US$15/21) is at the park entrance. It also has a **restaurant**, poolside terrace (visitors can use the pool for ZW$200) and petrol supplies.

National Park Campground (camping per person ZW$125-250) is not inviting, so you're better off camping at the **Orange Grove Motel** (camping per person US$2, singles/doubles with breakfast US$18/23) in Chinhoyi town.

The park entrance is right alongside the Harare–Chirundu road and 6km northwest of Chinhoyi town. From Harare, take any bus to Kariba or Chirundu and get off at the Caves Motel.

Eastern Highlands

Few travellers to Zimbabwe expect to find anything like the Eastern Highlands, but once they discover them, fewer still can get enough. The narrow strip of mountain country that makes up Manicaland isn't the Africa that normally crops up in armchair travellers' fantasies. It's a land of mountains, national parks, botanical gardens, rivers, dams and secluded getaways.

MUTARE

☎ 020 • pop 200,000

Mutare is Zimbabwe's third-largest city and the capital of the Manicaland province. The

Border Concerns

Although the civil war in Mozambique stopped years ago, the border areas of the Eastern Highlands are still volatile. Although the chances of standing on an unexploded land mine are negligible if you keep to well-worn tourist tracks, crime is on the increase. With the close proximity of the Mozambique border it's easy for thieves to mug a tourist and disappear back over the border. Authorities and the local community have made concerted efforts to counter the problem, such as setting up effective neighbourhood-watch-style programmes, but crime is still rife. There's no call for paranoia, but be aware of what's happening around you.

city has an odd northern European feel, with its pine forests, mountains and misty clouds. It's a charming town and an ideal base from which to explore the Eastern Highlands.

Information

The well-organised **Manicaland Publicity Bureau** (☎ 64711; cnr Herbert Chitepo St & Robert Mugabe Rd; open 8.30am-12.45pm & 2pm-4pm Mon-Fri) is one of the best tourist offices in Zimbabwe. It also offers a book exchange and informal left-luggage facility. And don't forget to pick up a free copy of the entertaining monthly *Mountain Digest* magazine.

The best exchange rates are available at **OFEB Bureau de Change** (Cecil Chambers, Herbert Chitepo St) and **CFX Bureau de Change** (cnr Herbert Chitepo & Robert Mugabe Rd), inside the CABS Bank. If you don't have cash, go to **Barclays Bank** (90 Herbert Chitepo St).

The **main post office** (Robert Mugabe Rd) has a few telephone booths. Otherwise, visit **Mr Fon** in the market area not far from the tourist office. The best place to surf the Net is **Internet Cyber Cafe** (67 Fourth St). **Kingston's** bookshop (93 Herbert Chitepo St) sells local maps and international magazines.

Things to See

The **Mutare Museum** (Aerodrome Rd; admission ZW$400; open 9am-5pm daily) offers a well-mounted agglomeration of geological, historical, anthropological, technological and zoological exhibits. The highlights are probably the collection of snakes, the stone, iron and agricultural-age relics, the transportation gallery and the aviary.

The **Utopia House Museum** (Jason Moyo Dr; admission by donation; open 8am-4.30pm daily) was the home of Rhys and Rosalie Fairbridge and their son Kingsley (1885–1924), a colonial poet and founder of the Fairbridge Farm Schools for homeless and neglected children. The home was built in 1897 but has been restored and refurnished in a style reminiscent of the 1920s. Admission includes a guided tour, after which you'll be asked for a donation (ZW$100 is enough). Walk up Herbert Chitepo St from the corner of Aerodrome Rd for 600m, turn left at Jason Moyo Dr, and the museum is on your right after 200m.

The **National Gallery of Zimbabwe in Mutare** (122 Upper Third St; admission ZW$200; open 8am-4.30pm daily) is housed in the city's first hospital. This private gallery hosts a worthwhile collection of art and sculptures, all of which are for sale. The attached **craft shop** also sells some charming and reasonably priced souvenirs. The museum is 300m up Third St from the corner of Aerodrome Rd.

It's easy to spend a day exploring the National Trust nature reserve on **Murahwa's Hill** (admission free; permanently open). The complex encloses some **rock paintings** and the crumbled **ruins** of an Iron Age village (part of which is in the Mutare Museum), but the real attractions are the **views** and natural landscapes. Look for the *mujejeje* (rocks that resonate when struck). Walk north up Robert Mugabe Rd from the corner of Aerodrome Road for 1km, turn left at Magamba Drive, and then continue for another 1km.

At the eastern end of Mutare is a small hill, **Cross Kopje** (admission free; permanently open), which looks over into Mozambique. The 10m-high cross on the summit is a **memorial** to black Zimbabweans and Mozambicans who died in WWI. Follow Robert Mugabe Rd to the southeast from the tourist office for 600m, turn left up Park Rd and take a right at the next block to Vincent Ave. This soon turns into Rekayi Tangwena (Circular) Drive, which passes near the foot of Cross Kopje after about 1.2km. Be careful about muggings.

ZIMBABWE

ZIMBABWE

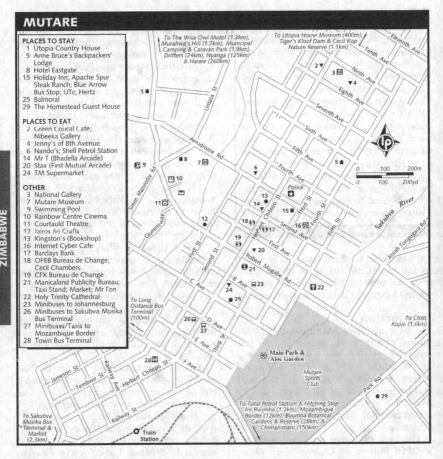

MUTARE

PLACES TO STAY
1 Utopia Country House
5 Anne Bruce's Backpackers'
   Lodge
8 Hotel Eastgate
15 Holiday Inn; Apache Spur
   Steak Ranch; Blue Arrow
   Bus Stop; UTc; Hertz
25 Balmoral
29 The Homestead Guest House

PLACES TO EAT
2 Green Coucal Café;
   Nibeeka Gallery
4 Jenny's of 8th Avenue
6 Nando's; Shell Petrol Station
14 Mr T (Bhadella Arcade)
20 Stax (First Mutual Arcade)
24 TM Supermarket

OTHER
3 National Gallery
7 Mutare Museum
9 Swimming Pool
10 Rainbow Centre Cinema
11 Courtauld Theatre
12 Jairos Jiri Crafts
13 Kingston's (Bookshop)
16 Internet Cyber Cafe
17 Barclays Bank
18 OFEB Bureau de Change;
   Cecil Chambers
19 CFX Bureau de Change
21 Manicaland Publicity Bureau;
   Taxi Stand; Market; Mr Fon
22 Holy Trinity Cathedral
23 Minibuses to Johannesburg
26 Minibuses to Sakubva Musika
   Bus Terminal
27 Minibuses/Taxis to
   Mozambique Border
28 Town Bus Terminal

To The Wise Owl Motel (1.3km),
Murahwa's Hill (1.7km), Municipal
Camping & Caravan Park (1.9km),
Drifters (24km), Nyanga (125km)
& Harare (260km)

To Utopia House Museum (400m),
Tiger's Kloof Dam & Cecil Kop
Nature Reserve (1.1km)

Police

To Long
Distance Bus
Terminal
(100m)

To Sakubva
Musika Bus
Terminal &
Market
(2.3km)

Main Park &
Aloe Garden

Mutare
Sports
Club

To Cross
Kopje (1.6km)

To Total Petrol Station & Hitching Stop
for Bvumba (1.2km), Mozambique
Border (12km), Bvumba Botanical
Gardens & Reserve (28km) &
Chimanimani (150km)

Train
Station

The 1700-hectare **Cecil Kop Nature Reserve** *(admission to all areas US$2; open dawn-dusk daily)* wraps around the northern side of Mutare and abuts the Mozambique border. Without a vehicle, however, you're limited to **Tiger's Kloof Dam**, which is fed by springs. The best time to visit is about 4pm (daily) when antelopes, giraffes and zebras congregate at the dam for a feed. To reach the dam, follow Herbert Chitepo St (which turns into Arcadia Rd) from the corner of Aerodrome Rd for 1.5km.

Organised Tours
United Touring Company *(UTc; ☎/fax 64784; Holiday Inn, cnr Aerodrome Rd & Third St)* offers full-day tours of the Bvumba Mountains (US$9 per person) and Nyanga National

Park (US$20), but tours won't start without a minimum number of passengers (about four). Renting a car will be cheaper and heaps more fun (see Getting Around later).

Places to Stay – Budget
Municipal Camping & Caravan Park *(Harare Rd; camping per person US$1)* is unfortunately just metres from the noisy highway. You'll also have to share the site with picnickers during the day, so privacy and security cannot be guaranteed. Take a taxi from the city centre.

Anne Bruce's Backpackers Lodge *(☎ 63569; 99 Fourth St; dormitory beds per person US$1, doubles with shared bathroom US$3)* is convenient. It's a little cramped, and would be noisy if tourists ever return in

droves to Zimbabwe, but the whole place is convivial and the lounge with satellite TV may be an attraction. One reader claimed that Anne can 'whip up magnificent home-cooked meals at very reasonable prices'.

Drifters (☎ 62964, fax 62930; camping in provided tents per person US$4, dorm beds US$5, singles/doubles with shared bathroom US$6/8, with bathroom US$13/15) is on a small wildlife reserve 24km west of Mutare. It's a popular, laid-back place with a pool and large bar-restaurant. Drifters is just off the highway and accessible on any bus between Harare and Mutare.

Balmoral (☎ 61435; C Ave; doubles with shared bathroom US$2) is cheap, cheerful and central, but understandably fairly basic for this price. Look for the pink, colonial-style building with wooden floors.

Utopia Country House (☎/fax 66056; e utopia@aloe.co.zw; 13 Robert Mugabe Ave; doubles with/without bathroom US$3.50/3) offers small but comfortable rooms with a TV and fan. Guests can use the kitchen, though home cooked meals are available. It's quiet, friendly and only 100m north of the intersection of Robert Mugabe Ave and Aerodrome Rd.

Places to Stay – Mid-Range & Top End

Hotel Eastgate (☎/fax 65769; Simon Mazorodze Rd; singles/doubles with bathroom & breakfast US$7/8) offers some of the largest rooms in Zimbabwe, all with a kitchen, fan and satellite TV. With these prices and amenities, it's popular, so book ahead.

The Wise Owl Motel (☎ 64643, fax 64690; Christmas Pass Rd; singles/doubles with bathroom & breakfast US$9/12) is along the extension of Robert Mugabe Ave, about 1.6km north of the junction with Aerodrome Rd. This motel features large grounds and a swimming pool, and quiet rooms with a TV and fan. It's worth the short taxi ride up the hill from the city centre.

The Homestead Guest House (☎ 65870, fax 67191; 52 Park Rd; singles/doubles with shared bathroom US$2/3, with bathroom US$3/4) is a homely place with clean and comfortable rooms. The attractions are the saltwater swimming pool, TV lounge and delightful gardens. Breakfast and dinner both cost an extra US$1. It's a little inconvenient, but perfect for a family or anyone with a car.

Holiday Inn (☎ 64431; e mutholinn@zimsun .co.zw; cnr Aerodrome Rd & Third St; doubles with breakfast US$123) is more of a landmark than an affordable hotel because it charges 'foreigners rates' in US dollars.

Places to Eat

The variety of excellent restaurants and cafés is another reason to linger longer in Mutare.

Holiday Inn (☎ 64431; cnr Aerodrome Rd & Third St; breakfast/lunch buffet US$3/4) is the place to head for if you wake up really hungry one morning. The lunch buffet will also fill you up until the next day.

Apache Spur Steak Ranch (☎ 64431; Holiday Inn, cnr Aerodrome Rd & Third St; meals US$1-2) might be avoided by budget travellers because of its corny name and upmarket location, but the food is delicious and pleasingly cheap. The help-yourself 'Salad Valley' buffet (US$1) will delight vegetarians. The only downside is the obsequious service.

Stax (☎ 62653; First Mutual Arcade, Herbert Chitepo St; meals US$1-2; open 7.30am-9pm daily) is deservedly popular. It's hard to decide between the tasty pizzas, delicious club sandwiches, healthy salads and 'all-day breakfasts' (try the backpackers' version with bacon, sausage, eggs and waffles with syrup). You will no doubt return there time and time again.

Jenny's of 8th Avenue (☎ 67764; 130 Herbert Chitepo St; meals about US$1; open 8am-4.30pm Mon-Sat) offers cakes, sandwiches, 'real' coffee and daily lunch specials (such as lasagne) along a charming veranda setting. A flower nursery and craft shop are attached.

Green Coucal Café (☎ 65509; 111 Second St; meals US$1-2; open 8am-4.30pm Mon-Fri, 8am-2pm Sat) is very similar to Jenny's, but slightly more relaxed. It offers the best coffee in Mutare, and also has an arts and crafts shop (see Shopping later).

For spicy chicken head to **Nando's** (16 Aerodrome Rd) in the Shell petrol station. **Mr T** (Bhadella Arcade, 67 Herbert Chitepo St) offers a better-than-average range of greasy burgers and chicken. Self-caterers should stock up at the **TM Supermarket** (cnr Herbert Chitepo St & B Ave) or visit the large fruit and vegetable market at the Sakubva Musika Bus Terminal.

ZIMBABWE

ZIMBABWE

Entertainment

The **Rainbow Centre** cinema (Robert Mugabe Rd) shows rubbishy American films that fill in a rainy afternoon. On Friday and Saturday evenings, the **Courtauld Theatre** (Robert Mugabe Rd) provides a venue for amateur theatre productions.

Shopping

Jairos Jiri Crafts (41 First St) offers a number of cheap souvenirs, such as batiks, carvings, wall hangings and T-shirts, with the added bonus that all profits go to the disadvantaged.

Nibeeka Gallery (Green Coucal Café; 111 Second St) is more avant-garde, with hand-painted textiles and other crafts.

Getting There & Away

Refer to the relevant sections later for details about travelling by bus or minibus from Mutare to the Bvumba Mountains, Chimanimani village and Nyanga National Park.

Bus & Minibus A few local buses use the **Town Bus Terminal** (F Ave), but the only services of interest to visitors are those to Burma Valley and Bvumba Mountains. The **Long-Distance Bus Terminal** (Chipanda St) is more of a pick-up and drop-off spot for buses and minibuses to Harare and beyond, but has buses to Nyanga village.

Almost all long-distance buses actually start and finish at the main Sakubva Musika Bus Terminal, about 2.5km southwest of the train station. To Harare (US$3, five hours), buses leave about every hour, and to Bulawayo (US$3, four hours), via Masvingo (US$2, three hours), buses depart every 60 to 90 minutes.

A better alternative to Harare is the Blue Arrow luxury coach (US$6, four hours). It leaves from outside the Holiday Inn (cnr Aerodrome Rd & Third St) on Wednesday, Friday and Sunday. Book at the UTc/Hertz office inside the hotel.

Tenda provides comfortable buses to Jo'burg (US$6) from the Sakubva Musika Bus Terminal four times a week. Minibuses to Jo'burg (US$10) also leave at about 9am every day from a spot along B Ave.

Minibuses (ZW$150) and shared/chartered taxis (ZW$200/1000) to the Forbes Border Post (at Machipanda) with Mozambique leave from the southern corner of Herbert Chitepo St and D Ave. From the border, there's frequent transport to Chimoio in Mozambique.

Train The most comfortable – but most time-consuming – way to travel between Harare and Mutare is by overnight train. The Pungwe Express departs Mutare daily at 9pm (US$2/1/1 for sleeper/standard/economy class, 8½ hours). Book at the **ticket office** (☎ 62801; open 8am-12.30pm & 2pm-4pm Mon-Fri) inside the **train station** (Railway St).

Getting Around

Minibuses to the Sakubva Musika Bus Terminal leave from the western corner of Herbert Chitepo and D Ave. Taxis congregate at Sakubva Musika and outside the tourist office. Official taxis use meters that must be linked somehow to the rotation of the moon, because their fares seem to have no correlation whatsoever between time and distance. It's cheaper to negotiate a fare with an unofficial taxi.

Because of the long distances, infrequent and uncomfortable public transport, and scenic roads, driving a car is the perfect way to get around the Eastern Highlands. The best place to arrange this is **Hertz** (☎/fax 64784; Holiday Inn, cnr Aerodrome Rd & Third St), because it happily allows foreigners to pay the 'local rate' in Zimbabwe dollars. See Car & Motorcycle in the Getting Around section earlier in this chapter for details about costs and conditions.

BVUMBA MOUNTAINS

☎ 020

Just 28km southeast of Mutare, the Bvumba (Vumba) Mountains are characterised by cool, forested highlands alternating with deep, densely vegetated valleys. In the language of the Manyika Shona people, Bvumba means 'drizzle' and you'll probably have the opportunity to determine the name's validity. With its meadows, apple orchards, country gardens and teahouses, the area seems to recreate the British countryside. If you're staying for more than a few days, pick up Bvumba: Magic in the Mist by David Martin from any decent bookshop in Zimbabwe.

Bunga Forest Botanical Reserve

This sprawling 1558-hectare reserve (admission free; permanently open) is a rare pocket of

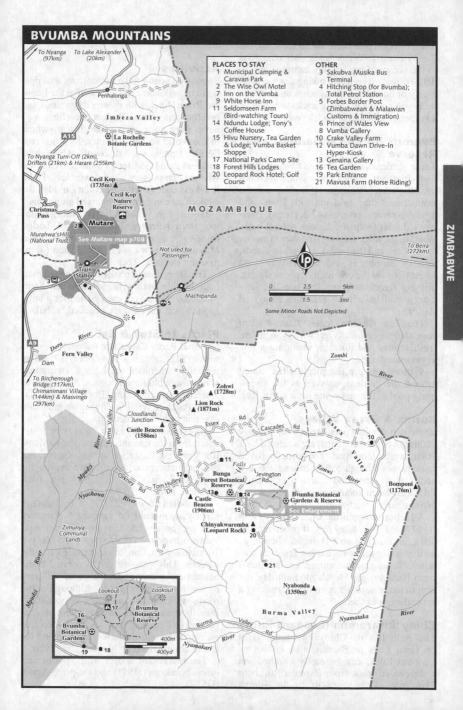

BVUMBA MOUNTAINS

PLACES TO STAY
1 Municipal Camping & Caravan Park
2 The Wise Owl Motel
7 Inn on the Vumba
9 White Horse Inn
11 Seldomseen Farm (Bird-watching Tours)
14 Ndundu Lodge; Tony's Coffee House
15 Hivu Nursery, Tea Garden & Lodge; Vumba Basket Shoppe
17 National Parks Camp Site
18 Forest Hills Lodges
20 Leopard Rock Hotel; Golf Course

OTHER
3 Sakubva Musika Bus Terminal
4 Hitching Stop (for Bvumba); Total Petrol Station
5 Forbes Border Post (Zimbabwean & Malawian Customs & Immigration)
6 Prince of Wales View
8 Vumba Gallery
10 Crake Valley Farm
12 Vumba Dawn Drive-In Hyper-Kiosk
13 Genaina Gallery
16 Tea Garden
19 Park Entrance
21 Mavusa Farm (Horse Riding)

To Nyanga (97km)
To Lake Alexander (20km)

Penhalonga

Imbeza Valley

A15

La Rochelle Botanic Gardens

To Nyanga Turn-Off (2km), Drifters (21km) & Harare (255km)

Cecil Kop (1735m)

Cecil Kop Nature Reserve

Christmas Pass

Murahwa's Hill (National Trust)

Mutare

See Mutare map p708

Train Station

MOZAMBIQUE

Not used for Passengers

Machipanda

To Beira (272km)

ZIMBABWE

0   2.5   5km
0   1.5   3mi

Some Minor Roads Not Depicted

A9

Dora   River

Fern Valley

Dam

To Birchenough Bridge (117km), Chimanimani Village (144km) & Masvingo (297km)

Zombi

River

Laurenceville Rd

Zohwi (1728m)

Lion Rock (1871m)

Cloudlands Junction

Castle Beacon (1586m)

Essex   Rd   Cascades   Rd

Essex Valley

10

Burma Valley   Rd

Orkney   Rd

Nyachowa River

Zimunya Communal Lands

Bunga Forest Botanical Reserve

Tom Hulley   Dr

Castle Beacon (1906m)

Falls

Jevington Rd

Zonwi   River

Bvumba Botanical Gardens & Reserve

See Enlargement

Chinyakwaremba (Leopard Rock)

Bomponi (1176m)

Essex Valley Road

Mpudzi   River

21

Nyabonda (1350m)

Burma   Valley

Nyamataka   River

Lookout   Lookout

17

Bvumba Botanical Reserve

16

Bvumba Botanical Gardens

19   18

400m
0   400yd

Burma   Valley   Rd

Nyamakari   River

forest that has not been (nor can be) chopped down or burnt off. There are no facilities, but the 39 hectares that straddle the main road to the botanical gardens do feature some ill-defined and overgrown hiking tracks, with plenty of butterflies, chameleons and birds to keep you company. These tracks are a bit of a crime spot, however, so take care.

Bvumba Botanical Gardens and Reserve

These gardens (admission US$10; open 7am-5pm daily) are divided into a landscaped botanical garden (159 hectares), with specimens from around the world and wide lawns, and a wild botanical reserve (42 hectares), criss-crossed with footpaths through natural bush. Wildlife includes samango monkeys (unique to the Eastern Highlands), as well as elands, duikers, bushbucks and sables. Watch the forest floor for the odd little elephant shrews, tiny but ferocious beasts that hop like kangaroos and have long ears and elongated snouts.

The Tea Garden (open 10am-4.30pm Tues-Sun) sells locally-grown Nyanga tea, fresh scones and lunches, including a few vegetarian dishes.

Visitors can use the picnic sites dotted around the gardens, as well as the swimming pool at the camp site for a small fee.

Burma & Essex Valleys

These two densely populated valleys, nearly 900m lower than Bvumba, are accessed by a 70km scenic loop road. The partially paved route passes through coffee, banana, tobacco and cotton plantations, and over beautiful forest-laden mountains with views into Mozambique.

A favourite stop is the Crake Valley Farm (☎ 61769; Essex Valley Rd). It produces and sells the famous, soft Bvumba cheese, as well as a dozen or more other regional varieties. Tours and samplings are available from 10am to 3pm Monday to Saturday, but ring to make sure it's open before making a special trip out there.

Chinyakwaremba (Leopard Rock)

The monolith of Chinyakwaremba (Hill of Tired Legs in Shona), also known as Leopard Rock, can be easily climbed via a signposted track from Bvumba Rd about 2km east of the turn-off to the Bunga

reserve. Of course, the views from the top are stunning.

Activities

Even if you can't tell a putter from a wedge, don't miss out on a round of golf at the Leopard Rock Hotel, with its superb grounds and breathtaking vistas. Budget travellers may never play on a course like this anywhere in the world so cheaply: nine/18 holes cost US$3/6 (guests get a discount), while clubs cost less than US$1 for 18 holes and caddies, who are compulsory, charge even less. There is a dress code (shirts with collar), though the authorities can be pretty relaxed about this.

If you fancy some horse riding, contact Hivu Nursery, Tea Garden & Lodge (☎ 66441); otherwise, arrange something at Mavusa Farm (☎ 68678), signposted (4km) past the Leopard Rock Hotel.

Twitchers should book (in advance) a two-hour birdlife walk with Seldomseen Farm (☎ 68482). Keep your eyes peeled for a buff-spotted fluff tail or stripe-cheeked bulbul.

Places to Stay & Eat

National Parks Camp Site (camping per person ZW$125, lodges with 4 beds US$2) offers welcome amenities, such as a swimming pool, clean ablutions block and braai pits, in a serene, natural setting. Book through National Parks & Wildlife Zimbabwe in Harare (see that section for details).

Forest Hills Lodges (☎ 62911) is 150m down from the entrance gate to the gardens. It's a private lodge set up for rangers, but they sometimes rent out spare rooms for negotiable rates (about US$4 per two-bedroom lodge).

Ndundu Lodge (☎ 63777; e ndundu@sys com.co.zw; Bvumba Rd; camping & dormitory beds per person US$1, singles/doubles with shared bathroom & breakfast from US$3/4) is a 10-minute walk from the entrance gate to the gardens. This imaginatively decorated home has superb views and a range of different rooms for different prices. Although some rooms are cramped and noisy, visitors don't mind because of the cosy lounge, convivial bar and self-catering facilities. Ring for a free pick-up from outside the tourist office in Mutare at around noon on Monday and Friday.

The restaurant is open to the public and offers breakfast (US$1) and set-price dinner (US$2).

Tony's Coffee House (Bvumba Rd; open 10am-5pm Wed-Mon), next to Ndundu Lodge, is a must. The menu, which is probably 50cm long, lists over 100 specialty teas and coffees, as well as a dozen cakes to die for. It doesn't serve any meals, however.

Inn on the Vumba (☎ 67449; e iotv@ innsofzimbabwe.co.zw; Bvumba Rd; singles/ doubles with bathroom, dinner & breakfast US$10/18) is the nearest place in the mountains to Mutare. This superb lodge offers rooms with a fan, huge bathroom and views, and two separate cottages with four beds and a kitchen for marginally more. The **restaurant** serves excellent table d'hôte dinners (US$3), including favourites like roast beef, and is worth the trip out from Mutare.

White Horse Inn (☎ 60138; e whi@mutare .mweb.co.zw; Laurenceville Rd; singles/doubles with bathroom & breakfast US$9/12) is an elegant hotel set in a deep valley amid trees about 2.5km from the main road. Overlooking the immaculate gardens and pool, each room is pleasantly trimmed in a different floral theme. The public can also enjoy fine cuisine at the **restaurant** (meals about US$2) and plunder the well-stocked cellar.

Hivu Nursery, Tea Garden & Lodge (Vumba Basket Shoppe; ☎ 66441; e hivu@sys com.co.zw; Bvumba Rd; singles/doubles with shared bathroom & breakfast US$1.50/3) is the cheapest place in the mountains. The singles are tiny, though the one double room is large and airy. The nursery is also one of the most scenic places in the mountains to enjoy a pot of tea and a plate of yummy scones (with jam and cream). It also offers full breakfasts and light lunches.

Leopard Rock Hotel (☎ 60115, fax 61165; singles/doubles with bathroom & breakfast US$90/140), below the flanks of Chinyakwaremba (Leopard Rock), is modelled on a French chateau. Built of stone by Italian prisoners of war during WWII, but destroyed in 1978 during the Second Chimurenga, it has been superbly renovated. The hotel also boasts a casino and golf course (see Activities earlier).

Shopping

Along Bvumba Rd you'll see women sitting underneath embroidered tablecloths, aprons and hankies, all strung up and swaying in the breeze. For other local specialities, such as pickles, honey, Bvumba cheese and Nyanga

tea, visit the sardonically-named **Vumba Dawn Drive-In Hyper-Kiosk** (Bvumba Rd). The **Vumba Basket Shoppe** (Hivu Nursery, Tea Garden & Lodge, Bvumba Rd) sells cheap basketware, as well as the famous Bvumba cheese.

The massive **Vumba Gallery** (Bvumba Rd) houses an extensive range of cheap T-shirts, baskets and pottery, while the **Genaina Gallery** (Bvumba Rd) sells more expensive, high-quality crafts from Zimbabwe and the region.

Getting There & Away

Without a vehicle, access to the mountains is limited. A bus usually (but not always) leaves the Town Bus Terminal (F Ave) in Mutare for Cloudlands Junction at about 10am, and returns about one hour later. Daily buses for the Essex Valley and Burma Valley circuit also leave irregularly from the same bus terminal.

It's not too hard to hitch a ride; start outside the Total petrol station on the corner of Park and Bvumba Rds in Mutare, about 1.5km down from the Town Bus Terminal. Alternatively, join a tour with UTc (see Organised Tours under Mutare earlier) or hire a car in Mutare.

NYANGA NATIONAL PARK
☎ 029

The 47,000-hectare Nyanga National Park (admission US$10; open 6am-6pm daily) is a scenically distinct enclave in the Eastern Highlands. Cecil Rhodes fell in love with the area, so he simply bought it for his own residence. Near Nyanga (Rhodes) Dam, he built a luxurious homestead and created an English-style garden with imported European hardwoods. His home has now been converted into the Rhodes Hotel.

Close to the old hotel is the **Main Gate** (☎ 8274) to Nyanga National Park. The **Nyanga Publicity Association** (☎ 8435; open 8am-1pm & 2pm-4pm Tues-Fri, 9am-11am Sat) is housed in the Nyanga village library, half-way between the village centre and the appropriately-named Village Inn.

Things to See & Do

The **Nyanga Historical Exhibition** (Rhodes Museum; admission ZW$50; open 9am-1pm & 2.30pm-5.30pm Thur-Tues) is housed in the old man's former stables in the grounds

ZIMBABWE

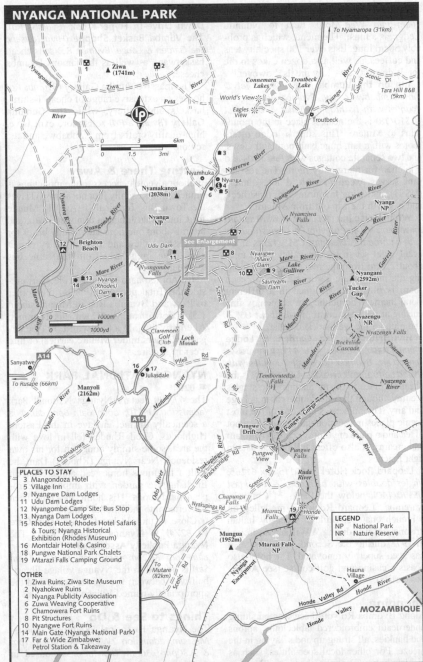

NYANGA NATIONAL PARK

To Nyamaropa (31km)

Ziwa (1741m)

Connemara Lakes

Troutbeck Lake

World's View

Eagles View

Tara Hill B&B (5km)

Troutbeck

Nyamhuka

Nyanga

Nyamakanga (2038m)

Nyanga NP

Nyamziwa Falls

Chirwe River

Nyanga NP

Nyangani (2592m)

See Enlargement

Nyangwe (Mare) Dam

Mare River

Lake Gulliver

Tucker Gap

Nyazengu NR

Nyazengu Falls

Saunyami Dam

Udu Dam

Nyangombe Falls

Rocklide Cascade

Brighton Beach

Nyanga (Rhodes) Dam

Claremont Golf Club

Loch Mhluie

Temborutedza Falls

Nyazengu River

Sanyatwe

To Rusape (66km)

Manyoli (2162m)

Juliasdale

Pifell Rd

Pungwe Gorge

Pungwe Drift

Pungwe View

Pungwe Falls

Ruda River

Chamakowa Rd

Nyakupinga Rd

Brackenridge

Chapungu Falls

Nyakupinga Rd

Mtarazi Falls

Honde View

To Mutare (82km)

Mungua (1952m)

Mtarazi Falls NP

Nyanga Escarpment

Hauna Village

Honde Valley Rd

Honde River

Honde Valley

MOZAMBIQUE

PLACES TO STAY
3 Mangondoza Hotel
5 Village Inn
9 Nyangwe Dam Lodges
11 Udu Dam Lodges
12 Nyangombe Camp Site; Bus Stop
13 Nyanga Dam Lodges
15 Rhodes Hotel; Rhodes Hotel Safaris & Tours; Nyanga Historical Exhibition (Rhodes Museum)
16 Montclair Hotel & Casino
18 Pungwe National Park Chalets
19 Mtarazi Falls Camping Ground

OTHER
1 Ziwa Ruins; Ziwa Site Museum
2 Nyahokwe Ruins
4 Nyanga Publicity Association
6 Zuwa Weaving Cooperative
7 Chamowera Fort Ruins
8 Pit Structures
10 Nyangwe Fort Ruins
14 Main Gate (Nyanga National Park)
17 Far & Wide Zimbabwe; Petrol Station & Takeaway

LEGEND
NP National Park
NR Nature Reserve

of what is now the Rhodes Hotel. It features displays about Rhodes, as well exhibits about black African history, the struggles of the Second Chimurenga and the admirable works of Zimbabwean war hero and philanthropist Rekayi Tangwena.

Near the Nyangombe Camp Site is a natural wide spot below a cascade in the Nyangombe River. The sandy beach, unofficially known as **Brighton Beach** (admission free; permanently open), features changing rooms, bilharzia-free swimming (if you're prepared to brave the chilly mountain water), and a green lawn.

Just outside the park's western boundary, the Nyangombe River tumbles over terraced stacks of cuboid boulders and plunges into a steep but shallow gorge called **Nyangombe Falls** (admission free; permanently open). Once you've seen the upper falls, have a look downstream where there's a higher and louder single drop into a deep river pool.

The reconstructed **pit structures** (admission free; open 8am-5pm daily), not far east of Nyanga Dam, may put the architecture of the many pit structures dotted around Nyanga into perspective. The most plausible explanation is that they were used as corrals for small livestock, and the animals were kept in by pales extending through the floor of the family hut that was built on a level stone platform above the tunnel. Smaller stone platforms surrounding the pit were probably used as foundations for grain-storage huts.

The ruins of **Chamowera Fort** (admission free; permanently open) is a pleasant 6km hike up the Nyangombe River from Brighton Beach – follow the well-defined path along the north bank (or drive from the road to Troutbeck).

The ruins of **Nyangwe Fort** (admission free; permanently open), a 3km walk east along a driveable road from Nyanga Dam, is better preserved. The main enclosure, which is full of storage-hut platforms and partially overgrown with aloes and msasa trees, is surrounded by five smaller fort-like enclosures.

These and other forts around the region, such as **Nyahokwe Ruins**, may resemble defence structures, but they probably served only as lookouts. Sentries posted in these hilltop structures, which are mutually visible on clear days, probably communicated by blowing on spiral kudu horns. The **Ziwa Site Museum** (admission US$1; open 8am-5pm daily), at the Ziwa Ruins, provides more explanations about the forts and other ruins in the Nyanga region.

World's View (admission ZW$150; permanently open) is perched atop the Troutbeck Massif on a precipice above Troutbeck. This National Trust site affords broad views of northern Zimbabwe, but not of the rest of the world! It's 11km up a winding, steep road from Troutbeck – follow the signposts.

The flat-topped and myth-shrouded **Nyangani** (2592m) is Zimbabwe's highest mountain. From the car park 14km east of Nyanga Dam, the climb to the summit takes two to three hours. Note that the weather can change abruptly, and when the mists drop the view becomes irrelevant. Local inhabitants even believe that the mountain devours hikers! Visitors must register at the main gate to the national park before setting off, and check back in on their return.

The tiny **Mtarazi Falls National Park** (admission US$5; open 6am-6pm daily) lies just south of Nyanga National Park and is, for all practical purposes, a part of the same park. The central attraction is the 762m-high **Mtarazi Falls**, but it's little more than a trickle of water that reaches the lip of the escarpment and nonchalantly plummets over the edge. It is, nevertheless, the highest waterfall in Zimbabwe. Along the main road from Mutare, turn right along the Honde Valley Rd and then turn left (northeast) after 2km for Scenic Rd. It's then 16km to the turn-off to the falls and another 7km to the car park.

Organised Tours

Rhodes Hotel Safaris & Tours (☎ 425, fax 477; Rhodes Hotel) offers a wide range of tours at reasonable prices: eg, a half-day tour to the Ziwa Ruins and museum (US$5 per person), and a full-day tour (U$7) to World's View (apparently a 'must for honeymooners'), Nyangani and a traditional African village.

Far & Wide Zimbabwe (☎ 3012; e farnwide@pci.co.zw, Juliasdale), just north of the petrol station, runs **rafting/canoeing trips** between December and April. Options range from one-day paddles (US$70 per person) to seven-day adventure camping expeditions along the Pungwe River.

Inquire at the main gate to the national park about **horse riding**, hiring **boats**, and trout **fishing**.

ZIMBABWE

Places to Stay & Eat

Many hotels listed here are popular with expats in Mutare, and business conferences from Harare, so it's worth booking ahead.

Juliasdale Montclair Hotel & Casino (☎ 2441, fax 2447; singles/doubles with bathroom & breakfast US$16/20) is a four-star place with luxurious trappings, such as a casino, swimming pool and mini-golf course, as well as tennis courts, croquet pitches and horse riding facilities. The rooms are large and cosy, and the roaring fires in the foyer are a nice touch. Bookings on weekends are essential.

The takeaway, at the petrol station just down from Far & Wide Zimbabwe, bakes excellent chicken pies.

Nyanga & Around Village Inn (☎ 336, fax 335; singles/doubles with bathroom, breakfast & dinner US$10/16) is a British-style country cottage set among gorgeous landscaped gardens. Although a little more expensive than it should be, it is worth every last dollar. The inn is at the end of a picturesque lane about 300m from the village centre.

Mangondoza Hotel (☎ 588; singles/doubles with bathroom & breakfast US$3/5), 3km north of Nyanga village, is worth considering if you're tired of the pseudo-British places around the highlands. The simple rooms contain grubby bathrooms, but the bar is cheap and friendly. Camping may be possible for about US$2 per person.

Several places in Nyanga village sell groceries, while the food stalls at the bus stop in Nyamhuka township provide another option.

Nyanga National Park The camp sites (ZW$300 per person), lodges (US$2/2.50 for one/two rooms) and chalets (US$4) are owned by National Parks & Wildlife Zimbabwe (NPWZ). They should be booked ahead at their offices in Harare or Bulawayo (see those sections for contact details).

Nyangombe Camp Site lies between the Nyangombe River and the road from Mutare. It's surrounded by dense pine forests and offers hot showers and *braai* pits. In the far south is the Mtarazi Falls Camping Ground. Camping elsewhere around the park is technically forbidden, but unofficially tolerated.

Lodges are at Udu Dam, Nyanga Dam and Nyangwe (Mare) Dam. In a remote section of Pungwe Drift, near the southern extreme of the park, are the **Pungwe National Park Chalets**. For all lodges and chalets, bring your own food.

Rhodes Hotel (☎ 425, fax 477; singles/doubles with breakfast US$15/19), with its tropical veranda and well-kept gardens overlooking the Nyanga Dam, was once the home of Cecil Rhodes. The charming colonial-style rooms are clean and well-furnished. If you're not staying there, at least visit for a meal or drink and admire the immaculate gardens.

Shopping

Zuwa Weaving Cooperative is opposite the post office and signposted (200m) from the centre of Nyanga village. It sells sturdy wool and cotton blankets and rugs, as well as mohair scarves. Nyamhuka township has a few shops and stalls, and a shabby **crafts village**.

Getting There & Away

From Mutare, buses leave every one or two hours from the Sakubva Musika Bus Terminal and Long-Distance Bus Terminal (Chipanda St) between 6am and 1pm for Nyanga village, via Juliasdale. (The buses sometimes continue to Troutbeck.) They stop outside the Montclair Hotel, in front of the Nyangombe Camp Site (close to the main gate of the national park), and in the centre of Nyanga village and Nyamhuka township.

From the Mbare Musika Bus Terminal in Harare, buses leave daily between 6am and 7am for Nyanga village, via Juliasdale and Nyamhuka. (This bus can also be caught from the corner of Glenara Ave and Robert Mugabe Rd in eastern Harare.) Alternatively, take a bus from Mbare to Rusape and another bus or minibus (every hour) to Juliasdale and Nyanga.

Otherwise, join an organised tour or rent a car – see the Mutare section earlier for details.

CHIMANIMANI
☎ 026

Chimanimani village, 150km south of Mutare, is enclosed by green hills on three sides, and opens on the fourth side to the dramatic wall of the Chimanimani Mountains. Even if you're not going to Chimanimani National Park (see later), the village is certainly worth visiting for its serenity and scenery.

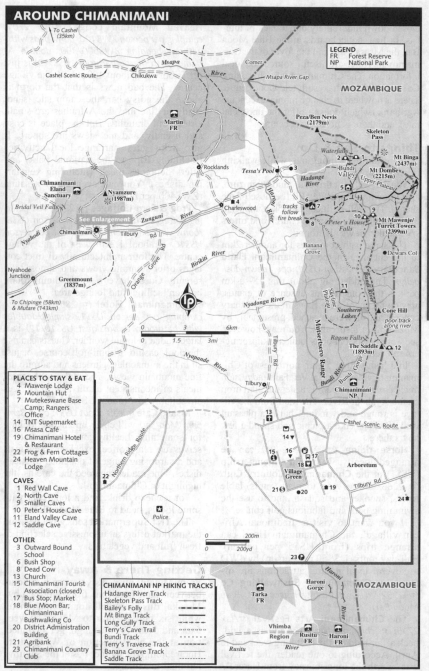

AROUND CHIMANIMANI

To Cashel (35km)

Cashel Scenic Route

Chikukwa

Msapa River

Corner

Msapa River Gap

MOZAMBIQUE

LEGEND
FR Forest Reserve
NP National Park

Martin FR

Rocklands

Peza/Ben Nevis (2179m)

Skeleton Pass

Waterfalls

Mt Binga (2437m)

Tessa's Pool

Bundi Valley

Mt Dombe (2215m)
Upper Plateau

Chimanimani Eland Sanctuary

Nyamzure (1987m)

Hadange River

Bridal Veil Falls

Charleswood

Zunguni River

See Enlargement

Chimanimani

Tilbury Rd

tracks follow fire break

Peter's House Falls

Mt Mawenje/ Turret Towers (2399m)

Banana Grove

Dewars Col

Nyahode Junction

Greenmount (1837m)

Orange Grove Rd

Birikiti River

Skyline Plateau

To Chipinge (58km) & Mutare (143km)

Nyadonga River

Southern Lakes

Cone Hill

Tilbury Rd

Ragon Falls

The Saddle (1893m)

Nyapande River

Mutsetsero Range

Bundi Gorge

Bundi River

Tilbury

Chimanimani NP

PLACES TO STAY & EAT
4 Mawenje Lodge
5 Mountain Hut
7 Mutekeswane Base Camp; Rangers Office
14 TNT Supermarket
16 Msasa Café
19 Chimanimani Hotel & Restaurant
22 Frog & Fern Cottages
24 Heaven Mountain Lodge

CAVES
1 Red Wall Cave
2 North Cave
9 Smaller Caves
10 Peter's House Cave
11 Eland Valley Cave
12 Saddle Cave

OTHER
3 Outward Bound School
6 Bush Shop
8 Dead Cow
13 Church
15 Chimanimani Tourist Association (closed)
17 Bus Stop; Market
18 Blue Moon Bar; Chimanimani Bushwalking Co
20 District Administration Building
21 Agribank
23 Chimanimani Country Club

0 3 6km
0 1.5 3mi

ZIMBABWE

Northern Ridge Route

Police

Cashel Scenic Route

13

14

15 16 17
18
Village Green

Arboretum

Tilbury Rd

21 20

19

24

0 200m
0 200yd

23

CHIMANIMANI NP HIKING TRACKS
Hadange River Track
Skeleton Pass Track
Bailey's Folly
Mt Binga Track
Long Gully Track
Terry's Cave Trail
Bundi Track
Terry's Traverse Track
Banana Grove Track
Saddle Track

Haroni Gorge

Tarka FR

MOZAMBIQUE

Haroni River

Vhimba Region

Rusitu FR

Haroni FR

Rusitu River

The **Chimanimani Tourist Association** has closed down indefinitely due to lack of tourists. In lieu, noticeboards in the Blue Moon Bar, the Msasa Cafe and the foyer of the Chimanimani Hotel are useful sources of local information. The **Chimanimani Bushwalking Co** (see later) is a makeshift telephone centre. There is nowhere to change money except the **Agribank** (which doesn't offer the unofficial rate), and there is no Internet centre.

Things to See & Do

Be careful about muggings while walking in remote areas.

You can walk (or drive) around **Nyamzure**, also known as Pork Pie Hill (because of the shape). The well-defined path (5km uphill) to the summit starts near the church and offers spectacular **views** all around.

The same path continues for another 2km to the entrance of the **Chimanimani Eland Sanctuary** *(admission US$1; open dawn-dusk daily)*. The odd thing about this 18-sq-km park is the conspicuous absence of elands; apparently, there were flaws in the sanctuary concept and all were poached, presumably by Mozambican insurgents. You may, however, see waterbucks, baboons, duikers, klipspringers and zebras.

In a lush setting 5.5km northwest of Chimanimani village, **Bridal Veil Falls** *(admission free; permanently open)* is a slender 50m drop on the Nyahodi River. The road from the village is rough and winding, but is a pleasant walk. Perhaps take a picnic and spend a few hours there.

Horse riding *(☎ 2294, 2496)* can be arranged locally. Temporary membership (US$1) at the **Chimanimani Country Club** *(☎ 2266)* allows you to play tennis, table tennis, snooker and squash, and to use the swimming pool and fabulous golf course.

If you want to visit a 'traditional African village', the Chimanimani Hotel can arrange trips (from US$5 per person). Full-day tours (US$50 per person) by 4WD to several local natural attractions are offered by **Chimanimani Bushwalking Co** *(☎ 2932; [W] www.bushwalkingco.com; Blue Moon Bar)*.

The **Chimanimani Arts Festival** *(☎/fax 2795; [e] chimaniart@aloe.co.zw)* is a laid-back affair held on the first long weekend in April. According to one reader, the festival was 'worth the long journey from Harare'.

Places to Stay & Eat

Heaven Mountain Lodge *(☎/fax 2701; camping per person ZW$100, dorm beds with/ without bedding ZW$500/300, double A-frames with shared bathroom US$2-3)* is just off Tilbury Rd, about 400m from the village centre. The bad news is that the dorm is above the noisy bar, the camp site is not shady or flat, and the A-frames are small, airless and draughty. But the place is cosy and friendly, and the views are superb. It also helps guests arrange local activities (including trips to the national park) and offers delicious meals (including vegetarian dishes). You can even enjoy a sauna (ZW$400 per hour).

Frog & Fern Cottages *(☎ 2294; self-catering cottages with bathroom per person US$8, rooms with bathroom & breakfast per person US$10)* is about 1.2km west of the village centre. The four architecturally distinct cottages offer stunning views and almost total serenity. Guests have use of the dining room, kitchen facilities and lounge area.

Chimanimani Hotel *(☎ 2851, fax 2515; camping per person US$1, singles/doubles with bathroom & breakfast US$10/12)* is a large, faded colonial wonder. Guests can use the pool, casino or mini golf course, or just sit in the immaculate gardens and admire the fine mountain views. The **restaurant** serves meals of inconsistent quality, but the prices are suitably low (about US$2).

Msasa Café *(meals about US$1; open 8am-5pm Mon-Sat)* will cheer up anyone looking for something healthy and wholesome. It serves up real coffee, excellent breakfasts and a surprising range of delicious Mexican dishes. One reader regarded the café as 'the highlight of Chimanimani'.

For a cheap drink, and a long chat with some locals, head to **Blue Moon Bar**.

The **TNT Supermarket** sells groceries, and the **market** offers an impressive selection of fresh fruit and vegetables.

Getting There & Away

From Mutare, buses leave every two hours between 5am and 1pm from the Sakubva Musika Bus Terminal for Chimanimani, while six buses return to Mutare between 5am and 5pm. To Masvingo, get a connection at the busy junction of Wengezi; to Harare, jump on another bus at the Sakubva terminal in Mutare.

Mines & Mozambique

Hikers climbing the higher peaks or bushwhacking through the back country must remain aware of the Mozambique border. It's marked only at Skeleton Pass and the Saddle, but there is a possibility (albeit very low) of encountering unexploded land mines, so stick to the defined tracks. The track to Chimanimani's southern extremes, which leaves Zimbabwe at the Saddle and passes through 8km of Mozambique territory before re-emerging at Dragon's Tooth, is dangerous and should be avoided. On the other hand, the popular climb up Mt Binga also loops briefly into Mozambique (in fact, Mt Binga is Mozambique's highest peak), but the track doesn't present any risks.

Hitching to and from Mutare isn't especially fruitful, and will probably entail a series of short lifts.

Seek advice before driving along the Cashel Scenic Route, because the track had already been closed for two years at the time of research.

CHIMANIMANI NATIONAL PARK

The formidable mountain wall that faces Chimanimani village is at the heart of a wilderness wonderland of steep sandstone peaks and towers, clear and safe swimming rivers, savanna valleys, and stone forests. Orchids, hibiscus and protea grow on the tangled slopes, and lobelia, heather and other wildflowers carpet the intermittent savanna plains. However, the readily visible wildlife is limited to baboons and a few antelopes.

In the midst of this wilderness is the 175-sq-km Chimanimani National Park (*admission US$10; open 6am-6pm daily*), which is only accessible on foot. Whether you're doing a day hike, or a five-day backcountry camping trip, this place is bound to get a grip on you.

Mutekeswane Base Camp, 16km east of Chimanimani village, is the entry point for most hikers. There's a rangers office, car park, camping ground and a welcome bush **shop** with cold drinks.

Organised Tours

Chimanimani Bushwalking Co (☎ 026-2932; ⓦ www.bushwalkingco.com; *Blue Moon Bar,*

Chimanimani village) is *the* major local trekking company. Guided trips around the park cost US$45/105/130/155 per person for one/two/three/four days, and US$170/210/240 (three/four/five days) for treks around Haroni Gorge in the south. Rates include guide(s), porter(s), transport, meals, camping gear and park admission fees. Camping is inside caves.

This outfit also rents full camping equipment for about US$1 per day. Local guides can be arranged through the Heaven Mountain Lodge, Chimanimani Hotel and Chimanimani Bushwalking Co (all in Chimanimani village) for about US$10 per guide per day.

Places to Stay & Eat

Only the Mutekeswane Base Camp should be booked in advance through National Parks & Wildlife Zimbabwe in Harare or Bulawayo (see those sections in this chapter for contact details). However, any guide (if you've hired one) in Chimanimani village should be able organise accommodation at the base camp easily.

If you had to walk to Mutekeswane from Chimanimani village, you'll probably wind up spending the night at **Mutekeswane Base Camp** (*per person ZW$125*). Hot baths and showers are available, but there's no electricity, so bring a torch.

Overlooking Bundi Valley, two or three hours walk from Mutekeswane, is a classic stone **mountain hut** (*per person ZW$250*) with bed frames, propane cooking rings and cold showers. It comfortably sleeps 20 to 30 people.

Fortunately, the Bundi Valley is riddled with **caves** and rock overhangs, which make ideal (free) camp sites. The most accessible caves lie near the valley's northern end. **North Cave**, a 30-minute walk north of the mountain hut, overlooks a waterfall and opens onto views of the highest peaks. Above the waterfall is a pool, ideal for a teeth-chattering dip, if you need some refreshment. **Red Wall Cave** lies 10 minutes further on.

A similar distance south of the mountain hut is **Peter's House Cave**, where the river provides a swimming hole. Further south (two hours from the hut), and 2.5km northwest of Southern Lakes, is **Eland Valley Cave**, which is divided into two 'rooms'

ZIMBABWE

Hiking In Chimanimani

Chimanimani National Park offers a wide choice of hiking routes and destinations, including

Bailey's Folly

Bailey's Folly is the shortest and most popular route between Mutekeswane and the mountain hut. The walk takes two to three hours – look for the rock piles that line the route.

Hadange River Track

The alternative route to the mountain hut begins near the Outward Bound School and follows the Hadange River up a shadowy ravine to connect with the Bundi River track just below North Cave. It gets very muddy and slippery.

Skeleton Pass

Skeleton Pass lies within an easy 3km walk from the mountain hut. Views are best in the late afternoon; on a clear day, the distant blue line of the Indian Ocean meets the horizon.

Mt Binga

The highest point in the Chimanimani Mountains, Mt Binga (2437m), right on the border, is also the highest point in Mozambique. It's a stiff two- or three-hour climb from the hut. Note: The last stream with drinking water is less than halfway between the hut and the summit.

The Saddle

The Saddle (1893m) is another pass into Mozambique. Cross the Bundi River between the first and second Southern Lakes and walk north along the river until you reach a steep track heading up the slope. From there, it's about an hour to the top.

Banana Grove & Long Gully

Both routes begin at Mutekeswane Base Camp. Descend steeply from the southern side of the road, about 250m west of the rangers office. At the bottom, slop your way through the small swamp, then follow the up-and-down fire swathe to the old base camp enigmatically known as Dead Cow. The track then turns sharply to the left and winds upward. At the fork above Dead Cow, you can choose between the two routes; the left one ascends Long Gully and the right one climbs to Banana Grove.

The Banana Grove route is more often used by hikers returning to Mutekeswane via the Southern Lakes. Coming from the mountain hut along the Bundi River, watch on your right as you approach the first Southern Lake and you'll see the red-earth track climbing steeply from the main river route before levelling off. Allow at least seven hours to walk from the mountain hut to Mutekeswane via Southern Lakes and Banana Grove.

---

by an artificial stone wall. At The Saddle is the imaginatively named **Saddle Cave**. Bring all your own food.

Getting There & Away

The road to the base camp is paved as far as Charleswood. An occasional bus leaves Chimanimani village for Charleswood, but it leaves in the evening – too late to get to the base camp before dark. Hitching is not easy because the competition for lifts to Charleswood at the turn-off along Tilbury Rd is *fierce* and the numbers of vehicles going to Mutekeswane is minimal these

days. Inquire at the Heaven Mountain Lodge, Chimanimani Hotel or Chimanimani Bushwalking Co about possible lifts to the national park.

In fact, it's easier to walk (16km) to Mutekeswane from Chimanimani village. The track is shadeless but fairly flat, and takes about four hours one way. Take the Tilbury road for 7.5km to Charleswood, turn left at the signpost and immediately take the right fork at the 'Mawenje' sign. After 4.5km, you'll pass the Outward Bound turn-off, which lies about 4km from Mutekeswane.

The Midlands & Southeastern Zimbabwe

Geographically, the Midlands are known as the highveld, while the warmer, lower-lying southeast is the lowveld. At the transition of the two regions is the appealing town of Masvingo. Nearby, is the expansive Lake Mutirikwe and the fabulous Great Zimbabwe, which gave its name to the country. The lowveld's finest attraction is the wildly beautiful but often-ignored Gonarezhou National Park.

KWE KWE
☎ 055 • pop 75,000

Kwe Kwe is a worthy place to break up the journey between Harare and Bulawayo, and offers more convenient and affordable accommodation than Gweru. The unusual name of this town is derived from the sound made by croaking frogs along the river banks.

The **Kwe Kwe/Red Cliff Publicity Association** (☎ 22301; Civic Centre, cnr Robert Mugabe Way & Gweru Rd) is worth a visit. All of the vital life-support systems, such as banks, bureaux de change and Internet centres, are along or just off the main road, ie, the Harare–Bulawayo highway, which is predictably renamed Robert Mugabe Way through the town centre. At the southern (Gweru) end of the main road is a useful landmark: the large (but not recommended) New Sebakwe (Security) Hotel.

The worthwhile **National Mining Museum** (First Ave; admission including guided tour US$2; open 9am-5pm daily) provides a fascinating introduction to commercial gold-mining in Zimbabwe, past and present. You're greeted by a working scale model of the Globe & Phoenix mine, which can be heard grinding away nearby. The Paper House, Zimbabwe's first prefabricated building, is also there. The museum is signposted from along the main road.

Places to Stay & Eat
Shamwari Hotel (☎ 22387; Robert Mugabe Way; singles/doubles with bathroom & TV US$7/8) is clean, popular and central (halfway along the main road). Breakfast costs an extra US$1.

Shumba Hotel (Nelson Mandela Way; doubles with shared bathroom US$3-4) offers very basic rooms with a sink, two beds and little else. It's in a central location, about one block northwest of the Shamwari, but is for some reason signposted 'Hotel Phoenix' from the main road.

Tropicana Guest Lodge (Gweru Rd; singles/doubles with bathroom & breakfast US$4/6) offers unpretentious, but clean and comfortable, rooms with a TV. It's 500m south of the New Sebakwe Hotel.

Several unappealing takeaways are dotted around the town centre, including **Wimpy** (Robert Mugabe Way), opposite the mosque.

Getting There & Away
Blue Arrow luxury coaches travel between Harare (US$5, three hours) and Bulawayo (US$5, three hours), via Kwe Kwe, three times a week in both directions. They stop at the Golden Mile Motel, 2km south of the New Sebakwe Hotel on the road towards Gweru. To avoid using the long-distance terminal in the eastern suburbs of Kwe Kwe, catch any bus to Gweru, Harare and Bulawayo from the bus stop along Fourth St, near the New Sebakwe Hotel.

The daily trains between Harare and Bulawayo stop at Kwe Kwe in the wee hours. Reservations are available at the **ticket office** (☎ 22327) inside the train station.

GWERU
☎ 054 • pop 128,000

Zimbabwe's fourth-largest city isn't a travellers' destination, though many pass through at some stage. It's worth stopping there, however, to visit the Antelope Game Park, one of the major attractions in the Midlands.

The **Gweru Publicity Association** (☎ 28606; cnr Eighth St & Robert Mugabe Way; open 8am-5pm Mon-Fri) is inside the front door of the grand Municipal Offices.

If you don't have cash, try **Barclays Bank** (cnr Main St & Robert Mugabe Way) or **Standard Chartered Bank** (Robert Mugabe Way), near the Kingston's bookshop. Better still, stock up on Zimbabwe dollars elsewhere, because Gweru has an alarming lack of bureaux de changes.

The **post office** (Robert Mugabe Way) is efficient. Several **Internet centres** are hidden away inside the Hajee Ismail Bahadur Centre (Main St), while international magazines are

ZIMBABWE

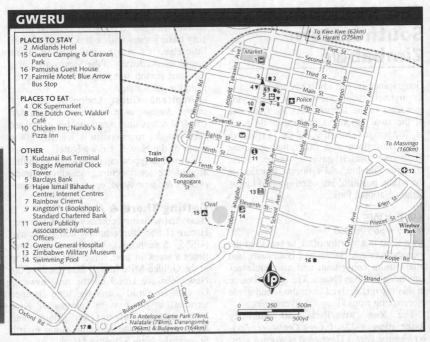

GWERU

PLACES TO STAY
2 Midlands Hotel
15 Gweru Camping & Caravan Park
16 Pamusha Guest House
17 Fairmile Motel; Blue Arrow Bus Stop

PLACES TO EAT
4 OK Supermarket
8 The Dutch Oven; Waldorf Café
10 Chicken Inn; Nando's & Pizza Inn

OTHER
1 Kudzanai Bus Terminal
3 Boggie Memorial Clock Tower
5 Barclays Bank
6 Hajee Ismail Bahadur Centre; Internet Centres
7 Rainbow Cinema
9 Kingston's (Bookshop); Standard Chartered Bank
11 Gweru Publicity Association; Municipal Offices
12 Gweru General Hospital
13 Zimbabwe Military Museum
14 Swimming Pool

available at the **Kingston's** bookshop (cnr Fifth St & Robert Mugabe Way).

Things to See

The **Zimbabwe Military Museum** (*Midlands Museum; Lobengula Ave; admission ZW$400; open 9am-5pm daily*) is the only one of its kind in the country. It houses a predictable collection of weapons, costumes and medals, as well as tanks, planes and other big toys.

The main attraction is the nearby **Antelope Game Park**. This privately-run park is one of the few places in Africa where you can literally (under supervision) 'walk with the lions' (US$20 per hour) and 'swim with the elephants' (US$35 per hour). Other comparatively mundane activities include **wildlife drives** (US$12 for two hours) and **horse riding** (US$12 per hour), while canoes (US$5 per half-day) and bicycles (US$5, half-day) can also be rented. If you book an activity (or accommodation) in advance, they may provide a free pick-up from Gweru.

Places to Stay & Eat

Antelope Game Park (*☎/fax 50374; e antelope@mweb.co.zw; camping per person US$5,* *pre-erected tents with shared bathroom per person US$15, lodges with bathroom per person from US$40; meals US$4-5*) offers accommodation in the middle of the wildlife sanctuary (mentioned earlier). The camp site is large and shady, and the lodges are comfortable though rustic. Other amenities include a swimming pool, communal kitchen and *braai* facilities. The rates for the pre-erected tents and lodges include breakfast. About 6km from central Gweru along the Bulawayo road is a signpost, from where it's 3km to the main gate. If you book accommodation in advance they may provide free transport from Gweru.

Gweru Camping & Caravan Park (*☎ 22929; off Robert Mugabe Way; camping per person US$1*) is not recommended because there's no fence or guard, so your privacy and security cannot be guaranteed. It's about 200m from the main road and next to the cricket oval.

Fairmile Motel (*☎ 24144; e fairmile@cajj.co.zw; Bulawayo Rd; standard singles/doubles with bathroom & breakfast US$14/19, suite US$20*) is probably named after the approximate distance from the city centre. It's like

a hundred bland motels found across North America, but is quiet and well-furnished, and the gardens and pool are inviting. All rooms feature satellite TV.

Pamusha Guest House (☎ *23535; 73 Kopje Rd; singles/doubles with shared bathroom US$8/10, with bathroom US$9/11)* offers the best value in town. It's quaint and friendly, some rooms contain massive, new bathrooms and all rooms come with breakfast.

Midlands Hotel (☎ *22581, fax 23784; cnr Main St & Robert Mugabe Way; singles/doubles with bathroom & breakfast US$15/25)* is a pretentious three-star place. It's ragged and overpriced, but the only option in the city centre.

The Dutch Oven (*56 Fifth St; meals about US$1; open 8am-8pm Mon-Sat)* is easily the best eatery in Gweru. It serves European-style food and is popular with expats.

Waldorf Café (*54 Fifth St; meals under US$1)*, next door, has a pretentious name, and serves African fare. The **bakery** inside is good.

A junk-food junction, with **Chicken Inn**, **Pizza Inn** and **Nando's**, is on the corner of Robert Mugabe Way and Sixth St. Otherwise, stock up at **OK Supermarket** (*Robert Mugabe Way)*.

Getting There & Away

From the **Kudzanai Bus Terminal** (*Robert Mugabe Way)*, between Second and Third Sts, local African buses or minibuses, and better express buses, travel every few minutes to Harare and Bulawayo. Before about 10am, minibuses are the only option to Bulawayo, and are always faster anyway.

Blue Arrow luxury coaches travel every day (in both directions) between Harare (US$6, four hours) and Bulawayo (US$4, two hours), and stop at the Fairmile Motel (Bulawayo road).

Daily trains between Harare and Bulawayo stop at Gweru between 11.30pm and 1.30am. Reservations are available at the **ticket office** (☎ *3711)* inside the **train station**, at the end of Tenth St.

AROUND GWERU

Nalatale (also spelt Nalatela or Nalatele) rates among the best of Zimbabwe's 150 walled ruins. This simple structure on a remote granite hilltop enjoys a commanding view across the hills, plains and *kopjes*.

The main feature, a decorated wall, exhibits in one collection all the primary decorative wall patterns found in Zimbabwe: chevron, chequer, cord, herringbone and ironstone.

The ruins are well signposted. From Gweru, turn south off the Bulawayo road at Daisyfield Siding and follow the gravel road approximately 27km to the signposted left turn-off. The site is 1km uphill from the parking area.

Commonly known as Dhlo Dhlo (approximate pronunciation: 'hshlo hshlo'), **Danangombe** isn't as lovely or as well preserved as Nalatale, but it is quiet and unspoilt. The most interesting feature is a crumbling enclosure formed partially by natural boulders, but the whole thing is overgrown by wandering tree roots and sheltered by large trees. Relics of Portuguese origin have been uncovered by amateur treasure hunters, but Danangombe's past largely remains a mystery. After the Ndebele invasions of the 1830s, the site was abandoned and only rediscovered by white settlers after the 1893 Ndebele uprising.

Danangombe is also well signposted, 32km south of Shangani, which is along the road to Bulawayo from Gweru.

There are no facilities at either site, but it is possible to camp in the wild.

MASVINGO
☎ 039 • pop 51,000

Masvingo emits a clean and routine small-town laziness, while Mucheke township, 2km to the southwest, is typically African – vibrant and chaotic. The name Masvingo, which was adopted after Zimbabwe independence, is derived from *rusvingo*, the Shona word for 'walled-in enclosures', in reference to the nearby Great Zimbabwe. Masvingo is easy-going and compact, and an obvious base for trips to Great Zimbabwe and Lake Mutirikwe (see the relevant sections later in this chapter for details).

Information

The helpful **Masvingo Publicity Association** (☎ *62643;* e *mgpa@mweb.co.zw; Robert Mugabe St; open 8am-5pm Mon-Fri, 9am-11am Sat)* sells a useful map of Lake Mutirikwe (ZW$40) and the informative *Masvingo Great Zimbabwe Bulletin* (ZW$10).

Staff at **Barclays Bank** (*Robert Mugabe St)* and **Standard Chartered Bank** (*22 Robert Mugabe St)* will just sneer if you ask about

ZIMBABWE

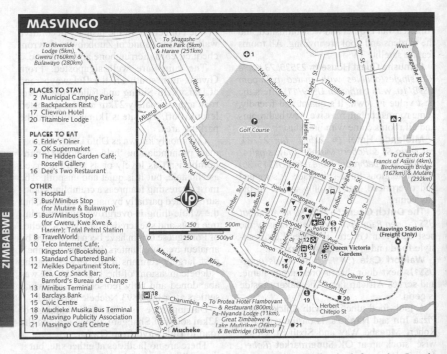

MASVINGO

PLACES TO STAY
2 Municipal Camping Park
4 Backpackers Rest
17 Chevron Hotel
20 Titambire Lodge

PLACES TO EAT
6 Eddie's Diner
7 OK Supermarket
9 The Hidden Garden Café;
  Rosselli Gallery
16 Dee's Two Restaurant

OTHER
1 Hospital
3 Bus/Minibus Stop
  (for Mutare & Bulawayo)
5 Bus/Minibus Stop
  (for Gweru, Kwe Kwe &
  Harare); Total Petrol Station
8 TravelWorld
10 Telco Internet Cafe;
  Kingston's (Bookshop)
11 Standard Chartered Bank
12 Meikles Department Store;
  Tea Cosy Snack Bar;
  Barnford's Bureau de Change
13 Minibus Terminal
14 Barclays Bank
15 Civic Centre
18 Mucheke Musika Bus Terminal
19 Masvingo Publicity Association
21 Masvingo Craft Centre

the unofficial exchange rate, so try **Barnford's Bureau de Change** (*Meikles Department Store, cnr Robert Mugabe St & Leopold Takawira Ave*).

Telco Internet Cafe (*shop 5, 2nd floor, Old Mutual Centre, Robert Mugabe St*) is the only place to surf the Net. Nearby, **Kingston's** bookshop (*Robert Mugabe St*) sells maps and international magazines.

For all travel-related information, including tickets for express buses and car hire, contact **TravelWorld** (☎ *62131;* e *trvl wld@mweb.co.zw; 14 Hughes St*), opposite the post office.

Things to See
The **Church of St Francis of Assisi** (*Italian Chapel; admission free; open 8am-6pm daily*) was constructed between 1942 and 1946 by Italian POWs to commemorate 71 of their compatriots who died in Zimbabwe during WWII. The simulated mosaics in the apse were the work of an Italian engineer, while the wall murals were completed 10 years later by Masvingo artists. Drive (or walk) 4km east towards Mutare from the caravan park, take the left turn at the signpost and

then turn immediately left again. Just in front of the military barracks, turn left yet again.

The small **Shagashe Game Park** (*admission US$1; open dawn-dusk daily*) lies 5km north of Masvingo along the road to Harare. You can either drive or charter a taxi from Masvingo, or take a guided tour at the park (the extra cost depends on the number of passengers). It's easy to spot wildlife from the viewing platforms during daily feeding times (usually at 4.30pm and 6pm).

Places to Stay
Municipal Camping Park (☎ *62431; off Mutare Rd; camping per person ZW$460, showers extra ZW$70*) has green lawns and a riverside setting. It's convenient, well maintained and secure (with decent fences and a night-time guard).

Backpackers Rest (☎ *63960; Josiah Tongogara Ave; dorm beds US$1, singles/doubles with breakfast & shared bathroom from US$2.50/5*) offers dark, musty and noisy rooms, but it is convenient and friendly. The hostel is upstairs and easy to miss; the entrance is along Robertson St.

Titambire Lodge (☎ 63858; 14 Kirton Rd; doubles with shared bathroom US$3) is basic, but clean, sunny and friendly.

Riverside Lodge (☎ 64725; e riversid@icon .co.zw; doubles US$5, with TV US$7) is about 7km from the town centre, just off the road to Bulawayo. It's quiet, welcoming and nicely set up for budget travellers. The extended house has a variety of rooms (some with bathroom, some without), as well as a TV lounge, communal kitchen, restaurant and two lively bars. All rooms come with breakfast. Contact them about free transfers from town.

Chevron Hotel (☎ 63581; e chevron@icon .co.zw; 2 Robert Mugabe St; singles/doubles with bathroom & breakfast US$9/12) is convenient and popular, so book ahead. The rooms are cosy, have a TV, and most overlook the pool and garden.

Protea Hotel Flamboyant (☎ 53085; e flamstel@mweb.co.zw; Beitbridge Rd; singles/doubles with bathroom & breakfast US$11/14) is better than the Chevron and only 20 minutes' walk south of the town centre. It offers a huge number of quiet rooms with TV, though most rooms look decidedly shabby these days. It's accessible by minibus from the terminal along Hughes St.

Pa-Nyanda Lodge (☎ 63412; e nrg-gr@ icon.co.zw; Beitbridge Rd; camping per person US$3, camping with evening meal/game walk US$5/8, cottages with bathroom & half board per person US$9) is easily the best value in and around Masvingo for as long as the manager can keep the rates so low for foreigners. The camp site is based around individual brick sheds with sinks and *braai* facilities. The lovely cottages are built in a traditional style, and the restaurant/bar is particularly appealing. The lodge is part of an ostrich farm, 11km south of Masvingo. Contact them in advance about transfers from town.

Places to Eat

The Hidden Garden Café (39 Hughes St; meals about US$1.50; open 8.30am-4.30pm Mon-Fri, 8.30am-1pm Sat) is an informal eatery with shady gardens. It offers daily specials at lunchtime, including vegetarian dishes, as well as all-day breakfasts (US$1). Drinks include delicious fruit juices and milkshakes. While waiting for your meal, perhaps stroll around the attached **Rosselli Gallery**, which

houses a diverse range of pottery, ceramics and carvings.

Tea Cosy Snack Bar (Meikles Department Store, cnr Robert Mugabe St & Leopold Takawira Ave; open 9am-5pm Mon-Sat) is, well, cosy, and serves tea, cakes and pastries.

Protea Hotel Flamboyant (☎ 53085; Beitbridge Rd; snacks US$1.50, meals US$2) is worth the trip even if you're staying somewhere else. The range of beef and fish meals is impressive, and the menu even lists a few vegetarian dishes. The lunch or dinner buffet (US$3) will keep you full for 24 hours.

Eddie's Diner (cnr Leopold Takawira Ave & Hellet St; meals ZW$250) is clean and friendly. It's perfect if you can't get enough of *sadza*-based meals or you're on a strict budget.

Dee's Two Restaurant (Simon Mazorodze Ave; meals about US$1) is arguably the best of the greasy spoons. It sells the usual array of chicken and burgers, all smothered with chips (French fries).

The **OK Supermarket** (Josiah Tongogara Ave) is well stocked.

Getting There & Away

Falcon Air (☎ Harare 04-780956, fax 780982) flies between Masvingo and Harare if at least seven passengers buy tickets. (This is so rare, however, that no-one at TravelWorld remembers Falcon Air ever flying to Masvingo.) So you'll probably have to take a bus.

Long-distance 'African' buses use the **Mucheke Musika Bus Terminal**, 1.5km southwest of the town centre, and accessible by minibus from the terminal along Hughes St. Masvingo is a stopover for all buses and minibuses travelling between Bulawayo (US$2, three hours) and Mutare (US$2, three hours) and Harare and Jo'burg, and for some buses and minibuses between Bulawayo and Harare (US$3, five hours), so there's plenty of public transport to choose from. It may be easier to catch a bus or minibus to Mutare or Bulawayo from along the top end of Robert Mugabe St; and to Gweru, Kwe Kwe and Harare from a spot next to the Total petrol station along Bradburn St.

For luxury coaches to Jo'burg, book tickets at TravelWorld (see Information earlier). Most buses between Harare and Jo'burg stop at the Shell petrol station, 6km south of Masvingo and at the turn-off to Great Zimbabwe.

ZIMBABWE

Getting Around

Consider renting a car to reach Great Zimbabwe and to explore Lake Mutirikwe. Riverside Lodge (see Places to Stay earlier) rents reliable 10- to 15-year-old vehicles for about US$12 per day, plus US$0.12 per kilometre. The rates include insurance, but not petrol. Otherwise, ask at TravelWorld or the tourist office.

GREAT ZIMBABWE
☎ 039

Great Zimbabwe *(admission US$13; open 6am-6pm daily)* is the greatest medieval city in sub-Saharan Africa and provides evidence that ancient Africa reached a level of civilisation not suspected by earlier scholars. As a religious and temporal capital, this city of 10,000 to 20,000 dominated a realm that stretched across eastern Zimbabwe and into modern-day Botswana, Mozambique and South Africa. The name is believed to come from one of two possible Shona origins; *dzimba dza mabwe* (great stone houses) or *dzimba woye* (esteemed houses). The grand setting and history-soaked walls certainly qualify as a highlight of Southern Africa.

If you need more information about the site than we can provide here, buy the *Great Zimbabwe* booklet (US$1) at the main gate or *A Trail Guide to the Great Zimbabwe National Monument* at any decent bookshop around Zimbabwe. Alternatively, arrange a two-hour guided tour (about US$1 per person) at the main gate or **Information Centre**, a grandly named open-air building at the start of the walking trails.

Inside the complex, **Matombo Curios** offers a huge selection of tacky souvenirs at reasonable prices. It also sells cold drinks, but the nearest place to eat is the Great Zimbabwe Hotel (see Places to Stay following).

Foreigners can pay admission fees to the site in Zimbabwe dollars (ie, ZW$2200).

History

Despite nearly one hundred years of effort by colonial governments to ascribe the origins of Great Zimbabwe to someone else (in fact, *anyone* else), conclusive proof of its Bantu origins was established in 1932 by British archaeologist Gertrude Caton-Thompson. Outside influences did, however, play a role in the development of Great Zimbabwe.

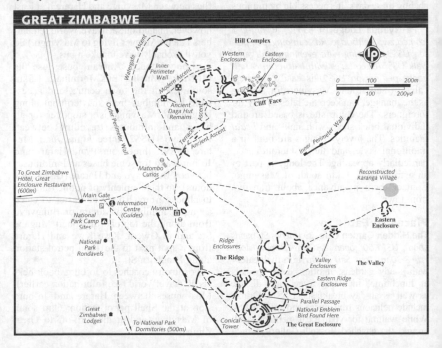

GREAT ZIMBABWE

Swahili traders were present along the Mozambique coast from the 10th century, and trade goods – Chinese porcelain, Persian crockery and beads, and Indian trinkets – have been found in the ruins.

Historians do know that what became Great Zimbabwe was first occupied in the 11th century. The settlers probably comprised several scattered groups that recognised the safety of numbers. Construction of the Hill Complex commenced in the 13th century, while the remainder was built over the next one hundred years.

Fuelled by Swahili gold trade, the city grew into a powerful religious and political capital, and became the heart of Rozwi culture. Royal herds increased and coffers overflowed. But eventually Great Zimbabwe probably became a victim of its own success: by the 15th century, the growing human and bovine population, and their associated environmental needs, had depleted local resources, necessitating emigration to more productive lands. Great Zimbabwe soon declined rapidly, and when the Portuguese arrived in the 16th century, the city was virtually deserted.

Things to See

The site is divided into several major ruins. Probably the first of the Great Zimbabwe structures to be completed, the **Hill Complex** (once known as the Acropolis) was a series of royal and ritual enclosures. Its most salient feature is the Western Enclosure, where the Ancient Ascent and Terrace Ascent converge.

The Valley is a series of 13th-century walls and *daga* hut platforms. The area yielded metal tools and the soapstone birds that became the national symbol of Zimbabwe.

The Great Enclosure, thought to have served as a royal compound, is the structure most identified with Great Zimbabwe. Nearly 100m wide and 255m in circumference, it's the largest ancient structure in sub-Saharan Africa. The mortar-less walls rise 11m and, in places, are 5m thick. The greatest source of speculation is the 10m-high **Conical Tower**, a solid and ceremonial structure that probably had phallic significance.

Leading north from the Conical Tower is the narrow 70m-long **Parallel Passage**. It may have been a means of moving from the northern entrance to the Conical Tower

without being detected by those within the enclosure. It may also have been that the construction skills of the builders had improved so dramatically over time that they decided to rebuild the entire wall in a superior manner. The outside wall of the Parallel Passage, perhaps the most architecturally advanced structure in Great Zimbabwe, is 6m thick at the base and 4m thick at the top, with each course of stone tapering to add stability to the 11m-high wall. This stretch is capped by three rings of decorative chevron patterns.

The **museum** *(admission included in the general ticket; open 8am-5pm daily)* houses (and explains) most of Great Zimbabwe's archaeological finds, and is worth visiting *before* you set off to explore the ruins. The soapstone Zimbabwe birds, which were probably Rozwi dynasty totems, are a highlight of the museum; other interesting exhibits include porcelain and glass goods brought by Swahili traders.

Organised Tours

Lowveld Heritage Tours & Safaris *(☎ 64274, fax 64884; Great Zimbabwe Hotel)* offers three-hour tours of the ruins (US$3 per person).

Places to Stay & Eat

National Park Accommodation *(camping per person US$1, dorm beds US$1.50, rondavels with shared bathroom per person US$3.50)* is strung out along a trail that heads south of the main gate. The rondavels are small, but cheap, while the camp site offers little shade or security. The dormitory building is fenced off, but isolated – about 1km from the main gate. These places are *not* run by National Parks & Wildlife Zimbabwe, so book at the main gate *(☎ 7055)*.

Great Zimbabwe Hotel *(☎ 64173, fax 64844; singles/doubles with bathroom & breakfast US$126/158)* is a luxurious place only 700m west of the main gate. It features a pool, shady gardens and tennis courts. With some gumption and negotiation skills, it *may* be possible to pay the 'local rate' (which works out at about US$30 per double if you change money at the unofficial rate).

The Great Enclosure Restaurant *(meals US$2, lunch/dinner buffet US$3/4)* offers delicious meals and reasonable prices considering the location and service. The

menu lists several tempting vegetarian dishes.

Great Zimbabwe Lodges (☎ 64173, fax 64844; with kitchen & TV per person US$43), run by the Great Zimbabwe Hotel, is a range of lodges about 400m south of the main gate. They are all charming and nicely furnished, and sleep up to six. Ask if you can pay the local rate (which works out at about US$20 per lodge). Guests can use the swimming pool at the parent hotel.

Getting There & Away
Buses and minibuses marked Morgenster, Nemanwa, Charumbira or Chatikobo leave about every hour from the Mucheke Musika Bus Terminal in Masvingo. Get off at the obvious turn-off to the Great Zimbabwe Hotel, walk about 1km to the hotel and then follow the trail (700m) through the hotel to the main gate. Otherwise, disembark at the official turn-off further east to the Great Zimbabwe site and walk 1.5km to the main gate. A taxi from Masvingo will cost about US$10 one way.

LAKE MUTIRIKWE (KYLE) RECREATIONAL PARK
☎ 039

In 1961, a 305m-wide wall was built across Mutirikwe River to create Lake Mutirikwe, Zimbabwe's second-largest dam (90 sq km). By the early 1990s, after nearly a decade of drought, the lake shrank to 1% of its capacity, but it's reasonably full these days.

The lake is part of the 22,000-hectare Lake Mutirikwe Recreational Park (still often called the Kyle Recreational Park). Along the northern shore, the **Lake Mutirikwe (Kyle) Game Park** (admission US$10; open 6am-6pm daily) hosts more species of antelopes than any other park in Zimbabwe, and is also home to a comparatively healthy number of white rhinos. Walking is only permitted around the **Vuchichu Walking Area** and the **Mushagashe Arm** (near the National Park camp site and lodges), but neither areas offer much wildlife because they're outside the game park fence.

About 200m above the **Kyle Dam Wall** is the delightful **St Andrew's Chapel** (not open to the public), probably the smallest of its kind in the country. It's next to a **lookout** offering wonderful views of the dam wall and lake.

A useful map (ZW$40) of the lake and parks is available from the tourist office in Masvingo.

Activities
Mutirikwi Lake Cruises (☎ 011-209516; per person US$4.50, or US$13 minimum for the boat) operates two-hour **cruises** to the game-park side of the lake from Mutirikwi Lake Shore Lodges. Not much wildlife can be seen from the lake, but the scenery, including an obligatory stop at the dam wall, makes it worthwhile. The cost includes soft drinks and snacks, but bring your own beer or wine (cool boxes and ice are provided). The same outfit rents boats for US$3.50 per hour (minimum of three hours), plus fuel.

Lowveld Heritage Tours & Safaris (☎ 64274, fax 6484, Great Zimbabwe Hotel) arranges **wildlife drives** (US$7, three hours) and **horse riding** (US$3 per hour) in the wildlife park, as well as **fishing** (US$4 per person, including equipment). **Horse riding** can also be arranged at the headquarters of the wildlife park, but should (in theory) be booked in advance at the National Parks & Wildlife Zimbabwe (NPWZ) office in Harare.

Places to Stay
National Parks Camp Site & Lodges (☎ 62913; camping per person ZW$125, lodges with 3/5 beds US$1.50/3), along the northern shore, has all the standard features, such as showers, toilets and braai pits. Book at the NPWZ offices in Harare or Bulawayo.

Kyle View Holiday Resort (☎/fax 64877; camping per person US$1, chalets with bathroom US$3, with bathroom & kitchen US$5-11) offers simple but clean chalets in a shady setting within 100m of the lake shore. Amenities include a swimming pool, bar and **restaurant**, and tennis courts.

Mutirikwi Lake Shore Lodges (☎/fax 64878; camping per person US$1, rondavels with bathroom & kitchen US$3.50-6) has several one- and two-storey rondavels huddled together along the lake shore. Each contains several beds and a TV. The pool is an uninviting green colour, but the shop, bottle shop and cruise operator (see Activities earlier) in the grounds are pluses.

Inn on Great Zimbabwe (☎/fax 64879; e iogz@innsofzimbabwe.co.zw; budget rooms with shared bathroom per person US$1.50, singles/doubles with bathroom, breakfast &

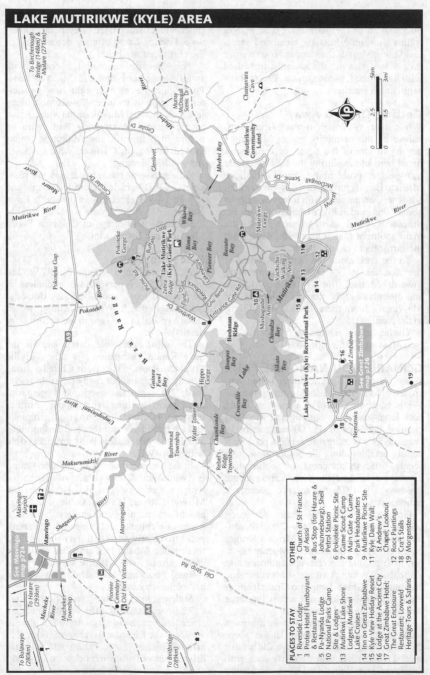

LAKE MUTIRIKWE (KYLE) AREA

0   2.5   5km
0   1.5   3mi

PLACES TO STAY
1 Riverside Lodge
3 Protea Hotel Flamboyant
   & Restaurant
5 Pa-Nyanda Lodge
10 National Parks Camp
   Site & Lodges
13 Mutirikwi Lake Shore
   Lodges; Mutirikwi
   Lake Cruises
14 Inn on Great Zimbabwe
15 Kyle View Holiday Resort
16 Lodge at the Ancient City
17 Great Zimbabwe Hotel;
   The Great Enclosure
   Restaurant; Lowveld
   Heritage Tours & Safaris

OTHER
2 Church of St Francis
   of Assisi
4 Bus Stop (for Harare &
   Johannesburg); Shell
   Petrol Station
6 Pokoteke Picnic Site
7 Game Scout Camp
8 Main Gate & Game
   Park Headquarters
9 Mutirikwe Picnic Site
11 Kyle Dam Wall;
   St Andrew's
   Chapel; Lookout
12 Rock Paintings
18 Craft Stalls
19 Morgenster

ZIMBABWE

dinner US$10/16) is a gorgeous place about 300m south of the main road. The budget rooms are simple, but new, clean and excellent value. Most of the standard rooms offer lake views, and all are lovingly furnished with a definite feminine touch. The **restaurant** is also excellent.

Getting There & Away

While it's easy enough to reach Great Zimbabwe by bus or minibus from Masvingo, getting to any of the hotels or camp sites listed here and exploring the lake by public transport is problematic. From Mucheke Musika Bus Terminal in Masvingo, catch a bus to Charumbira (which leaves daily at about 10am and 3pm) or Chatikobo (several times a day), and get off anywhere along the main southern road. Otherwise, walk from the turn-offs to Great Zimbabwe.

To the park along the northern shores of the lake, take a bus to Nyika, or anything towards Mutare, from Mucheke Musika, and disembark at the turn-off (16km east of Masvingo). From there, hitch a ride (17km) to the main gate.

The best idea is to hire a car from Masvingo (see Masvingo earlier for details).

GONAREZHOU NATIONAL PARK

When large-scale agriculture began encroaching on wildlife habitats during the late 1960s, tsetse-fly control measures (involving both large-scale bush-burning and shooting) claimed the lives of 55,000 large animals. Pressure for a wildlife refuge and a poaching-control corridor along the border grew, so a scenic, 5055-sq-km chunk of southeastern Zimbabwe became the Gonarezhou Game Reserve. (In 1975 the reserve became a national park.)

Gonarezhou National Park *(admission US$10; open 6am-6pm May-Oct)* is virtually an extension of South Africa's Kruger National Park and borders Mozambique. So, in late 2002 the relevant authorities in Zimbabwe, South Africa and Mozambique created the **Great Limpopo Transfrontier Park**, a 35,000-sq-km park across the three countries (with no boundaries).

The Save–Runde subregion is the most scenic section of Gonarezhou. This is where the rugged red sandstone **Chilojo Cliffs** (also spelt Tjolotjo) rise near its confluence with the Save River. With a 4WD, you can admire the majestic scenery from the **Chilojo Viewpoint** and **Chamuchinzu Viewpoint**. Otherwise, **Fishans Camp** offers a decent view of the cliff face from below.

The Mwenezi subregion is dotted with small, scenic pools and pans, such as **Rossi Pool**, which has an overnight viewing shelter. Other pools include: **Mwatomba** (deep in a rock shelter), **Mukokwani** (with a small picnic shelter), **Manyanda Pan** (with an overnight platform), and **Makonde** (overlooked by Wright's Tower, which is used for wildlife viewing).

Although some roads in the park are passable to 2WD vehicles, most are rough and require a 4WD, especially in the south. From November to April, access is not allowed to the national park camps at Chipinda Pools, Mbalauta and Swimuwini.

Places to Stay

The costs of camping range from ZW$250 to ZW$375 per person, while chalets at Swimuwini cost about US$2. Book at National Parks & Wildlife Zimbabwe in Harare or Bulawayo (see those sections for details).

The most accessible camp site in the Save–Runde subregion is the idyllic **Chipinda Pools**, 63km from Chiredzi along a badly corrugated but easily passable gravel road. The camp site overlooks vegetation-lined pools teeming with hippos. Further upstream is **Chinguli Camp**. Both Chipinda and Chinguli have showers and flush toilets, and in the dry season both are accessible without a 4WD.

In the Mwenezi subregion, the nicest camp is **Swimuwini Camp** (Place of Baobabs), which overlooks Buffalo Bend in the Mwenezi River. It's accessible in a 2WD and offers camping and chalets. It's also a haunt of elephants and lions, and the small pond frequently attracts thirsty nyalas. The more basic **Mbalauta Camp** has only five camp sites. Two wildlife-viewing hides – **Rossi Pools** and **Manyanda Pan** – serve as 'exclusive camps'.

Makwekwete Lodge (☎ *031-2865, fax 4178; lodges US$40)* offers self-contained stone and thatched lodges amid the granite *kopjes* of the Chiredzi River area. It can also arrange hiking, horse riding and wildlife drives, but only accommodates one group at a time, so ring in advance.

Getting There & Away

There is no public transport anywhere to, near or around the park, so you'll need a car – and a 4WD in the wet season.

Bulawayo

☎ 09 • pop 1 million

Zimbabwe's intriguing second city was originally called *Gu-Bulawayo* (Killing Place), which probably came about because of the executions undertaken on the Thabas Indunas (Hill of Chiefs) under Mzilikazi. These days, Bulawayo styles itself as the 'City of the Kings', a prosperous and historic metropolis with plenty of attractions and great places to stay and eat. Bulawayo is also a base for trips to nearby attractions, such as the Khami Ruins and Matobo National Park (see Around Bulawayo later). It's also an ideal staging point for trips to Hwange National Park, on the way to Victoria Falls.

Information

Tourist Offices The **Bulawayo & District Publicity Association** *(☎ 60867, fax 60868; e bulawayo@telconet.co.zw; Robert Mugabe Way; open 8.30am-4.45pm Mon-Fri, 8.30am-noon Sat)* is at the City Hall car park. It is probably the best tourist office in Zimbabwe, and also distributes accommodation lists and the free monthly *Bulawayo This Month* magazine. The noticeboard is a mine of local information.

The **Zimbabwe Tourism Authority** *(☎ 74055, 72338; e zta@byo.ztazim.co.zw; 74 George Silundika St)* is responsible for the rest of the country.

National Parks Office The **NP Bulawayo Office** *(☎ 63646, ☎/fax 65592; cnr Herbert Chitepo St & Tenth Ave; open 8am-4pm Mon-Fri)* doesn't inspire much confidence. The office is not computerised, so staff have to check manually with the head office anyway so you may as well deal with the office in Harare directly. The Bulawayo office does, however, accept direct accommodation bookings for Matobo National Park.

Wildlife & Environment Zimbabwe *(☎ 77309; 105 Fife St)*, just down from Haefel's Bakery, sells maps of Tshabalala Game Sanctuary and Matobo National Park, as well as a few souvenirs.

Immigration Office The **Department of Immigration Control** *(☎ 65621; cnr Herbert Chitepo St & Eleventh Ave; open 7.45am-1pm & 2pm-4.45pm Mon-Fri)* is where to go for a visa extension.

Money The city centre is crammed with banks, including the head offices of **Barclays Bank** *(cnr Leopold Takawira Ave & Fife St)* and **Standard Chartered Bank** *(cnr Eighth Ave & Fife St)*.

The numerous bureaux de change offer some of the best unofficial rates in the country. Try **CFX Bureau de Change** *(97 Robert Mugabe Way)* or **FXM Bureau de Change** *(Jairos Jiri Crafts, cnr Robert Mugabe Way & Leopold Takawira Ave)*. Several others are in the **Bulawayo Centre** *(cnr Main St & Ninth Ave)*.

Post & Communications The **main post office** *(cnr Eighth Ave & Main St)* has an efficient poste restante and fax service. Telephones booths are inside and around the post office.

For a large, prosperous city, there are surprisingly few places to surf the Net, which is why all Internet centres are crowded (so start early). The best places to go are **AfriNet Surfing** *(Bulawayo Centre, cnr Main St & Ninth Ave)* and **Digital CyberCom** *(mezzanine level, Parkade Centre, cnr Fife St & Ninth Ave)*.

Bookshops The ever-reliable **Kingston's** bookshop *(91 Jason Moyo St)* sells maps, novels and international magazines.

Camping Equipment **Eezee Kamping** *(☎ 62105; 95 George Silundika St)* is probably the best outdoors shop in Zimbabwe – which isn't saying much – but it only sells (not rents) camping equipment.

Emergency The best-equipped and most accessible public hospital is the **Bulawayo Central Hospital** *(☎ 72111; off St Lukes Ave)*, near the Ascot Racecourse. The privately-run **Galen House Emergency Medical Clinic** *(☎ 540051; cnr Josiah Tongogara St & Ninth Ave)* is better. For ambulance services, contact the **Medical Air Rescue Service** *(MARS; ☎ 60351; 42 Robert Mugabe Way)*. For other emergencies, contact the main **police** station *(☎ 72516; cnr Leopold Takawira Ave & Fife St)* or the smaller office in Central Park.

ZIMBABWE

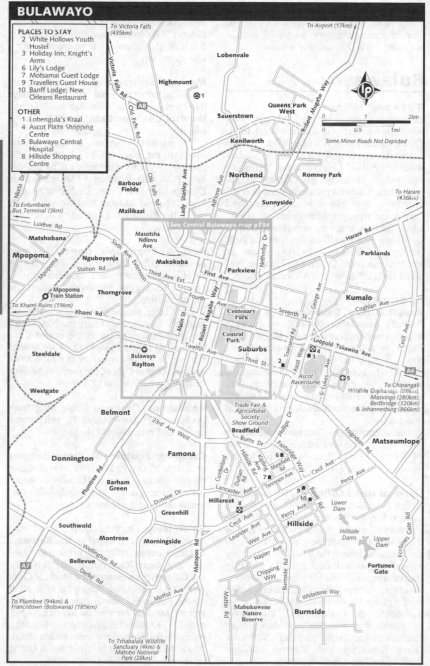

BULAWAYO

PLACES TO STAY
2 White Hollows Youth Hostel
3 Holiday Inn; Knight's Arms
6 Lily's Lodge
7 Motsamai Guest Lodge
9 Travellers Guest House
10 Banff Lodge; New Orleans Restaurant

OTHER
1 Lobengula's Kraal
4 Ascot Plaza Shopping Centre
5 Bulawayo Central Hospital
8 Hillside Shopping Centre

ZIMBABWE

Dangers & Annoyances Bulawayo is more laid-back than Harare, but women should avoid remote corners of Centenary and Central Parks. And *no-one* should walk alone along Caravan Way, between the centre and the Municipal Caravan Park & Camp Site after dark. (Some locals call this pathway the most dangerous spot in Zimbabwe.)

Things to See

The **Natural History Museum** *(off Park Rd; admission US$1.50; open 9am-5pm daily)* is the large circular building in Centenary Park. This is one of the best museums (and apparently the largest) in Southern Africa, and merits at least half a day's exploration. Nearly every type of wildlife indigenous to Zimbabwe and Southern Africa is represented – birds, antelopes, predators, fish, reptiles and even (they claim) the world's second-largest stuffed elephant. One room is also dedicated entirely to bugs. Historical displays deal with both African and European cultures, arts and artefacts, and an artificial mine explains extraction methods and contains rock and mineral specimens.

The **National Railways of Zimbabwe Museum** *(☎ 322452; Prospect Ave; admission ZW$50; open 9am-5pm Tues-Fri, 12pm-5pm Sat & Sun)* is obviously a labour of love for the ebullient manager. The extensive museum houses a collection of historic steam locomotives, old railway offices and buildings, and passenger carriages, most of which are over 100 years old. Don't miss Cecil Rhodes' opulent private carriage, which dates from the 1890s. (The museum's opening times are a little unreliable, so it's worth ringing ahead.)

The imposing **Douslin House** *(cnr Main St & Leopold Takawira Ave)* is one of Bulawayo's finest colonial buildings. Completed in 1900, it was originally known as the Willoughby building, after the mining and ranching firm that occupied it. In 1956 the building was taken over by African Associated Mines and given the riveting name of Asbestos House. It now houses **The National Gallery in Bulawayo** *(admission ZW$20; open 9am-5pm Tues-Sun)*, which exhibits a range of Zimbabwean and African art and sculpture.

The **Mzilikazi Arts & Crafts Centre** *(Taylor St; admission free; open 8.30am-12.30pm & 2pm-4pm Mon-Fri)* was established in 1963 to provide art training. This highlight of Bulawayo features various exhibits of art, pottery and sculpture, and seems more like a museum than a school. Free tours are conducted, but not during school holidays. Take the Mpilo or Barbour Fields (marked 'BF') bus from the Lobengula St Bus Terminal and get off at either the Bulawayo Home Industries Centre or Mzilikazi Primary School.

Organised Tours

A few companies offer tours that incorporate the major sites around Bulawayo, such as Matobo National Park. However, it's probably cheaper to rent a car (see Getting Around later) and explore the area yourself.

Adventure Travel (Tours for Africa, ☎/fax 66775, W www.toursforafrica.com) cnr Ninth Ave and George Silundika St, is a South-African based company with a full range of tours, eg, half-/full-day tours of Matobo (US$45/50) and half-day trips to Khami Ruins (US$35) and Chipangali Wildlife Orphanage (US$35). It also acts as an agency for adventure activities in Victoria Falls.

Adventure Trails offers local mountain bike tours for one day (US$60) or one/two nights (US$110/150), including bike rental, vehicle transport from Bulawayo, accommodation and meals. Make arrangements through the tourist office.

Circle Court Tours & Safaris (☎ 881309, fax 75230, W www.circtours.co.zw) cnr Main St and Ninth Ave, has been recommended by several readers. It offers full-day tours of Matobo by 4WD (US$50) and half-day trips to Khami (US$25) and Chipangali (US$25).

Madlala Tours (☎ 69060, e madlala@telconet .co.zw) 72 Josiah Tongogara St, is more down-market and affordable, but still reliable. It operates tours of lesser-known wildlife reserves and half-day trips around Tshabalala Game Sanctuary (US$25).

Touch the Wild (☎ 540944, fax 229088) cnr George Silundika St and Third Ave, is a safari company that runs various upmarket lodges in Hwange National Park, as well as trips to Matobo.

United Touring Company (UTC, ☎ 61402, fax 63383, e tours@utcbyo.co.zw) cnr Fourteenth Ave and George Silundika St, runs half-day city tours (US$25). Further out, it offers half-day excursions to Khami (US$25) and Chipangali (US$23), and half-/full-day tours of Matobo (US$45/55).

Special Events

The **Zimbabwe International Trade Fair** (one week in April or early May) gives Bulawayo an excuse to party, though the fair itself is of little interest to normal tourists. The **Inxusa**

CENTRAL BULAWAYO

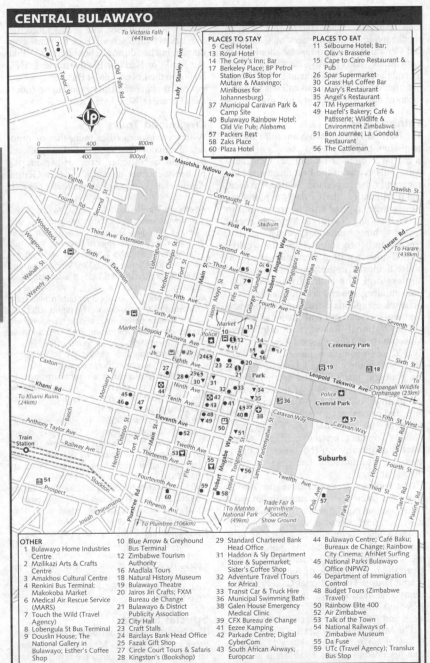

PLACES TO STAY
- 5 Cecil Hotel
- 13 Royal Hotel
- 14 The Grey's Inn; Bar
- 17 Berkeley Place; BP Petrol Station (Bus Stop for Mutare & Masvingo; Minibuses for Johannesburg)
- 37 Municipal Caravan Park & Camp Site
- 40 Bulawayo Rainbow Hotel; Old Vic Pub; Alabama
- 57 Packers Rest
- 58 Zaks Place
- 60 Plaza Hotel

PLACES TO EAT
- 11 Selbourne Hotel; Bar; Olav's Brasserie
- 15 Cape to Cairo Restaurant & Pub
- 26 Spar Supermarket
- 30 Grass Hut Coffee Bar
- 34 Mary's Restaurant
- 35 Angel's Restaurant
- 47 TM Hypermarket
- 49 Haefel's Bakery; Café & Patisserie; Wildlife & Environment Zimbabwe
- 51 Bon Journée; La Gondola Restaurant
- 56 The Cattleman

OTHER
- 1 Bulawayo Home Industries Centre
- 2 Mzilikazi Arts & Crafts Centre
- 3 Amakhosi Cultural Centre
- 4 Renkini Bus Terminal; Makokoba Market
- 5 Medical Air Rescue Service (MARS)
- 7 Touch the Wild (Travel Agency)
- 8 Lobengula St Bus Terminal
- 9 Douslin House; The National Gallery in Bulawayo; Esther's Coffee Shop
- 10 Blue Arrow & Greyhound Bus Terminal
- 12 Zimbabwe Tourism Authority
- 16 Madlala Tours
- 18 Natural History Museum
- 19 Bulawayo Theatre
- 20 Jairos Jiri Crafts; FXM Bureau de Change
- 21 Bulawayo & District Publicity Association
- 22 City Hall
- 23 Craft Stalls
- 24 Barclays Bank Head Office
- 25 Circle Court Tours & Safaris
- 27 Circle Court Tours & Safaris
- 28 Kingston's (Bookshop)
- 29 Standard Chartered Bank Head Office
- 31 Haddon & Sly Department Store & Supermarket; Sister's Coffee Shop
- 32 Adventure Travel (Tours for Africa)
- 33 Transit Car & Truck Hire
- 36 Municipal Swimming Bath
- 38 Galen House Emergency Medical Clinic
- 39 CFX Bureau de Change
- 41 Eezee Kamping
- 42 Parkade Centre; Digital CyberCom
- 43 South African Airways; Europcar
- 44 Bulawayo Centre; Café Baku; Bureaux de Change; Rainbow City Cinema; AfriNet Surfing
- 45 National Parks Bulawayo Office (NPWZ)
- 46 Department of Immigration Control
- 48 Budget Tours (Zimbabwe Travel)
- 50 Rainbow Elite 400
- 52 Air Zimbabwe
- 53 Talk of the Town
- 54 National Railways of Zimbabwe Museum
- 55 Da Fuse
- 59 UTc (Travel Agency); Translux Bus Stop

ZIMBABWE

Festival (June or July) is organised to revive old Lobengula traditions, and features music, dance, drama and theatre. The e'Nkundleni festival (one week at the end of November or early December) features traditional dances held at various venues in the city.

Places to Stay

All the budget and mid-range hotels, lodges and camp sites listed here allow foreigners to pay the local rate in Zimbabwe dollars. These places are listed according to standards and amenities, rather than prices.

Places to Stay – Budget

Municipal Caravan Park & Camp Site (☎ 63851; Caravan Way; camping per person ZW$200, single/double lodges with shared bathroom from US$1.50/3) is just a 10-minute walk from the city centre. It's the best place for anyone with a tent: the camp site is clean, shady, quiet and well-guarded, and the showers are hot. The lodges contain a mosquito net (in lieu of a fan), but are nothing special. Don't even *think* about walking to and from the camp site at night.

White Hollows Youth Hostel (☎ 256488; 52 Townsend Rd; separate-sex dorm beds US$0.50, singles/doubles with shared bathroom US$1/1.50) is the place to go if you're *really* on a tight budget – otherwise, pay a few extra Zimbabwe dollars and stay somewhere better. This big old house in the suburbs (easily accessible by minibus) contains a TV lounge, large dining room and kitchen for guests, and plenty of hot water.

Berkeley Place (☎/fax 67701; 71 Josiah Tongogara St; singles/doubles with shared toilet & breakfast US$3.50/7) is friendly, secure and central, and one of the best budget places in Zimbabwe. There's no bar or pool, but the quiet courtyard is convivial and the craft shop has an excellent range. Some rooms have a shower, but none of them have a toilet.

Packers Rest (☎ 71111; e packers@acacia .samara.co.zw; 1 Oak Ave; camping per person US$3, dorm beds US$4, singles/doubles with shared bathroom US$8/12) is a short walk from the city centre. The rooms are clean, but have thin walls, and the staff are helpful. It organises tours, offers free Internet access (for guests), provides a communal kitchen, and arranges bicycle hire.

Plaza Hotel (☎ 64280; Fourteenth Ave; doubles with breakfast & with/without bath-

room US$8/7) is a little inconvenient, but has a secure car park. The rooms are comfortable, if a little noisy, and contain a TV and fan.

Cecil Hotel (☎ 888539; cnr Third Ave & Fife St; doubles with/without bathroom US$5/4) is notable for the massive carvings lounging around the foyer and the confusing 'Hotel Mirage' sign above the door. The hotel is a bit musty, but good value and features a pleasant courtyard garden. Breakfast is US$1 per person.

The Grey's Inn (☎ 888318; 73 Robert Mugabe Way; singles/doubles with bathroom & breakfast US$9/11) is clean, comfortable and convenient. The rooms contain a TV and fan, and most are quiet. Other attractions are the swimming pool and popular pub.

Royal Hotel (☎ 65764, fax 79304; cnr Sixth Ave & George Silundika St; singles/doubles with bathroom & breakfast US$9/10) is similar to Grey's and Cecil's. It's in an ugly and, at times noisy, concrete block, but the rooms are large and feature a TV and balcony.

Places to Stay – Mid-Range

Lily's Lodge (☎ 245356; e nyararai@excite .com; 3 Masefield Rd; dorm beds US$5, singles/ doubles with shared bathroom & breakfast US$10/20) boasts a more 'African feel', with traditional meals and decor and the chance of some informal reggae jams. The rooms are large, though unexceptional, and the home contains a communal kitchen, dining room and TV lounge. It's poorly signed.

Banff Lodge (☎ 423176; e banff@acacia .samara.co.zw; Banff Rd; singles/doubles/suites with bathroom & breakfast US$8/9/10) is an elegant home in a quiet residential suburb. For as long as the management happily charges foreigners the local rates, this is one of *the* bargains in Zimbabwe – so book ahead. The suite is sensational, and the gardens and pool are inviting. The attached **New Orleans Restaurant** is classy and another reason to stay there.

Travellers Guest House (☎/fax 46059; 2 Banff Rd; doubles/suites with bathroom & breakfast US$25/30) is a blend of a B&B, guesthouse and backpackers hostel in and around a lovely home. It's popular, though the outside rooms are a bit cramped and it's comparatively overpriced. There is a communal kitchen, TV room, lounge and pool. Phone ahead for a pick-up from the city centre.

ZIMBABWE

Zaks Place (☎ 881129; e zaksplace@telconet.co.zw; 129 Robert Mugabe Way; doubles with breakfast US$20) is a friendly, four-storey place overlooking a courtyard. The decor in the rooms is as impressive as anything in the top-end range, and the rooms contain a satellite TV, walk-in cupboard, bathtub and fan.

Places to Stay – Top End

Motsamai Guest Lodge (☎/fax 246201; 17 Tennyson Ave; singles/doubles with shared bathroom & breakfast about US$30/50) is the nicest of the numerous lodges in the suburbs. It features immaculate lawns, an inviting pool, and elegant rooms with a fan. The bathrooms are glorious – but communal.

Bulawayo Rainbow Hotel (☎ 881273; e byorainb@internet.co.zw; cnr Tenth Ave & Josiah Tongogara St; singles/doubles US$90/114) is central and offers comfortable rooms with all the amenities expected at this price.

Holiday Inn (☎ 252460; e byoholinn@zimsun.co.zw; Milnerton Dr, off Ascot Way; doubles US$123) is next to the upmarket Ascot Plaza Shopping Centre. Extra amenities include a sauna and gymnasium, as well as billiard tables and several classy restaurants.

Places to Eat

Bulawayo boasts a veritable smorgasbord of eateries.

Restaurants Specialising in pizzas and pasta, La Gondola Restaurant (☎ 62986; 105 Robert Mugabe Way; meals about US$2; open Mon-Sat) also offers non-Italian 'pub specials' (US$1) every day. The menu is a little more exciting than the average Italian joint, and the service is hard to fault.

Cape to Cairo Restaurant & Pub (☎ 72387; 77 Robert Mugabe Way; starters/salads US$0.50, most meals US$2.50; open lunch Mon-Fri, dinner Mon-Sat) is almost a prerequisite for all visitors to Bulawayo. This tasteful, colonial-theme restaurant/bar specialises in game dishes, but the pub menu at lunchtime offers homesick Brits choices such as bangers and mash (US$1.50).

The Cattleman (☎ 76086; 117a Josiah Tongogara St; meals US$3) is a local favourite and better than The Cattleman outlets elsewhere in Zimbabwe. Lots of restaurants have kudu heads on the wall, but here, a reproachful bovine looks over people being served tender steaks by cowboys.

Olav's Brasserie (☎ 65741; Leopold Takawira Ave; starters US$1, mains US$2-3) is on the ground floor of the Selbourne Hotel. It serves mainly continental dishes, but Olav can also rustle up the occasional Chinese and Greek dish. The servings are large, and the prices are not as high as the decor and over-attentive waiters would suggest.

Mary's Restaurant (☎ 76721; 88 Josiah Tongogara St; mains US$1-2; open 9am-5pm Mon-Sat) offers pizzas and Chinese food, but most other dishes tend to have a Greek influence (which makes a nice change). It's very popular, so you'll find it almost impossible to get a table between 12.30pm and 2pm.

Angel's Restaurant (☎ 67068; cnr Ninth Ave & Josiah Tongogara St; mains US$1-2; open 8am-8pm Mon-Fri, 8am-1pm Sat) is a cosy place with a welcome array of tasty meals and daily specials (US$1).

It seems that there's a **fast-food** outlet on every street corner in the city centre, and several more in each shopping centre in the suburbs.

Cafés One of the few places in the city centre open on Sunday, Bon Journee (☎ 64839; 105 Robert Mugabe Way; meals US$1.50-2; open 8.30am-9pm Wed-Mon) is arguably the most authentic continental café in Zimbabwe – complete with checked tablecloths and noisy cappuccino machines. It's not cheap, but certainly worth trying for the Portuguese wine, delicious coffee, and range of European dishes (including breakfast).

Café Baku (Bulawayo Centre, cnr Main St & Ninth Ave; meals from US$1.50; open late Mon-Sat) heralded the arrival of the trendy café scene in Bulawayo. This air-conditioned eatery, complete with artworks on the wall, serves up so-so pasta, tasty baguettes and a medley of drinks. There's live music on the weekends.

Haefel's Bakery, Café & Patisserie (103 Fife St; open daily) offers healthy salad rolls, and not-so-healthy (but yummy) tarts and Danish pastries, as well as acceptable coffee. You can sit inside or at tables along a short, cobblestone section of the street.

Grass Hut Coffee Bar (☎ 63180; 88 Fife St; meals about US$1.50; open Mon-Sat) is an aptly-named eatery that will remind you that you are in Africa – that is, until the menu arrives with the usual selection of English-style dishes laden with chips (French fries).

Chip-less choices include sandwiches and omelettes.

Sister's Coffee Shop (☎ 60656; ground floor, Haddon & Sly Department Store, cnr Eighth Ave & Fife St; meals about US$1.50; open Mon-Sat) calls itself a 'wine bistro', so it's trendy (complete with uncomfortable chairs). The menu includes tempting treats such as jacket potatoes, salads and pastas, and the all-day breakfast could fill you up until dinner time.

Esther's Coffee Shop (☎ 816255; National Gallery, cnr Main St & Leopold Takawira Ave; meals about US$1; open 9am-5pm Tues-Sun) is at the back of the art gallery, overlooking a small garden. It's popular with well-heeled city workers and offers pastas, sandwiches and salads (including a pretty good attempt at a Waldorf salad).

Self-Catering For cheap fruit and vegetables, visit **Makokoba Market** (Walsall St), beyond the Renkini Bus Terminal. More convenient is the **Spar** supermarket (Herbert Chitepo St) and the truly massive **TM Hypermarket** (Eleventh Ave). If you have refined tastes (and deeper pockets), visit the supermarket on the ground floor of the **Haddon & Sly Department Store** (cnr Eight Ave & Fife St).

Entertainment

Bars & Clubs Almost all of the hotels listed under Places to Stay earlier have decent bars, and extensive research (!) reveals that some of the better hotel bars are attached to **The Grey's Inn** and the **Selbourne Hotel**. For a more Anglo–Zimbabwean atmosphere, try the **Old Vic Pub** (Bulawayo Rainbow Hotel) or the **Knight's Arms** (Holiday Inn).

Da Fuse (Robert Mugabe Way) usually thumps to the latest house and techno tunes, but may quieten down some evenings for some live rhythm and blues. **Alabama** (Bulawayo Rainbow Hotel; cnr Tenth Ave & Josiah Tongogara St) is a pleasant, but normally crowded, bar with live and diverse jazz styles. **Talk of the Town** (cnr Fife St & Twelfth Ave) offers something wild and wonderful on Saturday night, but is a little sleazy these days. Other haunts are advertised in the daily Chronicle.

Cinemas The multi-screen **Rainbow City Cinema** complex (Bulawayo Centre, cnr Main

St & Ninth Ave) is always popular, so line up early for tickets on weekends. **Rainbow Elite 400** (Robert Mugabe Way) offers less inviting flicks.

Theatre & Dance The **Bulawayo Theatre** (☎ 65393; Centenary Park, Leopold Takawira Ave) features dramatic productions, and occasionally hosts visiting troupes.

Amakhosi Cultural Centre (☎/fax 62652; Masotsha Ndlovu Ave) is a fabulous venue that organises the annual Inxusa Festival (see Special Events earlier) and cultural shows every Friday evening. More details are available from the cultural centre and tourist office.

Shopping

The footpath along Fife St near the City Hall is lined with **craft stalls**. The persistent vendors are annoying, however, so it's more relaxing to browse at any of the large retail shops in the city centre. All offer competitive prices, so Bulawayo is a great place to stock up on souvenirs.

Across the lawn from the Mzilikazi Arts & Crafts Centre (see Things to See earlier) is the **Bulawayo Home Industries Centre** (Taylor St; admission free; open 8.30am-12.30pm & 2pm-4pm Mon-Fri), where artisans weave rugs and produce other crafts. The country-wide **Jairos Jiri Crafts** (cnr Robert Mugabe Way & Leopold Takawira Ave) is also worth a visit. Profits from both outlets help the disadvantaged.

Fazak Gift Shop (79 Main St) is a massive place, where almost every item is engraved with the word 'Zimbabwe' or shaped like one of the Big Five.

Getting There & Away

Air To Harare **Air Zimbabwe** (☎ 72051, fax 6977; Treger House, Jason Moyo St) flies twice a day for US$142 one way (possibly US$53 on weekends). Air Zimbabwe and **South African Airways** (☎ 71338; Africa House, cnr Fife St & Tenth Ave) flies to Jo'burg twice a week.

Bus & Minibus

Domestic Most long-distance buses and minibuses use the manageable **Renkini Bus Terminal** (Sixth Ave Extension). From there, local 'African' buses and better express buses regularly travel to most places in Zimbabwe, including Harare (US$4, six hours) and

Mutare (US$3, four hours) about every hour or so. For Mutare and Masvingo (US$2, three hours), however, it's easier (though seats are not guaranteed) to catch a bus at the BP petrol station at the corner of Josiah Tongogara St and Leopold Takawira Ave (just around the corner from the Berkeley Place hotel).

The **Entumbane Bus Terminal** (*Luveve Rd*) is 6km northwest of the city centre. From there, buses and minibuses leave about 10 times a day for Victoria Falls (US$3, seven hours) between 5am and 7am and 1pm and 5pm (more on Friday), and minibuses depart for Hwange town and Binga. Entumbane is accessible on the Luveve minibus from in front of City Hall.

Blue Arrow (☎ *65548; 73a Fife St*) offers luxury coaches every day to Harare (US$10, six hours), via Gweru (US$4, two hours); and to Harare, via Kwe Kwe (US$5, three hours). Buses depart and arrive from outside its office.

Coaches run by Africa Link travel three times a week to Victoria Falls (US$17, five hours), via Hwange town and the Hwange Safari Lodge. They stop at the Holiday Inn in Bulawayo, but book at Zimbabwe Travel (see following).

For more information about travelling to places near Bulawayo, eg, Matobo National Park and the Khami Ruins, refer to the Around Bulawayo section later.

International Translux buses to Jo'burg (US$10) leave daily from the **UTc** office (☎ *61402, fax 63383;* e *tours@utcbyo.co.zw; cnr Fourteenth Ave & George Silundika St).* **Zimbabwe Travel** (☎ *76208;* w *www.gozim babwe.co.za; Budget Tours, cnr Tenth Ave & Fife St)* sells tickets for Africa Link buses to and from Jo'burg (US$52) on Wednesday and Sunday, which connect with the train to and from Victoria Falls. **Greyhound** (*Blue Arrow office, 73a Fife St)* also operates buses to Jo'burg (US$25) most days.

Quicker minibuses (US$17) to Jo'burg depart from outside the BP petrol station at the junction of Josiah Tongogara St and Leopold Takawira Ave (just around the corner from the Berkeley Place hotel).

To Botswana, you have three choices: a regular minibus to the border at Plumtree, from where other minibuses head to Francistown (the best option); a daily bus (at 8am, 11am or 3pm) to Francistown; or

a daily bus (at 1pm and, sometimes, 8am) to Gaborone (US$5). All leave from the Renkini Bus Terminal.

Train The *Manyame Express* to Harare (US$4/2/2 for sleeper/standard/economy class, nine hours) departs at 8pm every day and travels via Kwe Kwe and Gweru. The *Mosi-oa-Tunya* train to Victoria Falls (US$4/3/1 for 1st/2nd/economy class, 12 hours) departs daily at 7pm. Another train departs daily at 9.30pm for Chiredzi, but is of little interest to travellers.

Reservations are available in advance at the **ticket office** (☎ *322210; open 7am-9pm Mon-Fri, 7am-2pm Sat & Sun)* inside the **train station** (*Railway Ave).*

Getting Around

Check to see if **UTc** (☎ *61402; cnr Fourteenth Ave & George Silundika St)* or **Air Zimbabwe** (☎ *72051; Treger House, Jason Moyo St)* are offering minibuses (US$5 per person) to the airport. If not, a taxi between the airport and city centre shouldn't cost much more than US$5 anyway.

Bulawayo is one town in Southern Africa where using taxis is a joy: almost all drivers use meters, and fares are incredibly cheap, eg, from City Hall to the Renkini Bus Terminal costs about ZW$200. And cheap taxis obviate the need to use local minibuses.

Car & Motorcycle The **Transit Car & Truck Hire** (☎ *76495, fax 76394;* e *transit@acacia.sa mara.co.zw; 86 Robert Mugabe Way)* offers the cheapest car rental in Bulawayo. **Europcar** (☎ *74157;* e *fungayikatso@europcar.co.zw; Fife St),* just down from the South African Airways office, is the only major international car rental company to allow foreigners to pay the local rates in Zimbabwe dollars. See Car & Motorcycle in the Getting Around section earlier in this chapter for details about the costs and conditions of car rental.

Bicycle Mountain bikes can be rented from **Packers Rest** (☎ *71111; 1 Oak Ave)* for US$1/2 for a half/full day.

AROUND BULAWAYO
Tshabalala Game Sanctuary
This small sanctuary (*admission US$5; open daily 6am-6pm May to Oct, 8am-5pm*

Nov-April) is 9km south of central Bulawayo. It was established on land formerly owned by Fairburn Usher, a British sailor who arrived in 1883, and his Ndebele wife, one of Lobengula's daughters. The small **interpretative centre** at the main gate explains a bit more about the history and fauna.

Because Tshabalala doesn't contain any dangerous animals, **hiking** is allowed and **horse riding** (ZW$200/90 min) can be arranged at the main gate. Maps are available from **Wildlife & Environment Zimbabwe** (☎ 77309; 105 Fife St), or the tourist office, in Bulawayo. No private bicycles, or motorbikes, are allowed inside the park.

Adventure Trails (contact through the tourist office in Bulawayo) offers half-day mountain bike tours (US$25 per person) of the sanctuary, including transport to and from Bulawayo.

Buses to Kezi from the Renkini Bus Terminal in Bulawayo regularly pass the main gate. Hitching from Bulawayo isn't too difficult from the southern outskirts of Bulawayo.

Chipangali Wildlife Orphanage
☎ 09

Chipangali (☎ 72179; admission US$15; open 10am-5pm Tues-Sun), 23km east of central Bulawayo, was founded in 1973 to care for injured, sick, orphaned and illegally captured animals. The idea is to release them into the wild when they're able to cope, but some are inevitably destined for a life of captivity. The large walk-through aviaries house both large raptors and smaller birds. Staff feed the animals at 3.30pm most days (but check first).

If you can't bear to leave the cute little critters, the orphanage offers **accommodation** (☎ 287740; e chipanga@internet.co.zw; camping per person US$3, bungalows per person US$6, cabins per person US$10, all with shared bathroom). It's pretty basic, but the location is hard to beat. Guests can use the communal cooking facilities.

Chipangali lies 200m from the road to Beitbridge. Take the bus to Esigodini from the Renkini Bus Terminal. Hitching is best anywhere beyond the Ascot Plaza Shopping Centre.

Khami (Kame) Ruins
This Unesco World Heritage Site (admission US$1.50; open 8am-4.30pm daily), 22km west

of central Bulawayo, was built by the Torwa dynasty in the 16th century. But in the late 17th century, Torwa was apparently absorbed by the larger Rozwi state, which destroyed Khami.

At the northern end of the ruins, the **Hill Complex** served as the royal enclosure. The complex features several hut platforms and Khami's greatest concentration of stone walling. Also at the northern end is an odd platform with a stone Dominican cross, reputedly placed there by an early Portuguese missionary.

The scattered ruins of southern Khami contain several interesting sites. The **Vlei Platforms**, near the **museum**, are believed to have served as cattle *kraals*. Near the dam wall, a *mujejeje* (rock) rings like a bell when struck. The beautifully decorated 6m-high and 68m-long retaining wall of the **Precipice Platform** bears a chequerboard design along its entire length. For more information, pick up *A Trail Guide to the Khami National Monument*, available at the museum.

No buses ply the lonely (and flat) road to Khami, so some travellers hire bicycles in Bulawayo. Head out along Eleventh Ave beyond Lobengula St and follow the signposted route along Khami Rd. A taxi should cost around US$10 one way. Alternatively, hire a car or join an organised tour – see the Bulawayo section for details.

Matobo (Matopos) National Park
Matobo (☎ 083-8258; admission US$15; open 6am-6pm daily), 33km south of Bulawayo, is the oldest national park in the country. Dotted around the 425-sq-km park are 3000 officially registered **rock-art sites**, including one of the best collections in the world of San paintings (many over 20,000 years old). Some hidden niches still shelter clay ovens, which were used as iron smelters in making the infamous *assegais* (spears) used against the colonial hordes. Some peaks, such as Shumba Shaba and Imadzi (Bald One), are now considered sacred, and locals believe that even to point at them will bring misfortune.

With the history comes a superb array of **wildlife**, including leopards. The **birdlife** is also extensive. You may have the chance to see African hawk eagles or rare Cape eagle owls; in fact, Matobo is home to one-third of the world's species of eagles, including the greatest concentration of black eagles.

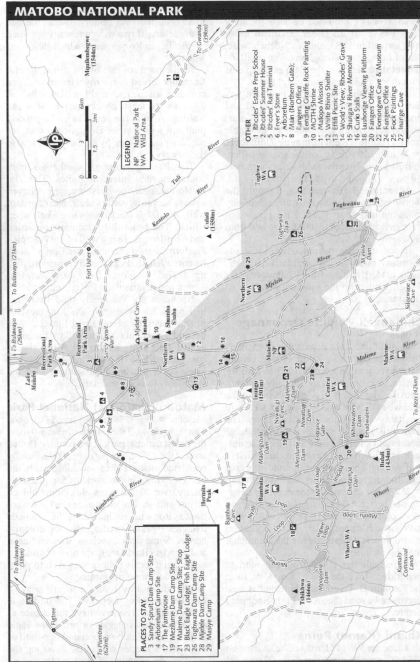

MATOBO NATIONAL PARK

ZIMBABWE

LEGEND
NP   National Park
WA   Wild Area

OTHER
1   Rhodes' Estate Prep School
2   Rhodes' Summer House
5   Rhodes' Rail Terminal
6   Fryer's Store
7   Arboretum
8   Main (Northern Gate);
    Rangers Office
9   Eending Giraffe Rock Painting
10 MCTH Shrine
11 Matopo Mission
12 White Rhino Shelter
13 Efifii Picnic Site
14 World's View; Rhodes' Grave
15 Shangani River Memorial
16 Curio Stalls
18 Lushonge Viewing Platform
20 Rangers Office
22 Fomongwe Cave & Museum
24 Rangers Office
25 Rock Paintings
27 Inarge Cave

PLACES TO STAY
3   Sandy Spruit Dam Camp Site
4   Arboretum Camp Site
17 The Farmhouse
19 Mezilume Dam Camp Site
21 Maleme Dam Camp Site; Shop
23 Black Eagle Lodge; Fish Eagle Lodge
26 Toghwana Dam Camp Site
28 Mjelele Dam Camp Site
29 Masiye Camp

Information Maps of the park are available from the main (northern) gate; or from **Wildlife & Environment Zimbabwe** (☎ 09-77309; *105 Fife St)*, or the tourist office, in Bulawayo. General admission (US$15) does not include access to any of caves or to World's View. These sites are all covered under one separate ticket (US$1 per day), available at Pomongwe Cave & Museum or World's View.

Things to See The busiest part of Matobo is **Maleme Dam**, with its camp site, general store, horse stables, rangers offices and picnic sites. The area west and northwest of Maleme Dam is home to antelopes, baboons, hyraxes and zebras.

An easy and scenic 7km walk northwest of Maleme Dam, and 200m up a steep track, will bring you to **Nswatugi Cave** and its well-preserved array of rock paintings. Note the accuracy in the motion of the galloping giraffes and running zebras, and the perspective giraffe paintings, kudus, hunting party, and eight (apparently sleeping) human figures. Excavations at Nswatugi have revealed human bones over 40,000 years old – possibly the oldest human remains yet uncovered in Zimbabwe.

During the 1920s a blotched attempt to preserve the gallery of ancient artwork from the elements was made at **Pomongwe Cave**, where an information board explains what was once depicted. The attached **museum** *(admission free; open 8am-5pm daily)* houses great piles of tools and pottery uncovered in several levels of archaeological deposits. The most recent layers were dated to about 6500 BC, while the lowest of these excavations has yielded artefacts over 35,000 years old.

The **Northern Wild Area** offers glorious views down the Mjelele Valley to the Mjelele Dam. Surprisingly, it's not unusual to see rhinos outside the park, grazing on the dry grasses of the valley floor. The **White Rhino Shelter** lies a short walk from the signposted car park. Rather than polychrome paintings, outline drawings are found here – a rare art form in Zimbabwe. Most prominent are the finely executed outlines of five white rhinos and the head of a black rhino, with human figures behind them, and five well-observed and exquisitely drawn wildebeest. On the basis of this painting, rhinos were successfully reintroduced into Matobo.

Cecil **Rhodes' Grave** is atop the mountain he called **World's View**, which the Ndebele people knew as Malindidzimu (Dwelling Place of Benevolent Spirits). The **Shangani River Memorial**, just downhill from Rhodes' Grave, was erected in 1904 to the memory of Allan Wilson and 33 soldiers of his Shangani River Patrol. (The entire troupe was wiped out by General Mtjaan and his 30,000 Ndebele warriors.) A display at the bottom of the hill outlines highlights of Rhodes' remarkable life and career.

The **Whovi Wild Area**, in the southwest of the park, is home to a full complement of antelopes, zebras and giraffes, as well as a relatively healthy population of white rhinos and more elusive black rhinos. What's more, the scenery, with Matobo's most precarious and imaginative pinnacles and boulder stacks, is as good as the wildlife. But you must stay in your vehicle (unless you're with a guide).

Toghwe Wild Area, in the east of Matobo, is a real wilderness area. It combines parts of the scenic Mjelele and Toghwana Valleys, which contain caves and fine collections of rock paintings. Roads there are rough, with some very steep sections, so ordinary cars with low clearance may have problems. After the rains, low-lying stretches may become impassable without a 4WD.

Atop a dwala dome, **Inange Cave** is a four- to six-hour (14km) return walk from the Toghwana Dam Camp Site. It's worth the effort, because inside the cave are some of Zimbabwe's most complex and well-executed **cave paintings**. Mixed herds of African animals march in confused profusion across the walls, interspersed with hunters and geometric and stylised designs. Most of the trail to Inange is marked by green-painted arrows and small rock cairns, but can become confusing as it passes over a series of nearly identical ridges and valleys.

Activities Guided **horse riding** (pony trails) is offered at the rangers offices near Whitewaters Dam and Maleme Dam, but advance booking is essential. Some rangers *may* charge you the local rate (about US$3), though others may want you to pay the 'foreigners rate' (US$20) for a 1½-hour gallop. **Walking safaris** (US$15 per person per hour) with an armed guard leave from the Maleme Dam Camp Site and from the rangers office at Whitewaters Dam. (Children under 12

ZIMBABWE

years are not permitted on walking safaris.) **Fishing** licences are also available; contact the tourist office in Bulawayo for details.

Places to Stay & Eat Camping costs ZW$125 per person; two/four bed lodges are US$2/3; and two/four bed chalets cost about US$1/2. The exceptions are the Black Eagle and Fish Eagle lodges where lodges (with five beds) cost US$6. Reservations are possible at the National Parks & Wildlife Zimbabwe (NPWZ) office in Bulawayo or Harare.

Most campers wind up at **Maleme Dam Camp Site**, 18km south of the main (northern) gate. During weekends and school holidays, this camp site can get quite crowded. (These are the easiest times to hitch a ride but maybe not be the most pleasant to actually *stay* there.) Maleme Dam offers camping, chalets and lodges, as well as a souvenir and grocery shop.

Near the main (northern) gate is the **Sandy Spruit Dam Camp Site**, which is close to the main road but convenient if you're arriving late. **Toghwana Dam Camp Site** (in the Toghwe Wild Area) and **Mjelele Dam Camp site** (8km south of Toghwana Dam) are both pleasant, but access can be difficult. The other options are the civilised **Arboretum Camp Site** (in the north of the park) and the small **Mezilume Dam Camp Site** (near Nswatugi Cave).

The combined **Black Eagle Lodge** and **Fish Eagle Lodge** both afford boulder-studded hilltop vistas. They're just south of Pomongwe Cave and easy to reach by road from the World's View. Advance bookings for both are essential.

Masiye Camp (☎ 09-60727; e masiyeca@ telconet.co.zw; with half-board per person US$50) is in a traditional village overlooking the Toghwana River. Rates include several activities, and profits are used to fund local community projects. The camp is just outside the southern boundary.

The Farmhouse (☎/fax 083-82506; with breakfast per person US$50) is the cheapest and most homely of the lodges scattered in and outside Matobo. This pleasant and low-key place, just outside the western boundary, offers self-contained cottages and a pool surrounded by bush. Meals are available.

Apart from the hotels and lodges, there are no restaurants in the national park. The only

supplies are at the basic **shop** at the Maleme Dam Camp Site and **Fryer's Store**, outside the western boundary and along the road between Bulawayo and Kezi.

Some drinking water in the park is treated – look for designated drinking taps. If you're unsure, boil or treat water before drinking. And note that all rivers, lakes and dams contain bilharzia so don't swim.

Getting There & Away Visiting Matobo on a budget is difficult without a vehicle; taxis are not permitted in the park and hitching can be slow and difficult. A more adventurous option is to hire a bicycle and ride from Bulawayo (along the fairly flat road) or possibly carry it on the bus; note that cyclists are not permitted in the Whovi Wild Area.

Alternatively, take the Kezi bus from the Renkini bus terminal in Bulawayo and disembark at any of the three turn-offs to the national park. From the first (most northern) turn-off, it's about 3km to the Sandy Spruit Dam Camp site; from the second (at Rhodes' Rail Terminal), the Arboretum Camp Site is 2km away; and from the third, less obvious turn-off near Whitewaters Dam, take the short cut (6km northeast) or the access road (12km) to the Maleme Dam Camp Site.

Better still, rent a car or join an organised tour from Bulawayo (see that section for details). Most travel agencies in Bulawayo can arrange half-/full-day trips to Matobo for about US$40/50 per person.

Western Zimbabwe

With three of the country's major attractions, Victoria Falls, Hwange National Park and Lake Kariba, western Zimbabwe looms large on most travellers' Southern African itineraries. Refer to the special Victoria Falls chapter for information about visiting the falls.

HWANGE
☎ 081

Hwange (sometimes still pronounced Wankie) is a reasonably charming town – well, as charming as a mining town could be. It's a stopover along the road between Bulawayo and Victoria Falls and a gateway (of sorts) to the Hwange National Park. It offers a few places to eat and drink, but nowhere to change money.

Baobab Hotel (☎ 32323; e hbaobab@mweb .co.zw; singles/doubles with bathroom & breakfast US$8/11) is on a hill overlooking the town. The rooms are smallish, but feature air-conditioning and views of the valley. It's also a great place to stop for a drink or meal. The hotel is 5km from Hwange town – look for the signs north up the hill past (west of) the turn-off to the town. The hotel is accessible by minibus or taxi from Hwange town.

The **train station** (☎ 2342) is in the town centre, but the daily services to Bulawayo and Victoria Falls arrive and depart between 10.30pm and 3am. Buses or minibuses between Bulawayo and Victoria Falls stop at Hwange town regularly. Taxis can be chartered in town to Hwange National Park.

HWANGE NATIONAL PARK
Hwange (admission US$15 per day; open about 6am-6pm daily) is the largest (14,651 sq km) and most wildlife-packed park in Zimbabwe. It's also the most accessible in the country, so hiring cars or arranging tours from Bulawayo or Victoria Falls is not difficult or too expensive.

Hwange is home to some 400 species of birds and 107 types of animals, including one of the largest numbers (30,000) of elephants in the world. The best time for wildlife viewing is July to October when animals congregate around the 60 water holes or 'pans' (most of which are artificially filled by noisy, petrol-powered pumps). But when the rains come and the rivers are flowing, successful viewing requires more diligence, because the animals spread across the park seeking a bit of trunk and antler room.

Access is possible in any sturdy vehicle between May and October, but seek advice if driving a 2WD during the wet season. And always consult a ranger (at any of the three camps) about road conditions before heading off too far into the park, regardless of what sort of vehicle you're driving.

Information and maps about the park are available at the rangers offices at the Hwange Main Camp, Sinamatella Camp and Robins Camp. The Tourist Map of Hwange National Park (available at bookshops throughout Zimbabwe) is adequate if you're sticking to the major trails, but get a decent map from the Surveyor General office in Harare (see that section for details) if you're taking a 4WD off the beaten track. Petrol supplies are (nor-

mally) available at Hwange Main Camp, Sinamatella Camp and Hwange Safari Lodge, but fuel sometimes runs out even if there's no countrywide shortage.

Robins Camp is 60km west of Sinamatella, and park regulations stipulate that you must leave Robins by 3pm to reach Sinamatella (and vice versa). Also, Robins is 150km west of Hwange Main Camp, so you must depart Robins by noon (and vice versa). Similarly, Sinamatella is 125km northwest of Hwange Main Camp, so you must leave Sinamatella by 2pm (and vice versa).

Activities
Two-hour **walking safaris** (per person US$30, no children under 12) with armed guards to Sedina Pan can be organised at Hwange Main Camp, and to Mandavu Dam from Sinamatella Camp. These walks must be booked in advance at Hwange Main Camp, Sinamatella Camp or Robins Camp. Two-hour **night drives** (per person US$30, no children under 12) are also available during (and about two days before and after) a full moon. These depart from Hwange Main Camp, where you must book in advance. Most lodges in and around the park offer **wildlife drives** during the day for guests and nonguests.

Organised Tours
A sign of the times is that many travel companies offering tours of Hwange National Park from Dete, Hwange town and lodges near the park have ceased operating. One exception is **United Touring Company** (UTc; ☎ 018-393, fax 367; Hwange Safari Lodge), which offers tours of the park from the lodge or Hwange Main Camp for US$25/50 (half/full day).

Most visitors will have to organise tours from Bulawayo (see that section for details) or Victoria Falls (see the Victoria Falls chapter for a list of tour operators there). One small operator in Victoria Falls that has been recommended by readers is **Reedbuck Adventures** (☎ 011-407119; Parkway), run by a former warden at Robins Camp.

Hwange Main Camp
The main camp (☎ 018-371, fax 378; office open 7am-6pm) is at the major park entrance. It offers most services, including a rangers office, grocery shop (open 7am to 7pm daily), souvenir shop and petrol station. **The Waterbuck's Head** (meals US$2) is

ZIMBABWE

HWANGE NATIONAL PARK

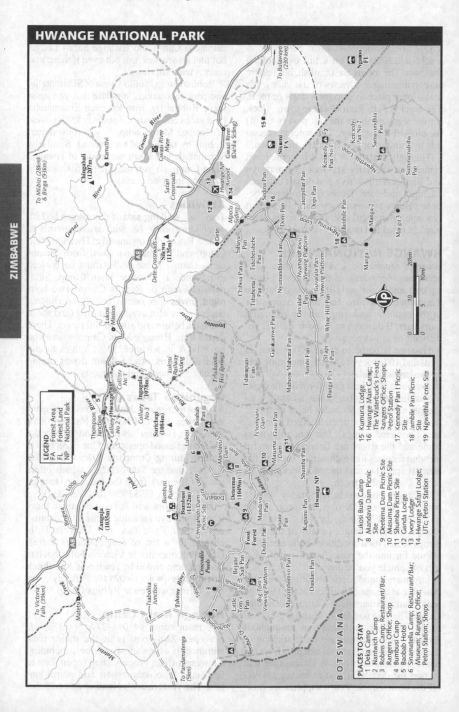

PLACES TO STAY
1 Deka Camp
2 Nantwich Camp
3 Robins Camp; Restaurant/Bar;
   Rangers Office; Shop
4 Bumbusi Camp
5 Baobab Hotel
6 Sinamatella Camp; Restaurant/Bar;
   Museum; Rangers Office;
   Petrol Station; Shops

7 Lukosi Bush Camp
8 Mandavu Dam Picnic
   Site
9 Deeteema Dam Picnic Site
10 Masuma Dam Picnic Site
11 Shumba Picnic Site
12 Ganda Lodge
13 Ivory Lodge
14 Hwange Safari Lodge;
    UTC; Petrol Station

15 Kumura Lodge
16 Hwange Main Camp;
    The Waterbuck's Head;
    Rangers Office; Shops;
    Petrol Station
17 Kennedy Pan I Picnic
    Site
18 Jambile Pan Picnic
    Site
19 Ngwethla Picnic Site

LEGEND
FA Forest Area
FL Forest Land
NP National Park

BOTSWANA

a charming bar/restaurant right outside the main gate and rangers office.

Most visitors make a few convenient loops starting near the Main Camp. One highlight is the **Nyamandhlovu Pan**, which features the high-rise **Nyamandhlovu Viewing Platform** overlooking a popular water hole. On the way from the Main Camp, check to see if there's any wildlife hanging around **Dom Pan**. South of the Main Camp is **Ngwethla Loop**, accessible to any vehicle. It passes the magnificent **Kennedy Pans**, particularly popular with elephants, though the greatest variety of wildlife can be found the **Ngwethla Picnic Site**.

Hwange Main Camp is accessible along two sealed roads from the highway between Bulawayo and Victoria Falls: via Dete, and via the airport and Hwange Safari Lodge.

Robins Camp

This camp (☎ 081-3503; office open 7am-6pm daily), at the western boundary, also has a sparsely stocked shop and **restaurant/bar**. The best wildlife viewing spots nearby are **Big Tom's Viewing Platform** and **Little Tom's Pan**. This camp is accessible along a good dirt road south from the turn-off at Matetsi. Robins remains open all year, but the roads used for local wildlife drives are usually closed from 1 November to 30 April.

Sinamatella Camp

Sinamatella (☎ 081-2775; office open 7am-6pm daily) is the nicest of the three main camps. It sits atop a 55m mesa with a commanding 50km panorama. By day, you'll see buffaloes and antelopes in the grassy patch below the camp, but it's at night time that Sinamatella really comes alive: expect to be haunted by the roaring of lions and the disconcerting howling of hyenas at the foot of the hill, along with a host of unidentified screeches, thumps and bumps. At any time, vicious little honey badgers skitter around the restaurant looking for hand-outs and even invade the chalets if given half a chance.

Amenities at Sinamatella include a rangers office, museum display, souvenir shop, grocery shop, petrol station and restaurant/bar. The popular **Mandavu Dam** is only 9km to the south.

Sinamatella is accessible by a sealed (and then gravel) road starting east of Hwange town along the Bulawayo–Victoria Falls highway.

Other more basic and remote camp sites are: **Bumbusi Camp** (24km northwest of Sinamatella and only accessible by 4WD in the wet); **Lukosi Bush Camp** (11km southeast of Sinamatella); and **Deka Camp** (25km southwest of Robins Camp), which is only accessible by 4WD, though the track may even be closed in the wet season. Safari operators often prefer these sites, so book ahead.

Places to Stay & Eat

The rates for accommodation at Hwange Main Camp, Robins Camp and Sinamatella Camp are: camp sites, US$1 per person; lodges (with two/four beds) US$2/3.50; cottages (two/four beds) US$1.50/3; and chalets (two beds) US$1 to US$2.

The larger lodges (with up to 12 beds) at Bumbusi and Nantwich camps cost US$4, while the lodge at Deka is US$9.

Hwange Main Camp has a camping ground, cottages, chalets and lodges. However, this is the only NPWZ camp in Zimbabwe where cottages do not contain a private kitchen, though the communal cooking facilities are perfectly adequate.

Sinamatella Camp also offers camping, chalets, cottages and lodges.

The amenities are not as good as **Robins Camp** and **Nantwich Camp**, but they are in prime wildlife areas (especially for lions, cheetahs and hyenas).

Ganda Lodge (☎ 09-61495; chalets with breakfast & dinner per person about US$10; transfers from Dete US$6.50) is in the Sikumi Forest Area overlooking the natural Ganda Pan. It offers **wildlife drives** (US$5 per person) and **walking safaris** (US$10) for guests and the public.

Hwange Safari Lodge (☎ 018-750, fax 337; including meals & activities per person US$155/209) is on a massive private estate within the Sikumi Forest Area. It looks more like a motel than a lodge, though all rooms thoughtfully overlook a popular water hole. Amenities include a **restaurant/bar** (open to nonguests) and swimming pool, and tours and activities are also available to the public.

Kumuna Lodge (☎/fax 018-295; including meals, activities & transfers from Dete or airport per person US$160) offers thatched rondavels in a shady area beside a mineral spring 20km from the park boundary. **Walking safaris** with knowledgeable guides are available, but only on the private estate.

ZIMBABWE

Children are welcome at the lodge with open arms.

Ivory Lodge (☎ 04-771915, fax 770641; including meals & activities per person US$250) is also in dense bushland on a private estate within Sikumi Forest Area. The rooms are actually thatched tree houses, with private bathrooms underneath.

Picnic sites are also available for camping, including **Shumba**, **Mandavu Dam**, **Masuma Dam**, **Ngwethla**, **Jambile Pan**, **Kennedy Pan I** and **Deteema Dam**. Each has its own attractions: eg, lions are frequently seen around Shumba (which means 'lion'); Mandavu Dam overlooks a charming expanse of water; Kennedy Pan I is home to hordes of elephants at night; Ngwethla is situated in an area of heavy wildlife concentration; and Masuma Dam is where you'll probably spend the night listening to belching hippos and trumpeting elephants. Each site is enclosed (ie, safe from wild animals) and has ablution blocks, but these are picnic grounds, so they're open to the public during the day.

Getting There & Away
Flights to and from the Hwange National Park Airport have been postponed indefinitely, so most travellers tie in a visit between Bulawayo and Victoria Falls.

Any of the numerous buses and minibuses between Bulawayo and Victoria Falls, and Bulawayo and Hwange town, can drop you at Safari Crossroads, 17km north of Hwange Main Camp. One or two buses or minibuses a day may detour via Dete – ask in advance at the bus stations. From wherever you get off you'll have to hitch to Hwange Main Camp, Robins Camp and Sinamatella Camp.

Better still is the Africa Link coach between Bulawayo and Victoria Falls (see those sections for details). It stops at Hwange town and the Hwange Safari Lodge. Also, **UTc** (☎ 018-393; Hwange Safari Lodge) runs daily shuttle buses to Bulawayo (US$36 per person, minimum of two).

The train between Bulawayo and Victoria Falls passes Dete far too early in the morning to be a real option. Dete is a dreary place with a few eateries and a grocery store. All hotels in the village have closed, but you may find somewhere to crash for the night if you ask around. Dete has no taxis, but it is possible to charter a taxi from Hwange town to Hwange Main Camp.

WESTERN LAKE KARIBA
The western half of Lake Kariba, which bears little resemblance to the eastern half (see the Northern Zimbabwe section earlier), is characterised by wilderness outposts, traditional Tonga culture and wild rolling hills.

Binga
The most interesting and accessible town along the western side of Lake Kariba is Binga. It was constructed expressly as a government administrative centre, with the purpose of resettling Tonga people displaced by the Lake Kariba dam. So, Binga is a good place to look for Tonga crafts, including decorative stools, headrests and drums. The town wanders sparsely from the shore to the hills, and without a vehicle getting around entails some hot and tiring walks.

Chibwatatata Hot Springs, uphill from the Bunga Rest Camp (see following), was long considered a 'power place' by the Tonga and once served as a rain-making site. A less violent spring nearby provides naturally heated water for the rest camp's swimming pool. Sadly, it's also used as a laundry and bath, and has become polluted. But there are plans to develop the springs for tourism, but when this will eventuate is anyone's guess.

Chilangililo Cooperative's Stilt Huts (☎ 015-563; huts per person US$5) built by the lakeshore about 1km up from the bus stop, is an interesting choice. Bring your own food and sleeping bag.

Binga Rest Camp (☎ 015-244, fax 245; camping per person US$1, dorm beds US$4, singles/doubles with shared bathroom US$6/7, chalets with 4/8 rooms & private bathroom US$12/15) offers basic accommodation, though the attractions are the pool and popular bar/restaurant under the shady trees.

Kulizwe Lodge (☎ 015-286; self-catering chalets per person US$20) offers several uninspiring but perfectly adequate holiday homes by the lake, 1km west of the rest camp. It also has boats for hire and sells firewood.

Although the road to Binga is sealed, hitching isn't easy due to the sparse traffic. Most minibuses from Bulawayo leave at about 6am, while those from Victoria Falls depart at about 11am. Buses to Victoria Falls and Bulawayo leave at about 5am from the bus stop in Binga, 4km southeast of the rest camp. Otherwise, get a connection at the larger town of Manjolo, 18km away by regular minibus.

Language

European Languages

Due to colonial influences, English is an official language in every Southern African country except Mozambique (where it's Portuguese). English-speaking visitors should have few communication problems.

Afrikaans is also widely used, and although it's often dismissed as the language of apart-heid, it's the first language of millions of people of diverse ethnic backgrounds.

In Mozambique and parts of northern Namibia along the Angola border, Portuguese is the European language of choice.

In parts of Namibia, German is also widely spoken, but is the first language of only about 2% of Namibians.

AFRIKAANS

Afrikaans is often used for communication between members of different groups (eg, Xhosa and Zulu, Herero and Nama, Owambo and Damara etc) who may not speak another common language. It's also used as a lingua franca in both South Africa and Namibia.

a	as the 'u' in 'pup'
g	halfway between English hard 'g' and 'h'
i	as the 'a' in 'ago'
r	rolled, as in Italian 'primo'
u	as the 'a' in 'ago', but with lips pouted
w	halfway between the English 'v' and 'f'
ae	like 'ah'
oe	as the 'oo' in 'loot'
oë	as the 'oe' in 'doer'
ooi	as 'oi'
oei	as the 'ooey' in 'phooey', preceded by 'w'
ui/y	as 'ay' in 'hay'
tj	as the 'ch' in 'chunk'
tjie	as 'kee' in 'keep'

Useful Words & Phrases

Hello.	*Hallo.*
Good morning.	*Goeie môre.*
Good afternoon.	*Goeie middag.*
Good evening.	*Goeienaand.*
Good night.	*Goeie nag.*
Please.	*Asseblief.*
Thank you.	*Dankie.*
How are you?	*Hoegaandit?*
Well, thank you.	*Goed dankie.*
Pardon.	*Ekskuus.*
Do you speak English?	*Praat u Engels?*
Yes.	*Ja.*
No.	*Nee.*
How many/much?	*Hoeveel?*

arrival	*aankoms*
departure	*vertrek*
to	*na*
from	*van*
single	*enkel*
return	*retoer*
ticket	*kaartjie*
am/pm	*vm/nm*
today	*vandag*
tomorrow	*môre*
yesterday	*gister*

information	*inligting*
left/right	*links/regs*
pharmacy/chemist	*apteek*
rooms	*kamers*
station	*stasie*
tourist bureau	*toeristeburo*

Food & Drinks

barbecue	*braaivleis* or *braai*
bar	*kroeg*
beer	*bier*
bread	*brood*
cheese	*kaas*
cup of coffee	*koppie koffie*
dried and salted meat	*biltong*
farm sausage	*boerewors*
fish	*vis*
fruit	*vrugte*
meat	*vleis*
vegetables	*groente*
wine	*wyn*

Days & Numbers

Monday	*Maandag/Ma*
Tuesday	*Dinsdag/Di*
Wednesday	*Woensdag/Wo*
Thursday	*Donderdag/Do*

Emergncies – Afrikaans

Help!	*Help!*
Call a doctor!	*Roep 'n doktor!*
Call the police!	*Roep die polisie!*
I'm lost.	*Ek is veloorer.*

Friday	*Vrydag/Vr*
Saturday	*Saterdag/Sa*
Sunday	*Sondag/So*

1	*een*
2	*twee*
3	*drie*
4	*vier*
5	*vyf*
6	*ses*
7	*sewe*
8	*agt*
9	*nege*
10	*tien*
100	*honderd*
1000	*duisend*

PORTUGUESE

Portuguese uses masculine and feminine word endings, usually '-o' and '-a' respectively - to say 'thank you', a man will therefore say *obrigado*, a woman, *obrigada*. Masculine/feminine are noted in this guide by the abbreviations 'm' and 'f' respectively.

Pronunciation

The following list should give you a rough idea of pronunciation, but listening to how local people speak will be your best guide.

ã	as the 'an' in 'fan' plus the '-ng' sound at the end of the word 'sing'
ão	as the 'ow' in 'how'
é	as the 'e' in 'whey'
ç	as the 'c'in 'celery'
c	as the 'k' in 'kit'
ch	as the 'sh' in 'shake'
h	usually silent; sometimes as in 'hot'
m	often silent; nasalises the preceding vowel
s	as in 'sun' when word-initial; as 'sh' before c, f, p, q or t; as in 'pleasure' before b, d, g, l, m, n, r and v
x	as the 'sh' in 'shake'
z	as 'jz' when word-final; elsewhere as 'sz'

Useful Words & Phrases

Good morning.	*Bom dia.*
Good afternoon.	*Boa tarde.*
Goodbye.	*Adeus/Ciao.*
See you later.	*Até mais logo.*
How are you?	*Como está?*
I'm fine, thank you.	*Muito bem, obrigado/a.* (m/f)
Yes.	*Sim.*
No.	*Não.*
Please.	*Por favor.*
Thank you.	*Obrigado/a.* (m/f)
You're welcome.	*De nada.*
I'm sorry.	*Desculpe.*
Excuse me.	*Com licença.*
I don't understand.	*Não compreendo.*
Could you write it down, please?	*Escrever, por favor.*
How much is it?	*Quanto custa?*
on the left	*à esquerda*
on the right	*à direita*
today	*hoje*
tomorrow	*amanhã*
yesterday	*ontem*
toilet/bathroom	*casa da banho*
Women	*Senhoras*
Men	*Senhors*
bus	*bus/machimbombo*
converted passenger truck	*chapa/chapa-cem*
ticket	*bilhete*
train	*comboio*

Accommodation & Food

hotel	*hotel/pousada*
cheap hotel	*pensão*
Is there a ... available?	*Tem um ...?*
room	*quarto*
single/double	*simple/duplo*
double-bed room	*casal*
bed	*cama*
market	*mercado*
snack bar	*quiosque*
street food stall	*barraca*
beer	*cerveja*
bread	*pão*
chicken	*frango/galinha*
chips/fries	*batatas fritas*
eggs	*ovos*
fish	*peixe*

Emergncies – Portuguese

Help!	*Socorro!*
Call the police!	*Chame a polícia!*
Call a doctor!	*Chame um médico!*
Go away!	*Deixe-me em paz!*
I'm lost.	*Estou perdido/a.*

fruit	*fruta*
meat	*carne*
mineral water	*agua mineral*
potatoes	*batatas*
rice	*arroz*
salt	*sal*
sugar	*açucar*
tea	*chá*
vegetables	*legumes*
water	*agua*

Numbers

1	*um/uma*
2	*dois/duas*
3	*três*
4	*quatro*
5	*cinco*
6	*seis*
7	*sete*
8	*oito*
9	*nove*
10	*dez*
100	*cem*
1000	*mil*

Bantu & Khoisan Languages

As a first language, most Southern Africans speak either a Bantu language – which would include a Zulu, Tswana, Owambo, Herero, Chewa etc language – or a Khoisan language, which may be Khoi-Khoi (Nama), Damara, or a San dialect. Due to common roots, several Bantu languages in the region, including Zulu and Ndebele languages, as well as Sotho and Tswana languages, are often mutually intelligible.

Many native Khoisan speakers also speak at least one Bantu and one European language, usually Afrikaans.

CHEWA (CHICHEWA)

Chichewa is the national language of Malawi and is also a very close relative of the Nyanja language spoken in Zambia – the two are

How to 'Click'

Khoisan dialects (as well as several Bantu languages, including the Xhosa and Ndebele languages) are characterised by 'click' elements that make them difficult to learn.

Clicks are made by compressing the tongue against different parts of the mouth to produce different sounds. Names that include an exclamation point (!) are of Khoisan origin and should be rendered as a sideways click sound, similar to the sound made when encouraging a horse, but with a hollow tone like that made when pulling a cork from a bottle. The other three clicks are formed by quickly drawing the tongue away from the front teeth (represented by /); the tutting sound made in English to indicate disapproval (represented by //); and a sharp pop formed by drawing the tongue down from the roof of the mouth (represented by ≠).

If the lingual gymnastics prove too much, just render all the clicks as a 'k' sound.

mutually intelligible. It is a complex language: word prefixes and suffixes change according to context, so one single word cannot always be given for its English equivalent. The most common forms are given here, but do remember that although these words and phrases may not be 'proper' Chichewa, you'll be understood. Most Malawians and Zambians will be pleased to hear even a few words spoken by a foreigner.

Greetings & Civilities

Bambo literally means 'father' but is a polite way to address any Malawian man. The female equivalent is *amai* or *mai*. *Mazungu* means 'white person', but isn't a derogatory term.

Hello.	*Moni.*
Hello, anybody in?	*Odi.* (knocking on door or calling at gate)
Come in/Welcome.	*Lowani.*
Goodbye.	*Tsala bwino.* (lit: 'stay well', when leaving)
Goodbye.	*Pitani bwino.* (lit: 'go well', when staying)
Good night.	*Gonani bwino.*
Please.	*Chonde.*
Thank you/ Excuse me.	*Zikomo.*

Getting it Right

The actual title of several Southern African languages can cause confusion for visitors. For example, the language of the Basotho people (from Lesotho) is SeSotho. Usually, the prefixes ('Chi', 'Se', 'Isi', 'Otji' etc) simply mean 'language', but they're only used when actually speaking that language. To say 'I can speak IsiZulu' is like saying 'I can speak Français'. When speaking English the prefixes are usually omitted. However, some languages, such as Chichewa, retain the prefix whatever language you're speaking.

Following are the the current official English designations for the predominant languages of Southern Africa (with their indigenous titles in brackets): Chichewa, Herero/Himba (Otjiherero/Otjihimba), Ndebele (Sindebele), North Sotho (SeSotho sa Lebowa), Owambo (Otjiwambo), South Sotho (SeSotho), Swati (SiSwati), Tsonga (Xitsonga), Tswana (Setswana), Venda (Tshivenda), Xhosa (Isi-Xhosa), Zulu (IsiZulu).

Thank you very much.	*Zikomo kwambile/ kwambiri.*
Yes.	*Inde.*
No.	*Iyayi.*
How are you?	*Muli bwanji?*
I'm fine.	*Ndili bwino.*
And you?	*Kaya-iwe?* (to one person)
	Kaya inu? (to several people)
Good/Fine/OK.	*Chabwino.*

Numbers

Chichewa speakers talking together will normally use English for numbers and prices. Similarly, time is nearly always expressed in English.

1	*chimonzi*
2	*ziwili*
3	*zitatu*
4	*zinayi*
5	*zitsano*

DAMARA/NAMA

The Damara and Nama peoples' traditional lands take in most of Namibia's wildest desert regions. Their languages belong to the Khoisan group, and as with the other San dialects, they feature several of the tricky 'click' elements (see the boxed text 'How to 'Click'').

Good Morning.	*!gai //oas*
How are you?	*matisa?*
Thank you.	*eio*
Do you speak English?	*engelsa !goa idu ra?*
Pardon	*mati*
What's your name?	*mati du/onha*
My name is ...	*ti /ons ge a ...*
I'm from ...	*tita ge a ...*
Yes.	*ii*
Goodbye.	*!gaise hare* (when leaving) or *!gure* (when staying)
How much is this?	*ne xu e matigo marie ni gan?*
Where is the ...?	*maha ... ha?*

Numbers

1	*/gui*
2	*/gam*
3	*!nona*
4	*haga*
5	*goro*
6	*!nani*
7	*hu*
8	*//khaisa*
9	*khoese*
10	*disi*

HERERO/HIMBA

The Herero and Himba languages are quite similar, and will be especially useful when travelling around Kaokoland and remote areas of north central Namibia, where Afrikaans remains a lingua franca and few people speak English. Most people, however, are delighted when foreign visitors attempt to communicate in Herero/Himba.

Useful Words & Phrases

Hello.	*Tjike.*
Good morning, sir.	*Wa penduka, mutengua.*
Good afternoon, madam.	*Wa uhara, serekaze.*
Good evening.	*Wa tokerua.*
Good night.	*Ongurova ombua.*
Please.	*Arikana.*
Thank you.	*Okuhepa.*
How are you?	*Kora?*
Fine.	*Naua.*
Well, thank you.	*Mbiri naua, okuhepa.*
Pardon.	*Makuvi.*

Remote Himba

The Himba living in remote areas speak a slightly different dialect. Again, people will greatly appreciate your efforts.

Hello/Good day.	*Moro.*
Good Evening.	*Huenda.*
How are you?	*Muwepe nduka?/Kora?*
Fine, thanks.	*Nawa.* or *Ami mbiri nawa.* (polite)
Yes.	*Eee.*
No.	*Kako.*
How much do you want for this?	*Imbi mokosisa vingapi?*
Do you know the road to ...?	*Motjiua ondjira ndjijenda ....?*
Where is the ...?	*... iripi?*
Goodbye.	*Kara/Karee nawa.* (to one person/many people)

Yes.	*Ii.*
No.	*Kako.*
Where are you from?	*Ove ua za pi?*
Do you speak ...?	*U hungira...?*
English	*Otjingirisa*
Herero/Himba	*Otjihimba*
Owambo	*Otjiwambo*
daughters	*ovanatje ovakazona*
sons	*ovanatje ovazandu*
wife	*omukazendu ngua kupua*
husband	*omurumendu ngua kupa*
mother	*mama*
father	*tate*
younger sister/ brother	*omuangu*
older sister/ brother	*erumbi*

Getting Around

caravan park	*omasuviro uo zo karavana*
game reserve	*orumbo ro vipuka*
hiking trail (long)	*okaira ko makaendero uo pehi (okare)*
hiking trail (short)	*okaira komakaendro uo pehi (okasupi)*
river (channel)	*omuramba*
road	*ondjiira*
rooms	*omatuuo*

Numbers

1	*iimue*
2	*imbari*
3	*indatu*
4	*iine*
5	*indano*
6	*hamboumue*
7	*hambomabari*
8	*hambondatu*
9	*imuvyu*
10	*omurongo*

LOZI

Lozi is the most common Caprivian dialect, and is spoken throughout much of western Zambia.

Greetings & Civilities

When greeting a close friend, use *Lumela, mwana* or *Lumela, wena.*

Hello.	*Eeni, sha* or *Lumela.*
Good morning.	*U zuhile.*
Good afternoon/ evening.	*Ki manzibuana*
Good night.	*Ki busihu*
Goodbye.	*Siala foo/Siala hande.*
Come in/Welcome.	*Kena.*
How are you?	*U cwang'/W'a pila/ W'a zuha?*
I'm fine.	*N'i teng'/N'a pila/ N'a zuha.*
And you?	*Wen'a bo?/Wena u cwang'?*
Please.	*Sha* (only used with people of higher social standing)
Thank you.	*N'itumezi.*
Excuse me.	*Ni swalele.* (informal) *Mu ni swalele.* (polite)
Thank you very much.	*N'i tumezi hahulu.*
Good/Fine.	*Ki hande.*
OK.	*Ku lukile.*
Yes.	*Ee.*
No.	*Awa.*
Do you speak English?	*Wa bulela sikuwa?*
How much?	*Ki bukai?*

Numbers

1	*il'ingw'i*
2	*z'e peli* or *bubeli*
3	*z'e t'alu* or *bulalu*
4	*z'e ne* or *bune*

The 'Other' Ndebele

The Ndebele language of South Africa is spoken in the country's northeastern region. It shares many linguistic features with North Sotho but is not mutually intelligible with the Ndebele language spoken in Zimbabwe. Here are a few phrases that may prove useful:

Hello.	Lotsha.
Goodbye.	Kharnaba kuhle/ Sala kuhle.
Yes.	I-ye.
No.	Awa.
Please.	Ngibawa.
Thank you.	Ngiyathokaza.
What's your name?	Ungubani ibizo lakho?
My name is ...	Ibizo lami ngu ...
I come from ...	Ngibuya e ...

5	z'e keta-lizoho
6	z'e keta-lizoho ka ka li kang'wi
7	supile
10	lishumi
20	mashumi a mabeli likiti

NDEBELE (SINDEBELE)

The language of Zimbabwe's Ndebele people is spoken primarily in Matabeleland in the western and southwestern parts of the country. It's derived from the Zulu group of languages and is not mutually intelligible with Shona.

The Ndebele of Zimbabwe and that of South Africa (also known as Southern Ndebele) are quite distinct languages. See the boxed text 'The Other Ndebele' for some useful phrases in the South African variety.

Greetings & Civilities

Hello. (on meeting)	Sawubona/Salibonani.
Hello. (reply)	Yebo.
Welcome.	Siyalemukela.
Good morning.	Livukenjani.
Good afternoon.	Litshonile.
Good evening.	Litshone njani.
How are you?	Linjani/Kunjani?
I'm well.	Sikona.
Goodbye.	Lisale kuhle. (when staying)
Goodbye.	Uhambe kuhle. (when leaving)
Yes.	Yebo
No.	Hayi.

Please.	Uxolo.
Thank you.	Siyabonga kakulu.
What's your name?	Ibizo lakho ngubani?
My name is ...	Elami igama ngingu ...
I'm from ...	Ngivela e ...
sir/madam	umnimzana/inkosikazi
How much?	Yimalini?
Where is the (station)?	Singapi (isiteshi)?

Numbers

1	okukodwa
2	okubili
3	okutathu
4	okune
5	okuyisihlanu
6	okuyisithupha
7	okuyisikhombisa
8	okuyisitshiyangalo mbila
9	okuyisitshiyangalo lunye
10	okuli tshumi

NORTH SOTHO (SESOTHO SA LEBOWA)

North Sotho is spoken in the northeastern provinces of South Africa.

Hello.	Thobela.
Goodbye.	Sala gabotse.
Yes.	Ee.
No.	Aowa.
Please.	Ke kgopela.
Thank you.	Ke ya leboga.
What's your name?	Ke mang lebitso la gago?
My name is ...	Lebitso laka ke ...
I come from ...	Ke bowa kwa ...

OWAMBO (OSHIWAMBO)

Oshiwambo – and specifically the Kwanyama dialect – is the first tongue of more Namibians than any other language, and also the language of the ruling SWAPO party. As a result, it's spoken as a second or third language by many non-Owambo Namibians of both Bantu and Khoisan origin.

Greetings & Civilities

Good Morning.	Wa lalapo.
Good Evening.	Wa tokelwapo.
How are you?	Owu li po ngiini?
I'm fine.	Ondi li nawa.
Thank you.	Tangi.
Please.	Ombili.
Do you speak English?	Oho popi Oshiingilisa?

How much is this?	*Ingapi tashi kotha?*
Yes.	*Eeno.*
No.	*Aawe.*
Maybe.	*andiya manga.*
Excuse me.	*Ombili manga.*
I'm sorry.	*Onde shi panda.*
I don't know.	*Ombili mwaa sho.*
I'm lost.	*Ombili, onda puka.*
Can you please help me.	*Eto vuluwu pukulule ndje?*

Getting Around

Where is the …?	*Openi pu na …?*
bank	*ombaanga*
hospital	*oshipangelo*
pharmacy	*oaputeka*
police station	*opolisi*
post office	*opoosa*
telephone	*ngodhi*
toilet	*kandjugo*
soft drink, soda pop	*pumbwa okanarnunate*
wine	*owaina*
beer	*ombiila*

Numbers

1	*yimwe*
2	*mbali*
3	*ndatu*
4	*ne*
5	*ntano*
6	*hamano*
7	*heyali*
8	*hetatu*
9	*omugoyi*
10	*omulongo*

SHONA

Shona is an amalgamation of several Bantu languages. It's spoken almost universally in the central and eastern parts of Zimbabwe. The 'high' dialect, used in broadcasts and other media, is Zezuru, which is indigenous to the Harare area.

Although most urban Zimbabweans have at least a little knowledge of English, many rural dwellers' English vocabulary is limited, so it helps to know a few words and phrases in Shona or Ndebele (see the 'Ndebele (Sindebele)' section in this chapter). Even those Zimbabweans who speak English well will be pleasantly surprised to hear a foreigner attempt a few words in the indigenous languages.

Where two translations are given for the same word or expression in the following section, the first is used when speaking to one person, the second, to more than one person.

Pronunciation

Shona, like Ndebele, was first written down by phonetic English transliteration, so most letters are pronounced as they would be in English. Differences of note are:

dya	pronounced 'jga', as near to one syllable as possible
tya	as 'chka', said quickly
sv	say 's' with your tongue near the roof of the mouth
zv	like the 's-v' sound in 'is very'
m	before a word-initial consonant, it's pronounced as a light hum
n	before a word-initial consonant, it's a hum with an 'n' sound

Greetings & Civilities

Hello. (initial)	*Mhoro/Mhoroi.*
Hello. (reply)	*Ahoi.*
Welcome.	*Titambire.*
How are you?	*Makadii/Makadi-ni?*
I'm well.	*Ndiripo.*
Good morning.	*Mangwanani.*
Good afternoon.	*Masikati.*
Good evening.	*Manheru.*
Goodbye.	*Chisarai zvakanaka.* (when staying)
Goodbye.	*Fambai zvakanaka.* (when leaving)
Please.	*Ndapota.*
Thank you.	*Ndatenda/Masvita.*
Yes.	*Ehe.*
No.	*Aiw.*
What's your name?	*Unonzi ani zita rako?*
My name is …	*Ndini …*
I'm from …	*Ndinobva ku …*
How much?	*I marii?*

Numbers

1	*potsi*
2	*piri*
3	*tatu*
4	*ina*
5	*shanu*
6	*tanhatu*
7	*nomwe*
8	*tsere*
9	*pfumbamwe*
10	*gumi*

SOUTH SOTHO (SESOTHO)

South Sotho is spoken by Basotho people in Lesotho. In South Africa it's spoken in the Free State, North-West Province and Gauteng. It's useful to know some words and phrases if you're planning to visit Lesotho, especially if you want to trek in remote areas.

Hello.	*Dumela.*
Greetings.	*Lumela.*
Peace.	*Khotso.*

Lumela and *khotso* will usually be followed by a title, eg, *Khotso, 'me* (lit: mother; said to an older woman). Other titles are:

ntate (lit: father)	to an older man
abuti (lit: brother)	to a young man
ausi (lit: sister)	to a young woman

| Yes. | *Ee.* |
| No. | *Tjhee.* |

There are three ways to say 'How are you?':

How are you?	*O kae?* (sg)
	Le kae? (pl)
How do you live?	*O phela joang?* (sg)
	Le phela joang? (pl)
How did you get up?	*O tsohele joang?* (sg)
	Le tsohele joang? (pl)

The responses (below) are interchangeable:

I'm here.	*Ke teng.* (sg)
	Re teng. (pl)
I live well.	*Ke phela hantle.* (sg)
	Re phela hantle. (pl)
I got up well.	*Ke tsohile hantle.* (sg)
	Re tsohile hantle. (pl)

When trekking, people always ask *Lea kae?* (Where are you going?) and *O tsoa kae?* or the plural *Le tsoa kae?* (Where have you come from?). When parting, use the following expressions:

Stay well.	*Sala hantle.* (sg)
	Salang hantle. (pl)
Go well.	*Tsamaea hantle.* (sg)
	Tsamaeang hantle. (pl)

'Thank you' is *kea leboha* (pronounced 'keya lebowah'). The herd boys often ask for *chelete* (money) or *lipompong* (sweets), pronounced 'dee-pom-pong'. If you want to say 'I don't have any', the answer is *ha dio* (pronounced 'ha dee-oh').

SWATI (SISWATI)

Swati is one of two official languages in Swaziland (the other is English). It's very similar to Zulu, and the two languages are mutually intelligible.

Yebo is often said as a casual greeting. It's the custom to greet everyone you meet. Often you will be asked *U ya phi?* (Where are you going?).

Hello. (to one person)	*Sawubona.* (lit:'I see you')
Hello. (more than one person)	*Sanibona.*
How are you?	*Kunjani?*
I'm fine.	*Kulungile.*
Goodbye. (when leaving)	*Sala kahle.* (lit:'stay well')
Goodbye. (when staying)	*Hamba kahle.* (lit: 'go well')
Please.	*Ngicela.*
I thank you.	*Ngiyabonga.*
We thank you.	*Siyabonga.*
Yes.	*Yebo.* (also an all-purpose greeting)
No.	*Cha.*
Sorry.	*Lucolo.*
What's your name?	*Ngubani libito lakho?*
My name is ...	*Libitolami ngingu ...*
I'm from ...	*Ngingewekubuya e ...*
How much?	*Malini?*

TSONGA (XITSONGA)

Tsonga is spoken in South Africa (north of Hluhluwe in KwaZulu-Natal) and in parts of Mozambique.

Hello.	*Avusheni.* (morning)
	Inhelekani. (afternoon)
	Riperile. (evening)
Goodbye.	*Salani kahle.*
Yes.	*Hi swona.*
No.	*A hi swona.*
Please.	*Nakombela.*
Thank you.	*I nkomu.*
What's your name?	*U mani vito ra wena?*
My name is ...	*Vito ra mina i ...*
I come from ...	*Ndzihuma e ...*

TSWANA (SETSWANA)

Setswana is widely spoken throughout Botswana and in some parts of South Africa (in

the eastern areas of Northern Cape, in the North-West Province and in western Free State). There are clear similarities in vocabulary between Tswana and the two Sotho languages, and the speakers of each can generally understand one another.

The letter **g** is pronounced as a 'ch' in Scottich *loch*; **th** is pronounced as a slightly aspirated 't'.

The greetings *dumela mma* or *dumela rra* are considered compliments and Batswana people appreciate their liberal usage. When addressing a group, say *dumelang*. Another useful phrase, which is normally placed at the end of a sentence or conversation is *go siame*, meaning the equivalent of 'all right, no problem'.

Greetings & Civilities

Hello.	*Dumela mma/rra.*
(to woman/man)	
Hello.	*Dumelang.*
(to group)	
Hello!	*Ko ko!*
(arrival outside a gate or house)	
Goodbye.	*Tsamaya sentle.*
(to person leaving)	
Goodbye.	*Sala sentle.*
(to person staying)	
Yes.	*Ee.*
No.	*Nnyaa.*
Please.	*Tsweetswee.*
Thank you.	*Kea leboga.*
Excuse me/Sorry.	*Intshwarele.*
Pardon me.	*Ke kopa tsela.*
	(lit: 'I want road')
OK/No problem.	*Go siame*
How are you?	*A o tsogile?* (lit: 'how
(morning)	did you wake up?')
How are you?	*O tlhotse jang?*
(afternoon/evening)	
Come on in!	*Tsena!*
Do you speak	*A o bua Sekgoa?*
English?	
Does anyone here	*A go na le o*
speak English?	*o bua Sekgoa?*
I understand.	*Ke a tlhaloganya.*
I don't understand.	*Ga ke tlhaloganye.*
How much is it?	*Ke bokae?*

Around Town

Where is a/the ...?	*E ko kae ...?*
I'm looking for	*Ke batla ...*
a/the ...	
bank	*ntlo ya polokelo*

market	*mmaraka*
post office	*poso*
public toilet	*matlwana a boitiketso*
tourist office	*ntlo ya bajanala*
hotel	*hotele*
guesthouse	*matlo a baeng*
camping ground	*lefelo la go robala mo tenteng*

Numbers

0	*lefela*
1	*bongwe*
2	*bobedi*
3	*borara*
4	*bone*
5	*botlhano*
6	*borataro*
7	*bosupa*
8	*boroba bobedi*
9	*boroba bongwe*
10	*lesome*

VENDA (TSHIVENDA)

Venda is spoken in the northeastern region of South Africa's Northern Province.

Hello.	*Ndi matseloni.*
	(morning)
	Ndi masiari.
	(afternoon)
	Ndi madekwana
	(evening)
Goodbye.	*Kha vha sale zwavhudi.*
Yes.	*Ndi zwone.*
No.	*A si zwone.*
Please.	*Ndikho u humbela.*
Thank you.	*Ndo livhuwa.*
What's your name?	*Zina lavho ndi nnyi?*
My name is ...	*Zina langa ndi ...*
I come from ...	*Ndi bva ...*

XHOSA (ISIXHOSA)

Xhosa is the language of the people of the same name. It's the dominant indigenous language in Eastern Cape in South Africa, although you'll meet Xhosa speakers throughout the region.

It's worth noting that *bawo* is a term of respect used when addressing an older man.

Hello.	*Molo.*
Goodbye.	*Sala kakuhle.*
Goodnight.	*Rhonanai.*

Tumbuka & Yao in Malawi

The two other principal indigenous languages of Malawi are Tumbuka (in the north) and Yao (in the south). Nearly all Tumbuka and Yao people also speak Chichewa, and many speak English as well. Nevertheless, a few simple words in Tumbuka and Yao will be most welcome.

English	Tumbuka	Yao
Hello.	Yewo.	Quamboni.
How are you?	Muliwuli?	Iliwuli?
Fine.	Nilimakola.	Ndiri chenene.
And you?	Manyi imwa?	Qualinimye?
Goodbye.	Pawemi.	Siagara gani ngwaula.
Thank you (very much).	Yewo (chomene).	Asante (sana).
What's your name?	Zinolinu ndimwenjani?	Mwe linachi?
My name is ...	Zinalane ndine ...	Une linaliangu ...
Where are you from?	Mukukhalankhu?	Ncutama qua?
I'm from ...	Nkhula khu ...	Gutama ku ...

Please,	Nceda.	Is it far?	Kukude yini?
Thankyou.	Enkosi.	left	ekhohlo
Do you speak	Uyakwazi ukuthetha	right	ekumene
English?	siNgesi?	food	ukudla
Are you well?	Uphilile na	water	amanzi
	namhlanje?		
Yes, I'm well.	Ewe, ndiphilile kanye.		
Yes.	Ewe.		
No.	Hayi.		
Where are you	Uvela phi na okanye		
from?	ngaphi na?		
I'm from ...	Ndivela ...		
I'm lost.	Ndilahlekile.		
Is this the road	Yindlela eya ... yini le?		
to ...?			
How much is it?	Idla mont na?		

ZULU (ISIZULU)

Zulu is spoken in South Africa by the people of the same name. As with several other Nguni languages, Zulu uses a variety of clicks (see the boxed text 'How to Click"). To ask a question, add *na* to the end of a sentence.

Hello.	Sawubona.
Goodbye.	Sala kahle.
Please.	Jabulisa.
Thank you.	Ngiyabonga.
Yes.	Yebo.
No.	Cha.
Where does this	Iqondaphi lendlela na?
road go?	
Which is the road	Iphi indlela yokuya
to ...?	ku ...?

!KUNG SAN

The click-ridden languages of the several San groups in Namibia and Botswana are surely among the world's most difficult for outsiders to learn (see the boxed text 'How to Click"). Perhaps the most useful dialect is that of the !Kung people, who are concentrated in eastern Bushmanland in Namibia and around northwestern Botswana.

To simplify matters, in the rudimentary phrase list that follows, all clicks are represented by !k, as locals will usually forgive you for ignoring the clicks and using a 'k' sound instead.

Greetings & Civilities

Hello.	!kao
Good Morning.	tuwa
What's your name?	!kang ya tsedia/tsidia?
	(to a man/woman)
How are you?	!ka tseya/tsiya?
	(to a man/woman)
My name is ...	!kang ya tse/tsi ...
	(man/woman speaking)
Thank you.	!ka
Thank you very	!kin!ka
much.	
Goodbye, go well.	!king se !kau

Glossary

Although English is widely spoken in most Southern African countries, native speakers from Australasia, North America and the UK will notice many words that have developed different meanings locally. There are also many unusual terms that have been borrowed from Afrikaans, Portuguese or indigenous languages. This Glossary includes many of these particular 'Afro-English' words, as well as other general terms and abbreviations that may not be understood.

In African English, repetition for emphasis is common: something that burnt you would be 'hot hot'; fields after the rains are 'green green'; a crowded minibus with no more room is 'full full', and so on.

For useful words and phrases in local languages, see the Language chapter.

ablutions block – found at camping grounds and caravan parks: a building that contains toilets, showers and washing-up area; also known as an amenities block

af – derogatory reference to a black person, as bad as 'nigger' or 'abo'

apartheid – 'separate development of the races'; a political system in which peoples were officially segregated according to their race

asimilados – Africans who assimilated to European ways (Mozambique)

ASL – above sea level

assegais – spears

ATVs – all terrain vehicles or 'four-wheelers'; locally called 'quad bikes'

baas – boss; subservient address reserved mainly for white males

babalass – a hangover (mainly Zimbabwe)

baixa – commercial area

bakkie – utility or pick-up truck (pronounced 'bucky')

barchan dunes – migrating crescent-shaped sand dunes

Basarwa – Batswana name for the San people

bashas – or 'bashers'; thatched A-frame chalets (mainly Zimbabwe)

Batswana – citizens of Botswana

bemanti – Swazi learned men

bhundu – the bush, the wilderness

bilharzia – water-borne disease caused by

blood flukes (parasitic flatworms) that are transmitted by freshwater snails

biltong – a normally delicious dried meat that can be anything from beef to kudu or ostrich

bioscope – Southern African English word for a cinema

bobotie – traditional Malay dish; delicately flavoured curry with a topping of beaten egg baked to a crust, served with stewed fruits and chutney

Boer – farmer in Afrikaans; a historic name for the Afrikaner people

boerewors – Afrikaner farmers' sausage of varying quality

bogobe – sorghum porridge, a staple in Botswana

bojalwa – an inexpensive sorghum beer drunk in Botswana that is also brewed commercially

boma – in Zambia, Malawi and some other countries, this is a local word for 'town'. In East Africa the same word means 'fortified stockade'. In Zimbabwe, Botswana, Namibia and much of South Africa, it's normally just a sunken campfire circle. It may be derived from the colonial term BOMA (British Overseas Military Administration), applied to any government building, such as offices or forts

boomslang – dangerous 2m-long tree snake

braai – a barbecue; a Southern African institution, particularly among whites

brötchen – small bread rolls (Namibia)

buppies – black yuppies

bushveld – flat grassy plain covered in thorn scrub

camarões – prawns (Mozambique)

camião – truck (Mozambique)

campeamento principal – main entrance (Mozambique)

capulanas – colourful cloth worn by women around their waist (Mozambique)

capuzinio – mission (Mozambique)

casal – room with a double bed, for married couples (Mozambique)

cascata – waterfall (Mozambique)

cassper – armoured vehicle; also used as slang for hippo

CBD – Central Business District; this rather scientific-sounding abbreviation is commonly

used where other English speakers might say city centre or downtown area

cell phone – mobile phone (wireless)

chapa – converted passenger truck or minivan (Mozambique, Malawi)

chibuku – local style mass-produced beer, stored in tanks served in buckets, or available in takeaway cartons (mostly in Zimbabwe and Malawi) and plastic bottles known as *scuds*. It's good for a quick cuphoria and a debilitating *hahalass*.

chili bites – spicy *biltong*, seasoned with *piri piri*

chiperone – damp misty weather which affects southern Malawi

chitenja – multicoloured piece of material used as a scarf and sarong

Concession – A communal land area governmentally designated for use by a given commercial entity for a set amount of time – usually five years; a popular concept in both Namibia and Botswana

Comrade – (or Cde) – a Marxist title used mainly by the media, referring to black Zimbabweans, especially government officials

coupé – two-person compartment on a train

cuca shops – small shops in northern Namibia; named for the Angolan beer once sold in them

daga hut – a traditional African round house consisting of a wooden frame, mud and straw walls and thatched roof (mainly Zimbabwe)

dagga – (pronounced **da**-kha) Southern African term for marijuana

danga – long turquoise necklace traditionally worn by the Xhosa

dambo – area of grass, reeds or swamp alongside a river course

dassies – herbivorous gopher-like mammals of two species: *Procavia capensis*, also called the rock hyrax; and *Dendrohyrax arborea* or tree hyrax. They're in fact not rodents, but are thought to be the closest living relatives of the elephant.

dhow – Arabic sailing vessel that dates from ancient times

difaqane – forced migration by several Southern African tribes in the face of Zulu aggression; also known as *mfecane*

djembe – a type of hand drum

dolfhout – wild teak

donga – steep-sided gully caused by soil erosion

donkey boiler – it may sound cruel, but this has nothing to do with donkeys; it's a water tank positioned over a fire and used to heat water for showers and other purposes

dorp – a small country settlement in South Africa

drankwinkel – literally 'drink shop'; a Namibian or South African off-licence or bottle shop

drift – a river ford; most are normally dry

dumpi – a 375ml bottle of beer (see also *pint* and *quart*)

duplo – a room with twin beds

Dutchman – term of abuse for an Afrikaner man

dwalas – bald knob-like domes of smooth rock

efundja – period of heavy rainfall in northern Namibia

eh – (rhymes with 'hay') all purpose ending to sentences, even very short ones such as 'Thanks, eh?'

ekipa – traditional medallion historically worn by Owambo women as a sign of wealth and status

eumbo – immaculate Owambo *kraal*; much like a small village enclosed within a pale fence

euphorbia – several species of cactus-like succulents; most are poisonous to humans

fathom – nautical measurement equal to six feet (1.83m)

flotty – a hat for canoe safaris, with a chin-strap and a bit of cork in a zippered pocket to ensure that it floats in case of a capsize

4WD – four-wheel drive; locally called 4x4

fynbos – fine bush, primarily proteas, heaths and ericas

game – formerly used for any animal hunted, now applies to all large, four-footed creatures

gap it – make a quick exit; often refers to emigration from troubled African countries

garni – a hotel that lacks a full dining room, but does offer a simple breakfast (Namibia)

gemütlichkeit – a distinctly German appreciation of comfort and hospitality

gudza – soft and pliable tree bark used to make blankets, mats and clothing

guti – dank, drizzly weather that afflicts Zimbabwe's Eastern Highlands in winter

half-bus – a bus with about 30 seats – to distinguish it from big buses or minibuses (Malawi)

heks – entrance gates, farm gates

high season – in most of Southern Africa, this refers to the dry season, from late June to late September; in South Africa's Cape regions, it refers to the dry season from late November to early April

Homelands – formerly self-governing black states (Transkei, Ciskei, Bophuthatswana, Venda etc) which were part of the apartheid regime's plan for a separate black and white South Africa

igqirha – Xhosa spiritual healer

impis – military regiments

Incwala – most sacred Swazi ceremony in which king gives permission to his people to eat the first crops of the new year

inselberg – isolated ranges and hills; literally 'island mountains'

ix-hwele – Xhosa herbalist

Izzit? – rhetorical question that most closely translates as 'Really?' and is used without regard to gender, person or number of subjects. Therefore, it could mean 'Is it?', 'Are you?', 'Is he?', 'Are they?', 'Is she?', 'Are we?' etc. Also 'How izzit?', for 'How's it going?'

jesse – dense, thorny scrub, normally impenetrable to humans

joala – sorghum beer (Lesotho)

jol – party, both verb and noun

Jugendstil – German Art-Nouveau architecture prevalent in Namibia, especially in Swakopmund and parts of Windhoek and Luderitz

jukskei – an Afrikaner game like horseshoe-tossing but using items associated with trek wagons

just now – refers to some time in the future but implies a certain degree of imminence; it could be half an hour from now or two days from now

kaffir – derogatory term for a black person

kalindula – rumba-inspired music of Zambia

kampango – catfish (Malawi)

kapenta – an anchovy-like fish (*Limnothrissa mioda*) caught in Lake Kariba and favoured by Zimbabweans

karakul – variety of Central Asian sheep, which produce high-grade wool and pelts; raised in Namibia and parts of Botswana

kerk – church in Afrikaans

kgadi – alcoholic drink found in Botswana; a brew of brown sugar and berries or fungus

kgosi – chief (Botswana)

Khoisan – language grouping taking in all Southern African indigenous languages, including San and Khoikhoi (Nama), as well as the language of the Damara (a Bantu people who speak a Khoikhoi dialect)

Kimberlite pipe – geological term for a type of igneous intrusion, in which extreme heat and pressure have turned coal into diamonds

kizomba – musical style popular in Namibia

kloof – a ravine or small valley

koeksesters – small gooey Afrikaner doughnuts dripping in honey or sugar syrup

kokerboom – quiver tree; grows mainly in southern Namibia and the Northern Cape province

konditorei – German pastry shops; found in larger Namibian towns

kopje – (pronounced 'koppie'); a small hill or rocky outcrop on an otherwise flat plain

kotu – king's court (Zambia)

kraal – Afrikaans version of the Portuguese word 'curral'; an enclosure for livestock, a fortified village of mud huts, or an Owambo homestead

kwacha – Zambian currency

kwasa kwasa – Congo-style rhumba music

laager – wagon circle

lagosta – crayfish

lapa – large, thatched common area; used for socialising

larney – posh, smart, high quality

lekker – (pronounced lak-ker) anything that's good, nice or tasty

liqhaga – grassware 'bottles'

litunga – king (Zambia)

location – alternative Namibian and South African word for township, usually affiliated with a rural town

lekolulo – a flute-like instrument played by herd boys in Lesotho

lupembe – wind instrument made from animal horn

lutindzi – type of grass

mabele – sorghum

machibombo – large bus

madila – thickened sour milk

mageu – a light and nonintoxicating drink made from *mielies* or sorghum mash

mahango – millet; a staple of the Owambo diet and used for brewing a favourite alcoholic beverage

majika – traditional rhythmic sound

makalani or **mokolane** – a type of palm tree that grows in the Kalahari region

make a plan – to sort things out; refers to anything from working through a complicated procedure to circumventing bureaucracy

makhosi – Zulu chiefs

makwaela – a dance characterised by a cappella singing and sophisticated foot percussion performed in southern Mozambique

makishi – a dance performed in Zambia featuring male dancers wearing masks of stylised human faces with grass skirts and anklets

Malawi shandy – nonalcoholic drink made from ginger beer, Angostura bitters, orange or lemon slices, soda and ice

mapiko – masked dance of the Makonde people

marimba – African xylophone, made from strips of resonant wood with various-sized gourds for sound boxes

marrabenta – typical Mozambican music, inspired by traditional *majika* rhythms

mataku – watermelon wine

matola – pick-up or van carrying passengers (Malawi)

mbanje – cannabis (Zimbabwe)

mbira – thumb piano; it consists of five to 24 narrow iron keys mounted in rows on a wooden sound board

mbongi – holders and performers of a Xhosa group's oral history; a cross between a bard and a court jester

mealie meal or **mielie pap** – maize porridge, which is a dietary staple throughout the region

mielies – cobs of maize

mfecane – see *difaqane*

miombo – dry open woodland, also called *Brachystegia* woodland; it's comprised mainly of mopane and acacia *bushveld*

mokoro (plural **mekoro**) – dugout canoe used in the Okavango Delta and other riverine areas; mekoro are propelled by a well-balanced poler who stands in the stern

mopane worms – the caterpillar of the moth *Gonimbrasiabelina*, eaten as a local delicacy throughout the region

morgen – unit of land measurement used by early Boer farmers, equal to about 1.25 hectares

moringa – thick-trunked 'ghost tree' of northwestern Namibia

mpasa – lake salmon (Malawi)

mujejeje – rocks that resonate when struck

multa – a fine (Mozambique)

murunge – see *muzungu*

mushe – the equivalent of 'very good' – used mostly in Zimbabwe

mushokolo – a beer made from small seeds

musika – a Zimbabwean market outside the town centre; also called *renkini* in Ndebele (Zimbabwe)

muti – traditional medicine

muzungu – white person, especially in Zambia and Malawi, or *murunge* in Zimbabwe

nganga – fortune teller

nalikwanda – huge wooden canoe, painted with black and white stripes, that carries the *litunga*

Nama – popular name for Namibians of Khoikhoi, Topnaar or Baster heritage

não faz mal – 'no problem' in Portuguese; useful in both Mozambique and Angola

!nara – type of melon that grows in desert areas; a dietary staple of the Topnaar people

nartjie – (pronounced 'narkie') South African tangerine

nchenl – lake tiger fish (Malawi)

Ngwenyama – The Lion; term given to the King of Swaziland

ngxowa yebokwe – goatskin bag carried over the left shoulder by Xhosa on important occasions

n!oresi – traditional San lands; literally, 'lands where one's heart is'

now now – definitely not now, but sometime sooner than 'just now'

nshima – filling maize porridge-like substance eaten in Zambia

nxum – the San people's 'life force'

nyama – meat or meat gravy

oke – bloke, guy (mainly South Africa)

omaeru – soured milk; a dietary staple of the Herero people

omulilo gwoshilongo – 'sacred fire' that serves as a shrine in each Owambo *kraal*; a mopane log that's kept burning around the clock

omuramba (plural **omiramba**) – fossil river channel in the Kalahari region of northern Namibia and northwestern Botswana

ondjongo – dance performed only by Himba cattle owners to demonstrate the care and ownership of their animals

oshana – normally dry river channel in northern Namibia and northwestern Botswana

oshikundu – tasty alcoholic beverage made from *mahango*; popular throughout traditional areas of northern Namibia

otjize – ochre used by the Himba women to protect their skin from the elements

otjizumba – natural perfume used by the Himba; normally derived from the commiphora (camphor) bush

outjina (for women) and **otjipirangi** (for men) – Herero dance where a plank is strapped to one foot in order to deliver a hollow, rhythmic percussion

padrão – tribute to a royal patron, normally a cross erected by early Portuguese navigators along the African coast

pan – dry flat area of grassland or salt, often a seasonal lake-bed

panveld – flat area containing many pans

participation safari – an inexpensive safari in which clients pitch their own tents, pack the vehicle and share cooking duties

peg – milepost

pensão – inexpensive hotel (Mozambique)

photographic safari – safari in which participants carry cameras rather than guns

pint – small bottle of beer or can of oil (or similar) usually around 300ml to 375ml (not necessarily equal to a British or US pint)

piri-piri or **peri-peri** – very hot pepper sauce of Portuguese/Angolan origin; the basis for the *Nando's* chain's chicken concoctions

plus-minus – meaning 'about'; this scientific/mathematical term has entered common parlance – eg, 'the bus will come in plus-minus 10 minutes'

pondo – 'pound', occasionally used in Botswana to refer to two pula, ostensibly because P2 once equalled £1

potjie – pronounced **poy**-kee; a three-legged pot used to make stew over an open fire. The word also refers to the stew itself, as well as a gathering in which a *potjie* forms the main dish

praça – town square (Mozambique)

praia – beach (Mozambique)

pronking – four-legged leaping, as done by some antelopes (particularly springboks); there is a variety of explanations of this behaviour, from protection, to observation, braking and sheer fun

pula – the Botswanan currency; meaning 'rain' in Setswana

pungwe – all night drinking and music party (Zimbabwe)

quart – about (but not necessarily exactly) twice the size of a pint

regulo – village chief (Mozambique)

relish – sauce of meat, vegetables, beans etc eaten with boiled *mielie* meal (*nsima*, *nshima*, *sadza*, *mealie pap* etc)

renkini – Ndebele version of *musika*

rhodey – a normally derogatory term for a white Zimbabwean; roughly the same as 'ocker' or 'redneck' in Australia and the US

robot – No, not R2D2 – it's just a traffic light

rondavel – round, African-style hut

rooibos – literally 'red bush' in Afrikaans; herbal tea that reputedly has therapeutic qualities

rubber duck – inflatable boat

rusks – solid bits of biscuit-like bread made edible by immersion in coffee or tea

rusvingo – Shona word for walled-in enclosures

sadza – maize-meal porridge

San – language-based name for indigenous people formerly known as Bushmen

sangoma – witchdoctor; herbalist

scud – plastic drinks bottle

seif dunes – prominent linear sand dunes, as found in the central Namib Desert

self-catering – term applied at camps where guests cook their own meals

setolo-tolo – a stringed instrument played with the mouth (Lesotho)

shame! – half-hearted expression of commiseration

shandy – refreshing mixed drink comprising lemonade, soda water and angostura bitters over ice; in one variation, the 'sneaky puff adder', vodka replaces the soda water

shebeen – an illegal township drinking establishment (which may also include a brothel)

shongololo – ubiquitous giant millipede; occasionally used to refer to a train

sibhaca – type of Swazi dance

slasher – hand tool with a curved blade used to cut grass or crops, hence 'to slash' means 'to cut grass'

slenter – fake diamond

Sperrgebiet – forbidden area; alluvial diamond region of southwestern Namibia

spruit – (pronounced 'sprait') a little streambed, which rarely contains any water

squaredavel – see *rondavel* and work out the rest

stiffy – removable computer disc

strandlopers – literally 'beach walkers'; term used to describe the ancient inhabitants of the Namib region, who may have been ancestors of the San or Nama peoples. Occasionally also refers to the brown desert hyena.

sua – salt as in Sua Pan (Botswana)

sungwa – a type of perch (Malawi)

swaartgevaar – Afrikaans for the 'black threat'

tackies – trainers, tennis shoes, gym shoes

tambo – fermented millet and sugar drink

thomo – a stringed instrument played by women in Lesotho

timbila – a form of xylophone played by Chope musicians

toasties – toasted sandwiches

toktokkie – Afrikaans for the fog-basking *tenebrionid* beetle, *Onomachris unguicularis*

tokoloshe – source of evil which lives in water but is also kept by Xhosa witches

tonkies – derogatory word for members of the Batonka tribe, and for anybody/thing basic, simple or 'gone bush'

township – indigenous suburb, typically a high-density black residential area

toxic sludge – disgusting mixed drink comprised of tequila or vodka combined with brandy or schnapps and hot cherry jelly (jello in the USA). To drink one is a badge of honour – fortunately, it hasn't spread outside of Southern Africa.

toy toy – jubilant dance

trypanosomiasis – sleeping sickness; disease transmitted by the bite of the tsetse fly

tsama – bitter desert melon historically eaten by the San people; it's also eaten by livestock

tsotsi – hoodlum, thief

tufo – traditional dance style from Ilha de Moçambique

tuk-tuk – Asian-style motorised three-wheel vehicle found in Durban

TWOGs – acronym for 'Third World groupies', used by white Zimbabweans in reference to foreigners who travel to underdeveloped countries and consciously sink to the lowest level of local society

uitlanders – (pronounced '**ait**-landers') foreigners

Umhlanga – Reed dance; sacred Swazi ceremony

umuzi – 'beehive' huts

upshwa – see *xima*

uri – desert-adapted vehicle that is produced in Namibia

UTC – Universal Time Coordinate (formerly GMT); the time at the prime meridian at Greenwich, UK

van der Merwe – archetypal Boer country bumpkin who is the butt of jokes throughout Southern Africa

vegetable ivory – fruit of the *makalani* palm (*Hyphaene petersiana*); hard, white palm nut used for carvings

veld – open grassland (pronounced 'felt'), normally in plateau regions; lowveld, highveld, bushveld, strandveld, panveld

veldskoens – comfortable bush shoes of soft leather, similar to moccasins; sometimes called 'vellics'

vetkoek – literally 'fat cake'; an Afrikaner doughnut

vlei – (pronounced 'flay') any low open landscape, sometimes marshy

wag 'n bietjie – (pronounced 'vak-n-bee-kee') literally 'wait a bit'; Afrikaans name for the buffalo thorn acacia

walende – a drink distilled from the *makaluni* palm that tastes like vodka

wandelpad – short hiking trail

watu – dugout canoe used in western Zambia and the Kavango and Caprivi regions of Namibia

welwitschia – bizarre cone-bearing shrub (*Welwitschia mirabilis*) native to the northern Namib plains

xima (or **upshwa**) – maize- or cassava-based staple, usually served with a sauce of beans, vegetables or fish (Mozambique)

zol – see *dagga*

Index

Abbreviations

B – Botswana
GP – Game Park
GR – Game Reserve
L – Lesotho
Mal – Malawi

Moz – Mozambique
N – Namibia
NP – National Park
RP – Recreational Park
SA – South Africa

Swa – Swaziland
WG – Wildlife Guide
Zam – Zambia
Zim – Zimbabwe

Text

A

aardwolf WG2
abseiling
  Victoria Falls (Zam) 601
accommodation 65-6, *see also
  individual country entries*
  national parks 27
activities, *see individual activ-
  ites and individual country
  entries*
Addo Elephant Park (SA) 486-7
Ae//Gams street festival (N) 330
African National Congress
  406-9, 612
Afrikaner people 311, 406
Aha Hills (B) 136-7
AIDS 51-2, 84, 414, 423, 581,
  665-6, 674
air travel
  Botswana 95-6, 97-8
  Lesotho 151
  Malawi 181, 183-4
  Mozambique 261, 263
  Namibia 321
  South Africa 428, 430
  Southern Africa to/from
    68-71
  Southern Africa within 75
  Swaziland 585
  Zambia 625-6, 627-8
  Zimbabwe 680-1
Aliwal North (SA) 496
Alliance for Democracy (Mal)
  166
Alte Feste (National Museum
  of Namibia) (N) 329
Alto Molócuè (Moz) 291
Amanzimtoti (SA) 510
Amatola Mountains (SA) 492
ANC, *see* African National
  Congress 406
Anglo-Boer War 83, 405, 559

Bold indicates maps.

Angoche (Moz) 293
animals, *see* wildlife
animism 29
antelope WG14
apartheid 27, 406-8, 545, 546
Apartheid Museum (SA) 546
Arnhem Cave (N) 337
arts, *see individual country
  entries*
Augrabies Falls National Park
  (SA) 478
Aus (N) 394

B

baboon WG15
badger WG7
Bainskloof Pass (SA) 460
Ballito (SA) 512
ballooning
  Swakopmund (N) 373
Banda, Dr Hastings 165-6
Bangué (Moz) 282
Bangweulu Wetlands (Zam) 640
Bantu people 18-20, 81, 162,
  306, 577, 665
Barberton (SA) 539
Barchan Dunes (N) 384
Barotseland (Zam) 653-7
Barra (Moz) 280
Basotho people 20, 147
Basotholand (L) 142
Baster people 311
Batswana people 82-3, 566
Battle of Blood River (SA) 404,
  514, 531, 557
Battle of Majuba (SA) 405
Bazaruto Archipelago (Moz)
  282-3
Bazaruto Island (Moz) 282
Beaufort West (SA) 495-6
Bechuanaland (B) 83
Bechuanaland Democratic
  Party (B) 84
Bechuanaland People's Party
  (B) 84

Beira (Moz) 283-6, **284**
Ben Lavin Nature Reserve (SA)
  571
Benguera (Moz) 282
Bergville (SA) 523
Bethlehem (SA) 564
bicycle travel, *see* cycling
Big Bend (Swa) 593
Big Trip, the 31, 88, 254, 313,
  417, 582, 617, 667, **34**
Biko, Steve 407-8
Bilene (Moz) 276
bilharzia 51, 178, 423, 584,
  592, 674
Binga (Zim) 746
birds, *see* wildlife
bird-watching 24-5, 150, 168,
  411, 425, 644
  Bangweulu Wetlands (Zam)
    640
  Bazaruto Archipelago (Moz)
    282
  Chinyakwaremba (Zim)
    712, 739
  Chobe National Park (B)
    121-4
  Elephant Marsh (Mal) 245
  Etosha National Park (N)
    345-9
  Gorongosa National Park
    (Moz) 286
  Kafue National Park (Zam)
    656
  Kruger National Park (SA)
    532
  Lake Chivero Recreational
    Park (Zim) 697
  Mamili National Park (N) 358
  Matobo (Matopos) National
    Park (Zim) 739-41
  Ondanhwa (N) 351
  Vwaza Marsh Wildlife
    Reserve (Mal) 204
  Walvis Bay (N) 377-8
  Xakanaxa Lediba (B) 133

Boxed Text & Special Sections

MAP LEGEND

CITY ROUTES

Freeway .... Freeway
Highway .... Primary Road
Road .... Secondary Road
Street .... Street
Lane .... Lane
.... On/Off Ramp
.... Unsealed Road
.... One Way Street
.... Pedestrian Street
.... Stepped Street
.... Footbridge

BOUNDARIES

.... International
.... State
.... Disputed
.... Fortified Wall

REGIONAL ROUTES

.... Tollway, Freeway
.... Primary Road
.... Secondary Road
.... Minor Road

AREA FEATURES

.... Building
.... Park, Gardens
.... Market
.... Sports Ground
.... Beach
+ + + ... Cemetery
.... Campus
.... Plaza

HYDROGRAPHY

.... River, Creek
.... Canal
.... Lake

.... Dry Lake; Salt Lake
.... Spring; Rapids
.... Waterfalls

TRANSPORT & STATIONS

.... Train
.... Tramway
.... Cable Car, Chairlift
.... Ferry
.... Walking Trail
.... Walking Tour
.... Path
.... Pier or Jetty

POPULATION SYMBOLS

○ CAPITAL .... National Capital
◉ CAPITAL .... State Capital

● CITY .... City
● Town .... Town

● Village .... Village
.... Urban Area

MAP SYMBOLS

● .... Place to Stay
▼ .... Place to Eat
● .... Point of Interest

.... Airfield; Airport
.... Anchorage
.... Archaeological Site
.... Bank; Battle Site
.... Bird Sanctuary; Zoo
.... Border Crossing
.... Bus Terminal/Stop
.... Camping; Hut
.... Caravan Park
.... Cave
.... Church

.... Cinema; Theatre
.... Dry Water Hole
.... Embassy/Consulate
.... Golf Course
.... Hindu Temple
.... Hospital
.... Internet Cafe
.... Kraal
.... Lighthouse
.... Lookout
.... Mine

.... Monument
.... Mountain
.... Mosque
.... Museum
.... National Park
.... Parking
.... Petrol
.... Police Station
.... Post Office
.... Pub or Bar
.... Shelter; Picnic Area

.... Shipwreck
.... Shopping Centre
.... Ski Field
.... Stately Home
.... Surf Beach
.... Swimming Pool
.... Taxi Rank
.... Telephone; Toilet
.... Tourist Information
.... Transport
.... Windmill

Note: not all symbols displayed above appear in this book

LONELY PLANET OFFICES

Australia
Locked Bag 1, Footscray, Victoria 3011
☎ 03 8379 8000   fax 03 8379 8111
email: talk2us@lonelyplanet.com.au

UK
72-82 Rosebery Ave, London, EC1R 4RW
☎ 020 7841 9000   fax 020 7841 9001
email: go@lonelyplanet.co.uk

USA
150 Linden St, Oakland, CA 94607
☎ 510 893 8555   TOLL FREE: 800 275 8555
fax 510 893 8572
email: info@lonelyplanet.com

France
1 rue du Dahomey, 75011 Paris
☎ 01 55 25 33 00   fax 01 55 25 33 01
email: bip@lonelyplanet.fr
www.lonelyplanet.fr

World Wide Web: www.lonelyplanet.com or AOL keyword: lp
Lonely Planet Images: lpi@lonelyplanetimages.com